Lecture Notes in Computer Science 5726

Commenced Publication in 1973
Founding and Former Series Editors:
Gerhard Goos, Juris Hartmanis, and Jan van Leeuwen

Tom Gross Jan Gulliksen
Paula Kotzé Lars Oestreicher
Philippe Palanque Raquel Oliveira Prates
Marco Winckler (Eds.)

Human-Computer Interaction – INTERACT 2009

12th IFIP TC 13 International Conference
Uppsala, Sweden, August 24-28, 2009
Proceedings, Part I

Springer

Volume Editors

Tom Gross
Bauhaus University Weimar, 99423 Weimar, Germany
E-mail: email@tomgross.net

Jan Gulliksen
Uppsala University, 75105 Uppsala, Sweden
E-mail: jan.gulliksen@it.uu.se

Paula Kotzé
Meraka Institute, 0001 Pretoria, South Africa
E-mail: paula.kotze@meraka.org.za

Lars Oestreicher
Uppsala University, 75120 Uppsala, Sweden
E-mail: larsoe@dis.uu.se

Philippe Palanque
Marco Winckler
University Paul Sabatier, 31062 Toulouse Cedex, France
E-mail: {palanque, winckler}@irit.fr

Raquel Oliveira Prates
Universidade Federal de Minas Gerais, 31270010 Belo Horizonte, MG, Brazil
E-mail: rprates@dcc.ufmg.br

Library of Congress Control Number: 2009932606

CR Subject Classification (1998): H.5.2, H.5.3, H.3-5, I.2.10, D.2, K.3-4, K.8

LNCS Sublibrary: SL 3 – Information Systems and Application, incl. Internet/Web and HCI

ISSN 0302-9743
ISBN-10 3-642-03654-6 Springer Berlin Heidelberg New York
ISBN-13 978-3-642-03654-5 Springer Berlin Heidelberg New York

springer.com

Printed in Germany

Typesetting: Camera-ready by author, data conversion by Scientific Publishing Services, Chennai, India
Printed on acid-free paper SPIN: 12734825 06/3180 5 4 3 2 1 0

Foreword

INTERACT 2009 was the 12th of a series of INTERACT international conferences supported by the IFIP Technical Committee 13 on Human–Computer Interaction. This year, INTERACT was held in Uppsala (Sweden), organized by the Swedish Interdisciplinary Interest Group for Human–Computer Interaction (STIMDI) in cooperation with the Department of Information Technology at Uppsala University.

Like its predecessors, INTERACT 2009 highlighted, both to the academic and to the industrial world, the importance of the human–computer interaction (HCI) area and its most recent breakthroughs on current applications. Both experienced HCI researchers and professionals, as well as newcomers to the HCI field, interested in designing or evaluating interactive software, developing new interaction technologies, or investigating overarching theories of HCI, found in INTERACT 2009 a great forum for communication with people of similar interests, to encourage collaboration and to learn.

INTERACT 2009 had Research and Practice as its special theme. The reason we selected this theme is that the research within the field has drifted away from the practical applicability of its results and that the HCI practice has come to disregard the knowledge and development within the academic community. However, to continue to develop and prosper, the HCI community needs to pay more attention to the cooperation and mutual learning between research and practice. We witness accidents happening in health care, airplanes crashing due to problems in their operation, we see tremendous money losses due to inefficiencies in computer support. On a smaller scale we find many tools and applications that are, if not difficult, annoying to use for reasons that are well known. At the same time we see an amazing development of new IT designs, games, robots and applications designed for pleasure and fun. IT is an essential source for efficiency and productivity in work as well as a large source of problems. For the future we need to learn from the positive development and reach for an understanding of the mechanisms behind the successes in order for us to let such processes influence the more challenged application domains. We hope that INTERACT 2009 provided such an inspiring meeting between research and implementation.

INTERACT 2009 brought the conference to Sweden and the Nordic countries. Through conferences such as NordiCHI, the Nordic countries have come to be recognized as one of the major local communities within the field of HCI. Nordic participants are one of the biggest regional participation categories at HCI conferences in the world. The Nordic tradition of HCI focuses on utility, equality, participation and quality of our everyday life and work. We aim at continuing these traditions while being in the forefront of development of the HCI field.

We hope that INTERACT 2009 will be remembered as a conference that brought research and practice closer together, focusing on making the computerized world a better place for everyone, regardless of functional abilities or particular requirements.

August 2009

Jan Gulliksen
Lars Oestreicher

Note from the Technical Co-chairs

You are holding the proceedings of the 12th Human–Computer Interaction Conference INTERACT 2009. The creation of this document is really a testament to the enthusiasm and collegial spirit amongst the HCI research and practitioner community worldwide. Thank you to all the authors who chose INTERACT 2009 as the vehicle to publish their research: a total of 723 submissions were received for the conference this year. Of these submissions, 244 were accepted for presentation at the conference. These include:

- 104 Full Research Papers
- 79 Short Research Papers
- 7 Interactive Poster Papers
- 17 Workshops
- 12 Tutorials
- 3 Special Interest Groups
- 6 Demonstrations
- 3 Panels
- 13 Doctoral Consortium Papers

The acceptance rate for the research papers was 29% of full papers submitted for review and 20% of initial abstracts submitted. The acceptance rate for the short research papers and interactive posters was 39%. Each research paper was reviewed by between three and six members of the International Programme Committee.

Our sincere gratitude goes to the all the International Programme Committee members who willingly helped out and ensured the high quality of the INTERACT Conference papers was properly maintained. Although some people had to be bullied into reviewing (sorry about that), everyone submitted their reviews on time without a murmur of complaint. Thank you all for the effort that you so obviously put into this task.

Finally we wish to express a special thank you to the Proceedings Publication Chair, Marco Winckler, who painstakingly put this volume together.

August 2009

Paula Kotzé
Tom Gross

IFIP TC13

Established in 1989, the International Federation for Information Processing Technical Committee on Human–Computer Interaction (IFIP TC13) is an international committee of 30 member national societies and 7 Working Groups, representing specialists in human factors, ergonomics, cognitive science, computer science, design and related disciplines. INTERACT is its flagship conference, staged biennially in different countries in the world.

IFIP TC13 aims to develop the science and technology of human–computer interaction (HCI) by encouraging empirical research, promoting the use of knowledge and methods from the human sciences in design and evaluation of computer systems; promoting better understanding of the relation between formal design methods and system usability and acceptability; developing guidelines, models and methods by which designers may provide better human-oriented computer systems; and, cooperating with other groups, inside and outside IFIP, to promote user-orientation and humanization in system design. Thus, TC13 seeks to improve interactions between people and computers, encourage the growth of HCI research and disseminate these benefits worldwide.

The main orientation is toward users, especially the non-computer professional users, and how to improve human–computer relations. Areas of study include: the problems people have with computers; the impact on people in individual and organizational contexts; the determinants of utility, usability and acceptability; the appropriate allocation of tasks between computers and users; modelling the user to aid better system design; and harmonizing the computer to user characteristics and needs.

While the scope is thus set wide, with a tendency toward general principles rather than particular systems, it is recognized that progress will only be achieved through both general studies to advance theoretical understanding and specific studies on practical issues (e.g., interface design standards, software system consistency, documentation, appropriateness of alternative communication media, human factors guidelines for dialogue design, the problems of integrating multimedia systems to match system needs and organizational practices, etc.).

IFIP TC13 stimulates working events and activities through its Working Groups (WGs). WGs consist of HCI experts from many countries, who seek to expand knowledge and find solutions to HCI issues and concerns within their domains, as outlined below.

In 1999, TC13 initiated a special IFIP Award, the Brian Shackel Award, for the most outstanding contribution in the form of a refereed paper submitted to and delivered at each INTERACT. The award draws attention to the need for a comprehensive human-centered approach in the design and use of information technology in which the human and social implications have been taken into account. Since the process to decide the award takes place after papers are submitted for publication, the award is not identified in the proceedings.

WG13.1 (Education in HCI and HCI Curricula) aims to improve HCI education at all levels of higher education, coordinate and unite efforts to develop HCI curricula and promote HCI teaching.

WG13.2 (Methodology for User-Centred System Design) aims to foster research, dissemination of information and good practice in the methodical application of HCI to software engineering.

WG13.3 (HCI and Disability) aims to make HCI designers aware of the needs of people with disabilities and encourage development of information systems and tools permitting adaptation of interfaces to specific users.

WG13.4 (also WG2.7) (User Interface Engineering) investigates the nature, concepts and construction of user interfaces for software systems, using a framework for reasoning about interactive systems and an engineering model for developing user interfaces.

WG13.5 (Human Error, Safety and System Development) seeks a framework for studying human factors relating to systems failure, develops leading edge techniques in hazard analysis and safety engineering of computer-based systems, and guides international accreditation activities for safety-critical systems.

WG13.6 (Human-Work Interaction Design) aims at establishing relationships between extensive empirical work-domain studies and HCI design. It will promote the use of knowledge, concepts, methods and techniques that enable user studies to procure a better apprehension of the complex interplay between individual, social and organizational contexts and thereby a better understanding of how and why people work in the ways that they do.

WG13.7 (Human–Computer Interaction and Visualization) is the newest of the working groups under the TC.13. It aims to establish a study and research program that will combine both scientific work and practical applications in the fields of Human–Computer Interaction and Visualization. It will integrate several additional aspects of further research areas, such as scientific visualization, data mining, information design, computer graphics, cognition sciences, perception theory, or psychology, into this approach.

New Working Groups are formed as areas of significance to HCI arise. Further information is available at the IFIP TC13 website: http://www.ifip-hci.org/

IFIP TC13 Members

Australia
Judy Hammond
Australian Computer Society

Austria
Horst Hörtner
Austrian Computer Society

Belgium
Monique Noirhomme-Fraiture
Federation des Associations Informatiques de Belgique

Brazil
Simone Diniz Junqueira Barbosa
Brazilian Computer Society (SBC)

Canada
Gitte Lindgaard (Secretary)
Canadian Information Processing Society

China
Chengguing Zong
Chinese Institute of Electronics

Czech Republic
Vaclav Matousek
Czech Society for Cybernetics and Informatics

Denmark
Annelise Mark Pejtersen (Chair)
Danish Federation for Information Processing

Finland
Kari-Jouko Räihä
Finnish Information Processing Association

France
Philippe Palanque
Societe des Electriciens et des Electroniciens (SEE)

Germany
Horst Oberquelle
Gesellschaft fur Informatik

Greece
Nikos Avouris
Greek Computer Society

Iceland
Marta Kristin Larusdottir
The Icelandic Society for Information Processing (ISIP)

India
Anirudha Joshi
Computer Society of India

Italy
Fabio Paternò
Italian Computer Society

Ireland
Liam J. Bannon
Irish Computer Society

Japan
Masaaki Kurosu
Information Processing Society of Japan

New Zealand
Mark Apperley
New Zeeland Computer Society (NZCS)

Nigeria
Chris C. Nwannenna
Nigeria Computer Society

Norway
Norwegian Computer Society

Poland
J. L. Kulikowski
Poland Academy of Sciences

Portugal
Joaquim A. Jorge
Associacao Portuguesa de Informatica

Singapore
Kee Yong Lim
Singabore Computer Society

South Africa
Janet L. Wesson (Vice chair)
The Computer Society of South Africa

Spain
Julio Abascal
Federacion Espanola de Sociedades de Informatica

Sweden
Lars Oestreicher
Swedish Computer Society

Switzerland
Ute Klotz
Swiss Federation for Information Processing

The Netherlands
Gerrit C. van der Veer
Nederlands Genootschap voor Informatica

UK
Phil Gray
British Computer Society

USA-Based
John Karat
Association for Computing Machinery (ACM)
Nahum Gershon
The Computer Society, Institute of Electrical & Electronics Engineers (IEEE-CS)

Expert Members
Jan Gulliksen
Sweden
Tom Gross
Germany

Working Group Chairpersons

WG13.1 (Education in HCI and HCI Curricula)
Paula Kotzé, *South Africa*

WG13.2 (Methodology for User-Centered System Design)
Peter Forbrig, *Germany*

WG13.3 (HCI and Disability)
Gerard Weber, *Germany*

WG13.4 (also 2.7) (User Interface Engineering)
Nick Graham, *Canada*

WG13.5 (Human Error, Safety, and System Development)
Philippe Palanque, *France*

WG13.6 (Human-Work Interaction Design)
Torkil Clemmensen, *Denmark*

WG13.7 (Human Computer Interaction and Visualization)
Mark Apperley, *New Zealand*

INTERACT 2009 Technical Committee

Conference Committee

General Co-chairs

Jan Gulliksen	*Uppsala university and KTH Royal Institute of Technology in Stockholm, Sweden*
Lars Oestreicher	*Uppsala University, Sweden*

Technical Programme Co-chairs

Paula Kotzé	*Meraka Institute, South Africa*
Tom Gross	*Bauhaus University Weimar, Germany*

Technical Programme Committee

Demonstrations Co-chairs

Olav W. Bertelsen	*University of Aarhus, Denmark*
Janet C. Read	*University of Central Lancashire, UK*

Doctoral Consortium Co-chairs

Else Nygren	*Uppsala University, Sweden*
Kasper Hornbæk	*University of Copenhagen, Denmark*

Full Paper Co-chairs

Paula Kotzé	*Meraka Institute, South Africa*
Tom Gross	*Bauhaus University Weimar, Germany*

Keynote Speaker Chair

Mats Edenius	*Uppsala University, Sweden*

Panel Co-chairs

John Karat	*IBM Research, USA*
Masaaki Kurosu	*The Open University of Japan, Japan*

Short Papers and Interactive Posters Co-chairs

Philippe Palanque	*University Paul Sabatier, France*
Raquel Oliveira Prates	*Federal University of Minas Gerais, Brazil*

Special Interest Groups Co-chairs

Ute Klotz	*University of Applied Sciences and Arts of Lucerne, Switzerland*
Nikolaos Avouris	*University of Patras, Greece*

Tutorial Co-chairs

Fabio Paternò	*ISTI-CNR, Italy*
Mats Lind	*Uppasala University, Sweden*

Workshop Co-chairs

Anders Jansson	*Uppsala University, Sweden*
Gitte Lindegaard	*Carleton University, Canada*

Organization

Proceedings Publication Chair

Marco Winckler	*University Paul Sabatier, France*

Program Chair

Bengt Sandblad	*Uppsala University, Sweden*

Sponsoring Co-chairs

Tomas Berns	*Ergolab, Sweden*
Bengt Sandblad	*Uppsala University, Sweden*

Students Volunteers Co-chairs

Elina Eriksson	*Uppsala University, Sweden*
Rebecka Janols	*Uppsala University, Sweden*

Website Co-chairs

Lars Oestreicher	*Uppsala University, Sweden*
Nils-Erik Gustafsson	*Frontwalker/IT-arkitekterna, Sweden*

Programme Committee Members

Julio Abascal, *Spain*
Silvia Abrahão, *Spain*
Heikki Ailisto, *Finland*
Xavier Alamán, *Spain*
Mir Farooq Ali, *USA*
Dima Aliakseyeu, *The Netherlands*
Margarita Anastassova, *France*
Elisabeth Andre, *Denmark*
Paul André, *UK*
Daniela Andrei, *Romania*
Jean-Yves Antoine, *France*
Mark Apperley, *New Zealand*
Cecilia Aragon, *USA*
Liliana Liliana, *Italy*
Carmelo Ardito, *Italy*
Myriam Arrue Recondo, *Spain*
Richard Atterer, *Germany*
Simon Attfield, *UK*
Juan Carlos Augusto, *UK*
Nikolaos Avouris, *Greece*
Cedric Bach, *France*
Jonathan Back, *UK*
Nilufar Baghaei, *Australia*
Sebastiano Bagnara, *Italy*
Rafael Ballagas, *USA*
Cecilia Baranauskas, *Brazil*
Simone Barbosa, *Brazil*
Javier Bargas-Avila, *Switzerland*
Louise Barkhuus, *USA*
Len Bass, *USA*
Konrad Baumann, *Austria*
Gordon Baxter, *UK*
Russell Beale, *UK*
Elke Beck, *Austria*
David Benyon, *UK*
Francois Berard, *France*
Regina Bernhaupt, *Austria*
Karsten Berns, *Germany*
Nadia Berthouze, *UK*
Nigel Bevan, *UK*
Nicola J Bidwell, *Australia*
Jacob Biehl, *USA*
Thomas Binder, *Denmark*
Jeremy Birnholtz, *USA*
Staffan Björk, *Sweden*
Renaud Blanch, *France*
Ann Blandford, *UK*
Eli Blevis, *USA*
Pieter Blignaut, *South Africa*
Florian Block, *UK*
Susanne Bodker, *Denmark*
Mads Bodker, *Denmark*
Davide Bolchini, *USA*
Marcela Borge, *USA*
Ron Boring, *USA*
Giorgio Brajnik, *Italy*
Emily Brown, *USA*
Mike Brown, *Isle of Man*
Mihaela Brut, *Romania*
Martin Brynskov, *Denmark*
George Buchanan, *UK*
Steffen Budweg, *Germany*
Sabin-Corneliu Buraga, *Romania*
Jamika Burge, *USA*
Andreas Butz, *Germany*
Jacob Buur, *Denmark*
M. Claudia Buzzi, *Italy*
Marina Buzzi, *Italy*
Daragh Byrne, *Isle of Man*
Paul Cairns, *UK*
Eduardo H. Calvillo, *UK*
José Campos, *Portugal*
Pedro Campos, *Portugal*
Stefan Carmien, *Spain*
Luis Carriço, *Portugal*
John M. Carroll, *USA*
Tiziana Catarci, *Italy*
Augusto Celentano, *Italy*
Anxo Cereijo Roibás, *UK*
Teresa Chambel, *Portugal*
Olivier Chapuis, *France*
Kelvin Cheng, *Australia*
Keith Cheverst, *UK*
Luca Chittaro, *Italy*
Luigina Ciolfi, *Isle of Man*
Torkil Clemmensen, *Denmark*

Nathalie Colineau, *Australia*
Karin Coninx, *Belgium*
Stéphane Conversy, *France*
Michael Cooke, *Isle of Man*
Nuno Correia, *Portugal*
Maria Francesca Costabile, *Italy*
Adrien Coyette, *Belgium*
Stefan Cronholm, *Sweden*
João Cunha, *Portugal*
Mary Czerwinski, *USA*
Carla Maria Dal Sasso Freitas, *Brazil*
Peter Dalsgaard, *Denmark*
Catalina Danis, *USA*
Peter Dannenmann, *Germany*
Nigel Davies, *UK*
Janet Davis, *USA*
Antonella De Angeli, *UK*
Oscar de Bruijn, *UK*
Berardina De Carolis, *Italy*
Alexander De Luca, *Germany*
Maria De Marsico, *Italy*
Giorgio De Michelis, *Italy*
Boris de Ruyter, *The Netherlands*
Clarisse de Souza, *Brazil*
Ruth de Villiers, *South Africa*
Andy Dearden, *UK*
Yogesh Deshpande, *India*
Francoise Detienne, *France*
Nicoletta Di Blas, *Italy*
Lily Diaz, *Finland*
Anke Dittmar, *Germany*
Tanja Döring, *Germany*
Carlos Duarte, *Portugal*
Emannuel Dubois, *France*
Casey Dugan, *USA*
Sophie Dupuy-Chessa, *France*
Achim Ebert, *Germany*
Niklas Elmqvist, *USA*
David England, *UK*
Paul Engelfield, *UK*
Thomas Erickson, *USA*
Vanessa Evers, *The Netherlands Antilles*
Giorgio Faconti, *Italy*
Stefano Faralli, *Italy*
Carla Faria Leitão, *Brazil*
William Farr, *UK*
Loe Feijs, *The Netherlands*
Daniel Felix, *Switzerland*
Ylva Fernaeus, *Sweden*
Amyris Fernandez, *Brazil*
Danyel Fisher, *USA*
Morten Fjeld, *Sweden*
Daniela Fogli, *Italy*
Eelke Folmer, *USA*
Joan Fons, *Spain*
Manuel Joao Fonseca, *Portugal*
Amanda Fonville, *USA*
Peter Forbrig, *Germany*
David Fourney, *Canada*
Silvia Gabrielli, *Italy*
Luigi Gallo, *Italy*
Craig Ganoe, *USA*
Nestor Garay-Vitoria, *Spain*
Roberto García, *Spain*
Stavros Garzonis, *UK*
Franca Garzotto, *Italy*
Jean-Marc Gauthier, *Singapore*
Miguel Gea, *Spain*
Helene Gelderblom, *South Africa*
Cristina Gena, *Italy*
Gautam Ghosh, *Norway*
Carlo Giovannella, *Italy*
Audrey Girouard, *USA*
Kentaro Go, *Japan*
Paula A. Gomes da Silva, *Portugal*
Daniel Gonçalves, *Portugal*
Maria Paula Gonzalez, *Argentina*
Connor Graham, *Australia*
Nicholas Graham, *Australia*
Raphael Grasset, *New Zealand*
Marianne Graves Petersen, *Denmark*
Phil Gray, *UK*
Marde Greefff, *South Africa*
William Green, *The Netherlands*
Joshua Gross, *USA*
Tom Gross, *Germany*
John Grundy, *New Zealand*
Nuno Guimaraes, *Portugal*
Jan Gulliksen, *Sweden*

Adriana Mihaela Guran, *Romania*
Francisco Luis Gutierrez Vela, *Spain*
Jörg Haake, *Germany*
Michael Haller, *Austria*
Lars Hallnäs, *Sweden*
Kim Halskov, *Denmark*
Morten Borup Harning, *Denmark*
Richard Harper, *UK*
Michael Harrison, *UK*
Steve Harrison, *USA*
Kirstie Hawkey, *Canada*
Steve Haynes, *USA*
Matthias L. Hemmje, *Germany*
Michael Herczeg, *Germany*
Morten Hertzum, *Denmark*
Martin Hitz, *Austria*
Wolfgang Hochleitner, *Austria*
Paul Holleis, *Germany*
Lars Erik Holmquist, *Sweden*
Kristina Höök, *Sweden*
John Hosking, *New Zealand*
Aaron Houssian, *USA*
Nancy Houston, *USA*
Stefan Hrastinski, *Sweden*
William Hudson, *UK*
Jina Huh, *USA*
Stéphane Huot, *France*
Duke Hutchings, *USA*
Ebba Hvannberg, *Iceland*
Netta Iivari, *Finland*
Shamshi Iqbal, *USA*
Poika Isokoski, *Finland*
Minna Isomursu, *Finland*
Giulio Jacucci, *Finland*
Lars-Erik Janlert, *Sweden*
Eva Jettmar, *USA*
Sune Alstrup, *Denmark*
Chris Johnson, *UK*
Matt Jones, *UK*
Steve Jones, *New Zealand*
Joaquim Jorge, *Portugal*
Anirudha Joshi, *India*
Christophe Jouffrais, *France*
Oskar Juhlin, *Sweden*
Anne Kaikkonen, *Finland*
Matthew Kam, *USA*
Bridget Kane, *Isle of Man*
Anne Marie Kanstrup, *Denmark*
Maurits Kaptein, *The Netherlands*
Victor Kaptelinin, *Sweden*
John Karat, *USA*
Kostas Karpouzis, *Greece*
Dinesh S. Katre, *India*
Rick Kazman, *USA*
Christina Keller, *Sweden*
Babak Khazaei, *UK*
Olga Khroustaleva, *USA*
Stephen Kimani, *Australia*
Alex Klippel, *USA*
Anders Kluge, *Norway*
Michael Koch, *Germany*
Christina Köffel, *Austria*
Christophe Kolski, *France*
Andreas Komninos, *UK*
Joseph A. Konstan, *USA*
Ilpo Koskenin, *Finland*
Paula Kotzé, *South Africa*
Kostas Koukouletsos, *Greece*
Matthias Kranz, *Germany*
Subramanian Krishnamurthy, *India*
Steinar Kristoffersen, *Norway*
Antonio Krüger, *Germany*
Sari Kujala, *Finland*
Juliusz Kulikowski, *Poland*
Kari Kuutti, *Finland*
Jennifer Lai, *USA*
Michael Lankes, *Austria*
Ann Lantz, *Sweden*
Rosa Lanzilotti, *Italy*
Andreas C. Larsson, *Sweden*
Marta Larusdottir, *Iceland*
Effie Law, *UK*
Marco Lazzari, *Italy*
Eric Lecolinet, *France*
Minkyung Lee, *New Zealand*
Jair Leite, *Brazil*
Barbara Leporini, *Italy*
Stefano Levialdi, *Spain*
Henry Lieberman, *USA*
Ann Light, *UK*

Cecile Paris, *Australia*
Timo Partala, *Finland*
Avi Parush, *Canada*
Oscar Pastor, *Spain*
Isabelle Pecci, *France*
Samuli Pekkola, *Finland*
Helen Petrie, *UK*
Emmanuel Pietriga, *France*
Marcelo Pimenta, *Brazil*
Ian Pitt, *Isle of Man*
Fabio Pittarello, *Italy*
Andreas Pleuss, *Germany*
Beryl Plimmer, *New Zealand*
Karolien Poels, *The Netherlands*
Klaus Pohl, *Germany*
Roberto Polillo, *Italy*
Vesna Popovic, *Australia*
Dorin Mircea Popovici, *Romania*
Chris Power, *UK*
Mathura Prasad Thapliyal, *India*
Marco Pretorius, *South Africa*
Costin Pribeanu, *Romania*
Angel Puerta, *USA*
Pernilla Qvarfordt, *USA*
Victor Ruiz Penichet, *Spain*
Kari-Jouko Raiha, *Finland*
Roope Raisamo, *Finland*
Nitendra Rajput, *USA*
Ismo Rakkolainen, *USA*
Roberto Ranon, *Italy*
Dimitrios Raptis, *Greece*
Matthias Rauterberg, *The Netherlands*
Madhu Reddy, *USA*
Johan Redström, *Sweden*
Karen Renaud, *UK*
Yann Riche, *USA*
Laurel D. Riek, *UK*
Thomas Rist, *Germany*
Chris Roast, *UK*
Markus Rohde, *Germany*
Teresa Roselli, *Italy*
Chiara Rossitto, *Sweden*
Ling Rothrock, *USA*
Amanda Rotondo, *USA*
Anne Roudaut, *France*
Jose Rouillard, *France*
Nicolas Roussel, *France*
Elisa Rubegni, *Switzerland*
Marco Sá, *Portugal*
Saqib Saeed, *Germany*
Antti Salovaara, *Finland*
Nithya Sambasivan, *USA*
Jaime Sanchez, *Chile*
Frode Eika Sandnes, *Norway*
Chris Sandor, *Australia*
Carmelina Santoro, *Italy*
Giuseppe Santucci, *Italy*
Corina Sas, *UK*
Anthony Savidis, *Greece*
Dominique Scapin, *France*
Chris Schmandt, *USA*
Albrecht Schmidt, *Germany*
Johannes Schöning, *Germany*
Gerhard Schwabe, *Switzerland*
Montserrat Sendin Veloso, *Spain*
Tacha Serif, *Turkey*
Cecília Sik Lányi, *Hungary*
Gavin Robert Sim, *UK*
Carla Simone, *Italy*
Mikael B. Skov, *Denmark*
Andy Smith, *UK*
Andrew Smith, *South Africa*
Marc Smith, *USA*
Eva Snee, *USA*
Hugo Solis, *USA*
Jan Stage, *Denmark*
Emil Stanescu, *Romania*
Christian Stary, *Austria*
Gunnar Stevens, *Germany*
Didier Stricker, *Denmark*
Sriram Subramanian, *UK*
Noi Sukaviriya, *USA*
S. Shyam Sundar, *USA*
Yngve E Sundblad, *Sweden*
John Tang, *USA*
Jean-Claude Tarby, *France*
Deborah Tatar, *USA*
Patrice Terrier, *France*
Nadia Thalmann, *Switzerland*
Jakob Tholander, *Sweden*

Michael Toomim, *USA*
Stefan Trausan-Matu, *Romania*
Daniela Trevisan, *Brazil*
Sanjay Tripathi, *India*
Manfred Tscheligi, *Austria*
Maurizio Tucci, *Italy*
Tuomo Tuikka, *Finland*
Phil Turner, *UK*
Susan Turner, *UK*
Jaime Urquiza-Fuentes, *Spain*
Kaisa Väänänen-Vainio-Mattila, *Finland*
Heli Väätäjä, *Finland*
Pedro Valderas, *Spain*
Judy van Biljon, *South Africa*
Elise van den Hoven, *The Netherlands*
Charles van der Mast, *The Netherlands*
Gerrit van der Veer, *The Netherlands*
Betsy van Dijk, *The Netherlands*
Darelle van Greunen, *South Africa*
Lex van Velsen, *The Netherlands*
Jean Vanderdonckt, *Belgium*
Alison Varey, *UK*
Radu-Daniel Vatavu, *Romania*
Angel Velázquez, *Spain*
Gina Venolia, *USA*
Markel Vigo, *Spain*
Giuliana Vitiello, *Italy*
Arnd Vitzthum, *Germany*
Jörg Voskamp, *Germany*
Ljiljana Vukelja, *Switzerland*
Dhaval Vyas, *The Netherlands*
Marion Walton, *South Africa*
Gerhard Weber, *Germany*
Carolyn Wei, *USA*
Alexandra Weilenmann, *Sweden*
Astrid Weiss, *Austria*
Janet Wesson, *South Africa*
Mikael Wiberg, *Sweden*
Daniel Wigdor, *USA*
David Wilfinger, *Austria*
Wolfgang Woerndl, *Germany*
William Wong, *UK*
Peta Wyeth, *Australia*
Heng Xu, *USA*
Diana Xu, *UK*
Pradeep G Yammiyavar, *India*
Alvin Yeo, *Malaysia*
Yeliz Yesilada, *UK*
Massimo Zancanaro, *Italy*
Luke Zhang, *USA*
Jürgen Ziegler, *Germany*
John Zimmerman, *USA*

Sponsors and Supporters

Gold

IT-arkitekterna

Swedish Foundation for Strategic Research

VINNOVA

Municipality of Uppsala

Silver

Microsoft Research

Bronze

IBM Research

ANTROP

Local Organizers

IFIP TC13

Uppsala University, Department of Information Technology

Swedish Interdisciplinary Organisation for Human-Computer Interaction (STIMDI)

Swedish Interdisciplinary Interest Group for Human–Computer Interaction

The Swedish Interdisciplinary Interest Group for Human–Computer Interaction (STIMDI) is a non-profit organization in Sweden that has the purpose of promoting cooperation between industry and academia within the field of HCI. STIMDI has been around since 1986 and also took the initiative of starting the NordiCHI conference series with NordiCHI 2000 in Stockholm. STIMDI is happy to be the co-organizer of INTERACT 2009 together with Uppsala University. More information can be found on www.stimdi.se

Uppsala University

Uppsala University is the oldest university in northern Europe. It was founded in 1477 and has about 40,000 students. Uppsala University is a complete university with all subjects that exist in its research area. It is the biggest center for HCI research in Sweden with three different departments of HCI at the Faculty of Science and Technology, at the Faculty of Social Science and at the Faculty of Medicine.

The research conducted by the HCI group at the department of Information Technology at Uppsala University concerns the analysis and design of computerized work environments. A goal is to ensure usability (satisfaction, efficiency and effectiveness) and reduce complexity for computer users. Most of the research is performed within governmental authorities, organizations and industrial settings, where the role is to guide the development of usable systems through user-centered design activities. A significant part of the research concerns complex computer systems intended for professional users in their everyday work. This also involves studying organizational aspects and work environment problems. Current research domains are:

- Human control of complex systems: high-speed ferry operation, train driver operation, train traffic control, simulators
- Administrative work environments: case-handling, call center operation
- Health care: decision support systems, tele-radiology, home health care
- Visualization: tactical control and command systems, virtual learning lab, 3D tools
- Work environment: Physical, psychosocial and cognitive work environment in computer supported work

Table of Contents – Part I

Part One: Keynote Speakers

Part Two: Long and Short Papers

Accessibility 1

Accessibility 2

Affective HCI and Emotion

Child Computer Interfaces

Ethics and Privacy

Evaluation 1

Evaluation 2

Games, Fun and Aesthetic Design 1

Games, Fun and Aesthetic Design 2

HCI and Web Applications 1

HCI and Web Applications 2

Human Cognition and Mental Load 1

Human Cognition and Mental Load 2

Human Error and Safety

Human-Work Interaction Design

Interaction with Small and Large Displays 1

Interaction with Small and Large Displays 2

International and Cultural Aspects of HCI

Mobile Computing 1

Mobile Computing 2

Mobile Computing 3

Mobile Computing 4

Model-Based Design of Interactive Systems

Table of Contents – Part II

Multimodal Interfaces 1

Multimodal Interfaces 2

Multimodal Interfaces 3

Multi-user Interaction and Cooperation 1

Multi-user Interaction and Cooperation 2

Novel User Interfaces and Interaction Techniques 4

Novel User Interfaces and Interaction Techniques 5

Novel User Interfaces and Interaction Techniques 6

Social Media/Social Networks

Tangible User Interfaces and Robotics

Tools for Design, Modelling and Evaluation 1

Tools for Design, Modelling and Evaluation 2

Usability Evaluation Methods

User Experience 1

User Experience 2

User Interfaces for Safety Critical Systems and Health Care 1

User Interfaces for Safety Critical Systems and Health Care 2

User Interfaces for Web Applications and E-commerce

Visualisation Techniques

Part Three: Demonstrations

Part Four: Doctoral Consortium

Part Five: Interactive Posters

Part Six: Panels

Part Seven: Special Interest Groups

Part Eight: Tutorials

Part Nine: Workshops

Mobile Life – Innovation in the Wild

Kristina Höök

Mobile Life
DSV, Stockholm University
Forum 100, 164 40 Kista, Sweden
kia@dsv.su.se
http://www.mobilelifecentre.org

Abstract. After a decade of work in our research labs on mobile and ubiquitous technology, often formed by the early visions of ubiquitous computing, with the urge to move interaction from the desktop out into the wild, these technologies have now moved out into the world – into the wild. We are in the middle of a second IT-revolution, caused by the spread of mobile and ubiquitous services, in combination with a broad consumer-oriented market pull. The first IT-revolution, the introduction and deployment of Internet and the World Wide Web during the 1990's, had a major impact on all parts of our society. As mobile, ubiquitous technology now becomes wide-spread, the design and evaluation of mobile services – i.e. information technology that can be accessed and used in virtually any setting – represents an important business arena for the IT- and telecom industry. Together we have to look for a sustainable web of work, leisure and ubiquitous technology we can call the mobile life.

But what impact does this have on HCI research? In particular, what is our role in innovating new services, new technologies, new interaction models and new ways of living with this technology? Obviously, new methods for design and evaluation of interfaces are needed, especially when those interfaces are not always clearly 'interfaces' anymore, but blend in with various new materials in our environments or even worn on our bodies. Usage situations are shifting, unstable, mobile settings – interaction in the wild. There is a need for design methods that help structure a multitude of different sources of inspiration and fieldwork, and synthesize it into concrete requirements and service or technology concepts. In our work we have used a variety of such methods, such as ethnography as a basis for design, Laban-notation to analyse body behaviours, novel forms of quick sketching of mobile service interaction, cultural probes to understand emotional processes in people's everyday lives, bodystorming for situating ideas in the real world, and the experience clip method for user self-evaluation to evaluate mobile services in their realistic setting. We have also developed our own methods, such as e.g. user-driven innovation - studying extreme or specialised user groups and then innovating services for other user groups based on those experiences.

But we also see trends that will turn these ways of approaching innovation upside down. Producers and consumers blend together in what we name Mobile 2.0-services, creating content dependent on the mobile setting. Sketching in hardware and software combinations becomes accessible not only to technology experts, but to all. How can HCI-practice change to make the 'digital materials' accessible to all rather than supporting only HCI-experts to develop innovative design?

T. Gross et al. (Eds.): INTERACT 2009, Part I, LNCS 5726, pp. 1–2, 2009.

As pointed out in the vision "Being Human: Human-Computer Interaction in the year 2020", HCI needs to orient towards the values shaped by the interaction between technology and people in our everyday lives. As digital, interactive technology enters every aspect of our lives we must do justice to the full complexity of actual human lived experience, where people actively and individually construct meaningful experiences around technology. We might even have to take responsibility for how society is shaped by this second digital revolution - making values such as privacy, autonomy or trust, but also living a good, rich life, explicitly part of our design processes and study methods, creating for a sustainable, human-friendly society.

In the Mobile Life centre, we work around a vision of a ludic society where work mixes with leisure, private with public – a society where enjoyment, experience and play are adopted into all aspects of life. It becomes important to recognise that private and leisure life should not have to be as polished and efficient as your work performance when practices and technology travel between these spheres of our life.

In my talk, I will discuss the implications for academic research in HCI as well as how this fosters a novel work practice in industry. The ICT and telecom industry will be less focused on identifying needs and more focused on values, in particular, ludic aspects of life.

Towards Human-Centred Design

Liam J. Bannon

Interaction Design Centre
Dept. of Computer Science & information Systems
University of Limerick
Ireland
liam.bannon@ul.ie

Abstract. The field of HCI has evolved and expanded dramatically since its origin in the early 1980's. The HCI community embraces a large community of researchers and practitioners around the world, from a variety of disciplinary backgrounds in the human and social sciences, engineering and informatics, and more recently, the arts and design disciplines. This kaleidoscope of cultures and disciplines as seen at INTERACT Conferences provides a rich pool of resources for examining our field. Applications are increasingly exploring our full range of sensory modalities, and merging the digital and physical worlds. WiFi has opened up a huge design space for mobile applications. A focus on usability of products and services has been complemented by an emphasis on engagement, enjoyment and experience. With the advent of ubiquitous computing, and the emergence of "The Internet of Things", new kinds of more open infrastructures make possible radically new kinds of applications. The sources of innovation have also broadened, to include human and social actors outside of the computing and design organizations. The question is to what extent is our mainstream thinking in the HCI field ready for the challenges of this Brave New World? Do the technological and social innovations that we see emerging require us to re-shape, or even, re-create, our field, or is it a case of a more gradual evolution and development of that which we already know? In this closing Keynote, I will provide a perspective on the evolution and development of the HCI field, looking backwards as well as forwards, in order to determine what are some of the changes of significance in the field. This "broad-brush" approach to what I term " human-centred design" will be complemented by the examination of specific projects and applications, to help anchor some of the discussion. Areas such as user-centred design, participatory design, computer-supported cooperative work and learning, and interaction design, in which I have had some involvement over the years, will be mentioned. I will discuss the themes of "ecologies of artefacts", appropriation, tinkering/bricolage, and the emergence of design anthropology, among other topics. The purpose of the talk is not to engage in a form of Futurism concerning the HCI field, but to examine some of the technical and social trends that can be observed, and to highlight some areas of particular significance that warrant further attention. I argue for a multi-layered approach that, while exploring new avenues of research concerning people's use of technology, does not necessarily dismiss the corpus of knowledge we have built up over the years concerning human-computer interaction. From a personal perspective, issues such as means and ends, our

T. Gross et al. (Eds.): INTERACT 2009, Part I, LNCS 5726, pp. 3–4, 2009.

underlying values, and concern for our fellow human beings in an increasingly fragile world, are issues that, while perhaps seen as outside the remit of a narrow HCI brief, impact on the field in significant ways. In this regard, discussions of our future should not be the preserve of techno-determinists, but be open to all. For example, ubiquitous computing can be involved in many scenarios, not only that of "Ambient Intelligence". We need to engage in the development and critique of these different perspectives and approaches. Being able to work in and with multidisciplinary teams embodying distint, and at times conflicting perspectives, being able to communicate ones ideas and information across a variety of social and institutional boundaries, will become of great importance. Of particular concern, in the context of an IFIP INTERACT event, is the need to balance the heterogeneity of concepts and methods being used in research and practice with some form of quality control. Despite the heterogeneity of perspectives and disciplines nowadays involved in the field, I will argue that the HCI community, as a community, still does have a significant role to play in the development and evolution of useful, usable and enaging ICT-enabled infrastructures and applications.

DTorial: An Interactive Tutorial Framework for Blind Users in a Web 2.0 World

Joshua Hailpern[1], Loretta Guarino Reid[2], and Richard Boardman[2]

[1] University of Illinois at Urbana Champaign, 201 N Goodwin Ave, Urbana, IL 61801
jhailpe2@cs.uiuc.edu
[2] Google, 1600 Amphitheatre Pky, Mtn. View, CA 94043, USA
{lorettaguarino,rickb}@google.com

Abstract. Effective tutorial systems can help promote products by reducing barriers of learning new applications. With dynamic web applications becoming as complex as desktop programs, there is a growing need for online tutorial/help systems. For visually impaired users the key limitations of traditional help systems are 1) poor access to help content with assistive technology, and 2) frequent reliance on videos/images to identify parts of web applications and demonstrate functionality. In this paper, we present a new interaction model, targeted towards screen-reader users, that describes how to embed an interactive tutorial within a web application. The interaction model is demonstrated within a system called DTorial, a fully functional dynamic audio-based tutorial with embedded content. While remaining within the web application, users can rapidly access any tutorial content, injected inline near relevant application controls, allowing them to quickly apply what they just heard to the application itself, without ever losing their position or having to shift windows. The model and implementation are grounded in sighted user help-systems literature and an analysis of screen-reader and Web-Application interactions. Lessons learned from the incremental design and evaluations indicate that providing visually impaired users with dynamic, embedded, interactive audio-based tutorial systems can reduce the barriers to new Web-Applications.

Keywords: Tutorial, Help Systems, Web 2.0, Screen Reader, Blind, Visually Impaired, Interactive Tutorial, Dynamic Content.

1 Introduction

There are many challenges that arise when ensuring equal opportunity access [6, 18, 25] for visually impaired and blind users. Even with state of the art tools (e.g., screen readers), one major hurdle for this community is the adoption of new software. Visually impaired users must rely upon recall to remember the available interface options. Creating such a mental model is a time consuming process. This process is complicated by industry's adoption of Web 2.0 applications (e.g. Dynamic Webmail, Web Document Editing, etc), complex and dynamic online programs that challenge users to use a computer in a completely new way: introducing multiple modes of

T. Gross et al. (Eds.): INTERACT 2009, Part I, LNCS 5726, pp. 5–18, 2009.

interaction, including one not in the vernacular of most screen-reader users. While literature would encourage the use of tutorials [23] existing mechanisms (e.g., video, flash and text+image) rely on visual presentations of context inaccessible to the VIU. Further, traditional Web-based tutorial systems provide poor access to content with assistive technology.

This paper addresses the unique challenges for visually impaired users using web-based tutorial and help systems. We have designed an interaction model specifically addressing the needs of audio-based tutorials systems for Web applications and screen readers. Our interaction model is demonstrated through our fully functional tutorial system, DTorial (**D**ynamic Tu**torial**). This model and implementation provide a mechanism allowing the VIU to learn the interface of a Web application through embedded tutorial information and an interactive control mechanism. The design is based on a set of interviews with visually-impaired computer users, best practices in existing literature, and an analysis of screen reader interaction with Web 2.0 applications. Our system was further informed through a rapid design and evaluation cycle with 17 VIUs. The foremost contribution of our model is the demonstration of a functional and accessible tutorial that can be integrated easily into the Web-application environment.

2 Definitions and Terminology

Visually impaired individuals range from those who are mildly near or far sighted, to those who are legally blind, to those who have no vision at all. Those with the most vision loss cannot rely upon sight at all to interact with the world around them. Approximately 1.5 million visually-impaired individuals live in the USA [3] and the worldwide statistics put the number at 161 million (about 2.6% of the world population [33]). For the purpose of this study, we define individuals who cannot rely upon sight for computer interaction as being ***V**isually **I**mpaired **U**sers* or VIUs.

Visually impaired individuals have learned to adapt to and augment many aspects of the world around them, for instance, with the Braille system [2]. As computer systems have become ubiquitous, technology also has adapted to meet the needs of these users [25]. One form of assistive technology, the Screen Reader, converts digital text to audio speech or Braille output. Common screen readers include Freedom Scientifics' JAWS, GW Micro's WindowEyes, and Apple's VoiceOver. This software allows users to navigate computer applications and web pages through a series of keyboard commands, while having the content read back to them. This content can be presented as either speech or on a refreshable Braille display [4]. For this experiment, we used audio feedback. We use the term "read" or "reading" to indicate the user is listening to a screen reader converting text to spoken audio. In this experiment we used the JAWS Screen Reader, the most popular screen reader [13].

3 Existing Technology and Limitations

Research in screen readers is ongoing in HCI. Jim Thatcher captured the philosophy best in 1994: "blind users must have access to the same computing environment as their sighted colleagues" [30]. Since then, much work has helped make computers accessible, with emphasis on improving Web accessibility [23, 26] for screen-reader users. There has also been rapid development of tools to help Web designers check for accessibility [14, 29]. Tools have also been developed to assist in the creation of more accessible Web pages [5, 10]. While new screen-reader based solutions may be invented, such solutions must be disseminated and adopted by the entire community to be effective. However, if new technologies are created and implemented server-side by Web developers, the burden of adopting new assistive technology will not be placed on the millions of existing screen-reader users.

While prior research into help systems and tutorials is rich and provides a strong foundation for future work, existing solutions do not take into account the unique needs and challenges of visually-impaired individuals. Research into tutorials and help systems [7, 19, 21, 22] has explored multimodal interfaces [16], behavior modeling [32], and intelligent help systems [1, 12, 27]. Many solutions have been created utilizing hypertext to provide easy access to help [11, 20]. Though some work has been done on web based help systems [8, 28], it has largely been based in the visual domain (images and Macromedia Flash [24]). Existing tutorials and help systems use video, PDF, Flash, and HTML, while relying heavily on pictures and animation. For VIUs, these modalities are inaccessible. The existing literature has not suitably addressed methods for embedded tutorials in Web 2.0 applications or targeted tutorial techniques for blind users.

The standard form of instruction for VIUs is a separate HTML page containing a tutorial (and discovering the location of said tutorial is not always easy). Most HTML tutorials are not screen-reader friendly, lacking appropriate HTML headings for easy navigation and poor description of how to access/find content with a screen reader. In addition, these tutorials lack context for the content and require frequent switching between windows, often causing users to loose their "place" in both the tutorial and application as they switch between the two windows.

With the advent of dynamic-asynchronous loading in 1999 [31], methods for users to interact with Web pages drastically changed from the world of static HTML. Dynamic Web pages, commonly referred to as Web 2.0 applications [15], often use AJAX to enable content to dynamically change without a page reloading. As a result, these Web applications function like a standard desktop application: the browser acts as a platform on which these new applications run. This facilitates dynamic content without page reloads and additional functionality such as application-based hot keys. Consider a Web e-mail application where a user uses the "c" key to compose an email or the "j" and "k" keys to cycle through the list of emails. Without JavaScript, this functionality would only be available via mouse interactions and not via hot-keys.

Though AJAX provides useful features, Web 2.0 applications add complexity to screen–reader users. Consider functionality in Appendix A, illustrating a JAWS screen-reader interacting with Web pages. A typical screen-reader user operates in two modes: *Forms Mode* (used for text input) and *Virtual Cursor Mode (VCM)* (for page navigation and reading). Interaction is conceptually segregated into these two modalities, making a natural division so users know when to switch modes.

Web 2.0 functionality (check marks in Appendix A) forces users to shift their interaction with the Web application to a third mode, *PC Cursor Mode (PCM),* to use Web-application specific keyboard commands. *PCM* stops JAWS from capturing keystrokes and allows the user to invoke application-specific hot keys. However, *PCM* is not familiar to the typical screen-reader user. This shift in the way the screen reader is operated is needed so that Web applications can capture user keyboard input (normally intercepted by JAWS for screen-reader functionality). Unfortunately *PCM*, also lacks audio feedback for users (see Appendix A).

For VIUs, Web 2.0 applications not only pose the common challenge of learning a new application, but also a burden in requiring new screen-reader interactions. VIUs must overcome both hurdles simultaneously. Thus, a Web-based tutorial system, designed for VIUs' needs, is critical for accessibility of ubiquitous Web Applications.

4 Interviews with Visually Impaired Users

There are many guides for creating tutorials on the desktop [7, 19, 21, 22] and for the Web [8, 28], but less is known about how VIUs approach computer usage and their concerns with adopting new software. To gain further insight, we conducted five 2-hour interviews with members of the visually impaired community. Participants were all screen-reader users from Silicon Valley (remunerated $75/hour). We attempted to recruit a representative user pool, individuals whose primary profession was not high technology. Each interview focused on participant's computer usage specifically, file organization, application management, and inter-personal communication.

Interviews were transcribed and video taped. All five participants reported large effort required to adopt new applications. However, each participant talked about new software adoption from a different perspective. One spoke about waiting to take a class to learn new software, while another said that she needed to wait for a large amount of time to be available to learn a new piece of software due to trial and error. Another individual wished to see a "guardian angel" that would show him around his programs and answer his questions. Participant issues revolved around the screen reader world-view that comes from memorization of key commands and Web page/application layout.

From our observations, we concluded that an accessible Web-based tutorial and help system would improve Web application adoption (akin to the findings of [23]). An examination of the existing practices of sighted users, detailed analysis of AJAX/screen-reader technologies, and comments from interviewees lead us to a proposed set of 4 key requirements that such a system should have:

- **Embedded Content** - Because layout and context is critical to users, any help system should provide its content in the context of the target application to reduce chances of losing position from window switching.
- **Interactive and Dynamic Content** - Users should be able to quickly gain access to and change their tutorial/help system content while in their application, thus reducing trial-and-error by allowing topic lookup as an easy alternative. *Note: while the concept of dynamic content is not new* [9], *the application to a non-visual domain is novel.*
- **Audio Based Content** - Because users rely entirely on audio cues, developers should ensure that content is presented in such a way to be fully understood through audio only and existing screen readers.

- **Mitigate AJAX** - Due to the complications created by screen reader interaction with Web 2.0 applications, tutorial systems must address this new complexity (for their own interaction model and the model of the target application).

5 DTorial and Incremental Design/Evaluation

In response to the complexity of learning new applications and the elaborate Web 2.0 + screen reader interaction techniques, we developed an initial design for embedded Web-based help systems for VIUs. In order to develop and evaluate our design, we built the DTorial system. By evaluating, testing and incrementally improving DTorial, we are able to analyze user behavior, reaction, and resulting design changes to create a higher-level interaction model.

5.1 DTorial

The DTorial system is a fully functional embedded tutorial, built using JavaScript. We used Grease Monkey to implement DTorial on top of Google's Web 2.0 Gmail, chosen because email is ubiquitous and is crucial to most individuals. Participants in our initial interviews said that email is empowering and central to their communications at work and at home. We used a set of JavaScript libraries called AxsJAX [10] to facilitate audio feedback and audio alerts.

DTorial works by moving a user around a Web page while simultaneously providing the user with audio feedback and describing the new content, what to expect, and how to interact. In other words, DTorial teaches the user how to interact with the computer while using the tool they are learning. As a result, the user is easily able to apply the skills learned without switching environments.

For example, consider a fictional VIU, Alice. When Alice wishes to understand the concept of the *Folders List* in Gmail (Inbox, Drafts, etc), she locates the *Drop Down List* on Gmail's webpage entitled "Tutorials." Alice selects the tutorial entitled "Folders" and then presses the *Go Button* to launch her content. The web browser's focus is automatically moved, via JavaScript, from her current element (e.g. *Go Button*) to the *Folder List* in Gmail. Simultaneously, tutorial text explaining *Folders* is injected into the DOM, at the top of the *Folder list*, within the now focused region. While having no visual impact to the layout of the page (using CSS markup), screen reader users like Alice can now access the entire body of injected text, including navigation by headings, lists, and other HTML elements. Alice can immediately explore the tutorial and test out her new knowledge without having to leave the instructional guide, because the guide AND environment, are side-by-side. DTorial further blurs the line between instruction and execution by ensuring a mechanism for re-reading the instructions at any time. It should be noted that the method for injecting text and re-reading content evolved through the incremental design process, and this example is representative of the final iteration of the DTorial system.

5.2 Incremental Design and Evaluation Methodology

In order to test learning via DTorial, we compared it against the standard form of instruction for VIUs, separate HTML web pages containing a tutorial. While most

HTML online tutorials are not screen-reader friendly, we eliminated bias towards DTorial by ensured that the HTML tutorial had marked headers, no references to video or images, and provided the same content as the interactive counterpart.

We followed a rapid cycle of evaluation and redesign. Visually impaired subjects were recruited from centers and organizations for the visually impaired in California's Silicon Valley and San Francisco. See Table 1 for demographics. Though we recruited 20 users, 17 individuals participated (eight men and nine women). Two were determined to be ineligible for the study when it was discovered that they were not visually impaired. One was removed from the study due to technical difficulties that arose during the session. A typical session with one subject lasted for one-and-a-half hours. Subjects were remunerated ($75/hour). Participants had no prior experience with Gmail, though some had accounts that were forwarded to desktop email clients.

Tutorial text was based on Gmail's Getting Started guide. We limited Gmail's feature set to Compose Mail, Inbox, Drafts, Spam, Trash, and Message Threads so we could focus on the tutorial and the learning experience. Because Web 2.0 applications require users to be in *PCM* when using hot-keys, we added audio feedback via AxsJAX, to increase accessibility (e.g., so that audio-based alerts were spoken when pages changed and updated).

During a session, a participant was exposed to each tutorial for approximately 30 minutes. The participant was instructed to "do as you normally would, as if trying this out for the first time on your own and as if we were not here." During a session with the HTML tutorial, a participant was provided with two windows, one pointing to Gmail and the other to the tutorial. After an exposure, each participant was asked a series of questions focusing on usability of the tutorial, accessibility of the tutorial content, how much the participant had learned about using the application, and methods for improvement. Following exposure to both tutorials, a series of questions were asked comparing the two methods. Participants were asked to indicate and justify a preference between the two tutorials.

The order of exposure was randomized to overcome learning effects. Overall, eight participants were shown DTorial as the first exposure, and nine were shown the HTML version as the first exposure. DTorial went through five iterations, and averaged four participants per cycle. Table 1 summarizes user demographics, experience, and conditions. DTorial went through five major design and evaluation cycles. Each cycle had 3-4 users. Revisions after each cycle were based directly upon user feedback and researcher observation.

Table 1. Demographic in Iterative Usability Study

Number of Users	17		
Mean Age	40 years		
Number of Users Per Age Group	20-29 (4)	30-39 (2)	40-49 (4)
	50-59 (3)	60-69 (4)	
Computer Experience (years)	1.5-23 Average 12.1 years		
JAWS Experience (years)	1.5-16 Average of 10.5 years		
Number of Users Exposed to DTorial First	8		
Number of Users Exposed to HTML Tutorial First	9		

6 Findings from Design and Evaluation Cycle

From the incremental design and evaluation with 17 real world users, we analyzed the behavior and design changes of DTorial and created a high-level interaction model. This set of design requirements is based on the results from our users and our iterative design and evaluation cycle.

At the conclusion of 17 studies, most participants were extremely positive about the prospect of using DTorial for their day-to-day learning. Through the design cycle, we noticed a distinctive shift in comments from users. Originally, feedback focused on the difficulty in switching modes and the complexity of Web 2.0 applications. At the conclusion of our studies, feedback was primarily about phrasing of the content, what topics to discuss, and adding additional functionality for a more robust user experience. Overall, 12 of our users wanted to use DTorial in their learning process. Out of the 5 who did not, all but one used the earliest versions of our software, without the benefits of our incremental improvements. Moreover, their concerns were addressed in iterative process of designing DTorial benefiting the later participants. One participant who teaches other VIUs said the following about DTorial:

> *This [interactive tutorial] is a very smoothly integrated environment for learning and getting your task accomplish... I think they are both good, but I think the learning curve will be a little bit more [steep] in [the HTML tutorial]. – P7*

The remainder of this section, we will focus on what Web 2.0 designers can do to help incorporate tutorials into their applications.

6.1 User Found 3 Modes of Interaction Confusing

The first requirement is based upon users' aggravation with the complexity of Gmail when using a screen reader: not all functionality was evenly distributed between the three Screen Reader modes. In Appendix A, we notice that users can **always** read in *VCM* and can control the Web application in **both** *VCM* and *PCM*. To control some features of Gmail, a mode switch was required (e.g., using a hot-key), while others times, mode switches were optional (e.g., accessing a check box). One user characterized this complexity by saying:

> *You have [the Virtual Cursor] off to read, and off to perform some of the keyboard commands, and you have other commands that you have to use when the virtual cursor is on, and then you have to remember that you have to have the virtual cursor on to turn forms mode on, which confused me a couple of times... it just seems to be a lot of steps. - PP1*

Because users relied on memory to recall hot keys and link locations, they were unable to remember every mechanism for content access, relying on a smattering of recalled access methods across the different modes.

> **RECOMMENDATION:**
> **Enable Interaction Based Modes (Reading & Control Mode)**

Due to the interaction limitations imposed upon screen-reader users when using Web 2.0 applications, user interaction must be simplified to easily categorized modes of interaction, to reduce user recall burden. To this end, we made a sharp division between control commands and reading commands to eliminate the mixing of metaphors (Appendix B). During the tutorial, we dubbed *PCM* as **Control Mode** and *VCM* as **Reading Mode** [17]. Navigation of Gmail was relegated to hot keys accessed in Control Mode. Though there may be multiple ways to achieve a goal (both with hot keys and by clicking links), tutorials (and applications) should clearly differentiate between reading (both tutorial and emails) and interacting with the application.

While audio feedback was limited in **Control Mode**, AxsJAX was used to provide audio feedback. Appendix B illustrates this modal breakdown. We ensured that all information and controls presented to users fit in one of two discrete modes. As the user becomes advanced, lines between the modes can be blurred. However, for novice Web 2.0 users, ensuring a clear distinction is essential. It will make the difference between the application seeming Accessible and Inaccessible.

6.2 Users wanted Non Linear Access to Content

Providing an easy mechanism for the user to navigate content by topic before reading is essential. If the user is presented with a long list of topics and their content (as in HTML tutorials), he can be overwhelmed and inclined to skim through rather than focus on learning specific details. One user summarized why she liked DTorial better:

> *If you got [the HTML tutorial] in one window and you are reading, you tend to zone out and read-read-read, and then you go back to the other window to try it out and say 'now what did I just read?'... I just read it and I forgot it! - PP12*

Initially, DTorial had users moved from topic to topic via hotkey (move forward, back, and repeat), forcing them to iterate over all topics in turn. However, this resulted in the same difficulty as iterating over the long HTML tutorial.

> **RECOMMENDATION:**
> **Facilitate Random Access to Tutorial Content via Quick Access Technique (e.g. Search, Drop Down List) within Application**

In a later iteration, DTorial avoided the nonlinear content access difficulty through a combo-box mechanism. Users could quickly iterate over possible tutorial topics, and from that list, select the instructional segment they wish to explore. This resulted in one of the most successful aspect of DTorial, the ability to quickly select and learn one specific aspect of a program via tutorial. The random content access system can be further enhanced through tutorial searching. Designers must remember that "finding" is universal. Blind or sighted, users want to find an answer to a specific question. Allowing random access to content ensure a quick resolution.

6.3 Users Felt That They Did Not Know What Was Occurring and Were Not in Control of Navigation

In an AJAX application where pages change dynamically without page reloads, the screen-reader user relies upon the application to notify him when content changes.

Though this is critical for Web 2.0 application design, it also influences the design of tutorials. For example, early in the DTorial design cycles, all tutorial content was injected directly to the screen reader. However, when text was injected in this manner, users were unable to reread in their traditional manner; reading by paragraph, sentence, or even words. One user stated that:

> *I didn't have to read a whole section at a time, I could go back through an read word by word, line by line... - PP1*

Lack of notifications when content changed, and the inability to read at one's own pace, caused considerable distress and made users feel like the "were not in control."

> **RECOMMENDATION:**
> **Always Keep Users Informed and in Control With Feedback**

Tutorials and Web 2.0 applications can address this problem though a solution like AxsJAX and inject content to be read when dynamic changes are made to the DOM. Further, when the screen-reader user wants to jump to a chapter, he must be able to select the new topic, and be notified that he is at a new location on the page. In addition, content in the tutorial must be book-ended, with both a header up front and a textual warning at the end that he is leaving the tutorial and returning to the Web application. This allows him to easily find the content again, and alerts him when he is leaving the tutorial information and reentering the application.

In the above example relating to DTorial content, we modified the system to inject tutorial text directly into the DOM, so that browsers treated it as actual page text, permitting users to read the tutorial content in the same manner as they read other web pages (whole text, line-by-line, and/or word-by-word). The text was inserted directly above the topic of discussion (e.g., the chapter on folders would be injected just before the folder list). As users moved from chapter to chapter, the old tutorial text would be removed and new text would be added. Yet as long as the user was in one section/chapter/topic of the tutorial, the content remained for reference at any point, so users could try out what they learned along the way. We further demonstrated that the text could be hidden with CSS and still be accessed by screen readers, thus making the tutorial only visible to a screen reader user.

6.4 Users Requested Both Upfront Tutorial and Embedded Help System

At the conclusion of our user studies many participants liked DTorial. However most requested an up-front tutorial document in HTML to give an overview of many or most of the topics. Getting a good all-in-one-read tour is necessary before exploring. The following quote illustrates why presenting a mental map of page content upfront is so important to users:

> *One key component of learning for a visually impaired person is orientation; I like to know where I am in the big picture* - PP4

However, an HTML tutorial alone still presents many of the difficulties experienced with the current state of online help systems.

> **RECOMMENDATION:**
> **Provide Tutorials with Embedded Quick Help**

Users explicitly requested a system design with both an upfront HTML tutorial (as a getting started guide) with embedded quick help system (that is accessable within the web application via search, list, or dropdown menu). Having a quick in-line reference like DTorial is a complement to facilitate trial and error, experimentation, quickly learning how to execute new functions, or get refreshers on forgotten features without leaving the application. One individual described having both systems as:

> *It would be the Cadillac, you would give me both of these... give it all to me and charge me not extra for it. – P4*

Another user described how having DTorial as a persistent element of the interface can provide constant support:

> *It seems like the fact that you have gotten rid of the complexity of having to change windows to do anything. I think the other thing is that this type of setup you could leave around, even if you, as you got more familiar with it, since it has the hide tutorial option, and if you did forget something... So basically, it seems that if you did temporary forget something, or want to go back look up a function that you didn't quite remember or didn't use often. The fact that you had that there would be really helpful – P17*

6.5 Users Complain about Readability

Since VIUs cannot skim a page visually, screen reader users are dependent on features in a screen reader to help them navigate the page to the textual content. Users must either listen to all the content in order, or use methods to stop and skip around on the page. One user specifically stated that:

> *The less irrelevant information the better... The less information, as long as you're deleting irrelevant information, I think it is better [or a JAWS user]*

Because listening is slower than reading, verbose language slows reading down, and if rushed, may skip sections not realizing where the vital material is located.

> **RECOMMENDATION:**
> **Facilitate Methods of Reading Content through Screen Readers**

Though often overlooked, following well-accepted accessibility practices when creating content is critical (e.g., bulleted lists that are clear, concise, terse, and to the point). For the visually impaired community, markers (such as headings and bullets) not only serve as demarcation between content and sections, but also facilitate aural skimming of content. Therefore, textual content should be well marked and language should be task based, in step-by-step format, simple, concise, and to the point to facilitate screen reader scanning.

7 Sighted Users and Future Work

We propose two main thrusts for future research to continue to explore this metaphor of the interactive tutorial. First, a system like DTorial should be tested in a full-scale system and deployed to numerous individuals. Testing the scalability and usability over a longer term will help validate this design in day-to-day scenarios.

Following the completion of the design cycle, we speculated on how a similar model on interactive tutorial could be applied to the sighted community. This form of DTorial would function by highlighting and enlarging the selected area, while providing an overlay of tutorial content for the user (Appendix C). This would provide the same functionality for the sighted user as for the screen-reader user, but in the modality that is most applicable. We created both an interactive prototype and a static visual mock-up of such a system. We took our design to the cafeteria of a large Silicon Valley, CA. company and asked both technical and non-technical employees their opinion was of such a model. Though many mentioned that they would like to have search capabilities and a version with all the content in one place (like the user of a screen reader), 100% of the 15 individuals asked felt this would be a "fantastic" solution. "Great idea, love it!" Others specifically mentioned that "[this tutorial] would be great for my parents." We encourage additional work to test the DTorial model for the sighted user and to examine how lessons learned from web accessibility can help all individuals learn to use new and complex web applications.

8 Conclusions

Equal accessibility for all users is a critical part in software design and deployment. With the advent of Web 2.0 technology, visually impaired individuals are forced to use their computer in new ways. One user described this paradigm shift as:

> *Driving on the opposite side in Europe. Because every time they go into this program they are going to have to junk everything that is in their head... - P10*

Because there is such a burden on these users for adopting new technology, it is incumbent upon us as researchers to explore new techniques and technologies to help educate and inform users on how to use new software and the changing Internet.

This paper presents a new interaction model and its demonstration, called DTorial. Unlike traditional tutorials that rely on images and video (inaccessible to VIUs), DTorial is an interactive guide to a Web 2.0 application. DTorial was iterated upon through five rounds of evaluation and redesign, with a total of 17 VIUs. Not only were VIUs excited by our design, but there are interesting applications to the sighted community as well.

Using the framework outlined by DTorial, we believe that Web 2.0 applications can move from inaccessible obstacles to the visually impaired user, to just another application to accomplish their goals. Our design cycle with visually impaired users, indicate the potential effectiveness of DTorial and our model for teaching screen-reader users new web applications.

Acknowledgements

We would like to thank all of our participants, Sensory Access Foundation, VISTA Center for the Blind, and Lighthouse for the Blind.

References

[1] Aaronson, A., Carroll, J.M.: Intelligent help in a one-shot dialog: a protocol study. In: Proceedings of the ACM SIGCHI Bulletin, Toronto, Ontario, Canada. ACM, New York (1987)

[2] American Foundation for the Blind. Braille, http://www.afb.org/Section.asp?SectionID=6 (Accessed, 2008)

[3] American Foundation for the Blind. Facts and Figures on Americans with Vision Loss, http://www.afb.org/Section.asp?SectionID=15&DocumentID=4398 (Accessed)

[4] Becker, J.V., Becker, D.A., Hinton, D.E., Anderson, H.G.: J. Braille computer monitor(6700553). Unites States Patent Office, USA (2004)

[5] Bigham, J.P., Ladner, R.E.: Accessmonkey: a collaborative scripting framework for web users and developers. In: Proceedings of the W4A 2007, Banff, Canada. ACM, New York (2007)

[6] Caldwell, B., Cooper, M., Guarino-Reid, L., Vanderheiden, G.: Web Content Accessibility Guidelines 2.0 (2008)

[7] Carroll, J.M., McKendree, J.: Interface design issues for advice-giving expert systems. Commun. ACM 30(1), 14–32 (1987)

[8] Chamberland, L.: Componentization of HTML-based online help. In: Proceedings of the International conference on Computer documentation, New Orleans, Louisiana, United States. ACM, New York (1999)

[9] Chang, B., Mackinlay, J., Zellweger, P., Igarashi, T.: A negotiation architecture for fluid documents. In: Proceedings of the UIST 1998, San Francisco, CA. ACM, New York (1998)

[10] Chen, C.L., Raman, T.V.: AxsJAX: a talking translation bot using google IM: bringing web-2.0 applications to life. In: Proceedings of the W4A, Beijing, China. ACM, New York (2008)

[11] Comeau, J.-M., Milton, P.R.: A window-based help, tutorial and documentation system. In: Proceedings of SIGDOC, Waterloo, Ontario, Canada. ACM, New York (1993)

[12] Fischer, G., Lemke, A., Schwab, T.: Knowledge-based help systems. In: Proceedings of CHI 1985, San Francisco, California, United States, ACM, New York (1985)

[13] Freedom Scientific. JAWS for Windows ® Screen Reading Software, http://www.freedomscientific.com/products/fs/jaws-product-page.asp (Accessed)

[14] Fukuda, K., Saito, S., Takagi, H., Asakawa, C.: Proposing new metrics to evaluate web usability for the blind. In: Proceedings of CHI 2005, Portland, OR. ACM, New York (2005)

[15] Garrett, J.J.: Ajax: A New Approach to Web Applications. adaptive path, February 18 (2005), http://www.adaptivepath.com/ideas/essays/archives/000385.php

[16] Greyling, J.H., Calitz, A.P.: The development of a computerised multimedia tutorial system for a diverse student population. In: Proceedings of AFRIGRAPH, Cape Town, South Africa. ACM, New York (2003)

[17] Hailpern, J., Guarino Reid, L., Boardman, R., Annam, S.: WEB 2.0: Blind to an Accessible New World. In: Proceedings of the WWW 2009, Madrid, Spain. ACM, New York (2009)

[18] Harkin, T.: Americans With Disabilities Act of 1990. U.S. Senate (1990)

[19] Houghton, R.C.: Online help systems: a conspectus. Commun. ACM 27(2), 126–133 (1984)
[20] Kantner, L., Rusinsky, L.: Designing a WinHelp project for quick conversion to lowest-common-denominator HTML-based help: a case study. In: Proceedings of SIGDOC, Quebec, Canada. ACM, New York (1998)
[21] Kearsley, G.: Online help systems: design and implementation. Ablex Publishing Corp., Greenwich (1988)
[22] Kearsley, G., Campbell, R.L., Elkerton, J., Judd, W., Walker, J.: Online help systems: design and implementation issues (panel). In: Proceedings of CHI 1988, Washington, D.C., United States, ACM, New York (1988)
[23] Landram, F.G.: Computer tutorials for introductory statistics. In: Proceedings of CCSC 2001, Branson, Missouri, United States. Consortium for Computing Sciences in Colleges (2001)
[24] Lee, K., Lee, D.H.: An online help framework for web applications. In: Proceedings of the International Conference on Design of Communication, El Paso, Texas, USA. ACM, New York (2007)
[25] McKeon, H.P.: The Rehabilitation Act Amendments (Section 508). U.S. Congress (1998)
[26] Miyashita, H., Sato, D., Takagi, H., Asakawa, C.: Making multimedia content accessible for screen reader users. In: Proceedings of the W4A 2007, Banff, Canada. ACM, New York (2007)
[27] Patrick, A., McGurgan, A.: One proven methodology for designing robust online help systems. In: Proceedings of the International conference on Systems documentation, Waterloo, Ontario, Canada. ACM, New York (1993)
[28] Rintjema, L., Warburton, K.: Creating an HTML help system for web-based products. In: Proceedings of SIGDOC, Quebec, Canada. ACM, New York (1998)
[29] Takagi, H., Asakawa, C., Fukuda, K., Maeda, J.: Accessibility designer: visualizing usability for the blind. In: Proceedings of the SIGACCESS 2004, Atlanta, GA, USA. ACM, New York (2004)
[30] Thatcher, J.: Screen reader/2: access to OS/2 and the graphical user interface. In: Proceedings of the Assets 1994, Marina Del Rey, CA. ACM, New York (1994)
[31] W3C. HTML 4.01 Specification - IFRAME (2008), `http://www.w3.org/TR/html4/present/frames.html#h-16.5` (Accessed, August 2008)
[32] Willis, M.: Building effective help systems: modelling human help seeking behaviour. In: Proceedings of the CHISIG of Australia 2006, Sydney, Australia. ACM, New York (2006)
[33] World Health Organization. WHO | Magnitude and causes of visual impairment (2008), `http://www.who.int/mediacentre/factsheets/fs282/en/` (Accessed, August 2008)

Appendix

Appendix A:
A breakdown of user functionality associated with providing technology and the Screen Reader Mode. Non-shaded region is tradition web browsing/computer usage. Shaded area is Web Application interaction.

Features	Virtual Cursor Mode	Forms Mode	PC Cursor Mode
Access Check Boxes	●	●	●
Navigate by TAB key	●	●	●
Access to Buttons	●	●	●
Execute Links	●	●	●
Read & Re-read Text *	●	●	
Access Combo Boxes	●	●	
Text Input		●	
JAWS Find	●		
Navigate by Element Type	●		
Navigate by Arrow Keys	●		
Navigate using Headings	●		
Navigate by page links	●		
Easy Tables Navigation	●		
JAWS Goto Line	●		
Read bold, italics, etc.	●		
Web Application Hot Keys **			✓
JavaScript caused Text input			✓
Move Focus via JavaScript			✓
JavaScript changes DOM ***			✓
Utilize JavaScript State			✓
Generate spoken text ****			✗

● JAWS Web Browsing ✓ Web 2.0 Features ✗ AxsJAX Features

* in forms mode, only re-read text in edit areas
** *Virtual Cursor Off* prevents conflict with Screen Reader Keys
*** without audio feedback
**** cannot go word-by-word or line by line

Appendix B:
Screen Reader modality and features associated with Control and Reading Mode metaphor. Shaded area represents features used to access tutorial content.

Features	Reading Mode	Control Mode
Access Check Boxes	●	
Navigate by TAB key	●	
Access to Buttons	●	
Execute Links	●	
Read & Re-read Text *	●	
Access Combo Boxes	●	
Text Input	✓	
JAWS Find	●	
Navigate by Element Type	●	
Navigate by Arrow Keys	●	
Navigate using Headings	●	
Navigate by page links	●	
Easy Tables Navigation	●	
JAWS Goto Line	●	
Read bold, italics, etc	●	
Web Application Hot Keys **		✗
JavaScript caused Text Input		✗
Move Focus via JavaScript		✗
JavaScript changes DOM ***		✗
Utilize JavaScript State		✗
Generate spoken text ****		✗

● Virtual Cursor Mode ✓ Forms Mode ✗ PC Cursor Mode

* in forms mode, only re-read text in edit areas
** *Virtual Cursor Off* prevents conflict with Screen Reader Keys
*** without audio feedback
**** cannot go word-by-word or line by line

Appendix C:
Mockup of DTorial in a visual domain. Notice how the folder list has been highlighted, and expanded in size, while the call out presents the tutorial's textual content.

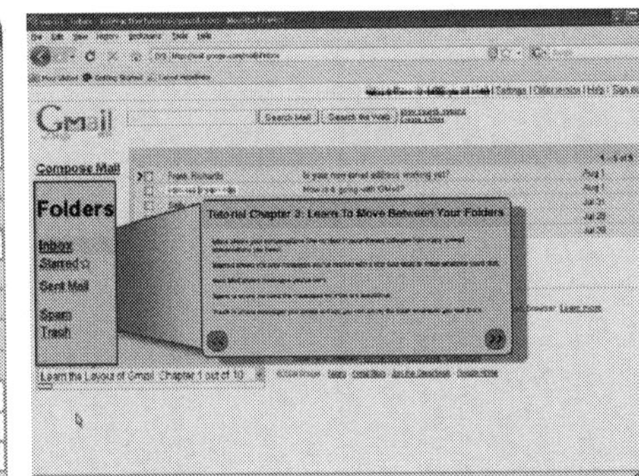

The Attentive Hearing Aid: Eye Selection of Auditory Sources for Hearing Impaired Users

Jamie Hart, Dumitru Onceanu, Changuk Sohn, Doug Wightman, and Roel Vertegaal

Human Media Lab
Queen's University
Kingston, Ontario
Canada K7L 3N6

Abstract. An often-heard complaint about hearing aids is that their amplification of environmental noise makes it difficult for users to focus on one particular speaker. In this paper, we present a new prototype Attentive Hearing Aid (AHA) based on ViewPointer, a wearable calibration-free eye tracker. With AHA, users need only look at the person they are listening to, to amplify that voice in their hearing aid. We present a preliminary evaluation of the use of eye input by hearing impaired users for switching between simultaneous speakers. We compared eye input with manual source selection through pointing and remote control buttons. Results show eye input was 73% faster than selection by pointing and 58% faster than button selection. In terms of recall of the material presented, eye input performed 80% better than traditional hearing aids, 54% better than buttons, and 37% better than pointing. Participants rated eye input as highest in the "easiest", "most natural", and "best overall" categories.

Keywords: Eye Tracking, Attentive User Interface, Assistive Technology, Hearing Impairment, Input Devices, Multi-Modal Input.

1 Introduction

The most common reason cited by hearing impaired individuals for rejecting the use of a hearing aid is intolerance of the large amount of background noise associated with such devices [14]. Traditional hearing aids amplify all sounds in the user's environment, whether the user is interested in them or not [5]. The problem of unwanted background noise has been shown to result in the avoidance of social situations, as well as negative physiological and psychological behavioral changes in users [15]. Over 80% of potential hearing aid wearers opt out of using a hearing aid altogether, reporting this as their chief reason [14]. Our Attentive Hearing Aid project hopes to address this problem by allowing users to target only the voices they wish to listen to, while attenuating background noise.

The technology behind AHA is based on ViewPointer calibration-free eye tracking [28]. It features a small wearable camera pointed at the eyes, which senses when users are looking at one of several infrared tags. These tags are mounted on lapel microphones that are handed out and worn by interlocutors during a conversation. It is

T. Gross et al. (Eds.): INTERACT 2009, Part I, LNCS 5726, pp. 19–35, 2009.

our hope that the ability to focus on individual speakers and sound sources allows AHA wearers to enjoy a better quality of life than they would with a traditional hearing aid.

Other directional hearing aid technologies exist, such as the Phonak Directional Hearing Aid [22], that help users direct their hearing towards one particular speaker in multiparty conversations. These technologies typically rely on a directional microphone mounted on the hearing aid, that is pointed toward the sound source via head orientation. While it has been shown to improve intelligibility of speech in simulated room conditions, benefits of directional hearing aids are limited, with one study quoting improvements in speech intelligibility of only about 20% over omni-directional aids [22]. The reason for this is that like omni-directional aids, directional hearing aids are not equipped to cut out extraneous environmental noise sources entirely. Instead, AHA switches microphone sources directly, allowing full control over potential sources in or outside of (visual) attention.

We designed a preliminary study into the performance of AHA as a mechanism for switching, rather than as a specific embodiment of any particular hearing aid technology. We did not include head orientation in our original study for several reasons. Multiple studies have confirmed that eye movements precede head movements when targets are not predictable by time and location [3]. The real world use cases and study addressed by this paper feature target selection that is not predictable by time and location. Head orientation is also known to be inaccurate in target selection tasks [19], users tend not to move their heads when visual targets are within 15 degrees of one another [7], and head orientation relies on neck muscles that are known to be some of the slowest in the human body [16]. The discussion section of this paper describes a subsequent study that further addresses head orientation input. In this study, we focused on comparing eye input with the switching of auditory sources via manual pointing, as well as with the kind of manual switches widely available in hearing aid controls. Performance of these manual input devices is known to be superior to that of head orientation, and we expected eye input to be superior to these manual inputs. The paper is structured as follows. First, we discuss existing literature on hearing impairment and on eye-based selection, after which we describe our prototype AHA. We then discuss our preliminary evaluation. We conclude by discussing possible implications of this technology for both hearing-impaired and normal hearing individuals.

2 Hearing Impairment

A recent survey [14] estimated that there are 31.5 million Americans with some form of hearing impairment, equaling about eight percent of the population. By 2050, it is estimated that about 50 million Americans will suffer from hearing loss [14]. Financially speaking, untreated hearing impairments cost the U.S. economy roughly $56 billion dollars: by way of medical care, lost productivity and special education and training [20].

2.1 Hearing Aids

A hearing aid is defined as “a compact electronic amplifier worn to improve one’s hearing, usually placed in or behind the ear” [12]. Hearing aids work by amplifying (and sometimes altering) sounds in the environment in order to compensate for the malfunctioning anatomy in the ear itself. Although there are several different styles of hearing aids on the market, most devices have the same four basic components [12]:

- A microphone that receives sounds in the environment and converts the sound into an electrical signal;
- An amplifier that makes the signal louder;
- A speaker that outputs the amplified signal into the ear;
- A small battery that powers the electrical parts of the hearing aid.

Research has shown that the use of hearing instruments dramatically improves the quality of life for hearing-impaired individuals. A survey of more than two thousand hearing impaired people found that hearing instrument users were more socially active, more emotionally stable, and both physically and emotionally healthier than non-users with a hearing loss [15]. A particularly disturbing reality is the fact that only one in five people who could benefit from a hearing aid actually wears one [14]. This begs the question: Why do so few hearing-impaired people take advantage of this technology?

2.2 Background Noise

One important reason is the inherent problem of standard hearing aids: they amplify everything in the environment, from useful sounds (voices, televisions, radios) to irrelevant sounds (background chatter, air conditioners). Although it is not entirely clear why, most hearing aids do not appear to allow users to separate the sounds that they want to focus on from unwanted sounds in the environment. Research has shown that the presence of background noise negatively affects people in terms of attention tasks, recognition, reaction time, and verbal memory [26], as well as blood pressure, heart rate, skin temperature, and hormone release [17]. Currently, there are three main ways of reducing background noise in commercial hearing aids:

• **Personal FM Systems.** Personal FM systems consist of a portable microphone that is placed near the person who is speaking, and an FM receiver worn by the hearing-impaired individual [10]. The microphone broadcasts a signal on a special frequency, which is picked up by the receiver. The receiver can either connect to the hearing aid via an induction loop, or can be used with a headset. These systems are very useful in settings where there is just one sound source; for example classrooms, churches, and cinemas. However, there may be issues with interference when multiple FM systems are used in the same location, and it can be difficult to select between multiple sources.

• **Directional Hearing Aids.** Directional hearing aids function by comparing the input from microphones at two (or more) different locations on the hearing aid. By summing the sound signals received from the multiple microphones, sounds in front of the user are emphasized and sounds from the sides or rear of the user are reduced. Directional hearing aids work on the assumption that most desirable sounds will be in front of the user. Research has shown that speech understanding in noisy environments can be improved in this way [30]. However, when noise and signal are diffuse, these hearing aids perform no better than conventional hearing aids [21].

Researchers recently unveiled a pair of "hearing-glasses" [31] that work similarly, with a total of eight microphones embedded in the arms.

• **Digital Noise Reduction Hearing Aids.** Digital noise reduction hearing aids take advantage of the frequency of speech, rather than its direction. Human speech has a frequency range of approximately 200 to 8000 Hz, and the range for common sounds is even narrower. Hearing aids equipped with digital noise reduction work by reducing sounds that fall outside of the frequency range of speech. There are two cases when these systems break down: when the noise falls in the same frequency range as speech and when the noise itself is unwanted speech [20]. Since background speech is the most difficult type of noise for humans to filter out [18], this is a very serious issue.

3 Eye-Based Selection

A large body of research exists on the use of eye input for selection tasks, both on-screen as well as in the real world. As detailed in [6], there are many arguments for the use of eye gaze for focus selection in hearing aids:

- The use of eye movements requires very little conscious or physical effort [13].
- Eye gaze is used in human-human communication to indicate whom the next speaker should be [34], and correlates very well with whom a person is listening to [34]. Hearing aid users would likely already be looking at a speaker, for example, to gauge responses or perform lip reading.
- Eye input prevents overloading of the hands because the eyes form a parallel input channel. It does not require hearing aid users to hold a pointing device.
- Eye movements precede head movements when targets are not predictable by time and location [3].
- Eye movements are much faster than either hand or head movements [7, 8].

Eye input also has its issues. Eye trackers are still expensive, requiring calibrations and bulky head gear when used in mobile scenarios [7]. However, new portable calibration-free technologies such as ViewPointer [28] have become available that address many, if not all of these problems. The Midas Touch problem is often cited in literature [24]. In auditory focus selection, it is easily avoided by not allowing binary selection: Using subtle amplification of selected sources, attenuating other sources of audio, eye input mimics the attentive mechanisms of the brain. Eye contact is known to trigger the very attentional processes that allow focusing on conversations [34], making eye input a natural technique.

3.1 Alternative Approaches

There have been many systems built upon the premise of using head orientation as a source of audio selection; we highlight only a small selection of systems in this review. Eye-R [23] is a glasses-mounted device that stores and communicates information based on both eye movement and infrared (IR) LEDs positioned in the environment. Users wear an IR receiver, and a transmitter that broadcasts a unique IR code. The receiver allows the system to determine when the wearer's head is oriented towards another user or device in the environment.

The Visual Resonator [37] is a recent project designed to be a realization of the so-called "Cocktail Party Phenomenon" first described by Cherry [5], and defined as "the ability to focus one's listening attention on a single talker among a cacophony of conversations and background noise" [1]. Similar to [2], Visual Resonator is an auditory interface that allows the user to hear sound only from the direction that she is facing. The device consists of a pair of headphones with a microphone and an infrared transmitter and receiver mounted on top. Visual Resonator is direction-sensitive because both the transmitter and receiver are always oriented in the direction that the user is facing. Incoming signals are received by the IR receiver, and then sent to the headphones where they are translated into sound. Outgoing speech sound is recorded by the microphone, translated into an infrared signal, and then beamed into the environment.

Most of these systems do not track where the user is actually looking. Therefore, if the user's head was oriented towards Person A, but he was actually listening to Person B; the system would incorrectly infer that the user was listening to Person A. This problem can be addressed by selecting targets using eye rather than head movement.

3.2 Performance of Eye Input

There have been many studies on the use of eye tracking as an input device for targeting in human-computer interaction. Ware and Mikaelian [35] compared three eye pointing styles for selecting targets on a CRT: (1) dwell time click, where the target was selected if the observers' gaze fixated on it for more than .4 s; (2) screen button, where the observer had to fixate on a button on the screen after looking at the target; and (3) hardware button, where the observers pushed a keyboard button while fixating on the target. Results showed click times compared favorably to those of the mouse, with an intercept approximately twice as small. Wang et al. [36] discussed an evaluation of eye-based selection of Chinese characters for text entry. In their task, users chose one of 8 on-screen Chinese characters by looking at the character while pressing the space bar. Results showed eye-based selection was not significantly faster than traditional key-based selection. They attributed this to the fact that the overall time required to complete their task was dominated by decision time, rather than movement time.

Zhai et al. [38] evaluated the use of eye input in gaze assisted manual pointing. In their MAGIC pointing technique, an isometric joystick was used to select targets on a screen. However, to speed up isometric pointing, they positioned the cursor at a location close to the current eye fixation point whenever the user initiated movement with the joystick. MAGIC pointing only marginally improved movement time in a Fitt's Law task. Sibert and Jacob [24] evaluated the use of a mouse and eye tracker with dwell-time activated click in a pointing task that involved selecting one of 16 circles on a screen. They found that trial completion time with the eye tracker was almost half that of the mouse. EyeWindows [8] compared the use of hotkeys for selection of windows with that of the mouse and two eye input techniques. Results showed that on average, eye input was about twice as fast as manual techniques when hands were overloaded with a typing task. LookPoint [6] is a system that allows for hands-free switching of input devices between multiple screens or computers. A multi-screen typing task was used to evaluate a basic version of the system, comparing eye input with multiple keyboards, hotkeys, and mouse. Results showed that eye input was 111% faster than the mouse, 75% faster than function keys, and 37% faster than multiple keyboards. User satisfaction surveys generally show that participants prefer using the eye input techniques over manual conditions. However, eye input is often inaccurate, with a proneness to wrongful selection.

4 The Attentive Hearing Aid

Our prototype Attentive Hearing Aid (AHA) consists of a wearable infrared camera, which is pointed at the user's eye and connected to a wearable Sony U70 computer (see Figure 1). The user also wears one or two hearing aid ear piece(s), while interlocators wear a lapel microphone that is augmented with an infrared tag (see Figure 2). These lapel mikes broadcast to a portable lapel receiver/mixer and/or induction loop system that connects to the ear piece(s) of the AHA wearer. The wearable camera is based on ViewPointer, a calibration-free eye sensor [27, 28]. The U70 processes images from this sensor and determines whether the corneal reflection of an infrared light source, in this case the tag on the lapel mike, is central to the pupil. This works as long as the camera is within 45 degrees of the visual axis of the eye. For a detailed technical discussion of ViewPointer, please refer to [27, 28]. The battery-powered IR tags on the lapel microphone (see Figure 2) consist of a bank of LEDs triggered by a microcontroller programmed with a binary code that allows tags to be identified through computer vision. When an AHA wearer is looking at another person wearing a tagged lapel microphone, AHA can thus identify the sound source and select it for amplification. Note that microphones need not be lapel microphones, but can be Bluetooth headsets commonly worn by users.

Fig. 1. The camera headpiece

Fig. 2. Lapel mike with wireless infrared tag

4.1 Video Conferencing Applications

If one does not accept that the above hardware is sufficiently practical for use in day-to-day conversations, there are many other cocktail-party situations, such as multi-person video conferencing, where participants are expected to have a microphone, and are represented within the confines of a screen. Due to the novelty of the equipment, and the large potential for measurement artifacts in a real-world setting, we used such a video conferencing setting during our experimentation.

5 Preliminary User Study

Initial evaluation consisted of hearing-impaired participants selecting targets on a videoconferencing screen in four conditions: ViewPointer input, pointing with a Nintendo Wii remote, button selection with a Nintendo Wii remote, and a control condition that simulated the use of an omni-directional hearing aid. Please note that this evaluation was preliminary, and aimed at determining the fastest and least disruptive technique for switching between sound sources. The participants' task was to follow a story told by three recorded actors on the screen, simulating turn taking in a videoconference. Every ten seconds, a switch occurred, and participants were required to select a new speaker as a source. This was done to mimic natural turn taking behavior in conversations in a controlled setting. We measured the time taken for the participant to select the new target (switch time) as well as participants' recall of the material presented in the story. We chose recall because it is indicative not just of the intelligibility of speech in various conditions, but the actual ability to comprehend that speech. For example, we expected this measure, but not intelligibility, to be sensitive to the mental load caused by the switching mechanism.

5.1 Recall Passages

We created nine passages on topics such as environmental issues, strange animals, and famous women in history. The passages were carefully structured to contain seven target items for recall testing at the end of each trial. Recall was thus measured on a scale from 1 to 7 after each trial.

We used seven of the nine passages as "foreground" stories in our actual experimentation, with the other two stories being used to simulate background conversation and noise. For each of our seven foreground passages, we created a seven-item multiple-choice questionnaire in order to test the recall of the material presented in that particular trial.

5.2 Task

The participant's task was to simply listen to a specific story told by the actors. The actor currently telling the target story was indicated with a red dot below his window. Each trial began with the audio of the target actor already amplified (i.e., a volume of 100%). The other two actors also spoke simultaneously, but at a reduced volume (of 10%) to simulate background chatter. After 10 seconds, the target randomly switched and the red dot moved to the next actor telling the story. The participant then had to

Fig. 3. Training screen in the Buttons condition. The numbers were displayed during training so the participant could memorize the actor-number mapping. IR tags for the eyes condition are also visible as yellow circles right below the actors.

select this new actor. This switching procedure repeated every 10 seconds for the entire duration of the trial. After each trial, the participant was immediately presented with a multiple-choice recall test. Seven recall tests were graded afterwards, and the results used as the measure for our recall variable.

5.3 Conditions: Switching Techniques

We compared eye input with two manual selection techniques, and a control condition consisting of an omni-directional hearing aid. For each participant, we ran one trial of the Control condition; and two trials of each of three experimental conditions. Each participant completed the trials in random order.

- **Control.** In this condition, participants were unable to select which actor they wanted amplified. This essentially represented performance of the most common of hearing aids, the omni-directional hearing aid. For consistency, the red dot still moved from window to window, but the volume of all three actors remained at 100% for the entire duration of the trial.
- **Pointing.** In this condition, participants used a Nintendo Wii remote to point at the target actor.
- **Buttons.** Here, participants used the buttons labeled 1, 2, and 3 on the Wiimote to select the target actor. In a real-world environment, interlocutors would not necessarily stay in one place, thus limiting the usefulness of a location-based button mapping. Participants were asked to select the person instead. Participants were required to first memorize which button (1, 2, or 3) corresponded to which actor before each trial began. We trained participants on the randomized actor-number mapping for a full practice trial before each trial began. During the practice trial, the numbers were displayed on the screen below the actors' window (see Figure 3), and the participants were encouraged to practice switching in order to memorize the mapping. No numbers appeared during the trial, so that participants had to rely on memory. In order to negate learning effects between trials, we used two different mappings in both Button trials.

- **Eye Input.** In this condition, the user simply had to look at the actor whose audio they wanted amplified. The IR tags mounted on the screen registered looks, and the audio of the corresponding actor was amplified within 0.5 seconds.

The participants knew they had selected the correct target actor when the narrative continued correctly across voices. We avoided visual selection feedback as participants would not receive such confirmation in real life scenarios either. Instead, to avoid confusion caused by subjects not recognizing the voice of an actor, in all conditions, audible switches would only take place after the correct target was selected. Thus, participants were allowed to make erroneous selections, but erroneous selection would not allow them to follow the focus conversation.

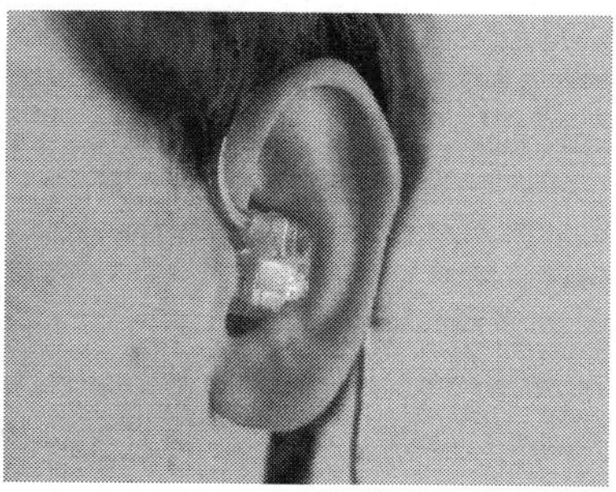

Fig. 4. Shure earpiece with foam insert

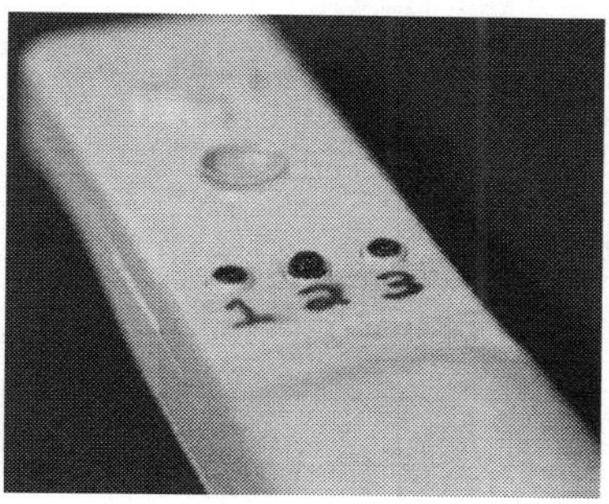

Fig. 5. Wii remote with modification and labeling

5.4 Participants and Experimental Design

We initially recruited 14 hearing-impaired individuals to participate in our preliminary evaluation. One volunteer had had three major eye surgeries, resulting in a large amount of scar tissue on his eyeball which caused inconsistent corneal tag reflections. Another was suffering from severe allergies and as a result, his eyes were watering profusely, again interfering with the corneal reflection. The third volunteer was hearing-impaired due to a deformity in her outer ear canal, so we were unable to successfully insert earphones. Our final participant group consisted of three males and eight females, ranging from age 13 to age 69 (average age of 48.5 years) (Please note that our subsequent significant findings indicated this sample size was in fact sufficiently large for an initial evaluation). We recruited participants with a wide range of hearing impairments, ranging from people with mild impairment who chose not to wear hearing aids on a daily basis, to people with profound hearing loss who cannot function without their hearing aids. We recruited participants who did not wear glasses, as the current ViewPointer form factor does not accommodate glasses. Each session took approximately one hour, and participants received $10 in compensation. A within-subjects design was employed, with the order of presentation randomized between participants.

5.5 Procedure

At the beginning of each session, the participants read and signed a Consent Form and filled out a questionnaire with details about their hearing impairment. Afterwards, the experimenter explained the procedure, and fitted the participant with sound-isolating earphones. Since hearing impairment varies immensely between individuals, participants first performed a short audio calibration task that we built into our software. We customized the audio by adjusting the overall volume, the balance between the left and right ear, and the relative volume of six different frequency bands. We also took participants' knowledge of their hearing loss into account during this calibration session. Once the briefing and calibration were completed, the experiment began. Before each of the seven randomly selected trials, the participant was allowed to practice with that selection technique until they were comfortable. After the experiment, we presented participants with a five-item questionnaire, asking their opinion on which condition they thought was best for Recall, fastest for Switching, easiest, most natural, and best overall.

5.6 Video and Audio Design

We recorded digital footage of three male actors each reading the nine passages, for a total of 27 movie files. We used movies rather than real conversations because it allowed for greater experimental control, particularly with regards to the turn switching process, that had to occur on a timed basis. We used a timed slideshow to present short phrases at the very top of a computer screen, placing the video camera directly above the screen. Thus actors appeared to maintain eye contact with participants for the entire duration of the recording. It also ensured that the timing and rhythm of the stories was the same between actors. When switching passages every ten seconds the story would continue seamlessly from one actor to the next. Audio was recorded, in stereo sound, with a lapel microphone clipped to the actor's collar. Before trials commenced, participants removed their hearing aids and were outfitted with Shure E5c sound-isolating earphones (see Figure 4) that eliminated all environmental noise. Trials were further conducted in a sound-proof usability lab.

5.7 Screen and Tag Design

Figure 3 shows the screen setup: a 52" plasma screen displaying three videos of actors telling stories. Below each of the three windows was a space where the red dot could appear, which helped participants identify the target window.

We affixed a total of five infrared tags to the screen. Two tags with four infrared LEDs each were centered about 3 cm apart on the upper frame of the screen. These tags emulated the sensor bar in the Nintendo Wii system, emitting solid infrared light to provide triangulation data for the Wii remote pointer. Three ViewPointer tags were mounted on the screen itself (see Figure 3), just below the actors' faces, and were activated in the eye input condition. These tags measured 3 cm in diameter and each consisted of six infrared LEDs. To not have to rely on battery power during experimentation, these tags were connected to a MacBook Pro and directly operated via a Phidget interface board [9]. The ViewPointer camera operated at 30 fps and the tags at 15 Hz. We used the following three eight-bit codes for our tags: 11111110, 11110000, and 10101010. Because we required three tags for this study, the user needed to look at each tag for approximately 0.5 seconds (or 15 frames) before the software recognized and identified the tag. This is well within the average human fixation, between 100 ms and 1 second [32].

During the evaluation, the participant sat in a straight-backed stationary chair that was placed 1.65 m from the screen. We placed a strip of black cardboard over the toolbar at the top of the screen so participants were not distracted.

5.8 Wii Remote

We adapted a Nintendo Wii remote ("Wiimote", see Figure 5) for the two manual input conditions of our evaluation. While we obviously do not expect hearing aid wearers to carry a Wiimote, it is representative for the kind of manual control device that could be considered optimal for this kind of real life task, as it is wireless, operates in 3-space, and relies on orientation only. In real-world conditions, we have observed hearing aid users using a similar small remote control to adjust their settings. Every time after using the remote, they would place it back in their pocket, or on their lap where it could easily be reached. Because it can be tiring to hold up a manual remote control, we allowed participants to relax their arm and place it on their lap in between selections, whenever they got tired of holding up the Wiimote. For the pointing condition, we switched the audio when the participant pointed at an activation box overlaid on the actor's window. For the button condition, we relabeled the –, HOME, and + buttons on the Wiimote to 1, 2, 3 and switched the audio when the participant pressed the correct button. Liquid plastic was applied to the buttons so they would be the same height, and have the same "feel". Figure 5 illustrates the relabeled buttons, as well as the physical modifications made to the Wiimote.

5.9 Software

Max/MSP/Jitter [4] is a graphical programming environment designed for use with multimedia. The program ran in one of three different "modes", with the mode randomly selected for every switch:

1. Same actor/different position – The same actor continues telling the story, but in a different position on the screen. In this case the red dot moves to the new position.
2. Different actor/same window – A different actor continues the story, but in the same window. In this case, the red dot stays in the same position.
3. Different actor/different window – Both the actor and the window position change. As in the first mode, the red dot moves to the new position in this case.

We did not allow for the same actor/same window mode because we needed to force participants to switch every 10 seconds.

5.10 Hardware

Our evaluation required three computers. A MacBook Pro was connected to the USB camera and ran computer vision software to analyze ViewPointer video. The MacBook Pro also ran the Phidget interface used to control and provide power for the infrared tags. The encoded tag number was sent to another PowerBook via the network connection. This PowerBook ran a Max/MSP/Jitter patch with an embedded Java program. This patch then sent out a single integer indicating the focus tag. An iMac ran the Max/MSP/Jitter software that controlled the audio and video switching based on which actor was identified as being in focus. This allowed the iMac to make full use of its processing resources to ensure that the three videos ran seamlessly, and in lip sync.

5.11 Hypotheses

To summarize, our independent variable was switching technique; either (1) None (Control), (2) Buttons, (3) Pointing, or (4) Eye Input. Our two dependent variables were recall (on a multiple choice test with seven questions), and switch time in milliseconds. We hypothesized that switch time would be best with eye input as pointing requires arm movement, and button presses imply a Hick's law selection. As a consequence, we predicted that participants would have the best recall with eye input, and the worst in the Control condition.

5.12 Data Analysis

For each participant, we had a total of six trials of data (two trials each of Buttons, Pointing, and Eye Input). As in [35], we defined switch time as the time between the instant the red dot flashed or appeared in a new location to the instant the user selected the correct actor. The switch time variable obviously could not be applied in the Control condition. For recall, we used the results of the multiple-choice test from each of the seven trials (one trial in Control condition, and two trials each of Buttons, Pointing, and Eye Input). The results indicated the number of correct answers out of a possible seven. Analyses of variance (ANOVAs) with the factor of selection method were performed separately on the switch time and recall variables.

This was followed by post-hoc pairwise comparisons between each condition, using Bonferroni correction to account for multiple comparisons. Questionnaire data was non-parametric and analyzed using Kruskal-Wallis tests. Significance level was assumed at $p < .05$ for all statistical analyses.

Table 1. Mean Switch Time and Recall per condition

	Control	**Buttons**	**Pointing**	**Eyes**
Mean Switch Time (ms) (s.e.)	n/a	2211.8 (151.6)	2424.6 (166.4)	1404.3 (113.7)
Mean Recall (s.e.)	.82 (.30)	1.91 (.28)	2.60 (.30)	4.14 (.46)

Table 2. User Experience results per condition

	Control	Buttons	Pointing	Eyes
Perceived Recall	0	5	1	5
Perceived Switch Time	0	4	1	6
Easiest	0	3	0	8
Most Natural	0	1	0	10
Overall	0	3	0	8

6 Results

Results show that Eye Input had a faster switch time than both manual techniques (see Table 1) ($F2, 30 = 13.14$, $p < .001$). Post-hoc pairwise comparisons with Bonferroni correction showed Eye Input was 73% faster than Pointing ($p < .001$) and 58% faster than Buttons ($p < .05$).

In terms of recall, Eye Input was 80% better than Control, 54% better than Buttons, and 37% better than Pointing (see Table 1) ($F3, 40 = 16.33$, $p < .001$). Post-hoc comparisons with Bonferroni correction revealed that Eye Input had significantly better recall than Pointing ($p < .05$), Buttons ($p < .001$), and Control ($p < .001$). In addition, recall in the Pointing condition was significantly better than in the Control condition ($p < .01$).

In terms of errors, we found that Eye Input had an average of 6.7 errors per condition, compared to 7 in the Buttons condition and 0 in the Pointing condition. These errors are mostly attributed to participants continuing to hold down a button at inappropriate times in the Button condition, or wrongful detection of a tag activation in the Eye Input condition.

6.1 User Experience

Table 2 shows the results of the five-item User Experience questionnaire across conditions. In terms of subjective ratings, results showed that the AHA was the easiest, the most natural, and the best overall. Kruskal-Wallis tests suggested differences for all five items: perceived recall ($p < .01$), perceived switch time ($p < .01$), easiest ($p < .001$), most natural ($p < .001$), and best overall ($p < .001$).

7 Discussion

Overall, the results obtained for both switch time and recall were in line with expectations. This section presents a discussion of what we believe are the two key explanations for these results: movement time and mental load.

7.1 Movement Time as a Limiting Factor

For switch time, Eye Input was 73% faster than Pointing, and 58% faster than Buttons. The chief reason for this is that there is very little movement, and mostly open-loop control involved in eye input. Selecting the actor required little to no cognitive processing, and the only movement required was a saccade. Similarly, in the Buttons condition, the only motion required was a thumb press to activate the correct button. However, it required a mental mapping and a Hick's style 3-way decision, which we will discuss in a subsequent section.

Pointing first typically involves an eye fixation, and a deliberate closed-loop coordination of the wrist and arm movement. We believe this resulted in a longer switch time. Both pointing and button conditions may have been affected by the need to lift up the arm in cases where participants were tired, and rested their arm prior to engaging in selections. However, we believe such bias is, in fact, reflective of real-world limitations of the device.

7.2 Mental Load as a Limiting Factor

In terms of our second dependent variable our results were again in line with our hypothesis; with Eye Input performing 80% better than Control, 54% better than Buttons, and 37% better than Pointing. We believe these results were in part due to switch time as well: the higher the switch time, the more of the story was missed. However, recall was 26% better in the Pointing condition than in the Buttons condition. We believe this difference was due to a higher mental load in the Buttons condition. In that condition, participants could not rely on deixis, or a spatial mapping (i.e., point wherever the dot is) to select the correct actor.[1] Every ten seconds, a Hick's law decision was required: a selection of one of three possible buttons, and a mapping needed to be made between the actor identity and the number to press. We argue this limitation is inherent with any non-spatial device in mobile scenarios, and it presents a distinct limitation for the use of remote control buttons to select persons in real world environments. Participants confirmed that mental load was the lowest in the Eye Input condition.

7.3 Difference between Perceived and Actual Recall

An interesting observation was a large difference between participants' self-reports and their actual data for the recall variable. Participants seemed to overestimate their recall ability in the Buttons condition; and conversely, underestimate their recall in the Pointing condition. One explanation could be that the mental load of remembering the actor-number mapping operates at a subconscious level, and participants therefore were unable to keep track of the extent to which memorization had affected their recall performance. Tognazzini presented a similar argument on perception vs. reality in [29].

7.4 Comparison with Head Orientation Input

Subsequent to the above study, and in response to reviewer feedback, we studied the movement time of selection in the same task using head orientation input. We used a high-resolution webcam tracking a fiducial marker affixed to the participants' heads,

[1] Note that this is a fundamental and inherent limitation that was specifically *not* designed to favour pointing or eye input conditions.

tracking their orientation towards the on-screen target. Although due to the post-hoc nature we cannot directly compare data between experiments, trends do indeed suggest that selection through head orientation is slower. Participant recall was about one full point lower than with eye input, which is what we expected, and which is consistent with findings in [3].

7.5 Pros and Cons of the Current Design

We would like to note that this represented a preliminary study aimed at evaluating the potential usefulness of eye input in such scenarios. Further studies are required in the field, in actual face-to-face conditions, and comparing other hearing aid technologies.

One of the main issues with the current AHA design, as well as other directional hearing aids is that the user must always be oriented towards the sound source that they wish to listen to. This means that it would be impossible to listen to the radio next to you, or hear your spouse when she is behind you. The big advantage of AHA over directional hearing aids is that AHA actually selects a sound source, obtaining a signal directly from a lapel microphone, thus eliminating background noise. The use of eye movement rather than head movement also follows more closely what actually occurs in conversations [33], an allocation of brain resources based on a tuning of visual attention. Our results show it to be much faster than hand movements, which in turn are known to be much faster than neck muscles.

In our evaluation, we chose a controlled environment, which effectively eliminated the Midas Touch Effect [13]. If the Attentive Hearing Aid were to be deployed in the real world, it would always amplify the audio of whoever the user would look at. However, users would also be familiar with the voices of their interlocutors, making wrongful selection easy to detect, and repair is as fast as a fixation on the correct speaker. Hypothesizing an error that occurs in every switch, adding another 500 ms to the mean measure would still find eye input significantly faster than either manual technique.

8 Conclusions

Research shows that the number one improvement sought by hearing aid users is better understanding of speech in noisy conditions. Most hearing aids, including directional hearing aids, have a relatively poor signal-to-noise ratio because they are unable to sufficiently differentiate desired sounds from unwanted noise. We presented the Attentive Hearing Aid, a system that uses eye input from a ViewPointer system to amplify tagged sound sources in the user's environment. We conducted a preliminary evaluation where hearing-impaired participants were asked to follow a story presented on screen by three actors. Participants selected the target actor every ten seconds in four different conditions: pressing a button, pointing with a remote control, using their eyes, and a Control condition in which actors were speaking simultaneously without filtering. Results suggest that selection with eye input was 73% faster than pointing, and 58% faster than buttons. In terms of recall of presented material, eye input was 80% better than control (no selection/omnidirectional hearing aid), 54% better than Buttons, and 37% better than Pointing. User experience reports were also very positive, with eye input receiving the highest rating in all categories. With proper miniaturization and optimization of components, we believe our results support the tremendous potential for AHA technology to improve the quality of life of users with hearing disabilities in future hearing aids.

References

1. Arons, B.: Review of the Cocktail Party Effect. Journal of the American Voice I/O Society 12, 35–50 (1992)
2. Basu, S., Pentland, A.: Smart Headphones. In: Ext. Abstracts of CHI 2001, Seattle, pp. 267–268 (2001)
3. Boyer, D.J.: The Relationship Among Eye Movements, Head Movement, and Manual Responses in a Simulated Air Traffic Control Task. Technical Report, US Department of Transportation, FAA (1995)
4. Cycling 1974. Max/MSP/Jitter, `http://www.cycling74.com`
5. Cherry, E.C.: Some Experiments on the Recognition of Speech, with One and with Two Ears. Journal of Acoustic Society of America 25, 975–979 (1953)
6. Dickie, C., Hart, J., Vertegaal, R., Eiser, A.: LookPoint: An Evaluation of Eye Input for Hands-Free Switching of Input Devices between Multiple Computers. In: Proc. of OzCHI 2006. ACM Press, New York (2006)
7. Duchowski, A.: Eye Tracking Methodology: Theory & Practice. Springer, London (2003)
8. Fono, D., Vertegaal, R.: EyeWindows: Evaluation of Eye-Controlled Zooming Windows for Focus Selection. In: Proc. of CHI 2005, pp. 151–160. ACM Press, New York (2005)
9. Greenberg, S., Fitchett, C.: Phidgets: Easy Development of Physical Interfaces through Physical Widgets. In: Proc. of UIST 2001. ACM Press, New York (2001)
10. Hawkins, D.B.: Comparisons of Speech Recognition in Noise by Mildly-to-Moderately Hearing-Impaired Children Using Hearing Aids and FM Systems. Journal of Speech and Hearing Disorders 49, 409–418 (1984)
11. Hearing Aid, `http://dictionary.reference.com`
12. Hearing Loss Education Center, `http://www.hearinglosseducation.com`
13. Jacob, R.J.K.: The Use of Eye Movements in Human-Computer Interaction Techniques: What You Look At Is What You Get. ACM Transactions on Information Systems 9(3), 152–169 (1991)
14. Kochkin, S.: Hearing Loss Population Tops 31 Million People. Hearing Review 12(7) (2005)
15. Kochkin, S., Rogin, C.: Quantifying the Obvious: The Impact of Hearing Aids on Quality of Life. The Hearing Review 7(1), 8–34 (2000)
16. Langolf, G.D., Chaffin, D.B., Foulke, J.A.: An investigation of Fitts' law using a wide range of movement amplitudes. Journal of Motor Behavior 8, 113–128 (1976)
17. Maschke, C., Rupp, T., Hecht, K.: The Influence of Stressors on Biochemical Reactions - A Review of Present Scientific Findings with Noise. International Journal of Hygiene and Environmental Health 203, 45–53 (2000)
18. Morrison, H.B., Casali, J.G.: Intelligibility of Synthesized Voice Messages in Commercial Truck Cab Noise for Normal-Hearing and Hearing-Impaired Listeners. International Journal of Speech Technology 2, 33–44 (1997)
19. Nickel, K., Stiefelhagen, R.: Pointing Gesture Recognition on 3d-Tracking of Face, Hands and Head Orientation. In: Proc. ICMI, pp. 380–400 (2003)

20. O'Neill, G., Summer, L., Shirey, L.: Hearing Loss: A Growing Problem that Affects Quality of Life. Challenges for the 21st Century: Chronic and Disabling Conditions 2, 1–6 (1999)
21. Ricketts, T.A., Mueller, H.G.: Making Sense of Directional Microphone Hearing Aids. American Journal of Audiology 8(2), 117–128 (1999)
22. Ricketts, T.A., Dhar, S.: Comparison of Performance across Three Directional Hearing Aids. American Journal of Audiology 8(10), 180–189 (1999)
23. Selker, T., Lockerd, A., Martinez, J.: Eye-R, A Glasses-Mounted Eye Motion Detection Interface. In: Ext. Abstracts of CHI 2001, pp. 179–180. ACM Press, New York (2001)
24. Sibert, L.E., Jacob, R.J.K.: Evaluation of Eye Gaze Interaction. In: Proc. of CHI 2000. ACM, New York (2000)
25. Smith, A.P.: Noise, Performance Efficiency and Safety. International Archives of Occupational and Environmental Health 62, 1–5 (1990)
26. Smith, A.P.: Noise and Aspects of Attention. British Journal of Psychology 82, 313–324 (1991)
27. Smith, J.D.: ViewPointer: Lightweight Calibration-Free Eye Tracking for Ubiquitous Handsfree Deixis. Master's Thesis, Queen's University (2005)
28. Smith, J.D., Vertegaal, R., Sohn, C.: ViewPointer: Lightweight Calibration-Free Eye Tracking for Ubiquitous Handsfree Deixis. In: Proc. of UIST 2005, pp. 53–61. ACM, New York (2005)
29. Tognazzini, B.: Tog on Interface. Addison-Wesley Longman Publishing Co., Boston (1992)
30. Valente, M., Fabry, D.A., Potts, L.G.: Recognition of Speech in Noise with Hearing Aids using Dual Microphones. Journal of the American Academy of Audiology 6(6), 440–449 (1995)
31. Varibel Hearing Glasses, `http://www.varibel.nl`
32. Velichkovsky, B.M., Hansen, J.P.: New Technological Windows into Mind: There is More in Eyes and Brain for Human-Computer Interaction. In: Proc. of CHI 1996, pp. 496–503. ACM Press, New York (1996)
33. Vertegaal, R., Ding, Y.: Explaining Effects of Eye Gaze on Mediated Group Conversations: Amount or synchronization? In: Proceedings of CSCW 2002, pp. 41–48. ACM Press, New Orleans (2002)
34. Vertegaal, R., Slagter, R., van der Veer, G., Nijholt, A.: Eye Gaze Patterns in Conversations: There is More to Conversational Agents Than Meets the Eyes. In: Proc. of CHI 2001, pp. 301–308. ACM, New York (2001)
35. Ware, C., Mikaelian, H.H.: An Evaluation of an Eye Tracker as a Device for Computer Input. In: Proc. of CHI+GI 1987, pp. 183–188. ACM Press, New York (1987)
36. Wang, J., Zhai, S., Su, H.: Chinese Input with Keyboard and Eye-Tracking - An Anatomical Study. In: Proceedings of ACM CHI 2001 Conference on Human Factors in Computing Systems, pp. 349–356 (2001)
37. Watanabe, J., Nii, H., Hashimoto, Y., Inami, M.: Visual Resonator: Interface for Interactive Cocktail Party Phenomenon. In: Ext. Abstracts of CHI 2006, pp. 1505–1510. ACM Press, New York (2006)
38. Zhai, S., Morimoto, C., Ihde, S.: Manual and gaze input cascaded (MAGIC) pointing. In: Proceedings of the ACM CHI 1999, pp. 246–253 (1999)

Video Gaming for Blind Learners School Integration in Science Classes

Jaime Sánchez and Mauricio Sáenz

Department of Computer Science, Center for Advanced Research in Education (CARE)
University of Chile
{jsanchez,msaenz}@dcc.uchile.cl

Abstract. In this study we evaluate how the use of audio-based technology can facilitate school integration of blind learners through the interaction with a science videogame. This experience consisted of designing and implementing *The Natomy's Journey Game* to be played by blind and sighted middle school students. The use of the videogame and its impact on the integration of blind learners into mainstream schools was also evaluated, through the participation of both teachers and learners. In the end, the goal was for blind learners to be able to interact and become socially integrated through active science video gaming and the application of specific science content. The results of this study provide initial data and evidence that the use of video games such as *The Natomy's Journey Game* can improve the process for the school integration of learners with visual disabilities.

Keywords: Visual disability, sound interface, school integration, science learning.

1 Introduction

The use and integration of ICTs into education has been the focus of discussion for many researchers and developers [2,6]. The use of this kind of technology in education, and in particular for complex content such as science, make its integration for use by the visually disabled through educational activities especially complicated. This is mainly due to the kind of resources required and these students' lack of one of the most important senses for the process of observing natural phenomenon: vision [9,14]. Children with visual disability have more problems accessing information, learning and putting basic operations into practice, and solving problems than their sighted peers [23,13]. However, the use of technology that is correctly adapted for this kind of disablement can lead to an efficient solution.

As such, we might ask: In what way can we create a context in which sighted and blind students could work collaboratively for effective science learning? In general, in several countries there are special schools for children with visual disabilities that work only with legally blind students as a segregated population. In these cases, there are usually scarce resources, which impede working in the same conditions as their peers in school integrated classes (mainstreaming).

T. Gross et al. (Eds.): INTERACT 2009, Part I, LNCS 5726, pp. 36–49, 2009.

Several studies have shown that audio interfaces can be used to foment learning and cognition in blind children [22,24,33]. The use of these audio-based applications stimulates the utilization of general cognitive processes, such as tempo-spatial orientation, abstract memory and haptic perception [22,24,27].

In recent years, video games have become a part of the daily life of children and school-aged youth [15,17]. With the progress of ICTs, video games have become a powerful force representing a part of the daily activities, concerns and interests of children and youth. In our country, 50% of students use the Internet to play games [1,32]. In the USA, young people between 8 and 18 years old play an average of 49 minutes of video games daily, almost the same amount of time dedicated to doing homework (50 minutes) and reading (43 minutes) [18].

In this way, computer-based video games represent an alternative that has penetrated distinct areas of education, mainly in their use in the classroom [12,30]. Such data demonstrates the potential importance of video games in education as a structure for the development of different cognitive abilities, such as problem solving, analysis, communication, collaboration and information management [29,31].

In taking into account the high degree of learners' motivation and interest in video games, the potential of these games to develop abilities and the need to integrate their use into the formal education of both blind and sighted users, we designed and developed a video game called *The Natomy's Journey Game*, for interactive collaboration between sighted and blind students. We also evaluated the usability of *The Natomy's Journey Game*, as well as its impact on the process of school integration between blind students and their sighted peers.

2 Related Work

In the last few years several software applications [20,22,24] have been developed involving blind users as the main participants, in order to assist them in their learning with interactive technology, focusing mainly on haptic interfaces [27] and desktop applications [22,24]. Also, there are several studies that show the importance of using video games for education [12,29,31]. Some important cognitive aspects that can be developed through the use of video games are the development of competition and concentration skills, mobility skills, language and mathematical skills, visual skills and problem-solving skills [3,4,25].

However, there is consensus in the literature that problem solving is the most important one of all, in that it provides students with tools that can be used not only in a school context, but in social and work contexts as well.

Polya [16] described the process for problem solving in four fundamental steps that consist of understanding the problem, devising a plan, carrying out the plan and examining the solution obtained. If this does not solve the problem, a new plan has to be devised.

The current literature includes several studies related to virtual environments and problem solving for the blind. In [5], an aid system is proposed for the mobility of a blind user through virtual reality mechanisms. In [26] the authors developed virtual reality tools so blind users could explore information constructively. In another study, a game with 3D navigation, Terraformers, was developed for stimulating development and solving tasks in an entertaining way [33]. Recently, some software programs for problem solving through interaction with virtual environments designed for users with visual disabilities have been developed [22,24]. These programs use labyrinths represented in different ways through spatial and stereo audio [34,35]. Access Invaders [36] is a video game that allows for online playing between blind users to solve a shared goal.

School integration is a very important subject nowadays. There are several studies about the present state of integration in the classroom as shown in [10,11,28]. On the other hand, several studies on the way that technology can aid in the school integration of users with different kinds of disabilities in the classroom have been developed [7,8]. In another example, in [19, p.57] it was concluded that, "With the large number of mildly disabled students in our schools, it is very important that teachers make every effort to educate their students as best as possible. Evidence has shown that technology is one of the best ways to implement this successfully. Using a variety of software and technology tools this process is becoming easier every day. Teachers must also make sure that they are educated in how to use these tools to better instruct their students' learning. As advancements in the field of technology continue to be made, more and more opportunities for this level of learning will be available to students and, as evidence has shown; more students will have better opportunities to receive the best education possible."

In this study, our proposal is *The Natomy's Journey Game*, a sound-based game that uses mobile technology so that blind and sighted children can interact, become socially integrated and learn science. In the following we present the main characteristics of the software, as well as an evaluation of its use by blind users and its impact on the process of school integration with their sighted peers.

3 The Video Game

3.1 Video Game Description

The Natomy's Journey Game represents four systems of the human body in which the student adopts a character with which he/she can interact with other characters in the game or in his/her work group, and thus complete the collaborative tasks necessary to achieve a main goal. These four systems are: the digestive system, the respiratory system, the cardiovascular system and the nervous system. The main problem to solve is to heal certain sicknesses by using the clues that are provided to the students through their interaction and investigation throughout the video game.

The video game was made to be used by workgroups of four students working simultaneously in a computer lab (with a maximum of 12 groups working at the same time).

The interaction with the legally blind students is based mainly on the use of the keyboard and feedback provided on their actions through a spatial sound system (4 or more speakers distributed in the end-user's surroundings) (see Figure 3).

The game can be played in an individual or a group mode. The user must interact with the characters and objects in the video game that provide clues and symptoms in order to solve the problem at hand. To these ends, the progress of each student depends on the progress of the rest of his/her team, thus creating a variety of interactions between the members of the group.

The game consists of two sicknesses to be discovered (Cholera and Rubella). As the player interacts with the characters, they provide information on the sickness and, at the same time, on the different organs and specific functions of the human body necessary to make decisions. The students must get to a place in the human body called the Center of Operations, where they enter an area of mini-video games that they must successfully complete in order to pass to the next level and to beat the game. Each system of the human body consists of 12 scenes that make up the totality of the virtual world with which the users must interact.

3.2 The Video Game Metaphor

The video game metaphor consists of a journey to within a sick human body. This journey is taken by a group of four friends who must go to the city of *Natomy*, where a crazy genius (Uncle Isaiah) provides them with a pill that they must take in order to shrink in size, to be able to enter the human body.

3.3 Video Game Architecture

This game was developed for a PC platform in Macromedia Director using Lingo language. The following system requirements are needed to run the game: 1 GHz processor or higher, Microsoft Windows XP SP2, 256 MB RAM, 32 MB DirectX 8 compatible video and sound card, 4 speakers or headphones for audio, and keyboard.

The software architecture upon which *The Natomy's Journey Game* is based has two main components: 1. Video game engine, responsible for controlling all the players' interactions, the logical relations and the dependencies between the different systems, 2. Interfaces module, responsible for receiving the users' actions through the keyboard and, at the same time, producing the necessary feedback through graphic objects and audio.

Each of the participating users interacts with the interfaces available in the video game. The users with visual disabilities (legally blind) mostly used the audio interfaces, which orients them and provides updated information on the state of the video game. On the other hand, the sighted users use both interfaces (audio and visual) to receive all the necessary information to be able to play the game correctly.

The information received through the interfaces is processed as input into the game's engine, which evaluates and processes the different logical interactions between all the software's components and the dependencies of these components. Afterwards, it takes the new information produced by the users' interaction, which is then sent to the interfaces to be provided to the users (see Figure 1).

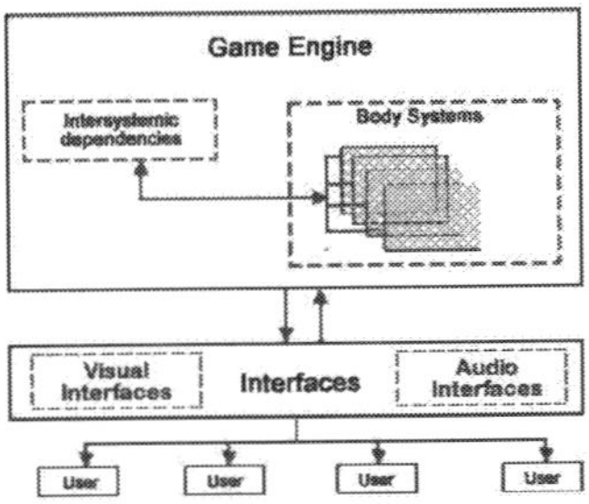

Fig. 1. Architecture of The Natomy's Journey Game

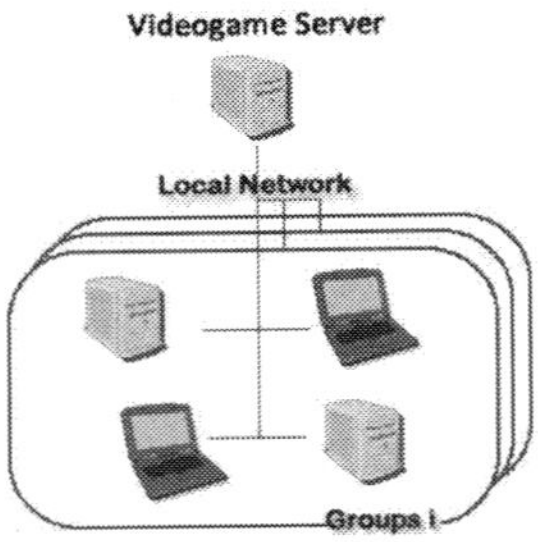

Fig. 2. Networking Architecture of The Natomy's Journey Game

3.4 Networking Architecture

The video game's multi-user interaction is carried out through architecture designed over a local network, in which both desktop computers and wireless mobile computers connected through WIFI can be used (see Figure 2).

3.5 Interfaces

Audio Interfaces. The audio interface developed for *The Natomy's Journey Game* consists of a combination of stereo and spatial sound. The stereo sound is utilized mostly for the voices in the game used for the instructions, the different menus, dialogues and some objects in the different scenes. The spatial sound is used mostly to identify the objects in the spatial environment (see Figure 3). This last system was designed so that the students with visual disabilities could orient themselves and recognize the position of the objects, doors and characters in the scene. This corresponds to certain audio elements that are constantly reproduced during the game, such as the entry, exit and doors to the systems of the human body, as well as other elements that are reproduced on-demand, such as the position of objects and characters.

To create a spatial immersion of the user into the virtual environment, the speaker system must be located properly. The front left and front right speakers must be placed in an angle of 45 or 60 degrees. In addition, the 3 frontal speakers must be placed at the same level. The rear speakers must be located behind the user and a little above his ears (see Figure 3). Depending upon how the sound was used, different levels of user immersion were attained. The use of the spatial sound attained the highest level of user's immersion allowing for a high fidelity representation of the audio in a real environment which points out to the user the position of objects and their location within the environment.

Audio interfaces were implemented using MS Directx, in particular the dxSound for Lingo library. This allowed for producing and controlling dynamically the spatial sound of the video game.

Fig. 3. Scenario for the use of the spatial sound

Visual Interfaces. The visual interfaces developed for the video game *The Natomy's Journey Game* correspond to caricaturized abstractions of the systems and organs of the human body as well as objects in the game.

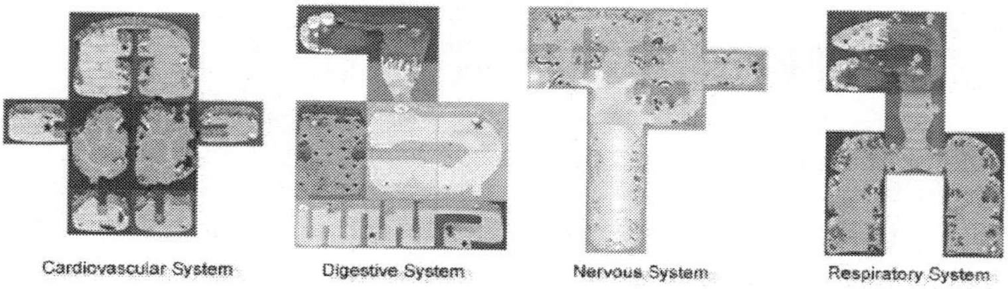

Fig. 4. Systems of the Human Body Representations in *The Natomy's Journey Game*

The graphic interfaces for the systems of the human body correspond to an integrated set of scenes that are coherently represented for the simulation of traveling through each of the systems. The figure 4 corresponds to the maps of each system of the human body, subdivided into 12 scenes with which the student interacts and through which he/she travels.

Fig. 5. Some Avatars and Characters in *The Natomy's Journey Game*

Avatars and Characters. Each student can pick from a total of 8 characters. The characters designed correspond mainly to organs of the human body, made into caricatures so that the students interact with them naturally and in the context of the system in which they are playing. Figure 5 shows some characters in the biological systems.

Main Interfaces. The game begins with an animated introduction according to the metaphor defined, which explains to the student the tasks that he/she has to undertake in the video game. Then there is an interface that corresponds to the main menu, where the user can select the kind of play (stand alone or group work), the group with which he/she will play in the game and the avatar, which will be the character that will represent him/her in the video game (see Figure 6a). After this, the student begins to play and can travel through the systems where he/she will be able to meet up with the other members of his/her group (see Figure 6b).

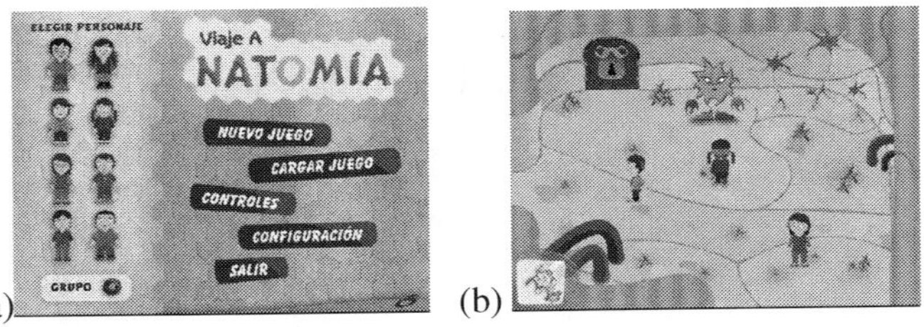

(a) (b)

Fig. 6. Visual Interfaces of the *The Natomy's Journey Game*

3.6 Model for the Virtual Environment

The navigation through different virtual environments and spaces replicates a successful model used for commercial videogames which follow a third-person metaphor with a camera view fixed from an above and behind position. This model of navigation has been adjusted to the needs of blind children, having added auditory cues of spatial sound which allows them to form a mental construction of the space.

The representation of the surroundings is described in a XML file in which all the attributes that characterize the different scenes can be found. The XML structure contains a series of elements that define the storylines, which can also be modified, extended or eliminated.

4 Evaluation

4.1 The Sample

To evaluate the impact of the use of *The Natomy's Journey Game*, a study was made with sixth and seventh-grade blind and sighted children between the ages of 11 and 14 years old. Tests were applied in seven mainstream public schools in Santiago de Chile during 4 months, with the participation of 15 teachers and 326 learners. Eight legally blind learners participated in this study (2 with partial vision and 6 totally blind).

4.2 Evaluation Instruments

End-user questionnaire: This instrument was applied to evaluate the interface of *The Natomy's Journey Game* through 4 dimensions: game satisfaction, control and use, images and sounds quality [21]. This questionnaire consisted of 18 sentences for which the users must define to what degree each of them was fulfilled, on a scale from A Little to A Lot, with quantitative values from 1 (a little) to 10 (a lot). Some of the sentences were: "I like the videogame", "The videogame makes me active", "I felt

I could control the videogame's situations", "The videogame is interactive", "The videogame allowed me to understand new things", "I like the sounds in the videogame", "The sounds in the videogame are clearly identifiable", and "The sounds in the videogame provide me with information"

Written guideline for the evaluation of school integration: To evaluate the level of integration, a written guideline was applied in which each participating student had to answer with opinions regarding the following four dimensions:

- *Autonomy* refers to the help that the students received to carry out the activities, such as tasks or movements (on a scale of 1 to 5, the higher the score, the higher the autonomy).
- *Teaching/learning style* refers to how the students perceived their learning style in relation to the way in which classes are held in the school (scale of 1 to 5, the higher the score the lower the agreement with the teaching style).
- *Belonging to the school* refers to the sense of belonging that the students had regarding their school; this asked if they felt integrated and if they identified with their class and school (on a scale of 1 to 5, the higher the score the higher the sense of belonging).
- *School Integration* refers to the opinion that they had on discriminatory practices or practices of school integration (on a scale of 1 to 5, the higher the score, the higher their disagreement with discrimination).

4.3 Procedure

The entire intervention lasted for 4 months in each school. This period was divided into 24 work sessions: 12 of group work with the software in the computer lab in each school, and 12 of group work in the classroom using material designed specifically for the study (board games, models and activities involving the building of objects having to do with the concepts of the human body).

All throughout the execution of the study we also performed constant monitoring of the participating schools, which implied visits to the classrooms and computer labs, as well as communicating the activities through telephone and email. By the end of the fourth month of intervention and after the last gaming session, the students answered the end-user questionnaire.

Among the methods for evaluating the results, a series of both qualitative and quantitative applications were used, collecting data from the actors involved in the development of the study, teachers and the participating students. In the case of the students, quantitative instruments were applied at the beginning and the end of the study, in order to obtain opinions on the development of the stuffy and to prove that the users accepted the video game, and that it motivated them to use these virtual tools.

4.4 Results

Usability Results: The results obtained from the application of the end user usability test could be grouped into 4 dimensions: Game satisfaction, control and use of the videogame, sound quality, and image and color quality.

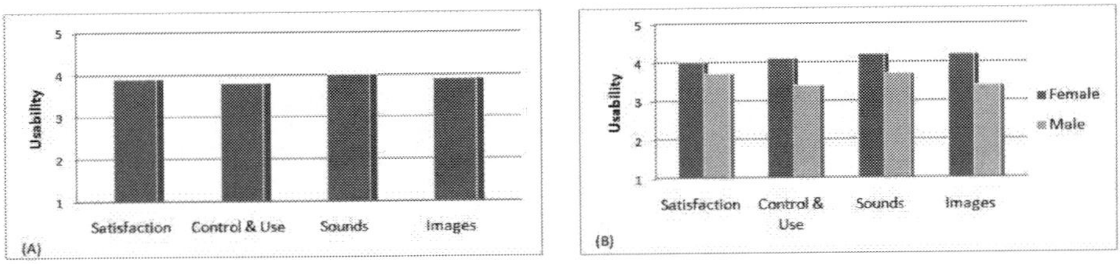

Fig. 7. (a) Usability Results by Dimension. (b) Usability Results by Gender.

As can be seen in the figure 7a, the means obtained in each of the dimensions were high and showed that there were no big differences between the learners´ valuations of the different areas analyzed regarding the usability of the software, as all the answers were located in the "agree" category.

Although there were no big differences, it could be observed that the area with the highest score was that related to the quality of the game's sounds (mean of 4 points out of a maximum of 5), which were agreeable and identifiable for the users. This ends up being very important considering that the game was designed so that learners with visual disabilities could participate. The game's images and the satisfaction with the game came in a close second, having obtained 3.9 points, which indicated that the design of the images helped to transmit information to the user and that the students liked the software in general, had fun with it, were challenged by it, believed that they learned from it and that it was able to capture their attention. The evaluation of the control and use of the game was similar (3.8 points), based on the fact that the users felt in control of the game, that they could perform different actions or stop performing actions whenever they wanted to, and on their perception that the game was interactive and easy to play, easy to use, motivating and with an interface that allowed the users to do anything simply and quickly.

It is important to point out the differentiation between the results obtained for the men and the women (figure 7b), as statistically significant differences were found in 3 of the 4 dimensions. In all 4 dimensions the women presented higher means than the men, and it was in the areas concerning use and control of the game ($t = 3.905$; $p<0.05$), sound quality ($t = 4.202$; $p<0.05$) and image quality ($t = 2.322$; $p<0.05$) that the differences were statistically significant. As for the dimension having to do with "game satisfaction", although the women presented a higher mean score than the men, this difference was not significant ($t = 1.915$; $p>0.05$).

To better understand the result of the usability evaluation is necessary to do a context analysis where the game was used. As a collaborative game, learners played in a group of 4 students and synchronically, sometimes saturating the audio between the four games. In general, the game contained heavy load of speech audio; audio that could be boring for the sighted gamers. Although there were high quality graphics in *The Natomy's Journey Game* including significant details, color and animation, they were not 3D graphics as learners are used today. Being primarily oriented to legally blind learners, the interaction relied strongly on keyboard, leaving aside devices such as mouse, joystick or gamepad.

School Integration Results: Regarding the items that referred to the students' autonomy in carrying out their activities, we focused on the students with visual disabilities. As shown in the figure 8a, there was an increase in the score between the pretest and the posttest for each one of the items. For the statement indicating that the students carried out most of their activities without assistance, there was an increase of 1.1 points between the pretest and the posttest (pretest = 2.2 points; posttest = 3.3 points). For the item indicating that the students tried to carry out their activities without help, there was an increase of 0.9 points (pretest = 2.9 points; posttest = 3.8 points); and for the item on whether or not the student studied with help from his/her parents or another person, there was an increase of 0.2 points (pretest = 4.2 points; posttest = 4.4 points).

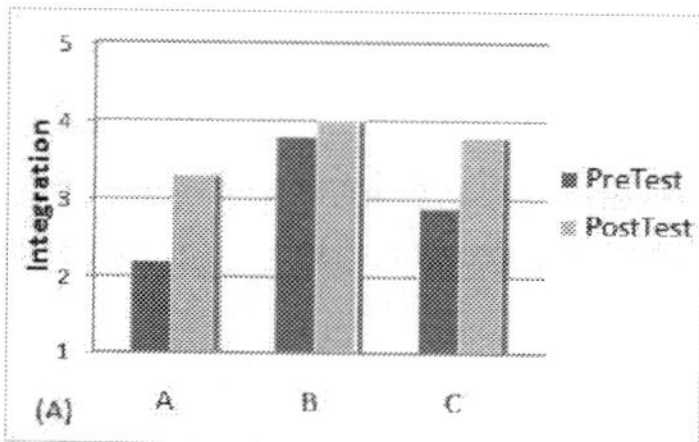

A. I carry out most of my activities without the help of my parents or another person.

B. I study with the help of my parents or another person.

C. I try to carry out my activities without help.

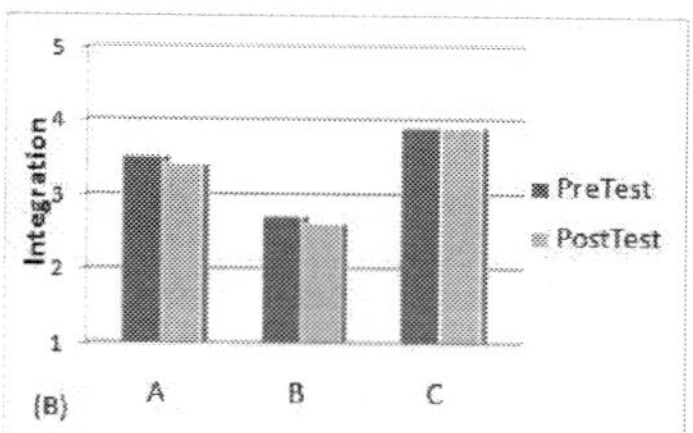

A. I feel that my way of learning is different from that of my classmates.

B. My way of learning has nothing to do with the classes taught by the teachers.

C. I wish the classes were different

Fig. 8. Integration Results. (a) Autonomy. (b) Learning Style.

As for the proximity between the classes and the students' learning styles, the figure 8b shows the means obtained from the students before and after having participated in the study, demonstrating very similar means. Only for the item that indicated that the students felt that their way of learning was different from their classmates was there a decrease pretest-posttest of 0.2 points (pretest = 3.6 points; posttest = 3.4 points) with a significant difference ($t = 2.431$; $p<0.05$; $df= 546$). This showed that after the study the blind students considered their way of learning to be closer to those of their sighted classmates than when they first began to use the video game.

Regarding the sense of belonging that the students had with their class and their school, there were no major differences in the opinions provided before and after the study (see Figure 9). For the item indicating that they felt identified with the majority of their classmates, a higher mean was obtained (a difference of 0.4 points between the pretest and the posttest, pretest=2.2 points; posttest=2.6 points), which was also statistically significant ($t= -2.374$; $p<0.05$; $df= 538$). This is to say that by the end of the study the students' experienced a higher degree of identification with their class, even though this was one of the lowest scoring items. The other items in which there was a pretest – posttest gain were: "I don't feel that my classmates bother me" (0.1 points difference, pretest=3.1 points; posttest=3.2 points; $t= -0.077$; $p<0.05$; $df= 539$)

and "I feel a part of my class" (0.2 points difference, pretest=3.7 points; posttest=3.9 points; t= -1.610; p<0.05; df= 536). The items that had no variation were: "I identify with my group of classmates" (mean of 3.5 points in both tests, t= 2.793; p<0.05; df= 538) and "I like my classmates" (mean of 3.1 points in both tests, t= 0.022; p<0.05; df= 538).

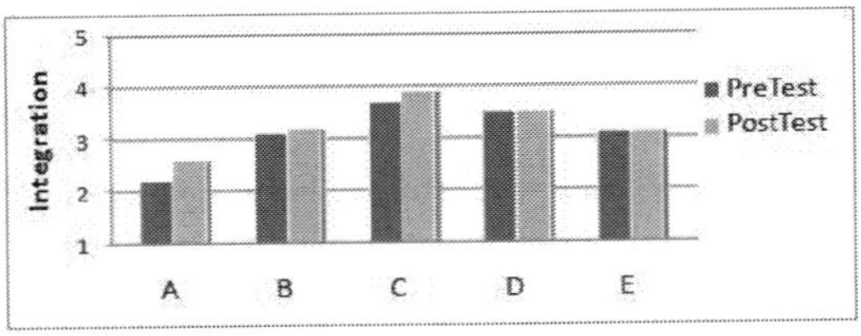

A. I feel like I identify with most of my classmates.
B. I don't feel that my classmates bother me.
C. I feel a part of my class.
D. I identify with my group of classmates.
E. I like my classmates.

Fig. 9. Integration Results. Sense of belonging to their school.

The scores obtained for the opinions provided on the students' perspectives on school integration or discriminatory practices did not present any pretest – posttest gains (see Figure 10). It is important to point out that the students' opinions, both before and after the intervention, had means higher than 4.4 points, which indicated their rejection of discriminatory practices and their approval of the idea that all students have the right to an education and that everyone is different.

As for the opinions provided by the participating teachers regarding school integration, measurements were taken both at the beginning of the study and at the end, to be able to compare the possible changes that took place. One important situation that was observed is that there was an increase in the percentage of teachers that stated having had experience with school integration, from 60% at the beginning to 72.7% at the end, so considering this experience with *The Natomy's Journey Game* as school integration with technology.

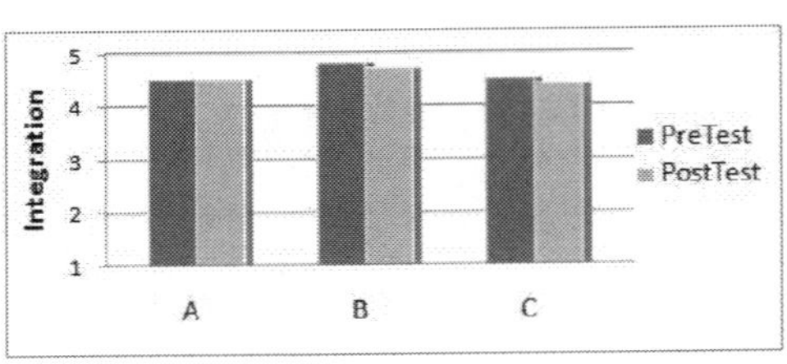

A. Discrimination is a bad thing.
B. All of us students have a right to education.
C. All of us students are different.

Fig. 10. Integration Results. School Integration.

In asking the teachers if they had implemented some strategy in the past three months for the integration of a student with visual disability, we also found that there was an increase in the final measurement, in that while initially 77.8% of the teachers had indicated "yes", at the end of the study 90.9% responded with a "yes".

Finally, in asking the teachers about how they felt working in the classroom with visually disabled students, an increase in those teachers that indicated feeling self-assured was observed, going from 50% for the initial measurement to 63.7% in the final measurement.

It is important to mention that the integration of learners with visual disabilities with the classroom and school classmates requires extended and sustained amount of work time that must be transversal at all school activities. Even though this fact it was possible to observe some advances as some participating teachers mentioned: " I felt that in some moments he (the blind child) became part of something", "I saw him for the first time integrated to a team work…and the group accepted him for sharing purposes", "I saw him integrated and a little more respected by their classmates because he tend to establish a negative relation with his classmates, in a defensive mode, but at the end of this experience his classmates accepted him well". All this assertions evidence qualitative relevant changes for the learner's integration considering that at the beginning it was observed that students were mostly excluded from their class, ending up as a result of participating in this study, with a more egalitarian participation in the project.

5 Conclusions

As a result of this study a video game for science learning by middle school blind and sighted learners was constructed and evaluated, to judge whether blind learners can interact and become socially integrated through the use of problem-solving skills and the application of specific science content.

The results of this study provide initial data and evidence that the use of video games such as *The Natomy's Journey Game* can improve the process for the school integration of learners with visual disabilities.

During the implementation process we made a non-participant observation to collect information about how learners and teachers appropriated and learned the methodology used. From these observations we could detect similar behaviors between learners during video gaming, as far as understanding controls and discovering new paths and goals. The participation of blind learners in particular was active and with high motivation.

The Natomy's Journey Game proposes a new way to learn science, especially the systems of the human body. The main achievement after using this game is that learners take an active role, learning in an interactive and motivated way. The learners enjoyed this new way of learning, felt motivated and participated actively and collaboratively in the tasks they had to undertake in the game.

In terms of school integration, this game helps to create a work environment in which differences are forgotten and children interact freely. They share ideas on how to solve the proposed problem as well as content knowledge among all four members of each team.

The Natomy's Journey Game allows blind children to become more socially integrated with their sighted classmates, to participate actively in society, and to be interested in the active learning of contents and new pedagogical ways of learning such as digital mobile gaming. Based on the children's comments, we point to the fact that the game allowed legally blind children to work together with their sighted peers, feeling part of the group, and this is very important issue in order to achieve a better and more complete education not only in terms of learning contents, but of school integration and teamwork skills as well.

Acknowledgments. This report was funded by the Chilean Ministry of Education, Innovation Program, Project "Digital Inclusion for the Science Learning" and Project CIE-05 Program Center Education PBCT-CONICYT.

References

1. Adimark, VTR, & EducarChile. Indice de generación digital 2006 (2006), `http://www.educarchile.cl/UserFiles/P0001/File/IGD%202006%20seminario` (Last Accessed July, 2007)
2. Balanskat, A., Blamire, R., Kefala, S.: A Review of Studies of ICT Impact on Schools in Europe. Europan SchoolNet (December 2006)
3. Cavazos, J.: Computer games. Crossroads 3(2) (Winter 1996)
4. Ellis, J.: Computer games and aggressive behavior: A review of the literature. Educational Technology 30(2), 37–40 (1990)
5. Everingham, M., Thomas, B., Troscianko, T., Easty, D.: Neural-network virtual reality mobility aid for the severely visually impaired. In: Proceedings of 2nd European Conference on Disability, Virtual Reality and Associated Technologies, pp. 183–192 (1998)
6. Facer, K., Joiner, R., Stanton, D., Reid, J., Hull, R., Kirk, D.: Savannah: mobile gaming and learning? Journal of Computer Assisted Learning 20, 399–409 (2004)
7. Feyerer, E.: Computer and Inclusive Education. In: Miesenberger, K., Klaus, J., Zagler, W.L. (eds.) ICCHP 2002. LNCS, vol. 2398, pp. 64–67. Springer, Heidelberg (2002)
8. Feyerer, E., Miesenberger, K., Wohlhart, D.: ICT and Assistive Technology in Teachers Education and Training. In: Miesenberger, K., Klaus, J., Zagler, W.L. (eds.) ICCHP 2002. LNCS, vol. 2398, pp. 297–334. Springer, Heidelberg (2002)
9. Hand, B., Alvermann, D., Gee, J., Guzzetti, B., Norris, S., Phillips, L., Prain, V., Yore, L.: Message from the "Island Group": What is literacy in science literacy? Journal of Research in Science Teaching 40(7), 607–615 (2003)
10. DeSimone, J.R., Parmar, R.S.: Middle School Mathematics Teachers' Beliefs About Inclusion of Students with Learning Disabilities. Learning Disabilities Research & Practice 21(2), 98–110 (2006)
11. Kalyanpur, M., Kirmani, M.: Diversity and Technology: Classroom Implications of the Digital Divide. Journal of Special Education Technology 20(4), 9–18 (Fall 2005)
12. Kirriemuir, J., McFarlane, A.E.: Use of Computer and Video Games in the Classroom. Presentation to DiGRA, Utrecht (2003b)
13. Kulyukin, V., Gharpure, C., Nicholson, J., Pavithran, S.: RFID in robot-assisted indoor navigation for the visually impaired. In: Kulyukin, V., Gharpure, C., Nicholson, J., Pavithran, S. (eds.) IEEE/RSJ Intelligent Robots and Systems (IROS 2004) Conference, September - October 2004, pp. 1979–1984. Sendai Kyodo Printing, Sendai (2004)
14. Kumar, D., Ramasamy, R., Stefanich, G.: Science instruction for students with visual impairments. In: ERIC 464805, pp. 1–2 (2001)
15. Mayo, M.: Games for Science and Engineering Education. Communications of the ACM 30(35), 30–35 (2007)
16. Polya, G.: How to Sove It, A new Aspect of Mathematical Method. Princeton University Press, New Jersey (1973)
17. Prensky, M.: Digital game-based learning. Computers in Entertainment 1(1), 21 (2003)
18. Rideout, V., Roberts, D., Foehr, U.: Generation m: Media in the lives of 8-18 year-olds, pp. 8–18. Henry Kayser Family Foundation, Menlo Park (2005)

19. Roper, R.: Using technology to teach students with mild disabilities: current trends and future technologies. Law and Disorder, Undergraduate Journal in Special Education Law (1), 54–58 (2006)
20. Sahyun, S., Gardner, S., Gardner, C.: Audio and Haptic Access to Math and Science - Audio graphs, Triangle, the MathPlus Toolbox, and the Tiger printer. In: Proceedings of the 15th IFIP World Computer Congress, Vienna, September 1998, pp. 78–86 (1998)
21. Sánchez, J.: End-user and facilitator questionnaire for Software Usability. In: Usability evaluation test, Santiago, University of Chile (2003)
22. Sánchez, J.: Mobile Science Learning and Inclusion for Blind People. In: 13th Annual CyberTherapy Conference, San Diego, CA, June 23-25 (2008)
23. Sánchez, J., Sáenz, M.: Developing Mathematics Skills through Audio Interfaces. In: Proceedings of 11th International Conference on Human-Computer Interaction, HCI 2005, Las Vegas, Nevada, USA, July 22-27 (2005) (to be published)
24. Sánchez, J., Sáenz, M.: Usability of Audio-Based Virtual Environments for Users with Visual Disabilities. In: Virtual Reality and Human Behavior Symposium, LAVAL Virtual 2007, Laval, France, April 18-22 (2007)
25. Sánchez, J., Salinas, A.: Science Problem Solving Learning through Mobile Gaming. In: MindTrek 2008 Conference, Tampere, Finland, October 8-9, pp. 49–53 (2008)
26. Schneider, J., Strothotte, T.: Constructive Exploration of Spatial Information by Blind Users. In: Proceedings of ACM ASSETS 2000, Arlington, Virginia, November 13-15, pp. 188–192 (2000)
27. Sjostrom, C.: Using haptics in computer interfaces for blind people. In: Sjostrom, C. (ed.) Proceeding of the ACM CHI 2001, Seattle, Washington, USA, March 31 – April 5, pp. 245–246 (2001)
28. Sloan, D., Phipps, L.: Helping to avoid e-discrimination in UK tertiary education. In: Proceedings of the 2003 conference on Universal usability, Vancouver, British Columbia, Canada, pp. 150–151 (2003)
29. Squire, K.: Video Games In Education. International Journal of Intelligent Simulations and Gaming 2(1), 49–62 (2003)
30. Squire, K.: Video games in education. International Journal of Intelligent Simulations and Gaming 2(1), 49–62 (2003)
31. Steinkuehler, C.: Learning in massively multiplayer online games. In: Kafai, Y.B., Sandoval, W.A., Enyedy, N., Nixon, A.S., Herrera, F. (eds.) Proceedings of the 6th International Conference of the Learning Sciences, pp. 521–528. Erlbaum, Mahwah (2004)
32. El Mercurio Newspaper (Chile), Edition of Sunday, Section C (June 15, 2008)
33. Westin, T.: Game accessibility case study: Terraformers – a real-time 3D graphic game. In: Proceedings of the 5th International Conference on Disability, Virtual Reality and Associated Technologies, ICDVRAT 2004, Oxford, UK, pp. 95–100 (2004)
34. Eriksson, Y., Gärdenfors, D.: Computer games for children with visual impairments. In: Proceedings of the 5th International conference on Disability, Virtual Reality and Associated Technologies, New College, Oxford, UK, September 20-22, pp. 79–86 (2004)
35. Archambault, D., Olivier, D.: How to make games for visually impaired children. In: Proceedings of the 2005 ACM SIGCHI international Conference on Advances in Computer Entertainment Technology. ACE 2005, June 15 - 17, vol. 265, pp. 450–453. ACM, New York (2005)
36. Grammenos, D., Savidis, A., Georgalis, Y., Stephanidis, C.: Access Invaders: Developing a Universally Accessible Action Game. In: Miesenberger, K., et al. (eds.) ICCHP 2006. LNCS, vol. 4061, pp. 388–395. Springer, Heidelberg (2006)

Speech-Based Navigation: Improving Grid-Based Solutions

Shaojian Zhu[1], Yao Ma[2], Jinjuan Feng[2], and Andrew Sears[1]

[1] UMBC, 1000 Hilltop Circle, Baltimore, MD, USA, 21250
{szhu1,asears}@umbc.edu
[2] Towson University, 7800 York Road, Towson, MD, USA, 21252
{yma1,jfeng}@towson.edu

Abstract. Speech-based technology is a useful alternative to traditional input techniques such as the keyboard and mouse. For people with disabilities that hinder use of traditional input devices, a hands-free speech-based interaction solution is highly desirable. Various speech-based navigation techniques have been discussed in the literature and employed in commercial software applications. Among them, grid-based navigation has shown both potential and limitations. Grid-based solutions allow users to position the cursor using recursive grids to 'drill down' until the cursor is in the desired location. We report the results of an empirical study that assessed the efficacy of two enhancements to the grid-based navigation technique: magnification and fine-tuning. Both mechanisms were designed to facilitate the process of selecting small targets. The results suggest that both the magnification and the fine-tuning capabilities significantly improved the participants' performance when selecting small targets and that fine-tuning also has benefits when selecting larger targets. Participants preferred the solution that provided both enhancements.

Keywords: MouseGrid, Speech-based Cursor Control, Accessibility.

1 Introduction

Speech recognition technology enables people to use speech as an alternative input method when interacting with computers. Some commercial operating systems like Windows Vista™ provide speech functions for a variety of graphical interface-based tasks such as interacting with the desktop applications and browsing the web [1]. When using computers, two types of tasks account for the vast majority of user activity: text generation and navigation [2]. Previous research has confirmed that modern speech recognition technology can be quite effective for text generation tasks [3], but it remains difficult for users to complete spatial navigation tasks using speech [4]. A number of researchers suggested that the use of pointing devices should not be completely eliminated when people use speech recognition to interact with computers [5]. Multimodal solutions that use speech for text generation and pointing devices for

T. Gross et al. (Eds.): INTERACT 2009, Part I, LNCS 5726, pp. 50–62, 2009.

spatial navigation are often recommended for people who can use their hands effectively [6].

However, people with disabilities experience lots of difficulties when using traditional input devices like the mouse. Therefore, a hands-free speech-based solution is likely to be more effective for disabled people. For example, there are a number of diseases and conditions that can affect the hands and arms, such as high level Spinal Cord Injuries (SCI), Amyotrophic Lateral Sclerosis (ALS), or stroke, making a mouse difficult to use [7]. Compared with other alternatives such as head-controlled devices, eye-controlled interactions, or electrophysiological solutions, speech-based solutions are less expensive, provide a more natural interaction style, and can be easier to learn. In order for speech technologies to be widely adopted by users with disabilities that affect their hands or arms, more effective speech-based cursor control solutions are highly desired.

Resources have been invested in this area, seeking to identify better ways for people to use speech recognition to easily complete the cursor control tasks. Grid-based solutions, developed by Kamel for blind users [8], and subsequently evaluated by sighted users [9], provide a flexible, reliable, alternative but opportunities for improvement remain. The grid-based method allows the user to select targets on screen by 'drilling-down' to a smaller grid until the cursor is positioned in the desired location. However, in a recent field study that focused on how people interact with speech technologies in realistic environments, we found the widely adopted version of grid-based cursor control is inadequate, resulting in poor performance and satisfaction ratings [10].

Based on our previous research [10], we proposed two enhancements to the grid-based solution: magnification and fine-tuning. A software prototype was developed integrating the two enhancements, and an empirical study was conducted to evaluate the efficacy of the enhancements. The results confirm that both fine-tuning and magnification resulted in significant improvements. In this paper, we discuss the motivation behind the two enhancements, how the empirical study was conducted, and the major results. Implications and directions for future research are discussed at the end of the paper.

2 Related Research

There are a number of research projects that used speech as one of the interface modalities. Substantial advancements have been made in speech recognition systems regarding both recognition speed and accuracy, with dictation accuracy reaching as high as 98% in controlled environments [11, 12]. However, a hands-free speech-enabled system must support both dictation and cursor control [2] and difficulties dealing with spatial tasks using speech have been discussed for years [6].

There are two main categories of cursor control for speech-enabled systems: direction-based and target-based solutions. Alternative speech-based cursor control solutions can also be discussed based on the type of movement that results: discrete or continuous movements [9]. For discrete direction-based navigation, users specify the movement direction and distance, such as ‘Move left three words’. The distance can be specified in inches, centimeters, words or other units that are appropriate for the situation. In some situations, a default distance such as one word or line is assumed. For continuous direction-based solutions, users must begin by issuing a command that initiates the movement (e.g., move left). Responding to the command, the cursor moves smoothly in the specified direction at a fixed speed until being stopped by another command (e.g., ‘stop’). The direction-based approach can allow users to control the movement direction and distance, but it also has substantial disadvantages. First, performance is influenced by the relative position of the cursor and target location. Second, the interaction is not natural for many users. Third, it does not provide enough flexibility for different contexts. Fourth, selection of small targets can be both slow and error prone.

Compared to direction-based navigation, target-based cursor control takes advantage of contextual information, allowing users to select targets by specifying the name of the desired object. For example, ‘select Friday’ could move the cursor to the word ‘Friday’ in a text document. For many users, this technique is more natural and direct, but it only works when all possible target have a name that is known by the user [13]. As graphical interfaces become more complex, many potential targets may not have clearly visible label accompanying them and the use of existing target-based techniques can become difficult. When the label is not visible, and multiple targets share the same name, target-based solutions become more difficult and less efficient.

A number of studies have focused on making speech-based navigation techniques more effective. Some focused on speech-based navigation techniques in the context of text documents [3, 14] while others focused on general target-selection tasks [13]. In general, target-based navigation has proven effective in the context of text documents, but less effective in the context of desktop interaction when the names of icons or targets are not clearly labeled. Direction-based techniques that result in continuous cursor movement have been reported to be both slow and error prone [13], and direction-based techniques that use contextual information (e.g., number of lines and words) may prove challenging since the only units available to specify distances are pixels or physical distances (e.g., inches or centimeters) both of which users are likely to have difficulty estimating accurately.

The grid-based technique was proposed as a way to select target without contextual information. Using this technique, the user recursively drills down through each grid until the cursor is placed on the desired object. Kamel and Landay [8, 15, 16] developed a speech-based grid drawing tool for blind people, employing a 3x3 grid, demonstrating the potential of grid-based speech cursor control. Dai [2] built on these results and evaluated two alternatives: the traditional solution with a single cursor in the middle of the grid and an alternative which placed a cursor in the center of each of the nine cells of the grid. The results indicated that the nine cursor solution was faster but resulted in more errors. To date, the grid-based approach has shown potential for desktop interactions when the target is fairly large (e.g., desktop icons), but it becomes increasingly cumbersome as targets get smaller (e.g., word, menu icons, letters). When targets are sufficiently small, grid-based navigation becomes slow and error prone. Some commercial speech-based business systems like Windows Vista™ provide variants of grid based cursor control. Within Windows Vista™, grid-based navigation is available through the MouseGrid command.

Compared to the target-based technique, grid-based solutions should result in less cognitive load because the grid numbers can be both visible and intuitive and the target selection procedure is straight forward. Another advantage is that the grid-based technique can position the cursor anywhere on the screen (e.g., a blank space on the screen), something that is not possible with target-based solutions. As discussed by Dai et al. [9], grid-based cursor control can place the cursor at any point on screen in N steps which can be calculated based on Formula 1:

$$N = Log_n(D/A). \tag{1}$$

In the formula, n is the number of grid rows/columns (normally three), D is the resolution of screen and A is the size of the target. The effectiveness of the grid-based approach is affected by the relative position of the cursor and target. If a target is located near the center of a grid, the user may be able to select it easily. More importantly, selecting small targets using the grid-based approach tends to be problematic. When the targets are small, the user may need to issue five or more commands to focus on smaller portions of the screen, with each command making it somewhat harder to determine the relative position of the target and the grid [13]. At the same time, grid lines and the numbers in the cells of the grid can become distracting. To address these challenges, we proposed the following two enhancements, magnification and fine-tuning to the grid-based approach.

3 Software Prototypes

To make it easier for users to select small targets, we proposed two enhancements to the grid-based technique: magnification and fine-tuning. Once the grid becomes sufficiently small, the magnification function shows the user a magnified version of the grid making it easier to see small targets. The fine-tuning function allows the user to fine-tune the cursor location using four simple commands: 'up, down, right, and left'. Each command moves the cursor to the specific direction by a specific number of pre-defined units, making it easy to shift the cursor small distances when that is all that is required to select a target.

The first version implements the basic grid-based navigation technique. The second implements the magnification capability. When user zooms a third time, the magnification capability is automatically activated simplifying the selection of small targets (See fig. 1a and 1b). The user can continue zooming if desired, with the selected cell being magnified each time. The third version implements the fine-tuning capability. After zooming a third time, the application stops zooming. Instead, a new cursor is presented indicating the current location (See fig. 1c and 1d). This cursor can be repositioned using the four fine-tuning commands. The fourth condition implements both magnification and fine-tuning (see fig. 1e and 1f).

Fig 1a and fig 1b show the transition after the user issued the command 'seven' with the magnification capability. The standard technique would shrink the focus into the seventh cell of the grid. With the magnification capability, the system will not only focus on cell seven, but also magnifies that region to make it more visible.

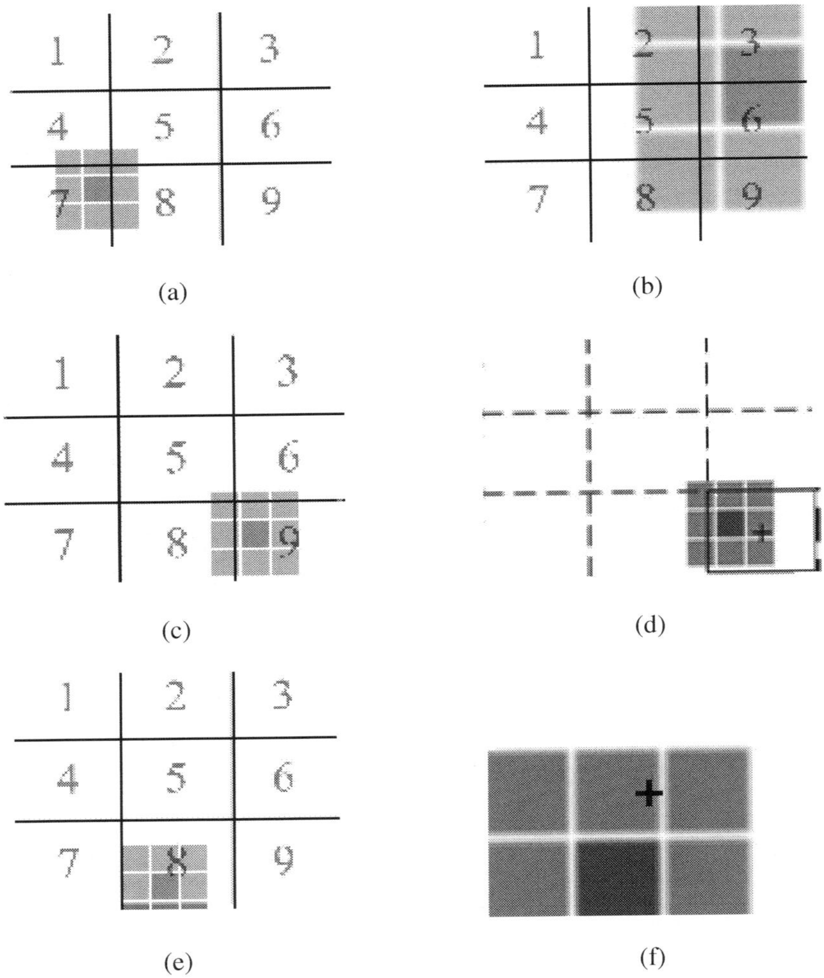

Fig. 1. (a) Before magnification. (b) After magnification. (c) Before fine-tuning. (d) After fine-tuning. (e) Before magnification & fine-tuning. (f) After magnification & fine-tuning.

Fig 1c and fig 1d show the transition after the user issued the command 'nine' with the fine-tuning capability. The basic grid-based technique just focuses on the ninth cell. With the fine-tuning function, the system focuses on cell three, then enables the direction-based fine-tuning commands (up, down, left, and right). The actual cursor is visualized using a black cross.

Fig 1e and fig 1f show the transition after the user issued the command 'eight' with both magnification and fine-tuning capabilities.

4 Methods

4.1 Participants

Twenty native English speakers (12 Males, 8 Females) volunteered to participate in our experiment. None of them had any cognitive or motor impairments. The average age of our participants was 21.3 (stdev = 3.36), and the average computer experience was 13.3 years (stdev = 4.09). Most of the participants had information technology related backgrounds. Each participant completed all four conditions with each condition requiring the selection of 40 targets.

4.2 Equipments

A PC running Windows XP was used for this study. A 17-inch LCD non-wide screen monitor was used for the visual output with the resolution set to 1024x768. Participants sat at a comfortable distance from the display. Voice commands were processed using the Microsoft SAPI5.1 speech recognition engine. Each participant used the same Andrea NC61 headset microphone to complete the study. A C# application was used to implement the prototypes with logging functions that recorded interaction activities including task completion times and target/cursor positions.

4.3 Experiment Design

A within-group experiment design was adopted. Each participant finished all four conditions listed in table 1. Condition 1 was the baseline condition in which neither of the enhancements was offered. The order in which participants completed the conditions was randomized.

Table 1. Four Experimental Conditions with different settings

	Without magnification	**With magnification**
Without fine-tuning	C1	C2
With fine-tuning	C3	C4

At the beginning of the study, the participant was given a training session with four target selection tasks to allow them to become familiar with the speech-based cursor control solution. Multiple training sessions were given upon request. After the training session, the participant completed 40 target selection tasks as part of each condition. For each task, the location of the target was randomly defined. The target size was randomly selected among four choices: 10x10, 20x20, 40x40 and 80x80 pixels (i.e., square targets 3.37, 6.74, 13.49 and 26.98 millimeters respectively). The four possible sizes were selected to represent the sizes of common graphical user interface components: letters (10), words/menus/small icons (20), buttons (40), and desktop icons (80). Under each condition, the participant selected a total of ten targets of each size.

4.4 Independent and Dependent Variables

The independent variables of interest include the type of grid-based navigation supported and target size. The dependent variables examined include target selection time, error rates, and subjective satisfaction ratings. An error was documented when a participant issued the 'ok' command to select a target and the cursor was located outside of the target area.

A questionnaire using a 5-point Likert-scale (1 as most positive and 5 as most negative) assessed the participants' subjective perceptions of speed, accuracy, and comfort level after each condition. A general questionnaire was completed after all conditions asking the participants to rank order the four alternative solutions (1 as most favorable and 4 as least favorable). Demographical information was also collected via the general questionnaire.

4.5 Hypothesis

We investigated the impact of magnification and fine-tuning capabilities on user performance and user satisfaction. User performance is measured by task completion time and error rates. User satisfaction is measured via subjective ratings collected through questionnaire. We tested the following hypotheses:

H1a: Task completion time will be shorter in the magnification condition than the baseline condition.

H1b: Task completion time will be shorter in the fine-tuning condition than the baseline condition.

H1c: Task completion time will be the shortest for the condition providing both magnification and fine tuning.

H2a: Error rate will be lower in the magnification condition than the baseline condition.

H2b: Error rate will be lower in the fine-tuning condition than the baseline condition.

H2c: Error rate will be the lowest for the conditions providing both magnification and fine tuning.

We expect that the size of targets play an important role for user performance, with smaller targets being harder to select. The following hypotheses are proposed with regard to target size and user performance.

H3a: Participants will spend longer selecting smaller targets.

H3b: Participants' error rates will be higher when selecting smaller targets.

Finally we examine whether there is significant difference in user satisfaction among the four conditions. The following hypotheses are proposed related to user satisfaction:

H4a: The magnification and fine-tuning capabilities will lead to more positive subjective assessments.

H4b: Users will prefer conditions with magnification and fine-tuning capabilities as compared to the control condition.

5 Results

5.1 Selection Time

Mean target selection times for each target size under each condition are reported in Table 2 and illustrated in Fig 2. A repeated measures ANOVA with target selection time as the dependent variable and target size and condition as independent variables confirmed a significant effect for both condition ($F(3, 57) = 4.85$, $p < 0.005$) and target size ($F(3, 57) = 183.4$, $p < 0.001$). The interaction between size and condition is not significant ($F(9, 171) = 1.72$, n.s.).

Table 2. Average task completion time for each condition/size (standard deviations in parentheses)

	size 10	size 20	size 40	size 80
Basic (N/A)	143.1 (37.9)	109.2 (22.7)	92.8 (11.5)	89.0 (15.9)
Magnification Only	125.4 (22.6)	100.9 (12.8)	92.7 (13.7)	87.3 (16.2)
Fine-tuning Only	126.1 (11.0)	103.9 (8.4)	82.7 (6.2)	79.9 (6.2)
Both	125.7 (15.4)	101.7 (10.6)	83.9 (8.9)	81.3 (6.6)

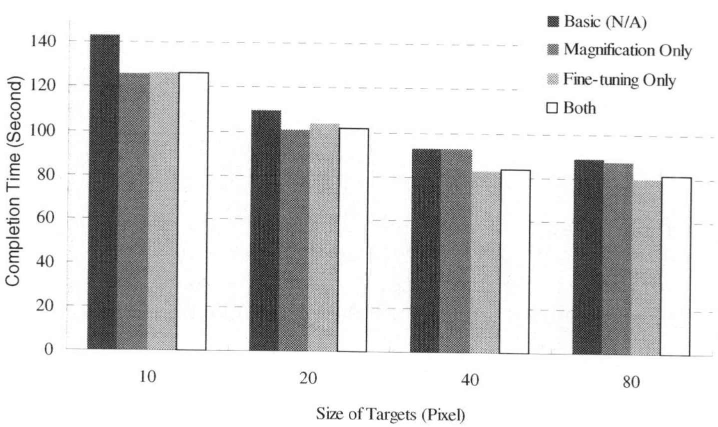

Fig. 2. Average task completion time for each condition/size

The different grid-based solutions resulted in significantly different target selection times for targets of size 10, 40 and 80 ($F(3, 57) = 2.91$, $p < 0.05$; $F(3, 57) = 6.39$, $p < 0.001$; $F(3, 57) = 3.90$, $p < 0.05$). However, difference for targets of size 20 was not significant ($F(3, 57) = 1.51$, n.s.). Table 3 summarizes the results of the one tailed Post Hoc tests comparing specific condition/target size combinations. When the target size was 10, participants spent significantly longer with the baseline solution as compared to any of the other solutions, suggesting both magnification and fine-tuning improved performance. When the targets were size 40 or 80, participants spent significantly less time in conditions that offered the fine-tuning enhancement as compared to those that did not. Overall, the results suggest that the magnification function did not improve performance for relatively large targets, but when targets are sufficiently small magnification is beneficial. In contrast, fine-tuning was useful for both large and small targets. Therefore, H1a is supported for small targets only. H1b is supported for both large and small targets. H1c was not supported (i.e., the benefits of magnification and fine-tuning were not additive).

Table 3. Summary of Post Hoc tests for Repeated Measure ANOVA

Conditions under comparison	Size 10	Size 40	Size 80
Baseline vs. Magnification	$p < 0.05$	n.s.	n.s.
Baseline vs. Fine-tuning	$p < 0.05$	$p < 0.001$	$p < 0.05$
Baseline vs. M & F-T	$p < 0.05$	$p < 0.05$	$p < 0.05$
Magnification vs. Fine-tuning	n.s.	$p < 0.05$	$p < 0.05$
Magnification vs. M& F-T	n.s.	$p < 0.05$	$p < 0.05$
Fine-tuning vs. M & F-T	n.s.	n.s.	n.s.

A regression analysis with time as the dependent variable and condition and target size as independent variables show a significant impact of both condition and size. Size explained substantially more variance in task time than condition (48.6% vs. 2.5%). So H3a is supported.

5.2 Accuracy

The mean error rate for each target size and condition combination are reported in Table 4 and illustrated in Fig 3. A repeated measures ANOVA with error rates as the dependent variable and size and condition as independent variables confirms that condition did not have a significant effect on error rates ($F(3, 57)=0.57$, n.s.). H2a, H2b, and H2c are not supported.

Target size did have a significant effect on error rates ($F(3, 57)=6.84$, $p < 0.01$) with participants making more errors when selecting smaller targets. The interaction between size and condition was not significant ($F(9, 171) = 0.87$, n.s.). H3b is supported.

Table 4. Average error rates (%) for each condition/size (standard deviations in parentheses)

	size 10	size 20	size 40	size 80
Basic (N/A)	4.5 (8.8)	1.0 (3.0)	0.0 (0.0)	1.5 (3.6)
Magnification Only	5.0 (0.0)	1.0 (4.4)	0.5 (2.2)	1.5 (4.8)
Fine-tuning Only	2.5 (5.5)	1.5 (4.8)	0.0 (0.0)	0.0 (0.0)
Both	2.0 (4.1)	0.5 (2.2)	1.5 (3.6)	1.0 (3.0)

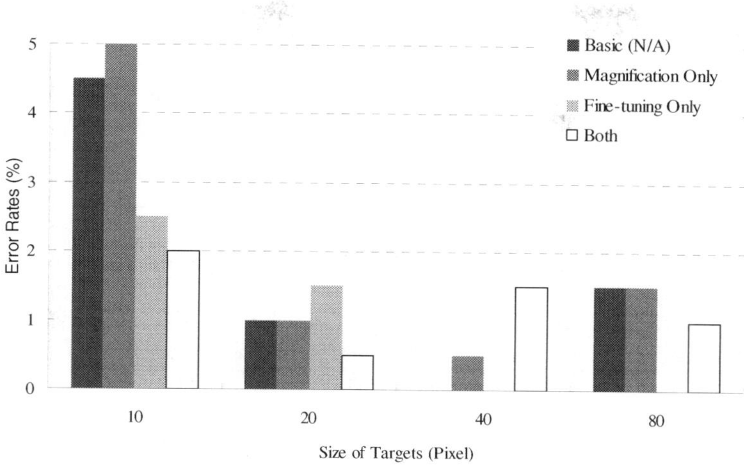

Fig. 3. Average error rates (%) for each condition/size

5.3 User Satisfaction Rating

Mean user ratings concerning speed, accuracy and comfort are reported in Table 5. A repeated measures ANOVA confirmed that condition did not have a significant effect on user satisfaction with speed (F(3, 57)=1.5, n.s.), accuracy (F(3, 57)=3.0, n.s.), and or comfort (F(3, 57)=1.2, n.s.). H4a is not supported.

A CHI squared test did identify a significant difference among the rankings provided for the four solutions (X^2 (9) = 35.6, p < 0.001). Table 6 indicates the

Table 5. Subjective rating or speed, accuracy, and ease of use Ratings were provided from 1 (most positive) to 5 (most negative) (Standard deviations in parentheses)

	Speed	**Accuracy**	**Comfort**
Basic (N/A)	2.05 (0.75)	1.55 (0.68)	1.55 (0.60)
Magnification Only	1.80 (1.00)	1.50 (0.82)	1.40 (0.59)
Fine-tuning Only	1.80 (0.69)	1.35 (0.58)	1.35 (0.58)
Both	1.75 (0.78)	1.40 (0.50)	1.40 (0.50)

Table 6. The number of participants who rated each solution as their first, second, third, or fourth preference

	First	**Second**	**Third**	**Fourth**
Basic (N/A)	3	1	5	11
Magnification Only	3	8	5	4
Fine-tuning Only	3	4	10	3
Both	11	7	0	2

number of participants who rated each condition as their first, second, third, or fourth preference. Eleven participants rated the solution that offered both magnification and fine-tuning as the best. Only three participants rated each of the other solutions as the best. H4b is supported.

6 Discussion

The data confirmed that the new capabilities (magnification and fine-tuning) did result in improved performance. Both magnification and fine-tuning significantly decreased task completion times compared to the baseline condition. However, neither magnification nor fine-tuning decrease the error rate significantly. We believe one possible reason is that the participants completed the tasks without time pressure. Therefore, they could spend as much time as necessary to achieve a desired level of accuracy. As we can see from Table 4, the highest error rate occurred under the magnification condition for targets of size 10, but even under this condition the participants' average error rate was just 5%. In general, users rarely made mistakes even for the smallest targets. It will be interesting to examine accuracy and efficiency in more detail. For example, it may prove useful to analyze the number of commands participants issued and the minimum number of commands required to select each target as well as the specific commands used.

Participants preferred the solution that provided both magnification and fine-tuning. While performance measures reveal no differences between this condition and those that provide a single enhancement, these results confirm that participants preferred to have both options available to be used if and when they desired. By providing both capabilities, users could fine-tune the cursor location as necessary including some situations when they were selecting large targets and the cursor was very close to being on the target. Similarly, users could take advantage of the magnification function when selecting small targets.

As expected, target size plays an important role with regard to performance, having a significant effect on both task completion times and error rates, which is consistent with the existing literature [9]. In addition, size explained a large portion of the variance in task completion time. While more effective grid-based navigation solutions can make selecting small target significantly faster, small targets will still require more time than larger targets. Therefore, designers of graphical user interfaces should still pay attention to the size of interface component to facilitate smooth interactions.

The pattern of results for task completion times is interesting. Clearly, magnification provided no benefit when selecting the two largest targets. For targets of size 20, a difference begins to emerge but it is not significant. Finally, when selecting the smallest targets, magnification allowed for significantly faster task completion times as compared to the baseline condition. It is possible that the lack of benefit for larger targets may be due directly to the size of the target or because users did not zoom in enough to activate magnification. A more detailed analysis of the specific commands issued may provide useful insights. For example, such an analysis may help provide a more definitive answer as to how small a target must be before magnification is useful.

The pattern of results is quite different for the solutions that provided the fine-tuning capability. In these conditions, users were able to select both large and small targets faster than they could with the baseline solution. While magnification was not useful when selecting large targets, it appears that there are some situations where the cursor may be close enough to a target that fine-tuning is still a useful alternative.

The results for the targets of size 20 may suggest that these targets are near the threshold where magnification first becomes useful. If this is the case, it could be that users end up spending more time deciding which enhancement to use, slowing the overall process of selecting the target. In future studies, we plan to examine the effect of target size in more detail by using a larger variety of target sizes.

While the solution that provided both magnification and fine-tuning was no more efficient than the solution that provided just fine-tuning, more than half of the participants rated the solution with both enhancements as the best. We suggest that this may be because this solution provides more flexibility than any of the other alternatives. Magnification is likely to be useful only for small targets, but fine-tuning could prove useful regardless of target size. Most importantly, users are free to use both magnification and fine-tuning if and when they believe it would be useful.

7 Conclusions

To address the limitations of existing grid-based navigation solutions, especially inefficiencies when selecting small targets, we proposed, implemented, and evaluated two enhancements: magnification and fine-tuning. Our empirical evaluation with 20 participants suggests that the fine-tuning function significantly reduced target selection time for both large and small targets while magnification was only useful when selecting small targets. Neither enhancement had a significant effect on error rates. Importantly, there was a clear preference for the solution that provided both magnification and fine-tuning. Besides, the results from this study imply the possible benefits for people with disabilities who are not able to use traditional input devices. We are currently conducting a study that involves individuals with physical disabilities to evaluate whether the results observed with able-bodied users can be generalized to users with disabilities.

Acknowledgments. This material is based upon work supported by the National Science Foundation (NSF) under Grant No. CNS-0619379 and National Institute on Disabilities and Rehabilitation Research (NIDRR) under grant number H133G050354. Any opinions, findings and conclusions or recommendations expressed in this material are those of the authors and do not necessarily reflect the views of the NSF and the NIDRR.

References

1. Vista™ Speech Recognition, `http://en.wikipedia.org/wiki/Windows_Speech_Recognition`
2. Oviatt, S.L.: Multimodal interactive maps: Designing for human performance. In: Human-Computer Interaction, vol. 12, pp. 93–129. Springer, Heidelberg (1997)

3. Feng, J., Sears, A.: Using confidence scores to improve hands-free speech based navigation in continuous dictation systems. ACM Trans. Comput.-Hum. Interact. 11(4), 329–356 (2004)
4. Lai, J., Yankelovich, N.: Conversational speech interfaces. In: Jacko, J.A., Sears, A. (eds.) The Human-Computer interaction Handbook: Fundamentals, Evolving Technologies and Emerging Applications. Human Factors and Ergonomics, pp. 698–713. L. Erlbaum Associates, Hillsdale (2007)
5. Cohen, M.H., Giangola, J.P., Balogh, J.: Voice User Interface Design. Addison Wesley Longman Publishing Co., Inc., Redwood City (2004)
6. Oviatt, S.: Multimodal Interfaces. In: Jacko, J.A., Sears, A. (eds.) The Human-Computer interaction Handbook: Fundamentals, Evolving Technologies and Emerging Applications, pp. 413–432. L. Erlbaum Associates, Hillsdale (2007)
7. Sears, A., Young, M., Feng, J.: Physical Disabilities and Computing Technologies: An Analysis of Impairments. In: Jacko, J.A., Sears, A. (eds.) The Human-Computer interaction Handbook: Fundamentals, Evolving Technologies and Emerging Applications. Human Factors and Ergonomics, pp. 829–852. L. Erlbaum Associates, Hillsdale (2007)
8. Kamel, H., Landay, J.: The Integrated Communication 2 Draw (IC2D): A drawing program for the visually impaired. In: CHI 1999 (1999)
9. Dai, L., Goldman, R., Sears, A., Lozier, J.: Speech-based cursor control: a study of grid-based solutions. In: Assets 2004: Proceedings of the 6th international ACM SIGACCESS conference on Computers and accessibility, pp. 94–101. ACM, New York (2004)
10. Feng, J., Zhu, S., Hu, R., Sears, A.: Speech technology in real world environment: early results from a long term study. In: Assets 2008: Proceedings of the 10th international ACM SIGACCESS conference on Computers and accessibility, pp. 233–234. ACM, New York (2008)
11. Halverson, C., Horn, D., Karat, C., Karat, J.: The Beauty of Errors: Patterns of Error Correction in Desktop Speech systems. In: Proc. INTERACT 1999, pp. 1–9 (1999)
12. Karat, C., Vergo, J., Nahamoo, D.: Conversational Interface Technologies. In: Jacko, J., Sears, A. (eds.) The Human-Computer Interaction Handbook, pp. 169–186. LEA, NJ (2003)
13. Karimullah, A.S., Sears, A.: Speech-based cursor control. In: Proceedings of Assets 2002, pp. 178–185 (2002)
14. Sears, A., Feng, J., Oseitutu, K., Karat, C.: Hands-free, speech-based navigation during dictation: difficulties, consequences, and solutions. Hum.-Comput. Interact. 18(3), 229–257 (2003)
15. Kamel, H., Landay, J.: A study of blind drawing practice: Creating graphical information without the visual channel. In: ASSETS 2000 (2000)
16. Kamel, H., Landay, J.: Sketching images eyes-free: A grid-based dynamic drawing tool for the blind. In: ASSETS 2002 (2002)

Useful, Social and Enjoyable: Mobile Phone Adoption by Older People

Mario Conci, Fabio Pianesi, and Massimo Zancanaro

FBK-irst,
38123 Trento, Italy
{mconci,pianesi,zancana}@fbk.eu

Abstract. The paper presents an empirical model of acceptance of mobile phones by elderly people. It is based on an extension of the widely used TAM-Technology Acceptance Model and aims specifically at investigating the relationship among intrinsic and extrinsic motivations to use. The data consists of 740 questionnaires from people over 65 years old. The validated model shows that intrinsic motivations play an important role albeit always mediated by utilitarian motives. Similarly, it emerges a strong influence of the reference social group (children and relatives) in increasing the utilitarian values of the use of mobile phones. These findings suggest that mobile phone usage by elderly might not be, after all, too much different, from a motivational point of view, from that of younger or adult people.

Keywords: TAM, mobile phones, elders, intrinsic motivation.

1 Introduction

Currently, people aged over 65 represent approximately 13% of the population, a figure that is expected to increase by 2030 [8]. Although the elderly is still under-considered in the technology world and seen as a "non technological" person, a substantial amount of studies contend this stereotype [see for example 9]. Indeed, there is no evidence that older people reject technology more than people of other ages; elderly, as anyone else, accept and adopt technology when the latter meets their needs and expectations [49]. Older people can be expected to have a different approach to technology from younger people. Because of sensory, motor, and cognitive changes due to ageing, older people might need more time to learn, be more error-prone, and need more steps to operate the system.

In this paper, we first propose and then investigate on a large group of elderly people living in northern Italy, a model for the acceptance of mobile phones (MP), operationalizing acceptance as the "intention to use" the technology. A major goal of the proposed model is to empirically investigate the motivational structure underlying MP acceptance, by considering both extrinsic (utilitarian) and intrinsic (hedonic) motivations. The results confirm the importance of utilitarian considerations, and particularly of the perceived usefulness, as a driving factor for the intention to use the MP. Yet they also show how intrinsic motivations, and in particular those concerning

T. Gross et al. (Eds.): INTERACT 2009, Part I, LNCS 5726, pp. 63–76, 2009.

self-realization and enjoyment, play an important role, even if the latter is still mediated by utilitarian consideration. Much as for younger people, social pressure is important also for older people, the difference mostly concerns the type of reference group: the children and the relatives for the elders and the peers for young people.

Another important aspect emerging from our study is that the perceived ease of use and the need for support to use MP persist even after years of usage. Compared with the evidence found in the literature showing that those relationships are typical of early stages of technology usage, our findings suggest that older people do not go beyond an initial approach to the MP, but maintain a certain distance with respect to it, even after years of frequent usage.

2 Related Works

Despite its enormous growth and social diffusion, the amount of studies in the area of acceptance of mobile phones is relatively small. In recent years, however, researchers have started to focus on the social and psychological aspects of the MP diffusion, and on its impact on people's daily lives and relationships. In consideration of the enormous adoption of the MP among young people, most efforts have been devoted to this age group, with only few studies at present targeting older people. Indeed, younger people have for long been the most active MP users, but in the last few years its usage by people over 60 has also been growing very rapidly. According to a recent survey, in Italy 58.5% of the people between 65 and 74 and 26.6% of those above 75 use the MP, with a much higher growth trend in this age group than in others [21].

According to Ling et al. [28] MPs gained so much popularity because they allow people to stay in touch and have easy access to information anywhere and anytime. Among younger people, the motivations towards the use of the MP are social and psychological [10]. Adolescents feel the power of the group, need to be part of a social network, and through the mobile phone they can nurture active networks of social relationships, and prevents the exclusion from the group. With adult users, the initial adoption of the MP seems to rest on safety and job-related reasons rather than social and hedonic ones. The flexible access to information has permitted both an increased productivity, and a timely access to help and support in case of need, improving users' feeling of personal and family security. Safety and security are recognized as most important reasons for MP adoption also among frailer (older and disabled) people, with a positive impact on personal independence [1] and self-image [35]. Aecent work in the tradition of acceptance modelling [45] has highlighted the importance of the distinction between utilitarian and hedonic technologies, and of the related distinction between intrinsic and extrinsic motivations, for the construction of explicit models of technology acceptance. Utilitarian technologies are meant to provide outcomes that go beyond the interaction with the system, usually aiming to provide as much instrumental added value as possible in terms of efficiency and performance. In contrast, hedonic-oriented technologies provide self-fulfilling value to the user; people do not have specific objectives to accomplish, nor do they worry about how and/or when to achieve it. In typical hedonic scenarios e.g. computer games, the focus is not on the instrumental function, but on the interaction with the system, whose value is as higher as greater is the fun experienced by the user during the interaction. The distinction between hedonic and utilitarian technologies reflects in the kind of motivations people have when interacting with them. Intrinsic motivations underlie the execution of an activity for the very sake of the execution itself, and not for the attainment of separable consequences; hence, they typically support the usage of hedonic systems. On the other hand, if separable consequences are a target of the activity (hence, with utilitarian systems), extrinsic motivations come into play [45]. It is not straightforward to map the dimensions taken into considerations by the studies mentioned above onto the intrinsic/extrinsic distinction. However, at a first attempt we might suggest that the main motivations for younger people to use the MP are of the extrinsic type: improve and nurture own social network [51]. As to older people, the literature suggests that they prioritize intrinsic motivations (quality of experience, self-image, etc.).

3 The Model

The model we propose builds on the Technology Acceptance Model (TAM) [11]. TAM aims to discover the impact of external variables on internal beliefs, attitudes and intentions. It assumes that the actual usage of a technology depends on the individual's intention to use it, which is, in turn, influenced by the perception of the advantages and of the easiness related with technology usage. TAM has been widely used in the literature for investigating technology acceptance, receiving extensive empirical support, as well as extensions to make it more capable to cope with different aspects of technology acceptance. According to Davis et al. [12] we used a modified version of TAM, where the intention to use a system (BI) is directly and significantly influenced both by the Perceived Usefulness of it (PU) and the Perceived Ease of Use it (PEU), without passing through attitude as in the original TAM. This version has been named Parsimonious TAM (pTAM) by Sharp [41]. Below we briefly review studies that modified TAM to account for mobile technology acceptance; none of them targeted a specific age group.

Kwon and Chidambaram' [24] model included: individual characteristics, Perceived Ease of Use, Perceived Usefulness, Enjoyment (an intrinsic motivation), and Social Pressure. Results pointed out a non significant general effect of individual characteristics (gender, income, occupation) on BI to use the mobile phone; age had a significant and positive association with Social Pressure, meaning that older people experience more social pressure in their usage of the MP. The Perceived Ease of Use was also an important factor influencing MP acceptance, and was strongly associated with Enjoyment. Nysveen et al. [34] studied the acceptance of mobile services by extending TAM with Perceived Enjoyment as an antecedent of Attitude and Intention to Use. The results supported a stronger effect of Perceived Usefulness and Perceived Ease of Use for utilitarian than for hedonic services. The situation was reversed for Perceived Enjoyment and Expressiveness. Hong and Tam [19] used Need of Uniqueness and Perceived Enjoyment as antecedents of Perceived Usefulness and Intention to Use in a study about acceptance of mobile data services. Van Biljon and Kotzé [44] proposed a Mobile Phone Technology Adoption Model (MOPTAM), which emphasises the importance of Social Influence and Facilitating Conditions like system service, costs and quality.

In building our model, we have focused on: a) the motivational structure of MP acceptance (intrinsic vs. extrinsic motivations), b) the influence of the social environment, c) facilitating conditions that may make the usage of the MP easier for the older person and, d) a specific outcome of MP usage consisting of an increased sense of safety. Here follows a review of works that have considered similar constructs in the investigation of the relationship between older people and advanced technologies. According to Ling and Haddon [30], there are several motives associated with the acceptance of the mobile phone, both for young and older people, including accessibility to information, display characteristics, arranging appointments, and safety that is a relevant factor especially for older people. Oksman [35] investigated the use of, and opinions about, the mobile phone by Finnish older people, reporting that many of them wanted to purchase it to increase security and communication, mostly with family member; recently, however, the usage of the mobile phone for communications with friends and acquaintances has increased. Kurniawan [23] reported that older people find the mobile phone more useful if it supports personal communication and provides sense of security, acting as a means of social integration and enhancing autonomy. Phang et al. [37] used TAM to examine the acceptance of an e-government system by older people. They introduced another intrinsic motivator, Self-Actualization as antecedent of Perceived Usefulness. They also investigated the effect of declining physiological conditions on Perceived Ease of Use, failing to find any, probably because of adaptive/compensatory behaviours by older people.

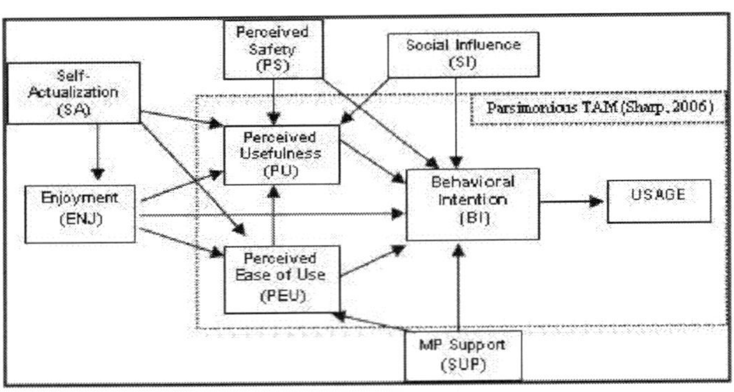

Fig. 1. The research model

The proposed model is displayed in Figure 1. It integrates a pTAM core with Social Influence (SI), Enjoyment (ENJ; an intrinsic motivation), Perceived safety (PS, a relevant outcome), Support to the use of mobile phone (SUP, a facilitating condition) and Self-actualization (SA, another intrinsic motivator). The next subsections discuss the model in greater detail.

3.1 pTAM Constructs: Behavioural Intention to Use (BI), Perceived Usefulness (PU), and Perceived Ease of Use (PEU)

Following a common practice, we operationalize the notion of acceptance by means of the construct of Behavioural Intention to use the system (BI) [13].

To capture extrinsic motivation we exploit TAM's Perceived Usefulness (PU), defined as the extent to which a person believes that using the given technology will enhance his/her performance [12]. PU picks up utilitarian concerns and the instrumental value attributed to the technology. A significant body of research has shown that PU is a strong determinant of BI [48]. Initial evidence that the PU→BI relationships might hold for elderly was provided by Phang et al. [37], though with a different technology (e-government systems).

Perceived Ease of Use (PEU) is defined as the degree to which a person believes that using a system will be free of effort [12]; in a way, it measures the degree of perceived workload due to the usage of the system: the higher PEU, the lower the perceived workload, and vice versa. Several studies pointed out the influence of PEU on BI and on PU [26], providing support to the idea that an easier technology is felt as more useful, and induces a stronger intention to use the system. It should be noted, however, that there is a certain consensus that the PEU→PU relationships holds mainly at the initial stages of technology usage, vanishing when acquaintance with it solidifies. Initial confirmation for the PEU→BI link with the MP was provided by Kwon and Chidambaram [24]. Phang et al.[37], in turn, found support for both PEU→BI and PEU→PU relations for seniors in their study on e-government services acceptance. In the context of our study, these hypotheses assume that a lower perceived workload when using the mobile phone will make elders keener to use it, and will increase its instrumental value.

H1. Perceived Usefulness has a positive effect on BI.
H2. Perceived Ease of use has a positive effect on PU.
H3. Perceived Ease of use has a positive effect on BI.

3.2 Social Influence (SI)

We define Social Influence as the degree to which an individual believes that people who are important to her think she should perform the behaviour in question [48]. We understand it as the feeling of being influenced by relatives and friends (Significant Others) in own usage of the MP. Several works [25, 43, 48] have investigated the possibility that SI affect BI, both directly and indirectly through the mediation of PU. Lee et al. [25] concluded that SI has an unclear effect on BI appearing as a weak predictor in some studies, while having a significant relevance in others. Concerning the mobile phone, SI has been investigated by Teo and Pok [43] as a construct influencing the adoption of a WAP mobile phone among Internet users. They found a positive association between SI and BI, suggesting that people's BI towards adopting a WAP-enable mobile phone is positively related to the influence of their reference groups. Teo and Pok [43] reported that Social Influence has greater effect when the behaviour is new and at the initial stages of adoption. Hypothesising that older people are little experienced with technology in general, they might be expected to follow relatives' opinions in their adoption choices.

H4. Social Influence has a positive effect on PU.
H5. Social Influence has a positive effect on BI.

3.3 Enjoyment (ENJ)

Enjoyment (ENJ), an intrinsic motivation, refers to the extent to which the interaction with the system is perceived to be enjoyable in its own right, apart from any performance consequence that may be anticipated [13].

A growing number of studies suggest that people purchase a mobile phone not just as a business tool but also as a source of enjoyment [24]. Usually ENJ has been studied in relation to technology adoption by young people. We hypothesise that it plays an important role also with older people. Many studies [2, 45] use Enjoyment as an antecedent of PEU and PU, meaning that an enjoyable system is also easier to use and more useful. That is, a high level of Enjoyment increases the instrumental value of the technology [2] and lowers the cognitive burden (the more I enjoy, the more the technology is easy to use). In this work we extend these considerations to the relationship between older people and the MP. Several authors [e.g. 49] found that there is no direct effect of Enjoyment on BI. Chesney [5], however, pointed out the importance for this relation of the system (hedonic vs utilitarian) and of the context where it is used. Following Heerink et al. [17], we assume that with mobile phones (being them at least partially hedonic), enjoyment directly influences the intention to use the mobile phone.

H6. Enjoyment has a positive effect on PU.
H7. Enjoyment has a positive effect on PEU.
H8. Enjoyment has effect on the BI.

3.4 Perceived Safety (PS)

Safety is the state of being "safe", the condition of being protected against physical, social, financial, psychological, etc., damages. In this study we consider the possibility that with seniors such a feeling is supported by the usage of the MP, e.g., to face unwelcome situations.

According to Aoki and Downes [3], personal safety is the initial motivation for many young people to obtain a mobile phone from their parents. The few studies about older people and the mobile phone [23] confirm that one of its most important functions is securing a sense of safety. We hypothesize that PS unfolds its effects by directly affecting both PU and BI, so that the more the MP fosters a sense of safety, the more people will find it useful and the more willing to use it they will be.

H9. Perceived Safety has a positive effect on Perceived Usefulness.
H10. Perceived Safety has a positive effect on Behavioural Intention.

3.5 Mobile Phone Support (SUP)

Originally, Support referred to the help provided by others to the person in her usage of a computer, in form of resources and knowledge [21]. This definition readily extends to the MP and older people. Getting support is very important to help users to overcome barriers with technology, especially during the early stages of use [48]. Igbaria et al [21], Venkatesh and Morris [48], and Phang et al [37] all showed that Support is positively linked to PEU with several technologies. Richardson et al. [39]

found similar results for older people's use of internet in non-workplace settings, where participants expressed their explicit need for support from relatives and friends.

We hypothesize that, since older people may be relatively unfamiliar and unsure of mobile phone usage, support by other people such as family members or friends can be a facilitating condition that increases PEU. Following Nysveen et al. [34], we also speculate that receiving support in using the MP increases the intention to use it.

H11. Support has a positive effect on PEU.
H12. Support has a positive effect on BI.

3.6 Self-Actualization (SA)

Self-actualization refers to the motivation to achieve everything one is capable of [31]. In Maslow's pyramid of needs, SA sits on the top, meaning that it is one of the most important needs to satisfy, by attempting to develop one's identity, increasing expectations and potentials, and achieving a significant social status. A high level of self-actualization co-occurs with people openness to new experiences and to the learning of new ideas and skills [37]. New technologies, in particular computers, allow people to exchange and gather information, and explore more and more of the world, contributing to actualize the self. Technologies that connect individuals, peers and social groups (as the MP does) hold great potential for learning, personal growth and life enhancement. Finally, the self-actualization tends to be more salient in later adulthood [31].

Following Phang et al [37] we exploit SA as a potential antecedent of PU, hypothesising that a higher SA increases the instrumental value of the mobile phone. Moreover, since SA is connected to intrinsic motivation [4], we theorize that it will also affect Enjoyment in MP usage. Finally, we hypothesise that a highly motivated person who wants to actualize herself by using a MP will experience less effort in using it.

H13. Self-actualization has a positive effect on PU.
H14. Self-actualization has a positive effect on Enjoyment.
H15. Self-actualization has a positive effect on PEU.

4 The Study

To explore the model presented above, a survey was conducted by means of mailed questionnaires. Each participant received an envelope containing the questionnaire, a letter of presentation and a second pre-stamped envelope for returning the filled questionnaire. No replying incentive was provided.

Each construct of the research model was measured using standard scales from the literature; when necessary, the scales were adapted to the domain of the study. Subjects were asked to indicate the extent of their agreement/disagreement with each statement of the various scales by means of seven-point Likert scales, anchored to 0="strongly disagree" and 7="strongly agree". Social Influence was measured by the three-item scale used by Hong and Tam [19] to investigate the adoption of mobile data services. We measured Perceived Usefulness through Venkatesh and Morris' scale [48, cit. in 26]. Perceived Ease of Use was investigated by means of the scale by Nysveen et al.[34]. Safety was measured by the seven-item scale used by Aoki and Downes [3]. To address Enjoyment we used a three-item scale by Davis et al.[13]. Support was measured by a four-item scale found in [14]. For BI we used Wixom and Todd's [52] scale, while for Self-Actualization, Porter's scale [cit. in 37] was exploited. More details about the scales can be found at the following url: http://www.mediafire.com/?mytwmyrz4cl.

A pilot study was conducted to assess the content of the questionnaire in terms of intelligibility, format and wording. The study involved 24 senior citizens (mean age: 70 years) who were contacted in several Elders Aggregation Centres in Trento, Italy. They compiled the questionnaire together with an experimenter who took notes of doubts and observations. The subjects were then interviewed about their personal experiences with mobile phones and their attitude towards them, reasons for use and not use and anecdotal facts. The results of this pilot study were used to finalize the questionnaire.

4.1 Participants

The sample consisted of 2970 people participating in the activities of the Third Age University of Trento. We received 1193 replies, with a response rate of 40%. After discarding incomplete questionnaires, 740 of them were retained for analysis. Among the respondents, 26% of them were male and 74% female. The distribution according to age was: (65-69) 33%, (70-74) 37%, (75-79) 20%, (≥80) 10%. The majority reported to own a mobile phone for longer than one year; 33% of the subjects declared to use it every day, 40% several times per week, 24% several times per month, and 3% to never use it.

4.2 Data Analysis

To analyze the model, PLS-Graph [7] was used. The assessment of the validity of the measurement model (convergent and discriminant validity; reliability) was conducted according to guidelines in [16]. All the relevant criteria were satisfied. For reasons of space, the details of the analysis of the measurement model (including loadings and cross loadings, values of average variance extracted, composite reliability and so on) are not presented here but can be found at http://www.mediafire.com/?mytwmyrz4cl.

The structural model was assessed by computing the significance of the path coefficients through t-testing the results of a bootstrap procedure (200 iterations); the results are reported in Table 1. As can be seen, all the relations are significant except for PS→BI and ENJ→BI. Perceived Usefulness, Perceived Ease of Use, Social Influence, and Support were significantly related to the Behavioural Intention to use the MP, hence supporting H1, H3, H5, and H12; the hypothesised influences of Perceived Safety and Enjoyment on BI were not supported (H8 and H10). Perceived Usefulness was significantly affected by Social Influence, Perceived Safety, Self-Actualization, Enjoyment, and Ease to use (H2, H4, H6, H9, and H13). Perceived Ease of Use is significantly influenced by Enjoyment (H7), Support (H11) and Self-Actualization (H15). Though, since the relation between SUP and PEU is negative,

Table 1. Results of Hypothesis Testing* $p<0.05$; ** $p<0.01$; *** $p<0.001$

Hypothesis	Path Coefficient	T-Value	Support
H1. PU → BI	0.236	3.734***	Yes
H2. PEU → PU	0.111	2.923**	Yes
H3. PEU → BI	0.225	5.798***	Yes
H4. SI → PU	0.196	3.904***	Yes
H5. SI → BI	0.155	3.014**	Yes
H6. ENJ → PU	0.118	2.894**	Yes
H7. ENJ → PEU	0.448	10.329***	Yes
H8. ENJ → BI	0.088	2.132	No
H9. PS → PU	0.398	8.095***	Yes
H10. PS → BI	0.089	1.548	No
H11. SUP → PEU	-0.198	5.822***	No
H12. SUP → BI	0.191	4.180***	Yes
H13. SA → PU	0.146	4.318***	Yes
H14. SA → ENJ	0.541	17.820***	Yes
H15. SA → PEU.	0.166	3.534***	Yes

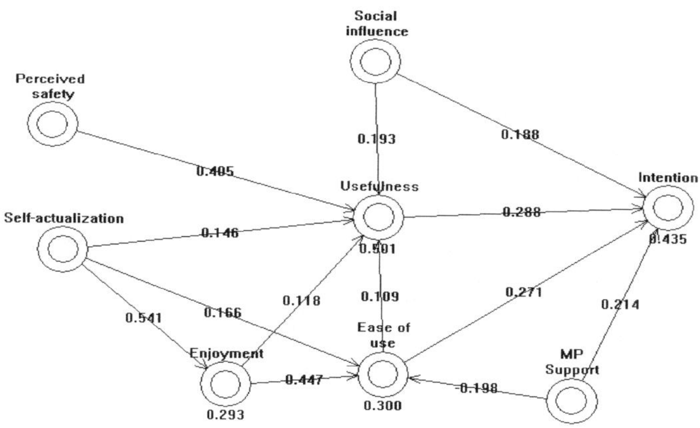

Fig. 2. Final Model

H11 is not supported. Finally, the strong relation between Self-Actualization and Enjoyment supports H14. Once non-significant relationships are dropped, the final model reproduced in Figure 2 is obtained, which reports both the path coefficients and the values of the explained variance, R^2.

4.3 Discussion

In accordance with the results reported in the literature, feeling safe is a crucial issue for older people; it acts on the intention to use the MP only indirectly, by increasing its utilitarian value. Intrinsic motivations are important factors for older people's adoption of the mobile phone. Enjoyment, which has mostly been studied in relation to young people, has the hypothesised effects of increasing the utilitarian value of the mobile phone, as well as its perceived ease of use. Hence, experiential aspects (enjoyment, fun, etc.) are efficacious on mobile phone acceptance in so much as a) they acquire an instrumental value ("I enjoy myself using the mobile phone, hence it is useful, hence I intend to use it"), and b) they contribute to lower the perceived cognitive load. Acceptance of the MP by the elder seem to be built up from utilitarian considerations [3], which are, however, strongly modulated by experiential aspects. Self actualization, the other intrinsic motivator, plays a very similar role to that of Enjoyment: it increases the utilitarian value (PU), lowers the cognitive load and improves the quality of experience (Enjoyment), providing support to Burleson's theory about the synergy among self-actualization, creativity and intrinsic motivations. Thanks to these influences, SA has an important, even if indirect, impact on BI, mediated again by utilitarian considerations.

There is distance between the old person and the mobile phone, though. This is shown by the highly significant relationship between PEU and BI. From the literature we know that in the adoption of technology in organizational settings the perceived ease of use is an important factor at the early stage of adoption, losing its force later on. This is a variety of the novelty effect: technologies that are new, and with a mainly utilitarian value (as the MP, as it turns out), motivate the users to carefully consider the ease of use of the technology when forming their intentions to use it. This effect tends to disappear with practice and with the increase in proficiency in technology usage. Our subjects patterned like early and non-proficient users of utilitarian technologies, in spite of the high frequency of use, and the fact that almost the totality of our subjects has owned a MP for more than 4 years. These findings suggest that even after years of frequent usage, the MP is still perceived as a new and distant technology by older people. This conclusion finds further support in the confirmed effect of SUP on BI. Much as PEU, also the need for support is typically more important at the initial stages of technology adoption. The persistence of its importance for the intention to use the MP (and its inverse relationship to PEU) is coherent with the idea of a stable distance between the MP and older people. Finally, the importance of the pressure from the social environment (in our case, mainly children and other relatives) is confirmed, both as a determinant of extrinsic motivation (PU) and, directly, on the intention to use the MP.

5 Conclusion

The contribution of this study is the development and testing of a model addressing a number of dimensions that the literature indicates as potentially relevant to the acceptance of mobile phones by older people. The model builds on pTAM, extending it with constructs that a) complete the motivational structure (Enjoyment and Self Actualization), b) consider the roles of relevant outcomes of the MP usage (Perceived Safety), facilitating condition (Mobile Phone Support) and social environment. As far as we know, this is one of the first attempts aimed at developing and testing a comprehensive model of older people acceptance of the MP.

We believe that the conclusions of this study are quite robust, because of both the statistical method used to analyse the data (PLS) and the size of the sample exploited (740 valid questionnaires). In this connection, we notice that no attempt was made to make the sample representative of the population of reference (e.g., through stratified sampling), and, indeed, it would be advisable that our study be replicated by adopting sampling procedures granting representativity. Still, due to the characteristics of the sample, which includes people from urban and rural areas, with different socio-economical conditions, and an age distribution that is very close to that of the population of reference, we believe our study provides a good and reliable account of the factors underlying MP acceptance by older people.

A key contribution of this study is that it highlights and details the role that intrinsic motivations play in MP acceptance by older people and their interplay with extrinsic ones. Although the basic motivational structure of MP usage turned out to be utilitarian, the fact that extrinsic motivations are strongly modulated by intrinsic one is of the utmost importance for HCI research, suggesting that designers and producers of MPs *can* leverage on hedonic and self-realization aspects to increase the value of the MP usage and, ultimately, its acceptance. Finally, although it is not possible to draw any straightforward comparisons with other age populations, due to the lack of similar studies for younger or adult people, a comparison with the literature reviewed above suggests that the motivational structure for MP acceptance in older people might share with that of younger and adult ones the emphasis on extrinsic motivations. Nothing can be derived, from those studies, about the way (if any) extrinsic motivations are modulated by intrinsic ones. It might well be that the most interesting differences among age populations is at this level; further studies, based on explicit acceptance models, are needed to explain probable effects.

Another important contribution to the understanding of the factors affecting MP acceptance by older people is the fact that the need for support and the influence of perceived ease of use on intention to use persist even after years of frequent usage. Since these two aspects are typical of early stages of adoption, we have argued that their persistence suggests that older people do not go beyond an initial acquaintance with the MP always maintaining a certain distance with respect to it. According to our model there are at least two ways to improve the overall confidence of older people in the MP: a) contrasting the importance of ease of use by improving long term usability of the MP, and b) given the relationships of Enjoyment and Self Actualization to PEU, leveraging on hedonic and experiential aspect, and on functionalities enhancing self-realization in older people.

References

1. Abascal, J., Civit, A.: Universal access to mobile telephony as a way to enhance the autonomy of elderly people. In: WUAUC 2001 (2001)
2. Agarwal, R., Karahanna, E.: Time flies when you're having fun: cognitive absorption and beliefs about information technology usage. MIS Quarterly 24, 665–694 (2000)
3. Aoki, K., Downes, E.J.: An analysis of young people's use of and attitudes toward cell phones. Telematics and Informatics 20(4), 349–364 (2003)
4. Burleson, W.: Developing creativity, motivation, and self-actualization with learning systems. Int. Journal Human-Computer Studies 63(4-5), 436–451 (2005)
5. Chesney, T.: An acceptance model for useful and fun information systems. Human Technology 2(2), 225–235 (2006)

6. Chin, W.W.: The partial Least Square Approach to Structural Equation Modelling. In: Marcoulides, G.A. (ed.) Modern Methods for Business Research. Lawrence Erlbaum Associates, Mahwah (1998)
7. Chin, W.W., Frye, T.: PLS-Graph, Version 3.00 (Build 1026). University of Houston (2001)
8. Czaja, S.J., Hiltz, S.R.: Digital aids for an aging society. Communications of the ACM 48, 10 (2005)
9. Czaja, S.J., Lee, C.C.: The internet and older adults: design challenges and opportunities. In: Charness, N., Park, D.C., Sabel, B.A. (eds.) Communication, technology and aging: opportunities and challenges for the future. Springer, New York (2001)
10. Davie, R., Panting, C., Charlton, T.: Mobile phone ownership and usage among pre-adolescents. Telematics and Informatics 21, 359–373 (2004)
11. Davis, F.D.: Perceived usefulness, perceived ease of use and user acceptance of information technology. MIS Quarterly 13(3), 319–340 (1989)
12. Davis, F.D., Bagozzi, R.P., Warshaw, P.R.: User acceptance of computer technology: a comparison of two theoretical models. Management Science 35, 982–1002 (1989)
13. Davis, F.D., Bagozzi, R.P., Warshaw, P.R.: Extrinsic and intrinsic motivation to use computers in the workplace. Journal of Applied Social Psychology 22, 1111–1132 (1992)
14. Eisma, R., Dickinson, E.A., Goodman, J., Syme, A., Tiwari, L., Newell, A.F.: Early user involvement in the development of information technology-related products for older people. Univ. Access Inf. Soc. 3, 131–140 (2004)
15. Fornell, C., Larcker, D.F.: Evaluating Structural Equation Models with Unobservable Variables and Measurement Error. Journal of Marketing Research 18, 39–50 (1981)
16. Gefen, D., Straub, D.: A practical Guide to Factorial Validity Using PLS-Graph: Tutorial and annotated Example. Communications of the Association for Information Systems 16, 91–109 (2005)
17. Heerink, M., Kröse, B., Wielinga, B., Evers, V.: Enjoyment, Intention to Use and Actual Use of a Conversational Robot by Elderly People. In: HRI 2008 (2008)
18. Höflich, J.R., Rössler, P.: Mobile schriftliche Kommunikation oder: E-Mail für das Handy. Medien & Kommunikationswissenschaft 49, 437–461 (2001)
19. Hong, S.J., Tam, K.Y.: Understanding the Adoption of Multi-purpose Information Appliances: The Case of Mobile Data Services. Inf. Systems Research 17(2), 162–179 (2006)
20. Igbaria, M.: End-User computing effectiveness: A structural equation model. Omega 18(6), 637–652 (1990)
21. Igbaria, M., Zinatelli, N., Cragg, P., Cavaye, A.L.M.: Personal computing acceptance factors in small firms: a structural equation model. MIS Quarterly 21(3), 279–301 (1997)
22. Knowledge for business, `http://www.key4biz.it/News/2008/05/06/Tecnologie/cellulare_Istat_televisione_bambini.html`
23. Kurniawan, S.: Mobile phone design for older persons. Interactions 24(4), 24–25 (2007)
24. Kwon, H.S., Chidambaram, L.: A test of the Technology Acceptance Model: the case of cellular telephone adoption. In: Proc. of the 33rd Hawaii Int. Conf. on System Sciences (2000)
25. Lee, Y., Lee, J., Lee, Z.: The effect of self identity and social identity on technology acceptance. In: 22nd Int. Conference on Information Systems (2001)
26. Legris, P., Ingham, I., Collerette, P.: Why do people use information technology? A critical review of the technology acceptance model. Inf. Management 40(3), 191–204 (2003)

27. Lin, C.A.: Looking back: the contribution of Blumer and Katz's uses of mass communication research. Journal of Broadcasting and Electronic Media 40, 574–582 (1996)
28. Ling, C., Hwang, W., Salvendy, G.: Diversified users' satisfaction with advanced mobile phone features. Univ. Access Information Society 5, 239–249 (2006)
29. Ling, R.: It is 'In.' It doesn't matter if you need it or not, just that you have it: Fashion and the Domestication of the Mobile Telephone among teens in Norway. Telenor R&D, Norway (2001)
30. Ling, R., Haddon, L.: Mobile telephony, mobility and the coordination of everyday life. In: Katz, E. (ed.) Machines that Become Us. The Social Context of Personal Communication Technology. Transaction Publishers, New Brunswick (2002)
31. Maslow, A.H.: Motivation and Personality, 2nd edn. Harper & Row, New York (1970)
32. Mayhorn, C.B., Lanzolla, V.R., Wogalter, M.S., Watson, A.M.: Personal digital assistants as medication reminding tools: exploring age differences in usability. Gerontechnology 4(3), 128–140 (2005)
33. Nelson, B.D., Carey, A., Friedman, M.: Cell Phone Use by Adults With Intellectual Disabilities. Intellectual and Developmental Disabilities 45(1), 1–9 (2007)
34. Nysveen, H., Pedersen, P.E., Thorbjørnsen, H.: Intention to use Mobile Services: Antecedents and Cross-Service Comparisons. Journal of the Academy of Marketing Science 33(3), 330–346 (2005)
35. Oksman, V.: Young People and Seniors in Finnish 'Mobile Information Society'. Journal of Interactive Media in Education 2 (2006)
36. Pedersen, P.E., Ling, R.: Modifying Adoption Research for Mobile Internet Service Adoption: Cross-Disciplinary Interactions. In: Proc. HICSS 2003 (2003)
37. Phang, C.W., Sutanto, J., Kankanhalli, A., Li, Y., Tan, B.C.Y., Teo, H.H.: Senior Citizens' Acceptance of Information Systems: A Study in the Context of e-Government Services. IEEE Transactions on Engineering Management 53(4), 555–569 (2006)
38. Quadrello, T., Hurme, H., Menzinger, J., Smith, P.K., Veisson, M., Vidal, S., Westerback, S.: Grandparents use of new communication technologies in a European perspective. European Journal of Ageing 2, 200–207 (2005)
39. Richardson, M., Weaver, J.K., Zorn, T.E.: Getting on: older New Zelanders'perceptions of computing. New Media Society 7(2), 219–245 (2005)
40. Selwyn, N., Gorard, S., Furlong, J., Madden, L.: Older adults' use of information and communications technology in everyday life. Ageing & Society 23, 561–582 (2003)
41. Sharp, J.H.: Development, extension and application: a review of the technology acceptance model. In: Proc. ISECON 2006 (2006)
42. Skog, B.: Mobiles and the Norwegian Teen: Identity, Gender and Class. In: Katz, J.E., Aakhus, M.A. (eds.) Perpetual Contact, Mobile Communication, Private Talk, Public Performance. Cambridge University Press, Cambridge (2002)
43. Teo, T.S.H., Pok, S.H.: Adoption of WAP-Enabled Mobile Phones among Internet Users. Omega 31, 483–498 (2003)
44. Van Biljon, J., Kotzé, P.: Modelling the Factors that influence Mobile Phone Adoption. In: Proc. Annual research conference of the South African institute of computer scientists and information technologists on IT research in developing countries (2007)
45. Van der Heijden, H.: User acceptance of hedonic information systems. MIS Quart. 28(4), 695–704 (2004)
46. Venkatesh, V.: Determinants of perceived ease of use: integrating control, intrinsic motivation, and emotion into the technology acceptance model. Information System Research 11(4), 342–365 (2000)

47. Venkatesh, V., Davis, F.D.: A model of the antecedents of perceived ease of use: development and test. Decision Sciences 27, 451–481 (1996)
48. Venkatesh, V., Morris, M.G.: Why don't men ever stop to ask for directions? Gender, social influence and their role in technology acceptance and usage behaviour. MIS Quarterly 24(1), 115–139 (2000)
49. Venkatesh, V., Morris, M.G., Davis, G.B., Davis, F.D.: User acceptance of information technology: toward a unified view. MIS Quarterly 27, 3 (2003)
50. Wei, R.: Motivations for using the mobile phone for mass communications and entertainment. Telematics and Informatics 25, 36–46 (2008)
51. Wilska, T.A.: Mobile phone use as part of young people's consumption styles. Journal of Consumer Policy 26, 441–463 (2003)
52. Wixom, B.H., Todd, P.A.: A Theoretical Integration of User Satisfaction and Technology Acceptance. Information Systems Research 16(1), 85–102 (2005)
53. Zimmer, Z., Chappell, N.L.: Receptivity to new technology among older adults. Disability and Rehabilitation 21(5/6), 222–230 (1999)

Overview of Behaviour Characteristics of High and Low Literacy Users: Information Seeking of an Online Social Service System

Neesha Kodagoda, B.L. William Wong, and Nawaz Kahan

Interaction Design Centre
School of Computing Science,
Middlesex University, London, UK
{N.Kodagoda,W.Wong,N.Kahan}@mdx.ac.uk

Abstract. We investigated the differences in information seeking behaviours between low and high literacy users on an on-line social service system called the "Adviseguide" website. Ten volunteers participated in the study. Using the UK's National Skills for Life Survey, five were classified as high literate; five as low literate. Participants had four information search tasks that vary in difficulty: easy, medium and difficult. Observations, video recording, and a semi structured interview technique were used. The data were analysed using Grounded Theory and Emergent Themes Analysis approach. We identified eight information seeking behaviour characteristics; Reading/ Scanning, Focus, Satisfied, Verification, Recovery, Trajectories, Representation and Abandon. Results showed that low and high literacy users demonstrated critically different characteristics.

Keywords: Low & high literacy users, information search task, information seeking behaviour characteristics.

1 Introduction

The purpose of this study is to investigate information seeking behaviours of low and high literacy users of an online social service system called "Adviceguide". This system is part of the services provided by the Barnet Citizens' Advice Bureau which provide support to clients from socially disadvantaged backgrounds. Literacy is the ability to read, write and count in one's primary language, taking advantages of the information sources available to them [1-3]. An adult can be categorised as a low literate when unable to read, write above UKs' national curriculum level 4. Literacy is measured using the National Skills for Life Survey which evaluates a person ability to read, write and listen and answer to questions or instructions. According to the UKs' National Skills for Life survey carried out in 2003, 16% or equivalent to 5.2 million of the UK population presented low levels of literacy [4]. Research show low literacy users are more likely to be socially disadvantaged and also more likely to be unemployed [4, 5].

T. Gross et al. (Eds.): INTERACT 2009, Part I, LNCS 5726, pp. 77–80, 2009.

A study by [6] show that low literacy users perform significantly worse than high literacy users as they were unable to find the information they were searching for or users assumed to have found the relevant information.

A previous study investigating low-literacy users reading strategies and navigational behaviour characteristics showed that low literacy users tend to read word by word, have a narrow field of focus, skip chunks of text if confronted by long and dense pages, quickly being satisfied with information found, minimise the amount of reading by skipping from one link to the another, and avoid searching as it requires spelling and typing [7].

As government and social services information are placed online, the problems faced by the low literacy users should be considered to enable digital inclusion. We analyse the information seeking behaviour characteristics between low and high literacy users of the "Adviceguide" website.

2 Study

An overview of the study is described below for more information about the experiment, participants, design, methodology and procedure please read [8].

Ten clients of the Citizens Advice Bureau volunteered for the study. They comprised six females and four males with an average age of 45 years. Using UK's National Skills for Life literacy assessment survey, five participants were classified as high literate, and the remaining five were classified as low literate. Low literacy participants showed a reading level below UKs' National Curriculum Level 4 while high literate users showed reading levels above 5. None of the participants had used the "Adviceguide" website previously, although all the participants had some experience in using the Internet.

Four information search tasks were developed based on the highest type of advice provided to the clients of the Barnet Citizens' Advice Bureau during April 2005 to May 2007. Information search task required the participant to find a specific piece of information, such as eligibility to receive benefits, money advice, assistance on giving up smoking, details of local child care availability, information on children hospital, and advice on council tax arrears. Users were refrained from using any internal or external search.

Multiple Cognitive Task Analysis (CTA) methods were used to extract and understand the human decision process during their cognitive work [9]. CTA methods used in our study were process tracing, observation and interview methods. Users were prevented from using the sites or other search facilities, users were asked to follow the web site menu links. The qualitative data were transcribed using HyperRESEARCH, and analysed using [10] Grounded Theory (GT) and [11] Emergent Themes Analysis (ETA) approach.

3 Results

Eight information seeking behaviour characteristics were identified: Verification, Reading/ Scanning, Recovery, Trajectories, Focus, Satisfied, Representation and Abandon. For detail results read [8].

V*erification* when users find information they need and examine other related links to support the information found for correctness. We did not observe this behavior in low literacy. For the purpose of this study, *Reading* behaviour took place when users read word by word, while *Scanning* behaviour referred to, users glancing through headings and subheadings or start, middle of a paragraph until they found something relevant or interesting. We observed low literacy users read word by word and that do not scan. R*ecovery* refers to recuperate from a wrong or irrelevant information search to a more focused or relevant one resulting in finding the required information. We observed low literacy users were unable to recover from a mistake. The *trajectories* are information search paths taken by users. The paths taken by low literacy users were dissimilar. *Focus* when users are not likely to notice content above, below or to the side of their focus, results a narrow field of focus. We observed low literacy users had a narrow focus of attention. *Satisfied* as soon as the user assumes they have sufficient information and abandon the search task at an inappropriate place, due to being satisfied quickly. We observed low literacy users got satisfied with information quickly. *Representation* users' mental representation of information categories becomes a mismatch to system. We found low literacy users representations of information categories was a mismatch to the system. *Abandon*: when users show a higher tendency to give up their search due to many reasons. We found that low literacy users are likely to abandon an information search task.

4 Discussion and Conclusion

Our study was consistent with the findings of [7]. Both studies showed that low literacy users read word by word trying to make sense of information and do not present the ability to scan (*reading*). They have a narrow field of view and are not likely to notice content above, below or to the side of their focus (*focus*). They were likely to be satisfied and abandon the search early assuming they found relevant information (*satisfied*). However, we did not observed users tendency to skip chunks of text when faced with dense pages as described [7].

Our study found when users were presented with dense pages with anchor links, they were very likely to get lost and disoriented, this resulted low literacy users to abandon the search. We also identified the following characteristics: Low literacy users do not verify the information found for correctness (*verification*). They were unable to recover from a mistake even if they did identify wrong or irrelevant content *(recovery)*. They did not share similar clues that lead to very different *(trajectories)* during their search paths. Low literacy users mental representations of the categories were a mismatch to the system (*Representation*). Finally, low literacy users had several reasons to abandon an information search task, (a) unable to find the information, (b) unable to *recover* from a mistake, (c) mental representation of the categories being a mismatch to the systems *representation*, (d) being *satisfied* quickly.

In conclusion, low literacy users demonstrated a critically different strategy from high literacy users when searching information using the "Adviceguide" website. They spend a lot of time reading instead of scanning, usually terminating the search before finding the right information. Verification was inexistent and a recurrent attitude to give up and terminate the search was presented. Their ability to recover from encountering wrong information was very low and they demonstrated a very narrow focus in all the cases. These behavioural patterns provoked low literacy users to use different search paths or trajectories.

These characteristics might help understand the low literacy user information seeking behaviour. Better interfaces design should help reduce low literacy users memory load, while maintain their attention by presenting less textual information; use high level linked clusters to afford rapid scanning so that they can see overall relationship structure; text which is simple to read; use of visual and audio where appropriate; assist users to recover from a search; try to match users mental perception with the interface design.

References

1. Chlebowska, K.: Literacy for Rural Women in the Third World. United Nations Educational Scientific and Cultural Organization (1990)
2. Baynham, M.: Literacy Practices, U.K (1995)
3. Stifelman, L.J., Schmandt, C., Hulteen, E.A.: VoiceNotes: A Speech Interface for a Hand-Held Voice Notetaker. In: INTERCHI 1993 (1993)
4. Williams, J., et al.: The Skills for Life survey: A national needs and impact survey of literacy, numeracy and ICT skills. BMRB Social Research for the Department for education and Skills, London (2003)
5. Shalla, V., Schellenberg, G.: The Value of Words: Literacy and Economic Security in Canada. Catalogue No. 89-552-MPE. Statistics Canada, Ottawa (1998)
6. Kodagoda, N., Wong, B.L.W., Khan, N.: Effects of Low & High Literacy on User Performance in Information Search and Retrieval. In: Proceedings of the 22nd annual conference of Interaction a specialist group of the BCS. HCI Liverpool 2008, vol. 1, pp. 173–181 (2008)
7. Summers, K., Summers, M.: Reading and Navigational Strategies Of Web Users With Lower Literacy Skills. 2005. In: 68th Annual Meeting Of The American Society For Information Science and Technology (ASIST) (2005)
8. Kodagoda, N., Wong, B.L.W., Khan, N.: Identifying Information Seeking Behaviours of Low and High Literacy Users: Combined Cognitive Task Analysis. In: NDM9 2009 (2009)
9. Wong, B.L.W.: The Critical Decision Method. In: International Encyclopaedia of Human Factors and Ergonomics, pp. 3067–3073. CRC Press, Boca Raton (2006)
10. Strauss, A., Corbin, J.: Basics of qualitative research: Grounded theory, procedures and techniques. Sage, Newbury Park (1998)
11. Wong, B.L.W., Blandford, A.: Analysing Ambulance Dispatcher Decision Making: Trialing Emergent Themes Analysis. In: HF 2002, Design for the whole person - integrating physical, cognitive and social aspects. ESA & CHISIG 2002 (2002)

'I Have Something to Say': Supporting Aphasics for Organizing and Sharing Personal Experiences by Photos

Abdullah Al Mahmud and Jean-Bernard Martens

Department of Industrial Design, Eindhoven University of Technology
P.O. Box 513, 5600 MB Eindhoven, The Netherlands
{a.al-mahmud,j.b.o.s.martens}@tue.nl

Abstract. When a person, due to brain injury or other disease, suffers in his or her ability to speak, it becomes inherently cumbersome to share needs, emotions, and experiences through personal stories and social interaction. We report on our early design exploration to share everyday experiences by photos for people having expressive aphasia. We also introduce the concept of a multimodal narrative template to help persons with aphasia to reconstruct their experiences and hence promote face-to-face communication and social interaction from everyday activities.

Keywords: Aphasia, Sharing experiences, Contextual interview.

1 Introduction

Much of our social life consists of sharing daily stories with other people. However, sharing personal stories can be extremely difficult for people with limited verbal ability, such as those suffering from expressive aphasia. As a result, aphasia often leads to increased social isolation and possibly to depression. Enabling persons with aphasia to share their daily experiences will help them to become more socially active and to re-engage with their preferred life style. Aphasia is an acquired communication disorder that is caused by brain injury or trauma. Aphasia affects language comprehension and generation [4], such that people's ability to express themselves verbally suffers. Speech Generating Devices (SGD) such as TouchSpeak [6] are widely used in aphasia therapy as well as during the post-therapy period though there are various limitations of SGDs such as (a) They contain isolated symbols whose meanings have to be learned and need to retrieve phrases or words to construct meaning which supports very simple stories. Therefore, these activities pose cognitive challenges for the users. (b) SGDs support needs-based interaction for functional communication. They lack the support for sharing experiences based on real-life events, which are key aspects to social interaction.

Sharing experiences from real-life events require evidence captured in different forms such as photos. Photographs have several functions such as preserving memories about the past, narrating and organizing everyday experiences, and communicating and building social relations [3]. Photography has been proposed within 'Aphasia Talks' [5] as a way of facilitating self-expression in persons with aphasia for reintegration, improving socialization and allowing recreation. The issue of how people with special needs can be empowered to use photos to share experience

T. Gross et al. (Eds.): INTERACT 2009, Part I, LNCS 5726, pp. 81–84, 2009.

does not yet seem to have been explored in depth. A study has been reported to help persons with aphasia in building stories [2]. However, there were several limitations of the prototype such as the editing has to be done at the time of capture and lack of support for organizing the captured photos. Moreover, the story-building task was limited just by adding simple emoticons or sound and lacking the support to build a meaningful narrative for persons with aphasia. Therefore, our objective is to design a supporting system for sharing personal experiences by taking into account the limitations described above.

2 Design Process

Several design methods have been used to design for aphasics [1]. As a first step in the design process, it became essential to ascertain how aphasics and their partners are involved in the communication process. Moreover, we wanted to explore how photos could be used to share experience for aphasics and their communication partners.

Contextual Interview. We interviewed an aphasic (Gender: Male, Age: 65+) and his partner. He has been living with aphasia for seven years and he has problems in finding appropriate words and depends on his partner for confirmation. In response to the question of how the aphasic shared his past events, he said that he could not share due to his inability to express by words and lack of alternative support. Later on, his partner added that, *he could not retell anything that he heard, saw or experienced.* In such cases, captured photos could be helpful for sharing his experience. His partner also added, '…*You would have used it if you were not able to communicate as you are now*'. The aphasic also emphasized that it (i.e. sharing experience through photos) would be helpful for other aphasics who can barely speak.

Sharing Experience through Photos. The final part of the interview consisted of an experiment to explore how the aphasic would tell stories from photos. First, he was shown a single picture where an old woman was playing cards and we tried to find out what he would tell if he would show this picture to others. He expressed that if he finds that the other person ('who') in the picture is not familiar, he would tell that first and then 'what' he/she/it is doing. If the person or object displayed on the picture is familiar to him, then the most important thing is to tell 'what' it is or he/she is doing. When he used pictures that he was familiar with, he naturally started to narrate about these pictures such as who they were in the picture and how they were related to him. This was observed when he showed two pictures that were hanging on the wall, a picture of his partner and her sisters, and a picture of his partner and her tennis group. Therefore, providing personally relevant cues with 'who' and 'what' would help him to share if he was unable to find personal relevance of the pictures. Later on, a series of four pictures were shown in order to find out whether or not he would combine those pictures into a larger story. He reflected on the pictures separately, since he did not consider that there was a meaningful connection between them.

Insights from the Interview. The key implications are summarized below:

- Photos can be used to capture and report past events for aphasics. Identifying 'who' and 'what' property from photos would be the first step for building and narrating an experience.

- Contextually rich image could invoke memories of the aphasics and consequently could help them to express their experiences. The contextually rich image should have clear personal association for aphasics.
- Support should be provided for 'why' and 'how' questions, that is why a picture has been taken and how it relates to a particular experience of aphasics.

Concept Design and Evaluation. We realized that it was not easy to intensively engage aphasics and elicit design requirements. Therefore, we did an experiment with a non-aphasic person to understand aphasic's experience and sharing capabilities. Our goal was to generate design requirements and later validate those with speech therapists. A voluntary non-aphasic participant was asked to capture daily experiences, later share it with us in a less familiar language, and act as if that he could only use his left hand for gesturing like aphasics. The experiment was done over two days. After the participant shared the experience in French (since he was less familiar with French language) from the captured photos, we expressed what we understood from what the participant told. The photos captured were related to his daily activities such as having lunch with friends, doing household work etc. It was observed that the participants had difficulties in expressing. He clustered the photos according to related activities and time to reflect each of them as a coherent story. The participant took in total eleven pictures that constituted two different stories. Since he was having problem in narrating the experience, he was given a template (template contains a grid such as who, where, what, emotion etc.) to help building the narrative. It was deduced that it was much easier for him to add relevant picture(s) for indicating and for us to understand the context as a whole story. The participant realized that he could take some more relevant pictures to express the right thing. However, next day he took ten pictures to tell three different stories. He also realized that he missed some joining phrases to tell experience from photos. It was also revealed that not many pictures were required to share the key daily experiences.

Based on the above findings we have designed an application that could help persons with aphasia to organize, build and share personal experiences from everyday photos. Firstly, the application helps to organize captured photos according to clusters on date and time to find out related events. The right side panel shows the most recent captured information (date and time) which is extracted from digital photos. Moreover, photos can be retrieved according to different clusters such as 'who', 'where' 'what'. Each of these clusters are subdivided into some basic categories such as 'who' cluster contains picture of family, friends and others. To help in building narrative of experiences a template is provided. The template has the option to fill appropriate picture according to 'who', 'where', 'what' and 'emotion property' (see Fig. 1). The template is a guided approach to construct a particular experience. If required the user can edit individual picture with text or inbuilt icons. There is an option for adding other media such as sound, video fragments if they are captured since these will enrich the understanding of the target experience by contextualizing it to others. In Fig 1, an example is shown where a narrative is constructed using the template. The relevant part of the template is filled to tell about the person, Pintu who is in the birthday party and the narrator is enjoying. This template helps to build photo driven or event driven narrative depending on the preference of users.

Designing an appropriate interface for person with aphasia is challenging and needs iterations. We are still refining the conceptual prototype by evaluating it with speech therapists. Based on the feedback we will develop a working system. An appropriate capturing device will be designed to actively capture contextually rich images, which can easily be operated by one hand. The complete system (capturing, editing and sharing) will be evaluated in field tests with aphasics and their communication partner(s).

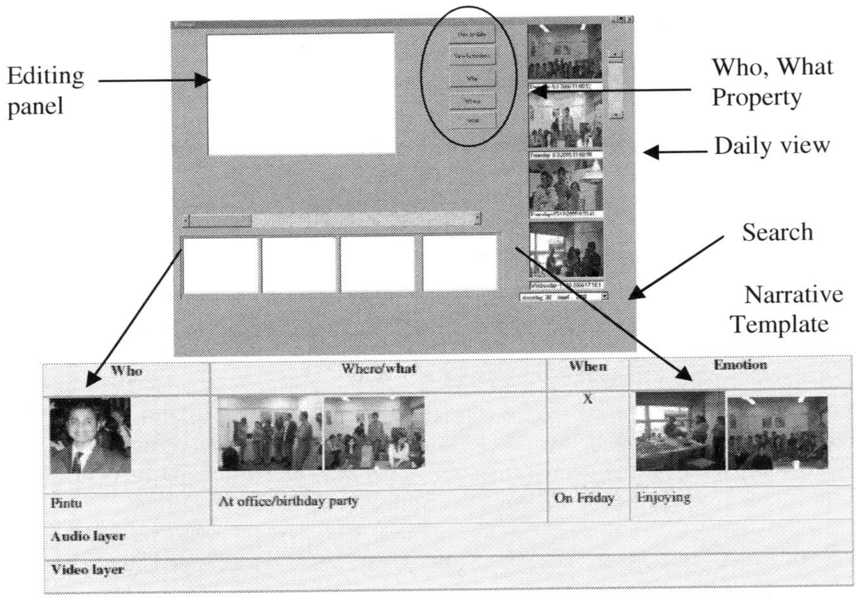

Fig. 1. Snapshot of the interface (top), a template to build a multimodal narrative of experiences (bottom)

References

1. Allen, M., McGrenere, J., Purves, B.: The Field Evaluation of a Mobile Digital Image Communication Application Designed for People with Aphasia. ACM Trans. Access. Comput. 1(1), 1–26 (2008)
2. Daemen, E., Dadlani, P., Du, J., Li, Y., Erik-Paker, P., Martens, J.B., de Ruyter, B.: Designing a free style, indirect, and interactive storytelling application for people with aphasia. In: Baranauskas, C., Palanque, P., Abascal, J., Barbosa, S.D.J. (eds.) INTERACT 2007. LNCS, vol. 4662, pp. 221–234. Springer, Heidelberg (2007)
3. Harrison, B.: Photographic visions and narrative inquiry. J. Narrative Inquiry 12(1), 87–111 (2002)
4. Hillis, A.A.: Progress in the last quarter of a century. Neurology 69, 200–213 (2007)
5. Levin, T., Scott, B., Borders, B., Hart, K., Lee, J., Decanini, A.: Aphasia Talks: photography as a means of communication, self-expression, and empowerment in persons with aphasia. J. Topics in stroke rehabilitation 14(1), 72–84 (2007)
6. TouchSpeak, `http://www.touchspeak.co.uk/`

The Attractiveness Stereotype in the Evaluation of Embodied Conversational Agents

Rabia Khan and Antonella De Angeli

Manchester Business School, University of Manchester, Booth Street West, Manchester, M15 6PB, UK
Rabia.Khan@postgrad.manchester.ac.uk,
Antonella.De-Angeli@mbs.ac.uk

Abstract. Physical attractiveness is an important cue for social interaction. Psychology studies have long shown that physical attractiveness can elicit positive personality attributions as well as positive behaviour towards other people. This effect is explained by the attractiveness stereotype. In this paper, we investigate whether this stereotype apply to the interaction with virtual agents. We report the results of two experiments where the attractiveness stereotype was tested with and without interaction with the agent. Results indicate a strong effect of the attractiveness stereotype, showing that users tend to form and maintain a better evaluation of attractive agents than of unattractive ones independent of actual interaction with the agent or the agents' ethnicity. Implications for design are discussed.

Keywords: Embodied conversational agents, user evaluation, virtual bodies.

1 Introduction

Since the media equation paradigm posited a link between computers and social actors [1], a large corpus of research has investigated the role of social cognition in HCI [2, 3]. Embodied Conversational Agents (ECA's) are a favourite target for this type of research as their anthropomorphic aspect tends to elicit social inference. There is evidence that virtual bodies carry with them stereotypical attributions and that users respond differently to ECA's based on their gender [4, 5], age [5, 6], and ethnicity [2, 5]. Stereotypes are widely shared generalisations about people as members of a social group, whereby group members are attributed similar characteristics on the basis of the categories to which they belong regardless of actual variation [8]. Stereotypes strongly influence social behaviour by providing default setting information for perception and action. Stereotype-based expectations are also believed to shape personality development due to social pressure [9].

In this paper, we investigate the effect of the attractiveness stereotype on the perception of, and behaviour with, ECA's. According to the attractiveness stereotype, nice looking people are perceived as more socially competent, more intelligent, friendlier, and more successful in life than less attractive people. Results of two experiments provided strong evidence that users apply the attractiveness stereotype in the evaluation of ECA's, independently of actual interaction with the agent or its ethnicity.

T. Gross et al. (Eds.): INTERACT 2009, Part I, LNCS 5726, pp. 85–97, 2009.

2 Related Work

Despite popular belief that "beauty is in the eye of the beholder", social scientists have demonstrated that attractiveness is defined by social consensus both within and across cultures and independently of gender [10]. Three main factors make a face attractive: symmetry, averageness and sexual dimorphism [11]. The more symmetrical a face is, then the more attractive it is perceived to be. Averageness refers to typicality of traits constituting a face, whereas sexual dimorphism signals the reproductive potential and sexual maturity of an individual. Research on sexual dimorphism suggests that attractive feminine traits corresponds to large eyes, high eyebrows, full lips, small nose, small chin, prominent cheekbones and narrow cheeks. Whilst, masculine traits such as square chins, thin lips, small eyes, and thick brows tend to signal dominance and status which enhance their mating value.

One of the earliest evidence of the attractiveness stereotype was reported by Dion and colleagues [12]. The authors asked participants to rate three photographs of fellow undergraduate students in terms of personality traits and behavioural characteristics. The stimuli differed on physical attractiveness: one picture represented an unattractive face, the second an average looking face, and the third an attractive face. Participants consistently attributed to attractive individuals more socially desirable traits than to unattractive individuals. Attractive individuals were also deemed to lead better lives in terms of occupational success and relationship satisfaction than their unattractive counterparts. Since this work, a large corpus of psychological research has investigated the reliability of the attractiveness stereotype. This research can be differentiated into three main streams according to objectives and methodology.

The first stream focused on the definition of the content of the stereotype adopting the stranger-attribution paradigm [7, 9]. Participants were invited to rate personality traits, as well as behavioural, social and emotional characteristics of hypothetical individuals depicted in photographs, sometimes enriched by minimal written information. Two independent meta-analyses of the stranger-attribution literature confirmed the strength of the attractiveness stereotype independently of gender and age of both evaluators and targets [7, 9]. Both meta-analyses concentrated on North American participants and highlighted very similar trait components of the stereotype [13]. Large to medium sized effects were found on all dimensions related to social behaviour, confirming that attractive people are perceived as possessing better social skills, and being more popular and more extrovert than unattractive individuals. Large effects also appeared in the perception of sexual warmth, suggesting that attractive people, and in particular attractive females, are perceived as being more sexually responsive. Medium sized effects were evinced for dimensions related to cognitive skills and dominance: attractive people are perceived as more intelligent, rational and bright, as well as being more dominant and assertive than unattractive people. No effect of attractiveness was found on character perception (e.g., trustworthiness, sincerity and honesty) or on concern for other. Negative effects emerged on modesty, implying that attractive people are perceived as vainer than unattractive people.

The second stream of research [9] investigated the objectivity of the attractiveness stereotype via correlational research looking at the relationship between self-rated attractiveness and measures of personality, social skills and mental ability. A meta-analysis of this research provided evidence in favour of the attractiveness stereotype only with regard to personality traits related to social behavior (e.g., loneliness, self-consciousness and social anxiety), social behavior measures (e.g., number of friends and popularity with the opposite sex), and self-reported measures of sexual permissiveness.

The third research stream extended the stranger-attribution literature to more ecologically valid situations [10] with studies of social interaction, whereby the attractiveness stereotype was measured after actual interaction with a target. A set of meta-analyses revealed the persistence of the attractiveness stereotype even when the perceiver could make an informed judgment [10]. Attractive individuals (child or adult) were evaluated and treated more favourably than unattractive individuals by other people, even by those who knew them. These meta-analyses also revealed that attractive adults and children tended to display significantly more positive behavior than unattractive individuals.

Several theoretical frameworks have been invoked to explain the attractiveness stereotype. Fitness-related evolutionary theories posit that attractiveness is linked to health and reproduction fitness [10]. On the contrary, social expectancy theories stress the influence of socialization mechanisms, claiming that expectations about an attractive person influence people's interaction with that person who eventually change their self-perception and behavior in line with the social expectations [10]. Although no individual theory seems to explain the complexity of the effect, there is no doubt that attractiveness is a powerful and cultural independent cue driving interaction [10, 13].

A growing number of studies have investigated social affordances of 'virtual bodies', showing that their demographics subtlety affect user behaviour. For example, people tended to be more influenced by a virtual agent of the opposite sex [4] and preferred interacting with an agent of their same ethnicity [2, 5]. Attractive agents were regarded by users as being more persuasive and effective sales agents in purchasing goods [14]. A relevant corpus of research has addressed the perception of avatars, as mediators of human-human interaction in virtual environments [15, 16]. Results showed that people tended to perceive feminine avatars as being more attractive than masculine avatars, and anthropomorphic avatars as being more credible and attractive [15]. In online dating environments, users tended to create more attractive avatars, and participants represented by attractive avatars were more willing to approach members of the opposite gender [17, 18]. Investigations into user behaviour in Second Life [19] have found that users report on making their avatars not only similar, but also somewhat more attractive than themselves. Such users with avatars that are more attractive than their real selves reported being more outgoing, extrovert, loud, and risk-takers in Second Life than in real life [19].

3 Experiment 1

This experiment was designed to test the reliability of the attractiveness stereotype in the evaluation of ECA's within the stranger-attribution paradigm. It applied as closely as possible the procedure proposed by [12] for stimuli selection and testing but it used pictures of agent faces instead of real faces. Similarly to the original study, which selected photographs from a University yearbook, the agent faces were selected from a large data-base of agent embodiments used in ECA research [6]. Contrary to [12], however, only female faces were tested as the variance in attractiveness and realism of male faces was more limited and did not allow proper differentiation between stimuli. Based on the face-to-face literature, we formulated the following hypothesis: (H1) *Attractiveness will affect the initial impressions on embodied conversational agents: the more attractive the virtual agent, the more positive the user evaluation.*

3.1 Method

Participants and Design. A total of 30 students at the University of Manchester (15 Male, 15 Female) took part in the experiment. Approximately 36% of participants were 18-25 years old, and the rest were between 26 and 35 years old. Attractiveness (3) was manipulated within–subjects. All participants evaluated three agents (attractive, average and unattractive).

Stimulus Materials. Six pictures of young female agents were used as stimuli in the study. These pictures were previously rated for attractiveness and realism by 545 independent evaluators. The 6 pictures were selected following the procedure applied in [12]. The 6 agents were assigned to one of two sets, each containing one attractive, one average and one unattractive face (Table 1).

Table 1. Agents used in the study

Agent Set 1		

Attractiveness: 1.68	**Attractiveness:** 3.09	**Attractiveness:** 4.63
Realism: 1.98	**Realism:** 3.71	**Realism:** 4.39
Agent Set 2		
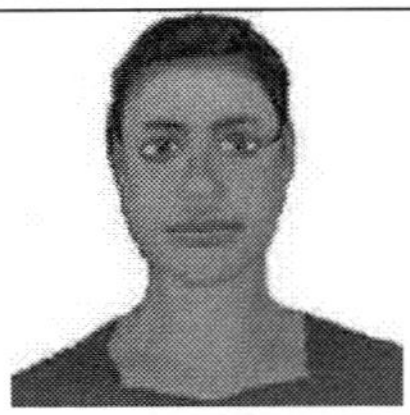	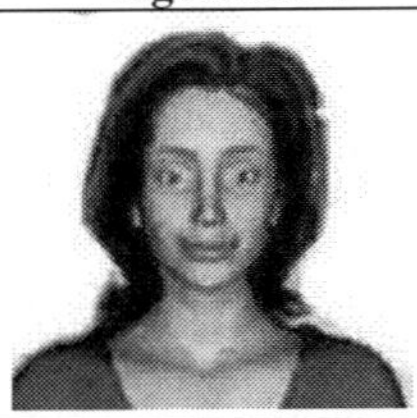	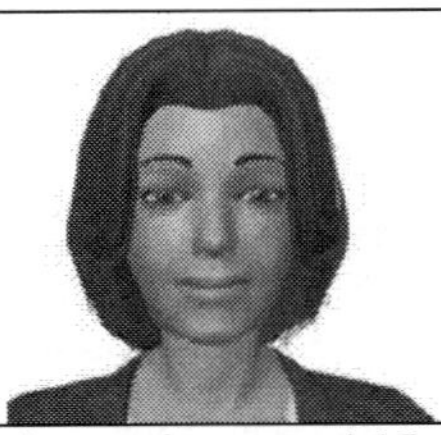
Attractiveness: 2.02	**Attractiveness:** 3.23	**Attractiveness:** 4.15
Realism: 2.39	**Realism:** 3.04	**Realism:** 3.37

The following selection criteria were applied: (*a*) human-looking faces from a white ethnic background; (*b*) high inter-rater agreement as to their physical attractiveness; (*c*) faces representing the very attractive and the very unattractive target were not at the extreme end of the attractiveness distribution; (*d*) faces had a neutral expression and; (*e*) neck and shoulders were displayed in the picture.

Procedure. The experiment took place in a usability laboratory. Participants were introduced to it as a study looking into the user's opinion of ECA's. Before the experiment, each participant was shown a short video giving examples of four online agents available on the Internet and invited to provide comments on them. They were then shown one of the three pictures from either agent set 1 or set 2 on a computer screen and invited to evaluate them filling an on-line questionnaire. Presentation order was randomized and each picture was visible in a prominent position of the screen until the participants submitted the questionnaire. On completion, participants were presented with all three images of the agents they had evaluated and asked further questions about their physical appearance.

Dependent Variables. Participants were invited to record their impressions of each face along 7 dimensions. A measure of *physical attractiveness* was collected to validate the reliability of the experimental manipulation. It was measured by the relevant sub-scale of the Interpersonal Interaction Scale [20]. *Social competence* (unsociable – sociable, unfriendly – friendly, introvert – extrovert), *intellectual competence* (unintelligent – intelligent, emotional - rational, unambitious – ambitious), *social adjustment* (unstable – stable, immature – mature, poorly adjusted – well adjusted), *potency* (weak – strong, unassertive – assertive, submissive – dominant) and *integrity* (dishonest – honest, untrustworthy – trustworthy, insincere – sincere) were measured for hypotheses testing. These dimensions are well-known components of the attractiveness stereotype [13] and were used in this study as they may also apply to the evaluation of ECA's. The items within this investigation were taken from [13]. A*nthropomorphism* was measured by two likert-items (The Agent is human Like, The agent is machine like) from [21].

3.2 Results

Reliability analyses returned satisfactory results for each dimension tested in the study and each level of attractiveness (Cronbach alpha > 0.80). Seven indexes were computed averaging scores on individual items for each attractiveness level. Mean scores were entered as dependent variables into seven 3*2 mixed-design ANOVAs, with attractiveness (3) as within-subjects factor and agent-set (2) as between-subjects factor. Linear contrasts were run to test the difference between consecutive values of attractiveness based on a linear model [22]. Partial eta-squared (η^2) was computed as estimate of effect size. Partial $\eta^2 = .01$ indicate small effects, partial $\eta^2 = .06$ medium effects, and partial $\eta^2 = 14$ large effects [23].

Manipulation Check. The ANOVA on physical attractiveness returned a very strong effect for agent attractiveness ($F_{(2,56)} = 135.88$, $p < 0.001$, partial $\eta^2 = .83$), and a significant interaction attractiveness * agent-set ($F_{(2,56)} = 12.29$, $p < 0.001$, partial $\eta^2 = .31$). The interaction was due to the unequal distribution of attractiveness levels

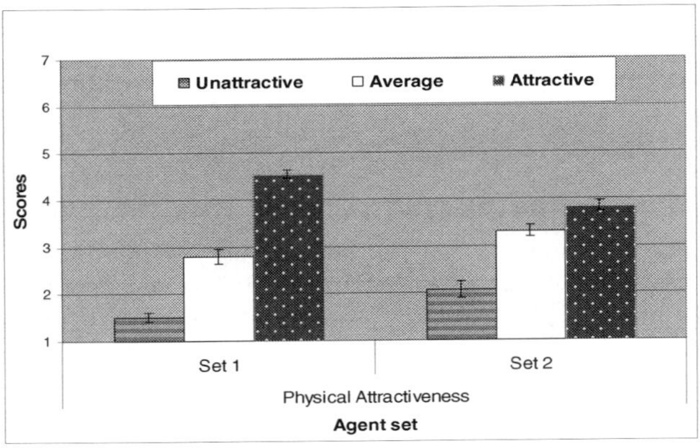

Fig. 1. Physical attractiveness scores as a function of experimental conditions

between the two agent-sets (Fig. 1). Although a significant linear trend was evident in each agent-set, the relative difference between attractiveness levels differed.

Test of Hypotheses. Perception of *social competence* was strongly influenced by attractiveness, $F_{(2,56)} = 97.68$, $p < 0.001$, partial $\eta^2 = .77$, with no interaction effect. Participants' evaluations increased linearly showing an improvement of about 1.5 points between consecutive levels of attractiveness.

The evaluation of *intellectual competence* and *social adjustment* revealed very similar patterns (Fig. 2). Both ANOVAs indicated a large main effect of attractiveness (in the order, $F_{(2,56)} = 51.99$, $p < 0.001$, partial $\eta^2 = .65$; $F_{(2,56)} = 45.52$, $p < 0.001$, partial $\eta^2 = .62$) and a significant 2-way interaction attractiveness * agent-set ($F_{(2,56)} = 7.22$, $p < 0.01$, partial $\eta^2 = .21$; $F_{(2,56)} = 9.19$, $p < 0.001$, partial $\eta^2 = .25$).

Although each agent set was affected by a significant linear trend, the increase between consecutive values of attractiveness was different. Set 2 followed a straight line, while the relative increase between the unattractive and the average looking agent in set1 was much larger than any other comparison, probably due to the lowest attractiveness scores of this agent.

Participants evaluated more attractive agents systematically better on the *integrity* dimension, $F_{(2,56)} = 54.5$, $p < 0.001$, partial $\eta^2 = .66$. The amount of improvement differed between the two agent-sets as reflected by the significant interaction attractiveness * agent set, $F_{(2,56)} = 3.3$, $p < 0.05$, partial $\eta^2 = .12$ (Fig. 3). The evaluation of agents in set 1 was more strongly affected by attractiveness than the evaluation of agents in set 2. Both sets however returned significant results to the linear trend test.

The ANOVA on *potency* as dependent variable displayed a different trend of results, due to the large interaction effect attractiveness * agent-set, $F_{(2,56)} = 7.52$, $p < 0.05$, partial $\eta^2 = .21$. Set 1 followed the linear trend evinced in all other analyses. In contrast, the most unattractive agent of set 2 was assigned the highest level on potency.

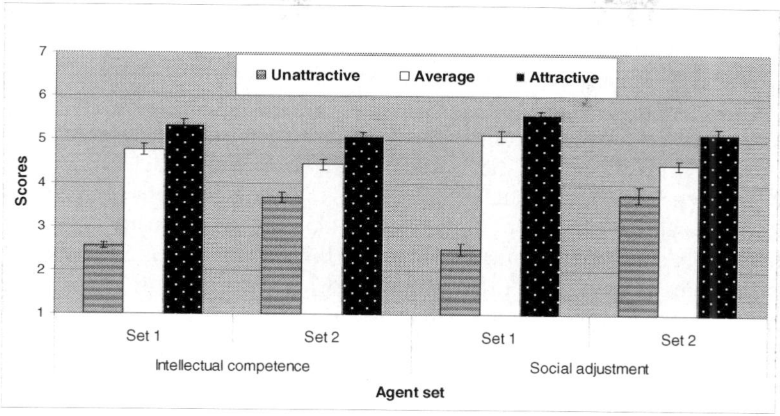

Fig. 2. Intellectual competence and social adjustment as a function of experimental conditions

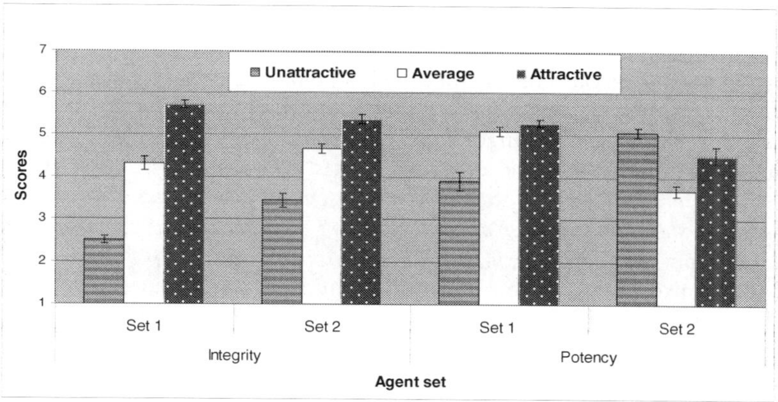

Fig. 3. Integrity and Potency scores as a function of experimental conditions

Anthropomorphism returned only a large main effect for attractiveness ($F_{(2,56)} = 41.59$, $p < 0.001$, partial $\eta^2 = .59$). Both agent set 1 and 2 indicated a significant linear trend, but the increase varied between consecutive values of attractiveness.

3.3 Conclusion

The study provided strong support to the hypothesis that the attractiveness stereotype applies to ECA's, following the stranger attribution paradigm [7, 9, 13]. The components of the stereotype closely mirrored those of real humans. The large effect sizes for social competence, social adjustment and intellectual competence equalled the effect sizes reported in social psychology experiments. On the contrary, the effect size for integrity was much larger than that reported in studies with real human-beings. This suggests that the association between trustworthiness and beauty may be exasperated when the target is artificial and thus susceptible to limited attributions of intentionality.

The only exception to the attractiveness stereotype was the dimension of potency. This variable was found to be subject to variation also in studies with real human beings and it was hypothesised to reflect the North American stereotype which may not apply to collectivistic cultures [13]. The sample tested in our study was evenly split between Europeans and people from Eastern countries who may pay more attention to collectivistic values. However, the lack of effect on potency may also be due to the specific target analysed in this study. Indeed, it is reasonable to believe that potency assumes differential valence when applied to artificial agents or to real human beings. Users want ECA's to serve them [24]. Hence, in this context, dominance, assertiveness and strength may be associated to negative traits rather than to positive ones. This hypothesis was supported by several comments reported by participants during the final interview which highlighted difficulties in understanding and rating the dimension.

4 Experiment 2

To address the reliability of the attractiveness stereotype towards ECA's in a more ecological setting, a second experiment was designed whereby evaluations were collected before and after actual interaction with the agent [10] Participants were invited to engage in a spontaneous conversation with an embodied chatterbot for 10 minutes. Given the very strong impact of attractiveness on first impression of ECA's evinced in experiment one, and following the interaction studies literature [10] we hypothesized that (H1) an *advantage of attractive agents over unattractive agents would be evident also after actual interaction with the agent.* However, we also expected that (H2) *the effect should be weaker after interaction as participants acquired more contextualized information to inform their evaluation.* Therefore, we predicted to find smaller differences between the evaluation of attractive and unattractive agents after usage. This decrease was expected to be associated to (H3) *a more negative view of the attractive agents after interaction,* as they may pay the price of the high expectations raised at first impressions.

To account for the problems evinced in study 1 using existing embodiments, the stimuli for experiment 2 were created by manipulating the appearance existing agents.

4.1 Method

Participants. Forty-eight students (21 female, and 27 male) at the University of Manchester participated in this experiment. Over 60% of participants were 26-35 years of age, and around 30% were 18-25. Participants were randomly assigned to experimental conditions in equal size groups.

Stimuli. Six Oddcast female agents of different races were systematically manipulated to decrease their physical attractiveness, based on the literature on facial attraction. Modification criteria are summarised in Table 2 below. A total of 15 agents were designed and pilot tested for attractiveness and realism with a sample of 58 participants. Four stimuli were selected from two models (one White and one Black female) which achieved the highest difference between the most and the least attractive pairs (Table 2).

Table 2. Attractive and Unattractive Agents

Attractive Agent	Unattractive Agent
Nose - Proportional to face.	Nose - Widened by 50%.
Lips - Full.	Lips - Thinned by 25%.
Symmetry - Head and shoulders proportional to each other.	Asymmetry - Head width reduced by 16.5%. Head height reduced by 25%. Shoulder width increased by 30%.

Attractiveness: 4.98	**Attractiveness: 2.86**
Realism: 4.78	**Realism: 3.31**

Attractiveness: 4.76	**Attractiveness: 2.76**
Realism: 4.28	**Realism: 3.28**

Design. The experiment was based on a 2*2*2 design. Agents' attractiveness (attractive vs. unattractive) and ethnicity (white vs. black) were manipulated between-subjects. Evaluations were collected prior and after interaction with the agents.

Procedure. Participants were introduced to the experiment as a user evaluation of ECA's. Prior interaction, participants were required to evaluate a static image of one of the four targets using the same array of instruments employed in experiment one. Then, they were invited to chat with the agent on any topic they pleased for 10 minutes and left alone in the laboratory. The user wrote their input into a conversation window, whereas the agent spoke its answer back. Finally, participants evaluated the agent image using all the evaluation instruments.

4.2 Results

Mean scores were computed for all 7 dimensions measured in the pre- and post-test (Cronbach alpha > 0.80). Mean scores were entered into 7 mixed-design ANOVAs with Attractiveness (2) and Ethnicity (2) as between-subjects factors and Time (2) as within-subjects factors.

Manipulation Check. The ANOVA on physical attractiveness returned only a strong main effect for attractiveness, F(1,44) = 46.23, p < 0.001, partial η2 = .51, supporting the reliability of the manipulation (mean difference = 1.15).

Test of Hypotheses. The analysis of *social competence* indicated a large main effect of attractiveness ($F_{(1,44)} = 48.38$, $p < 0.001$, partial $\eta^2 = .52$) and evaluation time ($F_{(1,44)} = 23.79$, $p < 0.001$, partial $\eta^2 = .35$). The interaction attractiveness * time was also significant, $F_{(1,44)} = 6.63$, $p < 0.001$, partial $\eta^2 = .13$. Fig. 4 reports mean and standard errors. (score values on social competence as a function of attractiveness and time). It is evident that participants gave better evaluation to the most attractive agents; and their evaluation improved after the interaction. However, this effect was mostly due to people who interacted with the unattractive agent, as they improved their evaluation significantly more (mean = difference .95) than participants who interacted with the attractive avatar (mean difference = .25).

The analysis on *integrity* returned similar results, although all effect sizes were smaller. The main effect of attractiveness ($F_{(1,44)} = 9.76$, $p < 0.01$, partial $\eta^2 = .18$) and evaluation time ($F_{(1,44)} = 16.25$, $p < 0.001$, partial $\eta^2 = .27$) were significant. Attractive agents were evaluated better than unattractive ones (Fig. 4). The evaluation improved with time especially for unattractive agents, although the interaction does not reach statistical significance ($p = .11$).

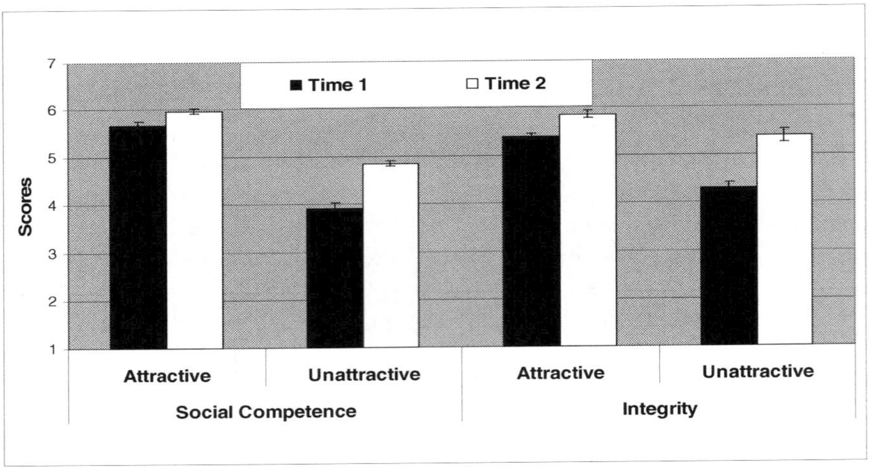

Fig. 4. Social competence and Integrity scores as a function of experimental conditions

The ANOVAs on *intellectual competence* (IC), *social adjustment* (SA) and *anthropomorphism* (A) returned significant effects for attractiveness (IC; $F_{(1,44)} = 10.14$, $p < 0.01$, partial $\eta^2 = .19$; SA: $F_{(1,44)} = 18.45$, $p < 0.001$, partial $\eta^2 = .29$; A: $F_{(1,44)} = 16.79$, $p < 0.001$, partial $\eta^2 = .28$) and time (IC: $F_{(1,44)} = 12.49$, $p < 0.01$, partial $\eta^2 = .16$; SA: $F_{(1,44)} = 8.64$, $p < 0.05$, partial $\eta^2 = .16$; A: $F_{(1,44)} = 152.69$, $p < 0.001$, partial $\eta^2 = .77$). Attractive agents were evaluated systematically better than unattractive agents in

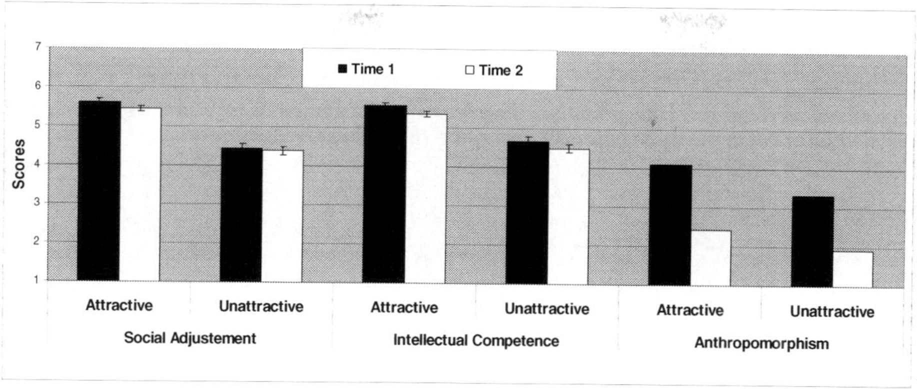

Fig. 5. Social Adjustment, Intellectual Competence and Anthropomorphism scores as a function of experimental conditions

all dimensions (Fig. 5). All evaluations significantly decreased after interaction. This drop was particular drastic in the case of anthropomorphism, as evinced by the higher effect size (A mean difference = .65).

The evaluation of potency followed a completely different pattern, showing a medium sized effect for ethnicity ($F_{(1,44)} = 7.54$, $p < 0.01$, partial $\eta^2 = .14$) and a marginally significant interaction ethnicity * attractiveness ($F_{(1,44)} = 3.74$, $p = 0.06$, partial $\eta^2 = .08$). The interaction effect was due to the unattractive white agent being scored lowest in potency and to the unattractive black agent being scored highest.

4.3 Conclusion

Results of study 2 are summarized in Table 3, which displays effect sizes of significant effects. The effect of attractiveness (A) is robust showing that attractive agents are regarded better in all experimental dimensions, confirming H1. Participants changed their evaluation over time (T), but the direction of this change differed according to the dimension. In particular, social competence and integrity increased, whereas intellectual competence, social adjustment and anthropomorphism decreased. Thus, we reject H2 and H3.

Table 3. Summary of Experiment 2 results

	A	T	E	A*T	A*E
Physical Attractiveness	.51				
Social Competence	.52	T1<T2 .35		.13	
Social Adjustment	.29	T1>T2 .16			
Intellectual Competence	.19	T1>T2 .22			
Potency			.15		
Integrity	.18	T1<T2 .27			
Anthropomorphism	.28	T1>T2 .77			

The only exception to the attractiveness stereotype was the dimension of potency, which also returned the only effect of ethnicity (E) found in the experiment. We argue that this dimension is rather subjective as participants may interpret it as being either a positive or negative trait in relation to an agent. It is worth noting that the agent's ethnicity did not have any major effect on the other dimensions.

5 Discussion

This paper contributes to the emerging literature on social implications of ECA's by showing that virtual bodies afford the attractiveness stereotype. This effect is very strong in first impressions (experiment 1 and experiment 2), but it pertains also to actual interaction (experiment 2). As in real life interaction, the stereotype particularly influences people's opinion of social competence, social adjustment and intellectual competence. The effect on integrity is generally stronger that in real life study, showing that appearance may influence character perception more strongly in ECA's than in real human beings, probably because ECA's are perceived as not to have hidden motives and agenda. Finally, the attributes of potency was found to be unaffected by attractiveness, probably because this is a culturally relevant attribute, or because of the specific target of judgment.

More research is needed to unveil the subtleties of user evaluation of embodied agents, this research provide some preliminary results and a methodology to foster this field.

References

1. Reeves, B., Nass, C.: The media equation: how people treat computers, television, and new media like real people and places. Cambridge University Press, Cambridge (1996)
2. Nass, C., Isbister, K., Lee, E.J.: Truth is beauty: researching embodied conversational agents. In: Cassell, J. (ed.) Embodied conversational agents. MIT Press, Cambridge (2000)
3. Moon, Y., Nass, C.: How 'Real' Are Computer Personalities? Psychological Responses to Personality Types in Human-Computer Interaction. Communication research 23(6), 651–674 (1996)
4. Zanbaka, C., Goolkasian, P., Hodges, L.: Can a virtual cat persuade you? The role of gender and realism in speaker persuasiveness. In: Proceedings of the SIGCHI conference on Human Factors in computing systems. ACM, Montreal (2006)
5. Baylor, A.L.: The impact of pedagogical agent image on affective outcomes. In: Proceedings of Workshop on Affective Interactions, Intelligent User Interface International Conference, San Diego, CA (2005)
6. Khan, R., De Angeli, A.: Mapping the Demographics of Virtual Humans. In: Proceedings of the 21st British HCI Group Conference HCI 2007. British Computer Society, Lancaster (2007)
7. Eagly, A.H., Ashmore, R.D., Makhijani, M.G., Longo, L.C.: What Is Beautiful Is Good: A Meta-Analytic Review of Research on the Physical Attractiveness Stereotype. Psychological Bulletin 110(1), 109–128 (1991)
8. Fiske, S.T.: Social cognition and social perception. In: Rosenzweig, M.R., Porter, L.W. (eds.) Annual review of psychology, vol. 44, pp. 155–194 (1993)

9. Feingold, A.: Good-looking people are not what we think. Psychological bulletin 111(2), 304–341 (1992)
10. Langlois, J.H., Kalakanis, L., Rubenstein, A.J., Larson, A., Hallam, M., Smoot, M.: Maxims or Myths of Beauty? A Meta-Analytic and Theoretical Review. Psychological bulletin 126(3), 390–423 (2000)
11. Rhodes, G.: The evolutionary psychology of facial beauty. Annual Review of Psychology 57, 199–226 (2006)
12. Dion, K., Berscheid, E., Walster, E.: What is beautiful is good. Journal of Personality and Social Psychology 24(3), 285–290 (1972)
13. Wheeler, L., Youngmee, K.: What is Beautiful is Culturally Good: The Physical Attractiveness Stereotype has Different Content in Collectivistic Cultures, 795–800 (1997)
14. Holzwarth, M., Janiszewski, C., Neumann, M.M.: The Influence of Avatars on Online Consumer Shopping Behavior. Journal of Marketing 70(4), 19–36 (2006)
15. Nowak, K.L., Rauh, C.: The Influence of the Avatar on Online Perceptions of Anthropomorphism, Androgyny, Credibility, Homophily, and Attraction. Journal of Computer-Mediated Communication 11(1), 153–178 (2006)
16. Nowak, K.L., Rauh, C.: Choose your 'buddy icon' carefully: The influence of avatar androgyny, anthropomorphism and credibility in online interactions. Computers in Human Behavior 24(4), 1473–1493 (2008)
17. Vasalou, A., Joinson, A.N., Banziger, T., Goldie, P., Pitt, J.: Avatars in social media: Balancing accuracy, playfulness and embodied messages. International Journal of Human-Computer Studies 66, 801–811 (2008)
18. Vasalou, A., Joinson, A.N.: Me, myself and I: The role of interactional context on self-presentation through avatars. Computers in Human Behavior 25, 510–520 (2009)
19. Messinger, P.R., Ge, X., Stroulia, E., Lyons, K., Smirnov, K., Bone, M.: On the Relationship between My Avatar and Myself. Journal of Virtual Worlds Research 1(2), 1–17 (2008)
20. McCroskey, J.C., McCain, T.A.: The measurement of interpersonal attraction. Paper presented at the Annual Convention of the Western Speech Communication Assn. Honolulu (1972)
21. Baylor, A.L., Ryu, J.: The psychometric structure of pedagogical agent persona. Tech., Inst., Cognition and Learning 2, 291–319 (2005)
22. Brace, N., Kemp, R., Snelgar, R.: SPSS for Psychologists: A guide to data analysis using SPSS using for windows (versions 12 and 13), 3rd edn. Palgrave MacMillan, Houndmills (2006)
23. Pallant, J.: SPSS Survival Manual: A step by step guide to data analysis using SPSS (2007)
24. De Angeli, A., Brahnam, S.: I hate you! Disinhibition with virtual partners. Interacting with computers 20(3), 302–310 (2008)

Interpreting Human and Avatar Facial Expressions

Sylvie Noël[1], Sarah Dumoulin[1], and Gitte Lindgaard[2]

[1] Communications Research Centre, 3701 Carling Ave. Ottawa, ON, Canada, K2H 8S2
[2] Carleton University, Department of Psychology, 1125 Colonel By Drive, Ottawa, ON, Canada, K1S 5B6
{sylvie.noel,sarah.dumoulin}@crc.ca,
glindgaa@connect.carleton.ca

Abstract. This paper investigates the impact of contradictory emotional content on people's ability to identify the emotion expressed on avatar faces as compared to human faces. Participants saw emotional faces (human or avatar) coupled with emotional texts. The face and text could either display the same or different emotions. Participants were asked to identify the emotion on the face and in the text. While they correctly identified the emotion on human faces more often than on avatar faces, this difference was mostly due to the neutral avatar face. People were no better at identifying a facial expression when emotional information coming from two sources was the same than when it was different, regardless of whether the facial expression was displayed on a human face or on an avatar face. Finally, people were more sensitive to context when trying to identify the emotion in the accompanying text.

Keywords: Emotions, avatars, virtual reality, collaborative virtual world, facial expression.

1 Introduction

The importance of emotional displays in face-to-face communication has led designers of virtual worlds and intelligent avatars to incorporate emotional states into their avatars. There have been various attempts to automate the recognition of a person's emotional state in order to animate that person's avatar with the proper emotional expression in real time. These attempts have included extracting the emotion from text [1], from voice cues [24] or through real-time facial tracking [2,9]. However, errors may potentially occur during these automated extractions – even real-time facial tracking could lead to errors if the person's face is occluded in some way. If such an error occurs, people might be confronted with contradictory emotional information from an avatar. How would they react in such a situation?

Researchers in human emotions have been studying the impact of contradictory emotional information for decades [10]. This early research was aimed at exploring the facial dominance theory. This theory, originally put forward in the 1960s by

T. Gross et al. (Eds.): INTERACT 2009, Part I, LNCS 5726, pp. 98–110, 2009.

Tomkins [27], states that there are a small number of prototypical facial expressions intrinsically associated with specific basic emotions (happiness, surprise, fear, anger, disgust, sadness, contempt) [see also 8,13,19]. According to this theory, people will use a person's facial expression to base their decision on what emotion that person is feeling above any other source of information, as long as the facial expression is one of the basic emotions. Early research on people's reactions to contradictions in emotional information seemed to support this theory [15]. However, Carroll and Russell [10] have suggested that this might at least partially be due to the experimental designs adopted. For example, by forcing participants to select an answer from a small set of prototypical emotions, previous researchers excluded the possibility that participants' responses could have been something other than one of the basic emotions. By modifying several elements of the experimental design, including offering more choices and presenting the context orally, Carroll and Russell were able to produce situations where their participants tended to describe the facial expression by using the emotion contained in the scene description rather than the emotion supposedly displayed by the face. These results supported their theory of limited situational dominance, which states that assigning an emotion to someone is based not only on the facial expression but also on the context, and that there are no prototypical emotional facial expressions.

More recently, De Gelder and Vroomen [12] presented a series of pictures ranging from happy to sad which they combined with a sad voice, a happy voice, or no voice. People responded more slowly when the emotions were mismatched. Voices had an impact on how a face was judged: a sad voice caused a happy face to be judged less happy and a happy voice caused a sad face to be judged less sad. This result appears to support the limited situational dominance theory.

These studies have looked at how people interpret information presented on real human faces. We turn now to studies that used synthetic humans as stimuli.

While research has shown that people can recognize emotions presented on avatar faces [6,21], results suggest that people have more difficulty identifying emotions that are presented on a virtual face as compared to a real human face [17,20,26; although see 3,4,5]. However, by varying the position of various facial elements, Fabri et al. [17] were able to find a virtual face whose recognition rate was similar to that of a human face for all of the emotions they tested. The only exception was that of disgust, which they attributed to the lack of detail in the avatar face, which couldn't display the wrinkled nose normally associated with this emotion.

Recent studies have investigated the impact of contradictory information in the presence of synthetic human faces or voices. Hong et al. [18], for example, paired neutral happy and sad voices with neutral happy and sad synthetic or real faces. Their results suggest that it was harder to identify emotions with contradictory than with congruent information. However, no statistical evidence was provided to support this hypothesis, which weakens the evidence considerably.

Nass et al. [22] paired emotional human and digitized voices (happy, sad) with emotional text (happy, sad) such that the two either had congruent or contradictory emotional content. When text and voice matched emotional content, people rated the content higher on emotion than when they did not match: happy stories were judged as happier and sad stories were judged as sadder. People also preferred content with matching stimuli, but found the stories more credible when the voice and text did not match.

Creed and Beale [11] investigated the impact of mismatches between facial emotional content and vocal emotional content, combining an animated avatar face with a female human voice. They used happy, warm, neutral, and 'concern' emotions. Mismatched stimuli that had either a happy or a warm element, be it in the voice or the face, were judged warmer and happier than those that had no such element.

The results from these three studies suggest that people viewing emotional avatar faces may be influenced by other contextual clues. However, the contradictory results from the studies concerning the impact of context on emotional identification for human faces and the paucity of studies on avatar faces leave us with many unanswered questions. In this paper, we set out to answer two main questions. Do people who are presented with contradictory emotional information identify the expression on a face differently than people who are presented with congruent emotional information? And does emotional information have a different impact depending on whether the displayed face is that of a human or that of an avatar?

2 Method

2.1 Participants

The 56 participants were recruited from the student population of a local university in return for course credit. Four participants were removed, two because English was not their first language[1] and two because they had made a mistake following instructions. The 52 remaining participants were placed randomly into four groups of nine females and four males each. Age varied between 17 and 51, with an average of 19.8 years.

2.2 Stimuli

Stimuli were static emotional images and short texts. The images were of a male avatar face and of a male human face showing five different emotions (anger, happiness, neutral, sadness, surprise). The avatar face (see Figure 1) is a Facial Action Coding System (FACS) [14] compliant face, originally created by Fabri et al. [17]. The facial expressions selected were based on an earlier experiment testing the recognition rate of various emotions [23].

The human face images (see Figure 1) were taken from DaFEx, a database of animated human facial expressions [7]. From the DaFEx's short clips, we selected single frames from movies made by the same actor. The selection criterion was to match as closely as possible the avatar's facial expressions.

[1] This was done in order to ensure that participants understood the list of emotion names presented to them.

Fig. 1. Surprised avatar and human faces

The texts were short two-sentence comments as told from the point of view of the person represented by the avatar or the human face (see Figure 2). For each of the emotions, we created five texts.

I applied for a really great job last week. They just called me to tell me that I got the job

Fig. 2. Happy text #5

We used 10 pictures (five avatar, five human) and 25 texts (5 for each emotion). Each facial emotion was associated with five texts of different emotional content. For example, the happy human face could be presented with a happy text (congruent situation) or with an angry, neutral, sad or surprised text (incongruent situations). The same texts were presented for the avatar and the human face in each condition (i.e., if sad text #4 was associated with a happy human face, it was also associated with a happy avatar face).

2.3 Measures

For each picture/text combination, participants were asked to accomplish two tasks. The ratings task consisted of judging each face on trustworthiness, sincerity, appropriateness, intensity, and convincingness. Because of the large amount of data created by this task, these results are not presented here. The identification task consisted of identifying the emotional content of the text and the image separately. This paper presents the results from the identification task only. The ratings and the identification tasks were presented on two different screens.

2.4 Procedure

Participants saw only human faces or avatar faces, but they all performed both the identification and the rating tasks. The order in which these tasks were presented was counter-balanced to avoid serial position effects. Thus the four groups of participants were as follows:

1. Avatar faces, identification first
2. Avatar faces, ratings first
3. Human faces, identification first
4. Human faces, ratings first

For the identification-first groups, the identification screen (Figure 3) was always presented first, followed immediately by the ratings screen (Figure 4). The order was reversed for the ratings-first groups. Participants were randomly assigned to one of these four groups.

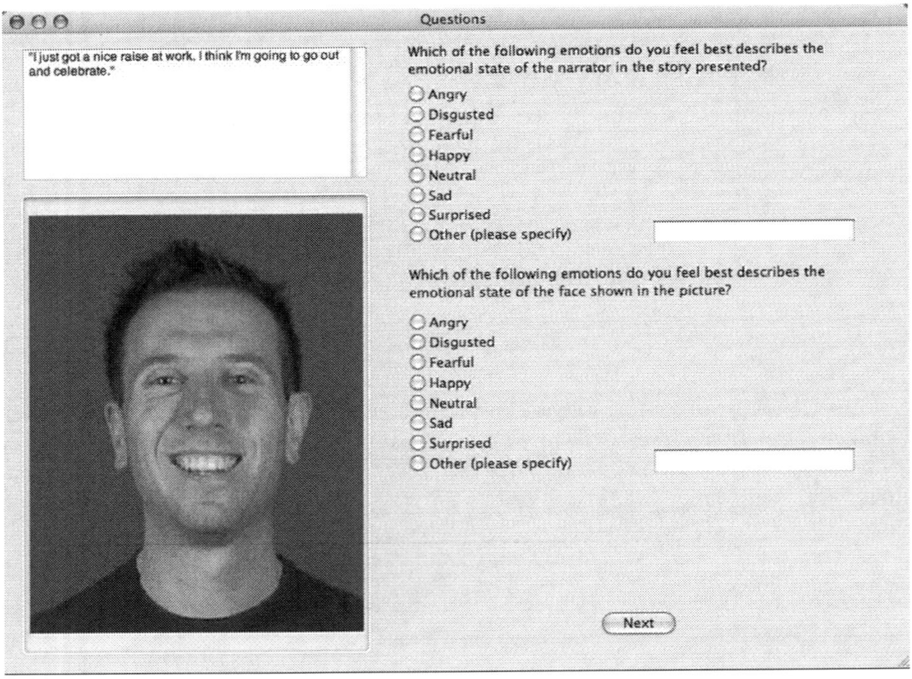

Fig. 3. Identification screen

After noting the participants' age and gender, the experimenter asked them to imagine either that they were using a text chat system that could display static images of chatters' faces (for the human face conditions) or that they were in a virtual world where people communicated through text (for the avatar face conditions). They were asked to imagine that the person they were talking to had just typed a short text message and displayed the image to go with it, and that they would be asked to answer a series of questions on that person.

For each of the five emotions tested, the participant saw five combinations of image and text (one congruent and four incongruent), for a total of 25 stimuli. The order of the combined text and image stimuli was randomized for each subject. A computer application was used to present the text-face combinations. There was no limit on the amount of time that participants could take to answer the questions.

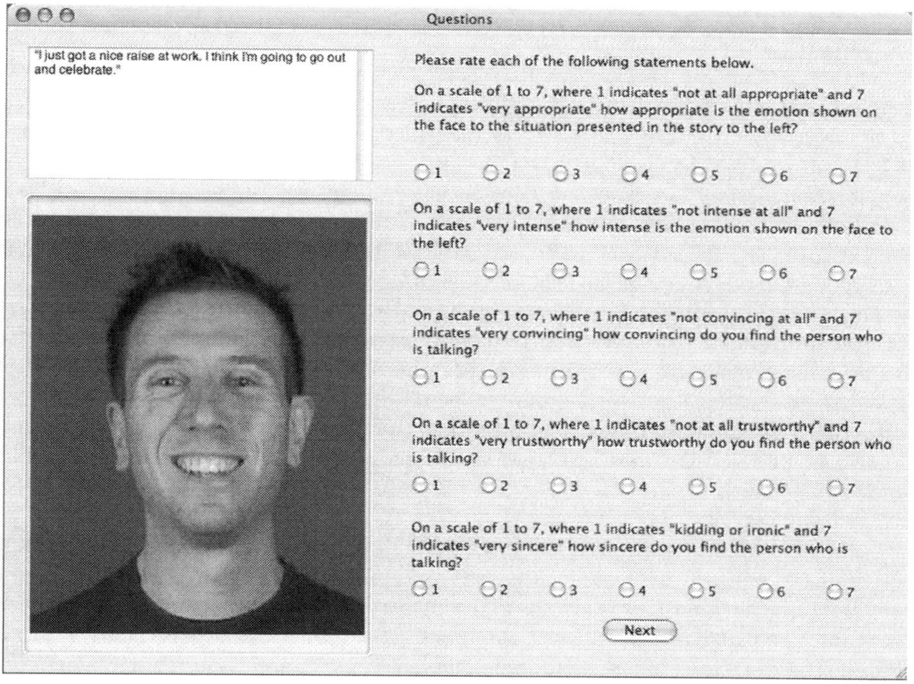

Fig. 4. Ratings screen

For the identification task, participants were asked to describe, separately, the emotional content of the text as well as of the face. To do this, they were asked to choose from a list of seven different possible emotions (angry, disgusted, fearful, happy, neutral, sad, surprised). There was also an "other" choice, in which case they were invited to type in the emotion they thought was displayed. In total, people entered an original emotion name that did not appear in the list 134 times for both faces and texts (approximately 5 percent of all answers).

2.5 Apparatus

The experiment was run on a Mac Powerbook G4 laptop with a 12-inch screen. A special application was created to present the stimuli and record the participants' answers. The screen size of the image was 8 cm wide by 10.5 cm high.

3 Results

In the following text, the "expected emotion" corresponds, for the faces, to the emotion typically associated to the facial expression according to Ekman and Friesen's [14] FACS coding; and, for the texts, to the emotion originally assigned to the text by the researchers.

3.1 Pictures

In this section, we present the results for the identification of the emotions presented on the faces. We begin by checking whether the order of the two tasks (identification first or ratings first) had an impact on the identification task. We then verify whether people are assigning the expected emotion more often than another emotion for both face types. We next test to see if there is a difference in the identification task depending on the face type. Finally, we explore the impact of the various emotional texts (congruent and incongruent) on the identification of each facial expression.

To test for any effects of presentation order, we compared the number of correct identifications made by participants in the groups who completed the ratings task first to the number made by participants in the groups who completed the identification task first. The ratings-task-first groups selected the expected emotion 559 times and some other emotion 91 times, while the identification-task-first group selected the expected emotion 535 times and some other emotion 115 times. This difference did not reach statistical significance (χ^2 (1) = 3.3, p>0.05). Therefore we have ignored the task order in the following analyses.

In order to ascertain the frequency with which participants assigned the expected emotions to the faces, we examined all participants' responses to all the stimuli, both congruent and incongruent. This showed that participants gave the expected answer 1094 times and gave another answer 206 times. This is significantly different (χ^2 (1) = 606.6, p<0.001). Contrary to Carroll and Russell's [10] results, but in agreement with other studies [15], our participants overwhelmingly described the face as displaying the emotion typically associated with the facial expression.

The data were then examined to determine if the performance of participants who saw a photorealistic face differed from that of participants who saw an avatar face. Participants in the photorealistic face condition selected the expected emotion 574 times and they selected another emotion 76 times, while those in the avatar condition selected the expected emotion 520 times and another emotion 130 times. This difference is significant (χ^2 (1) = 16.8, p<0.001). Participants in the photorealistic condition thus assigned the expected emotion to a human face more often than participants in the avatar condition.

Table 1 presents the percentage of time people gave the expected emotion for the human and the avatar faces for each stimulus combination. For both the human and the avatar faces, participants had a strong tendency to assign the expected emotion to the face, with the exception of the sad human face and the neutral avatar face.

In an effort to determine if performance differed between the human and the avatar faces on the various stimuli combinations, a series of Mann-Whitney U tests were performed. To take into account the numerous pairwise comparisons undertaken, we adjusted the threshold to 0.001. There were significant differences between the human and the avatar faces in the cases of the neutral face combined with an angry text ($U=169$, $p<0.000$) and the neutral face combined with a sad text ($U=143$, $p<0.000$). In both these cases, participants gave the expected emotion more often for the human face than for the avatar face. Perhaps this difference is due to our participants being more sensitive to context when presented with an avatar rather than a photorealistic face. Looking at the answers that people gave for the avatar face, we find that, for the neutral face combined with an angry text, the answers most often given were "neutral" (11 times) and "sad" (11 times), while for the neutral face combined with a sad text, the answers most often given were "sad" (14 times) and "neutral" (8 times). These results show that many people confused the avatar neutral face with a sad expression, particularly when the context was one of negative affect.

Table 1. Percentage of people assigning the expected emotion to a facial expression, according to facial type, facial emotion, and text emotion (congruent stimuli are in bold)

Face	Text: Angry	Happy	Neutral	Sad	Surprised	
			Human Face			*Average*
Angry	**84.6%**	84.6%	92.3%	96.2%	92.3%	*90.0%*
Happy	100%	**100%**	100%	100%	100%	*100%*
Neutral	92.3%	96.2%	**96.2%**	88.5%	96.2%	*93.9%*
Sad	69.2%	57.7%	57.7%	**80.7%**	65.4%	*66.2%*
Surprised	88.5%	92.3%	88.5%	100%	**88.5%**	*91.5%*
			Avatar Face			
Angry	**84.6%**	69.2%	65.4%	84.6%	80.8%	*76.9%*
Happy	88.5%	**100%**	96.2%	96.2%	84.6%	*93.1%*
Neutral	42.3%	69.2%	**69.2%**	30.8%	69.2%	*56.2%*
Sad	80.8%	92.3%	76.9%	**88.5%**	76.9%	*83.1%*
Surprised	92.3%	92.3%	88.5%	84.6%	**96.2%**	*90.8%*

The faces that showed the most variance in percentage of expected responses as the accompanying text differed are the human sad face and the avatar neutral face. A Cochrane Q was used to assess any differences between the various stimuli combinations. It revealed marginally significant differences between the various texts combined with the human sad face ($Q(4)=9.9$, $p=0.042$). For the sad human face, the congruent condition increased somewhat people's tendency to assign the expected emotion to that face as compared to incongruent conditions. In the case of the avatar neutral face, these differences were significant ($Q(4) = 16.6$, $p=0.002$). This appears to be due to the low recognition score for the sad text (30.8%). Removing this particular condition resulted in a non-significant Q ($Q(3)=6.8$, $p=0.079$). As noted earlier, when the neutral face was combined with a sad text, participants tended to assign a sad emotion as often as a neutral emotion to the avatar face.

In summary, our participants chose the expected emotion more than any other emotion, and they did this more often for the human than for the avatar face. The difference between the two face types was greatest with the neutral expression – people tended to confuse the neutral avatar face with a sad face, especially when the accompanying text contained a negative affect. Finally, the only face whose identification was different for congruent vs. incongruent emotion combinations was that of the human sad face, although this effect was marginal.

3.2 Texts

In this section, we look at how people perceived the emotions contained in the texts. As with the pictures, we begin by checking for any impact of task order on the text identification task. We then verify whether people were assigning the expected emotion to the texts and whether the facial type (human or avatar) had an impact on this identification task. Finally, we explore the impact of the accompanying facial expressions on the identification of each emotional text.

Does task presentation order have an impact on the identification of the emotions contained in each text? The two groups who completed the ratings task first selected the expected emotion 465 times and some other emotion 185 times, while the two groups who completed the identification task first selected the expected emotion 488 times and some other emotion 162 times. This difference was not significant (χ^2 (1) = 2.1, p>0.10). Therefore we ignored task order in the following analyses.

In order to determine the degree to which participants assigned the expected emotion to the texts, we examined all participants' responses to all of the congruent and incongruent stimuli. The expected emotion was assigned to the text 953 times and another emotion was provided 347 times. This difference was significant (χ^2 (1) = 282.5, p<0.001).

Participants in the human face group chose the expected emotion 476 times (and another emotion 174 times) while the avatar group chose the expected emotion 477 times (and another emotion 173 times). There is no significant difference between the two groups (χ^2 (1) = 0.004).

Since there was no difference between the two face-type conditions, we combined the data from the two conditions for the next analysis. Table 2 presents the percentage of participants who assigned the expected emotion to the texts for each stimulus combination. Was there a difference between the various emotion combinations for each emotional text? Assigning a threshold of 0.001, we found a significant difference between the various text and emotional face combinations for the angry text (Q(4)=18.9, p=0.001), the neutral text (Q(4) = 29.5, p<0.001), the sad text (Q(4)=61.8, p<0.001), and the surprised text (Q(4) =28.0, p<0.001). The only one that does not achieve significance is the happy text (Q(4)=10.9, p=0.027). Could these differences be due to people giving the expected emotion more often for the congruent stimuli as compared to the incongruent stimuli? In the case of the angry text, this appears to be the case. When the angry text is combined with an angry face, 75% of the people gave the expected answer, while the number drops below 54% for the surprised, happy, and sad faces. Although 73% of people assigned the expected emotion to the neutral face combined with the angry text, this is not a true counter-example, since the neutral face is de facto without an emotional expression. For that stimulus combination, the only source of emotional information should be the text, and so it is not surprising to see that the text emotion dominates. This pattern (high response rate for the congruent stimuli and the neutral face combined with the emotion text; low response rates for all other incongruent combinations) is also found for the sad text. However, this is not the case for the surprised text, where not only does the congruent combination (surprised text and surprised face) not receive the highest percentage of identification (this goes rather to the combination of surprised text and sad face), but the neutral face combination shows the lowest rate of identification of the expected emotion. Finally, in the case of the neutral text, the percentage of people who chose the expected emotion was similar when it was accompanied by either the angry, neutral or sad face.

Table 2. Percentage of people assigning the expected emotion to the text according to emotion in text and on face, for all groups (congruent stimuli are in bold)

	Text				
Face	Angry	Happy	Neutral	Sad	Surprised
Angry	**75.0%**	73.1%	100%	42.3%	75.0%
Happy	46.2%	**94.2%**	80.8%	44.2%	67.3%
Neutral	73.1%	80.8%	**98.1%**	88.5%	46.2%
Sad	46.2%	78.8%	96.2%	**88.5%**	88.5%
Surprised	53.9%	76.9%	75.0%	63.5%	**80.8%**
Average	*58.9%*	*80.8%*	*90.0%*	*65.4%*	*71.6%*

In summary, our participants chose the expected emotion for the text more than any other emotion. There was no difference between the groups that saw a human face and those that saw an avatar face. People were sensitive to context: the percentage of people who gave the expected emotion varied significantly according to the accompanying face, except in the case of the happy texts. Congruent stimuli combinations were better recognized than incongruent stimuli combinations in the case of the angry and the sad text (although when the facial expression was neutral, people also gave the expected emotion at a very high rate), but not in the case of the neutral or the surprised texts.

4 Discussion

The main goal of this experiment was to investigate the impact contradictory emotional information might have on people's ability to identify an emotion on a virtual or a human face.

Our participants overwhelmingly assigned the expected emotion to the face, regardless of whether that face was a photorealistic human face or an avatar face, although people in the avatar condition were somewhat less likely to do so. However, the difference between the human and the avatar face was only significant for two stimuli combinations: a neutral face with a sad text and a neutral face with an angry text. In these conditions, many people tended to interpret the neutral avatar face as sad. Finally, while we might have expected that people would assign the expected emotion more often in the congruent condition, this was not the case. The only emotional face that showed some difference between the various stimuli combinations was the neutral avatar face and this result was due solely to the very low recognition rate when that face was paired with a sad text.

These results are different from those obtained by Carroll and Russell [10]. One possible explanation for this is the differences in the design of the two experiments. Carroll and Russell limited their stimuli to a few combinations of text and face emotions that could be mistaken for each other, while our stimuli contained a variety of emotion combinations, including some that could not be confused (e.g., happy and angry). In addition, our text stimuli were very short and presented visually, while Carroll and Russell's were long and were read to the participants.

Our results also differ from others that studied the impact of contradictory emotions using synthetic human faces or voices [11,18,22]. While Hong et al. [18] thought that there was a difference between congruent and incongruent data, we found no such difference. Nass et al. [22] found that people judged a specific emotion as more intense when presented with two congruent sources of emotional information as opposed to two incongruent sources. Creed and Beale [11] found that people judged a specific emotion as more intense in incongruent stimuli when at least one of the two sources of emotion contained that emotion than when neither source contained the emotion. However, our research differed from these last two in that they asked their participants to judge the intensity of each emotion on a scale, whereas we asked participants to name the emotion being presented. It is possible that we might have obtained similar results if we had asked people to judge each individual emotion on a scale[2].

Our results agree with the predictions made by the facial dominance theory [27]. Apart from the neutral avatar face, the majority of our participants assigned the expected emotion to the facial expression. In the case of the neutral face, combining it with a text containing a negative emotion caused a large number of our participants to interpret the face as sad. It is possible that some of the neutral avatar traits are somewhat similar to those on the sad face such that the inclusion of text with negative affect was enough to push some people into interpreting the neutral face as sad. However, these results do not necessarily support Carroll and Russell's [10] limited situational dominance. If that had been the case, then the neutral face should have been interpreted as angry with the angry text and as sad with the sad text. This was not the case.

In the case of assigning emotions to the texts, although our participants generally selected the expected emotion, the various combinations of facial expressions and text had more impact on people's choices than they did when assigning emotions to the faces, except for the happy text. There were two cases where congruent stimuli (and a neutral face combined with an emotional text) were assigned the expected emotion more often than for incongruent stimuli: the angry text and the sad text. However, this was not the case for the surprised text or the neutral text. There are several possible explanations for these results. Our text stimuli were very short, using only two sentences to establish an emotion, compared to Carroll and Russell's [10] use of a full paragraph to set the mood in their experiment. This may have resulted in ambiguous text stimuli, which would explain why people were more sensitive to the various combinations of facial expressions and text emotions. Another potential explanation is that people interpret others' words based on several different input sources. Thus, if a person says they are angry and at the same time they are crying, the viewer may rightly

---

[2] While we did have a question in the ratings task on intensity, this was overall intensity of the facial expression, not the intensity of each of the possible emotions.

conclude that the speaker is hurt and sad. This may have had an impact on how people interpreted the text stimuli. However, it is important to note that, for most of the stimuli combinations, a majority of people did select the expected emotion for the texts.

In conclusion, people appear to interpret facial emotions in a similar way regardless of whether the face expressing the emotion is that of a human or of a medium fidelity avatar. The only exception was the avatar with a neutral face, which was more difficult to interpret in the presence of text with an unpleasant emotion. People are more sensitive to other sources of emotional information when trying to interpret the emotion in short texts, though people's reactions differ depending on the emotion presented in the text.

It is generally safe to use avatars for conveying emotions in an application, but care should be taken when attempting to convey neutrality. We cannot be sure if, in this case, the difficulty with the neutral avatar face was due to the particular avatar used. Independent testing of avatar facial expressions should therefore be performed prior to implementation.

Acknowledgements. We wish to thank Marc Fabri for the use of the avatar face and Alberto Battochi for the use of the DaFEx database.

References

1. Albrecht, I., Haber, J., Kähler, K., Schröder, M., Seider, H.-P.: May I talk to you?:-) – Facial animations from text. In: Proc. Pacific Graphics 2002, pp. 77–86. IEEE Computer Society, Los Alamitos (2002)
2. Bailenson, J.N., Yee, N., Merget, D., Schroeder, R.: The effect of behavioral realism and form realism of real-time avatar faces on verbal disclosure, nonverbal disclosure, emotion recognition, and copresence in dyadic interaction. Presence: Teleoperators and Virtual Environments 15(4), 359–372 (2006)
3. Bartneck, C.: Affective Expressions in Machines. Master's Thesis, Stan Ackerman Institute, Eindhoven (2000)
4. Bartneck, C.: Affective expressions in machines. In: Ext. Abstracts CHI 2001, pp. 189–190. ACM Press, New York (2001)
5. Bartneck, C.: How convincing is Mr. Data's smile: Affective expressions of machines. User Modeling and User-Adapted Interaction 11, 279–295 (2001)
6. Bartneck, C., Reichenbach, J.: Subtle emotional expressions of synthetic characters. Int. J. Human-Computer Studies 62, 179–192 (2005)
7. Battocchi, A., Pianesi, F., Goren-Bar, D.: The properties of DaFEx, a database of kinetic facial expressions. In: Tao, J., Tan, T., Picard, R.W. (eds.) ACII 2005. LNCS, vol. 3784, pp. 558–565. Springer, Heidelberg (2005)
8. Buck, R.: The Communication of Emotion. Guilford Press, New York (1984)
9. Burford, D., Blake, E.: Real-time facial animation for avatars in collaborative virtual environments. In: Proc. South African Telecommunications Networks and Applications Conference, pp. 178–183 (1999)
10. Carroll, J.M., Russell, J.A.: Do facial expressions signal specific emotions? Judging emotion from the face in context. J. Person. Soc. Psych. 70(2), 205–218 (1996)
11. Creed, C., Beale, R.: Psychological responses to simulated displays of mismatched emotion expressions. Interacting with Computers 20(2), 225–239 (2008)

12. De Gelder, B., Vroomen, J.: The perception of emotions by ear and by eye. Cognition and Emotion 14(3), 289–311 (2000)
13. Ekman, P.: Universals and cultural differences in facial expressions of emotion. In: Cole, J.K. (ed.) Nebraska Symp. On Motivation, vol. 19, pp. 207–283. University of Nebraska Press, Lincoln (1972)
14. Ekman, P., Friesen, W.: Facial Action Coding System. Consulting Psychologists Press (1978)
15. Ekman, P., Friesen, W., Ellsworth, P.: What are the relative contributions of facial behavior and contextual information to the judgment of emotion? In: Ekman, P. (ed.) Emotion in the Human Face, 2nd edn., pp. 111–127. Cambridge University Press, New York (1982)
16. Ehrlich, S.M., Shciano, D.J., Sheridan, K.: Communicating facial affect: It's not the realism, it's the motion. In: Proc. CHI 2000, pp. 252–253. ACM Press, New York (2000)
17. Fabri, M., Moore, D., Hobbs, D.: Mediating the expression of emotion in educational collaborative virtual environments: An experimental study. Int. J. of Virtual Reality 7, 66–81 (2004)
18. Hong, P., Wen, Z., Huang, T.S.: Real-time speech-driven face animation with expressions using neural networks. IEEE Transactions on Neural Networks 13(1), 100–111 (2002)
19. Izard, C.E.: The Face of Emotion. Appleton-Century-Crofts, New York (1971)
20. Kätsyri, J., Klucharev, V., Frydrych, M., Sams, M.: Identification of synthetic and natural emotional facial expressions. In: Proc. ITRW Audio Visual Speech Proc. Conference (2003)
21. Ku, J., et al.: Experimental results of affective valence and arousal to avatar's facial expressions. Cyberpsychology & Behavior 8(5), 493–503 (2005)
22. Nass, C., Foehr, U.G., Somoza, M.: The effects of emotion of voice in synthesized and recorded speech. In: Proc. AAAI Symp. Emotional and Intelligent II: The Tangled Knot of Social Cognition (2001)
23. Noël, S., Dumoulin, S., Whalen, T., Stewart, J.: Recognizing emotions on static and animated avatar faces. In: Proc. HAVE 2006 (2006)
24. Nogueiras, A., Moreno, A., Bonafonte, A., Marino, J.B.: Speech emotion recognition using hidden markov models. In: Proc. Eurospeech 2001 (2001)
25. Russell, J.A., Bacharowski, J.-A., Fernandez-Dols, J.M.: Facial and vocal expressions of emotion. Annu. Rev. Psychol. 54, 329–349 (2003)
26. Spencer-Smith, J., et al.: Making faces: Creating three-dimensional parameterized models of facial expression. Behavior Research Methods, Instruments & Computers 33(2), 115–123 (2001)
27. Tomkins, S.S.: Affect, Imagery, Consciousness, vol. 1, 2. Springer, New York (1962-1963)

Emotional Bandwidth: Information Theory Analysis of Affective Response Ratings Using a Continuous Slider

Danielle Lottridge and Mark Chignell

Interactive Media Lab, Mechanical & Industrial Engineering, University of Toronto, 5 King's College Rd, Toronto ON M5S3G8, Canada
danielle.lottridge@utoronto.ca, chignell@mie.utoronto.ca

Abstract. Emotions are an important part of the user experience in human machine interaction. More standardized methods of emotion measurement are required to assist in evaluating and comparing these experiences. This research introduces the concept of Emotional Bandwidth, a psychometric property of self-reported emotion measured through a continuous, quantitative slider. Emotional Bandwidth is illustrated in a videoconference watching case study. The Shannon-Weaver measure of informational entropy was used to quantify the rating usage bandwidth, which relates to the number of levels of emotional rating effectively utilized by participants. Significant differences in rating usage strategy were found, with four groups being identified; across the four experimental blocks, entropy either increased, decreased, remained constant or irregular. Emotional Bandwidth, the information-theoretic analysis of affect ratings collected with a continuous slider, may be used to characterize changes in participants' emotional self-rating during experiments and evaluations.

Keywords: Emotional Bandwidth, Psychometrics, Self-reported Emotion, Information Theory, Affective Responses, Sliders, Evaluation.

1 Introduction

There is increasing focus on affective interfaces and associated emotions such as delight or frustration (eg., [1])., and yet there is no standardized and well-accepted way to characterise participants' emotional responses. This work aims to contribute to a better understanding of self-reported emotion measurement using a continuous slider. Recent work has proposed sliders to measure self-reported emotion [2]. We wish to extend this work, to examine: what are the behavioural characteristics of how people self-report their emotions with continuous sliders?

Rating scales are often used to report participant experiences in tasks. Examples of self-reported scales include the NASA-TLX scale for mental workload assessment and Likert scales of agreement. These are often used to measure subjective effects after an experience. However, drawbacks of this method are that respondents are required to provide a summary of their experience, which may correspond to mode, average or end feelings [3]. Current methods of continuous self-report use sliders [2,4,5] and dials [6]. While continuous sliders have been used quite frequently to measure affective responses, relatively little attention has been paid to the properties of the ratings that are made using sliders. In this paper we introduce Emotional

T. Gross et al. (Eds.): INTERACT 2009, Part I, LNCS 5726, pp. 111–114, 2009.

Bandwidth, an entropy measure of informational complexity of rating scale usage that can reveal important properties of the scale and individual differences in its use. We report the results of a case study where self-reported ratings of affect (satisfaction) were collected using a slider, and where participants' emotional bandwidth demonstrated differences in rating scale usage.

2 Emotion Bandwidth

The capacity of participants' scale usage is one type of behavioural characteristic concerning how people self-report their emotions[7]. Individuals can display varying capacities, which may change over time in response to the stimuli, environment and context. We use the Shannon-Weaver measure of informational entropy to quantify the rating usage bandwidth, which we refer to as Emotional Bandwidth. In this paper, the emotional bandwidth corresponds to the effective number of rating points or levels utilized on the continuous slider scale[1].

Equations 1 and 2 show the informational entropy formula to determine Emotional Bandwidth: the number of levels utilized on the continuous slider scale. In this formula, n refers to the total number of levels on the scale, and p, to the proportion of the total time (x) spent at that level.

$$\text{entropy} = -\sum_{i=1}^{n} p(x_i) \log_2 p(x_i) \tag{1}$$

$$\text{emotional bandwidth} = 2^{\text{entropy}} \tag{2}$$

For example, if a scale has 7 levels and a participant used all levels equally often, the bandwidth score is 7. Those who use the equivalent of two levels would receive a bandwidth of two, regardless of whether those levels are -3 and -2, 1 and 5, or -3 and +3. These patterns are similar in their bandwidth capacity (binary view of emotional state) and that they differ in the strength of the levels reported. Other behavioural characteristics complement bandwidth, such as whether the individual tends to dwell on the positive or negative end of the scale (average), and whether the individual tends to use extreme or neutral levels (variance).

Variance in ratings can be displayed as a histogram, or as an average with standard deviations. A relative advantage of the emotional bandwidth score is that it is a single number, comparable across individuals, and across temporal blocks as participants progress through an experiment or evaluation. Moreover, bandwidth does not depend on the level placement in the scale. In the case mentioned above, the variance of the first individual would be large (moving between -3 and 3) and the second (moving between -1 and 1) would be small, which misses their similar binary capacity.

3 Case Study

Ranjan, Birnholz and Balakrishnan [8] carried out a study to compare the effectiveness of automatic multi-camera capture of a meeting with cinematographic rules

[1] Emotion Bandwidth has been used to refer to the richness of a media channel such as video or text. For e.g., http://www.kapor.com/writing/Emotional-Bandwdith.htm

versus capture using a professional film crew. Participants watched two 15 minute videos of 3 people discussing a 'survival scenario', where a group chooses the most useful 3 out of 10 tools for survival purposes. The videos were similar in terms of their overall patterns of interaction and artifact usage. A professional crew filmed one video; the other was filmed automatically.

11 participants (7 males, mean age = 26 years) were instructed to pay attention to both the content and the quality of the recording. They were provided with a physical slider to continuously express their satisfaction (on a 7 point scale that varied from -3 to +3, with a neutral (0) center). Participants were instructed to move the slider as often as necessary to best represent their affective feelings of satisfaction with the video coverage. A small window on the screen showed the numerical slider position.

The information complexity was calculated for each participant in terms of bits, based on the frequencies with which each point on the rating scale was used. Roughly 30 minutes of data was collected for each participant with slider positions being sampled at a rate of once per second for a total of about 1800 slider position assessments per participant. Data from one participant (ID = 3) was removed because it was incomplete. If a level was dwelled on for one second or less, it was treated as an intermediate level, and not included in the bandwidth calculations.

For number of bits H, the equivalent number of rating points used was then calculated as 2^H. The corresponding rating bandwidths had an average of 5.44 (std dev =.77). These rating bandwidths are interpreted as the effective number of rating points used by each participant. For this sample, they ranged from just under 4.2 rating points to just over 6.5 rating points.

Blocks. The consistency of rating scale usage was then assessed by dividing the data into four blocks each of approximately 7.5 minutes in duration. While some participants showed a relatively constant level of rating bandwidth across the four blocks, others show more variability. Five participants were selected as having relatively constant rating bandwidth across blocks. Based on visual inspection of the data, we classified remaining participants into three groups: two participants with a decreasing trend across the blocks, one with an increasing trend, and three with a blip (i.e., a temporary drop in one of the blocks followed by recovery).

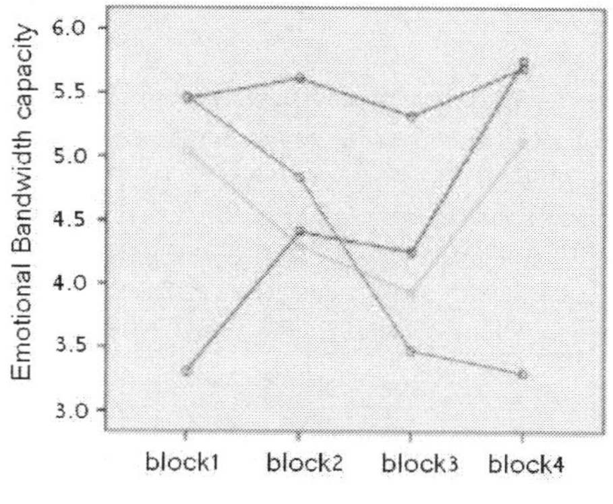

Fig. 1. Average rating bandwidths across four blocks for four groups of participants

We carried out repeated measures ANOVA to examine the interaction between blocks, and found a significant interaction effect of subject group and block on rating bandwidths ($F[3,7]=12.74$, $p<.005$). Using Mauchly's test, sphericity was not found to be violated.

This statistic should be interpreted cautiously since the groups were extracted from visual inspection of the data. This result suggest that the type of information theoretic analysis used here on slider data can be used to capture meaningful differences between participants in terms of how rating scales are used. Figure 1 shows the average rating bandwidths across the blocks for the four inferred groups.

Conclusions. Continuous sliders collect individual's impressions of their affective state. We contribute a novel application of information theory to characterize those ratings: emotional bandwidth. Emotional bandwidth is a psychometric property that represents participants' capacity, or the number of scale rating points that he or she is effectively utilizing. A case study showed variations in emotional bandwidth that distinguished different styles of rating scale usage. The present work is a first step in terms of research on the use of continuous sliders to collect detailed information on participants' motivation, affect, and capacity during experiments and evaluations.

References

1. Norman, D.: Emotional Design: Why we Love (or Hate) Everyday Things. Basic Books, New York (2004)
2. Laurens, G., Desmet, P.: Designing a research tool: A case-study in how design and research can cross-fertilize each other. In: DRS 2008 Design Research Society Biennial Conference, pp. 362(1)–362(10). DRS digital archive (2008)
3. Kahneman, D.: Objective happiness. In: Kahneman, D., Diener, E., Schwarz, N. (eds.) Well-being: The foundations of hedonic psychology, pp. 3–25. Russell Sage Foundation, New York (1999)
4. Baumgartner, H., Sujan, M., Padgett, D.: Patterns of Affective Reactions to Advertisements: The Integration of Moment-to-Moment Responses into Overall Judgments. J. of Market'g Research 34(2), 219–232 (1997)
5. Mauss, I.B., Levenson, R.W., McCarter, L., Wilhelm, F.H., Gross, J.J.: The tie that binds? Coherence among emotional experience, behavior, and autonomic physiology. Emotion 5, 175–190 (2005)
6. Gottman, J.M., Levenson, R.W.: A valid procedure for obtaining self-report of affect in marital interaction. J. of Consult'g & Clin. Psych. 53(2), 151–160 (1985)
7. Attneave, F.: Applications of Information Theory to Psychology. Holt, Rinehart and Winston, New York (1959)
8. Ranjan, A., Birnholtz, J., Balakrishnan, R.: Improving Meeting Capture by Applying Television Production Principles with Audio and Motion Detection. In: SIGCHI Conf. on Human Factors in Comp. Sys. CHI 2008, pp. 227–236. ACM Press, New York (2008)

Can You Be Persuaded? Individual Differences in Susceptibility to Persuasion

Maurits Kaptein[1], Panos Markopoulos[1], Boris de Ruyter[2], and Emile Aarts[2]

[1] Eindhoven University of Technology
Den Dolech 2, HG 2.38
5600MB Eindhoven, The Netherlands
{m.c.kaptein,p.markopoulos}@tue.nl
[2] Philips Research
High Tech Campus 34 -WB-5.27
5656 AE Eindhoven, The Netherlands
{boris.de.ruyter,emile.aarts}@philips.com

Abstract. Persuasive technologies are growing in popularity and many designers create systems which intentionally change users attitudes or behaviors. This study shows that peoples individual differences in susceptibility to persuasion, as implemented using the six persuasion principles proposed by Cialdini 2, relates to their compliance to a persuasive request which is accompanied by a persuasive cue. This result is a starting point for designers to start incorporating individual differences in susceptibility to persuasive cues in their adaptive persuasive systems.

Keywords: Persuasion, Persuasive technologies, Individual differences.

1 Introduction

Persuasive technologies are defined as a class of technologies that are intentionally designed to change a person's attitude or behavior 4. Roughly a decade after the seminal work of B. J. Fogg 5 the field of persuasive technologies has taken a big flight and the literature is increasingly populated by records of persuasive applications and case studies to demonstrate their persuasive powers 6. This literature though has not yet provided us with appropriate tools to characterize different individuals as subjects of persuasion; we set out to address this limitation.

In this paper we focus on the idea that people differ in their susceptibility to persuasion; their compliance to specific persuasive cues. We believe that for persuasive technologies to be effective, adaptivity to individual users is of great importance; like in interpersonal contacts the persuader has to choose a different strategy to approach different individuals. In the remainder of the paper we first summarize Cialdini's six principles of persuasion 23 - six ways of framing a persuasive request to increase behavioral compliance - and then show individual susceptibility to these cues to be related to compliance to a persuasive request. The six principles are summarized below:

T. Gross et al. (Eds.): INTERACT 2009, Part I, LNCS 5726, pp. 115–118, 2009.

1. *Principle of reciprocation*: People feel obligated to return a favor.
2. *Principle of scarcity*: When something is scarce, people will value it more.
3. *Principle of authority*: When a request is made by a legitimate authority, people are inclined to follow / believe the request.
4. *Principle of commitment and consistency*: People do as they told they would.
5. *Principle of consensus*: People do as other people do.
6. *Principle of liking*: We say 'yes' to people we like.

Individual differences in effective methods to increase compliance have been studied previously 78. Studies in the field of attitude change have identified personality and mood characteristics, as well as individual need for cognition 1 as moderating variables in compliance to a persuasive request. However, these works do not provide concrete guidance in choosing the most appropriate persuasion strategy.

We create a questionnaire to measure individual susceptibility to the six persuasion principles. Next, we conduct an experiment showing that people differ in their susceptibility to persuasive requests and that this measurement correlates to compliance. In this experiment we hypothesize the following:

1. Compliance to a persuasive request is *increased by using a persuasive cue.*
2. Compliance when a cue is present depends on *participant's susceptibility to persuasion.*

2 Method

To test our hypothesis we set up a study in which respondents were asked to fill in an online questionnaire. Respondents were recruited from a HCI mailing list, and consisted mainly of undergraduate and graduate students in the HCI field. The questionnaire consisted of 42 items and contained 12 items measuring respondent's susceptibility to persuasion and 30 dummy questions – the dummy questions where of use for another research project. After filling in the questionnaire respondents were asked to provide the experimenter with email addresses of friends that might be willing to participate in the same study. This request was either not cued (Condition 1 – *No-Cue*) or cued (Condition 2 – *Cue*) with 2 persuasive arguments. The first cue relied on the principle of consensus: "*All of the other participants provided several email addresses to us*". The second statement relied on the principle of reciprocation: "*In return for providing us with your friend's addresses, we will send you a copy of the results of our study*".

The twelve items used to measure susceptibility to persuasion were derived from the six principles of persuasion. For each of these principles two items were created to measure respondents' susceptibility. This resulted in the items presented in table 1 to be rated on a 7 point scale (*1 totally disagree to 7 totally agree*).

3 Results

Out of the 454 initially invited participants 82 took part in the study leading to a response rate of 18.1%. Of the people who responded, and thus completely filled in the

Table 1. The 12 item susceptibility questionnaire

Reciprocation	*1.* When a family member does me a favor, I am very inclined to return this favor. *2.* I always pay back a favor.
Scarcity	*1.* I believe rare products (scarce) are more valuable than mass products. *2.* When my favorite shop is about to close, I would visit it since it is my last chance.
Authority	*1.* I always follow advice from my general practitioner. *2.* When a professor tells me something I tend to believe it is true.
Commitment	*1.* Whenever I commit to an appointment I do as I told. *2.* I try to do everything I have promised to do.
Consensus	*1.* If someone from my social network notifies me about a good book, I tend to read it. *2.* When I am in a new situation I look at others to see what I should do.
Liking	*1.* I accept advice from my social network. *2.* When I like someone, I am more inclined to believe him or her.

study, 57.3% were males and 43.7% were females. The average age of the respondents was 37 years (SD = 13.3).

We first tested the 12 susceptibility to persuasion items on their internal consistency. Using reliability analysis we obtained a Cronbach's Alpha of 0.609; just sufficient to assume that the items measured one scale. Omission of items did not increase Cronbach's Alpha and we decided to continue the analysis using one averaged susceptibility score for each respondent.

The distribution of our dependent variable significantly deviated from the normal distribution. (KS=.319, $p<0.001$; KW=.651, $p<0.001$). Thus we used nonparametric statistics to test our two hypotheses.

To test hypothesis one a Mann-Whitney U test was performed on the number of email addresses provided. This resulted in a higher mean rank score for the *Cue* condition (50.35) than in the *No-cue* condition (31.74). This difference in mean rank was significant ($p < 0.001$) and confirmed hypothesis one.

To test hypothesis two we looked at the Spearman Rho coefficient of the correlation between individual susceptibility scores and the number of email addresses provided. There was a significant positive relationship between individuals susceptibility to persuasive cues and the number of email addresses provided ($r_s = .227$, $p < .05$).

Hypothesis two states explicitly an interaction effect: The relationship between susceptibility to persuasive cues and the number of email addresses provided is only present in the *Cue* condition. In the *No-cue* condition the relationship between participants persuasion scores and the number of email addresses provided was low and not significant ($r_s = .161$, $p = .328$). In the *Cue* condition the correlation was higher, but not significant. ($r_s = .236$, $p < .128$). The effect in the *Cue* condition was stronger than in the *No-cue* condition.

4 Discussion

Our results show that incorporating a persuasive cue can increase the compliance to a persuasive request. This in itself is not surprising: it is in line with the work of Cialdini 2 and confirms the persuasive powers of a technological artifact in line with the Fogg 5. We also showed that respondent's susceptibility to cues related to their compliance to a request. Additional ad hoc analysis of individual items showed that the correlations between scores on specific items of the questionnaire corresponding to the cues that were used were much higher than analysis of the full scale. For example the rating on susceptibility to consensus cues was strongly related to the number of email addresses provided in the *Cue* condition ($r_s = .672$, $p < .000$). Future work should thus focus on developing a more detailed scale to measure subject's susceptibility to specific cues.

Designers of persuasive systems should adapt their persuasive strategies to their users to increase compliance to their behavioral request. This article showed that participant's susceptibility to persuasive cues can be measured and relates to their compliance. Incorporating a user profile of susceptibility to specific cues, and adopting the persuasive strategy deployed by a persuasive system, could greatly enhance its effectiveness.

References

1. Cacioppo, J.T., Petty, R.E.: The need for Cognition. Journal of Personality and Social Psychology (1982)
2. Cialdini, R.: Influence, Science and Practice. Allyn and Bacon (2001)
3. Cialdini, R.: The science of persuasion. Scientific American Mind (2004)
4. Fogg, B.J.: Persuasive technologies: Introduction. Communications of the ACM archive 42(5) (1999)
5. Fogg, B.J.: Persuasive Technology: Using Computers to Change what We Think and Do. Morgan Kaufmann, San Francisco (2002)
6. Ijsselsteijn, W., de Kort, Y., Midden, C., Eggen, B., van den Hoven, E.: Persuasive Technology for Human Well-Being: Setting the Scene. In: IJsselsteijn, W.A., de Kort, Y.A.W., Midden, C., Eggen, B., van den Hoven, E. (eds.) PERSUASIVE 2006. LNCS, vol. 3962, pp. 1–5. Springer, Heidelberg (2006)
7. Petty, R.E., Cacioppo, J.T.: Attitudes and persuasion: Classic and contemporary approaches. Dubuque (1981)
8. Petty, R.E., Wegener, D.T.: The Elaboration Likelihood Model: Current Status and Controversies. In: Dual-process Theories in Social Psychology (1999)

The Subjective and Objective Nature of Website Aesthetic Impressions

Eleftherios Papachristos and Nikolaos Avouris

Human-Computer Interaction Group, E&CE Department, University of Patras, University Ypatias Str., GR-26500, Greece
epap@ece.upatras.gr, avouris@upatras.gr

Abstract. This paper explores the possibility to predict positive aesthetic impression and user preference of website design through a combination of objective and subjective factors. The objective factors used are symmetry, order, balance, complexity while the subjective ones include familiarity - novelty ratings. The advantages of such an approach is the reduction of user involvement since the ratings of objective factors may be provided by a small number of design experts. We found indications that balance between certain factors maximize the possibility of users having a positive aesthetic impression.

Keywords: Aesthetic evaluation, website preference, visual appeal.

1 Introduction

One of the main goals of a website's homepage is to attract users and to elicit positive first impressions. First impressions are based mainly on usefulness of content, information structure, visual attractiveness and are influenced by user expectations, experience and training [1]. Research suggests that aesthetic factors are detected first and impressions based on them can influence subsequent website judgments [2]. However, the question on how to design for or how to measure positive aesthetic impressions seems to raise the ancient argument about whether beauty lays on the eye of the viewer or in the object itself.

According to Coates [3] balance between the opposing factors of "*Information*" and "*Concinnity*" creates a positive aesthetic impression. *Concinnity* relates to the order and sense while *information* relates to contrast and novelty perceived in design. Both constructs have objective (e.g. symmetry, contrast) as well as subjective (e.g. novelty) components. Perception of attractiveness is expected to reach a maximum, if a design is balanced in regard to these constructs. High *concinnity* results in boring and well structured designs and high *information* in very novel but confusing designs. Coates assumptions bear similarities to Berlyne's theory of experimental aesthetics [4] which suggest that there is an inverted–U shape relationship between *preference* and *psychological arousal*. Berlyne investigated the impact of a number of collative variables such as complexity, ambiguity and novelty on pleasure. In a more recent study Lavie and Tractinsky [5] identified two dimensions of website aesthetics: "*Classical*" and "*Expressive*". The "*Classical*" dimension of aesthetics relates to concepts such as symmetry, order and clear design while the "*Expressive*" dimension

T. Gross et al. (Eds.): INTERACT 2009, Part I, LNCS 5726, pp. 119–122, 2009.

relates to creativity and originality. There are similarities between the two dimensions and the notions of *information* and *concinnity*; however Lavie and Tractinsky do not see their dimensions as two ends of the same continuum. Additionally, they do not distinguish between objective and subjective components in their dimensions.

The goal of this study is to explore the usefulness of Coates "Information – Concinnity" theory for website aesthetic impression predictions. There are clear advantages for such an approach since predictions could be made with less user involvement. Objective components of *information* and *concinnity* such as *symmetry* and *contrast* can be investigated by design experts and user involvement could be reduced to familiarity - novelty judgments. Although *symmetry*, *contrast* and *complexity* have been labeled as objective factors, users could perceive them subjectively due to differences in background or training. Therefore agreement between experts and user's as well as within users for these factors needs also to be investigated.

2 Methodology

In order to explore the usefulness of Coates theory an experiment was conducted in which the participants evaluated three alternative homepage designs of a university department's website. Each design was prior assigned to one of the high *concinnity*, high *information* and balanced areas of the "Information –Concinnity" continuum (figure 1). In the initial phase of the study the three experimental designs were selected out of the six homepages which were identical in terms of text, images and logo but they differed in accordance to form, color, general layout and style. The homepages were designed with the intent to differ considerably in the "Information - Concinnity" scale. Given the complexity of the *information* and *concinnity* constructs we had the participants to evaluate their constituent components and then we calculated a score for each design. To that end forty four volunteer students (28 male, 16 female) of the university department in question evaluated the six homepages on *Symmetry*, *Order*, *Contrast*, *Balance*, *Complexity* and *Novelty* on a 9 point scale.

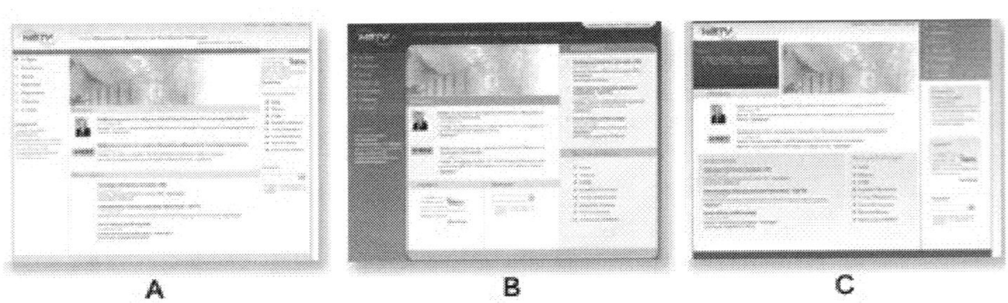

Fig. 1. University departments home page designs used in the experiment. Design A represents the *high concinnity* condition, B the *balance* condition, and C the *high information*.

From these factors the "Information – Concinnity" construct was computed for each design. Equal weight has been assigned to subjective and objective factors. In addition three design experts were asked to do the same in order to detect inconsistencies between them and website users without visual design training.

In the second phase another group of fifty three volunteer students (35 male, 18 female, age: mean = 22.2 SD = 0.92) from the same department evaluated the three selected designs. The evaluation took place on an eye-tracking device on which the three designs were presented randomly, first in pairs and then one by one. In the pair condition users had to choose which design they preferred most while eye-tracking data were simultaneously collected. Shortly afterwards, participants had to evaluate each design on *visual appeal*, *overall preference* and *novelty* on a 9 point scale.

3 Results

Factorial Repeated measures ANOVA for visual appeal and preference was performed with gender as a between subject factor. There was a significant main effect of "Information – Concinnity" on preference $F(2,168) = 33.364$, $p < .001$ as well as for visual appeal $F(2,168) = 29.650$, $p < .001$. Preference and visual appeal judgment peaked in the B (balance between "Information – Concinnity") condition as predicted by the theory.

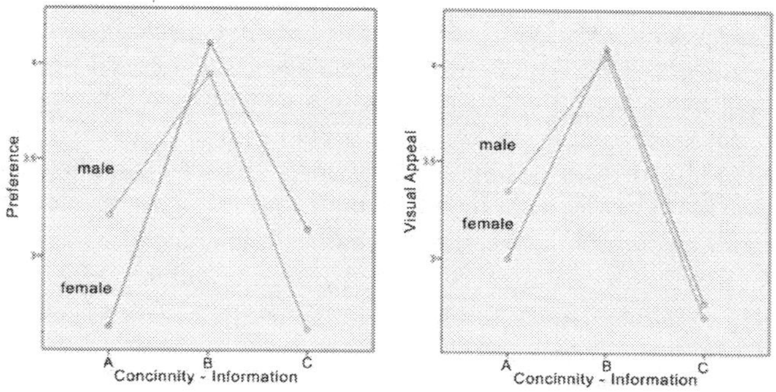

Fig. 2. Preference (left) and Visual appeal (right) ratings for Designs **A** (high concinnity), **B** (balanced) and **C** (high information), for male and female ratings

The A (*high concinnity*) design was perceived slightly better in visual appeal than C (*high information)* design. Although, there was agreement between gender in overall design preference we found an interaction effect between gender and "Information –Concinnity" "$F(2,166) = 5.033$, $p < .008$ for preference. In figure 2 we can see that male participants were more tolerant to the high concinnity design than female in both preference and appeal judgments. The eye-tracking data collected showed that design A had a smaller number of fixations and less observation time (mean 2.95 sec) in the pairwise comparison than the other designs. The design with the lengthiest observation duration was design B (mean 3.705 sec) followed by design C (mean 3.612 sec). Gaze time and fixation number can be indicators of attractiveness as well as for difficulty of the user to make sense of the stimuli. We used the eye-tracking data to confirm "objectively" that the designs were correctly assigned to each experimental condition. Although, the eye-tracking data confirmed our assumptions for the *concinnity* and *information* condition it is difficult to differentiate between attractiveness and *information* as a cause for high values in the balanced condition.

In order to investigate inter-rater agreement in the objective factors ratings of the first phase we transformed them into rankings and Kendall's W was calculated. Kendall's coefficient of concordance takes values from zero (total disagreement) to one (total agreement). Results on all factors were significant, however agreement varied from moderate to high with *balance* achieving the lowest agreement (0.372, df = 5, $p < .001$) and *symmetry* the highest (0.723, df = 5, $p < .001$). It could be argued that low agreement levels indicates that some factors shouldn't be labeled "objective" since judgments about them were influenced by individual perceptions. However, agreement levels between average user ratings and expert evaluations were considerably high (Kendall's W from 0.886 -0.971). This means that safe results about the objective constructs can be achieved by a small number of design experts or a large number of users with no experience in design.

4 Conclusions

In the presented study Coates "*Information – Concinnity*" theory has been explored for its ability to predict user's positive aesthetics impressions of websites. The advantage of this theory is that it recognizes both subjective and objective components of its constructs. In our study we found evidence that balance between *information* and *concinnity* results in higher attractiveness and higher preference ratings. Results also suggest that preference criteria for females differ from males in that they appreciate creativity and novelty in web design more in contrast to males who are in favor of *order* and *symmetry*. It could be argued that males prefer websites that are perceived as usable since "*Concinnity*" as well as Lavie's dimension of *Classical* aesthetics have striking similarities to usability advocated design principles. However the design that successfully combines form and function, sense and novelty seems to be preferred overall by both genders.

References

1. Hartmann, J., Sutcliffe, A., De Angeli, A.: Investigating attractiveness in web user interfaces. In: Proceedings of the SIGCHI conference on Human factors in computing systems, San Jose, California, USA, April 28-May 03 (2007)
2. Lindgaard, G., Fernandes, G.J., Dudek, C., Brownet, J.: Attention web designers: You have 50 milliseconds to make a good first impression! Behavior and Information Technology 25(2), 115–126 (2006)
3. Coates, D.: Watches tell more than time: product design, information and the quest for elegance. McGraw-Hill, London (2003)
4. Berlyne, D.E.: Studies in the new experimental aesthetics. Hemisphere Publishing Corporation, Washington (1974)
5. Lavie, T., Tractinsky, N.: Assessing dimensions of perceived visual aesthetics of web sites. International Journal of Human-Computer Studies 60(3), 269–298 (2004)

Biting, Whirling, Crawling – Children's Embodied Interaction with Walk-through Displays

Satu Jumisko-Pyykkö, Mandy Weitzel, and Ismo Rakkolainen

Tampere University of Technology, PO Box 553, 33101 Tampere, Finland
{satu.jumisko-pyykko,ismo.rakkolainen}@tut.fi

Abstract. Understanding of embodied interaction in the context of walk-through displays and designing for it is very limited. This study examined children's intuitive embodied interaction with a large, semi-visible, projective walk-through display and space around it using observation. We identified several interaction patterns for passing, staying and moving inside the screen, using whole body and its parts for manipulating surface and content on the screen, and ways of expanding the actual interaction environment outside of the projected screen. We summarize the interaction patterns in the form of palette for rich embodied interaction with projected walk-through displays.

Keywords: Human factors, Interaction, Design, Experimentation, Displays, FogScreen, Embodied interaction.

1 Introduction

Interaction research has shifted its focus from hand-mouse interaction to wider areas such as embodied techniques, which enables the user to interact with applications by using bodily movements. For the development of new input techniques that overcome hand-mouse interaction, the understanding of embodied actions is a starting point of the design process.

Various frameworks have been presented to understand, model and design human embodied actions or physical interaction in different levels of details. For example, a design-oriented framework for sensing-based interaction, presented by Benford et al. [1] categorizes user's movements to expected, sensed by system and desired by application. Similarly, an analytic framework developed by Suchman [2] aims at highlighting asymmetrical resources available to user and to machine. Both of these frameworks require a relatively well understood interaction design problem to be modeled or finalized application to be retrospectively analyzed. Instead of focusing on interaction design, the third approach called labanotation [3] focuses on detailed analysis of movements providing a comprehensive description of the movement including the analysis of body and its parts, space, time and dynamics. However, the approach has been criticized being overly specific in the embodied interaction design process [4]. All of these frameworks have been applied in the different phases of interaction design process [3] but none of them can easily be adapted for understanding embodied interaction with novel display technologies.

T. Gross et al. (Eds.): INTERACT 2009, Part I, LNCS 5726, pp. 123–136, 2009.

Walk-through displays are non-solid displays that the viewer can reach through or even walk through them. They can facilitate a new type of embodied interaction by enabling the user to penetrate the display. Different types of walk-through displays, e.g., water screens have existed for decades, but their use is very limited. With the advent of dry and high image quality mid-air FogScreens™ [5, 6], the walk-through displays are becoming applicable for wider exploitation and more applications. The emerging mid-air displays have created an opportunity also for novel user interfaces and direct interaction techniques, as the images floating in thin air are reachable. The user occupies the same space as the image, and the mid-air displays can also be room-sized. Even though the walk-through displays are increasingly used in various applications and venues, there are no previous studies aiming at understanding the patterns for embodied interaction and design for it in these novel environments.

The use of interactive technology has an important role in the life of children. Children encounter and use software technologies in their daily lives, e.g. cellular phones to communicate, computer games for individual or collaborative entertainment, or educational technologies for learning [7]. Thus, children have been involved as users in the design process of new hardware and software products in recent years since the early work of Druin [8] and Kafai [9]. In various studies [e.g. 7, 10, 11, 12, 13] research methods have been developed or adapted to children's technology design. Studies have been conducted both, in natural setting environments and in the lab to design or to evaluate new products.

This paper targets on understanding children's intuitive embodied interaction with a walk-through display and space around it. We use a term intuitive interaction to emphasize that our research interest is constrained to spontaneous or natural way of starting the interaction. We present an observational study of children's embodied interaction with multimedia material on a walk-through display. The results are summarized in the form of palette of interaction patterns. The results benefit both academia and practitioners. For the former, it increases the understanding of forms of embodied interaction in the context of walk-through display and its space. For the latter, our results inform design and development of applications and interaction techniques to promote and enable rich embodied interaction in such novel environments.

The paper is structured in the following way: In Section 2 we give an overview on embodied interaction and its frameworks. Walk-through displays are defined and a user study on children's game experiences with walk-through displays is outlined in Section 3. After describing our research method and the used study setup in Section 4, we present the results in Section 5. Finally, in Section 6 conclusions are given and the paper closes with some open issues that are discussed.

2 Interaction and Its Frameworks

To define interaction, the modern human-computer interaction has taken classical J.J. Gibson's ecological approach to perception as one aspect to interaction [14]. According to him we perceive objects as affordances showing possibilities for acting in the environment. Later, Norman [15] has introduced as a slightly modified version of affordances for interaction design but still highlighting properties and cues that object can offer for use. However, affordances are only one point of view to interaction.

Human interactions with the environment can be modeled using continuous output-input chain from user's perspective. This chain has the aspects to user goals, execution of goals in environment to evaluation of actions in relation to goals [15]. These definitions of interaction originate mainly from desktop computing.

During last ten years the research focus has emerged from hand-mouse interaction to embodied interaction. Embodied interaction emphasizes the role of action. The work of phenomenological philosopher Merleau-Ponty [16] has motivated interaction researchers [e.g. 3, 17, 18, 19, 20]. He described that our bodily experiences enable us to access the world of objects. For example, Svanaes [20] emphasizes that our lived body and its relation to environment is a key factor for understanding user's perspective in system development. Dourish [17] continues that, embodied interaction "is creation, manipulation, and shearing of meaning through engaged interaction with meaning through engaged interaction with artifacts". Finally, Hornecker [21] has underlined a more practical approach to embodied interaction. She calls it as embodied facilitation in which any technology can provide a structure for implicitly guiding user behavior by making some actions easier while constraining the others. Recently, Jacobs et al. [22] have developed a framework for Reality Based Interaction (RBI) aiming at understanding, comparing and analyzing all emerging interaction styles which go beyond conventional desktop computing. RBI includes four layers from identifying 1) naive physics, 2) body awareness and skills, 3) environment awareness and skills and 4) social awareness and skills. Taken together, embodied interaction sets the bodily actions into the focus of interaction and underlines that these actions enable us to be especially inside or engaged in the world. For the practitioners, understanding the embodied actions is a key factor for system design.

2.1 Frameworks of Studying and Designing for Embodied Actions

For studying and designing for embodied actions, different frameworks offer fruitfully different insight. Benford et al. [1] have presented framework for sensing-based interaction by categorizing user's movements to expected, sensed and desired. The natural movements of user, like walking, are expected movements. Sensed movements are recognized by a computer whereas desired movements are required from user by an application. Their framework underlines the possible overlaps between expected, sensed and desired movements. It can help for identifying the potential source of the problems in interaction, inspire for new design ideas as well as applied to analyze existing taxonomies of input and output devices.

The pioneering work of Suchman [2] emphasizes that action is situated, has improvisatory nature, and is constantly constructed and reconstructed in interaction. Embodied interaction, like movements, replicates contextual characteristics like other actions. Suchman composed an analytic framework for highlighting asymmetrical resources available to user and to machine in her work. Later, Loke et al. [18] have adapted the framework for interaction analysis in physical gaming applications. They differentiated user's actions/activities available and not available for machine and machines effects available for user.

Labanotation, created by Rudolf Laban in the 1920's [3], concentrates on careful analysis of movements. The method provides a symbolic notation, similar to music notation, for writing the symbols of body movements and their expressive quality (e.g. weight, time, space). For example, the structural form of labanotation provides the broadest and most detailed description of the movement including the analysis of body and its parts, space (direction, level, distance, degree of motion), time (meter and duration) and dynamics (quality, texture, strong, elastic, accented). The labanotation is popular in dance in which it is used for observing and exploring natural and choreographed movements but it has also been applied in physical gaming [3, 18]. While Labanotation offers systematic language for the analysis of bodily movements in space and time, it has been criticized being too laborious, difficult and detailed to be used in iterative game design process for children [4].

In addition to the analytical models presented, the recent research has also described the frameworks for designers to explore expressive and movement based interaction. The main idea behind the development work relies on Gibsonian way of thinking and is summarized by Hummels et al [23] from the viewpoint of designer as follows: "interaction creates meaning and it can stimulate designers to explore, study and design the relationship between variety of aspects such as sensation, dynamic character, story, interaction style, experience, emotion, function, form and semantics".For designer, the imaginations of ideas and temporally constrained sketching are not enough for searching and designing for expressive and rich behavior. To go beyond these limitations, design movement provides multidimensional tools and techniques including tasks of choreography of interaction, gestural design tools, interactive installations and interactive tangible sketching [23]. The aim is to facilitate the construction of meaning through interaction, capture richness of it, design by moving, and explore the support movement. This approach offers emphatic design aspect, but its appropriateness for designing for certain user groups, like children, might be questioned.

To sum up, there is variety of frameworks for understanding, modeling and designing human embodied actions or physical interaction. To use the frameworks of sensing-based interaction and Suchman's analytic frameworks, it requires relatively well-understood design problem to be proactively modeled or finalized application to be retrospectively analyzed. While these models focus on the input-output modeling, labanotation provides an insight for movement analysis. Its use is independent on the phase of system development. However, it might provide too detailed information for iterative system design and information which is possible not related to actual users' actions with the system. Our approach is to examine children's embodied interaction and movements with a large walk-through display. Instead of applying any actual input techniques or sensors, we are interested in children's natural way of starting embodied interaction and movements resembling the input part of the interaction. The work aims at identifying interaction patterns and design ideas for further system development.

3 Walk-through Displays

Various stereoscopic, autostereoscopic, volumetric, holographic, and effect screens [24] can give an illusion of objects floating in mid-air, but they are not truly walk-through displays. All these displays have their proper uses and applications.

Nevertheless, walk-through displays are an intriguing new category of displays, which may have wide application potential.

Large walk-through displays offer a good base for studying embodied interaction. Walk-through displays are non-solid displays that look and feel immaterial for the viewer, to the extent that the viewer can reach through or even walk through them. Examples of such displays are water screens, some particle screens such as smoke screens, and specifically the FogScreens, which enable high-quality projected images to hover in thin air and a dry walk-through experience. These mid-air displays attract the audience to move around and in front of the display, while offering a chance to touch the immaterial display medium. Example of such a display is given in Figure 1.

In terms of dryness, ease of employment and image quality, the FogScreen is generally the best walk-through display option. The core of the invention is how to form a thin, planar and non-turbulent image plane, which has a paramount effect on image quality. It usually employs dry, tiny fog droplets as a scattering medium. It is also a short-cut technology to create StarWars™-type mid-air displays [25]. The FogScreen requires rear projection, as it produces about 100-fold brighter image than front projection. While the side being viewed towards the projector has a bright image, the other side of the screen is nearly transparent. This enables also to create independent two-sided projection without noticeable interference.

Jumisko-Pyykkö et al. [26] examined children's game experiences between physical gaming on the mid-air FogScreen with hand-held pointer interaction technique and a conventional desktop computing. Their results underlined that the players were delighted in novel gaming environment, its stimulation for moving around and naturalness, but the interaction with the display was very demanding.

Previous results are good triggers for our work. Instead of focusing on certain applications or interaction techniques, we aim at understanding natural or intuitive way of approaching walk-through display and space around it. We argue that the knowledge about these factors is beneficial in two ways. Firstly, they increase the awareness of affordance that the walk-through display and its space can offer. These factors might likely differ from conventional displays in which user activities takes a place in front of the display. Secondly, they inform the design and development of applications and interaction techniques for maximizing the possibilities for embodied

Fig. 1. The Whack-a-mole-type game played on FogScreen

interaction in such novel environments. Our study employs only the FogScreen, but the results should be applicable also for the other types of walk-through displays, apart from their more material substance and/or worse image quality.

4 Research Method

The nature of the research problem required an open-ended and exploratory method. We conducted an observational study in a laboratory environment by taking notes and using visual technology. The observation was non-participating, unstructured and open, since the children were informed about being observed during the experiment. The collected qualitative data should offer insights into children's actions in different circumstances, while exploring and playing with the mid-air FogScreen, which is conceptually a new kind of a display and media platform.

Participants. Ten children participated in the observational study (6 girls and 4 boys. The youngest child was 5 years old and the oldest child was 10 years old. Two children were each at the age of 7 and 8 years and four children at the age of 9 years. Our sample was also multi-cultural, as the participating children originally came from several countries and could speak at least English or German. None of the children had seen or played with the FogScreen before. The study was conducted in pairs of siblings or friends to make the experimental situation more relaxed for the children [27].

Study Setup. The exploratory study was carried out at Tampere University of Technology which has a fully functional FogScreen with the screen width of 1.4 meters. The content was projected with an Epson EMP-74 projector (1024x768, 2000 ANSI lumen) on one side of the screen. For rendering, a PC (Intel Core 2 Duo, 1.86 GHz, 1GB RAM, Windows XP, Intel Graphics Media Accelerator 3000) was used.

The FogScreen was mounted in such a height that the children could reach the whole screen area. In front of the screen and behind the screen there was 2-3 meters of free space as well as on one side of the screen. For the interaction with projected 2D or 3D graphics objects, a Sick™ infrared laser range scanner (for plain hand pointing) and a modified eBeam™ whiteboard tracker (employing a hand-held pointer) were used. The contents, especially the games, required an audio presentation that was realized through a stereo loudspeaker setup behind the screen.

Procedure. Before actual starting, the experimenter engaged the children in some small talk to find out more about one another, showed the lab and explained in a child-friendly parlance how the FogScreen works and briefly explained the procedure. Children were given the task to explore and play with the fog while different contents appeared on the FogScreen. We allowed them to do whatever crossed to their minds and avoided to restrict and direct their movements and actions in any way. Therewith this part had a more exploratory and open-ended than task-oriented character.

Various contents were projected on the FogScreen to motivate the children to interact and get in touch with the screen. During the exploring part the complexity of the content increased (see Figure 2). First, still pictures of single and multiple colors were presented, followed by pictures that showed surface textures (mushroom, feather, snailshell, shamrock, ice cubes). Especially images with bright colors brought

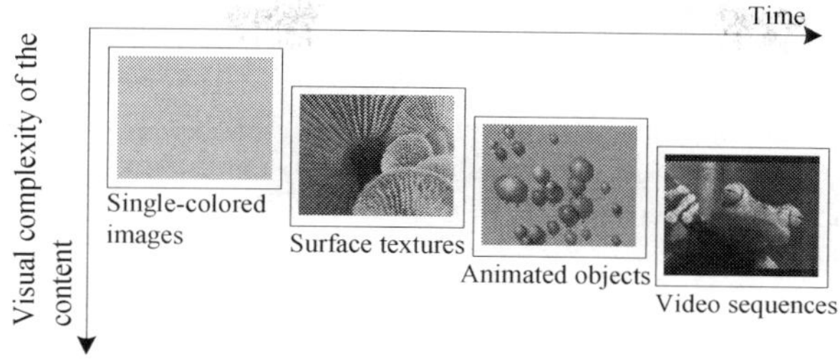

Fig. 2. The visual complexity of the presented content in the exploration phase was increased over the time

out the fog turbulence and the projected surface textures motivated the children to reach for and touch the projection. Subsequently, animated objects on black background (rain, fireworks, spirals, kaleidoscope, moving bubbles, flying balloons and butterflies) that gave the impression to be in mid-air were also shown. Finally, we presented short video sequences of moving carrousels and animals as well as short clips from Ice Age and Finding Nemo. The contents were shown one by one and children were allowed to play as long as they were interested in particular content. Exploration took about 20 minutes.

Children's interaction with the FogScreen was video recorded using indirect observation with two cameras for coverage in breadth. In addition the experimenter observed the children and made hand-written notes to focus on special areas of interest. At the end of session, the children together with the experimenter filled a short questionnaire about their age, gender, PC gaming and TV watching habits.

Method of analysis. Qualitative analysis following the principles of grounded theory was applied on the observational data. Grounded theory can be applied for data-driven analysis and to the phenomenon which are not well-understood [28]. The data obtained from the observation through video tapes and hand-written notes were analyzed. In the open coding process the video recordings were reviewed by marking

Table 1. The number of concepts and total frequency of codes for each category

Category	Nr. of concepts	Nr. of codes
Pass projection plane	4	47
Manipulate fog surface	6	50
Inside-fog motion/gesture	10	105
Hand movements	11	91
Natural/intuitive gestures/motion	9	58
Sidestep projection	2	9
Catch/reach for objects	7	71
Oral interaction	3	9
Shadow games	1	14
Expand game environment	2	5

meaningful segments of the recordings and concepts were assigned to observed children's movements. Based on actual codes we further hierarchically categorized them to higher level concepts and finally to categories. All categories, number of concepts, and frequency codes are shown in Table 1. The whole data set was analyzed by one researcher. Concepts and coding were reviewed by one independent researcher to improve the reliability of analysis.

5 Results

Children were eager to play with the fog and the projected 2D and 3D objects both on their own and together as a pair. The children played next to each other in front of the screen or on opposing sides of the screen, whatever they preferred. We observed small games such as catching as many objects as possible, parcour or shadow games. The majority of the movements were similar across all participants. In the following the gathered children's movement styles during the "exploring" part of the study are presented. Various gestures and motion ranged from movements of the upper body (e.g. hand, head, and torso) to holistic (full body) movements such as jumping, running and crawling. Figure 3 shows examples of some of the actions.

Pass projection plane. Passing the plane of fog contained various movement styles. Children walked and ran through the plane of fog and also targeted through projected objects from the front side of the screen to the back side and the other way around, thereby the children flapped their arms and hands up and down or stretched them to the side or upwards. The body stood up straight or was ducked by doing these movements. Moreover, projected objects were crossed or avoided by walking through the screen. To reach the other side of the screen, children also crawled under the fog so that the body touched the floor. In addition, jumping in or through the plane of fog or targeted through a projected object was observed. Hereby, the arms were near to the body, to the fore or stretched to the top of the projection plane.

Manipulate fog surface. Children used various hand movements to change the surface of the fog. For example, hands were run over the fog; the fog was moved and pushed aside with the hands like moving a curtain away. Children compressed the fog with both hands or performed wheels in the fog. The fog was whirled to and fro, up and down with one hand, both hands and the whole arm. Furthermore, some children put their mouth near to the plane of fog and blew strongly, causing the fog to whirl.

Inside-fog motion and gesture. The children spent couple of minutes in the fog. Thereby, they walked inside the plane of fog from the left to the right side and backwards respectively, jumped, span with stretched arms or stood straight for a while in line with the projection plane or rotated 90 degrees. One girl started dancing in the fog. Other children lay down on the floor horizontal to the fog plane and viewed to the fog. Thereby, their legs and arms were stretched towards the fog. Children put also their hands inside the fog and moved them in various ways. The hands were folded, rubbed or built to a plane and beckoned. While standing on one side of the screen children put their head in or through the fog, through projected objects.

Movement of the hand. The children performed various movements with hands and fingers. They waved hand over the fog, put hand into fog and beckon to shadow

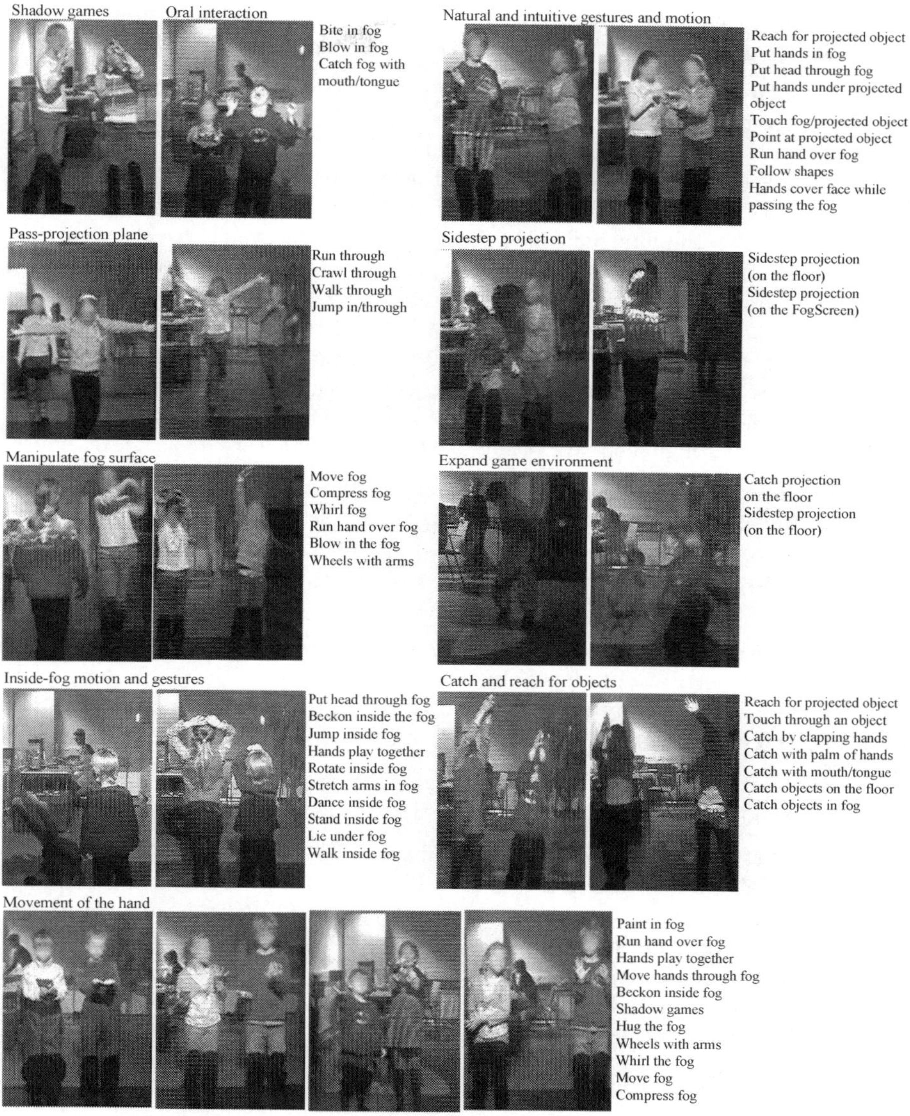

Fig. 3. Movements and gestures with walk-through display (the projected images are nearly invisible in order to highlight interaction in great detail)

games with their hands. The children used their hands and fingers like a pen and paint in the fog. They fold their hands, rubbed them and built a plane with them on the fog. The hands were moved through the fog up and down, whereas the movements were fast, slow or careful. The children opened their arms and hugged the fog either to touch or to catch it. The fog and projected objects were whirled to and fro, up and down with one hand, both hands or whole arm and fast movements. Children moved, pushed the fog aside with the hands and tried to compress the fog with hands.

Natural and intuitive gestures and motion. Several gestures and motion that the children performed while interacting with the walk-through display remind us of natural and intuitive movements that normally can be observed with real objects. Children ran their hands over the plane of fog, over projected objects and followed shapes and structures of projected objects with their fingers. When 2D or 3D objects were shown on the screen, the children pointed a finger at those objects or reached with their hands for them. While standing on one side of the screen hands and fingers were put in the fog or touched projected objects. Thereby the palms of hands were to the top, built a plane or the backs of hands were to the top. Furthermore, some children put their hands carefully in the fog under projected objects as if they wanted to collect them. While walking through the fog some children covered their face with their hands. We could observe that some children put their head in the fog, through projected objects or through the plane of fog like through a window.

Sidestep projection. Children sidestepped the projected content with the whole body while crawling or walking through the fog from one side to the other. In addition they tried to avoid touching selected projections on the floor. Also while standing in front of the fog, children sidestepped the objects with whole body movements that were shown on the screen.

Catch and reach for objects. Children tried to catch objects that were shown on the fog with palm of one or both hands by putting or moving the hands in the fog. To catch the objects, hands were clapped or moved through the fog whereas the palms of hands built a bowl. The tongue was also used to catch the fog or projected objects.

Mouth interaction. To catch the flowing fog or the projected objects, many children opened their mouth and stick the tongue out, blew strongly or bit in the fog.

Shadow games. While staying in front of the FogScreen, one hand or both hands were put through the fog, resulting as a dark shadow on the projection plane. Children varied the shape of the shadow through different positions of the hands and fingers. Shadow games reached from just putting the palm or back of a hand through the fog to imitate shapes of animals. Hereby, the arms were stretched through the fog and sometimes moved behind the fog. During this game children did not pay attention to the content that was projected on the screen.

Expanded game environment. In front of the FogScreen the projection eventually landed on the floor. Children used this projection to extend their gaming environment. While starting to run from the space behind the screen and jumping through the screen to the front side of the screen they sidestepped the projected content on the screen and on the floor with the whole body. Some children tried to catch the projection on the floor with their feet or hands. Use of physical space is summarized in Fig. 4.

5.1 Summary – Palette for Rich Embodied Interactions with Walk-through Displays

To summarize the results, we provide a palette for rich embodied interaction with a projected walk-through display. It can be used in interaction research and design

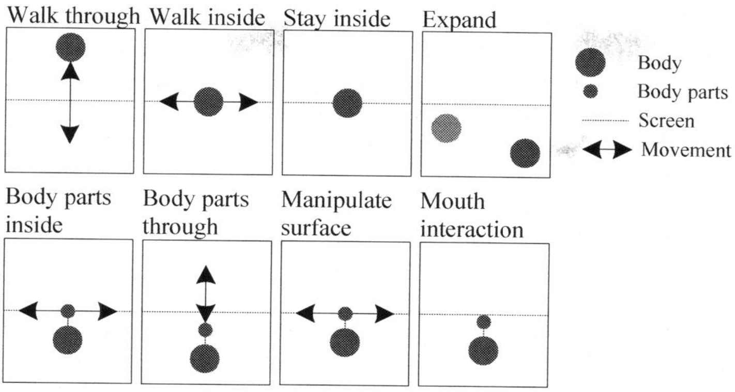

Fig. 4. Physical space children used while performing the movements and actions

(designers, developers and content producers), and applied for other type of walk-through displays, like water screens. Designing rich embodied interaction with walk-through displays offers multiple ways for the following:

1. **Passing the projection plane** vertically from crawling to stretched body from one side to other side.
2. **Manipulating surface** from running over, whirling, smoothing down, compressing, to destroying display medium.
3. **Staying inside** of fog from lying, standing, moving along to putting some parts of body outside of it.
4. **Using whole body** for touching, catching, following or manipulating objects.
5. **Using different parts of body** with the natural ways of acting for touching, catching, following or manipulating objects from mouth and tongue to head, from fingers to arm and from foot to leg. For mouth design affordances for blowing, catching with mouth and biting. For hands, design affordances also for two-handed actions like clapping and hugging.
6. **Expanding the interaction space** outside the screen space, e.g. to the floor.

6 Conclusions

This study examined children's intuitive embodied interaction with walk-through displays and space around it. We identified several interaction patterns for passing, staying and moving inside screen, using whole body and its parts for manipulating surface and content on the screen, and ways of expanding the actual interaction environment outside of the projected screen. We summarized the interaction patterns as a palette for rich embodied interaction with projected walk-through displays.

The results of our study highlighted that intuitive embodied interaction with walk-through displays is rich, vivid and multi-faceted. Even though the display category is named as a walk-through display, it offers more diverse affordances for moving through, manipulating and staying in than the name let us understand. Our results also underline that the affordances from such environment can be different from existing standing in-front-of displays. For designers it is important not to restrict their mind to the conventional displays when designing for this novel environment.

Our results show that input techniques for walk-through displays should allow natural and intuitive movements and actions for body and its parts. Besides using the upper body (e.g. hand, head, and torso), children enjoyed acting with full body movements such as jumping, running and crawling. Additionally, the large walk-through displays motivated to play and perform physical activities. Children included the projected image landing on ground through the screen in their play with the FogScreen. The projection on the floor, unintentionally made by the projecting system, is not necessarily a drawback, but can be a feature which can be taken advantage of. By tracking the floor also, the application area can be extended to the floor instead of being confined to the screen area, thus creating more engagement and physical challenge. Especially physically challenging games for children are imaginable applications, e.g. sports-like activities or action games [29, 30] or adventure games with possibilities of physical sensor-based interaction [31]. Children's movements could be used to remotely control the displayed game or avatars like it was done in Höysniemi's vision-based action games for children [27].

Our results of mouth-related interaction as well as staying under the flow of the display highlighted novel aspects for design. Mouth, especially biting as action, and tongue was used to catch the flowing fog and presented objects. These identified patterns can inspire design for taste-based interaction which as a research area is still rare in human-computer-interaction [32]. Walk-through displays with scented air or water flows could also provide a possible ground for prototyping. Staying or moving under the display stream triggered also to think the role of different modalities in interaction. To design for this interaction pattern, the use of different temperatures in streams could be an interesting issue to try out. Similarly, further work may also examine the possibilities to use scent in interaction design with these environments.

Our results are promising, underlining new interaction patterns for intuitive embodied interaction. However, the limitations of the current study and the need for further work are worth mentioning. Firstly, our study focused on the children's intuitive or natural way of starting interaction resulting that it mainly covered just part of the input-output chain. However, these interaction patterns can be used by designers for thinking the whole chain of interaction. Secondly, our work aimed at identifying the interaction patterns in relatively general level, but we did neither identify issues in multimodality or relation between content and interaction nor the co-play of children in detail. This was left for further work. Thirdly, participants of our study were children. Even though children are curious to try out different things and approach world through play using several senses, we assume that many ideas presented here can be utilized also in entertaining applications for older user groups. The further work needs to confirm this assumption.

To conclude, our study carried out with children has identified novel ways for embodied interaction with semi-visible walk-through displays. There has not been previous work aiming at understand embodied interaction in such context. Our results presented various vivid interaction patterns for acting in different positions in relation to screen (passing, staying and moving inside screen) and expanding the actual interaction environment, and finally using whole body and its parts in interaction. The results presented can be exploited for further design of interaction techniques for walk-through displays and for designing entertainment or physically demanding applications.

Acknowledgments. This work is in part supported by Academy of Finland under Grant 114006 and the Finnish Cultural Foundation. We thank all our participants.

References

1. Benford, S., Schnädelbach, H., Koleva, B., Anastasi, R., Greenhalgh, C., Rodden, T., Green, J., Ghali, A., Pridmore, T., Gaver, B., Boucher, A., Walker, B., Pennington, S., Schmidt, A., Gellersen, H., Steed, A.: Expected, sensed, and desired: A framework for designing sensing-based interaction. ACM Trans. Comput.-Hum. Interact. 12(1), 3–30 (2005)
2. Suchman, L.: Plans and Situated Actions: The Problem of Human-Machine Communication. Cambridge University Press, Cambridge (1987)
3. Loke, L., Larssen, A., Robertson, T.: Laba-notation for design of movement-based interaction. In: IE 2005 interactive entertainment, Sydney (2005)
4. Höysniemi, J., Hämäläinen, P.: Describing children's intuitive movements in a perceptive adventure game. In: Workshop on Multimodal Corpora., Lisbon, Portugal, pp. 21–24 (2004)
5. FogScreen Inc., `http://www.fogscreen.com`
6. Rakkolainen, I., Palovuori, K.: A Walk-thru Screen. In: Electronic Imaging 2002, Proc. of Conf. on Projection Displays VIII, pp. 17–22. IS&T/Spie (2002)
7. Jensen, J., Skov, M.: A review of research methods in children's technology design. In: The 2005 Conf. on Interaction Design and Children, pp. 80–87. ACM, New York (2005)
8. Druin, A.: The Design of Children's technology. Morgan Kaufmann Publishers, San Francisco (1999)
9. Kafai, Y.: Children as designers, testers, and evaluators of educational software. In: The design of children's technology, pp. 123–145. Morgan Kaufmann, San Francisco (1999)
10. Hourcade, J.: Design for Children. In: Handbook of Human Factors and Ergonomics, pp. 1446–1459. John Wiley, Hoboken (2006)
11. Markopoulos, P., Bekker, M.: Interaction design and children. Interacting with Computers 15(2), 141–149 (2003)
12. Nesset, V., Large, A.: Children in the information technology design process: A review of theories and their applications. Library & Information Science Research 26(2), 140–161 (2004)
13. Höysniemi, J.: Design and Evaluation of Physically Interactive Games. University of Tampere, Dissertation (2006)
14. Gibson, J.: The Ecological Approach to Visual Perception, Houghton Mifflin, Boston. Lawrence Erlbaum, Mahwah (1979)
15. Norman, D.: The Design of Everyday Things. Doubleday, New York (1988)
16. Merleau-Ponty, M.: Phenomenology of perception. English transl. Routledge, London (1962)
17. Dourish, P.: Where the action is: The foundations of embodied interaction. MIT Press, Cambridge (2001)
18. Loke, L., Larssen, A., Robertson, T., Edwards, J.: Understanding Movement for Interaction Design: Frameworks and Approaches. Pers. Ubiquit. Comput. 11, 691–701 (2007)

19. Robertson, T.: Cooperative work and lived cognition. A taxonomy of embodied actions. In: Proc. of E-CSCW 1997 (1997)
20. Svanaes, D.: Context-Aware Technology: A Phenomenological Perspective. J. Hum.-Comput. Interaction 16(2-4), 379 (2001)
21. Hornecker, E.: A design theme for tangible interaction: embodied facilitation. In: Proc. of 9th E-CSCW (2005)
22. Jacob, R.J., Girouard, A., Hirshfield, L.M., Horn, M.S., Shaer, O., Solovey, E.T., Zigelbaum, J.: Reality-based interaction: a framework for post-WIMP interfaces. In: Proceedins of CHI 2008, pp. 201–210. ACM, New York (2008)
23. Hummels, C., Overbeeke, K., Klooster, S.: Move to get moved: a search for methods, tools and knowledge to design for expressive and rich movement-based interaction. Pers. Ubiquit. Comput. 11, 677–690 (2007)
24. Benzie, P., Watson, J., Surman, J., Rakkolainen, I., Hopf, K., Urey, H., Sainov, V., von Kopylow, C.: 3DTV Displays: Techniques and Technologies. IEEE Trans. Circuits Syst. Video Technol., special issue on Multi-view Coding and 3DTV 17(11), 1647–1658 (2007)
25. Rakkolainen, I.: How Feasible Are Star Wars Mid-air Displays? In: 11th International Conf. on Information Visualization, pp. 935–942 (2007)
26. Jumisko-Pyykkö, S., Hellsten, S., Weitzel, M., Rakkolainen, I.: Children's Game Experiences in Different Settings. In: The 2nd IEEE 3DTV Conference. IEEE Press, Los Alamitos (2008)
27. Höysniemi, J., Hämäläinen, P., Turkki, L., Rouvi, T.: Children's intuitive gestures in vision-based action games. Commun. ACM 48(1), 44–50 (2005)
28. Strauss, A., Corbin, J.: Basics of Qualitative Research: Techniques and Procedures for Developing Grounded Theory. Sage Publications, Inc., Thousand Oaks (1998)
29. Bekker, T., Eggen, B.: Designing for children's physical play. In: CHI 2008 extended abstracts on Human Factors in Computing Systems, pp. 2871–2876. ACM, New York (2008)
30. Bekker, M., van der Hoven, E., Peters, P., klein Hemmink, B.: Stimulating Children's Physical Play through Interactive Games: Two Exploratory Case Studies. In: Interaction Design and Children proceedings, pp. 163–164. ACM Press, New York (2007)
31. Rogers, Y., Muller, H.: A framework for designing sensor-based interactions to promote exploration and reflection in play. Int. J. Hum.-Comput. Stud. 64(1), 1–14 (2006)
32. Kortum, P. (ed.): HCI Beyond the GUI. Design for Haptic, Speech, Olfactory, and Other Nontraditional Interfaces. Morgan Kaufmann, San Francisco (2008)

Causes of Simultaneous Keystrokes in Children and Adults

Akiyo Kano and Janet C. Read

ChiCI Research Group, University of Central Lancashire,
Preston, PR2 2XD, England
{Akano,jcread}@uclan.ac.uk

Abstract. Simultaneously pressing two keys on a keyboard (Zero Time keystrokes) is a unique typing occurrence. To understand the cause of Zero Time keystrokes, typing data were collected from young children and undergraduate computing students. The results show that, in both students and children, the most frequent cause of Zero Time keystrokes were errors in aiming for the intended key, resulting in the intended and an adjacent key being pressed together. The second most frequent errors were Transposition Errors, which were errors in the ordering of the intended two letters.

Keywords: Typing error analysis, Simultaneous keystrokes, Zero Time keystrokes, Adjacent letter Errors, Transposition Error.

1 Introduction

In text input evaluation experiments, key loggers with timestamps are often used to record which keys were pressed and when they were pressed [1]. The logger records the time of each key pressed and allows researchers to see how long a participant took to complete a typing task and the time taken between each keystroke. Timing of keystrokes has been widely used in text input analysis for various purposes.

Using timestamps, Grudin [2] analysed behavioural differences between experts and novices (8 novices and 6 experts) and found that potentially, more than half of Insertion Errors examined (e.g. 'fox' for 'foix') involved two keys struck by the same finger. This led him to conclude that the error was in the execution, because it is assumed to be the result of faulty implementation of the keystroke. Salthouse [3] found that 54% of his Intrusion Errors were adjacent letters to the intended key. He used timestamps to investigate pauses in typing around Intrusion Errors and found that when an adjacent key is struck with the intended key, the timing between the two keystrokes was much shorter (less than 0.1 second) than average. He thus concluded that adjacent insertions occurred by a finger being incorrectly positioned between two keys, resulting in the two keys being pressed together.

Kano & Read [1] defined the Zero Time keystroke as a keystroke where the time between it and the keystroke before it is recorded as 0.000 seconds by a key logger recording to the nearest 0.001 seconds. The NT/CT rules states that if the two keys had Zero Time interval, and they were Next-To or Close-To to each other, it can be

T. Gross et al. (Eds.): INTERACT 2009, Part I, LNCS 5726, pp. 137–140, 2009.

assumed that the two keys were pressed with one finger and at the same time. They used this rule to decide whether the letter insertion occurred simultaneously with intended letters, or on its own, and were able to resolve ambiguities between insertion errors.

So far, an analysis of what error types could result in Zero Time keystrokes is yet to be found in literature. This paper focuses on Zero Time keystrokes to understand the causes of this unique typing anomaly.

2 Experimental Design

Two large studies using phrase copy typing were conducted to gather Zero Time keystrokes from undergraduate students and young children. Phrase copying was preferred to free text creation as it enables researchers to know what the participant intended to type [4].

A four day study was carried out with undergraduate first year students from the computer science department at the authors' university. Out of the 92 participants, there were 80 male and 12 female students, the majority (86) of whom were between the ages of 18-30, with 6 students in their 30s and 40s. All experiments were carried out in quiet computing labs, equipped with the same model of keyboard (HP KB-0316). The investigator went into 7 practical classes of the same computing module and asked for volunteers to take part. There were less than 20 students per lab, and each had access to a PC. The procedure was explained to them fully before they started the task.

A second, five day study was also carried out in three schools in the local area, with children aged 6 to 10 years old. Of the 94 participants from 3 different schools, 58 were boys and 36 were girls. The children were from year 2 (6 to 7 year olds), year 3 (7 to 8 year olds) and year 5 (9 to 10 year olds) with the majority of the participants (79 children) from year 5. The children had half an hour to carry out the typing in their schools' ICT suites, which could hold 10 to 15 children. The procedure was explained to them fully beforehand and they worked on individual computers. As the child study was carried out in three schools, the equipment varied a little, with different makes and models of keyboards (Labtec Y-SAM64, Dell SK-8115 and HP KB-0136) However, they were all full sized, white letters on black keyboards with British keyboard layout.

In both studies a data-collecting tool GetItAll [1] was used to collect personal information about the participants, present the phrases and collect the typing data. Although adjustments were made between the students and the children in gathering personal information, the copy typing task itself was kept the same so the data remained comparable. Each participant ran an individual copy of GetItAll on his or her PC, and had 10 randomly selected phrases from the CPSet [5] to copy. The phrases were shown one at a time in font style Verdana at size point 14, with a space for the participant to copy the phrase underneath. The data collector logged what phrases were shown, each key that was pressed, recorded its timestamp and the time between the keystrokes.

The key logs were analysed for any keystrokes that were Zero Time. If the Zero Time key press did not cause an error, e.g. the two keys pressed simultaneously were the correct letters in the correct order, then it was classified as No Error.

For those Zero Time keystrokes that caused an error, these were divided according to what letters were involved. If the two letters pressed simultaneously were adjacent to each other, then they were categorised as NT-Mu or CT-Mu. *Next To Error Multiple Key Presses* (NT-Mu) refers to when a key directly next to the intended key is pressed along with the intended key (e.g. 'ourt' for 'out'). *Close To error Multiple key presses* (CT-Mu) refers to when one or more keys 'close to' but not next to the intended key are pressed together with the intended key (e.g. 'onl7y6' for 'only').

For the remaining Zero Time keystrokes, which caused an error but did not involve letters that were Next-To or Close-To each other, they were further divided into Transposition Errors (TE) or not. Transposition Errors (TE) refers to when consecutive letters are switched, such as 'tiem' for 'time'.

3 Experimental Results

23668 keystrokes were collected from the student study, of which 72 were Zero Time keystrokes. 22224 keystrokes were collected from the child study, of which 54 were Zero Time keystrokes. Figure 1 shows the number of Zero Time keystrokes found in each category for both students (shown in bold) and children (shown in italics) in percentages of the total Zero Time keystrokes found.

There were 6 Zero Time keystrokes in the student study and 12 in the child study that resulted in No Error. These No Errors occurred when the two letters pressed

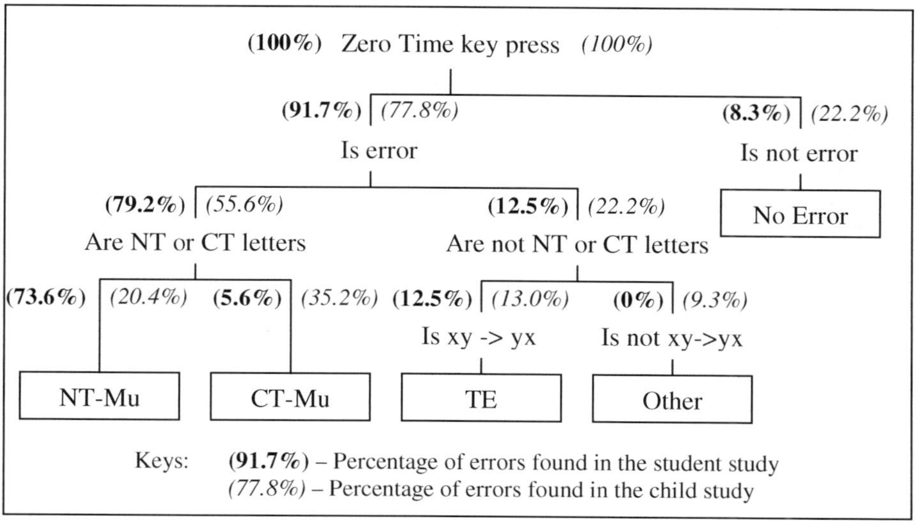

Fig. 1. Percentage of Zero Time Keystrokes Found in Each Category of Typing Errors for Students and Children

together were the correct letters, and despite the Zero Time, were recorded by the keyboard to have been pressed in the right order.

Interestingly, the students had made considerably more NT-Mu errors (73.6%) than CT-Mu errors (5.6%), while children made higher number of CT-Mu (35.2%) than NT-Mu (20.4%). One possible explanation is that some children resting their hands below the keyboard between keystrokes, and to reach any key, their hands must move vertically first, whereas adults tend to hover their hands over the keyboard and move more sideways. It is hard to conclude a cause for this observation, without a detailed study on the starting position of hands in between keystrokes in both children and adults.

Of all Zero Time keystrokes found, 91.7% in student study and 77.8% were either NT-Mu or CT-Mu. This suggests that the majority of Zero Time keystrokes are caused by pressing two adjacent keys when only one was intended. The next major group of errors were the Transposition Error at 12.5% for students and 13.0% children.

4 Conclusion

Zero Time keystrokes were collected from young children and undergraduate computing students and analysed. The results show that the in both children and students, the vast majority (average of 84%) of Zero Time keystrokes were due to misaim of the finger, resulting in the one finger pressing two keys together.

With respect to ratio of the different error types found, there were some interesting variations between the student and children study, such as the children's NT-Mu and CT-Mu ratio that were reversed in the student study. These variations require further investigation as to the causes.

References

1. Kano, A., Read, J.C.: Text Input Error Categorisation: Solving Character Level Insertion Ambiguities Using Zero Time Analysis. In: HCI 2009. ACM, Cambridge (2009)
2. Grudin, J.T.: Error Patterns in Novice and Skilled Transcription Typing. In: Cooper, W.E. (ed.) Cognitive Aspects of Skilled Typing, pp. 121–139. Springer, New York (1983)
3. Salthouse, T.A.: Perceptual, Cognitive, and Motoric Aspects of Transcription Typing. Psychological Bulletin 99(3), 303–319 (1986)
4. MacKenzie, I.S., Soukoreff, R.W.: Phrase Sets for Evaluating Text Entry Techniques. In: Extended Abstracts of the ACM Conference on Human Factors in Computing Systems - CHI 2003. ACM Press, New York (2003)
5. Kano, A., Read, J.C., Dix, A.: Children's Phrase Set for Text Input Method Evaluations. In: Proceedings of the Fourth Nordic Conference on Human-Computer Interaction - NordiCHI. ACM Press, Oslo (2006)

Evaluating a Tangible Game Video Console for Kids

Javier Marco, Eva Cerezo, and Sandra Baldassarri

Advanced Computer Graphics Group (GIGA)
Computer Science Department, Engineering Research Institute of Aragon (I3A)
University of Zaragoza, Spain
{javi.marco,ecerezo,sandra}@unizar.es

Abstract. Tangible and tabletop interaction can be suitable for kindergarten children as educational material, expressive tool, or merely for fun. But only playfully interactive experiences will happen if technologies include aspects that are relevant to the child's development, incorporating social experiences and easy control. Observation of children using these technologies is an important feedback to improve designs but an appropriated method has to be used in the evaluations. The Structured Expert Evaluation Method (SEEM) not only assesses technologies' usability but also fun aspects. This paper presents our research about the design and evaluation of a tabletop prototype oriented to children between 3 and 6 years, and the analysis of observations of children using our games.

Keywords: Tangible Interaction, Children Usability, Tabletop, User Center Design, SEEM, Games, Augmented reality.

1 Introduction

The educational and playful possibilities offered by tangible technologies are nowadays clear [8]. For the youngest, sympathetic interfaces such as "StoryMat" [4] and "Swamped!" [5] make use of toys in physical storytelling games. Other works, such as the "I/O Brush" [7] technologically enhance children toys for creativity and fun. Tabletop applications suitable for kindergarten children are less common, since interaction usually requires fine hand control that children less than 6 years old have not already achieved [6].

Our research intends to explore tabletop interaction possibilities with children between 3 and 6 years through the manipulation of physical toys avoiding multi-touch interaction problems. The design prototype described in this paper goes beyond common tabletop constraints with a low cost hardware, easily mountable and dismountable on kindergarten and schools rooms. During the design process periodical evaluation sessions were performed with small groups of children in order to observe and analyze the usability and fun of the tabletop prototype and games. The sessions were structured with the SEEM method [1] and after analysing their results general design recommendations can be obtained.

T. Gross et al. (Eds.): INTERACT 2009, Part I, LNCS 5726, pp. 141–144, 2009.

2 NIKVision Description

As our prototype would be mainly used by small children, it was needed to be robust, safe, and suitable in size: 70 cm x 70cm surface table and a height of 45 cm (see fig.1). Interaction is carried out manipulating toys over the table surface. Visual recognition software [3] translates the physical condition of the table into a 3D virtual environment implemented with [2] and shown on the TV. In addition, it is possible to project images on the tabletop in order to georeference guidance.

Fig. 1. Left: Tabletop prototype sketch: 1. Diffuse tabletop surface with toys. 2. USB webcam. 3. PC computer with Tabletop software. 4. Video projector for tabletop image output. 5. Mirror for projection under the table surface. 6. TV set with speakers for image and audio output. Center: Tabletop working. Right: Toys with fiducials used by recognition software.

3 Evaluating Tabletop Games with SEEM

While designing our tabletop and games one of our worries was to bring up, as soon as possible, usability problems. Therefore, we carried out periodical tests with children, that were structured with the help of SEEM questionnaires. SEEM questions focus on game goals, and how children perceive them in two aspects: usability and fun (see Table 1).

Table 1. SEEM questionnaire by categories

Category	Usability questions	Fun questions
GOAL	Can children perceive and understand the goal?	Do children think the goal is fun?
PLANNING ACTIONS	Children perceive and understand the actions they have to execute in order to reach the goal?	Do children think the actions they have to execute in order to reach the goal are fun?
PHYSICAL ACTIONS	Are children able to perform the physical actions easily?	
FEEDBACK	Can children perceive and understand the feedback (if any)?	Is the negative / positive feedback motivating?

Sessions were video recorded with two cameras: one took the TV image of the game evolution, and the other took the children actions with the toys over the tabletop. Additionally, the software recorded the toy's paths on the table during the game.

A competitive game, "Collecting strawberries", was used to detect interaction problems. The 3D scenery is a field with several plants (see fig. 2). Each of the two players chooses one farm animal to play with. Some plants hide strawberries and children compete for collecting them. To do this, children have to move the toy animals onto a plant location. Here, we will briefly explain the problems observed during the test sessions, grouped by the SEEM category, and the solutions that were carried out to solve them.

Fig. 2. The "Collecting strawberries" game

Physical actions: It is important that children can handily play on the tabletop. At the beginning, children showed difficulties in reaching the far side of the table. Several modifications of the tabletop design were carried out in order to improve this. On the other hand, children had doubts on how to move the animals to collect the strawberries. On the original game version, strawberries were collected by simply getting closer to the plants. Therefore, in the game final version the children shake the virtual plants with the toys in order to drop the fruits. This kind of movements, that have to be natural, improves the fun element of the game.

Planning actions: In the first tests, children did not have georeferenced help on the table surface to locate the plants, only the virtual scene on the TV. Children showed difficulties on moving the animals to the right place (see fig.3.left). So, tabletop projection on the game with georeferenced help was implemented to locate the plants. In the new tests, children were able to locate plants faster (see fig.3.right), and fun was improved.

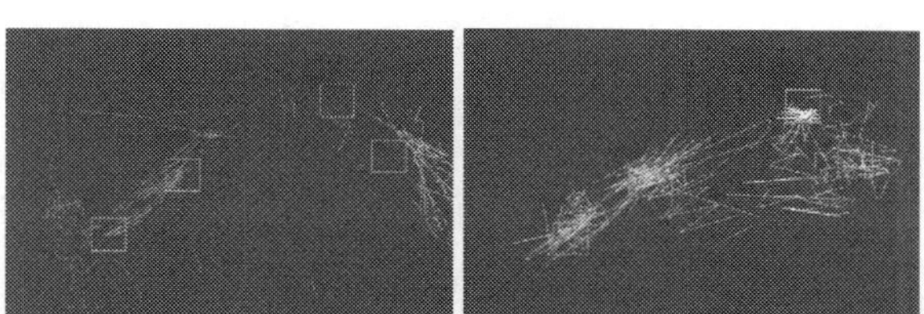

Fig. 3. Recorded graphs showing the paths followed by the toys in the strawberries game. Left: No georeferenced game. Right: Georeferenced game. The squares represent the plants location.

Feedback: With very young children, positive and negative feedback becomes one of the main design aspects to consider. In our tabletop, as children need to divide their visual attention between tabletop image feedback and TV 3D scenery, sound becomes the best way of giving feedback. Short and funny sounds indicates if a strawberry has been found (positive feedback), or the plant is empty (negative feedback).

4 Conclusions

The main conclusions of our test sessions are the following:

- Test sessions must be carried out as soon as possible during the development of the games to detect misconceptions on the designs.
- It is important that children understand clearly the goals of the game. However, giving to much details and instructions rests fun as they would only follow the steps. Letting them to explore and discover enhances fun and thus, learning.
- In this freely conditions, feedback (sound and georeference) is crucial, enabling the children to know in every moment if they are doing right or wrong.

Acknowledgements

This work has been partly financed by the Spanish "Dirección General de Investigación", contract number Nº TIN2007-63025 and by the Aragon Government through the Cooperation Projects between University and Secondary Education Departments (2008-2009) and the IAF Nº2008/0574 and CyT Nº2008/0486 agreements. We want to thank Janet Read, Emanuela Mazzone and Diana Xu of the ChiCI Group, at UCLAN University (UK) for their constant help and guidance.

References

1. Baauw, E., Bekker, M.M., Markopoulos, P.: Assessing the applicability of the structured expert evaluation method (SEEM) for a wider age group. In: Proceedings of the 2006 Conference on interaction Design and Children (2006)
2. Baldassarri, S., Cerezo, E., Serón, F.: Maxine: A platform for embodied animated agents. Computer & Graphics 32(4), 430–437 (2008)
3. Bencina, R., Kaltenbrunner, M.: The Design and Evolution of Fiducials for the reacTIVision System. In: Proceedings of the Third International Conference on Generative Systems in the Electronic Arts (2005)
4. Cassell, J., Ryokai, K.: Making Space for Voice: Technologies to Support Children's Fantasy and Storytelling. Personal Technologies 5(3), 203–224 (2001)
5. Johnson, M.P., Wilson, A., Blumberg, B., Kline, C., Bobick, A.: Sympathetic interfaces: using a plush toy to direct synthetic characters. In: Proceedings of the SIGCHI Conference on Human Factors in Computing Systems (1999)
6. Mansor, E.I., De Angeli, A., De Bruijn, O.: Little fingers on the tabletop: A usability evaluation in the kindergarten. In: Horizontal Interactive Human Computer Systems (2008)
7. Ryokai, K., Marti, S., Ishii, H.: I/O brush: beyond static collages. In: CHI 2007 Extended Abstracts on Human Factors in Computing Systems (2007)
8. Zuckerman, O., Arida, S., Resnick, M.: Extending tangible interfaces for education: Digital Montessori inspired manipulatives. In: Proc. of CHI 2005, pp. 859–868. ACM Press, New York (2005)

Exploring Geometric Shapes with Touch

Thomas Pietrzak[1], Andrew Crossan[2], Stephen A. Brewster[2], Benoît Martin[1], and Isabelle Pecci[1]

[1] Université Paul Verlaine, Metz, UFR MIM, île du Saulcy
57006 Metz, France
[2] University of Glasgow, Department of Computing Science
18 Lilybank Gardens, Glasgow, UK
{Thomas.pietrzak,benoit.martin,isabelle.pecci}@univ-metz.fr,
{ac,stephen}@dcs.gla.ac.uk

Abstract. We propose a new technique to help users to explore geometric shapes without vision. This technique is based on a guidance using directional cues with a pin array. This is an alternative to the usual technique that consists of raising the pins corresponding to dark pixels around the cursor. In this paper we compare the exploration of geometric shapes with our new technique in unimanual and bimanual conditions. The users made fewer errors in unimanual condition than in bimanual condition. However they did not explore the shapes more quickly and there was no difference in confidence in their answer.

Keywords: Tactile interaction, Tactons, geometry, non-visual interaction.

1 Introduction

Many subjects at school rely on structured data such as schematics. These are essentially visual representations, which are difficult to interpret for children with visual impairment. Children with some residual vision may be able to use magnified schematics, but those who are blind or have little residual vision have to use another sense. Raised paper is widely used for this purpose. Children can explore raised paper schematics by running their fingers over the paper to feel the raised sections of the image. However this technique provides a static representation of the schematic and cannot easily benefit from the advantages of a computer-based system. Large Braille displays could potentially provide similar functionality for a computer-based system, but are prohibitively expensive for most situations. The goal of our research is to identify techniques that can provide accessible representations of structured data such as shapes or schematics, and both take advantage of the benefits of the technology-based approaches without being too expensive. The VTPlayer mouse (figure 1) is an example of such a display, which has two 4x4 pin arrays on the top. It has previously been used to display tactile icons, which appeared to be a good way of conveying information [4]. We are interested in two aspects concerning the display of schematics with touch. The first one is the way the information is presented, and the second one is the way the schematic is explored. In this paper we propose a new presentation method, and will compare two exploration methods for it.

T. Gross et al. (Eds.): INTERACT 2009, Part I, LNCS 5726, pp. 145–148, 2009.

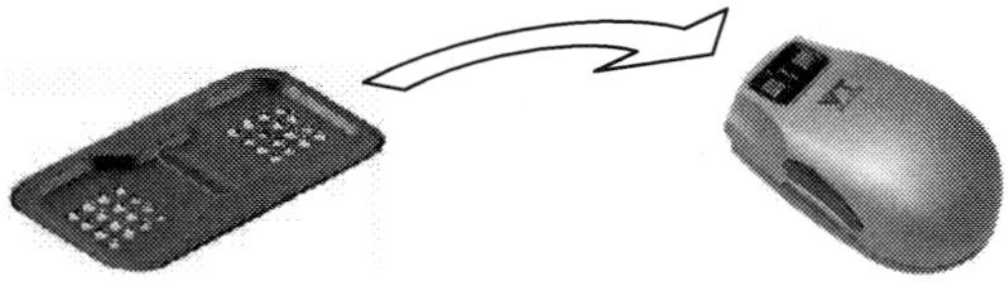

Fig. 1. VTPlayer mouse, with two 4×4 pins matrices on the top

2 Presentation and Exploration Methods

The common method to display schematics with pin arrays is a visual translation method that is a simple mapping of dark pixels into raised pins. It has been shown to be an inefficient method [2], unless it is enhanced by a guidance system [1,3].

The new method we propose consists of guiding users along the shape in order to help them explore it completely. It is based on a vectorial representation of the shape to explore. The shape is divided into line segments, which the user is guided around using directional Tactons. Tactons are structured tactile cues that convey information [4]. We use Tactons presented through one 4x4 pin array of a VTPlayer, which has been shown to be able to represent efficiently 8 directions (figure 2) [5]. A preliminary study of shape exploration with pin array Tactons in unimanual condition [6] shows that users were able to explore shapes with this technique. However they only provided directional information. The next step would be to enhance this system with more information. According to initial tests on Tactons, we can transmit successfully several pieces of information by varying several parameters on one Tacton [5]. For example, dynamic "blinking" Tactons are made with two individual animated frames. The Tacton is displayed by alternating a frame with a pattern made with raised pins and another frame with no raised pins with both frames being displayed the same duration.

Fig. 2. Patterns used to encode direction

Here we can display one piece of information through the pattern and another through the blink speed. We still use the pattern to encode the direction of the next vertex, and we use the blink speed to encode the distance to the next vertex. Initial studies varying blink speed showed that 3 blink speed values can be distinguished by participants with a high level of accuracy [5]. Here, we map increasing blink speed to decreasing distance to the start of the next line segment. Finally, we use a simple binary mapping on the second pin array of the VTPlayer which rests under the user's middle finger to encode whether the user's cursor is on the shape or outside the shape. The segments have a thickness, fixed after pilot studies. The opposite vertex is called the target. It is represented by a half-circle whose radius is equal to the segment's thickness (figure 3). The user is guided from one vertex to the next one in a loop, and can move around the shape as many times as is required. The Tacton is displayed under the index finger, and its characteristics depend on the user's position with respect to the current segment's position. If the user is on the segment, the Tacton's pattern aims at the target. Otherwise, it aims at the nearest point on the segment.

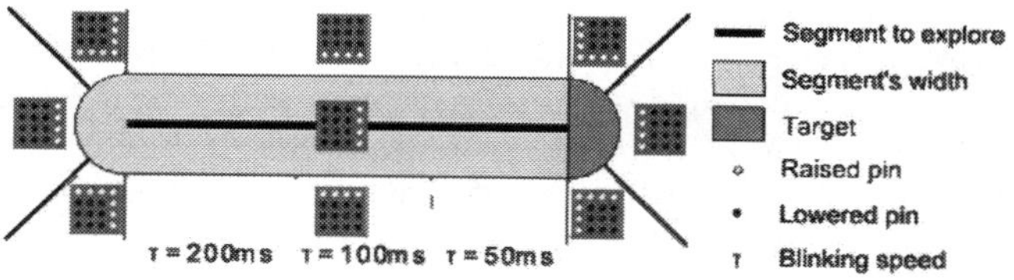

Fig. 3. Guidance on a segment

We explore two conditions: unimanual and bimanual. In the unimanual condition, users both navigates with the VT Player and feels the Tactons through their dominant hand, In the bimanual conditions, users navigate using a stylus in their dominant hand, while feeling the stimulus on their non-dominant hand resting on a static VT Player (as in [1,3]). The advantage of the first one is that the kinesthetic sensation provided by the movement of the pointing device comes from the same part of the body as the tactile stimulation. The advantage of the second method is that it could provide an alternative solution for blind users, for whom previous work has suggested that the use of the mouse can be problematic [2]. The use of an absolute referential provided by a tablet could resolve these problems.

3 Experiment

In this preliminary experiment we will search for the best exploration methods for our new presentation method. The task was to identify a series of shapes as quickly and accurately as possible. Eight sighted but blindfolded users took part of this experiment. They were 26 to 28 years old, and none of them suffers from a known tactile perception problem. All of them were regular computer users, but none had significant experience of using tablets. Half of the users explored the shapes with the VTPlayer, and the others with the tablet. All participants explored one training shape until they felt comfortable with the system, and 10 shapes (including a square, a triangle, a rectangle and simple polygons) they had 3 minutes to recognize. Response times as well as a confidence rate (on a scale of 1 to 7) were recorded for each shape. We make the hypothesis that users will make less errors, answer more quickly and will be more confident in their answers when exploring with the VTPlayer mouse rather than with the tablet.

We notice that the users who used the tablet made more errors (8/40) than the others who used the VTPlayer mouse to explore (4/40). Users who explored the shapes in unimanual condition gave a mean confidence of 5.85/7 (sd=1.28), compared to 5.6 (sd=1.62) for users who explored in bimanual condition. A Wilcoxon rank sum test does not show any significant difference (W=878, p=0.43). Concerning answer times, users who explored in the unimanual condition answered with a mean of 95.95s (sd=42.77s) compared to a mean of 93.45s (sd=52.54s) in the bimanual condition. Once again a Wilcoxon rank sum test doesn't show any difference (W=881.5, p=0.43).

According to these results we cannot accept our hypothesis about the error rate, the confidence rate and the exploration time. Indeed users made few errors with the VTPlayer and with the tablet. Moreover the exploration method did not have any impact on the answer times nor on the confidence of the users on their answers. However, some users reported it was disturbing to explore with one hand and feel the shape with the other one. These results are encouraging for the Tacton representation method as users were able to achieve a low error rate in both mouse and tablet exploration modes with very little training. We must be aware however that results might differ for visually impaired users.

4 Conclusion

We proposed a new presentation method for geometrical shapes. In this preliminary study we have tested the difference between two exploration methods with this new presentation method. Our results show that sighted users could use a Tacton representation to successfully explore shapes non visually. There were no significant differences in time or confidence when exploring shapes in unimanual condition or in bimanual conditions. The similar performance of these exploration methods encourages us to concentrate on exploration with a tablet as an input as this may be more suitable for visually impaired users due to the absolute positioning method used by this device. In future studies we will compare the efficiency of the new presentation method with the traditional tactile presentation method that consists of raising pins corresponding to dark pixels around the cursor, with sighted and visually impaired users.

References

1. Wall, S.A., Brewster, S.A.: Tac-tiles: multimodal pie charts for visually impaired users. In: Proceedings of NordiCHI 2006, Oslo, Norway, October 2006, pp. 9–18. ACM Press, New York (2006)
2. Jansson, G., Pedersen, P.: Obtaining geographical information from a virtual map with a haptic mouse. In: International Cartographic Conference, La Coruña, Spain (July 2005)
3. Ziat, M., Gapenne, O., Stewart, J., Lenay, C.: Haptic recognition of shapes at different scales: A comparison of two methods of interaction. Interacting with Computers 19(1), 121–132 (2007)
4. Brewster, S.A., Brown, L.M.: Non-visual information display using tactons. In: CHI 2004: Extended abstracts on Human factors in computing systems, Vienna, Austria, April 2004, pp. 787–788. ACM Press, Vienna (2004)
5. Pietrzak, T., Crossan, A., Brewster, S.A., Martin, B., Pecci, I.: Creating Usable Pin Array Tactons for Non-Visual Information. In: Transactions on Haptics, 12 pages (to appear)
6. Noble, N., Martin, B.: Shape discovering using tactile guidance. In: Proceeding of the 6th International Conference EuroHaptics 2006, Paris, France (July 2006)

Gender and Cultural Differences in Perceiving Game Characters of Digital Educational Games

Effie Lai-Chong Law[1], Tim Gamble[1], and Daniel Schwarz[2]

[1] Departmen of Computer Science, University of Leicester, LE1 7RH, UK
[2] TAKOMAT GmbH, Neptunplatz 6b, 50823 Köln, Germany
{elaw,gamble}@mcs.le.ac.uk, dan@takomat.com

Abstract. A survey on the initial design of a digital educational game was developed and administered to the target group in Germany and England. Some significant gender and cultural differences in game play habit, game type preferences and game character perceptions were observed.

1 Introduction

Developing digital educational games (DEGs) that can cost-effectively foster learning with fun and pleasure is a *vision* for researchers and practitioners in the field of HCI and technology-enhanced learning. DEGs offer exciting and dynamic environments which engage players in meaningful and motivating learning activities, inspiring them to explore a variety of topics and tasks. Nonetheless, previous research suggests that children in general tend to find educational games uninteresting, and that gender difference existed with boys holding a more negative attitude towards edutainment games than girls [1]. Interestingly, while the number of girls playing computer games has been increasing, they still tend to be perceived as masculine activity that more boys than girls prefer and spend time on. Such a disparity is attributable to the stereotypical presentation within games and to a general lack of female characters in games [2]. Even children in elementary schools perceive that software is gendered by design. The implication is more than just the attitude towards games; more serious impacts are girls' low confidence in working with computers and avoidance from technology-related fields, adversely affecting their employability. Specifically, Kinzie and Joseph [1] identified some interesting gender issues in game character preferences, for instance, the children in their study preferred characters to be of their same gender and ethnicity. Presumably, culture with its values, beliefs and norms plays an important role in shaping children's perceptions of game characters.

We are motivated to study gender and culture differences in the context of a DEG under development. The prototype topic is based on geography. An initial game design concept, prior to any implementation, was developed. Put briefly, the game story was about an alien kidnapping a boy and their flying round the world to collect relevant geographical information. A survey was designed with three objectives: (i) to evaluate the acceptance of the representative users of the game towards the game design; (ii) to evaluate if there are any gender and cultural differences in perceiving

T. Gross et al. (Eds.): INTERACT 2009, Part I, LNCS 5726, pp. 149–153, 2009.

the game characters; (iii) to elicit feedback on improving the game concept; a practical means to gather user requirements. It was administered in two countries.

2 Method and Procedure

Design of the Questionnaire. The questionnaire consists of two major parts. Part A contains five close-end questions on the respondent's gender, age, gameplay habit, gametype preference, and affinity for geography. Specifically, four gametypes – learning, action, strategic and sport – are provided as options to reduce the possible confusion in children; the other taxonomies are deemed rather complex (e.g. [3]). Part B addresses different aspects of the game. First a synopsis of the game story is presented. Then two close-end questions on the perceived interestingness of stories about aliens/UFO in general and of the game story in particular. An open-end question on describing improvement suggestions is presented. A set of four questions on understanding how respondents identify themselves with the story's main play characters are given. Another set of three questions on the preference of non-play character is posed. The last question is to assess the respondent's intention to play the game in the future.

Participants. Two samples from Germany and England were involved in the survey. They were school children aged between 11 and 14, the target group of the game. In Germany, the survey was conducted in the context of computer games fair. In England, the survey was administered in the classrooms of the five participating schools. Due to organizational constraints, the survey could only be conducted by the school teachers, who were asked to read aloud a script with similar wordings used in the German event. This step was taken to maximize the comparability of the data collected from the two settings.

Table 1. Demographic data of the survey respondents in the two countries

Country	Number/Age	Girls	Boys	Sub-total
German	Number	78	61	139
	Mean Age (SD)	12.6 (1.1)	12.8 (1.1)	12.7 (1.1)
British	Number	59	83	142
	Mean Age (SD)	12.5 (0.9)	12.7(0.9)	12.6 (0.9)
	Sub-total	137	144	281

3 Results, Discussions and Concluding Remarks

Results show that half of the British boys (52%) play games everyday and half of the German boys (51%) play games more than twice per week. Interestingly, 14% and 12% of the British and German girls report that they have never played games, whereas all of the British boys have played games. 45% of the German girls play games less than once per week whilst 44% of their British girls play more than twice per week. These figures seem to suggest that (i) Boys tend to play games more frequently than girls, irrespective of the country of residence; (ii) the British children tend to play games more frequently than their German counterparts. To investigate whether these observations are statistically significant, we performed the linear categorical regression analysis. The value of $R^2 = .25$ indicates that the two predictor variables *gender* and *country* can explain only 25% of the variations of the gameplay frequencies. Results show the significant effect of the predictor *gender* (beta = .49, $t = 9.32$, $p<.001$)) and the non-significant effect of the covariate *country* (beta = -.017, $t =-.136$, $p>0.05$). Boys tend to play games more frequently than girls, and the country of residence does not have a strong effect on the children's gameplay frequency.

Cramer's V was used to evaluate if *gender* was associated with *gametype preferences*. The most preferable gametype for both the British girls (51.7%) and boys (49.5%) are Action, followed by Strategic and Sport. The least preferable gametype is Learning with only 3.2% and 2.2% for the girls and boys, respectively. The value of the Pearson chi-square equals 0.581 (p =. 901), indicating that *gender* and *gametype preference* for the British sample are **not** significantly related. In contrast, the German sample demonstrates a slightly different pattern from their British counterparts. The most preferable gametype for the German girls is Strategic (40.7%), followed by Action and then Sport; the most preferable gametype for the German boys is Action (54.3%), followed by Strategic and then Sport. The least preferable gametype is Learning with 13.2% and 3.2% for the girls and boys, respectively. The value of the Pearson chi-square equals 13.972 ($p = .003$), indicating that *gender* and *gametype preference* for the German sample are significantly related.

With the aim of evaluating to what extent the respondents tended to associate the Boy's (the main play character) attributes with their own, they were asked to rate first the Boy and then themselves, using a 7-point scale, with respect to six pairs of contrasting adjectives adapted from the instrument Speech Evaluation Instrument [4] consisting of three subscales – superiority, attractiveness and dynamism, against which the entity of interest is evaluated:

- *Superiority*: Intelligent vs. Unintelligent; Uneducated vs. Educated;
- *Attractiveness*: Friendly vs. Unfriendly; Cold vs. Warm;
- *Dynamism*: Peaceable vs. Aggressive; Talkative vs. Shy

The exercises resulted in a set of so-called "Boy-based ratings" and another set of "Me-based ratings". We computed the correlations among them independently for the German and British samples. A number of statistically significant correlations are found. Nonetheless, based on our research interest, we explore to see whether there are gender differences in perceiving the relationships between the Boy's attributes, between the Me attributes, and between these two sets. Interestingly, results consistently show that the German female respondents tended to perceive the attribute interrelations, be they applied to the Boy or themselves, in a more complicated manner than did their male counterparts. Presumably, the German male respondents may associate their own attributes with the Boy's (same gender) more strongly than the female respondents (opposite gender) do; the empirical results indicate otherwise. In contrast, the British respondents' perceptions, irrespective of gender, are less complicated than those of their German counterparts. Interestingly, the British male respondents tend to perceive the associations in a more complex way than their female ones – a reversed trend demonstrated by the German sample. Fig. 1 illustrate the results how the respondents perceive the associations between the game main play character ("Boy") and themselves ("Me"). Contrasts are observed across gender and culture. We also aim to find out whether those who perceived a stronger "Boy-Me" association might have a higher tendency to play the game in the future (i.e. the last question of the survey) by summing the absolute differences in ratings over the six pairs of adjectives. While there is a moderately significant correlation for the British sample ($r = -.24$, $N = 199$, $p < .05$), it is not significant for the German sample.

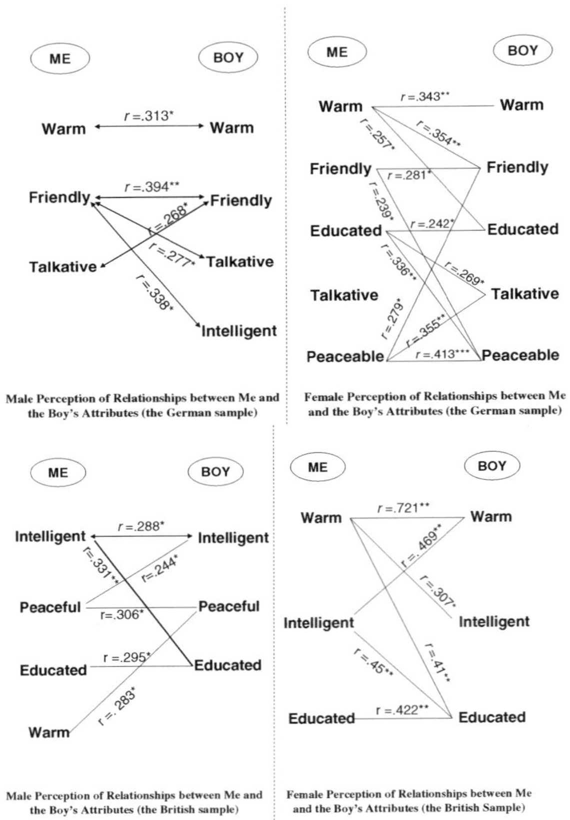

Fig. 1. The British (left) and German (right) children perceptions of the main game character. On both diagrams, boys are on the left and girls on the right.

Concluding Remarks: Previous research suggests that children, especially boys, tend to find learning games boring. It is corroborated by our findings that among the four gametypes learning game is least preferable and girls are more positive towards it than boys. Existing research also suggest that children tend to prefer game characters that are in some way "like me". Cultural preferences for normative personal qualities may influence children's preferences for the characters they play. While there are some very interesting gender and cultural differences in interpreting the main play character's qualities and in associating those qualities to theirs, such associations do not affect their intention to play the game. The setting where the survey was conducted could have impact on the children's perception and acceptance of the game: the relaxing atmosphere in the game fair with the exhibitors as opposed to the more structured classroom environment with the teacher. We explore psychosocial theories to explicate the phenomena observed and their implications on future work.

References

1. Kinzie, M.B., Joseph, D.R.D.: Gender differences in game activity preferences of middle school children. Educational Technology Research & Development 56, 643–663 (2008)
2. Gentry, M., Gable, R.K., Rizza, M.G.: Students' perceptions of classroom activities: Are there grade-level and gender differences? Journal of Educational Psychology 94(3), 539–544 (2002)
3. Apperley, T.H.: Genre and game studies: Toward a critical approach to video game geners. Simluation & Gaming 37(1), 6–23 (2006)
4. Zahn, C.J., Hopper, R.: Measuring language attitudes: The speech evaluation instrument. Journal of Language and Social Psychology 4, 113–122 (1985)

Staging Urban Interactions with Media Façades

Martin Brynskov, Peter Dalsgaard, Tobias Ebsen, Jonas Fritsch, Kim Halskov, and Rune Nielsen

Center for Digital Urban Living & Department of Information and Media Studies
Aarhus University, Helsingforsgade 14, DK-8200 Aarhus N, Denmark
{brynskov,dalsgaard,ebsen,fritsch,halskov,nrune}@imv.au.dk

Abstract. Using media façades as a subcategory of urban computing, this paper contributes to the understanding of spatial interaction, sense-making, and social mediation as part of identifying key characteristics of interaction with media façades. Our research addresses in particular the open-ended but framed nature of interaction, which in conjunction with varying interpretations enables individual sense-making. Moreover, we contribute to the understanding of flexible social interaction by addressing urban interaction in relation to distributed attention, shared focus, dialogue and collective action. Finally we address challenges for interaction designers encountered in a complex spatial setting calling for a need to take into account multiple viewing and action positions. Our research-through-design approach has included a real-life design intervention in terms of the design, implementation, and reflective evaluation of a 180 m^2 (1937 square feet) interactive media façade in operation 24/7 for more than 50 days.

Keywords: Media facades, urban screens, multi-user, public space.

1 Introduction

Research in human computer interaction has during the recent years progressed from predominantly focusing on the workplace setting [1], to other spheres of activity reflecting that only a fraction of the microprocessors produced today go into desktop computers whereas the majority become an integrated part of our physical environment [2]. Enabled in particular by ubiquitous computing technologies [3], HCI researchers have turned their attention to the expanding use of digital technologies as part of other aspects of human life including the home, entertainment, the school, museums etc. Urban life, with its social and cultural practices, differs from other aspects of human life, and has different kinds of spatial and material circumstances which pose new challenges for interaction designers. McCullough [4] has in his account of the intersection between architecture and interaction design drawn to attention the importance of addressing the situatedness of urban computing and has as part of that purpose compiled a tentative list of thirty situational types (e.g. watching, idling, cruising, attending, gazing) indicating the complexity and particularity of the urban setting. Greenfield & Shepard [5] have also explored the terrain of urban computing with a particular concern for the local and context sensitive aspects of what they call ambient informatics in contrast to urban computing.

T. Gross et al. (Eds.): INTERACT 2009, Part I, LNCS 5726, pp. 154–167, 2009.

In this paper, we focus on one particular kind of urban computing, media façades, which is the general term for incorporating displays as an integrated part of a building's façade [6]. Within the domain of media façades, a number of genres may be identified of which *advertising* together with *news* is by far the most common. The buildings surrounding Times Square in New York and Hachiko Square in Tokyo are some of the archetype examples of commercial advertising used as a media façade. *Architecture* has throughout history been constantly on the lookout for ways of renewing itself with new expressions and use of new materials. Use of mechanical devices are among the ways of dynamically altering the facade expression as seen on Institut du Monde Arabe in Paris [7], where iris-like shutters automatically open or close to adjust to the lighting conditions. *Art* is the genre where artists are the driving forces behind the creation of the media façade, like in the case of "Body Movies", an installation by artist Rafael Lozano-Hemmer [8]. *Games* are often used along with other genres such as art or community media. Blinkenlights [9] is a classical example of such an installation where artists placed lamps behind each window in a building in Berlin and used the pixel matrix as a screen for playing pong and displaying low resolution animations. *Community media* and *news* is the media façade version of community media and live events as explored as part of BBC Big Screens all over the UK leading up to the 2012 London Olympics. *Public Service* is driven by the need to provide information to citizens in urban areas, for instance in terms of bus schedules, weather forecasts or traffic info.

Using media façades as a subcategory of urban computing, our research focus revolves around coming to grip with sense-making and social mediation as part of identifying key characteristics of interaction with media façades in an urban setting. Our approach strongly relies on design research-through-design [10, 11] by conducting real-life design interventions where we have taken advantage of our engagement in specific design practices in order to explore aspects of urban computing. The specific case that provides the fuel for our discussion is *Aarhus by Light*.

Aarhus by Light was a two-month social experiment with an interactive media façade at the Concert Hall Aarhus in Denmark. In the façade lived small creatures of light. When you approached the concert hall, you entered their world, which was also a part of the city. They were social beings always (or mostly) happy to see you. On the central path leading visitors towards the concert hall were three illuminated zones, each covered with carpets in bright colors (pink, blue, and yellow). In these zones, camera tracking translated the visitors' presence and movements into digital silhouettes on the façade, and through the silhouettes, visitors could caress, push, lift and move the small creatures. The creatures would wave back, fight, sleep, climb, jump, kiss, and occasionally leave and come back, thereby creating a relation to the visitor which was not only physical and embodied but also emotional and narrative.

Our research proceeds along the path pursued by Peltonen and colleagues [12], who have drawn to attention the fact that interactions with large screens in urban settings is a new and fairly unexplored area of research. Their research is in many ways related to ours by focusing on the social organization of interaction but with notable differences in scale, location and duration: Peltonen et al. introduced a shop-window-sized display on a shopping street during an eight days period, whereas Aarhus by Light was an 180 m^2 (1937 square feet) interactive media façade in a central public park which ran 24/7 for more than 50 days. Another closely related study is that of Paay & Kjeldskov [13] who present a detailed examination of social interaction in urban space with a concern for the situated aspects of interaction which they use as the platform for the evaluation of a mobile prototyping system.

The structure of this paper unfolds as follows. First, we introduce our practice-based research methods followed by a presentation of our design intervention, Aarhus By Light. Following this, we account for our data collection consisting of observations, interviews and log data which provide the platform for our analysis of the emerging spatial interaction, sense-making and social mediation.

2 Method

Our research method has been a practice-based explorative approach known as research-through-design [10, 11] carried out as a reflective design practice, not only focusing on the design artifacts themselves but rather using design artifacts as a means to get insights into the kinds of interactions emerging in an urban context.

We have addressed our research question from a multidisciplinary perspective enabled by a series of collaborative workshops and other kinds of design activities, including field studies, experiments [14] and design workshops [15] that produced a series of materialized artifacts [16].

While navigating the research-through-design process, we selected various design methods and tools trying to overview, structure and foresee the consequences of the intervention. E.g., we conducted field studies to get insight into the complexity of the urban domain and existing use patterns, continuously refining design values for the design artifacts and using structured workshops to develop concepts for interventions; all in dialog with the materialization of sketches, 3D models, and prototypes.

We have studied and analyzed the interventions and their influence on the lived life in a specific urban context primarily using qualitative methods including observations and interviews [17]. In addition to video-logging of use during the entire period, the media façade software logged activation and other important events in terms of quantitative data which was used in the analysis of patterns of engagement and use.

In the subsequent analysis, we finally linked and summed up on all the material throughout our work to distil the findings in relation to our research question. Progressing from the research question toward the presented findings has not been an entirely linear process, neither a fully pre-designed research process in the narrow sense, but rather a continuously navigation through the design aspects uncovered. To a certain extent, the research activities have been iteratively interweaved through versions of design artifacts and workshops informing and shaping each other.

3 Design Intervention: Aarhus by Light

As mentioned briefly in the introduction, Aarhus by Light (AbL) was an interactive media façade, engaging local citizens in new kinds of public behavior in order to explore new possibilities of digital media in urban life. The large glass facade on the building was fitted with 180 square meters of semi-transparent LED screen that was distributed in a non-rectangular pattern behind the surface of the Concert Hall Aarhus towards to the adjacent public park. Visitors in the park were met with the spectacular view of animated creatures crawling around the structure of the glass facade along with a constantly moving outline of the skyline of Aarhus. When visitors walked through the park, they passed through three interaction zones marked with colored carpets. Once on the carpet, a sensor picked up the outlines of your body hereby creating a silhouette on the screen. This silhouette encouraged a curious and playful investigation of the expression among the users, while enabling them to interact with the creatures by pushing, lifting and dropping them.

The motivation behind AbL was driven by research interests and curiosity, but was also supported by the concert hall's interest in challenging its own rather conservative image. They did not, however, in any way want to influence the actual design.

As the platform for a systematic introduction to AbL, we apply a *design space explorer* [18] for media façades, a light-weight framework for addressing key aspects of media façades in an urban setting. The design space explorer consists of two parts: aspects listed in the top row and a number of design choices for each aspect in the columns below. As discussed in [18], the set of aspects may be adapted for each specific design case. In the case of AbL, the aspects are: Materials, Form, Location, Situation, Content, Interaction, and Values (Table 1).

Table 1. Design Space Explorer for Aarhus by Light

Materials	Form	Location	Situation	Content	Interaction	Values
Semi-transparent & low-res LED panels	Irregular	Façades	Visitors arriving	Creatures	Camera-tracking of movement and gestures	Playful
Carpets	Elongated	Public park	Passing by	Skyline		Integration
	Spatial	Lobby		Silhouette		Eye-catching
		Adjoining cultural institutions				Social

Material: AbL was based on 180 m^2 low-resolution LED panels. Each panel consisted of 25x50 pixels (4 cm dot pitch) that were assembled to a display counting 1250x150 pixels. The panels themselves were semi-transparent and were hardly visible from a distance. However, when the LEDs were lit, they constantly created awareness by emitting visuals in bright colors. In addition to the façade, a pink, a yellow, and a blue carpet were used in the park area to stage and call attention to the interaction zones.

Form: The rectangular LED panels in AbL matched the glass façade modules of the Concert Hall and were configured as a 50x6 meters irregular and elongated shape mainly placed alongside the main façade towards the park. The shape of the LED panels was deliberately designed to break away from a rectangular TV screen look, and a smaller part was wrapped around the facade corner in a spatial configuration.

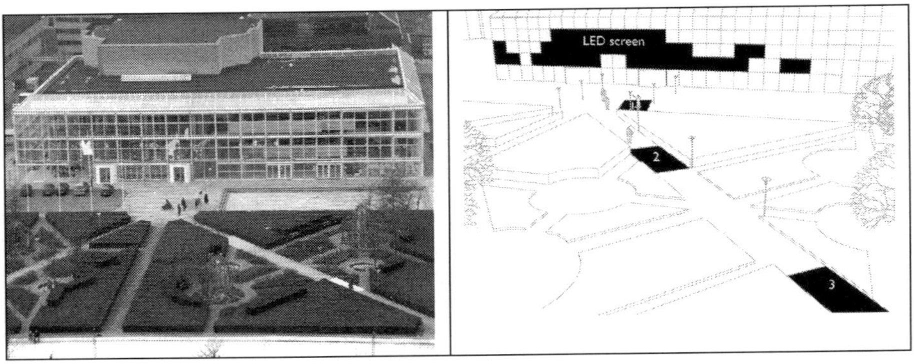

Fig. 1. Concert Hall Aarhus with the media facade installation and the three interaction zones

Location: Location is closely related to situation but refers to the spatial arrangement rather than the practices taking place within it. The LED panels that dominated the AbL installation were integrated in the 700 m2 glass façade of the Concert Hall, which is situated in the centre of Aarhus, the second largest city in Denmark. The public park in front of the Concert Hall is defined by a series of adjoining cultural buildings – among them an art museum, and the town hall. The panels were hung from the inside of the façade and the visual content was mainly visible from the park during daytime. But during night time, the light from the LED panels was mirrored in the glass façade visible from the foyer of the Concert Hall. The mirrored light hereby created a complex visual and spatial relation between the interplay of the panels and the glass façade together with the park and the foyer (Figs. 1 and 2).

Situation: Since AbL ran 24/7 for more than 50 days, it was designed to take multiple situations and use scenarios into account. Among them were people passing by versus dedicated visitors of the Concert Hall in relation to scheduled concerts and activities, all together with possible distances, perspectives, and visual obstacles in the public park and the lobby area.

Fig. 2. The installation in use. The LED panels themselves are almost invisible.

Content: There are three main content elements in AbL: (1) A one pixel wide lineart skyline of Aarhus landmarks which slowly emerge and disappear independently of other elements, (2) 30 luminous creatures which move around on the lattice of the facade; each creature is autonomous, though guided by specific rules which influence their behavior, and (3) silhouettes of users, which are displayed on specific parts of the facade in correlation with the users' position in the interaction zones in the park.

Interaction: In the case of AbL, users can interact by entering one of the three designated interaction zones in the park. When they do so, their silhouettes are tracked and displayed on set areas of the façade. The luminous creatures are drawn toward the silhouettes, and users can shove them around. The creatures will respond in a friendly manner – by waving at, dancing with, or crawling onto users – or hostile manner – by kicking the silhouettes. When no users are present, the creatures will go about their own routines, sleeping, kissing, fighting, crawling, and dancing. The intended duration of use ranges from <1-20 minutes. The interaction was implemented by having one big, digital canvas powered by a single PC running a custom-made C application. The canvas consisted of three layers. In the front most layer, the application processed input from the three cameras (one for each interaction zone) and produced silhouettes or rather blobs on three corresponding parts of the facade. The middle layer was populated with animated creatures, and the background layer held the changing skyline. The software ran unattended, calibrating the filter continuously for optimal silhouette-generation during shifting conditions.

Values: Values are the basic positive (or negative) considerations that have governed the design of the installation, reflecting the goals of the design and what is considered as important. AbL's final form and function is a crystallization of three main values which we have actively sought to incorporate into the installation: (1) *playfulness* as the key experiential quality which we sought to embed; this is reflected most evidently in the content-interaction fusion (use your bodily movement and gestures to play with the video game-like creatures, (2) *integration* into the existing setting, both relating to integration of the LEDs with the architecture of the Concert Hall, as well as the integration of the interaction into the existing practices and situations, and (3) an *eye-catching* expression making evident to passers-by that something new was afoot.

The design choices for each of the seven aspects have been interdependent. For instance, the choice of materials in terms of low resolution LED had implications for content in term of the line-art skyline and style of the luminous creatures. Likewise, the situational types of people passing by coincidentally or being on their way to an event at the Concert Hall Aarhus had implications for the interaction style.

4 Data Logs, Observations, and Interviews

In order to monitor the running status of the media façade and to capture events for later analysis, we set up a time-lapse camera as well as logged the activation of the interaction zone sensors. The time-lapse camera was placed in the bell tower of the nearby city hall. Throughout the duration of Aarhus by Light, it captured a still image every six minutes as an extra source of documentation (with no personal identification possible).

The media façade software produced a log recording every activation as well as other important aspects like for instance software updates. An activation is defined as a blob identified in a camera image by the software identified producing a corresponding silhouette on the facade. Figure 3 shows the number of activations of the three cameras summed up for each hour of the day during a 21 day period.

Activation of a camera generally indicates use, but there is no simple correlation between the number of activations and the number of persons triggering the activation. First of all, the number of activations each person generated varied greatly, since some only passed by whereas others spent considerable time interacting. Furthermore, there were some causes of activation that were not due to humans. In order to assess the proportion of human activation, we validated the log data by comparing selected time periods with two other sources: (1) the time lapse camera feed, and (2) a baseline of log data during and after the installation period where we knew positively no or very few people passed through the area. The validation revealed that when it was dark and wet, reflections from the media façade would feed back into the cameras and generate non-human activation. We also found that the yellow carpet was generating more non-human activations during dark and wet conditions even though it was farthest away from the facade.

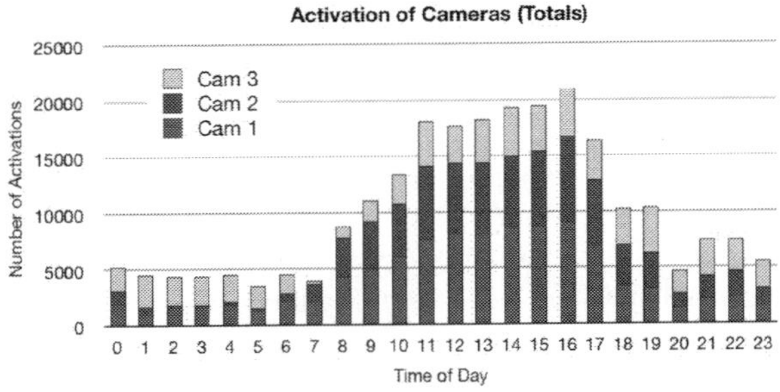

Fig. 3. Total number of activations of the three cameras over a period of 21 days

Having subtracted the estimated 'background', non-human activation, the overall use patterns that stand out from the validated log data is the following: People engage with installation primarily during daytime, beginning around 7 a.m. and increasing without dropping until 5 p.m. Then there is a significant dip until a second smaller peak between 9 and 11 p.m. The latter peak fits with the exit times from events in the concert hall, which are more concentrated than arrival times. During evenings without events in the concert hall, significantly less people are passing by the area.

Analyzing the data supports our thesis that the installation encouraged an interlude in the movements of the public. Especially the interaction zones generated a lot of movement, but also the area next to it seems to have been a popular spot for observing others interacting.

In addition to data logging, we carried out observations in two ways: First, we did a number of in-situ observations of the installation in use. These observations were often carried out in conjunction with qualitative interviews with users. The primary focus for these observations was on social interactions and exchanges as well as user experience, for instance if users displayed distaste or satisfaction with the installation. Second, we gathered video material of the installation in use for various purposes. The extensive amount of observations both from the interview sessions and video footage further highlights the rich variety of interaction forms and patterns spurred by the media façade. The observations show that all kinds of people interact with the façade, ranging from young boys and girls to older men and women. Observation video was shot quite openly with handheld cameras.

Last but not least, we carried out 25 structured interviews during the two months of operation. The interviews were carried out at different times of day and on different weekdays, and they were supplemented with observations before and after the interview itself in order to get a richer understanding of the interviewees' interaction with and experience of the installation.

Each interview consisted of 37 questions (not counting follow-up questions) and had a duration of 15-25 minutes. The questions were grouped into four categories: (1) occurrences prior to interaction, like the interviewees purpose for visiting the Concert Hall park, and whether they had heard of AbL before; (2) experiencing and interacting with AbL, for instance immediate impressions, accounts of what was represented on the façade and how to interact; (3) social aspects, including whether interviewees were interacting with other users, if these were strangers or familiar faces, and which types of social encounters this prompted; (4) identity and effect, like how AbL fit into the interviewees' general impression of the Concert Hall and the park, what kind of effect the installation had on the perception of a public space etc. Subsequently, the responses from the interviews were entered into spreadsheets for processing and comparison, and recurrent themes were condensed and analyzed.

5 Analysis and Discussion

Our analysis revolves around four themes: interaction patterns, space and interaction forms, sense-making and social mediation.

5.1 Interaction Patterns

During our analysis of the video and observation data, we have identified a number of recurrent interaction patterns. The most prominent patterns are shown in Table 2.

Table 2. Interaction patterns

Initiation	Interaction Style	Relation
Pass and notice	Basic exploration	Individual
Pass and interact	Visual engagement	Group
Walk-up-and-use	Embodied engagement	Family
Watch and join	Narrative and empathic engagement	Social
Watch and take over	Showing off	
Return	Hacking/unintended use	

Initiation refers to the ways in which people encountered and engaged with the installation. These span from passing and noticing the presence of Aarhus by Light through various modes of entering into interaction to returning after prior interactions.

Interaction style refers to the different modes in which people explored the installation when past the initiation phase. These encompass simple initial trials of the basic functionality and engagement in the visual expression, but also more immersive interaction through embodied interaction coupled with narrative and empathic interpretations; ultimately, a number of visitors appropriated the installation in unexpected ways, 'hacking' it and/or showing off in front of other users.

Relation denotes the social interaction patterns which we observed in the use of Aarhus by Light. Some users interacted with the installation individually, but, interestingly, the main part of users entered into social relations of some sort through interaction, either by being part of a previously formed group, possibly a family, or by entering into new social relations with strangers using the installation.

5.2 Space and Interaction Forms

An important part of understanding how people experienced AbL is to have a closer look at the interplay between the interactive media façade, the surrounding space, and the actual architecture. The integration of AbL into the Concert Hall's façade formed the basis of new use patterns in and around the Concert Hall. In this perspective, the interactive media façade, in combination with the Concert Hall and the park area, became a stage for new forms of interactions. Partly intentional interaction forms but also unforeseen and unintended use-patterns and consequences. In this section, we discuss the most important themes in relation to interactive and spatial aspects of AbL; among them, how people interacted with the media façade and how this affected the use of the park area and the very identity of the Concert Hall.

The park has gone from primarily being a place of transition with a few heated spots in connection to the entrance to a more diverse place where people still pass by, but with additional explicit hotspots in the interaction zones and the nearby areas. This indicates that the interactive zones have created new behaviors within the park, and based on the log data and the event program for the Concert Hall, we estimate that 500 persons have interacted with the installation during an average day. Furthermore, our observations as well as the log data specify that the interaction zone nearest to the concert hall has been the most used one, followed by the middle and furthest interaction zones in respective order. This is a strong indicator of the success of AbL as a new stage for urban interactions: The two latter zones were situated along what was prior to AbL the most used transitional path, whereas the interaction zone closest to the concert hall was previously almost not used at all. The new patterns thus reveal a strong interest for people to engage in interacting and experiencing the media façade.

Regarding the types of interactions, a clear pattern is that people attract more people: when there are already users interacting with the media façade, this attracts others to observe or engage in interaction. The people who interact thus become a part of the interactive installation attracting attention. Another characteristic is that a great number of people seem to return to the installation to try out new interaction forms, or to show other people how the façade works.

The interaction style patterns reveal a variety of use forms surrounding the media façade. A large group of the people who interact are primarily concerned with discovering the basic functionality, trying to identify the relation between the interaction zones and the media façade. Another dominant pattern of use is visual engagement in which the main focus of attention is the figures, the skyline, and the silhouettes on the façade, For many of the people interacting, the silhouettes they cast on the façade are more interesting than interacting with the figures; the silhouettes alone seem to make them want more, to explore how they can themselves be visualized on the screen. Another strong pattern of interaction is bodily engagement, interactions in which the focus is on the choreographic possibilities among the people who interact. People come together trying to coordinate movements on the carpet mimicking each others'silhouettes – or just to make choreographies on the carpet. It is clear that the carpet and the silhouettes legitimize physical activity in urban space that would otherwise have been seen as downright strange and inappropriate.

The above findings indicate that AbL did change the spatial relation in and around the Concert Hall, and by turning our attention towards how people came to think of the identity of the Concert Hall while the installation ran, it can help us get closer to how people experienced the space and the interaction forms. Especially the interviews indicate a new interpretation of the Concert Hall. With only a few exceptions, the interviewees found that the new interactive content augmented onto the façade, imparted a new view on the Concert Hall, ranging from more playful and inviting and in better contact with the younger visitors, to a more mystified impression balancing between the new and unknown and comparing it to other types of electronic media such as a 1980es computer game in an unexpected context.

These new interpretations of both the identity of the Concert Hall as well as the reading of the content of the media façade led to the next section where we will have a closer look at sense-making.

5.3 Making Sense of Large-Scale Urban Interactions

A particularly intriguing aspect of how people experienced AbL was their efforts to make sense of this strange intervention into the urban space. In their *Technology as Experience* [19], McCarthy & Wright propose that sense-making is at the core of how we experience technologies; following this line of thought, we will discuss the most salient sense-making themes relating to AbL in order to explore and elucidate users' experience and appropriation of large-scale urban installations.

Most notably, interviewees presented us with a number of varying interpretations of what the installation was about and how to interact with it. Every respondent was able to distinguish between the three different types of representations – silhouettes, luminous creatures, and skyline. Judging by the responses, the luminous creatures were of most interest to them, followed by the silhouettes and the skyline. The most general impression of the installation was that it was, or was similar to, a video game; this was attributed primarily to the general low-resolution visuals of the façade as well as the representation and behavior of the luminous creatures. This interpretation is evident in statements such as 'It is like Pacman meets the concert hall' and 'It reminds me of Commodore 64' (a popular home computer in the 1980s). This finding highlights two interesting aspects of interactive media façades. First, that the visuals of the installation, rather than the interaction form, architectural concerns, or social relations, were the most immediate point of reference in making sense of the installation. A particularly strong indicator of this tendency was that, when asked how the façade worked, interviewees answered along the lines of what it connoted – i.e. a computer game – rather than describing the technical and factual function of it. Secondly, that spectators clearly drew upon their repertoire of existing experiences with electronic media in order to understand what they were observing, and the computer game genre was deemed to have the closest resemblance to the installation. As Manovich [20] has examined, the development of new types of media lends extensively from genres and conventions from preceding media. This goes not only for media authors, developers, and designers, but also for the audience spectators and users. With regards to making sense of the interactive elements of the façade, people had fewer references to preceding media to draw upon. Since there were no explicit instructions of use, users had to adopt an experimental approach to understanding the installation, save for the instances when they could 'lurk' and observe already active users. As a result, many interviewees adopted an approach consisting of simultaneous trial-and-sense-making. The mirroring of users' silhouettes in three different colors corresponding to the three physical interaction zones functioned as a very direct introduction to the mode of interaction, and both interviews, in situ observations and video observations show strong evidence that users' understood this mapping easily.

Turning now to the relations between the three elements represented on the media façade, we observed a striking pattern of sense-making in interviewees' responses, namely that many of them presented us with accounts that went beyond what the installation was actually programmed to do. Most interviewees constructed narratives about what the creatures were doing, how they were interacting with each other, with users' silhouettes, and with the skyline. Some of these were in line with the programmed responses of the installation, e.g. how creatures would greet new users. Interestingly, however, many of these narratives went beyond what the installation was actually programmed to do. For instance, several interviewees presented us with narratives of social interactions among the creatures, or creature responses to visitors, which went beyond the programmed responses of the creatures. This finding is substantiated by studies in cognitive development which propose that we have a tendency to remember experiences in the form of narratives, and that we may in fact re-order components or fill out blanks in order to make the narrative conform to expectations (e.g. Nezworski et al. [21]). In the case of AbL, this tendency was in fact also evident not only in interviewees' subsequent accounts of what they had experienced, but also in the ongoing sense-making among interacting users. For instance, there was no pre-programmed interaction between the creatures and the skyline, yet several users told us how one had influenced the other. In one instance, a girl told that she was trying to crawl up on a tower on the LED to rescue the figures. In another instance, several children told us, while playing with the installation, that the creatures were building the skyline, and that they could tear it down with their silhouettes. This ascription of intentions and motivations mirrors Heider & Simmel's [22] seminal study of the attribution of causality, in which they demonstrated how observers of an animated clip of simple geometric shapes attributed behavior and intention to the shapes. For the children, this attribution of causality was reinforced by the ongoing sharing of their interpretations by which consensual narratives were created and maintained.

It should be noted that we do not view these potentially inaccurate accounts as problematic. Rather, we see this tendency to construct narratives beyond the designed ones as important input into a broader discussion of sense-making in complex urban environments. In such settings, heterogeneous factors, like architectural, habitual, technological, and social aspects, will almost always co-determine the experience of technological artifacts and installations. Thus it may in many situations be very hard, or even impossible, for designers to take into account all of these factors, let alone create an installation that commands the focused attention of users.

We propose that the balance between framing and open-endedness in AbL played an important part in its success. It presented users with recognizable representations in the shape of computer game-like creatures, the city skyline, and their own silhouettes, yet provided room for appropriation with regards to the emerging interactions. This proposition is in line with Thackara's [23] discussion of designers' proposing vs. imposing experiences and Greenfield's [24] similar examination of highly designed experiences.

5.4 Social Mediation

One aspiration of staging engagement in public space is often to provide a medium or a platform that invites people to connect socially. As we have seen, there are not many cases of interactive media façades facilitating social interaction, and there is no dominant, coherent framework to address the situation facing designers of interactive media façades. One reason is that the technology is still waiting to be deployed, but another and probably more important reason for the lack of interactive media façades is that they are not very easy to embed into the socio-cultural fabric of urban space. It is simply not obvious what kinds of social mediation are desirable and acceptable.

We may address this issue in the case of AbL by extracting observations and patterns in the interviews, observations, and log data, as we have seen above. As a platform for an attempt to further generalize and characterize these patterns and observations, we build on Ludvigsen's [25] framework of social use in public spaces, especially the notion of "situational interaction flexibility[1]", SIF. This framework is simpler than e.g. MIRANDA and SOPHIA [26], which are based on McCullough [4], but still captures salient features in a way that are easy to communicate and discuss.

SIF is based on Goffman's [27] concepts of behavior in public space: occasion, situation, and encounters. SIF then proposes another set of related concepts – levels of social interaction (Table 3) – that help answer the following types of questions when evaluating a design for social interaction: What is the level of social interaction? What do we want it to be? How is this specific level of social interaction supported? May the user(s) take the level of social interaction to another level?

Looking at quantitative and qualitative data through the optics of these levels, we may argue that the AbL is demonstrating a high degree of situational interaction flexibility. This means that not only is the installation mediating social interactions, it is facilitating a very wide range of social interactions and transition between these levels of interaction.

[1] We have rephrased the original term 'mobility' to 'flexibility' in order to reduce semantic confusion.

Table 3. Levels of social interaction according to Situational Interaction Flexibility

Level	Scope	Example
Distributed attention	Each person is in a separate 'bubble' of attention	People passing by
Shared focus	People observing the same thing, not unlike broadcast media	Watching, exploring together
Dialogue	"shared activity in which [people] are investing themselves and their opinions"	Showing off, intensive explorations
Collective action	People engage and work towards a shared goal	Choreography, mass explorations, hacking/unintended use

If we connect this claim with our initial question of how interactive media façades may embrace the socio-cultural practices of the occasion, to use Goffman's term, we get at least some answers in the form of qualified examples.

The relation patterns highlight the fact that most of the interactions are part of larger social relations. Even though there are examples of individuals interacting with the media façade alone (but still in public space), most of the interactions take place in different social groupings – families, groups hanging, or other social gatherings. The sociality of the interaction both relates to the carpet, where two or more people come together to interact, and when people are affecting other people by looking at or commenting their interactions.

6 Conclusions and Future Work

Using Aarhus by Light as the principal case, we have zeroed in on some of the challenges when designing for large media façades in urban space. We have in particular addressed the open-ended but framed nature of interaction, which in conjunction with varying interpretations enables individual sense-making. Moreover, we have contributed to the understanding of situational interaction flexibility by addressing urban interaction in relation to distributed attention, shared focus, dialogue, and collective action. In addition, we have elaborated on the challenges for interaction designers encountered in a complex spatial setting calling for a need to take into account multiple viewing and action positions. Space and time have only allowed us to build our argument around a single, though complex, case at the expense of having multiple cases to compare and generalize from. The complexity of the urban interaction surely calls for additional research into the distinctive spatial, material, and situational circumstances of urban interaction with media façades.

Acknowledgments. This research was funded by the Danish Council for Strategic Research grant number 2128-07-0011 (Digital Urban Living).

References

1. Greenbaum, J., Kyng, M. (eds.): Design at Work. LEA, Hillsdale (1991)
2. Thackara, J.: The Design Challenge of Pervasive Computing. Interactions 8, 46–52 (2001)
3. Weiser, M.: The Computer for the 21st century. Scientific American, 94–104 (September 1991)
4. McCullough, M.: Digital Ground. MIT Press, Cambridge (2004)
5. Greenfield, A., Shepard, M.: Urban Computing and Its Discontents. The Architectural League of New York, New York (2007)
6. ag4: Media Facades. daab, Cologne (2006)
7. Institut du Monde Arabe, `http://www.galinsky.com/buildings/ima`
8. Bullivant, L.: Responsive Environments: Architecture, art and design. V&A Publications, London (2006)
9. Blinkenlights, `http://www.blinkenlights.de`
10. Frayling, C.: Research in Art and Design. Royal College of Art Research Papers 1, 1–5 (1993)
11. Zimmerman, J., Forlizzi, J., Evenson, S.: Research through design as a method for interaction design research in HCI. In: CHI 2007, pp. 493–502. ACM Press, New York (2007)
12. Peltonen, P., Kurvinen, E., Salovaara, A., Jacucci, G., Ilmonen, T., Evans, J., Oulasvirta, A., Saarikko, P.: It's Mine, Don't Touch!: Interactions at a Large Multi-Touch Display in a City Centre. In: CHI 2008, pp. 1285–1294. ACM Press, New York (2008)
13. Paay, J., Kjeldskov, J.: Understanding Situated Social Interactions: A Case Study of Public Places in the City. Comput. Supported Coop. Work 17, 275–290 (2008)
14. Schön, D.: The Reflective Practitioner. Basic Books, New York (1983)
15. Halskov, K., Dalsgård, P.: Inspiration Card Workshops. In: DIS 2006, pp. 2–11. ACM Press, New York (2006)
16. Halskov, K., Nielsen, R.: Virtual Video Prototyping. Human-Computer Interaction 21, 199–233 (2006)
17. Patton, Q.M.: Qualitative Evaluation and Research Methods. Sage, Newbury Park (1990)
18. Dalsgård, P., Nielsen, R., Halskov, K.: A Design Space Explorer for Media Facades (accepted). In: OZCHI 2008 (2008)
19. McCarthy, J., Wright, P.: Technology as Experience. MIT Press, Cambridge (2004)
20. Manovich, L.: The Language of New Media. MIT Press, Cambridge (2002)
21. Nezworski, T., Stein, N.L., Trabasso, T.: Story Structure Versus Content in Childrens Recall. Journal of Verbal Learning and Verbal Behavior 21, 196–206 (1982)
22. Heider, F., Simmel, M.: An experimental study of apparent behavior. American Journal of Psychology 57, 243–259 (1944)
23. Thackara, J.: No more (design) heroes [interviewed by Pearlman, C.]. Wired (excerpt) (2000)
24. Greenfield, A.: On the ground running: Lessons from experience design. Adobe Think Tank (2008), `http://www.adobe.com/designcenter/thinktank/greenfield.html`
25. Ludvigsen, M.: Designing for Social Use in Public Places. In: DPPI 2005, pp. 389–408 (2005)
26. Paay, J.: Where We Met Last Time: A Study of Sociality in the City. In: OZCHI 2005 (2005)
27. Goffman, E.: Behavior in Public Spaces. Macmillan, Indianapolis (1963)

Location-Based Services and Privacy in Airports

John Paulin Hansen[1], Alexandre Alapetite[2], Henning Boje Andersen[2], Lone Malmborg[1], and Jacob Thommesen[2]

[1] IT University of Copenhagen
Rued Langgaards Vej 7
DK-2300 Copenhagen S, Denmark
{paulin,malmborg}@itu.dk
[2] Technical University of Denmark
Department of Management Engineering
Produktionstorvet 426
DK-2800 Kongens, Lyngby, Denmark
{alal,boje,jact}@man.dtu.dk

Abstract. This paper reports on a study of privacy concerns related to location-based services in an airport, where users who volunteer for the service will be tracked for a limited period and within a limited area. Reactions elicited from travellers at a field trial showed 60% feeling to some or to a large degree more secure with the system in operation. To provide a background for the privacy study we also describe services provided by the tracking facility and the infrastructure behind it as well as the design and evaluation activities we used. Based on project results including a large number of comments from passengers, we discuss factors influencing passengers' acceptance and appreciation of location-based services in airports.

Keywords: Location-based services, Mobile services, Tracking, Technology acceptance, Privacy, Transport.

1 Introduction

More and more mobile phone models appear with facilities that allow people to locate themselves, which in turn allow service providers to track the position of the phones. Similarly, future travel documents and photos may contain electronic tags that will make them traceable throughout the journey.

Privacy concerns for ubiquitous computing and location-based services have been examined in different contexts in earlier research (e.g. [1]). Design experiences reported in this paper come from the SPOPOS project [2], which has developed a technical infrastructure to track people and objects indoors and to provide location-based services to passengers and airport operators. Tracking data and user reactions have been collected during 2007-8 to direct the final design of services offered. The airport is using the location technology to improve its ability to predict the build-up of queues and – in the long run – to ensure that passengers get to their plane on time.

T. Gross et al. (Eds.): INTERACT 2009, Part I, LNCS 5726, pp. 168–181, 2009.

When departing from an airport, passengers want to have information about: 1) boarding time and gate number, including all relevant changes; 2) location of their gate and how to find it – in larger airports, way-finding may be a serious problem; and 3) the time it will take to go to their gate – depending on actual distance, internal airport transport service and queues on the way. To what extent can location-based services provide this information? Are passengers willing to give up some amount of privacy and be tracked in order to obtain the information when they are just passing through a transitional public place?

2 The Airport Case

An airport can be a challenging environment for both passengers and operators. Passengers may have positive as well as negative expectations, they may have some anxiety about delays, sudden change of gates and some may suffer from fear of flying. Frequent travellers need efficiency, and occasional passengers need security, the right information, and in general, peace of mind. But it is not easy to satisfy these needs. An airport is a very complex logistic system, and operators must deal with queues and transfer of baggage, they must guide passengers through a number of control points, provide services for different kinds of passengers during their stay, comply with strict security procedures and – most basically – they are running a business to generate a revenue for the airport owners.

2.1 Infrastructure

The SPOPOS system is an indoor, location-based platform developed to deliver transient services. The platform may be used at several public locations, for instance, railways, shopping malls, stadiums or museums. The service design was guided by our airport case while the technical infrastructure can be applied broadly.

Most people bring their mobile phones along when travelling – 93% according to a recent survey [3]. In a few years, electronic boarding passes may emigrate from kiosks and Web check-in into mobile phones (various approaches are being investigated by IATA – the International Air Transport Association [4]). The increased use of mobile phones for handling travel information prompted the project team to develop an integrated location-based service system for passengers, airlines and airport operators. The system deploys Bluetooth and RFID location detection to track passengers. Each detection method is able to show in which "zones" a passenger is located within a rough circle with a radius of roughly 30 meters (see Figure 1). The actual sizes of the zones vary widely because of signal reflections etc. However, due to privacy concerns we do not in fact seek to obtain any higher accuracy, although it would be possible to achieve this using, e.g., triangulation techniques.

Since 2001, Copenhagen airport has offered free SMS departure alerts to its Danish and Swedish customers. This service was used more than 1 million times in 2007. SPOPOS improves on existing communication and information by offering location-specific messages and additional information. The timing of SMS messages can now be relative to passenger location, and if the passenger is moving through zones towards the gate we can avoid sending a notification. If the passenger is not moving towards the gate (or moving in the wrong direction) the SMS system may be set to respond with increasing levels of urgency.

Since Internet access from mobile phones is now becoming more and more common (e.g., via 3G, Wi-Fi), the SPOPOS project proposes a simple Web interface combined with Bluetooth or RFID localisation. The main advantages of this solution is that it does not require the user to install any additional program, it works on all types of Web-enabled devices, and users are more skilled at and comfortable with using their Web browser than installing new programs on their mobile phone. The small drawback is the very modest cost of data traffic – in case the location does not offer free Wi-Fi.

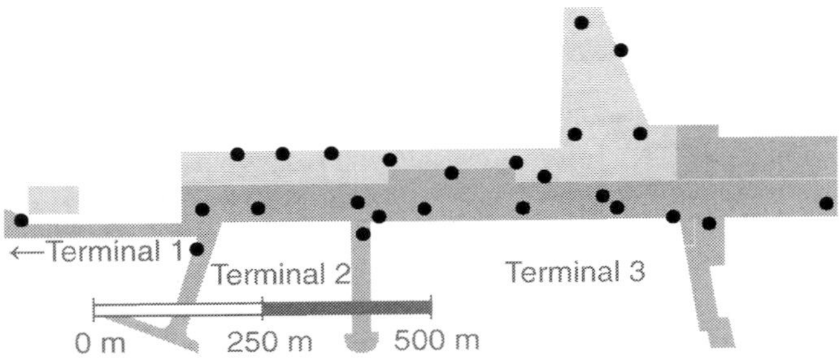

Fig. 1. Placement of Bluetooth and RFID antennas at Copenhagen Airport. Each zone is covered by both systems.

With each of the technologies, Bluetooth and RFID, a prior registration is needed to match a given passenger's mobile phone number with a tracking ID. The MAC address of the phone may be entered either from the passenger's home via the airport website or – in the near future – from a kiosk in the airport. Passengers with no registration may still provide some information to the airport operators, because if they have a Bluetooth equipped mobile phone that is turned on and which is not made invisible, they can then be tracked in an anonymous mode. This can accurately measure the time that passengers spend in particular areas and queues. However, since it is only a fraction of the passengers who keep their Bluetooth visible, this passive tracking is useful only for identifying common patterns in the flow of passengers.

In our field trials (see section 4) we used active RFID tags with batteries that emit a signal every 3 seconds when moved and every 20 minutes when not moved (they contain an accelerometer). RFID tags are an interesting technology for indoor tracking since they have a long battery-life (~4 years), a reasonable cost, and thus may be permanently mounted on e.g. baggage trolleys.

Initial measurements indicated an almost 100% success rate in detecting target passengers when they passed security, pier and gate, with both Bluetooth and RFID. Statistics for RFID and Bluetooth tracking looked similar, in particular with regard to the time difference between two detections of the same passenger. Most passengers inside a tracking zone are detected with intervals of less than 5 seconds and less than 5% remain unseen for more than a minute.

2.2 Location-Based Services for Operators

Increased security levels in airports increase the time passengers spend waiting for inspection and passport control. A queue can build up suddenly, and some passengers may become critically late while waiting in line. The SPOPOS tracking facilities make it possible for airport management to see passenger flow and congestions in real-time, and therefore, e.g., if and when a queue is accumulating at a particular control point. In turn, this overview provides airport staff with an option to increase the manning on the control point immediately (Figure 2).

Fig. 2. Tracking of Bluetooth mobile phones provides real-time information to passengers and security managers on waiting time. The information is also published at the airport's webpage.

Getting passengers on-board a flight is achieved by pushing information about departure time, gate number and boarding status to information displays. The push-approach has been optimized for decades but still it has some serious drawbacks. Passengers do not always pay attention to the information displayed; sometimes they misread the displays and sometimes they simply forget the information. Most modern airports are reluctant to use public loudspeakers and they do so only when passengers are about to miss their flight. Copenhagen Airport, with 21 million passengers departing per year (2008), is forced to make numerous public calls for late-at-gate passengers on a busy day, even though the airport strives hard to be a "silent airport".

The SPOPOS project was initiated by the commercial department of Copenhagen Airport for several reasons: Most importantly, it will generate large amounts of data needed for passenger flow analysis: How many people pass through a particular shop area? How long time do passengers dwell in specific rest areas? SPOPOS can accurately document, e.g., changes in passenger movements when new procedures for timing of announcements are introduced.

The airlines want passengers to arrive at their gate, if not as early as possible, then early enough to ensure that nobody is late. On the other hand the airport wants to keep passengers in the shopping area as long as possible and most passengers wish to spend as little time as possible waiting at the gate.

The observation that location-based systems may help passengers reach their gate in due time is not novel (e.g., [5]). However, as several researchers also have pointed out (e.g. [6]), location-based systems raise several privacy concerns, and if most passengers reject the system, it has little effect: i.e., the risk of delayed departures is only reduced substantially if a large proportion of passengers agree to use the system. So the big question is: can a system be designed which a large majority of passengers will accept?

2.3 Location-Based Services for Travellers

Airports invest considerable resources into putting out information about flight status. Unless passengers feel entirely updated about their flight, they are not relaxed and they may be uncertain about how much time they may spend on shopping, eating and leisure activities.

The design purpose of SPOPOS Gatecaller service is to reduce uncertainty that passengers experience and make them less liable to miss their flight. Airport operators will have fewer departures delayed due to missing passengers and, in the long run, more relaxed and satisfied passengers.

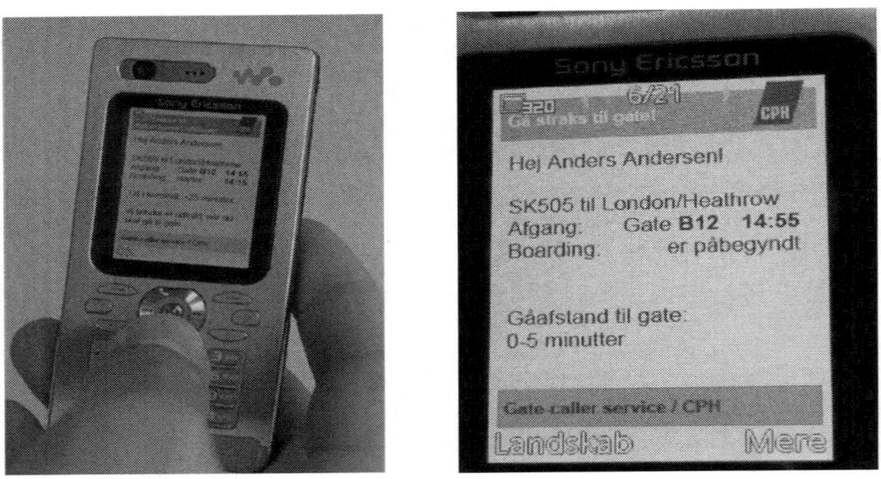

Fig. 3. The basic Gatecaller system informing passengers on when to go to gate, dependent on their current location. The picture to the right shows the message sent automatically when boarding has started to a passenger who has not yet shown up at the gate.

The basic Gatecaller is an automatic, observer-free, continuous and synchronous location system. No human observer (airport personnel) is involved. The service sends information about boarding and departure changes directly to the cell phone of the individual passenger, who will now no longer depend on access to information screens. Information and timing are based on the passenger's location and include estimated walking time to the gate (see Figure 3).

The extended Gatecaller allows gate personnel (i.e., a 'stranger') to locate and contact a passenger who is about to miss his or her departure. The gate personnel can monitor all passengers for a particular flight departure to check if anyone may be so far away that an alert is needed (see Figure 4).

The "Tag-along" expansion of the Gatecaller allows friends and relatives to observe the traveller's movements between zones from a password-protected Web page.

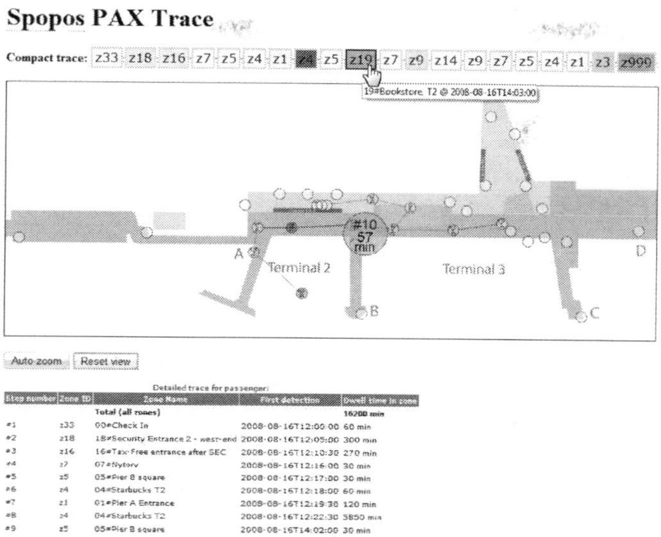

Step number	Zone ID	Zone Name	First detection	Dwell time in zone
		Total (all zones)		16200 min
#1	z33	00#Check In	2008-08-16T12:00:00	60 min
#2	z18	18#Security Entrance 2 - west-end	2008-08-16T12:05:00	300 min
#3	z16	16#Tax-Free entrance after SEC	2008-08-16T12:10:30	270 min
#4	z7	07#Nytorv	2008-08-16T12:16:00	30 min
#5	z5	05#Pier B square	2008-08-16T12:17:00	30 min
#6	z4	04#Starbucks T2	2008-08-16T12:18:00	60 min
#7	z1	01#Pier A Entrance	2008-08-16T12:19:30	120 min
#8	z4	04#Starbucks T2	2008-08-16T12:22:30	3850 min
#9	z5	05#Pier B square	2008-08-16T14:02:00	30 min

Fig. 4. Operators' view of a single passenger's route throughout the airport

For instance, one would be able to monitor, say, one's elderly parents or teenage children when they are airside. The interface is a simplified version of the map-view (Figure 4) provided to the airport professionals.

When a passenger who has used the SPOPOS services leaves the airport, all location data that refer to a specific mobile phone or ticket are deleted and only anonymous data are stored and used for statistical purposes – similar to current data capture by the airport of number of passenger by flight, airline, day and time etc.

2.4 Privacy Implications of the Gatecaller

Normally, privacy is used as a means for maintaining both security and maintaining social roles by managing the image that we present of ourselves to others (e.g. [7]). Thus, while we to a large extent share privacy with friends and relatives, we also require individual privacy by keeping secrets even within intimate relationships. A variety of 'domains' can be regarded as private and thus subject to potential invasions (or loss of privacy): a physical sphere such as a private home; sensitive personal information; personal relations and conversations; activities and decisions. Our privacy can be invaded by physical intrusion, by someone acquiring sensitive information about us, and/or by being observed and judged by others [8].

Even though the airport is not a private place, passenger may still expect some degree of privacy, not least because they are normally protected by anonymity, a basic means for privacy protection. They want to have private conversations without others' eavesdropping on them, or to meet people or make purchases without being profiled for some purpose.

Basically, the privacy implications of a service like the Gatecaller depend not only on the information provided, but also on the identity of the observer (e.g. [1]). Thus, on the one hand, location-based information may suggest behaviour (movements), purchasing and personal relationships (co-location with other passengers) – depending on the degree of accuracy. But the three services offered by the Gatecaller differ significantly in terms of the observer: the extended service seems to imply a greater loss of privacy, because the passenger is now being observed and to some extent judged by someone who will meet the passenger at the gate. The 'Tag-along' service may offer the comfort of being watched by close friends or relatives, but it also threatens the individual privacy that the passenger may wish to keep – by making it difficult to indulge secret habits.

3 Design Methods

We regard technology as a mediator in human activity. This implies acquiring a detailed understanding of the human activities that technological services will augment, i.e., passenger activities and operator activities. Passengers bring mobile phones, they care about surveillance and privacy, they pay only short visits to the airport, and some passenger activities in the airport are entirely "free" or up to the passengers themselves to decide on (shopping, sitting in a cafeteria, etc.). Operators work on standard personal computers and terminals on fixed locations in the airport, and they use a range of applications as part of their professional job function, required for specific tasks related to handling passengers in the airport.

Initially we developed a couple of short scenarios and personas to establish a shared understanding and starting point among the industrial and academic partners in the project. The topics of six extended scenarios were chosen in agreement with the site operator to span a range of important actors. Personas representing different passenger groups were then developed. They included a typical business traveller who aims at efficiency during his stay, seeking to minimize his waiting time and get the most possible work done while in the airport. At the other end of the user spectrum we developed an absent-minded teenager travelling on her own for the first time. For this persona the predominant design issue centred around feeling secure – and not least, letting her parents feel secure; and this sparked the idea of developing a "Tag-along" function in the Gatecaller that will allow people outside the airport to see the approximate location of friends or family inside the airport, provided they get the passengers' permission to do so. We also expanded on an idea of a location-dependent treasure hunt for this teenager. Time constraints soon forced us to abandon this idea, since the scenario made it clear how much additional system development it would take to implement it.

The personas and scenarios served to communicate and ultimately confirm the goals of SPOPOS. While presenting and discussing the scenarios with airport professionals in the project group, we were able to align researchers', technologists' and professional users' understanding of activities in the airport. Later, we used the scenarios to specify usability requirements, raise design issues and reveal open questions regarding the system architecture.

Observations in the airport helped us to detail and adjust our understanding of passenger and operator activities. We spent a long time in the airport observing passengers and staff. The area around the main information boards and the information desks in the transfer area turned out to be the most interesting places to observe passengers, since passengers would often come by and ask for directions, flight departures and other information, which we then later discussed as candidates for possible inclusion in the SPOPOS service.

Moreover, during our observations we often noticed passengers standing still for a very long time in front of the large information boards, simply waiting for the gate of their flight to be announced. As soon as the information appeared, they would begin to move, heading directly for their gate. This demonstrated to us that a not-so-small minority of passengers are seriously hampered by their concern not to miss their flight. For the airport as well as for the passengers this is not a favourable situation. The airport prefers the passengers to spend their waiting time in the shops or the restaurants or at least in the waiting areas and not thronged together in front of the boards and obstructing other traffic. Equally, for the passengers it is of course very tiring to be standing for a long time waiting for the gate announcement. They would have had a more pleasant stay in the airport if they had been given flight information on a mobile device, filtering out irrelevant information about other flights.

Understanding of operators' work processes at the airport was gained by interviewing staff in Copenhagen Airport, including in particular the marketing department, and by following service staff around and observing their professional activities for extended periods.

For several years the marketing department has collected large amounts of data about passenger flow, passenger segments (nationality, age, gender, business/pleasure, airline etc.), shopping behaviours, and dwell times. These data formed a useful ground for our work with personas. A number of the analytical methods developed by the marketing department could be implemented directly in the management module of SPOPOS.

When the Bluetooth / RFID antenna infrastructure became operational we developed passenger prototypes for the Gatecaller service (Figure 3). The prototypes served to give a better understanding of mobile interaction challenges in an airport. Some of these challenges include noise and strong sun light, the fact that passengers typically carry baggage and shopping bags, that they are concerned with following airport procedures (security, gate information, etc.), and that some of them are more or less occupied with taking care of other passengers (young children or elderly).

We made a first prototype of the Gatecaller service and tested it in the airport on three mobile phones in June 2007. It was based on real flight and passenger data, but pushing Bluetooth notifications with gate and departure information to passengers' mobile phones was simulated. Evaluation of the prototype was done by a Wizard-of-Oz session, a method that was a useful and needed substitute for an evaluation of a working prototype, since the connection between the Bluetooth server and the passenger and flight databases had not yet been established. Passenger notifications were pushed manually to the three mobile phones when required. The session was run as a real passenger situation, but with project members acting as passengers: The passengers checked in for a real departure (in a simulated check-in desk in the transfer area), and received departure information and information about their remaining time at appropriate points of time.

A second prototype evaluation with the same set-up, but adjusted according to the results from the first evaluation, was done in December 2007. This time, representatives from the press participated in the prototype evaluation, which was highly motivating and helped us making more precise the oral and written introduction given to passengers when asking them to sign up for the system.

The operator prototype has been tested by heuristic evaluations as well as think-aloud usability tests with airport personnel, providing several suggestions for improvements. Prototypes of the system modules for airline operators were tested at the departure gates in field tests (see next section). Prototypes for overall airport management have also been developed and tested in the final evaluation.

4 User Evaluation

Starting in March 2008, a series of test trials were launched with the collaboration of Scandinavian Airlines (SAS) involving passengers who accepted to participate in testing the Gatecaller. At the time of writing two such trials have been run, each involving the recruitment of passengers departing on an SAS charter flight from Copenhagen to Sharm El Sheik in Egypt. On these flights nearly all passengers are travelling in families or groups, and they often include a number of children or elderly family members.

At the check-in line, passengers were contacted by staff, wearing T-shirts with conspicuous SPOPOS logos, and asked if they would like to participate as volunteers in the testing of a new tracking and information service. Passengers who accepted our request were then asked to carry an RFID on their handbag or hand luggage till they reach their gate, and to register their mobile phone (if they have any). Passengers were also told that they would be asked to fill out a short questionnaire on arrival at gate.

Due to congestion at the check-in line, not all passengers could be approached, but nearly all who were so accepted to become volunteer subjects. The total number of successfully recruited subjects in the two field tests was 138, most of whom, 116, had time to complete the questionnaire at gate. The five staff members involved in recruiting passengers reported the ratio of passengers who either refused to participate (mean: 7%) or who were too busy with taking care of children or elderly friends (mean: 14%). No passengers were late at gate in the two trials. In the following we describe some of the questionnaire data including correlations with location data.

There are two significant findings from the passenger surveys. The first is the added comfort a number of passengers feel when they know that the Gatecaller service is running. (This service was not fully implemented for the first departure, so the question was asked to only passengers on the second departure, N=76.) We asked participants: "Has it made you feel more secure that the gate personnel now may find you if you are late?" As can be seen from their answers (table 1), a majority (60%) feels to some degree or to a large degree more secure with the knowledge that the Gatecaller function is available.

Table 1. Responses given by passengers at gate to the question "Has it made you feel more secure that the gate personnel now may find you if you are late?"

[N = 76]	No, not at all	No, hardly at all	Yes, to some degree	Yes, to a large degree
	20%	20%	39%	21%

The second most significant – and not foreseen – finding is that only a small minority of passengers seem to have felt their privacy affected during the time they have spent carrying the RFID tag that was traced (or had their Bluetooth cell phone traced). We asked respondents: "Have you felt yourself being monitored while you have been carrying the RFID tag?" As can be seen from table 2, few passengers feel themselves subject to monitoring.

Table 2. Responses given by passengers at gate to the question "Have you felt yourself being monitored while you have been carrying the RFID tag?"

[N =116]	No, not at all	No, hardly at all	Yes, to some degree	Yes, to a large degree
	86%	9%	4%	1%

We also asked participants if the time they spent on keeping themselves up to date influenced their movements in the airport.

Table 3. Responses given by passengers at gate to the question "Has time spent on information influenced your movements in the airport?"

[N = 98]	No not at all	No, hardly any time	Yes, some time	Yes, a lot of time
	38%	27%	24%	12%

At the same time, there is a significant though modest correlation (Spearman's rho=.26; p=.03) between time spent between security and before entering the pier and efforts spent on keeping up to date: i.e., the less passengers have felt their movements influenced by the need for keeping up to date on their departure, the more time they have been able to spend in the tax-free area before going to gate.

4.1 Evaluation by Airport Personnel

Staff at the gate is typically quite busy from the time they open the gate till the last passenger has embarked. One of the most critical tasks for the gate personnel today is to decide on the effort and time to spend on finding passengers who have checked in but who have not shown up at gate. The second greatest advantage of the SPOPOS Gatecaller is that it allows gate personnel an easy overview of where late passengers are and an opportunity to alert them or call them by phone. During the two trials that have been made so far, four persons from the SAS ground staff evaluated the system.

Staff reactions were uniformly and emphatically positive. At the present time, they have an entirely adequate overview of the number (and names etc.) of passengers who have checked and who have still not shown up at the boarding check-in. But they have no means of knowing where they are. The Gatecaller concept promises to change this. One of the senior gate staff participants stated that he "hoped that this technology will be implemented during my career". Another remarked that the boarding process could possibly be "turned 180° now". In our interpretation, she foresees a transition from the present push-approach towards a future 'pull-to-gate' procedure.

5 Discussion

There is now evidence that a large proportion of travellers in Copenhagen airport will accept and use the kind of location-based services that the Gatecaller will provide, if they are offered this. It is, however, an open question if this finding will generalize to other transitional spaces also. First and foremost, airports are special locations with regard to privacy. For many years, surveillance has been so prevalent in airports that we quietly accept it, as Adey [9] points out. Passengers are frequently asked to have their baggage examined, to take off their belt and shoes and they are used to technologies like CCTV cameras being part of an airport location. We got several comments from passengers interviewed at the gate, indicating that they are particular in their acceptance of being tracked by service providers in airports, but not in general:

"I don't mind using the tracking service (.....) in this airport. Here I can see the benefits. I would not use it in the shopping mall, where they would hunt me down with "offerings" all over the place" (Danish female, 40 years)

It is also important to people, that they have trust in the organization or people who requires information about their locations, cf. [1]. Copenhagen Airport is partly owned by a government that people trust in most other matters. One passenger addressed this:

"I have no worries that information handled within governmental institutions would ever be used in any harmful way" (Dutch male, 34 years).

Another passenger pointed out to us that trust is built on honesty that should be confirmed:

"Honesty is important for tracking. I would only allow companies that I trust to trace me and they should show themselves worthy of the trust..." (Danish male, 34 years)

A recent survey [3] asked passengers if they would "accept that an airline/ airport use their location sensing technology in order to locate you and better guide you through the airport terminal?" The percentages of people who answered "yes" to this differed dramatically from airport to airport. In one case (Charles de Gaulle, France) only 4 % would accept to be tracked, while the other 5 airports had acceptance rates between 40% and 69%. We do not have any data that can serve to explain the difference between the results of that survey with those we have obtained. However, it may be speculated that an approach to passengers that stresses openness and the fact that it is voluntary and that personal data will be deleted as soon as the passenger leaves the airport may play a role. The fact that people in our field test had actually experienced being tracked may have convinced them that this is rather harmless. In a recent study Tsai et al. [10] found that privacy concerns were reduced after people have had the experience of using a mobile location sharing system.

In the SPOPOS project we decided to invite the public news media to one of our field test. We also decided to implement the "Tag-along" service, partly because we wanted to make it commonly known how passenger's individual locations may be traced indoors, and partly because some passengers expressed great expectations to it.

The sensitivity of the private information increases with the accuracy of tracking, i.e., people are less concerned if their whereabouts are only roughly known. In the current version, the SPOPOS system is able to locate passengers only in wide zones, and the zones are so large that nobody will be able to tell which particular shop or cafeteria a passenger might be visiting. On passenger commented on the issue of granularity:

"I like the idea of this system. But I would not like it to know in detail when I am at the restroom" (Polish female, 24 years)

Brown et al. [11] deliberately designed the 'Whereabouts Clock' – a device to show the location of other family members – so that it would reveal their whereabouts in only coarse-grained terms (i.e. 'home', 'work', 'school' or 'elsewhere').

The SPOPOS Gatecaller is designed to track the passengers themselves. Nevertheless, there still is some room for anonymity, without inhibiting the underlying purpose of locating 'delayed' passengers. For most of the passengers, it would be sufficient only to be identified as an anonymous member of a group: the passenger list for a particular flight. It would be necessary to identify only the few passengers who do seem not to arrive in due time for boarding. Some passengers are aware of this:

"The system is a kind of surveillance. But there is a huge difference between [constantly] following a person on a screen or only gaining information when the gate is about to close." (Danish male, 34).

If location-based services are introduced at other public places, we expect that it would be acceptable to most potential users only if is able to justify itself by offering some services that are perceived useful. What those services might be are specific to the different places. Costumers in a shopping centre may appreciate it if they can easily find all the items they have on their shopping list. Spectators at a sports event may appreciate it that they can easily locate their seat. However, just as the "basic version" of the Gatecaller would work without any human monitors involved, we suggest that location-based services for other public spaces should also strive for anonymity if possible and should allow people to opt out, if they feel uncomfortable with the trustworthiness of the provider, cf. Kaasinen [6]. In quite a lot of cases where location based systems can be valuable, anonymity can simply be achieved by letting the device be aware of its own location, but without other parties tracking the location cf. Barkhuus & Day [12].

6 Conclusion

A majority of passengers who have tried the Gatecaller service report that they feel more secure knowing that it is working in the background, while only a small fraction of passengers report that they feel themselves monitored. Comments from passengers point to reasons for this high acceptance: people find the service useful; they have trust in the airport operators; they believe that data will be made anonymous after take-off; and they appreciate that it will only be possible for other people to see their approximate location in zones and only when they are about to be late at gate. Finally, airline handlers and airport management express enthusiasm about the information that this service will provide them.

Acknowledgements

We gratefully acknowledge the involvement from our industrial partners in the SPOPOS project: Lyngsoe Systems A/S, BLIP Systems A/S, Travelmarket A/S and Copenhagen Airports A/S. We also thank Scandinavian Airline Systems for their support in field trials. The research is supported by the Danish Research and Innovation Agency under the Danish Ministry for Knowledge, Technology and Development.

References

1. Lederer, S., Mankoff, J., Dey, A.K.: Who wants to know what when? privacy preference determinants in ubiquitous computing. In: CHI 2003 Extended Abstracts on Human Factors in Computing Systems. CHI 2003, pp. 724–725. ACM, New York (2003)
2. SPOPOS, `http://www.spopos.dk` (confirmed April 12, 2009)
3. SITA/air transport world passenger self-service survey, `http://www.sita.aero/files/resources/SITA_PSS_2008.pdf` (confirmed April 12, 2009)
4. IATA – International Air Transport Association, Simplifying the Business, `http://iata.org/stb/` (confirmed April 12, 2009)
5. Raper, J., Gartner, G., Karimi, H., Rizo, C.: A critical evaluation of location based services and their potential. Journal of Location Based Services 1(1), 5–45 (2007)
6. Kaasinen, E.: User needs for location-aware mobile services. Personal Ubiquitous Computing 7(1), 70–79 (2003)
7. Fried, C.: Privacy. Yale Law Journal 77(3), 475–493 (1968)
8. Introna, L.D.: Privacy and the Computer: Why We Need Privacy in the Information Society. Metaphilosophy 28(3), 259–275 (1997)
9. Adey, P.: Secured and Sorted Mobilities: Examples from the Airport. Surveillance & Society 1(4), 500–519 (2004)

10. Tsai, J.Y., Kelley, P., Drielsma, P., Cranor, L.F., Hong, J., Sadeh, N.: Who's viewed you?: the impact of feedback in a mobile location-sharing application. In: Proceedings of the 27th international Conference on Human Factors in Computing Systems. CHI 2009, pp. 2003–2012. ACM, New York (2009)
11. Brown, B., Taylor, A., Izadi, S., Sellen, A., Kaye, J.: Locating Family Values: A Field Trail of the Whereabouts Clock. In: Proc. of Ubi Comp 2007, pp. 354–371. Springer, Godalming (2007)
12. Barkhuus, L., Dey, A.K.: Location-based services for mobile telephony: a study of users' privacy concerns. In: Proceedings of INTERACT 2003, 9th IFIP TC13 International Conference on Human-Computer Interaction, pp. 709–712 (2003)

'I Know That You Know' – Ascertaining Mutual Awareness of Recipient's Availability Status in Instant Messaging Applications

Agnieszka Matysiak Szóstek and Berry Eggen

Department of Industrial Design,
Eindhoven University of Technology
Den Dolech 2, 5600MB Eindhoven,
The Netherlands
{A.Matysiak,N.H.Eggen}@tue.nl

Abstract. This study investigated ways to attain mutual, reciprocal awareness of recipient's availability status in Instant Messaging (IM) applications. For that purpose we designed, implemented and tested a prototype of an IM system named Do^{NT}Bother. The analysis of the quantitative and qualitative results showed that displaying status indication in the chat box encouraged participants to show more respect towards the communicative state of their colleagues comparing to situations, in which the status indication was presented only in the 'buddy list' view. These findings empirically confirm the importance of reciprocal awareness as defined by Erickson and Kellogg [12] who argued that, to stimulate social behaviours, systems need to maintain the mutual knowledge of who knows what of the information that is shared among users. The study also showed that mutual awareness needs to be maintained not only during communication initiation but also throughout the entire communication duration. To achieve that Instant Messaging systems need to: (i) support indicating the time frame for answering messages in situations when the recipient is not instantaneously able to engage in a conversation, (ii) support specifying the urgency of a message and also (iii) support indicating communication breakdowns especially if they are caused by a reason occurring outside the application domain.

Keywords: Instant Messaging systems, availability, mutual awareness.

1 Introduction

As there is no measurement regarding which behaviours are considered as socially acceptable people tend to develop their own conventions that define the best practices for different situations and different communities [5, 17, 9, 8, 16, 21, 23]. Current Instant Messaging (IM) systems are largely unaware of such social conventions and, therefore, do not account for the impact their functionality has on how people interact with each other [13]. Erickson and Kellogg [12] argued that, to stimulate social behaviours, systems supporting mediated communication need to maintain mutual

T. Gross et al. (Eds.): INTERACT 2009, Part I, LNCS 5726, pp. 182–195, 2009.

knowledge of who knows what of the information that is shared among communicators. By providing such cues people could be given the opportunity to attune to the communicative needs of others and act in ways that are both coherent and graceful.

The goal of this study was to investigate what is a successful way to ascertain mutual awareness about the recipient's availability status in IM applications. To reach this goal we implemented a prototype named Do^{NT}Bother, which was then evaluated in a web design company for a period of three weeks. The contributions of this research include the quantitative and qualitative measurements assessing the proposed solutions and a set of implications that promise to inform the design of future mechanisms supporting the attainment of mutual awareness in IM applications.

2 Related Work

IM systems are near-synchronous communication tools that facilitate one-to-one communication between a person and their 'buddy list' by supporting an exchange of short textual messages. The near-synchronous nature of the tool allows for communication to be paced according to the preferences of both communicators. The great success of IM can be attributed to its flexible nature [20] and low cost of interuptiveness [15]. However, as the use of IM is growing, particularly at work, the insufficient support for managing people's availability for communication tends to lead to communication breakdowns, which, in turn, can have negative effects on the social relationships between the system users [4]. The aforementioned problem is not new and a vast body of research was conducted in that subject [26, 3, 4, 18, 2, 34].

Prior works have shown that managing availability for communication is a dynamic and multidimensional process that depends on the continuously changing context [6, 13, 27, 4] and that technologies supporting mediated communication often disrupt the exchange of cues regarding that context [27]. Voida et al [34] observed that, in IM systems, while it might be convenient for the sender to initiate a conversation at a particular moment, it may be undesirable for the recipient to engage in that conversation at that moment. The recipient must then face a trade-of between continuing his/her current task and engaging in communication. Nardi et al [26] saw that information exchange can be successful only through subtle negotiations about availability as a way to establish connection by inhabiting and maintaining a shared communication zone. The process of negotiating availability binds people more tightly together for a specific interaction as they establish a particular attentional contract and is likely to have consequences for future communications. Dabbish and Kraut [10] argued that providing cues about recipient's availability prior to communication initiation should over a good prediction regarding the likelihood of accepting that communication and might even indicate how communication could proceed.

In the context of negotiating communications, the ability to provide awareness regarding availability status should be seen as one of the most important features of IM clients. They typically provide relevant information by indicating whether a user is online and whether (s)he is currently active or idle by measuring keyboard activity. Most IM clients also allow users to signal whether they are busy by entering short status messages that remain visible in the 'buddy list' view until changed or deleted. Szostek et al [29] showed that such contextual status indications are likely to allow communicators not only to see that their buddies are unavailable for communication but also to understand why they are unavailable. However, such manual solutions, although considered as rich and at the same time providing sufficient space for ambiguity, are imperfect: people tend to forget to update them when their situation changes [24, 29, 1]. Therefore, many works concentrated around designing systems deriving one's communicative state based on automatically detected availability cues [7, 6, 14, 31, 32, 30]. Availability indications were provided through video-streaming [11, 22], by representing the content of agendas or daily rhythms [7, 6, 32] or by showing computer activities and various sensory data captured from people's environments [13]. Evaluations of many systems showed, however, that presenting availability status alone appears to be insufficient for screening unwanted interruptions [7, 6, 31]. The study by Szostek et al [29] argued that it is crucial to introduce mechanisms stimulating mutual, reciprocal awareness regarding communicative needs of both the initiator and the recipient.

So far various mechanisms were designed allowing initiators to 'grab' recipient's attention through the use of various audio-visual alerts and alarms generally accessible in any IM client. Hsieh et al [18] and also Tang et al [33] recently showed that tagging of IM messages might be a valuable way for the initiator to indicate the importance of an incoming communication. However, as noticed by Nardi and Whittaker [25] an asymmetry can be seen in tools supporting mediated communication, where the initiator tends to have more control over the communicative exchange comparing to the recipient. Therefore, in this study, we focused on investigating attainment of a desirable level of mutual awareness regarding the communicative state of the recipient by attempting to answer the following question:

What is a successful way to achieve mutual, reciprocal awareness of recipient's communicative state in IM systems?

We aimed to answer this question by investigating the extent to which people were willing to comply with the availability status of others when provided with status indication during conversation initiation. Also, we looked into the possible effect of different status indications on their decision to initiate communication. Moreover, we were interested to see whether the mutual awareness of the recipient's status provided participants with a way to discard poorly timed communications. Finally, we aimed at eliciting design implications that help improve the attainment of the mutual awareness in IM systems.

3 Design

The Do^{NT}Bother system was implemented in Java and based on an open source Jabber client: JBother [37]. We chose JBother as it allowed for transport registration, so that participants could integrate their MSN client with the prototype and receive all IM messages through one unified application. In this way we wanted to lower the acceptance threshold for Do^{NT}Bother and assure that participants had the possibility to integrate all their contacts and to execute all their communications through Do^{NT}-Bother rather than using many separate IM applications.

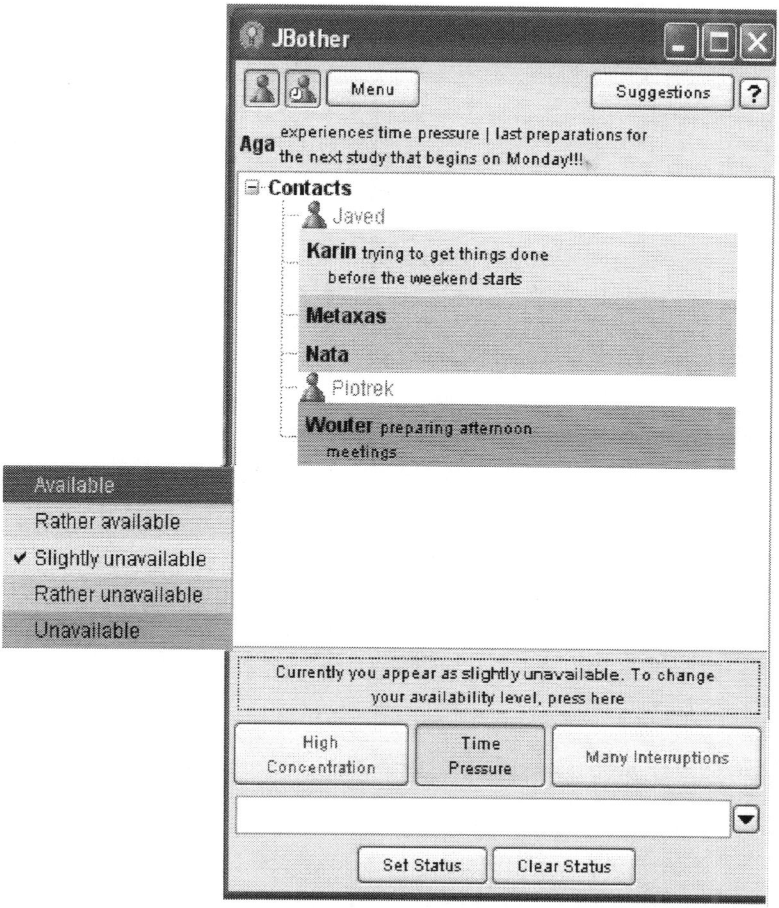

Fig. 1. Availability status representation consisting of: a expandable menu for indicating the *availability levels*, three *status buttons* and a text box to enter *a status message*

Based on the findings by Szostek et al. [29] we equipped DoNTBother with the following means of indicating its users' communicative state (see: Fig. 1). Participants could set their availability level on a 5-point scale ranging from available to unavailable and represented by colours spanning from green to red. Furthermore, they have at their disposal three status buttons ('Concentration', 'Time Pressure' and 'Many Interruptions'), each generating a predefined message ('Ann is concentrated', 'Ann experiences high time pressure', and 'Ann experienced many interruptions'). Finally, a text box was added in which a personalized status message of one's availability state could be entered.

The main difference between DoNTBother and conventional IM systems was that DoNTBother, besides showing contextual status information in the 'buddy list', also

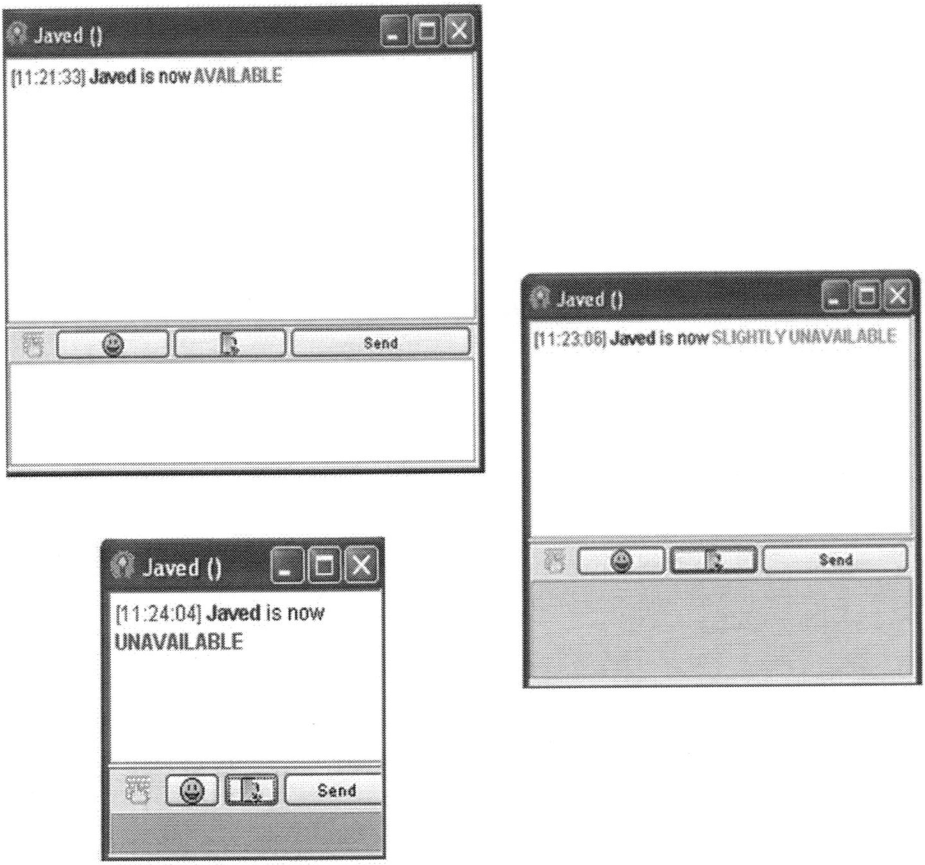

Fig. 2. Displaying recipient's status during communication initiation: a textual and graphical status update in the chat box

showed that information in every newly opened chat box. In such a way both communicators gained the opportunity to attain mutual awareness of the recipient's communicative state. DoNTBother provides two ways to achieve that (see: Fig. 2):

1. A textual status update: the recent recipient's status (including the availability level and the status description) was shown as a line of text appearing on the top of the chat box of a newly initiated IM conversation, so that both communicators could see it before engaging in a conversation. The colour of the text reflected the colour coding for recipient's current availability level.
2. A graphical status update: any newly open chat box changed its size depending on the availability level indicated by the recipient, so that it opened in full size if one indicated full availability and obtained a gradually smaller size if the status is set to the consecutive levels. Furthermore, the entry space of the chat box gradually changed colour from white to grey depending on recipient's availability. Change

in the physical parameters of the text entry box was intended to indicate to the initiator the possible cost of initiating communication. Nonetheless, the user was in no way prohibited from entering the text of any length. If necessary the chat box could be enlarged by dragging its right-bottom corner and the background colour could be changed by using the background-colour palette. Note that as soon as the reply to a message was received (meaning that the recipient showed interest in engaging in a conversation) the chat box returned to its original size and colour.

4 Participants

Ten employees (2 female) from a web design company, employing 35 people in total, agreed to participate in the study. Based on the data provided through the demographics questionnaire distributed prior to study initiation we noted that all participants were acquainted with at least one IM application (mostly MSN). An IM application was used only for professional purposes by 5 persons. The remaining participants used the IM for both professional and personal communications. 8 participants reported to use IM daily and 2 to use it a few times a week. Only 1 participant frequently updated her status, 6 did it sometimes and 3 persons never set their IM status before.

4.1 Study Setup

The system was presented to the participants during a one-hour presentation before the study initiation. All participants received a software package allowing them to install DoNTBother and also to integrate it with their other IM contacts. They were also provided with assistance during the application deployment and received a three-page document instructing them how to access features available in the system.

The study lasted three weeks (the first study week was treated as introductory and data collected during that week was removed from the dataset). Participants used both textual and graphical way of representing the recipient's availability status simultaneously. In such a way they could experience the proposed solutions and determine their preferences regarding both design proposals.

After the study completion, in two Focus Group sessions, participants were asked to compare the DoNTBother system to other IM systems with respect to: (i) ways to indicate communicators' availability status, and (ii) ways to stimulate mutual awareness of that status. Both sessions consisted of 5 participants. Each session lasted approximately one hour, was audio recorded and transcribed.

4.2 Data Analysis

In this study data was collected from two data sources. The summary of participants' interactions was intended to illustrate the relationship between their availability status and the initiated communications. For that purpose, we recorded the following data:

- time of communication initiation
- recipient's availability status at the moment of the initiation
- whether the initiation was executed or not
- whether the initiation was responded to or not.

The recipient's availability status at the moment of communication initiation was aimed to show the extent to which participants were willing to comply with the indicated availability status of their colleagues. The data about whether the initiation was executed gave insights into the possible effect of the status indication in the chat box on the decision to initiate communication. The data about whether the initiation was responded to showed the extent to which the mutual awareness of the recipient's status provided participants with an opportunity to discard poorly timed communications.

The analysis of the Focus Group sessions aimed at providing qualitative insights into participants' opinions and preferences regarding using the representations of the availability status as means to negotiate communication in IM systems. For that purpose, the transcripts from both sessions were analyzed using the Direct Content analysis [19]. 145 statements were coded by two independent coders in two iterations (Fleiss K = .82 [28] for the first iteration and Fleiss K = .91 for the second). In the analysis 47 statements were categorized as expressing participants' observations regarding the differences in setting the availability status between DoNTBother and other IM tools (specifically MSN). 69 statements reflected their opinions regarding attaining mutual awareness of the recipient's availability status. 39 statements were classified as providing inadequate motivation for expressed opinions (e.g., 'It all is just personal') and were removed from the data set.

5 Results

In this section, we describe the results from the two data sources. The summary of participants' interactions aimed at illustrating the ways they tended to initiate communications for different availability status indications. The analysis of the Focus Group sessions provided qualitative insights into subsequent participants' opinions regarding the advantages and disadvantages of DoNTBother in comparison to other IM applications, especially regarding ways of both presenting the availability status and invoking mutual awareness about that status.

5.1 Logs

During the study 173 communications were recorded (approximately 2 conversations per person per day). 73% of these initiations were commenced when participants' availability was indicated as available; 6%as rather available; 10% as slightly unavailable; 10% as rather unavailable and only 1% as unavailable. Such a result shows that, in general, communicators were willing to initiate communications at right moments based on the status information presented in the 'buddy list' view.

Interestingly, 30% of communication initiations recorded during the study were never responded to (n = 52). No relationship, however, was detected between lack of response and the availability status. Majority (n = 43) of unanswered communications were initiated when the recipient's status was indicated as available. From that observation we concluded that sending a message when the recipient appeared available did not necessarily guarantee receiving a reply. There might have been two reasons for lack of response: either the message itself did not require any or that the status indication visible in the system was not up to date and therefore the recipient was not able to answer the message. A detailed analysis of IM conversations would support further analysis of that observation.

Finally, we recorded 25 events, during which a chat box was opened but no communication was initiated. Majority of these events occurred when the recipient's availability status was other than available (for Level 2 - 6 cases, for Level 3 - 6 cases, for Level 4 - 2 cases and for Level 5 - 3 cases). This result shows the possible positive impact of the status update in the chat box on increasing awareness regarding the recipient's status at the point of communication initiation. Participants seemed to find additional means for verifying the communicative state of their colleagues and sometimes decide to withdraw from initiating communication when that status was set to somewhat unavailable.

5.2 Focus Groups

In the final part of the study opinions of ten participants added to our understanding regarding to what extent participants were aware of their communicators' availability status at the point of communication initiation.

Presenting Availability Status. Participants appreciated DoNTBother for allowing them to present their availability status in three different ways. The threefold way of defining one's status was perceived as providing an acceptable description about one's communicative state and at the same time as a way to disclose limited information about oneself (e.g., by only indicating one's availability level without providing any explanation of that level) or to exaggerate one's status (e.g., by setting the availability level to red and also pressing all status buttons). Different features allowed participants to control the amount of information they wanted to share with their colleagues. In line with findings by Nardi et al. [26], also in this study the system users reported to frequently use DoNTBother to check the status of a person whom they wanted to get in touch with through different communication means (e.g. Face-to-Face or through the phone).

> *'I think that what DoNTBother system has, as in opposite to MSN, is that it allows you to quickly tell others how busy you are and also on different levels, so not just only 'busy' or 'not busy'.'*

> *'Success of Do^{NT}Bother comparing to MSN is the way it allows me to set my status. You want to give others a correct feeling of what's going on with you. In a face-to-face situation if someone comes and I'm busy I give him a dark look and he should turn around and go away. In Do^{NT}Bother I set a very strong status.'*

The status indication did not always stop participants from contacting their colleagues in situations, in which they appeared unavailable. Participants based their decision of whether to interrupt or not on their knowledge regarding the current task of a co-worker. That knowledge was often supported by the status message stating the project a recipient was occupied with. Interestingly, we observed that a decision whether to interrupt someone or not was also based on how trustworthy the status appeared to the initiator. If the status indication seemed believable, participants were more likely to respect it. Participants considered as believable status indication that matched their own knowledge of another person's working situation (which was further rooted in their knowledge of others' workload derived from the fact of sharing a common physical space). However, whenever participants had doubts regarding status reliability they would easily discard it and initiate communication. Participants tended not to believe a status indication that seemed as intentional exaggeration or accidental overlooking to provide an updated value of one's communicative state.

> *'I find it handy when people set the status using messages so that I know that she is working on project X and she is really unavailable. Then if you are in the same project you know how to behave. I know that she is available for me. So any feature for setting the status and also for letting people know what they are working on is great.'*

> *'Some colleagues would set their status to unavailable from 8 a.m. to 5 p.m. If I checked it a few times, I would think: 'I don't believe that you had so many interruptions already at 8 a.m., you just pressed all buttons'. And I would contact him anyway.'*

Invoking Awareness of the Recipient's Status Among Communicators. Many participants considered both the textual and the graphical status update in the chat box as a successful reminder prompting them to either postpone communication or keep it short in situations when the recipient indicated limited availability. Participants felt that the status in the buddy list on its own was insu cient to assume that the communicator was aware of their communicative state. The textual status update was seen as a guarantee that one's status was seen and therefore one can use it as an excuse for delaying or deferring poorly timed communication. The graphical status indication was seen to counterbalance the possible negative impact that communication initiation could have on the recipient.

> *'If someone starts a conversation and gets my status, it is like a reminder: You started talking but I am under time pressure, so you should keep it short. And you can always ask this person to look at your status.'*

> *'It was very handy that the chat box got smaller if someone was unavailable. Sometimes you don't really check if he is available, you just want to talk to him. And then you see the chat box getting smaller.'*

Surprisingly, participants frequently reported misunderstandings regarding the meaning of sending a message at times when the recipient appeared unavailable. Often when participants sent a message to someone who displayed limited availability for communication they did not intend to compromise her need for solitude. Their goal was, instead, to indicate interest in communication. At the same time, initiators wanted to leave the initiative to the recipient as when to react to that message. However, while messages received at moments when the recipient was available could be easily deferred for later, those received while one's status was set to unavailable, were often seen as urgent and participants felt inclined to at least read and often also act on them immediately.

> *'If I see that someone is busy, I don't expect an answer right away. I already contacted him and it was enough for me to let him know what my problem is and that I would like a response sometime.'*

'When my status is set to available and something blinks then I don't care. But when my status is set to unavailable and there is something blinking I think: 'It must be really urgent'. I will answer both, of course, but my curiosity is higher when my status is unavailable and still someone tries to reach me.'

Finally, although they appreciated the status update in the chat box, participants felt that Do^{NT}Bother lacked support for communication breakdowns caused by a change in communicators' situation that occurred in the middle of the conversation and was often caused by a trigger happening outside the application (e.g., receiving a phone call). Participants needed to be able to quickly put an ongoing IM communication on hold if another situation needed their attention but at the same time they wanted to quickly provide an acceptable excuse explaining why they went into an idle state.

'It is important to define who should come back to that conversation because it may end up in a situation that someone is waiting for you and you are waiting for him to continue.'

'How many times I wrote: 'Wait a minute, phone'. It is an interruption in my conversation with this person and I want to put him on hold but I also want to tell him that I will be back in few minutes. It is better if somebody knows what is going on. But it is also annoying to have to type in the exact same message over and over again.'

6 Discussion

This study aimed at investigating what is a successful way to achieve mutual, reciprocal awareness of recipient's communicative state in IM systems. The analysis of both quantitative and qualitative results comparing the DoNTBother system with existing Instant Messaging applications (specifically: MSN) showed that providing current recipient's status in the chat box encouraged participants to respect the communicative state of their colleagues during communication initiation. Similarly to findings by Begole et al [6], also in this study we saw that users did not always refrain from initiating communications when their colleagues appeared unavailable. Therefore attaining mutual awareness about the recipient's status gave participants the opportunity to ignore untimely communications whenever necessary. The main advantage of the textual status update was its equal visibility to both the recipient and the initiator. Participants reflected that having the status message clearly visible in the chat box guaranteed that their communicative state was, indeed, seen by their communicators and provided them with the opportunity to use it as an excuse to withdraw from unwanted communication. The graphical representation was seen more as a 'defense mechanism' before the communication was, actually, initiated as it made the task of typing in the initial message more difficult. These findings confirm the importance of supporting reciprocal awareness that was already discussed by Erickson and Kellogg [12]. By ascertaining that all systems users know what information is shared among them people are likely to become more sensitive to the communicative needs of others and act in a way that is socially salient.

We can see that while the general idea of adding mechanisms to attain mutual awareness may seem to burden the IM users with additional effort when initiating communication, it should not be dismissed as these mechanisms bring clear benefits to the ways mediated communication unfolds. Such mechanisms, when well integrated in systems supporting mediated communication, are likely to provide several social benefits to communicators (like helping to formulate rules regarding when communication is desirable and when it is unwanted). However, for any awareness mechanism to be successful additional design implications need to be addressed: (i) support for indicating the time frame for answering a message in situations when the recipient is not instantaneously able to engage in a conversation, (ii) support for specifying the urgency of a message by the initiator and also (iii) support for indicating communication breakdowns especially if they are caused by a reason occurring outside the application domain.

The analysis of the results further identified a need for recipients to have the possibility to quickly and effortlessly indicate to the initiator when it is feasible to expect a response. Currently, the only way to delay conversations in IM applications is to temporarily ignore incoming communication, which then could stay up on the user's computer screen as a reminder [26]. Szostek et al. [29] reported that people wanted to be able to indicate to their colleagues that communication was poorly timed as a way to 'educate' them about the value of various availability indications. Wiberg and Whittaker [35] discussed that to avoid increasing of recipients' cognitive overload it is important to enable quick postponing of communications. Therefore, we argue that lightweight support for communication postponing could further support people in maintaining mutual awareness of their communicative state. Such a mechanism could resemble a 'Poke' functionality implemented in social networking applications like Facebook [36]. 'Poke' is a button that, once pressed, sends a predefined message to a selected recipient. A similar functionality deployed in an IM system could provide an effortless way to indicate to a colleague a delay in communication.

Moreover, the current study revealed the importance for the initiator to be able to indicate when a response to the message is likely to be expected. Mechanisms such as proposed by Hsieh et al [18] show their initial value in addressing this issue. The evaluation of their time and no popup tags showed their value as lightweight means to coordinate the intended pace of IM communications. We agree with the authors that message tagging is likely to facilitate different activities occurring in the IM systems. We, however, think that such tags should not only be provided for the communication initiators but also for the recipients.

Finally, an issue of a lightweight way of indicating communication breakdown especially if the breakdown is caused by an external factor (e.g., an appearance of a visitor or reception of a phone-call) is important to address. Current work-around for people is to send an explanatory message like: 'I am on the phone' and then leave the conversation. However, such a method is perceived neither efficient (people seem to be typing very similar messages every so often) nor lightweight (typing in a message requires time and may be very inconvenient especially if there is a visitor around). One possible solution would be to support users in creation of a list of 'delay' messages; a sort of an 'excuse repository', from which typical responses could be easily and efficiently retrieved. In such a way people would be supported in maintaining awareness of what is the availability state of communicators throughout the entire conversation duration.

7 Conclusions

In this study we empirically investigated ways to attain mutual awareness of recipient's availability for communication in Instant Messaging systems. For that purpose we tested a prototype of an IM system named Do^{NT}Bother. The analysis of the results showed that providing status indication during communication initiation encouraged participants to show more respect towards the communicative state of their colleagues comparing to similar situations when the availability status was visible only in the 'buddy list' view. These findings confirm the importance of supporting the attainment of reciprocal awareness as defined by Erickson and Kellogg [12]. Moreover, this study points as the fact that mutual awareness needs to be maintained not only during communication initiation but also throughout the entire communication duration. Within that context the following design implications were derived: IM systems need to allow for indicating the time frame for answering a message. IM systems should also support specifying the urgency of a message. Finally, IM systems must support indicating the reasons behind any communication breakdown especially if the breakdown is caused by a reason occurring outside the application domain.

Acknowledgments. We would like to acknowledge dr Jacques Terken and dr Natalia Romero from the Industrial Design department of Eindhoven University of Technology for their help in preparing this study. Furthermore, we would like to endorse Piotr Tamilla from Warsaw University of Technology in Poland for implementing the Do^{NT}Bother system. Above all, we would like to thank the study participants at Mirabeau B.V. (Daniel Peters, Hanneke Dam and Carmen Boekestein in particular) for their help in executing this research. This work is part of the Smart Surroundings project funded by the Ministry of Economic Affairs of The Netherlands (Contract no. 03060).

References

1. Aoki, P.M., Woodruff, A.: Making space for stories: Ambiguity in the design of personal communication systems, pp. 181–190. ACM Press, New York (2005)
2. Avrahami, D., Fussell, S.R., Hudson, S.E.: IM waiting: timing and responsiveness in semi-synchronous communication. In: CSCW, pp. 285–294. ACM Press, New York (2008)
3. Avrahami, D., Hudson, S.E.: Communication characteristics of instant messaging: effects and predictions of interpersonal relationships. In: CSCW, pp. 505–514. ACM Press, New York (2006)
4. Avrahami, D., Hudson, S.E.: Responsiveness in instant messaging: predictive models supporting inter-personal communication. In: CHI, pp. 731–740. ACM Press, New York (2006)
5. Barker, R.G.: Ecological psychology. Stanford University Press, Stanford (1968)
6. Begole, J., Matsakis, N.E., Tang, J.C.: Lilsys: Sensing unavailability. In: CSCW, pp. 511–514. ACM Press, New York (2004)

7. Begole, J., Tang, J.C., Hill, R.: Rhythm modeling, visualizations and applications. In: UIST, vol. 1, pp. 11–20. ACM Press, New York (2003)
8. Brown, P., Levinson, S.C.: Politeness: Some Universals in Language Usage. Cambridge University Press, Cambridge (1987)
9. Clark, H.: Using language. Cambridge University Press, New York (1996)
10. Dabbish, L., Kraut, R.: Controlling interruptions: Awareness displays and social motivation for coordination. In: CSCW, vol. 1, pp. 182–191. ACM Press, New York (2004)
11. Dourish, P., Bly, S.: Portholes: supporting awareness in a distributed work group. In: CHI, pp. 541–547. ACM Press, New York (1992)
12. Erickson, T., Kellogg, W.A.: Social translucence: An approach to designing systems that support social processes. ACM Transactions on Computer-Human Interaction 7(1), 59–83 (2000)
13. Fogarty, J., Hudson, S.E., Atkeson, C.G., Avrahami, D., Forlizzi, J., Kiesler, S., Lee, J.C., Yang, J.: Predicting human interruptability with sensors. ACM Transactions on Computer-Human Interaction 12(1), 119–146 (2005)
14. Fogarty, J., Lai, J., Christensen, J.: Presence versus availability: the design and evaluation of a context-aware communication client. International Journal of Human-Computer Studies 61(3), 299–317 (2004)
15. Garrett, R.K., Danziger, J.N.: IM= interruption management? instant messaging and disruption in the workplace. Journal of Computer-Mediated Communication 13(1), 23–42 (2007)
16. Goffman, E.: Interaction Ritual: Essays in Face-to-face Behavior. Random House Inc. (1967)
17. Hatch, M.J.: Physical barriers, task characteristics, and interaction activity in research and development firms. Administrative Science Quarterly 32(3), 387–399 (1987)
18. Hsieh, G., Hudson, S.E., Kraut, R.: Using tags to assist near-synchronous communication. In: CHI. ACM Press, New York (2008)
19. Hsieh, H.F., Shannon, S.E.: Three approaches to qualitative content analysis. Qualitative Health Research 15(9), 12–77 (2005)
20. Isaacs, E., Walendowski, A., Whittaker, S., Schiano, D.J., Kamm, C.: The character, functions, and styles of instant messaging in the workplace. In: CSCW, pp. 11–22. ACM Press, New York (2002)
21. Latorella, K.A.: Investigating Interruptions: Implications for Flightdeck Performance. PhD thesis, State University of New York at Buffalo (1996)
22. McEwan, G., Greenberg, S.: Community bar: Designing for awareness and interaction. In: CHI. ACM Press, New York (2005)
23. McFarlane, D.C., Latorella, K.A.: The scope and importance of human interruption in human-computer interaction design. Human-Computer Interaction 17(1), 1–61 (2002)
24. Milewski, A.E., Smith, T.M.: Providing presence cues to telephone users. In: CSCW, pp. 89–96. ACM Press, New York (2000)
25. Nardi, B.A., Whittaker, S.: The place of face-to-face communication in distributed work. In: Hinds, P., Kiesler, S. (eds.) Distributed Work. MIT Press, Cambridge (2001)
26. Nardi, B.A., Whittaker, S., Bradner, E.: Interaction and Outeraction: Instant Messaging in action. In: CSCW, pp. 79–88. ACM Press, New York (2000)
27. Palen, L., Dourish, P.: Unpacking "privacy" for a networked world. In: CHI, pp. 129–136. ACM Press, New York (2003)
28. Shrout, P.E., Fleiss, J.L.: Intraclass correlations: uses in assessing rater reliability. Psychology Bulletin 86(2), 420–428 (1979)

29. Szostek Matysiak, A., Karapanos, E., Eggen, B., Holenderski, M.: Understanding the implications of social translucence for systems supporting communication at work. In: CSCW. ACM Press, New York (2008)
30. Tang, J.C.: Approaching and leave-taking: Negotiating contact in computer-mediated communication. ACM Transactions on Computer-Human Interaction 14(1) (2007)
31. Tang, J.C., Isaacs, E.A., Rua, M.: Supporting distributed groups with a montage of lightweight interactions. In: CSCW, pp. 23–34. ACM Press, New York (1994)
32. Tang, J.C., Yankelovich, N., Begole, J., Van Kleek, M., Li, F., Bhalodia, J.: Connexus to Awarenex: extending awareness to mobile users. In: CHI, pp. 221–228. ACM Press, New York (2001)
33. Tang, J.C., Wilcox, E., Cerruti, J.A., Badenes, H., Nusser, S., Schoudt, J.: Tag-it, snag-it, or bag-it: combining tags, threads, and folders in e-mail. In: CHI. ACM Press, New York (2008)
34. Voida, A., Newstetter, W.C., Mynatt, E.D.: When conventions collide: the tensions of instant messaging attributed. In: CHI. ACM Press, New York (2002)
35. Wiberg, M., Whittaker, S.: Managing availability: supporting lightweight negotiations to handle interruptions. ACM Transactions on Computer Human Interaction 1(12) (2005)
36. http://www.facebook.com
37. http://www.jbother.org

Automatic Translation System to Spanish Sign Language with a Virtual Interpreter

Sandra Baldassarri, Eva Cerezo, and Francisco Royo-Santas

Advanced Computer Graphics Group (GIGA), Computer Science Department, Aragon Insittute for Engineering Research (I3A), University of Zaragoza, Spain
{sandra,ecerezo,497328}@unizar.es

Abstract. In this paper, an automatic translation system from Spanish language into Spanish Sign Language (LSE) performed by a virtual interpreter is presented. The translator is based on rules from Spanish grammar considering the syntactical and morphological characteristics of words and the semantics of their meaning. The system has been incorporated to an animation engine in which a virtual character acts as an interpreter that communicates using LSE. The mood of the interpreter is considered, so that the translation and the signs are modified depending on whether the interpreter is happy, angry, etc. The system has been tested with satisfactory results in speed and quality.

Keywords: Sign language translation, virtual characters, animation, emotion.

1 Introduction

In the last few years, the design of computer application interfaces has evolved in order to guarantee the accessibility of applications to everyone. Regarding the deaf community, a considerable amount of work has been done in the automatic translation into sign languages (SL). These languages, unfortunately, are not universal and each country has its own variety. In fact, most of the work done [1] is based on English grammar. This is the case of the works derived from ViSiCAST [2] and eSIGN [3] projects. Regarding Spanish Sign Language (LSE), San-Segundo et al. in [4] have developed a translator based on Spanish grammar that uses VGuido, an eSIGN avatar, but their application domain is very restricted (sentences spoken by an official when assisting people who are applying for their Identity Card).

None of the previous works includes mood. As in face-to-face communication, mood, emotions and facial expressions are an integral part of sign languages [5]. Words can considerable change their meaning depending on the mood/emotion of the speaker. Moreover, communicating in sign language without facial expressions would be like speaking in a monotonic voice: more boring, less expressive and, in some cases, ambiguous. The system presented in this paper is based on Spanish grammar, takes mood into account and has been integrated in an existing animation engine capable of managing expressive virtual characters to perform the signs.

T. Gross et al. (Eds.): INTERACT 2009, Part I, LNCS 5726, pp. 196–199, 2009.

2 Automatic Translation System to LSE

An automatic translation system from phrases in Spanish into LSE was developed as an independent module in C++ language. The system considers the syntactical and morphological characteristics of words and also the semantics of their meaning. The translation of a sentence or phrase is carried out by four modules (see Fig 1).

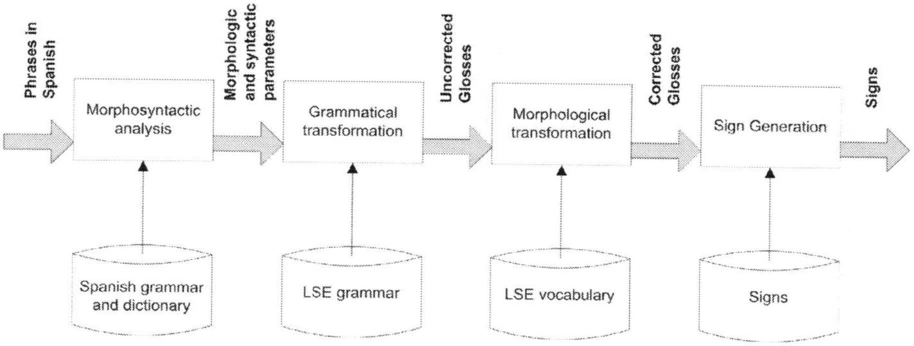

Fig. 1. Translation process

Morphosyntactic analysis: A phrase in Spanish is used as input. A series of parameters containing all the morphological information of the words as well as the relations and syntactical dependencies among them are drawn from it. This module uses the FreeLing analyzer [6], which was migrated to the Windows system.

Grammatical transformation: On the basis of the syntactic information gathered during the previous step, and through the application of grammatical rules, this module generates a series of glosses. The grammatical transformation module considers **mood** when it generates the translation, since mood influences the meaning and leads to the repetition of certain words, such as the nucleus, or to the appearance of new ones (similar to question tags or pet expressions). It can also be the case that certain blocks alter the order of the words to emphasize some of them.

Morphological transformation: Some of the glosses resulting from the previous step could be incorrect. This may occur when the original word in Spanish has no direct correlation to a term in LSE. Sometimes a synonym of that term will correlate directly to a term in LSE, but it can also occur that several signs are required in LSE to render a single word in Spanish. Or sometimes in Spanish several words can be used to express an idea that LSE expresses in a single sign. So, in this step, all the changes in the words are implemented, resulting in grammatically correct glosses.

Sign generation: Once the appropriate glosses have been produced (those which correspond directly to signs), in this step they are translated into a representation format that allows to generate the appropriated animations. **Mood** also influences the way in which specific words are signed. For example, the word "*no*" can be accompanied by different gestures. When the person signing is happy, he or she will move their finger, but if the person is angry, he or she usually resorts to dactylology and signs "N-O". In order to take these cases into account, the dictionary used for final translation of the glosses into signs has been modified, allowing a word to be translated differently depending on the mood parameter.

3 Managing the Virtual Interpreter

The translation system has been incorporated in a scripted animation engine called Maxine [7]. In Maxine, virtual actors are provided with full expressive body, facial animation and with an emotional state which can modify character's answers, expressions and behaviours.

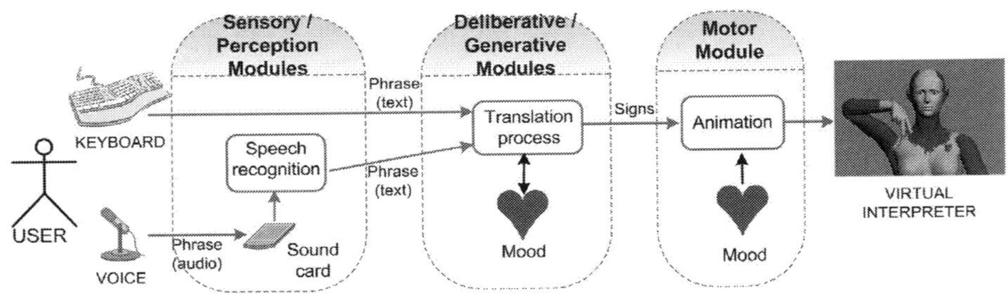

Fig. 2. Integration of the translation tool in the animation engine

The inputs of Maxine can be either written or spoken Spanish, generating phrases (see Fig 2). These phrases are given to the translation system, which returns the signs that must be animated. Also, the virtual character mood can be captured by a webcam [8] and it is supplied to the translator. The output consists in a virtual interpreter playing the signs corresponding to the translation, in Spanish Sign Language.

4 Assessment

Assessment was done by two teachers of a school of interpreters considering the accuracy of two aspects: the translation and the synthesis of the signs by the virtual interpreter.

The quality of translations was tested by means of a selection of phrases usually used during conversations.92 sentences with 561 words were selected. The phrases used in the measurement tests varied in length, ranging from simple phrases such as "How are you?" to more complex ones containing up to 25 words and several verbs along with subordination structures. The results obtained are: 539 well translated words (96%); 526 well translated and in the correct place inside the sentence (93.7%). 15 words were added without affecting the understanding of the sentences (2.7%), and 3 words were wrongly added affecting the meaning (0.6%). The results of the tests performed to check the translation speed were satisfactory and allowed to work in real time. The maximum time was 55 ms and the minimum 15 ms being the average for each sentence 19.59 ms.

Regarding sign synthesis, the results were validated video-recording a real interpreter signing different sentences and comparing with the same sentences performed

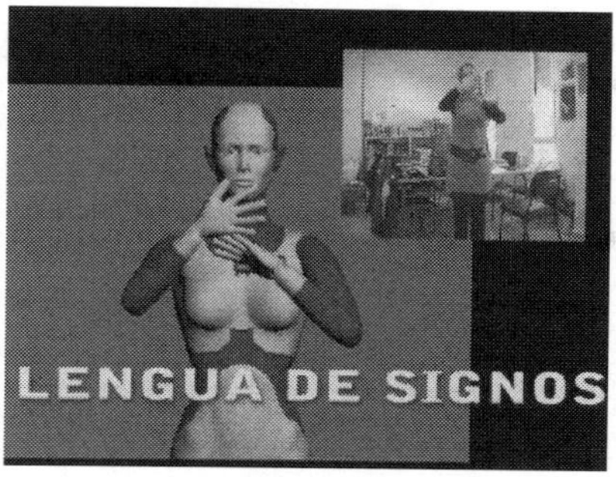

Fig. 3. Virtual and Real interpreters, signing the words "Sign Language" (in Spanish)

by the virtual interpreter in order to verify the visual quality of the sign animations (see Fig. 3).

5 Conclusions

The system presented performs automatic translation from Spanish to LSE and has been integrated in an animation platform that allows the signs to be performed by a virtual interpreter. This interpreter has a mood which may influence translations and signs. The quality of the results has been validated with sign language teachers, but in the near future a more formal evaluation with deaf people must be carried out

Acknowledgments. This work has been partly financed by the Spanish DGICYT', (contract NºTIN2007-63025) and by the Government of Aragon (Cooperation Project between University and Secondary Education Departments 2008-2009 and IAF Nº2008/0574 and CyT Nº2008/0486 agreement.

References

1. Ong, S., Ranganath, S.: Automatic sign language analysis: A survey and the future beyond lexical meaning. IEEE Trans Pattern Analysis and Machine Intelligence 27(6), 873–891 (2005)
2. `http://www.visicast.sys.uea.ac.uk/`
3. `http://www.sign-lang.uni-hamburg.de/esign/`
4. San-Segundo, R., Barra, R., Córdoba, R., D'Haro, L.F., Fernández, F., Ferreiros, J., Lucas, J.M., Macías-Guirasa, J., Monero, J.M., Pardo, J.M.: Speech to sign language translation system for Spanish. Speech Communication 50, 1009–1020 (2008)
5. Olivrin, G.: Composing Facial expressions with signing avatars. In: Speech and Face-to-Face Communication Workshop, Grenoble (2008)
6. FreeLing, `http://garraf.epsevg.upc.es/freeling`
7. Baldassarri, S., Cerezo, E., Seron, F.: Maxine: A platform for embodied animated agents. Computer & Graphics 32, 430–437 (2008)
8. Cerezo, E., Hupont, I., Manresa, C., Varona, J., Baldassarri, S., Perales, F., Seron, F.: Real-time Facial Expression Recognition for Natural Interaction. In: Martí, J., Benedí, J.M., Mendonça, A.M., Serrat, J. (eds.) IbPRIA 2007. LNCS, vol. 4478, pp. 40–47. Springer, Heidelberg (2007)

Towards an Approach to Ethics and HCI Development Based on Løgstrup's Ideas

Sandra Burri Gram-Hansen

Department of Communication and Psychology, Aalborg University, Denmark
burri@hum.aau.dk

Abstract. Concurrent with interactive technologies playing an increasingly large part of the lives of people all over the world, ethical reflections concerning the use of such technology are becoming more and more important. Most often ethical evaluations of a technology are based on either a utilitarian or a deontological approach. Both kinds of approaches to the ethics of information technology appear to be inadequate. This paper suggests an alternative based on the works of the Danish philosopher K.E. Løgstrup (1905-1981). On this basis it is argued that an attitude change is required amongst the developers of interactive technologies in order for new technologies to be developed in a truly ethical manner.

Keywords: Persuasive design, Ethics, Løgstrup.

1 Why Ethical Reflections Are Needed

Computers have become increasingly more pervasive over the years, and a technological approach is being taken to more and more areas where we would previously only have had solutions involving little or no technology. The motivation for this development is an attempt to ease the workload and increase the efficiency of the user by enabling technology to assist with great and small everyday tasks, thus allowing the user to concentrate on other things. However, the complexity of the modern technological society has given rise to a number of ethical considerations. For instance, in most cases the responsibilities for the changes in everyday life could previously be placed upon particular individuals, whereas the responsibility now has to be shared with a large number of rather anonymous developers of various technological devices – and who is then to blame when the new conditions turn out to be inadequate?

Amongst the areas of HCI technologies which in my opinion require special attention, is the field of persuasive design also known as captology. Persuasive design can be defined as a technological design which has an endogenous intent to change a person's behavior or attitude, without using coercion or deception [1]. This definition of captology is undoubtedly meant to clarify that the development theories presented within the field are meant to be applied when creating persuasive technologies which blatantly improve the user's quality of life in some way (for instance. health or educative benefits), without inflicting any negative consequences on the user or anyone else. Nonetheless, the definition is problematic as ethicality of any use of a product is dependent on the perspective of the evaluator. What might be considered ethically

T. Gross et al. (Eds.): INTERACT 2009, Part I, LNCS 5726, pp. 200–203, 2009.

sound to one person may be entirely unethical from the perspective of others. Ethics can, in other words, be considered a grey area, and it is the existence of such grey areas – in consideration of the increasing pervasiveness of HCI technology - which makes ethical reflections essential to the development process.

Similar to many other HCI fields, the ethical aspects of captology have been approached from a highly utilitarian perspective, which may not be entirely sufficient. Reflecting over possible consequences of using a technology or a design is without doubt important when trying to determine ethicality. It does however seem slightly inadequate to evaluate a technology solely on what may or may not be a possible consequence of its use, as designers and developers are not necessarily able to foresee every possible use of a technology whilst creating it. For instance, the developers of the Nintendo Wii console might not have predicted that the controller could also be used for making an interactive whiteboard[1].

For the field of captology, the utilitarian approach appears particularly scarce as the endogenous intention of the technology is the core of the design and should as a result be the main focus of an ethical evaluation, despite possible consequences of its use. Instead of referring to utilitarianism one might make use of the deontological perspective according to which ethics should be based on reason and idea that the notion of a good action is based on general principles and rules rather that an analysis of its consequence [2]. However, as we shall see in the following, K.E. Løgstrup was able to present rather strong arguments against this way of seeing the ethical demand of human life.

2 Introducing Løgstrup's Approach to Ethics

K.E. Løgstrup presented his approach to ethics as based on the so-called ontological tradition. According to this tradition humans are influenced by basic conditions which are inalterable. For instance, that the lives of humans are inevitably entangled with other humans from the very moment we are born, and that any type of interaction between humans results in a relation of ethical significance. Thereby, the third tradition distances itself from the previous two, by rejecting the possibility of evaluating ethics objectively (based on either actions or the consequences of such), and emphasising that ethics must be considered intuitive and open to be influenced by all humans.

Løgstrup argues that humans are born with several characteristic features such as benevolence, compassion, trust, love and open speech, and that these qualities are essential for the interaction between human beings. Caring for other humans is simply part of human nature, or as he calls it, *the ethical demand*. The spontaneous manifestations of life can as such be considered the features within human nature which are generally viewed as ethical, contrary to characteristics such as jealousy, hate, mistrust and injustice.

> "The demand, precisely because it is unspoken, is radical. This is true even though the thing to be done in any particular situation may be very insignificant. Why is this? Because the person confronted by the unspoken demand must him or herself determine how he or she is to take care of the other person's life."
>
> (Løgstrup 1997, 44)

[1] http://www.breakitdownblog.com/interactive-white-board-with-a-nintendo-wii/

The ethical demand in itself is silent; in the way that Løgstrup does not attempt to set up rules concerning ethical and unethical actions. Contrarily, Løgstrup argues that the assessment of the ethicality of actions taken in a given situation must be made by the individual performing the action, in accordance with the reality perception of that individual. Humans must be conscious that any type of human interaction results in a situation where one human becomes responsible for the life of another human being and in accordance with such acknowledgement; humans must strive towards doing to others as they trust others to do to them [3].

Taken into the perspective of technology development, every individual developer needs to be aware of the ethical responsibility which exists whenever a technology is designed and developed. Not only must a given design abide by possible general ethical restrictions and guidelines, but the developer must strive to create a product that will have impact on the user in a way which the developer himself accepts as ethically acceptable. The developer himself should respond to the ethical demand. The ethical evaluation should not be left to a rather distant utilitarian calculation or to an analysis based on rather abstract and general principles.

By defining ethics as an intuitive result of human nature, rather than moral rule based on reason, Løgstrup opposes one of the most recognized philosophers of deontological ethics; Immanuel Kant, who is known especially for introducing the categorical imperative which promotes the idea that ethics, is a matter of acting rationally. Løgstrup makes the argument that ethics based on the human ability to think freely, is problematic as this ability also enables the human mind to justify an action which at first hand does not appear ethical at all. Løgstrup states that humans in general have a clear sense of what is right and what is wrong, but that they also tend to end up in situations where conflict arises between the ethical choice and obligations bound in for instance legislation or profession. In such situations, humans tend to excuse acting against their ethical duty to an extent where the excuses themselves end up appearing as committing as the original ethical duty. The result is a balance between the ethical and the obligated action, which allows the human to choose freely between the two, and thus acting against the ethical duty [4].

3 Including Ethics in the Development Process

As mentioned previously, captology is currently defined as focused solely on technologies which are not manipulative or coercive – hence implying that persuasive technologies must be ethically acceptable. Although it seems clear that guidelines and universal codes of ethics are insufficient, the definition of persuasive technology does to a large extent make perfect sense in relation to Løgstrup's viewpoint on ethics. It seems perfectly applicable to define a persuasive technology as being a technology with an endogenous persuasive intention which can be related to the spontaneous manifestations of life, thus making it even more interesting to draw a connection between Løgstrup's perspective on ethics, and modern HCI technology development.

With the main point of Løgstrup's theory being that ethics is intuitive and personal rather than something based on calculations or abstract general principles, one essential aspect of ensuring an ethical approach to technology design must be to ensure that the developers are constantly aware of their individual ethical responsibility. Ethical reflections need to be an integrated element of the entire design process, rather than looked upon as an additional consideration once a technology has been put to use. In order to do so, ethical reflections must distinguish between intention in design and the use of technology, as the usage more often deviates from the original intention - a point which has been elaborated upon in more detail by Anders Albrechtslund in his perspective on ethics in a value sensitive design context [5].

As argued by Løgstrup, people are inevitably ontologically connected through their actions, and through the development of HCI technologies, developers become connected and as such responsible for the users via the technologies they produce. In acknowledgement of the impact modern technology has on people worldwide, such responsibility ought not to be taken lightly, but the handling of the responsibility is entirely dependent on the ethical awareness of the individual developer.

Undoubtedly, the commonly taken utilitarian approach to ethically evaluating HCI technologies requires supplement by a more nuanced perspective. In addition to attempting to create guidelines and rules concerning the development and use of HCI devices[2], developers and researchers should aim to place ethical reflections as a central focus area within any design process. Acknowledgement of the ethical considerations enables the developers to include them within their own range of the process, thus making it more likely that the technologies they design will evoke an ethically acceptable usage.

References

1. Fogg, B.: Persuasive Technology - Using Computers to Change What We Think and Do. Morgan Kaufmann Publishers, San Francisco (2003)
2. Andersen, S.: Som dig selv - En indføring i etik, Aarhus Universitetsforlag (2003)
3. Løgstrup, K.E.: The Ethical Demand. University of Notre Dame Press (1997)
4. Muckadell, C.S.d.: Løgstrups etik. København, Nordisk Forlag - Gyldendal (1997)
5. Albrechtslund, A.: Ethics and Technology Design. Ethics and Information Technology 9, 63–72 (2007)

[2] For instance the ACM code of ethics - http://www.acm.org/about/code-of-ethics

Evidence Based Design of Heuristics for Computer Assisted Assessment

Gavin Sim[1], Janet C. Read[1], and Gilbert Cockton[2]

[1] School of Computing Engineering and Physical Sciences
University of Central Lancashire, Preston, UK
grsim@uclan.ac.uk, jcread@uclan.ac.uk
[2] Department of Computing, Engineering and Technology
University of Sunderland Sunderland, UK
gilbert.cockton@sunderland.ac.uk

Abstract. The use of heuristics for the evaluation of interfaces is a well studied area. Currently there appear to be two main research areas in relation to heuristics: the analysis of methods to improve the effectiveness of heuristic evaluations; and the development of new heuristic sets for novel and specialised domains. This paper proposes an evidence based design approach to the development of domain specific heuristics and shows how this method was applied within the context of computer assisted assessment. A corpus of usability problems was created through a series of student surveys, heuristic evaluations, and a review of the literature. This corpus was then used to synthesise a set of domain specific heuristics for evaluating CAA applications. The paper describes the process, and presents a new set of heuristics for evaluating CAA applications.

Keywords: Heuristics, usability, computer assisted assessment.

1 Introduction

The process of conducting a heuristic evaluation has been well researched and is widely understood. Currently there are two main research areas in relation to heuristics: analysing methods to improve their effectiveness [1, 2]; and developing domain specific heuristics [3, 4]: this paper concentrates on the later.

The relevant literature contains no consensus over the most effective approach to developing domain specific heuristics. Paddison and Englefield [4] suggests two main methods for developing heuristics; examination of literature; and analysis of data from prior studies. Nielsen [5] used factor analysis and a explanatory coverage process to devise a set of 9 heuristics from a list of 249 problems. In their definition, Paddison and Englefield [4] did not especially clarify the meaning of analysing the data from prior studies, which could be interpreted as conducting primary research or carrying out a meta-analysis of other peoples' results. More clarity is found in [6], which identified three methods for developing heuristics highlighting previous research (Literature), modification of existing (Nielsen's) heuristics and from evaluation results (Primary Research). These more explicit criteria guided the research reported below.

T. Gross et al. (Eds.): INTERACT 2009, Part I, LNCS 5726, pp. 204–216, 2009.

A criticism of the approaches used to create heuristics is the method used for validating the heuristics. The raw count of the number of usability problems identified may not be an appropriate indicator of the effectiveness of a set of heuristics [7]. To validate heuristics, certain criteria are used including thoroughness [8], correctness, coverage and terminology [4]. Correctness refers to the terminology used in the specifications of the heuristics, and whether the descriptions provide sufficient information. Coverage and thoroughness are concerned with the extent to which heuristics adequately represent the domain being evaluated (both terms are used to describe the same construct). Effectiveness relates to the ability of heuristics to capture all significant problems within a domain. Ease of use is concerned with the application of heuristics by evaluators. To establish the effectiveness of a method, the formula proposed by [9] should be applied, however no new domain specific heuristics have had their effectiveness calculated by this method. For example the e-learning heuristic devised by [10] only used literature to synthesise the heuristic set. Reliance on a single method for developing heuristics may result in some important aspects being overlooked or biasing results based on the evaluator's experience.

Within the literature regarding Computer Assisted Assessment (CAA), there is a lack of consensus regarding terminology. Even so, Bull and McKenna [11] argue that CAA is the common term for the use of computers in the assessment of students and the other terminology tends to focus on broader e-learning. Therefore, the definition used here will be: CAA encompasses the use of computers to deliver, mark or analyse assignments or exams. CAA applications range from bespoke applications to off-the-shelf (ready-made) commercial systems. CAA embraces a wide variety of assessment techniques. However, this paper concentrates on devising heuristics for evaluating usability within CAA applications that incorporate *objective tests,* these are questions where the answer is predefined, for example multiple choice questions. With the increased adoption of CAA within educational institutions, there has been a rise in the number of ready-made systems available for delivery of objective tests. These include Questionmark Perception, TRIADS, and TIOA in addition to assessment tools that are incorporated into learning management systems like WebCT and Moodle.

There is limited research surrounding usability of assessment tools relative to studies investigating usability of educational technology environments [12-14]. Usability is important in CAA. Usability problems can cause users difficulties and dissatisfaction with unacceptable consequences. For example, in a multiple choice question with negative marking applied [15], inability to deselect a radio button could result in losing marks. Within CAA, student experience is also affected by pedagogy.

Instructors have preferred pedagogies, but in some instances the technology dictates the pedagogy with respect to test design, as this is governed by the question styles available. Therefore what instructors want may not necessarily be what they get. Their preferred examination may have to be modified to accommodate the constraints of the software. For example, WebCT® in 2005 only offered a limited range of styles compared to dedicated systems such as Questionmark®, therefore, the test experience of the user is dictated by the application. However in bespoke systems, the pedagogical challenge has driven the technology. This is evident for [16], who wished to address issues of guessing within MCQ tests and devised his own system. Regardless of the approach, poorly developed software or pedagogy may have a negative impact for the test take causing problems with unacceptable consequences.

When problems are identified in a heuristic evaluation they are often given a severity rating, using a scale such as the following [17]:

0. I don't think that this is a usability problem
1. Cosmetic problem only: need not be fixed unless time is available
2. Minor usability problem: fixing this should be given low priority
3. Major usability problem: important to fix, so should be given high priority
4. Usability catastrophe: Imperative to fix so should be given high priority

In devising domain specific heuristics, severity rating scales are often overlooked. Domain specific heuristics are synthesized, such as those for the playability of games [18], but complementary severity rating scales are not considered. Evaluators may have difficulty in distinguishing between a problem that is rated as a Major Usability Problem and a Usability Catastrophe when using playability heuristics. When comparing evaluator's classification of problems to severity ratings research has shown that inter-rater reliability tends to be low [19]. This may be due to the difficulty evaluators have in distinguishing the boundaries between scales. Within the CAA domain, the loss of one mark due to inability to select an answer may be difficult to classify using Nielsen's severity scale, therefore domain specific severity ratings may need to be devised to accompany new heuristic sets.

This paper proposes an evidence-based approach to synthesis of domain specific heuristics and associated severity ratings, with the aim of providing better coverage than Nielsen's heuristic set within the CAA domain. This evidence-based approach is also a mixed method research approach, whereby data is gathered from several studies including student surveys, heuristics and analysis of the literature to inform design of new heuristics. While Nielsen's heuristics may be regarded as dated, and inspection methods as inadequate, the latter remains the best option for CAA, where we cannot possibly submit every authored test to user testing, or even thoroughly user test e-learning tools with CAA features before buying and installing them. Heuristics are thus essential for purchasing decisions, as well as for instructor training. Even where user testing of CAA is possible, it cannot be associated with genuine summative assessments for clear ethical reasons, nor can reliable results be expected from assessments carried out solely for the purpose of user testing, since student motivations and moods will differ between true and artificial testing contexts.

2 Evidence Based Design

Reliance on a single method for developing heuristics may result in some important aspects being overlooked or yielding biased results based on evaluator experience. A mixed method approach to developing heuristics may address shortcomings of creating and validating based on a single method. The approach described here focuses on three areas: determining the effectiveness of Nielsen's heuristics within the domain; corpus building of usability problems within the domain; and synthesis of domain specific heuristics. Determining what constitutes acceptable evidence is a key challenge for evidence-based methods. A meta-analysis approach would use sources of evidence including guidelines, journal papers or grounded theory based on primary research, but in each instance careful attention must be paid to credibility and validity of data to ensure corpus quality.

2.1 Method

There are several heuristic sets that can be used for heuristic evaluations; two examples are the Squires and Preece e-learning heuristics [10] and Nielsen's heuristics [20]. Nielsen's heuristics have been applied to a wide variety of domains, including hypermedia browsers [21], edutainment applications [22] and to improve the hardware of musical products [23]. This suggested that the effectiveness of Nielsen's heuristics is worth evaluating in the context of CAA. Therefore in this study, the decision was made to use Nielsen's heuristics as they are the most generic and widely applied. Also Ling and Salvendy [6] suggested that it is naïve to develop domain specific heuristics without first considering Nielsen's original heuristic set. Even so, we anticipated that Nielsen's heuristic set and severity rating scale would need to be adapted and extended for CAA. Thus a series of evaluations using a mixed method approach was used to determine the effectiveness of the heuristic set.

2.2 Research Design

In establishing the effectiveness of the heuristics, a corpus building strategy was adopted with the intention of collecting problems with broad coverage of the CAA domain that would lead to unacceptable consequences. This corpus was then used to synthesise a revised and extended CAA-specific heuristic set. By combining student surveys, heuristic evaluations and literature analysis, the following known factors were addressed to ensure corpus quality:

- A range of CAA applications
- Different question styles
- Context of the examination, i.e., summative or formative assessment
- Cohorts – different year groups of students
- Evaluator Effect– different experience and expertise

In each study, different questions styles were addressed. The question styles predominately used were Multiple Choice, Multiple Response and Text Entry. Using an evidence-based approach, the corpus was developed over several studies and any remaining gaps were addressed through a CAA literature review to create the final comprehensive reliable corpus of unacceptable usability problems for CAA.

2.2.1 Surveys

The first stage involved using a survey method to establish if there were severe usability problems within a CAA application that would have unacceptable consequences. Over 300 questionnaires were distributed to students following CAA exams within the first authors' institution. The initial studies were also designed to form a corpus of reported usability problems [24, 25] that could be later used to establish the effectiveness of Nielsen's heuristic set. The survey method dealt with the following corpus quality factors: question styles; CAA applications and cohorts.

2.2.2 Heuristic Evaluations

The next stage involved a heuristic evaluation (Study A) of a CAA application using Nielsen's heuristic set to establish the effectiveness of the heuristic set within the CAA domain and expand the corpus. The evaluation was a between-subjects single factor study with two conditions: formative and summative assessment. The evaluators examined the software based on the potential academic use for formative assessment to support their learning or summative assessment to award a grade.

The evaluators were 11 HCI practitioners of both genders and a diverse age range. Group X consisted of 5 evaluators and Group Y, 6. Both groups completed the same test but evaluated the application within different contexts, Group X considered summative test conditions whilst group Y considered formative ones.

Questionmark® for Windows® was used to deliver the test; this was a standalone application and did not rely upon Internet access. The application was loaded onto the evaluators' laptops which varied in specification. However, the application was designed to be portable and operate under Windows® operating systems, so the evaluators' experiences resembled real usage. The evaluation dealt with the following corpus quality factors: *question styles* and *context*.

A further two additional heuristic evaluations were performed in order to expand the corpus. The next heuristic evaluation (Study B) was designed to expand the corpus and to improve coverage of the following factors; *question styles*, *contexts* and *evaluator* effects. This study used 4 novices and 4 expert evaluators who performed a heuristic evaluation of Questionmark Perception® using Nielsen's heuristic.

After the first two heuristic evaluations, it was clear that Nielsen's heuristics could not fully cover the CAA domain, so the emphasis in this study (Study C) was on extending the corpus as a basis for synthesising a new heuristic set. The study addressed the corpus quality factors of *CAA applications* (by looking at Questionmark, WebCT and TRIADS) and *question styles* [26]. Over 90 evaluators were used, and were split into groups of between 3 and 5 and each group evaluated a single CAA application.

2.2.3 Literature Review

Two literature reviews on CAA [27, 28], were used as the initial focal point along with searches in digital libraries. The purpose of the review was to expand the corpus to incorporate additional problems that had not been identified in the previous studies. This helped to address further factors which may reduce corpus quality, such as the limited range of CAA applications evaluated. The final heuristic set needed to have appropriate domain coverage.

2.3 Coding and Filtering Problems

In order to manage the corpus, each problem was given a unique code to ensure that problems could be cross referenced with other studies. In addition, each problem was coded with a task code based on what user task they would be performing when they encountered this problem and finally a code determining whether it would lead to unacceptable consequences. The unacceptable consequences codes were based on the implications that a problem would have on a student's test performance. They are:

- Dissatisfied – a student could be dissatisfied, but this is unlikely to affect their overall test performance
- Possible – there is a possibility that the problem may affect a student's test performance
- Probable – it would probably affect a student's test performance
- Certain – It would definitely affect students' test performances

The first two authors examined the raw data from each study and allocated task step and unacceptable consequence codes. Many issues identified were based on personal preferences without real adverse consequences for students, for example '*The order of the buttons previous, next, flag is not right – should be next, previous and flag*'. Ideally falsification testing would have been performed to eliminate problems from the corpus but this is not feasible within the CAA domain as it requires user testing. Therefore problems were filtered based on the unacceptable consequences scale above. Any problem judged to be 'Dissatisfied' was removed from the corpus. This would ensure that the corpus only comprised problems that would lead to unacceptable consequences. For example, an evaluator reported the problem of '*no question marks*'. This was judged to be *dissatisfied* as it would not affect the student grades and was removed from the corpus. Once the corpus was filtered, the remaining problems were merged removing duplicate problems by the first author and an educational technologist. The final corpus consisted of 34 problems which would have unacceptable consequences within the CAA domain. This corpus was then further analysed by two lecturers in HCI, two research students and the first author of this paper. A further card sorting exercise was performed. Each participant had to identify a maximum of 12 themes and match each problem independently to their own themes. Following discussion (sometimes vigorous), the themes were then merged with a summary statement. The final stage consisted of the first author and educational technologist examining the themes, re-examining Nielsen's original heuristic set and then devising an appropriate heuristic.

3 Results

A rationale for the new domain specific heuristics depends on the potential ineffectiveness of existing heuristic sets, which thus must be established.

3.1 Student Evaluations

From student post-test surveys, a total of 22 problems were reported. The problems were further filtered, with any problem judged to be 'Dissatisfied' removed. The 13 remaining problems formed the initial corpus that would be systematically extended to assess the effectiveness of Nielsen's heuristics for CAA.

3.2 Heuristic Evaluation Study A

The results from the first heuristic evaluation are presented in Table 1.

Table 1. Number of problems reported in the first heuristic evaluation

	Group X Summative	Group Y Formative
Raw Data	50	44
Removed	39	32
Total	11	12
Final Problem Set	17	

Raw Data is the count of problems reported by evaluators before any aggregation of the data. *Removed* is the count of problems removed after card sorting and filtering as described in Section 2.3. The raw data contained 7 problems that could not be matched to one of Nielsen's heuristics, indicating that they were not comprehensive for CAA. Evaluators were unable to attach generic severity ratings to 8 problems in both contexts; which confirms the need for context specific severity ratings.

To determine whether a problem identified in the heuristic evaluation was also reported in the user studies, an additional card sorting exercise was performed. A corpus of usability problems from student surveys in a summative context had previously been created, so this corpus was compared with the problems from the summative evaluation by the HCI experts. The first two authors performed this card sorting exercise. Each recorded problem from the heuristic evaluation was compared with the reported problems from student surveys to establish if the same problems were revealed using both methods. If both researchers agreed that the problems were the same, they were judged to match. In some instances, there was disagreement. To resolve this, there was a discussion about the problem and agreement was reached. Of 11 problems identified using heuristics in the context of summative assessment, card sorting revealed only 3 problems that had been identified in the student surveys.

Using the formula for establishing effectiveness [9] the final data was used to calculate the effectiveness of Nielsen's heuristics relative to the student data studies. Survey data is used in lieu of falsification testing, hence there 3 problems identified in both the user studies and heuristics constitute the problems found, and the 13 problems from the survey are the problems that exist, with 11 problems identified via heuristics. This gives a thoroughness score of 0.23 (3/13), a validity score of 0.27 (3/11) and an effectiveness score of 0.0621 (0.23 x 0.27). This indicates that Nielsen's heuristics are ineffective within the CAA domain. However, thoroughness is a maximum and validity is a minimum, since, had falsification user testing been performed, this would reduce thoroughness but could increase validity. This thus leaves open the issue of false alarms. Jeffries and Desurvire [29] suggest that if development resources are used to correct false alarms, then this may make the application less usable. Hence false alarms could affect the validity of the evaluation method and results [30]. Despite the ineffectiveness of the heuristics set, 17 problems remained after filtering and these were then used to expand the corpus.

3.3 Heuristic Evaluation Study B

The results of this study are reported in [31] and the results demonstrated that, in line with other studies, expert evaluators were better at finding problems than novices. An analysis of the raw data revealed that there were also 7 problems that the evaluators could not classify with an appropriate heuristic in a context of formative assessment, and 6 in a summative context. The results supported the finding from the first heuristic evaluation (Study A) that Nielsen's heuristics do not offer sufficient coverage of the CAA domain. The number of problems that were added to the evolving corpus is shown in Table 2.

Table 2. Problems from the second heuristic evaluation

	Summative	Formative
Raw Data	50	44
Removed	13	21
Total	28	34
Final Problem Set	24	

3.4 Heuristic Evaluation Study C

There was a total of 24 groups. Each group identified problems unique to their specific CAA environments, so it is questionable whether five evaluators, as suggested by [32] would find the majority of known problems. Some major usability problems such as browser buttons terminating the exam within Questionmark® may not have been reported with a much smaller number of evaluators.

Table 3. Data from heuristic evaluation of 3 CAA applications

	Questionmark	TRIADS	WebCT
Raw Data	41	51	44
Removed	20	26	23
Total	21	25	21
Final Problem Set	38		

Many problems were unique to a particular CAA application. Only five problems were reported for all three, making it clear that to further expand the corpus, other CAA applications would need to be evaluated. It was not possible to access all CAA applications, thus a literature review would address remaining gaps in coverage.

3.5 Literature Review

The literature revealed 24 problems identified in a range of CAA applications including TOIA and V32. They also identified issues with question styles not identified in the student surveys or heuristic evaluations.

Table 4. Themes identified and merged following the card sorting exercise

Final Theme	Individual themes
TH1. Moving through the test	Navigation x3 Clear Navigation Exiting the test
TH2. Interface / Visual Design	Bad Interface Layout Readability
TH3. Reduce Errors	Reduce errors – auto save Errors
TH4. Intuitive Input	Input Issues Answering questions Input
TH5. User Freedom	Match real world e.g. chance to review and edit objective test answers
TH6. Protecting Answers	Saving Issues
TH7. Access	Access Accessing Test
TH8. Test Design	Unclear Information in test Teacher Issues x2 Test related
TH9. Psychological / Perception	Comparability with paper Trust Stupidity Perception
TH10. Physical	Online Issues Hardware x2
TH11. System Feedback	Provide Help x2 Feedback x3 Confirm all actions Inadequate information for users Feedback and support

4 Synthesis of Heuristics

Table 4 presents themes that emerged as a result of the card sorting exercise. The final themes were then used to synthesise a set of heuristics for CAA. The first author and an educational technologist then re-examined Nielsen's heuristic set and the themes that had emerged to compare and contrast. The purpose was to guide synthesis of CAA heuristics through close attention to terminology before translating the themes into a heuristic set. For example, having a heuristic called 'access' (TH4, Table 4) would be ambiguous and not aid evaluators when using this heuristic.

Table 5. Final Heuristic Set and Descriptions, Retained and Modified Nielsen's

Theme	Heuristic	Description
Same as Nielsen's Heuristics		
TH3. Reduce Errors	H3. Error prevention and recovery	Prevent errors from affecting test performance and enable the student to recover from mistakes.
TH5. User Freedom	H5. User control and freedom	The test should match real world experience e.g. chance to review and edit
TH11. System Feedback	H11. Ensure appropriate help and feedback	System feedback should be clear about what action is required. For complex actions help should be provided.
Modification of Nielsen's Heuristics		
TH2. Interface/ Visual Design	H2. Ensure appropriate interface design characteristics	Interface should match standards and design should support user tasks.
TH4. Intuitive Input	H4. Answering question should be intuitive	Clear distinction between question styles and the process of answering the question should not be demanding. Answering the question should be matched to interface components.

Of the 11 heuristics, 3 were based on Nielsen's original set, 2 were modifications, and 6 were new heuristics specific to CAA. The process of creating heuristics from themes was rather complex. Appropriate terminology was important to encapsulate problems in the way that breaches of a heuristic could be clearly established. For example, *Psychological and Perception* (TH9) did not allow the researcher or educational technologist to establish whether a violation of this had occurred when conducting a heuristic evaluation. This would be influenced by the evaluators' prior experience of CAA or exams and understanding of the technology. However in Nielsen's heuristic set, Aesthetics and Minimalist Design would give rise to similar issues, so therefore the heuristic *Design should inspire trust and not unfairly penalise* was named to capture the psychological theme.

With the initial CAA heuristic set synthesized, the first author and educational technologist then went through the process of cross-checking every problem in the final corpus against the new CAA heuristics. Each heuristic was numbered from 1 to 11 and every problem was successfully mapped to a heuristic. A decision was made to let a problem be mapped to more than one heuristic. During this process, one heuristic was extended to enable incorporation of the problem *Recovery from errors*. Heuristic H3 *error prevention* was extended to become *error prevention and recovery*.

Table 6. Final Heuristic Set and Descriptions, New Heuristics not in Nielsen's Set

New Heuristics		
TH1. Moving through the test	H1. Navigating within the application and terminating the exam should be intuitive	Navigation should be intuitive enabling the user to identify where they have been, where they are and where they want to go. Options to exit should be identifiable.
TH6. Protecting Answers	H6. Prevent loss of input data	When answers are input the data should not be lost or corrupted.
TH7. Access	H7. Accessing the test should be clear and intuitive	Students should not encounter any difficulty in accessing the test.
TH8. Test Design	H8. Use clear language and grammar within questions and ensure the score is clearly displayed.	Text should be grammatically correct and make sense. It should be obvious to students what the score is for a particular question and the scoring algorithm applied (e.g. if negative marking is used). Question feedback should assist the learning process.
TH9. Psychological/ Perception	H9. Design should inspire trust and not unfairly penalize	Students should feel confident that the system will not fail. Ensure test mode does not impact on fairness and performance within the test. For example it should be clear if marks would be lost for incorrect spelling.
TH10. Physical	H10. Minimise external factors which could affect the user	Ensure that there is minimal latency when moving between questions or saving answers. Also ensure delivery platform is secure and robust.

To ensure that the heuristics offered better coverage than Nielsen's heuristic set it was important that each problem could be classified to at least one heuristic, which was achieved.

5 Conclusions

This paper has presented an evidence based approach to the development of a set of heuristics for CAA. Through a process of student surveys and heuristic evaluation a corpus of usability problems was created. However, the process of creating a corpus was time consuming and required a significant amount of time for filtering and merging the data sets. In total, over 300 problems were reported in the various studies and this corpus was filtered and merged to leave 34 problems that would lead to unacceptable consequences for students in CAA.

The heuristic set that was synthesized offers enhanced coverage of the CAA domain. Further studies are required with the heuristic set to establish ease of use, with a focus on the adequacy of the terminology. In addition unacceptable consequences have potential for use within severity rating scales. The reliability of this will be evaluated and compared to establish if inter-rater reliability is greater than when using Nielsen's scale. However, the validity of the new heuristics cannot be validated against user testing (as, e.g., in [1]), as user testing is not well suited to the CAA domain, as argued early in this paper. Claims for the adequacy of the new CAA heuristics are thus based on their systematic inspectable derivation from relevant examples based on over 300 reported usability problems for real world CAA applications (in contrast, the 249 problems used in [5] were far more heterogeneous). The whole process of derivation is inspectable, focused well grounded and diverse, having involved a good range of HCI and e-learning expertise. Given this, we are confident that our new set of CAA heuristics can reliably support CAA authors in the elimination of potential unacceptable usability problems through well informed procurement of CAA applications and revisions to specific objective test designs.

References

1. Cockton, G., Woolrych, A., Hindmarch, M.: Reconditioned Merchandise: Extending Structured Report Formats in Usability Inspection. In: CHI 2004, Vienna (2004)
2. Coyle, C.L., et al.: Heuristic Evaluations at Bell Labs: Analyses of Evaluator Overlap and Group Sessions. In: CHI 2007. ACM Press, San Jose (2007)
3. Korhonen, H., Koivisto, E.M.: Playability Heuristics for Mobile Games. In: MobileHCI 2006. ACM, Helsinki (2006)
4. Paddison, C., Englefield, P.: Applying heuristics to accessibility inspections. Interacting with Computers 16(2), 507–521 (2004)
5. Nielsen, J.: Enhancing the Explanatory Power of Usability Heuristics. In: Proceedings of the SIGCHI conference on Human factors in computing systems: celebrating interdependence. ACM, Boston (1994)
6. Ling, C., Salvendy, G.: Extension of Heuristic evaluation method: a review and reaapraisal. International Journal of Ergonomics and Human Factors 27(3), 179–197 (2005)
7. Gray, W.D., Salzman, M.C.: Damaged Merchandise? Journal of Human-Computer Interaction 13(4), 203–262 (1998)
8. Somervell, J., McCrickard, D.: Better discount evaluation: illustrating how critical parameters support heuristic creation. Interacting with Computers 17(5), 592–612 (2005)
9. Hartson, H.R., Andre, T.S., Williges, R.C.: Criteria for Evaluating Usability Evaluation Methods. International Journal Human Computer Interaction 15(1), 145–181 (2003)
10. Squires, D., Preece, J.: Predicting quality in educational software: Evaluating for learning, usability and the synergy between them. Interacting with Computers 11, 467–483 (1999)
11. Bull, J., McKenna, C.: Blueprint for computer-assisted assessment, p. 168. Loughborough University (2001)

12. Parlangeli, O., Marchigiani, E., Bagnara, S.: Multimedia systems in distance education: effects of usability on learning. Interacting with Computers 12(1), 37–49 (1999)
13. Piguet, A., Peraya, D.: Creating web-integrated learning environments: An analysis of WebCT authoring tools in respect to usability. Australian Journal of Educational Technology 16(3), 302–314 (2000)
14. Berg, G.A.: Human-Computer Interaction (HCI) in Educational Environments: Implications of Understanding Computers as Media. Journal of Educational Multimedia and Hypermedia 9(4), 347–368 (2000)
15. Sim, G., Horton, M., Strong, S.: Interfaces for online assessment: friend or foe? In: 7th HCI Educators Workshop. LTSN, Preston (2004)
16. Davies, P.: There's no confidence in multiple-choice testing. In: Sixth International Computer Assisted Assessment Conference, Loughborough (2002)
17. Nielsen, J., Mack, R.L.: Usability Inspection Methods. John Wiley & Sons, New York (1994)
18. Desurvire, H., Caplan, M., Toth, J.A.: Using heuristics to Evaluate the Playability of Games. In: CHI 2004. ACM, Vienne (2004)
19. Jacobsen, N.E., John, B.E.: The evaluator effect in usability studies: problem detection and severity judgements. In: Proceeding of the Human Factors and Ergonomics Society 42nd Annual Meeting. HFES, Chicago (1998)
20. Nielsen, J.: Usability Engineering. Morgan Kaufmann, San Francisco (1994)
21. Connell, I.W., Hammond, N.V.: Comparing usability evaluation principles with heuristics: problem instances versus problem types. In: Human-Computer Interaction - INTERACT 1999. IOS Press, Edinburgh (1999)
22. Embi, Z.C., Hussain, H.: Analysis of local and foreign edutainment products- and effort to implement the design framework for an edutainment environment in Malaysia. Journal of Computers in Mathematics and Science Teaching 24(1), 27–42 (2005)
23. Fernandes, G., Holmes, C.: Applying HCI to music related hardware. In: CHI 2002. ACM, Minneapolis (2002)
24. Sim, G., Holifield, P.: Computer Assisted Assessment: All those in favour tick here. In: World Conference on Educational Multimedia, Hypermedia and Telecommunications. AACE, Lugano (2004)
25. Sim, G., Holifield, P.: Piloting CAA:All aboard. In: 8th International Computer Assisted Assessment Conference, Loughborough (2004)
26. Sim, G., et al.: Heuristic Evaluations of Computer Assisted Assessment Environments. In: World Conference on Educational Multimedia, Hypermedia and Telecommunications. AACE, Vancouver (2007)
27. Conole, G., Warburton, B.: A review of computer-assisted assessment. ALT-J 13(1), 19–33 (2005)
28. Sim, G., Holifield, P., Brown, M.: Implementation of computer assisted assessment: lessons from the literature. ALT-J 12(3), 215–229 (2004)
29. Jeffries, R., Desurvire, H.: Usability Testing vs Heuristic Evaluation: Was there a contest? SIGCHI Bulletin 24(4), 39–41 (1992)
30. Lavery, D., Cockton, G.: Representing Predicted and Actual Usability Problems. In: Workshop on Representation in Interactive Software Development. Queen Mary and Westfield College, University of London (1997)
31. Sim, G., Read, J.C., Holifield, P.: Evaluating the user experience in CAA Environments: What affects user satisfaction? In: 10th International Computer Assisted Assessment Conference, Loughborough (2006)
32. Nielsen, J.: Finding usability problems through heuristic evaluation. In: Proceedings of the SIGCHI conference on Human factors in computing systems. ACM, Monterey (1992)

Physical Fidelity: Exploring the Importance of Physicality on Physical-Digital Conceptual Prototyping

Joanna Hare[1], Steve Gill[1], Gareth Loudon[1], Devina Ramduny-Ellis[2], and Alan Dix[2]

[1] The National Centre for Product Design and Development Research (PDR), The University of Wales Institutue, Cardiff (UWIC), Western Avenue, Cardiff, CF5 2YB, UK
{juhare-pdr,sjgill,gloudon}@uwic.ac.uk
[2] InfoLab21, Lancaster University, Lancaster, LA1 4WA, UK
devina@comp.lancs.ac.uk, alan@hcibook.com

Abstract. The physicality of digital-physical devices is an essential part of our interaction and understanding of information appliances. This paper draws on the findings of an empirical study investigating the effect of physical fidelity on a series of user trials. Three prototypes of a single design intent were built, the standard of their construction dictated by the time imposed on the designer. In choosing this constraint, the authors present the argument that the most important driver in decisions that dictate fidelity levels is the available and/or necessary time required for making a prototype in order to generate information of the right quality. This paper presents the empirical and qualitative results of the trials, which suggest that there is little effect of fidelity on user performance, but the user's ability to give constructive feedback on the design was influenced by the nature of the prototypes.

Keywords: Physicality, prototyping, fidelity, information appliance, product design, tangible interface, low fidelity prototyping.

1 Introduction

This paper focuses on *information appliances,* devices designed to do one task, but do it well. The design of these devices poses interesting challenges to the design community because not only do information appliances have physical considerations (size, shape, buttons, etc.), they also have digital considerations (dedicated computer running software menus, features, function etc.). The digital and the physical are therefore inescapably linked in information appliances.

Prototypes are used to physically explore an idea very early on in the design process and *interactive* prototypes can be used to explore the digital considerations integrated with the physical form. However, prototypes at this initial stage are inherently 'quick and dirty': they should not require a lot of time to make and should be an exploration of an idea rather than a refined model (what Schrage [1] describes as *'Serious Play'*).

T. Gross et al. (Eds.): INTERACT 2009, Part I, LNCS 5726, pp. 217–230, 2009.

There are many academic and industry research groups working on tools and techniques for rapid interactive prototyping. These include:

- *Paper Prototyping* [2] – a very low tech approach requiring no technical skills; the user usually interacts with a paper-based version of the interface on a physical model and the screen is adjusted by a facilitator, acting as the 'computer'.
- *D.tools* [3] – a toolkit with bespoke hardware and software.
- *Phidgets* [4] and *Arduino* [5] – both provide electronic 'building blocks' to integrate into a prototype.
- *IE (Information Ergonomics) System* [6] – a flexible system of hardware and software linking a prototype to a PC.

One of the underlying recognitions that tie all this work together is that prototypes need to be made quickly in order to evaluate the tangible interactions.

The *fidelity* of a prototype is usually considered to be the resolution (the refinement and detail) of the model. A number of publications have been focused on the effect of fidelity and the advantages and disadvantages of different prototyping techniques. Sefelin et al. [7] looked at the user's willingness to criticize paper prototypes versus their willingness to criticize computer based models. Virzi et al. [8] found that there was little difference in usability data for high and low fidelity models of standard two dimensional graphical interfaces and an interactive voice response system. McCurdy et al. [9] argued for a mixed approach that allowed various aspects of a prototype to be built at different fidelity levels according to the design component being prototyped. They go on to suggest that there are five 'dimensions' or fidelity aspects that can be defined as somewhere between high and low within the same prototype, namely, aesthetics, depth of functionality, breadth of functionality, richness of data and richness of interactivity. So far this concept of mixed fidelity has been trialed with software but not physical prototypes.

Information appliances and therefore prototypes of information appliances are inherently physical. Physicality as a term, is becoming more recognized with two International Workshops on Physicality [10, 11] held recently, plus Don Norman's article on Physicality [12]. Physicality is loosely understood as being the physical nature of something, for example, a form, process or button.

This paper seeks to contribute to our understanding of the nature of physicality in the design of information appliances so that designers can become more aware of when and how to use it. To this end, we explore physicality in the context of fidelity through user trials conducted on a conceptual information appliance.

2 Background

Gill et al. [13] conducted a number of trials on a wireless home phone. They demonstrated that low fidelity physical prototypes can produce similar usability results as the end product, thus significantly outperforming touch screen mock-ups. They went on to test prototypes of decreasing fidelity until they reached a point where the similarity of user test results started to differ significantly from the results produced from the real product. They concluded that if prototypes compromise on the physical attributes of a design, such as removing the tactile feedback of the buttons, then the performance data was affected. They state that "it is not the level of fidelity that is important but rather the considerations of tangibility and physicality".

Lim et al. [14] conducted trials on a mobile phone in order to understand the effect of fidelity levels on usability data. Three prototypes were tested: the final device, a software representation and a paper prototype. All models picked up major usability issues, but only the final device and software models facilitated the collection of comments regarding the concept's comparison with other products and performance.

In our study, we interpret user data from a trial of a conceptual device as there is no completed device to compare it to. The considerations that have driven the fidelity level and its effects on the physicality of the model have been purely time based. The designer had to decide on the best way to prototype the technical aspects within the allocated time.

User trials were chosen as a means of exploring the effects of fidelity and the resultant physicality on the prototypes. The research of Gill et al. [13] and Lim et al. [14] demonstrate that user trials are an effective way of highlighting design issues by comparing low fidelity models with the final design. Those results gave us the confidence to use similar trials on a conceptual device where there is no 'end product' to compare it to. The aim of comparing the prototypes in this manner was to gather data that enabled a review of the differences in the *way* the prototypes function as each of the prototypes has the same *level* of functionality.

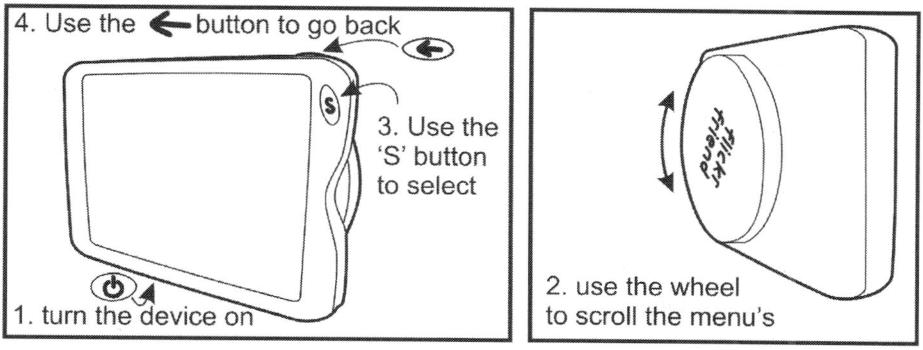

Fig. 1. Different ways of interacting with the device

3 Our Approach

The trials were conducted on a conceptual device. None of the users had been exposed to the device previously. The concept originated from an undergraduate design brief and was based on the design of a hard drive equipped device offering users the ability to wirelessly view their Flickr [15] web pages and store photos. Flickr is an online photo management and sharing application.

Some initial design work was undertaken in order to develop the physical and digital components of the concept, in order to reach a stage where, in a real design process, an interactive prototype would be the next natural step (see Figure 1 which shows the different ways of interacting with the concept). Each of the resulting prototypes used this initial design work as the starting point, therefore only the time to construct the prototype differed.

3.1 The Resulting Prototypes

'Lowest Level': Time allowed = 4 hours (actual time taken = 3 hours 30 minutes)
Method used: Paper prototyping

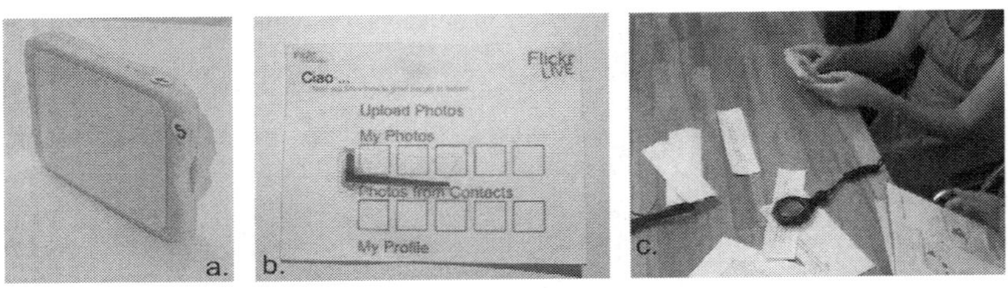

Fig. 2. Lowest level prototype: a) the foam model, b) a paper screen c) the trial set up

As noted earlier, Paper Prototyping is a very simple technique which provides a very fast method for creating low fidelity prototypes. A foam model was constructed to create the physical form to scale. The foam was sanded to produce a smooth finish with white cardboard depicting the buttons and screen (Fig. 2a). For the digital aspect a series of paper screens were created with a small red box to indicate which menu item is active (Fig. 2b). The participant held the physical model, the facilitator changed the screens and adjusted the 'select box' during user trials (Fig. 2c).

'Mid Level': Time allowed = 14 hours (actual time taken = 12 hours)
Method used: IE System

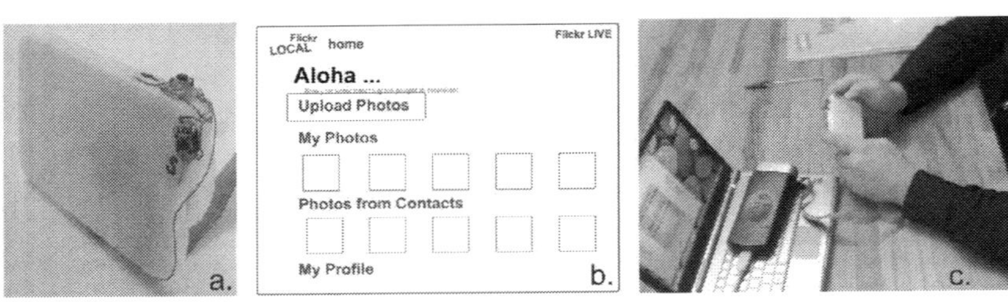

Fig. 3. Mid level prototype: a) the FDM model b) the basic flash interface c) the trial set up

The IE System was chosen to create the mid level prototype due to the simplicity it offered. The system allows a PC to receive keyboard inputs so that when a user interacts with a switch in the physical model, the PC will respond to the perceived keyboard input and a keyboard-triggered GUI is activated on the PC. A model was created in a Computer Aided Design (CAD) system and was constructed to scale using a Fused Deposition Modeling (FDM) machine (Fig. 3a). FDM is a rapid prototyping technique where the machine builds the material up layer by layer. A basic menu structure was created in Adobe Flash (Fig. 3b). The Flash animation used keyboard presses activated by off-the-shelf buttons for the screen changes, these were crudely tacked onto the outside of the model and a mechanical rotary dial was glued inside the model for the 'wheel' interaction. For the trial, the physical model was connected, with a cable, to a PC via the IE Unit (Fig. 3c) and the visual feedback was on a desktop monitor.

'Highest Level': Time allowed = 5 days (actual time taken = 5 days)
Method used: IE system and Phidgets

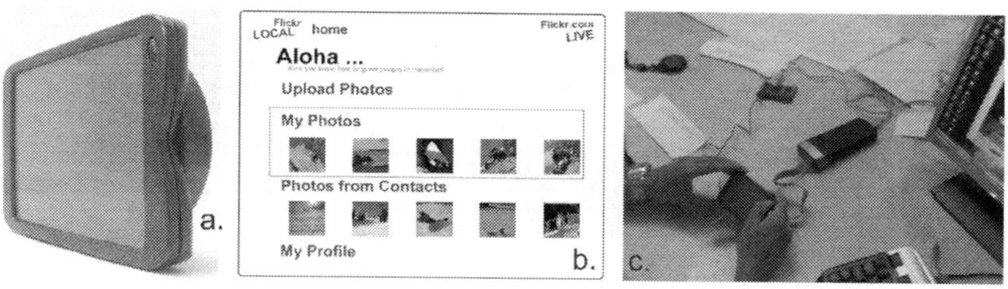

Fig. 4. Highest level prototype: a) the sprayed FDM model b) the flash interface c) the trial set up

The extra time allowed for the highest level prototype was used to develop the following three areas: the prototype was given a realistic finish, the wheel interaction was made to feel smooth and the Flash animation was developed to operate more like the intended design. Again a CAD model was created with design details such as shaped buttons and ports included. Once the FDM model had been made it was sanded and sprayed (Fig. 4a). Dome switches that produce positive tactile feedback with a low profile were used for the buttons triggering the Flash animation through the IE Unit. The smooth feeling analogue dial was an off-the-shelf Phidget component. This reflected the intended physical-digital interaction of the design intent better than the rotary dial used in the mid level prototype. The Flash animation had more realistic menus and a smoother transition between screens (Fig. 4b). For this trial, the physical model needed to be connected through both an IE Unit and a Phidget Interface Kit with wires (Fig. 4c), and the visual feedback was on a desktop monitor.

3.2 Initial Analysis of the Prototypes Created

The resulting prototypes differed considerably and their properties are reviewed in relation to McCurdy et al. [9] five dimensions of fidelity, as shown in Table 1. A similar technique is applied in Table 2 to analyse the subsequent effects on physicality, which are considered to fall under two areas: the physicality of the device itself (e.g. form, finish, weight) and the physicality of the interaction (feel of the buttons and wheel in this case).

Table 1. Properties of each prototype in relation to the five dimensions of fidelity (McCurdy et al. [9])

Dimension of fidelity	Driving factors	Lowest level 3 hrs 30min	Mid level 12 hours	Highest level 5 days
Aesthetics	Model material Model finish	**Blue foam** (both material and finish differ considerably from intended design)	**Unfinished FDM** (similar material but finish differs considerably from intended design)	**Sanded & sprayed FDM** (similar material and finish to intended design)
Richness of interactivity	Wheel mechanism	**Free rotating** (similar to intended design but no real-time feedback given)	**'Clunky', clicking mechanism with end points** (very different from intended design but gives real-time feedback)	**Smooth mechanism with end points** (very similar to intended design and gives real-time feedback)
	Buttons	**Cardboard representations** (very different in feel and aesthetics from intended design)	**Switches tacked onto model** (very different to intended design but gives real-time feedback)	**Integrated switches** (very similar to intended design in look and feel gives real-time feedback)
	Screen operation	**Paper screens** (no real-time feedback so very different from intended design)	**Basic Flash animation** (real-time feedback but sketchy interface, differs slightly from intended design)	**More advanced Flash animation** (real-time feedback and graphics similar to intended design)
Depth of functionality	Screen operation	All have identical features enabled, feature will appear 'unavailable' if it is not part of a task		
Breadth of Functionality	Screen operation	All have identical menu structures, the tasks chosen highlighted the breadth of functionality in the intended design		
Richness of Data	Data used	**Sketch data used** (different from intended design)	**Sketch data used** (different from intended design)	**Photos used** (very similar to intended design)

Table 2. Properties of each prototype in relation to the areas of physicality

Area of Physicality	Driving factors	Lowest level 3hrs 30min	Mid level 12 hours	Highest level 5 days
Physicality of the device	Scale Model material Screen material Weight	**1:1, made from blue foam with a cardboard screen** (form is very similar to intended design, finish and weight is considerably different)	**1:1, unfinished FDM with screen placement suggested on model (no colour difference)** (form is very similar to intended design, weight and finish are considerably different)	**1:1, finished and sprayed FDM with a colour difference depicting the screen** (form and surface finish is very similar to intended design, weight is different)
Physicality of the interaction	Wheel mechanism	**Wheel freely rotates** (as intended in design) **with no real-time physical or digital feedback** (extremely different from intended design)	**Mechanism feels clunky and cannot rotate continuously** (considerably different from intended design) **gives real-time physical** (not part of intended design) **and digital feedback** (part of intended design)	**Mechanism feels smooth** (very similar to intended design), **cannot rotate continuously** (not part of intended design) **gives real-time physical and digital feedback** (similar to intended design)
	Buttons	**Buttons are depicted with cardboard and give no physical or digital feedback** (very different to intended design)	**Buttons are off-the-shelf and tacked onto the model** (very different to intended design) **but give real-time physical and digital feedback** (similar to intended design).	**Buttons are integrated dome switches with real-time digital and physical feedback** (very similar to intended design)

4 Method

The set of trials and rating scale used to classify the severity of problems, was based on recommendations by Redish et al. [16]. Participants were divided into three independent groups, with each group using one level of prototype (low, mid or high). Each participant was given a series of 5 scripted tasks [17]:

Task 1: turn the device on
Task 2: find a photo on the *Flickr* website
Task 3: find a friend photo on the *Flickr* website
Task 4: find a photo from the hard-drive
Task 5: transfer a photo from a camera

4.1 Structure of the Trials

The following structure was applied to every participant for each of the three prototypes trialed:

i. Participant fills in a demographic questionnaire covering age and gender plus existing technology usage. Note the prototype is not in sight at this stage.
ii. Participant is given a written description of the product.
iii. Facilitator uncovers the model and records if the participant picks it up and her reaction in relation to the fidelity of the aesthetics.
iv. Participant is given the 5 tasks (as described above) to carry out. Facilitator records the time taken for each task and whether the user experienced a success, minor problem, serious problem, or a catastrophe (see Table 3).
v. Participant fills in a questionnaire and is asked to rate certain aspects of their experience with the device.

4.2 The Empirical Study

A pilot study was first carried out with 9 undergraduate participants from the University of Wales Institute, Cardiff (UWIC), which uncovered some problems, including hardware stability issues, and these were then fixed.

The main study was conducted using 48 participants recruited from UWIC staff who have used digital cameras (including cameras on their mobile phones). The participants were divided into three groups of 16, one for each fidelity level, to eliminate possible learning effects. 23 females and 25 males were trialed with ages ranging from 19 to 50, thus an average age of 29. All trials were videotaped for further qualitative analysis.

5 Quantitative Analysis

The quantitative data of interest is the 'performance' data, which shows whether the task was a success, had minor or major problems or was a catastrophe. The data was recorded at the time of each trial based on the criteria shown in Table 3.

Table 3. Description of performance rating and examples

Performance rating	Definition	Examples
Success	Task completed without error	User finds all the correct buttons and menus when needed
Minor problem	Task completed with small error	User goes into the wrong menu, user cannot find a button
Major problem	Task completed with major error/s	User repeatedly tries the wrong menus or buttons
Catastrophe	Task is not completed	User has not completed a task (even if he/she thinks they have), user gives up.

The quantitative analysis was conducted in order compare the results of the prototypes for each of the separate tasks (repeated measures). The performance data was converted into interval data (3 = success; 2 = minor problem; 1 = major problem; 0 = catastrophe) and analysis was conducted using a 3 (prototype level) by 5 (tasks) mixed analysis of variance (ANOVA) with the alpha level set to 0.05.

Figure 5 shows the performance data, a line has been included between the marks to aid interpretation of the graph. No significant overall differences were found between the prototypes. The plots suggest that the prototypes performed similarly for

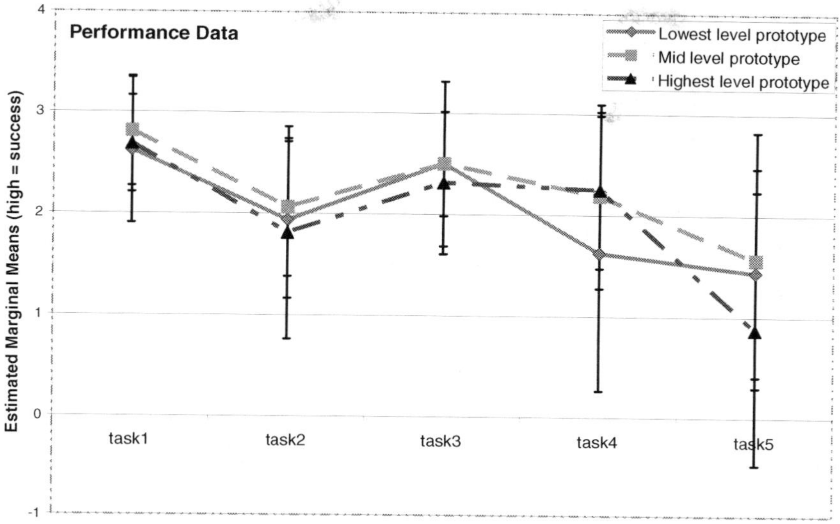

Fig. 5. Performance ratings for each of the 5 tasks as a function of device type

Tasks 1-3, but Tasks 4 & 5 appear to show some differences. Upon further analysis (simple effects) these differences were found to be not significant.

The quantitative data on its own did not reveal any differences, which suggests that neither differences in physicality nor in fidelity have an effect, or that this is not a reliable way of analyzing this effect.

6 Qualitative Analysis

The qualitative analysis was conducted by reviewing the video recordings of each participant after the trials. The qualitative analysis was twofold: firstly, identifying problems that participants may have encountered while performing each task (Part 1 Analysis) and secondly, assessing whether participants were influenced by the fidelity and physicality of the prototypes (Part 2 Analysis).

Part 1 Analysis: This was conducted to find out where participants were having problems performing each task (*types of usability problems*). During the trials, the main errors were observed and noted in a table. Later, while reviewing the video, each error made by the participant was recorded. If an error had not been listed before, it was added to the table. However, if a participant kept repeating the same error, it was recorded several times, this highlighted particular areas of concern. The errors were then condensed into four problem areas, which we identified as being of hindrance to a user in completing a task. The problems areas are:

a. Unclear meanings of symbols
b. Difficulty locating appropriate interface elements
c. Unexpected feedback from software (mental model mismatch)
d. Unintentional interaction with software (wanted to interact in a way that was not intended)

Table 4. Number of times usability problems occurred at different prototype level

Task	Usability problems	Prototype level		
		low	med	high
1	Locating appropriate interface element	9	4	9
	Got it right first time	12	14	11
2	Unclear meanings of symbols	2	1	5
	Locating appropriate interface element	32	13	18
	Unexpected feedback from software (mental model mismatch)	2	6	18
	Unintentional interaction with software	4	0	9
	Got it right first time	2	5	6
3	Unclear meanings of symbols	2	4	1
	Locating appropriate interface element	2	2	8
	Unexpected feedback from software (mental model mismatch)	12	2	16
	Got it right first time	10	9	8
4	Locating appropriate interface element	2	0	2
	Unexpected feedback from software (mental model mismatch)	22	17	12
	Unintentional interaction with software	6	4	4
	Got it right first time	7	8	6
5	Locating appropriate interface element	0	8	3
	Unexpected feedback from software (mental model mismatch)	23	18	16
	Unintentional interaction with software	1	4	8
	Got it right first time	3	4	4

Table 4 shows the number of times users encountered usability problems for each task at different prototype levels. The results that are of particular interest are those that differ across the prototypes. So, for example, during Task 2 there were 2 problems recorded by the lowest level prototype due to unexpected feedback from the software but. The same task resulted in 18 problems for the highest level prototype. Other notable results are again for Task 2 where users could not locate the appropriate interface 32 times for the lowest level, 13 times for the mid level and 18 times for the highest level. Interestingly for Task 5, there were 0 problems for the lowest level prototype in locating the appropriate interface elements, but 8 problems for the mid level and 3 problems for the highest level.

Further analysis of the problems related to Task 2 suggests that users of the lowest level prototype had so much trouble identifying the correct interaction (32) that there were very few mental model mismatch issues (2). Compare this to the highest level prototype, where users were able to find the interaction better (18 errors), but they had difficulty with the mental model of the device (18). The inability to identify the correct interaction could arise either because of a lack of understanding of the symbols (which were the same across the prototypes) or a complete misunderstanding of the results of that form of interaction. The mid level prototype instead has the lowest number of problems related to 'identifying the interaction' (13) and an average range of problems with the mental model (6). So what could be the reason behind these problems? From Table 2, we can see that the lowest level prototype has no tactile feedback on pressing the buttons (just the facilitator moving a screen), while the mid level prototype has very pronounced buttons that give both tactile and on screen feedback, and the highest level prototype has more subtle visual properties with subtle tactile feedback plus on screen feedback. The number of problems linked with locating the appropriate interface element in Task 5 could have arisen due to the same issues as in Task 2, in other words, users of the lowest level prototype had already made so many mistakes early on that they are less likely to make mistakes in the later tasks, unlike users of the highest level prototype who are still experiencing problems even in the later tasks.

Part 2 Analysis: This was undertaken to assess whether participants were affected by the fidelity and physicality of the prototypes based on the related comments made, for example, 'wheel mapping not natural'. A similar recording procedure was followed as in Part 1 Analysis using the errors noted during the trials plus the video review. The comments were then sorted and the ones related to the following areas were selected:

1. physicality of the device (e.g. size in the hand, screen position and size)
2. physicality of the interaction (e.g. the button is in the wrong place, how the wheel feels etc.)
3. feedback about the design and idea in general

The results are shown in Table 5. The general feedback on the design and concept is roughly the same across the prototypes. The lowest level prototype seems to differ in the number of comments about both the physicality of the *device* (22 at the lowest level compared to 13 at the mid level and 16 at the highest level) plus the physicality of the *interaction,* 42 at the lowest level compared to 52 at the mid level and 57 at the highest level. These results suggest that the test was set up in a way that entices generally attracted more comments about the physicality of the interaction rather than the physicality of the device. However, the lowest level prototype received more comments about the physicality of the device unlike the mid and highest levels. This could be because the physicality of the interaction was so far removed in the lowest level prototype from that intended, hence it was harder for users to judge this aspect of the design and as a result, they made more comments about the physicality of the device itself.

Table 5. number of comments related to the physicality and fidelity at different prototype levels

	Lowest level	Mid level	Highest level
Physicality of the device	22	13	16
Physicality of the interaction	42	52	57
General feedback on the design and	19	17	18

7 Discussion

Each of the prototypes created represented the same design intent and enabled the same functionality. Time constraints governed the fidelity level and each prototype was tested for usability and physicality issues. The prototypes needed to convey enough information to the users so they were able to get a feel for the design intent of the product. The initial hypothesis was that fidelity and subsequently physicality would have an effect on the users understanding of the product and therefore user feedback and usability would be affected. The analysis of the user trials showed the following results:

1. All prototypes achieved similar results for the performance test.

There was in fact little difference in performance across the prototypes with different fidelity levels (which would seem to agree with the research by Lim et al. [14]). This in itself is an important result showing that in the early stages of the design process, the fidelity level might not have a significant impact. Despite the mid level prototype being physically different from the intended design in a number of seemingly important ways (the wheel clicked, could not rotate 360º and felt very 'clunky'), it still produced valid feedback about the concept. Furthermore, the mid level prototype took less than half the time to build compared to the highest level prototype. Even the lowest level paper prototype seemed to produce usability data in line with the higher fidelity ones.

2. Users of the mid and highest level prototypes, with real time tactile and digital (on screen) feedback, had fewer problems in locating the appropriate interface element.

Even when all the prototypes had the same graphical symbols, the lowest level prototype users had a lot of problems identifying the appropriate interface elements. This may be because many users worked out what interactions did by 'experimenting' with them instead of understanding the symbols and thus made their decisions based on the feedback they received. This approach was only supported by those prototypes that had real time feedback, whereas the lowest level paper prototype required the facilitator to find the correct feedback and change the screen.

3. Users of the mid and highest level prototypes had more problems with the mental model of the device early on in the trial whereas the lowest level prototype users encountered these issues later on in the trial.

This is an unexpected outcome. Table 4 shows that, even after completing 4 tasks, users still made errors due to a mental model mismatch for task 5. Users who had real time tactile and digital feedback from their interactions had more difficulty in understanding how the device worked. The most likely explanation for this is that users of the lowest level prototype were so distracted by not locating the appropriate interface element that this overshadowed their understanding of the device. By the end of the trial, users of the lowest level prototype were having less problems locating the interface element but more difficulty in understanding the device (their mental model). This could possibly be due to the users' inability to fully engage with the device and therefore following a 'more luck than judgment' approach.

4. The mid and highest level prototypes gave more feedback about the physicality of the interaction.

This was not unexpected as in order to get valid feedback about an interaction, one needs to approximate the intended interaction, which the lowest level paper prototype did not facilitate.

8 Conclusion and Further Work

This paper has reported on a preliminary investigation into the effects of physicality and fidelity on the prototypes used for front end product design development. The trials suggest that there is no effect of fidelity at the early stage of the design process in terms of user performance, however a deeper analysis is required. As expected, the qualitative analysis showed that prototypes that gave real time interaction and feedback allowed users to get a more realistic appreciation of how the device worked, and also generated more useful comments about how the device feels to hold and to interact with.

From these results, we can draw that for the initial exploration of a design idea, very low fidelity prototyping is a fast and low cost method of getting reliable feedback. On the other hand, if more specific feedback about the intended design and interaction is required, then a prototype that can produce immediate feedback is essential. However, there are many more factors at play and these need to be researched further to inform design guidelines in relation to the needs of the early design process.

The nature of physicality seems to have an impact on the user trials of these prototypes, but a very in-depth analysis had to be carried out to tease out these effects. It would be more useful if such effects could be found and explored using faster quantitative analysis. Further work needs to be undertaken to explore how these effects of physicality can be tested in a quantifiable way and therefore fully explore the wider implications for designers in practice building.

Acknowledgments. This work has been supported by the AHRC/EPSRC funded DEPtH "Designing for Physicality" (www.physicality.org) project which is part of the "Designing for the 21st Century" research initiative (http://www.design21.dundee.ac.uk/).

References

1. Schrage, M.: Serious Play: How the World's Best Companies Simulate to Innovate. Harvard Business School Press, Boston (1999)
2. Snyder, C.: Paper Prototyping: The Fast and Easy Way to Design and Refine User Interfaces. Morgan Kaufmann, San Francisco (2003)
3. Hartmann, B., Klemmer, S.R., Bernstein, M., Abdulla, L., Burr, B., Robinson-Mosher, A., Gee, J.: Reflective physical prototyping through integrated design, test, and analysis. In: Proceedings of the 19th annual ACM symposium on User interface software and technology. ACM, Montreux (2006)
4. Greenberg, S., Fitchett, C.: Phidgets: easy development of physical interfaces through physical widgets. In: Proceedings of the 14th annual ACM symposium on User interface software and technology. ACM, Orlando (2001)
5. Burleson, W., Jensen, C.N., Raaschou, T., Frohold, S.: Sprock-it: a physically interactive play system. In: Proceedings of the 6th international conference on Interaction design and children. ACM, Aalborg (2007)
6. Gill, S.: Developing Information Appliance Design Tools for Designers. In: 1st Appliance Design Conference, Bristol, UK (2003)

7. Sefelin, R., Tscheligi, M., Giller, V.: Paper prototyping - what is it good for?: a comparison of paper- and computer-based low-fidelity prototyping. In: CHI 2003 extended abstracts on Human factors in computing systems. ACM, Ft. Lauderdale (2003)
8. Virzi, R.A., Sokolov, J.L., Karis, D.: Usability problem identification using both low- and high-fidelity prototypes. In: Proceedings of the SIGCHI conference on Human factors in computing systems: common ground. ACM, Vancouver (1996)
9. McCurdy, M., Connors, C., Pyrzak, G., Kanefsky, B., Vera, A.: Breaking the fidelity barrier: an examination of our current characterization of prototypes and an example of a mixed-fidelity success. In: Proceedings of the SIGCHI conference on Human Factors in computing systems. ACM, Montreal (2006)
10. Ghazali, M., Ramduny-Ellis, D., Hornecker, E., Dix, A. (eds.): Proceedings of the First International Workshop on Physicality, Physicality 2006, Lancaster University, UK, February 6-7 (2006)
11. Ramduny-Ellis, D., Dix, A., Hare, J., Gill, S.: Proceedings of the Second International Workshop on Physicality, Physicality 2007, Lancaster University, UK, September 2-3. UWIC Press (2007)
12. Norman, D.A.: The next UI breakthrough, part 2: physicality, vol. 14, pp. 46–47. ACM, New York (2007)
13. Gill, S., Walker, D., Loudon, G., Dix, A., Woolley, A., Ramduny-Ellis, D., Hare, J.: Rapid Development of Tangible Interactive Appliance: Achieving the Fidelity/Time Balance. International Journal of Arts and Technology (IJART) Special Issue on Tangible and Embedded Interaction 1, 309–331 (2008)
14. Lim, Y.-k., Pangam, A., Periyasami, S., Aneja, S.: Comparative analysis of high- and low-fidelity prototypes for more valid usability evaluations of mobile devices. In: Proceedings of the 4th Nordic conference on Human-computer interaction: changing roles. ACM, Oslo (2006)
15. Flickr (2004), `http://www.flickr.com`
16. Redish, J., Bias, R.G., Bailey, R., Molich, R., Dumas, J., Spool, J.M.: Usability in practice: formative usability evaluations - evolution and revolution. In: CHI 2002 extended abstracts on Human factors in computing systems. ACM, Minneapolis (2002)
17. Rubin, J.: Handbook of Usability Testing. John Wiley & Sons, Chichester (1994)

Considering Cost in Usability Evaluation of Mobile Applications: Who, Where and When

Georgios Fiotakis, Dimitrios Raptis, and Nikolaos Avouris

Human-Computer Interaction Group, E&CE Department, University of Patras, Ypatias Str., GR-26500, Greece
{fiotakis,draptis}@ece.upatras.gr, avouris@upatras.gr

Abstract. As computing moves from desktop to outdoor everyday life activities, usability evaluation must take into account new aspects, related with mobility and space. In this paper the effectiveness of established usability evaluation methods is examined through an extensive case study. The usability of an educational mobile museum application was tested using three different methods: inspection by experts, use in lab setting and use in the field. Results indicate that each method uncovers different types of problems at different cost. We believe that a combination of these methods may be worthwhile since their produced results seem to be complementary.

Keywords: Usability evaluation methods, mobile applications, user studies, expert evaluation, lab, field, cost, severity, effort.

1 Introduction

In many cases mobile applications are designed to facilitate everyday activities, related to specific contexts of use. Such mobile applications inherently require from their users not to limit their interaction to the device screen but additionally to interact through the application with the typical environment of use. Since mobile applications support everyday activities that in many cases take place in diverse environments, their design needs to take into account and cope with situations where the user's attention is allocated to stimuli diffused in the environment. Designers need to understand all these aspects and design mobile applications aiming to be embedded smoothly both in the human activity and the environment. An additional challenge is to tackle the problems that inherently characterize mobile technology, such as ergonomics of devices, difficulty with data entry, low processing capabilities, unreliable connectivity, etc., [7]. All these design considerations force us to adapt the traditional methods used for formative evaluation of desktop applications in order to effectively evaluate the mobile ones.

In this paper, we discuss a case study of usability evaluation of a mobile application that involved three different approaches. The application is a collaborative mobile game for a cultural museum. Three different evaluation studies of this application were performed and their findings are discussed in the following sections.

T. Gross et al. (Eds.): INTERACT 2009, Part I, LNCS 5726, pp. 231–234, 2009.

2 Questions Related to the Cost of Mobile Usability Evaluation

Due to the continuous evolution of mobile technology and the extensive competition of new mobile services and applications, their design life-cycle tends to be short. By considering that evaluation is a fundamental part of design, it seems that the optimization of the evaluation process is of high importance. Optimization can be achieved by providing appropriate answers to three fundamental questions related to the *cost*. Cost is perceived in terms of time, effort and efficiency.

The first two questions are: *Who*? and *When*? We propose the introduction of expert inspection techniques in early design phases prior to methods that involve typical users. The hypothesis is that a few experts can discover a significant number of problems and require a minimal amount of human and time resources. Then, after correcting the usability problems that the experts have identified, representative users can be involved in order to evaluate the updated version of the application and identify additional possible usability problems, of different nature sometimes, relating, often, with unexpected use of the application. Although the idea of combining user and expert based methods has already been suggested, its effectiveness has not been extensively verified in empirical research of mobile evaluation studies [5]. Another issue is related to the types of the problems that expert-based and user techniques can track. For example, expert based methods have not received much attention in the literature of mobile usability evaluation due to their inadequacy to record contextual influences over use [6].

The third question is: *Where*? Due to the dynamic context in which mobile applications are used many researchers have noted the importance of field evaluation ([3], [6]). However, some claim that there is little added value of performing the evaluation in the field, considering the required resources [4]. A recent survey shows that the situation tends to change as field studies gain considerable ground [2]. We've tried to answer these questions through the empirical study discussed next.

3 Case Study: Evaluating an Educational Mobile Application

The study consisted of three different tests. Study S#1 took place in a usability laboratory where three usability experts inspected the interface by following a given scenario. The experts interacted with the interface through an emulator in a desktop computer. Each expert coded the problems found according to a predefined coding (heuristics) and a severity scheme. Study S#2 involved users in the laboratory. A team of 8 primary school students were asked to follow the same scenario using the mobile application on a Tablet PC that contained a 2D map of the museum and a simulator of the PDA screen. The students manipulated a virtual character on the map, moved across rooms, selected exhibits, and the consequences of their actions to the mobile application were presented on the simulator. Each student interacted alone with the application. Study S#3 took place in the typical environment, inside the museum. A group of 8 primary school students (different than S#2) were requested to accomplish the same scenario using the mobile application on PDAs. In these last two tests users were asked to follow the think aloud protocol. For each one of S#2 and S#3, three usability experts were asked to evaluate the usability of the mobile application, by observing user activity recorded in the form of logfiles and video. Data analysis was facilitated by the ActivityLens tool [1]. All experts that used ActivityLens had prior experience with the tool.

The three experiments identified 32 usability problems overall. 20, 17 and 18 usability problems were identified in studies S#1, S#2, S#3 respectively. The contribution of each method is shown in figure 1b. Considering the severity, in relation to the users, of these usability problems, we see that the expert based method identified more critical and serious problems than the others (figure 1a). Moreover, most problems found solely by field evaluation were categorized as cosmetic (80%) and none of them as critical.

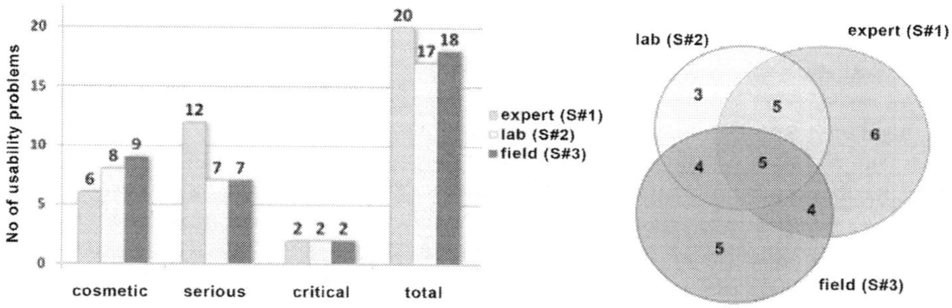

Fig. 1. (a) Severity ratings of usability problems per method, (b) Method performance

If we consider cost as the time consumed to perform the usability evaluation, then we found that the field evaluation (S#3) proved to be the most time consuming method requiring almost triple the time (310 min) than the lab evaluation (S#2) (110 min), while the first study (S#1) required just 32 min. Times mentioned include experiment preparation and analysis time. These differences in time is due to the fact that the experts had to deal with large amounts of observation data and that required considerable effort. The field evaluation required analysis of more sources of observation data (5 video files + logfiles) to capture the continuous movement of users in the field compared to the laboratory evaluation (2 video files + logfiles).

27 usability problems were found in relation to the user interface (84.3% of identified problems), 20 of them were located during S#1, 7 new ones were produced by S#2. From these figures, one might assume that field experiments are useless since they require a lot of effort and produce little results compared to other methods. But, if we consider that a mobile application extends outside the PDA's screen then there are going to be cases that these few and in our case characterized by evaluators as cosmetic problems, might have a significant impact on the design. The field experiment produced 3 problems related to environmental aspects (server delays, certain positions with low WiFi signal and problems in scanning the RFID tags), 1 problem characterized as "using the application in unexpected way" (a group of students developed a game strategy that allowed them to win by violating the purpose of the game) and 1 cosmetic problem related to the position of three RFID tags at a height that many children could not reach. The last, cosmetic for the evaluators but severe for the users, problem proved very significant since it changed many design decisions

concerning the use of RFID tags in the museum. Until then, all RFID tags were placed next to the exhibits. To cope with the identified usability problem some of them were moved lower and that introduced the problem of finding a mechanism to visually indicate to which exhibit each RFID tag corresponded. To solve this problem many different visual cues were placed on the RFID tags and at least three independent tests were performed in order to reach the final solution.

An in-depth inspection of the categories of problems revealed that the ones that are related to the PDA's interface (navigation and consistency problems) were mostly found by experts. On the contrary, the problems that concern the affordances of the interface objects, the visibility of services and the interaction with the surrounding space were found by methods that involved users.

4 Conclusions

In this paper we presented the results from evaluating a mobile application using three different methods: expert evaluation, laboratory and field user studies. The results indicate that the optimization of the evaluation process can be achieved through the sequential application of different evaluation methods throughout the design life cycle of a mobile application. Expert based techniques can locate, at low cost, various crucial usability problems related to the user interface in early development phases. Lab experiments can also identify at low cost many problems related to the user interface and some related to the activity as a whole. The most time consuming and hard-to-apply methods are the field experiments. However, they can deliver significant qualitative results concerning the real practices of users and the effects of the environment on the activity that cannot be found by other methods. As a conclusion, it seems that if all methods are combined they can give an explicit view of usability problems since their outcomes are in great extend complementary.

References

1. ActivityLens, `http://hci.ece.upatras.gr/activitylens`
2. Avouris, N., Fiotakis, G., Raptis, D.: On measuring usability of mobile applications. In: VUUM 2008 Workshop, pp. 38–44. IRIT Press, Toulouse (2008)
3. Goodman, J., Brewster, S., Gray, P.: Using Field Experiments to Evaluate Mobile Guides. In: HCI in Mobile Guides. Workshop at Mobile HCI 2004, Glasgow (2004)
4. Kjeldskov, J., Skov, M.B., Als, B.S., Høegh, R.T.: Is It Worth the Hassle? Exploring the Added Value of Evaluating the Usability of Context-Aware Mobile Systems in the Field. In: Brewster, S., Dunlop, M.D. (eds.) Mobile HCI 2004. LNCS, vol. 3160, pp. 61–73. Springer, Heidelberg (2004)
5. Nielsen, J.: Heuristic evaluation. In: Nielsen, J., Mack, R.L. (eds.) Usability Inspection Methods, pp. 25–62. John Wiley & Sons, Chichester (1993)
6. Po, S., Howard, S., Vetere, F., Skov, M.: Heuristic Evaluation and Mobile Usability: Bridging the Realism Gap. In: Brewster, S., Dunlop, M.D. (eds.) Mobile HCI 2004. LNCS, vol. 3160, pp. 49–60. Springer, Heidelberg (2004)
7. Zhang, D., Adipat, B.: Challenges, Methodologies, and Issues in the Usability Testing of Mobile Applications. Int. Journal of Human-Computer Interaction 18(3), 293–308 (2005)

Is the 'Figure of Merit' Really That Meritorious?

Jarinee Chattratichart[1] and Gitte Lindgaard[2]

[1] Faculty of Computing, Information Systems and Mathematics, Kingston University, London, United Kingdom
[2] HOTLab, Psychology Department, Carleton University, Ottawa, Canada

Abstract. Studies comparing performance of Usability Evaluation Methods (UEMs) led to three standard metrics, namely, validity, thoroughness, and effectiveness, calculated from lab-based usability test results. The effectiveness metric, E = T x V, was proposed as the 'figure of merit' [7] that would give a balanced account of validity and thoroughness. This paper provides an analysis of the formula to caution future researchers and usability practitioners against its use, proposes an alternative formula, and discusses the limitations of the common baseline approach to UEM comparison.

Keywords: Comparative usability evaluation, UEM, metrics.

1 Background

In the early 1990s when usability inspection methods (UIMs) were introduced as quicker and cheaper alternatives to usability testing, there was a surge of comparative studies of such methods. However, these studies yielded inconclusive results due to poor research design [6], a lack of standard measures, and a baseline for fair comparison [13]. Subsequently, three UEM performance metrics based on a common baseline were introduced and employed in Sears' [13] study. These metrics, namely, validity, thoroughness, and reliability, are computed from results of a usability test of the same interface using the following formulas:

$$\text{Thoroughness, T} = \frac{\text{\# of Real Problems Found}}{\text{\# of Real Problems that Exist}}$$

$$\text{Validity, V} = \frac{\text{\# of Real Problems Found}}{\text{\# of Issues Identified as Problems}}$$

$$\text{Reliability, R} = \max(0, R_{temp}), \text{ where } R_{temp} = \frac{\text{1-stdev(\# Real Problems Found)}}{\text{average (\#Real Problems Found)}}$$

Hartson, et al. [7] support Sears' common baseline approach to UEM comparison but raise a concern that neither T nor V alone "is sufficient for *[assessing]* UEM effectiveness" (p.394). They propose a 'figure of merit' for measuring UEM effectiveness that takes into account both T and V, "reflecting a more balanced overview of UEM performance" (p.394). The 'figure of merit' is defined as Effectiveness, E = TxV. Additionally, by way of analogy to the concept of precision (P) and recall (R) in Information Retrieval (IR) and Natural Language Processing (NLP), they propose "a

T. Gross et al. (Eds.): INTERACT 2009, Part I, LNCS 5726, pp. 235–238, 2009.

weighted measure for UEM performance" (F) using the F-measure formula [10] that is a well-known effectiveness metric used in those fields, but replacing the P and R variables in the formula by V and T, respectively:

$$F = \frac{1}{\alpha\,(1/V)+(1-\alpha)(1/T)}$$

where, α is "the factor used to set the weighting between thoroughness and validity".

After a decade of debate and uncertainty of how to compare UEMs fairly, that work [7, 13] is very valuable. Many studies have employed T, V, and/or E [1, 2, 3, 4, 7, 9, 13]. We provide arguments for and against the E formula, propose a new metric for E, and discuss the use of performance metrics to compare UEMs.

2 Arguments for and against the E Metric

The denominator of the T formula above has a constant value for a usability test. T is thus high when the number of predicted real problems is high. Yet, to achieve the latter, more evaluators must inspect the interface [12]. Increasing the number of evaluators allows more false alarms and in turn reduces V [4]. However, to increase V, requires fewer evaluators. More problems are therefore missed leading to a lower T. In short, T and V affect each other negatively. It is therefore unjustified to assess or compare UEMs using T or V alone. Hartson et al.'s [7] reason for a 'figure of merit' that gives an overall effect of T and V is thus justified. However, they did not explain why E should be equal to T times V, nor did they show the derivation of this formula.

The formula has since been used unquestioned. Empirical evidence from [1, 2, 3, 4, 9] shows that the E value is *'capped'* (i.e. it is always lower than the lower value between T and V). This raises our concern because if E is intended to reflect "a balanced overview of UEM performance" by taking into account both T and V [7], why should the balanced value be lower than the lower value of the two? Could these results be mere coincidence?

The above results were not coincidental. Mathematically, the E value is expected to be *'capped'*. T and V values are ratios, ranging from 0 to 1 [13]. When $0 < V < T$, and if we multiply both sides of the equation, $T \leq 1$, by V we get $TxV \leq V$. Replacing TxV by E results in $E \leq V$. Similarly, when $0<T<V$, it can be shown that $E \leq T$ by starting the same process with $V \leq 1$. There is no question that the E value is *'capped'*, but why should it be, especially if it aims to reflect a balance between T and V? We could not find a direct answer in [7], nor in the literature. However in [7], the F-measure was proposed as "a weighted measure for UEM performance" for the same purpose as E, in which case the two formulas should yield somewhat similar values. Our next question is whether the F value is *'capped'* also. A quick demonstration shows that this is not the case. Assuming that T and V have equal weight, $\alpha = 0.5$. Replacing this in the F formula yields $F = 2TV/(T+V)$, in other words, the harmonic mean (HM) of T and V. A mean value of A and B will always fall between A and B. Hence, the F formula gives a UEM effectiveness value that falls between T and V. Why, then, should the UEM's overall performance value be both between T and V (the F formula) and capped by the lower value between T and V? Which one should usability practitioners and researchers use if they wish to use a single composite metric to assess or compare UEMs?

The last argument against the E and in favor of the *F* formula is that E is ill-behaved while *F* is well-behaved. A standard metric should be well-behaved to avoid violation of statistical assumptions commonly required for data analyses. This is especially relevant to comparative UEM studies. A well-behaved variable has a normal distribution and no outliers [5]. We ran a simulation of 2501 values of E and HM of T and V (or *F* when $\alpha = 0.5$) from the 2501 (T, V) pairs of all possible combinations of T and of V values ranging from 0.02 to 1 with equal increments of 0.02 from one pair to the next. This yielded a total of 2500 pairs to which the (0, 0) pair was added. The (0, n) and (n, 0) pairs (where $0 < n <= 1$) were excluded because if one of the two metrics (T, V) is 0, i.e. no real problem exists or no real problem is predicted; the value of the other metric must therefore also be 0. The results revealed a positively skewed distribution and outliers for E, but a normal distribution, with no outliers for *F*. Skewness, mean and median were 1.0, 0.2 and 0.2 for E and 0.3, 0.4 and 0.4 for *F*, respectively. Hence, E is ill-behaved and in one half of the cases the E values do not exceed 0.2; on average, the value was only 0.2 on a scale 0 to 1.

3 Discussion

The above analysis suggests that the HM or weighted HM of T and V is safer than the E formula for giving an overview and a balanced value between T and V. However, the denominator of HM of T and V, T+V, violates a rule for addition. In mathematics, addition and subtraction can only be performed on like terms or same unit of measurements. Although both T and V are proportions, they differ semantically and their denominators are derived from different units. For T, the denominator is all real problems that exist; for V, it is all predicted problems including both real problems and false alarms. If the 'figure of merit' is to have a value between T and V, their geometric mean (GM) is a better option than HM because GM of T and V = $\sqrt{(T \times V)}$ and multiplying unlike terms in mathematics is allowed. The above GM simulation revealed a normal distribution with no outliers and a mean and median of 0.45 and 0.45, respectively. Our proposal for a new 'figure of merit' is hence, GM or weighted GM: $E = \sqrt{(T \times V)}$ or $E = T^{\alpha} \times V^{(1-\alpha)}$, where α is the weighted ratio of T.

Using a common baseline approach to compare UEMs should only be done within the same study, using the data from the same usability tests. This is because it is unlikely that a usability test will reveal all problems that exist or that different tests would yield the same results [11], making comparisons across studies unfair.

How does this analysis affect previous research using this approach? It does not affect conclusions about UEM performance as all figures are relative and have a common baseline. Yet, with E values calculated using the new formula would be higher than those published, fall between T and V, and they do not violate statistical assumptions commonly required for data analysis.

Another limitation of this common baseline approach is that it is performance-focused. However, there are many aspects of usability to measure and, at present, the choice, validity and reliability of usability measures used in usability tests is a pressing issue awaiting future research [8]. Performance metrics alone are not sufficient for assessing UEMs. Future studies should also compare UEMs on other usability aspects such as retention, learning, user satisfaction and perception.

4 Conclusion

We have presented arguments against future use of the E formula and suggested that the geometric mean of T and V be used instead. Limitations of the common baseline approach to UEM comparison and future directions were also discussed.

References

1. Andre, T.R., Hartson, R., Williges, R.C.: Determining the effectiveness of the Usability Problem Inspector: A theory-based model and tool for finding usability problems. Human Factors 45(3), 455–482 (2003)
2. Chattratichart, J., Brodie, J.: Applying user testing data to UEM performance metrics. In: CHI 2004 extended abstracts on Human factors in computing systems, pp. 1119–1122. ACM, New York (2004)
3. Chattratichart, J., Lindgaard, G.: A comparative evaluation of heuristic-based usability inspection methods. In: CHI 2008 extended abstracts on Human factors in computing systems, pp. 2213–2220. ACM, New York (2008)
4. Cockton, G., Woolwich, A.: Sale must end: Should discount methods be cleared off HCI's shelves? Interactions 9(5), 13–18 (2002)
5. Gray, A.R., MacDonell, S.G.: A comparison of techniques for developing predictive models of software metrics. Information and Software Technology 39, 425–437 (1997)
6. Gray, W.D., Salzman, M.C.: Damaged merchandise? A review of experiments that compare usability evaluation methods. Human-Computer Interaction 13, 203–262 (1998)
7. Hartson, H.R., Andre, T.S., Williges, R.W.: Criteria for evaluating usability evaluation methods. International Journal of Human-Computer Interaction 13, 373–410 (2001)
8. Hornbaek, K.: Current practice in measuring usability: Challenges to usability studies and research. International Journal of Human-Computer Studies 64, 79–102 (2006)
9. Howarth, J., Smith-Jackson, T., Hartson, R.: Supporting novice usability practitioners with usability engineering tools. International Journal of Human-Computer Studies (2009) (in press) (Available online February 27, 2009)
10. Manning, C., Schütze, H.: Foundations of statistical natural language processing. MIT Press, Cambridge (1999)
11. Molich, R., Ede, M.R., Kaasgaard, K., Karyukin, B.: Comparative usability evaluation. Behaviour & Information Technology 23(1), 65–74 (2004)
12. Nielsen, J., Landauer, T.K.: A mathematical model of the finding of usability problems. In: Proceedings of INTERCHI Conferences on Human Factors in Computing Systems, pp. 206–213. Association for Computing Machinery, Amsterdam (1993)
13. Sears, A.: Heuristic Walkthroughs: Finding the problems without the noise. International Journal of Human-Computer Interaction 9(3), 213–234 (1997)

User-Centered Evaluation of the Responsiveness of Applications

Gerd Waloszek and Ulrich Kreichgauer

SAP User Experience, SAP AG, Germany

Abstract. This paper presents an approach to evaluating the responsiveness of software applications from a 'user's perspective, which has been developed and applied at SAP AG, Germany, a leading manufacturer of business software. The approach is based on human time ranges and compares actual with tolerable response times, measured using standardized application scenarios.

Keywords: System responsiveness, perceived performance, human time ranges.

1 Introduction

Making software applications highly responsive is a usability and quality goal of utmost importance for software companies: It determines how efficient the users of a software application can be. Usually responsiveness is approached from a technical perspective. At SAP AG, a leading manufacturer of business software, dedicated technical teams measure the responsiveness of applications in clearly defined test environments, using step-by-step scenarios to compare different software versions by evaluating the effects of technical fine-tuning to improve responsiveness. However, these measurements tell us little about how users experience an application's responsiveness. Therefore SAP's User Experience team initiated the "Perceived Performance (PeP)" project to devise a user-centered method and apply it to the scenario-based measurements of the technical performance teams.

2 User-Related Criteria for Evaluating Responsiveness

2.1 The Challenge

The technical performance teams at SAP evaluate the responsiveness of applications by monitoring a number of parameters, one of these being the overall response time for user-initiated user interface (UI) events. The teams use a one-second threshold as a criterion for whether an application achieves SAP's performance goals. From a user-centered perspective, however, the one-second rule does not reflect expectations or behaviors. Some actions should take less than a second, others may take longer. The challenge is to develop an evaluation method that provides better insight into the actual user experience, and to identify areas needing improvement.

T. Gross et al. (Eds.): INTERACT 2009, Part I, LNCS 5726, pp. 239–242, 2009.

2.2 The Initial Concept: Human Time Ranges

The concept of human time ranges that refer to the psychological dimensions perception, operations, and cognition (thinking, attention, motivation) looked promising as a starting point for developing such a methodology.

Allen Newell's time scales of human action seem to be the original source, even though these were published after related work. In several papers from the end of the 1980s to the beginning of the 1990s, Card, Robertson, and Mackinlay applied the time ranges to human-machine interaction. A number of authors, including Jakob Nielsen (1993), Alan Cooper (2007), and, most notably, Jeff Johnson (2007), adopted the original table and adapted it to their needs. In their most basic and cited form, the time ranges are defined as follows:

- 0.1 sec.: Perception – cause-and-effect, animation > direct manipulation tasks
- 1 sec.: Operation – focused man-machine dialog > simple tasks
- 10 sec.: Cognition – focus on task lost > complex or compound tasks

Shneiderman and Plaisant (2004) mention an additional category of "common tasks" of about three seconds. This category is useful because it also marks two effects that "waiting" has on users. After three seconds (according to some authors, even after one or two seconds), users start to feel that the system is slow and loose their task focus. Nonetheless, they can maintain a degree of focus until up to 10 seconds. The authors also introduce a further relevant time: After waiting 15 seconds, users become annoyed. The PeP team integrated both categories into its time ranges.

2.3 PeP Application of Time Ranges

The basic idea behind the PeP method is to classify observed response times according to time ranges, and thus the psychological effects on users of waiting. This

Table 1. PeP adaptation of human time ranges table, including variations in ()

Time Range	**Human Aspect**	**Application / User Interface (UI): Acceptable Response**	**User: Response When Feedback Does Not Meet Time Range**
0.1 sec. (0.0-0.2)	Perception	Acknowledges user input	Perception of smooth animations and cause-and-effect relationship breaks down
1.0 sec. (0.2-2.0)	Dialog, action	Presents result of simple task	Engaged user-system dialog breaks down
3 sec. (2.0-5.0)	Cognition, attention, motivation	Presents result of common task	User has time to think – the system is perceived as slow, the user's focus starts to wander, and the user may turn to other tasks
10 sec. (5.0-15)		Presents result of complex tasks	User looses focus on task and may turn to other tasks
>15 sec.		Presents result of very complex task	User becomes annoyed – the system is detrimental to productivity and motivation

requires extending and connecting the time ranges from 0 to beyond 15 seconds, without leaving any gaps. The PeP team adopted Shneiderman's and Plaisant's (2004) values for the variation of the time ranges wherever possible, but a few decisions could not be backed up with data from the literature. We therefore initially set fairly conservative upper limits for the time ranges: See the first column in table 1.

2.4 PeP Assignment of UI Events to Time Ranges

By assigning UI events to the time ranges, you get a clearer picture of the response time a user with some experience would expect, and thus tolerate. The above-mentioned authors provide some suggestions for assignments, but for practical use in its evaluations, the PeP team created the following list:

- *Level 0: 0.1 (0-0.2) seconds – Perceptual Level:* Feedback after UI input involving direct manipulation/hand-eye coordination, such as mouse click, mouse/pointer movement, key press, button press, menu open/close.
- *Level 1: 1 (0.2-2) seconds – Dialog Level:* Finishing simple tasks, that is, most user-requested operations and ordinary user commands, finishing unrequested and system-initiated operations, opening a window (navigation) or dialog box, closing a window, completing a simple search.
- *Level 2: 3 (2-5) seconds – Cognitive Level:* Finishing common tasks, such as logging in to a system.
- *Level 3: 10 (5-15) seconds, Level 4: >15 seconds – Cognitive Level:* Completing complex tasks, that is, one task or one step of a multi-step task, completing one step in a wizard, completing a complex search or calculation.

3 The PeP Methodology

The PeP methodology is based on three steps:

1. *Preparation*: We break the use scenarios into task steps, or technically, UI events. These we categorize according to what response time would be tolerable for users. This (preliminary) assignment is based on the complexity of interactions, that is, the workload for the computer that experienced users would expect.
2. *Measurement*: We time the UI events and assign them to the time ranges. This assignment is based on the events' actual duration, and thus on the users' perception, not their expectations.
3. *Evaluation*: This data leads to a frequency matrix of tolerable versus observed time ranges (see table 2), which can be interpreted from a user's perspective.

Since for users' perceptions and reactions, the time ranges have distinct implications (directness, appropriateness, slowness, waning or lost focus, annoyance), the PeP evaluation matrix demonstrates a more detailed evaluation of how users perceive the performance of a software application than an evaluation that is based solely on one fixed time limit. This type of evaluation is particularly valuable if an application is considerably slower than expected or exhibits wide response-time variations.

In the (fictional) example, 30.1% fulfillment rate for simple tasks has a strong negative impact on user satisfaction. Generally, we would argue that the fulfillment rate should be highest for simple tasks, that is, tasks that need to be accomplished at a fast pace, and can be lowest for complex tasks. In our regular work, we measure many standardized scenarios. Our typical goal is to speed up processes so that observed UI events are at least as fast as the category they have been assigned to (diagonal in matrix); however, goals may be lower or more ambitious.

Table 2. Example of a PeP evaluation matrix (fictional data)

Tolerable Range	**Observed Range (Number of Times Measured)**				**Total**	**Fulfillment Rate (%)**
Type of Interaction	0.2-2.0 s	2.0-5.0 s	5.0-15 s	> 15 s		
Simple Tasks (0.2-2.0 s.)	22	26	20	5	73	30.1
Common Tasks (2.0-5.0 s.)	3	13	9	9	34	47.1
Complex Tasks (5.0-15.0 s.)	0	1	2	1	4	75.0
Overall	25	40	31	15	111	36.9

4 Future Research Directions

Further validation is needed of the assumptions on which the PeP evaluations are grounded. Currently, UI events are assigned to time ranges on a preliminary basis; a systematic investigation is required of actual UI events and their assignment to time ranges. Secondly, the transition points between the time ranges are based on data from the literature and on heuristic assumptions. These should be verified in systematic experiments involving users who rate the timeliness of selected UI events.

Another idea is to investigate the value of developing performance-oriented guidelines. This would entail defining high-level rules on top of UI guidelines for specific applications. Another idea is to measure the time costs of UI controls and suggest alternative designs to reduce screen rendering times.

References

1. Card, S., Robertson, G., Mackinlay, J.: The information visualizer: An information workspace. In: Proc. ACM CHI 1991 Conf., pp. 181–188 (1991)
2. Cooper, A., Reimann, R.M., Cronin, D.: About Face 3.0: The Essentials of Design, pp. 220–221. John Wiley & Sons, Chichester (2007)
3. Johnson, J.: GUI Bloopers 2.0: Common User Interface Design Don'ts and Do's, ch. 1 & 7. Morgan Kaufmann Publishers, San Francisco (2007)
4. Newell, A.: Unified Theories of Cognition. Harvard University Press, Cambridge (1994)
5. Shneiderman, B., Plaisant, C.: Designing the User Interface, 4th edn., ch. 11, p. 454. Pearson Addison-Wesley (2004)
6. Nielsen, J.: Usability Engineering, ch. 5. Academic Press, San Diego (1993)
7. Robertson, G., Card, S., Mackinlay, J.: The Cognitive Co-Processor Architecture for Interactive User Interfaces. In: Proceedings of the ACM Conference on User Interface Software and Technology (UIST 1989), pp. 10–18. ACM Press, New York (1989)
8. Robertson, G., Card, S., Mackinlay, J.: Information Visualization Using 3D Interactive Animation. Communications of the ACM 36(4), 56–71 (1993)

Evaluation of User Interface Design and Input Methods for Applications on Mobile Touch Screen Devices

Florence Balagtas-Fernandez, Jenny Forrai, and Heinrich Hussmann

Media Informatics Group, Department of Computer Science,
University of Munich, Germany
florence.balagtas@ifi.lmu.de, forrai@cip.ifi.lmu.de,
heinrich.hussmann@ifi.lmu.de

Abstract. With the advent of touch screen phones, good UI design and simplified input methods for applications running on such devices are important factors that contribute to its popularity and success. The goal of this research is to evaluate different user interface designs and input methods for mobile phones with touch screen capability. In order to do this, two prototypes of a simple social networking application were implemented using a G1 phone that runs the Android platform. A user study has been conducted to compare different input techniques and UI designs and evaluate their usability.

1 Introduction and Motivation

Mobile phones with advanced capabilities often employ touch screen as one of the main interaction methods. By adding touch screen capability, it is easier for users to carry out certain actions depending on the task they want to accomplish. However, even with the emergence of such technologies and input capabilities, the design of applications running on such devices is critical for the success of both the device and the application. Usability still plays a big role in its acceptance in the mobile market. It may be difficult to change the design of the actual hardware itself, but a well-designed application can be a big help in order to overcome such limitations.

Weiss [1] provided a list of guidelines for designing user-interfaces for handheld devices. However, these guidelines are very general and do not have concrete examples of UI components to be used based on specific models of handheld devices. Oehl et al. [2] looked into the correlation between the size of a screen's display to the difficulty of the pointing task influenced by the size of the target for touch screen displays using a stylus pen. This differs from our research since instead of evaluating the sizes of target components on the screen, we focus on the actual UI components that should be used in order to easily input information. The investigation done by Hoggan et al. [3] regarding the interaction with mobile devices without physical keyboards resulted in the conclusion that performance improved when tactile feedback is involved.

The research reported here differs from the mentioned existing researches in a way that we would like to focus on investigating which specific UI components promote ease-of-use. The three factors investigated were the overall interface layout, information input and menu accessibility. In particular, the focus of the work was on comparing a scrollable view versus a tabbed view for the layout, direct input using a

T. Gross et al. (Eds.): INTERACT 2009, Part I, LNCS 5726, pp. 243–246, 2009.

keyboard versus input by tapping on the screen through a modal dialog, and menu accessibility through the device menu versus the context menu. The G1 phone that runs the Android platform was used as the sample device for this research.

2 BDroid Protoype Designs

For the purpose of this study, an application called BDroid was developed. BDroid is a social networking application similar to its web-based counterparts such as Facebook and LinkedIn. Features of BDroid includes: an editable user profile, friends list with links to other friends' profile, sending/receiving messages, ability to share pictures, calendar and a search function to look for other registered BDroid users. Two versions of BDroid were developed, each featuring a different kind of user interface design and input methods. Fig. 1 describes the different layouts, input methods and menus used for both prototypes.

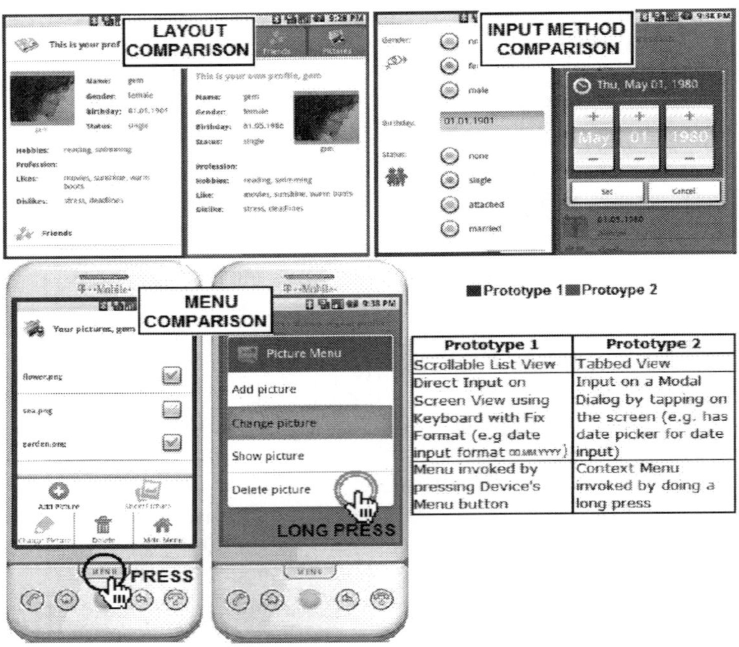

Prototype 1	Prototype 2
Scrollable List View	Tabbed View
Direct Input on Screen View using Keyboard with Fix Format (e.g date input format DD.MM.YYYY)	Input on a Modal Dialog by tapping on the screen (e.g. has date picker for date input)
Menu invoked by pressing Device's Menu button	Context Menu invoked by doing a long press

Fig. 1. BDroid prototypes and feature comparison

3 User Study Evaluation and Results

Ten people participated in the user study whose ages ranged from 23 to 53 years old (40% female, 60% male). All of the participants own a mobile device, and the average length of ownership is nine years. Out of the ten participants, only 10% own a mobile device with touch screen capability. In terms of experience with mobile device usage,

40% of the participants claim to have very good experience in using mobile devices, while 30% only rated themselves average and the rest said they are inexperienced with mobile device usage. The design of the user study was a within-subjects factorial design. The order in which the two prototypes were used was counterbalanced to minimize learning effects.

In the beginning of the user study, the participants were briefly taught how to use the phone such as accessing the context menu by doing a long press on the screen, changing the orientation of the phone to view the screen in landscape or portrait view, using the hardware components (e.g. keyboard, device menu, trackball), etc. The independent variables were the two different versions of the prototypes, which differed in terms of the layout of components (tabs vs. list view) and information input (keyboard input on non-modal screen vs. tapping on modal screen, context menu vs. device menu). Task times were measured through a logging system within the BDroid prototypes. Qualitative information was also collected in a form of a questionnaire at the end of each set of tasks.

The Tasks. Each participant was asked to perform specific tasks for each prototype of the BDroid application. For both prototypes, each task can be optimally accomplished in the same number of steps and basically differ in terms of how the user interface components are displayed and which components are used for input. The subtasks that we concentrated on looking into and the specific factors evaluated are: navigating from the main profile to the edit profile section (evaluate layout), editing profile (evaluate input methods) and, searching and adding/viewing a user (evaluate menu accessibility).

Results, Analysis and Empirical Observations. For the *Navigate task*, the average time to navigate using the scrollable view was significantly faster (M = 16.40 seconds, SE = 2.56) as compared to the tabbed view (M = 42.80 seconds SE = 13.58, $t(9)=-1.868$, $p<0.05$). This correlates to the users' preference in which 80% of them said it was easier to navigate using the scroll view as compared to the tabbed view. However, in terms of layout, 80% chose the tabbed view.

Through our empirical observation of how the users interacted with the prototypes, the probable reason why it was easier for them to navigate using the scrollable view was that, most of them used the trackball on the device. When the user was grasping the device with both hands when in horizontal position, there was no need to release their hold on the device since the trackball was easily accessible with the thumb. In contrast to navigating with the tabbed view, the user had to move the dominant hand in order to tap the tabs on the screen, or move one of the fingers closer to the screen which was relatively unreachable as compared to the trackball especially when both hands were grasping the device. An exception to easy navigation using the scroll view was when the user tried to scroll using the onscreen scrollbar by dragging their fingers on the screen. The problem with the onscreen scrollbar was that, it was too thin and tends to be occluded for users with large fingers. Another problem which was more hardware oriented was that, the screen itself was not too responsive to the touch.

For the *Edit task*, using the keyboard was faster (M = 108.30 seconds, SE =17.57) compared to inputting information by tapping on the screen (M = 130.00 seconds, SE = 20.72). Again, problems encountered were similar to the reasons previously mentioned which was basically influenced by the insensitivity of the screen to touch.

Other probable reasons why keyboard entry was faster was that, it uses the common QWERTY keyboard layout and also the tactile feedback [3] it provided. Changing the orientation of the device horizontally every time a user inputs something also proved to be time consuming and inconvenient.

For the *Search and Add/View task*, using the device menu was faster (M = 48.40 seconds, SE = 14.04) as compared to the one using the context menu (M = 79.40 seconds, SE = 23.04). Accessing the context menu via long press was also counterintuitive which most users mentioned in the post-test questionnaire.

For the last two tasks mentioned, the average times in which the two prototypes differ were not statistically significant. However, it can be concluded that most users preferred the prototype that allowed the tasks to be carried out faster as seen in Fig. 2.

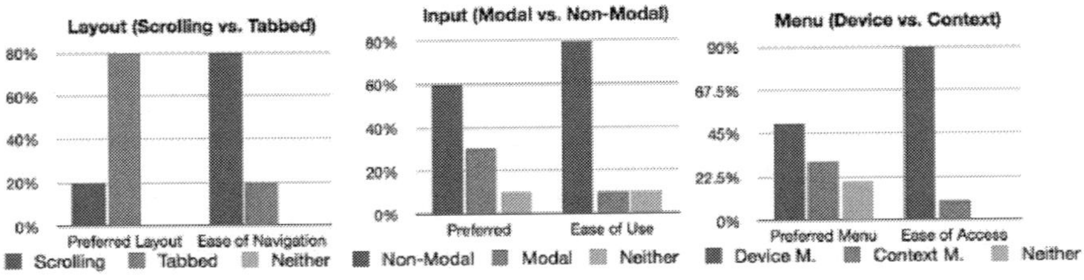

Fig. 2. Qualitative results of the post-test questionnaire

4 Summary and Conclusion

Two different prototypes that feature different styles of UI and input methods for mobile devices with touch screen capability were presented. Evaluation was done in order to see which design provided the user better ease-of-use. However, the user interface components and input methods described in this paper are just part of a bigger work that should be done to create a complete catalog of comparisons of different UI controls that promote usability. Automated tool support which gives the developer assistance on which specific UI elements to use with their applications would also be useful. It should be noted that, even though general design guidelines are helpful, specific examples that applies these guidelines for a specialized range of devices (e.g. using specific UI components for devices with touch screen capability) is more beneficial for the developers and designers whose goal is to create beautiful and usable applications.

References

1. Weiss, S.: Handheld Usability. John Wiley and Sons Ltd., Chichester (2002)
2. Oehl, M., Sutter, C., Ziefle, M.: Considerations on efficient touch interfaces – how display size influences the performance in an applied pointing task. In: Smith, M.J., Salvendy, G. (eds.) HCII 2007. LNCS, vol. 4557, pp. 136–143. Springer, Heidelberg (2007)
3. Hoggan, E., Brewster, S.A., Johnston, J.: Investigating the effectiveness of tactile feedback for mobile touchscreens. In: Proceeding of the twenty-sixth annual SIGCHI conference on Human factors in computing systems. ACM, Florence (2008)

Multi-format Notifications for Multi-tasking

Julie S. Weber[1], Mark W. Newman[2], and Martha E. Pollack[1,2]

[1] Computer Science & Engineering
[2] School of Information, University of Michigan
Ann Arbor, MI USA
{weberjs,mwnewman,pollackm}@umich.edu

Abstract. We studied people's perception of and response to a set of visual and auditory notifications issued in a multi-task environment. Primary findings show that participants' reactive preference ratings of notifications delivered in various contexts during experimentation appear to contradict their reflective, overall ratings of the notification formats when elicited independently of contextual information, indicating a potential difficulty in people's abilities to articulate their preferences in the absence of context. We also found people to vary considerably in their preferences for different notification formats delivered in different contexts, such that simple approaches to selecting notification delivery formats will be dissatisfying to users a substantial portion of the time. These findings can inform the designs of future systems: rather than target the general user alone, they should strive to better understand each user individually.

Keywords: Notification interfaces, multi-format notification, user preferences.

1 Introduction

With technology becoming ubiquitous and our attention constantly shifting among numerous devices and applications, notification technology is growing increasingly important. Notifications may be spawned by an instant messaging service, a calendar system, or myriad other applications that deliver new or updated information to their users. While useful, notifications also have the potential to adversely affect task performance, increase users' stress or frustration levels, and degrade the overall user experience.

Much research has addressed both the *timing* and *format* of notifications as a potential fix to these negative effects of computerized notifications, especially those that interrupt an ongoing task (e.g., [1,2,7]). Such research has focused primarily on the effects of notifications on user *performance* and only occasionally considers user *preferences* for notifications. Furthermore, when user preferences *are* included in an evaluation, they are often used as a secondary measure of a system's effectiveness, after performance.

Because it has been shown that annoyance is an underlying cause for displeasure with an intelligent computerized assistant [10], which may be grounds for discontinued use of such systems, we are interested in accounting for user preferences for notifications. We will describe two methods we use for measuring user preferences for

T. Gross et al. (Eds.): INTERACT 2009, Part I, LNCS 5726, pp. 247–260, 2009.

notifications: *reactive* ratings (positive or negative feedback issued directly upon receipt of a notification) and *reflective* ratings (a ranked list of preferred notifications, provided during post-session interviews).

Our primary hypotheses were that (1) certain contextual features, including specific features related to the tasks at hand and the notification being delivered, will influence a user's preferences for different notification formats, and (2) people will have the ability to accurately report their own notification preferences. In keeping with prior work, we regard as "contextual features" those aspects of notification delivery and a user's tasks that have been found, in various representations and combinations, to influence certain effects of a notification. These features are the cognitive task load, or attentional focus requirements, imposed by the task being performed when a notification is received, and the importance and urgency (jointly referred to as *utility*) of the topic of the notification. We ask whether these features themselves also influence the desirability of several different types of notification delivery formats: (1) occluding, or highly intrusive visual notifications; (2) peripheral, or mildly intrusive visual notifications; and (3) an auditory notification that is presented repeatedly until acknowledged.

To begin to understand the space of notification preferences as they apply to multi-format notifications delivered in a multi-task environment, we conducted a pair of experimental user studies. A preliminary study focused on a specific type of notification: reminders. It asked participants to indicate their format preferences for the delivery of reminders, both in the absence of contextual information and then via a set of hypothetical scenarios. Our second study asked users to rate three different notification delivery formats while participating in an actual multi-task setting.

Our central results indicate that contextual setting does influence the desirability of notification delivery formats, but not exclusively: people's preferences for individual notification formats vary among individuals and across contextual settings. We also found conflicting responses to the different notification formats delivered in a multi-task setting: participants' *reflective* feedback indicated an overall distaste for occluding notifications, yet that particular format was most positively rated when *reactive* feedback was provided. This conflict indicates that preferences for notification interfaces, at least in a multi-task setting, are difficult for users to articulate without access to an explicit contextual description.

Our contribution, then, is the result of a shift in focus toward the examination of *individual* user *preferences*, focusing on the individual rather than the general user, and studying users' affective reactions to notifications rather than any impacts on performance.

2 Related Work

Notifications have been evaluated both in the home and in the workplace. Vastenburg, *et al.* [15] showed that in the home, the desirability of notifications hinged on the contextual feature of urgency alone. Other researchers focus on other features, aside from urgency. In particular, McCrickard and Chewar [12] considered the potential effects of adapting notification delivery formats to contextual setting and inferred user goals. They suggest different types of animations that would be most suitable to different situations.

However, animations tend to be disruptive, as do notifications that arrive at inopportune times. Many researchers have addressed the issue of notification *timing* and how best to adjust it relative to a user's current task, e.g., [1,3]. Iqbal and Bailey [9] first developed a system to detect breakpoints within ongoing tasks, and then they examined the effects of deferring notifications to appropriate breakpoints based on the content of the notification. They found that people reacted faster and with less frustration when notifications were issued at breakpoints than at other points within the task. Fogarty, et al. [5] that simple sensors can provide accurate estimates of human interruptibility such that notifications can be scheduled accordingly. However, there may be certain situations in which the timing of a notification cannot be modified, in which case modifying notification format may be particularly useful.

Two recent studies are similar to our own in their evaluation of multi-format notifications. Gluck, *et al.* [7] studied the effects of correlating the utility of a notification with its relative level of attentional draw. While they also considered multi-format notifications, their study involved one single task per session: not a multi-task setting as investigated in our study. Consequently, they assumed that utility and attentional draw are perceived by users solely based on relevance to a user's *current task*, while we consider incoming notifications to be associated with a particular *secondary task* with the potential to be addressed concurrently. We therefore consider utility to comprise both a notification's level of importance and also the urgency with which the information within the notification must be digested.

Mark, *et al.* [11] studied the effects of different types of interruptions on user performance on a set of office tasks. They, like many of the others described above, primarily considered the disruption costs (here relative to performance and emotional effects, i.e., stress and frustration) of notifications rather than general user desirability of, or preferences for, the format of interruption delivery.

We are thus breaking new ground in studying attention management, with respect to multi-format notifications, with a primary focus on *preferences* rather than performance.

3 User Study 1: Situated Reminders

We performed a preliminary study, summarized here and described in more detail in [16], that laid a foundation for the experiment that is the primary focus of this paper. Sparked by informal interviews with users of intelligent systems, and public sentiment about commercial systems (e.g., [10]) this preliminary study first aimed to characterize notification delivery formats with respect to annoyance. Then, a second phase of the study was conducted to evaluate the correlation between annoyance, or intrusiveness, of a delivery format and its contextual acceptability corresponding to a given set of hypothetical scenarios.

We acquired user preference data from a set of twenty participants. In the first phase of Study 1, participants were asked to rate each of eight reminder delivery formats on their perceived annoyance level on a scale from 0 to 10. In the second phase of the study, participants were asked to classify each reminder format as being best, acceptable or unacceptable based on its content and the given situation. From this initial phase of the study, we learned that our reminder delivery formats can be grouped into two distinct categories based on their relative levels of perceived *intrusiveness*. This categorization influenced the design decisions for our second study, described in the following section. In particular, we note that the set of "highly intrusive" reminders, or more generally notifications, included any notification delivered via an occluding window, and "moderately intrusive" notifications all appeared in the periphery of the screen.

The second phase of Study 1 involved rating reminder delivery formats by their relative acceptability across various contextual scenarios, which sampled the space of high and low notification urgency, event importance, and user attention. It showed, first, that acceptability ratings for reminder formats were more positive when attention requirements were low and notification utility was high. It also showed that there was significant individual variability in the specific types of reminder formats preferred. Finally, it showed that often people expressed preferences for the types of reminder formats that had been consistently viewed as annoying in the first phase of the study. These preliminary findings encouraged us to further examine how preferences vary for different notification formats delivered in different contexts.

4 User Study 2: Multi-format Notifications in a Multi-task Environment

We conducted an experimental user study to explore the relative desirability of a set of three notification delivery formats when issued in different contexts. The study involved two computer games. One game, which was always available to the user to play, was the Memory game adapted from Gluck, *et al.* [7]; the other was called the "Alien" game and was an adaptation of the popular arcade game "Space Invaders" [13].[1] For ease of exposition, we adopt the terminology of Trafton, *et al.* [14] and refer to the Memory game as the "primary task" and the Alien game as "secondary."

There were two sessions of the primary task, during which notifications were issued to alert participants to the availability of the secondary task. Upon receipt of a notification, participants were at liberty to switch to the secondary task or maintain focus on the primary task. Beforehand, we conducted an initial phase of the study that was used to inform our design decisions regarding the primary task load.

4.1 Differentiating Task Load

For this first phase of the study, we needed to establish whether there is a significant difference in the workload requirements of various configurations of game boards used in the Memory task. Each of ten participants played four versions of Memory. In two versions, the board was small (6x6), and the other two versions comprised larger boards of size 8x8. Within each size category, we varied the similarity of the images to be matched: they were either very distinct (different colors, shapes, sizes) or similar (with a shared color scheme or image theme). The order of the boards was counterbalanced among participants, and an interview was conducted after each set of two Memory boards.

---

[1] In our version of Space Invaders, there were no obstacles or shots fired back by the aliens: participants merely targeted and eliminated 2D moving alien spacecraft.

To evaluate the relative task load requirements of the different boards, NASA Task Load Index (TLX) [8] ratings, also used in [1,7,11] among others, were analyzed between each pair of boards using a paired t-test with an alpha-adjustment to account for multiple evaluations per board. We found no recognizable difference, statistically, between the two smaller boards on mental demand, effort or frustration (with all $p>0.4$). However, all other board pairings led to significant differences in these work-load ratings ($p<0.05$ in all cases). Qualitative findings supported these results.

4.2 Multi-format Notifications in a Multi-task Environment

The purpose of our primary study was to measure the desirability of notifications delivered in different formats in a multi-task environment. As such, participants were asked to provide positive or negative feedback for each notification as it was delivered throughout the study.

Participants. We recruited 28 participants (9 female) between the ages of 18 and 49, all of whom reported that they use a computer for over an hour a day. Upon recruitment, participants were informed that they would receive compensation of $5 per hour of participation and a $10 bonus if they were more successful than two-thirds of participants at playing a set of computerized games.

Tasks. Similar to the first phase of our study described above, the objective of the Memory game was to find all pairs of matching images on each game board. Every match was worth 10 points toward the user's total score. Informed by findings from the initial phase of this study above, we divided Memory game boards into two levels of task load: one, the low-focus level, included twenty size 6x6 boards hiding 9 images (such that there were four identical instances of each image hidden on any given board); and another, the high-focus level, included five size 8x8 boards each hiding 32 image pairs that were much more similar to one another, with each matching pair differing only by a few minor visual characteristics from every other matching pair. In the Alien game, the user's objective was to remove as many aliens as possible from the screen during the time the game was active. There were two versions of the Alien game: the basic Alien game, in which all aliens were white in color and worth one point each, and the Bonus game, in which a handful of aliens were colored blue or red. Participants were informed that blue aliens were worth 20 points each, and that red aliens were worth 100 points. We designed these two games in such a way as to model two levels of importance, and with a variable amount of time for which a game is available, they represent two levels of urgency as well.

Notifications. Notifications were used to alert a user to a secondary task becoming available. A notification named the newly-available secondary task (either the Alien or Bonus game) and the exact amount of time for which it was to be available (either thirty seconds or three minutes). This was our method of representing the contextual features related to a notification: importance is high when the Bonus game is available (because it is worth far more points than can be attained in the Alien game) and low when the notification specifies the availability of the Alien game; and urgency is high when the game is available only for the next 30 seconds, whereas it is considered low if the user need not attend to the secondary task immediately.

Notifications were issued in one of three formats: two visual and one auditory. Our choice of visual notifications was informed by the two categories of reminder delivery formats from our initial experiment, Study 1. One visual notification was a large, occluding window that popped up in the center of the screen in which the user was playing the Memory game. The other visual notification was smaller and appeared toward the bottom right-hand corner of the screen. The design of these notification formats was strongly influenced by our initial experiment (Study 1) in which notification formats were grouped into two distinct equivalence classes (based on their relative levels of perceived intrusiveness). A third, auditory notification was a woman's voice dictating the same information that is presented in the visual notifications. We included this notification format to examine an alternative modality for information delivery. Fig. 1 depicts a low-focus board and an occluding notification on the left, and a high-focus board and a peripheral notification on the right.

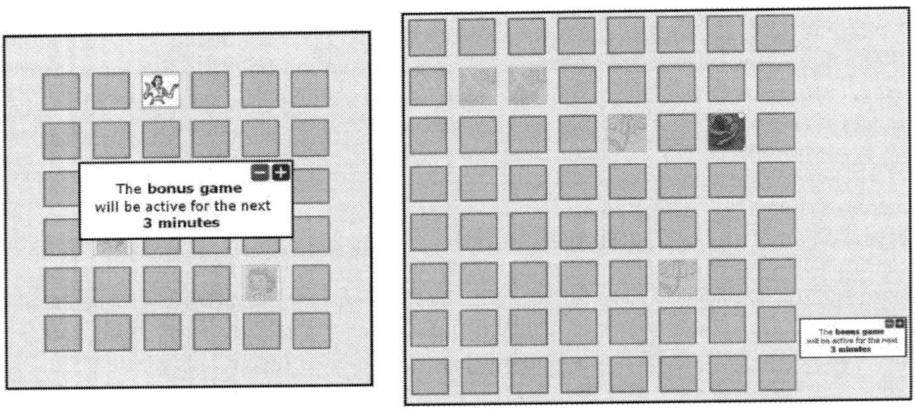

Fig. 1. A small Memory board displaying an occluding notification (left), and a large Memory board with a peripheral notification (right)

Upon receipt of a notification, it was requested that participants rate the notification using a pair of positive and negative feedback buttons. A positive rating indicated a desirable notification format in the given context and content of the notification, and vice versa. To capture the positive and negative feedback that was requested of the participants upon receipt of each individual notification, the feedback buttons (depicted in Fig. 2) were placed to the left of the keyboard: a blue smiling face was used for positive feedback, and a red frowning face was used as negative feedback.

Experimental Design. This study comprised a 2 Task load (high- and low-focus Memory task) X 2 Importance (high, low) X 2 Urgency (high, low) X 3 Notification format (occluding, peripheral, auditory) mixed design. All of the treatments were within subjects, so that user preference information could be compared across all users, scenarios and notification types. We used a Williams design [5] to counterbalance all of the treatment combinations.

4.3 Protocol and Evaluation Metrics

Procedure. Participants were first presented with a consent form, a pre-study demographics questionnaire, and verbal and written instructions for participating in the study. Then they were familiarized with each of the notification formats and administered a practice session in which they were walked through the process of playing the Memory game, receiving a notification, providing feedback, and addressing the secondary task (the Alien or Bonus game). Participants were encouraged to ask questions throughout this orientation process.

Fig. 2. The feedback buttons used for rating each delivery format upon receipt of a notification

Each user then participated in two 30-minute task sessions. One session involved the low-focus Memory task, and the other the high-focus task. During each session, each of twelve possible notifications was issued. After providing feedback to a notification using one of the feedback buttons in Fig. 2, a virtual button would appear in the upper right corner of the screen that, upon being clicked, would start the secondary game.

In addition to the workload assessment, a structured interview was conducted after each session of the study. Participants were asked to describe the desirability of the three notification delivery formats, and to rank order each of them to the degree possible. Participants were also asked whether certain notifications seemed generally more helpful than others, and whether there were certain times during the session in which notifications were more useful. We were also interested in participants' perceptions of their attentiveness to notifications and whether there were occasions on which they chose to defer attendance to a secondary task or ignore it altogether.

Subjective Measures[2]. Along with positive and negative (reactive) feedback ratings for each notification, our subjective measures also include users' responses to the NASA Task Load Index survey, which was completed in the first phase of our study as well as after each session of our experiment, both for the primary and secondary tasks. We also conducted an interview after each session of the experiment, asking participants about their perceptions of notifications delivered during the session, both

[2] Objective measures were taken for the sake of comparison with prior work, but accounting for space, they will not be reported here.

alone and in combination with contextual features of the multi-task environment in which the study was conducted.

4.4 Hypotheses

Our central hypotheses postulated that having access to a user's task context and the content of a notification will be enough to predict user response to the delivery format of that notification, and that users can accurately articulate their notification preferences both with and in the absence of contextual information.

H1: Contextual features (i.e., relative task load and notification utility information) will be sufficient to determine the desirability of each notification delivery format.

H2: Reactive ratings will correspond to reflective ratings; people who indicate an overall preference for a certain delivery format will provide more positive ratings to that format than to others. Furthermore, a delivery format that is favored by users overall (reflectively) will be provided the most positive ratings in a reactive setting.

5 Results

To address our first hypothesis, we analyze participants' reactive ratings in each scenario. Findings are displayed in Fig. 3, which depicts the number of positive ratings (on the y-axis) for the three notification formats in each of the eight contextual scenarios (the x-axis).

It can be noted that, contrary to the findings in the prior study, there is no strict trend in relative desirability from the low-load, high-utility scenario toward the high-load, low-utility scenario. The total number of positive ratings over all three notification formats was fairly stable over all eight scenarios, and it was even more stable when considering only visual notifications (to compare with Study 1): there was an approximately equal number of positive ratings over both occluding and peripheral notifications in every scenario. It is also the case that occluding notifications were almost always preferred to the other notification delivery formats, with peripheral notifications least positively rated in all scenarios. On the surface, this suggests that there is no support for hypothesis **H1**: the contextual features we examine do not seem to influence notification preferences, because occluding notifications are most preferred independent of contextual information.

Most importantly, we also found that there is again high individuality of preference ratings. Here, with only one type of notification style per category (highly intrusive, moderately intrusive and auditory), preference variation is exhibited between participants over the three notification categories. In particular, despite occluding notifications receiving the most positive ratings across scenarios (see Fig. 3), it is not the same set of users that provided those positive ratings in each scenario. Further, in the reflective setting, there was little overlap in the set of participants preferring, e.g., occluding notifications, across the high and low focus task sessions. Finally, for a majority of users, context does in a variety of ways affect their reactive ratings: only two participants in this study had static preferences across scenarios (and in both cases every notification was positively rated). It is thus *not* the case that there is any sort of uniform function from contextual features to preferences across users.

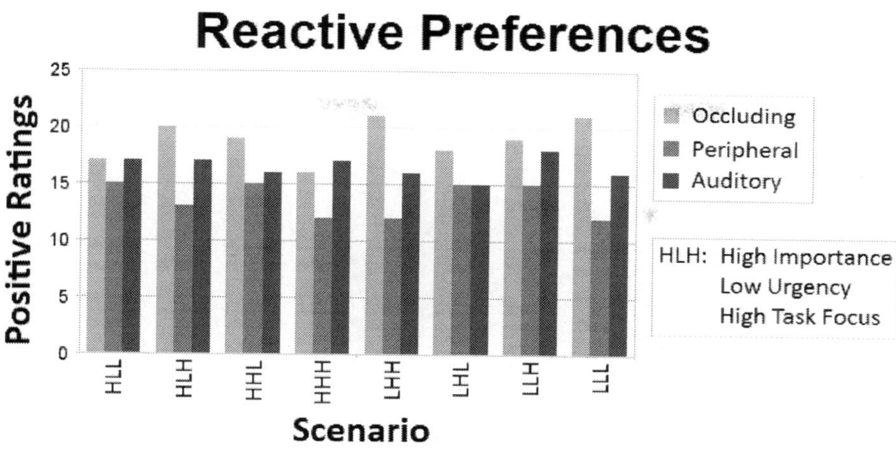

Fig. 3. The number of positive reactive ratings for each type of notification delivered in each of the eight contextual scenarios: {high, low} task load x {high, low} importance x {high, low} urgency. Each notification was rated individually; with 28 participants, any notification in any context could receive up to 28 positive ratings.

To address hypothesis **H2**, we compare reflective user ratings to the reactive ratings in Fig. 3, first on an aggregate basis and then individually. Aggregated reflective ratings are presented in Fig. 4, where ratings are grouped by partial orderings of the three notification delivery formats, as they were rank-ordered by participants during post-session interviews. With twenty-eight participants, we expected to accumulate 56 ranked orderings because each participant was interviewed twice: once after each of the two study sessions; however in two cases preference rankings could not be easily articulated,[3] which left us with 54 total rankings. With this in mind, from here forward, data will report the equivalent of twenty-seven participants rather than twenty-eight. The data presented in the graph shows the number of times a particular notification format was indicated to be preferred to the others after each session of the experiment.

When we categorize user preference ratings with respect to which type of notification was considered best, or most preferred, and which notification format was considered worst, or least preferred, overall, a resounding half of the user ratings placed occluding notifications last in their preferred list of notification formats. Further, Fig. 4 shows pictorially that occluding notifications were seldom preferred to both other types of notifications used in the study.

Individual user preferences—both reactive and reflective—are displayed in Fig. 5. The figure shows two rectangular diagrams, one displaying preference information elicited during the high-focus task session (upper diagram), and the other displaying preferences from the low-focus task session (lower diagram). Each column in the diagrams describes one individual user: the first row of both diagrams depicts that user's reflective preference for that task session, and the four boxes below a user's reflective preference describe that user's reactive ratings from each of the four contexts associated with that task session (all combinations of high and low importance and urgency). Users

[3] Two study participants believed their preferences to be directly linked with context and thus could not establish an overall ranking in one of the two sessions each.

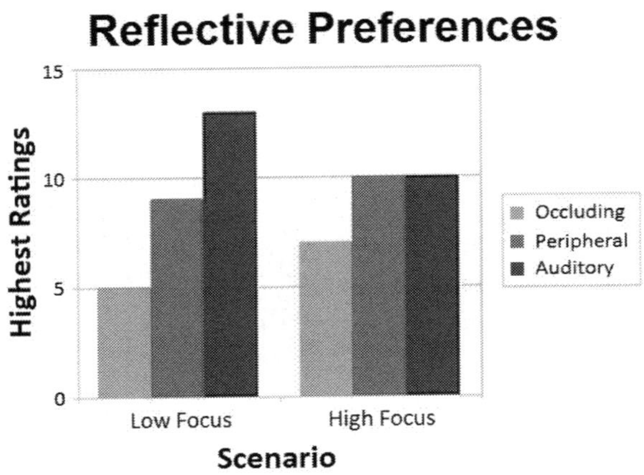

Fig. 4. The number of times Occluding, Peripheral and Auditory notifications were ranked highest in participants' reflective ratings, in all contexts with the low focus task (left) and high focus task (right)

are grouped by their reflective ratings: there are three groups, representing a reflective preference for occluding (in light blue, and corresponding to the first row of boxes), peripheral (in orange, of a middle shade), and auditory (colored dark blue). As an example of reading the top diagram (the high focus session), it indicates by its last column of ratings that one user reflectively preferred auditory notifications to occluding and peripheral during the post-session interview, but during that particular task session the user only provided positive ratings to occluding notifications.

As an aid in understanding the data depicted in the diagram, we will define three preference conditions: *complete match*, *partial match*, and *total mismatch*. A user whose data falls into the complete match category has provided positive feedback in every scenario of the reactive setting to that notification format deemed most preferred in the reflective setting. This does not preclude other formats having been provided positive ratings as well – e.g., someone who prefers auditory to visual notifications may appreciate any type of notification format under certain conditions. In Fig. 5 above, the first participant (column) of each category of reflective preferences, both in the high and low focus scenarios, is representative of a complete match: in all six of these cases, that user consistently provided a positive rating to the notification for which he or she indicated highest overall preference.

On the other end of the spectrum, a total mismatch describes a participant who indicated an overall preference for a notification format that did not receive a single positive rating in any of the scenarios within a given session. One example from Fig. 5 is the rightmost column in both sessions, describing a participant who indicated an overall preference for auditory notifications but only provided positive ratings to occluding notifications.

Finally, a partial match describes those participants who provided some but not a complete set of positive rating(s) to the notification format for which they indicated highest preference. This encapsulates all participants whose ratings do not fall into either the complete match or total mismatch categories (and it thus comprises the set complement of the union of the complete match and total mismatch sets).

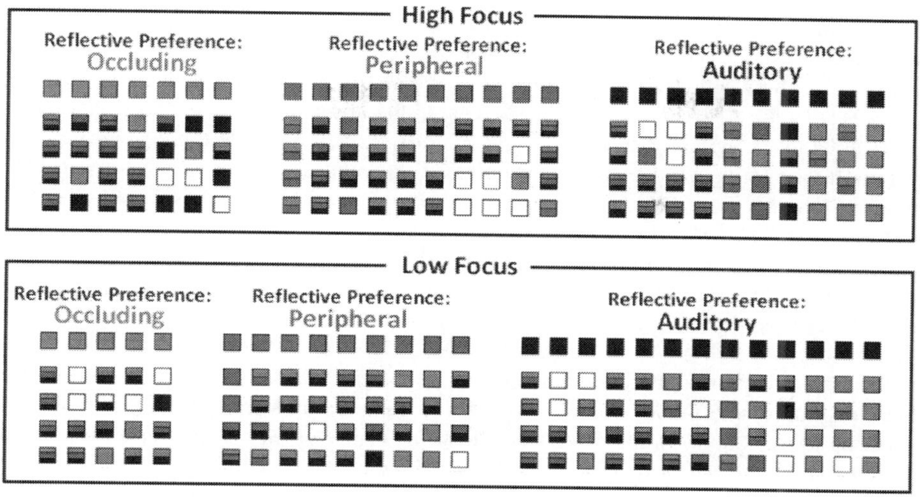

Fig. 5. Individual reflective preferences paired with reactive preference ratings, grouped by task session (high and low focus): each column represents a single user; the top row of boxes in each session displays individual users' format preferences during that session (corresponding to the groupings indicated by the reflectively preferred notification format), and the four boxes beneath each user's reflective preference present a visual description of that user's reactive preference ratings: light blue signifies a positive rating for the occluding notification delivered in the given context, orange indicates a positive rating for the peripheral notification, and dark blue indicates a positive rating for the auditory notification. If more than one notification was rated positively, multiple colors share the space. Empty spaces (i.e., white boxes) indicate that no notification was rated positively in that context.

Upon first glance at the pair of diagrams in Fig. 5, there is very little correlation between reflective and reactive user ratings. There are twenty-two complete match cases, in which people's reactive preferences correspond to their reflective preferences. Yet, this does not even account for half of the 54 sets of preferences that were acquired, suggesting that there is only a weak, if any, basis for supporting hypothesis **H2**. More notably, in fact, is the number of people whose preferences differ between reactive and reflective ratings. The number of participants who fall into the total mismatch category across both sessions is seventeen, almost as many as there are complete matches; and in total there are thirty cases (15 in each session, accounting for more than half of the participants) in which the reflectively-preferred notification format was not the one to receive the greatest number of positive ratings in the reactive stage (this includes fifteen cases of the partial match condition).

6 Discussion

Our results imply that the desirability of a notification delivery format cannot be generalized across either computer users or contextual settings. While feedback ratings provided directly in response to each notification indicated that occluding notifications would satisfy more users than either of the other two delivery formats, more participants rated the peripheral and auditory notifications most desirable overall (i.e., across contexts). And a number of participants provided contradictory preference information between the reactive and reflective settings. This suggests that user preferences may not be easily articulated, at least in the absence of contextual grounding.

Results also suggest that designers wishing to embed user preferences into intelligent software tools could potentially elicit that information by asking users to provide reactive feedback to explicit contextual scenarios (similar to the second phase of Study 1), but exhaustively enumerating all possible contexts would be a cumbersome if not intractable undertaking. Furthermore, because context does not appear to influence user preferences in a similar way across the majority of users, information acquired from one user would not necessarily generalize to any other user, meaning that the process would have to be replicated for each individual user. Instead, we propose that machine learning and user modelling techniques can perform this preference learning automatically, by learning the contextual features most relevant in understanding the effects of context and notification format on individual user preference patterns and then customizing notification delivery accordingly.

One important limitation of our primary study is that it was conducted by way of a pair of computer games. A gaming environment is not necessarily representative of an actual workplace, toward which much of our work is targeted. While our long-term goal is to understand notification preferences in real-world settings, we used a game-playing scenario as an initial test of our hypotheses within a controlled experimental setting. Further studies are currently underway in a technical support center, where actual notifications are being judged by actual employees toward our goal of understanding the similarities and differences among individual user preferences for notification delivery.

Unlike [9], I did not control the timing of a notification by matching task interruptions to known task breakpoints or otherwise. However, a number of participants commented (independently of the interview question regarding timing) on timing as a factor influencing their reactions to notifications. Interestingly, however, these comments pointed in different directions, with some users indicating a preference to receive notifications at the beginning or end of the primary task and others preferring notifications to arrive in the middle, with specific comments relating to effects of the games on that user's emotional state. This indicates that the tasks in which a user is engaged or has the opportunity to be engaged may themselves be important factors influencing user preferences for different notification delivery formats.

7 Conclusion and Future Work

With the surge in technology use over the past decade, people's attention is becoming more scarce; we are more often interrupted from our daily activities, both computer-based and not, and thus potentially inured to the effects of certain notifications, essentially making us less susceptible to them causing a disturbance in our daily routine. As a result, it is likely that people may be affected by notifications in a variety of different ways. Our results support this claim by suggesting that different people react and respond in different ways to different types of computerized notifications. Using only the contextual task and notification information selected for consideration in this study, our experiments with a non-adaptive, non-personalized system led to the satisfaction of between half and three-quarters of users, by way of issuing notifications in an intrusive manner across all contextual settings. User satisfaction levels can likely be improved, supporting the need for user modelling and/or machine learning tools, e.g., similar to those used in [6, 7] that have the ability to learn desirability of notification formats directly from user response and feedback.

The findings from our experiment motivate future study into the desirability and performance effects of a broader selection of notifications, from computer-based to mobile platforms, taking into consideration a broader selection of contextual features. Considering notification utility and a single aspect of task context (attentional focus requirements of the current task) is just one combination of contextual features that may influence a user's notification preferences. An exploration of other features, in a wider range of granularities, will be useful for understanding whether other aspects of context are better predictors of user preferences.

Acknowledgments. The authors would like to especially thank Jennifer Gluck for her kind support of this project, both in discussions and for materials that she donated for the sake of standardization and comparison. Thanks are also due to Dr. Joanna McGrenere for her early assistance with the statistical analysis of our results. And a special thanks to our blind reviewers for their insightful comments and suggestions, as well as our study participants for the time and energy they each devoted to the project.

References

1. Adamczyk, P.D., Bailey, B.P.: If not now, when?: the effects of interruption at different moments within task execution. In: CHI 2004: Proceedings of the SIGCHI conference on Human factors in computing systems, pp. 271–278. ACM, New York (2004)
2. Cutrell, E., Czerwinski, M., Horvitz, E.: Notification, disruption, and memory: Effects of messaging interruptions on memory and performance. In: Interact (2001)
3. Czerwinski, M., Cutrell, E., Horvitz, E.: Instant messaging: Effects of relevance and time. In: People and Computers XIV: Proceedings of HCI 2000, vol. 2, pp. 71–76. British Computer Society (2000)
4. Edwards, A.: Balanced latin-square designs in psychological research. American Journal of Psychology, 598–603 (1951)
5. Fogarty, J., Hudson, S.E., Atkeson, C.G., Avrahami, D., Forlizzi, J., Kiesler, S., Lee, J.C., Yang, J.: Predicting human interruptibility with sensors. ACM Trans. Comput.-Hum. Interact. 12(1), 119–146 (2005)
6. Gajos, K.: Automatically generating personalized user interfaces, phd dissertation (2008)
7. Gluck, J., Bunt, A., McGrenere, J.: Matching attentional draw with utility in interruption. In: Proceedings of CHI 2007, pp. 41–50 (2007)
8. Hart, S.G., Staveland, L.E.: Development of NASA-TLX (Task Load Index): Results of Empirical and Theoretical Research. In: Hancock, P., Meshkati, N. (eds.), Elsevier Science, Amsterdam (1988)
9. Iqbal, S.T., Bailey, B.P.: Effects of intelligent notification management on users and their tasks. In: Proceedings of the ACM Conference on Human Factors in Computing Systems (CHI 2008), Florence, Italy (2008)

10. Levitt, J.: Internet zone: Good help is hard to find. Information Week: Listening Post (2001), http://www.informationweek.com/835/35uwjl.htm
11. Mark, G., Gudith, D., Klocke, U.: The cost of interrupted work: more speed and stress. In: CHI 2008: Proceeding of the twenty-sixth annual SIGCHI conference on Human factors in computing systems, pp. 107–110. ACM, New York (2008)
12. McCrickard, D.S., Chewar, C.M.: Attuning notification design to user goals and attention costs. Communications of the ACM 46, 67–72 (2003)
13. Nishikado, T.: Space invaders (1978)
14. Trafton, J.G., Altmann, E.M., Brock, D.P., Mintz, F.E.: Preparing to resume an interrupted task: effects of prospective goal encoding and retrospective rehearsal. Int. J. Hum.-Comput. Stud. 58(5), 583–603 (2003)
15. Vastenburg, M.H., Keyson, D.V., de Ridder, H.: Considerate home notification systems: A field study of acceptability of notifications in the home. Personal and Ubiquitous Computing (2007)
16. Weber, J.S., Pollack, M.E.: Evaluating user preferences for adaptive reminding. In: CHI Extended Abstracts (2008)

Making Pen-Based Operation More Seamless and Continuous

Chuanyi Liu and Xiangshi Ren

School of Information Kochi University of Technology,
Kami-shi, 782-8502 Japan
{renlab,ren.xiangshi}@kochi-tech.ac.jp

Abstract. The feature of continuous interaction in pen-based system is critically significant. Seamless mode switch can effectively enhance the fluency of interaction. The interface which incorporated the advantages of seamless and continuous operation has the potential of enhancing the efficiency of operation and concentrating the users' attention. In this paper, we present a seamless and continuous operation paradigm based on pen's multiple-input parameters. A prototype which can support seamless and continuous (SC) operation is designed to compare the performance with MS Word 2007 system. The subjects were requested to select target components, activate the command menus and color the targets with a given flowchart in two systems respectively. The experiment results report the SC operation paradigm outperformed the standard ways in MS Word in both operation speed and cursor footprint length (CFL).

Keywords: Pen-based system, pressure, twist angle, continuous, seamless.

1 Introduction

Pen devices such as PDAs and Tablet PCs, have been used more and more widely because of the natural pen input. However, the current operation systems (OS) and applications for pen devices still remain the style of OS initially designed for Mice. There are various studies on exploring pen-suitable UI design. In these studies, how to improve the switch efficiency in selection-action patterns is an important research topic. Various techniques and paradigms on selection-action patterns have been presented lately (e.g., [1-3]). Most of these studies utilizing the same input channel for inking and gesturing. In some cases, it is rather difficult to eliminate the ambiguity of stroke recognition completely. And the use of these proposed techniques in pen-based systems is greatly limited for the lack of flexibility and ubiquity. On the other way, a commercial electronic pen commonly possesses multiple input channels. So our basic motivation is to find out an unambiguous and ubiquitously applicable method utilizing extra pen input channels with which users can perform selection-action patterns continuously, fluidly and unambiguously.

In this paper, we present a pen-suitable operation paradigm, under which fluid and continuous operations and seamless switch between different types of operation become possible throughout a computer task. To evaluate the proposed methods, a

T. Gross et al. (Eds.): INTERACT 2009, Part I, LNCS 5726, pp. 261–273, 2009.

drawing prototype system was implemented as a Java^{TM} program. And a comparative experiment was done to compare the operation paradigm and the corresponding ways in MS Word 2007 system. In the experiment, the subjects were asked to select the target components of a given flowchart, activate the command menus and color the targets. The results show that the proposed operation methods outperform MS Word in both speed and CFL, despite a little higher error rate.

2 Related Work

In this section, we discuss related work regarding both the studies on pen input parameters and these on seamless and continuous operations in pen-based systems.

2.1 Previous Work on Pen Input Parameters

To date, there are many studies on the utilization of pen input parameters. These studies can be roughly divided into two categories. One category investigates the general human ability to control pen input parameters; the other category aims at enhancing performance of human and computer interaction by implementing novel applications or techniques which exploit particular input parameters.

Up to now, pressure parameter has been explored extensively. Herot and Weinzapfel [4] studied the human capability of the finger to apply pressure and torque to a computer screen. Buxton [5] investigated the use of touch-sensitive technologies and the potential for interaction that they suggested. Ramos et al. [6] explored the human ability to vary pen-tip pressure as an additional channel of access to information. Ramos and Balakrishnan introduced *pressure marks* [1] and *Zliding* [7]. Pressure marks can encode selection-action patterns in a concurrent, parallel interaction. In pen strokes, variations in pressure make it possible to indicate both a selection and an action simultaneously. *Zliding* explores integrated panning and zooming by concurrently controlling input pressure while sliding in X-Y space. Li et al. [8] investigated the use of pressure as a possible method to delimit the input phases in pen-based interactions. Harada et al. presented a set of interaction techniques that leveraged the combination of human voice and pen pressure and position input when performing both creative 2D drawing and object manipulation tasks [9].

Input angles (i.e. tilt angle, twist angle and azimuth) are often used as UI clues for natural and intuitive interaction. Balakrishnan et al. [10] introduced the *Rockin'Mouse*. The *Rockin'Mouse* is a promising device for both 2D and 3D interaction that uses tilt input to facilitate 3D manipulation on a plane. Tian et al. [11] explored the *Tilt Menu*. The *Tilt Menu* is implemented by using 3D orientation information of pen devices for better extending selection capabilities of pen-based interfaces. Some other studies such as *TiltType* [12] and *TiltText* [13] focus on using the tilt information of mobile phones to affect text entry tasks in mobile devices. Bi et al. [14] explored rolling angle on general human being control ability. They suggested that both rolling amplitude and speed should be taken into account for rolling-based interact techniques.

As for sketch-based techniques, Davis et al. [15] introduced their *SketchWizard*, which is about wizard of Oz prototyping of pen-based user interfaces. Apitz and Guimbretire [16] presented their *CrossY*, in which pen stroke did all the drawing operations.

2.2 Previous Work on Seamless and Continuous Operations

Hinckley et al. [3] presented their pigtail delimiters, with which selection-action patterns can be performed in one continuous fluid stroke. A pigtail is created explicitly by intersecting one stroke itself and an action is specified or an object manipulated by the stroke's direction. Pigtails provide a way to integrate an explicit command invocation in a fluid stroke following the selection specification. But it is rather difficult to manipulate multiple targets in an irregular layout, since the targets are selected by a lasso. Furthermore, there is ambiguity between pigtail delimiters and freeform drawings.

Baudisch et al. [17] introduced *marquee menus*, which are a technique where the selection-action pattern occurs concurrently. The marquee menu's selection is specified by a rectangular area, which is defined by the start and the end points of a straight stroke; its action is determined by one of four movement directions of the stroke. *Marquee menus* are sensitive to both a mark's point of origin and direction while providing a compact interaction phase. The technique is promising for web browsing in small screens. But it has not been elaborated to show whether and how this technique scales for non-straight strokes with arbitrary orientations. Regardless of these considerations, this kind of technique is not suitable for multiple targets in an irregular layout and ambiguity between gesture strokes and freeform drawings limits its practical applicability in other scenarios.

Ramos and Balakrishnan [1] introduced their *pressure marks*, where variations in pressure are used as metaphors for actions. The marks of pressure variation are integrated into selection strokes, and then the selection-action patterns can be performed concurrently and seamlessly. However, there are some limitations with *pressure marks*' variation, e.g. once the user begins to slide a pen slightly then the HL (pressure variation signature, high-low, defined in the original) or HH (high-high) pressure mark may not appear in the following stroke. Furthermore, the number of simple pressure marks is limited, and compound marks are difficult to memorize and control. Again, this kind of technique is only useful for targets arranged in a regular layout.

3 The Proposed Operation Methods

From the previous work, we can see that the selection-action patterns have been explored extensively, but the use of these techniques are limited to some specific narrow scenarios. Furthermore, it is rather difficult to eliminate the ambiguity between gesture strokes and freeform drawings, since both are based on the same input channel. In this paper, we present an operation paradigm with extra input channels, which allows fluid target selection and continuous and seamless switching from selection to action. Commonly, a computer task includes three phases, i.e. object selection, command selection and object property setting phases. Under the operation paradigm, a computer task can be performed in one continuous and fluid stroke. In the target selection phase, users are allowed to string and select the targets with a pen stroke. Pen pressure input is used as a delimiter to distinguish between selection strokes and freeform drawings. When all the targets have been selected by a pen stroke, users can activate a pie menu by rolling the pen. If the rolling angle and speed exceed the respective thresholds, the pie menu will be activated and displayed with its center under the cursor. And then the user slides the pen tip, an action will be performed when the pen tip crossed a menu item. Throughout the whole process, the pen tip need not to be lifted from the screen. All the operations can be performed in one continuous and fluid stroke. The design of the three phases under the operation paradigm will be introduced in detail in the next section.

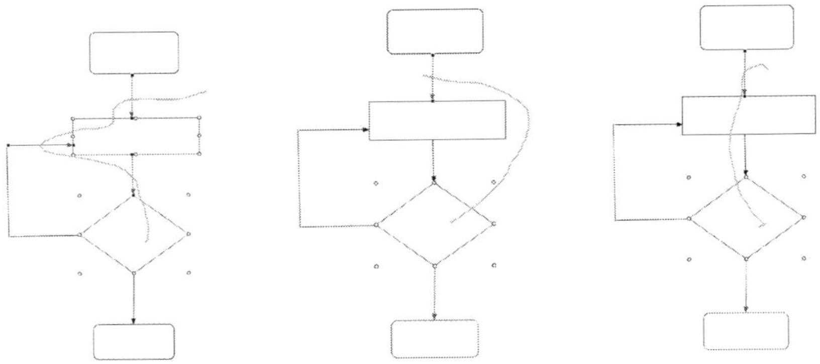

(a) String & select objects with one stroke (b) Steer clear of an object (c) Ignore an object crossed by the stroke

Fig. 1. Pressure-based line-string selection (the blue line is the cursor footprint; the objects with sizing handles are selected)

3.1 Target Selection

As suggested by [16, 18, 19] crossing performs better than pointing-and-clicking in UI design, especially for pen-based input devices. In the prototype system, we present a pressure-based line-string selection method. During a pen being slid on the screen, the objects stringed by the stroke are selected when the pen input pressure exceeds a given threshold.

Pressure Coupling Normal Stroke and Line-string Selection. In the application, pressure is used as a delimiter to couple normal stroke and line-string selection. A pilot study was done to determine the right pressure spectra for normal stroke and line-string selection. In our experiment, 12 participants were asked to draw with light pressure, normal pressure and heavier pressure alternately on a WACOM tablet combined display, which has 1024 levels of pressure. The results showed a statistically significant difference on the *maximum pressure scale* of a stroke between the light, the normal and the heavier pressure conditions. In our implementation, the heavy spectrum of pressure was employed for line-string selection, and the normal spectrum for normal stroke; for low end pressure, the spectrum is more difficult to control [7], therefore, it was omitted from the technique design.

Object Selection. The user strokes the pen starting from a blank area, where there is no object. If the pressure input exceeds the specified threshold, the stroke will be pressure-based line-string selection; otherwise it will be normal stroke. Under this selection mode, the user only needs to stroke the pen on a screen and all the objects stringed by the pen will be selected (see Fig. 1a). A blue footprint line following the path of the pen is used as visual feedback for the selection state. If there are some objects that the user does not want to select in the path of the selection stroke, s/he can steer clear of them (Fig. 1b) or reduce the pressure on the pen to below the threshold without lifting the pen tip from the screen, until the blue footprint line disappears. Then the figure will be crossed by the stroke without being selected (Fig. 1c).

Undoing Selection. The user can stroke the pen back and cross the footprint line on a selected object to undo selecting it. If the user lifts the pen and taps in a *blank area*, selection of all the items will be canceled.

3.2 Activating the Menu

Although, there are various studies on the select-action patterns, but most of these techniques use the same pen input channel for both command gesture and freeform drawings. So it is rather difficult to eliminate the recognition ambiguity completely. In the following section, we introduce a smooth and unambiguous technique for switching smoothly between selection and action by introducing extra pen input channels.

Li et al. [8] investigated five different mode switching techniques in pen-based UI design. They suggested that *non-preferred hand* is the most promising mode switching technique. In their experiment, a physical button mounted at the top-left corner of a Tablet PC screen was employed as a *mode switching button*. It was called a *non-preferred hand* mode switch that users tapped on the *mode switching button* with their *non-preferred hands* to perform a mode switch. In their study, they did not explore angle input channels, e.g., tilt angle, azimuth or twist angle. To determine the most suitable extra input channel that can serve as a switching trigger to activate the menu, we performed a pilot study to investigate all the possible input channels of a pen for mode switching techniques. After the first block of tests using the non-preferred hand section of the trials, we noticed that the subjects tended to keep one finger of their *non-preferred hands* on the *mode switching button*. Taking into account the practical application scenarios, it is impossible to keep the non-preferred hand on a specific button all the time. And under most conditions, the keyboard or such a button is not available in a pen-based system. In our implement, twist angle of pen input was used as an extra input channel for mode switch.

Bi et al. [14] presented their study on rolling (twist) angle for pen input. They suggested that the rolling can be identified as incidental if the rolling speed of a data event is between -30°/s and 30 °/s or the rolling angle is between -10 ° and 10 °. And -90 ° to 90 ° can be exploited as the usable rolling range. Based on their study results, rolling is employed in our experiment design to activate the pie menu if the rolling speed exceeds the range of [-50 °/s, 50 °/s], and rolling angle exceeds [-50 °, 50 °]. After selecting all the targets, the user intentionally rolls the pen. If the rolling angle and speed exceed the specific thresholds, the pie menu will be activated and displayed with its center under the cursor.

3.3 Performing an Action

We employed crossing to activate a menu command, for crossing performs better than pointing-and-clicking in UI design [16, 18, 19]. When the pie menu is activated, the user slides the pen tip across a menu item, the corresponding action is performed.

4 Experiment

To investigate the performance of SC operation paradigm, a quantitative experiment was conducted, the corresponding operation in MS Word 2007 served as a baseline.

4.1 Apparatus

The hardware used in the experiment was a WACOM Cintiq 21UX flat panel LCD graphics display tablet with a resolution of 1,600×1,200 pixels (1 pixel= 0.297mm), using a wireless pen with a pressure, tilt angle, azimuth and twist angle sensitive isometric tip (the width of the pen-tip is 1.76mm). It reports 1024 levels (ranging from 0 to 1023, the minimum unit is 1) of pressure and 360° (ranging from 0° to 359°, the minimum unit is 1°) of twist angle. The experimental program was implemented with Java^{TM} 6.0 running on a 3.2 GHz P4 PC with the Windows XP SP2 Professional operating system.

4.2 Participants

Six participants (two female and four male ranging in age from 27 to 36 years old, none paid) were all volunteers from the local university community. All of them were right-handed. One of them has two years of experience of using a digital pen and the other five have no such experience.

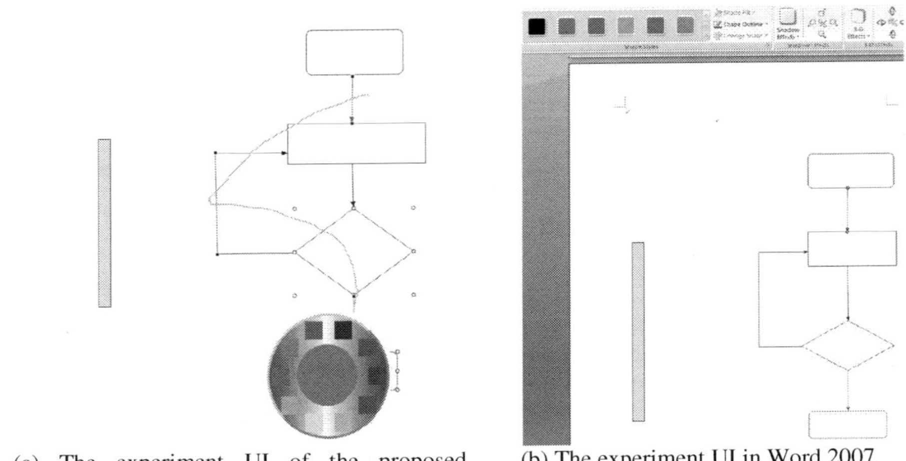

(a) The experiment UI of the proposed methods.

(b) The experiment UI in Word 2007

Fig. 2. The experiment UI design

4.3 Task

In the experiment, the subjects were asked to perform for both types of interface (SC operation UI and Word operation UI). For each trial in both types of interface, the subjects were given a flowchart (Fig. 2) composed of 10 components. Five out of the 10 components were randomly chosen as targets (displayed in red). And the target color was shown as a rectangular bar to the left side of the flowchart. For each corresponding trial; the flowchart size, component number, location in the screen as well as the targets are kept the same in both kinds of interface. The subjects were requested to color the outlines of the target components with the given target color. Each trial includes three operation phases, object selection phase (called as *selection phase*), menu trigger phase (called as *trigger phase*) and object property setting phase (called as *setting phase*). Under the proposed paradigm, the subjects selected the targets using pressure-based line-string selection (this process is computed as its *selection phase*), rolled the pen to activate the pie menu (this process is computed as its *trigger phase*) and slid the pen tip across a menu item to color the targets (this process is computed as its *setting phase*). The experimental program recorded the time and accuracy of each phase, and the CFL per trial. With Word 2007, the subjects tapped the pen tip on each target to select it with the (*Shift* or *Ctrl* key being pressed, this process is computed as its selection phase), moved the pen tip from the last target and pointed to the toolbar (this process is computed as its *trigger phase*) and tapped the pen tip to color the targets (this process is computed as its *setting phase*). Running in the background, the experimental program analyzed and recorded the time and accuracy of each phase, and the CFL per trial.

4.4 Procedure and Design

Each subject was asked to complete 5 blocks of trials. Each block consisted of 6 selection-action trails. A trial was erroneous if there is any error caused in any of the three phases. The program recorded one *selection phase* error if any target component was omitted or any non-target component was selected. One *trigger phase* error happened when the menu was activated incidentally under SC paradigm, or when the wrong toolbar is tapped in Word 2007. If the target components were not colored with the target color, a *setting phase error* was generated. The errors caused in the *selection phase*, *trigger phase* and *setting phase* are called as *selection error*, *trigger error* and *setting error* respectively. And the time elapsed in the *selection phase*, *trigger phase* and *setting phase* was computed respectively as *selection time*, *trigger time* and *setting time*. A within-subject design was used. The dimensions of all the flowcharts were displayed at a resolution of 297×622 pixels. In the SC operation UI, there are ten standard colors arranged in the same order as the standard color arrangement in the color toolbar of Word 2007. Before the task in Word 2007 began, the subjects were conducted to activate the standard color toolbar as a quick access toolbar, and to scroll the Word page to keep the flowchart directly under the toolbar. The dependent variables were trial time, CFL, error rate and subjective preference. Prior to the study, the experimenter explained and demonstrated the task to the participants. The participants were asked to do the trials as quickly and accurately as possible. At the end of the experiment, participants were instructed to give their subjective comments by completing a questionnaire, which consisted of four questions regarding "usability", "fatigue", "preference" and "attention concentration" on 1-to-7 scale (1=lowest preference, and 7 =highest preference). "Attention concentration" is a promising degree that takes into account the users' ability to focus on the targets themselves.

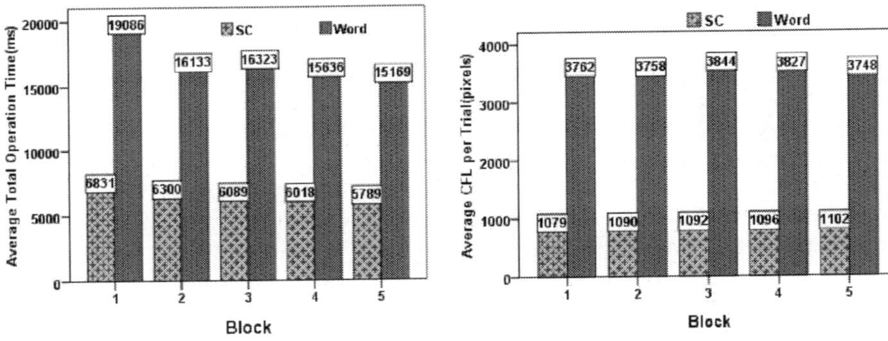

(a) The average total operation time (b) The average CFL

Fig. 3. The average total operation time and CFL

4.5 Results

Trial time for each participant averaged thirty minutes. A RM-ANOVA (repeated measures analysis of variance) was used to analyze the performance in terms of operation time, CFL, accuracy and subjective preference.

Total Operation Time and CFL

There was a significant difference in the overall mean operation time ($F(1,5) = 41.832$, $p = 0.001$) and CFL ($F(1,5) = 50.394$, $p = 0.001$) between the two operation paradigms. The overall mean operation time per trial was 6309.945 ms of SC operation, 16562.46 ms of operation in Word 2007. And the overall CFL per trial was 1084.172 pixels for SC operation, 3805.964 pixels for the operation in Word 2007. There were no main effects for blocks on overall mean operation time for either SC operation ($F(4,20) = 1.718$, $p = 0.186$) nor Word operation ($F(4,20) = 1.663$, $p = 0.198$). There were no main effects for blocks on CFL for either SC operation ($F(4,20) = 0.247$, $p = 0.908$) or Word Operation($F(4,20) = 0.058$, $p = 0.993$). However, as Fig. 3a illustrates, we observed a little improvement in speed. No significant effect was found for paradigm*block on overall mean time ($F(4,20) = 1.029$, $p = 0.417$) or overall CFL ($F(4,20) = 0.094$, $p = 0.983$), which indicated that the improvement in learning did not significantly affect relative performance on the two kinds of operation paradigm.

Selection Time. There was a significant difference in the overall mean selection time ($F(1,5) = 88.284$, $p < 0.0001$) between the two different kinds of operation paradigms. The overall mean selection time per trial was 3700.110 ms for SC operation and

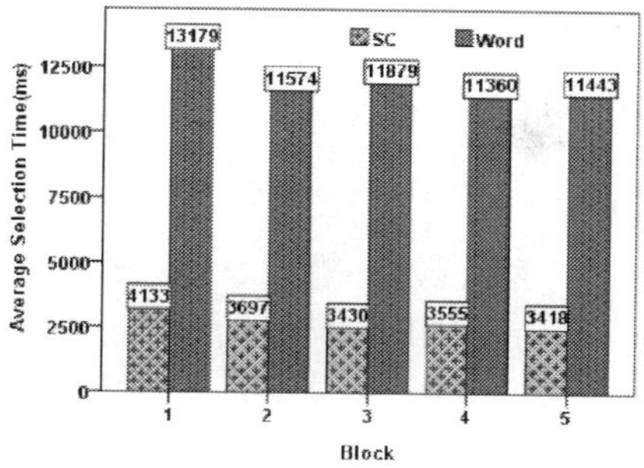

Fig. 4. The average selection time

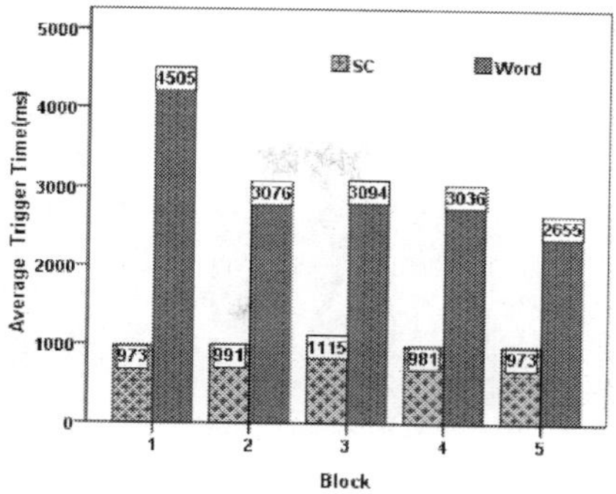

Fig. 5. The average trigger time

11955.45 ms for Word operation. There were no main effects for blocks for the operation of SC (F(4,20) = 1.164, p = 0.356) or Word 2007 (F(4,20) = 0.625, p = 0.650), on overall mean selection time. A small speed improvement in selection time for both SC and Word operation was also observed in Fig. 4. No significant effect was found for paradigm*block on the overall mean selection time (F(4,20) = 0.307, p = 0.870), which indicated the learning improvement did not significantly affect the relative performance of the two kinds of operation paradigm on selection time.

Trigger Time. There was a significant difference (F(1,5) = 6.991, p = 0.046) in the overall mean trigger time per trial between the two different kinds of operation paradigms. The overall mean trigger time per trial was 1030.373 ms for SC operation and 3297.632 ms for Word operation. There was no main effect for the operation of either SC (F(4,20) = 0.885, p = 0.491) or Word (F(4,20) = 1.570, p = 0.221), for blocks on overall mean trigger time. Fig. 5 also illustrates a small improvement in selection time for both SC and Word operation. No significant effect was found for paradigm*block on overall mean trigger time (F(4,20) = 1.562, p = 0.223), which indicated learning improvement did not significantly affect the relative performance of the two kinds of operation paradigm on trigger time.

Setting Time. There was a significant difference (F(1,5) = 12.973, p = 0.016) in the overall mean setting time per trial between the two different kinds of operation paradigms. The overall mean setting time was 1579.463 ms for SC operation and 1309.381 ms for Word operation. For the operation of both SC(F(4,20) = 2.896, p = 0.048) and Word (F(4,20) = 2.994, p = 0.043), there were main effects for blocks on overall mean setting time. Fig. 6 illustrates a little improvement in setting time for both SC and Word operation. No significant effect was found for paradigm*block on the overall mean trigger time (F(4,20) = 0.417, p = 0.794), which indicated the learning improvement did not significantly affect the relative performance of the two kinds of operation paradigm on setting time.

Errors. The results showed a significant difference in the overall mean error rate (F(1,5) = 24.306, p = 0.014) between the two different kinds of operation paradigm. The overall mean error rate was 2.458% of SC operation and 1.606% of Word operation. There were main effects for blocks on overall mean errors for SC operation

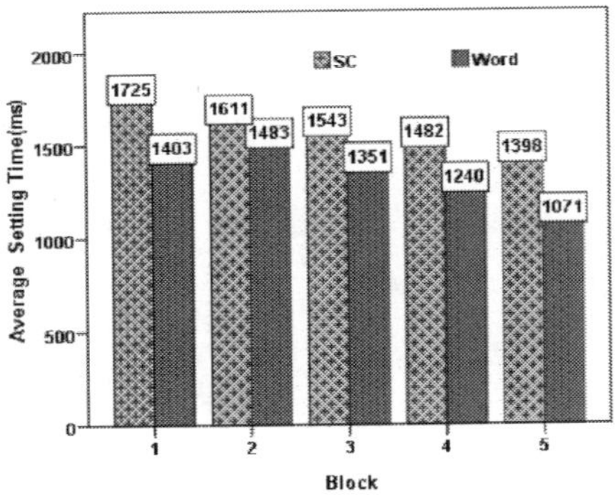

Fig. 6. The average setting time

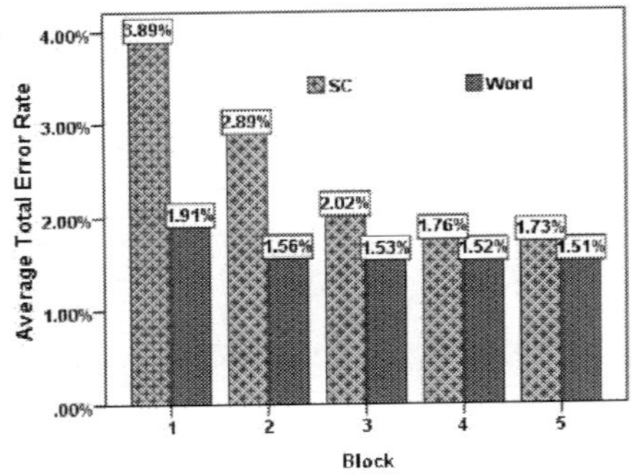

Fig. 7. The average total error rates

(F(4,20) = 6.332, p = 0.002), but no main effects for blocks on overall mean errors for Word operation (F(4,20) = 1.010, p = 0.043). As Fig. 7 illustrates, we observed a significant decrease in errors for SC and a marginal one in Word operation. Significant effects were found for paradigms*block on the overall mean errors (F(4,20) = 5.588, p = 0.003), which indicated the learning improvement significantly affected the relative performance of the two kinds of operation paradigm regarding errors.

Selection Error. The experimental analysis reported a significant difference in the overall mean selection error rate (F(1,5) = 9.423, p = 0.028) between the two different kinds of operation paradigm. The overall mean selection error rate was 0.864% of SC operation, 0.540% of Word operation. There were main effects for blocks on overall mean selection error rate for SC operation (F(4,20) = 1.650, p = 0.021), but no main effects for blocks on the overall mean selection error rate for Word operation (F(4,20) = 0.625, p = 0.650). Fig. 8 illustrates a big improvement in selection errors for SC operation and a marginal improvement for Word operation. Significant effect was found for paradigm*block on the overall mean trigger time (F(4,20) = 5.058, p = 0.037), which indicated the learning improvement significantly affected the relative performance of the two kinds of operation paradigm on selection errors.

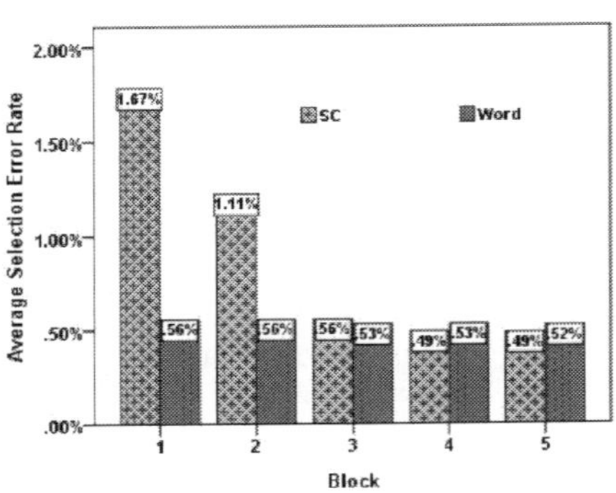

Fig. 8. The average selection error rates

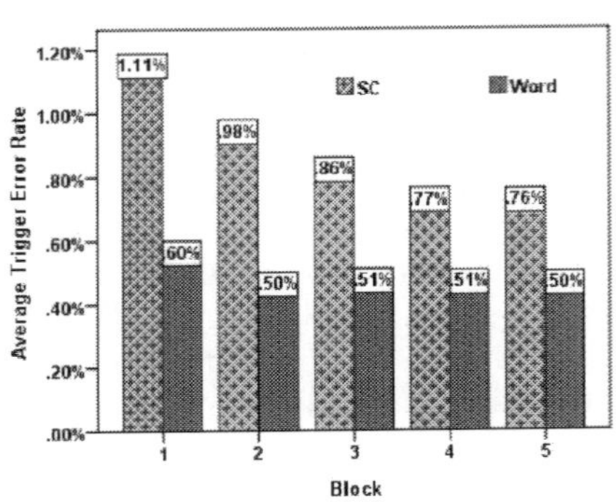

Fig. 9. The average trigger error rates

Trigger Error. There was a significant difference in the overall mean trigger error rate ($F(1,5) = 20.000$, $p = 0.007$) between the two different kinds of operation paradigm. The overall mean trigger error rate was 0.896% for SC operation and 0.524% for Word. There were main effects for blocks on overall mean trigger error rate for SC operation ($F(4,20) = 17.857$, $p = 0.001$), but no main effects for blocks on overall mean trigger error rate in Word 2007 ($F(4,20) = 0.250$, $p = 0.906$). Fig. 9 illustrates a significant decrease in trigger error rate for SC operation and a little decrease for Word 2007. Significant effect was found for paradigm*block on the overall mean trigger time ($F(4,20) = 9.062$, $p < 0.0001$), which indicated the learning improvement significantly affected the relative performance of the two kinds of operation paradigm on trigger error rate.

Setting Error. There was no significant difference in the overall mean setting error rate ($F(1,5) = 5.000$, $p = 0.076$) between the two operation paradigms. The overall mean setting error rate was 0.7% for SC operation and 0.534% for Word operation. There were main effects for blocks on overall mean setting error rate for SC operation ($F(4,20) = 5.000$, $p = 0.006$), but no main effects for operation in Word 2007 ($F(4,20) = 2.742$, $p = 0.057$). Fig. 10 illustrates the improvement in setting errors of both SC and Word operation. No significant effect was found for paradigm*block on the overall mean setting error rate ($F(4,20) = 2.619$, $p = 0.066$), which indicated the learning improvement did not significantly affect the relative performance of the two kinds of operation paradigm on trigger errors.

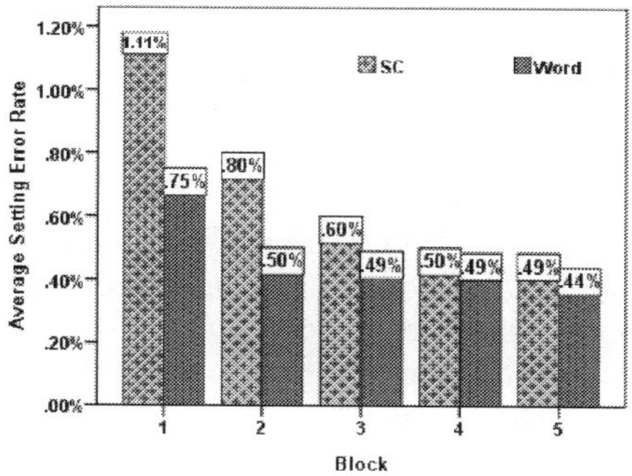

Fig. 10. The average object property setting error rates

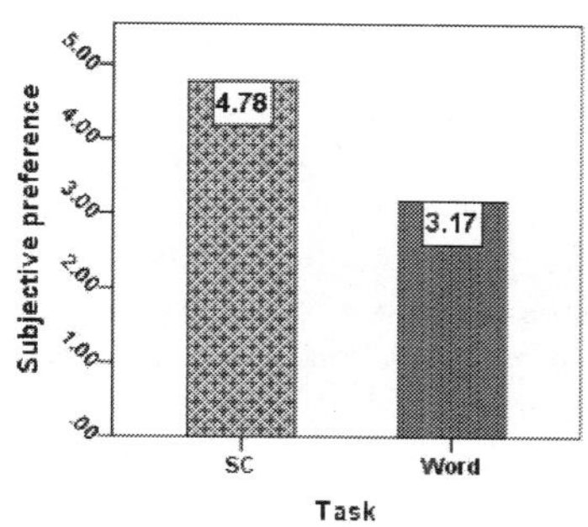

Fig. 11. The subjective preference

Subjective Comments. Fig. 11 shows the subjective ratings for the two kinds of operation paradigm. These ratings were based on the average value of the answers given by the subjects to the four questions. Significant main effects were observed between the two operation paradigms ($F(1,5) = 9.365$, $p = 0.028$). The average preference for SC operation paradigm is 4.8, and for MS Word it is 3.2.

5 Discussion

Various contrastive techniques (e.g., lassoing + pigtailing [3]) were taken into account, but none of the presented techniques for pen-based systems is suitable for the wide range of common computer tasks. Thus, MS Word was chosen as the baseline because it is the most widely used semantic paradigm. At the beginning of the experiment, we noticed that the participants stroked the pen rather cautiously and slowly to select the targets, rolled the pen nervously to activate the pie menu, and wanted to lift the pen tip to tap the target menu item. But after several trials, they stroked and rolled the pen fluidly and confidently. They commented that the SC operation was enjoyable; some of them said that performing the SC operation was like playing games.

The results illustrate that the selection and trigger speed of SC operation are significantly faster than that of MS Word. But the setting speed of SC operation is a little slower than that of MS Word. This is probably due to that part of the pie menu was visually occluded by the hand in the setting phase. We observed that some of the participants tended to adjust their hands when crossing a target menu item, others tended to hold the pen at a little higher position to facilitate crossing the menu item after the first block. From the experiment results, we also noted that the error rates for the three phases of SC operation were much higher than for MS Word in the first two blocks. But the difference between SC and MS Word operation in error rates was not much different from the third block, except for the average trigger error rate. During the experiment, we observed that some participants tended to trigger the pie menu accidentally much more often than others. This is probably due to the participants' different ways of holding the pen. Fig. 3b illustrates that the CFL for SC is much shorter than for MS Word, which proves that the cursor needs to be moved less in SC operation then in MS Word. This can further indicate that, in SC operation, the participants can concentrate their attention on the targets much better than with the standard interfaces.

6 Conclusion and Future Research

In this paper, we present an operation paradigm that is suitable for seamless and continuous operation in pen-based systems. The results of SC operation are rather promising in both speed and CFL, and the accuracy is not significantly different to the standard operation in MS Word after the second block. In our future research, we will explore which combination of pen input parameters is most promising, and the possible maximum number of pen input channels that the subjects can comfortably cope with.

References

1. Ramos, G., Balakrishnan, R.: Pressure marks. In: Proc. CHI 2007, pp. 1375–1384 (2007)
2. François, G., Andrew, M., Terry, W.: Bene_ts of merging command selection and direct manipulation. ACM Trans. Comput.-Hum. Interact. 12(3), 460–476 (2005)
3. Hinckley, K., Baudisch, P., Ramos, G., Guimbretiere, F.: Design and analysis of delimiters for selection-action pen gesture phrases in scriboli. In: Proc. CHI 2005, pp. 451–460 (2005)
4. Herot, C.F., Weinzapfel, G.: One-point touch input of vector information for computer displays. In: Proc. SIGGRAPH 1978, pp. 210–216 (1978)
5. Buxton, W., Hill, R., Rowley, P.: Issues and techniques in touch-sensitive tablet input. In: Proc. SIGGRAPH 1985, pp. 215–224 (1985)

6. Ramos, G., Boulos, M., Balakrishnan, R.: Pressure widgets. In: Proc. CHI 2004, pp. 487–494 (2004)
7. Ramos, G., Balakrishnan, R.: Zliding: Fluid zooming and sliding for high precision parameter manipulation. In: Proc. UIST 2005, pp. 143–152 (2005)
8. Li, Y., Hinckley, K., Guan, Z., Landay, J.A.: Experimental analysis of mode switching techniques in pen-based user interfaces. In: Proc. CHI 2005, pp. 461–470 (2005)
9. Harada, S., Saponas, T.S., Landay, J.A.: Voicepen: Augmenting pen input with simultaneous non-linguistic vocalization. In: Proc. ICMI 2007, pp. 178–185 (2007)
10. Balakrishnan, R., Baudel, T., Kurtenbach, G., Fitzmaurice, G.: The rockin'mouse: integral 3d manipulation on a plane. In: Proc. SIGCHI 1997, pp. 311–318 (1997)
11. Tian, F., Xu, L., Wang, H., Zhang, X., Liu, Y., Setlur, V., Dai, G.: Tilt menu: Using the 3d orientation information of pen devices to extend the selection capability of pen-based user interfaces. In: Proc. CHI 2008, pp.1371–1380 (2008)
12. Partridge, K., Chatterjee, S., Sazawal, V., Borriello, G., Want, R.: Tilttype: Accelerometer supported text entry for very small devices. In: Proc. UIST 2002, pp. 201–204 (2002)
13. Wigdor, D., Balakrishnan, R.: Tilttext: Using tilt for text input to mobile phones. In: Proc. UIST 2003, pp. 81–90 (2003)
14. Bi, X., Moscovich, T., Ramos, G., Balakrishnan, R., Hinckley, K.: An exploration of pen rolling for pen-based interaction. In: Proc. UIST 2008, pp. 191–200 (2008)
15. Davis, R.C., Saponas, T.S., Shilman, M., Landay, J.A.: Sketchwizard: Wizard of oz prototyping of pen-based user interfaces. In: Proc. UIST 2007, pp. 119–128 (2007)
16. Apitz, G., Guimbretire, F.: Crossy: A crossing-based drawing application. In: Proc. UIST 2004, pp. 1–10 (2004)
17. Baudisch, P., Xie, X., Wang, C., Ma, W.Y.: Collapse-to-zoom: viewing web pages on small screen devices by interactively removing irrelevant content. In: Proc. UIST 2004, pp. 91–94 (2004)
18. Accot, J., Zhai, S.: More than dotting the i's- foundations for crossing-based interfaces. In: Proc. CHI 2002, pp. 73–80 (2002)
19. Ren, X., Moriya, S.: Improving selection performance on pen-based systems: a study of pen-based interaction for selection tasks. ACM Trans. Comput.-Hum. Interact. 7(3), 384–416 (2000)

Insight into Goal-Directed Movements: Beyond Fitts' Law

Karin Nieuwenhuizen[1], Dzmitry Aliakseyeu[2], and Jean-Bernard Martens[1]

[1] Eindhoven University of Technology, Department of Industrial Design, Den Dolech 2, 5600 MB Eindhoven, The Netherlands
{C.J.H.Nieuwenhuizen,J.B.O.S.Martens}@tue.nl

[2] Philips Research, Media Interaction, High Tech Campus 5, 5656 AE Eindhoven, The Netherlands
Dzmitry.Aliakseyeu@philips.com

Abstract. Various methods and measures have been developed to assess the quality of input devices and interaction techniques. One approach to investigating the performance of input devices and interaction techniques is to focus on the quality of the produced movements. The current paper proposes a new method of analyzing goal-directed movements by dividing them into meaningful phases. In addition to the proposed analysis method a selection of measures is suggested to assess different aspects of rapidly aimed movements. In order to evaluate the added value of the proposed analysis method an experiment has been conducted to compare two input devices (mouse versus stylus with tablet) with respect to their performance on a multi-directional pointing task. The results show that the analysis into several phases reveals clear differences in the movement strategy.

Keywords: Input devices, interaction techniques, movement analysis, performance measures.

1 Introduction

A key aspect of human-computer interaction is the use of input devices, such as keyboard, mouse, or tablet with stylus. Since millions of people use computers on a daily basis it is important that input devices are well tailored to users' needs. This is especially true when devices are designed for people with disabilities [9, 11], or when devices are used within challenging environments, such as virtual reality. To improve existing input devices or in the process of developing new ones it is necessary to identify the reasons for variations in performance.

Several studies have compared input devices or interaction techniques by observing characteristics of movement paths during the execution of basic tasks such as pointing, selecting or steering [4, 10, 15, 14, 9, 8]. From these comparative studies two different approaches towards movement analysis can be discerned. The first approach considers characteristics of the overall movement, such as total time or throughput (Fitts' Law). The second approach, mostly found in human movement research, assumes that a movement consists of several submovements and that this

T. Gross et al. (Eds.): INTERACT 2009, Part I, LNCS 5726, pp. 274–287, 2009.

division may reveal distinct information about the quality of the overall movement [10, 16]. Although both approaches have proven to be helpful in comparing input devices or interaction techniques [15, 1, 9, 18] it is difficult to use them to distinguish different movement strategies and to apply these approaches to the design of input devices and interaction techniques.

In the current paper, we first explain why we believe it is necessary to develop a new method to analyze interaction movements. Subsequently, we propose new parsing rules for decomposing an overall movement into several meaningful movement phases. To illustrate the added value of this new analysis method it is used to compare indirect mouse interactions with direct stylus interactions. It will be demonstrated that a more detailed description of how interaction movements are influenced by the input device can be obtained by dividing the movements into meaningful phases. Finally, a large number of existing and newly proposed measures were applied to assess the characteristics of the identified movement phases. The method that we propose for identifying complementary measures is another contribution of the current paper.

2 Movement Analysis

2.1 Overall Movement Characteristics

Early studies on input devices based the analysis of movements on characteristics of the overall movement. The best-known example is Fitts' law [5], which states that the time to move to a target (MT) is logarithmically related to the ratio of the distance to the target (A) over the width of the target (W), i.e.,

$$MT = a + b * \log_2 (A/W + 1). \quad (1)$$

The logarithmic term is called the index of difficulty (ID) in "bits". It increases with a larger distance to the target or a smaller target width. The reciprocal of b is the index of performance (IP) or bandwidth in "bits/s", which is one of the summary statistics that is frequently used to compare movements made under different conditions. The most popular (and standardized) summary statistic used in most recent studies is *throughput* (IDe/MT), where the effective width (We) of the target is used instead of the actual target width (W) in the definition of the index of difficulty [14, 17].

Although Fitts' law can establish that there are differences between input devices or interaction techniques, it cannot provide much insight into the factors that are responsible for these differences. MacKenzie et al. [14] acknowledged that Fitts' law measures are "gross measures" and that they lack "any information on movement during a trial". Therefore, they proposed several alternative measures, based on the path being traced during the movement, to get a more accurate measure of efficiency and to get a better idea of why some devices are more efficient than others. Although their measures reveal some of the problems experienced with input devices when pointing to a target, they still do not take into account the detailed course of the movement as a function of time, i.e., they are still characteristics of the overall movement.

2.2 Movement Phases

According to Woodworth [19] rapidly aimed movements consist of an initial impulse, or ballistic phase, and a perceptually guided final control, or correction phase. The initial part of the movement is relatively fast, but as people get close to the target the movement becomes slower and is characterized by irregularities in the time-displacement profile. In other words, the ballistic phase is programmed to reach the target and the unintended errors are corrected during the correction phase, based on sensory feedback [16, 18]. These two phases can indeed be observed in actual displacement velocity profiles of goal-directed movements, as shown in Figure 1.

Based on this model, Meyer et al. [16] proposed parsing criteria to indicate the end of the first submovement, or ballistic phase: a) a zero-crossing of the displacement velocity from positive to negative (type 1); b) a zero-crossing of the acceleration, which is the derivative of velocity, from negative to positive (type 2); c) a zero-crossing of jerk, which is the derivative of acceleration, from positive to negative (type 3). Recent comparative studies used these criteria to divide movements into submovements in order to look at movements in more detail [9, 8, 18]. We will show that the above parsing rules often produce a subdivision into submovements that is not very meaningful. This means that the observed differences in submovement patterns obtained with this method should also be questioned.

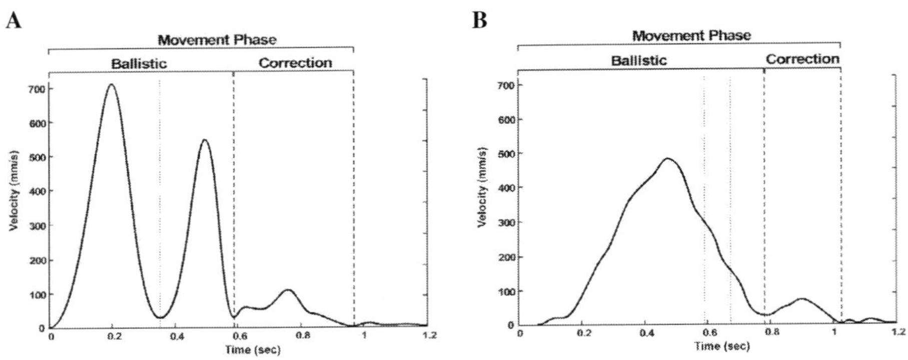

Fig. 1. Examples of velocity profiles of goal directed movements: A) executed with a mouse; B) executed with a stylus, indicating the ballistic phase and the correction phase

Although Woodworth's model formed the basis for Meyer's optimized dual-submovement model, the criteria that Meyer et al. [16] proposed do not necessarily divide the movement into a ballistic phase and a correction phase. They assumed that goal directed movements consisted of maximally two submovements and that the ballistic phase ends after the first submovement. If one examines the velocity profiles of rapidly aimed movements, one can observe that this is frequently not the case. For example, Figure 1A shows an example of a velocity profile of a goal directed movement carried out with a mouse. This graph shows that not one but two large submovements were necessary to get into the neighborhood of the target. Another example is shown in Figure 1B, which demonstrates that when using a stylus subtle changes in the deceleration rate, also called type-3 submovements, can occur. According to Wisleder and Dounskaia [18] type-3 submovements occur during relatively smooth motions and are only an indication of subtle accuracy regulation. In other words, they are not believed to signal actual interruptions in the ballistic movement and, therefore, they are not likely to indicate the end of the ballistic phase.

Both graphs illustrate that the assumption that a movement maximally consists of two submovements often does not hold for two-dimensional goal directed movements. The method Meyer et al. [16] proposed was based on 1D rotation movements, for which it is more plausible that they consist of maximally two submovements. Other studies investigating 2D interactions have also demonstrated that more than two submovements occur frequently when using Meyer's criteria [9, 8, 18]. Therefore, we may conclude that the division of two-dimensional movements into submovements should be reconsidered.

2.3 Parsing Rules

Although Meyer's criteria allow for a more detailed analysis of movements into submovements, these criteria require adjustments to address the problems described above. We therefore propose a modified method that is more stable and reliable with respect to the differentiation between the ballistic phase and the correction phase of a movement. The method has been tested on a large number of aimed movements, executed in both 2D and 3D, with a diversity of input devices (mouse, trackball, stylus in 2D and magnetically and optically tracked stylus in 3D). The method has been proven to be more robust than the parsing rules proposed by Meyer et al. [16].

Input data filtering. We start by filtering the position data as a function of time since taking derivatives of noisy signals easily gives rise to spurious details. The data is filtered using a Gaussian time filter with a standard deviation of 25 ms, which is comparable to the 7 Hz low-pass filter proposed in earlier studies. The advantage of a Gaussian filter is that it is known not to introduce spurious details, as explained in the theory of scale space filtering [12]. For this reason, Gaussian filters are used very frequently in computer vision.

Movement interval parsing. First, we identify the intervals in which actual movements occur. We define the latency phase and the verification phase as the intervals at the beginning and end of the trial where no significant movement occurs (interval in which the first and last 0.1 mm of the path is traveled, respectively). The latency phase can provide information about the time it takes to plan the movement towards the target. The verification phase can reveal problems with making the actual selection once the pointer has arrived at the target position (see Figure 2).

Second, the interval between the latency phase and the verification phase is divided into distinct movement intervals. These distinct movement intervals are separated by pauses in which no or only minimal movement of the pointer occurs. A pause is defined as an interval in which the speed of the pointer remains below 0.02 times the movement's peak speed. In contrast to earlier studies we propose to determine the speed of the pointer along the movement path instead of considering the parallel displacement of the pointer. Path length is used to determine the pointer's speed because the displacement velocity profile cannot discern real pauses from intervals in which the pointer moves perpendicular to the task axis. In addition, the analysis based on path length does not require a known task axis like the analysis based on parallel displacement, which makes it easier to extend the method to other tasks (such as circular steering tasks).

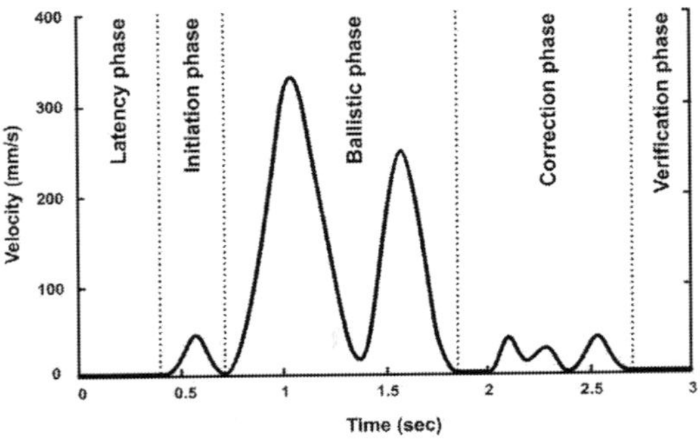

Fig. 2. Example of a velocity profile containing all 5 movement phases

Third, we determine for each identified movement interval whether or not it makes a considerable contribution to approaching the target. If the path length of a movement interval is contributing more than 25% to the total path length it is considered to be part of the ballistic phase. This criterion is introduced to be able to deal with cases where several movements are required to reach the target, such as the one depicted in Figure 1A. If a movement interval does not make a considerable contribution it is considered to be part of either the correction phase or the initiation phase. The movement interval will be considered part of the correction phase when it occurs after the last ballistic movement and it will be considered part of the initiation phase when it occurs before the first ballistic movement.

Finally, we divide the separate movement intervals into submovements. We do this for two reasons. First, we use this division to get more detailed information on how the movement was performed (i.e., fluently or with corrections). Second, we use this division to determine whether or not the last movement interval of the ballistic phase contains some correction submovements at the end. The criteria proposed by Meyer et al. [16] were adjusted so they could be applied to speed profiles based on path length:

a) a type-1 submovement occurs when the speed becomes (almost) zero (less than 0.02 times the movement's peak speed, which only occurs at the beginning of a movement interval);
b) a type-2 submovement occurs at a zero-crossing of acceleration from negative to positive (in combination with a positive jerk that exceeds 0.01 times the maximally observed jerk);
c) a type-3 submovement occurs at a zero-crossing of jerk from positive to negative (in combination with a negative value of its derivative that exceeds 0.01 times the maximally observed value).

The thresholds on the slopes of the zero crossings are incorporated to avoid submovement detection during small involuntary tremor or slow drift. The minimal requirements for submovements that were proposed by Meyer et al. [16] were specific for their 1D rotation task, and needed to be adapted for the case of 2D movement path. The following minimal requirements for a submovement (to avoid the division of movements into meaningless small submovements) are: a submovement should traverse a distance of at least 2 mm and last for at least 75 ms, while the maximum velocity should exceed 0.02 times the maximally observed velocity. Submovements that do not meet this requirement are combined with bordering submovements.

If the last movement in the ballistic phase consists of multiple submovements the ballistic phase ends at the first type-2 submovement that occurs in the last 75%-95% of the traveled path length. The corrective submovements that occur during the final part of the interaction movement are considered to assist in positioning the pointer within the target boundaries. They should hence be considered as being part of the correction phase. As mentioned before, type-3 submovements are only considered to be indications of subtle accuracy regulation and are therefore not used to signal the end of the ballistic phase. If the last ballistic movement consists of only one submovement the end of this movement coincides with the end of the ballistic phase.

2.4 Performance Measures

In order to draw meaningful conclusions from interaction movements a division of movements into meaningful components is not sufficient. We also need summary measures to assess the key characteristics of the phases that have been distinguished. A review of 43 studies in the field of 2D interaction and human movement science resulted in a set of 63 measures that can be applied to evaluate 2D interaction techniques. These findings indicate that there is no consensus about which measures are best to use when evaluating input devices and interaction techniques. It is highly likely, however, that several proposed measures assess similar qualities of the movement. It is argued that from this large list of measures only a few measures should be retained, i.e. those that are complementary to each other.

In the current study only measures that can extract information from a single movement path were applied to the movement data. We made an exception for throughput, which extracts the effective width from a series of trials in the same condition, for it is included in the ISO standard (ISO 9241-9). Time is one of the most frequently used measures to assess movement quality and therefore it was applied to the total trial and to each of the movement phases (latency, initiation, ballistic, correction and verification phase). Besides time and phase occurrence, 47 measures were applied to the overall movement, the ballistic phase and/or the correction phase. A short description of these measures can be found in Appendix 1. As indicated in the appendix some of the measures were applied to the overall movement as well as to the ballistic phase and the correction phase and some of the measures were applied to only the overall movement, the ballistic phase or the correction phase. As a result, a total of 99 movement characteristics were obtained from the data.

As mentioned before, the study described in the current paper compares indirect mouse interactions with direct stylus interactions. The reason for this choice is that previous studies comparing mouse interactions with stylus and tablet interactions were only able to find minor differences between the mouse and the stylus [15, 1], especially with respect to movement time. We will show how the application of the new division method in combination with the use of alternative measures can indeed provide a more detailed description of indirect mouse interaction movements and direct stylus interaction movements.

3 Experiment

3.1 Participants

Eight university employees voluntarily participated in the study that we undertook to test the proposed measures. The group consisted of 5 males and 3 females. Their age ranged from 30 to 35 years (M = 32.4 years). All participants indicated that their right hand was their preferred hand when using the mouse. Two participants indicated that their left hand was the preferred hand when using the stylus.

3.2 Task

The task used in the experiment was a multi-directional pointing task. In this task 8 "target" circles are arranged in larger circles with a diameter of 48, 96 and 144 mm around a central "home" circle (see Figure 3A). The targets have three different sizes, 3mm, 6mm and 9mm. The 9 combinations of target size and target distance resulted in 7 different levels of difficulty (ID = 2.7, 3.2, 3.5, 4.1, 4.6, 5 and 5.6 bits). At the beginning of a new trial, the target was presented together with the home circle (3 mm). The targets were presented in random order, with the restriction that subsequent targets were never positioned in the same direction in order to prevent learning effects. The data collection started when the home-circle was selected and continued until the target was correctly selected.

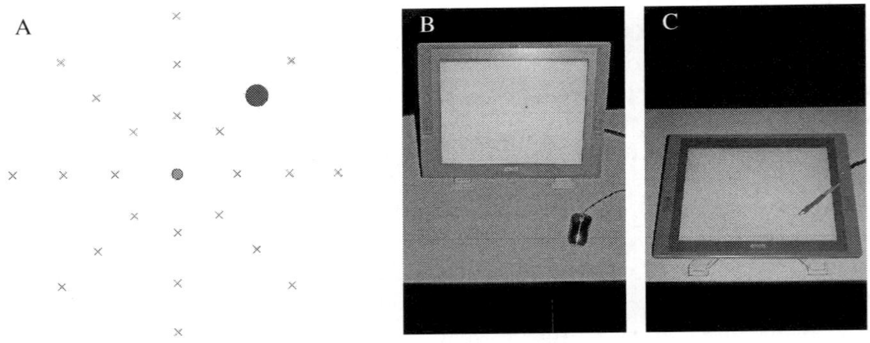

Fig. 3. Multi-directional pointing task: A) target layout, indicating home-circle (middle), target-circle and the other possible target positions; B) screen set-up when using mouse; C) screen set-up when using stylus

3.3 Procedure

The selection task was presented on a 21-inch WACOM Cintiq 21UX tablet, with integrated display. The resolution of the screen was set at 1600x1200 pixels. The position of the screen was changed in between sessions: when participants were using the mouse the screen was positioned vertically (see Figure 3B) and when they were using the stylus the screen was tilted horizontally so that the screen would face up (see Figure 3C). The position of the screen was adjusted to simulate the normal way of use as much as possible. The mouse had a constant CD-ratio of 1:4, while the CD-ratio was 1:1 in case of the stylus with integrated display.

Before participants started the experiment they were provided with a short instruction about the task. The experiment consisted of two sessions, each containing 72 trials, i.e., 8 target directions combined with 3 different target sizes and 3 different target distances. A practice session with 27 trials, i.e., 3 target directions combined with 3 different target sizes and 3 different target distances, preceded each actual experimental session. The order of the two experimental sessions was balanced so that the number of participants using the mouse during the first session was equal to the number of participants using the stylus during the first session.

4 Results

Although target size and target distance were included in the statistical model, the analysis reported here will focus on the influence of input device on phase duration and phase occurrence. Before analyses were carried out log transformations were applied to time measures and square root transformations were applied to counts. These transformations accomplished that the distributions of the data were closer to the normal distribution assumed by the applied statistical methods (such as ANOVA).

4.1 Overall Movement vs. Movement Phases

Figure 4A shows the duration of the total trial, ballistic phase and correction phase as a function of the input device. We averaged the times for the 8 different directions and applied a within-subject correction for subject, target size and target distance as proposed by Loftus and Masson [13]. As can be seen from this figure there is no difference in total trial duration between the mouse and the stylus. However, it also shows that there are considerable differences in the duration of the ballistic phase, correction phase and verification phases between the mouse and the stylus.

The repeated measures analysis with target size (3mm/6mm/9mm) and target distance (48mm/96mm/144mm) as within-subjects variables confirmed that there was no significant difference in total trial time as a function of input device (mouse/stylus), $F(1,7)=.08$, $p=.79$. It also confirmed that there were significant differences in duration of the ballistic phase and the correction phase between the mouse and the stylus. The ballistic phase was shorter when participants were using the mouse ($M=.41$; $SE=.02$) than when they were using the stylus (M=.64; $SE=.02$), $F(1,7)=137.73$, $p<.01$. On the other hand, the correction phase was longer when participants were using the mouse ($M=.34$; $SE=.01$) than when they were using the stylus ($M=.23$; $SE=.01$), $F(1,7)=72.38$, $p<.01$.

Repeated measures were also carried out to test the effect of input device on the duration of the latency phase, start phase and verification phase. Only the duration of the verification phase showed a significant effect of input device. The verification phase was longer when using the mouse ($M=.18$; $SE=.01$) than when using the stylus ($M=.07$; $SE=.01$), $F(1,7)=97.16$, $p<.01$. Due to the infrequent occurrence of the initiation phase when participants were using the mouse (see Figure 4B) the repeated measures analysis could not be carried out on the duration of the initiation phase.

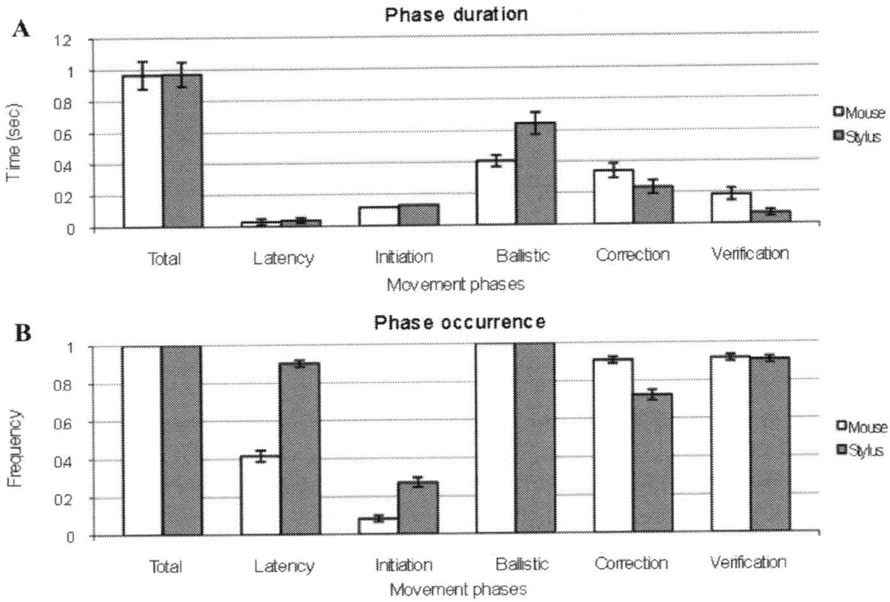

Fig. 4. The duration and phase occurrence (with 95% confidence intervals) are shown as a function of input device (mouse/stylus) for each movement phase

Figure 4B shows the frequency of occurrence for each of the movement phases as a function of the input device. This figure clearly illustrates that the latency phase and the initiation phase occur more often when participants were using the stylus than when they were using the mouse. However, the correction phase occurs more frequently when participants were using the mouse.

4.2 Measure Selection

To select only a few measures to assess the quality of the interaction movements a principal components factor analysis with varimax rotation was carried out. Fourteen of the 99 movement characteristics (such as initiation time, number of pauses during the ballistic phase, number of target misses and number of slip-offs) were excluded from the factor analysis because the data distributions were strongly skewed. By default, factor analysis retains factors with an eigenvalue larger than 1. However, this method resulted in the extraction of 15 factors, which would imply a relatively large selection of measures. Therefore, we chose to increase the eigenvalue boundary to 4, which resulted in the extraction of 4 factors, with eigenvalues equal to 22.4, 19.0, 8.0 and 4.9. Together, these factors explain almost 65% of the variance, with the last factor still making a considerable contribution to the explained variance (5.8%).

Table 1. Factor loadings after varimax rotation on the 4 extracted factors

Factor 1	Factor 2	Factor 3	Factor 4
Duration ballistic phase .94	Peak speed ballistic phase .92	Pauses >100ms correction phase .74	Orthogonal direction change overall movement .76
Mouse M=.41; SE=.02 *Stylus M=.64; SE=.02* $F(1,7)=137.73; p<.01$	*Mouse M=547.3; SE=17.2* *Stylus M=334.4 SE=26.9* $F(1,7)=57.95 ; p<.01$	*Mouse M=.29; SE=.02* *Stylus M=.32 SE=.03* $F(1,7)=.26 ; p=.63$	*Mouse M=.66; SE=.05* *Stylus M=.97; SE=.10* $F(1,7)=2.34 ; p=.17$
Relative accuracy ballistic phase -.87	Path length overall movement .91	Duration correction phase .73	Movement offset overall movement .66
Mouse M=.12; SE=.005 *Stylus M=.05; SE=.003* $F(1,7)=251.60; p <$	*Mouse M=107.4; SE=2.8* *Stylus M=101.6; SE=1.9* $F(1,7)=5.83, p<.05$	*Mouse M=.34; SE=.01* *Stylus M=.23; SE=.01* $F(1,7)=72.38; p<.01$	*Mouse M=3.0; SE=.18* *Stylus M=2.8; SE=.64* $F(1,7)=.14 ; p=.72$
Number of type 3 submovements ballistic phase .84	Mean speed ballistic phase .91	Mean duration of pauses correction phase .67	Path length efficiency ballistic phase -.60
Mouse M=.08; SE=.01 *Stylus M=.54; SE=.04* $F(1,7)=30.47; p<.01$	*Mouse M=234.8; SE=11.0* *Stylus M=146.0; SE=7.7* $F(1,7)=75.31; p<.01$	*Mouse M=.15; SE=.01* *Stylus M=.13; SE=.01* $F(1,7)=10.25; p<.05$	*Mouse M=.99; SE=.05* *Stylus M=.98; SE=.09* $F(1,7)=16.81; p<.01$

As can be observed in Table 1, the groups of measures loading high on the 4 resulting factors focus on different aspects of the goal directed movement. The first factor mostly contains measures that assess features of the ballistic phase and how it is related to the overall movement. The second factor focuses on how the movement is executed in terms of the length of the traveled path and speed. The third factor typically contains measures that assess the quality of the correction phase, e.g. the number and duration of pauses. The final factor includes measures that mainly focus on the efficiency of the movement path, like the number of orthogonal direction changes and the movement offset. This fourth factor hence resembles the measures proposed by MacKenzie et al. [14].

Table 1 also shows the results of repeated measures analyses which were carried out to test the main effect of input device. The results show that the duration of the ballistic phase was longer when participants were using the stylus, mainly because they were moving slower. Although more online adjustments were made during the ballistic movement and the ballistic phase ended closer to the target, the path length efficiency of the ballistic phase was somewhat lower when participants were using the stylus. When looking at the correction phase, there is no difference between input devices with respect to the number of pauses. However the duration of pauses is somewhat longer when participants use the mouse. Finally, there are also no differences between the input devices with respect to the number of orthogonal direction changes and the movement offset.

The measures extracted by the factor analysis were able to provide a well-founded explanation for the differences found in the duration of the distinct movement phases. The measures that proved useful in the analysis besides movement time and phase occurrence (frequency) are therefore proposed to assess the characteristics of aimed movements, especially with respect to differentiating between input devices:

- Mean speed
- Peak speed
- Path length
- Path efficiency
- Relative accuracy ballistic phase
- Orthogonal direction change
- Movement offset
- Number of submovements (type 3)
- Number and duration of pauses

Most of the proposed measures can be applied to the total trial as well as the ballistic phase and the correction phase, like mean speed, path length and movement offset. This means that these measures are also able to specify differences between these phases.

5 Conclusion and Discussion

This paper has introduced parsing criteria that divide a goal-directed movement not only into a ballistic and a correction phase, but also into an initiation phase, latency phase and verification phase. Although the criteria we proposed deviate from Meyer's criteria and might seem arbitrary it is not our primary aim to provide criteria that can be theoretically founded. It is our aim to provide a method that is able to divide goal-directed movements into meaningful parts. We believe that the division into the five phases described above is a meaningful and intuitive division. In addition, since the analysis method is applied to the cursor position this analysis method of goal directed movements can also be applied to assess the performance of other input device or interaction techniques in 2D as well as 3D environments.

We have demonstrated that the analysis of rapidly aimed movements into five movement phases (latency phase, initiation phase, ballistic phase, correction phase and verification phase) provides insights that cannot be obtained from the analysis of the overall movement. Due to the reverse effects of the input devices on the duration of the different phases, no main effects for input device can be found when looking at the overall movement duration. It is expected that such effects do not only occur with respect to movement time but also with respect to other measures. Even with an observed difference in the overall movement it is very well possible that the effect can be solely attributed to a particular phase. For example, the measure *number of pauses* reveals significant differences between the mouse and the stylus when looking at the overall movement. However, pauses are mainly found in the correction phase and not in the ballistic phase. Therefore, the application of a range of measures to the separate movement phases enables us to better understand the root causes of the differences between input devices. In this way the proposed analysis method is especially helpful in the design and improvement of input devices and interaction techniques.

The other contribution of the current paper is that we reduced the list of measures that can be applied to goal-directed movements to just a few measures. This selection was carried out because some measures assess similar aspects of the movements and are therefore redundant and some measures are better in discriminating between variables than others. It is thought that the selected measures have some face validity and they assisted very much in explaining the differences between mouse and stylus interactions. For example, from the selected measures it can be concluded that, when using the stylus, the ballistic movement is considerably slower and more online adjustments are made. As a result, the execution is more precise and, therefore, less time is required to enter the target region, which is shown by the shorter correction phase. A different strategy is applied when participants are using the mouse. Not only the short duration of the ballistic phase but also the absence of the latency phase and initiation phase indicate that participants using the mouse want to get into the neighborhood of the target as fast as possible. However, since the movement is fast and less controlled more time is required to make the final corrections in order to enter the target area.

Although the precise outcome may somewhat depend on the difference in CD-ratio for the mouse and stylus, it still shows areas where the mouse and stylus interactions can be improved. For the improvement of the mouse interactions, the focus should lie on increasing the end-point accuracy of the ballistic movement and on facilitating the execution of the correction movements, for example by automation techniques. On the other hand, for the improvement of the stylus interactions more focus should lie on increasing the movement speed, while maintaining the movement accuracy. Another issue with respect to direct stylus interactions is that participants sometimes covered the targets with their arm and as a result started moving in the wrong direction. This is also shown by a lower path length efficiency when participants were using the stylus. Solving the problem of covering important content would also increase performance of direct stylus interactions.

The proposed analysis method is tailored to assess the quality of rapidly aimed selection movements. Steering is another interaction technique that is frequently used in computer interactions (e.g. navigation through menu-structures). A major difference between selection and steering tasks is that steering tasks require a more continuous control of pointer precision. As a result, steering movements will most likely be subject to ongoing corrections and might have different characteristics than goal directed movements. Future work will focus on the question how the analysis method can be adjusted so that it can also be applied to these more controlled movements. Besides selection and navigating though menu-structures, there are other tasks that are important with respect to computer interactions such as changing an object's position and/or its orientation (e.g. in graphical applications). These tasks have not been standardized yet and future work should also focus on designing simple tasks that have similar characteristics as the ISO 9241-9 pointing task. In order to investigate the performance on these different tasks in a systematic way, it should also be investigated whether similar factors and measures will be extracted when different interaction techniques or tasks are applied.

Acknowledgments

This research was supported by The Netherlands Organization for Scientific Research (NWO). We would like to thank Victor Vloemans for the technical assistance.

References

1. Accot, J., Zhai, S.: Performance Evaluation of Input Devices in Trajectory-Based Tasks: An Application of the Steering Law. In: Proceedings of CHI 1999, pp. 466–472 (1999)
2. Akamastu, M., MacKenzie, I.S., Hasbrouq, T.: A Comparison of Tactile, Auditory, and Visual Feedback in a Pointing Task Using a Mouse-Type Device. Ergonomics 38, 816–827 (1995)
3. Behbehani, K., Kondraske, G.V., Richmond, J.R.: Investigation of Upper Extremity Visuomotor Control Performance Measures. IEEE Transactions on Biomedical Engineering 35, 518–525 (1988)
4. Card, S.K., English, W.K., Burr, B.J.: Evaluation of Mouse, Rate-Controlled Isometric Joystick, Step Keys, and Text Keys for Text Selection on a CRT. Ergonomics 21, 601–613 (1978)
5. Fitts, P.M.: The Information Capacity of the Human Motor System in Controlling the Amplitude of Movement. Journal of Experimental Psychology 47, 381–391 (1954)
6. Goldvasser, D., McGibbon, C.A., Krebs, D.E.: High Curvature and Jerk Analyses of Arm Ataxia. Biological Cybernetics 84, 85–90 (2001)
7. Hansen, S., Tremblay, L., Elliott, D.: Real-Time Manipulation of Visual Displacement during manual aiming. Human Movement Science 27, 1–11 (2008)
8. Hourcade, J.P.: Learning from Preschool Children's Pointing Submovements. In: Proceedings of IDC 2006, pp. 65–72 (2006)
9. Hwang, F., Keates, S., Langdon, P., Clarkson, J.: A Submovement Analysis of Pointer Trajectories. Behaviour and Information Technology 24, 205–217 (2005)
10. Jagacinski, R.J., Repperger, D.W., Moran, M.S., Ward, S.L., Glass, B.: Fitts' Law and the Microstructure of Rapid Discrete Movements. Journal of Experimental Psychology: Human Perception and Performance 6, 309–320 (1980)
11. Keates, S., Trewin, S.: Effect of Age and Parkinson's Disease on Cursor Positioning Using a Mouse. In: Proceedings of ASSETS 2005, pp. 68–75 (2005)
12. Koenderink, J.J.: The Structure of Images. Biological Cybernetics 50, 363–370 (1984)
13. Loftus, G.R., Masson, M.E.J.: Using Confidence Intervals in Within-Subject Designs. Psychonomic Bulletin & Review 4, 476–490 (1994)
14. MacKenzie, I.S., Kauppinen, T., Silfverberg, M.: Accuracy Measures for Evaluating Computer Pointing Devices. In: Proceedings of CHI 2001, pp. 9–16 (2001)
15. MacKenzie, I.S., Sellen, A., Buxton, W.A.: Comparison of Input Devices in Elemental Pointing and Dragging Tasks. In: Proceedings of CHI 1991, pp. 161–166 (1991)
16. Meyer, D.E., Abrams, R.A., Kornblum, S., Wright, J.E., Smith, J.E.K.: Optimality in Human Motor Performance: Ideal Control of Rapid Aimed Movements. Psychological Review 95, 340–370 (1988)
17. Soukoreff, R.W., MacKenzie, I.S.: Towards a Standard for Pointing Device Evaluation, Perspective on 27 Years of Fitts' Law Research in HCI. International Journal of Human-Computer Studies 61, 751–789 (2004)
18. Wisleder, D., Dounskaia, N.: The Role of Different Submovement Types During Pointing to a Target. Experimental Brain Research 176, 132–149 (2007)
19. Woodworth, R.S.: Accuracy of voluntary movement. Psychological Review, Monograph Supplement 3, 1–114 (1899)

Appendix 1. Measures with Descriptions

Acceleration time: Time interval during which the pointer was accelerating[1] [18]
Angle offset: Angle between the vector from the beginning of the ballistic phase to the end of the ballistic phase and the task axis[2] [8]
Average speed: Average speed in mm/sec, i.e. total path length divided by total time[1]
Counter-productive submovements: Number of times the coincident error is negative with a magnitude larger than the submovement's starting distance[1] [9]
Deceleration time: Time interval during which the pointer was decelerating[1] [18]
Distance to peak speed: Distance traveled from movement onset to the moment peak speed is reached[2]
Error magnitude: Distance from the position of the target miss (button click) to the target edge[3]
Final positioning time: Interval from target entry until the end of the trial[3] [2]
Goal distance correction phase: Distance to the target at the start of the correction phase[3]
High curvature occurrence: Number of times the angle between 3 sample points is less than 80 deg[1] [6]
Length offset: Difference between the length of the ballistic phase and 'distance to target' at the beginning of the ballistic phase[2] [8]
Max percent overshoot: largest percent deviation from the target once the pointer passes the target[2] [3]
Movement direction change: Number of times the tangent to the path gets parallel to the task axis[1] [14]
Movement error: Mean of absolute distances of the path from the task axis[1] [14]
Movement offset: Overall mean distances of the path from the task axis[1] [14]
Movement time: time interval from movement onset to movement offset[4] [16]
Movement variability: Extent to which the path lies in a straight line parallel to the task axis[1] [14]
Orthogonal direction change: Number of times the tangent to the path becomes perpendicular to the task axis[1] [14]
Overshoot: the frequency and duration (time interval from the moment the pointer passes the target edge to movement offset) of overshoots[2] [9,3]
Path length: Length of the path in mm[1]
Path length efficiency: Ratio between the shortest path and the traveled path[1] [11]
Pauses: Number of pauses (>0ms; >100ms; >250ms) [11] and mean duration of the pauses[1] [9]
Peak acceleration: Maximum acceleration reached during the overall movement[2] [7]
Peak deceleration: Maximum deceleration reached during the overall movement[2] [7]
Peak speed: Maximum speed reached during the movement[2] [11]
Peak time: time at which maximum overshoot is reached[2] [3]
Perpendicular error: Distance between the endpoint of the ballistic phase and the task axis, measured in the direction normal to the task axis[2] [9]
Relative accuracy: Ratio between 'distance to target' at the end of the ballistic phase and at movement onset[2] [10]
Relative parallel displacement: Ratio between parallel displacement of the ballistic phase and the overall movement[2]
Relative path length: Ratio between path length of the ballistic phase and the overall movement[2] [11]
Relative time: Ratio between duration of the ballistic phase and the overall movement[2] [18]
Relative time to peak speed: Ratio between time from movement onset to peak speed and the overall movement[2] [11]
Slip-off: Number of submovements that begin inside the target but end outside the target[3] [9]
Submovements: Number of submovements [9] and number of type 1, 2 and 3 submovements[1] [18]
Submovements after target entry: Number of additional submovements after the pointer has landed inside the target until movement offset[3] [9]
Target miss: Frequency of trials in which the mouse button is clicked outside the target area[3] [9]
Target re-entry: Number of times the pointer enters the target after the first target entry[3] [14]
Task axis crossing: Number of times the path crosses task axis[1] [14]
Throughput: IDe/MT ($IDe = \log_2[D/We + 1]$, where $We = 4.133*\sigma)$[4] [17]
Time to peak speed: Time interval from movement onset to the moment the peak speed is reached[2] [11]

---

[1] Applied to the overall movement, the ballistic phase and the correction phase.
[2] Applied to only the ballistic phase.
[3] Applied to only the correction phase.
[4] Applied to only the overall movement.

A Model to Simulate Web Users' Eye Movements

Myriam Chanceaux[1], Anne Guérin-Dugué[2], Benoît Lemaire[1], and Thierry Baccino[3]

[1] University of Grenoble, France
first name.last name@imag.fr
[2] University of Grenoble, France
Anne.guerin@gipsa-lab.inpg.fr
[3] Laboratoire LUTIN, Paris, France
baccino@lutin-userlab.fr

Abstract. One of the most important tasks on the Web is foraging information. In this study, we present a computational model which simulates human eye movements during information seeking in Web pages. Human visual scanpaths are guided by their information needs, by the visual features of the stimuli and by what they previously processed. Our model takes into account both semantic (top-down) and visual (bottom-up) information, as well as a memory model in order to predict the focus of attention. Our model operates at the block level, but also at the word level. To validate this model, both participants and model were asked to seek information in a pseudo online newspaper. We find good correspondence between simulated and empirically observed scanpaths. Knowing where the user is looking at while searching for information is crucial for evaluating the usability of Web sites and contribute to the design of Web pages.

Keywords: Computational model, Information foraging, Web page, Usability, Semantic, Visual saliency, Memory.

1 Introduction

A central concern of HCI research is how to determine the *usability* of user interfaces during both the design and final evaluation phases [1]. This usability assessment can be done by qualitative, criteria oriented and model-based methods (e.g., interview study, checklist, and cognitive model). Most of the time, cognitive models are missing and ergonomists have to rely on qualitative data to assess a user interface. The problem with such qualitative evaluation is that it is both expensive and time consuming. Model-based methods enable more detailed predictions of quantitative parameters, for example error rates, times and sequences of actions compared to qualitative and criteria based methods [2]. This allows to apply model-based methods in early phases of system-development processes, to detect usability problems and to change the examined user interface. Integrating these aspects, cognitive models additionally take into account the cognitive abilities and characteristics of human beings [3]. There are a number of cognitive models that have been used for usability assessment with the earliest GOMS [4] or CCT [5] and more recent work using

T. Gross et al. (Eds.): INTERACT 2009, Part I, LNCS 5726, pp. 288–300, 2009.

architecture like ACT-R [6] to test usability by means of simulated users [7]. These models may be outlines of tasks written on paper or computer programs which enable us to predict the time it takes for people to perform tasks, the kinds of errors they make, the decisions they make, or what buttons and menu items they choose. To sum up, cognitive models can be used in several ways: to determine ways of improving the user interface so that a person's task has fewer errors or takes less time, to build into the user interface to make software that reacts more effectively to help people use the system by anticipating their behavior or inferring their mental state, or as a means of testing current psychological theory. The goal is to radically reduce the time and cost of designing and evaluating usable systems through developing analytic engineering models for usability based on validated computational models of human cognition and performance.

Following the same approach of model-based methods for measuring the usability of a user interface, we present a computational cognitive model of Information Foraging on the Web. This model simulates the search for information on the Web (by combining the visual, semantic and memory processing) starting from realistic tasks and ill-defined goals. It is intended to explain how the visual exploration is made on Web pages containing both texts and images and as a consequence to provide fruitful information to any interface designers. The information seeking process implemented in our model is currently mainly based on textual information processing on one Web page without navigation.

2 Task

Our model is simulating a user searching for information on a pseudo online newspaper. Before explaining our model in details, we now describe the task, which will be performed by both humans and model.

This task consists in searching a piece of information in a simulated Web page representing an online newspaper. The goal is to find the block of text that best corresponds to an expression given beforehand. In this article we will refer to this expression as the *theme*. Examples of themes are *global warming, rise in the stock market, soccer players' win...* Since the goal is to find the block which *best* corresponds to the theme, users are encouraged to scan all blocks although they already found an interesting one, because the next one may be better. In addition, this design also encourages users to revisit previously visited blocks, which makes the overall scanpath quite complex.

Pages are composed of seven texts, one of them being associated with a picture. Texts are divided into 3 categories: 2 texts are semantically very close to the theme and are therefore potential targets; 2 texts are related to the theme, and 3 texts have no semantic link with the theme.

Figure 1 shows an example of a page. The theme is "planet observation". One text deals with the giant planets rings, another with a study of the solar system; they are the Strong Association texts (SA). Another text is on the problems of a spacecraft's antenna and another one on a software for aerial photographs; these two texts have Low Association (LA) with the theme. The three others do not have any association with the theme (Without Association, WA). They are about a complaint filled by a

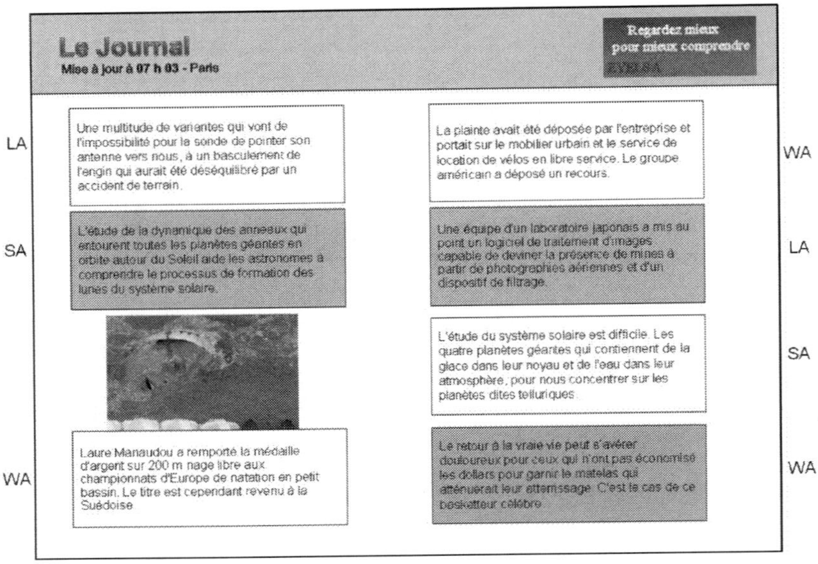

Fig. 1. Example of page, theme is *planet observation*. During experiment, block types are not visible (SA, LA and WA).

company; about the French swimmer Laure Manaudou and about the after-career of a basketball player.

To design these pages, we used the semantic measures provided by Latent Semantic Analysis (LSA) [8]. A semantic space was constructed from a 24-million word corpus composed of articles from the French newspaper *Le Monde* (year 1999). Once this space was constructed, we chose 20 themes and represented all of them by a 300-dimensional vector. Then, we selected for each of them 2 SA texts, 2 LA texts and 3 WA texts according to their cosine with the theme vector. A high cosine corresponds to a high semantic similarity. We sometimes had to manually revise the texts in order to keep an approximately constant length. Here are the semantic similarity statistics. SA: mean 0.7, max 0.92, min 0.45; LA: mean 0.19, max 0.46, min 0.14; WA: mean 0.01, max 0.13, min -0.05.

Since our model is intended to simulate the user conflict between semantic and visual attraction, we added visual information to our pages in addition to their semantic organizations. Therefore, blocks can have a white or colored background. There are three possible colors per image. The colors were chosen in order (1) to show iso-luminance (same contrast with the white background and black text) so that they all have the same readability and (2) to have the same color contrast between them (they form the apex of a triangle in the Lab color space). In each page one SA, one LA and one WA have colored backgrounds.

In order to be closer to a real Web page and have more variability in the semantic and visual ways of eye attraction, we added a picture to each page. This picture can be either associated with a SA block (4 out of 20 pages) or a WA block. There is no picture associated with a LA block. This avoids situations of reinforcement of the semantic link from the combination of textual and visual information. This link would not have been quantitatively controlled, with a risk that the semantic link between the theme and the LA block would have been greatly modified to the point of changing its semantic class (from LA to SA).

We designed 20 pages for 20 themes of information search (one theme per page). A randomized procedure (Latin square) on the colors and places created 6 lists (a participant only sees one list).

3 Model

Our model is intended to reproduce the average sequence of eye fixations a user is likely to do, given a page and a theme. The model output is therefore a sequence of fixations which are XY coordinates. We assumed that there are two distinct levels of navigation in the page. The first one consists in going from block to block (block level) whereas the second one operates within each paragraph (word level).

Basically at the block level this spatio-temporal model is based on the dynamic integration of visual and memory information. Each of these components is implemented by means of a conditional heat map of the current image, in which each of its elements is assigned a weight representing its relevance for the given component. The visual map is conditional on the location of the current fixation. It tends to reinforce local and visually salient regions. The memory map is conditional on the entire scanpath. It tends to penalize already seen regions. These maps are continuously updated during the simulated visual search. The two maps are integrated by a weighted sum and the simulated gaze is moved towards the best-weighted block. Once the new fixation has been selected, the second part of the model is required, and then maps are updated accordingly, a new block is chosen, and so on. From an initial fixation point, our model thus produces a path between block.

At the word level, the model is based on semantic information contained in the sequence of words fixated and compared with the theme of information foraging. This level enables the model to modulate the memory weight of the block, for further visits.

We now detail these two modeling levels.

3.1 Block Level

As we mentioned earlier, selecting the next block to process is based on two cognitive processes: a visual one and a memory one. Those two processes may be conflicting: the visual process may suggest visiting a close block whereas the memory process may indicate that it has already been seen recently. Our model therefore includes a mechanism to integrate those two sources of information. At this level, each process dynamically and independently determines a weight for each block.

Visual Process. The human eye is such that it has a local visual acuity which prevents it processing items that are far from the current location. Since long saccades are also physiologically costly, the human eye tends to operate locally. However, there might be visually salient items that could attract the attention. Sophisticated models of visual saliency have been proposed in the literature, mainly for natural scenes. These models are often based on the Feature Integration Theory [9]. Among them, the most popular is proposed by Itti and Koch [10]. It is based on a feature decomposition of the visual stimuli and generates a visual saliency map. The highest salient regions are then segmented and sorted according to their saliency value. For the first eye fixations on a picture, these models fit well the eye movements data when the visual stimuli have little semantic information and when the task is free without explicit task driving the scene exploration [11]. In the case of more demanding visual search, the visual saliency is progressively modulated over time by semantic and cognitive controls, depending of the type of the scene (a priori knowledge of the scene) and the task [12]. Our page is simple and here we just dynamically determined visual values for each block (B) by taking into account the spatial proximity with the current fixated block following the classical curve of visual acuity as a function of eccentricity [13].

In its current version, our model does not take into account visual features such as the various background colors of blocks.

Memory Process. The memory map also contains eight values representing the weight of each block. Human generally do not move back to locations previously visited. This mechanism is close to the Inhibition of Return (IOR) principle [14], which is often used in visual attention model. Here this process is used between blocks and not for each fixation, but the mechanism is quite similar. The IOR refers to an increased difficulty of orienting attention to a location to which attention has previously been directed.

Therefore, in our model the current block is given a weight of 0, meaning that it would be better not to go back to it. We also implemented a forgetting mechanism which enables to go back to previous location after a while. Actually, humans may visit again blocks that were considered interesting (see Results section). This level of interest is given to our model by the semantic similarity between the theme and the part of block that have been processed at the word level (see next section). Basically, blocks that have never been seen receive a maximum weight, blocks already seen but irrelevant are assigned a minimum weight and blocks already seen and interesting receive an intermediate weight according to their interest. All these weight are decreased at each step to simulate a forgetting mechanism. At each transition from one block to another one, the memory weight of each previously seen block B_i is calculated following this equation:

$$\text{MemoryWeight}(B_i) = \text{MemoryWeight}(B_{i-1}) + (1 - \text{MemoryWeight}(B_{i-1})) / \delta \quad (1)$$

δ was experimentally set to 6.

Integration. Each of these two processes can be viewed as computing a map, with exactly 8 distinct areas in our design. At each step, these two maps are summed to form the general map from which the best-weighted block is going to be fixated next. The sum is, for each block B_i:

$$\text{IntegrationMap}(B_i) = \alpha_M * \text{MemoryWeight}(B_i) + \alpha_V * \text{VisualWeight}(B_i) \quad (2)$$

These two processes do not have the same role. In fact in a previous version of this model we showed that the most important component in such a model is the memory process (see [15] for more details). In this previous experiment, the stimuli were very different (isolated words), but the involved processes were not. What was at the level of words in the previous experience is now at a block-level. α_M and α_V were set respectively to 0.65 and 0.35. In this new study we keep these parameter values.

Although limited to 8 areas in the current task, this mechanism can be extended to the larger number of distinct items that are usually found in real Web pages. As we will see in the following sections, this simple combination of maps reproduces the typical participant course. In fact, memory will always encourage new blocks and the visual map will promote the blocks nearby.

3.2 Word Level

At the level of the words inside a block, the model operates differently. The process by which humans gather information in a block of text is simulated by considering a word by word scanning. Some users do not actually read paragraphs linearly and prefer to pick words here and there, but most of our participants process a paragraph from its first word. However, what is very important to simulate is the fact that users do not read completely a paragraph if they realize after a while that it does not correspond to what they are looking for. All users stop reading uninteresting paragraphs and the challenge is to model that decision appropriately.

There are three conditions which seem to govern the decision to stop or to continue reading a paragraph:

- If the words processed so far are *unrelated* to the theme (using the LSA semantic measures), then the paragraph is abandoned with a zero value, so that the block is not likely to be visited again by the block level process;
- If the words processed so far are semantically *highly similar* to the theme, then the block is abandoned, but it is memorized as a potential solution by weighting it for the block level process with its semantic similarity with the theme;
- If the words processed so far are neither highly related nor semantically unrelated to the theme, then the next word is processed: the model keeps reading until it can take a decision.

Two thresholds of semantic similarity were defined for that purpose, one for defining what is a high similarity and one for the unrelatedness. These thresholds depend on the number of words already processed in the block: the more words the model sees, the more confident it can be in its decision. For example, if only two words are processed, the highly-similar-threshold is very high because the decision to abandon the block should only be done if the similarity between those two words and the theme is very very high. However, if 25 words have been processed, the threshold can be lowered because there are enough words to have a high confidence in the semantic measure. Thresholds are defined in the following way (P is a paragraph, W is the sequence of words processed so far and T is the current theme):

$$\text{Abandon (P) if similarity (W,T)} < \log(\text{nbWords(W)}) / 20 . \quad (3)$$

$$\text{Abandon (P) if similarity (W,T)} > 1\text{-}\log(\text{nbWords(W)}) / 5 . \quad (4)$$

These functions were defined experimentally and provided an appropriate behavior. Figure 2 presents these thresholds as the function of the number of words

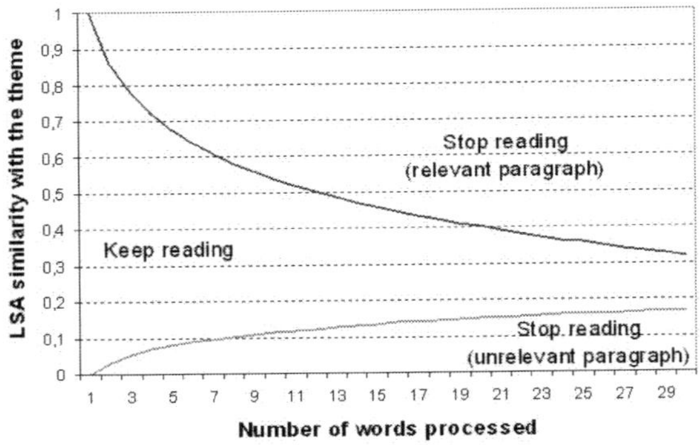

Fig. 2. Similarity thresholds as a function of the number of words

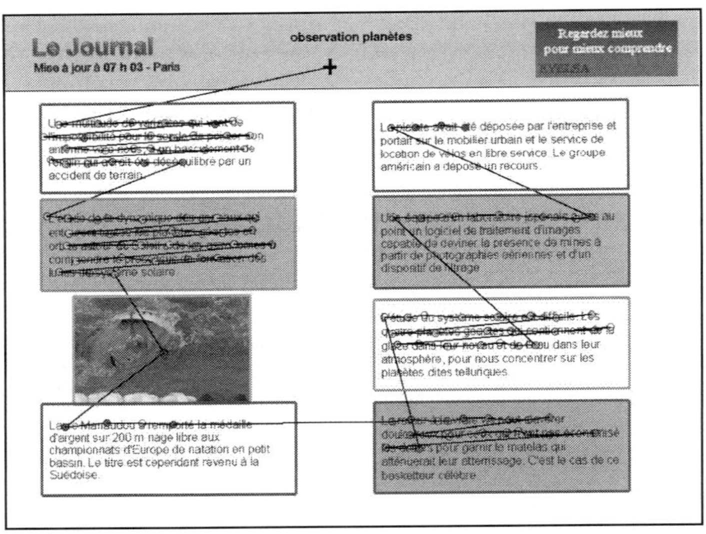

Fig. 3. Example of a scanpath generated by the model. Blocks abandoned because of high similarity with the theme are encircled with a green (gray)rectangle. Blocks abandoned because of unrelatedness are encircled with a red (black) rectangle.

processed so far. If the similarity with the theme is in-between the two lines, the model keeps reading and checks the next word. In the other cases, the block is abandoned and the block level part of the model determines which block will be fixated next.

Our model does not analyze the picture, nor does it takes into account its visual saliency. Therefore, it considers it as a block and just makes one fixation on the middle of the image.

Figure 3 presents an example of scanpath on the image presented earlier. Obviously, the model does not run on an image: it knows exactly the XY location of each word of each paragraph.

4 Test of the Model

In order to test the validity of our model, we recorded the visual scanpaths of human participants and compared their behavior with the model.

4.1 Experiment

Participants. Thirty-eight participants took part in the experiment. All had normal or correct-to-normal vision.

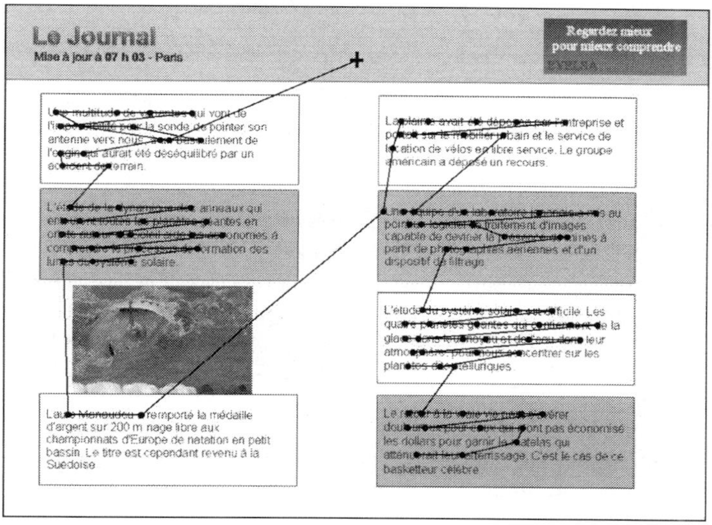

Fig. 4. Example of an experimental scanpath from a human being

Apparatus. Eye movements were recorded using a SR research EyeLink II eye tracker, sampling pupil position at 500 Hz. Eye position data were collected only for the guiding eye. Search displays subtended 40 horizontal deg. of visual angle (1024 * 768 pixels). Head position and viewing distance were fixed to 50 cm. A chin-rest was also used to keep the subject's head stable. This apparatus records horizontal and vertical gaze position data (x and y) in screen coordinates (pixels) for the guiding eye. From these coordinates, saccades and fixations are determined, leading to an experimental scanpath, as shown in figure 4.

Procedure. Each trial begins with an instruction followed by a cross fixation. This crosshair is positioned at the top of the page to be far from the text, in a non-informative area. After the participant gazed on this point an image appeared. Participants had to find the best block according to their opinion without maximum delay, then click on the selected block and give their confidence in their choice. Participants were asked to respond as quickly as possible without sacrificing accuracy and were told that many answers were possible. Figure 5 illustrates the process.

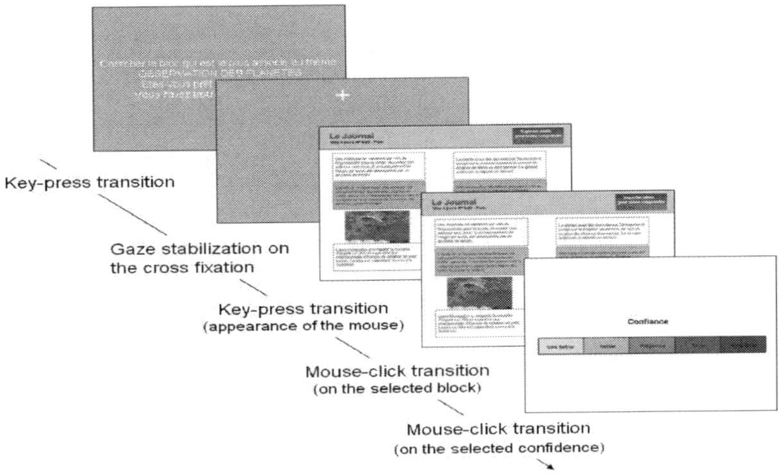

Fig. 5. Experimental process

There are 20 different experimental pages, and each of the 38 users saw all the pages, leading to 760 scanpaths. A scan on one page takes on average 36,298 ms (SD 22,841), 89.33 fixations (SD 52.63), into on average 11.36 blocks (SD 6.06).

4.2 Model Data

Our model performs the same task as humans, on the 120 (20 themes * 6 lists) pseudo Web pages. As it is deterministic, we obtained exactly 120 scanpaths we compared with empirical data.

For each page, we stopped the model when it reaches the average number of blocks seen by participants on this particular page.

4.3 Humans and Model Comparisons

Block Level. At this level, we looked at whether the participants and the model have systematic *block by block* paths.

The first column (the left one) is almost always visited from top to down, for both human (79.07%) and model (81.67%). Then, we noticed different behaviors: the matrix of transitions (Figure 6) between blocks showed us that the И path is the most common for humans, and the U path for our model. Indeed, humans are going down on the left and the right column. This might be due to the habit of reading from left to right and top to down, and the fact that the blocks are closer vertically than horizontally. On the contrary, the model goes up the second column (the right one) because its visual process prevents a large saccade from lower left to upper right.

Once all blocks have been fixated, participants often returned to the most interesting blocks, those which are semantically closest to the theme, as did the model. Figure 7 shows these rates of refixations, which are, as expected, significantly

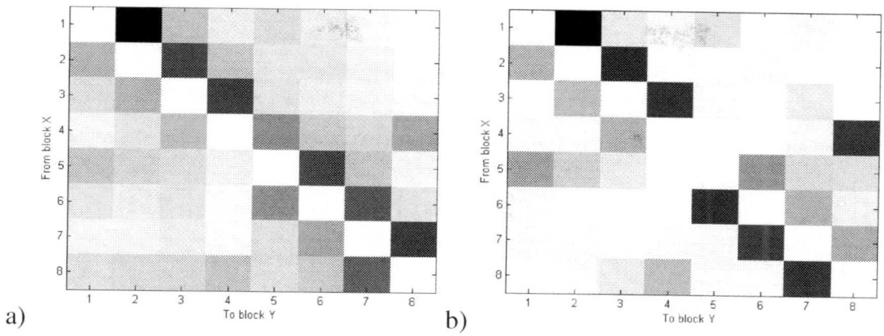

Fig. 6. Transitions matrices for human a) and model b). Blocks are numbered from upper left to lower left (1 to 4), then from upper right to lower right (5 to 8). The darker the cell, the more frequent the corresponding transition.

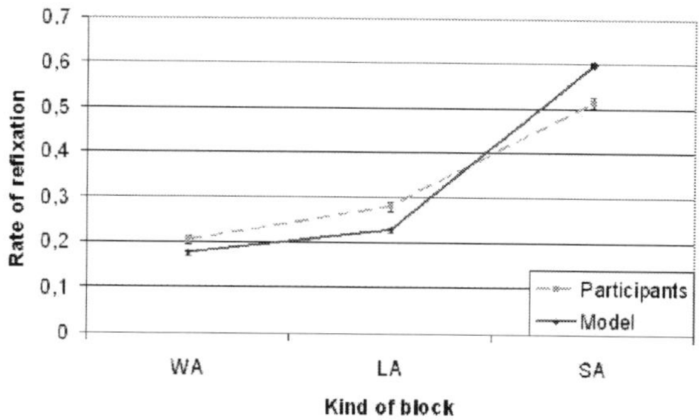

Fig. 7. Rate of blocks revisited for human and model according to the kind of block (Without Association, Law Association and Strong Association)

higher for SA blocks than for others and especially WA ones. (F tests, all $p<0.01$) This high rate of refixation for interesting blocks could be due to the fact that the goal in this information seeking task is ill-defined, and that two blocks are potential targets. There is therefore a choice to make between these two blocks, and to do it, reading them again could be necessary.

Last comparisons at this level will be for the background color of the block. Even if the model does not take into account this feature for the moment, it seems interesting to know how human deals with that.

What we observed on all data is that human gazed more often on colored block than others (Figure 8), $T(37)=12.92$, $p<0.01$. We plan to slightly improve our model in the future to account for that phenomenon.

Word Level. At this level we looked at the number of fixations in a block for each block category (SA, LA or WA) during the first visit of the block. These data were normalized by the number of words in the paragraph. The results showed that the WA blocks are sooner left than the others. That means that people do not need to read a lot

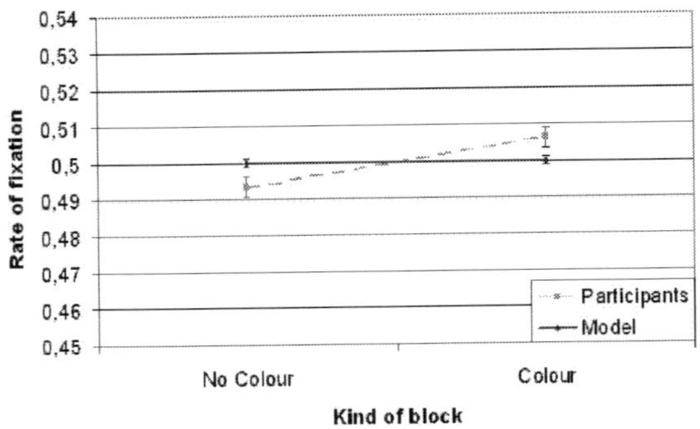

Fig. 8. Rate of blocks visited according to the kind of background, for model and participants

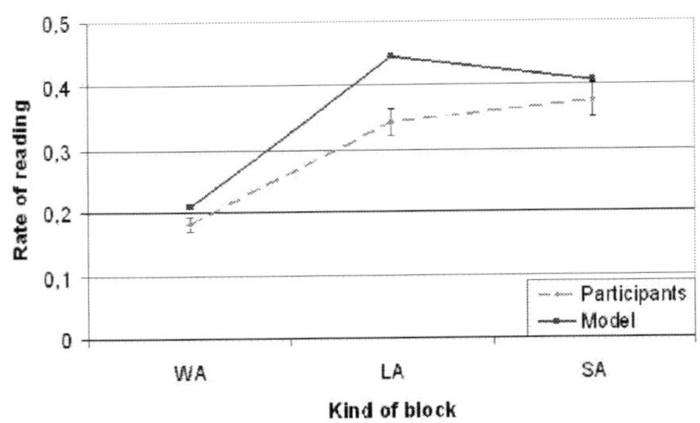

Fig. 9. Rate of reading (number of fixations divided by number of words) for human and model according to the kind of block

of words to decide that this block is unrelated to the goal. For instance, Figure 4 showed that only two fixations were necessary for that user to decide that the lower left block was unrelated to the theme. The others blocks (LA and SA) are read in more details, as shown in Figure 9. The rate of reading is significantly lower for WA than SA and LA blocks (T tests, both $p<0.01$) but there is no significant difference between SA and LA blocks ($T(37)=1.44$, $p=0.16$).

Our model obtains quite the same results, even if it reads more words before leaving the LA block, all differences are significant (F test, all $p<0.01$). This is a bias in the model conception, indeed when a block is interesting but not very interesting the model does not leave it because it does not know how to consider it, and need to process more information.

5 Discussion

Our model of a user searching information on a Web page can be compared to two systems, SNIF-ACT and CoLiDeS, which are considered complementary in the literature [16]. SNIF-ACT [17-18] was implemented using the ACT-R architecture. It simulates the navigation from pages to pages, considering each page as a whole. Basically, SNIF-ACT computes the utility of staying in the current page compared to going back to the previous page, clicking a link to go to another page or leaving the website. This model is using environmental regularities as explained in [19]. When searching for information on one Web page, the model evaluates the probability for each link to lead to the desired information. It includes an adaptive link selection mechanism that sequentially evaluates links on a Web page according to their position. At each step SNIF-ACT is faced on the exploration/exploitation trade-off problem: how to balance exploration of new actions against exploitation of actions that are known to be good. There are three possible actions: attend to the next link (exploration), click on a link (exploitation) or return to the previous page.

Our model is only simulating a single Web page. It is therefore closer to CoLiDeS [20]. This system first segments the Web page into regions called patches. Then it uses user preferences or LSA semantic similarities between regions and the current user's goal to select the object which will be the focus of attention. Then it performs an action, generally clicking on an hyperlink.

Our model also takes as input a Web page and a user's goal. The main difference is that our approach is intended to be more cognitively plausible. For instance, instead of segmenting the whole page into relevant patches, our model operates more locally because it reproduces the human visual system which cannot process the entire page in a detailed way in one shot. In addition, our model attempts to predict at a lower level since it simulates eye fixations. However, the limit of our system is that it cannot for the moment deal with complex interface objects such as buttons, links or menus that CoLiDeS can manage. To apply the model to a larger number of Web pages, to deal with more realistic web pages, it must take into account these different objects. It could then be applied in Web design, enabling designers to have an idea of what users will read according to what they want, which areas of the screen will be visited, in what order, etc. Various information searches could be tested, helping designers to validate Web pages and information content of the pages.

Taking as input a simple Web page, our model is able to predict the course from block to block, and also the rate of reading in each paragraph according to an ill-defined goal.

Further steps in the development of the model will also focus on adding a visual saliency model considering that human tend to fixate more often the colored blocks, and to be able to deal with the picture. Another issue will be to diversify the visual features, and to change the distribution map of the blocks, to prevent the systematic block by block strategy, and add a more global strategy, with preferred directions and/or locations. Finally to extend the model we should add a navigation process between several Web pages instead of dealing with just one page.

Acknowledgements

We would like to thank Gelu IONESCU for providing us LisEyeLink software; and Olivier SZARZENSKI for his work during the experiment. We also thank participants who accepted to pass the experiment.

References

1. Baccino, T., Bellino, C., Colombi, T.: Mesure de l'utilisabilité des Interfaces. Hermès Science Publisher (Lavoisier), Paris (2005)
2. Dix, A.J., Finlay, J.E., Abowd, G.D., Beale, R.: Human-Computer Interaction. Prentice Hall Europe, London (1998)
3. Newell, A.: Unified Theories of Cognition. Harvard University Press, Cambridge (1990)
4. Card, S.K., Moran, T.P., Newell, A.: The Psychology of Human-Computer Interaction. Lawrence Erlbaum Associates, Hillsdale (1983)
5. Kieras, D.E., Polson, P.: An approach to the formal analysis of user complexity. International Journal of Man-Machine Studies 22(4), 365–394 (1985)
6. Anderson, J.R., Matessa, M., Lebiere, C.: ACT-R: A theory of higher level cognition and its relation to visual attention. Human-Computer Interaction [Special Issue: Cognitive Architectures and Human-Computer Interaction] 12(4), 439–462 (1997)
7. West, R.L., Emond, B.: Can cognitive modeling improve usability testing and rapid prototyping? In: Proceedings of the Fourth International Conference on Cognitive Modeling, pp. 271–273. Lawrence Erlbaum Associates, Mahwah (2001)
8. Landauer, T., McNamara, D., Dennis, S., Kintsch, W. (eds.): Handbook of Latent Semantic Analysis. Lawrence Erlbaum Associates, Mahwah (2007)
9. Treisman, A., Gelade, G.: A feature-integration theory of attention. Cognitive Psychology 12(1), 97–13614 (1980)
10. Itti, L., Koch, C.: Computational modelling of visual attention. Nature Reviews Neuroscience 2(3), 194–203 (2001)
11. Mannan, S.K., Ruddock, K.H., Wooding, D.S.: The relationship between the locations of spatial features and those of fixation made during visual examination of briefly presented images. Spatial Vision 10, 165–188 (1996)
12. Henderson, J., Brockmole, J., Castelhano, M., Mack, M.: Visual saliency does not account for eye movements during visual search in real-world scenes. In: van Gompel, R., Fischer, M., Murray, W., Hill, R. (eds.) Eye movements: A window on mind and brain, pp. 537–562. Elsevier, Oxford (2007)
13. Geisler, W.S., Perry, J.S.: Real-time simulation of arbitrary visual fields. In: Proceedings of the 2002 symposium on eye tracking research & applications, pp. 83–87. ACM, New York (2002)
14. Klein, R.M., MacInnes, J.W.: Inhibition of return is a foraging facilitator in visual search. Psychological Science 10(4), 346–352 (1999)
15. Chanceaux, M., Guérin-Dugué, A., Lemaire, B., Baccino, T.: Towards a model of information seeking by integrating visual, semantic and memory maps. In: Caputo, B., Vincze, M. (eds.) ICVW 2008. LNCS, vol. 5329. Springer, Heidelberg (2008)
16. Kitajima, M., Polson, P.G., Blackmon, M.H.: CoLiDeS and SNIF-ACT: Complementary Models for Searching and Sensemaking on the Web. In: Human Computer Interaction Consortium (HCIC) 2007 Winter Workshop (2007)
17. Pirolli, P.L., Fu, W.-T.: SNIF-ACT: a model of information foraging on the World Wide Web. In: Brusilovsky, P., Corbett, A.T., de Rosis, F. (eds.) UM 2003. LNCS (LNAI), vol. 2702, pp. 45–54. Springer, Heidelberg (2003)
18. Fu, W., Pirolli, P.: SNIF-ACT: a cognitive model of user navigation on the World Wide Web. Human-Computer Interaction 22(4), 355–412 (2007)
19. Fu, W.-T.: Adaptive Tradeoffs between Exploration and Exploitation: A Rational-ecological Approach. Exploitation: A Rational-Ecological Approach. In: Gray, W.D. (ed.) Integrated Models of Cognitive Systems. Oxford University Press, Oxford (2007)
20. Kitajima, M., Blackmon, M.H., Polson, P.G.: Cognitive architectures for website design and usability evaluation: comprehension and information scent in performing by exploration. In: Proceedings of HCI-International, vol. 4, Theories, Models and Processes in HCI (paper 2005)

Balancing Skills to Optimize Fun in Interactive Board Games

Eva Kraaijenbrink, Frank van Gils, Quan Cheng, Robert van Herk, and Elise van den Hoven

Eindhoven University of Technology, P.O. box 513, 5600 MB Eindhoven
e.v.d.hoven@tue.nl

Abstract. Playing games against people with a different skill level can be boring or frustrating, which decreases fun. A solution is to introduce specific rules that balance a game. In this paper we describe a study in which we used an electronic board game with tangible interaction to investigate whether balancing a game indeed increases fun experienced. We also investigate whether balancing skill levels implicitly (players are unaware) or explicitly (players are aware) has an influence on the fun experienced. We found that players who lost a game felt more successful in the balanced game compared to the unbalanced game. The balanced game also offered the players more fun experience than they expected beforehand. Finally, players preferred to play an explicitly balanced game because it increased the feeling of effort and challenge.

Keywords: Balancing skills, board games, tangible interaction, game balance, interaction design, fun experience, and social interaction.

1 Introduction

In this paper we present a study that focuses on the balancing of differences in players' skill levels in a game.

Fun in games is influenced by three factors: fantasy, challenge and curiosity [14]. Offering a suitable amount of challenge can be difficult when people with different skills play together. When no effort is needed to beat an opponent a game is boring. Conversely, when an opponent is too challenging a game is frustrating. Boredom or frustration decreases fun, because challenge is not optimal.

When players are kept away from states where the game is boring or frustrating they are guided through the so-called 'flow channel' (see Figure 1), first described by Csikszentmihalyi [5] and put into a gaming context by Koster [9]. Balancing a game can be done implicitly or explicitly. In an *implicitly* balanced game, the players are not aware of the balancing mechanism. In an *explicitly* balanced game, they are. We further distinguish *statically* balanced games (based on skill level before the game) and *dynamically* balanced games (based on performance during the game).

First, we studied whether balancing a game changes the *fun experience* people have during the game in comparison to an unbalanced version. Second, we explored whether people prefer implicitly or explicitly balanced games. It could be argued that making the difference in skill level explicit encourages the weaker player to improve

T. Gross et al. (Eds.): INTERACT 2009, Part I, LNCS 5726, pp. 301–313, 2009.

his/her skills in order to participate at the same level. It might, however, also reduce the willingness of people to play because they do not want to be identified as the weaker player among other players. To answer these questions a digital tabletop game with tangible interaction, featuring a balancing mechanism, was developed. Because we used new technology, we were able to create a dynamically and implicitly balanced game: the game constantly assesses the player's skill levels and dynamically applies balancing rules. The players themselves remained unaware of this balancing mechanism until we told them it was in place.

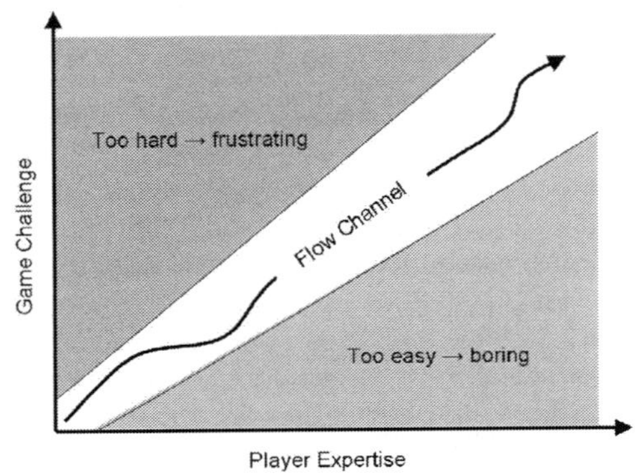

Fig. 1. The Flow Channel is the right balance between a challenge being too easy *(leads to boredom)* and too hard *(leads to anxiety)*

Balancing a game for players with different skill levels is not something new. The game 'Go', which originated in China more than 2500 years ago, already contained the possibility for two players with different expertise to play an equal match that is challenging for both. The balancing mechanism is explicit and static: the less experienced player is allowed to place one to nine stones already on the board at the start of the game, depending on the difference in expertise between the two players. Another well-known example of explicit static balancing is the 'handicap rule' in golf. Players that are less skilled clearly have a disadvantage, which is referred to as a 'handicap'. Their net score is calculated by subtracting the handicap from the gross score to be able to compare them to other players. Players that are less experienced can play against players that are more experienced and still have a challenging, competitive game.

An example of a balancing mechanism that is explicit and dynamic is the board game Wildlife [3]. In this game the player is helped by the rules of the game when falling behind during the game. It can be argued that the game is implicitly balanced because players can be unaware of the goal of the rules. The rules, however, are explicitly stated and explain the balancing mechanism.

Two examples of board games that use the possibilities of technology to create suitable challenges for players are a game called Tagtiles [34] that uses technology to offer children a challenge that is appropriate for their skill level and a tangible tabletop game that support therapy of children with cerebral palsy [35].

To set the right challenge in computer games, people can often adjust the difficulty before a game starts. Computer games typically offer different levels of difficulty (e.g., easy, normal and difficult) and adjust their challenge depending on the selection (explicitit static balancing). A new development is that the artificial intelligence of the game can analyze the expertise based on performance of the player and adjust the game implicitly [7][17] (implicit dynamic balancing). Research is also being done on the balancing of a game by recognizing emotions of a player [19]. The game is based on a number of emotion-data features like skin response, which are monitored continuously during the game (implicit dynamic balancing).

Combining traditional games and computer games give rise to interesting possibilities for mixing different ways to balance games. The expertise of a player of a tabletop game, for example, could be automatically assessed based on the placement of the game pieces on the game board before a game starts or during the game based on the amount of pieces that a player has lost.

1.1 Pervasive Games

There is a growing trend in today's games where the benefits of traditional games (physical movement and social interaction) and computer games (detailed graphics, animation and interactivity) are being combined [13]. This crossover is called pervasive gaming. To give insight in the various kinds of pervasive games some examples are described.

A first group of games is called computer augmented tabletop games that make use of a display as game board to create an interactive experience. Examples are 'KnightMage' on the STARS platform [12] and 'Weathergods' on the Entertaible platform [2]. These games use a display to show information and to create dynamically changing board configurations.

The second group consists of traditional boards that are augmented with electronics. Commercial examples of board games with very basic technology were already available in the seventies (e.g. Operation [3] and Electro [3]). Later examples are Vampire Hunter [3], where the game environment is completely changed based on the light that shines from a tower on the middle of the board and King Arthur [3] where the game board gives audio cues, tracks how you play and, adjusts the game accordingly.

Next to augmenting already existing traditional board games, such as the Settlers of Catan with an automatically changing board configuration and digital dice [4], games using advantages of technology are developed such as The MarbleGame that actually has an automatically and physically changing 'game board' [11]. Games that use the possibilities of technology to create challenges for players with different needs are called Tagtiles [21]. These games use technology to offer children a challenge that is appropriate for their skill level and a tangible tabletop game that support therapy of children with cerebral palsy [10].

Another group of pervasive games makes use of augmented reality. In these games the real world is combined with virtual reality. This makes it possible to play with tangibles, while using visually rich animations. An example is BattleBoard 3D [1], which uses physical flat markers that are recognized by a webcam, then 'translated' and shown as three-dimensional figures on a computer screen or via virtual reality goggles.

Finally, Head Up Games [16] such as Camelot [20] focus on social interaction, use interactive technologies but try to limit the use of displays. This is to create an interactive experience during which players keep there 'heads up'. A commercial product for Head Up games is Swinx [18]. Swinx is a game console focusing on active outdoor and indoor games. The base station gives feedback via lights and sound. Players can interact with the base station through bracelets containing RFID-tags. The base station can identify and track each individual player.

2 User Requirements

Before we could start with the design of the tangible board game we gathered user requirements that are defined based on an exploratory questionnaire.

2.1 Questionnaire

The questionnaire consisted of 4 parts: 1- *Demographics*: Gender, age and the frequency of play; 2- *Best game features*: The respondent could give 15 points, (1, 2, 3, 4 and 5 points) to their favorite top 5 out of 12 game features; 3- *Thoughts about skill balancing in games*: The respondent had to specify his/her level of agreement on a 5-point Likert scale to 18 statements about the preferred opponent's skill level, help and hinder and implicit and explicit balancing experience during a board game; 4- *Added value of digital elements* in board games: The respondent judged based on a 5-point scale, the added value of 10 digital elements in board games.

2.2 Results

The age of the respondents (n=53) ranged between 18 and 39 years, 42% females and 58% males. The respondents showed a wide variety in the frequency of playing computer and/or board games. There were three large groups that play 'once a week' 28% followed by 'less than once a month' (26%) and 'once a month' (23%). The minority plays 'once a day or more' (14%) or 'never' (9%).

First, the three preferred game elements out of 12 features were tactical insight (17%), problem solving (14%) and intelligence (12%). Second, the respondents liked the idea that the game was balanced for differences in game expertise between opponents, because they preferred a suitable challenge for both players during the game. Respondents indicated that they prefer balancing methods that help the weaker player (e.g., by giving him/her clues) instead of those that hinder the stronger player (e.g., giving him obstacles on the board). Third, helping the weaker player should be done implicitly instead of explicitly, because respondents indicated that they do not like to be explicitly identified as the weaker player. Players did not want to receive help at the very last moment because that would obviously show that they were losing. Visual feedback from the board and the playing pieces was perceived as an added value to traditional board games.

Based on these findings the following user requirements were defined: 1- The game should include at least one of the following game elements: tactical insight, problem solving or intelligence; 2- Weaker players are implicitly helped throughout the game; 3- The game board and playing pieces should give visual feedback.

3 Concept

Based on the defined user requirements two concepts were developed and made into paper prototypes. Seven pairs of people played both concepts. Afterwards people filled out a questionnaire about each concept and the winning concept was developed into the final concept.

Last Blood (see Figure 2) is the first paper prototype which is similar to the famous board game called Stratego [3], but augmented with technology. The pieces are set up on the four rows nearest to each player, one piece at a square with the backs of the pieces facing the opponent. The two central rows (with the small lake and wood) stay empty; the players are not allowed to deploy any pieces here. On the playing pieces an illustration of a number is shown that depicts the value of the rank (see Figure 2). The piece with five dots is the highest rank, the piece with one dot is the lowest rank and the bomb has no number, because it has a special role. Setting up is an important part of the game; victory or defeat can depend on it. In turns, players are allowed to move one piece one or two squares. Players can hit pieces of the opponent, resulting in a so-called battle. The piece with the highest rank wins a battle. Pieces die together when they have the same rank or if either piece is the bomb. After a battle is played, the losing player has to remove the playing piece from the game board. The players have won when s/he enters the red base of the opponent with one of his/her remaining pieces. Game rules are added that balance the game dynamically and implicitly: every time a player looses a piece, a `bonus' appears near another game piece of that player. The players can collect these bonuses by stepping on it with a game piece. Players can use the collected bonuses in battles to raise the strength of a piece by one rank. If more bonuses are collected the strength of a piece can also be raised during a battle by two ranks. Since bonuses pop up near game pieces of players that loose battles, it is easier for loosing players to collect them, and hence the game is balanced. An additional feature that technology allowed us to implement is that, contrary to Stratego, players do not have to show pieces that are involved in battles to each other in order to decide which piece won. Using an electronic game board it is possible to automatically indicate which piece wins in order to keep its exact level hidden and the tactics a mystery.

Pyromaniac (see Figure 2) is the second paper prototype that was developed. The game is based on tactical insight and problem solving. The goal of the game is to arrest a pyromaniac who is on the loose in the forest. The electronic board controls the pyromaniac. The pyromaniac is not visible and hides 'inside' the board. Players have to make use of a police man playing piece to find and arrest the pyromaniac and firemen playing pieces to extinguish any fires the pyromaniac lights. The game is dynamically and implicitly balanced by the artificial intelligence of the pyromaniac.

The two games were played by 14 people to test the concepts. A questionnaire was filled out about the amount of fun and excitement they experienced within each concept. The players also had to give a grade and indicate which concept they liked

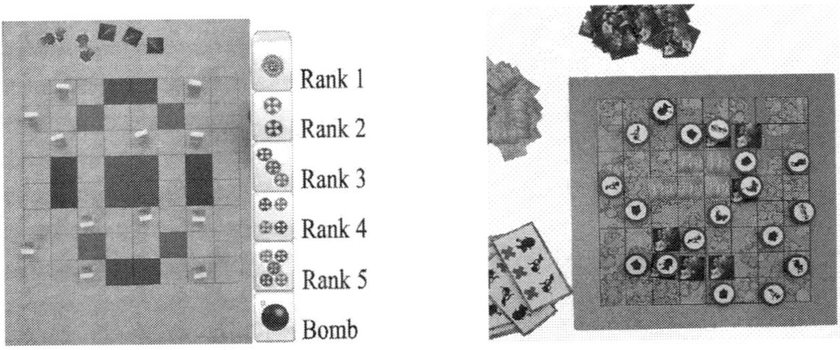

Fig. 2. Last Blood *(left)* and Pyromaniac *(right)* paper prototypes

the most. The preference for each concept was equally divided: 7 players (3 male, 4 female) chose Last Blood as their most favourite game and 7 payers (5 male, 2 female) chose for Pyromaniac. The average grade was a 7.1 on a 10-point scale for both concepts. Players pointed out that the amount of fun was the same for both concepts, but 64% of the players experienced more excitement during Last Blood. This result can be explained by the nature of both games. With Last Blood your opponent is the 'enemy' and therefore a competitive game. With Pyromaniac you try to find the same 'enemy', which makes it a collaborative game and hence moves of the opponent are of lesser importance. In addition, the rules of Last Blood were easier to understand and the duration of the game was shorter. Based on these findings Last Blood was chosen as a basis for the final concepts.

4 Final Concept Last Ice

A working prototype, with a new theme (see Figure 3) was built on the Edutainment Sensor Platform (ESP). This is a platform that is developed by Philips Research [6]. It can receive a variety of inputs (e.g., motion sensing, proximity detection and 2D object localization). On the basis of these inputs, it can then trigger a variety of outputs (including audio, LED arrays and amBX [15]). Applications for ESP are created with the ESPranto SDK, which is tailored towards allowing non-technical domain experts (e.g. game designers) to create their own content with little or no help from a software engineer [6].

The basic rules of the game Last Blood were implemented. Two versions of the game were programmed, namely the balanced and unbalanced game. In the balanced game a bonus was placed on the board near a piece that is on the side of the player that just lost a piece. In this way the game is assisting the weaker player by giving them extra points. The players will not change their strategy because they are unaware of this balancing mechanism. In the unbalanced game the bonus was randomly placed over the board. The board can decide who wins a battle and detect whether a player used a bonus. The board lights up where pieces are placed and indicates whose turn it is.

The game board was designed and printed on thick paper and put on top of the electronic board. The icebergs, shelters and bases were made of white wax to create an 'icy' look and were placed on top of the game board. The game pieces itself were made of Perspex. This material was chosen because of its transparency: colored light indicating which player owns which piece shines through the pieces. Coils were put inside the objects so that the 2D location detection electronics can track the pieces on the gaming board. Holes were drilled into the Perspex to fit the coils and pieces of paper handkerchiefs were used inside the hole to prevent the coils from moving. The hole was closed with transparent tape. Images of animals, which show the different ranks and weapons in the game, were attached to the Perspex game pieces with transparent tape (see figure 3).

Originally, we wanted to allow players to apply their collected bonuses and upgrade their pieces by physically shaking weapon pieces to create a feeling of 'powering-up'. The shake detection device used a wireless communication module using a specified radio frequency. However, the prototype shake detection device reached an accuracy of only 80% due to the quality of the radio transmission. Therefore, we decided not to use the shake detection in our user evaluation. Instead, players activated bonuses by placing a weapon piece on their own base within three seconds before a battle starts.

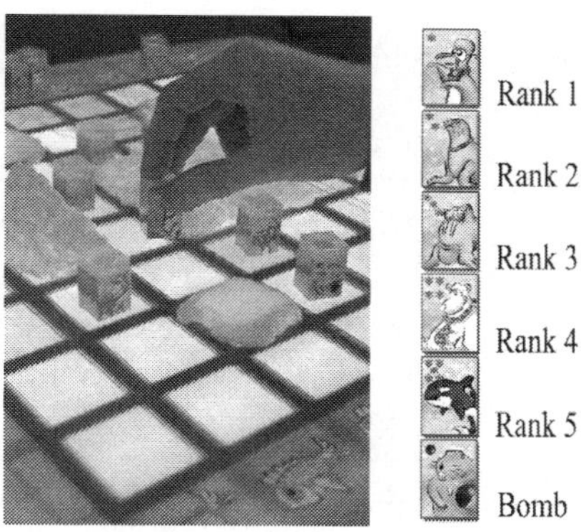

Theme
Due to the serious problem of global warming, the ice on the Arctic is melting fast. The animals living there have to fight for the last ice to live on. In order to survive, they have to put aside their differences and unite and infiltrate the base of a rivaling group of animals.

Fig. 3. Working prototype of the Last Ice concept and its tangible play pieces

5 Experiment

Based on the results of the first exploratory questionnaire, where the majority of the respondents indicated to prefer an equal challenge and that the weaker player was implicitly helped, the following hypotheses were tested:

Hypothesis 1: If the game is balanced then players will experience more fun compared to when the game is not balanced.

Hypothesis 2: If the game is implicitly balanced then players will experience more fun compared to an explicitly balanced game.

The procedure and timing of the experiment was checked with a pilot experiment done with four participants. As a result of this pilot experiment, programming was improved and rules of the game were printed on paper.

The improved experiment was performed with a group of 40 participants (29 males, 11 females) with ages ranging from 22 to 40. There were 16 frequent game players (12 male, 4 female) who played more than once a week, 14 participants (11 male, 3 female) were non-frequent game players, playing less than once a month. Seven participants played about once a month (5 male, 2 female) and three participants (1 male and 2 female) never played board games. We asked the participants about their experience in strategy games which require strategic thinking and planning. We decided to call players 'familiar' with strategic games when they played them at least 15 times. We found that 58% of the players were familiar with these games. A minority of 15% never played strategy games. In the experiment, each participant played the game twice against the same participant. Board games are most often played against a friend. We wanted to resemble reality and picked pairs that were familiar to one another. However, the ideal situation would suggest pairs where one player was much more skilled, but this was logically not feasible.

After filling in the pre-questionnaire and reading the rules, the game was practiced and explained by the experimenter. Half of the participants started with the unbalanced game and continued with the balanced game, the other half vice versa. After each game was finished a questionnaire was filled out. At the end of the two games the participants were told that they played a balanced and an unbalanced game. We asked them to give their opinion on implicitly and explicitly balancing a game and a post questionnaire was handed out. The experimental steps are described in Table 1 with an averaged time span.

Table 1. Experimental steps for the group, which started with the unbalanced game and continued with the balanced game

Time	Explanation
00.00h	The participant fills out a *pre-questionnaire* for demographic information and questions regarding previous experience in games and expectations.
00.03h	The participant reads the rules of the game.
00.06h	The participant starts *practicing* the unbalanced version of the game and the experimenter gives instructions.
00.10h	The participant *starts playing the unbalanced version* of the game.
00.18h	The participant fills out a *questionnaire I*, with questions regarding the fun experience during the game.
00.21h	The participant *starts with the balanced version* of the game.
00.29h	The participant fills out a *questionnaire II,* with questions regarding the experienced fun during the game and their preference for game 1 or 2.
00.32h	The participant is *interviewed* about the notability of a balanced and unbalanced game, about his/her preference regarding the two different games and his/her opinion about implicitly and explicitly balancing a game.
00.36h	The participant fills out a post-questionnaire regarding the experienced fun now s/he knows the second game was balanced for expertise.
00.40h	End of the experiment

The validated Game Experience Questionnaire (GEQ) [8] was used to measure the fun experienced during the balanced and unbalanced game. The questionnaire consisted of 22 questions. A typical question would be: 'I felt successful' and the participant could indicate how s/he felt during the game with the use of a 5 point Likert scale ranging from 1 (Totally disagree) to 5 (Totally agree). The players were also asked to indicate their fun experienced after each game and in which game, the first or second, they experienced more fun and competition.

In the interview, open questions were asked about the players' opinion about implicit or explicit balancing of games. The post-questionnaire consisted out of 11 questions of the GEQ questionnaire to investigate whether the fun experienced changed after the participant knew one game was balanced. An example question was: 'Now I know that I played a balanced game my experienced fun..' which participant's had to complete on a 5 point scale ranging from 1 (..decreased al lot) to 5 (..increased a lot). During the experiment the concrete differences between the two games (amount of pieces left, collected and used bonuses, and playtime) were also recorded.

6 Results

6.1 Difference between the Balanced and Unbalanced Game

The results of the individual questions of the Game Experience Questionnaire shows that there was a significant difference in *feeling successful* between the balanced and unbalanced game as tested by paired sample t-test on a 0.05 level (-2.7; 39, 0.01). This means that players felt more successful during the balanced game (M=3.8, SD=0.92) compared to the unbalanced game (M=3.3, SD=1.13). If we look closer (see figure 4), we see that the player that lost felt more successful during a balanced game compared to the unbalanced game as tested with the one way Anova-test on a 0.05 level (14.8; 38, 0.00). In contrary, the winner felt equally successful during the two games (one way Anova 0.03; 40, 0.86). In general, winners felt more successful than the players that lost a game as tested with the one way Anova (balanced 11.4; 39, 0.00, unbalanced 72; 39, 0.00).

Before the players started to play 83% expected to have *more fun* than average (M=3.98, SD=0.73). After they have played the balanced game the amount of fun based on the question 'I had fun during this game' significantly increased to 93% (balanced M=4.27, SD=0.60) as tested by the paired samples t-test on a 0.05 level (5.2; 38, 0.004). In the unbalanced game the fun experience increased slightly to 85%, which was insignificant (M=4.22, SD= 0.77). This means that the fun experience during the balanced game was more than the players expected it to be beforehand, while the fun experience in the unbalanced game remained the same.

During the interview 75% of the players preferred a balanced game because they expect it would give them more *competition, challenge* and *excitement* compared to a unbalanced game. However, many of the players (66% from the 75% that preferred a balanced game) commented that they would like to decide themselves which type of game to play, because this depends on the skills of the opponent. When they play

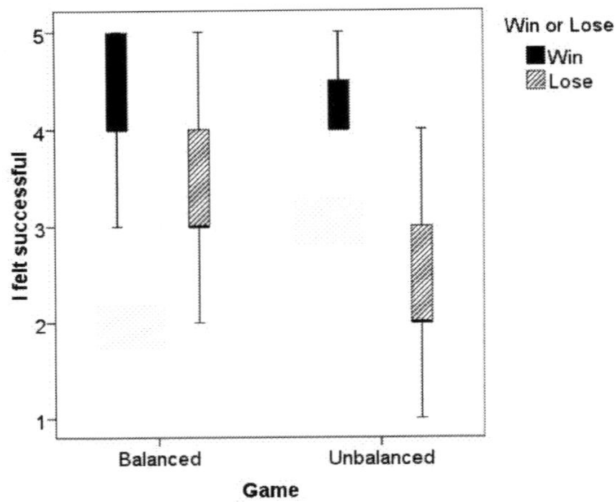

Fig. 4. The feeling of success after winning and losing a balanced and unbalanced game

against a child or an inexperienced player, they would choose a balanced game, but when they play against an opponent with the same game experience they would choose for an unbalanced game.

There were no differences between the total amount of play pieces that remained on the board after the game had ended (1.32, 39, 0.20), also the collected bonuses (-1.15, 39, 0.26), the used bonuses (-1.1, 39, 0.28) and the playing time (1.48, 37, 0.15) between the unbalanced and balanced game were the same.

Except for the question about feeling successful in the Game Experience Questionnaire, the difference in fun experienced during the balanced and unbalanced game of all questions in the GEQ were not significant as tested with a paired sample t–test on a 0.05 level. Thus the players experienced the same amount of fun in both games. The first hypothesis, that players experienced more fun when the game is balanced compared to when the game is not balanced, was therefore rejected.

The gaming skills of a participant (based on self-proclaimed experience in the pre-questionnaire) does not significantly influence the amount of fun experienced during the balanced or unbalanced game as measured with a one way Anova-test on a 0.05 level (balanced 0.23; 35, 0.93, unbalanced 0.92; 35, 0.46). This means that players with more gaming expertise experienced the same amount of fun during the games.

6.2 Implicit and Explicit Balancing of Expertise

In the interview the players were told one game was balanced and almost all players (95%) did not notice it. Players were asked in the post-questionnaire to indicate if the experienced fun changed now they were aware that a game was balanced. Explicitly balancing the game led to a significantly increase in the experienced amount of *effort* (2.08, 39, 0.04) and amount of *challenge* (2.69, 39, 0.01). This indicates that when players know that the game was being balanced based on their skill levels it will increase their experienced effort and challenge. The second hypothesis that players experience more fun when the game is balanced implicitly compared to explicitly was therefore rejected; players experienced more fun in the explicitly instead of implicitly balanced game.

Balancing a game could be kept secret, but many players think it would be unfair if they discover after many games that the weaker player was helped. Therefore, most players (82%) did not prefer implicit balancing and suggested balancing a game explicitly.

7 Discussion

The study presented in this paper raised some points for discussion. Sometimes the game had to be restarted due to errors. As a consequence the collected bonuses were lost, but the game could continue where the players had left off. This happened in 10 of the 40 games, but in only four games collected bonuses were lost (in the other games the participants did not have bonuses at that moment). This did not influence their games, because the four errors occurred in the beginning of the game when only one battle was played and the difference in play pieces was still small.

Players told that they prefer explicitly balanced games: they would like to know when the game is being balanced. However, if we would have made explicit that our game has a balancing mechanism, the stronger player actually could adjust his tactics (lose weak game pieces in order to use bonuses on the stronger game pieces) and abuse the balancing mechanics (i.e. bonuses are meant for the weaker player).

The balancing mechanism of the game was unfortunately not always effective enough. This was especially apparent when players with a big difference in expertise would play against each other. While the bonus appeared near the player that just lost a piece, it might be that this player still had more pieces than the other player and actually should not get help. Also the importance of the piece that was just lost was not taken into account by the balancing mechanism. Balancing the game would have been more effective if these two aspects also would have been considered.

We observed a learning effect considering the comprehensibility of the game. When the game was played for the second time, players appeared more conscious about their own tactics and experienced more competition because they became more absorbed in the game. Nevertheless, a learning effect was counterbalanced because half of the participants started with the balanced game and the other half with the unbalanced game to control for order effects. However, the players could have practiced the game more often, because after the second game the players indicated that they would change their tactics if they played again. This does not influence our results because all the players did not play this game before and had to find out which tactics they wanted to use.

The results of the GEQ questionnaire showed that players that lost a game, experienced more success in the balanced game compared to the unbalanced game. Although the feeling of success would suggest that it was influenced by the amount of play pieces that remained on the board after the game had ended, and the collected and used bonuses, there was no significant difference for these factors between these two conditions. This would imply that the feeling of success is influenced by something else besides the variables that were measured in this study. For future study it would be interesting to investigate which factors in a balanced game are responsible for feeling successful. Games should have the possibility to balance because it decreases differences in skill and brings diverse players closer together.

8 Conclusion

In this study it was investigated whether players experienced more fun when the game was balanced compared to when the game was not balanced. Also whether people preferred an implicitly or explicitly balanced game was examined.

The results of the GEQ questionnaire revealed that players that lost a game felt more successful during the balanced game compared to the unbalanced game, while the feeling of success for the players who won remained the same. The balanced game also elicits more fun experience than the players expected to have beforehand, while in the unbalanced game the fun experience was as they expected it to be.

During the interview players indicated that they preferred a balanced over an unbalanced game. They thought a balanced game would give more competition, challenge and excitement compared to an unbalanced game. However, players would like to have an option which game they want to play depending on the skills of the opponent.

According to the results of the Game Experience Questionnaire no difference was found between the unbalanced and balanced game in terms of the experienced fun during the games. Also the experienced fun of players with different gaming skills was the same for the balanced and unbalanced games, so regardless whether the weaker player was helped or not.

The players experienced more effort and challenge when they knew beforehand that the game was balanced (explicit balancing). The players preferred an explicitly over an implicitly balanced game. They believed it would be better when all players knew the weaker player was helped instead of keeping it secret (implicitly balancing). It was very important that balancing rules do not make a game feel completely random, because this would leave skillful players feeling cheated, while weak players would not feel the drive to learn. It was also important to construct balancing mechanics in such a way that players are not able to abuse them. This would defy the purpose of the balancing and make it an even more unbalanced game.

Through the use of technology we can create dynamically balanced games that reduce differences in skills between players and are proven to have a positive impact on the feeling of success. Balancing also offers players more fun than they expected beforehand and finally brings players of diverse abilities closer together.

References

1. Andersen, T.L., Kristensen, S., Nielsen, B.W., Grønbæk, K.: Designing an Augmented Reality Board Game with Children: The BattleBoard 3D Experience. In: Proceedings of OZCHI, pp. 22–24 (2004)
2. Bakker, S., Vorstenbosch, D., van den Hoven, E., Hollemans, G., Bergman, T.: Weathergods: tangible interaction in a digital tabletop game. In: Proceedings of Tangible and Embedded Interaction Conference, pp. 151–152 (2007)

3. BoardGameGeek, http://www.boardgamegeek.com (last accessed on December 2008)
4. de Boer, C.J., Lamers, M.H.: Electronic augmentation of traditional board games. In: Rauterberg, M. (ed.) ICEC 2004. LNCS, vol. 3166, pp. 441–444. Springer, Heidelberg (2004)
5. Csikszentmihalyi, M.: Flow: The Psychology of Optimal Experience. Harper and Row, New York (1990)
6. Herk, R., van Verhaegh, J., Fontijn, W.: ESPranto SDK: An adaptive programming environment for tangible applications. In: To be published in CHI 2009, proceedings. ACM, New York (2009)
7. Hunicke, R., Chapman, V.: AI for dynamic difficulty adjustment in games. In: Challenges in Game Artificial Intelligence AAAI Workshop, pp. 91–96 (2004)
8. IJsselsteijn, W.A., de Kort, Y.A.W., Poels, K.: The Game Experience Questionnaire, GEQ (2008)
9. Koster, R.: Theory of Fun for Game Design. Paraglyph Press, Phoenix (2004)
10. Li, Y., Fontijn, W., Markopoulos, P.: A tangible tabletop game supporting therapy of children with cerebral palsy. In: Markopoulos, P., de Ruyter, B., IJsselsteijn, W.A., Rowland, D. (eds.) Fun and Games 2008. LNCS, vol. 5294, pp. 182–193. Springer, Heidelberg (2008)
11. Lundgren, S.: Joining Bits and Pieces - How to Make Entirely New Board Games Using Embedded Computer Technology. Computing Science, IT (2002)
12. Magerkurth, C., Memisoglu, M., Engelke, T., Streitz, N.: Towards the next generation of tabletop gaming experiences. ACM Proceedings of Graphics Interface 62, 73–80 (2004)
13. Magerkurth, C.: Pervasive Games: Bringing Computer Entertainment Back to the Real World. ACM Computers in Entertainment 3(3), 11–29 (2005)
14. Malone, T.W.: Toward a theory of intrinsically motivating instructions. Cognitive Science 4(13), 333–369 (1981)
15. Philips Research Technology Backgrounder - Tangible Interaction Console, http://www.research.philips.com/newscenter/archive/2007/backgrounders/070830-tagtiles.html (last accessed on December 2008)
16. Soute, I.: HUGs: head-up games. In: Proceedings of Interaction Design and Children conference, pp. 205–208 (2007)
17. Spronck, P., Sprinkhuizen-Kuyper, I., Postma, E.: Difficulty Scaling of Game AI. In: Proceedings of Intelligent Games and Simulation Conference, pp. 33–37 (2004)
18. Swinx, BV: Swinx. Swinx Information Leaflet, http://www.swinxs.com/en/cmsmadesimple/uploads/ (last accessed on December 2008)
19. Tijs, T.J.W., Brokken, D., IJsselsteijn, W.A.: Dynamic game balancing by recognizing affect. In: Markopoulos, P., de Ruyter, B., IJsselsteijn, W.A., Rowland, D. (eds.) Fun and Games 2008. LNCS, vol. 5294, pp. 88–93. Springer, Heidelberg (2008)
20. Verhaegh, J., Soute, I., Kessels, A., Markopoulos, P.: On the design of Camelot, an outdoor game for children. In: Proceedings of Interaction Design and Children Conference, pp. 9–16 (2006)
21. Verhaegh, J., Fontijn, W., Hoonhout, J.: TagTiles: optimal challenge in educational electronics. In: Proceedings Tangible and Embedded Interaction Conference, pp. 187–190. ACM, New York (2007)

For Your Eyes Only: Controlling 3D Online Games by Eye-Gaze

Howell Istance[1,2], Aulikki Hyrskykari[2],
Stephen Vickers[1], and Thiago Chaves[2]

[1] Human-Computer Interaction Research Group, De Montfort University,
The Gateway, Leicester, LE1 9BH, UK
{hoi,svickers}@dmu.ac.uk
[2] Human-Computer Interaction Unit (TAUCHI), Department of Computer Sciences,
FIN-33014 University of Tampere, Finland
ah@cs.uta.fi, thiago.chaves@uta.fi

Abstract. Massively multiplayer online role-playing games, such as World of Warcraft, have become the most widespread 3D graphical environments with millions of active subscribers worldwide. People with severe motor impairments should be able to take part in these games without the extent of their disability being apparent to others online. Eye gaze is a high bandwidth modality that can support this. We have developed a software device that uses gaze input in different modes for emulating mouse and keyboard events appropriate for interacting with on-line games. We report an evaluation study that investigated gaze-based interaction with World of Warcraft using the device. We have found that it is feasible to carry out tasks representative of game play at a beginners skill level using gaze alone. The results from the locomotion task part of the study show similar performance for gaze-based interaction compared with a keyboard and mouse. We discuss the usability issues that arose when completing three types of tasks in the game and the implications of these for playing of this type of game using gaze as the only input modality.

Keywords: Gaze interfaces, games, evaluation, virtual communities, MMOGs.

1 Introduction

The popularity of Massively Multi-player Online Games (MMOGs) has increased enormously in recent years. World of Warcraft, probably the most popular fantasy role playing game, has 11 million monthly subscribers [1]. This has been accompanied by a similarly massive increase on the graphics capabilities of home machines that run the clients for these games and online worlds.

People with severe motor disabilities can derive much enjoyment from playing these games and taking part in virtual communities. Participation can be challenging and fun, it gives opportunities for social interaction, and the extent of the player's disability need not be apparent to other players. For some groups of people, eye gaze offers the only input modality with the potential for sufficiently high bandwidth to support the range of time-critical interaction tasks required to play.

T. Gross et al. (Eds.): INTERACT 2009, Part I, LNCS 5726, pp. 314–327, 2009.

There has been much work on eye gaze interaction with 2D desktop interfaces [2,3]; there has been only a little work on eye gaze interaction with virtual environments, and even less work on real-time interaction with multiplayer graphical worlds. There has been some work on how eye gaze can be integrated with other input modalities for games playing by able-bodied users, but no work to our knowledge on how far gaze can be used as the only input modality to play MMOGs. Understanding how gaze can be used as a single modality for motor impaired users will have a positive carry-over for understanding how to use it as an additional modality for able-bodied users too.

A number of general problems exist with using gaze-based interaction techniques developed for 2D desktop applications for the control of 3D worlds [4]. In addition, the player is under time pressure, which poses additional demands on gaze interaction techniques. Our aim is to design a software device that will enable game playing for the users who are not able to use traditional keyboard/mouse/gamepad input devices.

In this paper we report an evaluation study of the gaze interaction techniques developed so far carried out with World of Warcraft using able-bodied participants. We present a comparison of performance data from user trials with gaze and with keyboard/mouse as the input modalities. We also discuss the main usability issues associated with the gaze condition that arose during the game playing tasks.

2 Related Work

Interest in using gaze-input in games has been increasing due to the naturalness of pointing, and the potential for additional attentive input that the user's gaze can provide.

Isokoski et al. [5,6] used a first person shooter (FPS) style game in order to assess the performance of eye gaze as an extra input modality to mouse and keyboard. Their first findings showed that using eye gaze for aiming will not always improve the performance of the players when compared to using the game controller for aiming. However they did find that the number of hits from gaze is comparable to using the game controller alone, and that using gaze to play was more entertaining. The possibility of using eye gaze for controlling player direction was briefly examined but due to the necessity of the user constantly needing to change direction it was deemed not feasible.

Smith and Graham [7] performed an experiment using a similar control system on an open source port of the FPS Quake 2 called Jake2. Similar to Isokoski, the authors did not find any advantage in performance with gaze. However, their subjective user results showed that using eye gaze offered a much more immersive experience than using a mouse and keyboard.

Increased levels of immersion and enjoyment were also found by Jönsson [8] during trials using a combination of eye gaze and mouse within the FPS Half Life. Smith and Graham also performed trials using a version of the 80's arcade game Missile Command. Participants were required to use eye gaze to target missiles that were falling from the top of the screen and press a button to shoot them. They found that there is a need to fire ahead of the missile for a successful hit and this is easily achievable using a mouse. However, it is extremely difficult when using eye gaze to fire ahead as there is a constant distraction of the missile itself (the users looked at the missile rather than where they wished the missile to go). Thus, the majority of eye gaze shots missed and fell behind the missile, demonstrating the importance to disambiguate between a users attention and their intention when implementing interaction techniques.

Various implementations of different gaze driven paddle games (e.g. [9,10]) where simply following the ball by gaze gives the paddle the optimal coordinates show how effective gaze can be when used in a natural way. This point was made long ago by Jacob who advocated using gaze for non-command-based interaction, rather than deliberate command-based interaction [11]. Good task candidates are the ones where the user has to make a move to a point of interest (bat to ball in this case), or perhaps in World of Warcraft, move from 'here' to a target object, such as an enemy character, by simply looking at that target object.

Recently, Isokoski et al. [12] has reviewed the potential of using eye gaze in different genres of gaming as an additional modality for able bodied gamers. They identify features of each genre that are favourable or unfavourable for gaze control. They raise the important point that modifying a game to facilitate gaze control may remove some of the challenges and requisite skills that make playing the game interesting.

In context of immersive virtual environments (rather than games) Tanriverdi and Jacob [13] investigated gaze-based interaction techniques for selecting objects and compared performance using gaze with using a handheld pointer. Objects were assigned an index of interest determined by how long and often the user looked at them and were automatically selected and zoomed in upon. Significant performance benefits were found particularly for objects distant from the user in virtual space. They also found there was a cost in terms of poorer spatial memory of the locations of objects in the world in the gaze conditions. This is of particular interest for gaze-based interaction with games, when a significant amount of a user's visual attention may be allocated to interacting with the game, rather than observing the environment.

3 Design of the Eye-Gaze Based Games Interaction Device

Our overall objective is to produce a software device that uses eye position and gaze patterns as input, and produces keystroke and mouse events as output. The game client reacts to these events as if they had come from the keyboard and mouse hardware devices. In this way the device can be used with any game that can be operated by a keyboard and mouse. When the user gets a new game or joins a new on-line community, it should be easy to configure the eye device for the new game. Consequently the device should not require any modifications to the game client software.

Pointing using gaze measurement is inherently inaccurate. The eye is being used for interacting with on-screen objects as well as looking at the game. Normal keyboard and mouse use utilizes both hands for very precise rapid movements in parallel with the use of the eyes. We have no expectation that gaze interaction will be as good as keyboard and mouse for all aspects of games playing and all skill levels of players. However we do want to understand which parts of playing a particular genre of game, and at which skill level of play, gaze based interaction comes close to conventional input devices. For these tasks and at this skill level at least, the player supported by gaze need not appear to be different when on-line from their able-bodied counterparts.

3.1 Principles of the Design Solution

Our device [4] maps patterns of gaze behavior into various keyboard and mouse events. Each mapping corresponds to a mode which defines how the user's gaze behavior is interpreted. We can select four modes at any one time, which are then assigned to the four edges of the screen (see Fig. 1). The user can switch between modes by glancing off a particular edge of the screen and back again. Feedback about the currently active mode is given by a green strip that appears along the edge of the screen indicating the active mode. Additional feedback is given by changing the system cursor but this is unreliable as some games will define their own cursors.

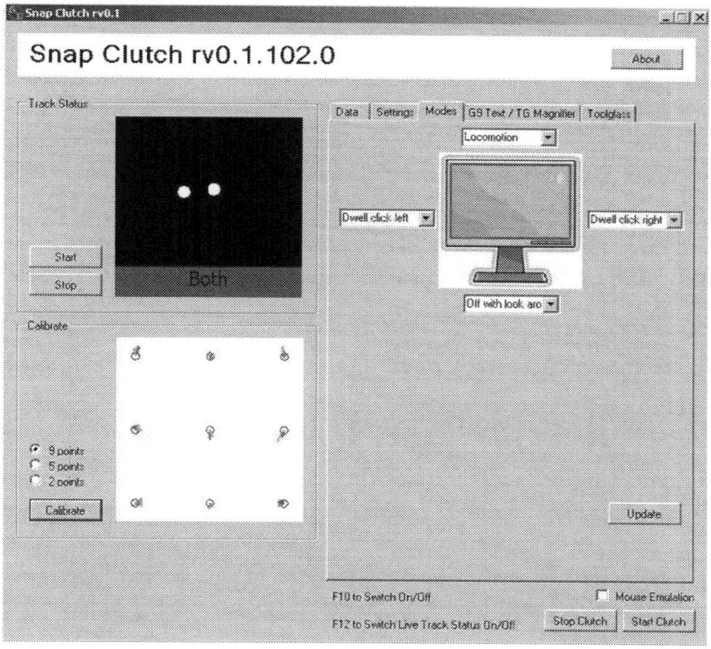

Fig. 1. The configuration window of the device in which the user defines the mapping of the desired modes

3.2 Gaze Interaction Performance Estimates

We obtained performance data for gaze interaction with a previous version of the device from an evaluation study using Second Life [14]. Twelve participants were required to do set of three tasks with keyboard and mouse and a similar set of three tasks with gaze. The tasks were designed to represent locomotion, object manipulation and application control.

The results were encouraging and showed that all participants were able to complete all tasks, after only a brief introduction and training with Second Life and with gaze interaction. Task times between gaze and keyboard/mouse were compared for each task, and these were partitioned into 'error time' and 'non-error' time. The proportions of each type of error enabled predictions to be made about the performance benefits that could be expected if the respective causes of each type of error were to be designed out. The main error types found were locomotion errors and accuracy errors. The first type resulted from a lack of sufficient control over the avatar's direction and speed of movement in the virtual world. The second type resulted from difficulty in positioning the cursor over small targets in interface control objects long enough for the dwell period to expire and the click event to be generated. The latter problem is common with gaze-based interaction. Table 1 shows the ratios of the task times with and without the error time component. In the present study we wished to see whether the non-error time performance ratios were achievable following modifications to our software device when using World of Warcraft (as an example of a popular MMORPG).

Table 1. Ratio of task time components from first evaluation study

Second Life Task	Total task times KB/Mouse : Gaze	Non-error time KB/Mouse : Gaze
Locomotion	1 : 1.6	1 : 1.2
In-World Object Manipulation	1 : 4.6	1 : 2.0
Application Control	1 : 2.8	1 : 2.5

3.3 The Present Design of the Gaze Interaction Device

The *locomotion mode* uses 'active regions' of the screen. When the user is in this mode, different keystroke events – which control locomotion – are automatically generated and sent to the game client application. Many games use the convention that the 'w' key moves the character forward, the 'a' key to the left, the 'd' key to the right, and the 's' moves the character backwards. The cursor control keys usually have the same function. We found that a player's eye movements using a mouse and keyboard in World of Warcraft, stayed in quite a distinctive area in front of the avatar. In Fig. 2 there is a heat map visualization [15] of a player's gaze positions during a period of movement around in an unfamiliar part of a world. On the basis of this we defined regions of the screen that the user does not usually look into during normal navigation. These are also shown overlaid on Fig. 2, although these are not visible to the player during use.

When the user looks at the regions, 'w', 'wa', 'a', 's', 'd', and 'wd' keystrokes respectively are streamed to the games client application. The first evaluation in Second Life showed that turning using gaze was very sensitive and often caused overshooting that required a steering correction in the opposite direction. To smoothen

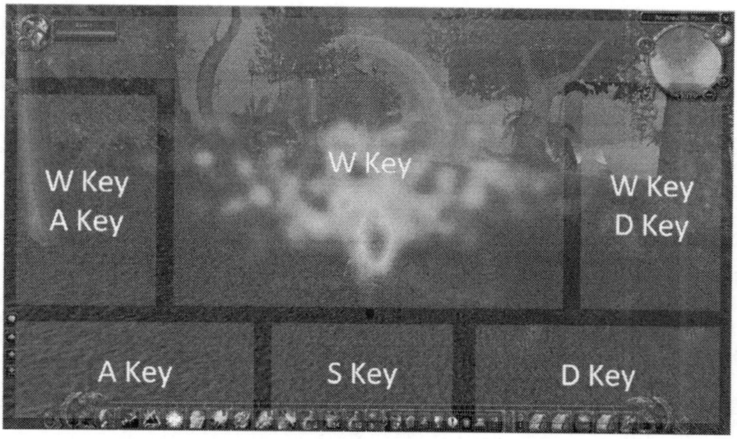

Fig. 2. Heat map illustrating the gaze behavior of a player when moving around in a part of the world in World of Warcraft that he was unfamiliar with

the turn, regions on the right and left send the 'w' key interleaved with the turning 'a' and 'd' keys. Looking down and left (/ right) still sent just a (/ d) keys to the application, and seemed to match surprisingly well the participants' intuitive expectations. To stop locomotion, the participant glanced down to switch into 'no action' mode.

Fig. 3. The magnifier glass can be dropped by dwell to a location where a close-up manipulation is needed

The *magnifier glass* (see Fig. 3) was designed to counteract the accuracy problem. The user can pick up the magnifier glass by a dwell on a semi-transparent icon placed on the game window. The magnifier glass then follows the point of gaze until the user drops it with another dwell. When the magnifier glass is dropped the user can then dwell within the magnifier area and send other interaction events within the magnifier glass area. A dwell outside the magnifier area moves the glass to a new position, and a subsequent dwell on the magnifier icon turns the magnifier off. The transparency, location and size of the magnifier icon can be configured from the device settings (Fig. 2) to reduce its interference with the underlying screen.

4 Testing the Modified Device with World of Warcraft

We carried out a series of user trials with the modified gaze interaction device to study its usability when playing World of Warcraft. Unlike the first study in Second Life, this study included time-constrained interaction with other characters. We also wanted to see whether we could obtain similar performance ratios of keyboard (and mouse) to gaze to those expected from the first study. World of Warcraft is an MMORPG in which the player's character or avatar plays alone or with other players to complete quests. The play involves fights with monsters or other players. These fights involve the use of hand-held weapons or spells which can be cast on opponents. The player has a collection of equipment which can be worn or sold and which can be taken, or 'looted', from opponents when they have been defeated in a fight. A player can have increasing levels of experience as a result of acquiring skills and using them to defeat opponents. In this study, we were only interested in tasks representative of beginners' level experience. The rationale here was that if these are achievable by gaze only, then we can progressively increase the difficulty of the tasks to establish the limits of what is possible using gaze interaction only. A character was created with a medium experience level (level 16) and all trials were carried with this character in the same virtual space around a village. We used a public server so there were other characters in the same space. We wanted the tasks to be conducted in a realistic play environment with a reasonable level of random distraction caused by external events in the game.

4.1 Device Configuration

For the user trials we used the following modes. **(1) Glance Up:** *'Locomotion'* mode, which functions as described in Section 3.3. **(2) Glance Down:** *'No action with look around'* mode, in which gaze dwell invokes no action, but the character rotates when the user looks inside the left and right hand edges of the screen. **(3) Glance Left:** *'Left mouse button click'* mode, in which a dwell causes a left button click event. **(4) Glance Right:** *'Right mouse button click'* mode, in which a dwell causes a right button click event. **(5) Glance at Magnifier icon:** *'Magnifier'* mode, whose operation was described in Section 3.3.

4.2 User Trials

Tasks. We designed four tasks representative of beginner level play in the game. The tasks were chosen following a task analysis of a period of beginners play in an MMORPG. These were:

- *Locomotion task* to walk to a location identified on the inset map, to turn around and return the starting point; and then to repeat the task running. There was no control over character speed and the participant was asked to stay on the path and complete the task as quickly as possible.
- *Fighting task* to find and fight a level 3 monster. The participant was asked to cast the same spell as many times as possible during the fight (by left clicking on an icon located on the shelf in the centre bottom of the screen). The difference in levels assured the participant would always win. After the fight, the participant was asked to loot the corpse (by right clicking on it) of one item (by left clicking on the list of treasure).
- *Equipment task* to put on or wear four items of equipment by opening a pouch (left clicking its icon in the bottom right of the screen); then opening the character sheet (left clicking its icon also in the bottom right of the screen); then selecting an item from the pouch (left clicking on its icon in the pouch); then selecting the highlighted slot in the character sheet which was open in the upper left part of the screen (again by left clicking in the empty slot); then closing both windows (left click in the close box in the top right of the window)
- *Communication task* to greet an object by typing a sentence using a predictive text keypad and then respond to the objects reply by typing another sentence and a closing abbreviated remark. We had designed and implemented the keypad to support communication with other players. There were a number of problems that arose during the trials with this part of the device and the outcomes of this task are not presented in this paper.

Participants. Ten participants were recruited for the trials, aged between 18 and 44. These were 9 males and 1 female, all were able-bodied, and all were students or staff at the computer science department at the university (biased gender distribution is justified on the basis that gamers are mostly males). None had taken part in the first experiment. Five had current extensive games playing experience with MMORPGs, three with World of Warcraft. All of the other 5 had played computer games, but did not consider themselves to be experienced MMORPG players. Participants were given cinema tickets in return for taking part.

Procedure. We carried out the trials in a usability laboratory equipped so that the trials could be observed from an adjacent room, separated by a one-way glass window. A Tobii T60 was used for the trials. The screen image from the trial machine was visible in the viewing room and it was recorded for subsequent video analysis.

Each trial consisted of a training phase (50 to 60 minutes), a break (20 to 30 minutes), and the data collection phase (about 30 minutes). The first part of the training covered the use of the gaze device, the magnifier, and locomotion mode. The second part of the training consisted of a structured introduction to World of Warcraft and completing a set of standard tasks. This was done first by keyboard and mouse, and then with gaze. After a break, all the four tasks were recorded with the keyboard and mouse. The same four tasks were then carried out using gaze. After the fourth task there was a 10 minute interview. The order of conditions during the trials was not counterbalanced as we wanted to increase the practice obtained before the gaze trial. We had no expectation that gaze would perform better than keyboard and mouse.

5 Results

5.1 Locomotion Task

In the present study, the locomotion task was carried out both running and walking. All participants completed the task in both conditions. Table 2 shows the means and standard deviations of the task completion times for the 9 participants. Data from one participant was omitted from the quantitative analysis but retained in the analysis of subjective data. This was due to problems calibrating the eyetracker. Willcoxen's Matched Pairs Signed Ranks Test shows the difference between the two conditions not to be significant ($p(\alpha) > 0.05$) when participants were walking. Running however took significantly longer in the gaze condition (($p(\alpha) \approx 0.01$) compared with the keyboard and mouse condition.

Table 2. Locomotion total task times for Kb/M and gaze

Locomotion		**Kb/M** (s)	**Gaze** (s)	**Kb/M:gaze** (ratio)
	mean	80.9	83.2	1 : 1.0
walk	stdev	2.6	7.5	
	n	9	9	
	mean	29.6	32.7	1 : 1.1
run	stdev	1.4	2.5	
	n	9	9	

In both cases the keyboard and mouse to gaze performance ratio was better than expected from the locomotion task in the Second Life trials (Table 1).

In the subjective evaluation, 7 participants of the 10 participants said controlling the rate of turn of the character was especially difficult in the gaze condition. Fine control of changes in direction was said by some participants to be much easier with the keyboard than with gaze. The other control issue reported by 3 was the difficulty in starting and stopping movement quickly in the gaze condition (by glancing over the bottom edge of the screen). Also searching for a type of monster required reading the labels over the heads of characters as they appeared on screen. If these appeared on the right or left sides, reading the labels would cause unintentional turns in that direction. Another participant referred to the problem of feedback where it was difficult to see whether the characters had turned far enough when looking at the bottom left or right hand corners of the screen. Three participants rated gaze control of locomotion to be easier than keyboard and mouse as there was no need to keep pressing a key to move.

We tried to rectify the 'turn overshoot' problem identified in the Second Life evaluation study by interleaving forward and sideways key events during a turn. However we still observed many instances of this error, particularly in the gaze condition. These did not result in significant recovery time loss but they did lead to more deviations from the centre of a forward path movement. Another observed gaze specific error was a 'distraction' error, where another character took the participant's visual attention to part of the screen which caused the own character to turn. This also caused path deviation, which had to be corrected.

5.2 Fighting Task

All participants completed the task in both conditions. The data from the fighting task is shown in Table 3. This shows the duration of the fight and the numbers of spells cast during the fight. The duration was measured from when the own character first engaged the monster until the monster died. The gaze fight lasted twice as long as the fight in the keyboard/mouse condition because the number of spells cast was fewer.

Table 3. Time taken and numbers of spells cast during the fighting task

Fighting		Kb/M	Gaze	Kb/M:gaze (ratio)
number of spells cast	median	5	3	
	n	9	9	
time	mean	15.1	31.69	1 : 2.1
	stdev	2.67	17.82	
	n	9	9	

In this simplified fighting task, the main requirement was to click the spell icon continuously to cast as many spells as possible. Willcoxen's Matched Pairs Signed Ranks Test shows the difference in the tasks times between the two conditions to be significant ($p\ (\alpha) < 0.01$)

In the subjective evaluation, 5 of the 10 subjects considered the size and location of the spell buttons to be a major factor with the difficulty of the task in the gaze condition. The magnifier was not used by any of the participants. When asked whether they considered using this to select the spell, one participant said that the number of actions to get the magnifier, drop it and then select the spell was simply too distracting from the action during the fight. This is an important indicator for the design of gaze interaction techniques for this type of task which involves interaction with other characters.

Two participants said it was difficult to control the character during the fight as it was not possible to do multiple actions at the same time, such as moving and casting spells. This is a requirement for some classes of character but not for others. There is one class of character that has an agent (a pet) that can fight on its behalf, which offers one type of solution to the issue of gaze-controlled fighting. Another participant pointed to the difficulty of gaze selecting a monster to engage in a fight while it was moving as the location for the dwell event has to be anticipated before the dwell begins. Another participant noted how difficult it was not to look at the battle while they needed to keep looking at the spell button in the tool bar at the bottom of the screen.

This task required rapid changing between modes to move, engage the character with a right click and then to cast spells with a left click. Three participants noted that they found changing modes quickly by glancing off screen difficult, although they thought the situation might improve with more practice.

5.3 Equipment Task

All participants completed the task in both conditions. The results are shown in Tables 4 and 5. The task has been split into 2 parts, opening the pouch window and the character sheet window (Table 4), and moving each of the four items from the pouch to the character sheet (Table 5). The icons to open the two windows were situated at the edge of the screen and some participants found selecting these by gaze particularly difficult due to the tracking accuracy near the edge of the calibrated area.

Table 4. Number of clicks and time taken for the first part of the equipment task

Opening 2 windows		**Kb/M**	**Gaze**	**Kb/M:gaze** (ratio)
number of clicks	median	2	3	
	n	9	9	
time	mean	3.4	17.2	1 : 5
	stdev	1.1	14.6	
	n	9	9	

Table 5. Number of clicks and time taken for the second part of the equipment task

Moves 4 items		**Kb/M**	**Gaze**	**Kb/M:gaze** (ratio)
number of clicks	median	8	14	
	n	9	9	
time	mean	17.4	45.4	1: 2.6
	stdev	5.4	23.0	
	n	9	9	

The keyboard/mouse to gaze performance ratios for the first and second parts of the tasks were 1:5 and 1:2.6 respectively. This gives a measure of the difference in difficulty between the two parts. Some participants used the magnifier in the gaze condition but only after they had tried to select the targets unaided. This resulted in long times on task and the standard deviations in both of the tables above reflect the large variability in task times. Also dropping the magnifier at the bottom of the screen meant that half of the magnifier was clipped, which could, in some cases, obscure the enlarged view of the target icon.

In the subjective evaluation, opinion was divided between those who thought the task was easy to complete and those who found the first part (opening the equipment windows) and consequently the whole task difficult. 4 of the 10 participants rated the ease of the task completion with gaze as being either as easy as or easier than with mouse and keyboard. There may be an order effect as this task always followed the fighting task in both the gaze and the keyboard and mouse conditions, and may have been considered easier overall.

6 Discussion

The outcomes of the trials have demonstrated the feasibility of gaze control of MMORPGs in as much that all participants were able to complete all of the tasks.

There is no universal definition of 'beginner' in terms of skills. Once a player knows what to do in the game, how to level the character, where to buy equipment and what spells do, he or she is no longer a beginner but a novice. Getting to that stage does not take very long (perhaps 30 minutes of play), but getting beyond this stage takes a much longer time. We believe that we demonstrated that gaze control of novice play is achievable.

We have used the ratio of task time using gaze to the time taken to complete the same task with keyboard and mouse as the main quantitative performance indicator. This allows some comparisons to be made between games (or worlds) provided the limits of similarities between the games and their tasks are recognized. The first experiment carried out with Second Life suggested that if the causes of identified problems in controlling locomotion could be designed out, then a performance ratio of keyboard/mouse to gaze in the region of 1 : 1.2 could be expected. We obtained performance ratios of 1 : 1.1 or better in these trials. The main problem with gaze control of locomotion is the lack of fine control over the rate of turn of the character. To some extent, this is a problem with the game client as well as with gaze, and there have been some discussions on forums about the need for better rate of turn control when using keyboard and mouse control with the World of Warcraft client. We recognise that the task given to participants was restricted to moving in a fixed path, and not moving in response to dynamic events in the game.

The fighting task shows some of the real limitations of using gaze to emulate normal mouse and keyboard without modifying the interface. The fighting task was deliberately chosen so that the participant character would always win and casting the same spell repeatedly is a very simplified view of fighting. The trials also revealed the limited nature of moded interaction in the present configuration of the interface, that is, that the player could either move, or cast spells, but not do both at the same time.

There was a 'midas-touch' like problem when the participant looked at a character that appeared at the edge of the screen when looking for monsters which also caused an unwanted change in direction.

The equipment and the fighting task were both hampered by the familiar problem of the difficulty of selecting small targets using gaze. A number of icons in the interface configuration we used were located right at the bottom of the screen, which lead to problems with the eye tracker calibration accuracy. The version of the magnifier that we developed as a means of overcoming accuracy problems apparent from the first experiment was not an effective solution to these. Some of these problems could be attributed to specific implementation issues and some to the lack of training the participants had with the interaction technique. However the main problem appeared to be the means invoking the magnifier, moving it, dropping it, and clicking through it were just too distracting and time consuming for it to be effective in a time-constrained game playing situation. An alternative means of using the magnifier needs to be found, or an alternative solution altogether to the accuracy issue is needed.

The equipment changing task shared some similarities with the appearance tasking changing task in Second Life. That experiment suggested that if the accuracy issues with gaze selection could be resolved then a performance ratio of 1 : 2.5 could be expected. The part of the equipment task involving object selection away from the edge of the screen in these trials had a keyboard/mouse to gaze ratio of 1 : 2.6. The similarity in these ratios gives encouragement to the idea that gaze performance across games can be quantified using the ratio as a metric, and that there is some consistency between similar types of task.

There are also broader interaction issues that the study has raised. In normal interaction in World of Warcraft, information about characters or equipment, for example, is displayed as text in a pop-up box in response to a mouse rollover. Dwell is fundamentally unsuitable as a means of rolling the mouse pointer over elements. The player will read what the box contains and in so doing will move the gaze point off the element. Alternative gaze actions for selecting elements, other than dwell, are needed.

The trials show that where we have time constrained game play, then gaze based emulation of mouse actions using dwell on standard interfaces is too limited. An interface configuration which allows the player to issue rapid commands with visual attention being diverted from the centre of the screen as little as possible is needed. Our ideas here involve using gaze based gestures, and a prototype gaze gesture driven interface to World of Warcraft has been built, and is currently being tested.

7 Conclusions

This work should be considered as a first step towards gaze-based game interaction for motor impaired users. We have not yet tested the interface with such users nor have we explored fully the range of design variables necessary to accommodate different types of motor impairment. We do, however, believe that the objective of total gaze control is achievable for a large proportion of users with motor impairments. The same interface works with an example of an MMORPG (World of Warcraft) and with an example of a multi-user virtual community (Second Life) and we expect it will work, with minor adjustments, with other games in each of these genres.

The difference between this project and others that have investigated eye gaze as a modality for game playing is the emphasis in this work on gaze as the sole input modality to enable motor impaired people to play MMORPGs. Others have studied how gaze can be used to complement other input modalities for use by able-bodied gamers. We have been able to demonstrate that it is feasible to carry simple locomotion, fighting and equipment manipulation tasks using gaze alone in World of Warcraft. From earlier work with gaze control of Second Life, we generated some expected performance differences between gaze and keyboard/mouse interaction using task time ratios for similar types of task. In this study we found good agreement with these expected values. The study has also highlighted the limitations of the current approach to using gaze for time-constrained interaction with World of Warcraft as an example of an MMORPG. If gaze-based interaction with MMORPGs is to be realised then interaction techniques which are lightweight, rapid and allow the user to maintain their attention on the centre of the screen are needed. This leads to alternative approaches to gaze interaction that embody these requirements, which are currently under investigation.

Acknowledgments. This work is supported by: Communication by Gaze Interaction (COGAIN) FP6 Network of Excellence, the Institute of Creative Technologies (IOCT) at De Montfort University, the Royal Academy of Engineering London and the Academy of Finland.

References

1. WoW Insider (2008), `http://www.wowinsider.com/2008/10/28/world-of-warcraft-hits-11-million-subscribers-worldwide/`
2. Hyrskykari, A., Majaranta, P., Räihä, K.-J.: From Gaze Control to Attentive Interfaces. In: Proc. HCII 2005, Las Vegas, NV (July 2005), `http://www.cs.uta.fi/hci/gaze/docs/Hyrskykari-HCII2005.pdf`
3. Majaranta, P., Räihä, K.-J.: Twenty years of eye typing: systems and design issues. In: Proc. Symposium on Eye Tracking Research & Applications (ETRA 2002), pp. 15–22. ACM Press, New York (2002)
4. Istance, H., Bates, R., Hyrskykari, A., Vickers, S.: Snap clutch, a moded approach to solving the Midas touch problem. In: Proc. Symposium on Eye Tracking Research & Applications (ETRA 2008), pp. 221–228. ACM, New York (2008)
5. Isokoski, P., Martin, B.: Eye tracker input in first person shooter games. In: Proc. Communication by Gaze Interaction; COGAIN Conference 2006, pp. 76–79 (2006)
6. Isokoski, P., Hyrskykari, A., Kotkaluoto, S., Martin, B.: Gamepad and eye tracker input in fps games; data for the first 50 minutes. In: Proc. Communication by Gaze Interaction; COGAIN Conference 2007, pp. 11–15 (2007)
7. Smith, J., Graham, T.C.N.: Use of eye movements for video game control. In: Proc. ACM SIGCHI international conference on Advances in computer entertainment technology (ACE 2006). ACM, New York (2006)
8. Jönsson, E.: If looks could kill - an evaluation of eye tracking in computer games, Master's thesis, Royal Institute of Technology, Stockholm (2005)
9. LC Technologies, Eyegaze software (2009), `http://www.eyegaze.com/content/programs-eyegaze-edge-communication-system`
10. Dorr, M., Bohme, M., Martinetz, T., Barth, E.: Gaze beats mouse: a case study. In: Proc. Communication by Gaze Interaction; COGAIN Conference (2007)
11. Jacob, R.J.K.: Eye Movement-Based Human-Computer Interaction Techniques: Toward Non-Command Interfaces. In: Hartson, H.R., Hix, D. (eds.) Advances in Human-Computer Interaction, vol. 4, pp. 151–190. Ablex Publishing Co., Norwood (1993)
12. Isokoski, P., Joos, M., Spakov, O., Martin, B.: Gaze Controlled Games, to appear in UAIS. Journal of Universal Access in the Information Society (2009)
13. Tanriverdi, V., Jacob, R.: Interacting with eye movements in virtual environments. In: Proc. SIGCHI Conference on Human Factors in Computing Systems (CHI 2000). ACM Press, New York (2000)
14. Istance, H., Hyrskykari, A., Vickers, S., Ali, N.: User Performance of Gaze-based Interaction with On-line Virtual Communities. In: Proc. COGAIN Conference 2008, pp. 28–32 (2008)
15. Wooding, D.: Fixation maps: Quantifying eye-movement traces. In: Proceedings of the Symposium on Eye Tracking Research & Applications, pp. 31–36. ACM Press, New York (2002)

Situating Productive Play: Online Gaming Practices and *Guanxi* in China

Silvia Lindtner[1], Scott Mainwaring[2], Paul Dourish[1], and Yang Wang[1]

[1] Department of Informatics,
University of California, Irvine,
Irvine, CA 92697-3440, USA
lindtner@ics.uci.edu, jpd@ics.uci.edu, yangwang@uci.edu
[2] People and Practices Research,
Intel Research, 20720 NW Amberglen Ct, MS,
Beaverton, OR 97006, USA
scott.mainwaring@intel.com

Abstract. Economic activities in and around online gaming in China are often correlated in the West with practices of gold farming, or selling in-game currency to players for real money in online games. What can we learn about online gaming in China and about online gaming and online sociality more broadly when we look at economic and other "pragmatic" practices through which online gaming becomes meaningful to players? In this paper, we present findings from an ethnographic study of online gaming in China's urban Internet cafes to discuss implications for game design, and HCI design more broadly. Considering the ties between socio-economic practices, development of trust and culturally situated imaginings of self-hood and otherness, brings to the fore how online gaming in and of itself constitutes the means for practical achievements in day-to-day management of *guanxi* (social connection).

Keywords: Online game, China, productive play, serious gaming, guanxi.

1 Introduction

In an Internet café in Hangzhou, a city in the Eastern region of China and an hour train ride from Shanghai, we met Tao, a 27 year-old player of the online game World of Warcraft. We were sitting next to Tao informally conversing about the happenings on his screen, when he told us, while pointing to one of the virtual characters that kept re-appearing next to his own: *I have a few close friends* [like this] *in the game. We have very good guanxi... I trust him and he trusts me... We all shared our phone numbers. We look after each others'* [in-game] *characters.*

During a 6-week long ethnographic study on online gaming in China in 2007, we encountered many players like Tao who invoked *guanxi* when describing the various types of relationships they developed in online games like World of Warcraft and at the physical locations where game play took place. *Guanxi* is a Chinese construct of social relations and reciprocal exchange [10, 23]. It is an important but complex frame in which certain social practices of material and emotional exchange are understood.

T. Gross et al. (Eds.): INTERACT 2009, Part I, LNCS 5726, pp. 328–341, 2009.

Often, *guanxi* is practiced and experienced through both the flow of material gifts (or capital-as-gift) and favors and the build-up of emotional and moral values such as trust or resentment within a network of dyadic relationships [4]. How and to what extent *guanxi* in Chinese societies differs from more general and culturally widespread processes of social networking and social capitalism remains a contentious issue [6]. From the perspective of HCI, however, even if *guanxi* is no more than an exemplar of a more generic phenomenon, it provides a particularly useful and culturally specific vantage point from which to consider how the design of online games (and online social spaces more generally) can become implicated within larger practices of currying favor, building networks, managing reputation, and leveraging social capital.

In recent years the HCI community has become increasingly invested in online gaming research. For example, previous research efforts have drawn our attention to the affordances of online gaming technology for complex social dynamics such as the formation of stable groups over longer periods of time, management of and collaboration within large collectives of people, and facilitating social action and flexible game play [2, 5, 15, 17]. More broadly, it has also been acknowledged that online sociality and play can have quite serious meanings for players and often impact players' lives and decision-making processes outside of the game [3, 5, 15, 17, 21] – especially in disruptive situations such as cheating in the game [21], shut down of game servers [17], break up of online groups [5], or when in-game activities take on the shape of work-like performances [22]. Edward Castronova, T.L. Taylor and Nick Yee, in particular, have highlighted how boundaries between play and work break down, how players make productive use of games (*e.g.* to earn money) or how gaming can also feel like work.

What happens, however, when playing the game is not just productive based on value generated within the game, but in fact fulfills pragmatic concerns beyond game play? Nowhere is this more evident, perhaps, than in the domain of online gaming in China. Though it is possible to approach this domain as a growing market, a cultural phenomenon, a state- and corporate-regulated infrastructure of hardware and software services, an online community, or even a challenging opportunity for user interface/experience design, it is more usefully considered a combination of all of these (and more). We argue in this paper for the efficacy of an approach that considers the contingency of the serious and playful [13] by applying it to an important theme that emerged from our ethnographic investigation of Chinese online gamers: how *guanxi* is shaping and being shaped by these gamers' perceptions, motivations, and behavior.

What we found in China were aspects of online gaming that render game play in and of itself a means for practical achievement, even when the online game is understood as exactly that: a game. We encountered gaming practices that were driven by pragmatic and socio-economic concerns such as maintaining and extending one's *guanxi* network, navigation around governmental restrictions of game play, and how to gain and/or maintain status and reputation in as well as outside of the game. Anthropologist Thomas Malaby insightfully points out that "...[games] are certainly, at times, productive of pleasure, but they can also be productive of many other emotional states"[13]. In line with Malaby's observations, an important aspect of understanding the complexities of online gaming in China required understanding the game's role within its wider material, social, and economic contexts. In previous work [11], we have provided an in-depth analysis of how game play in the Chinese Internet café spanned online and offline sites embedded in larger webs of political and socio-economic structures. Building on this previous work, this paper expands concurrent notions of productive play [5, 17, 24] in that we incorporate a wider range of serious practices including accomplishments within the larger society such as building one's career and social network (*guanxi wang*). The starting point of our analysis in this paper, thus, is to think through what "seriously" playing an online game such as World of Warcraft means not just in terms of instrumental activities *in* the game (that certainly also do have "serious" meanings beyond the game space), but also how the instrumental and serious are achieved and maintained *through* and *around* playing the game.

1.1 *Guanxi*

First, we wish to highlight that the work presented here acknowledges Chinese cultural particularities in relation to online gaming practices, while refraining from describing these practices as intrinsically Chinese [6, 10]. Our goal was to examine the ways in which instrumentalism and sentiment come together in *guanxi* networks that are developed and/or maintained *through* online gaming practices in China, and *not* how *guanxi* practices we observed in and around online gaming in China might be similar or different from social capital in online games in the U.S. Emotional aspects of the material and instrumental exchanges that come together in *guanxi* are not easily visible to outside observers, and the combination of instrumentalism and sentiment thus often appears contradictory [6] and leads to associations with corruption and bribing. We have thus refrained from a direct comparison between the "here" and "there" and rather focused on the practical contingencies of entertainment and its situated uses in the cultural context of urban China. For the scope of this paper, we consider *guanxi* as a useful framework in its own terms, independent of how one might theorize its relationship to larger concepts such as individualism/collectivism. In our work, we followed the lead of scholarly experts in China studies [*e.g.* 1, 10] in refraining from direct comparison between guanxi and understanding of individualism/collectivism in order to avoid an orientalist framing of "Chineseness."

Guanxi and its related socio-cultural constructs have been widely studied in anthropology, sociology, and business [1, 4, 6, 9, 10, 23]. For purposes of this paper, we schematize the key concepts as follows: First, *guanxi*, in its most basic form, is a social connection between two individuals over which gifts and favors (and, conversely, obligations for future reciprocation) flow [4, 10, 23]. Quite complex and far-flung *guanxiwang* (*guanxi* networks) are assembled out of these dyadic links. A *guanxi* link may be strong or "quality" (trustworthy, mutual, or genuine) or weak (unreliable, coercive, or perfunctory). Second, *guanxi* is built upon a mutually recognized "*guanxi* base" or common ground. In common practice, a *guanxi* base may take the form of a kinship relation (a family tie), a shared birthplace, a shared school or workplace, a shared acquaintance with whom both people have *guanxi*, or shared playing of the same game [4]. Third, *guanxi* must be cultivated and maintained. Without active attention, *guanxi* may decay over time; preventing such decay requires token or substantive gift-giving and -receiving over extended periods of time.

What underlies these general features is a diverse range of *guanxi*: in addition to good or bad, or strong or weak, it can be commodified, political, or friendly [10]. In each of these cases, however, *guanxi* is understood in distinction from a particular way of acting in the world, a way based on subsuming one's interests to institutions and their rules and ideologies. Indeed, a line of scholarly research has interpreted *guanxi* as a form of "navigation around the system" [1].

The art of doing *guanxi* resembles a kind of game play, a skilled activity that is marked as social, not work, amateur not professional, personal not official [6]. And so, a-priori, one might expect *guanxi* to be quite compatible with online gaming: a place in which to make social connections, feel human closeness, and maintain friendships over time, with a distinct feeling of being apart from the "non-game" "official" "real life" world, however, deeply intertwined with one's everyday life. While some researchers speculated that economic changes might cause a decline of *guanxi*, recent research also shows that *guanxi*, instead of diminishing, has found new territory in which to evolve [23]. Online gaming, with its analogies to artful practice of *guanxi*, in this light, is a particularly fertile ground for *guanxi*'s colonization and evolution. In this paper, then, we analyze how online gaming can provide exactly such a new territory for *guanxi* to be built and maintained.

2 Method

In the summer of 2007, we conducted ethnographic fieldwork in Beijing, Hangzhou, and Shanghai. Our main focus was the online game World of Warcraft (WoW), one of the most successful online games in China. In WoW, players create and develop an animated character in a setting derived from the fantasy game Dungeons and Dragons. Game activities include slaying monsters, fighting other players, and participating in a vibrant in-game economy. Although the game can be played alone, WoW is fundamentally a social game. We also encountered players of other popular games including Tencent's popular QQ Games, the Legend of Miracle 2 and With Your Destiny. Most fieldwork took place in physical sites of game play. We collected our data from observations, informal conversations, semi-structured interviews, and focus groups. Sometimes we asked our study participants to think aloud while they were playing or interviewed them during a game session. We conducted interviews in low- to high-end Internet cafés (*wang ba*), in restaurants, and in workplaces, dorms, and homes. Usually, we interviewed players at their preferred game location or at a place nearby. Most interviews lasted about an hour although some were longer.

In the semi-structured interviews we questioned study participants about many dimensions of their gaming experience. We asked players how they got started playing, about their previous gaming experience, what they liked and disliked about WoW, whether they played with people they knew in real life, whether they had made friends online and in *wang ba,* whether they belong to a guild, and if so, the kinds of experiences they had in their guild. We discussed the use of game-related software extensions and websites, forums, and wikis external to the game. We asked game-specific questions about character choice, naming of characters, game activities participants liked. We asked what players would change about the game if they could. We followed up conversational leads as they arose, consistent with standard ethnographic practice. We emphasize that this research was not intended to be a systematic study of the nature of *guanxi* around online gaming, rather *guanxi* emerged from the field work.

Study participants were acquired through our own social networks and through serendipitous encounters in Internet cafes or places where game-related merchandises such as game magazines were sold, *e.g.* shopping malls or small street vendors. We interviewed 80 players, 56 male, with diverse backgrounds including students, young professionals, a factory worker, a middle school teacher, senior players in their 50's, a marketing supervisor for a Chinese game company, a vice president of design for a Chinese game company, and owners of software stores, news kiosks and Internet cafes. We use pseudonyms for all study participants mentioned. We approached players in the *wang ba* and asked if they would have time for an interview.

3 Establishing and Maintaining *Guanxi*

We observed a wide range of opportunities where a shared gaming context was used to build *guanxi*. One of the techniques to establish *guanxi*, for example, was the reciprocal exchange of favors and gifts. Lian, a 50-year old player, told us about her experiences with a fellow player: *I chat with people in QQ games… there was a time that my computer got real slow in accessing the Internet, so I asked a favor from a friend I got to know in QQ games… he is very nice and he told me he is a computer science major, so I asked him to remotely control my computer and he fixed the problem.* In asking another player for computer support, Lian requested a favor, a gesture that rendered the relationship mutual and trustworthy. Even though the two players had never met offline, Lian allowed the other player to remotely control her computer to help her find a solution to the hardware problem. Through the offer of support and the sequential development of expectation to receive future support from Lian if needed, however, a reciprocal exchange took place that strengthened the *guanxi* that had been based on the shared online gaming context.

Besides playing games together online, physical proximity and shared context outside of the game could provide context for a *guanxi* base. Many of our study participants felt closer to online friends who lived in the same neighborhood or to in-game friends whom they met regularly at the same physical location, like the Internet cafe or student dormitories. Chenguang, for example, expressed feelings of safety and familiarity to other players who were living in her neighborhood: *The ones I feel comfortable meeting offline are the ones that live close to me and we have played together for a long time… Just because we are good online friends doesn't mean we are good friends in real world as well.* Another option to build *guanxi* was to rely on the referral of other players to whom *guanxi* was already established and maintained, as one of our study participants described: *you find out about who is trustworthy from a third party/recommendation by people you know. If you get ripped off, you only get ripped off once. You wouldn't fall for it again.*

3.1 Maintaining Pre-existing *Guanxi*

Online gaming in China also supported the maintenance of *guanxi* that had been developed prior to the game, as was the case for coworkers, couples, parents and children. Ming, for example, a 37-year-old gamer and employee at a publishing house in Chengdu, described that he would sometimes give his female colleagues QQ pets (an online casual game): *Sometimes, my QQ pets bore baby QQ pets. And, I already have too many QQ pets [he has 4 QQ pets], so I gave them to my female colleagues as gifts.* Interviewer: *Why did you give it to them?*

Ming: *la* [literally means to pull, figuratively means to actively build] *guanxi. I might need to ask them for help in the future.*

Jun and Wei are a young couple in Chengdu. WoW became increasingly important to their *guanxi*: *before WoW, Jun and I hardly had any interests in common. He has his friends and circle, and so do I. I wasn't interested in WoW when Jun first started playing the game. But, then I read some books about the stories behind the game and then started playing and fell in love with it. Now, we have this common hobby. I feel we are more connected.* In this example, the online game provided a shared context that allowed the couple to connect in new ways through spending time together online, in the Internet cafe and in their home. Similar to Wei and Jun, we found it common practice that "real life" friends started playing the game together. Extending from their *guanxi* existent prior to the game, they often established in-game groups and/or guilds that were highly successful and thus prestigious for others to join.

3.2 Leveraging Pre-existing *Guanxi*

At times, players who knew each other prior to the game leveraged their *guanxi* for in-game profit making. It was, then, often challenging for outsiders to join their activities. Often they also found themselves taken advantage of by the powerful and closely knitted group of *guanxi* friends. Many players referred to these guild members or player friends as "gold groups," because they would invite others outside the guild to join in-game activities and then take advantage of them. For example: *They recruit players from outside the guild to participate in gold raids. At the end of the gold raid, the people from the guild get offline and don't share the gold with the people from outside of the guild.* Bing, a software engineer from Beijing commented similarly on his experiences of joining the most prestigious guild on his server: *My guild is the best one on the server. Other people might not be able to get some of the equipment, but they succeed at it. But the relationships in the guild are not very good. If you are an outsider looking at this guild, you want to be added, because you see how fast they advance. After you get into this guild, you regret it.*

This example illustrates that online gaming did not necessarily always support "good" *guanxi*. While it was often easy for a group of friends to extend from pre-established *guanxi* and leverage their *guanxi* for in-game success, for others these pre-existing networks could also lead to the feeling of disconnectedness and exclusion. As in Bing's example, guild structures did not necessarily always provide the familiarity and continuity of interaction that players found so necessary for quality *guanxi* to develop. Building and maintaining "quality" *guanxi*, then, usually meant more than just acquiring the right equipment or participating in a stable and prestigious guild. Fen, for example, explained that for *guanxi* socializing in the game could be more important than equipment: *The bad aspect of the guild is that many people join the guild for the equipment and seldom have opportunity for sitting and chatting together, like you would have in real life. This is a change to humanity.*

Most of the players we talked to, however, were able to build new *guanxi* networks, mainly through leveraging a mix of online and offline resources and connections to others. They developed *guanxi* with other players in Internet cafes, with other Chinese players on foreign and private servers and when they met others while soloing in the game. Rui, for example, an employee at an Internet cafe in Beijing, told us that he considered some of the players he met in the Internet cafe as part of a trusted circle of friends. Rui moved to Beijing two years ago, which meant leaving friends and family on the one hand and building a new social network on the other. The Internet cafe, a place where he worked, slept and played, provided social and economic infrastructure to gain ground in the new environment.

4 Developing Quality *Guanxi*

Thus far, we have illustrated how online gaming provided the context for a shared *guanxi* base and have provided insights into the kinds of techniques players deployed to build and maintain *guanxi*. We will now focus on how dependable and trustworthy relationships were formed in and around online gaming in China, something that players often referred to as "quality" *guanxi*.

As it happened, our fieldwork took place at a time of considerable turmoil, at least for players of WoW in China. "The Burning Crusade" (TBC), an attractive expansion to WoW in 2007 that introduced among other features the increase in level cap to 70 (60 before), new zones and high-level dungeons, was released on January 16 in Europe, the U.S., and Australia, and on April 20 in regions of Taiwan, Hong Kong, and Macau. In Mainland China, however, TBC was not released until September 2007. Many players found work-arounds to play the TBC. For example, some created accounts on a server outside of Mainland China, *e.g.* in Taiwan or the U.S. Others accessed unlicensed game servers that provided access to TBC. Players moving to foreign servers or temporarily leaving the game while waiting for the upgrade to be released changed several dynamics in the game. Guilds (in-game groupings of players to help advance in game play) broke apart because of the decreased number of online members. As a result, many WoW players we talked to expressed having difficulty bonding with other online players, because of the increased instability in players' online patterns and the reduced number of players on servers in Mainland China. While these control mechanisms certainly structured the game space, we also found players building trustworthy relationships and quality *guanxi* in innovative ways, thus finding their own ways around certain restrictions.

[4] observed that *"Chinese societies are described as high in particularistic trust, such as among family members, but low in general trust in larger collectives. To the extent that* guanxi *building represents efforts by individuals to deal with an environment lacking general trust, interpersonal trust is essential in building a quality* guanxi*."* Some of our study participants referred to online gaming environments as lacking general trust. In other words, some players expressed low trust if they were strangers. Others, however, were able to develop trustworthy relationships that often lasted beyond game play. We were, then, intrigued by the question of whether and how online gamers developed interpersonal trust and quality *guanxi* in and beyond virtual environments.

Ming, for example, told us that he didn't like to play with strangers in the game and that building trust takes time and resources outside of the game: *I usually only play with my work colleagues, but sometimes they have other things to do and cannot play, so I have to play with other people that I don't know. Right after quests, they just grab the loots and run away. I was enraged! Loot should be equally divided. And we usually explicitly agree on that... I hardly trust strangers in games.* Lack of trust also occurred in transactions of game resources conducted online. He Peng, a 25 year-old IT consultant in Shanghai, reminisced about an incident of being cheated in WoW: *Once I didn't have much time left on my account, so I was in a rush. Somebody next to me* [in the game] *just happened to sell game point cards and I bought it immediately. The person told me to wait for a minute to activate the card. Later, I learned that he gave the same number to everybody.*

In general, low trust in online games was exacerbated by the widespread use of spyware and viruses. Several of our study participants had their game accounts stolen on a PC in an Internet cafe. Many players thus did not trust machines in the Internet cafe. Ming, who we introduced earlier, told us that he bought game objects through face-to-face cash transactions and sometimes both parties needed to log into the game to transfer game objects. Instead of using a computer in the Internet cafe to perform the transaction, he called his wife to log in the game using their home computer.

How did players generally tackle this trust issue and develop quality *guanxi*? Tao, a 27-year-old gamer in Hangzhou, had played the *With Your Destiny* game for 4 years and made close friends in the game. He commented: *People who seem nice in reality may not be nice online, but people who seem nice online are most likely to be nice in reality as well...*[because] *it's really hard for someone to pretend* [to be nice online] *for a long time.* During long-term interactions many players started to exchange game accounts and phone numbers as an expression of trust in each other. Tao, whom we introduced in the introduction section, for example, told us how he built strong trust and quality *guanxi* to other players: *We have very good guanxi... We shared our game accounts with each other. When I had already started working, he was still in college. We called each other to talk about games as well as other things. I discussed with him how to prepare in school to find jobs...we played as a highly organized team. We looked after each others' characters... when my account got stolen, my friends immediately offered to buy me a premium account that was worth several thousand RMB* (1 Yuan Renminbi is ~ 0.15 US$) *at that time.* The story of Tao and his close game friends is a telling example of how trust and quality *guanxi* were built through self-disclosure and external communication, long-term collaborations, exchange of favors, and a strong sense of comradeship and shared honor. We begin to see then that quality *guanxi* embodies both deeply emotional values, *e.g.* Tao's comment *"the saddest thing in the game is to see when [our character] was stolen and our enemy bought it"*, and support in practical manners, e.g. *"they offered to buy me a premium account that was worth several thousand RMB..."*

4.1 From *Guanxi* Base to Quality *Guanxi*

Another example of quality *guanxi* that we found in the context of online gaming was the *guanxi* between a software shop owner who sells point cards for online games and a gamer who buys point cards from the vendor. Game point cards serve as an economic bridge between the real world and game worlds. They convert public currencies into game values. Some of them are time-based, *e.g.* WoW point cards (30 RMB buys 66 hours of in-game time). Others are in form of game points that can be used to purchase virtual objects and services in the game worlds.

One of our study participants, Lin, ran a software shop that sold game, anti-virus and enterprise software as well as game point cards. Customers could purchase pre-paid scratch game cards from Lin. A typical game card came with its sales price in RMB and the value of the corresponding in-game value printed on the front side of the card. After purchase of a game card, customers could then redeem the value of the card into their game accounts using the card number and the password. Alternatively, customers could acquire game point directly from Lin. Lin would then log in as a vendor into a third party online game card sales system and conduct the purchase for her customer. After the customer paid her back, Lin would often write down the card number and password on a piece of paper and give it to the customer. This option required mutual trust and was thus reserved for Lin's quality *guanxi* customers: *Some of my old customers call me to buy game points. Usually, they transfer money directly to my bank account and I put the game money directly to their game accounts. Since they have been my customers for many years, we are very familiar with each other. I know their game accounts and they know my bank account. We have good guanxi. We are friends and help each other if needed. Once, my shop fell short of cash... I called them and asked them for help. They gave me several thousand RMB...*

Lin's example illustrates how interaction through the context of the online game served as a *guanxi* base for cultivating quality *guanxi*. If *guanxi* was to be maintained and turned into quality *guanxi* as in Lin's case, usually the game-related interactions extended beyond the game, connecting to real-life assets such as the bank account or face-to-face meetings for a transaction.

4.2 Assessing *Guanxi* and Interpreting Face

So far, we have looked at how players built *guanxi* to engage in trustworthy online and offline interactions and to develop mutual respect for each other. Another aspect that is commonly associated with *guanxi* in China is *mianzi*, or face in English. Face refers to one's social status in the eyes of others, which can be accumulated, lost or given to one another and is said to be a key principal guiding relations between Chinese people, rural or urban [9]. While some have speculated about the deterioration of *guanxi* practices due to industrialization and economic changes [10, 23] recent work has provided insight into how *guanxi* continues to evolve and might even counter-act feelings of anonymity or facelessness [1, 9]. Hertz, for example, argues that "*guanxi* locates its practitioners in webs of communitarian contacts and distinguishes them as individuals from the faceless universalized monads who make up the crowd" [9]. Players commented quite frequently on the importance of showing and receiving face through their relationships in and beyond the game. Ju, a student from Beijing, for example, explained how he gained face through his guild, when we asked him what he thought the advantages of being in a guild were: *If you can join a strong guild on your server, that is very good... You will feel more face brought by it... For example, your guild is No1 on your server. It is always your guild who wins difficult raids, you will feel honored. When you chat with others, you can mention "I am from..." In the game, if players apply to join our guild, they may be refused by the guild, while I can join the top guild, because I have friends in it.*

Often, players took specific actions in order to find out about other players' moral attitude and face online. They would, for example, use their secondary characters in order to see others' "true faces", as one player phrased it. Most of the online game players we talked to had several characters distributed across different guilds, sometimes having two or more characters in one guild without revealing to their team members that they are all owned by one player. He Peng explained: *Why I have different characters in different guilds? Most players do that. If you have a secondary character, I wouldn't tell others in the guild that it is a secondary character – to protect myself. You use the secondary character to understand what else is going on or to find out about another player's personality and his intentions. If you have really good equipment, people respect you. I use my secondary character to see who still is nice even though I don't have a lot of equipment.*

He Peng considered this action a strategy "to protect himself." If a *guanxi* partner looses face it might also entail loss of face for oneself or one's guild: *If people go and do something bad in the name of the guild, for example, they take stuff from the guild which is supposed to be distributed among the members. Others will critique the whole guild for having members like this. The fame of the whole guild is destroyed.* Quality *guanxi* is often associated with a moral and ethical attitude, as well as mutual reliance on each other, which converts into face/status for both *guanxi* partners when exposed to others [9, 10]. In confronting a trusted *guanxi* partner in the guise of a less-advanced character, the moral attitude of the other player could be evaluated.

5 Discussion

While *guanxi* practices in and around online gaming in China provide a telling example of the combination of the instrumental and emotional, it is not something unique to China or online gaming. A series of ethnographic studies in domestic settings, for example, draws attention to the ways in which pragmatic routines of keeping things in order and "configuring" the home bring to the fore symbolic and emotional properties of artifacts and their arrangements in the home [18, 20]. In a quite different context, we thus found a similar line of reasoning: that through pragmatic means quite emotionally intense outcomes can be generated. In addition, our findings also illustrated how leisure and fun can affect instrumental accomplishment. Bing's example of prestigious but exclusionary guilds brought to the fore how the ability to establish connections to other players outside the in-game structure of the guild or even beyond the game in China's Internet cafes provided opportunity to develop quality *guanxi*. In contrast, the decision to join a prestigious guild was motivated by the desire to gain reputation and status. Many players established just like Bing a myriad of *guanxi* connections, offline and online, and hybrids of both, varying in intensity and quality. While in some *guanxi* networks the emotional aspects prevailed, in others the instrumental aspect came to the fore. However, never did we find a sharp distinction between the instrumental and emotional aspects. Lian built a trustworthy connection to a fellow player and could rely on him for technical support. Chenguang and many others shared game accounts to express trust and mutual reliance, but also to gain knowledge about unfamiliar player classes. Similarly, the exchange of QQ pets strengthened the *guanxi* at stake, while at the same time helping advance the gifted player.

Previous HCI research has highlighted the importance of in-game infrastructures such as guilds and social action around virtual artifacts to support a stable social backdrop to many game activities [2, 5]. Consistent with this previous work, we found that members of well-run and successful guilds associated feelings of prestige and belonging. But we also came across a range of game practices that fulfilled pragmatic means beyond built-in grouping mechanisms, similar to findings in [15]. For example, despite political decisions such as the delay of the TBC and the pervasive lack of trust in online spaces and Internet cafes, players were able to develop and sustain a myriad of *guanxi* networks. Here, a pervasive aspect of making the game function for one's own needs was to exploit both digital and physical resources. We have argued elsewhere [11] that a crucial aspect of online gaming in China is the ability to act across an ecology of physical and digital infrastructures and artifacts. The maintenance and development of *guanxi* flourished exactly because players were able to make use of a mix of digital and physical resources. This evidenced in the cases of Lin and Tao. Lin conducted online transactions, interacted face-to-face, and exchanged bank account information with her customers. Her customers displayed loyalty and trust lending her several thousand RMB when Lin's business underwent a moment of crisis. Similarly, Tao made use of digital and physical resources to build *guanxi* to his fellow online game players. In exchanging game accounts and phone numbers, he and his online friends expressed trust in one another, eventually allowing for quality *guanxi* to emerge.

Practices of gold groups (closely knit networks of players who exploit others to gain advantage in the game), on the other hand, evidenced that a functioning social infrastructure in the game is not necessarily always about fair play or mutual support. Rather these groups often functioned so well because of exactly that: demolition of the functioning of others through, for example, exploitation and cheating. Members of gold groups leveraged their pre-existing *guanxi* networks to form strong and highly collaborative groups in the game. Exploiting both digital interaction and *guanxi* established outside the game, they not only engaged in highly successful in-game practices, but also strengthened their pre-existing "real life" *guanxi*. These examples illustrate that functioning in the game meant to artfully interweave online practices with contexts and artifacts that were valued beyond the game. We suggest that if we subscribe a myth of functioning of social groups in online gaming and online communities more broadly that is based on continuity, stability and structure within the online game, we might overlook these other much messier, but quite productive ways of navigating and playing around a regulated game space.

What we take away from these intersections of reciprocal exchange, expression of trust and achievement of instrumental means through game play is an alternate framing of productive and serious gaming. Serious gaming is often associated with the usage of games for educational settings[1], where through "doing" things in the game, lessons are learned for one's "serious" aspects of life. Thus, serious gaming often implies that gaming can be used as a test bed for the actual "real" that is happening outside of the game. The concept of productive play, on the other hand, is used to

[1] See for example: http://www.seriousgames.org

describe work that gets done in the game or relationships that are formed online, which are impacting players' behavior and attitudes outside of the game. Productive play thus has often been used to describe how boundaries between play and work increasingly blur [3, 5, 17, 22]. Yee, for example, comments on the irony of online players paying money to game companies for working hard in the game and refers to companies such as IGE that make money from selling virtual currency [22].

What we have found in our research in China is a form of productive play where fun and entertainment were tied to political and social contexts, thus not only producing value within, but accomplishment extrinsic to game play. Online gaming in China was not so much a test bed, as it was an integral part of people's functioning lives. Too often game design for education and work purposes stops with the online space or the assumption of a bounded game space. By expanding our scope and beginning to design entertainment services and games that take into account how people cross and exploit these boundaries, or how they maintain them in order to make games fit their own needs, we begin to leverage the meaningful serious and productive usages of the entertainment space.

6 Conclusion

The concept of *guanxi* arose repeatedly in our encounters with Chinese players of networked games. We might immediately be led to attempt to translate this an apparently equivalent Western understanding of "trust" or perhaps "social capital," but we have deliberately resisted that temptation here. These terms do not capture the way in which *guanxi* functions and manifests itself as an aspect of everyday social practice for the gamers we worked with. Our concern with "situating" play, then, is not one that attempts to look at the ways that a "Western" game is re-encountered by Chinese players, nor one that attempts to highlight particular issues as somehow essentially Chinese. Rather, we want to draw attention to the ways that the game is encountered and operationalized as a site for the further elaboration of already-existing social relationships and practices. *Guanxi* does not need to be "implemented" in WoW; for the Chinese players, it is already there as it is in everyday life. In this way, WoW is productive of everyday social relations even as it offers a place of enjoyment and entertainment.

While *guanxi* is "already" part of WoW, it lives in the margins and the fringes and in the ways WoW is encountered; it is not a designed-in feature of the game. In this way, the creative work-arounds and "productive" ways of play that we have found in the context of online gaming resemble findings from previous research in work-related settings. Studies of organizational work note that organizational structures, rather than prescribing the ways in which work gets accomplished, are the product of orderly work and situated workarounds [7, 12, 19]. Similarly, what we mean by "productive" play is not the ability to support stable social groups over time or to define univocally what efficient in-game collaboration might entail. Rather what we refer to are practices of creatively navigating around managed infrastructures, exploiting messy socio-technical settings and leveraging functionalities of a technological system in innovative ways. *Guanxi* in and around online gaming in China was about cohesive social relations through exchange of trust and favors. *Guanxi* practice, however, did not necessarily lead to the formation of stable groups within the game. Rather, making the game work meant to artfully interweave online practices with contexts and physical artifacts that were valued beyond the game. The "productive" use of the game was not something encoded into the game or planned in advance, rather arose out of the practical contingencies of the actual interaction, both online and offline.

In conclusion, we would like to offer a speculative and provocative outlook. Chinese and U.S. players [14] both rendered Chinese game play at times to be dishonest and lower in status than what was supposedly the case for the West. One might infer that the use of *guanxi* in game play may be responsible for this, as *guanxi* might be interpreted as "backward" or "corrupt", something that can be stamped out. One might also suggest that China, characterized as an emerging market, a nation often branded as being in "development", might eventually catch up with the U.S., causing the two game cultures to equalize. The research we presented in this paper, however, casts doubt on such an analysis. Online gaming in China is embedded in a culture that greatly values *guanxi* and teaches the importance of artful *guanxi*. The vigorous culture of *guanxi* tends to strongly intertwine game activities with real life activities. It is here that gaming and the digital and physical sites it engages become arenas for contrived contingency [13]. Considering the growth of social networking technologies in the U.S., China may, instead of lagging behind the U.S., also in certain cases illustrate a precursor of U.S. technology culture in the future.

Acknowledgements

We would like to thank Bonnie Nardi, Charlotte Lee, Gillian Hayes, Ken Anderson, Thomas Malaby, Lisa Nakamura, Tom Boellstorff, Johanna Brewer and Lilly Irani for their valuable input. We also thank our participants, the Intel Corporation and Intel's People and Practices Research group who supported this work. This work was supported in part by the National Science Foundation under awards 0527729, 0712890, 0838601, and 0838499.

References

1. Anagnost, A.: National Past-Times. Narrative, Representation, and Power in Modern China. Duke University Press (1997)
2. Brown, B., Bell, M.: CSCW at play: 'There' as a collaborative virtual environment. In: Proc. CSCW 2004, pp. 350–359. ACM Press, New York (2004)
3. Castronova, E.: Synthetic Worlds. The Business and Culture of Online Games. University of Chicago Press (2005)
4. Chen, X., Chen, C.: On the Intricacies of the Chinese Guanxi: A Process Model of Guanxi Development. Asia Pacific Journal of Management 21, 305–324 (2004)
5. Dibbel, J.: Play Money. Or, how I quit my day job and made millions trading virtual loot. Basic Books (2006)
6. Ducheneaut, N., Yee, N., Nickell, E., Moore, R.: The Life and Death of Online Gaming Communities: A Look at Guilds in World of Warcraft. In: Proc. of CHI 2007. ACM Press, New York (2007)

7. Gerson, E.M., Leigh Star, S.: Analyzing Due Process in the Workplace. ACM Transactions on Office Information Systems 4(3), 257–270 (1986)
8. Gold, T., Guthrie, D., Wank, D.: Social Connections in China. Institutions, Culture and the Changinq Nature of Guanxi. Cambridge University Press, Cambridge (2002)
9. Hertz, E.: Face in the Crowd: The Cultural Construction. In: Chen, N., Clark, C. (eds.) China Urban. Ethnographies of Contemporary Culture. Duke Univ. Press (2001)
10. Kipnis, A.: The Language of Gifts: Managing Guanxi in a North China Village. Modern China 22, 285–314 (1996)
11. Lindtner, S., Nardi, B., Wang, Y., Mainwaring, S., Jing, H., Liang, W.: A Hybrid Cultural Ecology: World of Warcraft in China. In: Proc. of CSCW 2008 (2008)
12. Lutters, W., Ackerman, M.: Beyond Boundary Objects: Collaborative Reuse in Aircraft Technical Support. Computer Supported Cooperative Work 16, 341–372 (2007)
13. Malaby, T.: Beyond Play: A New Approach to Games. Games and Culture 2, 95–113 (2007)
14. Nakamura, L.: Don't Hate the Player, Hate the Game: the Racialization of Labor in World of Warcraft. In: GLS Conference, Madison, Wisconsin (2008)
15. Nardi, B., Harris, J.: Strangers and Friends: Collaborative Play in World of Warcraft. In: Proc. CSCW (2006)
16. Ong, A.: Flexible Citizenship. The Cultural Logics of Transnationality. Duke University Press (1998)
17. Pearce, C.: Productive Play: Game Culture from the Bottom Up. Games and Culture 1(1), 17–24 (2006)
18. Rodden, T., et al.: Between the Dazzle of a New Building and its Eventual Corpse: Assembling the Ubiquitous Home. In: Proc. of Dis 2004, pp. 71–80 (2004)
19. Suchman, L.A.: Office Procedure as Practical Action: Models of Work and System Design. ACM Transactions on Office Information Systems 1(4), 320–328 (1983)
20. Swan, L., Taylor, A., Harper, R.: Making Place for Clutter and Other Ideas of Home. ACM Transactionson Computer-Human Interaction 15(2), Article 9 (2008)
21. Taylor, T.L.: Play Between Worlds: Exploring Online Game Culture. MIT Press, Cambridge (2006)
22. Williams, D., Ducheneaut, N., Xiong, L., Zhang, Y., Yee, N., Nickell, E.: From tree house to barracks: The social life of guilds in World of Warcraft. Games & Culture 1(4) (2006)
23. Yang, M.: Gifts, Favors and Banquets. The Art of Social Relationships in China. Cornell University Press (1995)
24. Yee, N.: The Labor of Fun: How Video Games Blur the Boundaries of Work and Play. Games and Culture 1, 68 (2006)

Head Tracking in First-Person Games: Interaction Using a Web-Camera

Torben Sko and Henry J. Gardner

School of Computer Science, College of Engineering and Computer Science
The Australian National University, Canberra, ACT, 0200, Australia
Torben.Sko@gmail.com, Henry.Gardner@anu.edu.au

Abstract. Recent advances in face-tracking technology have made it possible to recognize head movements using a commodity web-camera. This development has created exciting possibilities for enhancing player enjoyment during computer game play. In order to ascertain the real-world potential for head gestural input to First Person Shooter games, we have developed seven diverse interaction techniques and integrated these with a modern games engine. Evaluation of the techniques was carried out with four focus groups made up of expert games developers and experienced end-users. One of the techniques was further refined and subjected to a follow-up comparison test with promising results. A set of guidelines for the future development of head interaction techniques for computer games has been derived from the studies. All of the techniques have been built upon freely available software and open-sourced to encourage further research in this area.

Keywords: Input and interaction technology, face tracking, head tracking, computer game, game engine, first person shooter.

1 Introduction

Although real-time head tracking has been an interaction technology for many decades [1], its use as a commodity input mechanism for desktop computing is only just being realized. Thanks in large part to advances in computer vision (for example [2]), head tracking can now be achieved using an off-the-shelf web-camera and face-tracking software (for example [3]).

In light of these advances, HCI researchers have begun to study face-tracked head gestures as input to computer games. In their 2006 paper, Wang et al. studied two basic interaction techniques in two game contexts [4]. They showed that test participants experienced a greater "sense of presence" and satisfaction with their head-tracked techniques. Likewise, in 2008, Yim at al. [5] proposed a head tracking game built upon the popular work of Johnny Lee [6]. Continuing this line of research, we look to more systematically develop a set of interaction techniques, which map out important parts of the design space of head-gestural input to First-Person Shooter (FPS) games and then evaluate the real-world potential for the techniques using focus groups.

In the following section, we present a simple taxonomy for head-tracked interaction in games and use this to position and describe the collection of seven head-tracked

T. Gross et al. (Eds.): INTERACT 2009, Part I, LNCS 5726, pp. 342–355, 2009.

techniques that we have developed. We describe further aspects of the implementation of these techniques, and their integration into a game engine, in Section 3. The conduct and overall observations arising from the focus-group evaluation of these techniques is described in Section 4, which includes a technique-by-technique summary of the results. One of the techniques, singled out for its market potential, was subjected to a follow-up comparison test as described in Section 5. In Section 6, we present some preliminary design guidelines for head-tracked interaction techniques in games. Overall conclusions and future work are presented in Section 7.

2 Interaction Techniques

The complete design space for head-tracked interaction with games is huge. One needs to consider genres [7] (shooters, driving, role playing...), platforms (PC, console...), virtual dimensions (2D, 3D), perspectives (first-person, third-person, top-down...) and players (single, multiple local, multiple remote). As such, it is necessary to consider just a subset of this space. In our work, we chose to specialize to *single-user, first-person-shooter* (FPS) games due to their wide popularity and the natural correlation between the user's head and the first-person-view. We chose to work on the *Windows PC platform* due to its popularity, large software support and the ideal manner (for face tracking) in which users sit front-on to the screen. We also chose to specialize to techniques, which demanded only *light integration with the underlying games engine*, implying that the underlying game logic was only augmented, rather than substantially altered, by use of the new techniques. This last restriction meant that the new techniques should be applicable beyond a particular game scenario and other researchers could more easily emulate their implementation.

In their 2006 paper, Wang et al. [4] describe what appears to have been the first serious research into the design and development of face and head-tracked interaction techniques for computer games. They used a three-level design focus with categories of "presence", "role-playing" and "control" all related to the cognitive processes or activities of the user. They developed two basic interaction techniques: avatar appearance and control in a third person game and dodging-and-peeking (which they referred to as "bullet time") in a FPS game. Their evaluation showed the techniques to enhance end-user experience in various ways. In particular both were shown to significantly increase player presence.

When we came to consider techniques for our own work, we wished to position them in the context of a taxonomy. While the categorization of [4] was interesting, its focus on the effect on the player meant that techniques often overlapped categories. For instance, the dodging-and-peeking technique of [4] could arguably fall under all of their three categories, resulting in a poor classification. Our approach was to take a designer's perspective to derive a taxonomy that regards the effects the techniques have on the game rather than on the player. We present a simple two-level taxonomy, which categorizes techniques into either "ambient" or "control" techniques. Ambient (or perceptual) techniques have no effect on the state of the virtual world and are designed simply to enhance the visual and/or audio feedback based on the user's head position. Control techniques are focused on the controlling the state of the game. We can further refine this category into social and non-social (or gameplay) control techniques. Social control techniques are those concerned with communicating with avatars and other players. They are generally more relevant to other game types such as role-playing games and, by default, require a deep integration with the game engine. Given that we are only considering lightly integrated techniques, they have been excluded from this work. Gameplay control techniques pertain to all other forms of in-game control, such as looking and aiming in FPS games. With our new taxonomy the dodging-and-peeking technique of [4] can now be unambiguously described as a gameplay control technique. For the sake of brevity, we refer to "gameplay control" techniques simply as "control" techniques in this paper.

When considering the category of "control" techniques, we observed that head-gestures are most naturally associated to the concept of looking. Natural movements of the head, and natural *looking* metaphors, motivate controls such as *zooming* (leaning into the screen) and *peering* (leaning and tilting). For these techniques it is natural to map camera position to head position in a continuous manner, which is what we did with our first two interaction techniques: a *continuous zoom* technique and a *peering* technique.

Head movements can also be used as triggers for controls. We studied trigger controls by implementing three techniques: a *spinning* technique which causes a rapid camera rotation (by 180°) in response to flicking the head, a *threshold zooming* technique which activates when the head comes within a preset proximity of the screen, and an *iron sighting* technique. This last technique was inspired by the engaging metaphor of iron sighting (aiming down the barrel of a weapon).

The "ambient" techniques consisted of two techniques: *head-coupled perspective* (HPC) [8,9] which provides a 3D effect by making the desktop display replicate the appearance of a window, and a new ambient technique motivated by the unsteady effect created by a *hand-held camera* (the "Handy-Cam" technique). All of the seven interaction techniques are described in more detail in the following subsections and, with the exception of spinning, are illustrated in Fig. 1. A video of these techniques is also provided online [10].

2.1 Continuous and Threshold Zooming

The two zooming techniques let the user zoom into the scene by moving their head towards the screen. Whilst previous work explored the use of a head-controlled, *staggered* zoom to enhance browsing on a laptop [11], our work chose to explore the idea of *continuous* and *threshold* zooming. For the continuous zooming, the amount of zoom was directly and continuously proportional to the distance between the user's head and the screen as defined by the following function:

$$\text{cam.FOV} -= \text{zoom}_{max} \cdot \text{f}(\text{learnt.depth} - \text{head.depth}, \alpha, \beta)^{\nu} \quad (1)$$

In this equation, cam.FOV corresponds the field of view of the virtual camera while f() represents a function that normalizes its first argument over the second two, which in this case corresponds to the range [α, β]. The constants parameterized the shape of the mapping. In our default implementation, $\alpha = 0.05$m, $\beta = 0.3$m, $\text{zoom}_{max} = 40^{\circ}$, $\nu = 2.0$ (meaning the scaling was parabolic rather than linear) and learnt.depth initially starts at 0.7m, implying that 30cm forward lean would result in a 40° reduction in the

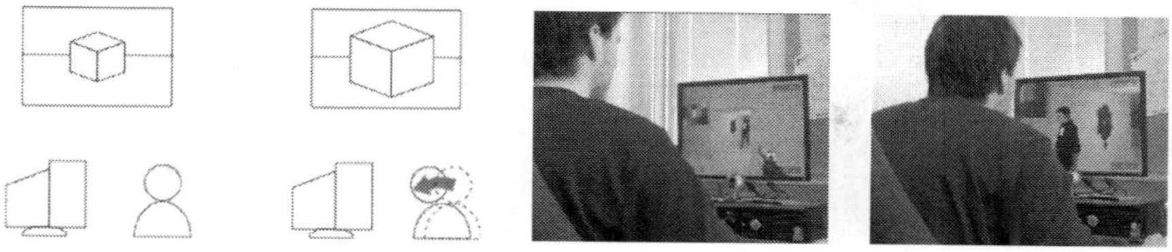

Zooming a scene by leaning towards the screen

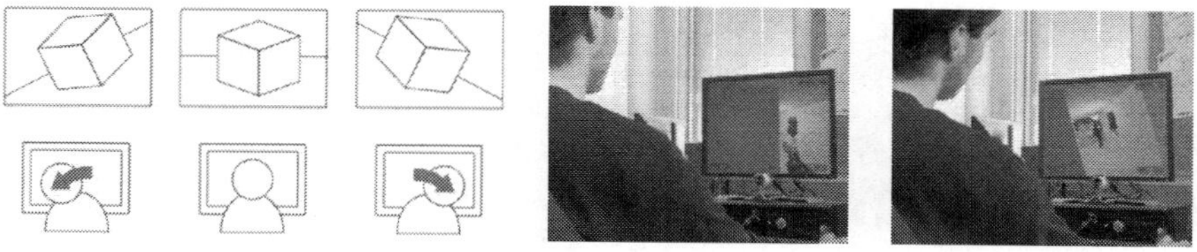

Peering around obstacles by tilting the head

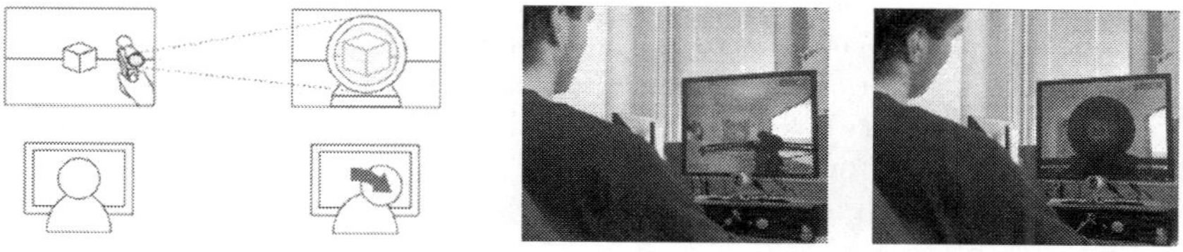

Iron Sighting through a telescopic sight by cocking the head

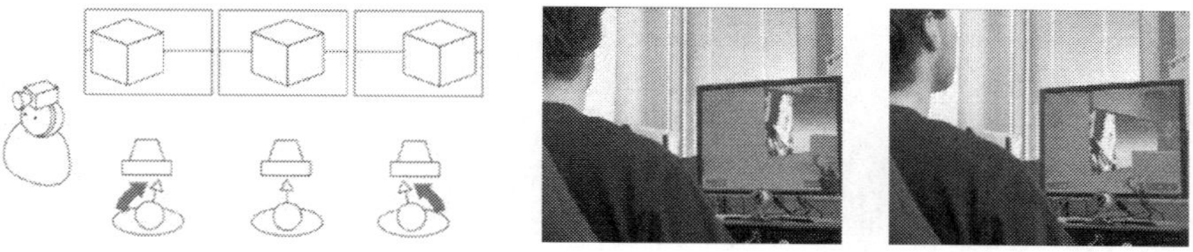

Subtle movements of the scene in response to changes in head position – similar to the effect of a hand-held camera (the Handy-Cam technique)

Head-Coupled Perspective. Notice the difference in the angle of the handgun

Fig. 1. Illustration of the techniques discussed in the paper, excluding the spinning technique. Head and body movements have been exaggerated for the sake of demonstration.

FOV. A full implementation would also induce some form of disadvantage, such accuracy reduction, to ensure the use of the technique was fair.

The threshold zooming induced a full zoom ($zoom_{max}$) when the user's head crossed a proximity threshold. If described using the same function as before, then $\alpha = \beta$, where both represent the threshold point. Worth noting was that users were unable to shoot whilst using the threshold zoom.

2.2 Spinning

The spinning technique allows the user to perform a rotation of the camera – defaulted to 180° – in response to a rapid flick of their head beyond an angular threshold. A subsequent spin could only be performed once the user had re-centered their head. This technique was designed for when the player was attacked from behind and appears to be new in the literature.

2.3 Peering

The peering technique lets the player look around objects in the virtual world by physically leaning their head to either side, following a similar concept implemented by Wang et al. [4] for dodging bullets. Unlike their technique, which only considers the *horizontal offset* of the user's head, we also considered the *roll*. The following formula describes how our version of peering-to-the-right functions (a similar equation would be employed for peering-to-the-left):

$$p^{+} = f(\ f(\text{head.roll}, \alpha, \beta\ ) + f(\text{head.off}, \gamma, \delta), 0, 1)^{v} \tag{2}$$

$$\text{cam.sideways} \mathrel{+}= \ \textit{check\_collisions}(p^{+}.\ \text{peer.sideways}) \tag{3}$$

$$\text{cam.height} \mathrel{+}= p^{+}.\ \text{peer.lower} \tag{4}$$

$$\text{cam.roll} \mathrel{+}= p^{+}.\ \text{peer.roll} \tag{5}$$

In these equations, α and β represent the minimum and maximum amount of required head roll (radians) respectively, while γ and δ represent the minimum and maximum amount of required sideways head movement (meters) respectively. As with before, f() is a normalizing function. In our default implementation, $\alpha = 0.15$ (rad), $\beta = 0.3$ (rad), $\gamma = 0.05$m, $\delta = 0.1$m, $v = 2.0$, peer.lower = 10, peer.sideways = 30, peer.roll = 15°. To avoid allowing the player to peer through the walls, we needed to ensure that we checked for collisions. A complete implementation would also alter the player's hit boxes and aiming position in an effort to maintain game balance.

2.4 Iron Sighting

The iron sighting technique allows the user to aim down the barrel of their weapon by tilting their head to the right, similar to how they would iron sight in real life. As the user rolls their head past a threshold, the virtual weapon is raised up and a slight zoom occurs. To enhance this effect, the sniper rifle was modified to feature a real-time scope, allowing the user to realistically target a far off enemy using the actual weapon model, rather just using a decreased FOV. As with other games that feature iron sighting, a full implementation would also induce an increase in accuracy and a reduction in player speed, to ensure the technique was balanced. This technique appears to be new in the literature.

2.5 Head-Coupled Perspective

The first of the two ambient techniques, Head-Coupled Perspective (HCP), is a classic enabling technology for fish-tank virtual reality [8,9] and has recently been publicized by the work of Johnny Lee [6] and has been subsequently used by Yim et al. [5] to develop a "Dodge It" game. Based on the user's head position, the parallax of the 3D scene is altered by varying the virtual camera's field of view, offset, orientation and vanishing point. Given that we have followed a standard implementation, the equations for this technique have been excluded.

2.6 Handy-Cam

The handy-cam technique adds natural movement to the view in an effort to replicate the unsteady appearance of movies filmed using a hand-held camera. This was achieved by coupling the rotation (and upon the request of one participant, the offset) of the player's head to those of the virtual camera using equations of the form:

Rotation:

$$\text{cam.yaw} \mathrel{+}= \alpha\,(\text{head.yaw}^{\nu}) \tag{6}$$

$$\text{cam.pitch} \mathrel{-}= \alpha\,((\text{head.pitch} - \text{learnt.pitch})^{\nu}) \tag{7}$$

Offsets:

$$\text{cam.height} \mathrel{+}= h\ .\ \text{head.height} \tag{8}$$

$$\text{cam.sideways} \mathrel{+}= s\ .\ \text{head.sideways} \tag{9}$$

$$\text{cam.depth} \mathrel{-}= d\,(\text{head.depth} - \text{learnt.depth}) \tag{10}$$

Where $\alpha = 40^{o}$, $\nu = 1.1$, $h = 10$, $s = 10$, $d = 20$, learnt.pitch initially equals 0.15 (rad), and, as with before, learnt.depth initially starts at 0.7m. Although existing FPS games sometimes simulate a hand-held camera motion to represent player movement through a scene, our handy-cam technique also works when the player is stationary. Furthermore, it imparts a subtle and responsive movement to the scene. It has not been previously reported in the literature.

3 Implementation

The head tracking was performed using a standard web camera and v2.1 of Seeing Machine's FaceAPI [3], which tracks the head with 6 degrees of freedom without the use of markers. This avoids the need to have the user wear specialized equipment (which, as Yim et al. [5] mention, could deter users). This software was integrated into Valve's Source [12] game engine via the use of client code and library calls. The overall system is shown in Fig. 2 and is freely available online [13]. The integration process required the game engine to be modified in a number of ways:

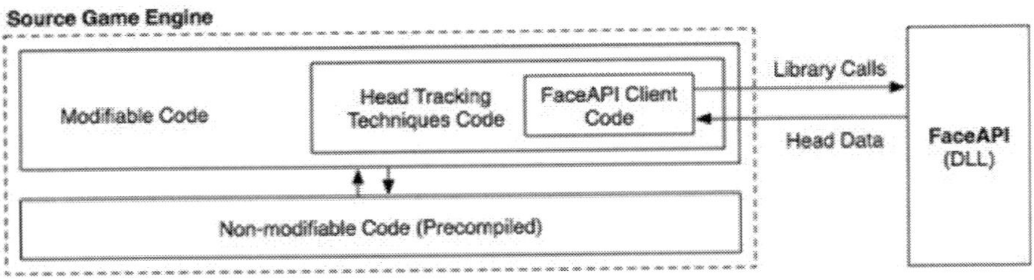

Fig. 2. System diagram for the implementation of the head-tracked interaction techniques in the Source game engine

Firstly, some of the techniques required functionality not already present in the engine including peering, spinning and iron sighting. Additionally, the rifle's scope was modified to show a real-time magnification of the view for use with iron sighting. Advice on these modifications was obtained from Value's support resources [14, 15].

Secondly, a layer of supporting logic was developed for the techniques. This included smoothing the head data over a specified number of data frames, learning the neutral position of the head, gracefully resetting to the neutral position following a tracking loss, resetting the tracking when the system suspected it to be inaccurate, and correcting for an arcing effect when moving the head directly towards the screen.

Finally, to get the most from the focus group evaluation, it was important that the techniques were of a near-commercial quality. For example, most techniques featured an ease-in (v) to avoid abrupt movements and the crosshair's position was made to be dynamic to ensure that it remained accurate in spite of moving the camera. Likewise for the iron-sighting technique, the modified rifle was refined until it was at a high level of aesthetic quality.

4 Focus Group Evaluation

The primary usability attribute of a computer game is that of *fun*. However, the mere concept of head-gestural input to an FPS game is a *fun* idea in itself. We therefore expected that the novelty value of our new techniques would be high but we wished to look beyond their immediate reception to get feedback about their potential for commercial FPS games in the near future. We chose a focus group approach with a double-layer design [16] to explicitly compare and contrast the views of two classes of *experts*: games developers and experienced end-users. This form of analysis was chosen due to the freedom it provided. Not only were we keen to collect feedback, we also wanted to gather the participant's suggestions and ideas.

A set of four focus groups were conducted: two with developers and two with end users with 15 participants in total. The two industry focus-groups included staff from two games companies of international reach. One of these focus groups also included staff from the company which produced the face-tracking software. Occupations included lead designer, lead software engineer, technical developer, marketing communications officer and a game producer. The end-user groups were conducted with university students all of whom had considerable experience with FPS games. Prior to the focus group interview, each participant completed informal tasks (such as exploration or combat) with each technique separately. This was followed by using three of the techniques simultaneously, namely handy cam, peering and zooming. The platform used was a 2.13GHz machine, with 2.00GB of memory and a nVidia GeForce 7600 GS graphics card. The video signal was provided by a USB Logitech QuickCam Pro 4000, placed directly under a 17" monitor as shown in Figure 1. The familiarization phase was conducted with all members of the group being present and the ensuing discussion was recorded and combined with the interview process.

The focus group interview was conducted away from the computer and was driven by a set of guiding questions. These questions started out by asking about the background of the participants including their experience and preferences. Questions about the techniques started at a general level (What is your impression of each of the techniques?) and then moved to cover specific issues such as the commercial viability of head tracking (Do you see head tracking as being something that may appear in games in the future?), the viability the techniques (Could you see yourself continually using any of these techniques or are they just a novelty?), and suggestions as to how they might be improved (Do you think any of the techniques could be improved?). Between one and a half and two hours were needed for each focus group (with 4 participants in most of the groups) and the study was conducted over a week.

Each of the authors conducted an independent analysis of the abridged focus group transcripts [16], which comprised a total of 144 pages of single-spaced text. General observations derived from these analyses were then pooled and are summarized in the next subsection. This is then followed by subsection 4.2, which provides an individual critiquing of all the techniques. In keeping with advice from the focus group literature [16] we report qualitative trends rather than quoting statistics.

4.1 General Observations

Considerable excitement was evinced in all of the focus groups, which confirmed our caution about the novelty effect of head-mounted interaction. One of the industry participants stated, "You've done a good job. I'm really impressed" while an end-user stated, "…when I first came into the room, I found that you actually control by your head, I was really impressed". As such, this initial reaction justified and the strong need for follow-up probing about their real-world potential as a commercial product.

The general excitement did not mean that group participants felt that head-mounted interaction had an immediate future with FPS games. To the contrary, a large amount of discussion time considered other genres of games which appeared to be more suited to the techniques – stealth games (much like "Thief" [17]) were particularly mentioned as well on-rails shooters and games which include the visible control of avatars.

Many participants reflected that they would not use any of the techniques for fast paced or competitive gameplay, as echoed by the statement of one end user who said, "when it's quick in competition, it's all buttons".

The reliability of our head-tracking system (the software/hardware configuration, camera and lighting conditions) was a particular concern when participants were first getting used to it. Our set-up had occasional problems with certain facial characteristics such as beards. In many cases the system tuned itself over time but there were still occasional drop-outs. It was pointed out in discussion that there is little room for tolerance for tracking drop-outs in a commercial product – particularly if the technique is to be used for control. In such cases, users will turn head-tracking off and use the keyboard alternatives. There was only one direct mention of latency as an issue of the system and this was with respect to the implementation of the Head-Coupled Perspective technique.

4.2 Technique Critiques

Although several participants provided some form of preferential ordering for the techniques, drawing out a clear ordering across all groups of the focus study was difficult. As, such, the following discusses the merits, criticisms and the potential of each technique separately, as reflected across all participants.

Peering. This technique clearly received the greatest amount of positive feedback of all of the control techniques, with several end users naming it as their favorite technique. Suggested improvements for the technique included providing a finer level of control, as well as allowing the player to shoot from the peering position. Of all the techniques, it was felt that peering could benefit the most from focusing the game content around its use.

Iron sighting. This technique caused the greatest split among participants. While one participant with a firearms background showed great fondness for the technique, most others expressed reservations about it. These comments included that it induced neck pain, that it placed the head in an awkward playing position, that a mouse click would be taken in preference to a head gesture, and finally that peering, which shares a similar action, would be chosen in preference. Some attributed these issues to the frequency, urgency, duration and extent of the action required. We feel that introducing some feedback could help alleviate these issues, given that most participants tilted their heads further than was required. Some participants suggested that closing one eye may be a more appropriate gesture.

Zooming. This technique generally received less attention than the others, but on the whole, the feedback for both zooming techniques was positive. Of the two, the continuous zooming was preferred, as it provided a greater level of control, although many participants felt the movement range was too large and that it lacked feedback regarding the end of this range. To improve the technique, some users suggested adding a depth of field and making the zoom length dependent on the gun.

Spinning. This technique, as a concept, received a large amount of positive feedback, although only a few participants noted that they would use a head gesture in preference to a keystroke. Many reflected that they felt the technique would be better suited to games consoles, where there is a greater tradeoff between the speed required for turning verses that for aiming. Many also suggested that the spin be 90° as this would be more natural and less disorientating. One participant voiced concerns about the effect of false positives, as these would significantly disadvantage the player.

Head-Coupled Perspective. This technique generally received an enthusiastic response. However, as the technique requires a low latency, accurate tracking and quite some tuning to accurately create the 3D effect, it places unrealistic expectations on the tracking system. As such, some participants reflected that they felt the technique to be ineffective, and one participant stated they would discard it altogether. Despite failing to create a real sense of depth, many participants still liked the way that it injected life into the scene, and some suggested that it would be better suited to either special moments during a first person game, such as peering through a virtual window, or for use in viewing the map in a top-down, strategy game.

Handy-cam. In spite of its subtle nature, this technique received only positive feedback from all participants, with several stating that it added *life* to the game and made it *more realistic*. One industry representative was particularly receptive to the technique and felt that it had market potential. Unlike the similar HCP technique, the handy cam technique places fewer expectations on the system, catering for a small level of latency and inaccuracy. As reported in the next section, only 2 of the 8 participants of the follow up study noted of any issues to do with the response of the technique. It was felt that this technique could be improved by making it work with relative, rather than absolute, head positions. In contrast, the level of integration was not raised as an issue, boding well in regards to the ease in which this technique could be integrated into other games.

Combining Techniques. Where requested, the handy-cam, peering and continuous zooming techniques were simultaneously activated. Whilst most participants noted that this combination of techniques was overwhelming, they enjoyed the increased freedom that this combined technique introduced to the game. Some felt they could become acclimatized to the combined technique in event they were provided with more time with a better-tuned version of it.

5 Follow-Up Test of the Handy Cam Technique

Given the large amount of positive feedback the handy-cam technique received, we felt it warranted further testing to see whether players indicated a preference for having this ambient technique switched on during play. We conducted a brief comparison test using our modified game engine and some early levels from the game Half-Life 2 [18]. For this study, the handy-cam technique was modified to include roll, with the following replacing Eqns. 6 and 7 from Sec. 2.6:

$$\text{cam.roll} \mathrel{-}= r\,(\text{head.roll}^{\,v}) \tag{11}$$

$$\text{cam.yaw} \mathrel{+}= y\,(\text{head.yaw}^{\,v}) \tag{12}$$

$$\text{cam.pitch} \mathrel{-}= p\,((\text{head.pitch} - \text{learnt.pitch})^{\,v}) \tag{13}$$

In this tuned version r = 65°, $y = 90°$, $p = 150°$, $w = 100$, $h = 50$, $d = 75$, learnt.pitch initially equals 0.15 (rad), and, learnt.depth initially equals at 0.7m. From the variables it can be seen that this version is much more accentuated than the version used in the focus group study.

Eight new end-user participants were asked to spend a total of 20 minutes playing the game for order-balanced conditions with and without the handy-cam switched on.

They were then asked four questions using Likert scales between one and five: Which condition did they prefer? How immersed in the game experience did they feel? How realistic was the experience? How aware were they of the ambient head-tracking technique being in operation? The median rating for the preference question was 4, showing a slight preference for having the handy cam on, and the median rating for awareness was 2, showing a low awareness of the head tracking system. Taken together, these two results argue well for the use of the handy-cam as an unobtrusive add-on for FPS games. We note however, that one outlier participant greatly preferred playing with the handy cam technique off, suggesting that this variant of the technique would still benefit from being an optional component. Additionally, some tracking issues occurred. In particular, the system failed to properly recognize one of the participants, implying the need to further refine the technique to make it more robust. The immersion and realism questions showed no significant difference between the two conditions.

6 Derived Design Guidelines

Despite being somewhat preliminary work, the four focus groups and follow up testing continually raised several important issues to do with the design of head-tracked interaction techniques. We have abstracted these observations, and combined them with our own experience in developing and testing these techniques to derive draft guidelines for others wishing to develop commercially viable (i.e. based on hardware that is affordable, intuitive, unimposing, etc), head-tracking techniques for use with computer games:

Cater for a lack of reliability. Unlike a keyboard and mouse, webcamera-based head tracking will, arguably, always suffer from some issues of reliability - be it latency, inaccuracy or simply dropping out altogether. As such, one should avoid using head tracking for performing critical control functions, given that the game would either need to be paused or feedback would need to be provided, in the event the system becomes unreliable. Such occurrences might detract from the user experience if they occur too frequently. A preferred approach is to use the head tracking to supplement the experience so that gameplay could continue without significant impact following a tracking loss.

Help the tracking system. Given the issues of reliability, avoid inducing movements that the head tracking system may find harder to accurately interpret. From our experience with our system, avoid large rotations, rapid movements, or requiring movements near the edge of the usage region. For the latter point, we suggest softening out an effect so the outer regions have less impact than the center, making the user more inclined to stay within a reliable usage region.

Make it natural. A technique should try to cater towards a natural affordance or action, allowing for them to be performed either unwittingly or intuitively. In the latter case, one must then consider what is considered intuitive for *most* people.

Do not strain the user. A technique should avoid placing a player under any form of physical duress. In particular, avoid making the player continuously hold awkward poses or perform quick, snapping actions. Developers must be responsible for the safety of their users, especially if a game is to be released to market.

Emphasize the continuous nature of the head data. A great advantage of the head data is that it provides continuous information, which allows the player to conduct partial movements. Given the difficulty in replicating this using buttons, head tracking can provide a finer level of control than a keyboard or mouse click.

Induce and reward the player. Thought should be given in focusing the game content around the techniques, particularly for control techniques, to induce the player into using them. If a technique requires something of the player, ensure that their efforts are rewarded. A player will cease to use something if it gives them no benefit. Worth noting, is that guideline must be considered in regards to the first guideline.

Make it general. In developing a technique, ensure that its implementation does not discriminate against particular users. For example, some users sit back, some slouch and others may be just be interpreted oddly by the head tracking. As such, avoid *preset* options. Either allow the user to set where they wish to, say, invoke an action, or preferably, refine and develop the technique until it works uniformly across all user types. Part of this will probably require making the technique work on *relative* movements, rather than *absolute* ones.

Be unobtrusive. A successful technique cannot expect too much of the user. Techniques that require a setup process, continual resetting, or any other form of inconvenience will deter users.

Feedback. In an effort to train the player in using a technique, feedback is very important to make players aware of the limits. For example, letting the user know how close they are to the edge of the working camera range, or how close they are to fully completing or activating an action will avoid them moving further than required. Auditory feedback is particularly good as it avoids cluttering the screen, however, elegant visual feedback could also be effective.

Unintentional movements. Unlike other forms of input, head tracking is susceptible to unintentional input. Sources of these may include external distractions, causing the player to turns their head away from the screen, and uncontrollable physiological responses, such as jumping during a scary, in-game moment. Techniques that do not reverse the actions of an unintentional movement upon returning to a neutral head position may cause the player frustration.

7 Conclusion

We have continued work initiated by others to more systematically explore the design space of head-tracked interaction with computer games. We have developed five interaction techniques for control and two for ambient interaction.

While, on the whole, the feedback received from the focus groups was positive, we conclude that the control techniques (peering, zooming, iron sighting and spinning) are most useful for games with specially designed, head-centric content or as an optional control for more mainstream games. This is primarily because of the high performance demands that gamers place on control devices, which, unfortunately, commercial head tracking systems do not seem to meet at this time.

By contrast, we see a greater potential for the ambient techniques in the FPS game genre, given the energy and realism they bring to the game. Given that these techniques provide nonessential functionality (at least in the form we propose) they better at catering for the unreliable nature of the head tracking system. Unfortunately though, the HCP technique still places unreasonable demands on the latency and configuration of the system. In contrast, the handy-cam technique, a technique first proposed in this paper, does not place these requirements on the system but still achieves a similar effect. Follow up testing showed that the majority of users preferred playing with the handy-cam technique switched on. For this reason, we believe this technique has the potential for the greatest immediate, commercial impact of all of the techniques studied here.

In the future, we hope to conduct more substantial and quantitative analysis of the handy-cam technique. We also wish to study the natural movement of players during gameplay as this will aid in utilizing the head-tracking data in future work.

Finally, to encourage further research in this field of work, the techniques discussed in this paper haven been open-sourced and can be downloaded from [13].

Acknowledgements. The authors gratefully acknowledge the donation of v2.1 of the FaceAPI from the Seeing Machines company for the purposes of this study. No commercial funding was received for this research.

References

1. Sutherland, I.E.: A Head-Mounted Three-Dimensional Display. In: Proceedings of the December 9-11, 1968, fall joint computer conference, part I, pp. 757–764. ACM, New York (1968)
2. Viola, P., Jones, M.T.: Robust Real-Time Face Detection. J. Computer Vision 57(2), 137–154 (2004)
3. Face-API, `http://www.faceapi.com`
4. Wang, S., Ziong, X., Zu, Y., Wang, C., Zhang, W., Dai, X., Zhang, D.: Face-Tracking as an Augmented Input in Video Games: Enhancing Presence, Role-Playing and Control. In: Proceedings of the SIGCHI conference on Human Factors in computing systems, pp. 1097–1106. ACM, New York (2006)
5. Yim, J., Qiu, E., Graham, T.C.N.: Experience in the Design and Development of a Game Based on Head-Tracking Input. In: Proceedings of the 2008 Conference on Future Play: Research, Play, Share, pp. 236–239. ACM, New York (2008)
6. Lee, J.C.: Hacking the Nintendo Wii Remote. J. IEEE Pervasive Computing 7(3), 39–45 (2008)
7. Crawford, C.: The Art of Computer Game Design. McGraw-Hill/Osborne Media, Berkeley (1984)

8. Arthur, K.W., Booth, K.S., Ware, C.: Evaluating 3D Task Performance for Fish Tank Virtual Worlds. J. ACM Transactions on Information Systems (TOIS) 11(3), 239–265 (1993)
9. Reikimoto, J.: A Vision-Based Head Tracker for Fish Tank Virtual Reality – VR without Head Gear. In: Proceedings of the Virtual Reality Annual International Symposium (VRAIS 1995), pp. 94–100. IEEE Computer Society, Washington (1995)
10. Video Demonstration of the Techniques, `http://www.youtube.com/watch?v=qWkpdtFZoBE`
11. Harrison, C., Dey, A.K.: Lean and Zoom: Proximity-Aware User Interface and Content Magnification. In: Proceeding of the twenty-sixth annual SIGCHI conference on Human factors in computing systems, pp. 507–510. ACM, New York (2008)
12. Valve Corporation, `http://www.valvesoftware.com`
13. Software Download Page, `http://www.torbensko.com/software/head_tracking`
14. Source Engine SDK Developer Wiki, `http://developer.valvesoftware.com/wiki/SDK_Docs`
15. Valve Support Forums, `http://store.steampowered.com/forums`
16. Krueger, R.A., Casey, M.A.: Focus Groups: A Practical Guide for Applied Research. Sage Publications Inc., Thousand Oaks (2000)
17. Thief Product Information, `http://www.eidosinteractive.co.uk/games/info.html?gmid=148`
18. Half-Life 2 Information Page, `http://orange.half-life2.com/hl2.html`

Playability: How to Identify the Player Experience in a Video Game

J.L. González Sánchez, N. Padilla Zea, and F.L. Gutiérrez

Software Engineering Department, University of Granada, E-18071, Spain
{joseluisgs,npadilla,fgutierr}@ugr.es

Abstract. Nowadays Video Games occupy a privileged position in the leisure and entertainment market, representing the fastest-growing industry globally. In this paper we will analyse how, in video game development, Usability alone is not sufficient to achieve the optimum Player Experience. We argue that the concept of Usability needs broadening and deepening, to embrace further attributes and properties that identify and describe the Player Experience. We present our proposed means of defining Playability, its attributes and properties and how associate them with the different elements of a video game.

Keywords: Playability, Usability, User Experience, Video Games.

1 Introduction

Throughout history, humans have had the capacity to manage their own leisure time, this being a significant driver in cultural development. Nowadays, video games and entertainment systems collectively make up the biggest industry in terms of turnover, more so than music and cinema. From this we can deduce that video games have become the preferred game of choice, exerting significant social and cultural influence over children, teens and adults [1]. In this paper we analyse why Usability is therefore not sufficient to describe the full User Experience in relation to video games. Secondly, we present a definition of Playability, its attributes and properties, to characterise and measure the Player Experience with these kinds of systems. Finally, we introduce the notion of Facets of Playability that will allow us to study Playability easily across the different video game elements, testing and analysing each attribute and its properties throughout the video game development process.

2 Playability in Entertainment Systems

When a *Desktop System (DS)* such as a word processor, is developed, the main objective is that *users can execute a set of tasks* in a predetermined context, for example working in an office. Usability is a measure of product use whereby users achieve concrete objectives in varying degrees of *effectiveness*, *efficiency* and *satisfaction*, within a specific context of use [2]. The *User Experience* (UX) [3] is facilitated by the Usability. It has two principal points of view, which characterize it: *process* (of use) and *product*. *Video Games* can be considered a 'special' interactive system, they have

T. Gross et al. (Eds.): INTERACT 2009, Part I, LNCS 5726, pp. 356–359, 2009.

a very specific objective: *to make the player feel good when playing it.* We propose that analysing the quality of a video game purely in terms of its Usability is not sufficient – we need to consider not only functional values but also non-functional values, given the specific properties of video games. In other words, the Player Experience (PX) could be much more complex than the UX. It entails to extend and complete formally the UX characteristics with *players' dimensions* (user and group) using a broad set of attributes and properties in order to identify and measure the experience of players playing a video game, *PX*. These properties indicate to us whether a game is 'playable' or not – that is, they will identify the *Playability* of the video game.

Although *Playability* is a live topic in the scientific community, it has been studied from different points of view and with different objectives without consensus on its definition or the attributes or properties to characterize it: *Playability* as only Usability in video games context [4, 5,6] or in the quality of game elements [7, 8].

We define *Playability* as: '*a set of properties that describe the Player Experience using a specific game system whose main objective is to provide enjoyment and entertainment, by being credible and satisfying, when the player plays alone or in company*'. Playability is characterised by attributes that exist in Usability but that have different meanings in video game context (Fig. 1). *Playability represents the degree to which specified users can achieve specified goals with effectiveness, efficiency and specially satisfaction and fun in a playable context of use.* We propose a set of seven attributes to characterise Playability and some examples of properties of *Playability*, to subsequently measure them:

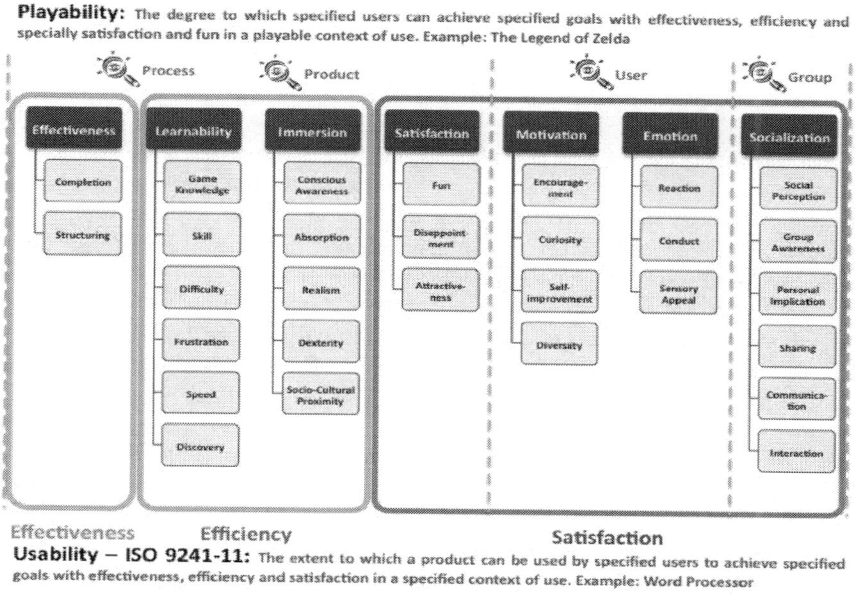

Fig. 1. Playability Model: attributes and properties to measure it

Satisfaction*:** We define this as the gratification or pleasure derived from playing a complete video game or from some aspect of it. We characterise it using the following properties: Game *Fun*, Contents *Disappointment* and *Attractiveness*. ***Learnability: We define this as the player's capacity to understand and master the game's system and mechanics (objectives, rules, how to interact with the video game, and so on). We propose the following properties to characterise it: *Game Knowledge*, Player *Skill*, Game *Difficulty*, Player *Frustration*, *Speed* of Learning and *Discovery* Techniques. ***Effectiveness*:** We define this as the time and resources necessary to offer players a fun and entertaining experience whilst they achieve the game's various objectives and reach the final goal. We identify Effectiveness as having the following properties: Game *Completion* and the *Structuring* of the Game Resources. ***Immersion***: We define this as the capacity of the video game contents to be believable, such that the player becomes directly involved in the virtual game world. To characterise Immersion we propose the following properties: *Conscious Awareness*, *Absorption* in game, Game *Realism*, Control *Dexterity* and *Socio-Cultural Proximity* with the game. ***Motivation***: We define this as the set of game characteristics that prompt a player to realise specific actions and continue undertaking them until they are completed. We characterise Motivation as having the following properties: *Encouragement* Techniques, *Curiosity* about the game, *Player Self-Improvement* and *Diversity* of game resources. ***Emotion***: This refers to the player's involuntary impulse in response to the stimulus of the video game that induces feelings or a chain reaction of automatic behaviours. We characterise Emotion as having the following properties: Player *Reaction*, Game *Conduct* and *Sensory Appeal* for game elements. ***Socialization***: We define this as the set of game attributes, elements and resources that promote the social dimension of the game experience in a group scenario. We propose that Socialization has the following properties: *Social Perception*, *Group Awareness*, *Personal Implication*, the *Sharing* of the Social Resources, *Communication* Techniques and *Interaction* Rules of the socialization game.

Playability analysis is a very complex process due to the different perspectives that we can use to analyse the various parts of video game architecture. In this work, we propose a classification of these perspectives based on six *Facets of Playability*. Each facet allows us to identify the different attributes and properties of *Playability* that are affected by the different elements of video game architecture [9]. The first facet is ***Intrinsic Playability***: this is the *Playability* inherent in the nature of the video game itself and how it is presented to the player. ***Mechanical Playability***: it is related to the quality of the video game as a software system. ***Interactive Playability***: this is associated with player interaction and video game user interface development. ***Artistic Playability***: this facet relates to the quality of the artistic and aesthetic game elements and how these elements are executed in the video game. ***Intrapersonal Playability*** or *Personal Playability*: This refers to the individual outlook, perceptions and feelings that the video game produces in each player when they play, and as such has a high subjective value. ***Interpersonal Playability*** or *Social Playability*: This refers to the feelings and perceptions of users, and the group awareness that arise when a game is played in company, be it in a competitive, cooperative or collaborative way.

The overall Playability of a video game, then, is the sum total of values across all attributes in the different Facets of Playability. It is crucial to optimise Playability across the different facets in order to guarantee the best Player Experience.

3 Conclusions and Future Work

In this paper we have presented video games as special interactive systems developed to entertain the user, concluding that Usability alone is an insufficient measure for determining the full Player Experience. We have presented the concept of *Playability* outlining the attributes that characterise it and their properties, in order to measure and guarantee an optimum Player Experience. To facilitate the analysis of *Playability*, we have proposed the *Facets of Playability* to study every property in each attribute in order to identify the elements necessary to achieve overall *Playability* in different video games. *Playability* must be taken into account in every phase of the game development, in order to, amongst other things, anticipate any unexpected or negative results for the developer and guarantee a high quality of playability and improve the Player Experience in the final product.

Currently we are designing a conceptual model of a video game which will enable us to specify and analyse *Playability* characteristics in the design phase, and to incorporate *Playability* techniques into software patterns, style guides and heuristic techniques, thus ensuring optimum *Playability* of the end-product. We are also adapting techniques used in Usability Engineering and User-Centred Design in order to include *Playability* in a quality model to enhance the Player Experience throughout the different phases of video game development.

Acknowledgments. This research is financed by: the Spanish International Commission for Science and Technology (CICYT); the DESACO Project (TIN2008-06596-C02-2); and the F.P.U. Programme of the Ministry of Science and Innovation, Spain.

References

1. Provenzo, E.: Video kids. Harvard University Press, Cambridge (1991)
2. ISO 9241-11: Guidance on Usability, also issued by the International Organization for Standardization (1998)
3. Hassenzahl, M., Tractinsky, N.: User Experience – A Research Agenda. Behaviour and Information Technology 25(2), 91–97 (2006)
4. Federoff, M.: Heuristic and Usability Guidelines for the Creation and Evaluation of Fun Video Games. Master Thesis, Department of Telecommunications, Indiana University (2002)
5. Desuvire, H., Capñan, M., Toth, J.: Using Heuristic to Evaluate The Playability in Games. In: CHI 2004. ACM, New York (2004)
6. Fabricatore, C., Nussbaum, M., Rosas, R.: Playability in Action Video Games: A Qualitative Design Model. Human-Computer Interaction 17, 311–368 (2002)
7. Rollings, A., Morris, D.: Game Architecture and Design. Ed. New Riders Games (2003)
8. Salen, K., Zimmerman, E.: Rules of Play: Game Design Fundamentals. Ed. The MIT Press, Cambridge (2003)
9. González Sánchez, J.L., Padilla Zea, N., Gutiérrez, F.L.: From Usability to Playability: Itroduction to the Player-Centred Video Game Development Procces. In: Procedings of HCI International (Forthcoming 2009)

SimCompany: An Educational Game Created through a Human-Work Interaction Design Approach

Pedro Campos[1] and Ana Campos[2]

[1] University of Madeira,
Campus Universitário da Penteada, 9000-390 Funchal, Portugal
ISEG School of Economics and Management, Technical University of Lisbon
[2] WowSystems
Rua da Alfândega, 78, 3º, 9000-059 Funchal, Portugal
pcampos@uma.pt, ana.campos@wowsystems.pt

Abstract. We present a novel children's educational game, which was created through a human-work interaction design – an emerging research field which advocates a better understanding of the relationship between work-domain based empirical studies and iterative design of prototypes and new technologies. We describe how "SimCompany", a game for teaching children about business management concepts, was created. SimCompany proved effective as a teaching tool about business management concepts, and initial evaluation showed a positive increase in students' rate of learning, compared to traditional teaching methods.

Keywords: Human work interaction design, sensor-based installations, field observations, educational games, interface design.

1 Introduction

In this paper, we describe a novel educational game that uses concepts from Human-Work Interaction Design [1]. This is an emerging research field, which was born under the auspices of IFIP's Working Group 13.6. In a recent workshop [1], new themes and directions of research on human work analysis and design to support it have been outlined. The main target of the work group is the analysis of and the design for the variety of complex work and life contexts found in different business. We argue in this paper that such analysis can be useful when designing childrens' educational games, in particular SimCompany, a game designed and produced with the goal of teaching children management and entrepreneurship concepts.

2 Related Work

One good way to motivate children to learn using technology is to apply games, which are well known, exploiting the power of popular TV shows. With the goal of minimizing the amount of effort and requirements to set up a situated learning environment, Lin [2] integrated scenarios of the popular video game Pokemon in classroom education of 2nd grade math concepts. Observations showed that, in such arrangement, they could

T. Gross et al. (Eds.): INTERACT 2009, Part I, LNCS 5726, pp. 360–363, 2009.

engage some students into the scenarios where math is applied. Since most children inevitably spend much time playing digital games, it is argued that digital game-based learning is one way to involve kids to do the right things with computer [2].

Lee et al. [3] performed a study to investigate whether educational video games could be integrated into a classroom with positive effects for the teacher and students. They conducted the study with 39 2nd grade students using their mathematic drill software "Skills Arena" [3]. Early data from the study suggested that not only do teachers and students enjoy using "Skills Arena", students even exceeded expectations by doing three times more math problems in 19 days than they would have using traditional worksheets. Regardless of the popularity that games exhibit when it comes to teaching children, there is a lack of research towards *design approaches* that can prove useful when conceiving and designing such games.

3 "SimCompany" and Its Design Process

"SimCompany" is a fun game designed to instill in children (9-14 years old) the entrepreneurship spirit. As the young player progresses in the game, the basic concepts of consumer behavior, marketing and strategic management are described, illustrated and reinforced in a fun, easy and engaging way.

The goal of the game is to reach the last level and complete it with the greatest amount of points accumulated and before time expires. As an example, we provide a brief description of three levels of this game, taken from the game's script, which was outlined through a human-work design approach.

Level 1: Getting to know the consumer. At the first level, the young player will be faced with a roll of different people (consumers). Based on the description of these characters (age, sex, social class, profession, interests, etc.), the player will have to associate the various products that appear onscreen (e.g. skateboards, neckties, candies, etc.) to the most likely consumer. Figure 1 illustrates this level's user interface.

Fig. 1. Overall aspect of the "SimCompany" game, Level 1

The learning objective is to show the player that there are various factors (demographic, geographic, personal tastes, lifestyle, etc.) that determine the choices of consumption, the ways that each person chooses to spend time and money and that should be taken into account when attempting to open the right business. To move to the next level, the player must accumulate a minimum number of points directly related to the number of correct associations made between consumer-product.

Level 9: Competition. At this level, the competition increases… New organizations start to emerge, which are direct competitors… To worsen the situation there is also an increase on the number of substitute products. The player must be able to identify situations where the threat of substitutes and rivalry in the industry increases and choose the scenario where his/her organization will have better chances to survive. The learning objective is to demonstrate the importance of being aware of the threats of direct competitors and substitute products for the survival of the business.

Level 10: Let's make a trip! The big finale! The business has been a success and now the player has the opportunity to diversify it in geographic terms. But, how? Several scenarios and advice will be given and the player must use his incredible management abilities to internationalize his business in the best possible manner... It will be a difficult task but we know that he will make it...trying is all that matters!

The learning objective of this level is to show children, in very simple and captivating way, the most basic concepts of internationalization of a business.

Human-Work Design Approach. The approach we followed was based on analyzing the work that managers do when conducting their business and from that point we established a creative game script aimed at engaging children but also making them learn the day-to-day *real work* of a businessman. The approach followed for each of the game's levels was divided into three stages: (i) cognitive analysis, (ii) definition of learning objectives and (iii) translation into a game script.

Stage (i) was directly concerned with outlining the kind of decisions that are made by business managers and entrepreneurs, when leading their operations. Stage (ii) focused on the learning objectives, which were derived after consulting with different business managing experts in the field and also according to some interviews with business leaders and general research literature on the subject. The final stage, translation into a game script, was focused on writing a compelling script that children would enjoy. At the same time, the script would need to meet the learning objectives stated during stage (ii). The final game script document served as a game design document and formed the basis for the user interface design of the game.

4 Evaluation and Discussion

The evaluation of this game has been initially conducted with two classes (children aged 9-11) at a local school. Overall there were 28 females and 21 males. In both classes, participants were randomly divided into two groups of equal dimension: a control group, composed of students who took a lesson on managing a business using traditional methods – blackboard, books and the lecture itself – and the experimental group, composed of students who played "SimCompany". Each class was divided into three phases: a pretest phase, when students answered a random set of questions about the subject being taught (management) without being taught anything about it. Then came the learning phase itself. It consisted of a traditional lesson in the control group and a "SimCompany" playing session, in the experimental group.

At the end of the class, students performed a similar posttest, so that we could quantify their average degree of learning obtained by each of the groups. One way to measure the *degree of learning* (how much the students knowledge improved) obtained through a particular mode of education is quantified by the <g> score [4], which is calculated the following way:

$$\langle g\rangle = (\text{posttest\%} - \text{pretest\%}) / (100\% - \text{pretest\%})$$

where posttest% is the percentage of correct answers in the posttest and pretest% is the percentage of correct answers in the pretest. The procedure for the control groups was similar, except that the teacher was asked to give the class about the exact same subject but using traditional methods like the whiteboard.

Table 1 shows the evolution from pre-tests to post-tests for each of these groups of students. The results refer to the pre and post-test percentage of correct answers; the right-most column shows the <g> value.

Table 1. Evolution of the students' degree of learning <g>

	Pre-Test	Post-Test	<g>
Control Group (without SimCompany)	59.1	70.3	27%
Experimental Group (playing SimCompany)	57.2	77.4	47%

From this initial evaluation, it became clear that SimCompany is an effective game for teaching children general business management concepts: results showed a higher <g> value for the experimental group than the control group. This is a step forward in designing technology that really helps children learn. Future work will include evaluating the game in more schools and students, as well as outlining general principles that can prove useful when designing this kind of games. This will also contribute to a growing body of knowledge based on human-work interaction design.

References

1. Clemmensen, T., Orngreen, R., Pejtersen, A.M.: Describing Users in Contexts: Perspectives on Human-Work Interaction Design. In: Workshop Proceedings of Interact 2005 (2005)
2. Lin, Y.-H.: Integrating Scenarios of Video Games into Classroom Instruction. In: Information Technologies and Applications in Education, ISITAE 2007 (2007)
3. Lee, J., Luchini, K., Michael, B., Norris, C., Soloway, E.: More than just fun and games: assessing the value of educational video games in the classroom. In: CHI 2004 Extended Abstracts on Human Factors in Computing Systems, Vienna, Austria, April 24 - 29 (2004)
4. Mayo, M.J.: Games for science and engineering education. Communications of the ACM 50(7), 30–35 (2007)

What's Next? A Visual Editor for Correcting Reading Order

Daisuke Sato, Masatomo Kobayashi, Hironobu Takagi, and Chieko Asakawa

Tokyo Research Laboratory, IBM Japan, 1623-14, Shimo-tsuruma,
Yamato City, Kanagawa, Japan, 242-8502
{dsato,mstm,takagih,chie}@jp.ibm.com

Abstract. The reading order, i.e. the serialized form, of the webpage should be a meaningful order for alternative representations such as the audible forms needed for visually impaired users. However, the serialized form rarely receives attention because it is visually elusive for authors using the existing WISIWYG authoring environments. Therefore we propose a new visualization technique called "reading flow" that visualizes the order of the serialized form with variable granularity by using a visible path extending through the elements in the content. This allows the authors to instantly evaluate the ordering by the visual pattern of the path. Our approach also allows them to interactively and intuitively reorganize the order of the serialized form. The results of two comparative experiments show that our reading flow greatly increases the ability of the authors to understand and organize the ordering compared to the existing techniques.

Keywords: Reading flow, reading order, Web accessibility, ARIA flowto.

1 Introduction

With advances in Web technology, there are increasing demands for highly visual webpages. At the same time, it's extremely helpful if the serialized form of each webpage appears in a meaningful order for alternative representations, such as the audible forms used by visually impaired users or the transcoded forms used on small devices. For example, when a set of lists and headings for the lists are arranged in multiple columns in a table, all of the headings are read first, and then each of the lists is read sequentially (see Figure 1). Each list is separated from its title, and the intended semantics are hidden in the audible form. This is a well known, common, and severe accessibility problem. Authors should make the order meaningful at authoring time. This is mentioned in major accessibility guidelines and regulations. For example, the W3C Web Content Accessibility Guidelines (WCAG) 1.0 [1] rate the reading order adjustments at conformance level "A", the highest priority. Section 508 of the U.S. Rehabilitation Act [2], JIS X 8341-3 in Japan [3], and the eEurope Action Plan 2002 [4] all mention reading order.

However, the order of the serialized form (which reflects the order in the source code) is rarely noticed, because the existing WYSIWYG authoring tools allow authors to edit the content without considering the underlying source code order. The authors would have to modify the source code directly to control the ordering. Although there are many

T. Gross et al. (Eds.): INTERACT 2009, Part I, LNCS 5726, pp. 364–377, 2009.

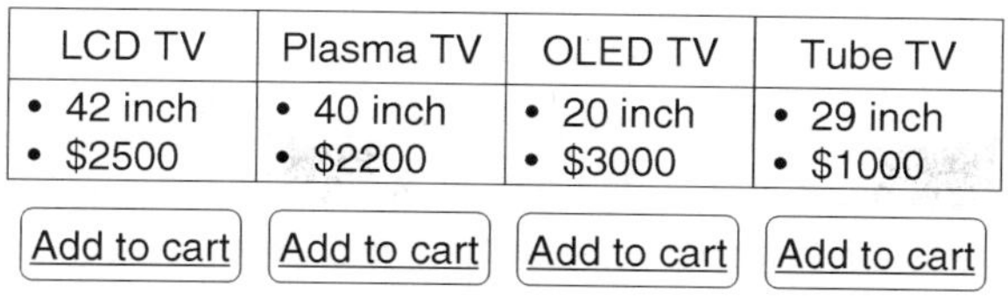

Fig. 1. An example of an inaccessible layout using a table. This would be read as "LCD TV, Plasma TV, OLED TV, Tube TV, 42 inch, $2500, 40 inch, $2200, 20 inch, $3000, 29 inch, $1000, link add to cart, link add to cart, link add to cart, link add to cart."

types of accessibility checking tools, the order of the serialized forms is rarely evaluated automatically because of the essential difficulty of algorithmically defining an appropriate reading order. Existing tools force authors to manually inspect the order of the serialized forms, but this is not intuitive and the tools do not support changing the order.

Therefore we propose a new visualization technique called "reading flow" that visualizes the order of the serialized form by using a visible path extended through the elements in the content. The reading flow represents the visual flow of reading the corresponding elements, and can represent fine or coarse granularity of the flow of the content. This allows an author to immediately see the serialized form and easily adjust it. The technique reduces the work for authors and developers when they build the webpages, since they can freely modify the reading order separately from the page design tasks. Going beyond webpages, our technique can potentially be applied to other types of documents where the reading order causes problems, such as presentation documents, PDF documents, and Flash content, and can help improve their accessibility.

The rest of this paper is organized as follows: Section 2 describes related work, Section 3 presents the proposed reading flow technique, Section 4 describes our implementation of reading flow, Section 5 reports on user experiments with reading flow, and Section 6 discusses the results of the experiments and some residual problems, and then concludes this paper.

2 Related Work

2.1 Transcoding

One major approach that can control the reading order without modifying the original content involves transcoding on a proxy server [5, 6]. This modifies the original content en route to a browser by using predefined metadata that can adjust the priority of each part of the content for blind users. There are also client-side techniques without proxies that generate alternative user interfaces for blind users by using predefined metadata [7, 8]. These techniques can also exploit a visual metadata editor but there is no interface to visually organize the reading order. The HearSay browser analyzes the content and the history of the link navigation on the fly to assess the most important parts of the content for the blind users, and then reorders the content by considering each part's importance to the users [9]. One of the interesting flexible aspects is that the resulting reading order may change depending on the links that access the page, since those links may reflect different purposes and thus importance. All of these techniques could use our reading flow metadata when modifying or reordering the content.

2.2 Accessibility Checking Tools

There are various types of automated tools to check whether or not a document complies with the accessibility standards such as WCAG [1]. Some of them also have functions to simulate or visualize the serialized forms of the content.

Textualization is the basic function provided by WAVE [10, 11], aDesigner [12], and many other tools. The textualizing functions provide text-only views that simulate the serialized forms of the content. However, this function does not offer an intuitive way for users to evaluate the appropriateness of the content order because it loses the positional information of the display. The users must struggle to understand the relationships between the text and the original visual layout.

Numbering is an advanced function provided by WAVE. It visualizes the content order by showing the sequence as a number with each element. Although the number is clear about the order of the content, it is still hard to get an overview of the reading order. The aDesigner tool also provides a function to visualize the content order using gradations of the background color, thus showing the reaching time from the top of the webpage in the screen readers, but there is no easy way for users to determine which elements come first in the content. These tools are mainly used for checking the accessibility, and they don't have functions to organize the order of the content.

2.3 Tools for Optical Character Recognition (OCR)

In the field of OCR, there are also problems with the reading order of the content resulting in a lot of research. Various technologies predict the reading order based on layout analysis [13] or machine learning techniques [14]. Those automatic predictions may not be perfect. Therefore tools to visualize the results and to allow users to correct the results are provided. Such tools also include functions that allow users to adjust the reading order, which is important when validating OCR results [15, 16, and 17]. One system visualized the order between pairs of recognized text zones in the captured image by using arrows. Our reading flow was motivated by these techniques. We have extended the functions to handle the specific accessibility problems of HTML documents, and also improved the usability and the presentation.

3 Reading Flow

Our reading flow can be regarded as an interaction technique to obtain and organize the order of the serialized forms of the webpages. This section describes three major features of the reading flow: visualization, authoring, and granularity control of the reading flow.

3.1 Visualization of Reading Flow

The reading flow visualizes the order of the serialized forms of the webpages by using a traversal path aligned with the elements of the content. Figure 2 shows an example of the visualization of our reading flow on the webpage of INTERACT 2009. Our reading flow will be displayed over the rendered image of the content, which can be scaled to any size. The reading flow is represented by smoothly connected arrows that indicate the visual flow of reading the corresponding elements. The visual flow of reading each element is determined by its content and the mode of the characters, which can be left-to-right and top-to-bottom, top-to-bottom and right-to-left or some other order. Not all of the elements need to be included on the path. Multi-granularity visualization is an extension of this approach (Section 3.3). In the finest-grain visualization, three properties of the element are considered to support skipping unnecessary elements. First, whether or not the element is audible for reading by screen readers. Second, whether the element is visible or hidden. Third, whether or not the element is located in the visible part of the screen (see Table 1). The traversable path of the reading flow must pass through all audible, visible, and on-screen elements. The parts of the path for the hidden elements and the visible but off-screen elements can be collapsed and displayed as special tags at appropriate positions on the complete path. By clicking the tags, the corresponding collapsed paths can be displayed.

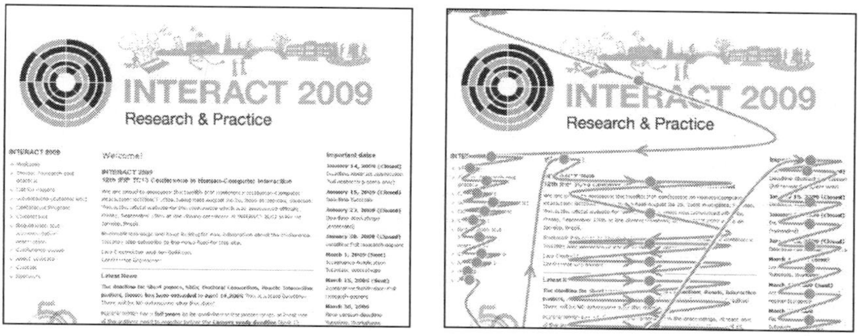

Fig. 2. A fine-grain visualization of the reading flow of the INTERACT 2009 webpage. Each distinguished element has a knob (shown as a circle) on the path of the reading flow.

Table 1. The relationships between the properties of elements and their visualization

	Audible		Not audible
	On the screen	**Off the screen**	**On and off the screen**
Visible	Displayed	Collapsed	Not Displayed
Hidden	Collapsed	Collapsed	

3.2 Authoring of Reading Flow

The reading flow also provides a knob on each element so that the author can explicitly and visually change the ordering by connecting each knob to the next one. Figure 3 shows an example of reordering. If a user finds an incorrect order on the reading flow at an element (Figure 3a), the user can easily change the flow by dragging the knob on that element to the knob of the proper next element. During the dragging operation, the prior path of the dragged knob is highlighted and the rest of the path is temporally hidden (Figure 3b and 3c). The interface uses three constraints to maintain the consistency of the reading order in spite of the reordering and to make the interface as simple as

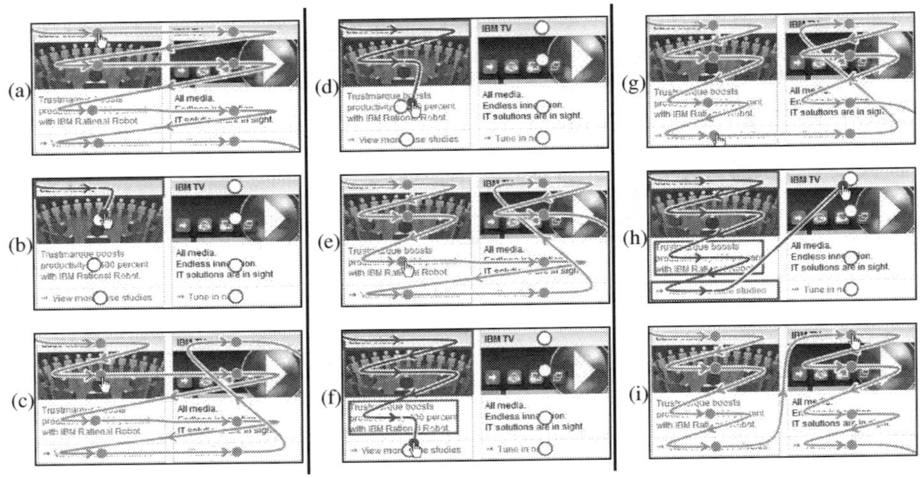

Fig. 3. An example of organizing the reading flow. Part (a) shows the original reading flow of the content, (b), (d), (f), and (h) show snapshots while the dragging the knobs. By dragging the first knob at the upper left to the knob below it (b), the skipped knob at the upper right is moved to the end of the path (c). The pairs (d) – (e), (f) – (g), and (h) – (i) show similar reordering operations to create a two-column layout in this example.

possible (so even novice users can use it). (1) A knob can only be connected to another knob going forward. In other words, the user connects a knob to some later element or an unlinked element, not to an earlier element. (2) A knob cannot be connected to make a loop in the reordered path. (3) If a group of elements becomes disconnected, then that segment is moved to the end of the current path.

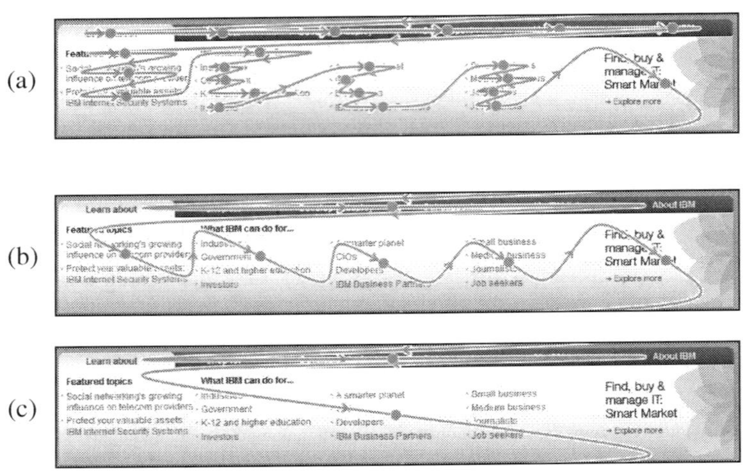

Fig. 4. (a) Shows the most details of the reading flow, (b) shows a medium abstraction level, and (c) shows the highest level of abstraction of the reading flow

3.3 Granularity Control of Reading Flow

Our tool has a slider that allows users to determine the granularity level of the reading flow. Figure 4 shows an example of controlling the granularity of the reading flow. With the fine-grain reading flow the users can check the path to each element in the content (Figure 4a). By selecting a higher granularity level, the users can grasp the overview quality of the reading order in the page. For example, the items of a list now have a left-to-right flow and are aligned at the left side of the list (Figure 4b), and at the highest level, the entire series of lists is regarded as one object (Figure 4c). The reordering in a granularity level affects the other levels of granularity, so that the users can edit the order of the flow at any granularity level that is displayed.

The granularity control is implemented as a grouping of elements by using geometric similarities in the tree structure of the content, because the layout of the content is often separated from the tree structure by the style sheets. The system calculates the linkability between adjacent elements in the flow, and then assembles the pairs of elements having highest linkability into a group. The linkability is determined by the geometric similarity and the size of the elements, and the more similar and smaller elements get the higher linkability scores. The system continues this step of prioritizing elements until the number of elements is greater than a target number determined by the setting of the slider for the granularity control. In this process certain pairs are excluded, such as a pair of widely separated elements or a pair that causes an unnatural flow (as when the second element of a pair is above the other element within a top-to-bottom block of text).

4 Implementation

Our reading flow is currently implemented as a function in a Firefox extension written in JavaScript. The metadata generated by the tool is in the Accessibility Commons format [18] and can be shared through the Web service as XML or JSON.

The current implementation handles the order of the content in a semantic layer separated from the original content to reduce the complexity and to allow for sharing the order information as accessibility metadata. When a user modifies an order, the modification is stored as a set of metadata to change the reading. The metadata is created with a "flowto" concept, which is defined in the working draft of the Accessible Rich Internet Applications (WAI-ARIA) version 1.0 [19]. Each flowto attribute has an ID for a target element to be read next.

It is easy to add flowto attributes to the content, but currently (January 2009) there are no screen readers that can directly use the flowto attributes to control the order of the content. Therefore currently the flowto metadata is applied to the content inside browser on the client side to simply change the order in the DOM tree of the original content, and ignoring possible disruptions of the appearance. The flowto metadata also can be converted into metadata for other systems that seek to change the reading order, such as transcoding systems.

5 Experiments

We carried out a two-task experiment to empirically evaluate user performance using our reading flow technique. The first task involved finding problems in the reading order. The second task studied the editing process for the reading order. In the experiment we compared our technique with a baseline numerical sequence display, controlled by entering sequence numbers into the interface.

5.1 Participants

Twelve computer science researchers (9 males and 3 females) from 25 to 33 years of age participated in the experiment. (One participant's age was unknown.) All had experience with graphical user interfaces. Seven had professional or partial knowledge of accessibility. Four had prior knowledge of the reading order problem. We made a selection of the participants and focused on their expertise in accessibility, because the target users of these user interfaces are people who want to correct accessibility problems, such as Web designers and Internet volunteers.

5.2 Apparatus

We used a 3.8 GHz Xeon workstation running Windows XP, connected to a 17-inch LCD display with a resolution of 1280 × 1024 pixels and a standard optical mouse. In the tests involving our reading flow system, the reading order was visualized as arrows displayed on top of the target webpage and modified by the mouse operations described in Section 3.

In the numerical interface, the positions were presented as sequence numbers on each element in the page. Each number was displayed using black digits in a small white rectangle. An input dialog for modifying the number popped up when the user clicked on a button next to the number. If the user entered an existing number, the other elements with that number and the following numbers were automatically incremented so that each element always had a unique number. All of the target webpages in the experiment were small webpages that could be displayed in the experimental window without scrolling.

5.3 Task 1: Determining the Quality of the Reading Order

Each accessibility trial involved five steps: (1) Before beginning the trial, each participant saw a screenshot of the target webpage. The participant was allowed to study the structure of the page until satisfied. (2) The participant clicked anywhere on the screen to start the timed portion of the actual trial. (3) The reading order was displayed on top of the page. (4) The participant clicked on the screen again after deciding whether or not the reading order of the target webpage was accessible. (5) The participant then recorded the decision by clicking on a good or bad button. The participants were instructed to complete each trial as quickly as possible.

We measured task completion time as the time between Steps 2 and 4 and the error rate was defined as the percentage of trials in which participants failed to correctly assess the quality of the reading order.

We used a within-participant design. The independent variables were the interface (fine-grain reading flow, coarse-grain reading flow, or sequence number display), reading order quality (good, somewhat problematic, or very problematic), and target webpage (e-commerce or airport). We tested 18 combinations in total. Each participant performed one trial for each combination. The presentation order of the interfaces was counterbalanced. The quality of the reading order and the target webpage were presented in a random order.

To introduce this task, we instructed participants about accessible and inaccessible reading orders, including several good and bad examples. The participants also had a training trial for each interface to become familiar with the task. Each session took approximately 10 minutes, including the training.

5.4 Task 2: Revising the Reading Order of Contents

Each editing trial involved four steps: (1) Before beginning the trial, each participant saw two screenshots, one with the initial reading order and another with the desired reading order. The participant was also told about the specific problems of the initial order and given instructions how to fix the problems. (2) The participant clicked on a start button to begin the trial. (3) The participant modified the reading order to change it to the desired order using one of the two interfaces. (4) The trial ended as soon as the modified reading order matched the desired order. During this task, the granularity slider was set to "fine" because several steps in this task required low-level changes in the reading order, which could only be performed with the fine-grain arrows. The participants were asked to complete each trial as quickly as possible. We defined the task completion time as the time between Steps 2 and 4. We did not measure error rates because each trial continued until the reading order matched the desired order.

We again used a within-participant design. The independent variables were the interface (reading flow or sequence number entry), reading order quality (somewhat problematic or very problematic), and target webpage (e-commerce or airport). We tested eight combinations in total. Each participant performed one trial for each combination. Half of the participants had four trials of the reading flow interface first, followed by four trials of the number sequence entry interface. The other half of the participants had the reverse order. The quality of the reading order and the target webpage were presented in a random order.

At the beginning of each session, both interfaces were described. The participants also received a training trial for each interface to familiarize them with this task. Each series of sessions took approximately 20 minutes, including training. After finishing all of the sessions, the participants filled in a questionnaire that covered both tasks.

5.5 Results

Figure 5a shows the task completion times for each reading order quality and target webpage combination in Task 1. In this data, we excluded all of the trials with errors. The average values were 6.63 seconds for fine-grain reading flows, 4.99 seconds for coarse-grain reading flows, and 10.18 seconds for numerical displays. The numerical display interface took 53% longer than the fine-grain reading flow and 104% longer than the coarse-grain reading flows. Analysis of variance showed significant primary effects of the interface ($F_{2,178} = 36.69$, $p < .001$), reading order quality ($F_{2,178} = 14.55$, $p < .001$), and target webpage ($F_{1,178} = 8.529$, $p < .005$). There were interaction effects for the interface × reading order quality. A post hoc analysis indicated that the coarse reading flow is significantly faster than the fine reading flow ($p < .05$) and reading flows are significantly faster then the sequence number display ($p < .001$). It also indicated that the good reading order took a significantly longer time to confirm than to detect problematic conditions ($p < .001$). There was no significant difference between the degrees of problems.

Figure 5b shows the incorrect assessment rate for each combination of reading order quality and target webpage in Task 1. The overall values were 4.2% for each interface. Most errors involved the less problematic conditions. Analysis of variance showed a significant primary effect of the reading order quality on the error rate ($F_{2,187} = 6.872$, $p < .005$). The interface and target website had no significant effects, and there were no interaction effects. A post hoc analysis indicated that somewhat problematic conditions caused significantly more errors than good or very problematic conditions.

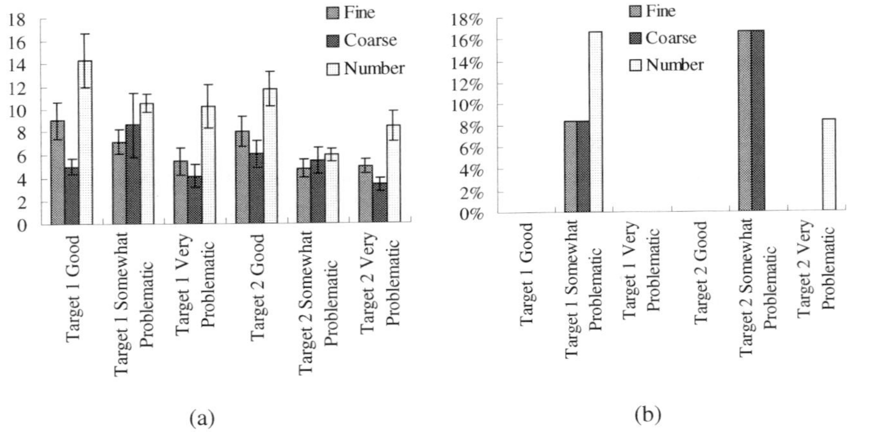

Fig. 5. (a) Task completion times (seconds) with standard errors and (b) error rate (%) for quality assessment

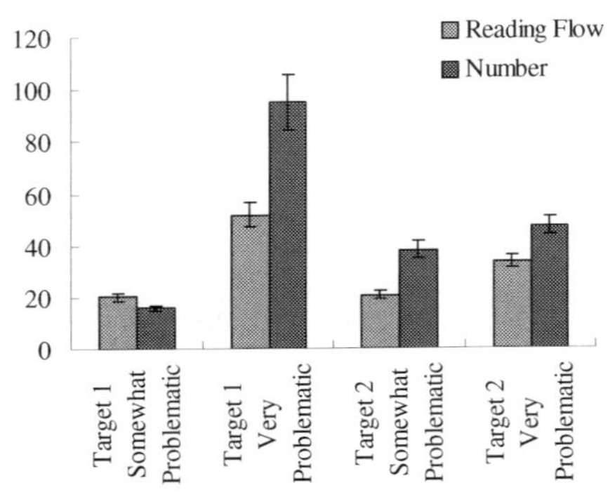

Fig. 6. Task completion times (seconds) with standard errors for reading order revising

Figure 6 shows the task completion time for each combination of reading order quality and target webpage in Task 2. The overall average values were 31.6 seconds for reading flows and 49.1 seconds for numerical entries. The numerical entry interface took 56% longer than the reading flow interface. The reading flow interface generally outperformed the numerical entry interface except for the e-commerce website in the somewhat problematic condition. Analysis of variance showed a significant primary effect of the interface on this value ($F_{1,77} = 9.226$, $p < .005$). The reading order quality and target website had no significant effects and there were no interaction effects.

The post experiment questionnaire asked for subjective evaluations of our reading flow interface. All eleven participants preferred the reading flow interface to the numerical display interface for both tasks. For Task 1, six participants preferred coarse-grain reading flows, two preferred fine-grain reading flows, and the others had no preference between the reading flows granularities.

6 Discussion

6.1 Effectiveness and Visual Patterns

The results clearly show the effectiveness of this new visualization method. Subjects could perform the tasks in significantly shorter times (Figure 5a) by using the visualization than by using the sequence number display. Also, the subjects preferred the visualization over the sequence number display (Figure 6). The coarse-grain visualization also accelerated the performance. In most cases, coarse-grain visualizations achieved significantly faster performance than fine-grain visualizations (Figure 5a), even though the error rates were the same (Figure 5b).

The differences in task completion time were significant between visualization and sequence number display in all cases, but the degree varied depending on the quality of each target page. When a page did not have any problems ("good" in Figure 5a) or when a page had many problems ("very problematic"), the difference is much larger than for pages with a smaller numbers of problems ("somewhat problematic").

One possible interpretation of the result is that subjects could recognize visual patterns for good or very problematic pages at a glance. The visual patterns are not clear from the interview comments, but we think that one of cues is the number of crossing points in the visualization. The line traverses the content with fewer crossing points if the reading flow matches smoothly with the visual semantics, otherwise the line becomes tangled with many crossing points (Figure 7a). In contrast, for "somewhat problematic" pages, the problem is elusive in the smooth reading flow line, which is not visually obvious in comparison to good pages (Figure 7b). The error rate was significantly higher in those tasks, even though subjects spent substantial time with somewhat problematic pages (Figure 5b). This may indicate that subjects overlooked small visual patterns with problems.

If this hypothesis is true, it should be possible to improve the visualization by highlighting the characteristic visual patterns of problems on a page. For example, the color gradation for each segment of the flow line from the top to the end of a page could improve the visibility of visual patterns by giving a sense of the distance for each intersection. A more direct enhancement might be the highlighting of each crossing point with a red flag on the background. If a visualization is filled with red, then the page may have many problems. Another type of improvement involves few crossing points. For example, Figure 7b looks like a good example with a smooth line and no crossing points, but it has the table layout problem. This example resulted in the highest error ratio (Figure 5b "Target 2 Somewhat Problematic"). This type of problem can be easily recognized by comparing the reading order with the original content without considering the visual patterns. Therefore, it is necessary to warn about potential problems in the visualization. For example, if knobs have different colors for table elements, that could warn users to carefully compare the semantic reading order with visualization.

6.2 Interface for Correction

The result of Task 2 shows the significance of the visualization for correction tasks compared with the numerical interface. However, the difference is not clear in some cases. For example, the somewhat problematic example for target 1 had results that were reversed from the other cases (Figure 6). Subjects commented that they consistently tried to scan the numbers from the top of a page, and changed the values to satisfy the semantic ordering. For the reversed results, the page can be fixed by changing only a few numbers close to the top of the page. Then the subjects could finish more quickly, since the time duration for each repair operation is shorter than the visualization. One subject also commented that the temporary intermediate visualizations during a sequence of repair operations were often hard to interpret as the lines became tangled.

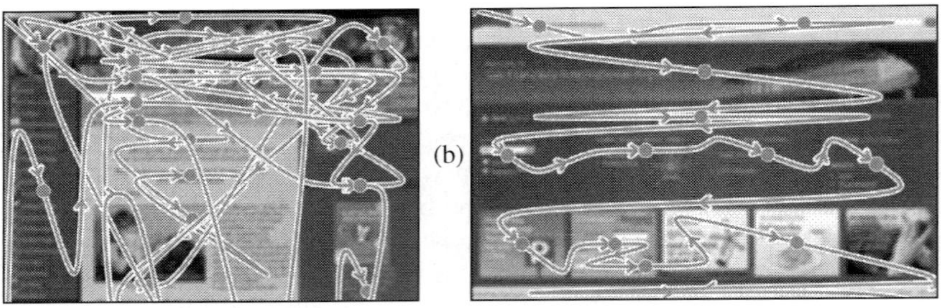

Fig. 7. Examples of reading flows with problems. (a) Is very problematic, and (b) has a problem related to table heading order, and is somewhat problematic.

These results give insights into the characteristics of the repair operations. The visualization was very quick and effective when subjects could recognize the problems in a page, and the improved recognition times also contributed to the improvements in the correction task (Task 2). However, the correction operation based on mouse dragging was relatively less time effective and also the method for temporary intermediate visualization was not completely effective for the subjects during the task.

Several areas for possible improvements appear in these results. The biggest area might be a combination interface with both sequence numbers and the visualization. The numbering of each element would be the simplest combination and also temporary and local numbering may improve the usability when changing the order of a series of elements. The number-based correction also can be integrated into the visualization along with the mouse-based interface that uses dragging and clicking. We will consider these improvements as future work.

6.3 Possibility for Collaborative Correction

It is clear from the experiment that the visualization allows users to correct reading order significantly faster. If the method becomes sufficiently easy for average Web users, collaborative accessibility improvements for ordering by community volunteers will become possible in the near future. This would be part of a new strategy to make a wide range of Web content accessible by gathering the power of Web users, based on the same social computing techniques as used in the widely accepted wikis and social bookmarking services. Projects by Takagi et al. [20] and Jeffly et al. [21] are leading projects in this area, allowing volunteers to fix various accessibility problems, such as missing alternative texts and missing heading tags. Currently, the services do not have any function to allow volunteers to reorganize reading order, mainly because the existing reordering interfaces (e.g. sequence number display) are far too difficult for typical Web users to understand without special training. The reading flow will be one of the key technologies for such services to provide ideally accessible webpages for the blind. We plan to deploy these functions to help blind users who face difficulties in the current visual Web environment.

6.4 Feedback to the Original Content

Although the metadata for reading order is completely separated from the original content in our current implementation, there is a various possibilities for applying the metadata to improve the content. The metadata can be used to modify the source of the content or to change the live DOM on the client browsers, but the feedback system for the reading order without affecting its appearance and the usability is a challenging problem because the structure of the content and the style sheets influence the appearance and the usability. However this is a final piece when trying to realize a full ecosystem of checking and organizing the reading order for the collaborative corrections that help the blind users.

7 Conclusion

A new method to visualize the reading order of webpages was introduced. Our "reading flow" approach allows Web authors to easily and intuitively evaluate the appropriateness of the reading order or their webpages. We have shown how the reading flow visually exposes the order of webpages with a variable granularity, supporting functions for visually reordering the elements, and generates reading order metadata that is separate from the original content. Two sets of user experiments were conducted comparing the performance in recognition and the performance of repair tasks in the reading order (against a numerical interface). The results show that the reading flow technique is significantly faster than a numerical interface. The result also suggested several areas for improvement, both in visualization and in the interface for repairs.

As future work, we are planning to implement improvements and investigate feedback mechanisms for applying the reading order metadata inside the original content and the effectiveness for the blind users. The visualization will be a key technology to allow average Web users to work on improving Web accessibility in the social approach. We hope to deploy the visualization function to broader audiences, and to provide the benefits of this new metadata for correcting reading order for blind users worldwide.

References

1. Web content accessibility guidelines (WCAG) 1.0. W3C Recommendation May 5 (1999), http://www.w3.org/TR/WCAG10/
2. Section 508 of the rehabilitation act, http://www.section508.gov/
3. Japanese Standard Association. JIS X 8341-3:2004 guideline for older persons and persons with disabilities -information and communications equipment, software and services-part3 Web content
4. Council of the European Union. eEurope 2002 -an information society for all -action plan (2002)
5. Takagi, H., Asakawa, C., Fukuda, K., Maeda, J.: Site-wide annotation: reconstructing existing pages to be accessible. In: ASSETS 2002: Proceedings of the Fifth international ACM conference on Assistive technologies, pp. 81–88 (2002)
6. Harper, S., Bechhofer, S.: Sadie: Structural semantics for accessibility and device independence. ACM Trans. Comput.-Hum. Interact. 14(2), 10 (2007)
7. Miyashita, H., Sato, D., Takagi, H., Asakawa, C.: Aibrowser for multimedia: introducing multimedia content accessibility for visually impaired users. In: ASSETS 2007: Proceedings of the 9th international ACM SIGACCESS conference on Computers and accessibility, pp. 91–98 (2007)
8. Kouroupetroglou, C., Salampasis, M., Manitsaris, A.: A semantic-Web-based framework for developing applications to improve accessibility in the www. In: W4A: Proceedings of the 2006 international cross-disciplinary workshop on Web accessibility (W4A), pp. 98–108 (2006)
9. Ramakrishnan, I.V., Stent, A., Yang, G.: HearSay: enabling audio browsing on hypertext content. In: WWW 2004: Proceedings of the 13th international conference on World Wide Web, pp. 80–89 (2004)
10. WAVE 4.0 accessibility tool, http://wave.webaim.org/
11. Kasday, L.R.: A tool to evaluate universal Web accessibility. In: CUU 2000: Proceedings on the 2000 conference on Universal Usability, pp. 161–162 (2000)
12. Takagi, H., Asakawa, C., Fukuda, K., Maeda, J.: Accessibility designer: visualizing usability for the blind. In: ASSETS 2004: Proceedings of the 6th international ACM SIGACCESS conference on Computers and accessibility, pp. 177–184 (2004)
13. Meunier, J.-L.: Optimized xy-cut for determining a page reading order. In: ICDAR 2005: Proceedings of the Eighth International Conference on Document Analysis and Recognition, pp. 347–351 (2005)
14. Malerba, D., Ceci, M., Berardi, M.: Machine Learning for Reading Order Detection in Document Image Understanding. Machine Learning in Document Analysis and Recognition (2008)

15. Yacoub, S., Saxena, V., Sami, S.N.: Perfectdoc: A ground truthing environment for complex documents. In: ICDAR 2005: Proceedings of the Eighth International Conference on Document Analysis and Recognition, pp. 452–457 (2005)
16. Yanikoglu, B.A., Vincent, L.: Pink panther: a complete environment for ground-truthing and benchmarking document page segmentation. Pattern Recognition 31(9), 1191–1204 (1998)
17. Kanungo, T., Lee, C.H., Czorapinski, J., Bella, I.: TRUEVIZ: a groundtruth/metadata editing and visualizing toolkit for OCR. In: Proc. SPIE Document Recognition and Retrieval VIII, vol. 4307, pp. 1–12
18. Kawanaka, S., Borodin, Y., Bigham, J.P., Lunn, D., Takagi, H., Asakawa, C.: Accessibility commons: a metadata infrastructure for Web accessibility. In: ASSETS 2008: Proceedings of the 10th international ACM SIGACCESS conference on Computers and accessibility, pp. 153–160 (2008)
19. Accessible rich internet applications (WAI-ARIA) version 1.0. W3C Working Draft, August 6 (2008), `http://www.w3.org/TR/wai-aria`
20. Takagi, H., Kawanaka, S., Kobayashi, M., Itoh, T., Asakawa, C.: Social accessibility: achieving accessibility through collaborative metadata authoring. In: ASSETS 2008: Proceedings of the 10th international ACM SIGACCESS conference on Computers and accessibility, pp. 193–200 (2008)
21. Bigham, J.P., Ladner, R.E.: Accessmonkey: a collaborative scripting framework for Web users and developers. In: W4A 2007: Proceedings of the 2007 international cross-disciplinary conference on Web accessibility (W4A), pp. 25–34 (2007)

Looking Ahead: A Comparison of Page Preview Techniques for Goal-Directed Web Navigation

Aaron Genest[1], Carl Gutwin[1], Adrian Reetz[1], Regan Mandryk[1], David Pinelle[2], and Andre Doucette[1]

[1] Department of Computer Science, University of Saskatchewan, 110 Science Place, Saskatoon, SK, Canada, S7N 5C9
{aaron.genest,regan.mandryk,adrian.reetz,carl.guwin, andre.doucette}@usask.ca
[2] National Research Council, 46 Dineen Dr., Fredericton, NB, Canada, E3B 9W4
david.pinelle@nrc-cnrc.gc.ca

Abstract. On the World Wide Web, page previews augment hyperlinks to provide extra information about each link's destination. These previews can reduce navigation time and errors in goal-directed navigation tasks when the information provided by the text and context of links is inadequate. A number of different types of page previews have been proposed, and some are already in use; however, little is known about which preview types will consistently help users make good navigation decisions. Our study compares six preview techniques (title, URL, subject category, page genre, genre symbol, and thumbnail), two delivery mechanisms (inline and popup), and two page load times (fast and slow). We found that previews showing the genre of the page (e.g., whether the page is an information page or a search page) yielded significantly faster performance than other preview techniques, and participants also preferred the genre-based previews. Our study is the first to compare the performance of a wide range of page previews in a naturalistic, non-search environment, and provides empirical data that can improve support for goal-directed navigation.

Keywords: Goal-directed browsing, information scent, page previews.

1 Introduction

Goal-directed browsing – in which users look for information that satisfies a specific information need – is a common activity on the World Wide Web (WWW). In these tasks, people try to move towards their goal by navigating through successive Web pages, making a decision at each page about where to go next. If the user has experience with a page or destination, these decisions could be based on prior knowledge, but in the majority of cases, a page will be unfamiliar to the user, so they will have to choose an outgoing link based on information presented on the current page.

This local information about where links will take the user is called *information scent* – that is, proximal information that gives cues about distal information sources (i.e., other Web pages) [4]. The primary means for providing information scent in a Web page is through the link text itself – and in many cases, link text does an adequate

T. Gross et al. (Eds.): INTERACT 2009, Part I, LNCS 5726, pp. 378–391, 2009.

job of indicating where the link goes: e.g., "For more information, visit the SuperCorp website". However, many other pages have links with poor information scent, and provide few clues about where links will take the user. Many blogs, news sites, and review sites suffer from this problem of hyperlinks with low scent.

When links have low information scent, it becomes difficult for users to make good navigation decisions; as a result, people need more time to decide which link to follow, and may make more navigation errors. In high-cost environments (such as a slow network link, or an expensive roaming data plan), extra time and more errors can quickly lead to frustration and added expense.

To deal with this problem, Web designers can incorporate better information scent into the links on their pages (e.g., [18, 25]); however, automatic provision of additional scent could be an important alternative for existing pages, or for pages that do not follow ideal design principles. Insertion of additional scent is a realistic possibility – because browsers can retrieve information about the destination page, it is possible to add a *destination preview* as part of the information scent for each link on the page. Most browsers already provide a limited form of this kind of preview, by showing the link URL in the window's status bar. There are also several other types of previews that are possible. For example, some pages augment links with an icon to indicate that the link will take the user offsite (e.g., "example link ⧉"), and page scripts can allow the display of a thumbnail image of the actual destination page on mouseover (as in Figure 1B). Other possibilities include showing the page title, a text summary of the page, or a word or symbol indicating the page type or subject.

Although destination previews are already possible, little is known about what preview type will work best – that is, which kind of preview will most consistently help users make good decisions about where to go. Prior work has tested previews for search results pages, but no research has looked at preview techniques in naturalistic Web pages such as blogs or reviews. To address this limitation, we carried out an empirical study that compared the performance of six different preview types in realistic goal-directed navigation tasks, and tested them with fast and slow page load times and in both pop-up and inline formats.

Three of our destination previews can be derived from the destination page itself: URL, page title, and thumbnail. Three others involve human or automatic classification of pages into categories – in our study, either the subject category of the page or the page's genre (e.g., information, shopping, or search).

Our study showed that there were significant differences between the preview types: performance with genre-based previews was significantly faster than with the other preview types, and participants preferred genre-based previews. In addition, thumbnails had the slowest task times of all the methods, and were the least-liked technique. In this paper, we provide details of these findings and present guidelines for the design of Web pages and page preview techniques.

2 Related Work

Information foraging theory considers how people navigate as they seek information in spaces like the WWW [4]. An important part of information foraging is the idea of information scent – 'proximal clues to distal content' that help the user understand the likely outcome of each navigation action [4, 20]. When information scent is poor, users exhibit indecision and hesitation when deciding between hyperlinks. When they do not have the information that they need to make good navigation decisions, users often randomly click on links, and must backtrack to correct their mistakes [25].

Poor information scent is common on the Web, and evidence for the errors that this can cause can be seen in recent studies of backtracking behaviour [2, 14, 23]. For example, Obendorf et al. found that backtracking accounted for 31% of page revisits, and they also suggest that people actively spend time trying to avoid backtracking [19]. In recent years, developers have released software aimed at reducing backtracking and related navigation errors. For example, Berkun [1] stated that navigation errors helped to motivate the development of the Explorer bar, which helps manage favorites, browsing history, and search results.

Navigation errors can be frustrating and potentially expensive since each page view can cost time or money. For example, navigation errors are particularly time consuming for visually impaired users: it can take up to 120 seconds to interpret a new page [10]. Similarly, users on pay-per-bit networks or networks with bandwidth constraints pay substantial penalties when they make hyperlink selection errors.

Providing users with information about the destination of a hyperlink can improve navigation [9, 17, 26]. Adding this preview information enhances information scent so users can make more accurate decisions about target pages [25]. Nielsen [18] suggests that Web designers should strive to improve information scent by using links and category text that accurately characterize the destination page, but others have taken this idea further, considering several different presentation techniques, including thumbnails, symbols, and genre information [16, 24, 26].

Weinreich and Lamersedorf [24] list several types of information that can be used to provide previews of destination pages, including basic information about the page (such as the title, author, language, or last visit), the direction of navigation (forward or backward), the expected access time, the target file type, the behavior of the link (will the link open a new window, replace the current one, or change a frame), the location of the page (remote or local), and the status of the link. Drori [7] found that a combined preview of the title, relevant text from the target page, common words, and keywords in context was effective at improving completion times during search tasks.

Another preview approach is to use high-level semantic categories to describe target pages. Matsuda and Fukushima [16] developed a system that classifies pages based on keywords and the page's internal structure. They classify pages according to common page genres, such as 'product catalog,' 'investigation report,' and 'advertisement.' Other research developed similar genre classifications, with different criteria, including fine-grained information about the style and layout of page content [15], and information about the placement of links on pages and their URLs [22]. Clustering search results based on subject categories can improve speed and accuracy for search tasks [3]. Generating subject or genre classifications accurately and efficiently is still an active research area [27], but explorations into syntactic classification [16] and semantic hierarchical classifications [8] have shown promise.

A third common preview technique is to provide thumbnails that show a miniature representation of the destination page. Some researchers have found that thumbnails improve recognition during bookmarking tasks [5, 13]. More recently, Woodruff et al. [26] evaluated an enhanced thumbnail technique that highlights page text, and found that people were able to complete certain search tasks more quickly with the enhanced thumbnail than with either text alone or standard thumbnails.

Researchers have also developed preview techniques to dynamically modify the current page to provide information about destination pages. Faaborg et al. found that determining the user's goals and adaptively altering or adding to the content of the current Web page can reduce completion times in goal-directed navigation [9]. Miura et al. [17] expand potential page targets within the current browser window to create documents within documents. However, this technique can create large unmanageable spaces that force users to scroll extensively within a page.

There are several examples of page previews already used on the Web: most browsers show URLs in the status bar when the user hovers over a link; plug-ins and page scripts are available for adding thumbnails; and Web sites such as Wikipedia add a symbol to indicate that a link will take the user to an external page.

Previous studies have compared performance differences between page preview techniques, but these evaluations have focused on Web search scenarios [8, 16, 26]. For example, Woodruff et al. [26] compared the performance and subjective differences when people use thumbnails, enhanced thumbnails, and text summaries in Web searches. Dumais et al. [8] compared several different search interfaces, which combined different preview techniques, including category names, text summaries, and page titles, using both inline and hover presentations.

Unlike past studies, we are interested in evaluating preview techniques when they are used with realistic Web pages. Our goal is to extend the understanding of preview performance to tasks and situations that more closely reflect general goal-directed navigation on the WWW.

3 A Comparison Study of Page Preview Techniques

To determine performance and preference differences between different types of page previews, we carried out a study that asked participants to make navigation decisions in realistic Web pages with six different preview techniques. In particular, we wanted to answer the following questions:

1. Does the preview type affect the time needed to navigate to the correct page?
2. Does the preview type affect the number of navigation errors?
3. Which preview types do users prefer?
4. Do people use the previews or the page content when making navigation decisions in low-scent situations?
5. Does changing the presentation method (inline or popup) change the performance of any preview type?
6. Does changing the page load time change the way people use previews?

To answer these questions, we manipulated three independent variables in our study: preview content, presentation method, and page load time.

3.1 Independent Variables

We tested six different kinds of preview content: destination page title, URL, thumbnail image, subject category, genre category, and genre symbol.

Title. Title previews showed the full title of the destination page, as retrieved from the page's HTML header.

URL. The full URL of the destination page.

Thumbnail image. Thumbnail previews showed 128x128-pixel images of the destination page (similar to that shown in Figure 1B).

Subject category. Subject previews are short tags (one to three words) describing the semantic category of the destination page (e.g., 'hockey' or 'politics'). We selected subject categories from Google Directories (www.google.com/dirhp); for example, www.golfknickers.com has a directory path of Shopping > Sports > Golf > Apparel, so we used the tag 'Golf apparel shopping.'

Text genre category. Text genre categories are a single word that describes the genre of the destination page; they classify the page type, but not the page subject. Eight genre categories – developed through a series of pilot studies – were used in the study: login, news, shopping, search results, blog, forum, corporate, and information.

Genre symbols. Genre symbols use the same categories as genre text, but use a symbolic representation (see Figure 2).

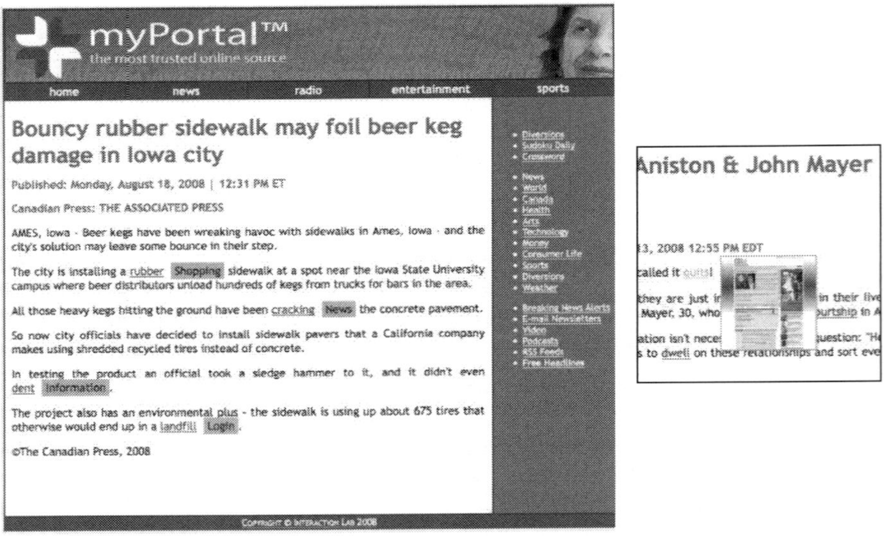

Fig. 1. A) Sample of page with inline genre text links; B) Popup thumbnail preview

Fig. 2. Genre symbols and names

Two presentation mechanisms, inline and popup, were used in the study. Inline presentation showed the preview content at all times, located to the right of target links (Figure 1A). Inline URLs and titles were truncated to 30 characters. Popup presentation showed previews when the mouse pointer was over the link (Figure 1B).

Two page load times were simulated to determine whether delay influenced the performance or preference of the preview types. In the slow page-load condition, there was a 10-second delay between clicking on a link and the delivery of the destination page. The fast-load condition had no delay.

3.2 Task

The previews were deployed in a series of custom-built Web pages that resembled simple blog or news sites. In all pages, we manipulated the content so that the links on the page had poor information scent. We equalized the amount of text shown in links, and the amount of information provided by the surrounding text and the link text. Each hyperlink was reduced to one word. These manipulations were determined through pilot studies where users judged the link scent on each page.

Source pages provided the same set of sidebar and topbar links (these links appeared live, but returned the participant to the source page). There were no animations or advanced visual objects (e.g., Flash) on the source pages.

Participants were asked to carry out short navigation tasks in which they had to decide which link on a source page would move them towards a given information goal. Participants carried out 30 of these tasks in different experimental conditions, but in all cases the source page had links with poor information scent. An example source page is shown in Figure 1A. The task for this page was to select the link that would best allow them to "find out the average impact resistance of a rubber sidewalk slab." Participants were told to decide as quickly as possible while minimizing errors. The information goal was always available in a separate browser window.

Articles were actual posts found in news and blog sites. The text was approximately the same length for each article, and all pages could be read without scrolling the browser window. Links were added or removed to achieve a uniform four links per article, and only one link was the correct choice for each task.

After participants selected a link from the source page, they were shown a form asking what influenced their decision (the article's content, the link preview information, both, or neither). Participants were then told whether they had chosen the correct page; if they were incorrect, they were reminded of the information goal and directed back to the source page. Participants continued until they chose the correct link.

To simulate expert performance with the symbols in the 'genre symbols' condition, participants could see a reminder window with the symbols and their names.

3.3 Study Design and Procedures

The study used a mixed factorial design with both between- and within-participants factors to reduce the length of the study to under an hour per participant. The within-participants factor was preview type (page title, URL, thumbnail image, subject category, genre text, genre symbol). The two between-participants factors were presentation method (inline or popup) and page load time (fast or slow), since pilots suggested that both factors would have easily measurable differences between conditions.

Each participant used each technique on five Web pages (for a total of 30 pages). Each technique was shown as a block: a participant would see five pages in a row for each preview type before moving on to a different type. The order of the six preview techniques was counterbalanced using a Latin square, but tasks and pages were presented in the same order for all participants, balancing the six preview techniques across the 30 task pages.

Presentation method and page load time were between-participants factors. Half the participants saw preview techniques inline, and the other half saw them as popups. In addition, half the participants were assigned to the slow-loading condition, and half to the fast-loading condition. In the slow-load condition, participants were redirected to a page that indicated that the content was loading during the 10-second delay; the loading page was not used in the fast-loading condition.

Participants began by completing a demographic survey and an informed consent form. Participants read a short description of the study procedure and viewed examples of each of the preview techniques using the appropriate presentation method. Following the orientation, participants completed the set of 30 navigation tasks using the Firefox Web browser. At the end of the session, participants completed a post-experiment questionnaire that asked them to rate and rank the techniques according to preference and usefulness. The questionnaire also asked whether participants used the text of the page, the previews, or both in their navigation decisions. Participants were also permitted open-ended responses.

Twenty-four participants, 14 female and 10 male, were recruited from a local university. Participants ranged in age from 18 to 28 years (mean of 22). All participants reported either using a computer 'often' (1) or 'every day' (23), and reported using a Web browser 'occasionally' (1), 'often' (1), or 'every day' (22). As there were two between-participants factors, there were four groups of users (6 users per group): popup-delay, popup-no-delay, inline-delay, and inline-no-delay. Kruskal-Wallis tests on 4-independent samples showed no differences between the groups in terms of their expertise with computers (χ^2=3.0, p=.392), video games (χ^2=2.6, p=.451), Web browsers (χ^2=2.1, p=.553) or e-mail (χ^2=2.1, p=.554), or with their choice of primary Web browser (χ^2=6.2, p=.101) or primary input device (χ^2=1.8, p=.614).

Computer logs were used to track completion time, error rates, and participants' mouse movement over target links. Completion time was measured from the moment the task page loaded to the moment the participant selected a target link. In the delay condition, the 10-second delay was not included in the completion time measure. Pages were served from a machine connected on a local area network, so additional latency was negligible. Incorrect links selected during a task were logged as errors.

We performed a Repeated Measures Multivariate Analysis of Variance (MANOVA) on the completion time and error data for the six preview types, with presentation method and page load time included as between-subjects factors. All main effects and interactions were tested at α=.05 and Least Significant Differences were used for all post-hoc pairwise comparisons. The sphericity assumption was not violated, thus the degrees of freedom were not adjusted. Questionnaire data were analyzed using non-parametric statistical techniques appropriate for rankings data.

4 Results

4.1 Empirical Results

Does preview technique affect task completion time? Preview technique had a significant effect on the task completion time ($F_{5,100}$=3.50, p=.006, η^2=.15; see Figure 3A). Pairwise comparisons showed genre text yielded significantly faster performance than all other preview types (all p<.025), while there were no differences between the other preview types. Table 1 shows the means and standard errors for each preview type.

Does preview technique affect error rates during tasks? Although error rates for the six preview types showed similar trends as completion time, there were no statistically significant differences between the preview techniques with respect to their error rates ($F_{5,100}$=1.16, p=.337, η^2=.06), see Figure 3B.

Does page load time affect task completion time, error rate, or mouse movements? There were no main effects on completion time ($F_{1,20}$=.315, p=.581, η^2=.02) or error rate ($F_{1,20}$=.749, p=.397, η^2=.04) by varying the simulated network delay. The 10-second delay between clicking the link and discovering whether or not the answer was correct appeared to have no effect on user behavior (see Table 1).

For participants who saw the preview techniques as popups, we investigated whether page load time impacted the number of times participants hovered over the links before making a decision. An RM-ANOVA on the preview types with delay as a between-subjects factor showed no significant difference ($F_{1,10}$=0.67, p=.432, η^2=.06).

Does the presentation method affect completion time? There were no effects of the presentation method on completion time ($F_{1,20}$=2.15, p=.158, η^2=.10) (see Table 1).

Does the presentation method affect the error rate? Error rate did vary significantly with respect to presentation method ($F_{1,20}$=4.62, p=.044, η^2=.19). Participants who were presented with the preview techniques inline had a higher error rate than those who saw popups (means and standard errors are presented in Table 1).

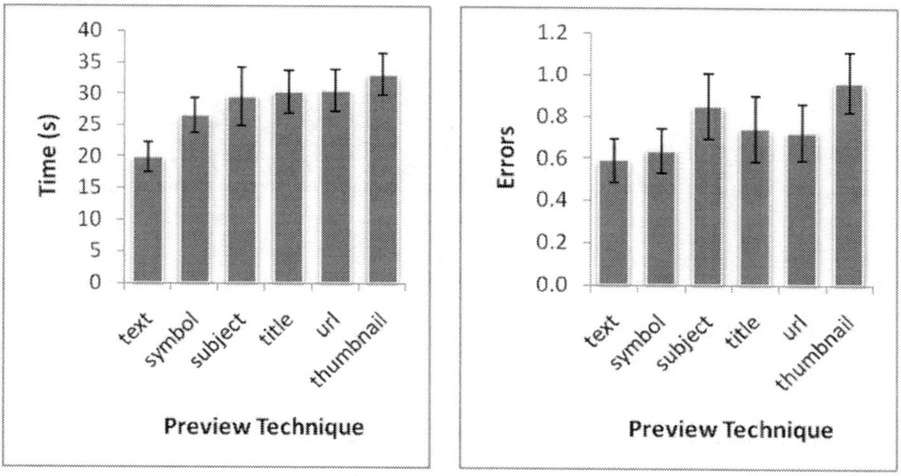

Fig. 3. A) Mean time (±SE) per task by preview technique; B) Mean errors (±SE) per task by preview technique

Table 1. Means ±SE for time (s) and errors by page load time and presentation method

	Presentation Method		Page Load Time	
Time	popup	24.6 (36.1)	delay	29.8 (36.1)
	inline	32.1 (36.1)	no-delay	26.9 (36.1)
Errors	popup	0.6 (0.1)	delay	0.8 (0.1)
	inline	0.9 (0.1)	no-delay	0.7 (0.1)

Does preview type interact with the between-subject factors (page load time, presentation method)? There were no significant interactions between preview type and page load time (Time:$F_{1,20}$=1.0, p=.425, η^2=.05; Error:$F_{1,20}$=1.11, p=.358, η^2=.06), preview type and presentation method (Time:$F_{1,20}$=.69, p=.635, η^2=.03; Error:$F_{1,20}$=.1.24, p=.295, η^2=.06), or presentation method and page load time (Time:$F_{1,20}$=1.37, p=.256, η^2=.06; Error:$F_{1,20}$=.18, p=.675, η^2=.01).

4.2 Subjective Results

Which preview techniques were most liked and disliked? Participants rated their agreement with the statement "I liked this preview technique" on a 5-point scale (see Figure 4). The ratings were significantly different for the six preview techniques ($\chi^2(5)$=15.6, p=.008), and pairwise comparisons showed that participants liked thumbnails less than all other techniques (all p<0.05). There were no significant differences in the ratings between users in the slow page load versus the fast page load condition; however, users who saw the preview techniques inline liked page titles less than those who saw the previews in the popup condition (p=.027).

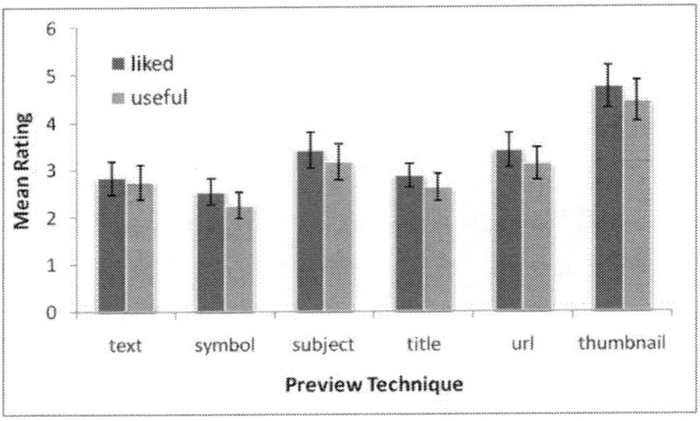

Fig. 4. Mean ratings (± SE) for how liked and how useful the preview techniques were on a 5-pt scale (lower rating = more liked and more useful)

In addition, participants chose the preview techniques that they liked the most and the least. The most liked techniques were genre symbol (9 people) and genre text (7). In followup comments, participants suggested that they found the symbolic representation faster than reading text: one participant said "once you learn the symbols it's the fastest and easiest approach" and another stated "recognizing symbols when searching was a lot simpler than reading words."

The least liked technique was thumbnails (9 people), followed by URLs (8). Comments suggested that the fidelity of the thumbnails made it difficult to gain useful information: one person said "I could usually not tell what the page was, or even the type of page." and another said "The thumbnails were small and I could only [get] a general impression of what the website was." Reasons for disliking URLs included difficulty in reading and interpreting the URLs, and the lack of useful information: "It does not really tell me whether it is related to what I am searching for."

Did participants find the preview techniques to be useful? Participants rated their agreement with the statement "This preview technique was useful" on a 5-point scale (see Figure 4). The ratings were significantly different for the six preview techniques ($\chi^2(5)=12.4$, $p=.030$), and pairwise comparisons showed that participants thought thumbnails were less useful than all other techniques (all $p<0.05$).

Did participants use the preview techniques or the page content to make their navigation decisions? After each link selection, we asked participants to report what information they used to make their navigation decision. Participants most often stated that they used previews (51%), followed by page content (22%), then both (16%), and neither (11%).

4.3 Summary of Results for Preview Types and Presentation Method

Genre Information. Participants were significantly faster when using the genre techniques, and fastest with text-only genre labels. There were few individual pages where this preview type performed badly. We believe that this indicates an important aspect of goal-directed navigation: users want to know what they can *accomplish* at a destination page, and that information is not currently conveyed by other page preview techniques. When describing the genre techniques, people used words like "simple", "easy", and "quick", and many participants identified the relationship between the task and the genre text as being particularly helpful. One participant wrote, "if I was to look for something to buy, it would obviously be in the link that had the genre text 'shopping' rather than 'forum'."

Subject Categories. Subject categories appeared to work well with some tasks, and poorly with others, and overall this technique was slower than genre information. Inspection of individual pages suggested that although the category accurately represented the topic of the destination pages, it was not often a good fit for the task.

URLs. Participants' performance with URLs was comparable to performance with subjects, titles, and thumbnails. This technique was most successful when there was a fortuitous match between an aspect of the task and an element of the preview. For example, one task asked people to find out how a person's name could be easily changed, and the URL of the correct target contained "www.namechange.com;" similarly, a task asked participants to determine a property of a type of concrete block, and the correct destination page's title was "Building Materials." These fortuitous correspondences were infrequent; URLs usually provided very little information that was relevant to the task. Although URL preview information is included in most browser implementations, no users identified it as their favorite technique and several ranked it last. Our results also suggest that 're-written' URLs (such as tinyurl.com or dynamic javascript links) will detract from the browser's existing default page preview technique (showing link URLs in the status bar).

Page Titles. User performance with page titles was also relatively poor, and this technique was not preferred by any participants. One problem with page titles is that title information is set by Web designers, so some pages can have titles that contain poor information scent—either accidentally or through intentional misdirection. The pages used in this study were carefully chosen to include valid titles, but the titles were not necessarily good matches for users' tasks.

Thumbnails. Completion times using thumbnails was the slowest of all techniques. People also gave thumbnails the lowest ratings for usefulness and preference – significantly lower than all other preview types. There was, however, a wide variance in performance with this technique. Thumbnails appeared to work well when the destination page contained distinctive visual elements (e.g., a company logo), and when the title of the page was large enough to be readable. When destination pages were less recognizable, however, thumbnails performed very poorly: in several tasks, all of the four destinations had similar visual appearances, making it difficult for participants to make a choice based on thumbnail alone. The value of having readable text in a thumbnail suggests that the technique could be improved by creating better thumbnails – for example, using textually-enhanced thumbnails (e.g., [26]).

Presentation Method. The popup presentation of previews performed better overall than inline previews – there was no time difference, but popups led to fewer errors. The good performance of popups is valuable for designers, since many available preview techniques cannot feasibly be placed inline, since they clutter the display and may change the author's intended page layout.

5 Discussion

In this section, we identify lessons for designers, and comment on issues that must be considered in a more widespread deployment of page previews.

First, our work provides guidelines that should be considered by designers of Web pages and browser add-ons.

- *Previews are valuable in low-scent environments.* It is clear from the study that all the preview techniques led to decisions that were much better than chance, and all of our participants reported using the previews in their decisions. Therefore, browsers should continue to make standard previews available, and should continue to investigate previews that are more effective than simple URLs.
- *Genre categories are valuable.* The genre of a page provided our participants with useful information for goal-directed browsing, but genre is not used in any current system. There is still considerable work to be done to achieve accurate and automatic genre classification, but this is an area that shows considerable potential for improving navigation support.
- *Use popup presentations.* User-controlled delivery of previews, such as a popup, is better than inline presentations for several reasons: they led to fewer errors, they do not alter the source page, and they do not add scent where none is needed. They

give Web designers more control over the look and feel of their pages because previews are delivered on demand without changing the page layout.

- *Thumbnails alone perform poorly.* Our study reinforces earlier findings [24] suggesting that thumbnail images alone should not be used as primary previews – they performed poorly and were disliked by participants. This is an important result, since several existing tools provide exactly this type of preview. Designers who wish to use thumbnails should include additional information such as title along with the image.

Second, our experiences with page previews suggest several questions that must be considered when deploying page preview techniques more widely.

- *Will previews clutter or detract from some Web pages?* In situations where the page presents adequate information scent, or where the page author has carefully designed the visual appearance, extra information could distract the user or clutter the page. This possibility argues strongly for popup presentations, which avoid showing preview information until explicitly requested, and which do not change layout.
- *Will automatic information scent clash with intrinsic scent?* Designers may have carefully added information scent to links in their page in order to create a particular impression on the user, and may not want additional previews. Although in general it is always legitimate to provide more information to users who want it, this situation raises the larger issue of whether preview information can be trusted.
- *Can preview information be manipulated?* If the authors of destination pages know how previews are being generated, they could manipulate their pages to change their preview. In some cases, this understanding will be beneficial, in that it will lead to better previews (e.g., readable text in a thumbnail, accurate page titles). However, authors could also create a falsely attractive preview to try and get more traffic.
- *Would combination previews work well?* Several types of previews seemed to work well in different situations, suggesting that multiple information sources could provide better performance. To test this possibility, we recorded the minimum times for any of the thumbnail, URL, and title previews. This hypothetical combined preview would have ranked second in performance. Combined previews have been previously explored in the context of search tasks and were found to be effective [7, 26].
- *Is automatic genre categorization feasible?* The performance of genre as a preview is dependent on being able to correctly categorize pages. Our study categorized pages by hand, but research on automatic classification is underway [8,16]. Assigning a genre is hard for some types of pages, but is easy for others (such as login or search pages) that give clear cues. It is also possible that authors could supply the page genre (although with the same manipulation risks discussed above), or by a community effort such as that for subject categories (the Open Directory).

6 Conclusions and Directions for Future Work

During task-based navigation on the World Wide Web, links with low information scent can cause navigation problems for users. Page previews can help address these problems by improving navigation time and accuracy, but little is known about the effectiveness of various proposed preview techniques. We evaluated six different preview techniques with two page load time conditions and with two presentation methods. Our study is the first to move beyond search results pages to investigate preview performance in realistic Web sites.

We found that participant performance was best using genre-related preview techniques, and that this technique was preferred by the majority of users. Performance was slowest using thumbnail previews, and most participants disliked this technique. Our results suggest that while any preview information is valuable in low-scent environments, previews that consider the user's activity can be particularly useful. In addition, the study showed that popup presentations have advantages over inline previews, and that page load times do not change performance or preferences.

There are several possible directions for future work in this area. First, we plan to explore other preview techniques and combinations of the methods investigated here, and test them with a larger pool of participants. Second, we will continue to develop the genre preview technique. Preliminary efforts have been made on automated genre classification [8,16], and we are currently working towards low-cost techniques for classifying Web pages with genre information, through both automated and social approaches. Third, we will investigate the longitudinal effects that page previews have on browsing behaviour, through an experiment that logs navigation activity with and without page previews. Fourth, it is worth determining whether the presence of previews might actually hinder navigation when the information scent contained in links is adequate: we will investigate the relationship between information scent and page previews in navigation tasks. Last, we plan to carry out further studies with eye tracking systems to obtain more detailed information about the way that users interact with page previews.

References

1. Berkun, S.: The Explorer Bar: Unifying and Improving Web Navigation. In: Proc. Interact, pp. 156–162. IOS Press, Amsterdam (1999)
2. Catledge, L.D., Pitkow, J.E.: Characterizing Browsing Strategies in the World-Wide Web. Computer Networks and ISDN Systems 27, 1065–1073 (1995)
3. Chen, H., Fan, H., Chau, M., Zeng, D.: MetaSpider: Meta-Searching and Categorization on the Web. J. Am. Soc. Information Science and Technology 52(13), 1134–1147 (2001)
4. Chi, E.H., Pirolli, P., Chen, K., Pitkow, J.: Using information scent to model user information needs and actions and the Web. In: Proc. CHI, pp. 490–497. ACM Press, New York (2001)
5. Cockburn, A., Greenberg, S., McKenzie, B., Jasonsmith, M., Kaasten, S.: WebView: A Graphical Aid for Revisiting Web Pages. In: Proc. OZCHI (1999)
6. Drori, O.: Display of Search Results in Google-based Yahoo! vs. LCC&K Interfaces: A Comparison Study. In: Proc. Informing Science, pp. 309–320 (2003)
7. Drori, O.: How to Display Search Results in Digital Libraries-User Study. In: Proc. Workshop on New Developments in Digital Libraries, pp. 13–28 (2003)
8. Dumais, S., Chen, H.: Hierarchical Classification of Web Content. In: Proc. SIGIR, pp. 256–263. ACM Press, New York (2000)
9. Faaborg, A., Lieberman, H.: A Goal-Oriented Web Browser. In: Proc. CHI 2006, pp. 751–760 (2006)

10. Harper, S., Goble, C., Stevens, R.: A Pilot Study to Examine the Mobility Problems of Visually Impaired Users Traveling the Web. Computers and the Physically Handicapped 68, 10–19 (2000)
11. Huck, S., Cormier, W.: Reading Statistics and Research. HarperCollins, New York (1996)
12. Hurst, M.: The Page Paradigm (2004), http://www.goodexperience.com/blog/archives/000028.php (accessed 8/15/2008)
13. Kaasten, S., Greenberg, S., Edwards, C.: How People Recognize Previously Seen Web Pages from Titles, URLs and Thumbnails. In: Proc. HCI, pp. 247–265 (2002)
14. Kellar, M., Watters, C., Shepherd, M.: The Impact of task on the Usage of Web Browser Navigation Mechanisms. In: Proc. Graphics Interface, pp. 235–242 (2006)
15. Lee, C.H., Kan, M.Y., Lai, S.: Stylistic and Lexical Co-training for Web Block Classification. In: Proc. Web Information and Data Management, pp. 136–143 (2004)
16. Matsuda, K., Fukushima, T.: Task-oriented World Wide Web Retrieval by Document Type Classification. In: Proc. Information and Knowledge Management, pp. 109–113 (1999)
17. Miura, M., Shizuki, B., Tanaka, J.: inlineLink: Inline Expansion Link Methods in Hypertext Browsing. In: Proc. Internet Computing, pp. 653–659 (2001)
18. Nielsen, N.: Alertbox: Information foraging: Why Google makes people leave your site faster (2003), http://www.useit.com/alertbox/20030630.html (accessed 8/31/08)
19. Obendorf, H., Weinreich, H., Herder, E., Mayer, M.: Web Page Revisitation Revisited: Implications of a Long-term Click-stream Study of Browser Usage. In: CHI, pp. 597–606 (2007)
20. Pirolli, P., Card, S.K.: Information foraging. Psychological Review 106(4), 643–675 (1999)
21. Plaisant, C., Shneiderman, B., Doan, K., Bruns, T.: Interface and Data Architecture for Query Preview in Networked Information Systems. Transactions on Information Systems 17(3), 320–341 (1999)
22. Shih, L.K., Karger, D.R.: Using URLs and Table Layout for Web Classification Tasks. In: Proc. World Wide Web 2004, pp. 193–202 (2004)
23. Tauscher, L., Greenberg, S.: Revisitation Patterns in World Wide Web Navigation. In: CHI, pp. 399–406 (1997)
24. Weinreich, H., Lamersdorf, W.: Concepts for Improved Visualization of Web Link Attributes. Computer Networks 33, 403–416 (2000)
25. Withrow, J.: Do your links stink? Techniques for good Web information scent. Bulletin of the American Society for Information Science and Technology 28(5) (2002)
26. Woodruff, A., Faulring, A., Rosenholtz, R., Morrsion, J., Pirolli, P.: Using Thumbnails to Search the Web. In: CHI, pp. 198–205 (2001)
27. Zamir, O., Etzioni, O.: Grouper: A Dynamic Clustering Interface to Web Search Results. Computer Networks 31(11-16), 1361–1374 (1999)

Comparison of Tag Cloud Layouts: Task-Related Performance and Visual Exploration

Steffen Lohmann, Jürgen Ziegler, and Lena Tetzlaff

University of Duisburg-Essen,
Lotharstrasse 65, 47057 Duisburg, Germany
{steffen.lohmann,juergen.ziegler,lena.tetzlaff}@uni-due.de

Abstract. Tag clouds have become a popular visualization and navigation interface on the Web. Despite their popularity, little is known about tag cloud perception and performance with respect to different user goals. This paper presents results from a comparative study of several tag cloud layouts. The results show differences in task performance, leading to the conclusion that interface designers should carefully select the appropriate tag cloud layout according to the expected user goals. Furthermore, the analysis of eye tracking data provides insights into the visual exploration strategies of tag cloud users.

Keywords: Tag Clouds, Tagging, Performance, Perception, Eye Tracking, Visualization, User Goals, Navigation, Evaluation, Folksonomy.

1 Introduction

With the advent and great success of a new generation of community-oriented websites in domains such as Media Sharing (e.g., Flickr, YouTube) or Social Bookmarking and Citation (e.g., Delicious, Connotea), a new way of metadata creation has emerged, commonly known as *tagging*. Tagging-based systems enable users to add *tags* – freely chosen keywords – to Web resources to organize these resources for themselves and/or others. Visual browsing in the tag collections is realized in different ways; often, websites offer an interface element known as *tag cloud*. Usually, a tag cloud presents a certain number of most often used tags in a defined area of the user interface. A tag's popularity is expressed by its font size (relative to the other tags) and is therefore easily recognized. Sometimes, further visual properties, such as the font color, intensity, or weight, are manipulated (for an overview see [2]). Next to their visualization function, tag clouds are also navigation interfaces as the tags are usually hyperlinks leading to a collection of items they are associated with.

However, tag clouds are not only used to display tag sets but are also increasingly applied in other contexts and for various data sets, for instance, in the areas of information visualization or text summarization (cp. [11]). Furthermore, several layout variations emerged on the basic design principles of tag clouds. Most popular is the 'classic' rectangular tag arrangement with alphabetical sorting in a sequential line-by-line layout. Fig. 1a shows an example of this well-known type of tag cloud from the photo sharing website Flickr [12]. One reason for the popularity of this tag cloud layout might be its

T. Gross et al. (Eds.): INTERACT 2009, Part I, LNCS 5726, pp. 392–404, 2009.

easy implementation. However, a sequential arrangement of tags may not provide optimal support for all purposes a user consults a tag cloud for. A wide range of alternative layouts, such as circular or clustered tag clouds (see Fig. 1b), have been proposed.

Although little is known about the benefits of tag clouds and the situations in which website visitors use them, some typical user goals have been identified – from getting an overview or general impression of a website's contents to searching for specific topics or tags (cp. [5, 9, 10]). It has also been conjectured that tag clouds serve a social purpose by conveying a sense of activity in a Web community [7]. The ability of different tag cloud layouts to support certain user goals and information needs, however, is still a largely open research issue.

This paper takes a closer look at tag cloud performance and perception by investigating different tag cloud layouts in their ability to support users in typical information seeking tasks. In Sec. 2, we give a short overview of related work and summarize recent research findings. We then describe the experimental setup and the systematic generation of tag clouds, user tasks, and scenarios in Sec. 3, followed by a description of the experimental procedure in Sec. 4. Sec. 5 and 6 report and discuss results of task-layout-performance and perceptual patterns that could be analyzed from the eye tracking data. Based on these results, we draw some general conclusions in Sec. 7.

(a) (b)

Fig. 1. Tag cloud examples: (a) sequential layout with alphabetical sorting, showing the "all time most popular tags" of the photo sharing website Flickr [12], (b) statistically clustered tag cloud, presenting keywords of the famous speech "I Have a Dream" by M. L. King Jr. [3]

2 Related Work

Most existing studies evaluate tag clouds at a general level by comparing them with other types of user interfaces. For instance, Halvey and Keane compared tag clouds with unweighted, horizontal and vertical lists by asking participants to find and select specific tags in both interface types [5]. The results indicate that unweighted lists perform better than tag clouds and that alphabetical sorting further accelerates search. In addition, the tags' font sizes had a strong effect on search speed and tags in the upper left corner of the cloud were found most quickly. Based on the times the study participants needed to find tags in specific target regions of the cloud, the authors also concluded that tag clouds are rather scanned than read. Kuo et al. got similar performance results by comparing tag clouds and lists as alternative presentation forms for search result summarization in the biomedical domain [8]. Though the study participants solved the descriptive tasks more quickly with the lists they attributed the tag clouds a higher level of satisfaction.

Sinclair and Cardew-Hall [10] conducted an experiment in which the subjects could either use a tag cloud or a traditional search interface to answer questions. They found that the subjects preferred the search interface for specific information retrieval tasks whereas the tag cloud was preferred for more open-ended questions. They concluded that tag clouds are not a replacement but a valuable extension to other types of user interfaces.

Other work takes a closer look at the visual features of tag clouds. Bateman et al. varied eight tag cloud properties and measured their effects on tag selection [2]. Their results show that some properties, such as font size and font weight, have stronger effects on tag selection than others, such as the intensity of a tag's color or its number of characters. Furthermore, the authors observed a central tendency: Tags in the middle of the cloud were selected more often than tags in the top and bottom areas.

Rivadeneira et al. conducted two experiments [9]: The first examined the effects of font size, location, and proximity-to-the-largest-tag. The user task was to recall terms that were previously presented in tag clouds. In accordance with [5] and [2], a strong effect of font size was observed, while proximity-to-the-largest-tag had no significant impact. Furthermore, tags in the upper left quadrant were recalled more often, but the authors attributed this to the sparseness of the tag clouds that were used in the study. In the second experiment, Rivadeneira et al. investigated the effects of font size and tag cloud layout on impression formation and recognition. Again, font size had a strong effect on the results. The tag cloud layouts had no impact on recognition but affected the accuracy of impression formation. In accordance with [5] and [8] it showed that an unweighted, one-dimensional list performs slightly better than a tag cloud.

2.1 Discussion of Related Work

While the presented studies provide valuable findings on tag cloud performance and are first steps towards a better understanding of tag cloud perception, they mainly focused on a sequential layout without considering further ways to arrange tags. The only study that evaluates different tag cloud layouts [9] is very limited in its conclusions as these layouts were highly diverse leading to many interdependencies in the visual features. Moreover, layout performance was only examined regarding recognition and impression formation in this study but not with respect to more typical situations of tag cloud interaction.

In many of the studies, the experimental material was comparatively unusual and artificial. For instance, in some cases the tag clouds consisted of a very limited number of tags (e.g., only 10 tags [5] or 13 tags [9] in total) or few font size variations (e.g., only 3 different font sizes [5]). In other cases, the used tag corpus was rather untypical for Web contexts [2, 9].

Most important, none of the studies addressed the visual exploration of tag clouds directly. All conclusions regarding tag cloud perception have been indirectly inferred from the tags that were either selected or recalled by the study participants. None of the studies recorded any gaze data or considered visual exploration strategies.

3 Experimental Setup

In contrast to related work, we pursued the following objectives with our study:

- Defining user tasks that simulate situations of nearly realistic tag cloud interaction.
- Presenting tag clouds with a common number of tags and font size variations.
- Generating tag cloud layouts that differ only in tag arrangement but no other visual properties.
- Using eye tracking to measure the actual attention areas and perception patterns of tag clouds.

3.1 User Tasks

From the range of purposes tag clouds might be used for, we selected three search tasks that are very common according to the literature [2, 5, 8, 9, 10]:

1. Finding a specific tag
2. Finding the most popular tags
3. Finding tags that belong to a certain topic

By providing a scenario along with the tasks, a somewhat realistic interaction situation was simulated. For example, one text for the first task was: "You always wanted to visit Nizza. At the moment, you have not enough money for travelling and can only dream about it... Please click on the term 'Nizza' in the following tag cloud." Thus, the participants were asked to search for a target tag and click on it in this task. In the second and third task, the participants had to search and select three tags of choice that were either among the most popular ones (task 2) or related to a given topic (task 3). All study participants reported that they had understood the tasks; none needed further explanation or complained in the post-test questionnaire.

3.2 Tag Cloud Layouts

In order to reduce the countless variations of possible tag arrangements to a manageable and reasonably representative number, we made the following assumption: Many user interfaces are based on a two-dimensional grid layout that conceptually divides the interface into a number of rectangles by horizontal and vertical lines [1]. Thus, a typical requirement for a balanced integration of tag clouds into user interfaces is that they (1) are displayed in a rectangular area and (2) fill this area with tags as completely as possible. Based on these requirements, three main ordering principles can be distinguished:

1. *Sequential layout,* with either a horizontal or vertical arrangement of tags, sorted alphabetically or by some other criteria (e.g., popularity, chronology, etc.)
2. *Circular layout,* with the most popular tags in the center and tags with decreasing popularities towards the borders (or vice versa)
3. *Clustered layout,* in which the distance between tags follows a certain clustering criteria (e.g., semantic relatedness) and related tags are positioned in close proximity [3, 6]

We generated one prototypical tag cloud for each of these three layout strategies. In addition, we created a forth tag cloud with no variation in the tags' font sizes as reference layout (see Fig. 2).

3.3 Tag Corpora

Since we aimed to compare the different tag cloud layouts independently of interpersonal differences, we decided to present all four layouts in a series to every study participant. We used tag corpora from four different domains to prevent learning effects that could likely result from presenting the same tags in each layout.

Tag corpora from "real" Web contexts were not well suited for our controlled experiment as they usually contain terms with heterogeneous connotations and little semantic consistency. We aimed at minimizing any bias caused by personally affecting or political terms (such as "terrorist"). Furthermore, we wanted to present tags that are well-known to the study participants to avoid effects that result from different interests and educational backgrounds. Additional requirements for the tag corpora included a reasonable way of categorizing the tags for the clustered tag cloud and the usage of terms that are common in Germany, since the study participants were all German-speaking. For these reasons (and due to a lack of alternatives) we decided to develop our own tag corpora for the study that consisted of neutral terms from common knowledge areas (France, sports, furniture, animals) and could be used to create somewhat realistic interaction scenarios. Each corpus consisted of 100 tags with varying popularity values.

3.4 Generation of the Tag Clouds

Since our goal was to evaluate general layout types and not specific algorithms, we decided to generate the tag cloud layouts by our own instead of using available algorithms. That way, we could apply the same design guidelines for all tag clouds and strictly control tag distribution. Nevertheless, the tag clouds were designed to largely follow typical algorithms and were not perceived as artificial or unusual by the study participants.

We generated the tag clouds for all four layouts as follows: We used an equally sized rectangle with an aspect ratio of 3:2 and filled it with the 100 tags of one of the four corpora. We mapped the tags' popularity values on six discrete font sizes, resulting in one tag of 30 pt up to 27 tags of 15 pt for each tag cloud. Every quadrant of the tag cloud got the same number of tags of each font size to avoid biases caused by an unbalanced presentation. In accordance with the ordering principle of the circular layout, the 30 pt tag was placed in the middle of the cloud. In the sequential and clustered layout, the 30 pt tag was placed in another quadrant for each of the four corpora. We also considered the different user tasks in the tags' distribution: We varied the size and quadrant position of the tags the participants were asked for in the first task. Likewise, we distributed the thematic clusters that were of interest in the third task among all four quadrants of the tag clouds. We kept all other visual features, such as font styles, weights, colors, or intensities, constant in order to avoid interdependencies as reported in [2].

Fig. 2 shows the resulting four layouts that were generated for the corpus 'France'. The colored lines, circles, and arrows indicate quadrant separations and ordering principles of the layouts (not visible for the study participants).

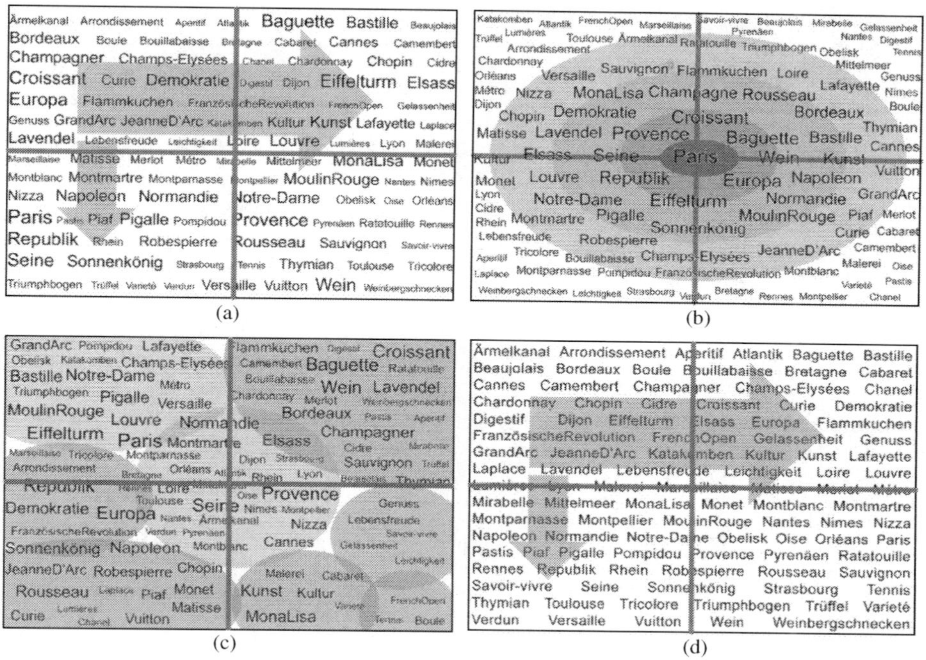

Fig. 2. Tag cloud layouts for the corpus 'France': (a) sequential (alphabetical sorting), (b) circular (decreasing popularity), (c) clustered (thematic clusters), (d) reference (sequential, alphabetical sorting, no weighting of tags)

4 Experimental Procedure

36 participants, mainly students, with an average age of 26 (min 17, max 57) took part in the experiment. All had normal or corrected-to-normal vision. The general familiarity with tag clouds was given with a median of 4 on a scale of 1 to 10. Five participants could not remember having seen any tag clouds before.

In order to create a nearly identical understanding of tagging and tag clouds, the experiment started with a short introduction into these topics, consisting of an oral explanation accompanied by a paper demonstration (see Fig. 3). In addition, we presented three tag clouds from popular websites (flickr, delicious, last.fm) that all followed a sequential layout with alphabetical sorting. We expected that many participants had already come across this well-known layout – effects caused by a higher familiarity cannot be avoided but somewhat compensated by presenting this type of tag cloud to all participants in advance.

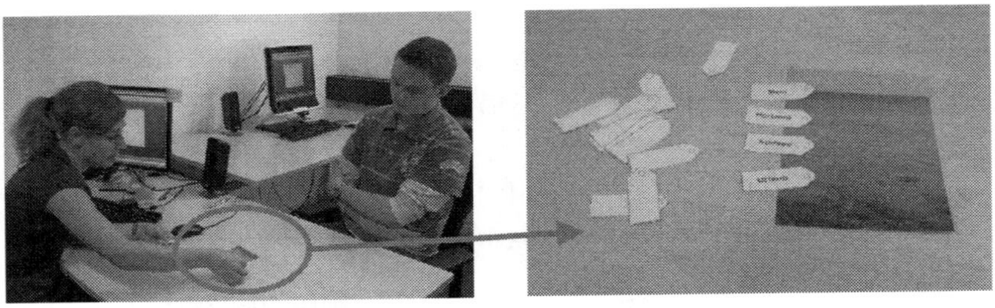

Fig. 3. Introduction into tagging and tag clouds by oral explanation and a paper demonstration

After the introduction, the participants were randomly assigned to one of the three tasks, resulting in 12 participants per task. We applied a Graeco-Latin square design to counterbalance the layout-corpus-combinations in the series of trials for each experimental group. Table 1 shows the resulting four series for task 1. The second and third experimental groups (task 2 and 3) were assigned to corresponding layout-corpus-combinations that also followed a Graeco-Latin square design.

Table 1. Graeco-Latin square design for the first task (group 1): Systematizing tag cloud layout (L) and tag corpus (C) for the four subgroups (SG) and four trials (Tr)

SG	Tr1	Tr2	Tr3	Tr4
1	L1 / C1	L2 / C3	L3 / C4	L4 / C2
2	L2 / C2	L1 / C4	L4 / C3	L3 / C1
3	L3 / C3	L4 / C1	L1 / C2	L2 / C4
4	L4 / C4	L3 / C2	L2 / C1	L1 / C3

The tag clouds were presented on a 17" TFT monitor with a screen resolution of 1280 x 1024 px. They were placed in the middle of a blank screen in an area of 20 x 13.3 cm. Before the presentation of each layout, a short text was displayed explaining the scenario and task. The text of the task was identical within each group; the scenario was adapted to the corresponding tag corpus. The participants should carefully read the task and the scenario before moving on. When one layout was completed by clicking on the tags, the group's task was again displayed along with the next scenario and tag cloud layout. After all four layouts had been presented, the participants filled out a questionnaire in which they chose their preferred layout among others. All four layouts were again shown in the questionnaire to aid recognition. The click times were recorded by the presentation software. Gaze data was captured by an eye tracking system that was embedded in the TFT monitor.

5 Results of Task-Layout-Performance

We measured the task-layout-performance as the time the participants needed to accomplish the tasks. For the first task, we measured the time until the target tag was selected. For the second and third tasks, we calculated the mean value of the time needed for the three selections as indicator for task-layout-performance.

We ran a Kruskal-Wallis test on the data to get an objective ranking on how the layouts perform for each of the three tasks. In addition, we calculated a subjective ranking by counting the study participants' votes for the layouts in the post-test questionnaire. Table 2 shows these values for all three tasks along with the means, medians, minima, and maxima (all in seconds) of the times needed. In the following, we discuss the results for each task in more detail.

Table 2. Performance values of the tag cloud layouts for the 12 participants (N) of each task: Kruskal-Wallis (KW) mean rank, user votes, mean, median, minimum, and maximum (in sec)

Task	Layout	N	KW Mean Rank	User Votes	Mean	Median	Min	Max
1 p=.131 3df χ^2=5,6	sequential	12	22.5	8	8.6	6.5	2.5	18.8
	circular	12	27.8	1	13.6	12.8	3.3	42.3
	clustered	12	30.0	0	14.3	12.2	2.8	33.5
	reference	12	17.8	3	6.9	5.3	2.3	18.7
2 p=.036 3df χ^2=8,5	sequential	12	20.8	1	2.6	1.6	1.0	6.6
	circular	12	18.7	8	2.2	1.8	0.8	4.7
	clustered	12	24.4	3	3.1	2.3	1.0	7.8
	reference	12	34.1	0	4.5	3.4	1.2	9.8
3 p=.239 3df χ^2=4,2	sequential	12	26.5	4	7.3	5.0	1.7	23.0
	circular	12	22.0	3	5.4	4.7	1.9	12.2
	clustered	12	19.4	5	4.9	3.7	1.5	13.2
	reference	12	30.2	0	6.9	6.5	3.0	11.5

5.1 Results for Task 1

For the first task (finding a specific tag), the reference layout (the layout without any weighting of tags) performed best with a value of 17.8 when comparing the mean ranks, followed by the sequential tag cloud (mean rank: 22.5). Since both layouts were alphabetically sorted and hence highly supported scanning for a particular term, we expected these layouts to score well in this task, though the differences were not significant (p=.131). Furthermore, we found some evidence that tags with large font sizes are selected more quickly than small tags in this task. However, we cannot provide reliable values as this effect seemed to be influenced by other visual features, such as a tag's number of characters or its position and neighboring tags in the cloud.

Interestingly, only 3 of this group's 12 participants voted for the reference layout in the questionnaire (two of them have never come in contact with tag clouds before). Although the font sizes did not provide additional value in this task, most participants (8 of 12) preferred the sequential tag cloud layout. It seems that their choice was not only driven by rational factors but largely influenced by aesthetic aspects, since many subjects mentioned the more appealing appearance of the tag clouds compared to the reference layout in the questionnaire.

5.2 Results for Task 2

In the second task (finding the most popular tags), the circular layout showed the significantly best performance results (mean rank of 18.7, p=.036). It was also selected as the preferred layout by most participants (8 of 12). Unsurprisingly, the reference layout failed both in click times and user ratings as it does not provide any information about tag popularity.

Interestingly, the two participants that needed the longest time to accomplish the task preferred the clustered layout – it seems as if the circular layout supports the identification of objectively popular tags (i.e., tags with large font sizes) whereas the clustered layout encourages subjective decision making on most important tags (i.e., considering not only a tag's font size but also its position in the clustered layout). However, this interpretation needs further validation.

5.3 Results for Task 3

The results of the third task (finding tags that belong to a given topic) also met our expectations as the clustered tag cloud layout performed best (though not significantly, p=.239). However, not all participants seem to recognize its ordering principle; some even selected tags from topic areas that were not asked for in the task. Interestingly, most participants that chose tags in accordance with the task also voted for the clustered tag cloud in the questionnaire.

Again, font size had a strong effect on tag selection, as the selected tags had a mean size of 23.6 pt (median: 25 pt) compared to a mean size of 19.6 pt (median: 18 pt) for all tags, even though the study participants could freely choose any tags that belong to the given topic area, independently of their font size.

6 Analysis of Eye Tracking Data

The analysis of the eye tracking data was performed in an exploratory manner looking for typical patterns in the visual search. We focused on the spatial distribution of fixations over the three tag cloud layouts (the reference layout was not of interest here). All fixations of the subjects' eyes with a minimum duration of 100 ms were considered, using a fixation radius (i.e., the smallest distance that separates fixations) of 50 px. We analyzed the fixation data of the first six seconds of each trial, which represent well the main phase of the search process.

In a first analysis, we divided the whole tag cloud areas into 5 x 5 rectangular, equally sized subareas and counted fixations in these areas. Fig. 4 shows the distribution of fixations over the 25 subareas. In the circular layout, fixations are quite strongly focused on the central part of the tag cloud. They are more dispersed and oriented towards the upper left quadrant in the sequential layout. In the clustered layout, they are more evenly distributed. The lower right attracts less attention in all layouts.

The uneven distribution of fixations among the quadrants becomes even more apparent when aggregating the 25 subareas into partly overlapping quadrants (see Fig. 5a). Compared to a strict quadrant separation, fixations near the quadrant borders are counted for more than one quadrant in this variant what further strengthens the results in our case. Interestingly, the distribution of fixations over the quadrants varies only

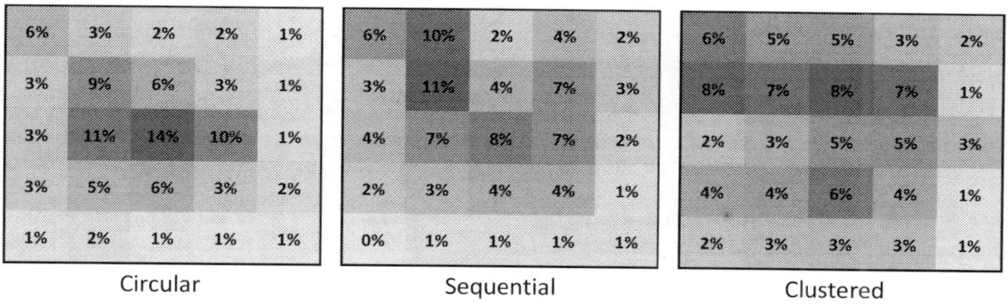

Fig. 4. Distribution of fixations in percent over the 5 x 5 subareas for the three tag cloud layouts. The five-level coloring illustrates the pattern of the distribution.

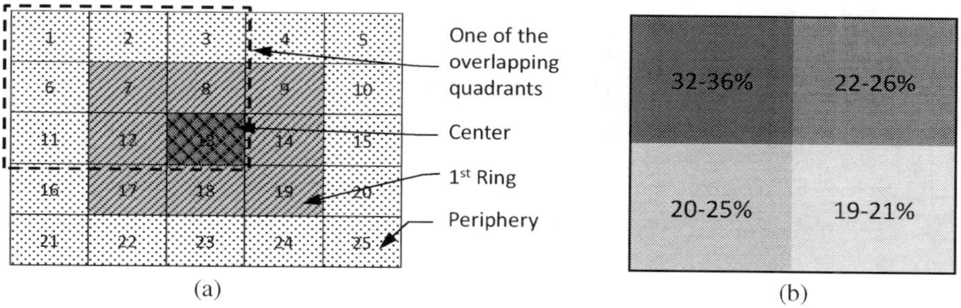

Fig. 5. a) Definition of areas of interest, b) Distribution of fixations over the quadrants

marginally among the layouts (see Fig. 5b). In all layouts, the upper left quadrant got the most fixations (32-36%) and the bottom-right the fewest (19-21%). This might be explained by Western reading habits.

To further analyze the tendency towards the center we aggregated the 25 subareas to three larger, concentric zones as illustrated in Fig. 5a: 1) a center zone consisting of the single rectangle in the middle, 2) a 1st ring of rectangles around the center, and 3) a 2nd ring of rectangles ('periphery'). In this case, we calculated the number of fixations per unit of area (fixation density). The data for the center, 1st ring, and peripheral zones show that the highest proportion of fixations lies in the central parts of the cloud (center + 1st ring), regardless of the layout (see Fig. 6). For the circular layout, the small center rectangle has even more than double the fixation density than the surrounding 1st ring, indicating a very strong central focus.

In order to gain insight into the temporal variation of the gaze focus, we divided the overall time interval analyzed (sec 0-6) into three subintervals: sec 0-1 (period 1), sec 1-3 (period 2), and sec 3-6 (period 3). We chose three periods of increasing length since we were interested in contrasting a short initial phase indicative of a subject's orientation at the beginning of the trial with the gaze focus in later intervals where the visual search becomes more expansive and covers larger areas. Fig. 7 shows the gaze distribution over the center-to-periphery zones for the three time periods. As already observed in the overall gaze distribution, the circular layout generates the highest central orientation, which is slightly decreasing over time for the benefit of the 1st ring

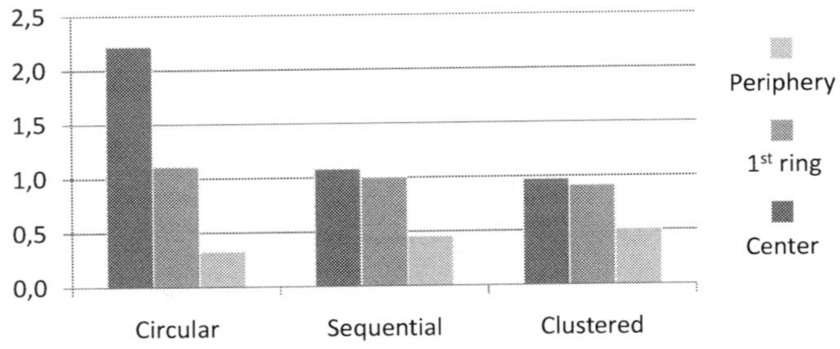

Fig. 6. Fixation density for the central-to-peripheral zones

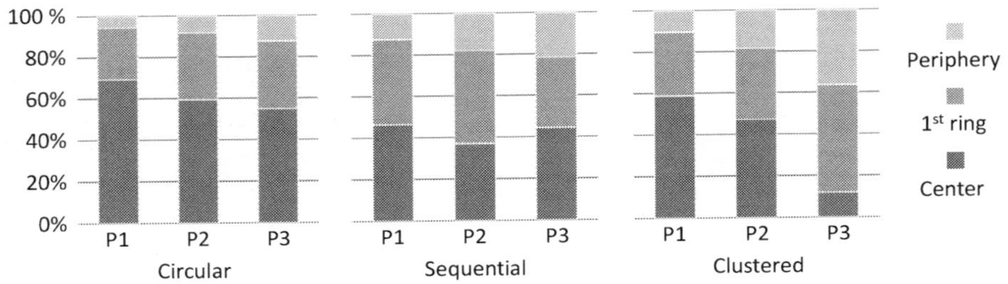

Fig. 7. Distribution of fixation density in the center, 1st ring and periphery zones for the three time periods

and peripheral zones. The change in distribution is less pronounced for the sequential layout. In the clustered layout, the decrease in central orientation is strongest. A possible explanation is that the gaze tends to stay in the target cluster once the thematic relation with it has been recognized.

7 Conclusions

The results of our comparative study on tag cloud layouts show clearly that there exists no single best way to arrange weighted terms in a cloud – as common in interaction design, the optimal solution depends strongly on the specific user goals and intentions of the designer. However, regarding the layout classes and user goals investigated in our experiment, the following task-layout-matchings are supported by our results:

1. Finding a specific tag: Sequential layout with alphabetical sorting.
2. Finding the most popular tags: Circular layout with decreasing popularity.
3. Finding tags that belong to a certain topic: Thematically clustered layout.

Generalizing from the layouts and tasks, we got some results that are largely in line with the findings and assumptions made in related work. Table 3 summarizes the findings by contrasting the general results of our study with the results of related work (cp. Sec. 2): As already indicated in previous studies [2, 5, 9], we also found that tags with large font sizes seem to 'pop out' to the viewers – they were on average

Table 3. Summarization of the research findings on tag cloud perception and performance contrasting related work and our own study (encompassing both quantitative and qualitative observations)

Abbreviation	Description & literature source	Evaluation based on our results
Tag size	Large tags attract more user attention than small tags [2, 9] and are found more quickly [5].	Basically, our results support these findings, though they also indicate that further properties, such as the number of characters, the position of a tag in the cloud, or neighboring tags, influence this effect (cp. [2]).
Scanning	Users scan rather than read tag clouds [2, 5].	The eye tracking data support this finding. However, in contrast to the assumption of [5], no general scanning direction could be identified.
Centering	Tags in the middle of the cloud attract more user attention than tags near the borders [2].	This seems to be true for most kinds of tag clouds though the layout can increase (e.g., circular) or decrease (e.g., clustered) this effect.
Position	Tags in the upper left quadrant are better recalled [9] and are found more quickly [2].	The eye tracking data show that the upper left quadrant receives the most fixations in all layouts.
Layout	The layout of a tag cloud influences its perception [9].	This finding is strongly supported by our eye tracking data.
Exploration	Tag clouds provide suboptimal support when searching for specific tags [5, 8, 10].	In general, we support this finding. However, very popular tags can be found comparatively quickly.

identified more quickly in the first task and more often selected in the third. Although tag clouds perform worse than unweighted lists on average [5, 8] they seem to accelerate the identification of very popular tags.

When aggregating the eye tracking data of all layouts and tasks, we observed a tendency towards the center: Tags in the middle of the cloud attracted more user attention than tags near the borders. Also, an effect of position could be observed in the eye tracking data: The upper-left quadrant received more fixations than the others. Thus, a tag's general visibility is largely influenced by its position in the tag cloud, which might be used by designers to direct users' attention to certain tags.

The feedback and ratings of the study participants suggest that fun and aesthetic aspects largely affect the user's interaction with tag clouds. Participants partly preferred layouts that did not yield the best performance. Thus, such aspects should be included in any design decision and usability evaluation of tag clouds. A holistic approach must furthermore consider the general nature of tags and the characteristics of tagging systems [4] that were not within the focus of this paper. As shown by our findings, interface designers must also and foremost consider the possible user tasks before deciding for a certain type of tag cloud or using tag clouds at all.

References

[1] Ambrose, G., Harris, P.: Grids. Ava Acedemia, Lausanne (2008)
[2] Bateman, S., Gutwin, C., Nacenta, M.: Seeing Things in the Clouds: The Effect of Visual Features on Tag Cloud Selections. In: Proc. of the 19th ACM conference on Hypertext and Hypermedia, pp. 193–202. ACM Press, New York (2008)
[3] Clark, J.: Clustered Word Clouds (2008), `http://www.neoformix.com/2008/ClusteredWordClouds.html` (retrieved on 2009-01-30)
[4] Golder, S., Huberman, B.A.: Usage Patterns of Collaborative Tagging Systems. Journal of Information Science 32(2), 198–208 (2006)
[5] Halvey, M., Keane, M.T.: An Assessment of Tag Presentation Techniques. In: Proc. of the 16th International Conference on World Wide Web, pp. 1313–1314. ACM Press, New York (2007)
[6] Hassan-Montero, Y., Herrero-Solana, V.: Improving Tag-Clouds as Visual Information Retrieval Interfaces. In: Proc. of International Conference on Multidisciplinary Information Sciences and Technologies. INSTAC, Mérida (2006)
[7] Hearst, M.A., Rosner, D.: Tag Clouds: Data Analysis Tool or Social Signaller? In: Proc. of the 41st Annual Hawaii International Conference on System Sciences. IEEE Press, New York (2008)
[8] Kuo, B.Y.-L., Hentrich, T., Good, B.M., Wilkinson, M.D.: Tag Clouds for Summarizing Web Search Results. In: Proc. of the 16th International Conference on World Wide Web, pp. 1203–1204. ACM Press, New York (2007)
[9] Rivadeneira, A.W., Gruen, D.M., Muller, M.J., Millen, D.R.: Getting our Head in the Clouds: Toward Evaluation Studies of Tagclouds. In: Proc. of the SIGCHI Conference on Human Factors in Computing Systems, pp. 995–998. ACM Press, New York (2007)
[10] Sinclair, J., Cardew-Hall, M.: The Folksonomy Tag Cloud: When is it Useful? Journal of Information Science 34(1), 15–29 (2008)
[11] Viégas, F.B., Wattenberg, M.: Tag Clouds and the Case for Vernacular Visualization. Interactions 15(1), 49–52 (2008)
[12] Popular Tags on Flickr, `http://www.flickr.com/photos/tags/` (retrieved on 2009-01-30)

Bringing Web 2.0 to the Old Web: A Platform for Parasitic Applications

Florian Alt[1], Albrecht Schmidt[1], Richard Atterer[2], and Paul Holleis[3]

[1] Pervasive Computing Group, University of Duisburg-Essen, Germany
{florian.alt,albrecht.schmidt}@uni-due.de
[2] Media Informatics Group, Ludwig-Maximilians-University Munich, Germany
richard.atterer@ifi.lmu.de
[3] DOCOMO Euro Labs, Munich, Germany
holleis@docomolab-euro.com

Abstract. It is possible to create interactive, responsive web applications that allow user-generated contributions. However, the relevant technologies have to be explicitly deployed by the authors of the web pages. In this work we present the concept of parasitic and symbiotic web applications which can be deployed on arbitrary web pages by means of a proxy-based application platform. Such applications are capable of inserting, editing and deleting the content of web pages. We use an HTTP proxy in order to insert JavaScript code on each web page that is delivered from the web server to the browser. Additionally we use a database server hosting user-generated scripts as well as high-level APIs allowing for implementing customized web applications. Our approach is capable of cooperating with existing web pages by using shared standards (e.g. formatting of the structure on DOM level) and common APIs but also allows for user-generated (parasitic) applications on arbitrary web pages without the need for cooperation by the page owner.

1 Introduction

A drawback of the WWW has always been that information only flows in one direction i.e. from the author of a web page to its readers. To resolve this shortcoming, several approaches have been proposed, such as guest books, bookmarks and discussion boards. However, most of these approaches are not capable of providing a true two-way flow of information, neither by modifying the information resource itself nor by extending the unidirectional flow in a way that indirectly associates separately stored additional information with the original source. A popular solution which allows interaction and shared working on documents is Wikis. However, they still require installation of the Wiki software on the server side and are hence limited to specific web sites. Especially with the advent of Web 2.0 technology, annotation systems and tools supporting automation and customization of rendered web pages have become popular. Yet, those approaches are static in a sense that the applications cannot be easily distributed and made available to other users or programmers.

Our contribution in this paper is twofold. First, we provide a modular technical platform which permits novel types of applications to be deployed on top of existing web applications. This is possible using statically added components which are implemented

T. Gross et al. (Eds.): INTERACT 2009, Part I, LNCS 5726, pp. 405–418, 2009.

directly within the platform, such as a tool which allows users to leave annotations on arbitrary web pages. More advanced applications are customizable and dynamic, e.g. a voting tool allowing the user to specify questions, options and the pages to deploy the tool on. Finally, user-generated applications are also possible, they allow programmers to execute code of their choice on arbitrary pages. The platform is based on an HTTP proxy which modifies page content before sending it to the browser, together with an application/database server for storage of code and data of the deployed applications.

Existing solutions in this area rely on client-side software installation, which has the unfortunate effect that only users who install the software can use the application. In comparison, our solution merely requires the user to reconfigure their browser's HTTP proxy setting. Additionally, existing efforts cannot easily support dynamic applications requiring for example a database connection due to the same origin policy. We solve this problem by providing users a simple high-level API that offers methods for database access and XMLHttpRequests.

Our second contribution is at the conceptual level: The abovementioned applications can be deployed in a symbiotic or a parasitic way. In the first case, they can use the existing API of the web application they extend. In contrast, parasitic applications can be built on top of any web page without the need of cooperation of the site owner. This enables many interesting application concepts to be realized, and allows new user interface components to be added to many sites in a consistent way.

This paper is organized as follows: First, we introduce challenges arising from the use of parasitic code on arbitrary web pages. Based on this we present a technical approach for allowing the deployment of static, dynamic, and user-generated code. In chapter 4 and 5 we present to case studies, demonstrating how our platform can be used to augment web pages with annotations and dynamic code and which issues arise thereof. Finally we present related work in chapter 6.

2 Challenges of Parasitic Applications

In contrast to Berners-Lee's vision of the WWW, the web as we experience it today has many restrictions and follows standards only to a certain degree. This makes it difficult to build applications on top of web documents which enhance those documents.

2.1 One-Way Information Exchange

When considering the flow of information of web documents on the World Wide Web, it is obvious that a one-way information exchange from the author to the reader prevails, since the user sitting in front of the browser has read-only access to web documents. Many different tools are available for the document author to visualize his information, while the interaction of the reader is limited to viewing the page, clicking on hyperlinks and creating bookmarks. Other types of communication on the web, such as forms or email, do not have these restrictions. It is apparent that the unidirectional information exchange limits the system in its communication potential.

Tools supporting the deployment of user-generated code on web pages can partly help to overcome this problem by providing the readers a form of backchannel. With the help of such a backchannel, they can not only address the author but also provide others with tools to embed information and thus modify the page.

2.2 Structural Diversity

Another problem of web documents is the lack of a structural layout standard, which leads to the use of arbitrary layouts. As an example, a margin is not any longer a mandatory element of each document. While numerous web pages have a fixed width, which results in a margin being displayed if the browser window size is large, there are also a lot of web pages that adjust automatically to the window width.

This raises severe problems when it comes to implementing applications that try to interact with the web page's static code. Our approach tries to overcome this problem by providing a way to symbiotically interact with pages, e.g. based on a common standard, but also explores ways of how to interact with pages without knowledge about their structure.

2.3 Multidimensionality of Web Documents

In contrast to traditional documents, digital documents allow to overcome the two-dimensionality of documents by adding new layers. The use of CSS offers the chance to position elements above each other, thus providing content to be added similar to post-its that are stuck to a sheet of paper. This way, an almost unlimited amount of additional space is available for new content. However, this raises several issues such as how to create a relation between this content and the original document, and how to define and display an anchor in the original text.

2.4 Reliable Modifications to Existing Page Layouts

At a more technical level, adding new code and layout elements to existing web pages is a non-trivial task if we consider that the existing page may change subtly over time. For example, if an annotation was placed on a page, it should still be attached to the sentence it was added to, even if other parts of the text content change. This makes it necessary to define different levels on which positioning of added content is possible, and to extract high-quality anchor information which allows proper repositioning even in case the source document is modified [11, 25].

3 A Platform for Parasitic Applications

Existing systems supporting client side interaction need to make a trade-off between several advantages and disadvantages. Systems requiring client side software installation tend to have a more intuitive and responsive user interface since they benefit from the tight integration with the browser and client side integration of the features. On the other hand, the main advantage of server-based approaches is that site visitors do not need to install software on their computer. Instead, they can start using the server side system immediately to deploy any changes.

It is the aim of our work to combine both aspects. Even though no software installation should be required, the user interface should be intuitive to use and responsive, for example by avoiding re-downloading and redisplaying the entire page during working. This is achieved by combining an AJAX-based architecture for responsive client side performance with an HTTP proxy approach which allows the deployment of code on arbitrary pages.

3.1 Requirements

In our experience, the following requirements were important for such a system:

- In the same way as the other technologies of the WWW, our implementation should achieve platform independence on the server side (i.e. with arbitrary web server solutions) and the client side (different browsers and operating systems).
- Furthermore, it should be minimally invasive in terms of required client and server side changes. In contrast to systems that require the installation of software, which is always a possible source of errors and implies an additional burden to the user, this approach reduces the users' effort: they only need to change the browser preferences for the HTTP proxy. (Moreover, by deploying the proxy as a transparent proxy for a whole network, even this small change can be eliminated.)
- Maintainability of code for the platform and for applications should be ensured. Because the JavaScript code for the application platform is delivered by the proxy each time a page is loaded by the user, the code can be modified at any time without requiring the user to make an explicit software update. Also, the strong conceptual isolation of the web server, proxy and browser makes it easier to replace any of these components.
- The platform should support different types of applications, such as static applications provided by the platform owner, dynamic applications that can be configured by the user and user-generated applications.
- Finally, the result should be responsive despite the fact that loading and storing of modifications requires a lot of traffic between the client and scripting/database server. An efficient implementation using AJAX technology is essential to avoid negative effects of the platform on the user experience.

3.2 Supported Types of Applications

Especially since the advent of Web 2.0 technology, a lot of research has gone on into the area of automating and customizing web pages based on user-generated code and content. Widely available examples are tools for annotation, adding links, building custom portals, and making alternative queries (see related work). All those tools have in common that they allow users to add content to web pages without any programming knowledge. On a lower level, several approaches allow users to execute their code on arbitrary web pages. Prominent examples are toolkits such as Greasemonkey and WBI [4] or high-level programming languages such as WebL [15] or Chickenfoot [6].

However those applications have major drawbacks. First, high level applications (such as annotation tools) are static in the sense that they do not allow for customizing or modifying by the user. Second, solutions allowing the deployment of user-generated code are not easily available, since first, the toolkit itself has to be installed as a plug-in which limits its use to certain browsers, and second, the scripts are not centrally available. Finally, existing approaches cannot easily be extended or modified though probably intended by the author, since placing user-generated content requires the use of, e.g., a database. This is difficult due to the same origin policy of modern browsers.

Our system tries to integrate the advantages of different approaches. First, we support pre-implemented applications deployable by users without any programming knowledge. Second, we allow providing applications that can easily be customized, and finally we provide means to implement JavaScript-based applications.

Static Applications: As mentioned before, a lot of effort has been put into the development of technologies supporting the deployment of applications on top of web pages, hence easing the automation and customization for users. The challenging part for such applications is the storage of data, since web pages are only virtually modified. Most of those applications are static because extending the functionality would require major changes on the provider side and cannot be simply achieved by writing client side code. Yet such applications are very useful, since no programming knowledge is required for their deployment. An example for a static application that can be distributed via an application platform such as the one presented in this work are annotation tools. In chapter 5 we explain how such a system can be integrated with our platform.

Dynamic Applications: A similar, yet more generic approach is the support of dynamic applications. Although those applications also have to be deployed within the application platform, they leave more space for customization. An example would be an application allowing for generating customized surveys. Connections to external storage such as a database server again have to be implemented within the application platform. Yet the code for the application itself is created dynamically based on user requirements.

User-Implemented Applications: Finally we also support applications implemented by users. We provide a module which allows for inserting arbitrary JavaScript code in any web page through the application platform. The JavaScript code is stored in a database and can be fetched and executed on demand. In order to enable users to create dynamic applications, we further provide a simple high-level API realizing access to a database. The API provides methods such as `insert(key, value)` which writes a (key, value) pair into the database and `get(key)` which returns the value for a given key. `value` can be an arbitrary string which allows for storing 2-dimensional data sets. Programmers can simply parse the value variable in order to store multiple attributes. This provides an easy way of avoiding the same origin policy and additionally supports users in creating dynamic applications without the need to care either for XMLHttpRequests or for database connections.

In order to allow the use of the database by multiple applications, we use prefixing for the key values in the form `{app1}_{local|global}_key`. Hence it is not only possible to use multiple applications but also to determine between local and global entries in the database within one application. Taking the voting system as an example, local entries would be the available options (e.g. `votingApp_local_1 = "option 1"`), global entries would be the answers of the users (e.g. `votingApp_global_1 = "1"`).

3.3 Parasitic vs. Symbiotic Applications

We now introduce the concept of parasitic and symbiotic applications. In the WWW, the client side has read-only access to web resources. To virtually take control over a web page, pages need to be manipulated directly before or after they are rendered in a browser. Hence an illusion for the users is created pretending that they are given the power to modify a web page itself.

We call a web application *parasitic* if it is capable of editing, inserting or destroying content on a web page without the need for server side cooperation. We call a web

Table 1. Classification of parasitic and symbiotic applications

	Non-cooperative (parasitic)	**Cooperative (symbiotic)**
Static applications	Annotations tool for arbitrary web pages	Annotation tool supported by web pages using common guidelines
Dynamic applications	Voting tool	Customized search tool
User-based applications	Script for increasing contrast of web pages	Websites using user-based APIs (e.g. drag and drop)

application *symbiotic* if it uses functionality provided by the server side or provides functionality that can be used by the server side to modify web content. Table 1 gives examples for the different types of applications that become possible with our platform.

Parasitic Applications: Parasitic applications interact with web pages without the explicit permission of the site's owner. This creates new opportunities since it allows users to adjust web sites to their needs.

While this may sound unattractive at first, parasitic code can be useful in a number of ways: an interested party can increase the accessibility and usability of the web application without having to coordinate this activity with the provider of the application. Furthermore, opposing goals of the application provider and of the users can be solved by users. At the simplest level, this can involve removing advertising, but more controversial changes are also possible, such as preventing users from accidentally signing up for a service they have to pay for. Finally, it is possible to enrich existing applications with new functionality, e.g. by interfacing it with other online services such as maps, dictionaries or even related services of competitors.

Symbiotic Applications: Web pages and applications deployed on top of them can also interact in a symbiotic way. Web page owners can support the use of applications provided by our platform in different ways:

- *Page formatting*: Repositioning of additional UI elements is not an easy task. Web pages that use identifiers for areas containing text can support applications in a way such that places where insertions or modifications happen can easily be retrieved once the page is loaded, especially if they moved to a different location.
- *Provide APIs*: Web site owners can provide APIs to be used by applications deployed via the platform. Hence, programmers can be supported and encouraged to write applications, thus increasing the value of a page. Like this, dynamic applications can be supported by providing them access to, e.g., a local database.

Further, page owners can also benefit from deploying platform-based applications:

- *Piggyback applications*: Page owners can use the APIs provided by the platform to implement applications outside their web server. This allows the use of applications among multiple page owners. An example would be a rating system supported among a company's web pages. Hence a user-generated rating could be created based on comments and ratings and stored in a third party's location (in this case the application platform) thus increasing its credibility and liability.

- *Increasing usability/functionality*: The platform can offer scripts that increase the usability and add functionality to websites by offering tools to the user for customizing and formatting of web pages based on their needs. A simple example would be a script to adjust the font-size according to the users' preferences.

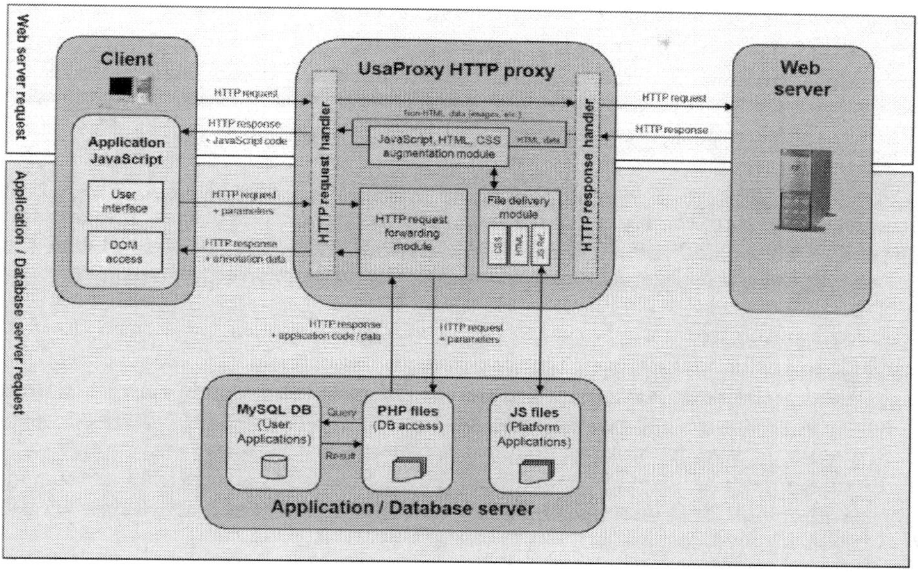

Fig. 1. Components of a proxy-based application platform: application server, HTTP proxy and client side JavaScript. With this approach, no installation of software is necessary on the client browser or the web server.

3.4 Implementation

The implemented application platform consists of three components: an HTTP proxy, an application/database server and the client side JavaScript code which supplies the main functionality as well as the user interfaces. Figure 1 gives a simplified overview of the interaction of the components during operation of the application platform.

HTTP Proxy: The HTTP proxy UsaProxy ([3, 4, 5]) forms the center of the application platform since it connects the client side JavaScript code and the application server. Its first task is to embed Java- Script code on-the-fly on any page that is sent from the web server to the client in response to a standard HTTP request. This makes it possible to realize the embedding of content on the client instead of the proxy. In order to add the JavaScript code, UsaProxy monitors all HTTP requests which pass through it. In case the server delivers HTML content to the browser, the content type of the server response is text/html or text/xhtml, and the returned document is modified. Other content types such as videos and images are forwarded without any changes. The modifications to the original HTML content are small: a <script> tag is added inside the document's <head>, and its src attribute references the annotation JavaScript. The same approach is used to include a CSS style sheet which controls the layout of the user interface for the application platform as well as the layout of the modifications themselves. Finally, the elements for the user interface and the API is inserted after the opening <body> tag.

To access the application (script) data in the database on the application server, the JavaScript which is run inside the browser as a result of the above modifications uses further HTTP requests. XMLHttpRequest objects provide a convenient way of downloading the data. A problem when doing so is that, for security reasons, modern browsers require that the requests are made to the same server which also supplied the original web page. This "same origin" policy is circumvented in the following way: the JavaScript simply makes a request to the same server that the HTML was requested from, which is allowed by the browser. The requested URL is special in that it apparently attempts to access the directory /usaproxylolo/httprequest/ on the server. However, in reality, the request never reaches the original web server. Instead, triggered by the special directory name, it is intercepted by UsaProxy and redirected to the application server, which answers the query and returns the required data.

Application and Database Server: The purpose of the application server is to store the code for both, platform-side applications and for client side JavaScripts in a database, and to retrieve it later upon request. The database is accessible via PHP scripts, which handle storage and retrieval of the data. Furthermore, they pre-process data before returning it to the browser, which simplifies the work of the JavaScript.

Based on the type of modification required by the deployed applications (annotations, voting tools, text marking), different types of information are stored. They can be separated into three classes:

- *Content information*: data such as the code for creating the voting tool or text that is selected by a marking.
- *Positioning information*: the topmost positioning information is the URL of the page an application or modification was created for. Additionally, x/y coordinates are stored for relatively positioned content whereas for selections, a string representation of the DOM path, the surrounding context, the actually marked text, and, if available, the ID of the node is stored.
- *Additional information*: all types of information not directly related to the content or the positioning such as the date a modification was inserted or updated, the author or the title of the page.

Client-side JavaScript: The client-side JavaScript code is inserted into every page by means of the HTTP proxy. Its purpose is to provide the interface for loading and executing available applications from the database. Access to the database is realized using XMLHttpRequest to server-side PHP scripts.

In a similar fashion, the API is made available to programmers using the platform for distributing their applications. The high-level functions that allow programmers to use the platform's database are written in JavaScript and by default delivered by the proxy by embedding a script tag in the page <script type='text/javascript' src='UsaAPI.js'>. Further methods can be simply added by updating the remote JavaScript source file. The API would be available immediately for all users hence meeting the requirement of easy maintainability.

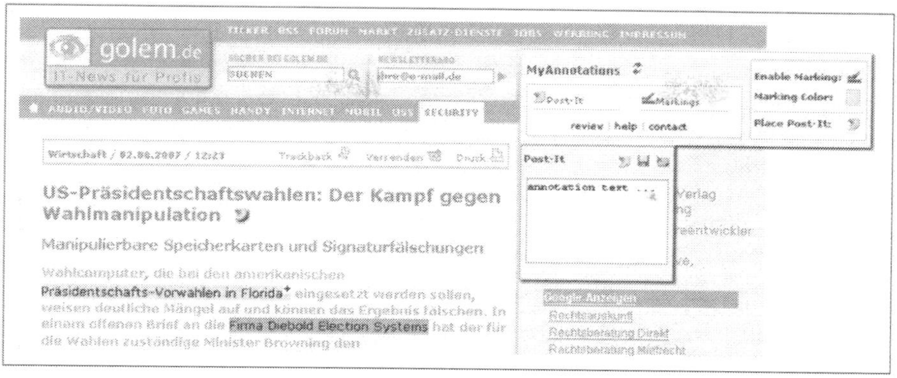

Fig. 2. Elements of the system's user interface: control panel, sticky notes, markings

Modifications to the Existing Page Layout: Modifications of the original HTML can happen at different granularity levels: The same change (e.g. adding a layer with UI elements) can be performed on all pages of a domain, or it can be tailored for exactly one page on a website. Within pages, the modification can apply to a certain node which must be identified. At the most accurate level, it is specific to individual characters, such as text that has been highlighted by the user.

To be able to implement applications capable of making changes on these levels, different types of information are needed for reinserting the changes correctly on a page. This includes anchor text information and surrounding context [8] as well as structural document information and absolute positioning information. Thus, the platform for deployment of applications supports not only the simple case that absolute positioning is used to add new elements at fixed positions on the page, but also that the positioning depends on the properties of a certain element in the existing document's Document Object Model (DOM) tree. To allow individual characters to be addressable, e.g. to ensure that an annotation for a part of the text appears next to the relevant words, the platform can identify the characters using the offset within their enclosing element. Alternatively, it can store the marked text, i.e. the words or sentences that the user selected when he created the annotation, and employ a substring search at a later time to find it again. This approach can be made more robust against changes on the page by not only storing the marked text, but also some of the text surrounding it.

4 Case Study 1: A Web Annotation Tool

One of the best-researched piggyback applications on the web are annotation tools. Hence we had a student implement such an annotation tool as a proof-of-concept for our application platform during a master thesis. An annotation tool is an example for a static application deployed on the platform side. However, we added several dynamic elements that allow for customization such as dynamically choosing the marking color.

In this section we give an overview of the design process and implementation and in a final step the evaluation in a user study and a real-world deployment.

4.1 Implementation

The annotation tool provides two basic forms of annotations: the marking of text, similar to the use of a highlighter, and placing sticky notes onto a website, similar to sticking paper post-its to a sheet of paper. Additionally, inline comments are introduced, which allow for associating comments with marked text passages. Figure 2 shows the different types of supported annotations and the expanded control panel.

The basic idea for the marking tool is to simply change the background color of the text selected by the mouse, thus creating a similar effect to using a highlighter in the real world. However this approach is technically limited to the marking of text so that it is not possible to highlight arbitrary page elements.

In order to offer the opportunity to create a text comment related to a marking, similar to notes scribbled between the lines or in the margin near the annotated text on physical paper, the marking concept is extended by so-called inline comments. Once created, they can be displayed either as tool tips or as text rendered next to the marked text. This way of displaying inline comments differs significantly from real-world annotations, so special attention was paid to it during the evaluation.

The use of sticky notes is similar to the real-world Post-It counterparts which can be placed everywhere on a page. To allow moving the sticky notes around a page, a drag-and-drop functionality is implemented so that sticky notes can easily be positioned in arbitrary locations. An interesting extension of this concept trying to deal with the limited space on a web page is to provide a minimize function which transforms sticky notes into small icons that can similarly be dragged around, but do not obscure any elements on the page.

To enable access to the previously described functions, it is necessary to provide a control panel, a layer that is automatically inserted on each page. The control panel offers access to other features such as hiding, displaying, expanding and collapsing the annotations, creating summaries or overviews, and using the notification tool.

The positioning of the control panel is a non-trivial problem. For automatic positioning, the system would have to interpret the structure and the content of the page in order to determine whether important areas of the page are obscured. To deal with this, the control panel can be dragged to any position on the page by the user. Additionally, a minimizing feature of the control panel is provided that reduces the control center to a small box showing only the most important functions.

4.2 Real World Usage Scenario

In order to assess the applicability of tools developed for the use with our application platform in WWW, we tested the annotation tool in the real world. The system was set up and adjusted for the online archive of the German weekly newspaper *Die Zeit*, in preparation for productive use with the pages which comprise the archive.

The goal of the evaluation was to discover potential issues that arise from using our system on pages in the World Wide Web. Therefore, we not only intensively tested all features of the system, but also closely examined the internal HTML structure of the page, the layout, and the use of CSS styles.

It turned out that the entire functionality of the annotation tool could be used throughout the website without any restrictions. However, we discovered some potential issues that might interfere with the use not only of the annotation system but also with other tools deployed via the application platform. Most of the issues are related to the modification of content and/or structure of web sites.

- *Dynamic URLs*: since each annotation is uniquely defined by the URL of the page it belongs to as well as its ID, the insertion algorithm relies upon the URL for correctness. Hence, URLs that change according to session IDs or dynamic parameters may lead to duplicate pages so that annotations can no longer be associated with a specific web page and get orphaned.
- *Dynamic page width*: while markings are positioned directly in the DOM structure, sticky notes strongly rely on the layout of a page since their position is recorded in pixel coordinates. This way, pages that do not have a fixed width and/or are not left-aligned lead to sticky notes being displayed in different locations for different browser window sizes.
- *Dynamic page content*: for pages with dynamic content, the DOM tree can change thus causing the positioning information of annotations to become invalid. This can be circumvented by predefining areas for dynamic content. Thus the DOM path will only be changed on a level where it does not affect the positioning algorithm for the annotations.
- *Overriding global style sheet settings*: the CSS rules which are intended for formatting the annotations should be designed with care to avoid that they influence the original site layout. This is achieved by defining a special class for all parts of the annotation UI, and assigning it to the UI elements.

4.3 Summary

The implementation of the annotation tool prototype helped us considerably in understanding issues and challenges arising from the deployment of piggyback applications. We think that applications provided via our platform could especially benefit in symbiotic scenarios by following common design guidelines or even standards. Applications will be most successful once they are well integrated and their functionality tailored towards specific tasks.

However, we also showed that such tools can be deployed as parasitic applications. Yet, creating reliable parasitic applications requires a lot of effort, such as the implementation of complex positioning algorithms.

5 Case Study 2: UsaScript

In a second case study, we implemented UsaScript, a tool for testing the deployment of user-generated code on arbitrary web pages. The tool uses the infrastructure of the application platform to store JavaScript code in the database and to make it available on any web page to any user.

A simple example would be a script that overcomes the very common problem of web pages with low contrast between background and text. A user could implement a script based on three lines of code that sets the background color of an arbitrary web page to white and the standard text color to black:

```
var bodyNode = document.getElementById('body');
bodyNode.style.background = '#FFF';
bodyNode.style.color = '#000';
```

A user who wants to use that piece of code can simply choose it from a list of available applications provided by the platform. The script is loaded into a <script> tag embedded in the page by the platform and executed immediately.

However, the tool also allows for writing more complex applications that provide, for example, a GUI. In order to prevent the code of being immediately executed once loaded, programmers can define JavaScript methods to be called later, even by other scripts. By following this approach, UsaScript does not only support the deployment of user-generated scripts, but also gives programmers the opportunity to provide APIs for other programmers or the site owners.

An example would be an API that enables drag and drop for page elements. This API could provide a function makeDraggable(id) which assigns drag and drop functionality to the element id. Page owners could then define page elements which should be draggable (e.g. products in an online store that could be dragged to the shopping cart). To users who are not using the application platform, the web page appears normal. However, once they use the application platform, they are able to drag and drop elements without any further required action since the API for the drag and drop functionality can be loaded based on the URL of the page.

6 Related Work

Since the advent of the World Wide Web, programmers try to realize Tim Berners-Lee's vision of its interactive and bidirectional use. There have been numerous attempts to build systems enabling users to customize and modify pages of the World Wide Web by adding content and controls. However, existing solutions require either a special server side setup or installation of software on the client machine, both of which limit the areas in which the system is useful.

First we focus on research in the area of customization and modification in general, second we look at research that has been carried out in order to achieve this through augmenting web pages by content and controls. As a third part we especially focus on annotation tools as an illustrative application.

Bolin et al [7] have proposed a categorization of tasks supported by tools that deal with the automation and customization of web pages on the client side. The categorization distinguishes between automating repetitive operations, integrating multiple websites (e.g., incorporating a map service inside a web page), and transforming a web site's appearance.

Suitable approaches for automation include scripting languages such as Perl, Python, or WebL [15] but also tools that support the recording of macros such as LiveAgent [16] or WebVCR [1]. Those tools allow for recording the actions necessary to access hard-to-reach content and replay it later.

Examples for approaches that deal with transforming a website's appearance are toolkits such as the browser extensions Greasemonkey and Platypus, as well as WBI [4], a pre Web 2.0 approach that observes user interactions by using different kinds of agents.WebL [15] and Chickenfoot [4] provide a high-level language to ease the manipulation of web pages. The advantage of Chickenfoot is that it supports the modification of web pages without requiring knowledge about HTML programming.

Concerning modifications of a page, mechanisms and strategies are required to insert content into the page. Bouvin et al [7] present an overview of web augmentation strategies. They define a tool as a hypermedia augmentation tool if "it through integration with a web browser, an HTTP proxy or a Web server adds content or controls [. . .] with the purpose to help users organize, associate or structure information found on the web." Such tools can be divided into four categories: structuring/spatial, link creation and traversal, guided tours, and annotations/discussion support.

First, spatial hypermedia describes applications where link structures are not shown explicitly any more but rather implicitly based on the spatial relationship between objects, hence providing a powerful tool for organizing and structuring the web. An example is Web Squirrel [20] that helps users to organize their URLs in information farms.

Second, example tools for link creation and traversal are Chimera and DLS. Chimera [1] is an experimental system that allows for displaying structural information of a page in a separate program (applet) or within the browser by hooking up a web server to the Chimera server hence translating the Chimera structures into HTML. The Distributed Link Service (DLS) [10] is based on the MicroCosm hypermedia system [13]. It allows for attaching a link service menu to the browser by using a wrapper. This wrapper would contact the link server once a link was clicked in this menu.

Third, tools supporting guided tours are mainly used in educational settings. Walden's path [11] uses a path authoring tool such as VIKI [19] to compose a trail that students have to pass. Trails are stored on a Path Server as well as CGI scripts to provide an interface to the path. A similar approach is followed by WebVise [12], an open hypermedia service which provides a link, annotation and guided tour authoring interface integrated with MSIE. It can be accessed in arbitrary Web browsers via a proxy server interface.

Finally, annotation tools such as implemented in the presented case study have been widely examined and numerous approaches of deploying them exist. Most common are client side browser extensions such as Yawas, Diigo, Fleck, and Stickis, or bookmarklets such as sharedcopy. Yet, also entire browsers have been implemented which support annotations such as comMentor [17]. On the other side, also several serverbased approaches exist such as CritLink [21] which works based on prefixed URLs or Dashnote which is, similar to Wikis, entirely deployed on web servers. Between those two solutions also hybrid approaches exist such as Annotea [14] which allows for storing the annotations locally or on an annotation server.

7 Conclusion

In this work, we have introduced the concept of parasitic and symbiotic applications capable of bringing Web 2.0 to any page of the World Wide Web. This was realized by implementing a proxy-based application platform. Our approach offers the opportunity to deploy static and dynamic applications provided by the platform owners as well as the deployment of user-based code.

For the implementation of the concept, UsaProxy served as a basis for inserting JavaScript code on-the-fly into each web page delivered from a web server to the client. This JavaScript code provides the basic functionality for inserting or editing the content of web pages. Furthermore, a HTTP proxy was extended to allow for XMLHttpRequests to a remote application server, thus avoiding the same origin policy of modern browsers. Hence, content can be dynamically loaded from or stored to the application/database server using AJAX technology.

As a proof-of-concept we presented two case studies. One focused on deploying a parasitic application supporting both static and dynamic elements in the form of an annotation tool. We presented challenges arising from dealing with arbitrary web pages and provided potential solutions either by complex client side mechanisms or by symbiotic deployment. Issues like scalability and extensibility still need further research.

Second, we presented UsaScript, a tool for deploying user-based scripts and APIs on web pages. We outlined how this approach can also be used among web site owners to cooperate with the application platform thus creating additional benefits for the user.

References

1. Anderson, K.M.: Integrating Open Hypermedia Systems with the World Wide Web. In: Hypertext 1997 (1997)
2. Atterer, R., Wnuk, M., Schmidt, A.: Knowing the User's Every Move - User Activity Tracking for Website Usability Evaluation and Implicit Interaction. In: WWW 2006 (2006)
3. Atterer, R., Schmidt, A., Wnuk, M.: A proxy-based infrastructure for web application sharing and remote collaboration on web pages. In: Baranauskas, C., Palanque, P., Abascal, J., Barbosa, S.D.J. (eds.) INTERACT 2007. LNCS, vol. 4662, pp. 74–87. Springer, Heidelberg (2007)
4. Barrett, R., Maglio, P.P., Kellem, D.C.: How to Personalize the Web. In: CHI 1997 (1997)
5. Bigham, J.P., Ladner, R.E.: Accessmonkey: a Collaborative Scripting Framework forWeb Users and Developers. In: W4a 2007 (2007)
6. Bolin, M., Webber, M., Rha, P., Wilson, T., Miller, R.C.: Automation and Customization of Rendered Web Pages. In: UIST 2005 (2005)
7. Bouvin, N.O.: Unifying Strategies for Web Augmenting. In: Hypertext 1999 (1999)
8. Brush, A.J., Bargeron, D., Gupta, A., Cadiz, J.J.: Robust Annotation Positioning in Digital Documents. In: CHI 2001 (2001)
9. Cadiz, J.J., Gupta, A., Grudin, J.: Using Web Annotations for Asynchronous Collaboration around Documents. In: CSCW 2000 (2000)
10. Carr, L.D., De Roure, W., Hall, W., Hill, G.: The Distributed Link Service: a Tool for Publishers, Authors and Readers. The Web Journal 1, 1 (1995)
11. Furuta, R., Shipman, F.M., Marshall, C.C., Brenner, D., Hsieh, H.: Hypertext Paths and the World-Wide Web: Experiences with Walden's Paths. In: Hypertext 1997 (1997)
12. Grønbæk, K., Sloth, L., Ørbæk, P.: Webvise: Browser and Proxy Support for Open Hypermedia Structuring Mechanisms on the WWW. In: WWW 1999 (1999)
13. Hall, W., Davis, H., Hutchings, G.: Rethinking Hypermedia: the Microcosm Approach. Kluwer Academic Publishers, Dordrecht (1996)
14. Kahan, J., Koivunen, M.-R.: Annotea: an Open RDF Infrastructure for Shared Web Annotations. In: WWW 2001 (2001)
15. Kistler, T., Marais, H.: WebL - a Programming Language for the Web. In: WWW 1998 (1998)
16. Krulwich, B.: Automating the Internet: Agents as User Surrogates. IEEE Internet Computing 1, 4 (1997)
17. Phelps, T.A., Wilensky, R.: Robust Intra-document Locations. University of California, Berkeley (2000), `http://www9.org/w9cdrom/312/312.html`
18. Röscheisen, M., Winograd, T., Paepcke, A.: Content Ratings and Other Third-Party Value-Added Information: Defining an Enabling Platform. Stanford University, Stanford (1995)
19. Shipman, F.M., Marshall, C.C.: Spatial Hypertext: an Alternative to Navigational and Semantic Links. ACM Comput. Surv. 31, 4 (1999)
20. Simpson, R.M.: Experiences withWeb Squirrel: my Life on the Information Farm. In: Hypertext 2001 (2001)
21. Yee, K.-P.: CritLink: Advanced Hyperlinks Enable Public Annotation on the Web, University of California, Berkeley (2002)

Are Ten Participants Enough for Evaluating Information Scent of Web Page Hyperlinks?

Christos Katsanos, Nikolaos Tselios, and Nikolaos Avouris

Human-Computer Interaction Group, Electrical and Computer Engineering Dept., University of Patras, GR-265 00 Rio Patras, Greece
{ckatsanos,nitse}@ece.upatras.gr, avouris@upatras.gr

Abstract. Information scent of hyperlinks, that is the user's assessment of semantic relevance of navigation options in a webpage, has been identified as a critical factor in Web navigation. An important question in this context is to identify the minimum number of participants required to measure reliably information scent. A two phase study was conducted in an attempt to provide an answer to this question. In the first phase, involving 101 participants, ratings produced by different size subsets of participants were compared to those of the whole set. In the second phase, the ratings of these different size subsets of participants where compared with measures of behavior of 54 participants, who performed the same information navigation tasks using a typical web browser. Results indicate that representative estimates of information scent can be obtained from 10 participants in both cases. This finding has important implications for future scent-related studies.

Keywords: Information scent, Web usability study, cost-benefit analysis.

1 Introduction

Recent models of user behavior while foraging for information in the Web have contributed to the better understanding of human-information interaction. A key concept in these models (e.g. SNIF-ACT, CoLiDeS, MESA - see [1] for a review) is *information scent*, defined as the user's assessment of semantic relevance of the provided navigation options. Recent studies rendered information scent as the most important factor in Web navigation [1], [2].

Various semantic similarity algorithms, such as LSA and PMI-IR, have been proposed as a computational model of information scent [3] and have been used in order to facilitate the task of measuring information scent [4], [5]. However, in certain cases, such as modeling users with considerable background knowledge and/or expertise, or assessing similarity of 'rare' or informal words, computational techniques may yield misleading results.

Therefore, often human raters are called to evaluate information scent [6], [7]. In a typical study, participants are presented with hyperlink options as well as the information goal and are asked to evaluate semantic similarity among them. A key question in this context is how many people to involve in such a study in order to obtain representative estimates of information scent. The current practice does not seem to follow a

T. Gross et al. (Eds.): INTERACT 2009, Part I, LNCS 5726, pp. 419–422, 2009.

clear pattern on this issue. For instance, Miller and Remington [6] used the assessments of three judges and Brumby and Howes [7] reported involvement of 13 participants, without discussing the quality of the results with respect to the number of raters.

A similar question has been asked in the context of general usability evaluation. As concluded by a variety of related studies, the required number of participants to unveil a specific percentage of usability errors is ruled by a cumulative function of the geometric distribution [8]. The question is of significant importance towards understanding quantitative aspects of human-information interaction on the Web.

In the study presented in this paper, we attempt to identify the number of required participants to evaluate information scent in a reliable way, using as reference the ratings of a large set of users first and objective user behavior measures in the second phase of the study. Such a finding could help both practitioners and researchers to manage the available resources in a more efficient way.

2 First Phase of the Study

In the first phase of the study we compared the ratings of different size groups of raters with the ratings produced by a large pool of raters, considered as reference case. The study involved 101 University students, 39 female, with a mean age of 22.2, who were asked to rate on a 1-5 scale the semantic relevance of all the links of a menu to the associated given goal (1=poor relevance, 5=high relevance). All eight menus consisted of eight links each and were selected from actual websites[1]. A total of 6464 ratings (=8 goals x 8 links x 101 raters) were gathered during this phase of the study.

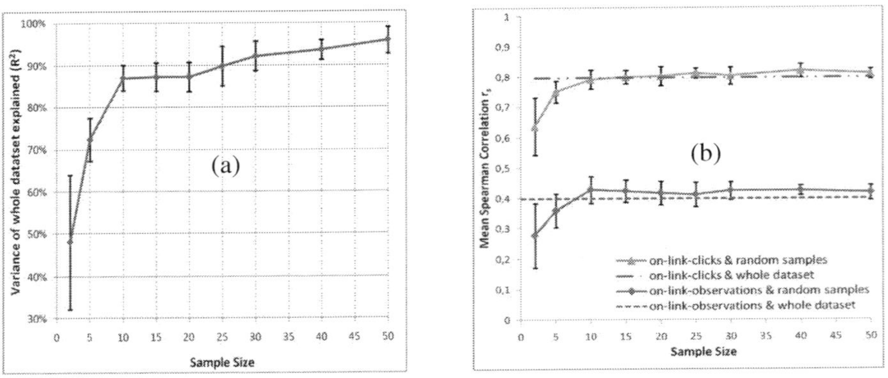

Fig. 1. (a) Total variance of 101 participants' scent-ratings explained as a function of sample size. (b) Mean spearman correlation between two measures of users' behavior (on-link-clicks, on-link-observations) and scent-ratings of random samples of raters. Note: Error bars represent standard deviation of the 10 random samples.

Then, subsets of various sizes were built and compared to the ratings of the whole group; an approach also used by Tullis and Wood [9 - page 223] who aimed at identifying the optimal number of users required for a card-sorting study. Ten subsets were

[1] Tasks and menus used can be found at http://hci.ece.upatras.gr/Katsanos_et_al_INT2009

randomly selected, of N raters each, for N=2, 5, 10, 15, 20, 25, 30, 40 and 50. Next, the average ratings of these subsets were compared to the ratings of the whole population of raters. The mean spearman correlation between the ratings of each sample size and the ratings of the 101 raters was calculated.

Fig. 1a presents the resulting total variance explained (R^2) as an increasing function of sample size. The error bars in the graph represent standard deviation of the values for the 10 random samples and were calculated as $(r_{MEAN} \pm r_{SD})^2$. As depicted in the graph, a sample size of 10 raters was found to explain 84-90% of the total variance of the ratings of all 101 participants. The lowest value observed for this sample size was 76% for the seventh goal, whereas the highest was 98% for the fifth goal[1]. After that point, there is a marginal gain in involving more participants. In specific, increasing to 15 or 20 participants does not have any impact and only when the raters are tripled the results get approximately 5% closer to the whole dataset. Thus, 10 raters appear to be a cost-effective solution to evaluate information scent without expense in the quality of results.

3 Second Phase of the Study

In the second phase, a new set of users was asked to perform the navigation tasks of the first phase using a typical Web browser. Fifty-four University students, 11 female, with a mean age of 24, all proficient in English, took part in this phase. First, users were presented with a goal-description screen. Next, they were presented with the associated menu and were asked to select a link as they would normally do. The presentation of the menus and the order of links were randomized to avoid serial order effects. An unobtrusive 17'' Tobii T60 eye tracker with minimum fixation duration set to 100ms was used to record users' eye movements. Two measures of users' behavior were gathered: a) *clicks on each link* and b) *observations on each link*. Observations were used instead of simple on-link fixations to avoid bias of higher fixations counts due to lengthier text descriptions [10].

Next, the ratings of the different size sets of raters of the first phase were correlated with these two measures of users' behavior, using mean spearman correlation. A non-parametric measure of association was used since the assumption of normality was violated for all variables. The question in this case was to identify the number of human raters that were enough to reach an acceptable rate of correlation with the two measures of users' behavior that were used as a reference.

Fig. 2b presents graphs of the resulting mean correlations. The dotted lines represent the mean correlation between measures of observed behavior and all participants' scent-ratings for the eight goals. This correlation coefficient is high for the on-link-clicks measure (r_s=0.80, $p<0.01$, one-tailed) and medium for the on-link-observations measure (r_s=0.40, ns). As depicted in Fig. 2b, 10 participants are enough to reach these values with 0.7% deviation for the on-link-clicks measure and 7.4% deviation for the on-link-observations measure. However, given the medium overall correlation between scent-ratings and on-link-observations found in this study, scent-ratings should be used only as a rough indicator of users' distribution of attention on the available navigation options.

4 Conclusions

The goal of this paper was to investigate the minimum number of participants required to representatively evaluate information scent. Analysis of the data collected in the reported study, suggest that 10 human raters can be enough to obtain representative results of users' link-selection behavior and distribution of attention on the available links. Involving more users increases the resources spent with marginal gain in the quality of results.

This is an important finding for both researchers designing future Web interaction studies, and practitioners evaluating the semantic appropriateness of hyperlinks in a webpage. Furthermore, it contributes to the overall debate on suitable number of users for a Web usability study. In addition, it was found that scent-ratings should be used only as a rough indicator of users' distribution of attention regardless of the number of raters involved, due to their medium overall correlation with on-link-observations (r_s=0.40, ns). In such cases, an eye-tracking study would be more suitable. Furthermore, it should be noted that if strong statistical inferences about the user population are required, then additional participants should be recruited.

Future work includes investigating the influence of task complexity on the optimal number of participants required, as well as investigating the presented finding in the context of highly specialized domains and/or varied user group composition [8].

References

1. Fu, W., Pirolli, P.: SNIF-ACT: a cognitive model of user navigation on the world wide web. Human-Computer Interaction 22(4), 355–412 (2007)
2. Spool, J., Perfetti, C., Brittan, D.: Design for the Scent of Information. UIE Fundamentals, User Interface Engineering (2004)
3. Kaur, I., Hornof, A.J.: A comparison of LSA, wordNet and PMI-IR for predicting user click behavior. In: Proceedings of CHI 2005, USA, pp. 51–60. ACM Press, New York (2005)
4. Blackmon, M., Kitajima, M., Polson, P.: Tool for accurately predicting website navigation problems, non-problems, problem severity, and effectiveness of repairs. In: Proceedings of CHI 2005, USA, pp. 31–40. ACM Press, New York (2005)
5. Katsanos, C., Tselios, N., Avouris, N.: InfoScent evaluator: a semi-automated tool to evaluate semantic appropriateness of hyperlinks in a web site. In: Proceedings of OZCHI, Sydney, Australia, pp. 373–376. ACM Press, New York (2006)
6. Miller, C.S., Remington, R.W.: Modeling information navigation: implications for information architecture. Human-Computer Interaction 19(3), 225–271 (2004)
7. Brumby, D., Howes, A.: Strategies for Guiding Interactive Search: An Empirical Investigation into the Consequences of Label Relevance for Assessment and Selection. Human-Computer Interaction 23(1), 1–46 (2008)
8. Caulton, D.A.: Relaxing the homogeneity assumption in usability testing. Behaviour & Information Technology 20(1), 1–7 (2001)
9. Tullis, T., Albert, W.: Measuring the User Experience: Collecting, Analyzing, and Presenting Usability Metrics. Morgan Kaufmann, San Francisco (2008)
10. Poole, A., Ball, L.J.: Eye Tracking in Human-Computer Interaction and Usability Research: Current Status and Future Prospects. In: Ghaoui, C. (ed.) Encyclopedia of Human Computer Interaction, pp. 211–219. Idea Group Reference (2006)

Navigational Consistency in Websites: What Does it Mean to Users?

Helen Petrie, George Papadofragkakis, Christopher Power, and David Swallow

Department of Computer Science, University of York, Heslington,
York YO10 5DD, United Kingdon
{helen.petrie,gp519,cpower,dswallow}@cs.york.ac.uk

Abstract. A study was conducted to investigate the effects of navigational inconsistencies in websites on users' perceptions and performance. Of four inconsistencies manipulated (position of navigational bar, order of elements in navigational bar, font type and size of elements), only the position of the bar had a substantial effect. However this affected both users' perception of their performance and their actual performance, in terms of the time spent on webpages. The mean time spent on the page with the inconsistently positioned navigational bar more than doubled and this effect persisted over subsequent pages. The methodology developed provides a useful way of investigating the effects of navigational inconsistency, an under-studied phenomenon.

Keywords: Website navigation, navigational consistency, website usability.

1 Introduction

Ever since we have had hypertext systems, people have been getting lost in them. The term "lost in hyperspace" was coined in the late 1980s [2] to describe this phenomenon, even before the advent of the World Wide Web. Many navigational aids have been proposed to users to assist in overcoming this problem, including breadcrumb trails [6, 13], site maps [1, 13] and tabs [13]. Nonetheless, users continue to get lost and feel disoriented, particularly on the Web.

In addition, numerous guidelines and design principles have been proposed to assist developers in creating websites that are easy to navigate [3, 4]. One such guideline is to use consistent navigation, which is of course simply a specific instantiation of the more general and widely cited principle of consistency in interface design [8, 10, 12]. But what do users actually notice in navigational consistency and what affects their performance? Surprisingly few empirical studies have been conducted on these questions. Studies have investigated the sense of "lostness" at a global level and created appropriate metrics [5, 9, 11] with interesting results, but less work has looked at the fine-grained detail of navigational consistency. Yet the few studies which have done so have produced surprising results. For example, Kalbach and Bosenick [7] found that users did not perform any more efficiently when the navigation was on the lefthand side of webpages, as recommended [13], than when they were on the righthand side of pages.

T. Gross et al. (Eds.): INTERACT 2009, Part I, LNCS 5726, pp. 423–427, 2009.

This study therefore set out to investigate both user perceptions and performance in relation to four aspects of navigational consistency on websites: position of the navigational bar on the webpage, order of elements in a navigational bar, size and font of navigational elements.

2 Method

Fourteen participants, nine men and five women were recruited from students at the University of York. Their mean age was 20.9 years (range: 19 to 25). They were all experienced Web users, with a mean of 8.3 years of experience (range: 3 to 11). They spent on average 35.1 hours a week using the Web (range: 10 to 70).

We have developed a website specifically to enable us conduct studies of navigation on websites. It is the website for a fictional university computer science department, the University of North Yorkshire. The website contains information about four MSc courses, each of which had one distinct subtree within the website's information architecture with no cross-linking between them. This means that when participants undertake a task about one MSc, a navigational inconsistency can be introduced and it is highly likely they will all encounter it after the same number of pages and will then continue to the task conclusion with the same number of pages with the new navigational style (data from participants who deviate from the expected path can be removed from analyses if necessary).

The navigational inconsistencies investigated in this study were:

- Position of navigational bar: changed from lefthand to righthand side of page;
- Order of elements in the navigational bar: the order of the 5 elements was altered;
- Font size: changed from 10 pt to 12pt;
- Font type: changed from sans serif (Arial) to serif (Times Roman).

10 and 12 point were chosen for font sizes, as although the difference in size is not great, an informal survey of 100 websites showed that these are the two most commonly used default font sizes. Although much is presented in Times Roman, there is a long running discussion about the readability of serif versus sans serif fonts, and this distinction is quite clear to readers, so a serif and a sans serif font were used.

A Windows XP Professional PC was used to conduct the study. Screen resolution was set at 1024 x 768, and no horizontal scrolling was necessary in accessing the study website. Participants were given the choice between using Internet Explorer 6.0.2900 and Mozilla Firefox 3.0.8, as it was known that the student population at York favour these two browsers. Thus any difficulties in navigation would not be attributable to lack of familiarity with the browser. Four chose Explorer and 10 chose Firefox. There was no difference in the website's appearance between the two browser configurations, so this choice did not affect the final results. Morae software[1] was used to record participants' interaction with the website.

---

[1] Techsmith. Morae customer experience software. Available at: www.techsmith.com/morae.asp

Participants undertook ten tasks, eight of which led the participant through a sequence of pages that introduced one navigational inconsistency. The remaining two tasks were control tasks and they led participants through a sequence of pages with no inconsistency, that is a consistent sequence of pages.

After each task the participant answered the following question: Did you notice any change in the navigation bars throughout this task? (answer yes or no). If they answered yes, they were asked two further questions: What was/were the change(s)? Did the change(s) affect your performance during the task? (on a scale from 1 = not at all to 5 = very much)

No feedback was given to the participant about the navigational (in)consistencies and the accuracy of their perceptions after each task. After all the tasks were completed, the participants were debriefed and were shown the inconsistencies.

3 Results

The extent to which participant noticed the navigational inconsistencies was analysed. The change in the position of the navigational bar was noticed on most occasions (85.7%), the change in font size of navigational elements was noticed on about half the occasions (42.9%) and the change in font type and the order of navigational elements was noticed on only about 20% of instances (21.4% in both cases). A Cochran's Q test showed that these percentages were significantly different from each other (test conducted on mean % per participant per inconsistency type, Cochran's Q $= 44.1$, df $= 3$, $p < 0.000$).

For those participants who noticed a navigational inconsistency, their perception of how it affected them was analysed, using their answers on the Lickert scale (1 = not at all to 5 = very much). The mean rating for the perception of the position inconsistency was 2.38, for the order and font type inconsistency it was 1.67 and for the font size inconsistency it was 1.38. Thus none of the mean ratings were higher than the midpoint on the rating scale.

To investigate how the inconsistencies affected participants' performance, the times they spent on the pages before the inconsistency (PagesB), the page where the inconsistency appeared (PageI) and the pages after the inconsistency (PagesA) were analysed. A one way repeated measures ANOVA was conducted on the mean time (in seconds) spent on the web pages with three variables: (1) the type of inconsistency, (2) the pages before/on/after the inconsistency, and (3) the task (first or second task for a particular inconsistency). This analysis found that there was a significant difference between the mean ratings for the five inconsistency conditions (F = 5.86, df = 4,

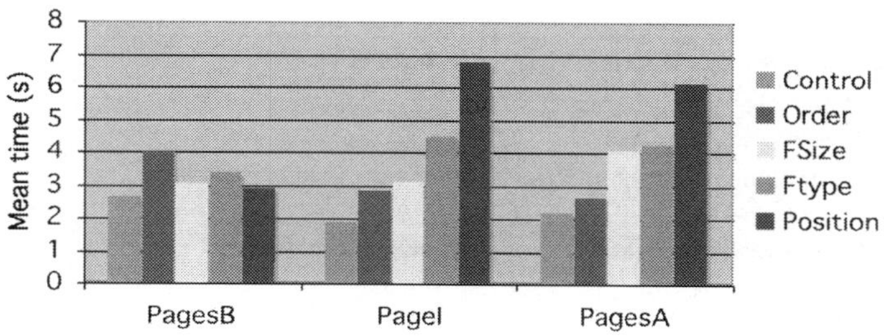

Fig. 1. Mean time on page for different navigational inconsistencies

52, $p < 0.03$). There was also a significant difference between the page conditions ($F = 10.44$, df = 2, 26, $p < 0.005$). There was also a significant interaction between inconsistency type and page type ($F= 4.26$, df = 8, 104, $p < 0.05$). From Fig 1, it can be seen that for the position inconsistency, the time spent on the page where the inconsistency occurs is much longer, and this increased time persists to subsequent pages.

4 Discussion and Conclusions

This study found that of the navigational inconsistencies investigated, only the position of the navigational bar had any noticeable influence, but that this affected both participants' perception and their performance. The effect on performance was very noticeable, with time spent on the page with the inconsistency more than doubling, and that effect persisting over subsequent pages. The persistence of the effect is interesting: it may be that once a position inconsistency occurs, web users become less confident about the layout of the navigation, and spend more time scanning the page when they land on this. We will follow up this possibility with a study of navigational inconsistencies that uses eye tracking to study the pattern of page scanning. We believe the methodology developed in this study will be useful for investigating the perception and performance implications of navigational inconsistencies, as well as the effectiveness of navigational aids such as breadcrumb trails. We are already undertaking a further study that investigates a larger range of navigational inconsistencies and will follow this up with an investigation of breadcrumb trails.

References

1. Billingsley, P.A.: Navigation through hierarchical menu structures: Does it help to have a map? In: Proc. Human Factors and Ergonomics Society Annual Meeting, pp. 103–107 (1982)
2. Edwards, Hardman: Lost in hyperspace: cognitive mapping and navigation in a hypertext environment. In: McAleese, R. (ed.) Hypertext: theory into practice. Intellect Books, Exeter (1989)
3. Farkas, D.K., Farkas, J.B.: Guidelines for designing web navigation. Technical Communication 47(3), 341–358 (2000)
4. Fleming, J.: Web navigation: designing the user experience. O'Reilly, Sebastopol (1998)
5. Gwizdka, J., Spence, I.: Implicit measures of lostness and success in web navigation. Interacting with Computers 19(3), 357–369 (2007)
6. Instone, K.: Location, path and attribute breadcrumbs. In: 3rd Annual Information Architecture Summit, Baltimore, March 16-17 (2002), `http://instone.org/breadcrumbs`
7. Kalbach, J., Bosenick, T.: Web page layout: a comparison between left- and right-justified site navigation menus. Journal of Digital Information 4(1) (2003), `http://jodi.tamu.edu/Articles/v04/i01/Kalbach/`
8. Nielsen, J.: Heuristic evaluation. In: Nielsen, J., Mack, R.L. (eds.) Usability Inspection Methods. John Wiley & Sons, New York (1994)
9. Otter, M., Johnson, H.: Lost in hyperspace: metrics and mental models. Interacting with Computers 13(1), 1–40 (2000)

10. Shneiderman, B.: Designing the user interface: Strategies for effective human-computer interaction, 3rd edn. Addison-Wesley Publishing, Reading (1998)
11. Smith, P.A.: Towards a practical measure of hypertext usability. Interacting with Computers 8(4), 365–381 (1996)
12. Tognazzini, B.: First principles of interaction design, `http://www.asktog.com/basics/firstPrinciples.html`
13. U.S. Department of Health and Human Services. Research-based web design and usability guidelines (2006), `http://www.usability.gov/pdfs/guidelines.html#1`

CloudMonster: Support Flexible Browsing and Searching within Music Collections

Ya-Xi Chen, Matthias Hoyer, and Andreas Butz

Media Informatics, University of Munich
Amalienstr. 17, 80333 Munich, Germany
yaxi.chen@ifi.lmu.de, matthias.hoyer@campus.lmu.de,
andreas.butz@ifi.lmu.de

Abstract. Studies in the field of Music Information Retrieval (MIR) have shown that users would like to use multiple criteria simultaneously and additional criteria besides the widely used metadata of artist, album and song. We present our prototype named CloudMonster, which supports flexible browsing and searching within music collections using multiple criteria. In a preliminary evaluation the added flexibility for browsing and searching was highly appreciated and we received valuable suggestions for future research.

1 Motivation and Formative Study

For Music Information Retrieval (MIR), there are additional criteria besides the widely used artist, album and song. These criteria, for example, similarity, mood and social activities, are less common but nonetheless desired [1]. Cunningham et al. [2] suggested that functionalities beyond explicit searching should be offered, to allow users to find unexpected but acceptable results. Some researchers have already built visualizations based on non-standard criteria, such as similarity [3] and mood [4].

In order to learn more about the actual criteria people wish to use, we conducted a formative study. We recruited 36 college students, 25 male and 11 female, with an average age of 22 years and investigated their current browsing behavior. From this, we learned that the most desired criteria for organization seem to be genre, year and cover art, while for playlist generation, they are gender, tempo, instrument and listening history. By combining the results of our survey with existing research, we selected the set of most desired criteria and integrated them into a prototype named CloudMonster for browsing and searching within music collections.

2 CloudMonster

CloudMonster is implemented based on Prefuse (http://www.prefuse.org/). The basic metadata, such as genre, duration, released time and cover art are extracted from ID3Tags. The content-based similarity is derived from low level features extracted with jAudio (http://jmir.sourceforge.net/jAudio.html). Contextual information such as artist popularity and similarity are derived from Last.fm (http://www.last.fm).

T. Gross et al. (Eds.): INTERACT 2009, Part I, LNCS 5726, pp. 428–431, 2009.

Figure 1 shows the CloudMonster interface, in which songs are represented as either nodes or cover art. Upon mouse-hover, more song detail is shown (see figure 3(b)). The whole collection is displayed with genre-, popularity- and similarity-based *initial views*. Five *color coding schemes* are provided: for ordinal parameters, each color presents one category such as artist, genre and gender and for quantitative parameters such as popularity and year, the transparency represents the popularity or recency.

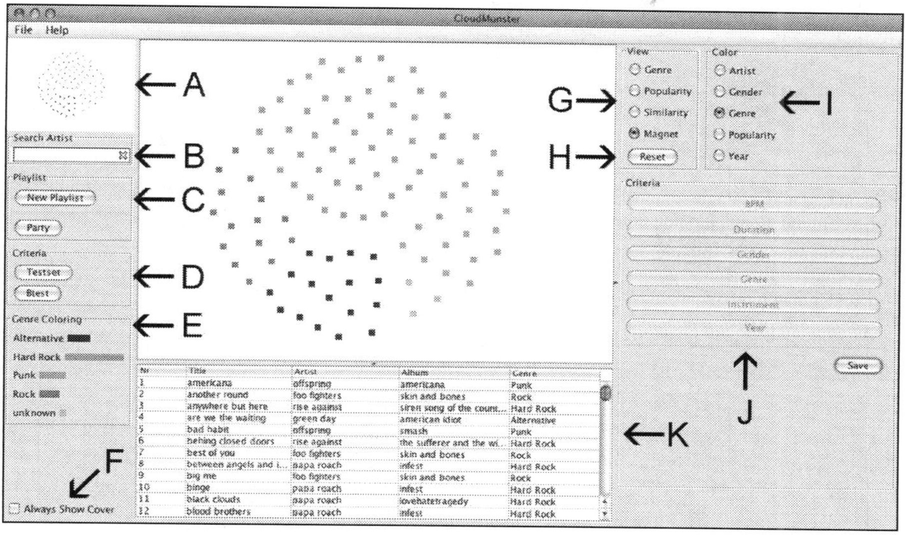

Fig. 1. CloudMonster with genre-based view and genre color coding. (A) Overview. (B) Keyword-based searching. (C) Saved playlist. (D) Saved criteria. (E) Genre histogram. (F) Cover art. (G) Initial views. (H) Reset button. (I) Color scheme. (J) Criteria list. (K) Song list.

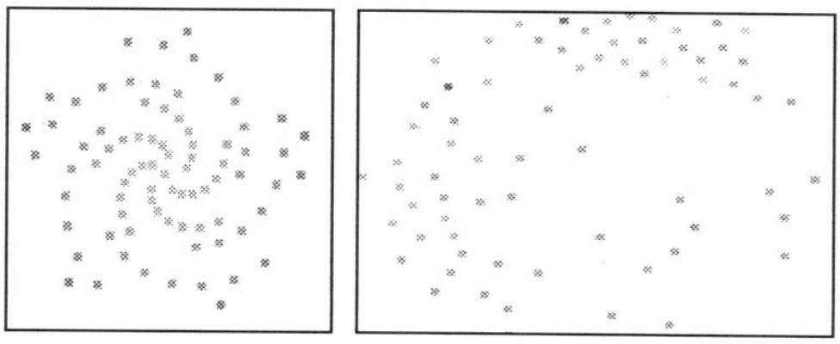

Fig. 2. (a) Popularity-based view with popularity color coding. (b) Similarity-based view with artist color coding.

Based on the Dust&Magnet metaphor[5], each criterion works as a *magnet* and attracts matching songs while repelling differing ones. The user can create or delete a magnet by double clicking a criterion in the criteria list. The magnet value can be set in the criteria list and its strength is presented as its size, which can be adjusted by mouse wheel. The user can then adjust the magnet position freely and the songs will move accordingly. For example, three magnets were chosen in figure 3(a): BPM, gender and genre. The values were set as 136-160, female and R&B. These magnets were place in a triangle. The matching songs were attracted in the center and shaped in a circle. The current configuration and visualization can be saved for future reuse. Similarly, one *song* can serve as an *example* and attract similar songs (see figure 3(b)). The weights for content- and context- similarity can be adjusted by a weight slider.

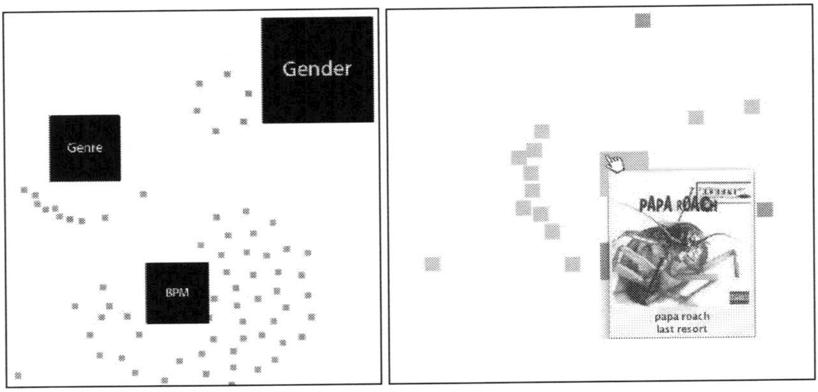

Fig. 3. (a) Multiple-magnets-based search. (b) Example-based search.

The user can *generate a playlist* by simply drawing a rectangle in the graph view. All the songs inside will then be included in a playlist, which can be saved. Once a saved playlist is chosen, the graphic for the moment this playlist was created will be re-visualized, which also improves the system reproducibility and speeds up learning.

3 Preliminary Evaluation

We recruited 12 users at (delete for blind review), 7 female and 5 male with an average age of 24 years, who regularly use music player software. The evaluation was conducted with the participants' own music collections. After a brief tutorial and freely playing around, participants were asked to conduct 5 tasks concerning browsing, searching and playlist generation, and then filled out a post-questionnaire.

The tasks were: Locate some personal favorite songs; from these, filter out faster songs; search for the songs similar to an example song; search for songs of the favorite genre and released in the same year; generate a playlist for a party.

Post-questionnaire: After completing the tasks, the participants were asked to score the initial views and color coding schemes (1 for not useful at all and 10 for very useful). The average scores for genre-, popularity- and similarity-based views were 8.75, 8.23 and 7.75. For the color coding schemes, the average scores for genre, popularity, gender, artist and year were 8.25, 8.16, 8, 7.8 and 7.125. The average score for the overall impression was 8.0. For helpfulness, enjoyments, feeling of control and understandability the average scores were 8.75, 8.5, 8, 8, and 7.5.

Results and implications: In task 1, all the participants conducted a keyword-based search. In task 2, they firstly conducted keyword-based search for the artist, and then used a BPM-magnet to attract songs with higher BPM value. The usage of keyword-based search illustrated its advantages with large collections. In task 3, the participants firstly chose the similarity-based view, and then chose one example song from the song list. This song was highlighted as an example in the graph and similar songs were attracted automatically. In task 4, the participants used the genre- and year-magnets. Without being prompted, all of them were able to make the right judgment of matching songs, which implied the understandability of the magnet metaphor. In task 5, the most frequently used criteria were BPM, genre, popularity and instrument. Generally positive feedback was received in the post-questionnaire. Although all the participants claimed that the magnet metaphor was easy to understand, the average score for the overall understandability was lower because of the attribute inconsistency in the views, color coding schemes and criteria list.

4 Conclusion and Future Work

In this paper we present CloudMonster, which supports flexible browsing and searching within music collections. CloudMonster received positive feedback in an initial evaluation and its multiple search options were highly appreciated. CloudMonster can be easily extended for example for browsing in large online music dataset or generalized for broad multi-criteria search. In our future work, we will address the problems revealed in the evaluation, for example, improve the systems consistency, allow duplicate magnets and multiple example songs, and enhance the histogram for color coding. Then we will conduct a formal user study concerning systems scalability, data reliability and look in detail at the behavior differences between different visualizations, such as list and graph.

Acknowledgement

This research was funded by the China Scholarship Council (CSC) and by the German state of Bavaria. We would like to thank Eric Rademacher and Ben Blaha for their dedication in the initial design and thank the participants of our user study.

References

1. Vignoli, F.: Digital Music Interaction concepts: a user study. In: Proc. of the 5th International Conference on Music Information Retrieval. ISMIR 2004, Barcelona, Spain (2004)
2. Cunningham, S., Reeves, N., Britland, M.: An Ethnographic Study of Music Information Seeking: Implications for the Design of a Music Digital Library. In: Proc. of ACM/IEEE joint conference on Digital libraries. JCDL 2003, Houston, TX, USA (2003)
3. Pampalk, E.: Islands of Music: Analysis, Organization, and Visualization of Music Archives. Journal of the Austrian Soc. for Artificial Intelligence (2003)
4. Gulik, R., van Vignoli, F.: Visual Playlist Generation on the Artist Map. In: Proc. of the 6th International Conference on Music Information Retrieval. ISMIR 2005, London, UK (2002)
5. Yi, J.S., Melton, R., Stasko, J., Jacko, J.: Dust & Magnet: multivariate information visualization using a magnet metaphor. In: Proc. of the international conference on Information Visualization. IV 2005, London, UK (2005)

Combinable Tabs: An Interactive Method of Information Comparison Using a Combinable Tabbed Document Interface

Gonglue Jiang[1], Chen Zhao[2], Matthew R. Scott[2], and Fang Zou[2]

[1] Zhejiang University, No.38, Zheda Road, Hangzhou, 10027, China
jianggonglue@hotmail.com
[2] Microsoft Research Asia
49, Zhichun Road, Haidian District, Beijing 100190, China
{chzha,mrscott,v-fzou}@microsoft.com

Abstract. The Tabbed Document Interface ("TDI") of today's web browsers is widely considered to be a usability improvement over the previously predominate Single Document Interface ("SDI"). TDI styled interfaces however, especially in mashups or other overlays of different information sets, suffer from a key usability limitation: they cannot show two or more tabbed documents simultaneously. Users are left with the task of quickly switching between tabs when trying to visually compare content. Our contribution is centered on intuitively enabling the comparison of tabbed content via what we coined a Combinable Tabbed Document Interface ("CTDI"). This interface extends TDI to allow tabs to be dragged and dropped onto one another to form a "master tab" whose data page renders a "side by side" view of its combined "sub tabs". The combined view will revert to the previous form when closing the master tab. It's a novel solution for those websites that needs to compare information, such as e-commerce sites, online dictionaries, etc. To test the effectiveness of CTDI, we developed an online dictionary called "Engkoo" which puts the concept to practice.

Keywords: Information comparison, TDI, CTDI, AIC, tabs, combinable tabs.

1 Introduction

With so much information available through the internet, one of the major issues in computing today is designing a browsing user interface that not only models page style data but also makes the experience of navigating and interacting with the data feel natural. We went about looking at this issue by focusing on one major scenario common on the internet today: information comparison[1]. From our user studies, we found the majority of people go about finding their target information by sorting through numerous data by a process of identification and comparison. However, users are required to open a new page and must switch back and forth between the original pages if they want to compare, which is cumbersome to many users because of the repetitive action and sizable number of clicks. Our design practice is based on a project whose aim was to build a breakthrough online English-Chinese dictionary website for Chinese people called Engkoo.

T. Gross et al. (Eds.): INTERACT 2009, Part I, LNCS 5726, pp. 432–435, 2009.

2 Process

We ran a user interview that contains 8 participants who frequently use online dictionary. Besides open questions, participants were also asked to show their "using" mode of online dictionary as they usually do and the procedure was tracked and recorded. A key finding from the interview, which is the underpinning of our Combinable Tabs work, can be coined "Appropriate Information Comparison" (AIC), as Figure1 shows. The AIC pattern was found when users needed to look up an English translation for a Chinese word. We observed the participants using the leading English-Chinese online dictionaries in Chinese market, Dict.cn, Youdao.com, and Iciba.com. For nearly all searched terms in these dictionaries, the results are multiple translations. We observed AIC when the participants copied and pasted the resulting translations, one by one, into the search box to execute further reverse dictionary look ups to verify their comprehension of the definitions and then switch back quickly between the tabs of the browser to compare the results of other definitions to find the most suitable one for their task, as Figure 1 shows. This user behavior pattern triggered us to think about how to support it in a more efficient way.

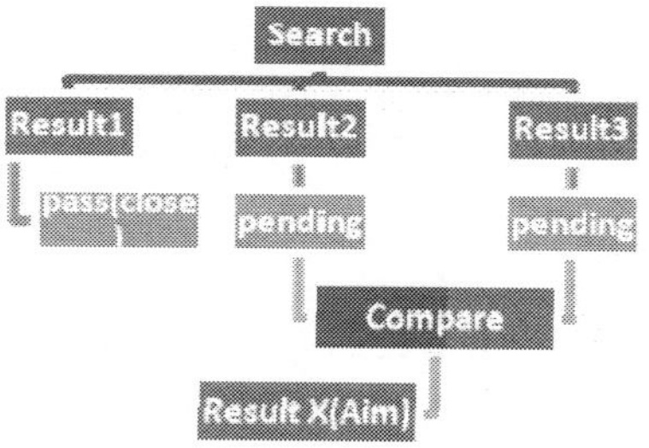

Fig. 1. AIC Model

2.1 Engkoo Prototype 1

We found that the users' requirement for comparison nearly always occurs when they search for synonyms or related words. The key intuition to prototype 1 is that these queries are always in sequential order. Therefore, our approach to enabling the entry point for comparison was to present the option for "compare" upon a subsequent search. The interface design was to enable the visibility of a compare button adjacent to the search button if another query is executed in the same session, as Figure 2 shows. When the compare button was clicked, the compare mode becomes activated, which presents a split view containing the definition results for the active query and the preceding query. Users can still type in new queries. When a new query typed and the compare button executed, it will be compared with the previous one, and the first one will be popped off. It is like a word comparison flow. The limitations with this approach are that it can't be used to compare non adjacent queries and also entering compare mode in this way isn't very intuitive.

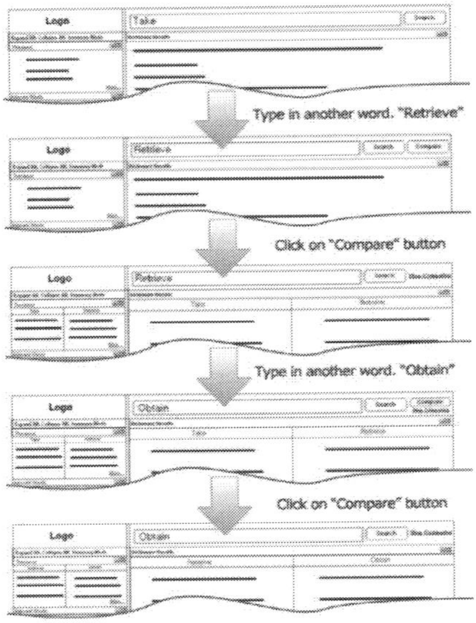

Fig. 2. Prototype 1

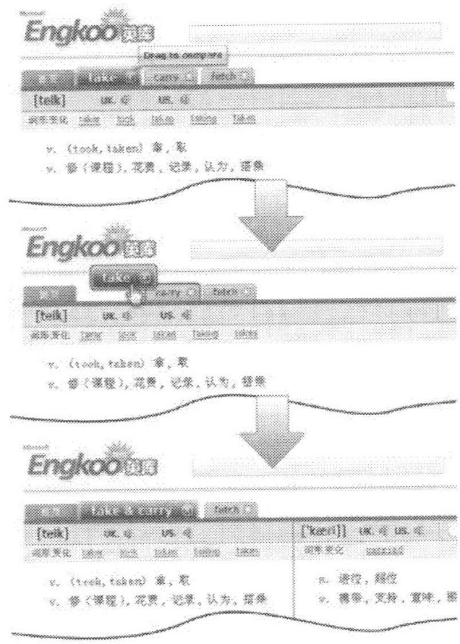

Fig. 3. Prototype 2

2.2 Engkoo Prototype 2

We brought the concept of a Tabbed Document Interface into our online dictionary design[2]. In our improved prototype 2, as Figure 3 shows, we innovated on the concept in an intuitive way by creating a Combinable Tabbed Document Interface which allows tabs to be dragged and dropped onto one another to form a *master tab* whose data page renders a side by side view of its combined *sub tabs*. When users click on an English translation to see the details (the same action as typing in a new query), a new tab is created. All the information of each tab, including definition, sample sentence, synonym, etc, is stored in the cache. Therefore, to the user, switching between tabs is an instantaneous operation. By just making the webpage TDI enabled – it would still carry all the same comparison usability problems generally associated with such an interface model. Our novel extension, CTDI, overcomes those usability problems by providing an intuitive method to enter into a comparison mode, which clearly shows the state is now in a compare mode, and allow for easy visual consumption of the information. To exit the comparison mode, users intuitively close the master tab – and the sub tabs will be released into their previous state. One key benefit of this approach that it allows comparison of any two queries executed, not just the current and preceding ones as in prototype 1.

3 Evaluation and Findings

For the evaluation, we design a task compared between our design and Iciba.com (#1 market leader) as competitor. The task followed AIC process-(1)Search Chinese word "拿" in Engkoo.com and iCiba.com. (2)Explore the details of three translations and compare three of them at one time, such as "Take vs. Catch vs. Carry". (3)We recorded the "number of new pages" and "clicks" as a measurement of the usability [3]. The result shows that Engkoo.com has a obvious advantage in this task-"number of new pages":Engkoo(0), iCiba(3); "clicks":Engkoo(8),iCiba(17). Engkoo performs more effective and usable in the AIC process compared to iCiba-the market leader.

To design this new kind of interface for solving the AIC problem, this concept could be extended to a further pattern: internet search. Such a domain is analogous to the usability problems found in dictionary lookup because there is usually more than one result from a search query. Users click on the resulting hyperlinks that may or may not match the user's intended search[4]. Modern implementations of web browsers have partially made this task less arduous by implementing TDI; however the issue of not being able to simultaneously view the contents of multiple resulting web page documents is a usability inhibitor. A CTDI approach provides a solution to this problem while maintaining the benefits of a TDI interface.

4 Conclusion and Future Work

We have designed a novel concept to mitigate the AIC pattern by comparing information using CTDI. There is no need to have a "compare mode view" button or open another page for compare. All the action is executed in an intuitive way; drag to combine and close to end. To demonstrate this design we built a website prototype called Engkoo, which is publically accessible at http://www.engkoo.com.

In future work, we will explore the possibility of extending CTDI to all users to open multiple tabs at one time. A powerful aspect of this design is that users can combine N tabs together for comparison. That is, they can continually drop tabs into the master tab to compare further, which continually subdivides the visual area, and if necessary a horizontal bar is enabled to scroll if data is pushed off-screen.

References

1. Baeza, R., Ribeiro, B.: Modern Information Retrieval. Practical Comparison, 214–215
2. Maximilian, V., Carsten, S., Vassil, G., Michal, S.: Relevance and Impact of Tabbed Browsing Behavior on Web Usage Mining. In: WI 2006. IEEE Computer Society Press, Los Alamitos (2006)
3. Hornbæk, K.: Current practice in measuring usability: Challenges to usability studies and research. International Journal of Human-Computer Studies 64, 79–102 (2006)
4. Jan, C.W.: Single-source indexing. In: SIGDOC 2001. ACM Press, New York (2001)

Web User Modeling via Negotiating Information Foraging Agent

Xuehong Tao[1], Yin-Leng Theng[1], and Terence Ting[2]

[1] Wee Kim Wee School of Communication and Information
[2] School of Mechanical and Aerospace Engineering
Nanyang Technological University, 50 Nanyang Avenue, Singapore 639798
{exhtao,tyltheng}@ntu.edu.sg, ekting@singnet.com.sg

Abstract. Information foraging theory lays a good foundation for web user modeling. However, the existing user modeling methods mainly focus on fixed information needs. In the real world, a user's information goal often evolves, and information foraging is a negotiation process between the user and the system. In this paper, we proposed an agent based approach that modeled the dynamic information seeking process of information foragers.

Keywords: Information foraging, information scent, information retrieval, user modeling, software agent.

1 Introduction

Usability evaluation is important in the software development lifecycle. However, it is usually difficult to afford a large number of real users to participate in the usability studies. Using software tools to simulate real users' behavior and therefore to conduct automated usability evaluation is a practical solution. There are some tools that based on information foraging theory for web usability evaluation, such as SNIF-ACT [1] and WUFIS [2]. They modeled web users' navigation from page to page searching for information with fixed information goals. However, a user's information goal may change based on what is learned during the seeking process. He/she may adapt to what the system has if the original information goal is not reached. The goal evolvement and the adaptation/negotiation process between searchers and systems have not been well addressed in the existing models.

This paper proposes an agent based web user model. The model distinguishes itself from the existing models in that it situated information goal in context and modeled the goal evolvement and the negotiation process of information seeking.

2 Information Foraging

Information foraging theory [3] is a foundation theory of web navigation. On the web, users typically forage for information by navigating from page to page along web links. The content of pages associated with these links is usually presented to the user by some snippets of text or graphic. Foragers use these proximal cues (snippets,

T. Gross et al. (Eds.): INTERACT 2009, Part I, LNCS 5726, pp. 436–439, 2009.

graphics) to assess the distal content (page pointed by the link). Information scent is a subjective perception of the value and cost of information sources obtained from proximal cues, such as web links, or icons representing the content sources [2]. The goal of the information forager is to use proximal information scent cues (eg. a web link) to predict the utility of distal sources of content (i.e. the web page associated with a web link), and to choose the links having the maximum expected utility [1]. Three important aspects of information foraging have not been well addressed in the existing web user modeling literature:

1) The goal of information foraging evolves. According to the berrypicking information seeking model [4], in real-life web search, users may begin with one feature of a broader topic, or a relevant reference, and move through a variety of sources. Each new piece of information encountered can offer new ideas and directions to follow, hence a new conception of query. The search goal evolves.

2) Information foraging is situated in context. Information foraging is usually a task embedded in the context of other tasks. Its value and cost structure is consequently defined in relation to the embedding task and often changes dynamically over time [5]. Such an embedding task can be choosing a good graduate school, developing a financial plan, or writing a scientific paper.

3) Information foraging is a negotiation process between the searcher and the system [6]. It is a trade-off between the value of information gained and the cost of performing a task to find the information. Therefore, foraging refers to the variety of strategies seekers exhibit in their quest for information and how humans adapt to their environments on a situational basis.

3 Negotiating Information Foraging Agent (NIF-Agent)

Software agents are autonomous entities that work towards their goals. They are suitable to work as representatives of human users. This section proposes a negotiating information foraging agent (NIF Agent) to simulate web information foragers. The NIF agent is able to model the goal evolvement, goal's context and the negotiation process of information foraging.

- **NIF Agent Knowledge Model**

Users may have different level of search goals. There can be four broad categories of goals: long term goal, leading search goal, current search goal and interactive intention [7]. For a specific search, higher level search goals may have different lower level options (sub goals). For example, to find out "why the baby is crying", the user may have a few search options in mind, such as "ear infection" or "infant colic". Lower level goals may further have next level of options. Different levels of goals form a hierarchical structure. The goals and their relationships form the knowledge base of a NIF agent, and it can be defined as a directed graph KB= <V, E>, where $V = \{ v_i \mid i = 1, 2, \ldots n. \}$, it is a set of all search goals $E = \{(v_i, v_j) \mid v_i$ is the higher level goal of $v_j \}$, it is a set of goal relationships, v_i is termed as father of v_j, v_j is termed as son of v_i.

- **Proximal Scent Matrix**

The scent of information comes from the linguistic relationships between words expressing an information need and words contained in links to web pages. People are more likely to select the link on a page that appears to have the highest probability of leading them to the page best matching their information need.

The proximal scent of a link is calculated as a degree of similarity between the proximal cues and the information need. Proximal Scent Matrix PS' and PS can be computed based on WUFIS (Web User Flow by Information Scent) algorithm [2, 8] which calculates the similarity based on the weight of word importance. Each PS'(i,j) describes the similarity degree between the proximal cues of a link (link from page j to page i) and the information need. Matrix PS is obtained by normalizing the PS' matrix so that each of the columns sums to 1. Each entry in PS(i,j) specifies the probability of a user flowing down the link from page j to page i.

- **Automation of Information Foraging**

Information goal evolves and is embedded in certain context. The knowledge base of NIF agent models the context. For an information goal (a node in KB), its higher level goals is the search purpose and sibling goals are other search options. When a user is not able to achieve a search goal, he/she may change to other options (sibling goals) or a more general goal (father goal). For example, for the purpose of finding out "why my baby is crying, and always draw up his knees against his abdomens", the user may search for the possible options, from "ear infection" to "rashes". He/she may also shift to a more general search about "crying baby". The shifting of goals models the dynamic evolvement of the information need.

A user might bring some initial information needs to start the foraging. However, the system may not be able to satisfy the user's needs exactly. Other information is still acceptable to the user if it has considerably strong information scent (satisfying certain threshold) to the user. This is the negotiation nature of information foraging. As in the "crying baby" example, if the user hasn't found the perfect explanation of the baby's situation, a link "infant colic" with high information scent may also catch his/her attention. In this case, "infant colic" is actually the most likely answer.

Algorithm *Forage* and *Find* is provided below. Algorithm *Forage* automates the information foraging processes with evolving goals, and the algorithm *Find* is a sub function that forages for a fixed information goal. In the algorithm, v.InfoNeed, v.father/v.son and v.visited are used to refer to the information need vector of goal v, the super/sub goal of v and whether v is processed respectively.

Algorithm. Forage ()
For all $v \in$ V in KB, v.visited = false
CurrentPage = n_1, add n_1 to the end of *PageLog //PageLog records the history*
v = *StartNode //Suppose the search starts from a goal StartNode*$\in$*V*
While ($v \neq \Phi$)
{ If Find(v.*InfoNeed*)= true Return true
Else
v.*visited* = true, v = v.*father*
if ($v \neq \Phi$) *// change goal to the most detailed level of other relevant goals*
while (exist v.*son* $\neq \Phi$ and v.*son.visited* = false) v = v.son
} Return false
End Forage.

Algorithm. Find (InformationNeed) *//forage for a fixed information need*
Step = 0, Build matrix PS' and PS based on *InformationNeed*
While (*Step* < *MaxSteps*) *// give up after a certain number of steps*
{ Randomly generate *NextPage* based on the probability, i.e. the value of
PS[1, *CurrentPage*], PS[2, *CurrentPage*],... ,PS[*n*, *CurrentPage*]
Put *NextPage* at the end of *PageLog*, *Step=Step*+1
If (PS'(*NextPage, CurrentPage*) $\geq \theta$) *//θ is the user satisfaction threshold*
CurrentPage = *NextPage*, Return true
// suppose the link cues are meaningful, i.e. if the link cue is similar with the
// user need, the page pointed by the link is also similar to the user need
Else *CurrentPage* = *NextPage //flow to the next page and continue foraging*
} Return false
End Find.

4 Conclusion and Future Works

The NIF agent we proposed models the exploratory search activity [9]. The model distinguishes from the existing models in that it models the evolvement of information need and the negotiation process of information seeking. Future works include the implementation of a NIF agent tool and evaluation of its effectiveness.

References

1. Pirolli, P.L., Fu, W., Chi, E.H., Farahat, A.: Information scent and Web navigation: theory, models and automated usability evaluation. The Next Wave: NSA's Review of Emerging Technologies 15(2), 5–12 (2006)
2. Chi, E.H., Pirolli, P., Chen, K., Pitkow, J.: Using information scent to model user information needs and actions on the Web. In: Proceedings of the SIGCHI conference on Human factors in computing systems, Seattle, USA, pp. 490–497 (2001)
3. Pirolli, P., Card, S.K.: Information foraging. Psychological review 106(4), 643–675 (1999)
4. Bates, M.J.: The design of browsing and berrypicking techniques for the online search interface. Online Review 13, 407–424 (1989)
5. Pirolli, P., Card, S.: Information foraging in information access environments. In: Proceedings of the SIGCHI conference on Human factors in computing systems, pp. 51–58 (1995)
6. Kalbach, J.: Designing for Information Foragers: A Behavioral Model for Information Seeking on the World Wide Web. Internetworking ITG Newsletter (3.3) (2000), `http://www.internettg.org/newsletter/dec00/article_information_foragers.html`
7. Xie, H.: Shifts of interactive intentions and information seeking strategies in interactive information retrieval. Journal of the Smerican Society for Information Science 51, 841–857 (2000)
8. Lawrance, J., Bellamy, R., Burnett, M., Rector, K.: Using information scent to model the dynamic foraging behavior of programmers in maintenance tasks. In: Proceeding of the twenty-sixth annual SIGCHI conference on Human factors in computing systems, Florence, Italy, pp. 1323–1332 (2008)
9. White, R.W., Drucker, S.M., Marchionini, G., Hearst, M., Schraefel, M.C.: Exploratory search and HCI: designing and evaluating interfaces to support exploratory search interaction. In: CHI 2007 extended abstracts on Human factors in computing systems, April 2007, San Jose, USA (2007)

Distinguishing Difficulty Levels with Non-invasive Brain Activity Measurements

Audrey Girouard[1], Erin Treacy Solovey[1], Leanne M. Hirshfield[1], Krysta Chauncey[1], Angelo Sassaroli[2], Sergio Fantini[2], and Robert J.K. Jacob[1]

[1] Computer Science Department
[2] Biomedical Engineering Department Tufts University
Medford, MA 02155, USA
{audrey.girouard,erin.solovey,leanne.hirshfield,krysta.chauncey, angelo.sassaroli,sergio.fantini,robert.jacob}@tufts.edu

Abstract. Passive brain-computer interfaces are designed to use brain activity as an additional input, allowing the adaptation of the interface in real time according to the user's mental state. The goal of the present study is to distinguish between different levels of game difficulty using non-invasive brain activity measurement with functional near-infrared spectroscopy (fNIRS). The study is designed to lead to adaptive interfaces that respond to the user's brain activity in real time. Nine subjects played two levels of the game Pacman while their brain activity was measured using fNIRS. Statistical analysis and machine learning classification results show that we can discriminate well between subjects playing or resting, and distinguish between the two levels of difficulty with some success. In contrast to most previous fNIRS studies which only distinguish brain activity from rest, we attempt to tell apart two levels of brain activity, and our results show potential for using fNIRS in an adaptive game or user interface.

Keywords: Brain-computer interface, human cognition, functional near-infrared spectroscopy, fNIRS, task classification, game, difficulty level.

1 Introduction

A brain-computer interface (BCI) can be loosely defined as an interface controlled directly or indirectly by brain activity of the user. While most BCI research is designed for direct use with disabled users, we instead focus on passive BCIs for healthy users. Passive BCIs are interfaces that use brain measurements as an additional input, in conjunction with standard devices such as keyboards and mice [1].

Unlike much BCI work which uses electroencephalography (EEG) [2], this research uses functional near-infrared spectroscopy (fNIRS), which is non-invasive, portable, and relatively impervious to user movement (Figure 1). It is also uniquely sensitive to changes in blood oxygenation, which can be used to extrapolate levels of brain activation. This tool has been used in the contexts of biomedical research and experimental psychology, but little has been done to take advantage of it in a human-computer interaction (HCI) context. Researchers have used fNIRS to investigate brain

T. Gross et al. (Eds.): INTERACT 2009, Part I, LNCS 5726, pp. 440–452, 2009.

patterns related to particular mental activities, such as motor imagery [3, 4], mental workload [5], deception [6], or emotions [7]. However, most of these studies concentrate on differentiating between no activity and one activity, while this experiment attempts to differentiate two levels of activity from each other, as well as each level of activity from a resting baseline.

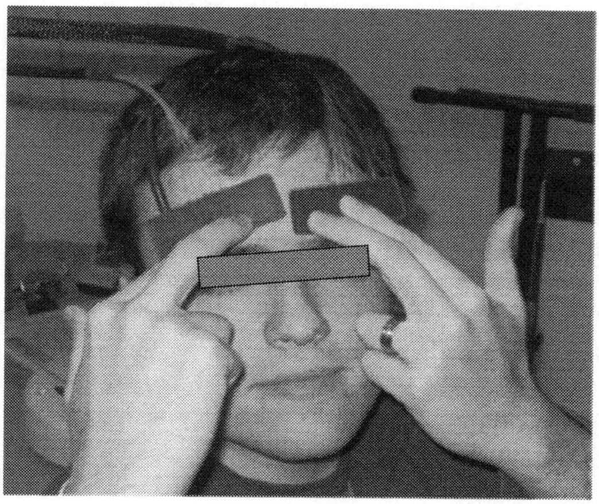

Fig. 1. A picture of a subject with the two probes (usually held by a headband)

The goal of the present study is to distinguish between different levels of game difficulty using fNIRS data collected while subjects played a computer game. The study is designed to ultimately lead to adaptive games and other interactive interfaces that respond to the user's brain activity in real time. Our results show that we can distinguish between the user playing Pacman or being at rest, as well as between two difficulty levels of Pacman.

2 Background and Related Work

2.1 Functional Near-Infrared Spectroscopy

fNIRS measures changes in hemoglobin concentrations [8]. At the near-infrared range, light can pass through most tissues, allowing them to be probed for depths up to 1-3 cm. By measuring the light sent at two wavelengths, we can calculate oxygenated and deoxygenated hemoglobin concentration. The slow hemodynamic changes measured by fNIRS occur in a time span of 6-8 sec [9]. fNIRS provides high temporal resolution (data points measured in the order of tenths of ms), and a spatial resolution of approximately 5mm. However, it can only measure the cortical surface of the brain. In comparison, fMRI has a low temporal resolution but allows whole-brain imaging, including both cortical and subcortical structures. EEG can gather information from electrodes placed all over the scalp, with a high temporal resolution. While there are many brain imaging techniques, each with advantages and disadvantages [2], we believe fNIRS to be a suitable brain sensing technology for HCI research because it is safe, non-invasive, easy to use, and relatively impervious to user movement, as compared to other brain techniques.

2.2 Psychophysiological Related Work

Game play has been measured using psychophysiological signals. For instance, Chen et. al used two physiological measures (heart rate variability and electromyogram) to measure the interruptibility of subjects in different tasks, including a game, and found a high correlation between those measures and the self-report of interruptibility [10]. Other researchers have measured the brain during game play using EEG and demonstrated the ability to distinguish the user resting, exploring the game environment or playing the video game [2]. Based on these results, we wanted to explore the fNIRS blood oxygenation response during different levels of video game play.

Task load and blood oxygenation have been shown to be correlated in a number of non-game environments [11] as well as in more directly relevant game-playing environments. Several fNIRS studies reported a significant variation in hemoglobin concentration in the prefrontal cortex in comparison to resting while playing an arcade game [12], a shooting game, a rhythm action game, a block puzzle and a dice puzzle [13]. Another study showed that one could differentiate between playing and not playing a computer game using functional magnetic resonance imagery (fMRI), by comparing three video games: Space Invaders, Othello and Tetris [14]. These studies all compare rest versus play, but never more than one level of difficulty.

These research papers show a prefrontal cortex response to video game playing, which lead us to believe that the video game Pacman could produce similar activations. However, note that most of the fNIRS studies measure a larger brain region, with probes that are much different than ours, although our current probe format has the advantage of a simple and comfortable setup. The present study applies fNIRS to the human forehead, measuring the anterior prefrontal cortex, a subset of the prefrontal cortex. The choice of Pacman was motivated by the fact that Pacman offers different difficulty levels that keep all other aspects identical, such as the scene and the characters' behavior. It was also desired to study an untested arcade video game with fNIRS, which we believe can be translated to other games of similar mental demand.

3 Experimental Protocol

The goal of this study was to measure brain activity using fNIRS during game play, and to differentiate the brain signal between different levels of a computer game. The arcade game Pacman was selected because of its customizable environment. We implemented a homemade computer version of the game, originally released by Namco (Japan). The user directs Pacman through a maze by pressing arrow keys, with the goal of eating as many fruits and enemies as possible, without being killed. Two levels of difficulty, differentiated by pace and quantity of enemies, were selected through pilot testing.

Participants were hypothesized to be able to distinguish these difficulty levels, so it was also hypothesized that brain measurements would show distinguishable differences in addition to observed differences in performance.

Nine subjects (4 females) participated in this study (mean age of 24.2 years; std 4.15). All were right-handed, with normal or corrected vision and no history of major head injury. Informed consent was obtained, and participants were compensated for their time. All knew of the game, and all but one had previously played it. Participants practiced the game for about one minute to familiarize themselves with our version.

3.1 Design and Procedure

Participants completed ten sets of two trials (one in each difficulty level) over a twenty minute period. In each trial, participants played the game for a period of thirty seconds, and rested for thirty seconds to allow their brain to return to baseline. Conditions within each set were randomized for each subject. The experimental protocol of alternating 30s-long windows of activation and rest was designed to take into account the slow hemodynamic changes that occur in a time span of 6-8 sec [9] as well as a short game cycle that nonetheless allowed performance to level off.

In addition to fNIRS data, we collected performance data—number of times Pacman is killed, as well as number of fruits and enemies eaten. At the end of the experiment, subjects were asked to rate the overall mental workload of each game level with the NASA Task Load Index (NASA-TLX) [15], a widely used measure of subjective mental workload used here as a manipulation check. NASA-TLX provides a ground truth measurement, a benchmark for comparing and validating fNIRS results. It is a collection of questions relating to the task's mental, physical, and temporal demands on the user, their performance, effort and frustration level when executing the task. The NASA-TLX for each level was administered using a paper version (two in total).

3.2 fNIRS Equipment

We collected fNIRS data using an OxiplexTS, from ISS, Inc. (Champaign, IL). Our setup is comprised of two probes (see Figure 2). Each source emits two wavelengths (690 and 830nm), with a sampling rate of 6.25Hz. The probes were placed in the middle of the forehead. We chose to use the data from the two last sources of each probe only (with source-detector distances of 2.5 and 3cm), because they reach deeper into the cortex. The shallower source-detector axes are thought to pick up primarily systemic responses happening in or on the skin.

Movement artifacts picked up by the fNIRS probes can include both general limb movement, and specific skin movements (e.g. frowning). The user was seated at ease, with their right hand positioned to reach the arrow keys of a standard keyboard comfortably, with the fingers resting on the keys, minimizing all movement of the arm and hand. We asked the users not to move their limbs, or to frown, but they were not constrained in any way. We did not measure their eye blinks or frowning, but we did visually observe their behavior. We did not find a visual correlation between such small movements and the preprocessed data. A pilot test indicated that small finger movements show up only minimally in our data, and this noise is mostly removed with filtering.

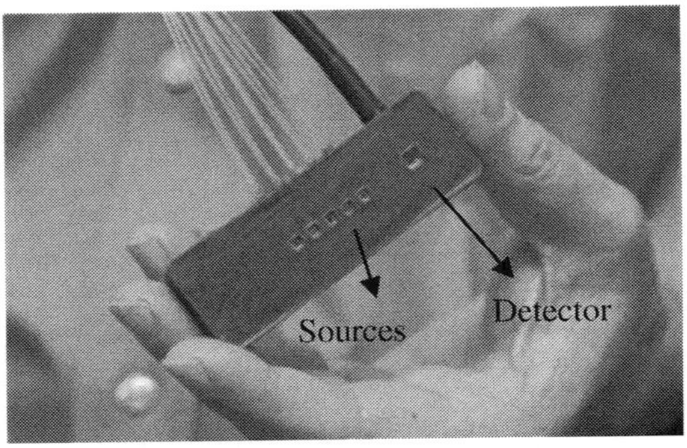

Fig. 2. A picture of the right probe. A probe includes a detector (larger square) and four light sources (smaller squares). While the probe has five possible light sources, only four sources can used at once because of hardware constraints. Moreover, we decided to only use data from two sources, the two furthest from the detector. The picture shows the side that will be on the forehead.

4 Analysis Techniques and Results

4.1 Behavioral Results and Performance Data

In this section, we performed an analysis on the non-brain data collected, such as the NASA-TLX results and the game performance statistics.

NASA-TLX. We analyzed results from the NASA-TLX data to confirm that users perceived the two difficulty levels as different. Results indicated an average mental workload index of 26 (std 12.9) for the easy level, and 69 (std 7.9) for the hard level, on a 100 point scale. This difference was significant according to a two sided t-test ($p<0.01$), and confirm our manipulation.

Performance Data. We also examined the performance data. Every data source collected showed a significant difference between the two difficulty levels ($p<0.05$). Figure 3 displays the average value of the data collected.

4.2 Brain Data

fNIRS is still a new methodology, and as such it lacks well-established preprocessing and analysis methods [16]. Each researcher is currently left to his or her better judgment to find a method that works best. Some researchers choose to do a visual inspection of the data to determine patterns [17], while most use some sort of statistical analysis of the data, with no real consensus on how to perform this analysis. Many perform paired t-test on averaged concentration change for each trial [18], while others average all the trials at each time point and performs t-test to compare each point with a baseline point [5, 12]. Additionally, a small number of researchers perform machine learning classification and clustering on fNIRS data [4, 5].

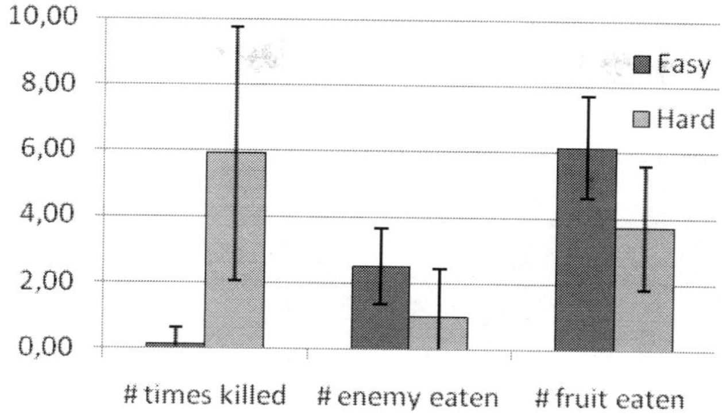

Fig. 3. Graph of data collected, with standard deviation, for each difficulty level, averaged over trials and subjects. The difference between each level is significant for each data type.

We performed two analyses of the brain data to confirm the presence of differences in hemoglobin concentrations for the different conditions: a classic statistical analysis to establish the differences between conditions, and a more novel task classification that will show the possibility of using this data in a real-time adaptive system.

Data Preprocessing. We preprocessed the raw data to remove artifacts and transform it into concentration of oxygenated and deoxygenated hemoglobin. To remove motion artifacts, and optical changes due to breathing and heart beat, we applied a folding average filter using a non-recursive time-domain band pass filter, keeping frequencies between 0.01Hz and 0.5Hz. The filtered raw data was then transformed into oxygenated hemoglobin and deoxygenated hemoglobin concentrations (respectively [HbO] and [Hb]), using the modified Beer-Lambert law [8].

Given the assumption that the brain returns to a baseline state during each rest period following the stimuli, even though it may not be the same baseline state in each rest period, we shift each trial so that the initial value is zero to control for differences in initial state. Finally, we separate each trial according to *Activeness*—whether the user was playing or resting. Figure 4 illustrates trials of data for a particular stimulus.

Statistical Analysis. For the statistical analysis, we average each trial of each condition to get a mean value of [HbO] and [Hb], for each difficulty level, activeness, hemisphere and channel. We then apply a factorial repeated measures analysis of variance (ANOVA) on *Difficulty level* (2) x *Activeness* (2) x *Hemoglobin Type* (2) x *Hemisphere* (2) x *Channel* (2) x *Subject* (9). This factorial ANOVA will observe differences within each participant, and determine if they are significant across participants. If the end result is to construct a system that can respond to different individuals with a minimum of training, we need to know how different we should expect individuals to be—hence including subjects as a factor in the analysis. Given the novelty of the fNIRS method, and the lack of well established analysis methods in previous work in this area, the cortical distribution of the(combination of channel and hemoglobin type effects cannot yet be predicted beforehand. In addition to the statistical significance, we report the effect size of the interaction (ω^2), which is the magnitude of the observed interaction,

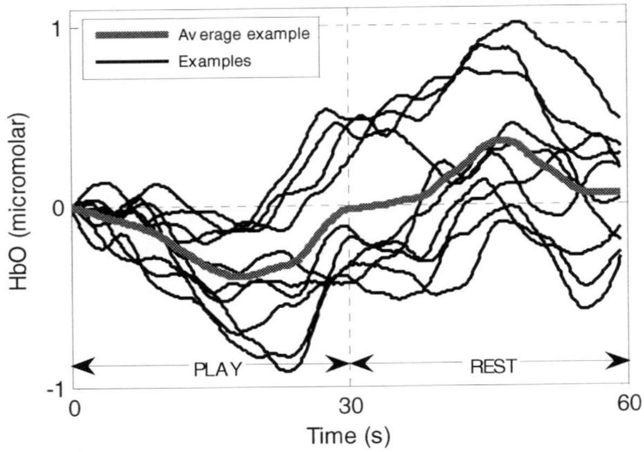

Fig. 4. Example of fNIRS data. The data displayed is subject 2's [HbO], from source 3 of the right probe, filtered. The red, ticker line indicates the mean of all trials. The left half of the data was taken when the user was playing the easy Pacman, and the right half was the rest period following.

and indicates practical significance. An omega-squared measure of 0.1 indicates a small effect, 0.3 a medium effect and 0.5 a large effect [19].

We found that the *Hemoglobin Type* was a significant factor, with a medium effect ($F(1, 8)=6.819$, $p<0.05$, $\omega^2=0.39$). This was expected, because [Hb] and [HbO] are present in different concentrations in the blood. The interaction of *Channel* x *Hemoglobin Type* is also significant, with a medium effect ($F(1, 8)=5.468$, $p<0.05$, $\omega^2= 0.33$), indicating that [Hb] and [HbO] are not the same at a given channel.

Game-playing compared to resting are significantly different as an interaction with channel with a large effect size (*Activeness* x *Channel*, $F(1, 8)=27.767$, $p<0.001$, $\omega^2= 0.75$), showing that there is a difference between playing Pacman and resting, and that this difference varies as a function of the cortical depth of the measurement (that is, the source-detector distance). We also observed that the interaction of *Activeness* x *Channel* x *Hemoglobin Type* is significant, with a medium effect ($F(1, 8)=5.412$, $p<0.05$, $\omega^2= 0.32$).

Finally, we observed a significant interaction of *Difficulty Level* x *Activeness* x *Channel* x *Hemoglobin Type*, with a small effect size ($F(1, 8)= 7.645$, $p<0.05$, $\omega^2= 0.18$). This interaction shows that we can significantly distinguish between the activeness of the participant, and the degree of difficulty of the current game when we take into account the channel and the hemoglobin type. This confirms our initial hypothesis.

Machine Learning Classification. Statistical analysis confirmed our hypothesis that the brain signals in the different conditions were significantly different. We then wanted to determine whether this signal could be used in an adaptive user interface. To do this, we used machine learning to train a classifier.

We chose sequence classification [20] because of its simple nature. Sequence classification applies a label to an entire sequence of data, and uses each data point as a feature. In our case, a sequence is one trial, containing 180 points. We used the same preprocessing as for the statistical analysis, but we use non-zeroed data, as it is more similar to data we would have in a real time brain-computer interface.

Because we have multivariate data (8 recordings for each time point: 2 probes x 2 channels x 2 hemoglobin types), we classify each channel individually first. To combine the results of all these classifications, each classifier votes for the label of the example. We used a weighted voting technique that takes into account the probability distribution of each example by each classifier.

The classification algorithm used is k-nearest-neighbors (kNN), with k=3. kNN uses the label of the three most similar examples (the closest neighbors) to the example to classify, and assigns a label based on the weighted average of their labels. We used a random 10-fold cross-validation in all classifications. We trained the classifier on part of one subject's data, and then tested for this specific subject with the left out data. This procedure was repeated for each subject.

We attempted three types of classification: (a) *Activeness* (Play versus Rest), (b) *Difficulty level* (Easy versus Hard), and (c) *Two difficulty levels and rest* (Easy versus Hard versus Rest). To accomplish each classification, we selected and/or grouped the trials differently. For *Activeness*, we combined all playing trials into one class, and all resting trials into another to form two classes. For *Difficulty Level*, we compared the easy and hard levels using the play trials only. Finally, in *Two difficulty levels and rest*, we compared three conditions: the play period of the easy level, the play period of the hard level, and all rest periods. Figure 5 shows the average accuracy of each type of classification (accuracy averaged over subjects).

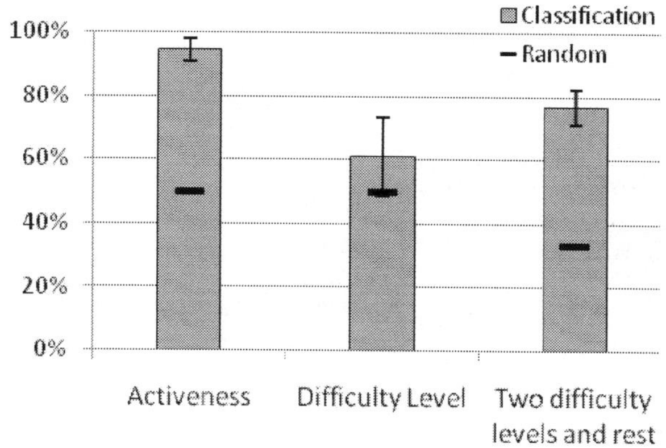

Fig. 5. Average accuracy for different classifications, with the standard variation and the random classification accuracy. *Activeness* compares the playing trials to the resting trials; *Difficulty Level* compares the easy and hard levels using the play trials only; *Two difficulty levels and rest* compares the easy playing trials versus the hard playing trials versus the resting trials.

5 Discussion

Our analyses show that we can distinguish between subjects being active and passive in their mental state (*Activeness*), as well as between different levels of game complexity (*Difficulty Level*) in this particular task when combined with the activeness of the participant, the channel and hemoglobin type measured. The classic statistical analysis confirmed that these conditions produced different patterns in blood oxygenation level, and the machine-learning analysis confirms that these patterns can be distinguished by the classifiers used.

While some might argue that performance data is sufficient to classify the difficulty level of a game and can be obtained without interference, the goal of this study is to investigate the use of the brain measurements with fNIRS as a new input device. In a more complex problem, performance and brain data coming from fNIRS might not be as related, e.g. if the user is working hard yet performing poorly at some point. In addition, distractions may also produce workload increases that would not obvious from monitoring game settings and performance, and thus may necessitate brain measurements. That is, a participant playing a simple game while answering difficult questions might also show brain activity relating to increased workload that would be incomprehensible based only on performance data (e.g. [21]). In real, non gaming situations, we might not have performance data like in the present case, as we don't always know what to measure— how hard is an air traffic controller working, or a person creating a budget on a spreadsheet? The use of the brain signal as an auxiliary input could provide better results in these situations.

5.1 Brain Activation When Playing Pacman: Play versus Rest

Results indicate the presence of a distinct brain signal when playing Pacman, in comparison to the rest periods. The *Activeness* classification in Figure 5 yields an average accuracy of 94.4%. It indicates a noticeable difference between the playing signal, and the resting signal. This corresponds to the results obtained with the statistical analysis, where *Activeness* was a significant factor in multiple interactions. This provides real time measurements that could be used in an adaptive interface. Our results corroborate those of previous studies that showed prefrontal cortex activity related to video games, measured with fNIRS.

5.2 Difficulty Levels: Easy versus Hard

The *Difficulty level* of the game was shown to be a significant factor in this experiment in both types of analyses. This is supported with the fact that users perceived the two levels as being significantly different according to the NASA-TLX. Hence, we can say that there was a significant cognitive difference between the two levels. Previous fNIRS game experiments [12, 13] only analyzed stimuli versus non-stimuli periods (which in this experiment we have called activeness), and not two levels of difficulty, making this result an advance over prior work.

However, the statistically significant interaction that included *Difficulty Level* had a small effect size, and classifying the difficulty of playing periods yields an average accuracy of 61.1%. This relatively low accuracy indicates that it is difficult with this classifier to differentiate between the two levels, which relate to the small effect size found in the statistical analysis. We also observed significant inter-subject variability: four participants scored between 65% and 85%. This indicates that the two difficulty levels might be significantly different with only part of the participants. As everyone's brain varies greatly, this is not a surprising result.

A comparison of three types of conditions (*Two difficulty levels and rest*) indicates an encouraging average accuracy of 76.7%, explained by the low differentiation between the difficulty levels, and the high separation between the activeness of the subjects. We must note that the difference in brain signal measure is not strong. One explanation may be that the difference in mental processes between each level manifests itself in other brain locations besides the anterior prefrontal cortex (location measured), such as in the dorsolateral prefrontal cortex. It could also be that the difference between the two difficulty levels was not big enough to cause strong changes in activation.

Results are consistent with prior work. Distinguishing work from rest was relatively easy, but discriminating different workload levels was harder, with significant inter-subject variability. Similar results have been found over decades of EEG work (e.g. [22, 23]), which may suggest fundamental limitations in making fine discriminations between two similar workload levels.

5.3 Subject Movement

We noted earlier that subjects' motions can sometimes be picked up by fNIRS devices. We believe that by simply asking the subjects to restrain their movement (major limb movements, as well as yawning and frowning), and by applying a filtering algorithm, we can minimize these motion artifacts. The data showed in this paper corroborates this hypothesis. The experiment was located in a quiet work environment, our subjects did use the keyboard, and significant differences between conditions were still obtained. This is good news for the use of fNIRS in HCI, as it shows the feasibility of using such tool in a real setting. We hypothesize that the use of the mouse would also be acceptable because those movements are usually minimal.

Overall, the findings indicate the presence of brain activation in the anterior prefrontal cortex when playing Pacman. Because the activation of the different levels of difficulty is correlated with mental workload (measured with NASA-TLX), we can presume that the difficulty level in this experiment is also correlated with mental workload.

The machine learning results show that fNIRS data can be classified easily, suggesting great potential as an auxiliary input for an adaptive interface. In the long run, our goal is to be able to classify data in real time.

6 Future Work

There is much interesting work to be done with fNIRS that could benefit the HCI community. Next steps include converting an offline classifier into a real-time algorithm that accepts streaming data for use in an adaptive interactive user interface. Additional data analysis could further resolve the temporal dynamics of classification efficacy, such as detecting workload changes within the first 2, 5, or 10 seconds instead of 30. Furthermore, a probe with more sensors, placed differently, could lead to a stronger signal, as it would pick up changes in blood oxygenation in more locations.

Saito et al observed a larger activation cluster in the dorsolateral prefrontal cortex with the games of Othello and Tetris than with Space Invaders [14]. This was justified with the fact that Othello and Tetris require spatial logical thinking (planning and memory of prior moves). The game of Pacman relates more to Space Invaders than to Othello or Tetris, as both are arcade games, and not puzzles, suggesting the possibility of a stronger signal with a different game. In addition, previous work using fNIRS to study video games compare different types of games (e.g. shooter game versus puzzle game), which could be interesting to experiment with, such as contrasting different levels in other types of games. This could verify whether differentiating two levels of video games yield weak results in other game types, or that Pacman's main brain activation is located elsewhere.

In a larger research context, exploring the use of fNIRS in an adaptive interface would prove interesting for the HCI community. Pacman was chosen in this experiment because of its great potential for passive adaptability: it is easy to change the amount of enemies to maintain interest without overwhelming the user. Results of the comparison of two different levels could be applied to other games of similar mental demand. The correlation between mental workload and difficulty levels in this experiment indicates we could also apply the current results to general applications that respond to such measurements.

There are limitations to using fNIRS in real-time, such as the fact that the metabolic response measured by fNIRS occurs over a few seconds, and the difficulty of filtering out motion artifacts in real time. This suggests that a real time user interface would be hard-pressed to produce an immediate, perfect response. Using fNIRS as a passive supplemental input will avoid some of these issues since the interface would not be dependent on this signal for its interaction. The interface can be adapted in a subtle matter, when we have a high degree of certainty in the user's cognitive state. In the case of an adaptive Pacman, changing the difficulty level should not be clearly noticeable to the user.

7 Conclusion

In this experiment, we have shown that functional near-infrared spectroscopy can distinguish between the brain at rest and the brain activated when playing a video game, both using statistical analysis and machine learning classification. We also demonstrated that we can differentiate two levels of difficulty. The activation of the different levels of difficulty is correlated with mental workload, measured with NASA-TLX. Hence, we can presume that the difficulty level in this experiment is correlated with mental workload. However, our classification accuracy was low when distinguishing easy or hard levels.

We introduced fNIRS as a new input device to the HCI community. It shows potential by its ability to measure different brain signals, such as difficulty level and mental workload, and its ease of use, and quick setup time. This is a step forward, as previous work only studied the activeness of the user during video games using fNIRS. We believe this work to be a stepping stone to using fNIRS in an adaptive user interface, in this case a passive brain-computer interface. In a real time user interface, we could use fNIRS measurement as an additional input on which to adapt the interface. In the case of Pacman, it could be used to modify the game's difficulty level to keep the user in an ideal game level, always challenged without being overwhelmed.

Acknowledgements. The authors would like to thank our colleagues and alumni in the HCI research group at Tufts University; Michel Beaudoin-Lafon, Wendy Mackay, and the In|Situ| research group; and Desney Tan at Microsoft Research for their helpful inputs and encouragement. We thank the National Science Foundation (Grant Nos. IIS-0713506 and IIS-0414389), the US Air Force Research Laboratory, the Natural Sciences and Engineering Research Council of Canada, the US Army Natick Soldier Research, Development and Engineering Center for support of this research. Any opinions, findings, and conclusions or recommendations expressed in this article are those of the authors and do not necessarily reflect the views of these organizations.

References

1. Cutrell, E., Tan, D.S.: BCI for passive input in HCI. In: Proc. ACM CHI 2008 Conference on Human Factors in Computing Systems Workshop on Brain-Computer Interfaces for HCI and Games (2007)
2. Lee, J.C., Tan, D.S.: Using a Low-Cost Electroencephalograph for Task Classification in HCI Research. In: Proc. UIST 2006 (2006)
3. Coyle, S., Ward, T., Markham, C., McDarby, G.: On the Suitability of Near-Infrared Systems for Next Generation Brain Computer Interfaces. In: Proc. World Congress on Medical Physics and Biomedical Engineering, Sydney, Australia (2003)
4. Sitaram, R., Zhang, H., Guan, C., Thulasidas, M., Hoshi, Y., Ishikawa, A., Shimizu, K., Burbaumer, N.: Temporal classification of multichannel near-infrared spectroscopy signals of motor imagery for developing a brain-computer interface. NeuroImage 34, 1416–1427 (2007)
5. Hirshfield, L.M., Solovey, E.T., Girouard, A., Kebinger, J., Sassaroli, A., Tong, Y., Fantini, S., Jacob, R.J.K.: Brain Measurement for Usability Testing and Adaptive Interfaces: An Example of Uncovering Syntactic Workload with Functional Near Infrared Spectroscopy. In: Proceedings of CHI 2009 Conference on Human Factors in Computing Systems (2009)
6. Bunce, S., Devaraj, A., Izzetoglu, M., Onaral, B., Pourrezaei, K.: Detecting deception in the brain: a functional near-infrared spectroscopy study of neural correlates of intentional deception. In: Proceedings of the SPIE International Society for Optical Engineering, vol. 5769, pp. 24–32 (2005)
7. Herrmann, M.J., Ehlis, A.C., Fallgatter, A.J.: Prefrontal activation through task requirements of emotional induction measured with NIRS. Biological Psychology 64(3), 255 (2003)
8. Villringer, A., Chance, B.: Non-Invasive Optical Spectroscopy and Imaging of Human Brain Function. Trends in Neuroscience 20, 435–442 (1997)
9. Bunce, S.C., Izzetoglu, M., Izzetoglu, K., Onaral, B., Pourrezaei, K.: Functional Near Infrared Spectroscopy: An Emerging Neuroimaging Modality. IEEE Engineering in Medicine and Biology Magazine, Special issue on Clinical Neuroengineering 25(4), 54–62 (2006)
10. Chen, D., Hart, J., Vertegaal, R.: Towards a physiological model of user interruptability. In: Baranauskas, C., Palanque, P., Abascal, J., Barbosa, S.D.J. (eds.) INTERACT 2007. LNCS, vol. 4663, pp. 439–451. Springer, Heidelberg (2007)
11. Izzetoglu, K., Bunce, S., Onaral, B., Pourrezaei, K., Chance, B.: Functional Optical Brain Imaging Using Near-Infrared During Cognitive Tasks. International Journal of Human-Computer Interaction 17(2), 211–231 (2004)

12. Nagamitsu, S., Nagano, M., Tamashita, Y., Takashima, S., Matsuishi, T.: Prefrontal cerebral blood volume patterns while playing video games-A near-infrared spectroscopy study. Brain & Development 28, 315–321 (2006)
13. Matsuda, G., Hiraki, K.: Sustained decrease in oxygenated hemoglobin during video games in the dorsal prefrontal cortex: A NIRS study of children. NeuroImage 29(3), 706–711 (2006)
14. Saito, K., Mukawa, N., Saito, M.: Brain Activity Comparison of Different-Genre Video Game Players. In: Proceedings of ICICIC '07 International Conference on Innovative Computing Information and Control, pp. 402–406 (2007)
15. Hart, S.G., Staveland, L.E.: Development of NASA-TLX (Task Load Index): Results of empirical and theorical research. In: Hancock, P., Meshkati, N. (eds.) Human Mental Workload, Amsterdam, pp. 139–183 (1988)
16. Butti, M., Caffini, M., Merzagora, A.C., Bianchi, A.M., Baselli, G., Onaral, B., Secchi, P., Cerutti, S.: Non-invasive neuroimaging: Generalized Linear Models for interpreting functional Near Infrared Spectroscopy signals. In: Caffini, M. (ed.) Proceedings of CNE '07 Conference on Neural Engineering, pp. 461–464 (2007)
17. Nishimura, E., Stautzenberger, J.P., Robinson, W., Downs, T.H., Downs, J.H.: A new approach to functional near-infrared technology. IEEE Engineering in Medicine and Biology Magazine 26(4), 25–29 (2007)
18. Matsuda, G., Hiraki, K.: Prefrontal Cortex Deactivation During Video Game Play. In: Shiratori, R., Arai, K., Kato, F. (eds.) Gaming, Simulations, and Society: Research Scope and Perspective, pp. 101–109 (2005)
19. Field, A.P., Hole, G.: How to design and report experiments. Sage publications Ltd., Thousand Oaks (2003)
20. Dietterich, T.G.: Machine learning for sequential data: A review. In: Caelli, T.M., Amin, A., Duin, R.P.W., Kamel, M.S., de Ridder, D. (eds.) SPR 2002 and SSPR 2002. LNCS, vol. 2396, pp. 15–30. Springer, Heidelberg (2002)
21. Nijholt, A., Tan, D., Allison, B., Milan, J.d.R., Graimann, B.: Brain-computer interfaces for hci and games. In: CHI 2008 extended abstracts on Human factors in computing systems. ACM, Florence (2008)
22. Gevins, A., Smith, M.: Neurophysiological measures of cognitive workload during human-computer interaction. Theoretical Issues in Ergonomics Science 4, 113–131 (2003)
23. Allison, B.Z., Polich, J.: Workload assessment of computer gaming using a single-stimulus event-related potential paradigm. Biological Psychology 77(3), 277–283 (2008)

Memorization and Information-Retrieval Behaviors

Jun-ichiro Watanabe and Youichi Horry

Hitachi Human Interaction Laboratory
1-280, Higashi-koigakubo, Kokubunji, 185-8601, Tokyo, Japan
{junichiro.watanabe.ws,youichi.horii.jx}@hitachi.com

Abstract. What is the relationship between memorization of information and the behavior used to retrieve that information? Searching for photos stored on a media is a common activity. Chances are that it is easier to find some types of photos than others. To determine the reason for this, we conducted a user study to clarify the mechanisms people use to retrieve information. We found that the operational patterns differed with the degree of memorization and the types of target photos. In particular, we found that the overall relative positions of target contents and/or the order of the arrangement affect memorization. The difference in operational patterns can be interpreted as a difference in retrieval strategies. These findings should contribute to the field of computer-human interactions, enabling the mechanisms used to retrieve information to be better understood. This understanding should lead to interfaces that can dynamically and appropriately assess user intentions and situations.

Keywords: Information-retrieval, scrolling, memorization, operation patterns.

1 Introduction

Due to the rapid progress in information technologies, we live in a society where we can enjoy a rich variety of digital information. However, the complexity of the interfaces between digital information and potential users has increased, and accessibility to the information they require has been reduced. Even though a great deal of research on user interfaces has been done, and many excellent results have thus far been obtained, there have not been that many studies on the mechanisms people use to retrieve information. If we could understand them more clearly, novel and instinctive user interfaces based on these mechanisms could be attained.

In our user study, we focused on scrolling because this is one of the basic methods for retrieving digital information, and investigated how the degree of human memorization and the features of the targeted information affect the scrolling operation. For example, someone searching for a favorite photo in a folder may be able to find it immediately without straying because he/she remembers the folder's contents and the photo's whereabouts well. In contrast, someone searching for a friend's favorite photo in an unfamiliar folder will likely take longer to find it and may stray in the information space. This illustrates that the scrolling pattern used may be affected by the target information. We asked the participants to retrieve photos by scrolling, and we measured the time it took to find the target photo, recorded the identification numbers of

T. Gross et al. (Eds.): INTERACT 2009, Part I, LNCS 5726, pp. 453–466, 2009.

the photos viewed (the "scrolling position") for every time unit, and derived the velocity from the changes in position. We also asked them to complete a questionnaire that enabled us to estimate how well they remembered the target photos, not only their features but also their position in the arrangement.

The rest of this paper is organized as follows. After briefly introducing related work, we describe the motivating hypothesis in Section 3. Then we describe the user study we conducted in Section 4, and present some of the results in Section 5. In Section 6 we discuss the results, and finally describe our conclusion.

2 Related Work

Several cognitive psychological studies have investigated how people use Web browsers and their information-retrieval behaviors [4,5,6,7,15,16]. These have shown that a user's retrieval behavior is driven in part by the way information is presented. That is, the user interface design affects the retrieval behavior. The results of these studies have been used to develop tools for designing and evaluating Web pages, and techniques to improve browsing or searching content-rich information [14,17].

People are generally good at retrieving things stored spatially. Several groups have conducted studies aimed at organizing digital data spatially like we do in the physical world [1]. One approach has been to reproduce the arrangement of objects on a physical desk on the computer. Stacks of files are arranged at spatially different positions on a desktop-like GUI as groups of information.

An investigation of the relationship between scrolling distance and the required precision of scrolling [8] revealed that Fitts' Law models the scrolling behaviors well, though it is usually used to evaluate the performance of pointing devices. This investigation of how conventional scrolling techniques are actually used resulted in a paradigm that can be used for designing new retrieval techniques.

Various methods have been proposed for the scrolling operation. Igarashi et al. proposed a scrolling technique for browsing a large amount of content using a zoom function [9]. The pseudo speed of scrolling is kept constant by automatically zooming in and out in accordance with the speed of operation. This technique utilizes the scrolling speed to dynamically change the content presentation. However, it does not take the relationship between the types of content and scrolling operation into consideration.

Appert et al. proposed a technique for automatically adjusting the zoom level in accordance with the user's operation, not the operation speed. Their OrthoZoom Scroller [2] controls the zoom level by moving the pointer in the direction perpendicular to the scrolling direction. As the pointer approaches the scrollbar, the contents are presented with lower precision, and as the pointer moves away from the scroll bar, the contents are presented in higher precision.

Kumar et al. proposed using eye gaze to control scrolling [12]. They focused on the finding that scrolling is strongly coupled with a user's ability to catch information using his/her eyes. For example, the placement of a document being read on a screen can be maintained even when the page up or page down key is pressed by detecting the eye-gaze point and using it to limit the scrolling edge.

For supporting user operations, some studies have suggested using the users' operation tendencies to deduce their intentions. Asano et al. used the direction and peak speed of pointer movement to deduce the target and automatically scroll to it [3]. Kobayashi et al. proposed a technique for operating a cascaded menu [11]. The direction of pointer movement is mapped to the direction of the cascaded-menu items, and the user does not have to actually point to an item to open it. Ishak et al. described a scrolling method that depends on the content characteristics [10]. The speed of scrolling and zooming automatically changes in accordance with the context of the content. For example, if a document with two columns is being read, the scrolling operation is supported by a function for automatically jumping from the bottom of the left column to the top of the right column.

Improving the scrollbar has been another topic of interest regarding scrolling. In one study, a rubber band metaphor was used to control the scroll speed [13]. The speed changed with the distance between the pointer and the scrollbar slider. When the user drags the slider, the speed of scrolling is the same as that of the slider. When the user drags somewhere else in the scrollbar area, the speed of scrolling is higher the greater the distance between the mouse pointer and the slider. This enables more precise pointing to the desired contents because the closer the target content comes to the screen, the lower the scrolling speed.

Most previous studies focused on the functions or design of the user interface itself, not on the effect the target contents has on using the interface. In this study, we focused on how the contents affect a person's use of an interface. We attempted to clarify the mechanisms people use to retrieve information and explored the possibility of using them as a basis for novel computer-human interaction techniques.

3 Hypothesis

In this study, we investigated the relationship between memory and retrieval behavior by conducting a user study in which users retrieved target photos using scrolling. The scrolling speed was controlled by the user and was not constant during the retrieval process. The identification numbers on the photos scrolled through were recorded, and the number of photos scrolled through per time unit was used as a measure of the scrolling speed. The speed varied with the operation pattern, for example, how long keys were pressed or the speed at which the slider was moved. We hypothesized that the shape of the scrolling pattern (Fig. 1) depends on the user's memorization of the target contents and that the patterns can be categorized on the basis of their shapes.

The time it takes to find a target photo in a folder and the psychological load are affected by how well the searcher remembers the contents of the folder and their order. This means that the scrolling patterns for well-memorized photos should differ from those for poorly memorized ones. The memorization can be affected by both the features of the contents, that is, the contents themselves and their overall relative positions. Though a computer cannot directly calculate the degree of a person's memorization, there is a relationship between the degree of memorization and the features of the contents that a computer can calculate. There are characteristic differences between photos that tend to be well memorized and those that are not. A series of photos with the same theme taken on nearly the same date or at the same time can usually be easily distinguished in a folder of photos. Photos with strong features such as tone or composition can also usually be easily distinguished. Thus, we categorized the target photos into three types before conducting the user experiment: "series," "impressive," and "featureless." We investigated the relationship between photo type and ease of memorization and between photo type and operation pattern.

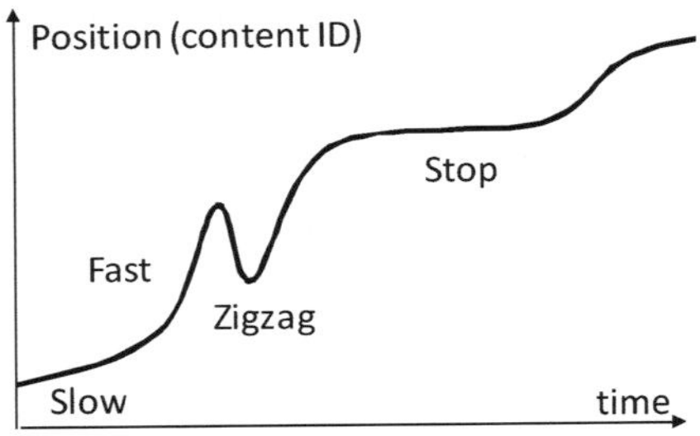

Fig. 1. Example plot of scroll track

4 User Study

The participants were asked to find a target photo from among 200 photos using two types of operation.

- Operation 1: Use only left and right arrow keys on keyboard to scroll.
- Operation 2: Use only mouse movements to drag scrollbar slider.

Eight people (two women and six men, 25 to 42 years old) familiar with computer operation participated. Photo browsing software was run on a desktop PC with a 24-inch display (Fig. 2 (a)). The photos were presented in one dimension horizontally across the middle line of the display. A fixed cursor was presented at the center of the display, and three photos were shown at once. The target photo was shown in the upper-center area. The participants scrolled through the photos by dragging the scrollbar slider using the mouse in operation 2. They could also scroll by pressing the left and right arrow keys on the keyboard (in operation 1), and the slider moved in accordance with how the keys were operated. There were five steps in the experimental process.

1. We gave the participants (one at time) 3 min to memorize the features of a total of 200 photos and their order.
2. The participant pressed the Enter key to start searching. The target photo was displayed, and the timer started. The participant scrolled by pressing keys (in operation 1) or dragging the scrollbar slider (in operation 2) to find the target.
3. The participant pressed the Enter key again when the target photo was apparently found in the fixed cursor. If the photo was the target one, the task was accomplished and the timer stopped. If not, a beep was sounded, and he/she resumed searching.
4. After the participant found the target photo, he/she answered three questions on a questionnaire.
5. Each participant repeated steps (1) to (4) for 12 photos, once using keyboard operation and once using mouse operation, i.e., 24 tasks in total.

(a) Photo browser.

Q1: Did you remember the photo itself?
1: Yes 2: No
Q2:Did you remember its position?
1: Yes (Accurately)
2: Yeah (Almost)
3: No, but remembered
(Remembered during the operation)
4: No (Not at all)
Q3: Did you find it where you expected it to be?
1: Yes (exactly) 2: No (different)

(b) Inquiries.

Fig. 2. Photo browser and inquiries for experiment

Each time the participants finished a task, they were asked to write their answers to three questions (Fig. 2 (b)). The first question ("Did you remember the photo itself?"; "yes" or "no") was used to investigate the effect remembering the photo itself had on the operation pattern. The second question ("Did you remember its position?"; "yes (accurately)," "yeah (mostly)," "no (but remembered during the operation)," or "no (not at all)") was used to investigate the effect remembering the photo's position had on the operation pattern. The difference between Q1 and Q2 was "position." Someone may remember the photo itself and the position as well. Others may remember the photo itself but not the position. The operation strategies may be different between these two. The third question ("Did you find it where you expected it to be?"; "yes (exactly)" or "no (different)") was used to confirm the accuracy of their memory. From the results of the last two questions, we defined a "memory score," which represented how memorable the photo was.

The same 24 of these photos were used as retrieval targets, and they were presented in the same order to all participants. The 24 photos were categorized into three types: "series," "impressive," and "featureless." The "series" type included photos that had been taken in close succession and had the same theme. The "impressive" type included photos that had strong, easily remembered features. They included photos that were striking in some way, such as photos with strong tones, an interesting composition, or a strange object. The "featureless" type included photos that were not in a particular series and had no strong features. For example, a photo between one series and another series could be of this type. In the experiment, we recorded the identification numbers of the photos located at the fixed cursor position during each time unit (100 ms). We then derived the velocity from the changes in position. The entire time it took to find the target photo was also measured.

5 Results

5.1 Classification of Scrolling Patterns

We gathered scrolling-pattern data, i.e., the ID numbers of the photos scrolled through (i.e., the scrolling position) and the derived velocity of scrolling for the eight participants for both the keyboard and mouse operations. Some of the patterns had a similar shape even though they were for different target photos or were for different participants. This indicates that the scrolling patterns can be classified using several typical patterns and their combinations. We found that we could use four typical patterns for each type of operation to classify all the patterns. All the gathered patterns can be one of the four patterns itself or the combination of them. As shown in figures 3 and 4, the patterns comprised two plots: position (ID) vs. time and velocity vs. time. The patterns in the figures are for actual data obtained from the user study.

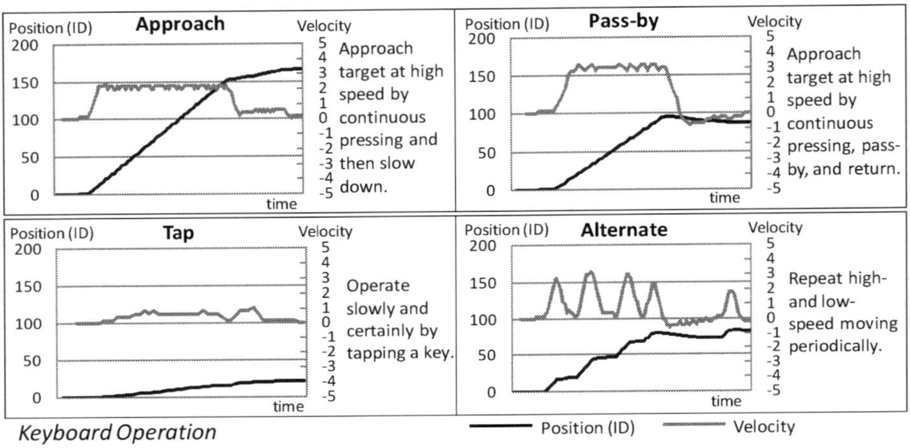

Fig. 3. Typical scrolling patterns for keyboard operation

Scrolling Patterns for Keyboard Operation (Fig. 3)

"Approach": The user continued pressing (key down) an arrow key until the target photo appeared. He/she then stopped pressing and started to tap the key to scroll slowly until the target photo was reached. That is, he/she approached the target at high speed by continuously pressing a key and then slowed down. The slope of the position plot is initially steep, and then it becomes gentle near the target; the velocity plot forms a trapezoid.

"Pass-by": The user continued pressing an arrow key until the target photo had been passed. He/she then stopped pressing and started to tap the key for moving in the opposite direction to scroll slowly back to the target photo. That is, he/she approached the target at high speed, passed the target, stopped suddenly, and returned to the photo. The slope of the position plot is initially steep, and then it becomes gentle with opposite inclination; the velocity plot forms a trapezoid.

"Tap": The user scrolled by continuously tapping an arrow key. That is, he/she operated slowly and certainly by tapping a key. The position plot remains fairly steady, and the velocity plot has a very gentle slope.

"Alternate": The user alternated between continuously pressing an arrow key and tapping an arrow key. That is, he/she periodically repeated high- and low-speed moving. The position plot has steps, and the velocity plot has spikes at semi-regular intervals.

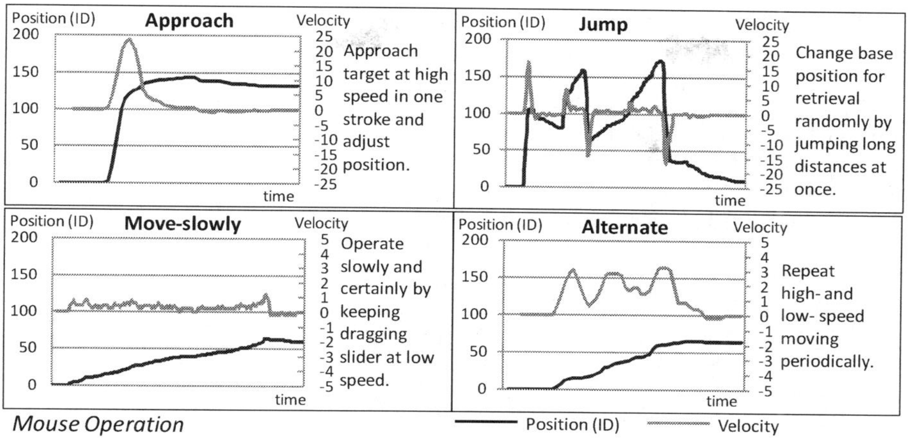

Fig. 4. Typical scrolling patterns for mouse operation

Scrolling Patterns for Mouse Operation (Fig. 4)

"Approach": The user initially dragged the slider quickly over a long distance, scrolling through numerous photos until the neighborhood of the target photo was reached. He/she then slowly searched through the neighboring photos until reaching the target. That is, he/she approached the target at high speed in one stroke and then carefully adjusted the position. The position plot has a very steep, almost vertical, slope, and the velocity plot has one sharp peak near the beginning and then remains flat.

"Jump": The user alternated between suddenly and rapidly moving the slider over a long distance and moving it very slowly until the target was reached. That is, he/she randomly changed the base position for retrieval by jumping long distances at once. Both the position plot and the velocity plot have discrete sharp peaks. This is a characteristic pattern of mouse operation and is not found in keyboard operation.

"Move-slowly": The user moved the slider slowly and continuously until reaching the target. That is, he/she operated slowly and certainly by dragging the slider. The average speed of scrolling was very low. The position plot remains fairly steady, and the velocity plot has a very gentle slope.

"Alternate": The user alternated between moving the slider over long and over short distances (or stopping). That is, he/she periodically repeated high- and low-speed moving. The position plot is stepped, and the velocity plot has spikes at semi-regular intervals.

We then defined representations for all the scrolling patterns. For example, if the scrolling pattern was simply "approach", (approach, pass-by, tap, alternate) was represented as (1,0,0,0). If the pattern included both "pass-by" and "tap," it was represented as (0,1,1,0). The former representation is interpreted as "approach 100%" (i.e., the rate of use was 100%); the latter is interpreted as "pass-by 50% and tap 50%" (i.e., the rates of use for both patterns was about 50%).

5.2 Degree of Memorization of Photo Itself and Operation Pattern

In the questionnaire (Fig. 2), we asked the participants whether they remembered the target photo itself. Using the answers to Q1 and the scrolling pattern representations, we identified the relationship between the degree of memorization of the photo itself and the operation pattern. As shown in Fig. 5 (a), finding unremembered photos took longer, and the difference in retrieval times is consistent with it being more difficult to find unremembered photos than to find remembered ones.

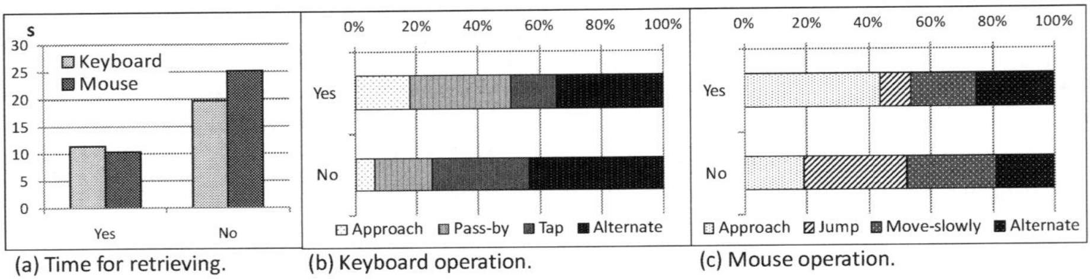

Fig. 5. Time for retrieving (a) and details of operations (b), (c) for the answers to Q1, "Did you remember the photo itself?"

Answer to Q1 and Keyboard Operation: As shown in Fig. 5 (b), the participants who answered "yes" to Q1 for keyboard operation used the "approach" and "pass-by" scrolling patterns at a combined rate of about 50%. Those who answered "no" used them at a combined rate of about 25%. This is consistent with the idea that a user who remembers the target photo will tend to scroll quickly because he/she can catch a rough impression of it even when the photos are scrolled rapidly. Additionally, a user who remembers the position of the photo can move toward it without straying. A user who does not remember the photo has no clues for finding it and will thus tend to scroll through the photos more slowly, with more dependence on visual feedback.

Answer to Q1 and Mouse Operation: As shown in Fig. 5 (c), the participants who answered "yes" to Q1 for mouse operation used the "approach" scrolling pattern at a rate of about 45%, while those who answered "no" used the "jump" pattern at a rate of about 35%. That is, someone who remembers the target photo can approach the target with one long movement. Someone who does not basically scrolls slowly, and, if he/she cannot find the target, he/she changes the base retrieval position by scrolling a long distance in one stroke. That is, they jump to a new position and start searching again slowly.

5.3 Degree of Memorization of Photo's Position and Operation Patterns

We have seen that differences in remembering the target photo caused significant differences in operation patterns and retrieval times. Next, we focus on the effect of remembering the target photo's position rather than the photo itself because this information could prove useful in finding the photo. The scrolling patterns for "remembering the photo but not the position" should differ from those for "remembering the photo and the position as well." We thus analyzed the representations for Q2 ("Did you remember its position?") for those participants who answered "yes" to Q1.

Fig. 6 (a) shows the retrieval time for each pattern. The participants who did not remember the position of the target photo (Q2: "no") even though they remembered the photo itself (Q1: "yes") took more than twice the time to find the photo than those who gave one of the other three answers.

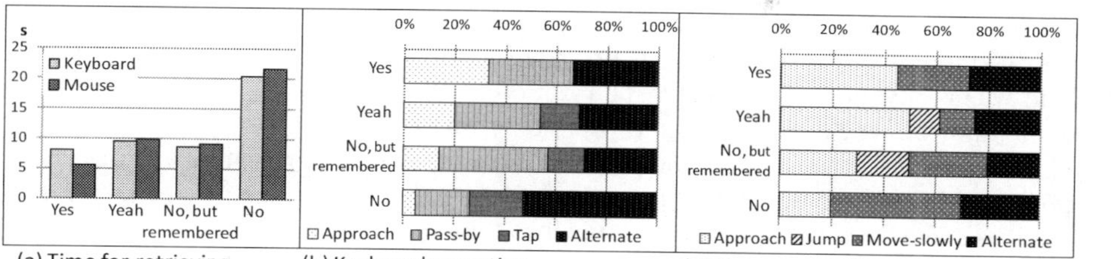

(a) Time for retrieving. (b) Keyboard operation. (c) Mouse operation.

Fig. 6. Time for retrieving (a) and details of operations (b), (c) for the answers to Q2, "Did you remember its position?"

Characteristic Tendencies for Keyboard Operation: As shown in Fig. 6 (b), the rate of using the "approach" scrolling pattern for keyboard operation was significantly reduced when the degree of memorization was lower. That is, the more accurately the participant remembered the position, the easier it was for him/her to recognize when he/she was close to the target. He/she was able to move directly and rapidly toward the target because he/she knew where it was. As he/she approached the target, he/she slowed down to be able to stop directly at the target. Interestingly, when the answer to Q2 was "yes" i.e., the user remembered the position exactly, the "tap" scrolling pattern was not used. The basic strategy was to keep pressing the arrow key and moving quickly until the neighbors of the target were reached.

The characteristics for users who answered "yeah (mostly)" or "no, but remembered" to Q2 were similar. In particular, the percentages for the "pass-by" pattern were high. This was because it was more difficult for them to recognize when they were close to the target because they approximately rather than accurately remembered the position. They could find the photo visually because they knew the photo itself, so, when they found it, they immediately stopped moving and went back to the target.

When they did not remember the position (Q2: "no"), the percentage for the "alternate" pattern was more than 50%, and the two "keep-on pressing" patterns ("approach" and "pass-by") had the smallest percentages. This can be interpreted to mean that these participants used a probabilistic search strategy. That is, by periodically changing the "base" position of retrieval, they hoped to more quickly approach and reach the target.

Characteristic Tendencies for Mouse Operation: As shown in Fig. 6 (c), when the participants remembered the position of the target exactly (Q2: "yes") or almost exactly ("yeah"), the rate of using the "approach" pattern for mouse operation was close to 50%. The "jump" pattern was virtually unused, especially for "yes." This means that, when the participants knew the position of the target, they moved toward it without hesitation. If they did not initially remember the position but remembered it during the operation ("no, but remembered"), the rate of using the "approach" pattern was lower, and that of using the "jump" pattern was higher. The "jump" pattern was also used by those who answered "yeah". As evident in the figure, the lower the degree of remembering the position, the higher the rate of using the "jump" and "move-slowly" patterns. However, when the participants did not remember the position at all (Q2: "no"), the "jump" pattern was not used, and the rate of "move-slowly" was close to 50%. This can be interpreted to mean that, when a participant roughly remembered the position, he/she used the strategy of frequently changing the base position of retrieval, aiming to accidentally and probabilistically find a location near the target. And when they did not remember the position at all, they used the strategy of slowly searching from one end of the photo list one-by-one.

As we have seen, the operation patterns varied with the degree of how well the target's position was remembered. In keyboard operation, when the participants remembered the position accurately, the typical pattern used was "approach"; when they remembered the position approximately, it was "pass-by"; and when their memory was poor, it was "alternate." In mouse operation, when they remembered the position exactly, the typical pattern used was "approach"; when they remembered the position approximately, the "jump" pattern had a larger rate; and when their memory was poor, "move-slowly" was dominant.

5.4 Types of Photos and Operation Patterns

We have seen that there is a relationship between the degree of memorization and the operation patterns used. Then, what kinds of photos are easy to memorize and what kinds of photos are difficult? We defined "memory score" (MS) for evaluating the ease with which the photos were memorized. It was calculated for the photos for which the answer to Q1 was "yes." MS makes use of the answers for Q2 and Q3 and is defined as

$$MS_{i,j} = \begin{cases} 3 \times q_{1,i,j} + 2 \times q_{2,i,j} + 1 \times q_{3,i,j} + 0 \times q_{4,i,j} & \text{(if answer to Q3 was "yes")} \\ 0 & \text{(if answer to Q3 was "no")} \end{cases}$$

where i stands for participants and j stands for photos. The $q_{1,i,j}$, $q_{2,i,j}$, $q_{3,i,j}$, and $q_{4,i,j}$ are the answers to Q2 ("yes," "yeah," "no, but remembered" and "no") and took a value of 1 if they corresponded and 0 if they did not. The more accurately the participants remembered the position of the target photo, the higher the score that was awarded. If the answer to Q3, which was to confirm how accurately they remembered the position after finding the target photo, was "no," a score of 0 was given because their memorization was not accurate. The higher the MS, the easier it was for participant i to memorize photo j.

The average MS for each photo type we used in the experiment is shown in Fig. 7 (a). The "series" photos tended to have higher scores, and the "featureless" ones tended to have lower scores. The results show a correlation between photo types and MS, i.e., ease of memorization.

We have seen that the operation patterns varied with the degree with which the photo itself and its position were remembered. Since the degree of remembrance is affected by the photo type, there must be a correlation between photo type and patterns used. This is supported by the finding that it took longer to find featureless photos (Fig. 7 (b)).

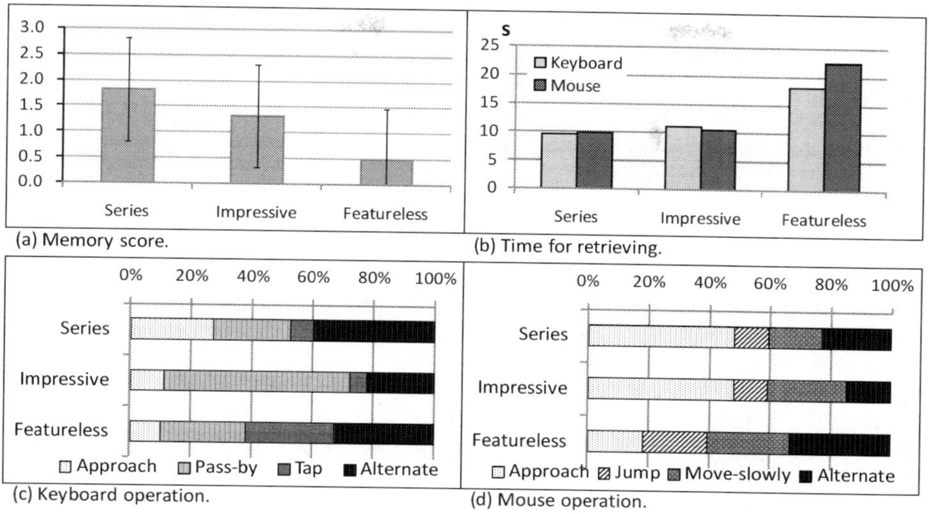

Fig. 7. Type of photo and (a) memory score, (b) time for retrieving, details of operation for (c) keyboard and (d) mouse operation

Photo Type and Keyboard Operation: As shown in Fig. 7 (c), when searching for "series" photos, the participants used the "approach" scrolling pattern at a higher rate than for the other two types of photos. This can be explained in the sense that, when searching for a "series" photo, it was easier for a participant to recognize when he/she was in the neighborhood of the target photo even when they approached it quickly because the similar photos in the series were easily recognized. It was surprising to find that the "alternate" pattern had the highest rate (~40%) for "series" photos. This could be because, when the participant did not remember the position of the series, he/she searched for the series of photos that included the target at a medium scrolling speed (not quickly by continually pressing the key, and not slowly by using the "tap" pattern). This would be more likely to happen when the series containing the target photo contained only a few photos, and the target photo itself was "featureless." When searching for "impressive" photos, the participants used the "pass-by" pattern at a rate of about 60%. This was because the "impressive" photos could be memorized more accurately, enabling the participants to move directly and quickly toward the target photo. However, since the target was not in a series, it was difficult to recognize when they were near the target so that they could slow down. They passed the target and then went back. The "tap" pattern was used more often to search for "featureless" photos. The participants tended to search for the target by scrolling slowly from one end of the photo list photo-by-photo because they had few clues for recognizing the photo.

Photo Type and Mouse Operation: As shown in Fig. 7 (d), the mouse operations used to search for "series" and "impressive" photos were mostly the same. In both cases, the "approach" pattern, i.e., moving the slider rapidly over a long distance toward the target, had a rate of about 50%. The difference is that the rates for "move-slowly" and "alternate" were reversed between "series" and "impressive." For "series," the rates were about 13 and 24%. For "impressive," they were about 26 and 15%. This indicates that, when the participants did not know the whereabouts of the target photo accurately and searched for a series of photos, they tended to use "alternate," so the average scrolling velocity was medium. When they searched for a single impressive photo without knowing its whereabouts, they tended to use "move-slowly," so the average velocity was low. For "featureless" photos, the rates for "jump" and "alternate" were higher (~21 and ~32%). The search strategy was to increase the probability of finding a neighbor of the target by changing the retrieval base periodically or by suddenly beginning to move the slider.

6 Discussion

Effects of Type of Photo and Degree of Memorization: We have seen that different scrolling patterns were used depending on the degree of memorization of the target photos and of their positions in an arrangement. There was also a relationship between the type of photo and the degree of memorization. This relationship was used to define a rule combining the patterns of operations and the type of target content. The differences in the scrolling patterns can be interpreted as difference in information-retrieval strategies.

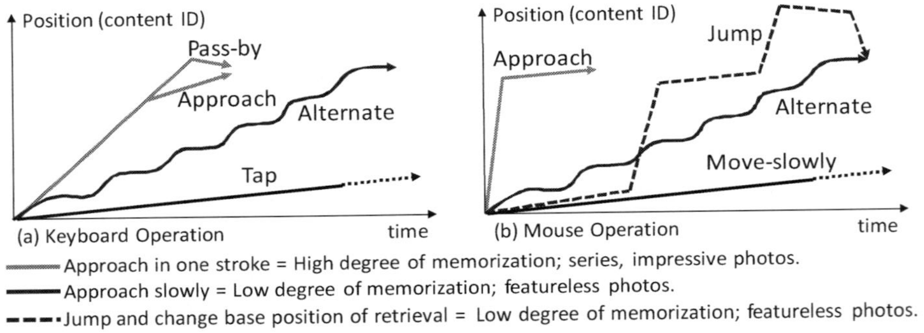

Fig. 8. Typical patterns of operations

In our user study, we found some typical patterns of operations (Fig. 8). The "approach" and "pass-by" patterns observed for keyboard operation were consistent with the "approach" pattern observed for mouse operation. They were generally used to search for well-memorized photos that were either in a "series" or "impressive" and were not used much to search for poorly memorized "featureless" photos. For "series" photos, the searcher tended to slow down and stop at the photo. For "impressive" photos, the searcher tended to go past the target and return to it. The "tap" and "move-slowly" patterns observed in keyboard and mouse operations, respectively, were used to search for unfamiliar photos (poorly memorized and/or "featureless").

The interesting and unexpected patterns we found were "alternate," observed for both keyboard and mouse operations, and "jump" for mouse operation. The "alternate" pattern was used for retrieving poorly memorized photos, especially in keyboard operation. The "jump" pattern was correspondingly used in mouse operation. It tended to be used to search for poorly memorized, "featureless" photos. With the "alternate" and "jump" patterns, the participants used a similar strategy for finding unfamiliar photos. They changed the base position of retrieval, aiming to accidentally and probabilistically come close to the target. The difference between the two is that with "alternate," the participants changed their base position periodically and generally continued scrolling in the same direction. With "jump," they changed the base position suddenly and did not necessarily continue scrolling in the same direction, so that the position (photo ID) plot zigzagged.

Effect of Arrangement Order: We received several useful comments regarding photo memorization. For example,

1. *"I memorized the photos on the basis of the clothes the people wore or the season."*
2. *"I knew that the target photo was not in the latter half of the photo list, even though I did not remember the photo itself. The target photo showed some houses, and although I did not remember any pictures with houses, I did recall that there were no photos with houses in the latter half of the photo list, only ones with beautiful beach scenes."*

The first 100 of the 200 photos used in the experiment were taken in May, and the other 100 were taken in October. People with short-sleeved shirts or trees with green foliage were included in the photos taken in May, reflecting the season becoming warm. Likewise, people with long-sleeved shirts or trees with foliage that had turned red were included in the photos taken in October. Comment 1 indicates that the participant had memorized photos by using a mental model of clothes and seasons. That is, a sense of the season of the photos was mapped onto the flow of time for all 200 photos and was used to estimate the position of the target photo. Comment 2 indicates that the position of the photo could be deduced even when the participant did not remember the photo itself. The participant searched for the photo by comparing it with the order or atmosphere of all the photos to estimate its position. These comments indicate that we make use of a mental model reflecting the atmosphere of all the photos, focusing on their features and order, rather than memorizing each photo exactly. If the order of photos is changed, the atmosphere generated by the whole collection of photos is also changed. This can change the scrolling patterns or time it takes to find the target photo.

7 Conclusion

We have demonstrated that the scrolling patterns used for retrieving photos differ significantly depending on how well the searcher memorizes them and their positions in the arrangement. We also demonstrated that a photo's characteristics affect the degree to which it is remembered. The difference in scrolling patterns can be interpreted as a difference in strategies for retrieving information. These findings enable the mechanisms used to retrieve information to be better understood, and lead to interfaces that can dynamically and appropriately assess user intentions. Our ultimate goal is to understand the mechanisms people use to retrieve information and to establish a method for designing user interfaces based on that understanding. To reach this goal, we plan to investigate the relationship between not only photos but also other contents, such as text or sound, and retrieval behaviors. In the study described in this paper, we investigated fundamentals of these mechanisms. We showed that it is possible to extract a principle of information retrieval that is based on memorization and to develop an algorithm for adapting user interfaces to human's behaviors. For example, an algorithm could be constructed that causes only photos in a series with high memorization potential to be presented with emphasis when a user scrolls through the photos rapidly and that causes featureless ones with low memorization potential to be presented with emphasis when the user scrolls slowly. Though this example is rough and the details must be worked out, if such algorithms were established, we could design interaction methods based on the natural behaviors of people rather than simply designing the outer layer or a brand-new input method or defining functions that treat the relationships between the various factors and the search behaviors in the same way.

References

1. Agarawala, A., Balakrishnan, R.: Keepin' It Real: Pushing the Desktop Metaphor with Physics, Piles and the Pen. In: Proc. CHI 2006, pp. 1283–1292 (2006)
2. Appert, C., Fekete, J.-D.: OrthoZoom Scroller: 1D Multi-Scale Navigation. In: Proc. CHI 2006, pp. 21–30 (2006)
3. Asano, T., Sharlin, E., Kitamura, Y., Takashima, K., Kishino, F.: Predictive Interaction Using the Delphian Desktop. In: Proc. UIST 2005, pp. 133–141 (2005)
4. Blackmon, M.H., Polson, P.G., Kitajima, M., Lewis, C.: Cognitive Walkthrough for the Web. In: Proc. CHI 2002, pp. 463–470 (2002)
5. Card, S.K., Pirolli, P., Wege, M.V.D., Morrison, J.B., Reeder, R.W., Schraedley, P.K., Boshart, J.: Information Scent as a Driver of Web Behavior Graphs: Results of a Protocol Analysis Method for Web Usability. In: Proc. CHI 2001, pp. 498–505 (2001)
6. Chi, E.H., Pirolli, P., Chen, K., Pitkow, J.: Using Information Scent to Model User Information Needs and Actions and the Web. In: Proc. CHI 2001, pp. 490–497 (2001)
7. Chi, E.H., Rosien, A., Supattanasiri, G., Williams, A., Royer, C., Chow, C., Robles, E., Dalal, B., Chen, J., Cousins, S.: The Bloodhound Project: Automating Discovery of Web Usability Issues Using the InfoScent™ Simulator. In: Proc. CHI 2003, pp. 505–512 (2003)
8. Hinckley, K., Cutrell, E., Bathiche, S., Muss, T.: Quantitative Analysis of Scrolling Techniques. In: Proc. CHI 2002, pp. 65–72 (2002)
9. Igarashi, T., Hinckley, K.: Speed-Dependent Automatic Zooming for Browsing Large Documents. In: Proc. UIST 2000, pp. 139–148 (2000)
10. Ishak, E.W., Feiner, S.K.: Content-Aware Scrolling. In: Proc. UIST 2006, pp. 155–158 (2006)
11. Kobayashi, M., Igarashi, T.: Considering the Direction of Cursor Movement for Efficient Traversal of Cascading Menus. In: Proc. UIST 2003, pp. 91–94 (2003)
12. Kumar, M., Winograd, T.: Gaze-Enhanced Scrolling Techniques. In: Proc. UIST 2007, pp. 213–216 (2007)
13. Masui, T., Kashiwagi, K., Borden IV, G.R.: Elastic Graphical Interfaces for Precise Data Manipulation. In: Proc. CHI 1995, pp. 143–144 (1995)
14. Olston, C., Chi, E.H.: ScentTrails: Integrating Browsing and Searching on the Web. Transactions on Computer-Human Interaction (TOCHI) 10(3), 177–197 (2003)
15. Pirolli, P.: Computational Models of Information Scent-Following in a Very Large Browsable Text Collection. In: Proc. CHI 1997, pp. 3–10 (1997)
16. Pirolli, P., Crad, S.: Information Foraging. Psychology Review 106(4), 643–675 (1999)
17. Pirolli, P., Card, S.K., Van Der Wege, M.M.: The Effects of Information Scent on Visual Search in the Hyperbolic Tree Browser. Transactions on Computer-Human Interaction (TOCHI) 10(1), 20–53 (2003)

Aspects of Auditory Perception and Cognition for Usable Display Resolution in Data Sonification

Johan Kildal

Nokia Research Center
P.O. Box 407, FI-00045 Nokia Group
johan.kildal@nokia.com

Abstract. Sonification of data via the mapping of values to frequency of sound is an auditory data analysis technique commonly used to display graph information. The goal for any form of graph is to display numerical information with accuracy and neutrality while exploiting perceptual and cognitive processes. Conveying information in frequency of sound is subject to aspects of pitch perception, largely overlooked to date, that can influence these properties of auditory graphing. This paper identifies some of these aspects and describes potential design limitations and opportunities derived from the musical nature of auditory data representations.

Keywords: Frequency categorization, auditory display, auditory graph, design.

1 Introduction

Parameter-mapping data sonification (PMDS) is an established data analysis technique in which numerical information is mapped to parameters of sound in order to perceptualise relations in the data [1]. As with any method to display quantified information, maximising the accuracy with which the information is made available to the senses is a desirable property. The accuracy that can be attained depends on the perceivable resolution of the information display, a function of the resolution of the display and the resolution of the senses involved. In data sonification, given the high pitch and temporal resolutions of the human auditory system (and the relatively large usable range for any of these parameters of sound), information mapped to frequency of sound and time can be conveyed with high accuracy. Research and experience have shown that optimum implementations of PMDS techniques are obtained by mapping relative numerical data to frequency of sound and laying them out temporally. This pairing of frequency and time has become the default design for auditory graphs [2].

An additional requirement is the uniformity of the psychophysical scaling used in the display. Focusing on the frequency-of-sound axis of the auditory displays considered here, the logarithm of the frequency offers a good approximation to a linear scale in the middle band of audible frequencies, within which equal increases of the logarithm of frequency are perceived as equal increases of pitch. This is particularly true for frequencies between 80 and 800Hz, where toneness is highest [3].

These characteristics of the frequency-of-sound scale are comparable – when not superior – to the most common visual quantitative data display scales, like distance on

T. Gross et al. (Eds.): INTERACT 2009, Part I, LNCS 5726, pp. 467–470, 2009.

an axis in a typical visual graph. In spite of this, this paper argues that there are aspects of human auditory perception and cognition which do not always permit representing numerical relations on a pitch scale in as neutral a way as with analogous visual scales. Furthermore, this paper argues that the way in which we interpret sounds in the frequency space can pose a limitation on the use of our fine frequency discrimination skills for the display of numerical information. These theses are grounded both on user experience observed with the use of frequency-and-time PMDS techniques (section 2), and on the current understanding of psychology of hearing (section 3).

2 Musical Nature of Sonified Data

In the many studies conducted in [4], users explored large numerical data sets interactively using frequency-and-time PMDS techniques, estimating magnitudes based on perceived pitch of piano notes and chords. The value-to-frequency mapping strategies employed in the sonifications made use of either the chromatic 12 tone equally tempered (12-TET) scale or the whole continuum of the frequency space. The participants that evaluated these techniques reached consistently high performance levels in overview and detail information-retrieval data-exploration tasks. During the interviews conducted to evaluate these techniques qualitatively (their usability and the exploratory strategies devised for different types of data sets), users often volunteered reports of their subjective experiences derived from listening to sonified data. A frequently-recorded comment was that upon extended use of these techniques the sonifications became more tiring to listen to. Many of their comments included aesthetic judgements regarding the audio representations of the data, with ratings ranging from appealing to (more frequently) ugly and even harsh. Both frequency spaces used (12-TET and whole continuum of frequency) received positive and negative aesthetic ratings.

The interesting aspect about receiving this kind of feedback was not the actual aesthetic tastes of the participants, but the fact that they volunteered them in interviews that dealt with pragmatic questions regarding interface usability and effective data mining. The frequent recording of such comments, together with multiple anecdotes about users attempting to improvise musical compositions during the more distended parts of the experiments (by searching for data that would render in particular frequency ranges, generating sonifications in rhythmic patterns, and even identifying elements of specific musical compositions and styles) provided enough anecdotal evidence to realise that the outcome of frequency-and-time PMDSs convey associated musical and aesthetic qualities, even when the tasks in hand are strictly analytical belonging to the domain of data mining. Indeed, research has already suggested that musical training can be an important factor in the use of PMDS techniques [5]. However, musical expertise is not required for users to be implicitly aware of the categories present in the different musical dimensions, and ultimately to be implicitly aware of the rules forming a particular musical context [6] that may arise from the sonification of data.

3 Cognitive Limitations on Usable Display Resolution

As stated above, we possess a very fine capacity to discriminate audible frequencies. The majority of the population can detect frequencies far smaller than a semitone, often of only a few cents, particularly across the middle range of audible frequencies (see [7] for a summary of related studies). This would suggest that the highest display resolution usable by most people is obtained by mapping values to the frequencies in the 12-TET scale, and that even the majority of users would benefit from the further-increased resolution obtained when values are mapped to the exact corresponding frequencies in the frequency continuum. In contrast, literature in musicology shows that, despite our fine frequency discrimination capabilities, no musical tradition makes structural use of more than 12 equal divisions in the octave[1]. Burns ([8] p.218), offers the following explanation for this: "*The most likely reason for the adoption of a relatively small number of discrete intervals as the tonal material for music is that discretization or categorization is a typical, if not universal, strategy used by animals in order to reduce information overload and facilitate processing when subjected to the high-information-content signals and/or high information rates from a highly developed sensory system*". Due to the categorical perception of pitch (for which frequency shifts of any size are reliably labelled as one of the discrete intervals in familiar musical scales, like the 12-TET scale [9]), making use of the whole frequency continuum for the mapping of values may not provide the fine display resolution that could be expected. Instead, and unless required for local detailed analysis of a few data points, it could often be beneficial to select a relatively small subset of intervals per octave, and represent values rounded to those discrete frequencies. Such mapping strategy would be useful for overview explorations of larger data sets, where sonifications could represent data with sufficient accuracy, while being 'easier' to listen to.

When considering subsets of intervals for value-to-frequency mappings, it is necessary to investigate whether the obvious division in 12 equal intervals is still too large. For instance, in music (at least in the western tradition), although with exceptions, diatonic scales are used to create melodies, and not the full chromatic scale [8]. If the selection of such small collections of intervals for musical expression are part of a strategy to cope with complexity of information, similar criteria could also be relevant for the implementation of PMDS techniques intended to extract knowledge from complex data. However, as smaller sets of intervals are used, the chances of obtaining musical phrases with a strong tonal identity would be higher. This gives rise to the question of whether musical context (which can significantly improve pitch judgements [10]) is a desirable factor in a display of numerical information or if, on the contrary, the sense of expectation of musical events that might arise [11] could interfere with the objective exploration of numerical information.

4 Conclusions

This paper has identified aspects of psychology of music and auditory perception and cognition that can be relevant for the design of value-to-frequency mapping strategies in auditory displays. Building on qualitative data collected from users of interactive

[1] While there are traditions that include quarter tones or other intervallic divisions that are smaller than the western semitone, as well as embellishments like glissandi, none of them seem to make use of intervals smaller than the western semitone to construct structural elements in music, such as intervals in melodic lines. See [8] for a comprehensive discussion on this topic.

sonification interfaces who explored large data sets, it is highlighted that auditory representations of data possess a musical nature that influences the subjective experience of data mining, even to an aesthetic level, and that they are generally rated as unpleasant if generated with relatively large sets of intervals per octave. The paper then discusses the implications of the categorical perception of the pitch space, arguing that, except for the cases in which detailed examination of data is required locally, most stages of the exploration cannot benefit from the complexity of information generated with very accurate mappings. These aspects of human auditory cognition should be included in the research agenda about PMDS techniques, and taken into account in their implementations. In particular, the effects of low-resolution displays in the performance and subjective experience with large auditory graphs should be investigated, including the implications of stronger tonal contexts that might arise as a result.

References

1. Hermann, T.: Taxonomy and Definitions for Sonification and Auditory Display. In: 14th International Conference on Auditory Display, Paris, France (2008)
2. Flowers, J.H.: Thirteen Years of Reflection on Auditory Graphing: Promises, Pitfalls, and Potential New Directions. In: First International Symposium on Auditory Graphs (AGS2005), 11th International Conference on Auditory Display, Limerick, Ireland (2005)
3. Huron, D.: Tone and Voice: A Derivation of the Rules of Voice-Leading from Perceptual Principles. Music Perception 19(1), 1–64 (2001)
4. Kildal, J.: Developing an Interactive Overview for Non-Visual Exploration of Tabular Numerical Information. PhD Thesis, Department of Computing Science, University of Glasgow, UK (2009)
5. Neuhoff, J., Wayward, J.: Pitch Change, Sonification, and Musical Expertise: Which Way Is Up? In: 8th International Conference on Auditory Display, Kyoto, Japan (2002)
6. Bigand, E.: Contributions of Music to Research on Human Auditory Cognition. In: McAdams, S., Bigand, E. (eds.) Thinking in Sound. The Cognitive Psychology of Human Audition, pp. 231–277. Oxford University Press, Oxford (1993)
7. Moore, B.C.J.: Pitch Perception. In: An Introduction to the Psychology of Hearing, pp. 195–232. Academic Press, London (2004)
8. Burns, E.M.: Intervals, Scales, and Tuning. In: Deutsch, D. (ed.) The Psychology of Music, pp. 215–264. Academic Press, London (1999)
9. Burns, E.M., Campbell, S.L.: Frequency and Frequency-Ratio Resolution by Possessors of Absolute and Relative Pitch: Examples of Categorical Perception? J. Acoust. Soc. Am. 96(5), 2704–2719 (1994)
10. Warrier, C.M., Zatorre, R.J.: Influence of Tonal Context and Timbral Variation on Perception of Pitch. Perception & Psychophysics 64(2), 198–207 (2002)
11. Huron, D.: Sweet Anticipation: Music and the Psychology of Expectation. MIT Press, Cambridge (2006)

Simulating Perceptive Processes of Pilots to Support System Design

Andreas Lüdtke and Jan-Patrick Osterloh

OFFIS Institute for Information Technology, Escherweg 2,
26127 Oldenburg, Germany
{luedtke,osterloh}@offis.de

Abstract. In this paper we present an approach towards supporting the ergonomic design of aircraft cockpits by predicting the probability that pilots might miss relevant information due to routine learning effects combined with non-adequate placement of display instruments. The approach is based on an executable cognitive pilot model. We focus on the cognitive interaction between (1) rule-based processing of flight procedures, (2) the pilot's mental model of the current situation and (3) pilot's attention. The cognitive model is coupled with a formal cockpit design to simulate human-machine interaction during flight procedures. As an example we analyze the perception of automatic flight mode changes.

Keywords: Human modeling for design, human (selective) attention, mental models, human behavior simulation.

1 Introduction

Today, human factor analysis of aircraft cockpit systems like autopilot or flight management systems is based on expert judgment and simulator-based tests with human subjects (e.g. test pilots) when first prototypes exist. This is in general a very expensive and time-consuming approach, because a number of subjects have to be hired for the simulation and necessary changes can only be realized with huge effort in the usually late stage of system development. In preceding papers an approach relying on cognitive models as partial substitutes of human subjects has been suggested (e.g. [5], [6]). In this paper latest extensions of the cognitive model are described.

Cognitive models were established in the early eighties as research tools to unify psychological models of particular cognitive processes. These early models neglected mental processes such as multitasking, perception and motor control that are essential for analysis of complex dynamic systems like aircraft cockpits. Models such as ACT-R [1] and SOAR [2] have been extended in this direction, but still have their main focus on processes suitable for static, non-interruptive environments. Other cognitive models like MIDAS [3] and APEX [4] were explicitly motivated by the needs of human-machine interaction. At OFFIS we developed a cognitive model with focus on how pilots adapt their mental knowledge about flight procedures while they gain experience of a particular system [5]. The phenomenon is called Learned Carelessness (LC).

T. Gross et al. (Eds.): INTERACT 2009, Part I, LNCS 5726, pp. 471–484, 2009.

In the EU funded project ISAAC the cognitive model was coupled with STATEMATE system design models to analyze pilot-autopilot interaction by human simulation to identify design structures where LC might have an impact on flight safety [6]. Case studies conducted in ISAAC already demonstrated plausible predictions of a number of erroneous pilot actions and provided insight in potential improvements of the analyzed autopilots. Based on these promising results it was suggested to extend the scope of covered psychological phenomena.

In this paper we present extensions towards simulation of human behavior on the level of perception and how these processes interact with rule-based processing of flight procedures and with the pilot's mental model of the current situation. This extended model shall be used to evaluate the ergonomics of cockpit layouts with regard to characteristics of human attention including a phenomenon called Selective Attention (SA) which may undermine the effect of graphical means used by designers to shift attention to critical events (like flashing annunciations). Both, LC and SA, may induce errors of omission. LC may lead to omitting displayed information, because routinely no relevant information is expected. SA may also lead to omitting displayed information because it is absorbed by other attention capturing displays in the neighborhood, e.g. a flashing warning signal may go undetected if it appears in the context of other dynamic elements.

In the following we first discuss LC and SA in the context of autopilot mode changes and mode annunciations during takeoff maneuvers. Afterwards, we present our model of these phenomena in the context of the OFFIS cognitive architecture. Then the model's operation including the interaction of LC and SA is illustrated based on three simulation run examples. The paper finishes with a brief overview of related work.

2 Monitoring Autopilot Modes

Aircraft cockpits are becoming increasingly information rich. Pilots have to take a lot of information into account in order to monitor the current aircraft status and to plan next actions. In this paper we focus on the autopilot (AP) of the Piper Cheyenne III PA42. The interaction with the AP is highly dependent on the actual AP mode. The modes indicate the current state of the system, what it is doing and what it is going to do. Because modes may change automatically during the flight, pilots are required to monitor the Mode Annunciation (MA). The MA is located in an instrument called the Primary Flight Display (PFD) which primarily indicates pitch and roll of the aircraft in a graphical way. Mode are indicated in form of letter codes, e.g. 'ALT' flashing in Green is an abbreviation for the Altitude Capture mode, in which the AP automatically decreases vertical speed in order to smoothly level off to an altitude previously dialed into the Alerter. 'ALT' flashes for approx. 6 seconds. Afterwards the annunciation is steady. On more modern flight decks a flashing box appears around the letter code and flashes for 10 seconds to attract pilots' attention.

Fig. 1 shows an excerpt of activities pilots have to perform during a takeoff maneuver with a Piper Cheyenne. The horizontal bars indicate what instruments have to be monitored at which time by the pilots according to the normative flight procedure. Parallel bars indicate that several instruments have to be monitored simultaneously.

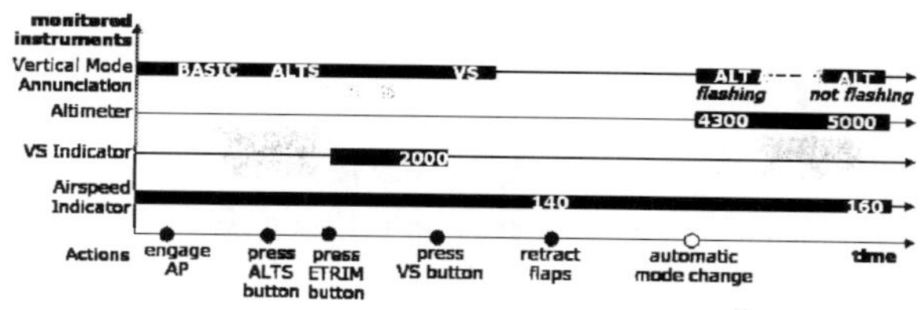

Fig. 1. Pilot activities after liftoff

The diagram refers to three subtasks pilots' have to perform after liftoff. *(1) Automatic climb:* the pilot has to engage and configure the AP in order to initiate an automatic climb to the initial altitude. The ALTS button has to be pressed to activate the target altitude dialed into the Alerter already as part of the preflight takeoff items. The ETRIM button has to be operated to adjust the vertical speed. At a vertical speed of 2000 ft/min the VS button has to be pressed to stabilize the climb. As soon as the aircraft is near to the target altitude the AP mode changes automatically to Altitude Capture mode ('ALT' flashes). *(2) Flaps retraction:* the pilot has to monitor the airspeed in order to retract the flaps at a speed of 140 knots. *(3) Leveloff monitoring:* as soon as the AP mode has changed to Altitude Capture mode the pilot has to monitor that the aircraft actually flies to the initial altitude and no error (for some reason) occurs.

One crucial point in this takeoff phase is that the pilots recognize the automatic mode change in order to begin monitoring the leveloff and because during automatic capture pressing the VS button (for stabilizing the automatic climb) is no longer allowed. Stabilizing the climb makes only sense before the mode change has occurred. If done afterwards it causes an altitude overshoot. The automatic mode change appears between 300 – 900 feet before reaching the target altitude. This paper considers two cognitive processes that may cause pilots to miss mode annunciations: Human (Selective) Attention and Learned Carelessness

3 Human Attention and Learned Carelessness

Human attention can be separated in top-down and bottom-up attention. Top-down attention is a deliberate process that shifts the gaze to current Areas of Interests, e.g. if an action depends on the actual airspeed, the eyes (and head) are moved to the airspeed indicator and attention is shifted accordingly.

Bottom-up attention, often referred to as *Selective Attention*, refers to the possibility that eye (and head) movements and a shift of attention are triggered by the onset of a salient stimulus [7]. Although eye movements and attention shifts can also be caused by acoustic and haptic stimuli, in this paper we investigate only visual stimuli. Thus, a salient stimulus means a discontinuity in space or time in the visual field. A discontinuity in space represents a difference in a static property, like color, brightness, form or orientation, e.g. a green dot in a set of red dots, or a circle in a set of quadrates. In contrast to this, a discontinuity in time (or dynamic discontinuity) denotes a dynamic change, like abrupt onset, flashing or moving of an object. In this paper we focus on dynamic discontinuities (like the flashing letter codes for modes), as this is commonly used by cockpit designers to capture the pilots' attention.

The flashing letter code 'ALT' is intended to take advantage of SA. But recent studies showed that the flashing annunciations have not always the intended effect of shifting the pilots' attention to changing modes. Mumaw, Sarter and Wickens [8] investigated mode changes in Boeing aircraft and found that 30 to 60 percent of pilots did not look at the Flight Mode Annunciation in an appropriate time after the mode had changed. On Boeing and other modern flight decks a flashing box (instead of flashing letter codes) is used to highlight mode changes. A successor study by Nikolic, Orr and Sarter [9] provides a hypothetical explanation: The context of the display, like color or dynamic elements can undermine the effect of attention capturing. The intended effect might be undermined by the data-rich and multiple-dynamic display context. As mentioned above, the PFD not only contains the MA, but, for example, also the artificial horizon which is moving according to the pitch and roll of the aircraft. Due to the colorful and dynamic neighborhood, the probability that the flashing 'ALT' captures the pilots' attention significantly decreases. Nikolic, Orr and Sarter [9] performed further more basic experiments which showed that the detection rate of the flashing box is about 0.649 (standard deviation 0.282), when the stimulus occurs in a colorful and dynamic context; in the control condition (solid black background) the detection rate is significantly higher (0.969, standard deviation 0.057). The results provide evidence that the salience of a stimulus depends on how much it differs from its surroundings.

Top-down and bottom-up attention compete against each other [7], e.g. a salient stimulus might detract the pilot from the task on which (s)he is currently concentrated, which is often intended, e.g. in case of warnings. The other way round, a salient stimulus might go undetected, because top-down attention causes the eyes to move to an Area of Interest where the stimulus is either out of the visual field or still in the visual field but absorbed by a dynamic neighborhood. Top-down processes drive attention while the pilot performs flight procedures. We assume that pilots have mental models of how to interact with the cockpit systems. While human pilots can partially substitute visual perception with other information from other resources, e.g. sense of balance, we assume for our modeling activities that pilots always move their visual attention to an instrument if one of the sub tasks that are currently performed requires the displayed information as an input according to the mental model of the flight procedure. Thus, the mental model drives the top-down attention, and is the main parameter that determines if a certain stimulus (like the flashing 'ALT') is in the visual field or not. Being in the visual field is certainly a precondition for being detected by bottom-up visual attention processes. The missing effect of resource substitution has to be considered in the model validation, e.g. one can conclude from the actions of the pilot that he perceived certain data, and this can be counted additional evidence for perception.

Obviously, considering the mental flight procedure model as the only driver of visual top-down attention is a simplification because it neglects scanning patterns pilots additionally use to get constant updates on the aircraft state. But, studies by Sarter [10] and others have shown that especially the autopilot modes are often not part of these scanning patterns. There is evidence that observing modes is more driven by mode change expectations.

While SA refers to the bottom-up aspect of human attention LC refers to the top-down aspect. The mental model of flight procedures is initially formed based on normative flight procedures acquired through handbooks and in simulator sessions. Then during line operation the mental model is modified by cognitive learning processes. LC describes the learning process on which we focused our investigations. The psychological theory "Learned Carelessness" [16] states that humans have a tendency to neglect safety precautions if this has immediate advantages, e.g. it saves time, and allegedly allows keeping the same safety level. In the context of avionics systems safety precautions may be understood as checking the current state or mode of the systems before performing critical actions. LC is characteristic for human nature because we have to implicitly simplify in order to be capable to perform efficiently in a complex environment. Resulting behavior is highly adapted to routine scenarios but, unfortunately, may lead to errors and hazards in non-routine situations.

Visual events like flashing indications on cockpit displays might be a countermeasure against the effects of LC but as described above this might be undermined by characteristics of SA. By modeling these two phenomena in the same executable model it is possible to simulate and analyze the interaction of LC and SA in specific scenarios with the goal to optimize normative flight procedures (with their resulting scanning paths) and the ergonomics of display designs.

4 The OFFIS Simulation Platform

Lüdtke and Möbus [5] developed a generic rule based cognitive architecture, which can be used to simulate pilot behavior (including pilot errors). The architecture is based on a flight procedure formalisation in the form of "if-then" rules. The rules formally describe a mental representation of flight procedures. Currently the procedure must contain the tasks of the pilot flying and non-flying, because the cognitive architecture in its present development state does not support task sharing between the two.

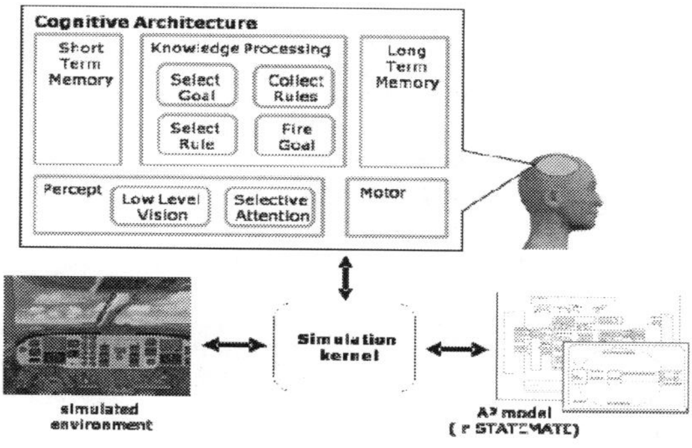

Fig. 2. Simulation platform with cognitive architecture

In order to perform the simulation the flight procedure rules are uploaded to the cognitive architecture (cf Fig. 2). A cognitive architecture with uploaded procedure rules is what we call a pilot model. The cognitive architecture can be understood as an interpreter or executor of formal flight procedure rules.

Within a simulation platform (Fig. 2) the pilot model interacts with a system under investigation (modeled in STATEMATE) and a simulated environment (including the aircraft). A simulation kernel synchronizes the different models and organizes the dataflow.

4.1 Modeling Flight Procedures with Rules

The format of our procedure rules is a Goal-State-Means (GSM) format (Fig. 3). All rules consist of a left-hand side (IF) and a right-hand side (THEN). The left-hand side consists of a goal in the Goal-Part and a State-part specifying Boolean conditions on the current state of the environment. Apart from the condition the State-part contains memory-read items to specify that in order to evaluate the condition the associated variables have to be retrieved from memory. The right-hand side consists of a Means-Part containing motor and percept actions (e.g. hand movements or attention shifts), memory-store items as well as a set of partial ordered sub-goals. In the GSM rule syntax variables are underlined.

The rule in Fig. 3 can be informally be read as "IF the actual goal is to retract the gear and the aircraft has lifted off, THEN pull the gear lever, shift attention to gear annunciation, pursue the goal to check if the gear actually retracts and afterwards pursue the goal to call out the gear state. This rule defines a goal-subgoal relation between GEAR_UP and subgoals CHECK_GEAR_UP, CALLOUT_GEAR_UP. Between the subgoals a temporal order is imposed (by "After").

During simulation the cognitive architecture selects rules based on their left-hand sides and executes the right-hand sides.

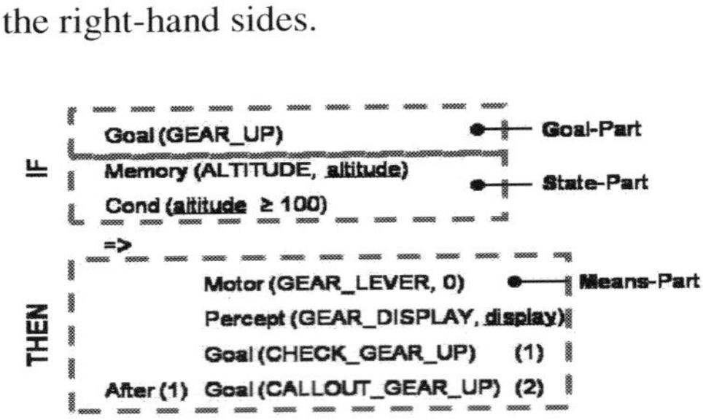

Fig. 3. Example GSM rule

Fig. 4 shows a subset of rules for the takeoff maneuver described above (Fig. 1) with its subtasks automatic climb, flaps retraction and leveloff monitoring. *(1) Automatic climb:* With rule 21 the pilot model prepares climb stabilization by looking at the flight mode annunciation and perceiving the displayed value. Rule 23 is a percept rule used directly after the percept action to store the perceived value into memory. Rule 24 and 25 retrieve the current mode from memory, in case it is Altitude Capture mode rule 24 prescribes to perform no action, in case it is not Altitude Capture mode rules 25 prescribes to press the VS button. "ALT-flash" is the symbol for the flashing letter code. *(2) Flaps retraction:* Rule 46 serves to prepare flaps retraction. With rule 47 and 48 the pilot model decides either to operate the flaps lever (rule 47) or to continue to monitor the speed annunciation (rule 48) by using rule 46 again. *(3) Leveloff monitoring:* Rule 52 serves to prepare monitoring the leveloff. It is fired as soon as

MA annunciates the transition to Capture mode. With rule 53 the pilot model decides if the aircraft has leveled off correctly. A further rule not shown here prescribes to continue monitoring the leveloff if the altitude has not yet been reached.

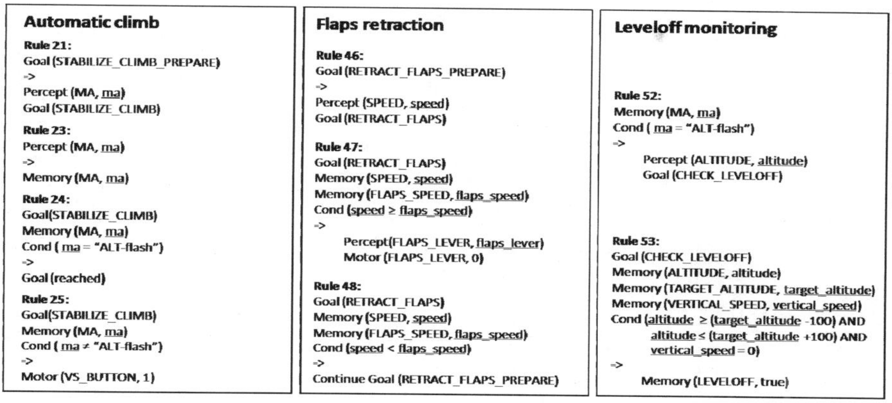

Fig. 4. Subset of rules for takeoff procedure

4.2 Processing Rules Inside a Cognitive Architecture

The human model has been developed in a modular way. It consists of a short-term and a long-term memory, knowledge processing, a learning component and components for perception and motor (Fig. 2). The percept and motor components serve to communicate with the simulated environment and the system model. All data entering the model via perception is stored in the short-term memory. Additionally the short-term memory stores a set of goals which the model has to process (goal agenda). The long-term memory stores procedural knowledge in form of GSM-rules. The following presentation of the cognitive architecture focuses on the data structures and processes that have been added in order to model human perception including Selective Attention (SA).

Simulated Environment: The cognitive model relies on a symbolic representation of the simulated world with which it is intended to interact. Most relevant are the topology of the cockpit as well as the ergonomic features and current values of the instruments. Every instrument is represented as an Area of Interest object (*AOI Object*) with the following structure: a name, e.g. "MA", the current value, the 3-dimensional position coordinates, the physical dimensions height, width and depth, the primary colors and a Boolean variable indicating, if the AOI is dynamic in the sense of dynamic discontinuity (like the MA with its flashing letter codes). As described above, dynamic AOIs might cause a shift of attention if their effect is not absorbed by other dynamic AOIs in the neighborhood. Changes of dynamic AOIs (e.g. flashing) are modeled as *Visual Events* that are sent to the cognitive model by the simulation kernel and are processed by the SA mechanism (see Perception below). A Visual Event is always associated to exactly one AOI Object and is furthermore specified by attributes that characterize the associated stimulus, e.g. type of event (e.g. flashing, moving), frequency of flashing, and duration of event. Visual Events are sent for example by the MA when the mode changes automatically to Altitude Capture mode and 'ALT' flashes and by the PFD when the artificial horizon moves while the aircraft is changing its attitude.

Memory: The memory component of the cognitive model stores the mental image of the current environmental state. Consequently, there is a corresponding Memory Object for every AOI Object. Memory Objects store a subset of the AOI Object attributes including name and the current value.

Rules: Additionally to the GSM-rules described above we added a second rule type, called reactive rules. Rule 52 in Fig. 4 is an example of this rule type. The only difference is that reactive rules have no Goal-Part. While GSM-rules represent deliberate behavior and are selected by the knowledge processing component during the execution of a flight procedure, reactive rules (State-Means (SM) rules) represent immediate or reactive behavior which is triggered by visual events in the environment (bottom-up perception).

Knowledge Processing: The knowledge processing component executes a four step cognitive cycle typical for production systems: (KP1) a goal is selected from the goal agenda in short-term memory, (KP2) all rules containing the selected goal in their goal-part are collected and a request for retrieving the current state of the variables contained in the Boolean conditions in the state-parts of the rules is sent to the memory component, (KP3) after the request has been answered one of the collected rules is selected by evaluating the condition-part, finally (KP4) the selected rule is fired, which means that the motor and percept actions are sent to the motor and percept component respectively, the subgoals are added to the goal agenda (together with the partial temporal order) and the values contained in memory items are sent to the memory component.

The cycle time is 50 ms like in ACT-R. This time may be prolonged depending on the memory retrieval in KP2. In KP2 all variables contained on the left-hand sides of the collected rules have to be retrieved from memory. The retrieval time is influenced by the number of variables.

In KP1 the goal agenda may contain several goals that are currently applicable according to the temporal order. We modeled a simple task switching mechanism in order to achieve an alternating between tasks. Our mechanism is similar to the multitasking general executive of Salvucci [17] and selects goals, based on a most-recently-used criterion. In KP2 reactive rules may be added to the set of collected rules if new values for the variables contained in the State-Part have been added to the memory component (by the percept component). In KP3, reactive rules are always preferred to non-reactive rules.

Vision: When modeling visual perception, the main focus is on *what can be perceived based on the visual constraints*, and *how much time is needed* to perceive something. In order to answer this, one needs to model visual focus, visual field, human attention, as well as head- and eye-movements. In our model we assume a visual field of 170 degree horizontal and 110 degree vertical around an optical axis (defined by the gaze direction of the eye). The focus is modeled with an expansion of seven degree around the optical axis. Eye-movements can be initiated either by the knowledge processing component or by Visual Events in the environment. Currently we do not distinguish between moving eyes and moving attention. We assume that if eyes are moved also the attention is moved. This is of course a simplification which does for example not allow simulating the phenomenon "seeing without noticing". For a validation of the model with human pilots, an extensive debriefing of the human pilots is necessary in order to identify seeing without noticing, and to enhance gaze data.

The visual component is split into *Low Level Vision* (LLV) and SA. LLV implements all basic functions of human vision: eye- and also head-movements (including focus and visual field). SA is modeled as a mechanism that computes for each Visual Event if it is detected or not. The two processes are performed in parallel. LLV is triggered either by the knowledge processing component when percept actions are sent to the percept component during rule firing in KP4 (top-down perception as explained above) or by the percept component itself if SA detects a salient stimulus (bottom-up perception). In both cases LLV performs the necessary steps to move the eyes and head to an Area of Interest (AOI). For top-down perception this is done in three (LLV1-3) and for bottom-up perception in two (LLV2, 3) steps:

- LLV1: For top-down perception the variable (e.g. ALTITUDE) contained in the percept action has to be transformed into an AOI by retrieving the position of the corresponding instrument from memory. Then the position of the instrument is transformed into the coordinate system of the eyes, so that the angle α between the actual optical axis of the eye V1 (e.g. pointing towards the MA) and the desired optical axis V2 (e.g. pointing toward the Airspeed Indicator, ASI) can be computed:

  - $$\alpha(V_1, V_2) = arcos\left(\frac{x_{MA} \cdot x_{ASI} + y_{MA} \cdot y_{ASI} + z_{MA} \cdot z_{ASI}}{\sqrt{{x_{MA}}^2 + {y_{MA}}^2 + {z_{MA}}^2} \cdot \sqrt{{x_{ASI}}^2 + {y_{ASI}}^2 + {z_{ASI}}^2}}\right) \quad (1)$$

- This preparatory step takes about 140 to 200 ms normally distributed around 170 ms. For bottom-up perception this step is skipped because the AOI is defined by a visual stimulus directly in the cockpit at a certain instrument position. Thus, no position has to be retrieved from memory.
- LLV2: Eyes and head are moved in order to focus the new AOI. Based on concepts of Freedman [11] we developed a model for a combined movement of head and eyes. The contribution of head and eye, respectively, to the total change α is calculated as follows:

  - $$EYE_{contrib}(\alpha) = \begin{cases} \alpha, & \alpha \leq 20 \\ \min(0.31 \cdot \alpha + 13.6,\ 40), & \alpha > 20 \end{cases} \quad (2)$$
  - $$HEAD_{contrib}(\alpha) = \alpha - EYE_{contrib}(\alpha) \quad (3)$$

- The eye contribution is limited to 40 degree, due to the physical design of the human eyes. The modeled speed of the eye and head are approximated functions from Freedman as well.
- LLV3: The AOI is fixated until LLV is triggered again. If fixation can be kept for at least 200 ms the actual value of the AOI Object is sent to the memory component and stored in the corresponding Memory Object. A shift of attention might be interrupted in LLV3 by a new attention shift request as soon as the centration of the eyes in the head is finished. Thus, it may happen that LLV3 is interrupted before the needed fixation time of 200 ms has passed. In such a case the AOI value is not written into memory.

Each Visual Event sent by the simulated environment is processed by the SA mechanism which is divided in three steps:

- SA1: Based on the actual eye and AOI position it is determined if the AOI to which the currently processed event belongs lies within the current focus or at least in current visual field. To be in the visual field the AOI must be within 85 degrees of the eye position. If the AOI is in the visual focus, then the associated event is marked as recognized and SA3 is started, skipping SA2. If it is outside the visual field the associated event is marked as unrecognized, the next event is retrieved and SA1 is restarted. If it is within the visual field but not in focus SA2 is initiated in order to determine recognition.
- SA2: It is determined if in a neighborhood of 15 degree around the AOI other Visual Events have occurred. The 15 degree neighborhood has been derived from the experimental setup of Nikolic, Orr and Sarter [9], so that the probabilities of their study can be used in our model. If the event indeed has a dynamic neighborhood, a probabilistic choice is computed to determine if the event is recognized or not: the probability to detect an event within a dynamic neighborhood is 0.649 with a standard deviation of 0.282. If the event is recognized SA3 is started else the next event is retrieved and SA1 is restarted.
- SA3: The Visual Event is sent to the memory component to be stored. LLV reacts to this event as soon as step LLV3 is entered. The other LLV steps cannot be interrupted.

Learning Component: The learning component implements our LC mechanism. Rule 25 in Fig. 4 specifies that the vertical speed must be stabilized as long as the target altitude has not been captured (MA ≠ 'ALT-flash'). Using rule 21 the current value of MA is perceived from the associated cockpit instrument. Rule 23 stores the perceived value into the memory. Most of the times when the pilot tries to press the VS button the mode change has not occurred, because the distance to the target altitude is long enough. Thus most of the time the percept action delivers 'ALTS' which indicates that the current mode is Altitude Select and not Altitude Capture. We hold the hypotheses that due to this regularity a pilot would simplify his mental model of the procedure into a version, where the MA value is no longer perceived from the cockpit instrument but is just retrieved from memory. This is modelled by melting two rules into one rule by means of *rule composition* [14]. A precondition for composing rules is that firing of the first rule has evoked the second rule, or more exact, the first rule derives a subgoal that is contained in the Goal-Part of the second rule. Melting the rules means building a *composite* rule by combing the left-hand sides of both rules and also combing both right-hand sides.

The crucial point is that in this process elements that are contained on the right-hand side of the first and also on the left hand side of the second rule are eliminated. This process cuts off intermediate knowledge processing steps. Fig. 5 shows the composite rule 112 that was formed by composition of rule 21 and 23. The percept action has been eliminated and the composite always stores the value 'ALTS' in memory. Rule 112 is appropriate in scenarios that are similar to those in which the rule has been learned (MA does not indicate Altitude Capture mode). In deviating scenarios (MA does indicates Altitude Capture mode) applying rule 112 results in careless behaviour: pressing the VS button independent from the current mode annunciation.

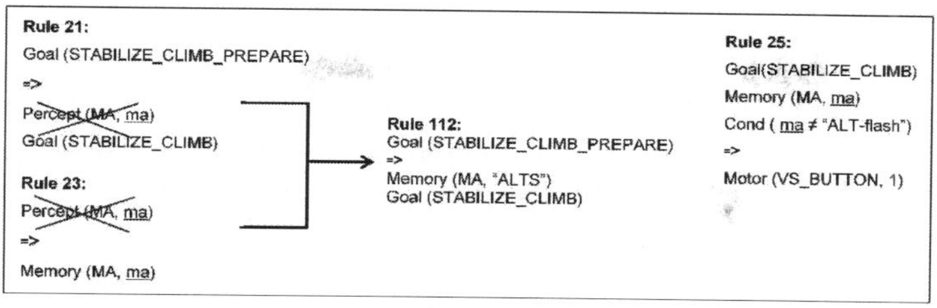

Fig. 5. Simplified rule

At the beginning of the simulation all procedure rules in the long-term memory component are normative, meaning that the application of these rules does not lead to an error.

5 Simulation Run Examples

In this section we present three simulation runs which we observed on the simulation platform. These runs serve to illustrate the interaction between the cognitive model and the Piper Cheyenne cockpit systems with a focus on the autopilot. All scenarios refer to the rules presented in Fig. 4 and thus to the takeoff phase after liftoff. In all scenarios the simulated pilot is careless with regard to the Altitude Capture mode annunciation because he has learned rule 112 (Fig. 5) during the preceding simulation runs. Simulation shall show if the annunciation of the automatic mode change is effective in capturing the pilot's attention and to alleviate the effect of LC.

Scenario 1: LC not alleviated due to other dynamic displays

The pilot model engages the AP and presses the ALTS button (Fig. 6). It looks at the VS Indicator in order to stabilize vertical speed as soon as 2000 feet are reached. In parallel it monitors the Airspeed Indicator to prepare flaps retraction. The automatic mode change occurs while the aircraft starts to fly a turn towards a heading of 50 degrees. The pilot model does not recognize the mode change annunciation. The PFD at this moment is highly dynamic because of the turn. Thus the mode change annunciation appears in a dynamic neighborhood and the probability that the visual event is not recognized is high. The VS button is pressed during Altitude Capture mode and finally the flaps are retracted when the flaps retraction speed is reached. The pilot model does not monitor the leveloff and thus does not recognize that the initial altitude is overshot. In the simulation the scenario ends with a failure as soon as the altitude is 300 feet above the prescribed altitude.

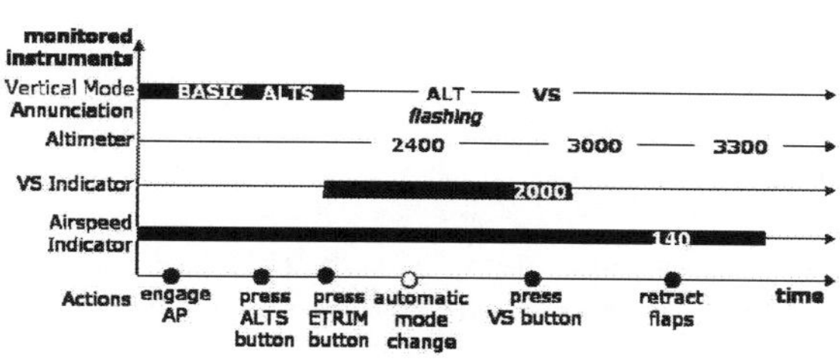

Fig. 6. Mode change not recognized due to dynamic PFD

Scenario 2: LC alleviated by successful SA
Scenario 2 (Fig. 7) is similar to scenario 1 but shortly before the change to Altitude Capture mode the airspeed is already close to flaps speed. When the mode change occurs the pilot model actually monitors the speed annunciation. The other annunciations on the PFD at that time are static thus the probability that the visual mode change event is detected is much higher than in scenario 1. The mode change annunciation is recognized in the visual field and enters the model's memory. The pilot model correctly initiates monitoring the leveloff. Furthermore the mode change information prevents the model from pressing the VS button. The scenario ends with a success because the altitude is reached and maintained.

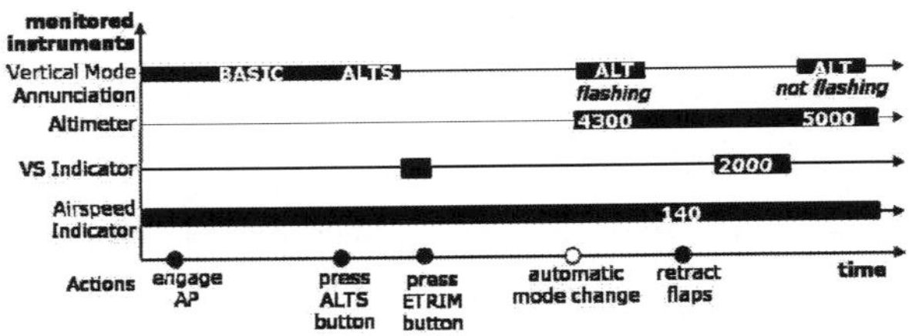

Fig. 7. Mode change recognized due to successful SA

Scenario 3: LC not alleviated due to limited visual field
In this scenario the airspeed of 140 knots is reached when the mode change occurs. The pilot model retracts the flaps and fixates the flaps lever at that time. Thus the mode change Visual Event cannot be recognized because it is out of the visual field. The result is similar to scenario 1: the VS button is pressed during Capture mode and because the leveloff is not monitored the altitude overshot is not recognized. The scenario ends with a failure.

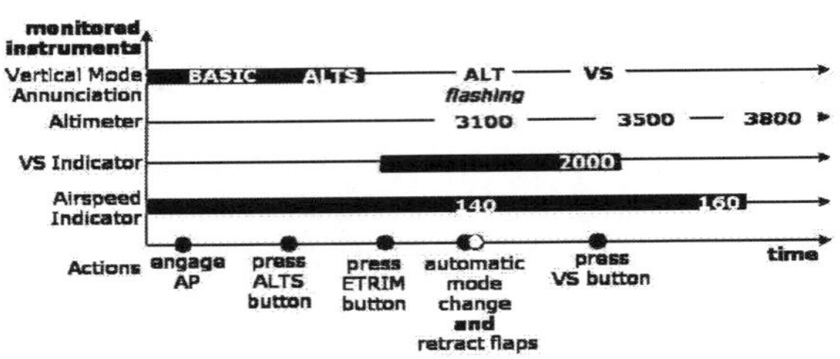

Fig. 8. Mode change annunciation outside visual field

6 Related Work

Processes of visual perception and attention have been modeled in other cognitive models like ACT-R, APEX and MIDAS as well. ACT-R has been extended over the last years to incorporate perception in form of visual focus that can be shifted by production rules (top-down attention [12]). EMMA [15], an ACT-R extension, simulates eye-movements taking into account the distance to the target for calculating eye movement time. MIDAS [13] is equipped with a complete anthropological model. APEX [4] was designed to model air traffic controllers, and has a detailed temporal model of the eyes. Unique for the OFFIS cognitive model is the consideration of Selective Attention especially in combination with Learned Carelessness. While APEX and MIDAS allow building dedicated rules for SA which reacts to dynamic stimuli, the OFFIS model has an architectural build-in SA model that takes the neighborhood of instruments into account to determine detection rates.

The OFFIS model does not consider visual search mechanisms like scanning cockpit instruments based on their contextual importance. General mechanisms of visual search are a major topic in the ACT-R field (e.g. [17]). Furthermore the OFFIS model does not distinguish between moving the eyes and moving attention. Within human cognition these are separate processes which have not always the same target, e.g. when the eyes of the pilot are fixed on the instrument, but (s)he actually thinks about a communication with the air traffic controller.

7 Summary and Future Work

We extended the OFFIS cognitive model with a sophisticated perception component. The new visual component models the basic concepts of human perception like visual field and focus, eye- and head movements as well as Selective Attention. This enables the prediction of eye movements and the analysis of the effectiveness of graphical stimuli used to trigger attention shifts in aircraft cockpits. The OFFIS model additionally allows simulating a routine learning process called Learned Carelessness causing pilots to neglect checking the current flight modes before performing actions. The integration of this learning process with the perceptive processes allows analyzing if the graphical attention capturing stimuli are sufficient to alleviate the effects of the routine learning process. Our intention is to use this model to develop a methodology to validate the ergonomics of cockpit layouts. Our future work will concentrate on a detailed validation and improvement of the perceptive processes as well as the model as a whole. The validation requires a complex design of experiments with real pilots. A series of scenarios is needed to induce routine learning effects. Afterwards dedicated scenarios to test the effect of graphical stimuli on attention shifts have to be investigated. This would allow comparing the detection rate of mode annunciations as well as eye-movements of real pilots with the corresponding data of the cognitive model. Such a complex experimental design is foreseen in the European project HUMAN which started in March 2008 in the 7th Framework Program of the EU (cf. www.human.aero).

References

1. Anderson, J.R., Bothell, D., Byrne, M.D., Douglass, S., Lebiere, C., Qin, Y.: An integrated theory of the mind. Psychological Review 111(4), 1036–1060 (2004)
2. Wray, R., Jones, R.: An introduction to Soar as an agent architecture. In: Sun, R. (ed.) Cognition and Multi-agent Interaction, pp. 53–78. Cambridge University Press, Cambridge (2005)

3. Corker, K.M.: Cognitive models and control: Human and system dynamics in advanced airspace operations. In: Sarter, N., Amalberti, R. (eds.) Cognitive Engineering in the Aviation Domain, pp. 13–42. Lawrence Erlbaum Associates, Mahwah (2000)
4. Freed, M.: Simulating Human Performance in Complex, Dynamic Environments. PhD thesis, Northwestern University (1998)
5. Lüdtke, A., Möbus, C.: A Cognitive Pilot Model to Predict Learned Carelessness for System Design. In: Pritchett, A., Jackson, A. (eds) Proceedings of the International Conference on Human-Computer Interaction in Aeronautics (HCI-Aero), 29.09.-01.10.2004. Cépaduès-Editions, Toulouse, France (2004) CD-ROM
6. Lüdtke, A., Cavallo, A., Christophe, L., Cifaldi, M., Fabbri, M., Javaux, D.: Human Error Analysis based on a Cognitive Architecture. In: Reuzeau, F., Corker, K., Boy, G. (eds) Proceedings of the International Conference on Human-Computer Interaction in Aeronautics (HCI-Aero), 20.-22.09.2006, Seattle, USA, Toulouse, pp. 40-47. Cépaduès-Editions, France (2006)
7. Knudsen, E.I.: Fundamental components of Attention. Journal of Annual Review of Neuroscience 30, 57–78 (2007)
8. Mumaw, R.J., Sarter, N.B., Wickens, C.D.: Analysis Of Pilot's Monitoring And Performance On An Automated Flight Deck. In: 11th International Symposium on Aviation Psychology. The Ohio State University (2001)
9. Nikolic, M.I., Orr, J.M., Sarter, N.B.: Why Pilots Miss the Green Box: How Display Context Undermines Attention Capture. The International Journal of Aviation Psychology 14, 39–52 (2004)
10. Sarter, N.B.: Knowing when to look where: Attention Allocation on advanced automated Flight Decks. In: Proceedings of the 5th International Symposium on Aviation Psychology, p. 239 (1995)
11. Freedman, E.G.: Interactions between eye and head control signals can account for movement kinematics. Biological Cybernetics 84, 453–462 (2001)
12. Byrne, M.D., Anderson, J.R.: Enhancing ACT-R's perceptual-motor abilites. In: Proceedings of the Nineteenth Annual Conference of the Cognitive Science Society, p. 880 (1997)
13. Hart, S.G., Dahn, D., Atencio, A., Dalal, K.M.: Evaluation and application of MIDAS v2.0. In: Proceedings of the Society of Automotive Engineers (SAE) World Aviation Congress (2001)
14. Möbus, C., Schröder, O., Thole, H.J.: Online Modeling the Novice-Expert Sift in Programming Skills on a Rule-Schema-Case Partial Order. In: Wender, K.F., Schmalhofer, F., Böcker, H.-D. (eds.) Cognition and Computer Programming. Ablex, Norwood (1995)
15. Salvucci, D.D.: A Model of Eye Movements and Visual Attention. In: Proceedings of the Third International Conference on Cognitive Modeling, pp. 252–259 (2000)
16. Frey, D., Schulz-Hardt, S.: Eine Theorie der Gelernten Sorglosigkeit. In: Mandl, H (Hrsg.) 40. Kongress der Deutschen Gesellschaft für Psychologie, pp. 604–611. Hogrefe Verlag für Psychologie Göttingen (1997)
17. Salvucci, D.D., Taatgen, N.A.: Threaded cognition: An integrated theory of concurrent multitasking. Psychological Review 115, 101–130 (2008)
18. Everett, S.P., Byrne, M.D.: Unintended Effects: Varying Icon Spacing Changes Users' Visual Search Strategy. In: Proceedings of ACM CHI 2004: Conference on Human Factors in Computing Systems. ACM, Vienna (2004)

Cognitive Load Measurement from User's Linguistic Speech Features for Adaptive Interaction Design

M. Asif Khawaja[1,2], Fang Chen[1,2,3], Christine Owen[4], and Gregory Hickey[4]

[1] Nicta, ATP, Sydney, Australia
[2] School of Computer Science and Engineering, UNSW, Sydney, Australia
[3] School of Electrical Engineering and Telecommunication, UNSW, Sydney, Australia
{asif.khawaja,fang.chen}@nicta.com.au
[4] University of Tasmania, Hobart, Australia
{christine.owen,gregory.hickey}@utas.edu.au

Abstract. An adaptive interaction system, which is aware of the user's current cognitive load (CL), can change its response, presentation and flow of interaction material accordingly, to improve user's experience and performance. We present a speech content analysis approach to CL measurement, which employs users' linguistic features of speech to determine their experienced CL level. We show analyses of several linguistic features, extracted from speech of personnel working in computerized incident control rooms and involved in highly complex bushfire management tasks in Australia. We present the results of linguistic features showing significant differences between the speech from the cognitively low load and high load tasks. We also discuss how the method may be used for user interface evaluation and interaction design improvement.

Keywords: Cognitive Load, Measurement, Linguistic Features, Language usage, Word Categories, Interaction Design, Bushfire Management.

1 Introduction

Cognitive load (CL) refers to the amount of mental load imposed on a person by a particular problem-solving task. It is attributable to the limited capacity of the person's working memory and his ability to process novel information [5,6]. In complex, time-critical, and data-intense situations, users of an interaction system can experience high cognitive demands, caused either by the complexity of the task being performed or by the complex interaction designs, as in multimodal or multimedia interfaces and improper amounts of contents presented at once [7]. For example high intensity control room work-situations, such as that found in high-reliability environments e.g. air traffic control, require users or operators to manage a number of such interfaces, switching from one application interface to another, often over multiple screens and in time-critical scenarios. Operators will frequently use radios or mobile phones, make and answer calls, and speak to their co-located colleagues while completing their tasks. This can result in extremely high cognitive load and interfere with users' ability to perform at the optimum level.

Adaptive interaction systems that are aware of the users' cognitive load (CL) could in fact alleviate these problems by implementing strategies to adjust the response, presentation and flow of interaction material as per users' experienced CL to help

T. Gross et al. (Eds.): INTERACT 2009, Part I, LNCS 5726, pp. 485–489, 2009.

them complete the task effectively. However, measuring a user's CL robustly is not a trivial task. Many studies have attempted to measure CL using several methods including physiological, performance, and self-reporting subjective measures [1-3,6]. Such measures, however, can be physically or psychologically intrusive and can disrupt the normal flow of the interaction. While they may be useful approaches in research situations, they are often unsuitable for deployment in real-life scenarios.

Behavioral measures such as some speech features, e.g. pitch, prosody, pauses, and disfluencies, have also been found to be changing under high levels of CL [4,8-10]. Such measures allow non-intrusive analysis as they are based on speech data generated by users while they complete the task. Linguistic and grammatical features may also be extracted from spoken or written input for the purpose. Such features have been used before for purposes other than CL measurement [11-13].

In this paper, we present a study that analyses linguistic features of speech as potential indices of CL. We analyze several linguistic features, extracted from speech of operators working in computerized incident control rooms and involved in highly complex bushfire management tasks around Australia. We present the results of linguistic features showing significant differences between the speech from the cognitively low load and high load tasks. We also discuss how this approach may be used for user interface evaluation and interaction design improvement.

2 Study and Method

2.1 Data and Participants

Australia is one of the most bushfire-prone regions in the world. As the impact of climate change results in more extreme weather events, fire and emergency service work is becoming increasingly important and needs to be managed in order to save the communities from their effects. The speech data used in this study was collected from operators of Incident Management Teams (IMTs) [14] involved in bushfire management in Australia. Three targeted roles comprised of Incident Controller (IC), Planner, and Operations (Ops), who participated in planned bushfire management training exercises simulated to be conducted in four states of Australia (New South Wales, Victoria, Queensland, and Tasmania).

The data was collected from 9 different exercises each about 5 hours in duration on average, resulting in 27 operators' speech data being available for our study. All operators had experience in bushfire management and were competent for their assigned roles. Each exercise was monitored by a bushfire management expert training in charge. During each exercise a fire is reported that escalates and threatens local assets. The operators co-located in a control room manage the fire and communicate information and resources needed to manage it with each other as well as with the field workers and volunteers. For this purpose they use different methods e.g. phone calls, map boards, computers often with multiple screens for updated fire maps and task checklists etc. All operators' speech was recorded using lapel microphones for each exercise and was later transcribed and coded using Transana [15].

2.2 Cognitive Load Coding and Data Cleaning

All exercises were monitored by bushfire management experts who manually marked speech transcriptions for cognitive and/or task load indication based on their observations and given subjective ratings by the operators. The transcriptions were marked for four different load levels: (1) 'low': non-bushfire activity, no time pressure; (2) 'medium': routine tasks; (3) 'high': challenging tasks, time constraints; and (4) 'very high': very challenging, lot of unexpected events and breakdowns happening. The transcribed data was later cleaned and parsed semi-automatically to bring it in a form usable by an automatic text analysis and extraction software tool. The cleaned data for each IMT role from each exercise was stored in a separate text file grouped as coded load levels resulting in 27 transcription text files.

2.3 Hypotheses

We expected several linguistic indices to be likely indicators of load including word count, negative emotions, perceptive and cognitive phrases, and inclusive words, etc. Across users, indices that we expected to increase with CL include negative emotions, number of long words, affective words (preposition and conjunction words), perceptive and cognitive phrases, and feelings and inclusive words. Indices that we expected to decrease with CL include total number of words spoken, and number of words per sentence.

3 Data Analysis and Results

During cleaning it was observed that for load levels 'low' (1) and 'very high' (4), there was insufficient data available, which could affect the results of our analysis. So to handle the problem of missing data, we combined two lower load tasks i.e. (1) and (2) into one as 'low' and two higher load tasks i.e. (3) and (4) into one as 'high' for all transcription files. These files were processed using a text analysis software called LIWC [16] that automatically extracted 85 predefined linguistic features from each transcript file for 'low' and 'high' load speech separately in that file. To take into account differences in verbosity, these were extracted as percentages of total words.

We analyzed extracted linguistic data for all three operator roles combined, as well as separately, resulting in four data sets for analysis. Tables 1 and 2 show linguistic features that showed consistent trends, i.e. either increased or decreased use of a feature between low load and high load tasks across four data sets, underscoring the importance of these features for measuring CL. The values show the usage difference in percentage for each feature, indicated by a plus sign for an increased usage and a minus sign for a decreased usage.

Table 1. Significant Linguistic Features

Features→ / ↓Data Sets	WPS	AW	NE	Per	Cog	Feel
Load-wise (All Roles)	+24%	-22%	+42%	+21%	+14%	+62%
Role-wise (IC)	+39%	-15%	+98%	+36%	+18%	+113%
Role-wise (Planning)	+22%	-48%	+80%	+20%	+4%	+20%
Role-wise (Operations)	+14%	-2%	+9%	+8%	+13%	+26%

Shaded cells = Statistically significant; $p < 0.03$

Table 2. Supporting Features

Features→ / ↓Data Sets	WC	LW	Inc
Load-wise (All Roles)	+12%	+5%	+4%
Role-wise (IC)	+4%	+13%	+5%
Role-wise (Planning)	+5%	+2%	+4%
Role-wise (Operations)	+7%	+5%	+11%

The linguistic features are listed below with few examples of each:

- WC: Total number of words spoken by the operator;
- WPS: Number of words used per sentence;
- AW: Affective words i.e. preposition and conjunction words, e.g. about, along, etc.
- NE: Words that denote negative emotions, e.g. annoy, angry, messy, afraid, etc.;
- Per: Perception words, e.g. vision, beauty, quite, rough, cold, etc.;
- Cog: Words that represent the human cognitive processes, i.e. think, consider etc.;
- Feel: Words that denote feelings, e.g. hard, difficult, heavy, loose, sharp, tight etc.
- LW: Number of long words, i.e. words with at least six letters;
- Inc: Inclusive words, e.g. and, both, each, including, plus, with etc.;

To test the significance of these features, we analyzed them for the differences between low and high load tasks for the four data sets using dependent-sample 2-tailed t-Test with 95% confidence level (alpha = 0.03 after Bonferroni adjustment). Table 1 shows test results for features with majority of them statistically significant (shaded; $p<0.03$). This implies that we can use these features to determine a user's level of CL from similar speech data robustly. Table 2 shows features that were found insignificant but may be used to support the significant features for better CL measurement due to their consistent trend across all roles.

4 Discussion

Analyses of bushfire operators speech showed consistent trends for selected linguistic features over a variety of data sets and roles, along with many significant results, and therefore, confirmed the robustness of these features for CL measurement. We remain optimistic about the lack of significant results for some roles, as this may have been due to insufficient amount of speech data. Additionally, although all operators are expected to have same language profile, some of them may not have used enough relevant words or terms for a particular linguistic feature category, due to possible difference in the nature of role.

It was interesting to find out that in contrast to our hypothesis about the WC and the WPS features, these showed increasing trends. This could be due to the complex and data-intense nature of the task. We expect same feature behavior in similar task situations but this trend may not persist with less critical task situations. Also, though the results apply across a variety of people and roles, they are specific for this combination of tasks, in a bushfire management scenario. Different linguistic features may be found to be robust for other types of application scenarios, e.g. in road or air traffic management, though it is expected to have common linguistic features across these application areas.

Adaptive interaction can be achieved with a system, which is able to determine user's experienced CL using the proposed approach. For example, in bushfire management control room scenario, the system can be able to adapt many things, from highlighting critical screen or window, to sorting and prioritizing task checklists, to showing controlled reminders, to filtering email messages, to redirecting phone calls to less cognitively loaded operators etc.

Besides the possible system adaptation, this linguistic approach to measuring CL may be used as a post-hoc analysis technique for user interface evaluation and interaction design improvement. For example, we may evaluate two different speech-enabled interfaces to see which one is resulting in higher CL. Based on the findings we may be able to improve the interaction design for the interface causing higher CL.

5 Conclusion and Future Work

This study has provided encouraging evidence for use of linguistic features of speech as indicators of increased CL. Though these features require further cross-application validation, analysis and evaluation, they offer a promising contribution to the set of potential interactive indices that may be used by human computer interaction systems.

For future work, we intend to include in our analyses the grammatical features for CL measurement, along with validation of all the potential features and development of a common feature set for different application areas. We also intend to develop a software application to demonstrate the concept using the proposed features.

References

1. Kramer, A.F.: Physiological metrics of mental workload: a review of recent progress. In: Damos, D.L. (ed.) Multiple-task performance, pp. 279–328. Taylor and Francis, London (1991)
2. Ark, W., et al.: The Emotion Mouse. In: Bullinger, Ziegler. (eds.) HCI: Ergonomics and User Interfaces 1, vol. 1, pp. 818–823. Lawrence Erlbaum Assoc., London (1999)
3. Windell, D., Wiebe, E.N.: A Comparison of Two Mental Workload Instruments in Multimedia Instruction. In: Proc. HFES 2006. Human Factors and Ergonomics Society Press, Santa Monica (2006)
4. Yin, B., Chen, F., Ruiz, N., Ambikairajah, E.: Speech-based Cognitive Load Monitoring System. In: Proc. ICASSP 2008, pp. 2041–2044. IEEE Press, Los Alamitos (2008)
5. Chandler, P., Sweller, J.: Cognitive load theory and the format of instruction. Cognition and Instruction 8(4), 293–332 (1991)
6. Paas, F., Tuovinen, J.E., et al.: Cognitive Load Measurement as a Means to Advance Cognitive Load Theory. Educational Psychologist 38(1), 63–71 (2003)
7. Mayer, R.E.: Multimedia learning. Cambridge University Press, Cambridge (2001)
8. Berthold, A., Jameson, A.: Interpreting Symptoms of Cognitive Load in Speech Input. In: User Modeling 1999. Springer, Wien (1999)
9. Khawaja, M.A., Ruiz, N., Chen, F.: Potential Speech Features for Cognitive Load Measurement. In: Proc. OzCHI 2007. ACM Press, New York (2007)
10. Muller, C., et al.: Recognizing time pressure and cognitive load on the basis of speech: An experimental study. In: Proc. 8th International Conf. User Modeling, pp. 24–33 (2001)
11. Sexton, J., Helmreich, R.: Analyzing Cockpit Communication: The links between language, performance, error, and workload. University of Texas Team Research Project, Austin, USA (2000)
12. Stirman, S.W., Pennebaker, J.W.: Word Use in the Poetry of Suicidal and Nonsuicidal Poets. In: Psychosomatic Medicine, vol. 63. American Psychosomatic Society Press (2001)
13. Kramer, A., Oh, L.M., Fussell, S.R.: Using Linguistic Features to Measure Presence in Computer-Mediated Communication. In: Proc. CHI 2006. ACM Press, New York (2006)
14. Australasian Fire Authorities Council, The Australasian Inter-service Incident Management System (AIIMS), AFAC Limited, 3rd edn. (2005), `http://www.afac.com.au`
15. Transana, University of Wisconsin-Madison Center for Education Research, `http://www.transana.org`
16. Pennebaker, J.W., et al.: The Development and Psychometric Properties of LIWC 2007 (2007), `http://www.liwc.net`

Using Psychophysiological Measurements in Physically Demanding Virtual Environments

Domen Novak, Matjaž Mihelj, and Marko Munih

University of Ljubljana, Faculty of Electrical Engineering,
Tržaška c. 25, 1000 Ljubljana, Slovenia
domen.novak@robo.fe.uni-lj.si

Abstract. Psychophysiological evaluation of mental workload in human-computer interaction has generally been limited to situations with little physical load. This paper examines the viability of using heart rate, skin conductance, respiration and peripheral skin temperature as psychophysiological indicators in a physically demanding task performed in a simple virtual environment. Respiratory rate was found to be a good indicator of arousal while respiratory rate variability and skin temperature indicated changes in valence.

Keywords: Affective HCI, Human Factors, Multi-Modal Interfaces.

1 Introduction

Human-computer interaction makes use of findings from many scientific fields to study the response of humans to technology. One such field is psychophysiology, which describes how a person's physiological responses reflect his or her psychological state. Physiological responses are a valuable tool for human-computer research since they provide an objective estimate of the user's psychological state. The most commonly used responses are those of the autonomic nervous system: heart rate, skin conductance, respiration and skin temperature. Unfortunately, they are not only influenced by a person's psychological state, but also by any physical activity. Thus, many studies of psychophysiological responses try to limit physical activity to a minimum. However, to some degree, responses of the autonomic nervous system may provide meaningful results even in physically demanding environments. Our goal was to determine which autonomic nervous system responses could be used to determine the level of mental activity, stress and frustration in tasks that require physical load.

2 Materials and Methods

This paper presents a study of a physically demanding hand-eye coordination task performed with different difficulty levels. Thirty healthy subjects (age 19-46 years, mean 26.2, 23 male, 7 female) participated in the study. They were presented with the classic inverted pendulum problem. An unstable pole standing atop a cart was shown on the screen, and participants had to balance the pole (pendulum) by moving the cart using a HapticMaster haptic interface (manufactured by Moog FCS) that also measured the

T. Gross et al. (Eds.): INTERACT 2009, Part I, LNCS 5726, pp. 490–493, 2009.

force exerted. The HapticMaster actively resisted movement, requiring a significant force to move. If the pole fell to a horizontal position, it was reset to a nearly vertical position. Figure 1 shows a participant balancing the pendulum.

Fig. 1. Participant performing the pendulum task

Three difficulty levels of the pendulum task (PT) were implemented. While the medium difficulty level (PT.M) was moderately challenging and the easy level (PT.E) was only slightly easier than the medium level, the hard level (PT.H) was intended to be difficult to the point of frustration. This was done by subtly manipulating the mathematical model describing the cart and pole in order to make the pole much less responsive to user input. In addition to the PT, a control task (CT) was introduced to evaluate the effect of physical load in the absence of mental load. During the CT, participants had to move the HapticMaster left and right at an even, moderate speed while nothing was shown on the screen. Participants were informed that they would need to perform the PT three times, but that there would be no change in difficulty.

The participants rested for five minutes in order to obtain baseline values. Afterwards, CT, PT.E, PT.M and PT.H were performed in random order for five minutes each. After each period, participants were presented with nine-point arousal and valence self-report scales from the self-assessment manikin [1].

The electrocardiogram was recorded using surface electrodes affixed to the chest and abdomen. Skin conductance was measured from the second and third fingers of the non-dominant hand using a g.GSR sensor (g.tec Medical Engineering GmbH). Respiratory rate was obtained using a thermistor-based SleepSense Flow sensor. Skin temperature was measured using a g.TEMP sensor (g.tec) attached to the distal phalanx of the fifth finger. All signals were sampled at 2.4 kHz. After the experiment, the following physiological parameters were calculated for each time period: mean heart rate (HR), two standardized measures of heart rate variability (SDNN and RMSSD [2]), mean skin conductance level (SCL), nonspecific skin conductance response frequency (SCRF), mean respiratory rate (RR), respiratory rate variance (RRV) and final skin temperature (ST). In addition to physiological measurements, the mean absolute force exerted by participants was calculated for each time period.

The purpose of the study was to determine how physiological responses are affected by psychological arousal and valence in the presence of physical load. Arousal is defined as general mental activity while valence indicates whether the person's emotions are positive or negative [3]. Comparing PT.M to CT was expected to show the effects of arousal. Since PT.H was designed to be frustratingly difficult, comparing it to PT.M was expected to primarily show the effects of negative valence. Significance was evaluated using a one-way repeated-measures ANOVA followed by the Tukey test in post-hoc analysis. Differences were significant for $p < 0.05$.

3 Results and Discussion

Results of the self-assessment manikin showed that self-reported arousal was higher during CT than during the baseline period ($p = 0.02$). Thus, we cannot rule out some influence of arousal during CT. Arousal during all three difficulty levels of PT was higher than during CT ($p < 0.001$). There were no significant differences in arousal between difficulty levels. Self-reported valence decreased from baseline during CT ($p = 0.02$) and PT.H ($p = 0.007$). Valence was lower during PT.H than during the other two difficulty levels ($p < 0.01$ for both comparisons). It was also lower during CT than during PT.E and PT.M ($p < 0.05$ for both comparisons).

Mean absolute force during CT was more than twice as high as during all three difficulty levels of PT ($p < 0.001$). It was also higher during PT.H than PT.E and PT.M ($p < 0.05$ for both comparisons). Thus, we must be cautious when comparing physiological responses. The change in a physiological response may not have been caused by changes in psychological state, but by the differences in physical load.

The following physiological parameters changed significantly from baseline to CT: HR (increased by 10.2%, $p < 0.001$), SDNN (incr. by 17.1%, $p < 0.01$), RMSSD (incr. by 23.9%, $p < 0.01$), SCL (incr. by 1 μS, $p < 0.001$), SCRF (incr. by 236.2%, $p < 0.001$), RR (incr. by 17.4%, $p < 0.001$) and RRV (decreased by 6%, $p = 0.04$). Thus, all physiological parameters other than ST were affected by physical load.

The following physiological parameters were significantly different between CT and PT.M: HR (lower in PT.M, $p < 0.001$), RMSSD (lower in PT.M, $p < 0.001$), RR (higher in PT.M, $p = 0.006$) and RRV (lower in PT.M, $p = 0.02$). The difference in SCRF approached significance (higher in PT.M, $p = 0.07$).

Since there was no significant difference in SCL between CT and PT.M, it appeared to be primarily affected by physical load and thus not useful in physically demanding tasks. Previous studies have noted a connection between SCRF and arousal [4]. However, since the difference in SCRF between CT and PT.M was not quite significant, SCRF is apparently only a reliable indicator of arousal if little physical load is involved. On the other hand, since SCRF increases with physical load, we can assume that it would have been much lower in CT if the mean absolute force exerted had been the same as in PT.M. In that case, the difference between CT and PT.M probably would have been significant. RR during CT was significantly higher than the baseline value, but RR during PT.M was higher still. Since mean absolute force was higher during CT, the changes in RR cannot be attributed solely to changes in physical load, but must be caused by arousal. Previous studies have indeed shown respiratory rate to be connected to arousal [5]. Similarly, RRV during CT was significantly lower than the baseline value, but was even lower during PT.M. Mental arousal thus apparently also decreases RRV. By far the highest increase in HR was during CT, where the exerted force was also the highest. Since there was no significant difference between difficulty levels, we can conclude that HR was mostly influenced by physical load. Similarly, though significant differences in SDNN and

RMSSD were observed between CT and PT.M, none can be reliably attributed to changes in psychological state – they may have been caused by physical load.

No physiological parameters showed significant differences between PT.E and PT.M. There were two significant differences between PT.M and PT.H: RRV was lower during PT.M ($p < 0.001$) while ST was higher during PT.M ($p = 0.01$).

Differences between CT and PT.M indicated that RRV decreases as arousal increases. The difference in RRV between PT.M and PT.H suggests that RRV also increases as valence decreases (i.e. as frustration increases). Since ST significantly decreased from baseline only during PT.H and was lower during PT.H than during PT.M, it apparently decreases as valence decreases. Other studies have linked decreases in fingertip temperature to anxiety and stress [6], supporting our findings. Again, it is worth noting that ST was the only psychophysiological response not influenced by physical load.

4 Conclusions

We demonstrated a significant influence of both mental arousal and emotional valence on skin conductance, respiration and skin temperature even in the presence of moderate physical load. However, our study only confirms the usefulness of psychophysiological responses up to a certain level of physical load. Strenuous physical activity would probably cause physiological responses that would completely overshadow the physiological responses caused by changes in psychological state.

Acknowledgments. The work was funded by the EU Information and Communication Technologies Collaborative Project MIMICS grant 215756.

References

1. Lang, P.J.: Behavioral treatment and bio-behavioral assessment: Computer applications. In: Sidowski, J.B., Johnson, J.H., Williams, T.A. (eds.) Technology in Mental Health Care Delivery Systems, pp. 119–137. Abbex, Norwood (1980)
2. Task Force of the European Society of Cardiology and the North American Society of Pacing and Electrophysiology: Heart rate variability: Standards of measurement, physiological interpretation, and clinical use. European Heart Journal 17, 354–381 (1996)
3. Russell, J.A.: A circumplex model of affect. Journal of Personality and Social Psychology 39, 1161–1178 (1980)
4. Nikula, R.: Psychological correlates of nonspecific skin conductance responses. Psychophysiology 28, 86–90 (1991)
5. Brookings, J.B., Wilson, G.F., Swain, C.R.: Psychophysiological responses to changes in workload during simulated air traffic control. Biological Psychology 42, 361–377 (1996)
6. Min, B.C., et al.: Autonomic responses of young passengers contingent to the speed and driving mode of a vehicle. International Journal of Industrial Ergonomics 29, 187–198 (2002)

Resilience of Interaction Techniques to Interrupts: A Formal Model-Based Approach*

Maurice H. ter Beek[1], Giorgio P. Faconti[1], Mieke Massink[1], Philippe A. Palanque[2], and Marco Winckler[2]

[1] Istituto di Scienza e Tecnologie dell'Informazione 'A. Faedo' (ISTI), CNR via G. Moruzzi 1, 56124 Pisa, Italy
{terbeek,faconti,massink}@isti.cnr.it

[2] Institute of Research in Informatics of Toulouse (IRIT), University Paul Sabatier 118, route de Narbonne, 31062 Toulouse cedex 9, France
{palanque,winckler}@irit.fr

Abstract. In many modern working environments interruptions are commonplace as users must temporarily suspend a task to complete an unexpected intervening activity. As users are faced with more and more sources of information competing for their attention, it is becoming increasingly important to understand how interruptions affect their abilities to complete tasks. This paper introduces a new perspective for research in this field by employing analytical, model-based techniques that are informed by well-established cognitive theories and empirical data available in the literature. We propose stochastic modelling and model checking to predict measures of the disruptive effects of interruptions to two well-known interaction techniques: Drag 'n Drop and Speak 'n Drop. The approach also provides a way to compare the resilience of different interaction techniques to the presence of external interruptions that users need to handle. The obtained results are in a form that allows validation with results obtained by empirical studies involving real users.

1 Introduction

In many modern working environments interruptions are commonplace as users must temporarily suspend a task to complete an unexpected intervening activity. Interruptions are unpredictable and quite often cannot be disregarded by users in working environments. Web page pop-ups, phone calls, emails, instant messaging and social events can also be disruptive when people need to concentrate on certain tasks. One of the interesting aspects of interruptions, according to O'Connaill and Frohlich [17], is that they reveal that the timespace of any individual is not owned and controlled in the same way as their workspace, but can collide and merge with that of another individual unexpectedly.

Research has shown that different types of interruptions can affect their disruptiveness. Quite often, interruptions are associated with negative effects:

* This work has been funded by the EU project Resist/Faerus (IST-2006-026764), by the RSTL project XXL of the Italian National Research Council (CNR) and by the PaCO and D-ASAP projects of the Italian Ministry of University and Research.

T. Gross et al. (Eds.): INTERACT 2009, Part I, LNCS 5726, pp. 494–509, 2009.

resuming a task after an interruption is difficult and may take a long time, interrupted tasks are perceived as harder than uninterrupted ones, interruptions cause more cognitive workload and they are quite often annoying and frustrating because they disrupt people from completing their work.

Interruptions can also lead to incidents due to human error. According to Trafton & Monk [22], pilots experiencing interruptions during preflight checklists have been blamed for multiple aviation crashes. In addition, recent studies have shown that interruptions may be an important factor in driving, emergency room care and nursing errors. Indeed, frequent interruptions can reduce user performance. However, not all interruptions have negative impact: awareness systems such as alarms and alert systems effectively shift our attention to matters that need immediate care and, at least for simple tasks, interruptions may actually increase performance.

As users are faced with more and more sources of information competing for their attention at any time, it is becoming increasingly important to understand how interruptions affect one's abilities to complete tasks [5]. Interruptions raise questions of non-exclusive practical and theoretical significance including: How many interruptions occur at work? How is performance affected by various interruption characteristics, like complexity, duration, timing and frequency? How many interruptions are disregarded rather than handled? Who benefits from the ensuing interactions? How disruptive are interruptions to prior tasks? What can be done to mitigate negative disruptive effects? Most current research tackles these questions by conducting empirical studies with users, either on controlled conditions (i.e. usability labs) or on working environments (e.g. ethnographical studies). This paper introduces a new perspective for the research in this field by employing stochastic model-based techniques during early phases (i.e. specification phases) of the development process of interactive systems to investigate potential disruptive effects of interruptions on user performance and the *resilience* of interaction techniques to such interruptions, i.e. the ability to sustain the impact of interruptions and recover and resume its operations [11].

Outline of the paper. We start by a review of the literature on interruptions in Sect. 2 followed by a description of our proposed methodology in Sect. 3. In Sect. 4 we briefly recall the cognitive theory ICS that we use to motivate the models of the user aspects of the interaction techniques presented in Sect. 5. The stochastic model addressing the multi-modal Speak 'n Drop interaction technique is presented in Sect. 6. In Sect. 7 the results of the performance analysis of the models are presented and their differences in resilience to external interrupts are discussed for different assumptions on the average number of interrupts that occur. Finally, in Sect. 8 we conclude the paper with some considerations on current work and a discussion of future research on this topic.

2 Task Interruptions

Interruptions occur when a person is working on a primary task (usually long-lasting) and an alert for a secondary task occurs [22]. Sources of alerts could be either internal (i.e. user thoughts) or external (e.g. a person coming into the room to ask the person a question, a fire alarm, instant messaging). An important aspect of alerts is that they create an interruption lag as the user has to turn her attention to the interruption. The person then starts the secondary task. After completing it, the person must resume the primary task. During the resumption lag, the person must figure out what she was doing during the primary task and what to do next. Finally, the person resumes the primary task. From this task analysis and real-world examples, it is clear that different aspects of the cognitive system are relevant to the study of interruptions and resumptions.

Since the seminal work of Zeigarnik [24], who was the first to publish the relations between interruption and selective memory, researchers have not ceased to document other effects of interruption in human behaviour.

There have been several attempts to formalise cognitive models describing the impact of interruptions in human behaviour. Only a few, however, address formal description techniques to describe the occurrence of interruptions in system specifications [12]. In fact, there seems to be a gap in the literature concerning predictive methods to system specifications towards hazardous effects of interruptions. A main problem is to identify suitable notation to formalise interruptions occurring in interactive systems. The unpredictability of interruptions would favour the use of declarative models to describe what should be accomplished by the user system (whatever happens) rather than describing the steps required (i.e. control flow) to accomplish it [21]. Nevertheless, there are situations where the interruption of an actual task should be considered part of the user goals, e.g. to cancel document printing. Indeed, task models like CTT [20] explicitly provide the operator suspend/resume to allow explicit modelling between tasks. Similarly, West and Nagy [23] have added theoretical structures to the notation GOMS to overcome its limitations for analysing interruptions when task switching is common. Jambon [12] has analysed the idiosyncrasies of relationships between tasks (e.g. parallelism and sequence) to derive a formal model (using automata) describing the semantics of interruptions in notations like MAD, UAN and Petri nets. However, none of these works has yet evolved to a systematic analysis approach to deal with interruptions during task execution.

3 Methodology

The methodology we propose and experiment in this paper exceeds the specific case of interruptions and can be used whenever it is necessary to make design decisions concerned with usability issues. For this purpose we address syndetic modelling [6], relevant human factor studies and formal specification with particular emphasis on stochastic techniques [4]. Syndetic modelling is a conceptual breakthrough in interactive system and man-machine interface design. It provides design and formal specification and verification techniques that take into account both human's capabilities and limitations together with robustness of interactive systems, thus enabling the study of the joint man-machine behaviour. Such joint models allow for the investigation of properties expressing requirements or expectations and provide insight in the extent to which an interactive system meets such requirements and constraints. The point of departure from known design methods is the requirement that the system should be usable. This is not just a mechanical property of the system, but a statement that implicitly or explicitly must embody some claim or understanding about human capabilities and limitations. In other words, in addition to being a (formally) provable consequence of the specification, the property must also be psychologically valid.

With a syndetic approach, capabilities of and constraints on user behaviour are expressed explicitly by representing a cognitive model (or an approximation) as a formal theory, which can then be integrated or combined with the model of system behaviour. In this way, the user model is explicit and it contains the theoretical basis for the claims based on it; the model is as correct as the theory it encapsulates. However, properties can be expressed and verified only at the level of abstraction at which available models describe cognitive behaviour. If this is not the case, we need to refine aspects of user behaviour in the model by addressing human factors and usability studies. Given a set of statistical characteristics of both system and user performance derived from literature and available empirical data, we can use stochastic modelling techniques to understand the character of the interaction between user and system. We can see the resulting specification as a means to make explicit the assumptions about the capabilities of both user and system, and to explore the behaviour of the combination of system and user based on these assumptions. In this way, answers to design questions can be both easier to relate to empirical performance data from human factors and usability studies, and the analysis results can be more meaningful for interpretation by human factors experts. Moreover, much modern and emerging user interface technology is stochastic in nature, which provides additional motivation to apply stochastic techniques to model interaction.

Our methodology uses a range of theories and techniques, from cognition to formal languages, to model interaction. For the purpose of the current work we make use of the following theories and techniques and, consequently, apply them: ICS theory [2]; studies on pointing gestures [14,8]; the PEPA process algebra [10]; the stochastic model checker PRISM [13]. We use these to develop a case study for comparing two interaction techniques to remove objects from a display in the presence of interrupts.

4 Interacting Cognitive Subsystems

Interacting Cognitive Subsystems (ICS) [2] is a comprehensive model of human information processing that describes cognition in terms of a collection of subsystems, each of which process different mental representations. There are three sensory subsystems (*visual, acoustic, body state*), four central subsystems composed of two structural subsystems (*morphonolexical, object*) and two meaning subsystems (*propositional, implicational*), and two effectors subsystems (*articulatory, limb*). These representational subsystems are supplemented by peripheral somatic and visceral response systems (Fig. 1).

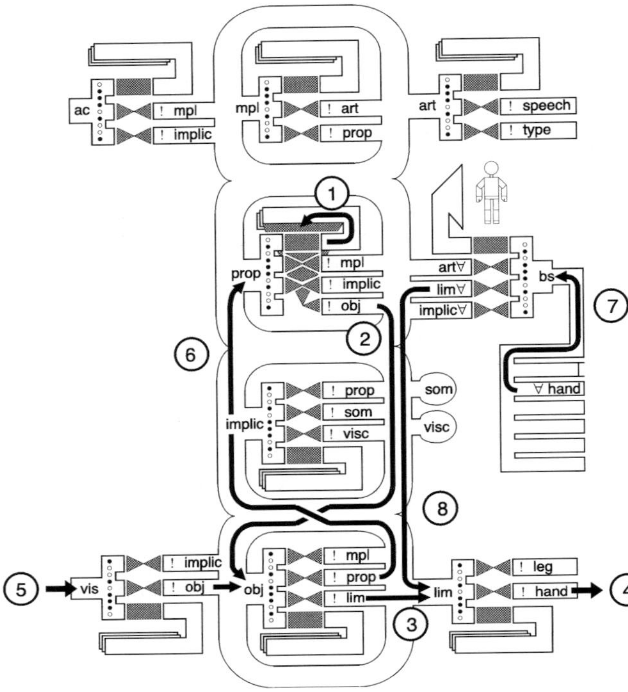

Fig. 1. ICS architecture configured for gestural interaction

The internal decomposition of all subsystems is identical. Incoming data streams arrive at an input array, from which they are copied to an image record representing an unbounded episodic store of all data received by that subsystem. In parallel with this copy process, each subsystem also contains transformation processes to convert incoming data to certain other mental codes. This output is passed through a data network to other subsystems. If the incoming data stream is incomplete or unstable, a process can augment it by accessing or *buffering* the data stream via the image record. However, only one transformation a time can be buffered in a given processing configuration. Coherent data streams may be blended at a subsystem's input array, as a result of which a process can *engage* and transform data streams derived from multiple input sources.

Overall behaviour of the cognitive system is constrained by the possible transformations and by several principles of processing. Visual information for instance cannot be translated directly into propositional code, but must be processed via the object system that addresses spatial structure. Although in principle all processes are continuously trying to generate code, only some of the processes will generate stable output that is relevant to a given task. This collection of processes is called a *configuration*. The thick lines in Fig. 1 show the configuration of resources deployed while using a hand-controlled input device to operate on some object within a visual scene.

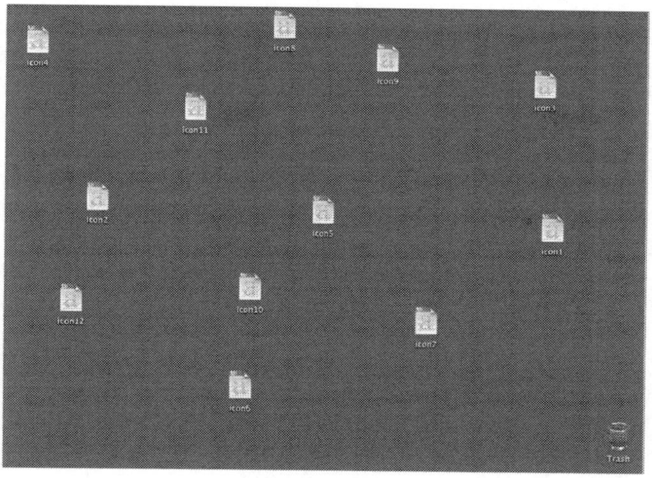

Fig. 2. Example of display

5 Case Study

We developed a case study in order to highlight the potential of the proposed methodology. The choice of the case study is motivated by the fact that a number of real-life applications require operators to remove objects from the current system presentation, such as, e.g., in multi-modal man-machine interfaces for space ground segment applications [19].

We assume the presentation to be composed of a set of icons on a display, the standard device for output communication in man-machine interfaces. It is well known from psychological theories [9] that design and layout of objects in a visual scene, as well as other (multi-)media structures, play a fundamental role in the way people perceive, think and react to sensorial stimuli. However, this level of detail is beyond the scope of our current work. We assume that the symbolic configuration or pattern of icons is based on a set of features that directs the structuring of the visual scene into a group of icons with one distinguished icon (the trash in our case). The user is asked to remove the icons from the display (see Fig. 2) using one of the following two interaction techniques.

Drag 'n Drop. This well-known technique works as follows: (i) by means of a mouse device, the user moves the cursor on the display over one of the icons; (ii) by pressing the appropriate button of the mouse, she selects that icon which gets highlighted and linked to the cursor; (iii) while keeping the button pressed, she moves the mouse dragging the icon over the trash; (iv) she releases the button causing the system to remove the icon from the display.

Speak 'n Drop. This multimodal technique uses a combination of mouse and voice commands: (i) the user selects one of the icons by positioning the cursor over it and by pressing and releasing (click) the appropriate button of the mouse;

(ii) she pronounces the word *delete* interpreted as a command by the system. When both the icon selection and the delete command are acquired by the system, that icon is removed from the display. No constraints are imposed on the users' behaviour, i.e. the modalities can be used in any order as well as concurrently, and the system must be designed to cope with this.

The performance of a user using a particular technique can be characterised by the number of items she is able to drop during a fixed period of time. We assume an interrupt to manifest itself as a pop-up window fully covering the display. The user has to click the mouse button over a push button positioned in the centre of the window to make it disappear and to resume the previous task.

6 Model Development

To illustrate the methodology, we first describe the general assumptions w.r.t. the case study, followed by the steps necessary to develop a stochastic model of it.

We include in the model only correct behaviour of both the user and the system. We do this deliberately in order to be able to separate two concerns: reduction of performance due to the occurrence of external interrupts and reduction of performance due to user and/or system errors. Although the consideration of the combination of erroneous behaviour and interrupts would be interesting too, it is useful to be able to study the effects of these two aspects first in separation. In fact, if both aspects would be included in the model from the beginning it would be no longer clear to which extent a certain outcome should be attributed to erroneous behaviour, to the effect of interrupts or to both. In this work we are mainly interested in the effect of interrupts and a formal model based methodology that allows one to compare the resilience to external interrupts of different interaction techniques.

A further concern is the level of abstraction used for modelling. We choose to keep the models relatively abstract, modelling observable events, and to refine the models only after a clear indication that this would lead to significantly better approximations. Finally, we use exponential distributions to approximate the average duration of activities. This way we make minimal assumptions on the exact shape of the distribution of the duration of individual actions.

6.1 User Model

In the first phase of model development, we consider an abstract view of the flow of information between interaction devices, system and user with the aim of getting insights in the cognitive resources required to perform the task at hand.

Referring to the ICS theory, features, such as colours and edges, contribute to form a mental *visual representation* derived from raw data acquired by the eyes. The structure of the visual scene in terms of icons is a more abstract *object representation* obtained by combining the visual representation with the knowledge and the experience the perceiver has of the world. This knowledge comes from a level of abstraction, where objects are named and their properties identified in terms of a *propositional representation*. Thus, the current structuring of the visual scene is used to augment the propositional knowledge about the objects being sensed. Visual and propositional representations can be combined to produce a further level, called *implicational representation*, where the general meaning of information is stated. Combining implicational and propositional knowledge, people are able to define goals and to act accordingly. Consequently, the object representation enriched by propositional data can be transformed into *limb representation* controlling physical actions performed, e.g., by hands and eyes. A continuous source of sensorial information, *body state representation*, provides feedback to the co-ordination of the physical actions. In the Drag 'n Drop case, this is thinking mentally of moving the cursor over one of the icons, push the mouse button to select it, drag it over the trash and release the button. The propositional knowledge can be transformed into a *morphonolexical representation* describing the phrases' structure. This is transformed into an *articulatory representation* controlling the physical production of speech. For Speak 'n Drop, this involves thinking mentally of moving the cursor over one of the icons on the display followed by a mouse click, while pronouncing the word delete.

The above reasoning is described by a set of subsystems, where knowledge is stored as representations, a set of processes transforming the knowledge from one representation into another, and a set of communication paths carrying the information from one subsystem to another. The set of transformations in place at a given moment in time, fully characterises the mental activity and is referred to as a *configuration*. The *reaction time* is the interval from the acquisition of sensorial data to the production of physical actions. It represents the time the user needs to put in place the appropriate mental configuration in order to react to sensorial data. From literature on cognitive psychology it is known that each transformation step in such a configuration takes approximately 40 milliseconds on average. Consequently, the time required to deploy the configuration for graphical interaction in Drag 'n Drop is at least 240 ms. The configurations for Drag 'n Drop and Speak 'n Drop, resp., are specified by

$$\text{DnDconfig} \supseteq \bigcup \begin{pmatrix} \{\text{:vis-implic:}, \text{:prop-implic:}\}, \\ \{\text{:obj-prop:}, \text{:implic-prop:}\}, \\ \{\text{:vis-obj:}, \text{:prop-obj:}\}, \{\text{:obj-lim:}, \text{:bs-lim:}\} \end{pmatrix} \quad \text{and}$$

$$\text{SnDconfig} \supseteq \bigcup \begin{pmatrix} \{\text{:ac-mpl:}, \text{:prop-mpl:}\}, \{\text{:mpl-art:}\}, \\ \{\text{:vis-implic:}, \text{:prop-implic:}\}, \\ \{\text{:obj-prop:}, \text{:implic-prop:}, \text{:mpl-prop:}\}, \\ \{\text{:vis-obj:}, \text{:prop-obj:}\}, \{\text{:obj-lim:}, \text{:bs-lim:}\} \end{pmatrix}$$

The ICS theory can be used also to describe which changes in mental configurations occur when unexpected events happen during a user's activity aiming at satisfying a specific goal. The mechanism put in action is the stopping of the activity of effector subsystems and the deployment of the following configuration:

$$\text{RecoveryConfig} \supseteq \bigcup \begin{pmatrix} \{\text{:ac-implic:}, \text{:bs-implic:}, \text{:vis-implic:}, \text{:prop-implic:}\}, \\ \{\text{:implic-prop:}\} \end{pmatrix}$$

The sensorial and propositional information is blended at the *implicational subsystem* and fed back into the *propositional subsystem*. This loop with information mutually exchanged between implicational and propositional subsystems, enables to get insights on what we know both as facts and feelings and to reason about the current context in which the unexpected event has occurred.

To get better insight in the user's performance in pointing movements, we need to refine the ICS model by addressing human factors and usability studies. It is well known that the duration of pointing movements is fairly well approximated by Fitts' law. Fitts' law based experiments show that the average time spent to point at an icon on a computer display by operating a mouse is in the order of 1000 ms [14]. Additionally, more recent findings [8] show that the movement itself can be distinguished into several phases including a *planning phase*, where the display is investigated and the propositional goal is formed; a *ballistic phase*, where the movement is based on low-level hand control (i.e. without buffering taking place at limb subsystem); an *approach phase*, performed under *visual control* requiring focus of attention (i.e. with buffering taking place at the limb subsystem [7]); and an *adjustment phase* to check that the target has been reached, similarly requiring the focus of attention. With this information, it is possible to refine the ICS analysis by splitting the pointing movement into two distinct phases: the first includes the planning phase plus the ballistic movement; the second consists of visual control. Consequently, the transfer of the buffer may occur later w.r.t the start of the movement and this will have important effects in the case of multimodal interaction.

6.2 Stochastic Automata

We move from the semi-formal and qualitative reasoning to a formal and quantitative one by specifying the identified user activity as PEPA (Performance Evaluation Process Algebra) models [10], described via a parallel composition of stochastic automata.

Configurations are modelled as states of the automata. Configuration changes usually identified by an observable action, are modelled as pairs *(action type, rate)* linking two states. *action type* denotes the type of the action and *rate* the negative exponential distribution of the activity duration; that is the average period of time during which a particular configuration (state) is in place. A special case are actions with infinite rates called *passive actions* as opposed to *active actions*. These play a special role in the parallel composition of the automata in which synchronisation on *(action type, rate)* pairs can be specified. The expected duration of a passive action cooperating with an active one is fully determined by the rate of the active one. The expected duration of a cooperation of active actions is a function of the expected durations of the corresponding activities in the components (typically corresponding to the longest one).

Due to lack of space, we only briefly describe one of the stochastic automata developed for the Speak 'n Drop interaction, shown in Fig. 3 (a); the interested reader is referred to [3] for details. To illustrate our approach to calculate the values of the rate parameters, consider transition $\mathrm{Usr} \stackrel{(\mathrm{move},im)}{\longrightarrow} \mathrm{UsrMve}$ modelling the initial part of the pointing movement. The value of rate im is composed of a planning phase of 240 ms, which is the time to deploy the relevant mental configuration, and the average time of the ballistic mouse movement, estimated to be 670 ms on average given the average distance that a user needs to cover to reach an icon on the screen obtained from empirical data available in the literature. Rate im then equals $1/(0.240+0.670) = 1.1$. Other values are obtained in similar ways, resulting in $ss = 1.6$, $vc = 3.4$ and $mc = 8.33$ for this case study.

Speak 'n Drop interaction is multimodal in nature, requiring both speech and gesture. In a *real setting*, where pointing gestures are performed in the same visual space where the referred objects exist, it will result in the performance of deictic references. In our case, the key question is whether users will be able to deploy the resources of the interface to achieve their tasks by performing a deixis or by using a sequential construct. Two major facts constrain user performance of Speak 'n Drop: the performance of the speech recognition system and the use of the mouse. Realistic speech recognition systems matching an acceptable performance accuracy operate at a rate in the range of $2/2.5 \times \mathit{real\ time}$. For the use of the mouse, it is known [7] that operating any device in a space different from the visual one, under visual control, requires the transfer of the buffer to the limb subsystem. Consequently, users will focus on operating the mouse device and they will be unable to initiate speech. However, they will be able to sustain previously initiated speech that is not in conflict with resource allocation.

In Fig. 3(a), transition $\mathrm{UsrMve} \overset{(\mathrm{startSpeak},ss)}{\longrightarrow} \mathrm{UsrSpeak1}$ defines a user that starts to speak while operating the mouse before entering visual control and that will achieve both goals in parallel. The alternate $\mathrm{UsrMve} \overset{(\mathrm{visualCtrl},vc)}{\longrightarrow} \mathrm{UsrOp1}$ refers to the case in which the visual control is entered before speech is started. Consequently, pointing occurs first and speaking is delayed.

It is interesting to note the duality of the states *UsrEndSpeakOp* and *UsrSel-Speak*. Both identify a condition in which one of the modalities has reached a stable point, in the sense that the task can be completed re-starting from that state after an interrupt has occurred. This requires special attention to be paid to the presentation of the system state in order to help the recovery of the propositional goal. For example, how do users know whether or not the system has already recognised the pronounced words? and by what means can this knowledge be made persistent over a period of time?

The system component is specified using the same formalism, allowing both user and system models to be combined to study the resulting conjoint behaviour. The system is split into two automata, similar in structure, specifying the selection and speaking tasks, as shown in Fig. 3(b–c). Both are always ready to reply to user's initiated actions as well as to interrupts. In addition, the *SysSpeak* automaton defines the rate at which speech is recognised with variable $es = 1$.

Interrupt generation rate and interrupts handling is specified by the automaton of Fig. 3(d). We assume that no nested interrupts occur. The Speak 'n Drop model is the parallel composition of the four automata described above:

$$\mathrm{Usr} \bowtie_{\{\mathrm{move},\mathrm{startSpeak},\mathrm{click},\mathrm{endSpeak},\mathrm{drop},\mathrm{interrupt},\mathrm{clickOK}\}}$$
$$((\mathrm{SysMouse} \bowtie_{\{\mathrm{drop},\mathrm{interrupt},\mathrm{clickOK}\}} \mathrm{SysSpeak}) \bowtie_{\{\mathrm{interrupt},\mathrm{clickOK}\}} \mathrm{Interrupt}),$$

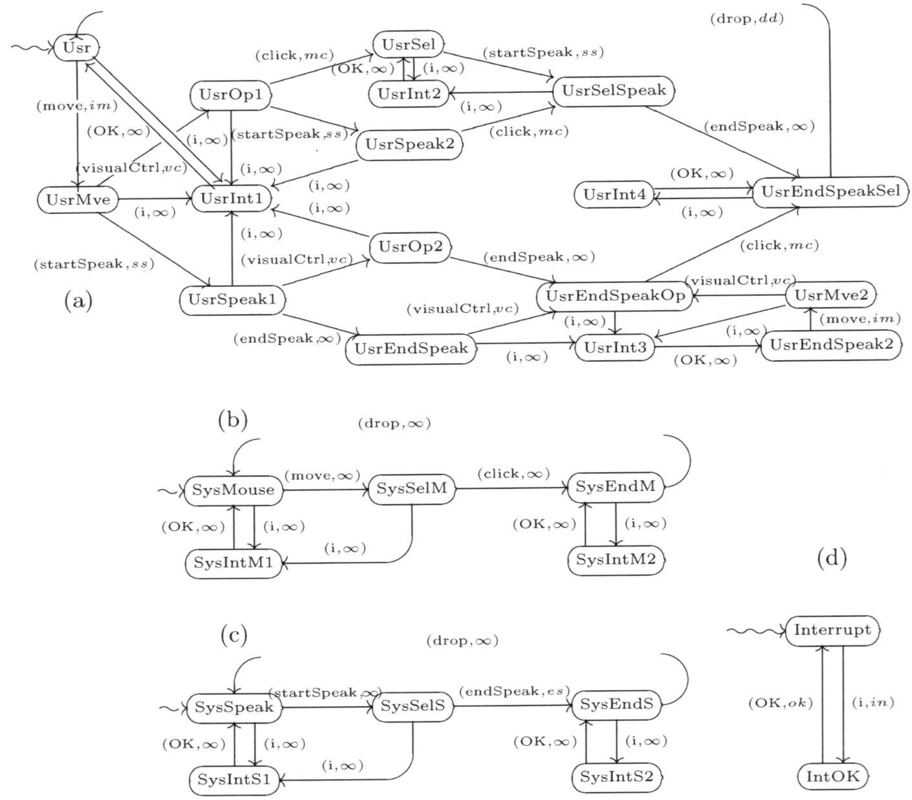

Fig. 3. Stochastic automata of (a) Usr, (b) SysMouse, (c) SysSpeak and (d) Interrupt, in which i=interrupt and OK=clickOK

where the sets of actions identify the synchronisation of automata over the named actions and ⋈ stands for the PEPA cooperation operator. Actions *interrupt* and *clickOK*, e.g., represent the occurrence of an interrupt and its handling. The above composition expresses that they may occur only with the participation (i.e. synchronisation) of *all* component automata. Action *drop* instead requires the participation of all except the Interrupt automaton, as it is not part of its synchronisation set at the cooperation operator. The resulting PEPA specification can be analysed with the stochastic model checker PRISM [13], a prototype tool that supports, e.g., the automatic verification of temporal logic properties and reward properties. One kind of reward property is particularly useful for the analysis of the effects of interrupts and will be explained in the next section. Reward formulae implicitly use reward structures that must be included in the specification to define those transitions that generate a certain amount of reward when executed. In our case, e.g., we have assigned a reward of 1 to each drop action to analyse the total number of such actions over a certain period of time.

7 Analysis Results

As an indicator of the resilience of an interaction technique to external interrupts we study the number of effective *drops* a user manages to perform during a fixed period of time under a varying number of interrupts occurring randomly during that period. The expected number of *drops* and *interrupts* occurring during an interval of 5 minutes (i.e. 300 s) are cumulative reward measures that can be formalised in reward stochastic temporal logic supported by the PRISM model checker as:

$$R\{\text{"}drops\text{"}\}_{=?}\ [C \leq 300] \qquad \text{and} \qquad R\{\text{"}interrupts\text{"}\}_{=?}\ [C \leq 300].$$

The notation $R\{\}_{=?}$ means that instead of comparing the results with a specific bound, the effective number of drops and interrupts is calculated.

Fig. 4(f) shows the expected number of drops a user manages to perform in the presence of a number of interrupts over the time span, for the Drag 'n Drop and Speak 'n Drop interaction techniques. The effective number of interrupts at rate 1 in Fig. 4(f) is 130 and not 300 because the user needs time to handle an interrupt (i.e. moving the cursor to a button and click on it). Recall that our model assumes no new interrupts arrive while a user is still handling a previous interrupt. With an interrupt rate close to 0, the user performs on average (given the values chosen for the model's parameters) 134 drops when using Drag 'n Drop and only 109 when using Speak 'n Drop. As expected, the user's performance decreases when the interrupt rate increases. In the presence of about 130 interrupts in 300 s, the user manages to perform only 27 and 33 drops.

Although the differences are relatively small, we can nevertheless make some observations. First of all, in the absence of interrupts Drag 'n Drop leads to a higher average number of drops. This is explained by the fact that we have assumed a time of recognition of spoken words equal to 2.5 × *real time* for the Speak 'n Drop model; this is a realistic assumption, but it limits the speed of interaction a user can reach. Furthermore, when the number of interrupts increases, Speak 'n Drop leads to better performance than Drag 'n Drop. The latter is more sensitive to interrupts because the total time involved in dragging is relatively long and when an interrupt occurs the user needs to start all over.

Apart from a basic comparison of the performance of the two techniques, we also investigated their sensitivity to the variation of the various action rates. In Fig. 4(a), the performance of Drag 'n Drop is shown for different user behaviour concerning the distribution of time between the various phases of a movement. As expected, when the percentage of time spent on the ballistic phase increases w.r.t. that spent on the visually-controlled phase, the performance improves slightly. However, a variation of 12% of splitting between the two phases accounts for only a 4% difference in the number of drops, showing that the model is not very sensitive to how the movement is partitioned over time in the two phases. Regarding Speak 'n Drop, the same analysis shows a negligible difference of performance: a variation of 12% in the distribution of the time accounts for only a 1% difference in the number of drops. Likewise, in Fig. 4(b) the line labelled *drops*

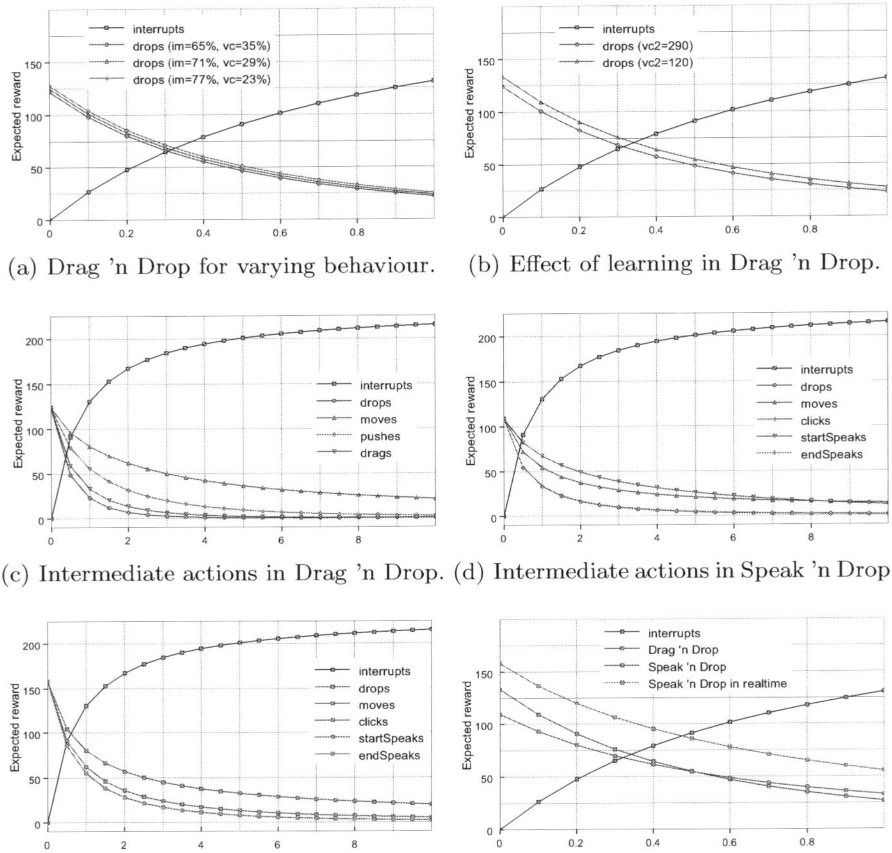

(a) Drag 'n Drop for varying behaviour. (b) Effect of learning in Drag 'n Drop.

(c) Intermediate actions in Drag 'n Drop. (d) Intermediate actions in Speak 'n Drop.

(e) Intermediate actions in Speak 'n Drop (with real-time speech recognition). (f) Drag 'n Drop vs. Speak 'n Drop (with and without real-time speech recognition).

Fig. 4. (a) Case study; (b)–(h) Results performance analyses performed for this paper (on the x-axes the values of the rate of interrupts used, ranging from 0 to 1 per second)

(vc2=1/0.120) shows the effect on performance of a user skilled in sustaining the overall propositional goal, while that labelled *drops (vc2=1/0.290)* shows the performance of a less skilled user. Clearly, in the former case the performance is uniformly better than in the latter; this describes the effect of learning due to frequent recurrence of the operation. According to the modelling experiments, an already skilled user can increase her performance by 8% with such a learning effect. This learning effect does not apply to Speak 'n Drop: there is no significant variation in performance when the user is behaving procedurally or not.

Fig. 4(c) relates the performance of various actions to the overall performance, i.e. it shows the total number of *move*, *push* and *drag* actions needed to obtain the corresponding number of drops for the given number of interrupts occurring in 300 s. About 50% of moves, 35% of pushes and 10% of drags are interrupted not leading to a successful drop. In fact, since the Drag 'n Drop technique is sequential, clearly actions that occur towards the beginning of the sequence fail more often than those close to the end. For Speak 'n Drop, it is particularly interesting to relate the intermediate actions to the number of drops. In Fig. 4(d) two facts show up clearly. First, the number of interrupted *startSpeak* actions keeps decreasing after the other actions have reached a more or less stable number. This is explained by the relatively slow speech recognition, which forces users to adapt themselves to the performance of the system. Second, the number of failures of the *click* and *endSpeak* actions is substantially equal to the number of *drops* for any number of interrupts considered. In fact, given the scale of Fig. 4(c), those actions collapse in the bottom curve and are not distinguishable. This is explained by the parallel execution of the subtasks and the very short time that passes between their respective completion, making the occurrence of an interrupt unlikely.

From these results, one might conclude that Drag 'n Drop is better suited for low interrupt rates while Speak 'n Drop takes the lead as the number of interrupts increases. On the other hand, the Speak 'n Drop proves to be more resilient, both to the number of interrupts and to the varying performance of users. Also, taking into account the percentage of failures of intermediate actions caused by interrupts, it can be expected that Speak 'n Drop might be more appreciated by users because they experience less frustration than with Drag 'n Drop, where for many interrupts they continuously need to restart their activity.

After these observations, we repeated the analysis specifying a *real-time* speech recogniser as shown in Fig. 4(e). In this case we observe that the number of *startSpeak* actions decreases in a similar way as for the other actions, the percentage of failing *clicks* and *endSpeaks* is very low, the increase of failing actions is moderate, and speech fails less often than selection. As before, the *click*, *endSpeak* and *drop* actions cannot be distinguished in Fig. 4(e) since they collapse in the bottom curve due to the scaling factor.

Finally, under the objective assumption that simple command languages can be recognised in real time by a speech recogniser, Fig. 4(f) shows the overall performance of the interaction techniques (i.e. number of *drops*) comparing Drag 'n Drop and Speak 'n Drop, both without and with real-time speech recognition. Real-time multimodal interaction clearly gives the best results for any number of interrupts.

8 Conclusions and Future Work

In this paper we have developed syndetic stochastic models of the Drag 'n Drop and Speak 'n Drop interaction techniques and analysed their resilience to the presence of external interrupts. We have modelled the human behaviour based on the well-established cognitive theory ICS and used literature on Fitts' law to obtain timing information on task execution. The models have been specified in the process algebra PEPA and analysed with the stochastic model checker PRISM. The models produce surprisingly plausible results given their level of abstraction and the fact that the parameter values come from published experiments each referring to different concerns of the overall user behaviour. To exactly what extent our models may serve to predict performance of human interaction in the presence of external interrupts requires further validation and is a topic for future research. This brings us to another issue: in reality human errors cannot be excluded and may clearly influence overall performance. Extending the models to cover erroneous behaviour is another interesting topic for future research. A particular challenge is to take into account the effects of cognitive load. A high cognitive load may result in more errors, but perhaps also in a slower capability of resuming the original task after an interrupt. A further topic for future research is the adaptation of the proposed methodology to the formalisms more commonly used in the HCI community, like ICO [18].

References

1. Bailey, B.P., Konstan, J.A., Carlis, J.V.: Measuring the effects of interruptions on task performance in the user interface. In: Proceedings SMC 2000, pp. 757–762. IEEE, Los Alamitos (2000)
2. Barnard, P.J.: Interacting Cognitive Subsystems: A Psycholinguistic Approach to Short-term Memory. In: Ellis, A. (ed.) Progress in the Psychology of Language, ch. 6, vol. 2, pp. 197–258. Lawrence Erlbaum, Mahwah (1985)
3. ter Beek, M.H., Faconti, G.P., Massink, M., Palanque, P.A., Winckler, M.: Resilience of Interaction Techniques to Interrupts: A Formal Model-based Approach—FULL VERSION. Technical Report, 2009-TR-001, ISTI–CNR (2009)
4. Brinksma, E., Hermanns, H., Katoen, J.-P. (eds.): EEF School 2000 and FMPA 2000. LNCS, vol. 2090. Springer, Heidelberg (2001)
5. Cades, D.M., Trafton, J.G., Boehm-Davis, D.A., Monk, C.A.: Does the difficulty of an interruption affect our ability to resume? In: Proceedings HFES 2007, Human Factors and Ergonomics Society, pp. 234–238 (2007)
6. Duke, D.J., Barnard, P.J., Duce, D.A., May, J.: Syndetic modelling. International Journal of Human Computer Interaction 13(4), 337–393 (1998)
7. Faconti, G.P., Duke, D.J.: Device models. In: Proceedings DSV-IS 1996, pp. 73–91. Springer, Heidelberg (1996)
8. Faconti, G., Massink, M.: Analysis of pointing tasks on a white board. In: Doherty, G., Blandford, A. (eds.) DSVIS 2006. LNCS, vol. 4323, pp. 185–198. Springer, Heidelberg (2007)
9. Gordon, I.E.: Theories of Visual Percept. Psychology Press (2004)
10. Hillston, J.: A Compositional Approach to Performance Modelling. Cambridge University Press, Cambridge (1996)
11. Hollnagel, E., Woods, D.D., Leveson, N. (eds.): Resilience Engineering: Concepts and Precepts. Ashgate (2006)
12. Jambon, F.: Formal modelling of task interruptions. In: Proceedings CHI 1996, pp. 45–46. ACM, New York (1996)
13. Kwiatkowska, M., Norman, G., Parker, D.: Probabilistic symbolic model checking with PRISM: A hybrid approach. In: Katoen, J.-P., Stevens, P. (eds.) TACAS 2002. LNCS, vol. 2280, pp. 52–66. Springer, Heidelberg (2002)
14. MacKenzie, I.S.: Fitts' law as a research and design tool in human-computer interaction. International Journal of Human Computer Interaction 7(1), 91–139 (1992)

15. McCrickard, D.S., Chewar, C.M.: Attuning notification design to user goals and attention costs. Communications of the ACM 46(3), 67–72 (2003)
16. McDaniel, M.A., Einstein, G.O., Graham, T., Rall, E.: Delaying execution of intentions: overcoming the costs of interruptions. Applied Cognitive Psychology 18(5), 533–547 (2004)
17. O'Conaill, B., Frohlich, D.: Timespace in the workplace: Dealing with interruptions. In: Proceedings CHI 1995, pp. 262–263. ACM, New York (1995)
18. Palanque, P.A., Bastide, R.: Petri net based Design of User-driven Interfaces Using the Interactive Cooperative Objects Formalism. In: Proceedings DSV-IS 1994, pp. 383–400. Springer, Heidelberg (1994)
19. Palanque, P.A., Bernhaupt, R., Navarre, D., Ould, M., Winckler, M.: Supporting usability evaluation of multimodal man-machine interfaces for space ground segment applications using Petri-net based formal specification. In: Proceedings SpaceOps 2006, American Institute of Aeronautics and Astronautics (2006)
20. Paternò, F., Mancini, C., Meniconi, S.: ConcurTaskTrees: A Diagrammatic Notation for Specifying Task Models. In: Proceedings INTERACT 1997, pp. 362–369. Chapman & Hall, Boca Raton (1997)
21. Pinheiro da Silva, P.: User interface declarative models and development environments: A survey. In: Palanque, P., Paternó, F. (eds.) DSV-IS 2000. LNCS, vol. 1946, pp. 207–226. Springer, Heidelberg (2001)
22. Trafton, J.G., Monk, C.A.: Task Interruptions. Reviews of Human Factors and Ergonomics 3, 111–126 (2007)
23. West, R.L., Nagy, G.: Using GOMS for Modeling Routine Tasks Within Complex Sociotechnical Systems: Connecting Macrocognitive Models to Microcognition. Journal of Cognitive Engineering and Decision Making 1(2), 186–211 (2007)
24. Zeigarnik, B.: Das behalten erledigter und unerledigter handlungen. Psychologische Forschung 9, 1–85 (1927)

Adaptive Security Dialogs for Improved Security Behavior of Users

Frederik De Keukelaere[1], Sachiko Yoshihama[1], Scott Trent[1], Yu Zhang[2], Lin Luo[2], and Mary Ellen Zurko[3]

[1] IBM Tokyo Research Laboratory, Kanagawa, Japan
[2] IBM China Research Laboratory, Beijing, China
[3] IBM Lotus, Massachusetts, USA
{frederik,sachikoy,trent}@jp.ibm.com,
{zyucrl,luolin}@cn.ibm.com, mzurko@us.ibm.com

Abstract. Despite the increasing awareness of the importance of security for daily computer users, we see that many users still fail to behave securely when confronted with a security-related decision. In this paper, we introduce a new approach to security-related dialogs called Adaptive Security Dialogs (ASD). This approach is a combination of a new architecture and a new way of interacting with users to provide them with appropriate and effective security dialogs. ASD realizes this goal by matching the complexity and intrusiveness of security-related dialogs to the risk associated with the decision the user is making. This results in an architecture in which users can focus on their tasks, get (immediate) feedback on their decisions, and interact with dialogs with an appropriate complexity and appearance for the decision's associated risk. This paper makes the following three contributions. First, we introduce a general architecture for handling security-related decisions. Second, through an empirical user study using a web-based e-mail client, we show significant improvement in the care exercised by our participants without sacrificing usability. Third, we describe how the different pieces of existing research fit into the bigger picture of improving users' behavior.

1 Introduction

In their daily life, computer users are frequently confronted with security-related decisions. However, even though most computer users are aware of the existence of security risks when using a computer, many do not make safe security decisions [15].

The underlying causes of this have been identified as: (1) most users are task driven and do not want to be bothered by distracting security questions [15], (2) dangerous security decisions usually go unpunished and undetected for long periods of time [2], (3) many security-related dialogs are too complicated for typical users [7, 16], and (4) it hard for the users to estimate the level of risk, since the dialogs look basically the same regardless of their security implication. For example, a dialog for saving a file and a dialog for running active content in a browser often look much alike [15]. We illustrate this with real world examples in Sec. 2.1.

T. Gross et al. (Eds.): INTERACT 2009, Part I, LNCS 5726, pp. 510–523, 2009.

To battle these problems, several approaches have preceded ours. To counter task-driven behavior, [7] concludes that the user's primary task should be clearly interrupted. To ensure users feel the impact of their security decisions, users were immediately punished in [2]. To simplify the user experience, a complex operation with many dialog boxes, required to connect to a secured wireless network, was simplified to a three-click operation [1]. In [5], dynamic security skins make a dialog or even an entire application appear differently to prevent phishing attacks.

However, to the best of our knowledge, none of these proposals have addressed the different levels of user risk and correspondingly adapted their dialogs. Nor did they change the appearances of the dialogs based on user behavior or external factors such as recent attacks. In this paper, we introduce an architecture which has a general model of a user with respect to security decisions. This model, when confronting a user with a security decision, takes into account: (1) the security risk associated with the decision, (2) the user's recent security performance, and (3) the external security situation and related factors. We show how adapting the security dialogs to these factors significantly improves security behavior. To test the effectiveness of our model, we implemented a prototype web mail client and performed a user study.

This paper makes the following three contributions. First, we introduce a general architecture for handling security-related decisions (Sec. 2). Second, through an empirical user study, we show significant improvement in user behavior when opening e-mail attachments in a web-based e-mail client. This improvement was quantified by a reduction in opened attachments, and an increase in time spent on the decision whether or not to open the attachments (Sec. 3 and 4). Third, we describe how the different pieces of existing research fit into the general architecture and what work is needed to complete the puzzle (Sec. 5 and 6).

2 Adaptive Security Dialogs

2.1 An Intuitive Feel

To get a better feel for the current user experience with security dialogs, let us briefly consider opening attachments in an e-mail program. When trying to open an attached text file the typical warning users are confronted with is "Opening attachments can be dangerous to your system. Click OK to open the attachment." When Bob, an inexperienced user, first sees this, he probably thinks "Is that so? Eh, what does that mean? What should I do?" and he quickly discovers that the message goes away by simply clicking OK. Alice, a more experienced user, will most likely think "I already know that, you have told me a thousand times. And by the way, text files are safe."

Now suppose they are confronted with a dangerous attachment, an executable file disguised as a text file. Bob, who has gained some experience by now, has learned that if he clicks OK, he can quickly open the attachment. "Why not?" he thinks, "The other times I clicked OK nothing bad happened." Alice, who is really in a hurry today, did not pay attention to the extension of the file name and is fooled by the icon of the attachment (which of course looked just like a text file). While unknowingly installing the latest malware on her system, she thinks, "Is it really necessary to have these useless warnings for text files?" and continues her work.

Our goal with Adaptive Security Dialogs (ASD) is to change the outcomes of these all-too-common scenarios. Since ASD adapts dialogs to the risk a user is exposed to, the appearance of the dialog when opening a text file and when opening an executable file will be obviously different. For Alice, this would have been a clear indicator that she was not opening a text file. Confronting Bob with a new type of dialog along with explanatory information, allows him to learn that different files have different risks.

Since ASD learns about the performance of each user as they are confronted with security dialogs, Alice, who always behaves securely, will receive fewer complex dialogs. This allows her to complete her tasks with minimal disturbance. For example, after behaving safely for some time she will no longer be informed of potential risks when opening a text file. But she will receive an appropriate dialog box for high risk attachments, warning that attention should be paid. In contrast, Bob will get the maximum of information about the risks he is being exposed to and more feedback on the choices he makes so that he can learn how to behave properly. As his knowledge evolves, so will his user performance and the ASD system will become less intrusive.

A third aspect of ASD is adaptation to external factors. Suppose, for example, a worm is spreading as a macro in an MS Word file. Typically these attachments can be identified by a certain fingerprint (e.g., the file name). By using an external source (e.g., an anti-virus program), ASD could identify high risk attachments and warn the user in the attachment-opening dialog. ASD could even offer to inform the sender of the possible infection. Other external sources influencing the security risk level could include compliance with company security policy, current best practices, and so on.

The core goal of ASD is therefore to provide an effective dialog with an appropriate level of intrusiveness to the user's tasks while providing a personally optimized user experience with the necessary feedback.

2.2 Architecture

In this section we describe the components of the ASD architecture. Since the focus of this paper is to demonstrate the feasibility of ASD using an empirical study of its effectiveness in a web mail application, we leave a detailed explanation of the algorithms to a future paper. This section provides the high level overview required to understand the overall system and interpret the results of the user experiment.

To realize the goal of the ASD, we designed the architecture in Fig. 1. The architecture is composed of several data stores, engines, and an end-user application. Security information is collected and stored in the data stores. The engines use this information to alter the behavior of the dialogs. The different types of data stores are:

- Decision Risk Data (DRD): This data store contains information that links program execution points and decision types to risk levels. E.g., a mail client would have a corresponding record stating that opening an attachment (a program execution point) that contains an executable file (a decision type) is a high risk operation.
- User Performance Data (UPD): This data store contains user performance regarding security dialogs. E.g., if a user opens any attachment regardless of type, this incautious security behavior would be stored here.
- Environmental Data (ED): This data store contains information from external sources which influence the engines. E.g., information about best practices, recent virus and malware trends, corporate policy, other users' behavior, and so on.

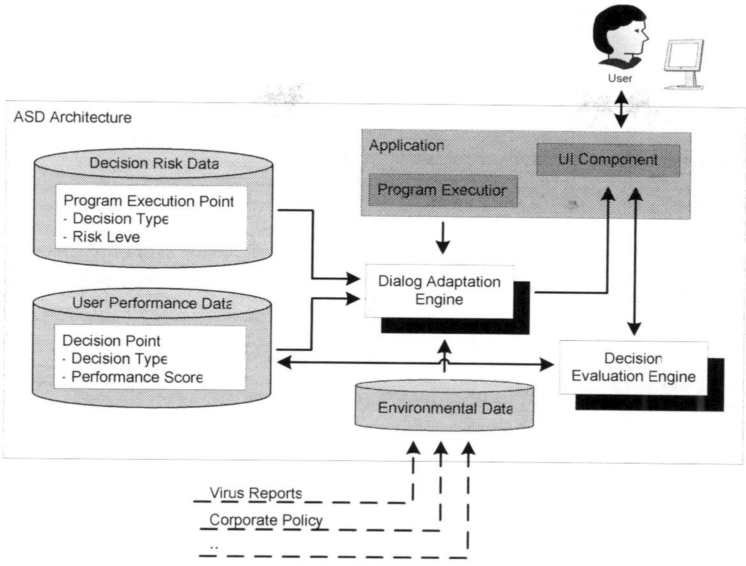

Fig. 1. ASD Architecture *The Dialog Adaptation Engine combines data sources to provide the user with an appropriate dialog. The user's decision is evaluated by the Decision Evaluation Engine which gives feedback to the user and loops the performance score back into the system.*

Based on information in these data stores, the engines will instruct the UI component to generate an appropriate dialog, track users' behavior, and provide user feedback. Feedback is used to train the user to make better decisions. The engines are:

- Dialog Adaptation Engine (DAE): This engine selects the appropriate dialog for a given security risk during program execution. E.g., for a normally cautious user who tries to open an text file attachment, a minimal dialog will be displayed.
- Decision Evaluation Engine (DEE): Users make decisions about each dialog, e.g., whether or not to open an attachment. The DEE tracks this and generates a user performance score, which is stored, and used to select dialogs. This engine guides the user by providing information, penalties, and or rewards.

2.3 Dialog Types

Although theoretically any type of dialog box can be used within our ASD system, we limited the dialog types in our empirical study to the following five classes of dialogs. These dialogs were selected based on the authors' estimation of three criteria: 1) understandability, 2) interference with the user's task, 3) estimated handling time.

- Warn-and-Continue (W&C) [2]: This is a dialog that warns the user and asks the user to confirm an action. This is currently the most used dialog in e-mail software. In the upper left of Fig. 2 a sample W&C dialog is shown for the situation in which a user wants to open an e-mail attachment containing a text document.

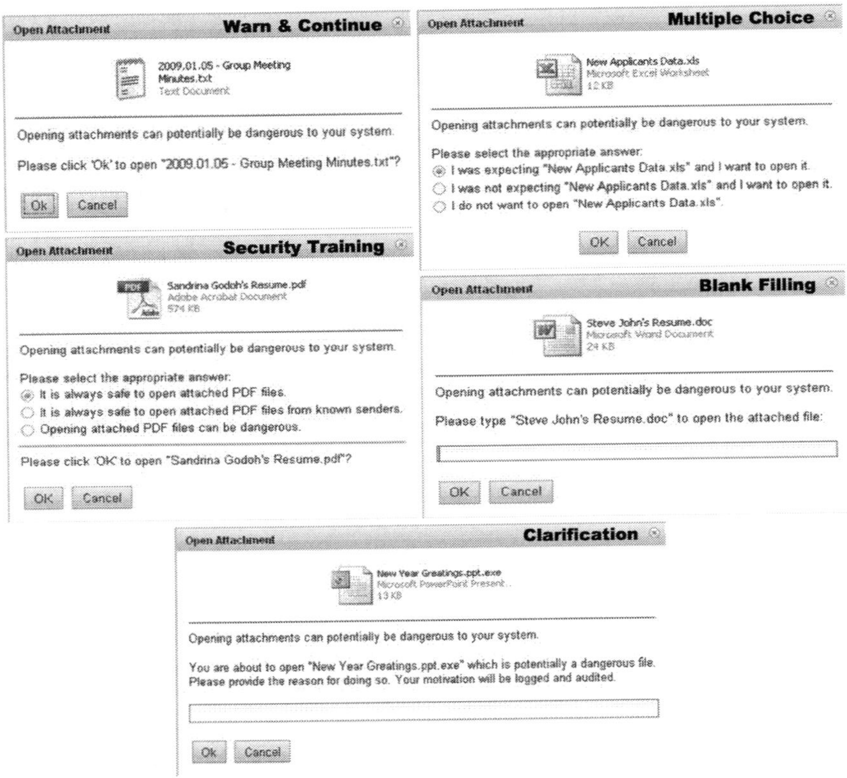

Fig. 2. Different types of dialog boxes *Warn-and-Continue, Multiple Choice, Security Training, Blank Filling, and Clarification Dialogs for attachments of different file types*

- Multiple Choice Dialog (MC): This type of dialog provides the user with different options from which to choose the correct one to open the attachment. At the upper right side of Fig. 2 a sample multiple-choice dialog is shown for the situation in which a user wants to open an e-mail attachment containing an MS Excel File[1].
- Security Training (ST): This type of dialog combines a W&C dialog with a related security question. This question is taken from a set of security training questions and selected based on the topic of the W&C dialog. With the ST dialog the user learns more about the background of the question and can therefore make more informed decisions. At the bottom left of Fig. 2 a sample ST dialog is shown for the situation in which a user wants to open a PDF file.
- Blank Filling (BF): To complete this dialog the user is asked to confirm the file to be opened by typing in the file name. This makes sure the user is fully aware of

[1] As an alternative a polymorphic dialog [2] could be used. Such a dialog changes the order of its elements each time it is presented, and provides step by step context-based guidance to the user. In our user experiment, we opted for the simpler multiple choice dialog to ensure that decisions can be made in one step.

which file he/she is being opened. At the bottom right of Fig. 2 a sample blank filling dialog is shown for the situation in which a user wants to open an e-mail attachment with the filename "Steve John's Resume.doc".

- Clarification Dialog (CD): In this dialog a user is required to type in the reason for opening the attachment. This reason is stored and later audited. This makes the user more aware of what he is doing and requires him to think about the motivation for doing it. At the bottom of Fig. 2 a dialog is shown for a situation in which a user is trying to open an executable attachment pretending to be an MS PowerPoint presentation[2].

3 Testing Methodology

3.1 Experiment Set-Up

To test the impact of ASD on the user tendency to open all attachments, we implemented a web-based e-mail client simulating ASD and performed user trials. To make sure that none of our participants would perform better than others due to familiarity with a certain e-mail client, we built a new mail application based on the DOJO Dijit Mail demo [14]. As a result, our participants performed the tests on a browser-based AJAX application similar to currently popular online mail clients such as GMail [8], Yahoo! Mail [18], and Hotmail [10].

We created three different versions of the e-mail application for this experiment: (1) a version in which all of the dialogs are W&C dialogs, referred to as W&C throughout the rest of this paper, (2) a version in which dialogs are selected using the ASD system, except that feedback is given to the participant, called ASD throughout the rest of this paper, (3) a version in which dialogs are selected using ASD and automatic feedback is provided to the participant, called ASDF throughout the rest of this paper. Feedback was given by using virus warnings and explanatory dialogs to help users to make better choices for later attachments.

The questions we wanted to answer with this experiment are:

1. Do our participants behave more carefully when using ASD or ASDF versus W&C?
2. Does the use of ASD or ASDF come with a cost in usability?
3. How do the participants experience each type of dialog as regards complexity and interference with their tasks?
4. What is the effectiveness of immediate feedback on a participants' tendency to open attachments?

We divided users into three equal groups to observe any differences in the behaviors of the participants using W&C, ASD, or ASDF. One group used the W&C dialog application, the second group ASD, and the third used ASDF. We tracked the decisions of each participant on whether or not to open attachments. In addition, we measured the time it took the user to answer each dialog. This time was measured by taking the difference between the time at which the dialog appeared and the time of

[2] This dialog can be considered a variation on the audited dialog introduced in [2]. Once again, we selected a simplification to maintain a single step decision process.

the user decision. Due to the length of the experiment, it was not possible to evaluate the influence of repeated appearances of the same dialog on the decision time. Therefore, the measured time should only be seen as a first indicator towards the amount of attention the participant paid to the dialog when confronted with the choice to open an attachment or not. We used an *unpaired t-test* to evaluate the significance of the differences between the three groups.

At the end of the test, we presented the participants with a feedback form in which they were asked to evaluate our application. The W&C group was presented with a general questionnaire about the overall usability. The ASD group received the same questionnaire with additional questions regarding the difficultly of understanding the dialogs and the interference of the dialogs with completing their tasks. The ASDF group was asked the same questions with one additional question about the usefulness of the feedback. These final results were later compared with the objective effects observed during the tests.

3.2 Role Playing Scenario

Our participants were provided with a URL which gave them access to our experiment website. On the first page they received instructions on how to complete the experiment. The instructions explained (1) that we were testing a new web-based mail client for its usability, (2) that they were supposed to play the role of Chris Baker, an office worker at a credit card application company[3], and (3) a set of tasks that Chris needed to complete. Note that we chose not to disclose that we were actually measuring the efficacy and usability of ASD to make sure that our participants were not security-biased while performing the experiment.

Chris' task list was given to the participants to make sure that everyone would perform the same actions. A welcomed side-effect of a task list is that having the tasks distracts people from the actual dialogs, more as if they were doing their daily tasks in their normal working environments, which made the test more realistic. The tasks required each participant to read the mails in the Inbox and to possibly open the attachments. The following email messages were present:

- A request from a coworker to extract deadlines from some meeting notes. The notes were attached as a text file.
- A request from a coworker to search for the applicant with the highest annual income in a new applicants list. The list was attached as an MS Excel file.
- A request from a coworker to check out a cool New Year's card. The card was attached as an executable disguised as an MS PowerPoint file.
- A resume of an unknown job applicant. Attached as a PDF file.
- A resume of an unknown job applicant. Attached as an MS Word file.

For the W&C group, all dialogs were of the W&C type. The dialogs for the ASD and ASDF groups are shown in Fig. 2. Due to the length of the test, it was not possible

[3] The authors acknowledge that providing participants with a scenario can influence their security behavior, as shown by Schechter et al. [11]. However, it was our intention to control the content of the messages and their attachments and therefore we could not allow our test subjects to answer their personal messages.

to study all aspects of the adaptive behavior of ASD. We studied adaptation based on the type of attachment (decision risk data) and the simulation of a recent outbreak of PDF exploits (environmental data). However, even with these limitations, we will show a significant improvement in behavior in Sec. 4. It is the authors' opinion that experimentally observing the educational benefit of ASD on user's behavior would improve the results even more. However, to obtain significant results regarding long-term user behavior improvement would require a longer observation period than in this experiment.

3.3 Participant Information

The participants in the experiment were all familiar with e-mail clients. However, we excluded potential participants with a background in computer science or engineering, or any person that had significant computer security expertise. Their security behavior is fundamentally different from the general computer users, for whom ASD was designed. After filtering, we had a total of 32 participants. From these, the results of 8 participants were excluded as incomplete. This could have been avoided if the tests were performed in a more controlled environment such as a fixed lab setting. However, for more natural behavior, we allowed participants to perform the tests in their own environments.

Table 1 summarizes the characteristics of the final participants and the survey summary results. A majority of our participants were female. This was not the authors' intention and we do not assign any significance to it. The other results depicted in Table 1 will be further discussed in the next section.

Table 1. Participants characteristics *Participant numbers, genders, average ages, and their feedback on the system*

	W&C	ASD	ASDF
Participants (#)	8	8	8
Female (#)	5	6	6
Male (#)	3	2	2
Age (avg.)	30	32	28
Overall Usability	2.75 / 5	2.62 / 5	2.75 / 5
std.dev.	0.71	0.74	0.89
Usefulness Feedback			2.37 / 5
std.dev.			0.52

4 Experimental Results

Tables 2 and 3 contain the main results of our experiment. We indicate the mean, standard deviation, effect size, and p-value of our experimental results. The effect sizes are expressed as Cohen's d-values [4, 13] which indicate the strength of the observed effect. A value larger than 0.8 is considered a large effect. The p-value of our *unpaired t-test* [3, 4] is used to indicate the statistical significance of our results.

A value smaller than 0.05 indicates that our results are statistically significant and that we accept our null hypothesizes that with ASD fewer people immediately open attachments and with ASD people spend more time considering their decisions.

Table 2. Comparison between W&C and ASD (unpaired t-test, n=8) *ASD shows a significant increase in the time participants spent analyzing the dialogs and a reduction in the percentage of attachments opened*

	mean	std. dev.	eff.size	p-value
attachments opened (%)				
W&C	92.50%	10.35%		
ASD	87.50%	10.35%		
difference	-5.00%	17.73%		not sig.
dialog response time (sec)				
W&C	3.85	1.76		
ASD	29.49	29.88		
difference	25.64	30.56	1.3	0.00004

Table 2 shows the comparison between W&C and ASD. It indicates that ASD causes an average 5% reduction in the number of attachments that our participants opened. The average time spent by users making a decision increased by an average of 25.64 seconds. This result was statistically significant and had a large effect (p=0.00004, d=1.3). Although the result for file openings was not statistically significant, combined with the decision times it indicates that our participants were more careful in ASD than in W&C when deciding to open an attachment. The large value for the standard deviation on the time measurements, 29.88 seconds, is caused by having five different types of dialogs with different average decision times, and representing a large variance in times.

Table 3. Comparison between W&C and ASDF (unpaired t-test, n=8) *ASDF shows a significant increase in the time participants spent analyzing the dialog and a significant reduction in the percentage of attachments opened*

	mean	std. dev.	eff.size	p-value
attachments opened (%)				
W&C	92.50%	10.35%		
ASDF	75.00%	14.14%		
difference	-17.50%	12.82%	1.51	0.01707
dialog response time (sec)				
W&C	3.85	1.76		
ASDF	35.80	29.28		
difference	31.96	30.23	1.65	< 0.00001

Table 3 shows the comparison between W&C and ASDF. In this case, the results indicate that ASDF causes an average 17.50% reduction in the number of attachments opened by our participants. The average time spent making decisions went up by

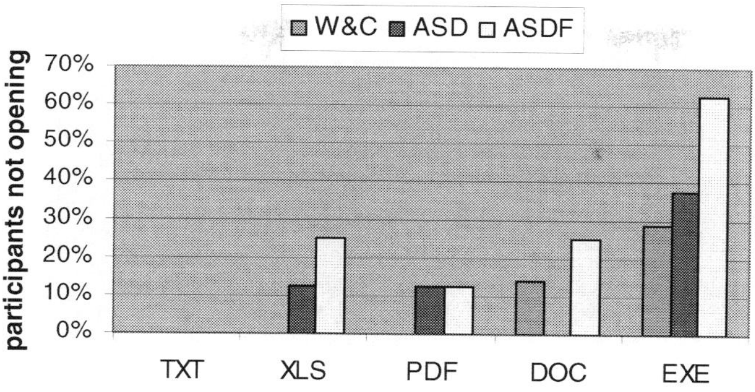

Fig. 3. Percentage of participants not opening attachments of varying file types *For W&C most participants opened all of the attachments, while for ASDF their behavior was more careful*

31.96 seconds. In this comparison both values were statically significant and had a large effect (p=0.01707, d=1.51 and p<0.00005, d=1.65 respectively). The large standard deviation for time measurements has the same cause as in Table 2.

Tables 2 and 3 indicate that ASDF causes an improvement in the care taken by our participants when opening attachments. Figure 3 reinforces this by showing the number of participants who did not open certain types of attachment using W&C, ASD, and ASDF. A percentage of zero indicates that all of the participant opened that attachment. With W&C, the participants tended to open almost every type of attachment. We see this is not the case for ASD and even more so for ASDF. An interesting result is that for BF (the dialog box used for opening a doc file) the performance of ASD is worse than W&C. The feedback we received from our participants is that they were not motivated to think about security when confronted with a blank to fill in. They simply performed the task they were asked to do, which was to type the file name so that they could open the attachment. In addition, interviews with our participants showed that to them file types had little security meaning. More education on the risks associated with certain file types could potentially improve the performance of this dialog box.

Figure 4 displays the participants' reported scores for difficulty and interference with their tasks. These values are expressed on a scale from 1 to 5, ranging from "easy to understand" to "difficult to understand" and "low interference" to "high interference." In addition, this figure also contains the relative time participants spent on different dialogs. These values are expressed on a scale from 1 to 5, where 1 is the dialog that took the least time to respond to and 5 is the one that took the longest time. The reported values become larger as the dialogs were more demanding of the users. Again, the score for BF is unusual, since it indicates that in spite of the fact that it is considered more complex and more intrusive than dialogs such as MC, it does not result in more careful security behavior. However, it does have a relative shorter decision time.

The bottom of Table 1 contains feedback we received from our participants regarding the relative overall usability of the application (compared to their current mail client) and on the usefulness of the feedback in ASDF. These values are expressed on a scale from 1 to 5, ranging from "much less usable" to "much more usable" and "not useful" to "very useful" respectively. A score of 3 should be considered equally usable and to have neutral usability, respectively.

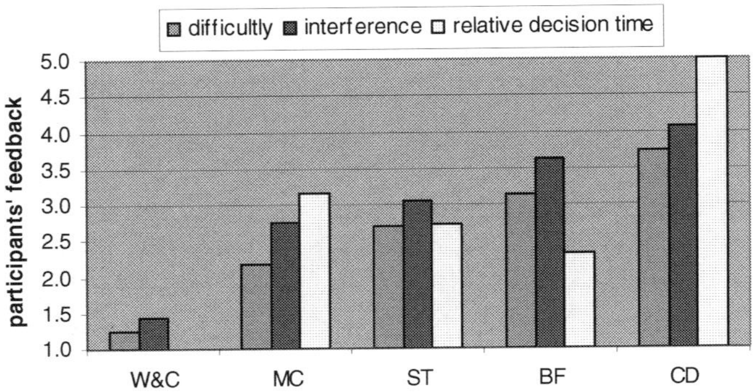

Fig. 4. Participants' experienced difficulty, interference and relative decision time for the different dialog types. *Paradoxically, little time was spent on the Blank Filling dialog despite the high difficulty and interference rating.*

The participants rated our mail application as slightly less usable (a score less than 3) compared to their current mail clients. The main complaint we received was that our application was missing functionality for forwarding mail and did not have a folder for sent mail. A more interesting aspect of the results was that they were all very similar to each other. This suggests that the dialogs are not a significant factor when deciding on the overall usability of a web based mail client. An alternative explanation could be that the dialogs in ASDF do not negatively influence the usability. In either case, the participants did not consider the ASDF versions to be (significantly) worse than the W&C version.

The participants in the ASDF test did not consider the feedback useful (a score less than 3). The main complaint we received was that the feedback came too late and had no impact on opening the attachment. For example, when a user was presented with a multiple choice question, he received feedback after making a decision. In this prototype, we did not provide any options to the user to change the decision. As a result, most of our participants spent little time reading the feedback and considered it to be interfering with their tasks. Despite this, the results for ASDF are slightly better than those for ASD.

5 Future Work

The biggest challenge in evaluating the efficacy of ASD(F) is to carry out a long-term experiment that fully resembles the day to day environment in which participants are confronted with security dialogs. Due to the limited timeframe in which we evaluated our system, we were only able to measure our system in its initial state. Therefore, it was not possible for us to test the effectiveness of using dialogs to educate the users and improve their long-term security behavior. The already promising ASD(F) could be further improved by such a study. Interesting aspects to measure would be: 1) the impact of using different machine-learning algorithms to profile the security awareness of the participant, 2) the improvement of the perceived usability of a system that adapt to the user's security knowledge, 3) the extent to which a user learns to associate risk levels with the appearance of certain types of dialogs.

As a result of various studies [6, 7, 9, 17], we are beginning to understand the factors that influence a user's interaction with a security dialog. Also in this experiment, we found that there is no single factor that influences users. Further study of the correlation of the different aspects of a security dialog and users' security behavior (such as the impact of difficulty, interference, decision time, layout, and attachment file type) could be used as a basis for improving the base set of dialogs in our ASD architecture.

6 Related Work

Although security usability is still a field in which a lot of future research must be done, several relevant experiments have preceded ours. In addition to the references to related work throughout the paper, we list some of the most relevant studies here and consider how they compare to our experiments. A recent publication by West [15] tries to answer the question: "Why do well-intending users make dangerous decisions?" His analysis looks at the psychology behind user behavior when confronted with security decisions. One of the main thoughts in this paper is that people are generally unmotivated when confronted with security decisions. This was confirmed in our experiments as our participants often choose the quickest path to complete their tasks. Paradoxically, making them spend more time on some of the security dialogs did not have a negative impact on their perception of the overall usability of our application. This hints that, for certain decisions, users find interruptions justified.

Another aspect contributing to users making dangerous decisions is that it is generally hard for security-naive users to understand security precautions. In [16] Whitten evaluates how difficult it is for ordinary users to integrate encryption and signing of e-mails into everyday tasks. This work shows that security user interfaces need their own design principle and should be considered separately from normal user interface design. This was confirmed by Zurko in [19], where she evaluated how users respond to dialogs in Lotus Notes and noted the difficulty they had in understanding and correctly evaluating the content of the dialogs. In our experiment, ASDF ensured that the security dialogs were treated differently from other dialogs. We designed the dialogs so that they provide the user with the necessary information to facilitate decision making. A thought-provoking finding was that making users spent time on a dialog can provide improved security behavior. There appears to be a correlation between the number of actions required to process a dialog and security performance.

Dangerous decisions are also often triggered when users do not spend sufficient time evaluating a security decision. Users tend to be task driven and any dialog that stands between them and the completion of their task is generally considered an obstacle that needs to be overcome as quickly as possible. In [12], Sharek wanted to evaluate if users differentiate between real pop-up messages and fake pop-up messages. Perhaps the most interesting result from this study was that up to 40% of the test users just wanted to get rid of a dialog as quickly as possible and had very little or no concern about the content or authenticity of the pop-up. By giving our test users a task driven scenario we evaluated the effectiveness of our solution against this potential problem.

In most applications, security dialogs are just one of many types of dialogs. This leads to the current situation where users tend to consider each dialog they encounter to be of equal importance. To the user, all dialogs appear the same [7]. For example, a warning that opening a suspicious attachment is dangerous and a dialog used for paragraph formatting often appear visually the same to users [15]. In [2] Brustoloni successfully introduced polymorphic and audited dialogs to make security dialogs stand out clearly from other dialogs. This idea was applied in Firefox 3 and Internet Explorer 7 to handle certificate problems more carefully. In our ASD architecture, we extended this idea to make the appearance of all security dialogs fundamentally different depending on the attachment type, user performance, and so on.

In [7], Egelman differentiates between active warnings and passive security indicators. Active warnings can be regarded as a form of dialog since they interrupt the user's task. Passive notices are just indicators on the users' screen of dangerous states. Egelman found that passive notices have very little effect on user behavior, so we designed our ASD architecture and experiment to use active security interruptions.

7 Conclusion

In this paper we introduced Adaptive Security Dialogs (ASD), a new architecture and approach to improve the security behavior of computer users. We made the following three contributions.

First, we introduced ASD, a general architecture for handling security-related decisions. We described the different components within ASD and illustrated how ASD adapts the type of dialog to (1) the risk associated with the security decision the user is about to make, (2) the user performance regarding previous security decisions, and (3) environmental factors such as virus reports, company policies, and so on.

Second, we studied the feasibility of our approach. We created several versions of a web-based e-mail prototype which we used to compare the current practice with ASD. We observed the security behavior of 24 participants while they were performing a set of e-mail-related tasks. With this empirical study we showed how our ASD prototype provides a significant improvement in the care exercised by the participants regarding opening attachments. Despite the high intrusiveness of our dialogs in certain risky situations, our participants rated the usability of all of the prototypes similarly, illustrating that ASD does not add significant overhead.

Third, the elements of our ASD architecture were compared to the current state of the art and we described how the different pieces of existing research fit into a bigger picture. In addition, we identified what work is needed to fill the gaps to build a fully adaptive security dialogs framework.

Acknowledgements. The authors would like to thank the anonymous reviewers for their valuable comments and suggestions. Their time and efforts have helped improving this paper. In addition, we would like to thank J. C. Brustoloni and R. Villamarin-Salomon for their permission to reuse their user scenario [2] in our experiments.

References

1. Balfanz, D., Durfee, G., Grinter, R.E., Smetters, D.K., Stewart, P.: Network-in-a-box: how to set up a secure wireless network in under a minute. In: SSYM 2004: Proceedings of the 13th conference on USENIX Security Symposium, Berkeley, CA, USA, p. 15. USENIX Association (2004)
2. Brustoloni, J.C., Villamarin-Salomon, R.: Improving security decisions with polymorphic and audited dialogs. In: SOUPS 2007: Proceedings of the 3rd symposium on Usable privacy and security, pp. 76–85. ACM Press, New York (2007)
3. Burton, R.: Using Excel to do basic statistical tests (2002), `http://depts.alverno.edu/nsmt/stats.htm`
4. Cohen, J.: Statistical Power Analysis for the Behavioral Sciences, 2nd edn. Lawrence Erlbaum, Mahwah (1988)
5. Dhamija, R., Tygar, J.D.: The battle against phishing: Dynamic security skins. In: SOUPS 2005: Proceedings of the 2005 symposium on Usable privacy and security, pp. 77–88. ACM, New York (2005)
6. Dhamija, R., Tygar, J.D., Hearst, M.: Why phishing works. In: CHI 2006: Proceedings of the SIGCHI conference on Human Factors in computing systems, pp. 581–590. ACM, New York (2006)
7. Egelman, S., Cranor, L.F., Hong, J.: You've been warned: an empirical study of the effectiveness of web browser phishing warnings. In: CHI 2008: Proceeding of the 26th Annual SIGCHI Conference on Human Factors in Computing Systems, pp. 1065–1074. ACM Press, New York (2008)
8. Google. Gmail, `http://mail.google.com`
9. Kumaraguru, P., Rhee, Y., Acquisti, A., Cranor, L.F., Hong, J., Nunge, E.: Protecting people from phishing: the design and evaluation of an embedded training email system. In: CHI 2007: Proceedings Of the SIGCHI Conference on Human Factors in Computing Systems, pp. 905–914. ACM Press, New York (2007)
10. Microsoft. Hotmail, `http://www.hotmail.com`
11. Schechter, S.E., Dhamija, R., Ozment, A., Fischer, I.: The emperor's new security indicators - an evaluation of website authentication and the effect of role playing on usability studies. In: IEEE Symposium on Security and Privacy, SP 2007 (2007)
12. Sharek, D., Swofford, C., Wogalter, M.: Failure to recognize fake internet pop-up warning messages. In: Proceedings of the Human Factors and Ergonomics Society 52nd Annual Meeting, pp. 557–560 (2008)
13. Thalheimer, W., Cook, S.: How to calculate effect sizes from published research articles: A simplifed methodology (2002), `http://worklearning.com/effectsizes.htm`
14. The DOJO Foundation. Dijit mail demo, `http://dojotoolkit.org/demos`
15. West, R.: The psychology of security. Communications of the ACM 51(4), 34–40 (2008)
16. Whitten, A., Tygar, J.D.: Why Johnny can't encrypt: a usability evaluation of pgp 5.0. In: SSYM 1999: Proceedings of the 8th Conference on USENIX Security Symposium, Berkeley, CA, USA, p. 14. USENIX Association (1999)
17. Wogalter, M.S.: Handbook of Warnings, Communication-Human Information Processing (C-HIP) Model, p. 5161. Lawrence Erlbaum Associates, Mahwah (2006)
18. Yahoo! Yahoo! mail, `http://mail.yahoo.com`
19. Zurko, M.E., Kaufman, C., Spanbauer, K., Bassett, C.: Did you ever have to make up your mind? What Notes users do when faced with a security decision. In: ACSAC 2002: Proceedings of the 18th Annual Computer Security Applications Conference, Washington, DC, USA, p. 371. IEEE Computer Society, Los Alamitos (2002)

Perceptions of Risk and Control: Understanding Acceptance of Advanced Driver Assistance Systems

Somya Joshi[1], Thierry Bellet[2], Vanessa Bodard[2], and Angelos Amditis[1]

[1] Institute for Communication & Computer Systems, 9 Iroon Politechniou Street, DECE - office 2131, Zografou, Athens 157 73, Greece
Tel.: +30 210 7721508; Fax: +30 210 7723557 -2291
[2] 25, Avenue François Mitterrand - Case 24, F-69675 BRON, Lyon, France
s.joshi@iccs.gr, a.amditis@iccs.gr, thierry.bellet@inrets.fr, vanessa.bodard@inrets.fr

Abstract. With a marked increase in advanced driver assistance systems (ADAS) being designed and deployed for cars, there is a logical emergence of studies that critically examine the influence these have on driver behavior and attitudes towards risk and safety. The research question addressed within this paper asks to what extent the level of perceived criticality or risk on the part of drivers influences their acceptance of advanced assistance.

1 Introduction

Presently, the technological feasibility of most ADAS is not the main issue for implementation anymore [1]. In fact, the first ADAS applications have already entered the market, such as adaptive cruise controls and collision warning systems. The focus in scientific research on ADAS in the past years has shifted from basic technology research and development towards the complexity and impacts of implementation of ADAS [2]. By focusing on the tools (both technological and conceptual) that mediate between our subject group of drivers and our augmented driving environment, this paper attempts to critically examine how diverse driver attitudes towards risk and control can be factored into the design of intelligent in-car systems.

2 Methodology and Experimental Design

This paper reports on the findings from two years of post-doctoral research that took place within the broader frame of a European network of excellence called HUMANIST[1]. Our methodology combined qualitative, interpretative analysis tools with simulator based study design, thereby allowing for a deeper, richer understanding of driver decision-making behaviour and subjective attitudes towards risk and safety, albeit within a controlled environment.

A total of 20 subjects participated in our study, who were selected from a diverse background, cutting across gender, age, driving experience, and license history. With

[1] http://www.noehumanist.org/

T. Gross et al. (Eds.): INTERACT 2009, Part I, LNCS 5726, pp. 524–527, 2009.

regard to the novice-elderly distribution, the subjects covered ages ranging from 24 to 66, their experience ranged from 1 to 48 years. In terms of mileage the subjects varied from below 3000 kms to 100000 kms. Finally, we had a mixture within the group of subjects that had points on their license and those that held a clean license history.

The simulator part of the experiment was divided into three main stages. These were: Orientation, Non-assistance and Assistance. This was further characterised by two series (1&2) where the driver experienced a range of critical and non-critical situations, but without any automation or assistance from the intelligent vehicle. Then in series (3&4) they once again experienced a range of critical driving condition, with assistance in the form of automatic breaking, steering control and speed reduction. Warning assistance was given by way of audio (beeps) and visual (flashing diode) signals. Finally the last section of series 4 ended with a near-collision scenario. After the simulator part, we again asked our subjects to fill in questionnaires and participate in semi-structured subjective interviews, where they had another opportunity to provide rich data on their perceptions of risk and control and their subsequent acceptance or need for ADAS.

3 Analysis

The environment that we refer to here concerns the physical features of the road (weather, geometry, signs and signals), the driver's own speed and direction, and the paths and speeds of other road users. As subject here we refer to the individual driver, while the instruments in question would be the ADAS and IVIS functions available within the experimental car. Our explicit goal here, or the object, would be to reduce accidents and injury on the road, thereby making the overall environment safer by endowing the subject with more informed decision-making powers. In Fig. 1 below we see this represented within the framework of the activity model.

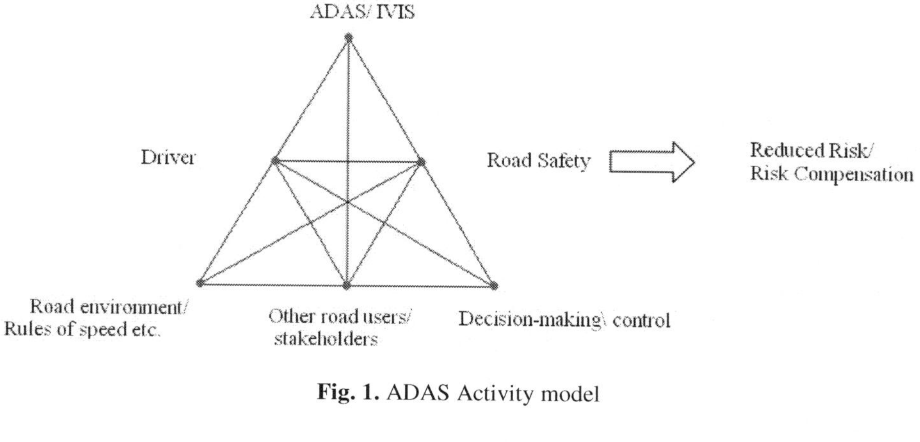

Fig. 1. ADAS Activity model

The outcome of the activity however is determined by the interactions between the various nodes. And given the subjective nature of risk it is not surprising that the final outcome of the activity could take form either in line with the desired object of activity or in tangent to it. For instance the perceived level of risk will be relatively low if the driver is confident about having the necessary coping skills, and higher in the case of those who doubt their abilities. This was precisely what was reported by one of our subjects during his self-assessment exercise:

"I consider myself a risk taker, however it is very important for me to be in control. Being in control for me means being aware of what is happening around me, to be at a speed that I can master and in general be in charge of the situation."

Thus our subject was implying that risk taking was acceptable, in so far as the some of the variables were under his control. Taking this a step further, it is logical to argue that individuals differ not only in the accident risk they are willing to accept but also in their ability to *perceive* accident risk and in their decision-making and executive skills in the face of risk. Individuals differ in both willingness (i.e. acceptance) and ability (skill). However as situation awareness varies amongst drivers, so does their subject evaluation of the posed risk. Burger et al. [3], have found that those with a high desire for control exhibited a greater illusion of control (perceived control over chance events). The primary functionality of ADAS, as is understood at present, is to facilitate the task performance of drivers by providing real-time advice, instruction and warnings. This type of systems is usually also described by the term "co-driver systems" or "driver support systems". Driver support systems may operate in advisory, semi-automatic or automatic mode [4], all of which may have different consequences for the driving task, and with that on traffic safety. Although the articulated object or goal of a driver support system is to have a positive effect on traffic safety, unintended effects have been shown on driver behaviour, indicative of negative effects on traffic safety [5]. Firstly, the provision of information potentially leads to a situation where the driver's attention is diverted from traffic. Secondly, taking over (part of) the driving task by a co-driver system may well produce behavioural adaptation. This behavioural adaptation, or compensation as it is called in a wider field, must be taken into account when investigating the conditions for introduction of ADAS [6]. When interviewed post simulation, one of our subjects outlined for us this very feature of compensation.

"When a system adds something that I don't have, for instance in the case of fog, or night-time if a systems takes control, due to my inability to see well in poor conditions, I can accept that."

The critical issue here is one of dependency on a technical artefact that could potentially lead to overlooking crucial variables and affecting the stakeholders in an adverse way. For instance there is now substantial evidence that the effect of risk compensation has been to shift part of the burden of risk from people in vehicles to vulnerable road users outside vehicles, leaving the total number killed in road accidents that could be attributed to seat belt legislation little changed [7].

4 Conclusion

Within this paper we've have seen how shifting perceptions on risk and control determine the efficacy and acceptance of ADAS systems. In terms of future directions for this research, we aim at continuing our analysis efforts both in terms of driver diversity in risk-taking, as well as in terms of user acceptance of ADAS. Parallel studies that were conducted using video tools and focusing on sensation-seekers and risk takers, will be integrated with the findings of this project at a wider level.

References

1. Van der Laan, J.D., Heino, A., De Waard, D.: A simple procedure for the acceptance of assistance of advanced transport telematics. Transportation Research C5(1), 1 (1997)
2. van der Heijden, R.E.C.M., Wiethoff, M. (eds.): Automation of Car driving. Exploring societal impacts and conditions. DUP, Delft (2000)
3. Burger, J.M.: Desire for control and the illusion of control: The effects of familiarity and sequence of outcomes. Journal of Research in Personality 20, 66–76 (1986); Burger, J. M.: The effects of desire for control in situations with chance-determined outcomes: Gambling behaviour in Lotto and bingo players. Journal of Research in Personality 25, 196–204 (1991)
4. Rosengren, L.G.: Driver assistance and co-operative driving. In: ERTICO (ed.) Towards an intelligent transport system. Proceedings of the First World Congress on Advanced Transport Telematics and Intelligent Vehicle Highway Systems, pp. 1613–1622. Artech House, London (1995)
5. Zwahlen, H.T., Adams, C.C., DeBald, D.P.: Safety aspects of CRT touch panel controls in automobiles. In: Gale, A.G., Freeman, M.H., Haslegrave, C.M., Smith, P., Taylor, S.H. (eds.) Vision in Vehicles - II, pp. 335–344. Elsevier, Amsterdam (1988)
6. Verwey, W.B., Brookhuis, K.A., Janssen, W.H.: Safety effects of in-vehicle information systems. Report TM-96-C002. TNO Human Factors Research Institute, Soesterberg, the Netherlands (1996)
7. Janssen, W.H.: The Effect of Seat Belt Legislation on Fatality Rates in a Number of West European Countries, Report Number 1ZF, 1989-13, TNO Institute for Perception, Soesterberg, Netherlands

Detection of Pilot Errors in Data by Combining Task Modeling and Model Checking

Florian Frische, Tomasz Mistrzyk, and Andreas Lüdtke

OFFIS e.V., Escherweg 2,Oldenburg, Germany
{Florian.Frische,Tomasz.Mistrzyk,Andreas.Luedtke}@offis.de

Abstract. In this paper we show a consistent approach of using Hierarchical Task Analysis together with model checking to identify pilot errors during the interaction with cockpit automation systems in aircraft. Task analysis is used to model flight procedures which describe how to operate a specific system in a particular situation. Afterwards model checking is used to identify deviations from these procedures in empirical simulator data. We envision applying this method to automatically detect pilot errors during flight tests or pilot training.

Keywords: Hierarchical Task Analysis, Model Checking, Error Analysis.

1 Hierarchical Tasks Analysis of Normative Pilot Activities

Our goal is to identify aircraft pilot errors (e.g. omission of actions) during the interaction with cockpit automation systems while performing specific flight tasks. This is done based on two inputs: (1) Information about how the flight task has to be performed normatively and (2) data on the actual performance (recorded in flight simulations) of the task. We define pilot errors as deviations from normative activities. To get the first input we perform a hierarchical task analysis to produce a hierarchical task model.

There are various approaches supporting analysis and modeling of tasks. Semi-formal task analysis and modeling approaches such as [5, 6] primarily concentrate on the hierarchical decomposition of tasks into subtasks and their temporal ordering. The models are semi-formal in the sense that they formally structure (hierarchy, temporal relations) informal elements (task descriptions in natural language). Formal task modeling approaches define a granular formal structure for the task descriptions, e.g. in form of Goals, Operators, Methods and Selection Rules (like in GOMS [4]). The result of a task analysis is a hierarchical task model. Task models are typically used in the early phases of system design [8] or user interface design [4] to get valuable information about task performance. They are also increasingly applied for the analysis of workplace situations, especially for human error analysis [1].

In our approach we implement a tool chain which combines semi-formal and formal task analysis and modeling. The tool chain begins with AMBOSS [5], a tool for the semi-formal level of task analysis and modeling. This modeling environment provides different abstraction levels in a hierarchical manner, represented graphically in a tree-like format. AMBOSS offers different features for task inspection like task

T. Gross et al. (Eds.): INTERACT 2009, Part I, LNCS 5726, pp. 528–531, 2009.

order specification, task duration and task criticality as well as the description of the task environment. Similar to other approaches [7] AMBOSS also provides simulation of semi-formal task models to support the experts in the analysis of the plausibility of such models. To go from semi-formal to formal task modeling AMBOSS supports the export of the task model as an XML output file which can be imported by PED.

PED (Procedure Editor) is a modeling environment for creating formal task models. With the formal task modeling the designer gets a highly precise description of the environment that the operator interacts with. To achieve such a fine granular level we developed a rule based language which is based on the well-known GOMS [4] language. Using PED we formalize procedures as a set of rules. Each rule contains a left- and a right-hand side. The left-hand side defines the conditional part. Every rule is assigned to exactly one goal and is applicable if the conditional part evaluates to true. Conditions contain system variables (e.g. current auto pilot mode) or environmental variables (e.g. current altitude of the aircraft). The right-hand side specifies the method, which is a sequence of different types of actions. Actions are functional entities distinguished in percept, motor, vocal, memory retrieval and memory store actions. This language allows us to organize a flight procedure in a tree-like structure of goals and sub-goals, methods and operators to achieve a certain goal on a fine granular level.

After we have analyzed and modeled the normative pilot activities we have to produce data on actual performance of pilots during a flight task. The normative activities and the data are then used to find deviations from normative activities and to derive actual pilot errors. These steps are described in the next section.

2 Identifying Actual Pilot Errors Based on Actual and Normative Pilot Activities

Data on actual task performance is recorded during experiments with pilots in flight simulations. The recorded data contain aircraft states (e.g. current speed), pilot actions (e.g. eye-movements) and environment states (e.g. weather conditions). The flight simulations and data recording will be performed by DLR (German Aerospace Center) with whom we cooperate in the European project HUMAN.

Based on the raw data we produce an activity trace. The activity trace consists of time stamped data rows. Each row in the activity trace represents a pilot action or the beginning / the ending of a task with the corresponding aircraft and environment states at a given time. Deviations from normative activities are detected by automatically comparing normative activities (rules) with actual activities (activity trace). These deviations are then classified in two types: (1) additional normative activities that have not been identified during the tasks analysis before - in this case the normative activities have to be extended - or (2) true errors. Experts have to decide whether deviations are the former or the latter.

Deviations of type (2) are classified with regard to error types (ETs), e.g. omission of actions or goals. The allocation of errors to an ET is done by interpreting an erroneous action in context of the task that a pilot is performing and environmental / aircraft conditions.

Model Checking is a powerful approach for automatic system verification. Meanwhile there are approaches which try to use model checking on user behaviour with the intention to enhance human-machine interfaces [2] and to analyze erroneous actions [3]. We are currently developing a method based on formal automata and model checking to perform the detection of pilot errors and ET classification automatically. This requires a transformation of the normative and actual activities into automata. In addition, we have chosen a set of ETs that have to be available in automata as well. These three types of automata are formally integrated into a comprehensive model in order to apply model checking techniques for the automatic detection of pilot errors. We use the model checking tool UPPAAL [9]. Fig. 1 depicts our approach.

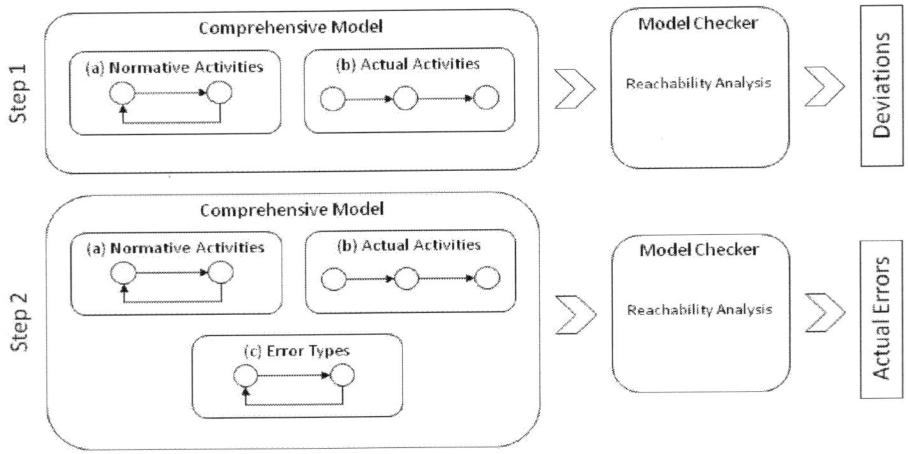

Fig. 1. Automatic detection of pilot errors by analyzing a comprehensive automata model of normative activities, actual activities and error types using a model checker

We perform the error detection in 2 steps: First, we only integrate the automata for the normative activities and a pilot activity trace (a and b in Fig. 1). We apply the model checker to test if the actual activity automaton can be successfully synchronized with the normative activity automata. This is done by a reachability analysis for the final state of the actual activity automaton. The synchronization between the automata is modeled by communication variables (channels in UPPAAL) for each pilot action. Every transition in the activity trace has a channel which sends a message to the normative automata. A transition is only possible if at least one normative activity automata can understand the message and perform a transition itself. In this way the reachability analysis will only be successful if the actions in the activity trace are normative.

The model checker denotes deviations from normative activities as deadlocks. In a second step we subsequently add the ET automata (c in Fig. 1) to the integrated model and run the query again (individually for each ET automaton). The ET automata include communication variables similar to those in the normative activity automata. A true pilot error has been identified if one of the ET automata solves the deadlock.

3 Conclusion

In this paper we presented a comprehensive approach to analyze and model normative flight procedures in a stepwise approach from semi-formal to formal. The resulting formal task model is used to automatically identify pilot errors in data that has been recorded in flight simulations. Preliminary tests with the model checking tool UPPAAL showed that the method produces results for some normative activities. But, we found that the current construction of the automata is not powerful enough to cover all aspects of normative flight procedures: information about tasks on a low level and some types of temporal relations between tasks could not be handled. We tackle these problems in the next steps by extending our task language as well as the automata structure. We envision applying our method for the automatic detection of pilot errors during flight tests in a simulator or during pilot training. In the first case the automatic identification of pilot errors can support highlighting weaknesses of the cockpit design to drive subsequent design improvements. In the second case the analysis of the trainees' performance and the design of individual training sessions can be supported.

The work described here is funded by the European Commission in the 7th Framework Programme within the project HUMAN (FP7-211988, www.human.aero).

References

1. Bastide, R., Basnyat, S.: Error patterns: Systematic investigation of deviations in task models. In: Coninx, K., Luyten, K., Schneider, K.A. (eds.) TAMODIA 2006. LNCS, vol. 4385, pp. 109–121. Springer, Heidelberg (2007)
2. Basuki, T.A., Cerone, A., Griesmayer, A., Schlatte, R.: Model-checking user behaviour using interacting components. Journal of Formal Aspects of Computing (FACS), Springer (2009)
3. Fields, R.E.: Analysis of erroneous actions in the design of critical systems, University of York (2001)
4. John, B.E., Kieras, D.E.: Using GOMS for user interface design and evaluation: which technique? ACM Trans. Comput.-Hum. Interact. 3, 287–319 (1996)
5. Giese, M., Mistrzyk, T., Pfau, A., Szwillus, G., von Detten, M.: AMBOSS: A Task Modeling Approach for Safety-Critical Systems. In: Forbrig, P., Paternò, F. (eds.) HCSE/TAMODIA 2008. LNCS, vol. 5247, pp. 98–109. Springer, Heidelberg (2008)
6. Lu, S., Paris, C., Vander Linden, K.: Tamot: Towards a Flexible Task Modeling Tool. In: The Proceedings of Human Factors, Melbourne, Australia, pp. 25–27 (2002)
7. Mori, G., Paternò, F., Santoro, C.: CTTE: support for developing and analyzing task models for interactive-system design. IEEE Transactions on Software Engineering, Bde. 28(8), 797–813 (2002)
8. Navarre, D., Palanque, P.A., Barboni, E., Mistrzyk, T.: On the benefit of synergistic model-based approach for safety critical interactive system testing. In: Winckler, M., Johnson, H., Palanque, P. (eds.) TAMODIA 2007. LNCS, vol. 4849, pp. 140–154. Springer, Heidelberg (2007)
9. UPPAAL. Project homepage, http://www.uppaal.com

Improving the Cost Structure of Sensemaking Tasks: Analysing User Concepts to Inform Information System Design

Simon Attfield and Ann Blandford

UCL Interaction Centre, MPEB 8th floor, University College London,
Gower Street, London WC1E 6BT, UK
{s.attfield,a.blandford}@cs.ucl.ac.uk

Abstract. In many everyday contexts people interact with information systems in order to make sense of a domain of interest. However, what this means and how it can best be supported are poorly understood. In particular, there has been little research on how to develop system representations that simplify naturally occurring sense making processes by matching people's conceptualizations of the domain. In this paper we draw on Klein et al.'s data-frame theory and Russell at al's notion of cost-structures in sensemaking to propose an approach to understanding sensemaking that supports reasoning about system requirements. The two key elements of the approach are the identification of the process and the transformational steps within that process that could benefit from support to reduce costs, and the identification of primary concepts which are cued by information in the context of a given sensemaking task and domain, and around which users integrate information to form a structured understanding. Our general principle is that by understanding a sensemaking transformation in terms of its source data and the integrating structures it creates, one is better able to anticipate the evolving information needs that it tends to invoke. We test this approach with a case study of fraud investigation performed by a team of lawyers and forensic accountants and consider how to support the elaboration of prototypical user-frames once they have been invoked.

Keywords: Sensemaking, conceptual design, fraud investigations.

1 Introduction

In many everyday professional and personal contexts, users interact with information systems in order to develop a 'picture' or 'model' of some domain [5, 19]. And yet ideas about what this means and how it can best be supported are still poorly formed. Consequently, guidance for the design of innteractive systems that support the development of user understanding is typically generalized, heuristic and based around exemplars. Whilst there is value in this, there is a need to understand the specifics of the cognitive processes people go through in different situations in order to reason about specific system design solutions.

The process of constructing understanding from information (in the widest sense) has been referred to as 'sensemaking'. People engage in sensemaking when they find

T. Gross et al. (Eds.): INTERACT 2009, Part I, LNCS 5726, pp. 532–545, 2009.

themselves in situations they want to understand. Sensemaking is a process of imposing structure on the unfamiliar in understanding it. There are many models of sensemaking, developed within different research traditions; examples include Dervin's Sensemaking Methodology as a means of eliciting users' information needs and their contexts [5], Pirolli and Card's model of sensemaking for intelligence analysis [14], Russell et al.'s learning loop complex [16] and Klein et al.'s data-frame theory [12].

In this paper we build on Klein et al.'s data-frame theory and Russell et al.'s ideas about cost structures in sensemaking to develop a theoretically informed approach to the analysis of sensemaking tasks in a way that yields specific system requirements. We focus on these two approaches because their semi-formalized descriptions of representational change provide useful accounts of the interplay between top-down and bottom-up cognitive processes which is central to sensemaking. However, they do not offer generalised leverage for information systems design; a question we consider here. We test our approach through a case study of a fraud investigation performed by a team of lawyers within a large law firm.

2 Background

'Sensemaking' is the process through which people make sense of their worlds. As a topic of research it spans a number of disciplines, including Human Computer Interaction, Organisational Studies, Naturalistic Decision Making, and Information Science. In Human Computer Interaction sensemaking research has tended to focus on sensemaking in electronic environments. This typically involves tasks that extend over time, and include searching and exploring large information collections or datasets, and integrating information into a coherent understanding. During such sensemaking tasks, people often create personalized, external, and often structured representations. These retain important information relevant to the task and can also be a resource for determining important elements and relationships. An interest in such representations has itself formed a significant focus in Human Computer Interaction research which identifies a concern with sensemaking (see, for example, [14, 15, 16]).

2.1 Data-Frame Symbiosis and the Learning Loop Complex

Klein et al.'s data-frame theory of sensemaking [12] evolved out of Klein's work on naturalistic decision making in relation assessment in command and control [11]. Klein et al. [12] focussed on sensemakers' internal, cognitive representations. Following Weick [23], they view sensemaking as a ubiquitous cognitive function.

According to the data-frame model, people react to information within their environments by accommodating it within 'frames'. A frame is seen as an integrating structure with slots for data. In this respect they draw a link with previous notions of frames [9], scripts [17] and schemata [2].

In outline, the data-frame model argues that when faced with a situation sensemaking involves abductively inferring a frame based on a few key cues or 'anchors' within that situation. The frame then 'connects the dots' and offers a plausible interpretation of what the situation is—an interpretation that can support explanation, prediction and decision response.

Importantly, frames are seen as extending beyond the cues. Consequently, they determine expectations about the world, including the possibility of specific kinds of information that could be found to elaborate the frame. In common with Starbuck and Milliken [20], Klein et al. argue that as an interpretation of a situation a frame can act as an information filter and determine what is subsequently noticed. Where information is noticed that conflicts with a current frame, however, the plausibility of the frame (or indeed the data) can be challenged and a new frame required. Hence, sensemaking is seen as a process of framing and re-framing.

Klein et al. argue that people have repertoires of frames derived from experience that they can apply to new situations and that this, for example, underlies the distinction between experts and novices. Experts, it is argued, reason in the same way as novices. The difference lies in the fact that experts have richer repertoires of frames that are better differentiated. These allow them to make sense of a greater variety of situations and to be more precise about expectations.

The data-frame model identifies seven kinds of frame-based operations applied in the sensemaking process. These are:

- *Connecting data and frame*: Identifying the situation with a frame.
- *Elaborating a frame*: The frame is elaborated with detail. New data does not challenge it.
- *Questioning the frame*: Expectations created by a frame are violated by unexpected data. The frame or the data can be questioned.
- *Preserving the frame*: Inconsistent data are explained away or simply ignored and the frame is maintained (significant for explaining confirmation bias).
- *Comparing multiple frames*: Multiple frames are explored. These may be similar but mutually inconsistent (for example, alternative medical diagnoses).
- *Reframing*: A replacement frame is adopted when it is suggested by data (a frame also defines what counts as data).
- *Seeking a frame*: Trying to find (recall) or construct an appropriate frame.

For Russell et al. [16], information representations also form a central component in sensemaking, although Russell et al. are concerned with the creation of external, user-generated representations. They observed a group of course designers who defined schemas within a hypertext system for capturing information relevant to the content of a new course. The instantiated schemas then provided a resource for automated clustering in order to identify core concepts within the material.

Russell et al. used findings from this study to motivate a model of sensemaking called the 'learning loop complex'. According to this model, a sensemaker generates representations (schemas) to capture salient information (generation loop), uses these to guide the identification of information of interest, and then encodes found information within the representations (data coverage loop). During data coverage, however, salient information can be discovered which does not fit the representational scheme (residue), and the representation can be changed to accommodate (representational shift loop), followed by further data coverage, etc.

In another example, they described a case study of someone making sense of the laptop market to decide which to buy. The sensemaker created a table to hold salient data (specifications etc.) and then explored available literature on different models to populate the table. During exploration, however, they made changes to the table according to new decisions about which properties were most relevant to their decision and the extent to which the relevant information was retrievable.

Despite the fact that Russell et al.'s model is concerned with external representations and Klein at al's model is concerned with internal representations, their accounts are strikingly similar. In both, representations reflect an understanding generated about some domain, and lead to an interplay between bottom-up and top-down processing. Accordingly, the representations evolve through encounters with information triggering and shaping the structures and these, in turn, guide subsequent encounters with information—affecting what is sought and what is noticed.

2.2 Cost Structures in Sensemaking

Russell et al. argued that sensemaking tasks can be decomposed into their constituent activities and that optimising sensemaking involves selecting methods to maximise the expected cost-to-gain ratio of individual steps. Given any particular method, there is a fixed cost-to-gain function according to which a given cost (or effort) provides a given gain. Adaptations that sensemakers make to their method change the characteristics of the cost-to-gain function (hopefully in their favour).

For example, they observed in their case-study of course designers that the main user-cost was incurred by the manual extraction of data (finding relevant documents, selecting the right information, transforming this into canonical form suitable for the external representation). The payoff for this investment of effort, however, came from the fact that extracting the data and encoding it into hypertext schemas allowed the course designers to use a computer to perform automated clustering; a powerful technique whereby they were able to reveal recurring concepts within the content. The payoff for adjustments (representational shifts) to the schemas that occurred during extraction was an improvement in the reliability of human encoding and the ultimate utility of the automated analysis.

They analysed the cost of sensemaking as the sum of the costs of generating representational schemas, finding relevant information and instantiating the schemas. They argued that technology that improves the cost-to-gain ratio of one step can free up time to invest in others.

3 An Approach to Identifying Costs and Representations

Understanding the internal processes of sensemaking in a given situation can highlight requirements for tools to support that process. Within our approach, there are two main steps:

1. *Identify opportunities for achieving the greatest benefit*. This involves analysing the sensemaking process and identifying the most expensive elements (in terms of time and effort). Identifying opportunities for achieving the greatest benefit involves developing a sensemaking process model for the activity to be supported and, within that, identifying opportunities for making local improvements that will have the greatest impact on the process as a whole. Russell et al. [16] and Attfield et al. [1] show that sensemaking tasks often involve users in sequences of external representational transformations. An approach to identifying opportunities for local improvement is to capture these in a 'process-resource' model [1]; this model includes explicit

representation of the key information transformations that users perform during sensemaking and the main information resources that each transformation uses and produces. Once a model has been developed, the next step is to identify the activities with greatest potential for cost saving.

2. *Understand the frames of significance to the sensemaker and optimise the conceptual fit between user and system* [3]. This begins with the ontology or 'frame of reference' with which a user understands and interprets a domain, and so will permeate the sensemaking process as that process moves from large amounts of unstructured information towards more concise and parsimonious representations. The significance of this is that the ontology with which the user understands and interprets a domain is not necessarily represented in the information system they use. Consequently, the burden is on the user to translate from one ontology to the other. Blandford et al. [1] recognize the importance of identifying the concepts that users are working with to design systems that support manipulation of and reasoning about those concepts, and in the more general problem-solving literature the roles of external representations are well recognised (e.g. [4]).

Klein et al.'s data frame symbiosis theory provides a useful framework here. In Klein et al.'s theory, a frame is a mental representation which corresponds to a domain concept. The concept might be anything that is salient to the user in terms of forming their understanding of the domain e.g. a product, a terrorist incident, a performance, a device, a company etc. Once instantiated through interaction with a situation—meaning that some cue identifies the frame as a plausible interpretation of some situation—a frame can become a 'centre of gravity' or focus around which relevant information can be related.

Frames themselves are determined by a priori knowledge, which itself arises from experience. Hence they not only integrate *known* information but suggest *unknown* elements too. For example, you may come to know that a terrorist incident took place in a particular location, but you may not know the time and the date or the number of casualties—facts which it may be useful to discover.

Frames evolve continuously as new situations are encountered, reasoned over and learned about. And the particular information elements or constituents that are considered relevant for a given purpose will vary depending on the sensemaker's broader interests and what information they see as usefully informing them. The existence of frame constituents, the fact that at any point in a sensemaking task these may be relatively well defined and yet unknown (i.e. known unknowns), and their possible importance for furthering the sensemaker's interests, means that frames offer a basis for explaining the content and evolution of information needs—an issue very significant to the design of information systems. Hence, analyzing typical frames within a given sensemaking context and how they are cued and evolve, provides a basis for reasoning about design.

In summary, our approach involves:

1. *Identify opportunities for achieving the greatest benefit.*
    a. Develop a 'process resource' model of the sensemaking process.
    b. Identify transformations that represent major overheads.

2. *Understand the frames of significance to the sensemaker and optimise the conceptual fit between user and system.*
   a. Understand transformations in terms of the users' frames.
   b. Design to reduce the costs involved in developing key frames.

4 A Case Study – Investigating Corporate Fraud

The case study was of a large fraud investigation undertaken by a corporate law firm in London. Ten in-depth interviews were conducted with nine lawyers who had worked on the case. For reasons of client confidentiality, it was not possible to gather real-time observational data, but key sense-making artefacts emerging from the case were made available for study. The interviews aimed at understanding global and local processes of the investigation, with a particular focus on the relationship between sensemaking and the use of external representations and automation.

Participants were recruited through a combination of snowball [10] and theoretical sampling [8]. Theoretical sampling was used to focus in on emerging issues. Following the practices of Grounded Theory [8], data gathering and analysis were interleaved. Data from the first five interviews were analysed to develop a preliminary model of the sensemaking processes of the legal team, covering both individual sensemaking and team co-ordination. This model was tested and refined with participants through subsequent interviews and analysis, and is the model presented in this paper (figure 1, below).

Interviews were conducted in an open and informal way. Each lasted from 45 minutes to 1hr 40 minutes. Early interviews focused on how the individual investigator had identified and worked with documents of interest, what tools they had used, what external representations they had generated and how they had used them, and how they coordinated their individual activities with those of the team. Many interviews were conducted using supporting artefacts. These included representations that had been generated by the investigators such as evidence tables from the investigators' final report, and software that had been used, loaded with the investigation data. These artefacts provided a reference point for discussing and reconstructing specific aspects of the investigations.

Interviews were transcribed and analysed through open coding [21] and the generation of process models used to describe the activities. Models decomposing the process were developed on an ongoing basis. Later interviews included discussion of these models. In this way, the models were verified and elaborated by participants on an ongoing basis and through constant comparison against the data [21].

4.1 Step 1a: Develop a 'Process Resource' Model of the Sensemaking Process

The investigation occupied a team of around 30 lawyers and forensic accountants for three months. Broadly, the objectives were to discover whether a particular kind of fraud had taken place in a company and, if so, who had been complicit. Figure 1 shows the investigation process in overview as a 'process-resource' model, as described above. In Figure 1, rectangular boxes represent processes. Arrows between them represent flow of information. This flow occurred through resources (marked against each arrow) created or modified by one process and used by another. In this way each process acted as a transformation.

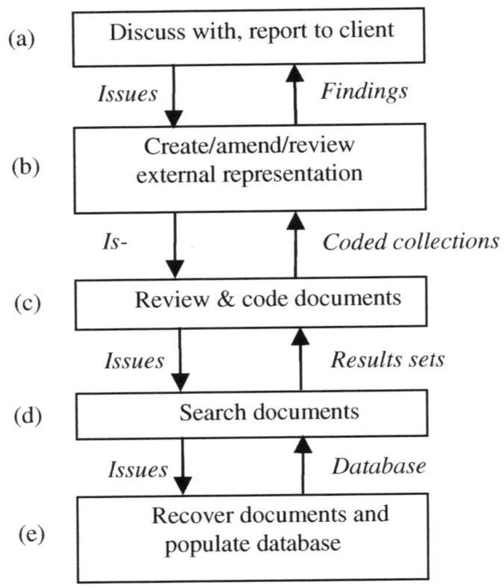

Fig. 1. An overview of the investigation process

The model begins and ends at the top with client discussion (a) where objectives are agreed and findings reported (client discussion was also returned to throughout). Following some early evidence review the objectives were explicitly characterised as set of relatively discrete investigation 'issues'. These were thematic lines or enquiry each of which had or developed associated theories, questions and facts.

In the model, issues propagate down as a resource influencing all other processes and can also be refined by any process in the light of discoveries. Processes can also be skipped depending on what resources are available and what are required at any one time. At the beginning of the investigation the issues informed the recovery of evidential documents (e). Documents (mostly electronic) were recovered from computers used by the company under investigation. Information was gathered from around 500 locations (including email servers) and the collection was ultimately equivalent in size to about 8.5 million novels. Evidence was also gathered through witness interviews (although here we focus on documents). Once recovered, documents were added to a database.

The database provided a resource for submitting searches (d), again guided by the investigation issues. Returned documents were then individually read and coded for relevance to the issues (within a document management system) (c). Relevant documents were then used as a resource for constructing integrated representations (b) which structured extracted facts relevant to the investigation and allowed connections to be seen between them. A number of representations were used, but most attention was given to chronologies which recorded meetings and other significant events. Chronologies were created for each issue by different groups within the investigation team and these were combined into a single master chronology for review by senior team members.

Significantly, the investigation process was not linear. By interacting with documents and external representations the investigators gradually made more sense of the company's activities and, in addition to discussions with the client, this led them to refine the issues with new theories and questions. For example, the chronologies provided a narrative which supported the identification of unexplained or suspicious events and showed overall timescales from which periods of particular interest could be identified. As the issues evolved into more specific sub-issues so these propagated down to motivate new searches or the recovery of new documents.

4.2 Step 1b: Identify Transformations that Represent Major Overheads

As discussed above, optimising sensemaking involves maximizing the cost-to-gain ratio of component tasks. That is, increasing the amount of gain obtained for a given level of expended effort. As with any task, when people perform sensemaking they design their activities in such a way as to achieve an optimal trade-off between cost and gain given the tools at their disposal [Russell et al., 1993]. Changing the tools, however, can enable more effective trade-offs (e.g. as a mode of transport, cycling has an improved cost-to-gain ratio compared to walking).

In considering where to focus attention to make improvements, we could consider any part of the process in figure 1. However, the investigators consistently cited document review (c) as imposing the major overhead in terms of time and effort. They submitted a total of 200 searches, each of which returned hundreds or even thousands of documents. The results were presented as date-ordered document lists from which documents were selected in turn and their full-text reviewed. Over the course of the investigation 130,000 documents were reviewed in all. This represents a significant reduction on the document universe, but is nevertheless a very significant number of documents to have reviewed.

4.3 Step 2a: Understand Transformations in Terms of Users' Frames

An answer to this lies in understanding the representational forms that the investigators were aiming to construct. Our general principle is that by understanding a sensemaking transformation in terms of its source data and the integrating structures it creates, one is better able to enable this transformation and anticipate the evolving information needs that it tends to invoke.

The chronologies were created using Microsoft Excel spreadsheets with entries corresponding to a pre-defined event schema. Russell et al. [16] refer to such instantiated schemas as *encodons*. The schema included the date and time of the event, a text account of it's important elements, a field for recording the people involved and the event's location, and a field for recording references to the supporting document(s). Where a document, such as an email, referred to a significant event, an entry would be raised. Events could, for example, represent a meeting between protagonists; the signing of a contract; or a protagonist travelling. A single document could potentially give rise to a number of records and a given record could be based on multiple documents.

Many of the chronologies the investigators created corresponded to events specific to particular business activities, such as those surrounding particular contracts. Even when the individual chronologies were combined in the master chronology this separation was maintained using metadata attached to each event.

In the following we elaborate two types of frame emerging from the study data (event frames and business activity frames) and the way in which processes of sensemaking were organized around them. What we see is frames at different levels of granularity invoked through discovery after which they act as foci for elaboration and validation.

Event frames

An event frame connects information (date, time, description, people) relating to a particular event. In developing the chronologies, the investigators reviewed documents (email messages in most cases) and drew inferences about events (connecting data to frame). An email might propose a meeting or it might discuss a meeting that had occurred in the past. It might provide details such as the time and location and who the participants were, and it might provide some evidence for what was discussed and the outcomes of the meeting.

A single email, however, would typically only provide partial and potentially inconclusive information about an event. Where a meeting was planned and discussed it may not have taken place or it may have been replaced by a telephone call. Hence, beliefs about events could be more or less speculative, at least initially. Inferring what had actually happened, as supported by the totality of the available evidence, required further investigation. As one participant reported:

P4: [...] So you put an entry down for November 20th and then you'd start looking for documents which relate, which might give evidence that that happened, that it actually happened [...] and if it did happen who else was involved, who were they meeting, what were they doing, what were they saying to each other?

Given the discovery of an email about an apparently significant event, an investigator would then want to elaborate and validate it (in Klein et al.'s terms). Each reviewer was presented with a display of document titles from which full-text could be selected. A problem was that this display provided no cues as to the comparative value of a given document at any given time over-and-above their responsiveness to a particular search. This did not account for evolution in the user's thought processes as described above.

Given the design of the system they used, this would present them with a choice. One option would be to temporarily pause the exhaustive review, and attempt to find further messages containing references to the event (using new searches, for example). Alternatively, they could record the event as a plausible conjecture in a chronology (e.g. 'possible meeting'...) and continue their review in the hope of finding further relevant information later, or that someone else would find it. Often the reviewers used this exhaustive strategy requiring them to maintain multiple, overlapping cognitive sub-threads of interest.

In terms of the data-frame model, this example (which was repeated many times throughout the investigation) this demonstrates a sensemaking process which begins with a message acting as an 'anchor' for an event frame. The occurrence of an event is a plausible interpretation or is at least suggested by the anchor. However, given knowledge that the investigator brings to the situation (about meetings and emails etc.), they also know that there may be more important information to discover and that this may show that the meeting did not occur at all.

The occurrence of the frame, then, motivates its own elaboration and validation (and potential questioning) as a plausible interpretation of the available data. Salient information may include location, a list of participants, motives, discussion topic, and outcomes. Information contained in the initial message may populate some of these and provide some level of guarantee about them. But the frame necessarily triggers further information requirements specific to the event. It extends beyond the given information, and so creates expectations which need to be tested and elaborated.

Once the frame is cued, the need for elaboration and validation gives rise to new information requirements and this gives new shape to the relative values of different documents. For the investigator in that situation, documents that also discuss the event become of greater value.

Business Activity Frames

A second kind of frame that emerged as being important in this study was a business activity frame, which connects information about a given business activity. This links work around a particular contract or negotiation and is made up of a sequence of separate but causally related event frames. In part, their structure depended upon the investigators' a priori knowledge of business processes augmented by specific modi operandi of the company as revealed during the investigation.

The determination that the investigators sought concerned potential malpractice in the business activities of a company. Naturally, the company had many business activities and part of the investigators' task early on was to identify activities of particular concern. The identification of an activity of concern was followed by the elaboration of events associated with it.

The investigators were aware that evidence for malpractice might ultimately arise in very few documents. Lawyers involved in regulatory investigation and litigations typically sift through thousands or even millions of documents in order find what may be just a few documents of significance to the questions of the case.

However, it was necessary for the investigators to develop a broader understanding first. The interpretation of an event, such as an email communication or a meeting, depended upon how it located within a wider context of activity. Hence, that context must be elaborated. People may meet, exchange information or even money, but what these mean in legal terms can only be determined in the light of a broader set of events. In this sense the events were indexical [22] with interpretation dependent on context. Having said that, the reverse is also true: understanding the context depends on understanding a series of individual events. And so the investigators were tied into a hermeneutic loop. Interpretation of the parts depended upon interpretation of the whole and vice versa [18].

In addition to supporting interpretation, elaborating the business activity contexts also enabled the investigators to identify and focus on key periods of concern. By a process that acts in reverse to the interpretation of the meaning of an event, by elaborating broader business activity sequences, the investigators were able to identify periods when fraud could technically have occurred. These could then form areas for more intense investigation. Given the size of the information universe, focusing attention on these periods was particularly important:

P5: we'd be thinking, well if we're right on this, this is a really important build up [...]. Or, we think money must have been sucked out of this business around this time. [...] And this is what we did, [Junior Partner] selected certain periods and posed certain questions in relation to those periods. And we would go back and interrogate the information further.

P6: So some time-periods where it was absolutely critical to know... because you're following this through forensically trying to figure out what's going on... it's absolutely critical to know minute-by-minute the exact chain of events.

A business activity is a frame that is triggered by information indicating an identifiable business activity which may be considered suspicious or 'vulnerable'. The frame then acts as a focus and generates expectations about what further information might be found. Like the event frame, the business activity frame extends beyond its anchor to create expectations about information to discover.

In terms of the goal of elaborating a business activity frame, some documents had higher value than others:

P4: You know a document may actually lead to five different entries on the chronology because for example it may be someone's email saying 'right I'm organising [contract]. These are key milestone dates [...] and on this day I'm planning on being in [overseas city].

Some documents made reference to events and some did not; those that did had higher value for elaborating the frame. Documents that discussed a series of dates were particularly useful. The system that the investigators used, however, did not provide any method for finding these documents beyond exhaustive reviewing.

4.4 Step 2b: Design to Reduce the Costs Involved in Developing Key Frames

We have used a frame-based approach to sensemaking as a method for elucidating the evolution of information needs of the investigators in our case study. In this section we consider how this translates into design requirements, focusing on finding relevant documents within a results list.

A results list offers the user a list of information objects from which to select items for inspection. By default, users in our case study were presented with linear, unstructured lists within which all documents were presented as equal. However, the need to elaborate or validate a frame changes the relative values of documents as the user progresses. Some documents become more important to find and others less so. Specifically, once an event frame is cued the user wants to find other documents about that event (as a nested sub-task), after which they will likely continue the search for other events. Consequently, continuity would be best served by two complementary organisation schemes at the interface; the first links documents in some default way (e.g. chronological), whilst the other links documents in virtue of reference to common events. Ideally, users would be able to move easily between the two schemes as they interweave the discovery of events with their detailed exploration.

Given that a business activity frame incorporates multiple events, reducing the cost of elaborating and validating single event frames will also reduce the cost of elaborating the business activity frame to which they belong. However, we saw from the case study that some documents had higher value than others for elaborating such frames.

In particular, documents containing references to many events (such as project milestones) could cue many related event frames. These helped in establishing broad frames of reference which allowed the investigators to focus in on specific periods in detail. Consequently, by drawing attention to the number of event references in a single document at the interface users would be better able to prioritise exploring those with potentially higher value for elaborating such a frame.

In terms of developing document results presentations, these needs could be addressed by providing structured results presentations or visualisations which indicate documents' chronological ordering, link documents according to common event references, and indicate the number of event references within each document. We anticipate that text processing techniques necessary to create such representations do not significantly extend beyond current capabilities; indeed progress has been made in the identification and normalization of temporal references in free texts [7]. Our aim, however, is to illustrate how understanding the frames that users work with in particular sensemaking tasks, and in particular how these are cued, elaborated and validated as information is encountered, can provide a basis for requirements for the design of more useful information systems.

5 Discussion

The approach we have proposed and illustrated for improving the efficiency of large-scale sensemaking tasks involves the identification of activities of high demand, and exploring these in terms of the sensemaker's typical cognitive frames involved in making resource transformations. By providing an analysis of related information needs and the way these develop, it provides a useful foundation for reasoning about the design of effective solutions using available technologies. By eliciting typical sensemaking activities and concepts, it is possible to identify design requirements that support them.

In relation to users' interactions with information systems, such an account has been lacking within both the Human Computer Interaction and Information Science literatures. In Information Science, in particular, it has long been recognised that users' information needs are broad and under-specified early on in a research task but become more specific and better defined later on [13]. One way of understanding the role of a frame, or (more generally) users' conceptual understanding of the domain of which sense is being made, is as a mechanism through which broad, under-specified information needs evolve to become needs that are more focussed. Consequently, a concept-based approach to understanding the evolution of users' domain models provides a basis for explaining this characteristic phenomenon.

We have also shown that frames can embed within each other. The business activity frames we described are constructed from multiple individual event frames. This extends beyond Klein et al.'s original model by revealing the stratification of sensemaking and the way in which addressing one frame can be a part of addressing another.

The applicability of the approach presented here depends upon the predictability of particular user concepts during sensemaking. Contexts of more variegated sensemaking may offer fewer opportunities. However, there is evidence that other domains offer the requisite predictability. For example, Russell et al.'s [16] case studies on course designers and laptop purchasing lend themselves to a concept-based analysis in terms of printer components and the attributes of laptop models respectively, and research on users' experiences with using information visualisations of research literatures shows that they tend to conceptualise this domain specifically in terms of papers, key ideas and people [6]. The extent to which sensemaking can be supported by explicitly representing such concepts in a way that facilitates user reasoning and information transformation remains a topic for future research.

To conclude, in order to design for sensemaking we need to understand it. Little attention has been given to the way people think about the domains they are trying to make sense of, or of how to provide targeted support for that sensemaking. In this paper, we have presented an approach to identifying the most costly elements of the sensemaking process. This involves generating a process description and reflecting on the challenges presented to the user by each step of that process and the possibilities of providing support for key steps. It also involves identifying the core concepts with which users are working and how they are structured. We have tested the approach with a case study of legal discovery processes: this paper therefore provides a domain-specific account of sensemaking in e-discovery as well as proposing some general principles about strategies for supporting sensemaking of large bodies of information.

Acknowledgments

We would like to thank Freshfields Bruckhaus Deringer for their kind help with this study. The work was funded under EPSRC grant EP/D056268.

References

1. Attfield, S., Fegan, S., Blandford, A.E.: Idea Generation and Material Consolidation: Tool Use and Intermediate Artefacts in Journalistic Writing. Int. J. of Cog. Tech. and Work (Online First Feburary 2008)
2. Bartlett, F.C.: Remembering: A Study in Experimental and Social Psychology. Camb. Univ. Press, England (1932)
3. Blandford, A., Green, T.R.G., Furniss, D., Makri, S.: Evaluating System Utility and Conceptual Fit Using CASSM. Int. J. of Hum.–Comp. St. 66, 393–409 (2008)
4. Cockayne, A., Wright, P.C., Fields, B.: Supporting Interaction Strategies Through the Externalization of Strategy Concepts. In: Sasse, M.A., Johnson, C. (eds.) Proceedings INTERACT 1999, pp. 582–588. IOP Press (1999)
5. Dervin, B.: An Overview of Sense-making Research: Concepts, Methods and Results. Paper presented at the Annual Meeting of the Int. Communication Assoc. Dallas, TX (May 1983)
6. Faisal, S., Cairns, P., Blandford, A.E.: Developing User Requirements for Visualizations of Literature Knowledge Domains. In: Proc. of the 10th Int. Conf. on Information Visualisation, London, UK, July 5-7 (2006)
7. Gaizauskas, R., Wilks, Y.: Information Extraction: Beyond Document Retrieval. J. Doc. 54(1), 70–105 (1998)

8. Glaser, B., Strauss, A.: The Discovery of Grounded Theory: Strategies for Qualitative Research. Aldine, Chicago (1967)
9. Goffman, E.: Frame Analysis: An Essay on the Organizational Experience. Harper, NY (1974)
10. Johnson, J.C.: Selecting Ethnographic Informants. Sage, Newbury Park (1990)
11. Klein, G.: Sources of Power: How People Make Decisions. MIT Press, Cambridge (1998)
12. Klein, G., Phillips, J.K., Rall, E.L., Peluso, D.A.: A Data-frame Theory of Sensemaking. In: Expertise Out of Context: Proc. of the Sixth International Conf. on Naturalistic Decision Making, Pensacola Beach, Florida, May 15-17, 2003, pp. 113–155. Lawrence Erlbaum Assoc. Inc., US (2007)
13. Kuhlthau, C.C.: A Principle of Uncertainty for Information Seeking. J. Doc. 49(4), 39–55 (1993)
14. Pirolli, P., Card, S.: The Sensemaking Process and Leverage Points for Analyst Technology as Identified Through Cognitive Task Analysis. In: Proc. Int. Conf. on Intelligence Analysis, McLean, VA, May 2-3 (2005), `https://analysis.mitre.org/proceedings/` (Accessed Feburary 11, 2008)
15. Qu, Y., Furnas, G.W.: Sources of Structure in Sensemaking. In: Proc. of the CHI 2005 Conf. on Hum. Factors in Comp. Sys (Extended Abstracts), Portland, OR, USA, pp. 1989–1992. ACM Press, New York (2005)
16. Russell, D.M., Stefik, M.J., Pirolli, P., Card, S.K.: The Cost Structure of Sensemaking. In: Proc. of the INTERACT 1993 and CHI 1993 Conf. on Hum. Factors in Comp. Sys., Amsterdam, The Netherlands, pp. 269–276. ACM Press, New York (1993)
17. Schank, R.C., Abelson, R.P.: Scripts, Plans Goals and Understanding: An Inquiry into Human Knowledge Structures. Lawrence Erlbaum Assoc., Mahwah (1977)
18. Schmidt, L.K.: Understanding Hermeneutics. Acumen, Stocksfield, UK (2006)
19. Spence, R.: A Framework for Navigation. Int. J. of Hum.-Comp. St. 51, 919–945 (1999)
20. Starbuck, W.H., Milliken, F.J.: Executives' Perceptual Filters: What They Notice and How they Make Sense. In: Hambrick (ed.) The Executive Effect: Concepts and Methods for Studying Top Managers, pp. 35–65. JAI Press, Greenwich (1988)
21. Strauss, A., Corbin, J.: Basics of Qualitative Research: Techniques and Procedures for Developing Grounded Theory, 2nd edn. Sage, London (1998)
22. Suchman, L.: Plans and Situated Actions: The problem of Human Machine Communication. Camb. Univ. Press, Cambridge (1987)
23. Weick, K.: Sensemaking in Organisations. Sage, London (1995)

Vote and Be Heard: Adding Back-Channel Signals to Social Mirrors

Tony Bergstrom and Karrie Karahalios

Department of Computer Science
University of Illinois at Urbana-Champaign
{abergst2,kkarahal}@cs.uiuc.edu

Abstract. In face-to-face group situations, social pressure and organizational hierarchy relegate the less outspoken to silence, often resulting in fewer voices, fewer ideas, and groupthink. However, in mediated interaction like email, more people join in the discussion to offer their opinion. With this work, we aim to combine the benefits of mediated communication with the benefits and affordances of face-to-face interaction by adding a mediated back-channel. We describe *Conversation Votes*, a tabletop system that augments verbal conversation with a shared anonymous back-channel to highlight agreement. We then discuss a study of our design with groups engaged in repeated discussion. Our results show that anonymous visual back-channels provide a medium for the underrepresented voices of a conversation and balances interaction among all participants.

Keywords: Anonymous, back-channel, collocated, debate, feedback, voting.

1 Introduction

This work introduces an anonymous visual back-channel as a cue to shape the understanding of conversation in groups. A cue is a non-verbal communication such as a gesture, a facial expression, body posture, movement, or tone of voice [1][2][3][4][5]. Visual cues can enhance words or make their own statement: the meaning of "I love to work" can be redefined by rolling one's eyes [4]. Similar cues allow us to successfully negotiate social interactions, save face [3], and to coordinate actions quickly and efficiently [6]. In some cases, such as communicating feelings, non-verbal and visual communications are significantly more reliable indicators than the spoken word alone [5].

Considerable work has investigated the creation and conveyance of new conversational cues in remote spaces [7][8][9][10]. However, less work investigates their use in collocated spaces. One goal for this work is to enable new back-channel cues that communicate as effectively as traditional back-channel cues [11] but at a lowered social cost via anonymity. When speaking or gesturing, an individual draws attention to himself and affects his social persona, for better or worse [2]. The weight of being judged and the stigma associated with a mistake regulates speakers to silence. As US President Abraham Lincoln said, "It is better to remain silent and be thought a fool than to speak out and remove all doubt." While a person's image could benefit by adhering to this advice, the net result encourages silence and reliance on the rest of the group [12].

T. Gross et al. (Eds.): INTERACT 2009, Part I, LNCS 5726, pp. 546–559, 2009.

(a) Table in use

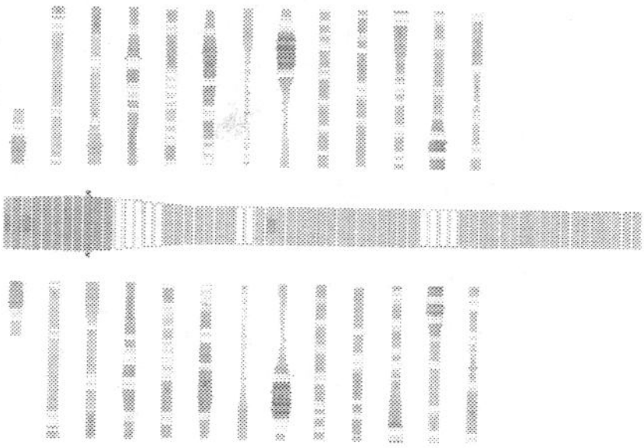

(b) Visualization

Fig. 1. Above we see a picture of the *Conversation Votes* table during a conversation. The most current interaction is highlighted by the larger horizontal central history. To provide a longer historical context, past minutes are mirrored in the historical stacks (more in Figures 2a, 2b).

The pressure to conform is less prevalent in anonymous and asynchronous interactions than in face-to-face or group interaction [13]. Employees in an organization withhold disagreements from employers in face-to-face meetings that they will divulge via email [10][14]. We designed *Conversation Votes* to allow similar, impersonal, feedback in a collocated environment (Figure 1a).

In the following sections, we will discuss previous work in face-to-face interaction, group awareness, and aural augmentation. We next describe the *Conversation Votes* visualization, focusing on design aspects for audio depiction and anonymous feedback in a face-to-face setting. This is followed by a study of the *Conversation Votes* that addresses questions of how participants utilize the visualization to understand their co-located peers. We conclude by discussing our results that show the underrepresented viewpoints become salient with a new anonymous 'visual voice.'

2 Related Work

Work related to *Conversation Votes* covers a wide range of areas. We briefly touch on three broad areas that are most relevant: Face to face interaction, group awareness, and aural augmentation.

2.1 Face to Face

With any social situation, appearance is important. A person changes behavior to fit the audience and make a good impression [2, 3]. In the workplace, coworkers might be casual with each other, but only when it does not reflect negatively on the individual employees. If a distinguished guest is introduced, social protocol becomes more formal and distant.

A person will adapt their persona to be seen as amiable and intelligent in the eyes of the guest [15][16]. Professional vocabulary and mannerisms replace the normal signals; individuals say 'sir' or are overly attentive as a sign of respect [17]. However, communication is many faceted and not limited to spoken words. When listening to the guest, back-channels show interest and attention. These could be short phrases like 'yeah' or 'really?' but could also be a non-verbal smile or a head nod acting as a signal.

Evolutionary biology derived signaling theory to acknowledge both intended and unintended signals. When speaking to the guest, the intention may be to come across as interested and engaged, but unintended actions can betray a facade [18]. For example, checking the time might demonstrate the desire to leave or tone of voice reveal displeasure in current company. It's left for the signal's receiver to judge the reliability of a signal. Though many of these signals are given without thought, they serve as efficient cues in groups.

Groups use signals to coordinate cooperative action. Organized groups, such as a baseball team or military unit, might actively establish gestures and most familiar groups naturally learn to recognize cues to anticipate the needs of others. Coordinating groups that require complicated orchestration often necessitates complex but intuitive non-verbal communication [6].

Conversation Votes, leverages the idea of visual cues in the interface. Cues remain interpretable and subtle, as is body language, while giving participants explicit opportunity to signal. With *Conversation Votes* we are not trying to eliminate or replace the face-to-face element, but to provide that extra back-channel in face-to-face interaction.

2.2 Group Awareness

Shared group displays can alter small group conversations. Simply, labeling individuals as over-participating, participating, and under-participating, participants seek a conversation balanced in contribution [19]. In follow-up work, a suite of conversation visualizations allowed participants to gain insight into their interaction after the session concluded [20]. Post meeting displays, designed to include the conversation history, were found to be more informative for the group as they included a detailed depiction of the verbal exchange.

Collocated and remote groups benefit from cues through heightened group awareness. In collocated programming environments, shared displays highlight changes and conflict in a development group [21]. This visual feedback allows the collocated groups to be more agile in their process: developers saw when they were both editing codependent files and could coordinate their changes more appropriately. In a remote setting, interfaces re-establish status cues that enable effortless coordination when face-to-face. Status cues have been used to indicate a remote presence, the desire to speak in a teleconference, or to indicate confusion in a meeting [22][23].

When introducing anonymity into group awareness, the issue of trusting the signal becomes more important. With fewer repercussions for creating animosity, an anonymous signal has been used to create discord for no reason other than to incite an argument [24]. In *Conversation Votes* we rely on collocation and mutual accountability to keep the anonymous signals meaningful. People are more trusting and cooperative with known individuals [25][26], and the cues gathered from the visualization are evaluated with knowledge of the all other personal cues in the space.

We explore group awareness in a collocated setting with a mixture of explicit feedback and anonymous cues. *Conversation Votes* simultaneously presents the aural interaction history annotated with perception cues.

2.3 Aural Augmentation

Sound and speech are experienced serially, one word after another, hindering the ability to review recorded sound more quickly. Searching through archived recordings to find a specific segment of desired information can require listening to the full recording. In research, some provide tags to index important moments for later review, a method similar to random access [27]. Others have hastened aural review by speeding up the playback speed, removing silence, and providing automatically generated transcripts [28][29][30].

Rather than focusing entirely on word content, others provide a visual display to summarize the aural contribution. Visiphone displayed a synchronous continuous depiction activity in each remote space by monitoring the volume at each end and combining them into a common visualization [8]. As conversational dominance was one of the most cited observations in Visiphone, it was recommended for use in marriage counseling sessions as a demonstration tool. Another project, the Conversation Clock, provided a persistent history of conversation [31]. The Conversation Clock produced augmented visual cues of conversation domination, interruption, turn taking, mimicry, and more based solely on the aural input of participants. Using this visualization, participants reported increased awareness of conversational patterns and found the visualized history revealed patterns that were otherwise undetected.

Audio augmentation and visualization has been explored in artistic works focused on collocated audio and the interaction of sound. These works use aural input to create continually changing visualizations. For example, Levin's work In-situ detects phonemes and produces depictions of each based on the aural characteristics of any utterance [32].

These works demonstrate the benefit visualization provides in understanding audio and interaction. *Conversation Votes* cues act as powerful tags to visually annotate audio during conversation. While we do not include text, transcripts, and speech recognition in our visualizations, the annotated visualization salient moments of conversation are highlighted through participant feedback.

3 Conversation Votes

Conversation Votes falls in a category of visualization called social mirrors [31]. By capturing and visualizing social activity back into a group. In the visualization, a shared image of the participants' changing interaction allows direct comparison between oneself and all others at the table.

We designed the anonymous back-channel as a medium for those with less social standing to offer their opinions [10]. In large groups, conference calls, or public meetings there is not always the opportunity for all to speak; participation favors those with higher social rank. The *Conversation Votes* visualization annotates aural activity with explicit voting feedback on the tabletop display. The resulting public image conveys the group's opinion of the conversation and denotes salient moments. Additionally, the anonymous votes further lower the social cost of entry into conversation allowing a wider swath of views to be discussed [33].

Conversation Votes extends the idea of the social mirror described in [31]. As a social mirror it provides a real-time common visualization for a group of four participants in a conversation. The visualization presents a structured timeline that highlights speech and voting activity integrated into the physical environment. Individuals can access additional knowledge and the cues in a small group without drawing visual attention away from the group.

3.1 The Timeline and History

In designing a table visualization integrated into conversation, we aim to convey the most important information at a glance. Our structured timeline highlights the most recent past while summarizing interaction history.

The *Conversation Votes* visualization presents the passage of time as a sequence of rectangular bars. The length of each rectangle represents the average audio sample for a single second. As shown in Figure 2a, rectangular samples progress through the table's center. This center progression shows one minute of elapsed conversation. Its central location on the table provides a detailed view of the interaction most recent in history.

Either side of the center progression depicts older minutes in the conversation (Figure 1b). Details are smaller and less visible; participants to get a higher-level view of who talks, how long people talk, and who received votes. The history stacks accumulate to 16 minutes, each stack showing one minute of samples. The leftmost stack of rectangles in our images indicates the most current minute. The full history is replicated above and below the central progression, making it easily visible from any seat at the table. As each minute ends, all completed minutes slide over to make room for a new minute (Figure 2b). The timeline and history provide the structure to view the individual contributions that make up conversational cues.

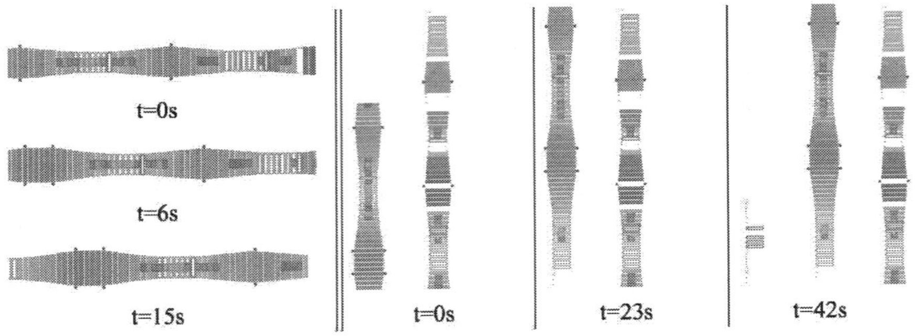

Fig. 2. Figure 2a shows the progression of the central history. Each second, a new sample is taken and appended to the leftmost end of the progression. All bars in the progression slide to the right to make room. Dotted rectangles mark the time a vote took place and simultaneous speech can be seen as multicolored bars. Figure 2b demonstrates how the historical stacks move over time. Each line of samples represents a single minute of time, the most recent picture furthest to the left. A line fills over the span of a minute and moves to the right to make room for the next.'

3.2 Contribution and Voting

Conversation Votes shows interaction by noting who spoke when and for how long. Individual microphones monitor each speaker, and unique colors identify each microphone in the visualization. With no votes, the visualization provides a simple color-coded view of who spoke in the conversation. Initially each sample is of uniform length, favoring no individual.

While the visualization automatically captures a conversation's aural features, it relies on the participants' votes to highlight a salient moment and provide feedback. Participants cast positive votes and negative votes (Figure 3) at any time during the conversation to indicate approval or disapproval respectively. A positive vote increases the size of the sampled bars while a negative vote has the opposite effect on the same set of samples. Additionally, a positive vote brightens the colored interior of the bar while a negative vote causes the color to fade into the background. The vote influences adjacent bars for visual impact while acknowledging the difficulty in pressing a button at the exact moment an utterance occurs. While a vote will always occur after the exact instance that inspired a participant to vote, adjacent bars are adjusted in both directions under the assumption that salient moments of conversation might continue after the button press.

Voting buttons can be held in one's hand discreetly and pressed with little effort. By using his or her two buttons, each listener alters the representation of the current speakers. A viewer sees which speakers provided a greater positive contribution to conversation by examining the full history. Larger and more saturated bars distinguish positive contribution at a glance. In our pilot study, participants found negative votes hurtful. Some voiced their concern about the animosity created. No one wanted to end his or her utterance on a negative note when in such a small group. These same participants agreed that it might be much more useful in larger, room-filling, groups and crowds. For this reason, we removed the negative voting button for our full study of small groups.

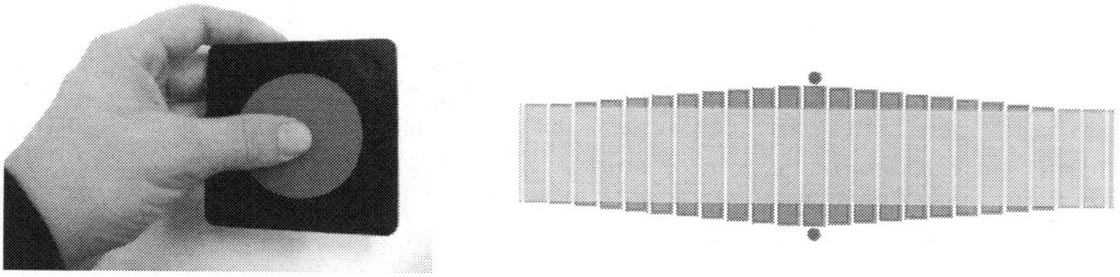

Fig. 3. The voting button (left) is a handheld plate with a colored circle indicating where to push. The button could be held discreetly under the table. There was no tactile feedback in this button, a light press was sufficient to vote and alter the visualization. The effect of a positive (right) lengthens the otherwise uniform bars.

3.3 Simultaneous Speakers

Moments of simultaneous vocalization, indicating excitement, agreement, or contention, proved to be among the most salient aural features portrayed by the Conversation

Clock [31]. We incorporated this visual cue into *Conversation Votes* by showing the two loudest active speakers in each sample bar. The speaker with greater volume determines the color of the outer bar while embedded rectangle represents the second speaker. Previously, overlapped bars would indicate relative amplitude of each speaker. As the bar length is no longer indicative of amplitude, the decision to only show two speakers makes the visualization more legible.

4 User Study

We set out to evaluate the following questions:

Q1: Do less talkative members provide more anonymous feedback?
Q2: Does receiving votes change a person's interactions?
Q3: Will positive feedback disrupt the trend to balance conversation?
Q4: Does voting convey participants' views in the conversation?

4.1 Method

We gathered 24 volunteers (13 male / 11 female) to meet in 6 groups. Participants consisted predominately of undergrad and graduate students in engineering disciplines. We asked each group to meet once in the our lab and take part in three debates.

The four participants of a group sat at our rectangular table, two per side on the long side. Prior to beginning the study, lapel microphones were clipped to each participant's collar before calibrating the microphone sensitivity. Participants were also given a single button and told to indicate their approval and encouragement of the current speaker by pressing it. As there is little sensory feedback when pressing the buttons, all participants first tested a button press before beginning the session.

A full session lasted about 1.5 hours and consisted of three 15-minute mini-session debates. In order to provide a base level of activity for comparison, the first mini sessions were conducted without the visualization projected. In this session, participants were not aware of the visualization's appearance and voted knowing only they were marking positive moments in conversation. The second mini-session began with a demonstration of the previous topic's visualization, an explanation of how conversation was depicted, and a live demonstration. The visualization was projected onto the table for the duration of the topic (Figure 1a). The final mini-session was without the visualization to offer a comparison with the baseline.

Topics for each mini-session were chosen from a collection of debate topics for youth debate groups that would be familiar and easily understood by most participants: the minimum age to allow voting, the establishment of national ID cards, and banning smoking in public places. The debate nature of the discussion was to provoke a confrontational style of conversation. Debate questions were assigned prior to each mini-session, and each group received a unique ordering. Participants were free to argue either side of the issue, explore a topic, and switch sides during discussion.

For each mini-session, we logged the aural activity and button presses used to generate the *Conversation Votes* visualization. For each individual we monitored their participation and noted how often they Lead conversation, how many Turns and the Turn Length, and the number of Votes. These measurements are all straightforward and simply logged during conversation. We also generated a measure of Voting Effect to represent the visual "bump" a participant receives (Figure 3). Voting effect can be calculated as the increase of a participant's graphical rendering from a baseline of no votes. All of these measures were normalized to be per minute for comparison across groups.

To measure individual perspective on the conversation, mini-sessions concluded with the same brief questionnaire. We presented participants with three, seven point, Likert Scales to measure how adequately everyone's viewpoints were Represented, how Comfortable participants were in the discussion, and how much their opinion was Altered due the discussion. Additionally, we asked all participants to notate the degree of contribution each group member made to the conversation.

The second session questionnaire included an additional set of seven point Likert scales to investigate the visualization awareness, visualization accuracy, level of voting anonymity, and degree of altered participation due to the visualization.

As part of the survey following each mini-session, participants were asked to estimate the total contribution during conversation. We compared this attribution to the logged lead data to calculate the Estimation Error in all conditions.

4.2 Results

Overall, our investigation demonstrates that anonymous voting creates an effective back-channel to enable some, though not all, to better assert themselves in conversation. Though this group was not the less talkative members that we expected, those enabled by the back-channel felt the un-augmented conversation was less inclusive of all viewpoints.

To investigate our hypotheses, participants were classified and divided for comparative analysis. Similar to prior work, groups are divided based on aural participation in the initial session; Heavy contributors spoke more than the leads per minute median value while light contributors spoke below that same threshold. To explore voting, participants were grouped into active voters and less active voters to examine how the voted and divided into heavily supported and lightly supported based on the visual effect of received votes.

Table 1. The table below summarizes the second session's likert scale survey. Participants reported being somewhat altered in their interaction and noticing alteration in others.

(a) Changes over Sessions

Measure	F value	p value
Leads	$F_{(2,21.3)} = 0.25$	$p < 0.79$
Turns	$F_{(2,20.3)} = 1.00$	$p < 0.39$
Turn Length	$F_{(2,24.1)} = 3.68$	$\mathbf{p < 0.04}$
Votes	$F_{(2,19.1)} = 0.65$	$p < 0.54$
V. Effect	$F_{(2,38.0)} = 1.04$	$p < 0.37$
Represented	$F_{(2,22.6)} = 2.13$	$p < 0.14$
Comfortable	$F_{(2,22.6)} = 0.55$	$p < 0.59$
Opinion	$F_{(2,22.5)} = 0.25$	$p < 0.79$
Error Est	$F_{(2,24.9)} = 3.10$	$p < 0.063$

(b) Likert Results

Measure	Result
Altered You	3.38
Altered Others	3.38
Anonymous	5.08
Comfortable Voting	4.33
Look at Vis	5.16
*Encouraged to Speak**	4.00

**ranged from 1-Less to 7-More*

For the statistical analysis, we fit our data to a Linear Mixed Effects Model using Hierarchical Linear Modeling with a repeated condition. A generalized linear model, it is commonly used to address hierarchical data models in social and behavioral sciences when analyzing groups with set hierarchies. Modeling our data as individuals who are a part of a group, we acknowledge individuals are not independent observations and account for the variance that naturally occurs between groups. To investigate Q1-Q4 posed earlier, the model also included variables indicating splits defined above.

Table 2. Splitting the participant groups on three different variables, the linear mixed effects model highlights the differing interaction emerging from our split categorizations over time and across the visualization conditions

	df	*Participation Split*		*Voting Split*		*Supported Split*	
Leads	(2, 21.3)	$F = 5.42$	$\mathbf{p < 0.012}$	$F = 5.35$	$p <$ **0.013**	$F = 2.85$	$p < 0.080$
Turns	(2, 20.3)	$F = 2.32$	$p < 0.13$	$F = 6.54$	$p <$ **0.006**	$F = 0.42$	$p < 0.67$
Turn Length	(2, 24.1)	$F = 0.21$	$p < 0.82$	$F = 0.55$	$p < 0.59$	$F = 1.08$	$p < 0.36$
Votes	(2, 19.1)	$F = 1.08$	$p < 0.36$	$F = 1.12$	$p < 0.35$	$F = 2.79$	$p < 0.087$
V. Effect	(2, 38.0)	$F = 0.30$	$p < 0.75$	$F = 0.48$	$p < 0.63$	$F = 0.03$	$p < 0.98$
Represented	(2, 22.6)	$F = 0.14$	$p < 0.88$	$F = 4.45$	$p <$ **0.021**	$F = 1.02$	$p < 0.38$
Comfortable	(2, 22.6)	$F = 0.64$	$p < 0.54$	$F = 0.05$	$p < 0.96$	$F = 0.59$	$p < 0.57$
Opinion	(2, 22.5)	$F = 0.91$	$p < 0.42$	$F = 0.25$	$p < 0.79$	$F = 0.63$	$p < 0.54$
Error Est	(2, 24.9)	$F = 0.23$	$p < 0.80$	$F = 0.04$	$p < 0.96$	$F = 0.65$	$p < 0.54$

Changes over Sessions, by sub-categorization

As can be seen in Table 1a, *Conversation Votes* only altered turn length consistently across all individuals ($F_{(2,24.1)} = 3.68$, $p < 0.04$). Follow-up investigation reveals that turn lengths decreased in the final mini-session. Table 1a also shows error estimation approached significance, indicating that people are modestly better at estimating contribution when they have a visual representation available. Surveys presented during the visualization session indicated participants were aware of stronger changes than these initial results reveal. They noted that both their own and others participation were altered from the previous session (Table 1b). This does turn out to be the case, but it is only after analyzing changes throughout the sessions when split that it becomes apparent.

Few differences could be found, outside of the defining characteristic, by making comparisons between the splits overall. Heavy participants tended to speak about 9 seconds more per minute than the less active participants ($F_{(1,25.1)} = 38.83$, $p < 0.001$) and take an additional turn every two minutes ($F_{(1,21.7)} = 19.83$, $p < 0.001$). Active voters pressed their buttons an additional time every 2 minutes ($F_{(1,23:0)} = 13.47$, $p < 0.001$), and heavily supported participants received 10% more increase in visual prominence than did the remaining participants ($F_{(1,28.2)} = 11.69$, $p < 0.002$). However, we see many more interesting differences when the splits are examined over the course of the sessions (Table 2).

The first split, between heavy and light participants, is motivated by previous work demonstrating visual feedback of group activity tends to balance contribution [19][31]. Our results with the *Conversation Votes* supports that finding ($F_{(2,21.3)} = 5.42$, $p < 0.012$). Participants noted a change in their debate, stating, "[it] more evenly dispersed conversation. I was less likely to interrupt." Overall, the visualization

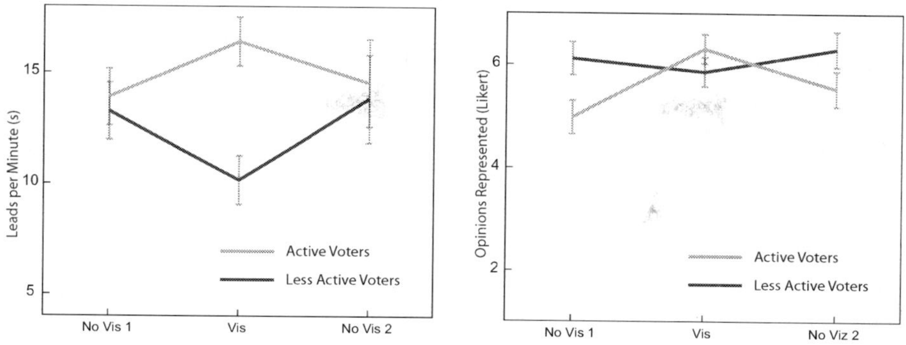

(a) Differences in voter speech (b) Differences in voter opinion

Fig. 4. Though similar contributions were seen without the visualization, Figure 4a shows active voters increased their contribution while less active voters significantly decreased during the visualization condition. Figure 4b shows that the most active voters did not feel representation was comparable until the visualization was present in mini-session two.

encourages a more equitable distribution of contribution and can be considered a balancing element in conversation.

An even more interesting story is told when examining differences between active and less active voters (Table 2). Unlike the balancing seen in the previous split, when active voters can see the results of their votes they drastically increase their lead in the conversation, diverging from the non-voters ($F_{(2,21.3)} = 5.35$, $p < 0.013$). Looking at Figure 4a, we see that both groups are essentially equals in leading conversation with no visualization present, but active voters speak about 30% more than less active voters with the visualization.

These same active voters reported better representation of opinions when the visualization was shown ($F_{(2,22.6)} = 4.45$, $p < 0.021$). Seen in Figure 4b, active participants were significantly less satisfied than their less active counterparts that conversation was providing a full representation of viewpoints. Feedback also indicated the back-channel could have been better utilized with a larger vocabulary of signals. One participant stated a negative vote would be particularly useful because he looked when he wanted to move on and "felt someone was talking too much." Though the channel was limited, the visualization allowed this group of active voters not only to speak more, but also to feel more satisfied with the group discussion.

Surprisingly, though voting enables activity and makes participants feel better about the debate, receiving a vote made little difference in our quantitative results. However, it inspired the most conversation amongst the participants.

> *"You could see when the others agreed with you, so it encouraged you to continue talking."*
>
> *"I could get a visual grasp of argument/conversation successes (i.e. winning others over)."*
>
> *"[I would] check if others were agreeing with the point presented (not necessarily by me)."*

In spite of our participants' receptive comments, the last split examining the heavily and lightly supported shows no significant differences, only two notable differences. These notable differences in leads ($F_{(2,21.3)} = 2.85$, $p < 0.080$) and votes ($F_{(2,19.1)} = 2.79$, $p < 0.087$) fall in line with the above quotes. However, a larger testing pool is needed to confirm those receiving votes become more talkative and more apt to vote during the *Conversation Votes* sessions.

5 Discussion

The results demonstrate that conversation visualization with a voting back-channel can influence conversation and perception. Below is a brief summary of highlights from the qualitative and quantitative highlights, noting how it relates to our original four questions.

Opening a back-channel: With Q1, we sought to show an anonymous back-channel offered an outlet for those reluctant to speak up. We had expected the light contributors would utilize the back-channel while heavy contributors favored speaking. However, our results do not show a significant difference in the voting patterns of heavy and light contributors.

Instead, active and unsatisfied voters increased their participation over the less active voters with the visual cues (Figure 4a) to ensure more opinions were represented (Figure 4b). Qualitative feedback also indicates the back-channel helped the group to better craft their arguments by understanding the group's overall sentiment.

The back-channel did not serve the purpose we had targeted, but it did create a new medium to better shape conversation contribution.

Participants strive for balance: The social mirror encourages people to have a balanced conversation as posed in Q3. Previous work found significant change towards balance when conversation is visualized. Presenting perceived contribution as opposed to raw data did not change this effect.

However, we cannot claim that a balanced conversation is a necessary goal of good conversation. A balanced conversation might be a result of silencing a more informed or provocative speaker. Further study is necessary to investigate the definition of quality in conversation, though our results for Q1 and opening a back-channel indicate that the balance did not lessen the quality of group conversation.

Awareness of Self and Others: With the visualization, participants reported being significantly more aware of others' contributions. They reported checking the visualization for agreements and approval of points. The visualization became a testing ground for ideas and feedback into one's success within the rest of the group. Participants also reported checking for reactions in response to other people's points. For Q4, we argue the visualization does adequately convey how participation view conversation.

The Voice of the Voter: The heaviest voters were less satisfied with the overall representation of ideas. Their voting could indicate pressure toward other topics. As one participant stated, the vocabulary of feedback needs to be expanded. While we removed negative votes for our study, our quantitative and qualitative results support an expanded set of cues. We have shown the visualization provides the necessary back-channel to send cues anonymously, however, the voters desired a back-channel with more than just the positive vote.

Social Mirror Karma: In examining Q2, we cannot definitively say receiving votes changed a person's interaction; our numbers are not strong enough to be certain. However, combined with the qualitative feedback, we hypothesize what further work might show.

Heavily supported individuals can be shown to be more talkative and more active in voting when visual feedback is present. Participating in the conversation and being active in the social mirror seem to correlate with receiving more votes from the remaining participants, in a sense one must give in order to receive. While a participant mentioned the possibility of gaming the system by anonymously voting for himself, an examination of the logs does indicate it occurred in our study.

From our own observation we posit both receiving and casting votes are influenced by engagement in the conversation. A participant in conversation is likely to speak more and vote more when a topic is close to his or her knowledge or interest, encouraging them to influence the social mirror to support their ideas. Future work should consider measuring prior knowledge and taking it into account.

6 Conclusion

Conversation is about more than relaying words. Rather than focusing on recreating face-to-face cues in a remote space, our work encourages the exploration of beneficial augmentations for collocated spaces.

We have shown that anonymous back-channels are used to better understand a group and balance participation while conversing. Participants responded in debates based on the feedback they received from the table and reported a heightened awareness of others opinions and their own interaction. Further, we have shown that the heaviest voting block are those who feel conversation is not adequately representing all viewpoints. Though our feedback is limited in vocabulary, *Conversation Votes* is our first step in enabling the underrepresented voices to be heard in a collocated setting.

References

1. Duncan, S.: Some signals and rules for taking speaking turns in conversation. Journ of Personality and Social Psyc. (1972)
2. Goffman, E.: The Presentation of Self in Everyday Life. Doubleday Anchor Books (1959)
3. Goffman, E.: On Face-Work. In: Interaction Ritual. Anchor Books (1963)
4. Levinson, S.C.: Pragmatics. Cambridge University Press, Cambridge (1983)
5. Mehrabian, A.: Silent Messages. Wadsworth (1971)
6. Heath, C., Luff, P.: Collaboration and control: Crisis management and multimedia technology in London underground line control rooms. Journal of Computer Supported Cooperative Work 1(1), 24–28 (1992)

7. Bly, S.A., Harrison, S.R., Irwin, S.: Media spaces: bringing people together in a video, audio, and computing environment. Comm. of ACM (1993)
8. Donath, J., Karahalios, K., Viegas, F.: Visiphone. In: ICAD 2000: International Conference on Auditory Display (2000)
9. Hollan, J., Stornetta, S.: Beyond being there. In: Proceedings of CHI (1992)
10. Sproull, L., Kiesler, S.: Connections: New Ways of Working in the Networked Organization. MIT Press, Cambridge (1991)
11. Saville-Troike, M.: The Ethnography of Communication. Basil Blackwell, Inc., New York (1989)
12. Jones, M.G., Gerig, T.M.: Silent Sixth-Grade Students: Characteristics, Achievement, and Teacher Expectations. The Elementary School Journal 95(2), 169–182 (1994)
13. Baltes, B.B., Dickson, M.W., Sherman, M.P., Bauer, C.C., LaGanke, J.S.: Computer-Mediated Communication and Group Decision Making: A Meta-Analysis. Organizational Behavior and Human Decision Processes 87(1), 156–179 (2002)
14. Markus, M.L.: Finding a happy medium: explaining the negative effects of electronic communication on social life at work. ACM Trans. Inf. Syst. 12(2), 119–149 (1994)
15. Tannen, D.: Teachers' Classroom Strategies Should Recognize That Men and Women Use Language Differently. The Chronicle of Higher Education (1991)
16. Tannen, D.: Gender and Discourse. Oxford University Press, Oxford (1994)
17. Chaika, E.: Language: The Social Mirror. Heinle and Heinle Publishers (1994)
18. Hauser, M.D., Chomsky, N., Fitch, W.T.: The Faculty of Language: What Is It, Who Has It, and How Did It Evolve? Science 298, 1569–1579 (2002)
19. DiMicco, J.M., Pandolfo, A., Bender, W.: Influencing group participation with a shared display. In: Proceedings of CSCW (2004)
20. DiMicco, J.M., Bender, W.: Group Reactions to Visual Feedback Tools. In: Persuasive Technology (2007)
21. Biehl, J.T., Czerwinski, M., Smith, G., Robertson, G.G.: FASTDash: a visual dashboard for fostering awareness in software teams. In: Proceedings of CHI (2007)
22. Ding, X., Erickson, T., Kellogg, W.A., Levy, S., Christensen, J.E., Sussman, J., Wolf, T.V., Bennett, W.E.: An empirical study of the use of visually enhanced voip audio conferencing: the case of IEAC. In: Proceedings of CHI (2007)
23. Yankelovich, N., Walker, W., Roberts, P., Wessler, M., Kaplan, J., Provino, J.: Meeting central: making distributed meetings more effective. In: Proceedings of CSCW (2004)
24. Donath, J.S.: Identity and deception in the virtual community. Communities in cyberspace (1999)
25. Bradner, E., Mark, G.: Why distance matters: effects on cooperation, persuasion and deception. In: Proceedings of CSCW (2002)
26. Rocco, E.: Trust breaks down in electronic contexts but can be repaired by some initial face-to-face contact. In: Proceedings of CHI (1998)
27. Degen, L., Mander, R., Salomon, G.: Working with audio: integrating personal tape recorders and desktop computers. In: Proceedings of CHI, New York, NY, USA (1992)
28. Arons, B.: SpeechSkimmer: interactively skimming recorded speech. In: Proceedings of UIST (1993)
29. Vemuri, S., DeCamp, P., Bender, W., Schmandt, C.: Improving speech playback using time-compression and speech recognition. In: Proceedings of CHI (2004)
30. Vemuri, S., Schmandt, C., Bender, W.: iRemember: a personal, long-term memory prosthesis. In: Proceedings on Continuous archival and retrival of personal experences, pp. 65–74. ACM, New York (2006)

31. Bergstrom, T., Karahalios, K.: Seeing More: Visualizing Audio Cues. In: Proceedings of Interact (2007)
32. Levin, G., Lieberman, Z.: In-situ speech visualization in real-time interactive installation and performance. In: Proceedings of the symposium on Non-photorealistic animation and rendering (2004)
33. Kiesler, S., Siegel, J., Timothy, W.M.: Social psychological aspects of computer-mediated communication, 657–682 (1988) (Reprint)

Ownership and Evolution of Local Process Representations

Thomas P. Moran[1], Tara L. Matthews[1], Laurian Vega[2], Barton Smith[1], James Lin[1], and Stephen Dill[1]

[1] IBM Almaden Research Center, San Jose, California, USA
{tpmoran,tlmatthe,n6hdn,jameslin,dill}@us.ibm.com
[2] Center for Computer-Human Interaction, Virginia Tech, Blacksburg, Virginia, USA
laurian@vt.edu

Abstract. Knowledge workers tailor collaborative business processes to local conditions. They own (i.e., create and maintain) representations of these local processes (such as checklists) to guide the work. Our goal is to design tools to support the ownership of collaborative local processes by enabling workers to flexibly adapt process representations to work situations. This paper focuses on how workers evolve representations for collaborative, locally-owned processes by updating them from situated experiences to keep up with changing business conditions. To understand this, we conducted a field study and a lab study. From the field study, we describe how factors like group roles and documentation purposes affect the evolution of process representations. Based on these observations, we propose a model of the practice of evolving local process representations that provides a framework for understanding activity documentation needs. The lab study then provides behavioral details on the ways people carried out the evolution practice. These studies yield design implications for collaborative activity support tools.

Keywords: Coordination, collaboration, business processes, activities, work practices, process evolution.

1 Introduction

Business processes are often treated as centrally-owned and mandated work [1,2]. However, various ethnographic studies of knowledge workers have shown that they formulate their own objectives for business processes and work out strategies and methods for attaining them [3,4,5,6]. We call these *locally-owned processes*. They are local in that they are adapted to local work situations and needs, even when workers are following centrally defined and mandated organizational processes, which we call *central processes*. Local processes are owned by the workers involved and responsible for doing the work. A number of studies show that people adapt central processes to local situations and needs, e.g., [2,7,8,9]. However, little is known about how workers actually go about evolving local process representations over time, an issue investigated in the studies presented in this paper.

T. Gross et al. (Eds.): INTERACT 2009, Part I, LNCS 5726, pp. 560–573, 2009.

1.1 Local Process Representations (LPRs)

In everyday, informal work practices, processes exist as verbal or even tacit knowledge. However, prior work has found that knowledge workers also create representational artifacts, or documentation, to help manage these processes – checklists, diagrams, charts, how-to's, instructions, etc. [3]. These local process representations (LPRs) help workers: (1) carry out activities by providing to-do reminders, critical how-to information, key resources, etc.; (2) manage and coordinate activities by representing the dynamic state of the processes; and (3) support adapting *activities* (i.e. instances of local processes) to specific situations by being flexibly changeable.

The key to the vitality of LPRs is that people not only create them, but also *maintain* them. LPRs are never perfect, and even if they were, they would degrade over time as conditions change [10]. We are investigating whether workers will adapt and evolve LPRs, under what circumstances they will do so, and what types of LPRs they see fit to evolve over extended periods of time. Throughout the paper, we use the terms *LPR* and *documentation* interchangeably.

1.2 Studying the Practice of Evolving LPRs

To study practices of evolving LPRs, we distinguish two aspects: (1) the organizational context and (2) cognitive capabilities and working styles of the workers involved. To explore the effects of the both aspects on practices of evolving LPRs, we conducted field interviews. Based on observations from the field, we propose a model of the practice of evolving LPRs that provides a vision and hypothesis for the lab study. To explore the second aspect in more detail, we conducted a lab study to gather behavioral data on the ways people carried out the practice of evolving LPRs. These studies yielded design implications for collaborative activity support tools.

2 Related Work

Process representations and their coordination and use are research topics that have an extensive and varied literature. Since we cannot cover all this research in detail, we will show how our work is positioned along with some key examples.

The first broad research area, *activity theory* [11], examines how people work communally with socially constructed tools to create situated outcomes. In this framework, central processes serve as a tool to help people negotiate their roles and actions as mandated by the community's rules. Local processes and their documentation is seen as fashioned from the local needs of in situ activity. Sachs [4] articulates this dichotomy as an "organizational, explicit" view of work (central process representations) versus an "activity-oriented, tacit" view (LPRs).

A second area of research, *distributed cognition*, examines how tools such as LPRs help mediate cooperation, learning, and error recovery. In a study of how groups coordinate with regular member attrition and on-the-job novices, Seifert and Hutchins showed how people organized the work of navigating a navel vessel with minimal errors [12]. The work on distributed cognition highlights the need to use tools, such as processes and LPRs, for shared understanding and cooperation.

A large body of *ethnographic work* examines how knowledge management systems – which can be considered as collections of process representations – came into being [13] and were reused [14]. Along with studies that were in-depth analyses of discrete yet complex work (e.g., call centers [15,16], ticket booking [5], and banking [17]), this research emphasizes that work is seen to follow a rote method, but is actually quite messy and locally adapted: "Study after study have demonstrated, unambiguously and beyond any doubt, that the status of these formal organizational constructs in the actual course of work is problematic in that these constructs are impoverished idealizations when taken as representations of actually unfolding activities" [5, p.166].

Another body of work studies *organizational routines* [18,19], which are "repeated patterns of behavior that are bound by rules and customs" that continuously change [18]. This literature also observes the "endless variations" of routines (e.g., in different departments) and the range of artifacts that enable and constrain them [19].

The literature on *articulation work* is another form of process reification. Articulation work is the detailing of who will do what and when. Articulation work is dintinguished from "cooperative work," which is the business of doing the work. (See [5] for theoretical postulates on the balance between the two.) This research reflects our findings about who, how, and when people go about revising documentation about both articulation work and cooperative work.

Suchman notes that central process technologies serve as "a basis for centralized assessments of the efficiency and correctness of the local operations in which the technologies are embedded" [2]. Similarly, Dourish argues that workflow technologies (which he describes as centrally-owned) act as "organizational accounting devices," rendering employees' work "observable and reportable" [1]. In contrast, the goal of our work is to inform the design of technologies to represent and coordinate locally-owned processes. While prior work shows that locally adapting processes is widespread, there are few studies of the systematic practices of evolving LPRs, the issue we explore here.

3 Field Study: The Practice of Evolving LPRs

Our field study's goal was to explore and discover the processes for which LPRs are created, the roles people had in updating LPRs, and the practices for revising LPRs.

3.1 Participants, Method, and Data

In order to focus on LPR evolution, we selected 14 participants who coordinated processes, since they would more likely own the documentation. Our participants came from diverse work contexts: they worked across two states, in three different organizations (a large business organization, a university, and a home owners association), in seven positions (administrator, director of development, program manager, HR, department manager, graduate student, professor, and fiscal technician) and in eight different departments. Ten participants were female.

All interviews were conducted in person, in the participant's working context. Interviews lasted 40-90 minutes and were audio-recorded. The interviews were semi-structured, based on questions designed to gather data about the processes they carried out, factors affecting how they carried out the processes, and how they and their teams used and evolved process representations. We also probed topics that arose during interviews, and we collected copies of process representations.

Because participants coordinated processes, our data does not represent a general office population. However, this enabled us to gather concentrated data on practices related to evolving LPRs. We focused on gathering in-depth data about processes that had some aspect of *local ownership*, were *collaborative*, and were *repeated.*

3.2 Results

We discussed various repeated, collaborative processes with participants (26 different processes in total), including on-boarding new hires, disclosing inventions, planning various events and programs, evaluating employees, creating products, moving offices, and teaching classes. For all of these processes, participants had 40 LPRs they and/or their teams maintained through evolving business conditions and local contingencies. We report three main findings in this section: (1) people spent effort to maintain LPRs for four specific purposes; (2) LPRs were updated at different times depending on the way they were used; and (3) roles emerged in teams for practices of evolving LPRs.

Purposes for Maintaining LPRs. We observed that participants took time to maintain and reuse LPRs for four different purposes. Six LPRs were coded as serving two purposes.

- *Explicit and complete how-to information for a complex activity* (8 of 40 LPRs). For example, two administrative assistants at the same global company maintained and used how-to checklists for only two processes (on-boarding new hires and organizing a colloquium), even though they carried out many other processes regularly. The difference in these two processes was that they were particularly complex or long, warranting the effort spent to maintain LPRs. For their remaining, simpler processes, they had memorized the steps. These two checklists included details missing from central documentation and local customizations to the way the process was carried out (e.g., adding new hires to departmental email lists).
- *Maintaining status information for a complex activity* (8 LPRs). Complex activities often require participants to develop LPRs to track status. Both the documentation that organizes status information and the status information itself can evolve over time and participants found these valuable to maintain. For example, one participant coordinated a patent disclosure process by placing post-its, each representing a disclosure, in the various boxes of a state diagram drawn on her whiteboard. The position of a post-it told her the status of the corresponding disclosure. The disclosure process had gone on continuously for years, and the diagram had evolved over that time as she learned more about the process (e.g., she added boxes upon learning of new disclosure states).
- *Informational documentation used during an activity* (22 LPRs). Informational documentation was referenced or shared during a process to help users learn or remember what to do and how to do it. Email archives were most commonly used for this purpose (14 LPRs). For example, one participant who organized volunteer programs at a large company, archived her informational emails sent to employees

about the programs each year and reused them next year, both to remind her about how to do the process and to revise and resend to employees.

- *Final product of a process* (8 LPRs). Products created as part of a process, such as papers or presentations, were commonly maintained and reused. For example, when planning and teaching a course a professor reused the previous year's syllabus, editing it for the current semester, and posting it for students.

Timing for LPR Updates. Participants updated LPRs at varying times in process life cycles, depending on the way the LPR was used and the process itself.

- *Just before reusing the documentation.* This was observed in cases when a participant was about to reuse old documentation, but knew that it was out-of-date or not specific and thus revised it first (7 processes). For example, a participant at a large global company kept archives of all the email she sent about the regular employee volunteer programs she coordinated. When a volunteer program was approaching, she would revise and then reuse her old emails about the program.
- *After completing the process.* This was observed in cases that the participant (1) discovered the existing documentation was inadequate or incorrect after using it and updated it for themselves (3 processes) or (2) wanted to keep a record of changes made to the process for people who would do the process in the future (1 process). For example, a participant who was working as a creator and coordinator knew that in the following year someone else in his club would have to coordinate a large yearly event that involved approximately twenty people. To help that future coordinator, he updated his LPR, an online to-do list with associated notes, a week after finishing while the details were still fresh in his mind.
- *While carrying out the process.* This was observed in two of the processes for which the documentation became a product of the process. For example, a wiki, used by a conference planning team of eight people at a large global company, was revised as part of the process: originally, the wiki was used to coordinate their activities that were discussed in meetings (e.g., who to invite as speakers). After the meetings people would keep track of the progress by looking at the artifacts people were working on that they had posted on the wiki. Some of these artifacts were eventually molded into final products, like the conference agenda and speaker list.
- *As new process information arose.* This was observed in four processes where changes to some aspect (planning, coordination, status) happened continuously or at particular times. For example, one participant created a state diagram for disclosing inventions, which she constantly updated whenever the legal department informed her of a new patent status. She revised the diagram as she learned about the process, regardless of the process' status as starting, completed, or in-progress.

Roles in the Practice of Evolving LPRs. Related studies on documentation practices have noted that experts tend to create documentation, because they have the knowledge needed to do so [12,14,15]. However, our results suggest that additional roles are important in LPR evolution: *creator*, *coordinator* (of various kinds: managerial, administrative, partial, and overall), *team member*, and *advisor*. Of course, not all processes had all of these roles.

Process *creators* usually generated the initial process documentation. For example, a participant was the first president of his homeowners association and created a format for organizational meetings. This format was documented as the meeting agenda, which was discussed in meetings, annotated, and republished with notes monthly to the other four association members through email.

If there was a process *coordinator*, this person usually did the bulk of the LPR updates. If there was a *managerial* and an *administrative* coordinator, the latter tended to be in charge of documentation. For example, SN co-coordinates a yearly conference, but he has an administrative assistant who helps him keep the documentation for the process up-to-date. Coordinators maintained LPRs since they were responsible for making sure the process was accomplished.

In the absence of an explicit coordinator, one or more *team members* will sometimes maintain documentation for collaborative activities. For example, SN describes a repeated process in which he collaboratively creates presentations with team members. The presentation slides are created by whoever takes responsibility first, and they are edited by all the team members.

An *advisor* was a person who instructed others how to complete a process, but was not directly involved in doing so. For example, TS keeps a set of how-to LPRs for managers in her local population. Whenever corporate HR sends an email instructing managers to do an HR process, TS sends a follow-up email with helpful instructions.

4 A Model for the Practice of Evolving LPRs

We articulate a general model for the practice of evolving LPRs to clarify what we mean and to serve as a hypothesis for a lab study exploring individual workers' capabilities and tendencies for evolving LPRs (presented in the next section).

A *locally-owned process* is an organization of the work required to accomplish a business objective, by some more or less specific method, with various *actors* and *resources*. The actors play different *roles* to carry out the process collaboratively. Example:

> *Patenting at an engineering firm is initiated with a central* Invention Disclosure Process, *which is the first legal documentation of an invention that could be patented. The actors in this process are an* Inventor, *the inventor's* Manager, *an* Attorney, *and an* Expediter. *The Expediter coordinates the others to make sure inventions are disclosed correctly and efficiently.*

A specific instance of a business process is called an *activity*. Every activity is carried out in the context of a specific work *situation*. A situation includes physical conditions, task constraints and requirements, and actor availability. A situation also includes the actors' knowledge of, experience with, and attitudes towards the activity being done. Situations vary because every work context is different. More importantly, there are trends in the variations. Situations *drift* over time as people, resources, organizations, and business conditions change and evolve. Local processes must also evolve to keep up with this drift, in order to remain relevant and effective. Example (continued):

Joe and Jane each invented a new technique that might be patentable. Though their disclosures are happening at the same time, their situations are different—the inventions are different (one is time critical), they have different Managers and Expediters (one is new to the role), and the shared files have been moved to a new server. These are local variations. The organizational context has also evolved: two months earlier, Managers were not part of the process, but they were given a role to reduce the burden on Inventors.

To help manage a process, actors can create a *local process representation (LPR)* or *documentation*, such as a checklist of steps describing the substantive work and coordination work needed to carry it out. Process representations can vary in detail, accuracy, and completeness, depending on how well actors maintain them. Example (continued):

The first Expediters worked together to create a 16-step set of instructions to describe the invention disclosure process, which they put in a shared file directory. The steps in the instructions are assigned to the different roles, and they are in the approximate order in which they should be carried out.

Documentation can be imperfect for a particular situation. There are discrepancies between the instructions and the situation. A *discrepancy* is a specific inconsistency between what the instructions say and what the situation demands. Two types of discrepancies involve people (actors failing in various ways and roles being unassigned or misassigned) and steps (being too difficult, vague, or just wrong). Example (continued):

The instructions assign Jane's Manager too many steps, but this Manager always delegates these to his senior engineer. When the Expediter encounters this discrepancy, he finds and works with the senior engineer to get the information needed.

In this model, we characterize a situation by its *delta*, the number of discrepancies between the situation and its documentation. Delta is the measure of the inaccuracy of the process representation in context.

As situations drift and processes evolve, the *documentation must evolve* to continue to be useful guidance for the process. In other words, documentation must be updated to keep the deltas manageable. It is the actors who must update them, since they own them. Thus the practice of evolving LPRs requires that actors not only carry out activities, but also update the process representations. Example (continued):

When the Managers assumed a role in the process, the instructions had to be altered to assign some of the Inventor's steps to the Manager, as well as to change some of the steps.

Actors must carry out activities in situations with discrepancies in the LPRs. When discrepancies are encountered, which can happen before or during a performance of the activity, actors must *reflect* on the discrepancy, *decide* whether it is useful to document their reflections, and actually *document* them by fixing the instructions. In some situations, discrepancies will cause a *breakdown* in the activity, with which actors must first *cope* (find a way around) and then *reflect* upon.

The model does not specify when revisions happen (since this varied based on field study results) or the roles of actors within the process (since these depend on the process). The focus of the model is how potential updates can arise from the experiences of carrying out processes in specific situations.

5 Lab Study: Individual Behaviors in Evolving LPRs

We conducted a lab study to explore people's capability to carry out a practice of evolving LPRs consistent with the model: Can they cope with the discrepancies? Can they fix documentation on the fly? What kinds of fixes do they make or not make?

Participants in the study carried out a typical local business process – an invention disclosure process (explained above). The participants used Google Talk to communicate and followed instructions on a single-page shared Google Document, which served as the LPR.

Each participant played a coordinator role (which we called the Expediter) in a single session, coordinating one complete invention disclosure activity. As Expediter, the participant's job was to gather information from the others, draft the disclosure, and coordinate the others in assessing, enhancing, and approving the disclosure. The researcher, using IM, played the roles of the collaborators – Attorney, Inventor, and Manager – according to predefined scripts that enacted various situations.

We varied deltas in different sessions by planting role discrepancies (unassigned and incorrectly assigned roles) and step discrepancies (incorrect, irrelevant, missing, and out-of-order steps). Participants encountered discrepancies while interacting with their collaborators. For example, if steps were listed in an incorrect order, the participant would notice this either when a collaborator did them in the correct order or when a collaborator would warn the participant that he did a step at the wrong time. Given these discrepancies, the participant was instructed to make sure the LPR (the instructions) were accurate for the next group doing this process.

5.1 Session Groups

Session situations were constructed to enact specific discrepancies to control the delta. We designed the situations as four related groups. Two groups had *stable situations*, where the situation was the same in each session; and two groups had *drifting situations*, where each session's situation had increasingly more discrepancies than the preceding session's. Two groups had *static instructions*, where the same instructions were used in each session; and two groups had *evolving instructions*, where the updated instructions from each session were passed on to the next session. See Figure 1. Our research questions were:

- *Stable-Static Group* (the situation and instructions are the same for each participant). How much variation is there in coping with and fixing discrepancies?
- *Drifting-Static Group* (subsequent situations have higher deltas, but the instructions are the same). What limits do people have for coping with discrepancies?
- *Stable-Evolving Group* (the situation stays the same, but evolved instructions are passed from one session to the next). Will the instructions become optimized to the specific situation, that is, will the deltas approach zero?
- *Drifting-Evolving Group* (subsequent situations have higher deltas, but evolved instructions are passed from one session to the next). Will the instructions evolve to keep up with drifting situations?

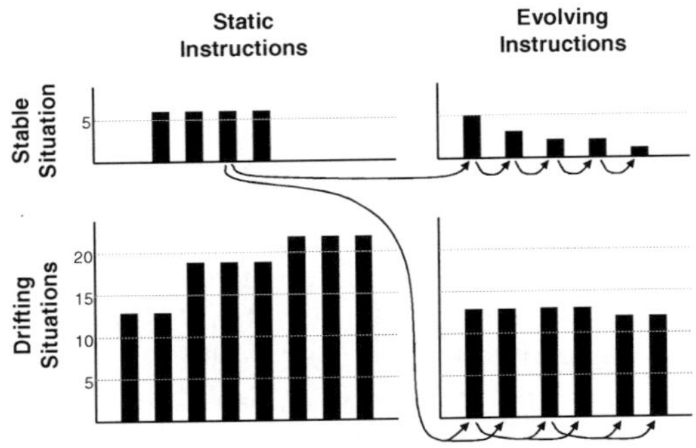

Fig. 1. The quadrants depict deltas for the four groups: the height of a bar represents the number of deltas a participant encountered during that session (only 23 out of 27 participants are portrayed, because data from the four participants who did not follow the practice of evolving LPRs were removed). Arrows show how updated instructions were passed between sessions in the two evolving-instructions groups.

Figure 1 shows the four groups: the height of a bar represents the number of deltas a participant encountered in that session (only 23 of 27 participants are portrayed, since data from 4 participants were removed for reasons described below). For example, in the Stable-Static Group (upper-right quadrant of Figure 1) the four participants started with the same instructions and faced the same discrepancies. The number of deltas participants encountered in the two evolving-instructions groups (right quadrants of Figure 1) was determined by how many discrepancies the previous participants actually fixed (and introduced) in the instructions, since instructions were passed from one participant to the next. Our prediction was that the deltas in these groups would be lower than those of the static-instructions groups.

5.2 Participants and Procedure

We recruited 27 study participants from a global company: 14 were employees, 13 were interns. Interns had little or no experience in patent disclosures. Employees had participated in some part of the patent process, either writing or reviewing patent disclosures. The process and LPR used in the study were significantly different from the process and LPR some participants were familiar with, so all participants were relative novices. Participants ranged in age from 23 to 60 years; 7 were female.

Each session was conducted as follows: The participant was (1) introduced to the tools; (2) read and discussed a document explaining the task, roles, and instructions; (3) began the invention disclosure activity with his collaborators, for which there was a one-hour limit; (4) took up to ten minutes to update the instructions for use by subsequent participants; (5) completed a survey about how he felt the activity went; and (6) was interviewed by the researcher to better understand how he felt the activity went, what changes he made to the instructions, and why. Participants were compensated for their time with lunch vouchers. The revised instructions and qualitative feedback were the raw data from the study.

A critical part of the procedure is how we conveyed the basic idea of the practice of evolving LPRs to the participants. In part (2) of the session procedure they read:

Edit the instructions to reflect how your group actually did the work. You can change, add, or delete; and you can add advice or notes as bullets under the steps—whatever you need to best reflect your work. These instructions are not perfect. People have worked on them before you. The previous groups could have added information that is useful. But they could also have added information that is not helpful or even wrong.

Further, they were told their revised instructions would be used by participants in the next session. We motivated participants to improve the instructions by offering them an extra lunch voucher if their revisions helped the next participant.

5.3 Results

The study verified that most participants could follow the practice of evolving LPRs. Specifically, participants experienced minor breakdowns when they faced discrepancies; but all of them, even those in high delta situations, were able to cope with the breakdowns and complete the activity correctly. Participants were able to reflect on breakdowns and document about half of them by fixing the instructions. Revised instructions had an impact on subsequent participants. However, we also observed that not all participants followed the practice of evolving LPRs.

Participants Not Following the Practice of Evolving LPRs. Our most basic question is whether people understand and agree to follow the LPR practice. This includes knowing that they own and can change the instructions, viewing the instructions as a valuable tool for completing the activity, and making changes that document their experience. Four out of 27 participants did not follow the LPR practice. In the lab study situation, these four participants did not update the LPR either because they did not find it was a useful practice, they did not feel they should change the LPR since they did not feel they owned it, or they felt that the LPR was ineffective and completely re-engineered the process by creating a new LPR. Overall, this finding indicates that not everyone will understand or agree with the practice of evolving LPRs.

Participants Following the LPR Practice. Of 27 participants, 23 followed the practice of evolving LPRs. Figure 1 depicts the number of deltas encountered during these 23 sessions. We focused our analysis on how well participants evolved the instructions, measured by the number of discrepancies they *fixed*. A *fix* removes a discrepancy from the instructions, and thus is a positive change. The grouping of sessions also enabled us to examine the effects of evolving instructions on the number of deltas, in both stable and drifting situations. Evolved instructions had the predicted effect: deltas for sessions using evolved instructions were lower than the corresponding static-instruction sessions (see Figure 1).

First, consider the two groups with stable situations. The Stable-Static group had a delta of 6 (same instructions, same situation). But the Stable-Evolving group showed that continually passing on revised instructions allowed participants to optimize the instructions to delta of 1. The final participant in this group said, "Everything was straightforward and really easy to follow, so I made no changes" to the instructions. The instructions could be continually optimized since the situation was a stable target.

Next, consider the groups with drifting situations, where the situations were designed to become more discrepant with the initial situation. The Drifting-Static group shows the continually increasing deltas in succeeding sessions. But the Drifting-Evolving group was able to hold the deltas down by passing on revised instructions. These situations were a distinct improvement compared to the deteriorating situations in the Drifting-Static group. (The fact that the deltas were held constant is an accidental artifact of our having made the situations drift at the same rate as the participants could fix discrepancies.) Regardless of delta, all participants could cope with all discrepancies to correctly complete the disclosure process, even if they did not fix all of them. As delta increased, the number of fixes also increased, but the percentage of discrepancies fixed remained constant, averaging 41%.

These results may seem obvious, but we think it is important to empirically demonstrate that most people can follow an effective practice of evolving LPRs. For example, participants might not have been able to cope or to revise instructions in a way that benefits succeeding participants.

How Participants Followed the Practice of Evolving LPRs. The lab study also revealed *how* people follow the practice of evolving LPRs.

First, participants did more than fix discrepancies. Participants had no way to distinguish our planted discrepancies from any other parts of the instructions that they felt could be improved. We use the term *enhancements* to label any changes participants made to the instructions that were not fixes of planted discrepancies. While we reserved the term *fix* for changes in the LPR that were positive remedies to planted discrepancies, enhancements could have negative effects: they could actually introduce discrepancies into the instructions (25% of enhancements were *incorrect*, thus increasing the deltas for the following participants) or could lead to verbose, confusing instructions (one participant in the Stable-Evolving group spoke about her instructions, which had been revised by three others: "Some of the notes … were lengthy and confusing…."). Overall, participants made six enhancements per session on average. We found that the number of enhancements did not depend on delta and did not vary across the different session groups. This is surprising, because intuitively one might expect fewer enhancements in sessions with more discrepancies to fix or with instructions that had already been enhanced.

Second, participants fixed different *types* of discrepancies with differing frequency. We planted two types of discrepancies into the study situations: role and step discrepancies. For sessions with deltas 6–22, participants fixed 60% of the role discrepancies and 40% of the step discrepancies. (In lower delta sessions, participants had fixed all role discrepancies.) The participants' enhancements can be classified into step-oriented (74% of all enhancements), role-oriented (21%), and other (5%). Editing a step was by far the most common (55% of all enhancements), and most of these were to add clarifying content to the step (43% of all enhancements).

Participants could revise the instructions while they worked on the activity (up to 60 minutes) or in a 10-minute period after the activity ended. Participants fixed discrepancies *during* the activity more often than *after* in the higher delta sessions (deltas 13-22): there was an average of 6 fixes during the activity and only 1 fix afterwards. Enhancements were made equally during and after the activity.

Participants fixed 41% of discrepancies on average. The most common reason for this (revealed in interviews) was that participants simply did not notice they had coped with a discrepancy (10 participants). Other reasons included: feeling like a novice in the disclosure task (5 participants); being confused by the instructions, which could have reduced their ability to document discrepancies (2); forgetting to fix a discrepancy (1); having limited time to make revisions (1); and believing that some discrepancies were so minor they were "not worth recording" (1). These results indicate that iterations over several sessions may be needed to optimize instructions, since some discrepancies will often be overlooked in each session.

6 Discussion and Design Implications

Our field interviews focused on practices and roles affecting the practice of evolving LPRs, while our lab study focused on the capabilities of individuals. Using two empirical methods to explore the same issue proved useful since results from each study provided data and design implications the other could not. One lab study finding was that there was a limit to the number of problems people could recognize and fix in the documentation (a fairly constant rate of 41% for the experimental situation). The lab study also helped us to identify a distinction between different kinds of revisions: *problem fixes* (which were more objective) and *enhancements* (which were more subjective) – a distinction designers may want to consider to help users maintain usable documentation.

The field study helped us explore contextual factors that were hard to simulate in the lab. We found that roles emerged for document evolution. Processes had a primary documenter (usually the coordinator), indicating that tools may need different functionality for documenters and other participants. We also identified four specific purposes motivating people to spend effort maintaining LPRs: how-to and status information for complex activities, informational documentation using during an activity, and final products of processes. A design implication is that tools should support creating and maintaining these types of LPRs. Specifically, *how-tos* should be findable and the audience should be explicit since LPRs are tailored for specific groups. To track *status* information, designers should enable the creation of custom status views, like state diagrams. Since email was so commonly used as *informational documentation*, it will be important for tools to tightly integrate with email. Finally, to help teams collaborate on *products*, tools need to support iterating and commenting on drafts and transitioning content to final product format.

Other results from the lab and field studies complement each other. Lab study participants were told they were in a coordinating role (the Expeditor) and were in charge of documentation. Even so, not all participants adopted this role (3 made no changes to the instructions). However, *all* participants edited the patent abstract. Similarly, we saw in our field study that more team members collaborated on deliverable documentation. Such documentation does provide some information about process status, though it is primarily a product of the process. For design, this implies that mixing general process documentation with the product of a process in tools may increase team participation in maintaining both.

In the lab, most people revised instructions *while doing* the activity, but we saw more varied behavior in the field. This difference may have been due to differences in processes and situations. For example, lab participants had no way of discovering problems before doing the activity, and revising. The high variability of processes in real contexts shows it is important that documentation can be easy to revise at any time.

7 Conclusion

Our goal is to inform the design of tools supporting ownership of local processes. We conducted a field study and learned how participants evolved LPRs: factors like group roles and purposes of documentation affect the evolution of process representation. Based on our findings, we developed a model of the practice of evolving LPRs to explore a specific vision of bottom-up ownership. We used a lab study to explore the cognitive issues of whether and how people understand and carry out the practice. The model and studies revealed implications for designing tools that can not only support coordination through process representations, but also make evolution of LPRs integral to such support.

References

1. Dourish, P.: Process descriptions as organisational accounting devices: the dual use of workflow technologies. In: Proceedings of the 2001 International ACM SIGGROUP Conference on Supporting Group Work, pp. 52–60. ACM, Boulder (2001)
2. Suchman, L.: Making work visible. Communications of the ACM, 56 (1995)
3. Kogan, S.L., Muller, M.J.: Ethnographic study of collaborative knowledge work. IBM Systems Journal 45(4) (2006)
4. Sachs, P.: Transforming work: collaboration, learning, and design. Communications of the ACM, 36–44 (1995)
5. Schmidt, K., Simone, C.: Coordination Mechanisms: Towards a Conceptual Foundation of CSCW Systems Design. In: Computer Supported Cooperative Work (CSCW), vol. 5, pp. 155–200 (1996)
6. Gerson, E.M., Star, S.L.: Analyzing due process in the workplace. ACM Trans. Inf. Syst., 257–270 (1986)
7. Suchman, L.A.: Office procedure as practical action: models of work and system design. ACM Trans. Inf. Syst. 1(4), 320–328 (1983)
8. Fischer, G., Ostwald, J.: Knowledge Management: Problems, Promises, Realities, and Challenges. IEEE Intelligent Systems 16(1), 60–72 (2001)
9. Hardstone, G., d'Adderio, L., Williams, R.: Standardization, Trust and Dependability. In: Clark, K., et al. (eds.) Trust in Technology: A Socio-technical Perspective, pp. 69–103. Springer, Dordrecht (2006)
10. Bertelsen, O.W.: Organisational learning is crystallised into artefacts. SIGOIS Bull. 17(3), 37–39 (1996)
11. Kuutti, K.: Activity theory as a potential framework for human-computer interaction research. In: Nardi, B.A. (ed.) Context and Consciousness: Activity Theory and Human-Computer Interaction, pp. 17–44. Massachusetts Institute of Technology, Cambridge (1995)

12. Seifert, C.M., Hutchins, E.L.: Error as opportunity: learning in a cooperative task. Human-Computer Interaction 7(4), 409–435 (1992)
13. Halverson, C.A., Erickson, T., Ackerman, M.S.: Behind the help desk: evolution of a knowledge management system in a large organization. In: Proceedings of the 2004 ACM conference on Computer supported cooperative work, pp. 304–313. ACM, Chicago (2004)
14. Markus, M.L.: Toward a Theory of Knowledge Reuse: Types of Knowledge Reuse Situations and Factors in Reuse Success. Journal of Management Information Systems 18(1), 57–93 (2001)
15. Ackerman, M.S., Halverson, C.: Considering an organization's memory. In: Proceedings of the 1998 ACM conference on Computer supported cooperative work, pp. 39–48. ACM, Seattle (1998)
16. Clancey, W.J., et al.: Brahms: simulating practice for work systems design. Int. J. Hum.-Comput. Stud. 49(6), 831–865 (1998)
17. Cluts, M.M.: The evolution of artifacts in cooperative work: constructing meaning through activity. In: Proceedings of the 2003 international ACM SIGGROUP conference on Supporting group work, pp. 144–152. ACM, Sanibel Island (2003)
18. Feldman, M.S.: Organizational Routines as a Source of Continuous Change. Organization Science 11(6), 611–629 (2000)
19. Pentland, B.T., Feldman, M.S.: Organizational routines as a unit of analysis. Industrial and Corporate Change 14(5), 793–815 (2005)
20. Wasserman, A.I., Shewmake, D.T.: Rapid prototyping of interactive information systems. In: Proceedings of the Workshop on Rapid Prototyping, Columbia, Maryland. ACM Press, New York (1982)

Designing for Improving Verbal Patient Transfer

Abdullah Al Mahmud, Max Eichenbrenner, and Omar Mubin

Department of Industrial Design,
Eindhoven University of Technology,
P.O. Box 513, 5600 MB Eindhoven, The Netherlands
a.al-mahmud@tue.nl, o.mubin@tue.nl

Abstract. The current verbal patient transfer between nurses and paramedics lacks communication, which leads to loss of information. During this operation, handwritten protocols are used to document the patient's personal data and the treatment given at several intervals. In order to encourage teamwork between the two parties (i.e. nurses and paramedics), the challenge is to present the patient information in a more accessible and feasible way. In this paper, we present the design and evaluation of an interactive and tangible presentation medium that aims to improve the verbal patient transfer by mediated communication. Our result shows that the concept would improve the current verbal patient transfer as evaluated by paramedics and nurses.

1 Introduction

In the pre-hospital phase of an emergency, medical technician and paramedics provide patients with treatment, care and qualified transport to the hospital. During this operation, handwritten protocols are used to document the patient's personal data, the anamnesis and the treatment given at several time intervals. The verbal patient transfer (VPT) is the crucial joint between the pre-hospital and hospital treatment of the patient where information in condensed form has to be presented and understood. It has been observed that the traditional form of VPT in hospitals leads to miscommunication and information loss between the emergency medical technician-paramedics, short paramedics, and nurses [3], [4]. It is stated that the majority of the VPT is only 'partly' performed according to a standard guidelines [2]. In perspective of the nurses, it is stated that most VPT would provide only 'partly' useful information and it is better to gather information on your own instead of listening to the paramedics. Currently used operation protocols would be designed for the information need of a doctor, whereas in hospital most VPT are performed between nurses and paramedics. Even sometimes verbal handover is done without filling the protocol [6]. Further, it is suggested that the communication between the two parties needs to be drastically intensified, to improve the VPT [1]. The goal for this work therefore is to design an interactive and tangible presentation medium to improve the verbal patient transfer by mediated communication. More precisely, the aim is to help improving the verbal patient transfer (VPT), to enhance the quality of the patient treatment and to prevent miscommunication and information loss that may lead to death of patients in worst cases.

T. Gross et al. (Eds.): INTERACT 2009, Part I, LNCS 5726, pp. 574–577, 2009.

2 Design Approach

It was necessary to understand the current workflow and verbal patient transfer (VPT). Therefore, two different research approaches have been followed namely, the Activity-Centered Design (ACD) and the User-Centered Design (UCD) approach [5]. Information was gathered through semi-structured interviews and observations in the work environment A total seven paramedics, seven nurses and two doctors from five hospitals and four fire departments were interviewed in several iterations to gather insights about the workflow and the social coherence of information during patient transfers.

Verbal Patient Transfer (VPT). The quality of the VPT is highly dependant on the presenter and the receiver type. In case a doctor is present, it was stated that the VPT was generally better performed by the paramedics. The interviewed paramedics had the belief that VPT performed with the nurses was problematic. Main sources of miscommunication and information loss could be defined as: the mental state of the presenter (i.e. nervous, less conscious and unmotivated), the missing structure (i.e. coherent story line) and missing abstraction (i.e. highlight level of importance). The paramedics stated confusion, caused by similar operations and forgetting details as the major sources of miscommunication and information loss. Concerning the interaction, the paramedics stated that they would miss the nurse's feedback, whether the information was understood.

Protocol. An interview with an experienced attendant revealed that the operation protocols are commonly thrown in the bin without putting an effort in evaluating them. Interviewed nurses stated "the changing status of the patient and the tendency of higher measurements during the transport" as the reason for neglecting the protocols. In summary, the nurses did not perceive the protocol as their responsibility. One interviewee mentioned she experienced frustration with the poorly written protocols. Generally, it can be stated that the current handwritten protocols find no acceptance by the nurses and thus are not suitable as supporting element of the VPT.

Concept Design and Implementation. Based on the above results, consultation with nurses and paramedics a concept of intelligent table named 'DACCORD' was developed. It uses a so-called data terminal, a laptop with a touch screen and UMTS/VPN connection, to send the patient information in the form of an .xml document from the ambulance directly to the hospital. The DACCORD concept (Fig. 1) transfers this .xml document into an interactive interface. Two different access points located opposite each other are designed to fit the individual tasks of the communication partners. Both sides are equipped with a separate screen showing the same content. The presenter's (paramedic) side uses a slider for navigating through the interface. The receiver's (nurse or doctor) side is equipped with a notepad, to add information and an accept buzzer. The accept buzzer allows the information receiver to give feedback whether he/she understands and agrees. An additional LED light on each side of the table, called side leafs, are depicting information of the level of emergence by color. The two table halves were positioned in a 15-degree angle, which allows good visibility of the screen in front and slight visibility of the other screen. Together with an expert from the fire department and the hospital, two cases were defined which were representative for the whole range of operations.

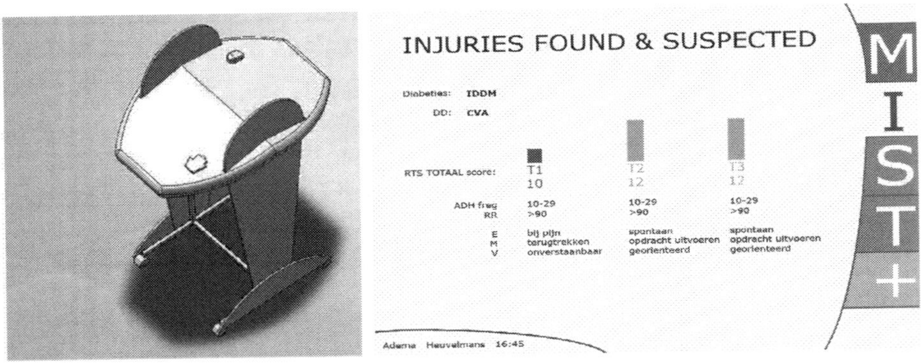

Fig. 1. Implementation: table (left), interface layout (right)

It was decided to define an emergent case, a poly-trauma, and a less emergent case in the form of a diabetes patient. To create the interface, the currently used handwritten protocol and the digital protocol were analyzed. The digital protocol was completed by an expert from the fire department according to the two cases. Furthermore, the official guideline in the Netherlands, called the 'MIST' (i.e. measurements, injuries, signs and treatment) schema, which describes content of the VPT was studied. Based on the documents, first versions of the interface were sketched. Depending on the sketches a digital version of the interface was created. To create the content, relevant information was filtered from the .xml document of the completed digital protocol and the handwritten protocol. This information was then sorted into the basic structure of the official 'MIST scheme'. The Revised Trauma Score (RTS), composed of a combination of results from Glasgow Coma Scale, Systolic Blood Pressure, and respiratory rate was transferred into a graph. This graph (Fig. 1) illustrates in form of bars by three different sizes and colors the condition of the patient over time.

3 Evaluation

In total two tests were performed with four users. For each user test one nurse or attendant and one paramedic participated. The user evaluation aimed for questions concerning usability and user experience that could possibly lead to improvements of the design. The user test was divided into two steps. Firstly, the system was introduced and time for one individual 'practice round' was given. Secondly, the participants got a real case and were asked to perform a VPT using the system. To make sure, the participants use the full range of functions, they received a task list beforehand. The session closed with an interview.

Overall, the DACCORD concept was understood by all of the medical staff. Based on the short instructions, the participants were able to perform the 'practice round' individually. The instruction including the 'practice round' of the system took 10 minutes and should be a part of the real deployment of the DACCORD table. The system helped the paramedics to present the information in a more structured manner. Statements such as "clear interface, you cannot miss it. It goes step by step", support this conclusion. The system aided the nurses in the VPT process. This can be reasoned by observing the following qualitative remarks: "I can see the told information", "No more information is presented than I need", "I do not have to search" and "I have control of accepting" (in reference to the accept button). The system demands to process auditory and visual information at the same time. This was considered as 'easy' by all participants. As an improvement, participants suggested a clear distinction between the two access points. Furthermore, the nurses and paramedics suggested being in control of the uploading of the patient data instead of the server. It should be noted that the total number of four users is not sufficient but we were restricted by the availability of the user group in a real setting. The test could not include a patient, who could cause interruptions and unexpected behavior during a natural VPT process. Furthermore, the test worked with an already filled out protocol. In future, we will compare previous systems with the DACCORD prototype.

4 Conclusions

The main benefit of the DACCORD concept lies in creating face-to-face communication through tangible interaction and in providing a modality to give or receive feedback. The paramedics valued that the concept would urge them to go through every step. Whereas the nurses valued that, the concept forces the communication partners to face each other at one location. Such a system would stimulate cooperation between the pre-hospital and hospital patient treatment by lending information accessibility and transparency. This newly created information chain would result in a faster and quality enhanced patient treatment and prevention of miscommunication and information loss which could be detrimental to the patients health.

References

1. Berger, B.: Patientenübergabe zwischen Rettungsdienst und Ambulanzpersonal aus Sicht des Rettungsdienstpersonals, XIII. Innsbrucker Notfallsymposium (2004)
2. Currie, J.: Improving the efficiency of patient handover. J. Emerg Nurse 10(3), 24–27 (2002)
3. Jenkin, A., Abelson-Mitchell, N., et al.: Patient handover: Time for a change? J. Accident & Emergency Nursing 15(3), 141–147 (2007)
4. Jones, J.S., Dwyer, P.R., et al.: Patient transfer from nursing home to emergency department: outcomes and policy implications. J. Acad Emerg Med 4(9), 908–915 (1997)
5. Saffer, D.: Designing for interaction; creating smart applications and clever devices (2007)
6. Yong, G., Dent, A., et al.: Handover from paramedics: Observations and emergency department clinician perceptions. J. Emergency Medicine Australasia 20(2), 149–155 (2008)

Exploring Manual Interaction and Social Behaviour Patterns in Intensely Collaborative Teamwork

Natalie Ruiz[1,2], Kelvin Cheng[1], and Markus Rittenbruch[1]

[1] NICTA
Level 5, 13 Garden Street, Eveleigh, NSW 2015, Australia
[2] UNSW
Sydney, NSW 2052, Australia
firstname.lastname@nicta.com.au

Abstract. This paper presents the results of a comparative study of 4-person collaborative teams working at a traditional table with pen and paper vs. a multi-touch table with digital keyboards and notepads. We compare the social behaviours of 'giving' and 'taking' during intensely collaborative teamwork, namely the differences between paper-based behaviour, digital-object based behaviour and a mixed condition behaviour where both paper and digital objects were used. Differences in sharing behaviour may be attributed to the degree of ownership afforded by digital objects on a touch display vs. paper objects. Additional visual metaphors to help tabletop users are recommended.

Keywords: Manual gestures, CSCW, Multi-touch table, paper vs. digital.

1 Introduction

The recent development of multitouch interactive surfaces (e.g. using Frustrated Total Internal Reflection) has introduced a new interaction paradigm that allows teams of people to manipulate digital artefacts simultaneously, in natural and intuitive ways. Ideally, no learning or training for specific gestures is required in such a scenario: users can treat digital artefacts just as they would paper artefacts, thus supporting intense collaboration, such that the technology becomes transparent.

Previous research has investigated paper-based group behaviour and space allocation on shared surfaces [1] in order to inform digital surface interaction design. Other literature examines ways to provide support for documents on digital tabletops such as orientation and surface interaction [2]; still others consider the suitability of specific gestures to be used for various digital document functions to inform manual gesture interaction design [3]. Nevertheless, paper and digital objects are fundamentally different, comprising disparate physical, visual and tangible characteristics. For this reason, the paper-based collaboration paradigm cannot simply be translated into a surface implementation of digital objects.

In one particular study we found in the literature, survey responses were used to capture hypothetical differences between the manipulation strategies of paper and digital objects [4]. We further this notion of artefacts shared on interactive surfaces with a comparative study between digital, paper and mixed artefact scenarios. We

T. Gross et al. (Eds.): INTERACT 2009, Part I, LNCS 5726, pp. 578–581, 2009.

investigate the social interaction within teams, naturally sharing and handling both paper and digital artefacts, during an intensely collaborative – and meaningful – task.

In this study, we look at the *giving and taking* differences in sharing digital and paper objects. We hypothesise that more *giving* behaviour would be seen in the paper only scenario compared to the digital objects scenario. Giving behaviour is exemplified by directly handing objects over to another team member or to the public arena. However, more *taking* behaviour would be evident in the scenario with digital objects than in the scenario with only paper objects. Taking behaviour comprises actively taking objects held by other individuals or taking objects from the group's common resource. Finally, we expected that paper-based behaviours would converge into mixed condition (paper and digital artefacts) behaviour. The reasons for this, we believe, are related to the degree of feelings of personal ownership of paper objects versus digital objects. Drawing from everyday sharing behaviours, when an object is considered to be under one's ownership, it is more easily 'given' than an object that is part of the public domain. Likewise, objects that are considered to be part of the public domain are more likely to be 'taken' by individual team members. We believe that giving and taking patterns can affect the relative individual contributions of each team member in a group task, and the overall team performance, during intensely collaborative tasks.

2 User Study Design

Ten teams of four friends participated in the study, members ranging from engineers to corporate staff. The task required subjects to compile five lists, each with as many semantically related words as possible. A single word was provided to start off the semantic list, e.g. NURSE. Single related words such as DOCTOR or PATIENT were added by group members one by one.

Fig. 1. Digital, paper and mixed conditions

Three conditions were administered. In the paper only condition, subjects were required to write words using five different coloured pens on five matching pieces of coloured cardboards. In the digital only condition, five different coloured keyboards were used to input the words into five matching coloured note windows. A Multi-touch Cell [5] surface was used for the implementation of this task, supporting natural manual movement of digital objects. Finally, in the mixed condition, subjects were required to use two digital item sets, as well as three coloured paper sets. Conditions were balanced to counter order effects (with the mixed condition always last). The paper condition was limited to 2 minutes duration, and the other two conditions limited to 3 minutes duration.

Annotations. We devised an annotation scheme to capture various *giving* and *taking* behaviours, as shown in Table 1. To begin with, we annotated a one-minute sample from the middle of the task of each condition, for each team, and each participant.

Table 1. Annotation Scheme of Sharing Behaviour

Sharing	*ID*	*Type*	*Description*
Giving	G1	Direct Give	Directly passing an object to another individual
	G2	Passive Give	Passing an object at someone's request
	G3	Give to Centre	Actively putting an object in the public domain
	G4	Reactive Give	Object in your personal space- allow others to take it
Taking	T1	Direct Take	Directly taking an object from another individual
	T2	Passive Receive	Taking an object given directly by someone else
	T3	Take from Centre	Actively taking an object from the public domain
	T4	Reactive Take	Taking an object that happened to be near you

3 Preliminary Findings

The analysis included a total of 882 instances of sharing behaviour across groups. Given the inter-group dependencies in terms of strategy and performance, each group was first assessed individually, before acquiring an average across groups of *give-to-take* ratios, and normalized with a log function (Figure 2). A ratio value of zero means equal give vs. take, positive values mean more giving, negatives more taking.

In the digital-only condition, the ratio of *give-to-take* behaviour in each group ranged from -0.41 to -0.05, with a collective average between groups of -0.19. This means that subjects were more likely to display *taking* behaviours than *giving* behaviours when using digital objects, substantiating our first hypothesis. In the paper-only scenario, the group ratios of *give-to-take* ranged from -0.08 to 0.06, with an average across groups of 0.01, indicating the proportion of *giving* and *taking* were roughly equal. Finally, in the mixed condition, the group ratios of *give-to-take* ranged from -0.2 to 0.15, with an average of -0.02, indicating that the sharing behaviour converged toward the paper condition as expected. A one-way, correlated samples, ANOVA shows significant differences between groups ($df=29$, $F=18.05$, $p<0.0001$). Subsequent Tukey HSD tests show significant differences at the 0.01 level between the mixed and digital only conditions; and between paper only and digital only conditions. Analyses specifically on person-to-person (G1 and T1) and person-to-public (G3) or public-to-person (T3) 'pro-active' behaviours, where subjects directly move objects, highlight very similar patterns.

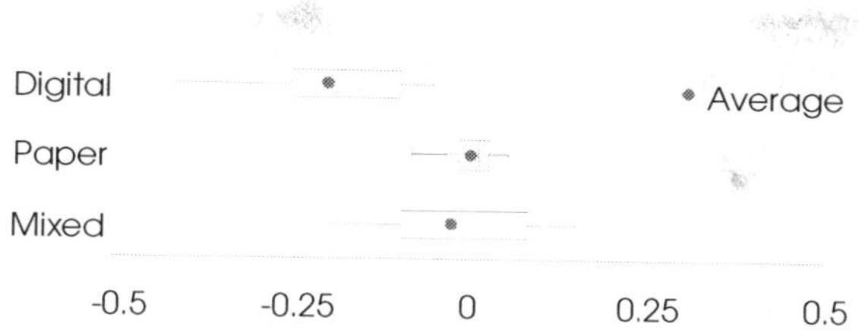

Fig. 2. Summary of *give-to-take* ratios across groups for each condition

4 Discussion and Future Work

As expected, subjects exhibited more *giving* behaviours in the digital only condition; likewise, more *taking* behaviours in the paper only condition, with the mixed condition converging to paper-like behaviour. Since the multi-touch table allows natural gesture to be used for movement of digital objects, these differences may be attributed to the feelings of ownership afforded by each set of materials. It is possible that tangible paper objects, due to their physical characteristics, *feel* more like the property of the individual manipulating them than digital objects. Proportionately fewer giving behaviours in the digital condition may be symptomatic of this. Though digital objects were far more malleable (could change in size and were more dynamic, bounced off the sides etc.), this plasticity did not seem to make any difference to their 'ownership status'. While they could be moved into each individual's personal space and into public spaces just like paper, they seemed to remain "behind the glass", engendering a feeling of perceptual distance between the team and the items.

Drawing more general design implications from this result, it seems that digital object scenarios may benefit from the implementation of visual effects or widgets that convey a greater sense of ownership. For example, 'magnetic personal areas' where objects are pulled towards, and attached to, personal spaces when passed around, may help encourage stronger notions of ownership between objects and participants. Future work includes further analysis of the social behaviour categories annotated.

References

1. Scott, S.D., Sheelagh, M., Carpendale, T., Inkpen, K.M.: Territoriality in collaborative tabletop workspaces. In: Proc.CSCW 2004, Chicago, November 6-10, pp. 294–303. ACM, New York (2004)
2. Shen, C., Everitt, K.M., Ryall, K.: UbiTable: Impromptu Face-to-Face Collaboration on Horizontal Interactive Surfaces. In: ACM Int. Conf. on UbiComp (October 2003)
3. Wobbrock, J.O., Morris, M.R., Wilson, A.D.: User-defined gestures for surface computing. In: Proc.CHI 2009, Boston, April 4-9, pp. 1083–1092. ACM, New York (2009)
4. Morris, M.R.: Supporting Effective Interaction With Tabletop Groupware. Stanford University Technical Report (April 2006)
5. Multitouch Cell, `http://multitouch.fi/`

A Comparison of Direct and Indirect Multi-touch Input for Large Surfaces

Dominik Schmidt, Florian Block, and Hans Gellersen

Computing Department, Lancaster University, Lancaster, UK
{schmidtd,block,hwg}@comp.lancs.ac.uk

Abstract. Multi-touch input on interactive surfaces has matured as a device for bimanual interaction and invoked widespread research interest. We contribute empirical work on direct versus indirect use multi-touch input, comparing direct input on a tabletop display with an indirect condition where the table is used as input surface to a separate, vertically arranged display surface. Users perform significantly better in the direct condition; however our experiments show that this is primarily the case for pointing with comparatively little difference for dragging tasks. We observe that an indirect input arrangement impacts strongly on the users' fluidity and comfort of 'hovering' movement over the surface, and suggest investigation of techniques that allow users to rest their hands on the surface as default position for interaction.

Keywords: Multi-touch interfaces, surface computing, indirect input.

1 Introduction

Multi-touch input on interactive surfaces has been studied for over 25 years, from early work on tablets as separate input device [14] to more recent direct multi- touch on interactive tabletops [7, 10]. Multi-touch supports natural use of both hands for bimanual tasks and greatly expands the range of gestural input that can be used in interaction [6, 26]. This is inspiring widespread research activity on multi-touch interactive tabletops [22], but empirical insight into multi-touch input performance is still limited.

Recent work on multi-touch input has tended to imply its use for direct interaction. As noted by Forlines et al. [9], it is commonly argued that direct touch is more "natural" or "compelling" than working with an indirect input de- vice. Forlines et al. took this to motivate a study comparing direct multi-touch with indirect mouse input (providing evidence for their respective advantages for bimanual and single-pointer tasks). We, in turn, ask how much the benefit of multi-touch for bimanual tasks depends on the directness of the input. Intuitively, direct multi-touch would appear superior to indirect multi-touch. However indirect interaction, where the hands are off the output medium, can have a variety of advantages depending on application context, for example interaction at-a-distance, separate input surfaces for multiple users, avoidance of occlusions [21], or one input surface to multiple displays [19].

The contribution of this paper is an empirical study of direct versus indirect use multi-touch input. The study compares direct input on a tabletop display with an

T. Gross et al. (Eds.): INTERACT 2009, Part I, LNCS 5726, pp. 582–594, 2009.

indirect condition where the table is used for input only, with output on separate display. Figure 1 illustrates the two conditions. In the direct condition, input and output space coincide. In the indirect condition, output is on a display arranged vertically behind the input surface; for reference between input and output space, the user's hand contours are displayed.

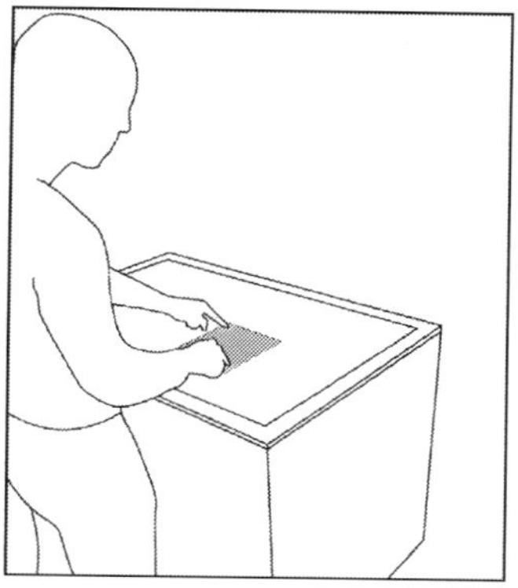

(a) *Direct multi-touch:* input and output space coincide

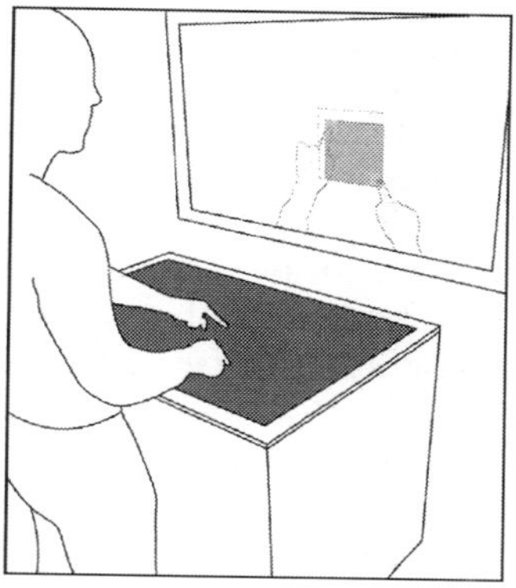

(b) *Indirect multi-touch:* separate output with display of hand contours

Fig. 1. Direct versus indirect multi-touch interaction

We describe an experiment that investigates direct versus indirect multi-touch for a symmetric bimanual task, in terms of quantitative performance, qualitative observations, and user preference. The results overall indicate that users are faster with multi-touch for direct interaction but are also able to use multi-touch efficiently for indirect input. A main observation was that users approach tasks differently in the two conditions, in the direct condition with fluid movement to a target, and in the indirect condition with hovering movement until a target has reached, resulting not only in longer selection time but also less comfort. The discomfort with hovering over the surface to avoid accidental touch suggests adoption of multi-touch techniques that would allow user to rest their hands on the surface for interaction.

2 Related Work

The performance of direct and indirect input modalities for bimanual tasks on interactive surfaces has been scarcely explored. Forlines et al. compared direct- touch with mouse input for bimanual and single-pointer tasks, highlighting their different advantages [9]. Barnert described a similar experiment on dual-mouse versus multi-touch [2]. These studies provide some insight into suitability for the respective interfaces for unimanual versus bimanual tasks. Our work, in contrast, is focused on a single input modality (multi-touch on interactive surfaces), to analyze its use and performance in direct versus indirect interaction.

Direct versus indirect input has been studied widely for single-pointer interaction, comparing indirect input devices with direct-touch or pen input (e.g., [20, 23]). A recent study is close to ours in spirit, as it focuses on a single in- put technology, here a stylus pen, which is compared for direct and indirect interaction showing that indirect use can perform as well for certain tasks [8].

Multi-touch technology has become closely associated with interactive displays and direct interaction, however a variety of recent systems have been based on multi-touch input separate from output. Malik et al. demonstrated a system that integrates multi-touch input for interaction with multiple displays in the environment [19]. In other work, Moscovich et al. investigate indirect multi- touch techniques aimed to overcome limitations of direct-touch interaction on touchscreens (e.g., limited precision, occlusion issues, and limitations on size and proximity of the display) [21].

In this work we focus on the use of multi-touch technology that has more recently evolved with interactive tabletops [10, 26]. However, our work also ties in with a large body of earlier work on bimanual interaction (e.g., [1, 5, 13, 15]).

To support indirect multi-touch, we track and display hand contours. This concept was first demonstrated in Krueger et al.'s Videoplace [12]. In recent work, a related technique was used for 'see-through' multi-touch input on the back of a mobile device, addressing occlusion and precision limitations of multi-touch 'on the front' of the device [24].

3 Experimental Design

The principal aim of our study was to gain insight into direct versus indirect use of multi-touch input for bimanual tasks. We specifically sought to understand performance differences (are users slower when input is indirect, and how much so?), principal obstacles in using multi-touch indirectly (are users able to use multi-touch effectively when input is displaced from output?), and potential qualitative differences in interaction behavior (do users approach tasks differently when input is separate from output?).

22 users took part in the study (10 female, 12 male). They were recruited from the local campus and compensated with £8 for their time. The age ranged from 18 to 53 years with an average of 27.23 years (SD = 7.79). All participants but one were right-handed and regular computer users without specific experience in bimanual interfaces.

3.1 Apparatus

The experiment was designed to compare direct and indirect multi-touch in the configuration we introduced in Figure 1. Both conditions use the same tabletop technology as input surface. In the direct condition, the surface doubles as display. In the indirect condition, the display is provided on a separate screen arranged vertically behind the input surface. In both conditions, the respective other display is turned off. The size of the vertical display is chosen to appear, from the user's perspective, to be the same size as the input surface. This preserves the 1:1 ratio of input and output spaces across the two conditions. Mapping between input and output is supported with a contour display of the user's hands, and with display of circles as feedback for points of touch.

(a) *Direct multi-touch* (b) *Indirect multi-touch*

Fig. 2. User interacting with multi-touch table and vertical screen

The experimental setup is shown in Figure 2. The tabletop had a surface diagonal of 100cm with rear projection display of 1280 × 768px. Touch detection was based on a diffused illumination principle, using a Point Grey Firefly MV camera with a resolution of 640 × 480px at 60fps to capture points of touch. The vertical display was provided by a 126cm plasma screen with the same resolution as the tabletop display. A second camera (same model) was mounted on the ceiling to track the position and contour of the user's hands over the tabletop. The hands were extracted from the captured image, processed by an edge detection algorithm, and mapped using homography.

3.2 Task

Figure 3 illustrates the 2D symmetric bimanual task used in this experiment. In order to build upon the literature, the task was designed according to the bimanual task in

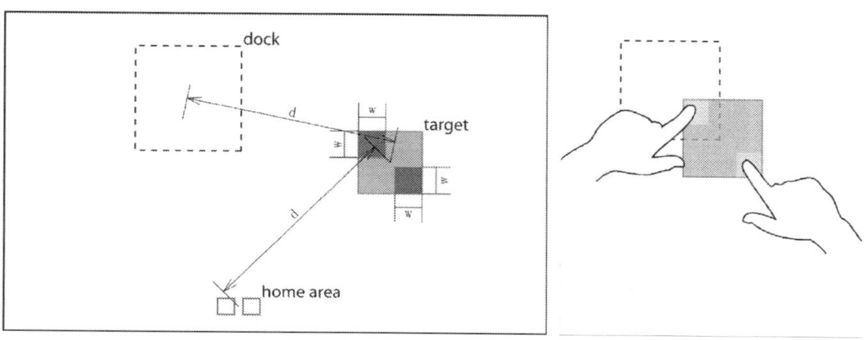

(a) Task layout: home area, target, and dock; same distance d between home area and target respectively target and dock; square handles of side length w

(b) Dragging and resizing selected target to match dock

Fig. 3. Task design: pointing (starting in home area) and dragging (target onto dock)

Forlines et al.'s [9] experiment. It consists of a pointing and a dragging subtask, both common interaction techniques in direct manipulation interfaces, but shown to yield difference performance behavior [18]. Additionally, the dragging subtask requires the user to simultaneously perform a resizing operation similar to the "stretchies" technique proposed by Kurtenbach et al. [13] but limited to translation and scaling.

At the beginning of each task, a home area is shown at an arbitrary location, consisting of two red, non-filled squares. Participants were instructed to touch these squares, using one finger of each hand. To prevent participants from rushing through tasks, a waiting time was introduced before target and dock appeared. To complete the pointing subtask, participants had to select the target's two handles. The target was rendered as blue, semi-transparent square with two square handles in the opposite corners. While the target had a fixed size of 150px square the handles' sizes were varied as part of the experiment. Providing visual feedback, selected handles were highlighted in a brighter color. Moreover, once both handles—and hence the target—were selected the target's color changed from blue to green.

To complete the dragging subtask, participants had to match the target with the dock by translating and scaling the target (compare figure 3(b)). The dock was rendered as outlined square with a dashed, black border at a fixed size of 250px square. The target's size could be adjusted by changing the handle's relative position. It was sufficient to match the four edges accurately within 10px each which was indicated by changing the dock's border and fill color. The dragging task was successfully completed once target and dock were matched and the user had released at least one of the handles.

Home area, target, and dock positions were randomized but precalculated for all trials, i.e. each user was presented with the same position constellations. In addition to the handle size, the distance between home area and target respectively target and dock was simultaneously varied as part of the experiment. Participants were instructed to perform the task as quickly and accurately as possible. It was not possible to move on to the next task before the matching and hence the task was completed successfully.

3.3 Design and Procedure

A repeated-measures design was used with the within participant independent variables *interaction condition* (direct, indirect), *handle width* (32, 48, 64px), and distance (300, 500, 700px). Every combination of handle width and distance was repeated three times. With 27 trials per block, every user performed five blocks resulting in 135 trials per user and condition and a total number of 5940 trials.

Participants were introduced to the interface and the concept of multi-touch interaction. The experiment started with two training blocks which were followed by the three blocks used in the analysis. Participants completed both input conditions in succession and their order was counterbalanced. Each participant was presented with the same set of precalculated trials. However, the presentation order of trials within a block was pseudo-randomized for every user. The same set of blocks was used for testing the direct and indirect conditions.

After each condition, participants were asked to state their agreement with eight items[1] selected from the *IBM Computer Usability Satisfaction Questionnaire* [16] on

[1] Statements 2, 4, 5, 6, 7, 9, 17, and 19 of the *Post-Study System Usability Questionnaire* were selected as applicable to the test system.

a seven point Likert scale ranging from "strongly agree" to "strongly disagree". In addition, participants were also asked to rate the amount of mental demand required to fulfill the task as well as their frustration level and to give a self-assessment of their performance, using three items from the *NASA Task Load Index* [11]. In the end of the experiment, participants were asked to state a preference and their subjective rating about performance and error rates for each condition.

The measured variables were overall trial time (pointing + dragging time), pointing time, dragging time, pointing errors, dragging errors, and handle selection delay. Additionally, we recorded video footage of all participants with the camera placed at the shorter side of the table slightly above its surface to capture arm and hand movements as well as hand postures.

4 Results

4.1 Quantitative Measurements

Trial Time. Trial time is the sum of pointing and dragging time. It was measured in milliseconds from the moment when the user left the home area to the moment when he or she completed the docking successfully. A 3-Way Repeated Measures ANOVA of the recorded data indicates a significant main effect of *condition* on the trial time, $F_{1,21} = 216.86$, $p < 0.001$. Participants completed a trial quicker in the direct condition ($M = 4311$, $SD = 1787$) than in the indirect condition ($M = 6700$, $SD = 2704$). Figure 4(a) shows mean trial times broken down by pointing and dragging time.

(a) Mean trial time for each *condition* broken down by pointing and dragging time

(b) Mean trial time for each *condition* broken down by *width*

Fig. 4. Mean trial times

Both, *width* and *distance* have main effects on trial time, $F_{2,42} = 45.05$, $p < 0.001$ and $F_{2,42} = 91.94$, $p < 0.001$ for *width* and *distance* respectively. The only significant interaction revealed by the analysis is *condition* × *width*, $F_{2,42} = 5.99$, $p = 0.005$, indicating that the effect of *width* on trial time differed for the two conditions. Contrasts on this interaction term revealed that when the difference in trial time between direct and indirect condition was compared for 32 and 48px there was no significant difference, $F_{2,42} = 0.56$, $p = 0.465$. However, comparing the difference in trial time between direct and indirect for 48 and 64px, a significant difference emerged ($F_{2,42} = 7.75$, $p = 0.011$) which indicates that the decline in trial time between 48 and 64px was significantly more pronounced in the indirect condition (compare figure 4).

Pointing Time. Pointing time was measured in milliseconds from the moment when the user left the home area to the moment when he or she had success- fully acquired both of the target's handles. As erroneous trials were not repeated the user continued until the selection was successful. Therefore, pointing time includes time required to correct errors. An ANOVA of the recorded data indicates that pointing time was significantly shorter in the direct ($M = 811$, $SD = 505$) than in the indirect condition ($M = 2386$, $SD = 995$), $F_{1,21} = 357.75$, $p < 0.001$.

Both, *width* and *distance*, have main effects on pointing time, $F_{1.63,34.14} = 162.26$, $p < 0.001$ (corrected degrees of freedom using Huynh-Feldt estimates of sphericity) and $F_{2,42} = 91.09$, $p < 0.001$ for *width* and *distance* respectively. The *condition* × *width* interaction is significant, $F_{1.6,33.61} = 37.86$, $p < 0.001$ (Huynh- Feldt), and so is the *condition* × *distance* interaction ($F_{2,42} = 19.06$, $p < 0.001$), indicating that the effect of *width* respectively *distance* on pointing time differed for the two conditions. No significant interaction between *condition*, *width*, and *distance* was found. Figure 5 shows the mean pointing time for each width and distance, separated for each condition.

Contrasts on the *condition* × *width* interaction term revealed that when the difference in pointing time between direct and indirect condition was compared for 32 and 48px respectively 48 and 64px, significant differences emerged in both comparisons ($F_{1,21} = 27.7$, $p < 0.001$ respectively $F_{1,21} = 19.73$, $p < 0.001$). Likewise, contrasts indicated a significant differences in pointing time between direct and indirect condition for 300 and 500px ($F_{1,21} = 5.47$, $p = 0.029$) and 500 and 700px ($F_{1,21} = 23.21$, $p < 0.001$). To sum up, the decline in pointing time for larger handles as well as shorter distances was significantly more pronounced in the indirect condition.

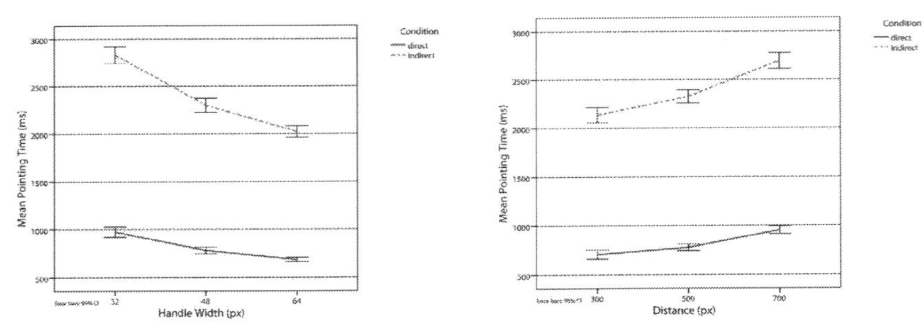

(a) Broken down by *width* (b) Broken down by *distance*

Fig. 5. Mean pointing time for each *condition*

Pointing Errors. A pointing error would be registered if the participant missed either handle. Multiple pointing errors could occur as the trial would not be reset if an error was made. An ANOVA shows that significantly fewer errors were made in the direct

($M = 0.16$, $SD = 0.6$) than in the indirect condition ($M = 0.57$, $SD = 1.21$), $F_{1,21} = 55.48$, $p < 0.001$.

Both, *width* and *distance*, have main effects on pointing error, $F_{2,42} = 14.66$, $p < 0.001$ and $F_{2,42} = 6.9$, $p = 0.003$ for *width* and *distance* respectively. No significant interaction between *condition* and *width* or *distance* was found.

Dragging Time. Dragging time was measured in milliseconds from the moment of successful acquisition of both handles to the moment the user released either handle while the target was accurately enough aligned with the dock. Time required to reacquire handles after errors is included in this measure. An ANOVA suggests that dragging time was significantly shorter in the direct ($M = 3500$, $SD = 1619$) than in the indirect condition ($M = 4315$, $SD = 2358$), $F_{1,21} = 31.39$, $p < 0.001$.

Both, *width* and *distance*, have main effects on dragging time, $F_{2,42} = 6.44$, $p = 0.004$ and $F_{2,42} = 43.23$, $p < 0.001$ for *width* and *distance* respectively. No significant interaction between any factors was found.

Dragging Errors. A dragging error occurred when either handle was left while dragging. Multiple dragging errors could occur within a single trial. An ANOVA indicates a significant main effect of *condition* on dragging errors, $F_{1,21} = 5.72$, $p = 0.026$. Participants completed the dragging subtask with fewer errors in the direct ($M = 0.36$, $SD = 1.3$) than in the indirect condition ($M = 0.68$, $SD = 2.64$). No further significant effects were found.

Handle Selection Delay. Furthermore, we measured the delay in milliseconds between the initial selection of the first and second handle. An ANOVA revealed that this delay was significantly lower ($F_{1,21} = 36.43$, $p < 0.001$) in the direct ($M = 133$, $SD = 317$) than indirect ($M = 525$, $SD = 595$) condition.

Both, *width* and *distance*, have main effects on handle selection delay, $F_{2,42} = 71.47$, $p < 0.001$ and $F_{2,42} = 7.7$, $p = 0.001$ for *width* and *distance* respectively. Additionally, the *condition* × *width* interaction is significant, $F_{1.6,34.75} = 11.51$, $p < 0.001$ (Huynh-Feldt). No further interactions were found.

4.2 Observations

The following descriptions are based on observations made during the experiment and on a post-hoc analysis of the recorded video. In general, the task was easily understood by the participants, independent of which condition was tested first.

However, a noticeable difference regarding the way users approached the surface with their arms and hands could be observed. While many participants relaxed their hands by slightly changing the hands' postures or moving them around the wrist in between trials when interacting directly on the table, their hands remained in a rather static posture, mostly hovering over the surface and already focusing on moving to the home area again when interacting with the screen. We also observed that users often maintained a more tense hand posture in the indirect than in the direct condition. In this context, several users were intuitively relaxing and shaking their hands in between blocks in the indirect condition.

In addition, we could observe that participants were more likely to break down the pointing movements in the indirect condition. First, they aligned their fingers with the target to point at. Second, they moved their fingers down to touch the surface. In the direct condition, the pointing task resembled more a fluid single movement. Moreover, it was obvious that many participants followed a sequential strategy to select the two handles of a target in the indirect condition. Only after they positioned their finger over one handle and then put it down to make the selection, they started to adjust the position of their other hand's finger.

We observed that several users tried to apply a different strategy in the pointing task when interacting with the screen. They left their fingers on the surface while sliding towards the target, then lift the fingers up and put them down again to select the target. In these cases, users were asked to perform the pointing as originally instructed.

A potential problem which we noted in this user study concerns long finger nails. They prevent users from touching the table in a steep angle which causes more unintended touches. Moreover, they make the fingers appear longer in the hand contour representation which results in a mismatch between the displayed fingertip and the actual point of touch.

4.3 User Feedback

Quantitative Feedback. Participants consistently rated the direct condition better in both, the satisfaction questionnaire and the task load index. Wilcoxon Signed-Rank Tests indicate that these differences are significant for each rating.

Results show that 3 out of 22 (13.64%) participants preferred the indirect condition. Moreover, three (different) participants stated that they were faster in the indirect condition; two of them also felt they made fewer errors in it. In addition, one of those who preferred the indirect condition also stated he made fewer errors in it. However, none of these ratings regarding time and error rate are reflected in the collected data.

Qualitative Feedback. In addition to the previous ratings, we asked participants to comment on positive as well as negative aspects of the tested conditions during and in the end of the experiment. Ten participants perceived the direct condition to be easier than the indirect condition. Five participants noted that more mental effort was required to complete the tasks in the indirect condition; they felt they had to concentrate and think more or were more tired afterwards. Twelve of the participating users stated that it was difficult to coordinate their hands with the respective contours displayed on the screen. In addition, two of them reported on having problems with distinguishing their fingers on the screen, hence they only used their index fingers in a pointing posture.

In the direct condition, two participants said they had experienced problems with occlusion due to their arms or hands covering parts of the table; three participants felt they had a better overview or visibility with the screen. We received five comments indicating that the indirect condition is more comfortable mainly due to problems that occur in the direct condition when looking down at the table for a prolonged period of time. However, further seven participants perceived the direct condition as more comfortable to work with; three of them noted that this is due to a higher amount of physical stress for the fingers in the indirect condition.

Further comments reached from describing the indirect setup as a fun system with an appealing idea that one user even could imagine to be working with comfortably in a job over the day, to statements about how nerve breaking this kind of interaction was perceived. One user noted that she hated the indirect condition while another saw it as a training tool for multitasking abilities.

5 Discussion

In general, completion times were shorter and error rates lower in the direct condition throughout all results. This difference in speed and accuracy was also perceived by most participants when asked for a comparative assessment of the two conditions. In addition, results of task load index show that participants rated their performance better in the direct than in the indirect condition. Furthermore, agreement with the two statements of the usability satisfaction questionnaire which are concerned with speed and efficiency also underlinesS these results.

One possible explanation for this measured and perceived performance decrease can be found in the additional cognitive load present in the indirect condition. Not only the task load evaluation revealed a higher demand for mental and perceptual activity in the indirect condition, also the qualitative feedback we received suggested that more concentration was required. In addition, the input hardware was identical in both conditions which suggests that observed differences are due to an added complexity of coordination. In summary, interacting indirectly with the system was more challenging for participants and resulted in a significantly higher frustration level.

5.1 Differences in Pointing and Dragging

Times. In accordance with findings of related studies [9, 18], dragging was slower than pointing, independent of the condition. It is noteworthy that the overall trial time was decreased by the same factor in our study as in the one by Forlines et al. [9], although different input techniques were used in the indirect condition. Additionally, it is important to acknowledge that the dragging was more demanding than the pointing task by design since it included positioning and scaling. However, while it took participants on average 2390ms (55%) longer to complete a trial in the indirect condition, the already shorter pointing time contributed 1575ms (66%) to this total time difference between direct and indirect interaction; only 815ms were due to differences in dragging performance. That is, it took participants about 200% longer to complete a pointing task in the indirect condition, while we only observed a time decrease of 23% for the dragging task. These results suggest that differences in the conditions had more impact on completion time for pointing than dragging.

Moreover, significant interactions between *condition* and *width* as well as *distance* were found for pointing time. Contrasts on these interaction terms reveal that the smaller the target is, the larger is the pointing time difference between direct and indirect condition. On the same lines, larger distances have a higher impact on pointing time in the indirect condition. That is, smaller targets respectively larger distances seem to render the pointing task unequally more time consuming in the indirect compared to the direct condition. In contrast to pointing time, there is no indication that *width* or *distance* had a significant influence on the difference in dragging time between conditions, suggesting that there is less complexity added in the indirect condition compared to pointing.

While our experiment was designed to include error trials it is still insightful to look at times without errors. A brief analysis of only those pointing tasks without errors reveals completion times which are around 11% lower in both conditions; indirect pointing is still about 200% slower. However, an analog analysis for dragging times shows that the speed advantage of direct over indirect interaction for dragging is further decreased. In trials without errors we only observed a time decrease of 13% for dragging between the direct and indirect condition, also indicating a smaller discrepancy in complexity between direct and indirect interaction.

Errors. Since a trial was not interrupted on errors but continued until successfully completed, it is no surprise to find a similar tendency of differences between interaction conditions as seen for completion times in the respective error rates, too. While participants were more than three times as likely to make a pointing error in the indirect than direct condition, a dragging error was only less than twice as likely made.

Yet it is important to account for the relatively high dragging error rates observed in our study compared to values found in literature for a similar task [9]. First, it was sufficient to position the target over the dock in the said study; matching was performed automatically. Our experiment required participants to actively release the handles, though, resulting in a more complex and error prone task. Second, we used a vision-based input technology which is more sensitive to touches and capable of detecting non-finger contacts, too. In specific, we observed that lifting the finger off the surface sometimes caused the selected target to move as described by Sears et al. [23]. Therefore, it was not properly aligned with the dock anymore which was counted as dragging error. Third, our prototype system sometimes lost momentarily track of fingers while dragging which is indicated by frequent handle reselection events within milliseconds. This happened in both conditions at about the same rate. It was post-hoc not possible to distinguish these errors from valid user activities.

Furthermore, it is interesting to note that no significant interactions were found between *width* or *distance* and *condition* for the pointing error rate. In the light of the findings about pointing time, this indicates that smaller targets or larger distances did not have a pronounced effect on pointing error rate in the indirect compared to the direct condition. In short, it appears that the time spent for aiming paid off.

5.2 Peculiarities of Indirect Interaction

In the following, we discuss observed behavior which gave indication to higher cognitive load in the indirect condition and helps to explain the varying performance differences between direct and indirect condition and pointing and dragging tasks. A first indicator for an increased mental demand is the less parallel approach of handle selection in the indirect condition. Analyzing the time which passed between selecting the first and second handle of a target shows that participants were about four times quicker to select the second handle in the direct condition, also contributing to the total shorter pointing time.

As described before, we observed that participants tended to split the pointing task into two separate movements. Only after positioning the fingers over the target they would move them down to touch the surface. A possible explanation for this behavior can be found in the increased difficulty of estimating the distance between hand and table surface when looking at the screen; the user interface did not provide three-dimensional hints. Therefore, it is arguably more difficult to perform a fluid movement consisting of a combined horizontal and vertical component to select a target in the indirect condition. Participants attempting to perform such a combined movement often touched the surface too early and slid into the target instead of pointing at it which accounted for a pointing error. To sum up, the missing perception of the hands' three-dimensional location above the surface seems to substantially add to the coordination load in the indirect condition. Clearly, no estimation of distance between hands and surface is required while dragging. In addition, observations of users who tried to apply a sliding and a "lift-and-tap" technique [17] instead of a pointing movement suggest that dragging was perceived to be more intuitive in the indirect condition. However, realizing selection by dragging raises challenges concerning the differentiation of input states as discussed by Buxton et al. [4]. Wilson et al. [25] present a pinching gestures which could serve as trigger for a state transition. On the same lines, Benko et al. [3] implemented *SimPress* to distinguish between mere touches and clicks.

In general, we could observe a more restricted usage of the indirect interaction technique with regard to hand postures and movements. Participants seemed to put more emphasis in maintaining certain hand postures over the trials in the indirect condition. A possible explanation for this behavior is the added complexity due to the mapping between the hand contours and the actual hands. This mapping can arguably be facilitated by having a clear and constant point of reference, such as the index finger in a pointing gesture.

6 Conclusions

Our results indicate that a simple replication and transfer of common interaction techniques from a direct multi-touch to an indirect multi-touch surface comes along with a substantial decrease in performance. Nevertheless, it is important to acknowledge that even unexperienced users understood the underlying principles of the studied indirect interaction modality instantly. In addition, our results indicate that performance loss between direct and indirect is mostly due to the requirement of blindly keeping arms and hands at distance to the input device. Allowing the user to stay in contact with the surface has been shown to decrease performance differences between direct and indirect interaction considerably. These findings motivate the design of interaction techniques that allow the user to keep permanent contact with the surface. The presented results provide a basic understanding of factors relevant to the design of indirect multi-touch systems and suggest that a significant potential for improving indirect multi-touch interaction exists. Further investigations with respect to the quality of indirect multi-touch interaction is clearly needed to gain a better understanding of costs and benefits of these techniques.

References

1. Balakrishnan, R.: The Role of Kinesthetic Reference Frames in Two-Handed Input Performance. In: Proc. UIST, pp. 171–178 (1999)
2. Barnert, W.C.: A Comparison of One-Handed and Two-Handed Direct and Indirect Computer Interaction. Technical report, Tufts University (2005)

3. Benko, H., Wilson, A.D., Baudisch, P.: Precise Selection Techniques for Multi-Touch Screens. In: Proc. CHI, pp. 1263–1272 (2006)
4. Buxton, W.: A Three-State Model of Graphical Input. In: Proc. INTERACT, pp. 449–456 (1990)
5. Buxton, W., Myers, B.: A Study in Two-Handed Input. In: Proc. CHI, pp. 321–326 (1986)
6. Cao, X., Wilson, A.D., Balakrishnan, R., Hinckley, K., Hudson, S.E.: ShapeTouch: Leveraging Contact Shape on Interactive Surfaces. In: Proc. TABLETOP (2008)
7. Dietz, P., Leigh, D.: DiamondTouch: A Multi-User Touch Technology. In: Proc. UIST, pp. 219–226 (2001)
8. Forlines, C., Balakrishnan, R.: Evaluating Tactile Feedback and Direct vs. Indirect Stylus Input in Pointing and Crossing Selection Tasks. In: Proc. CHI, pp. 1563–1572 (2008)
9. Forlines, C., Wigdor, D., Shen, C., Balakrishnan, R.: Direct-Touch vs. Mouse Input for Tabletop Displays. In: Proc. CHI, pp. 647–656 (2007)
10. Han, J.Y.: Low-Cost Multi-Touch Sensing Through Frustrated Total Internal Reflection. In: Proc. UIST, pp. 115–118 (2005)
11. Hart, S.G., Stavelan, L.E.: Development of NASA-TLX (Task Load Index): Results of Empirical and Theoretical Research. Human Mental Workload (1988)
12. Krueger, M.W., Gionfriddo, T., Hinrichsen, K.: VIDEOPLACE - An Artificial Reality. SIGCHI Bull. 16(4), 35–40 (1985)
13. Kurtenbach, G., Fitzmaurice, G., Baudel, T., Buxton, W.: The Design of a GUI Paradigm Based on Tablets, Two-Hands, and Transparency. In: Proc. CHI, pp. 35–42 (1997)
14. Lee, S.K., Buxton, W., Smith, K.C.: A Multi-Touch Three Dimensional Touch- Sensitive Tablet. SIGCHI Bull. 16(4), 21–25 (1985)
15. Leganchuk, A., Zhai, S., Buxton, W.: Manual and Cognitive Benefits of Two-Handed Input: An Experimental Study. ACM Trans. Comput.-Hum. Interact. 5(4), 326–359 (1998)
16. Lewis, J.R.: IBM Computer Usability Satisfaction Questionnaires: Psychometric Evaluation and Instructions for Use. Int. J. Hum.-Comput. Interact. 7(1), 57–78 (1995)
17. MacKenzie, I.S., Oniszczak, A.: A Comparison of Three Selection Techniques for Touchpads. In: Proc. CHI, pp. 336–343 (1998)
18. MacKenzie, I.S., Sellen, A., Buxton, W.: A Comparison of Input Devices in Elemental Pointing and Dragging Tasks. In: Proc. CHI, pp. 161–166 (1991)
19. Malik, S., Ranjan, A., Balakrishnan, R.: Interacting with Large Displays from a Distance with Vision-Tracked Multi-Finger Gestural Input. In: Proc. UIST, pp. 43–52 (2005)
20. Meyer, S., Cohen, O., Nilsen, E.: Device Comparisons for Goal-Directed Drawing Tasks. In: Proc. CHI, pp. 251–252 (1994)
21. Moscovich, T., Hughes, J.F.: Indirect Mappings of Multi-Touch Input Using One and Two Hands. In: Proc. CHI, pp. 1275–1284 (2008)
22. Scott, S.S., Carpendale, S.: Guest Editors' Introduction: Interacting with Digital Tabletops. IEEE Computer Graphics and Applications 26(5), 24–27 (2006)
23. Sears, A., Shneiderman, B.: High Precision Touchscreens: Design Strategies and Comparisons with a Mouse. IJMMS 34, 593–613 (1991)
24. Wigdor, D., Forlines, C., Baudisch, P., Barnwell, J., Shen, C.: Lucid Touch: A See-Through Mobile Device. In: Proc. UIST, pp. 269–278 (2007)
25. Wilson, A.D.: Robust Computer Vision-Based Detection of Pinching for One and Two-Handed Gesture Input. In: Proc. UIST, pp. 255–258 (2006)
26. Wu, M., Balakrishnan, R.: Multi-Finger and Whole Hand Gestural Interaction Techniques for Multi-User Tabletop Displays. In: Proc. UIST, pp. 193–202 (2003)

Evaluating Gaze and Touch Interaction and Two Feedback Techniques on a Large Display in a Shopping Environment

Angelique Kessels, Evert van Loenen, and Tatiana Lashina

Philips Research, User Experiences,
High Tech Campus 34,
5656 AE Eindhoven
{Angelique.Kessels,Evert.van.Loenen,Tatiana.Lashina}@Philips.com

Abstract. At Philips Research, an Intelligent Shop Window (ISW) was developed. With the ISW, a unique combination is made between a transparent display that is embedded in the window glass, and physical products presented in the shop window. In this paper, touch and gaze interaction with the large display in the ISW are investigated and evaluated. For sensing interfaces it is known that especially with gaze interaction, it is a challenge to communicate to the user that the system is ready and attending to the user, but also which part of the system the user can address. Therefore, two suitable feedback mechanisms for this interaction were designed and evaluated with users. The first was the 'polite products' concept, where products were placed on a turntable. When the user selects the product with either touch or gaze interaction, the product on the turntable turns towards the user. The second feedback method was a transparent light tile behind the products, which changed color when the product was selected. The evaluation results showed that the polite product concept was rated better than the light tile on almost every item related to hedonic values such as enjoyability and fun. Next to that it became clear that participants felt more in control when using touch interaction and that touch worked faster and more efficient than gaze interaction. However, gaze interaction was a fairly new and exotic interaction method for participants and they said they liked using gaze interaction. Especially the combination of gaze interaction with the polite products feedback method was very strong.

Keywords: Touch interaction, gaze interaction, feedback mechanisms, large displays, public space.

1 Introduction

To investigate the use and benefits of new technologies in the public domain and specifically in shops, Philips has built the experience lab "Shoplab" on the High Tech Campus in Eindhoven. This Shoplab embodies a fashion shop where many prototypes

T. Gross et al. (Eds.): INTERACT 2009, Part I, LNCS 5726, pp. 595–607, 2009.

that have associations with shopping are built in and can be tested with users. Shoplab also has a shop window [2, 3], which carries the name: "Intelligent Shop Window" (ISW). The Intelligent Shop Window responds to the presence, movement and input of shoppers near to the window, with light, sound, text, images and animations. It is also an interactive shop window where shoppers can obtain information about the products on display, using different interaction styles.

The research described in this paper focuses on the interactive part of the Intelligent Shop Window. Our first exploratory research question therefore is: *What is the best way to interact with a large shop window?* All interaction styles need to trigger some sort of feedback to clarify that the system responds to the input of the user. So from the first research question, a second one automatically arises: *What is the best form of feedback that gives the user a clear and understandable interaction experience?*

2 Concept Design of the Intelligent Shop Window

The sensors in the sensing environment around the ISW can be used as input devices for a user interface on the shop window. This way the interface can attend to what users need without getting explicit input from users [4]. These kind of interfaces are called *attentive* interfaces: user interfaces that dynamically prioritize the information they present to their users such that information processing resources of both user and system are optimally distributed across a set of tasks [5]. The design of the interface of the ISW is based on the attentive interface principle. Therefore we adopt the following hypothesis: in a shopping environment, an attentive interface on the shop window can attract customers, by dynamic adaptations to the information that is visible on the shop window. To this end, a differentiation will have to be made in various phases and states the shop window can be in. When a shopper is far away from the shop, the information on the shop window will obviously be different of content and size than when the user is near to the window. Also, it is essential that only information is given on products that are of interest to the user. When the user is very near to the shop window it is possible to see where he is looking at and only give information about that particular product. This implicit input should result in enhancing the appeal of the product and increasing the interest of the user.

2.1 Interaction Design

The interaction concept with the Intelligent Shop Window is based on the concept presented in [1]. Vogel et al. [1] present 4 interaction phases, related to distance of the user to the screen and body/head posture (figure 1):

- Ambient Display
- Subtle Interaction
- Implicit Interaction
- Personal Interaction

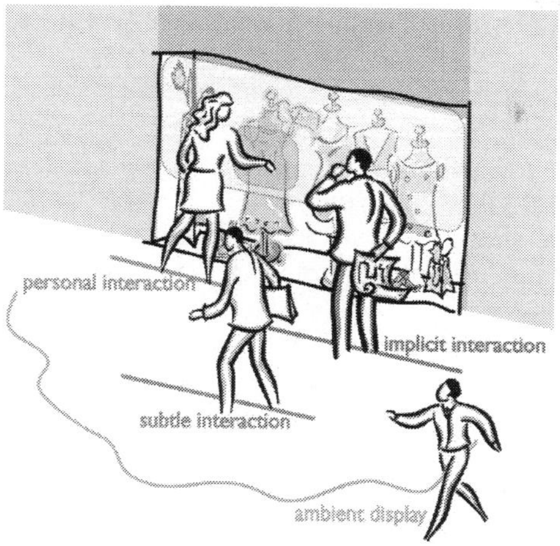

Fig. 1. Four phase interaction concept

The differentiation between the various phases is highly applicable to the ISW and will be further explained in the next paragraphs. Unfortunately Vogel et al. [1] only discuss the use of a screen with touch interaction and body orientation as implicit interaction with the system, while with the ISW the choice can be made between various sensors that can function as input devices, i.e. gaze, touch, position and direction of movement of the user. Also the products inside the shop window, combined with the screen provide an added dimension. Various adjustments to the implementation of the 4 phases are made and implemented in the ISW [2, 3].

2.2 The Ambient Display

The first interaction phase is the 'ambient display' phase according to Vogel et al. [1]. In the current ISW this is implemented as the 'attractor mode' of the window. This is the neutral stage of the screen when no shoppers are near to the shop. The screen is displaying the shop atmosphere and the message the shop wants to convey to the shopping people outside. Next to the current implementation of atmosphere creation, the system can show a range of information items like upcoming fashion shows, news updates and perhaps sale or discount information. A shopper that is walking by at a relative large distance should be able to get a sense of the overall information that is displayed at one glance.

2.3 Subtle Interaction

When a user walks parallel to the window, the system reacts to that. In the current implementation of the ISW, butterflies and text pop up on the screen at the position of the shopper. Also a range of audio devices produce a stream of directed audio. Both audio and visible attractors are moving along with the shopper as he walks along the shop window. The position and orientation of a user passing by or standing still in front of the shop window is determined by the use of a pressure sensitive floor in front of the ISW.

2.4 Implicit Interaction

When the user looks into the shop window, it is possible to track his gaze with cameras that are inside the shop window. In the current ISW, the gaze tracker gives the user the possibility to just look at an item in the shop and the system will give appropriate feedback on this product selection. To investigate which feedback is most appropriate, four feedback mechanisms are developed to give this feedback: the first feedback is information about the selected product, displayed on the screen of the shop window. Second, an audio feedback is given by a clearly audible 'click'. The third and fourth feedback mechanisms are developed to make the product more attractive: the 'polite products' concept and the 'light 'em up' concept.

Feedback method: Polite products

In the polite products concept, all products in the shop window are placed on a specially designed turntable. This turntable can rotate and tilt the product in any desired direction. The metaphor behind the concept is based on human behavior while having a conversation. When people talk to each other, they turn their body or at least their head towards the person they are talking to. It is often considered as polite to turn towards your speaking partner, so in the same manner, the products in the shop window will turn their 'faces' towards the customer when he/she looks at them. When the product is placed below the viewers eyes, the product will also be tilted, to give the customer the best view.

For the polite products concept, there were three design constraints:

1. The product in the shop window should be able show itself and turn towards the shopper who is in front of the window
2. The product can be placed anywhere in the shop window, and at any place, it should be able to show its front side.
3. The product has the size of a bag or a pair of shoes.

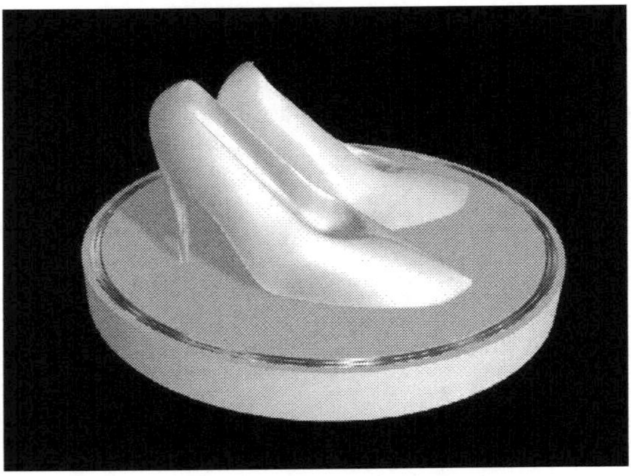

Fig. 2. 3D model of the turntable with a pair of shoes

A dedicated turntable was designed and manufactured. After consideration of various options, a cardan suspension was chosen. This suspension is a universal mounting which, by means of gimbals, allows the supported part to remain horizontal irrespective of the orientation of the rest of the instrument. This sort of mounting is often seen in compasses in old ships. In this case, the mounting is turned up side down, so the ground is the horizontal fixture and it is possible to position the upper part of the mounting in any desired angle. This results in a 35cm wide turntable that is 7 cm high. This size was chosen because the width ensures that it fits a pair of shoes and the height makes sure the shoes can be tilted for 20 degrees. The base part and the disc on top of the turntable are made of a plastic. The two inner rings are made of aluminum because more strength was needed to withstand the forces that would be put on them. The total weight of one turntable is about 8 kilos.

The positioning of the 2 rings and the disc is done with 3 servos: one for every angular degree of freedom. The model of the turntable is given in figure 2. To fit the turntable in the high-fashion look of the shop window, the plastic that is used is spray-painted with glossy white paint. The aluminum parts keep their original metal color. In total 3 identical turntables were manufactured.

The actuation of the servo motors is controlled with Phidgets™ [6]. In every turntable one control unit is built which is connected to the controlling pc. The control pc is on its turn connected to the gaze tracker and to the touch interface, so when a user selects a product on a turntable (either with gaze or touch), the 3 servos are actuated and turn the product towards the user. At the time of testing, the servos move from their starting position to their end position at a constant speed.

Fig. 3. Combined feedback mechanisms

Fig. 4. Touch interaction

Feedback method: Light 'em up
In many everyday interaction mechanisms, light is a powerful feedback from the system to the user. Lights also attract attention. This also holds for shop windows: the best lit products get the most attention. [2, 3].

Hence, light feedback is also currently implemented in the Intelligent Shop Window. When a shopper looks at a product or even points at it, a light behind the product changes color and keeps the attention of the user focused on the product. It gives the shopper feedback that the system knows where the interests of the shopper are at that particular moment. When the user walks away, or indicates that he/she is interested in something else in the shop window, the light returns to its regular state.

To be able to test both feedback mechanisms without altering the experimental setup, the two mechanisms are combined as indicated in figure 3. Three tables of different sizes and height are placed in the shop window. The turntables are placed in the middle on top of them and the light tiles are mounted at the back of the tables in such a way that the bottom of the light tile is at the same height as the top of the turntable.

2.5 Personal Interaction

In the personal interaction phase described in Vogel et al. [1], gesture and touch interaction is used. In the current ISW, both gaze and touch interaction can be used in this phase. A user can select products with gaze, but also point at them on the glass and browse through the information displayed on the screen using touch interaction. Here, gaze and touch interaction are the most logical interaction styles to use, because the user is standing close to the window which is already used as a screen. In contrast, other interaction styles like speech are less natural or useful in a noisy shopping environment.

When a user walks away after using the interface on the screen, the information that is displayed disappears and another interaction phase can be entered.

3 Evaluation of Interaction and Feedback Mechanisms

To be able to evaluate the two interaction methods and two feedback mechanisms described in the previous chapter, an evaluation with users has been done. In the following sections, the participants, setting, design, procedure and results will be discussed.

3.1 Participants, Setting and Design

The experiment involved 18 participants, (9 women and 9 men). Participants were selected in the range from 23-40 years old. The mean age was 31. They all indicated they go shopping from time to time. Participants were randomly assigned to the predefined sequence of the experimental conditions.

The experiment took place in front of the ISW of the ShopLab at the Philips High Tech Campus. Participants would be asked to step in front of window 3 (out of 4) of the shop window, whereas the experimenter would stand in front window 2, starting and ending the tasks with the touch interface on the window.

A camera was used to record the whole experiment and a small unobtrusive microphone was placed between the experimenter and the participant. The products in the shop window were dedicated female products for female participants and dedicated male products for male participants.

We adopted a within-subjects design in which the method of interaction and the feedback mechanism in the shop window was manipulated, as indicated in table 1. There were in total six conditions. We were interested in comparing gaze and touch interaction, as well as comparing the different feedback mechanisms.

Table 1. Interaction and feedback conditions

	Turntable feedback	**Light tile feedback**	**No feedback**
Gaze interaction	1.	2.	3.
Touch interaction	4.	5.	6.

The experiment consisted of 3 parts, in which participants were requested to perform several tasks.

- In the first part, participants would either use gaze or touch interaction (the order was balanced over user) and perform 3 tasks. A typical task in the experiment was: "Find the price of the white shoes in the shop window". By either looking at the product or pointing at it and using the touch interface, participants were able to find the requested information about the product. At the moment the product was 'selected', typical information about that product appeared on the glass of the shop window. We opted for three tasks in order to try out the two feedback conditions and the no feedback condition. Each tasks was then accompanied by a different form of feedback: 1. no feedback, 2. lighting the tile, 3. turning the product. After completing the tasks, the participant was asked to fill in a questionnaire about the interaction style that was used. This questionnaire enclosed multiple questions on hedonic values, perceived ease of use, perceived usefulness and affect (see §3.2).
- In the second set, again three tasks were carried out. The interaction style that was used changed but the feedback methods were not changed. After the three tasks the participant filled in the same questionnaire, but now about the interaction style in the second set of tasks.
- In the third set of tasks, participants could choose their preferred interaction style (touch or gaze interaction) and they were asked to elaborate on their choice. Only two tasks were given and only the feedback mechanisms 'light tile' and 'turntable' were presented. Before starting the third set of tasks, the experimenter told the participants that in the shop window two different feedbacks would be given and that questions would be asked about them after the tasks. After completing the two tasks, participants would be asked to fill in a questionnaire, directly comparing the light tile and turntable feedback mechanisms.
- A closing interview was done with all participants.

3.2 Measures

A multiple set of measures was used to test both the direct effects of the feedback mechanisms inside the shop window as well as the speed, effectiveness and ease of use of the interaction styles.

Time measurements. The time between the start and end of a task was measured.

The Unified Theory of Acceptance and the Use of Technology (UTAUT) [7,8,9] is a measure of technology acceptance. The UTAUT was used with some adaptations for the shopping domain. The scales perceived ease of use (PEOU) and perceived usefulness (PU) are adopted in this experiment.

The Affect scale (AF) [10] refers to the affective emotional considerations about the interaction.

The Hedonic part of the HED/UT scale of van der Heijden [11] which includes factors as enjoyability and fun.

The Users' preference for a feedback mechanism is a list of carefully composed questions, including comparing questions between the two feedback mechanisms, whether or not the response of the system is noticed and if it is and adequate feedback for interaction with the intelligent shop window.

An interview was done with all the participants about their general preference of interaction method and feedback mechanism. Also some questions about privacy (cameras) were asked.

3.3 Procedure

In order to calibrate the gaze tracker to each individual participant, a profile of the participants face had to be made. Because this profiling of participants was time consuming (approx. 1 hour), this occurred at least 3 days before the actual experiment. of time consuming profiling (approx. 1 hour), participants were asked to take part in the real experiment another time.

At the start of the experiment itself, the participants were again welcomed and they filled in an informed consent form, approving audio and video recordings. They were also explained what the purpose of Shoplab was and the goal of the experiment. Next, the participant was asked to step in front of window nr 3. At the glass of the window a large button was projected labelled 'START'. The experimenter stepped in front of the window next to the participant (window 2). On this window, the participant number could be chosen. With this choice, the sequence of interaction styles and feedback mechanism was also chosen which would be presented to the participant. The order of these sequences was balanced out over all participants.

After explaining that the interaction style with the interactive shop window was under investigation and not the actions of the participant, it was explained which interaction style should be used during the first tasks (touch or gaze interaction). Now, the first task of the first set was read out loud to the participant. After the task was read, the participant pressed the 'start' button on the touch-sensitive shop window (starting the time measurement) and carried out the task. When the participant read the correct answer out loud, the experimenter stopped the time measurement by pressing a button on window 2. After carrying out the three tasks of the set, the participant was asked to fill in a questionnaire about the interaction style that was just used. The second set of tasks was carried out in the same manner, with filling in the questionnaire shortly after that.

Before starting the third set of tasks, the preferred interaction style of the participant was indicated on window 2 by the experimenter. The participant was asked to pay close attention to what was happening inside the shop window when interacting with it. Then, the two tasks were carried out and again a questionnaire was filled in about the feedback mechanisms in the shop window. Afterwards, this questionnaire was used as a basis for an interview where the participants gave their impression of the experiment and the thoughts they had about the interaction styles and the feedback mechanisms.

3.4 Results

Hedonic scale

All questionnaires included the Hedonic part of the HED/UT scale by van der Heijden [9]. A T-test was used and Cronbach's alpha was calculated for the whole scale: α=0,92, indicating the set of items measures a single unidimensional latent construct. This calculation included all ratings from all participants on touch and gaze interaction and on the 2 feedback mechanisms.

Only the sub-item 'Boring/Fun' in the Hedonic scale shows a significant difference between touch and gaze interaction, meaning that touch was rated more fun than gaze. Also the item 'Disgusting/Delightful' shows a marginal significant result. On all the other items, no significant difference was found. Despite the significant difference in fun between the interaction styles, for the complete HED scale no significant difference was found. However, given the fact that touch interaction is known to many participants and that none of them ever worked with gaze interaction, this non-significant difference between the interaction styles is still a striking result.

In the results for the feedback mechanisms, in all cases, the median score is for the turntable feedback one point higher than the light tile rating. Also the variance for the turntable feedback is smaller than the variance in rating for the light tile, so participants were quite agreed in their opinions regarding the turntable.

Half of the items (dull/exciting, boring/fun, serious/playful, unthrilling/thrilling) in the HED scale indicate a significant difference ($p< 0.05$) between the turntable and the light tile, in favor of the turntable. All other items except the 'disgusting/delightful' item show a strong trend that the turntable is rated higher than the light tile. The results for the complete HED scale for the feedback mechanisms show a marginally significant difference in favor of the turntable (p=0,052, z=-1,941, n=18), so on the Hedonic scale, participants rated the turntable feedback higher than the light tile.

Perceived Ease of Use and Perceived Usefulness[2]

Next, the data for the scales 'perceived Ease of Use' (PEOU), 'perceived usefulness' (PU) and 'affect' (AF) is analyzed. The calculated Cronbach's alpha for PEOU is: α=0,943 and for PU: α=0,791.

In figure 5 it is striking to see that the mean of all answers of all participants on touch interaction is higher on all items in the PEOU and PU scale. For PU a higher variance

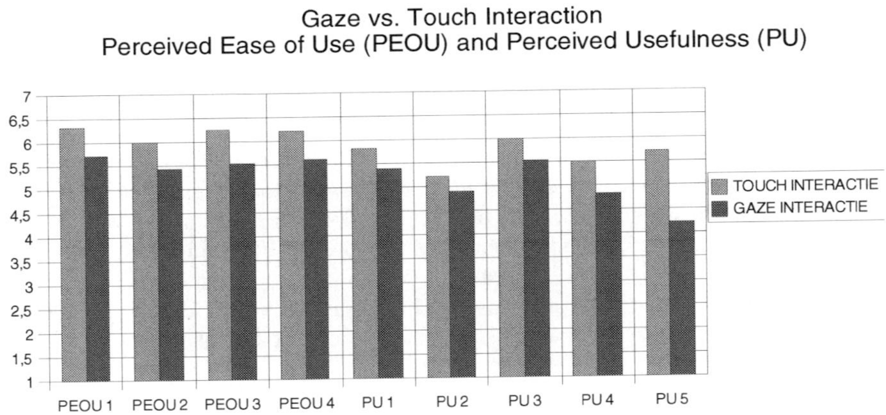

Fig. 5. Mean results for PEOU and PU scales for touch and gaze interaction

for gaze interaction is observed, but also that the median ratings for gaze are lower than for touch. A Wilcoxon signed ranks test is performed to see if this difference is significant. The difference in PU between touch and gaze interaction was only significant for PU5 ($z = -2.687$, $df = 17$, $p < 0.05$) indicating that participants rated the amount of control he/she had in operating the system higher with touch interaction. In total, touch interaction scores are significantly higher on perceived usefulness than gaze interaction.

The difference in PEOU between touch and gaze interaction was not significant. Not a single item scores significantly different in favor of touch or gaze, although the trend points out that touch interaction scores higher on Ease of Use.

Affect

From figure 6 it is clear that touch interaction scores higher on all items in the Affect scale. A Cronbach's alpha for the scale was calculated: $\alpha=0{,}889$. The variance for affect on gaze interaction is larger than for touch interaction.

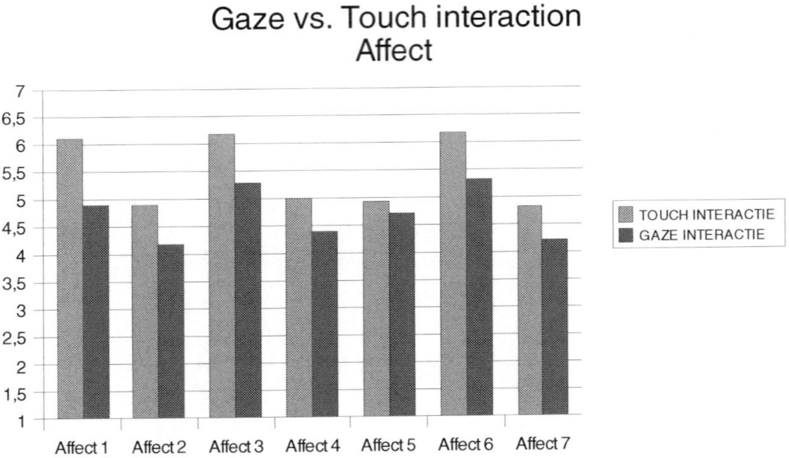

Fig. 6. Mean results for Affect scale for touch and gaze interaction

The difference in affect between touch and gaze interaction was in four out of seven items significant ($p< 0.05$) indicating that participants enjoyed working with touch interaction more than working with gaze. Some items in the affect scale are 'frustration' and 'awkwardness' of the interaction style. Also, regarding the complete affect scale the following result was obtained: p=0.007, z=-2.676, n=17, meaning that touch interaction scores significantly higher on affect than touch interaction.

Users' preference for a feedback mechanism

All users were asked to compare the two feedback mechanisms in the shop window with each other. In figure 7, the ratings are given for the 5 questions that are stated below. It is clear that the turntable is rated higher than the light tile on all questions. Also, when the light tile and the turntable were directly compared with the question 'Which form of feedback do you prefer?', 12 out of 18 participants answered they preferred the turntable.

1. I noticed that [sometimes lights went on/the products in the shop window were sometimes moving].
2. [A light behind the product/Moving a product] in the shop window is an adequate response of the system.
3. I find [a light behind the product/movement of the product] in the shop window useful
4. [A light behind a product/Movement of the product] is helpful for me in searching the shop window
5. [A light behind a product/Movement of the product] enhances my effectiveness in searching.

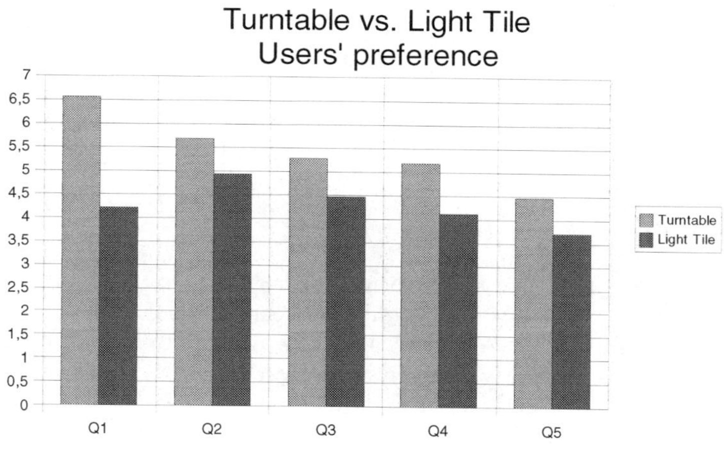

Fig. 7. Turntable vs. Light Tile, users' preference results

The opinions on the light tile were wider spread than opinions on the turntable. One explanation for this is that 5 out of 18 participants indicated that they did not see the light tile while performing the tasks. Only when they were explicitly instructed to look at the light tile, they saw the effect. A Cronbach alpha is calculated: α=0.573, so all items in this set were treated individually. Only the question if the feedback was noticed by the user during the tasks was significant in favor of the turntable (Z=-3,078, df=18, p<0,05). The other questions were not significant, although the trend showed that users had a slightly higher preference for the turntable.

Time measurements

During all the tasks in the experiment, a time measurement was done to get an indication on which interaction style gave the fastest results. The timer was started when the task was read out loud by the experimenter and the participant pushed the 'start' button on the glass of the shop window. When the correct solution to the task was read out loud by the participant, the timer was stopped by the experimenter. The participants were not aware that a time measurement was done. Per participant, 8 time measurements were done. 3 for every interaction style and another 2 with the interaction style of the participants' choice. For this comparison only the first three tasks for both interaction styles were investigated, because of a large learning effect.

For 7 out of 18 participants, the task that was performed fastest was with gaze interaction, for the remaining 11 participants this fastest task was performed with touch interaction. A mean time for carrying out a task was around 10 seconds. The tasks where it took longer than 30 seconds to complete were excluded from the data, because the participant was lost in the interface on the glass (using touch) or the gaze tracker did not work properly. When a task took longer than a minute, the task was stopped by the experimenter and skipped. A total of 6 records for gaze and 3 records for touch interaction were excluded because of the stated reasons. This exclusion was an indication that gaze interaction did not work as stable as touch interaction. With the data exclusion taken into account, for 10 participants, the mean time for the tasks with gaze interaction is shorter than the mean time for tasks with touch interaction. This result showed that gaze and touch interaction were very competitive in interaction speed, but it has to be emphasized that the participants were not trying to complete the tasks as quick as possible, nor were they told that they were going to be timed. To be conclusive on which interaction style works the fastest, another test has to be done, focusing on the time it takes to complete a task.

4 Conclusion

From the user study it became clear that participants think that gaze interaction is quite fun to work with, but from the interview it became clear that the loss of control is for many difficult to accept. Also it seemed to be difficult to find a solution when an unexpected or no response was given by the gaze system. Touch interaction is found to be robust and participants knew how to operate it immediately. However, drawbacks related to the public shopping environment (vandalism, fingerprints on the window) were mentioned very often.

Regarding our first research question: *What is the best way to interact with a large shop window?* we can conclude that touch interaction is at this moment a very robust and intuitive interaction method. However, when gaze tracking technology has become robust and stable and does not require a profile of a face anymore to be able to track it, gaze interaction can be a very attractive, vandalism proof and powerful interaction style in shop windows.

Regarding the second research question: *What is the best form of feedback that gives the user a clear and understandable interaction experience?* we can conclude that both feedback mechanisms that were investigated, provided the user with clear and understandable feedback that the system responded to the user. However, the polite products concept was rated higher than the light tile and especially in combination with gaze interaction, this form of feedback is a very strong one in the context of shopping environments. Shoppers do not need to touch anything to take a good look at a real product in a show window. The product automatically presents itself politely when looked at.

References

1. Vogel, D., Balakrishnan, R.: Interactive public ambient displays: transitioning from implicit to explicit, public to personal, interaction with multiple users (2004)
2. van Loenen, E., Lashina, T., van Doorn, M.: Interactive Shop Windows. In: Ambient Lifestyle: From Concept to Experience. Bis Publishers, Amsterdam (2006)
3. van Loenen, E., Lashina, T., van Doorn, M., van Gelder, K., Teeven, V., de Bruin, W., van Haasen, R.: DreamScreen: Intelligent Shop Window. In: New Business through User Centric Innovation, Philips Research Europe publication, ISBN 907444573X
4. Maglio, P.P., Barrett, R., Campbell, C.S., Selker, T.: SUITOR: an attentive information system (2000)
5. Vertegaal, R.: Principles & methodology: Designing attentive interfaces (2002)
6. Phidgets, `http://phidgets.com/`
7. Davis, F.D.: A technology acceptance model for empirically testing new end-user information systems: Theory and results (1986)
8. Davis, F.D., Bagozzi, R.P., Warshaw, P.R.: User acceptance of computer technology: A comparison of two theoretical models. Management Science (1989)
9. Venkatesh, V., Morris, M.G., Davis, G.B., Davis, F.D.: User acceptance of information technology: Toward a unified view (2003)
10. Keinonen, T.: Expected usability and product preference (1997)
11. Van der Heijden, H.: User Acceptance of Hedonic Information Systems (2004)

Design and Evaluation of a Large Interactive Display to Support Social Interaction at Work

Sanjin Pajo, Senka Zubić, Agnieszka Matysiak Szóstek, and Janienke Sturm

Eindhoven University of Technology, Den Dolech 2, 5612 EZ, Eindhoven, The Netherlands
{S.P.Pajo,Z.S.Zubic,J.Sturm,A.Matysiak}@tue.nl

Abstract. Social interaction at work has been shown to enhance creativity and productivity. This paper describes the design and evaluation of a large, interactive display that aims to stimulate social interaction amongst co-workers by providing food for talk in the form of activities, jokes, and music. User and system requirements were collected using Cultural Probes and Focus groups. The evaluation of our prototype system provides valuable insights that may guide the design of future systems supporting social interaction at work.

Keywords: Design, Large Touch-Screen Display, Social Interaction, BSCW.

1 Introduction

In recent years, much research has shown that social interaction can lead to a sense of cohesiveness and cooperation amongst employees. It can, also improve self-esteem, mental health and overall personal satisfaction by reducing anxiety and uncertainty [4]. Social interaction in the workplace can make the job more enjoyable and therefore, enhance creativity and productivity [2]. Moreover, social interaction has been shown to reduce stress and help build up relationships, which can lead to better access to resources and materials [1]. Our goal was to design a large interactive display that is specifically aimed at facilitating and stimulating social interaction among co-workers. This system will be referred to as the LID (Large Interactive Display) system. We elaborate and report on the initial set of requirements that was collected by using methods such as a Cultural Probes and Focus Groups [3] [5]. We also discuss a prototype system and describe the results of a first user test of this system.

2 Eliciting Requirements

The first step of the design process was to define the user and system requirements for the design. We decided to use cultural probes [3] as a requirements elicitation method, because they provide not only events but also people's feelings and impressions regarding interactions and preferences as to what parts of their social interactions could be supported by the system. For the cultural probes study we invited 13 participants from two companies: 10 from a small consultancy company and three from a research institute (8 male and 5 female). The study was carried out over a period of five working days. The materials that could be used by the participants (i.e. diary, posters for

T. Gross et al. (Eds.): INTERACT 2009, Part I, LNCS 5726, pp. 608–611, 2009.

illustrations and cameras) were designed to be engaging, to stimulate thought, and to capture emotions and experiences in a playful manner.

The information gathered from the probes was categorized and put into four main clusters: social awareness, ice breakers, cultural information and general information. The result of the cultural probes method was a list of 36 user requirements, spread across the different clusters.

To rank-order the initial requirements by their relative importance and to obtain initial design ideas we carried out two focus group sessions [5]. Six research office workers from the Technical University of Eindhoven participated in the first and 10 in the second session. A general overview of the session was sent to each participant in advance. The participants in each group were asked to discuss the list of requirements that was provided and to select the requirements they found most important for stimulating social interaction at work. Thereafter, they were asked to propose a possible design for a system that would support social interaction among co-workers, using the selected requirements.

The focus groups helped us deduce a set of significant system requirements regarding the input, presentation and management of the content.

The following are the selected user requirements:
Personal information: Each group member should be able to share their personal history through the system or build a personal profile for other group members to view.

Organizational information: Company events, such as conferences, trips, excursions, and birthdays are important for stimulating social behavior that should be presented by the system. Other organizational information such as complaints, suggestions, and opinions can further engage the group members in interacting and socializing.

Ice breakers: Brain teasers, jokes, multiplayer games, open questions, traffic and weather reports all give opportunities for people to talk about, discuss and share.

The following are the selected system requirements:
System self-management: The system must be able to gather and manage some of content automatically. Content for sections like jokes can be gathered by the system from various sources on the web.

Attractive content presentation: The shown content must be appealing and inviting. All presented information must automatically change or cycle in appropriate periods to attract passersby. It must draw attention but not distract from a professional or social interaction that might be occurring.

Context awareness: The displayed content should be appropriate for the surrounding space. Group members can change or define the theme or appearance of the information for special events or occasions. Awareness of users would further help in providing most engaging content.

Extendibility: The system should allow users to change the content. Users should be able to adapt the system to suit particular group needs and preferences; for example, they should be able to define their own categories.

"Walk-up-and-use": System must be easy to use and self explanatory. First-time computer-savvy users should not need extra training to use the system effectively.

3 The System

The main LID application, which shows the content on a touch screen, gathers content stored in the Basic Support for Collaborative Work (BSCW) database and from the web. The majority of the content is entered by group members through personal computers or other devices like Pocket PCs. The remaining content is retrieved automatically from the web by the LID application. The LID application makes frequent requests for user content, combines it with content from the web, and displays the interface on a large touch screen. Users registered in the workspace can access their workspace on the server and create, manage, and distribute documents, notes, links, etc [6]. The center of the LID screen displays the content selected. The tab bar section at the bottom of the screen contains ice breaker categories: jokes, games, questions, weather and traffic. The section on the right hand side of the screen contains the contents of the remaining user requirements, such as personal information sharing and organizational matter.

4 Validation of User Requirements

To validate user requirements a user evaluation was conducted. The goal was to find out if the user requirements were implemented in a way that is suitable for the working environment, and if the requirements would fit working routines and attract and keep the interest of the participants.

Set-up and procedure. The test took place at the Technical University of Eindhoven with 40 students of the post-graduate User System Interaction Program. The user test lasted for five days and was performed during working hours. To evaluate the use of the system, four different measures were taken. Interactions with the display were time-stamped and logged. Information regarding material uploaded to the BSCW system was logged, as well. Before and after the test participants filled in a questionnaire and 6 had a follow-up interview.

Results. *Quantitative results*: The total number of uploaded files was 46. The highest number of uploads was in the category of *pictures* or *images*. The lowest number was 0 for the *personal achievements* category. Popular categories were also *forum* (6), *non-university events* (6), *messages* (5), and *travel* (5). The category *music* was added after a request by some of the participants and it recorded 31 uploaded music files.

Analysis of the logging data showed that most interactions took place on the first day of the evaluation (almost 350 interactions), after which the number of interactions decreased to a steady 150 per day. The most popular category was *pictures* (selected 111 times during the testing period) and the least popular category, *Wikipedia* (38 selections).

Interviews: Data regarding the participants' general impression was positive. All six interviewed participants found that the information presented on the screen was interesting, and presented in a suitable manner. They characterized the Large Interactive Display as funny, easy to use, and attractive. Automatic changes of the content were positively evaluated. The participants felt that the application did not change the group's social behavior, but it improved their communication. It also stimulated them to learn more about their colleagues and to share information about themselves. The participants described the application as a conversation starter, it made the atmosphere in the common room cozy and they would love to have it at their disposal in the future.

Questionnaire: A validated questionnaire for the evaluation of group communication was used to evaluate the effect of the system on the group interaction [7]. We found no significant changes in social interaction as perceived by the participants.

5 Discussion and Conclusion

The goal of this study was to design and evaluate an interactive system supporting social interaction at work. The added value of such a system for the work floor could be inferred from the analysis of the interaction logs and confirmed during interviews with the participants. However, the analysis of the study questionnaire showed no significant change regarding how participants felt about their social interactions before and after using the system, which may be explained that the evaluation period was too short to generate visible impact on social interactions in this particular group. Despite the limitations we were able to derive several interesting design implications for systems supporting social interaction at work. Ice breakers were a very important part of the system. They served a double function: not only did they attract people's attention to the system, but they also fostered interaction between users. We realize that each working group has different needs and requirements that are specific for this particular group and are not likely extendable to other groups. However, the categories defined in the present study could serve as a backbone for similar systems, although those systems should stay open for customization by their users.

References

1. Buunk, B.P., Verhoeven, K.: Companionship and Support at Work: a Microanalysis of the Stress-Reducing Features of Social Interaction. Basic and Applied Social Psychology 12, 243–258 (1991)
2. Bryant, S.: Workplace Friendships: Asset or Liability. Monster Work/Life Balance, `http://content.monster.ca/9667_en-CA_p1.asp` (viewed September 8, 2008)
3. Gaver, W., Dunne, T., Pacenti, E.: Cultural probes. Interact: New Visions Hum. Comput. Interact. 1, 21–29 (1999)
4. Hodson, R.: Work Life and Social Fulfillment: Does Social Affiliation at Work Reflect a Carrot or a Stick. Social Science Quarterly 81, 221–239 (2004)
5. Krueger, R.A., Casey, M.A.: Focus Groups: A Practical Guide for Applied Research. Sage Publications, Inc., Thousand Oaks (2000)
6. OrbiTeam Software Gmbh & Co. BSCW – Version 4.4 Manual, OrbiTeam Sofware Gmbh & Co. KG, Bonn, Germany
7. Widmeyer, W.N., Brawley, L.R., Carron, A.B.: The measurement of cohesion in sport teams: The group environment questionnaire. London: Sports Dynamics 1 (1985)

Interactivity for Museums: Designing and Comparing Sensor-Based Installations

Pedro Campos[1], André Dória[1], and Magno Sousa[2]

[1] University of Madeira
Campus Universitário da Penteada, 9000-390 Funchal, Portugal
[2] WowSystems
R. da Alfândega, 78, 3°, 9000-059 Funchal, Portugal
pcampos@uma.pt, andredoria@netmadeira.com,
magno.sousa@wowsystems.pt

Abstract. Technology today provides exciting new possibilities for creating more appealing museum experiences, since we can exploit the surprise factor of innovative interaction styles to create an engaging experience that facilitates the learning process. This research was based on extensive in-site observation as well as surveys conducted at the scene, and it relates to a cultural interactive exhibition titled "*Cultural Tourism*". The issues were organized around usability problems detected, social interaction and differences between interaction styles, all of which contribute to increasing our knowledge regarding the use of interactive technology as a means to reduce the distance between visitors and cultural heritage.

Keywords: Interactive installations, museum exhibitions, sensor-based installations, kiosks, field observations.

1 Introduction

The use of sensor-based interactive installations, in particular installations involving infrared motion sensors as well as cameras coupled with real time video processing algorithms, have been receiving considerable interest both from industry and academia [1, 2, 3]. During the design and evaluation of interactive exhibitions, much can be learned about interaction design for public settings like these.

We describe our own experience designing and evaluating an interactive exhibition, which featured four different interaction styles to control digital contents: *touching*, *walking over*, *waving* and *page-flipping*. Our design approach was tailored to the exhibition's contents and makes a creative use of sensor-based technology, with the explicit goal of reducing the distance between visitors and cultural heritage [7].

The remainder of this paper is organized as follows: Section 2 describes related work with a particular emphasis on adding interactivity to cultural heritage exhibitions and museums. Section 3 describes the interactive installations designed as well as the interaction styles employed. Finally, Section 4 described the evaluation approach and results, drawing some conclusions organized around usability problems detected, social interaction among visitors and differences between interaction styles.

T. Gross et al. (Eds.): INTERACT 2009, Part I, LNCS 5726, pp. 612–615, 2009.

2 Related Work

Technology today provides exciting new possibilities to approach museum visitors to culture and heritage. Danks and colleagues [1] refer the focus shift towards using interactive artifacts to enhance the visiting experience, which contrasts with the traditional approach, centered on the museum's collection, display and storage of objects. They argue that today's museum visitor expects to learn while also having fun at the same time, therefore interactive storytelling and gaming have a great potential to improve modern museum's experiences [1].

Several experiences have been conducted to study how visitors experience novel interaction styles within museums and science centers. Explore@Bristol, for instance, was an interactive science museum, which was studied to analyze six of its exhibits according to three dimensions: Drama/Sensation, Challenge/Self expression and Social [5]. A "Walk in the Wired Woods" illustrates how to design an engaging experience through context-sensitive media and interaction. The visitors were invited to take a walk in which they were automatically presented with audio content appropriate to their physical location [6]. Other interesting studies have been performed, regarding novel interaction styles and schemes, applied both to leisure and educational activities. Such examples include "The Fire and the Mountain" exhibition, held in 2006 at the Civic Museum of Como, Italy [4] and the "Listen Reader" from Xerox PARC, an innovative and engaging reading experience installed in three different museums over a six-month exhibition period [3].

When studying visitors' interaction with museum digital installations, the problem of evaluation arises inevitably, since it's neither easy nor clear to establish the right set of methods in order to draw credible conclusions. Hornecker and Stifter [2], reporting on the evaluation of a digitally augmented exhibition on the history of modern media, based their conclusions on (i) logfiles' analysis, (ii) interviews and (iii) observation in the museum. We also followed this approach as a means to obtain a better understanding of the interactive installations, described in the next section.

3 The "Cultural Tourism" Exhibition

In April 2008, we designed a set of sensor-based installations in a cultural exhibition organized by the Direction of Cultural Affairs, which aimed at showing the visitor the cultural richness that formed the streets of Funchal (Portugal). The concepts of the exhibition revolved around *promoting awareness about*, and *fostering a better understanding of*, the cultural tourism that can be performed by simply walking through strategic streets and watching certain buildings, sites, and heritage. To better complement the exhibition's traditional large-format printed panels, the organizers wanted to have the interactivity factor as a means to add value to the visitor's experience.

The final set of installations included: (i) a virtual book that could be browsed by simple page-flipping gestures performed in mid-air; (ii) an interactive floor that illustrated the evolution of the transportation means along the years; (iii) an interactive timeline using a touch-screen and (iv) a panel with projected images that would change through waving. These installations are shown in Fig. 1.

Fig. 1. The installations and interaction styles employed throughout the exhibition (clockwise from top left): *waving*, *walking over*, *page-flipping* and *touching*

4 Results and Future Work

The evaluation of the exhibition was conducted during 30 days, from April to May (2008), and consisted in observing visitors interacting with the installations.

The interactions were observed both in presence and video-recorded. A subset of 74 out of more than 1000 visitors was also interviewed during a debriefing session after their visit. Of these 74 visitors, 32 were under 12 years old, 21 were above 60 years old and 51 were female visitors. Additionally, qualitative data analysis was applied to all data (observer notes, video recordings and survey results) in order to gain more insight regarding the visitors' experience. This insight was organized in three different issues: *usability problems found*, *social interaction among visitors*, *differences between interaction styles*. We found differences in all these issues to be correlated to age, e.g. younger visitors exhibited a much larger degree of social interaction than older visitors, and they also enjoyed one particular interaction style that wasn't as much appreciated by older visitors: walking over the interactive floor.

In general, visitors were very pleased with the interactive installations. In the debriefing interviews, we asked them to rate some aspects using a 5-point Likert scale:

– How much they enjoyed the exhibition – 4.7

– Interaction style rating: walking (4.8), page-flipping (4.2), touching (3.9) and waving (3.7). *(all values are an average over 74 answers)*

Usability problems found. In general, children had no difficulties interacting with the installations, even though they most of them had never used interactive installations of the kind. Older visitors were more averse to interacting and preferred to simply watch. Some visitors didn't immediately realize the installations were interactive: people are not used to this kind of exhibitions. Affordances are needed so that visitors know they can interact with the installations: this would have grabbed much more attention and visitors.

Social interaction. As we mentioned, there were much larger levels of social interaction among children than adults. But the most successful ones were clearly the page-flipping gestures performed at the virtual book and the interactive floor. The interactive floor, in particular, allowed collaborations between visitors that wanted to discover the images underneath them and sparked conversations (about culture) between visitors who interacted with the floor at the same time.

Differences between interaction styles. We observed that there was a tendency to "transport" interaction styles from one installation to the next, i.e. visitors trying to "page-flip" a touch-screen. The collaboration allowed by the interactive floor clearly enhanced the level of engagement and their focus. Regarding the virtual book, it was interesting to note the important role of affordances, which were adequate to the interaction style: you browse the *virtual* book the same way you browse a *real* book.

One of the main problems we face today, when trying to provide museum experiences incorporating interactive technologies, is to find out issues that could guide future designs: in this paper, we learned, for instance, the importance of showing visitors they can interact with screens and floors, since people aren't still used to this kind of interactive technologies. What the HCI community needs are more concrete design case studies coupled with observational analysis drawn from those case studies. In this sense, we believe our contribution is a first step towards bringing people closer to their cultural heritage.

References

1. Danks, M., Goodchild, M., Rodriguez-Echavarria, K., Arnold, D.B., Griffiths, R.N.: Interactive storytelling and gaming environments for museums: The interactive storytelling exhibition project. In: Hui, K.-c., Pan, Z., Chung, R.C.-k., Wang, C.C.L., Jin, X., Göbel, S., Li, E.C.-L. (eds.) EDUTAINMENT 2007. LNCS, vol. 4469, pp. 104–115. Springer, Heidelberg (2007)
2. Hornecker, E., Stifter, M.: Learning from interactive museum installations about interaction design for public settings. In: Kjeldskov, J., Paay, J. (eds.) Proceedings of the 18th Australia Conference on Computer-Human interaction. OZCHI 2006, vol. 206. ACM, New York (2006)
3. Back, M., Cohen, J., Gold, R., Harrison, S., Minneman, S.: Listen reader: an electronically augmented paper-based book. In: Proceedings of the SIGCHI conference on Human factors in computing systems, pp. 23–29. ACM Press, New York (2001)
4. Garzotto, F., Rizzo, F.: Interaction paradigms in technology-enhanced social spaces: a case study in museums. In: Proc. DPPI, pp. 343–356. ACM Press, New York (2007)
5. Kidd, A.: Technology experiences: What makes them compelling? Hewlett Packard Laboratories, Bristol, UK (2001)
6. Hull, R., Reid, J., Geelhoed, E.: Social impacts of computing: Codes of professional ethics. Pervasive Computing 1(4), 56–61 (2002)
7. Dória, A., Campos, P., Fernandes, E.: Designing an Interactive Forest through Sensor-based Installations. In: Proceedings of CHI 2008, Florence, Italy (2008)

Leaf Menus: Linear Menus with Stroke Shortcuts for Small Handheld Devices

Anne Roudaut[1], Gilles Bailly[1,2], Eric Lecolinet[1], and Laurence Nigay[2]

[1] Telecom ParisTech – CNRS LTCI UMR 5141, 46 rue Barrault, 75013, Paris, France
{anne.roudaut,gilles.bailly,eric.lecolinet}@telecom-paristech.fr
[2] LIG-IIHM, University of Grenoble 1, B.P. 53, F-38041 Grenoble Cedex 9, France
{gilles.bailly,Laurence.nigay}@imag.fr

Abstract. This paper presents Leaf menu, a new type of contextual linear menu that supports curved gesture shortcuts. By providing an alternative to keyboard shortcuts, the Leaf menus can be used for the selection of commands on tabletops, but its key benefit is its adequacy to small handheld touchscreen devices (PDA, Smartphone). Indeed Leaf menus define a compact and known layout inherited from linear menus, they support precise finger interaction, they manage occlusion and they can be used in close proximity to the screen borders. Moreover, by providing stroke shortcuts, they favour the selection of frequent commands in expert mode and make eye-free selection possible.

Keywords: Menu Techniques, Mobile Devices, One-handed Interaction.

1 Introduction

Although the command selection is a frequent task in interactive systems, few studies have been proposed to improve menus for the case of handheld touchscreen devices. The widespread menu techniques are still linear menus whereas they do not fit well with mobile device limitations. First, in comparison with the interface of a classical computer, those of mobile devices are dramatically impoverished: 1) the lack of screen real estate makes it difficult to display much information (especially in the widthways direction); 2) the user cannot use hotkeys (keyboard shortcuts) because there is often no keyboard; 3) there is no right click while using a touchscreen as opposed to a mouse. Moreover these devices are used in mobile situations and users very often interact with fingers and with only one hand [6]. In this case, they use their thumb and this has several implications on interaction including the occlusion of the thumb, the difficulty to reach the borders of the screen and the lack of accuracy as defined in [7].

To overcome these limitations, we introduce Leaf menu, a context linear menu with stroke shortcuts, which is designed for mobile touchscreen devices. Leaf menus provide a compact layout, support precise finger interaction, manage occlusion and can be used in close proximity to the screen borders.

2 Related Work

Thumb menus are dedicated to mobile devices [4]. Indeed they take into account the constraints of thumb interaction on mobile devices by avoiding occlusion and increasing

T. Gross et al. (Eds.): INTERACT 2009, Part I, LNCS 5726, pp. 616–619, 2009.

accuracy. However they do not have an expert mode (often no keyboard) and do not permit selections in close proximity to the borders of the screen. Moreover their semi-circular layout is not compact in comparison with a linear menu.

Gesturing strokes define an efficient alternative to increase the accuracy [8]. However, they have two limitations. First some strokes cannot be performed near the borders (such as a downward stroke in close proximity to the bottom border of the screen). Second this interaction style is not self-revealing [5]: the system does not provide information about what commands are available and how to invoke them.

One solution consists of displaying stroke shortcuts to items of menus attached to a menu bar [1,5]. However, as these menus are not contextual and stroke shortcuts must be explicitly learned, this forces users to interrupt his/her activity's flow. In the opposite way, Marking menus are context circular menus that offer a "fluid transition" from novice mode (selection in the menu) to expert mode (gestural interaction) because users execute the same gesture in these two functional modes. So, users learn the expert mode implicitly just by using the menu repeatedly in novice mode. However the circular representation of Marking menus does not fit well with small screen devices. Indeed, such menus require more horizontal space than two linear menus (items are laid out on both sides around the center point). Moreover, they do not solve the problem of strokes in close proximity to the borders of the screen.

3 Leaf Menu

Leaf menus are context linear menus with stroke shortcuts (Fig. 1). Leaf menus present five main differences with linear menus that overcome the previous limitations: 1) When the menu enters in *novice mode* (after a delay of 0.3 s), it appears by default on the south-west zone (for right-handed people) to avoid the occlusion of the hand on it, as recommended by [4]; 2) Each item has a corresponding stroke that can be used in expert mode (if the user does not wait and begins gesturing immediately); 3) Stroke shortcuts are drawn globally to the menu (instead of inside the items as in [1,5]) in order to be easily legible on small screens and to favour implicit learning as with the Making menus; 4) A visual feedback occurs after the activation of one item to help the learning of stroke shortcuts ; 5) The Leaf menu uses a *mirror effect*

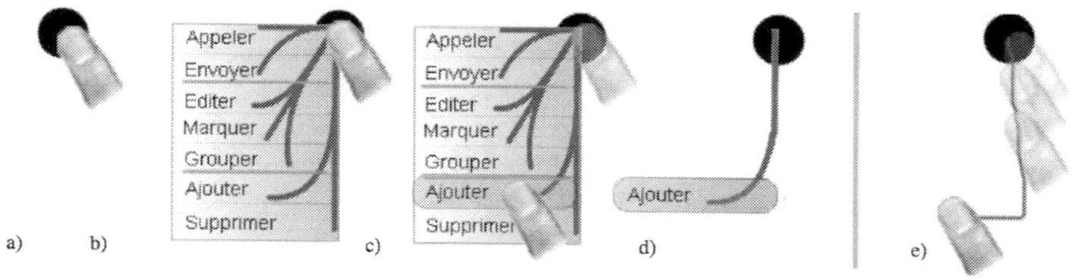

Fig. 1. Leaf menu. a) The user presses a target. b) The menu appears after 0.3 s. A stroke shortcut is defined for each item. c) When the user releases his finger, the command is executed. d) A visual feedback occurs to confirm the selection. e) The user selects the item in expert mode and draws the corresponding marks without waiting for the menu to appear.

(Fig. 2) when the space below the activation point is not sufficient to display the menu. The mirror effect (Fig.2) consists of displaying the menu above the activation point and to invert the order of items by a vertical symmetry. By doing so item 1 of Fig.2 is always the closest item of the activation point. The item 1 can then be quickly reached according to Fitt's law, no matter what the location of the menu on the screen. This contrasts with linear menus where item 1 is the furthest away item when the menu is activated close to the bottom border and is therefore shifted upward.

When the user does not wait and begins gesturing immediately, the menu is in *expert mode*. As Marking menus, the user must perform the appropriate stroke to select an item. Stroke shortcuts are mapped to items depending on their positions in the menu, so that the user can easily learn the expert mode. Indeed, this mapping helps the user to easily associate an item to a stroke or to predict the other strokes (by knowing the position of the item, in the menu or relatively to neighbor items). Since the Leaf menu layout corresponds to a quarter of the circular layout of a Marking menu, it is not possible to have more than 3 straight gestures for maintaining good performance (a limitation identified in Marking menus [5]). Leaf menus therefore support curved gestures as in Flower menus [2], an extension of Marking menus. The curved gestures are simple enough to be accurately executed and to permit eye-free selection, useful when visual modality is already used or impossible in mobility context. Leaf menus therefore support 3 straight and 4 curved gesture shortcuts used in the expert mode while allowing more items in the novice mode. The frequent items can therefore be mapped with the 7 gesture shortcuts. Moreover, Leaf menus are hierarchical. In novice mode, they work in the same way as linear menus: submenus appear on the left or on the right of the parent item. In expert mode, the user executes a series of "simple" overlapping marks, one mark by menu level [2].

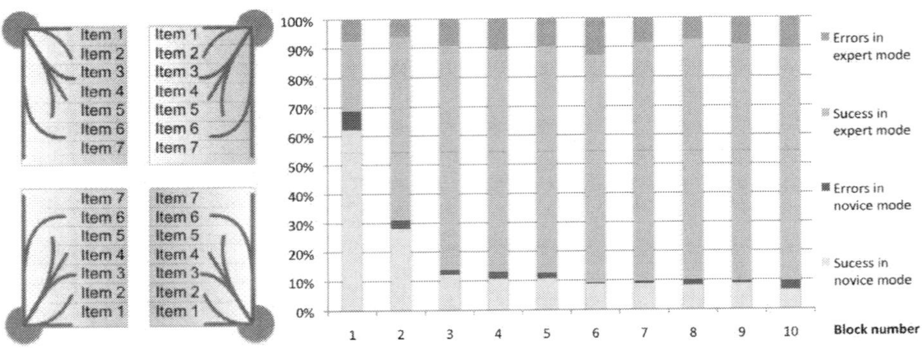

Fig. 2. Left, the four configurations of the Leaf menu (mirror effect). Right, experimental results of our pilot study: the type of selection [success or error] and the mode [novice or expert] per block number.

Finally a major difference with previous menus is that the expert mode of Leaf menus is always available wherever the menu is activated. Indeed, each item has several symmetrical stroke shortcuts, thanks to the mirror effect (Fig. 2). This flexibility that Leaf menus offer makes it possible to always have at least one available stroke shortcut everywhere on the small screen.

4 Pilot Study and Discussion

The experiment aims at evaluating if users can select and memorize commands in expert mode. The 8 participants were asked to activate items as quickly and accurately as possible on a target. Targets were located in the 4 corners of the screen to evaluate the Leaf menu in the worse scenario: indeed users were confronted with all horizontal and vertical symmetries. No instructions were given about the mode to use (novice or expert). Participants interacted on a HTC P3600 (supporting Windows Mobile 5.0) with the thumb of their dominant hand. The experiment was divided into 10 blocks of 28 trials (7 commands*4 target locations). The order of items was counter-balanced and the position of targets was randomized. The 4 results found are explained below.

Fig. 2 shows the type of selection (success or error) and the mode used (novice or expert) per block number. As expected, blocks have a significant effect on correct selections in expert mode ($F_{9,63}$=25.9, p<.0001) indicating that *participants learnt and correctly used the expert mode* (2 blocks of practice are sufficient). Moreover, these results can be improved by revisiting our basic recognition algorithm by taking into account the morphology of the thumb. For instance, simply by studying the recorded traces, 12% of selections in expert mode could be corrected for the item 3.

An analysis of the first block shows that more than 24% of correct selections were made in expert mode for items 1, 6, 7 and more than 15% for items 2 and 4. Then 5 commands can be quickly learned (< 4 trials) and it is not necessary to independently learn all gestures, because the symmetry of the menu helps to deduce them easily. This suggests that *the simplicity of a gesture may be as important as the repetition.* This result needs to be investigate further.

Most of participants said that once gestures are learned (number of blocks > 5), the expert mode (89.1% of correct selections) was more accurate that the novice mode (84.4%) because gestures are more accurate than a pointing task. So *gestures are not only faster but also less error-prone*, as previously highlighted in [8].

Finally, all our participants *enjoy the mirror effect and some of them found it more "logical"* than the linear menu. They also like drawing marks to select items.

References

1. Appert, C., Zhai, S.: Using Strokes as Command Shortcuts: Cognitive Benefits and Toolkit Support. In: ACM CHI 2009, pp. 2289–2298 (2009)
2. Bailly, G., Lecolinet, E., Nigay, L.: Flower Menus: A New Type of Marking Menus with Large Menu Breadth, within Groups and Efficient Expert Mode Memorization. In: ACM AVI 2008, pp. 15–22 (2008)
3. HanCock, M.S., Booth, K.S.: Improving menu placement strategies for pen input. In: ACM GI 2004, pp. 221–230 (2004)
4. Huot, S., Lecolinet, E.: ArchMenu et ThumbMenu: Contrôler son dispositif mobile "sur le pouce". In: ACM IHM 2007 (2007)
5. Kurtenbach, G.: The Design and Evaluation of Marking menus. University of Toronto. Ph.D., Thesis (1993)
6. Parhi, P., Karlson, A., Bederson, B.: Target Size Study for One-Handed Thumb Use on Small Touchscreen Devices. In: MobileHCI 2006, pp. 203–210 (2006)
7. Roudaut, A., Lecolinet, E., Huot, S.: Taptap and MagStick: Improving One-Handed Target Acquisition on Small Touch-screens. In: ACM AVI 2008, pp. 146–153 (2008)
8. Yatani, K., Partridge, K., Bern, M., Newman, M.W.: Escape: a target selection technique using visually-cued gestures. In: ACM CHI 2008, pp. 285–294 (2008)

Spatial Cues in Small Screen Devices: Benefit Or Handicap?

Martina Ziefle

Human Technology Centre (HUMTEC) Theaterplatz 14,
RWTH Aachen University, 52062 Aachen, Germany
ziefle@humtec.rwth-aachen.de

Abstract. Disorientation in small-screen-device menus is a frequent problem for many users. This study examines if navigation aids containing spatial information may reduce disorientation. Two aids were implemented into a simulated mobile phone: One aid contained spatial cues, providing an overview of menu locations and routes, the other delivered landmark knowledge, representing salient features on the route. Also, a condition without any aid was examined. 24 children and 24 adults solved four phone tasks twice. Dependent variables were navigation effectiveness and efficiency. Performance was lowest when users were not supported by any aid. The aid providing survey knowledge yielded the best performance. Though, the relative benefit by aids revealed to be age-related. While the aid providing survey knowledge was advantageous for all users, the aid delivering landmark knowledge was especially harmful for the children, which showed considerably more detouring in the menu. It is concluded that navigation aids reduce disorientation in small devices, especially those which support users to build up a spatial representation of the menu.

Keywords: Spatial orientation, navigation aids, small-screen-device.

1 Introduction

Recent studies examining the usability of small screen devices, as e.g. the mobile phone, show that users have considerable difficulties to navigate through the device menu [1,2]. Users get lost in a menu system, without knowing where they are, where to go next, and how to get back to previous navigation routes or known parts in the menu [2,3,4]. This especially applies for menus implemented in small screen devices, because of the restricted screen space, where users only see parts of the menu they have to navigate through (2,5). On the one hand, the hierarchical menu structure, still the most common form of interaction in communication technology devices, is advantageous as the functions are organized in smaller groups, thus rationing the multitude of options and keeping the information manageable. On the other hand, hierarchical menus also hold great potential for confusions and disorientation when menu structures are complex [4,5,6,7,8]. The screen only provides the functions currently available with only little information given about previous or subsequent menu levels. As depth of the phones' menu continuously increases with increasing number of functionalities, still more function labels intervene along the path and seduce the users to

T. Gross et al. (Eds.): INTERACT 2009, Part I, LNCS 5726, pp. 620–633, 2009.

take the wrong turnoff in the menu, if not being prevented from by excellent verbal memory abilities [2,6]. Users need to remember which functions they have already selected during the search and where they are located within menu hierarchy. The memorizing of salient features on the route supports the development of an adequate mental representation of the system structure. If short-term memory's capacity is exceeded, disorientation in the menu occurs, accompanied by additional meandering in search for the targeted function. Users report to loose their bearings in the menu, and, subsequently delve into distraction [2,3,4].

A considerable number of studies underline the importance of spatial orientation processes for the proper handling of technical devices [4,5,9,10,11,12,13], especially small screen devices [1,2,6]. When interacting with complex menu structures, users need to build up a mental representation of the spatial structure of that menu in order to orient themselves. The knowledge of how a menu is spatially structured guides users in their search through different levels in different menu depths. Theoretical concepts of spatial orientation [14,15] assume that orientation includes three major spatial knowledge types: route knowledge (the knowledge of the sequence of actions required to get from one point to another), landmark knowledge (representing salient features on the route), and survey knowledge (reflecting the overall structure and providing an overview of locations and routes in space). The concept had been successfully transferred to the navigation through different forms of hypertext [16,17,18], also for PDAs [1,19,20], and for mobile phones [2,6,8]. The navigation performance was superior when users had built up survey knowledge (hierarchical nature of the menu), route knowledge (which route to take through the menu), and also landmark knowledge (at which crossings to turn 'left' or 'right'). Spatial abilities specifically advantage navigation by developing a mental representation of the systems' structure [2,21,22,23], which helps users to harmonize their relative menu and to keep the menu structure in mind while navigating through the system.

Yet, an increasing number of studies have been dealing with the usability of computer interfaces and small screen devices for older adults [1,2,3,4,11,19,20,21], addressing the impact of the demographic change. Only few studies considered the difficulties children experience [8,24,25,26] when using mobile devices. Though the investigation of children is of specific interest. Children are an increasingly important user group of small screen devices, and therefore need usable designs. Also, children are supposed to easily master the interaction with technical devices and to understand the mode of operation of those devices much faster by virtue of their early contact with technology. Additionally, children's fascination for explorative and inquisitive activities is well known. According to recent studies [25,26] evidence is given that children showed considerable performance losses in suboptimal interface designs.

The present study examines the utility of two navigation aids, which were implemented into the phones' display. One type provides survey knowledge and the other landmark knowledge. In order to learn how user characteristics interact with navigation in mobile phones, children and younger adults were examined and verbal memory and spatial abilities were surveyed. The first question to be answered is if any navigation aid implemented in the small screen of a miniature device is helpful at all. The critical argument in this context refers to screen space restrictions and the limited amount of information to be displayed at a time. Any additional information on small screens also bears the danger of causing visual overload, possibly interfering with the visual encoding process and affecting information processing [27). As additional information load in the small display should be held as low as possible, maximizing the effectiveness of information access, the adding of information could also disadvantage performance by causing visual load . The second question is if there are differences respecting the type of information which is delivered by the navigation aid. Here, it is of interest if children, which have lower cognitive abilities due to their developmental status, can process the spatial information delivered by navigation aids.

2 Method

2.1 Independent and Dependent Variables

Two independent variables were examined. The first independent variable was the type of navigation aid. Two different navigation aids were implemented into a computer simulation of a real mobile phone. In one condition, the interface showed the name of the current category, as well as a list of its contents. This aid delivers mainly landmark knowledge without spatial information about the menu structure (Fig. 1, center). The other interface was identical to the first except that it showed the parents and parent-parents of the current of the category and that sub-categories were indented to emphasize the hierarchical structure (Fig. 1, right). This aid contained spatial cues, providing survey knowledge (structure of the menu). In addition, a control condition was examined, in which no navigation aid was given. Instead, the original interface was presented (Fig. 1, left). In each of the three cases shown in Figure 1, the top display is a higher level version of the bottom display.

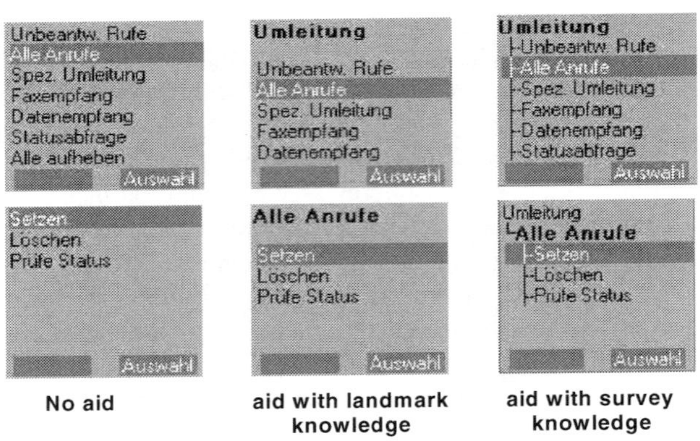

Fig. 1. Visualizations of the three different interface conditions of the mobile phone

The second independent variable was users' age, comparing the performance of children, and younger adults. In addition, verbal memory and spatial abilities were psychometrically determined and treated as between subject variables, possibly affecting navigation performance and interacting with the navigation aids.

Dependent variables were the effectiveness and efficiency of navigation [28]. For the task effectiveness, the number of successfully solved tasks (within the time limit of five minutes per task) was measured. A maximum of eight tasks (four tasks solved twice) were to be completed. For efficiency, three different measures were collected: The time needed to process the tasks was surveyed. Also, hierarchical returns to higher levels in menu hierarchy were analyzed. Returns in menu hierarchy occur when users in the belief of having taken the wrong path go back to a known menu position, consequently re-orientating themselves. In addition, returns to the top were determined. This measure was assumed to reflect utter disorientation, as users had to re-orientate by returning to the top menu level, beginning from scratch.

2.2 Experimental Tasks

Four typical and frequently used mobile phone tasks were selected. In order to determine learnability effects, the tasks had to be solved twice consecutively. The order of tasks in the two trials was held constant over participants. In total, a minimum of 47 steps was necessary to solve the four tasks. Participants had to

- *Call a number* (11 keystrokes).
- *Hide one's own number when calling someone* (14 keystrokes).
- *Send a text message* (11 keystrokes; the message was already provided and only had to be sent when participants had reached the adequate point in the menu).
- *Make a call divert to the mailbox* (11 keystrokes).

2.3 Participants

48 participants volunteered to take part. 24 children (nine boys, 11 girls), aged 9 - 10 years (M = 9.5; SD = 0.8) of age and 24 young adults (12 males, 12 females), aged 23 - 31 years (M = 24.9; SD= 2.9)). The children were pupils in their fourth school year; the adults were students of different academic fields. Participants' experience with mobile phones and other technical devices was studied as well as the reported ease of using them. They reported if and how often they use a mobile phone and a PC, using a 5-point scale (1 = several times per day, 2 = once per day, 3 = once or twice a week, 4 = once or twice per month and 5 = less than once or twice a month). Furthermore, they rated the ease of using these devices, using a scale (1= the usage is easy, 2 = the usage is rather easy, 3 = the usage is rather difficult and 4 = the usage is difficult). Finally, participants indicated their interest in technology, using a 4-point scale (1 = low interest; 2 = rather low interest, 3 = rather high interest, 4 = high interest).

2.4 Assessing User Characteristics Interacting with Navigation Performance

It was a major aim to learn how age groups were interacting with the mobile phone and, which user characteristics might be crucial for navigation performance. Therefore, participants were surveyed regarding spatial ability and verbal memory capacity; both cognitive abilities help to built up a mental representation of the system structure. For the children, two subtests of the HAWIK-R were carried out. In the spatial ability test ("Mosaic Test") the experimenter showed the child a picture (Fig. 2, left) and the child's task was to reproduce the picture using cubes having different patterns on each of the sides (max. 26 points). The test on short-term memory required the children to verbally repeat a row of numbers read aloud by the experimenter, which had to be reproduced directly after. The children were given two trials to correctly reproduce each row (max: 14 points). For the adult group, spatial abilities were assessed with the paper-folding test [29]). Each of the twenty items includes successive drawings of two or three folds made in a square sheet of paper. The final drawing shows a hole punched in the folded paper. Participants had to mentally rotate the paper from the folded into the fully opened form and to indicate which of a number of possibilities shows the correct drawing. The 20 items had to be solved within 180 s. In Figure 2 (right), an example item of the paper-folding test is given. To assess memory ability, the verbal memory test [6] was used.15 Turkish words (unknown to Germans) were presented in succession for 3 sec, each. Directly after, users had to recognize the target items among three distractors, each being phonologically or visually similar. The maximum score was 15.

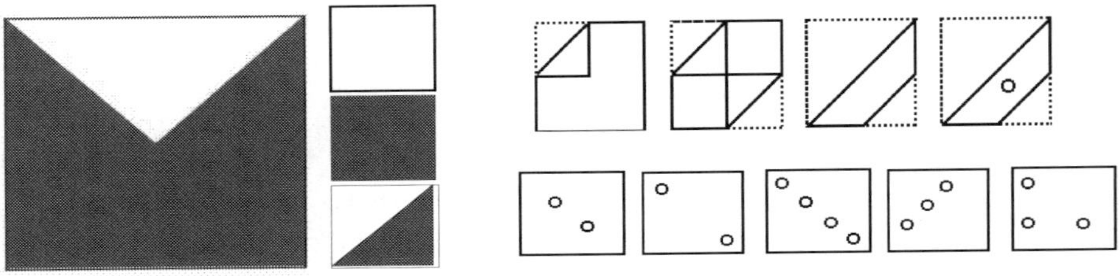

Fig. 2. Left: the Mosaic-Test to assess children's spatial visualization ability [30]; right: Item example of the Paperfolding test to assess adults' spatial visualization ability [29]

2.5 User Characteristics of Participants

In this section, the experience with technical devices, and the reported ease of using them are focused at. Also, the rated general interest in technology is illustrated. Furthermore, the participants' verbal memory and spatial abilities are described. It is of interest, if these variables are modulated by age or the gender of participants.

Technical experience. Users showed a high experience with technical devices, however, significant age differences were present ($F(1,40)=18.8$; $p<0.05$. In contrast to the adults which used mobile phones and PCs several times a day (phone: M = 1.3; SD = 0.5; PC: M = 1.4; SD = .48), the children used the mobile phone (M = 3.1; SD = 1.1) and the PC (M = 2.2; SD = 1.3) less frequently. The interest in technology was generally high, but also showed significant age differences ($F(1,40)=15.8$; $p<0.05$). Interestingly, the children's interest in technology (M = 3.5; SD = 0.6) was higher compared to the adults (M = 2.8; SD = 0.7). Also, gender differences were revealed ($F(1,40)=13.1$; $p<0.05$). Independently of age, male users reported a higher interest in technology (M = 3.5; SD = 0.8) than did female participants (M = 2.9; SD = 0.8).

Verbal memory. First, outcomes in children's verbal memory are reported. From the 14 points that could be attained at the most, the children reached, on average, 5.5 points (SD = 1.4). Apparently, the memorizing and recall of the digits was quite difficult for them, as none of the children was able to reach the maximum score. For the adults, the performance equaled 13.1 (SD = 1.9) points (out of 15). Gender differences were not present, neither in the children nor the adult group.

Spatial visualization abilities. The children differed considerably with respect to the extent of spatial abilities. The lowest performance in the mosaic test was 5 points, however, there were also children, who reached the maximum score of 26 points (M = 15.2; SD = 5.1). With respect to the performance of the adults, the spectrum of correct answers ranged between 9 and 19 (out of 20), reaching a mean performance of 13.3 (SD = 3.1). No gender differences in spatial visualization ability were found.

2.6 Apparatus and Materials

The utility of navigation aids is a rather generic question, which is quite independent of the device type. A simulation of a real mobile phone was used (Siemens S45). None of participants had used the specific model before. As individual navigation routes had to be analyzed in detail, the phone was simulated as software solution, run on a PC, and displayed on a touch screen (Iiyama TXA3841). The display corresponded to the original size, but the phone's chassis and the keys were enlarged enabling easy operation with the finger on the touch screen. Moreover, a logging software tool was developed, which logged any user interaction with the system. By this, the number and type of keys used, the functions selected, and the individual navigation routes taken through the menu could be reconstructed in detail. In order to assure a comfortable body posture, participants sat on a table and worked on the touch screen fixed to the edge of the table (Figure 3).

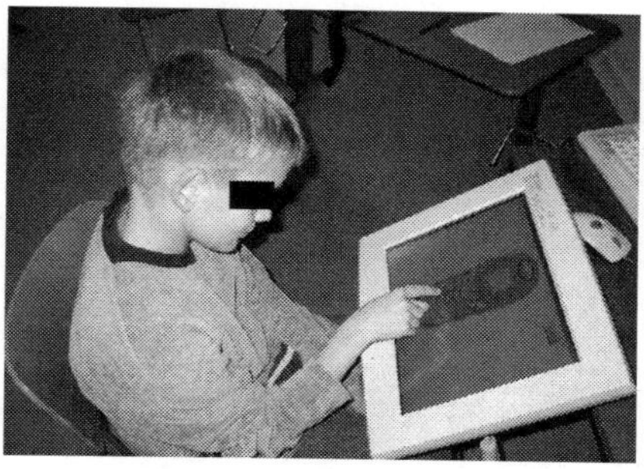

Fig. 3. Photo of a child using the simulated mobile phone on the touch screen

2.7 Design and Procedure

The study was based on a two-factorial design. Both main factors (navigation aid and age) were treated as between-subject variables. Gender was balanced. Spatial visualization and verbal memory abilities were treated as between subject variables.

In the beginning of the experiment, participants' technical experience was assessed and verbal memory and spatial abilities were determined. Then, the nine tasks were to be solved twice, in order to determine learnability effects. A time limit of five minutes per task was set (the appropriateness of the limit was tested in previous studies). A fast and thorough working style was instructed. If a task was solved successfully, a 'Congratulations' - message appeared on the display. To avoid any biases, the aids were neither explained nor mentioned. It was instructed that the experiment was concerned with the usability of mobile phones. All participants were told that -in case of a very difficult task- they should feel free to "give up", in order not to overly burden them. However, none of participants did so, but rather enjoyed the experiment. Depending on the individual working speed, the experiment lasted about 60 minutes.

3 Results

The results were analyzed by multivariate analyses of variance assessing effects of the type of navigation aid and age on effectiveness (tasks solved) and efficiency (time, hierarchical returns and returns to the top). The significance of the omnibus F-Tests was taken from Pillai values, followed by the description of the single F-tests. Also, learnability effects were analyzed, determining if performance improved from the first to the second trial). A final analysis was concerned with the impact of user characteristics for performance. The level of significance was set at $p < 0.05$.

Regarding the analysis of task efficiency, two strategies can be considered: One strategy only includes users that successfully accomplished the tasks; the other one includes all participants, independently from their tasks' success. Both strategies are basically "sensible". On a first sight, the selection of successful task performers for further analysis seems to be advantageous as their results can be directly related to effectiveness. However, if only a rather small proportion of participants were able to solve a certain task, only small and unequal samples would have entered statistical analyses. Moreover, from an ergonomic point of view, it is more insightful to learn about the ergonomic shortcomings and navigation difficulties and to consider all user actions -- even if users failed at the end. Analyses showed that result patterns for "task solvers" and "non-solvers" were quite similar. Therefore, task efficiency was statistically analyzed comprising the total group.

3.1 Effects of Navigation Aids

A first analysis was concerned with the different types of navigation aids. MANOVA analyses revealed a significant omnibus effect ($F(4,80) = 2.9$; $p<0.05$). On the single F-test level, the main effect of navigation aid was significant for the effectiveness ($F(2,42) = 5.4$; $p<0.05$), the returns in menu hierarchy ($F(2,42) = 3.6$; $p<0.05$), and the returns to the top. The descriptive outcomes can be seen in Figure 4.

From figure 4 it can be seen that the lowest performance was given in the condition where no navigation aid was given (white bars). The disadvantage of having no aid is especially prominent in the two disorientation measures, the returns in menu hierarchy and the returns to the top. However, the utility of the two different aids turned out to be different. The aid providing landmark knowledge did not differ from the no-aid condition, yielding about the same (low) level of performance, what is –again- very pronounced in the disorientation measures. Having the aid providing landmark knowledge as support, users spent 14 min on the tasks and stepped, on average, 61.5 times ($SD = 37$) back to higher levels in the menu. In contrast, supported by the aid delivering survey knowledge, this happened about half as often ($M = 29.9$; $SD = 23$). The difference yielded a significant effect ($F(2,42) = 3.6$; $p<0.05$). The same pattern can be seen in the number of returns to the top. In the landmark aid, users had to re-enter the menu, 6.6 times ($SD = 5.3$), while it occurred significantly less often ($M = 2.1$; $SD = 2.3$) in the navigation aid delivering survey knowledge ($F(2,42) = 4.2$; $p<0.05$).

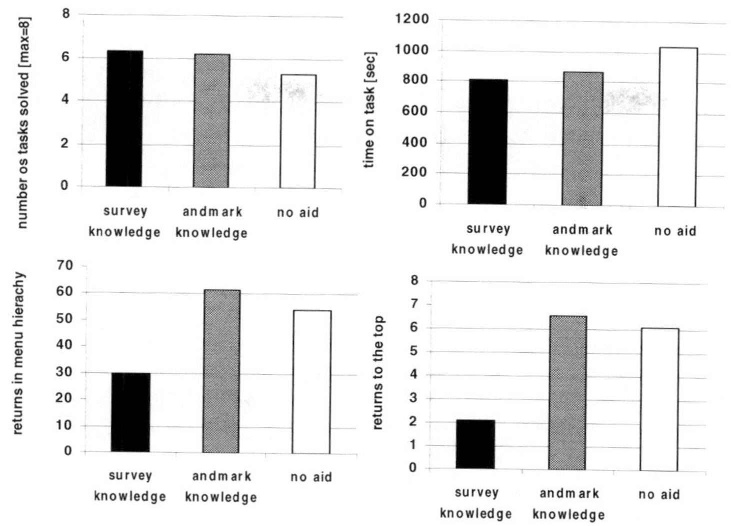

Fig. 4. Effects of navigation aid. Upper left: effectiveness; upper right: time on task; lower left: returns in menu hierarchy; lower right: returns to the top.

3.2 Effects of Age

Next, the performance of the children compared to the adults is focused. With respect to task effectiveness, significant ($F(1, 42) = 86.5$; $p < 0.05$) age effects were found. Of the eight tasks, children solved, on average, 4.2 tasks (SD = 1.7) successfully, and the adults 7.6 tasks (SD = 0.8). The age differences were even more prominent regarding efficiency: The adults needed, on average, 6 minutes (SD = 256 s) to process all tasks, while the children needed 24 minutes (SD = 416 s; $F(1, 42) = 118.5$; $p < 0.05$). When navigating through the menu, adults made 21.4 hierarchical returns (SD = 16.8), and, on average, 1.8 returns to the top (SD = 2.2). Again, children's efficiency was much lower, carrying out more than three times as many hierarchical steps back (M = 75.6; SD = 49) with, on average, more than four times as many returns to the top (M = 8.1; SD = 6.9). Age differences in both, hierarchical steps back ($F(1,42) = 28.9$; $p < 0.05$)

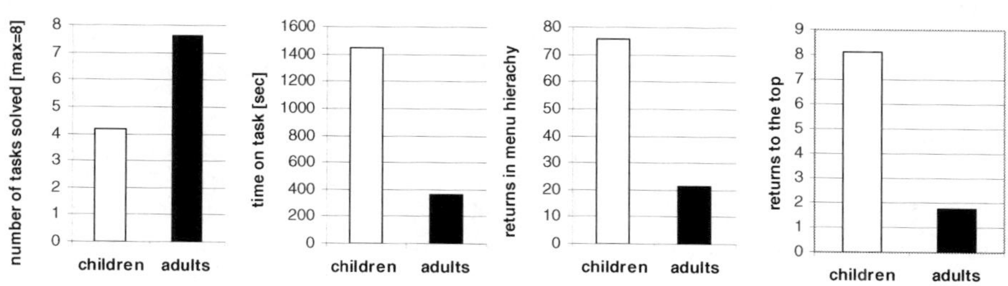

Fig. 5. Effects of age on all dependent measures

and returns to the top ($F(1, 42) = 21.3$; $p < 0.05$) yielded statistical significance. In Figure 5, age differences are pictured for all dependent measures.

The interaction of both variables, the type of navigation aid and users' age had shown to be significant ($F(8, 80) = 2.1$; $p<0.05$). The nature of the co-acting of navigation aid and age becomes evident from Figure 6.

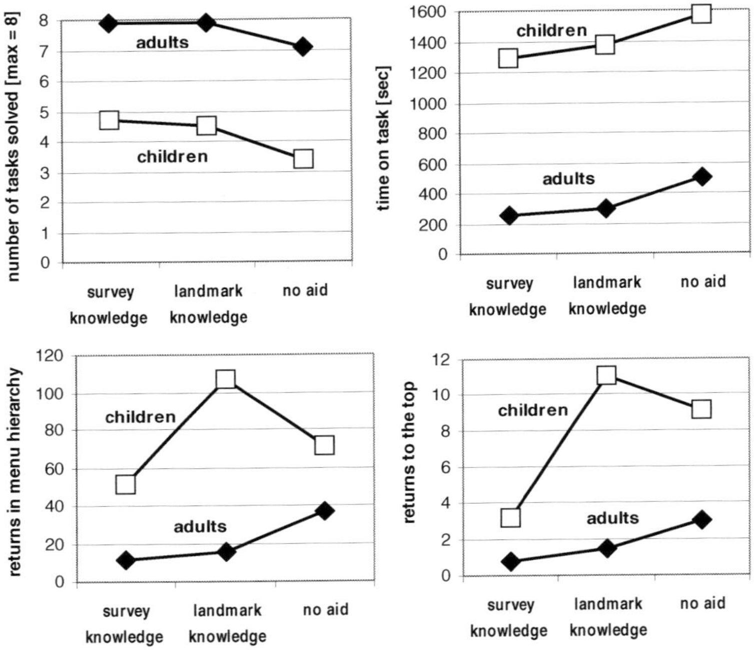

Fig. 6. Interacting effects between age and navigation aid for all dependent measures

The interaction mainly stems from the disorientation measures (returns in menu hierarchy, and returns to the top). While the aid with the survey knowledge yielded advantageous effects on the performance in both age groups, the aid delivering landmark knowledge showed detrimental effects for the children, as taken from the considerably higher detouring in the menu. With respect to the number of returns in menu hierarchy, the disadvantage of the landmark knowledge aid compared to the survey knowledge aid for the children was 55% and, for the number of returns to the top even 70%.

3.3 Learnability Effects

Can users improve their performance in the second trial? With respect to task effectiveness significant improvements were found (effectiveness: $F(1,36) = 4.4$; $p<0.05$), however, not differing between the navigation aids conditions (Figure7). In the first trial, 2.9 ($SD = 1.1$) of the four tasks were solved and 3.1 tasks ($SD = 1.1$) in the second. Looking at the time on task, also significant learnability effects were detected ($F(1, 36) = 22.3$; $p<0.05$). However, learnability differed between conditions, revealing a significant interacting effect ($F(2,36) = 3.3$; $p<0.05$, Figure 7).

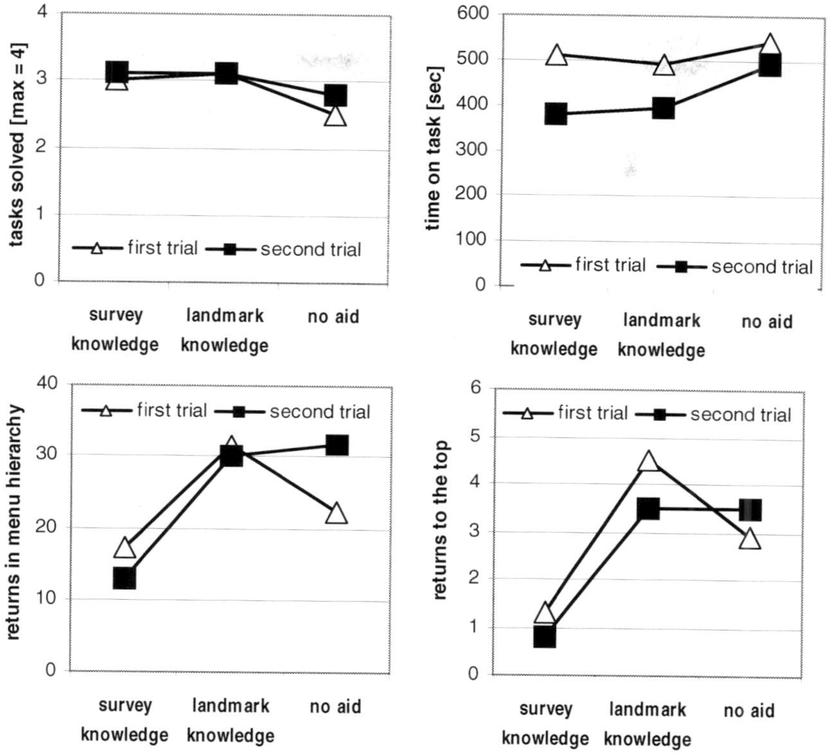

Fig. 7. Learnability effects in the three experimental conditions

From Figure 7 it can seen that, learnability effects were mainly limited to the time on task, showing that participants were considerably faster processing the phone tasks a second time. For the disorientation measures, performance did not significantly improve from the first to the second trial. Detailed analyses showed that the reason for the non-significant learnability effect is the low performance in the condition in which no aid was present. Here, the performance in the second trial was even lower than in the first trial. This negative learnability effect in the control condition corroborates that participants have major difficulties developing a mental representation of the menu without any navigation aid.

3.4 Impact of User Characteristics on Performance Outcomes

Finally it is analyzed whether there are crucial user characteristics to be considered which influence the navigation performance. Also it is of interest if user characteristics interact with the utility of the navigation aids. Answering the second question first, no interacting effect between user characteristics and the utility of navigation aids were found. Thus, we can assume that the benefit by the aids, and specifically the benefit of the aid providing survey knowledge is universal and thus can be recommended for a broad variety of users. However, there were significant correlations between user characteristics and navigation performance. For the adult group, spatial visualization ability was significantly correlated with the time needed to process the tasks ($r= -.57$; $p<0.05$), the number of returns in menu hierarchy ($r= -.51$; $p<0.05$), and the returns to the top ($r= -.47$; $p<0.05$). Thus, persons with high spatial abilities are considerably advantaged. Memory abilities and technical experience did not show a significant impact on performance. For the children group, task effectiveness turned out to be significantly related to the frequency of using a mobile phone ($r= -.39$; $p<0.05$) and the ease of using it ($r= -.44$; $p<0.05$). Also, time on task showed significant correlations with the frequency of using a mobile phone ($r= -.39$; $p<0.05$), as well as a PC ($r= -.44$; $p<0.05$), and also with the ease of using the mobile phone ($r= -.4$; $p<0.05$) and the PC ($r= -.4.2$; $p<0.05$). Thus, children with a high technical experience are advantaged in menu navigation. The level of verbal memory and spatial visualization, did not affect children's menu navigation.

4 Discussion and Conclusion

As disorientation is a frequent problem when using mobile small-screen devices with a hierarchical menu [e.g. 1,2,3,20], the utility of navigation aids implemented in the menu of a mobile phone menu was under study. The navigation aids contained different types of spatial knowledge. Based on the theoretical framework of spatial orientation [14,14], two types of spatial knowledge very varied within the navigation aids. One type represented an aid mainly containing landmark knowledge, which tells users salient features on the navigation route. The other type delivered spatial information and survey knowledge, which informs users about the menu structure and providing an overview of locations and routes in space. However, as any additional information on the restricted screens may also cause visual overload and interfere with the visual encoding process [27], affecting information processing, a control condition was examine122d, in which no aid was given. Here, participants used the original display design of the phone.

The results clearly showed that the handling of a common mobile phone is not easy to accomplish, but rather represents a high cognitive challenge for users. Especially the 9-10 years olds showed considerable difficulties to master the four common phone tasks on a common mobile phone. Tasks effectiveness ranged only at about 50%, accompanied by a huge number of detouring routes. Children executed many returns in menu hierarchy, re-orientating themselves, even returning frequently to the top menu level, beginning from scratch. Also the young adults, students, bright and technology-prone, which do not represent the average user, but a kind of "best case" user group, did not show a "perfect" performance, solving all the tasks without barriers. Taken from their detouring routes, they also experienced disorientation in the menu. Facing the increasing penetration of small screen devices in all parts of daily life, and considering the growing user diversity, this corroborates the enormous impact of usable designs. It must be concluded that current small screen devices are -- cognitively -- challenging to use. This is true for young adults, but it is even more valid for children, which –due to their developmental status- can be categorized as "weaker" users [8,24,25,26]. The fact that both navigation aids advantaged users' performance in the menu shows that the disorientation problem in small screen device menus can be basically relieved. It is an important finding that useful and usable designs do not necessarily require huge sums of additional costs with respect to the implementation in state-of-the-art mobile design. As shown here, very small software modifications can be very effective and in an ergonomic sense, successful.

The answer to the question which of both navigation aids is more helpful for users reveals both, universal and differential aspects to be considered for usable interface designs. The aid which delivered structural information and survey knowledge showed to have a universal benefit, advantaging performance for both, the children and the adults. Task success was higher and the detouring in the menu was distinctly reduced, taken from the smaller number of detour steps and returns to higher levels in menu hierarchy. It is assumed that the nature of the strong benefit by the survey knowledge lies in the fact that users are supported in constructing a proper mental representation of the systems' structure [4,9,12,21,23]. They are informed about their relative position in the menu and can keep the menu structure in mind while navigating through the system. Thus, by having an appropriate model and a structural concept of the mental 'room' that has to be navigated through, performance is distinctly increased. In the mobile phone, where the overall structure of the menu is not transparent, and the screen size is very limited this is even more crucial.

The aid delivering mainly landmark knowledge (showing the name of the current category and a list of its contents), though, turned out to be age-sensitive. While young adults simply showed a somewhat lower performance (compared to the aid delivering survey knowledge), the children had extremely difficulties handling the aid providing landmark knowledge. Apparently, the kids were not able to capitalize on the landmark information when searching for a specific function. In the contrary, their navigation was impeded by this aid, as taken from the fact that the detouring in the menu was dramatically increased when having the landmark aid as support.

The findings presented here do have implications for the design of mobile phones in general. First, it is important to learn that the way the information and menu of a system are structured seemed not to be fully transparent to children – even if they are used to working with programs such as Windows Explorer®, which is organized in the same fashion as our sample. Therefore, the constant visualization of the menu structure is of unobtrusive assistance. Another way of overcoming disorientation problems associated with hierarchical menu structures [31] is to use only one long alphabetical list of functions, where users can search by initial letters. This was evaluated with students. It is to be questioned whether this really helps users less experienced with mobiles as they often have no idea of the functions' naming in the menu and simple recognition of functions and categories – even though far from trivial – should be easier than active recall of the right term for a specific function.

From the outcomes of this study both, important knowledge about user groups as well as practical design recommendations can be derived.

- Even the children, which are broadly assumed to easily master the usage of small screen device, have serious difficulties to handle small screen devices.
- Applying a navigation aid in the small screen which informs users about the spatial structure of the menu can compensate for these difficulties.
- Designers and manufactures should take usability issues serious and implement spatial cues as navigation aids into the small screen of mobile devices.

- The utility of this kind of navigation aid is not restricted to phones, but can be easily transferred to any small screen device with a hierarchical menu, as MP3-Players, eHealth devices for medical care, wrist watches, fax machines, printers, banking and ticket machines or mobile gaming devices etc.

Future studies will have to extend this research by examining navigation aids that are not only visual, but use auditory and sonically enhanced navigational cues [32,22].

Acknowledgments. The author thanks Susanne Bay for valuable contributions to this research. Thanks also to Philipp Brauner, Eugen Yu, Thomas Michel, Luisa Bremen, Judith Strenk, and Fabia Tucht for their research support.

References

1. Goodman, J., Gray, P., Khammampad, K., Brewster, S.: Using landmarks to support older people in navigation. In: Brewster, S., Dunlop, M.D. (eds.) Mobile HCI 2004. LNCS, vol. 3160, pp. 38–48. Springer, Heidelberg (2004)
2. Ziefle, M., Bay, S.: How to overcome disorientation in mobile phone menus: A comparison of two different types of navigation aids. Human Computer Interaction 21(4), 393–432 (2006)
3. Arning, K., Ziefle, M.: Barriers of information access in small screen device applications: The relevance of user characteristics for a transgenerational design. In: Stephanidis, C., Pieper, M. (eds.) ERCIM Ws UI4ALL 2006. LNCS, vol. 4397, pp. 117–136. Springer, Heidelberg (2007)
4. Lin, D.-Y.: Hypertext for the aged. Computers in Human Behaviour 19(2), 201–209 (2003)
5. Edwards, D., Hardmann, L.: Lost in Hyperspace. Cognitive Mapping and Navigation in a Hypertext Environment. In: McAleese, R. (ed.) Hyperspace: Theory into practice, pp. 105–125. Intellect limited, Oxford (1989)
6. Bay, S., Ziefle, M.: Design for all: User characteristics to be considered for the design of phones with hierarchical menu structures. In: Luczak, H., Zink, K.J. (eds.) Human Factors in Organizational Design and Management, pp. 503–508. IEA Press, Santa Monica (2003)
7. Billingsley, P.A.: Navigation through hierarchical menu structures: Does it help to have a map? In: Proc Human Factors Society 26th Annual Meeting, pp. 103–107 (1982)
8. Bay, S., Ziefle, M.: Children using cellular phones. The effects of shortcomings in user interface design. Human Factors 47(1), 158–168 (2005)
9. Downing, R., Moore, J., Brown, S.: The effects of spatial visualization and domain expertise on information seeking. Computers in Human Behaviour 21, 195–209 (2005)
10. Norman, K.: Spatial visualization - a gateway to computer-based technology. Journal of Special Education Technology 12(3), 195–206 (1994)
11. Pak, R., Czaja, S., Sharit, J., Rogers, W., Fisk, A.: The role of spatial abilities and age in performance in an auditory computer navigation task. Computers in Human Behaviour 24(6), 3045–3051 (2008)
12. Allen, G.L.: Human Spatial memory. Remembering where. LEA, Mahwah, NJ (2004)
13. Westerman, S.J.: Individual differences in the use of command line and menu computer interfaces. Int. J. of Human Computer Interaction 9(2), 183–198 (1997)
14. Thorndyke, P.W., Goldin, S.: Spatial learning and reasoning skill. In: Pick, H.L., Acredolo, L.P. (eds.) Spatial orientation, pp. 195–217. Plenum, New York (1983)

15. Thorndyke, P.W., Hayes-Roth, B.H.: Differences in spatial knowledge acquired from maps and navigation. Cognitive Psychology 14, 560–589 (1982)
16. McDonald, J., Stevenson, R.: Navigation in Hyperspace: An evaluation of the effects of navigational tools and subject matter expertise on browsing and information retrieval in hypertext. Interacting with Computers 10, 129–142 (1998)
17. Vicente, K.J., Hayes, B.C., Williges, R.C.: Assaying and isolating individual differences in searching a hierarchical files system. Human Factors 29(3), 349–359 (1987)
18. Kim, H., Hirtle, S.C.: Spatial metaphors and disorientation in hypertext browsing. Behaviour and Information Technology 14(4), 239–250 (1995)
19. Arning, K., Ziefle, M.: Understanding differences in PDA acceptance and performance. Computers in Human Behaviour 23(6), 2904–2927 (2007)
20. Arning, K., Ziefle, M.: Cognitive and personal predictors for PDA navigation performance. Behaviour and Information Technology (2009), doi:10.1080/01449290701679395
21. Ziefle, M., Bay, S.: Mental models of a cellular phone menu. Comparing older and younger novice users. In: Brewster, S., Dunlop, M.D. (eds.) Mobile HCI 2004. LNCS, vol. 3160, pp. 25–37. Springer, Heidelberg (2004)
22. Mayer, R.E.: Models for Understanding. Review of Educational Research 59(1), 43–64 (1986)
23. Sein, M.K., Olfman, L., Bostrom, R.P., Davies, S.A.: Visualisation ability as a prediction of user learning success. Int. J. Man-Machine-Studies 39, 599–620 (1993)
24. Ziefle, M., Bay, S.: Transgenerational Designs in Mobile Technology. In: Lumsden, J. (ed.) Handbook of Research on User Interface Design and Evaluation for Mobile Technology, pp. 122–140. IGI Global, Hershey (2008)
25. Ziefle, M., Bay, S., Schwade, A.: On keys' meanings and modes: The impact of navigation key solutions on children's efficiency using a mobile phone. Behaviour and Information Technology 25(5), 413–431 (2006)
26. Bay, S., Ziefle, M.: Landmarks or surveys? The impact of different instructions on children's performance in hierarchical menu structures. Computers in Human Behaviour 24(3), 1246–1274 (2008)
27. Bay, S., Ziefle, M.: Effects of menu foresight on information access in small screen devices. In: 48th Annual Meeting of the Human Factors and Ergonomic Society, pp. 1841–1845. Human Factors Society, Santa Monica (2004)
28. EN ISO 9241-11, Ergonomic requirements for office work with visual display terminals. Part 11: Guidance on usability, Beuth, Berlin (1997)
29. Ekstrom, R.B., French, J.W., Harman, H.H., Dermen, D.: Manual for the Kit of Factor-Referenced Cognitive Tests. Educational Testing Service, Princeton (1976)
30. Tewes, U.: Hamburg-Wechsler-Intelligence Test. Huber, Bern, Switzerland (1983)
31. Marsden, G., Jones, M.: Ubiquitous computing and cellular handset interfaces – are menus the best way forward? South African Computer Journal 28, 67–76 (2002)
32. Chittaro, L., Burigat, S.: Augmenting audio messages with visual directions in mobile guides: an evaluation of three approaches. In: Proceedings of the 7th international conference on Human computer interaction with mobile devices & services, pp. 107–114 (2005)
33. Brewster, S.: Overcoming the Lack of Screen Space on Mobile Computers. Personal and Ubiquitious Computing 6(3), 188–205 (2002)

3DKey: An Accordion-Folding Based Virtual Keyboard for Small Screen

Khaldoun Al Faraj, Mustapha Mojahid, and Nadine Vigouroux

University of Toulouse,
118 Route de Narbonne,
31062 Toulouse Cedex 9, France
{alfaraj,mojahid,vigourou}@irit.fr

Abstract. Nowadays, handheld devices are more and more equipped with functionalities and applications so that they almost serve like a desktop computer. However users find them tedious and tiring to input text due the tiny keys of their virtual keyboard. In this paper, we discuss a new text entry method (3DKey) based on addition of a third dimension to traditional virtual keyboard to overcome the small screen constraint of handheld devices. In this context, the accordion-folding the virtual keyboard is used as a solution to expand keys leading to easier selection. Thus our 3DKey virtual keyboard can be seen as composed of two zones: an accordion-folded zone and a spread zone. Our study showed that users achieved more accurate and relatively faster text entry with 120° accordion-folding and predictive spreading virtual keyboard, which resulted in speed improvement of 37.71 %, than with traditional virtual keyboard.

Keywords: Text input, virtual keyboard, 3D key, accordion folds style, prediction system, mobile devices, handhelds, PDAs, UMPCs.

1 Introduction

The computing and telecommunication products are shrinking more and more in size. Nowadays, beside smart phones and Personal Digital Assistants (PDAs), Ultra Mobile Personal Computers (UMPCs) with 4.5" in display size also exist on the market. However their shrinking size has a great effect on text entry so the traditional full-size keyboard is no longer adequate to be used on. Furthermore, these handheld devices tend to be equipped with functionalities, applications and services (e.g. office applications, e-mail, and so on) so that they serve almost like a desktop PC.

In other words, today's mobile devices are not designed to just typing a short text like SMS (Short Message Service) and diary operations, but also a complex messages and small documents. As a result, a text entry method as efficient as on a desktop PC is required to make available handheld device technologies exploitable.

The most of these mobile devices are equipped with a touch screen that led to stylus-based text entry techniques like virtual keyboard and handwriting recognition instead of physical keyboard.

Virtual keyboard is a copy of physical keyboard at the bottom area of a touch screen that users can tap on using the stylus. However, mobile devices are too small to

T. Gross et al. (Eds.): INTERACT 2009, Part I, LNCS 5726, pp. 634–644, 2009.

have desktop or laptop virtual keyboard requiring its miniaturization that makes keys tiny, thus their selection becomes more difficult and tedious to typing a text.

Handwriting recognition systems do not require a significant portion of screen because entering a character or a word only needs to make its corresponding gesture. Although these systems can help to overcome screen-space constraint of handheld devices, they are still inherently limited by writing speed and need user learning to make their gestures.

In the case of virtual and hardware keyboards, the time required to type a character is the same regardless of its graphical shape. While in the case of handwriting input, the time of making a character varies according to its shape trajectory. The maximum time is attributed to complex gestures like “k”, while the minimum time is attributed to simple gesture such as “i”. As a result, thanks to keys, input time of character is always shorter for keyboard than that for handwriting input.

In short, while the document is the primary point of focus in a traditional desktop application, a document is often consumable and non-editable (read-only) on handheld devices. Therefore, a research of text entry method that enables users to author a complex messages and small documents on their handhelds has been one of the most prominent challenges in the world of mobile computing.

In this paper, we aim to make handheld devices usable for creating information though a new text entry solution based on accordion folding and predictive spreading virtual keyboard.

2 Related Work

Stylus-based text entry techniques for handheld devices generally fall into three main categories: virtual keyboards, handwriting recognitions and gesture-based input.

2.1 Virtual Keyboard

As we have mentioned in the introduction, virtual keyboard (sometimes called on-screen keyboard) is a graphical representation of physical keyboard on the screen of computing devices. It is originally designed to allow people with disabilities and special needs to access computes. Small screen devices have also used it as a text entry solution but with lower number of keys (nearly 105 keys for computer keyboard versus 80 keys for small screen device). Such reduction resulted in using modes to enter numbers and special characters. Furthermore, keys are always much smaller than those of desktop computer (26 versus 16 pixels in width) regardless this reduction, then with these tiny keys selection is getting more difficult and requires more focus of attention.

McGffin, M. & Balakrishnan, R. [1] proposed expanding targets when pointer approaches them as a solution to facilitate their selection. Fisheye [2] applied it, but distortion of whole keyboard with each stylus movement may annoy users and more attention is required to enter character. BigKey [3] makes virtual keyboard almost static through expanding the next entry i.e. the most probable next letters.

As stylus or cursor of mouse replaced ten fingers, many researches [4], [5] have been conducted to find the keyboard configuration minimizing stylus travel distances between characters as much as possible, thus speeding up entry. But users' familiarity with the QWERTY layout may slow down their ability to learn other layouts.

2.2 Handwriting Recognition

The first proposed gestural alphabet was Unistrokes alphabet [6]. Each letter is represented as a signal stroke to resolve the segmentation problem related to handwriting recognition. However, it was not similar enough to Latin alphabet, forcing users to learn a new alphabet. Palm OS popularized Graffiti® as a unistroke alphabet through its PDAs. The success of Graffiti alphabet is attributed to its high similarity to Latin alphabet. CIC (Communication Intelligence Cooperation) provided Jot alphabet as a mix of unistroke and multistroke letters on a wide range of handheld devices. However the two previous methods require accurate drawing of their strokes to be recognized, that makes a huge obstacle for novice users.

Feeltwood, M.D. et al. [7] compared Graffiti to the Palm OS stylus keyboard and found that novice were faster with the Keyboard (7 vs. 16 WPM) but experts were faster with Graffiti (21 vs. 18 WPM)

2.3 Gesture-Based Input

In contrast to unistroke alphabets, continuous gesture-based text entry techniques do not require lifting the stylus between characters. Given this, entire words or even sentences can be written with a single continuous gesture.

Quickwriting [8] defines nine letter zones through a grid (3×3). To enter a character, user moves the stylus from central zone to one of eight surrounded zones, possibly into two or even three adjacent zones, then returns to central zone. Isokoski et al. [9] conducted a formal longitudinal study of using Quickwriting with stylus, joystick, and keyboard. They found that it is difficult to learn and not particularly fast, but suitable for multi-device use.

In Cirrin [10], letters are arranged on the circumference of a circle, and their order is based on the common sequences in English language. A word is entered by pressing and moving the stylus over the letters. However, the small zone size of letter makes accurate selection difficult.

Dasher [11] uses a continuous gesture and a language model to predict the next entry. Each character is surrounded by dynamic rectangle, the size of which expands according to a letter's probability of entry. Characters are entered by moving the pointing device toward intended character. Although speed entry can be achieved with it, continuous motion of characters produces additional visual attention and cognitive load. Dasher consumes all screen space as well.

A combination of gesture and virtual keyboard to allow word level entry with keyboard has been constructed in Shark [12]. It defines a shorthand symbol for each word according to its movement pattern on optimized stylus keyboard ATOMIK.

3 3DKey Virtual Keyboard

We propose a new text entry method based on addition of a third dimension to traditional virtual keyboard to break the small screen obstacle of handheld devices.

Mackinlay J.D. et al. [13] have discussed 3D layout for visualizing linear information through the perspective wall. It has three panels: a panel in the center for viewing information details and two perspective panels on either side for viewing information context. When user selects an item; the wall moves that item to the center panel with a smooth animation.

As far as our 3D layout is concerned, we have noticed that the accordion folds "zigzag" help to overcome a small size constraint. In fact, accordion folds are used on many products such as a fan, brochures, maps, an accordion shutter system, mini accordion books, and so on. The principal reason of using such accordion folds is to adapt a large size object into a small spatial zone as shown in figure 1. Therefore, accordion-folding the virtual keyboard presents an adequate solution to expand or spread keys, leading to easier selection. In this way, the virtual keyboard can be seen as composed of two parts: a spread part (the active zone i.e. where user is typing) and an accordion-folded part (the inactive zone i.e. unused or free zone at the moment of typing). As a result, our proposal includes two key patterns: spread and folded keys. Note that, the key size in X and Y dimensions corresponding to spread key takes more area than that in X, Y and virtual Z dimensions corresponding to folded key.

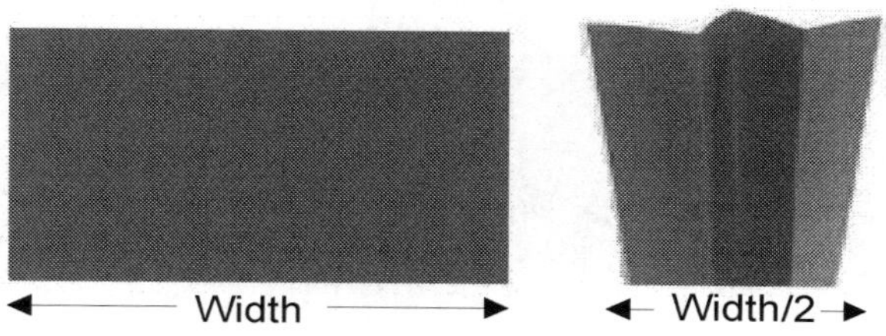

Fig. 1. Accordion-folding a sheet of paper

3.1 Accordion-Folding the Virtual Keyboard

Accordion-folding the virtual keyboard must consider following three factors: the folding dimension or direction, the folding angle or the oblique angle and the number of folds to be produced on small screen.

The keys of virtual keyboard are arranged in two dimensions: horizontal and vertical dimensions. We chose accordion-folding the virtual keyboard in the horizontal dimension for following two reasons. The first one, the virtual keyboard is having more number of the keys in the horizontal dimension than that in the vertical dimension. The second reason, handheld devices screen is greater in length than in width.

We all know that the shortest distance between two points is a straight line and the oblique line increases the distance between two points. The relationship between the length of straight line (Ls) and the length of oblique line (Lo) can be expressed by the following equation:

$$Lo = \frac{Ls}{\cos\theta} \tag{1}$$

Where $\theta \in [0, 90]$ is the oblique angle as shown in figure 2.

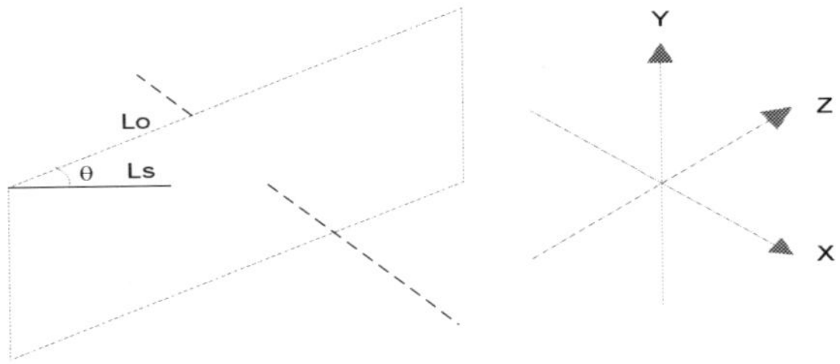

Fig. 2. The angle θ between the straight and oblique lines

Equation 1 indicates that the increasing amount of the length of straight line depends on the oblique angle. As a result, accordion folding style allows spreading (i.e. expanding) the size of keys as a function of the oblique angle or the folding angle. Smaller the folding angle (or bigger the oblique angle), bigger the size of spread key is. In our experiment, we chose 120° as a folding angle (e.g. 30° of oblique angle) because it meets our need in expanding keys to the same width of desktop virtual keyboard i.e. one and a half times bigger than their initial size (without spreading).

Figure 3 shows the number of folds taken to build our accordion virtual keyboard with 120° of folding angle.

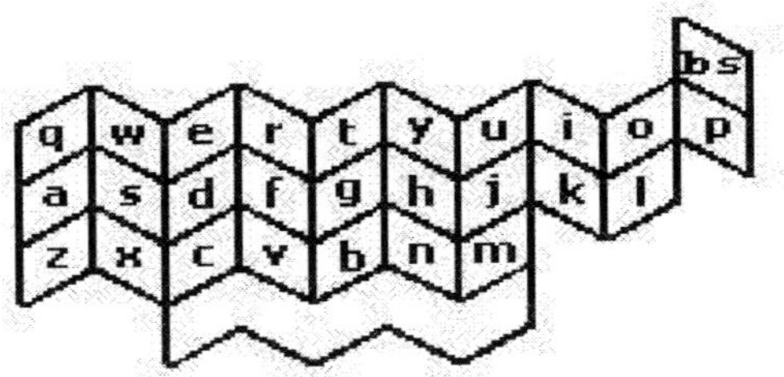

Fig. 3. The accordion virtual keyboard with 120° of folding angle

3.2 Spreading Accordion-Folding Virtual Keyboard

There are two strategies to spread accordion-folded keys. The first one when the stylus approaches target, the nearest folded keys are spread i.e. spreading keys with stylus movement. The major advantage of our 3D design is that there is no need to distort whole keyboard like Fisheye method but only spreading two columns with smooth animation.

The second strategy is based on letter prediction to spread the keys corresponding to the next entry so it reduces the distance between the key to be typed later and the key which is being typed by user at that moment of time.

In both cases, we can set a spread key width to that of desktop virtual keyboard. In this way, text entry task can be as efficient as with a desktop PC.

In our user study, the second strategy to spread accordion-folded keys is used for two following reasons. On the one hand, predicting the next entry can reduce the time of visual scanning keyboard to find letters that one is looking for. On the other hand, the first strategy, i.e. spreading keys with stylus movement requires touch-screen with electro-magnetic field that is unavailable for wide range of mobile devices.

To predict the next letter based on previous letters, we have used tables of single-letter and diagram frequency counts proposed by [14]. For each entry, the number of spread keys taken corresponds to two columns of accordion-folding virtual keyboard as seen in figure 4. They can contain up to four most probable next letters according to used prediction system.

Our choice of spreading two whole columns can be justified by following reasons. Fist is that with the replacement of ten fingers by stylus or other pointing devices, user achieves text entry task from area-to-area. A second reason is to offer as many spread keys as possible, because there isn't a perfect prediction system, and especially to include space character that is considered as the most probable letter. A third reason is to allow prefix and suffix completion like (th, er, ed, es, ng, was), thus reducing number of times a spreading is occurred and speeding up entry.

Our proposed solution also helps to increase a character visibility. In fact spreading can be considered as a *zoom-in tool* to make characters easier to read and then reducing the visual attention required to inputting them.

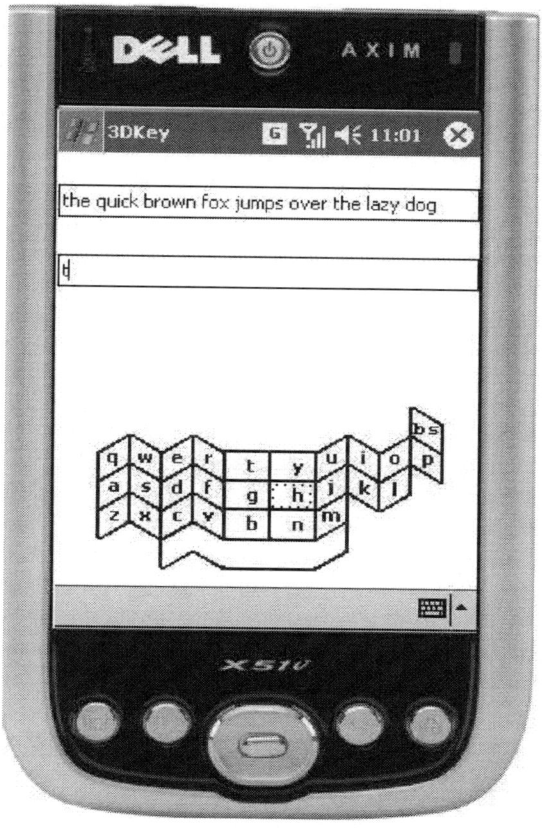

Fig. 4. The screenshot of 3DKey virtual keyboard

3.3 Fitts' Law and Accordion-Folding Virtual Keyboard

Fitts' law [15] predicts the time (MT) to acquire a target of width (W) which lies at a distance or amplitude (A) as given by the following relationship [16]:

$$MT = a + b\log_2(\frac{A}{W} + 1) \tag{2}$$

Where a & b are constants determined through linear regression. The logarithmic term is called the index of difficulty (ID) and is measured in "bits".

According to Fitts' law (2), the acquisition time of the target will be shorter if the size of the target is big in its size and the distance between the targets is smaller. Our proposed 3DKey virtual keyboard fulfills both requirements of Fitts' law i.e. spreading allows the targets to get bigger in size and the folding reduces the distance between targets.

4 Experiment

The aim of this study is to verify following hypothesis: the proposed accordion-folding and predictive spreading virtual keyboard may improve target acquisition for text entry task on handheld devices.

4.1 Subjects

Ten volunteers (6 male, 4 female) from our university campus participated as subjects in this study. Participants averaged 27.5 years of age (ranging from 24 to 32 years). They were all stylus-based text input novice users. All users had normal or corrected eyesight and were using a right-handed stylus as a pointing device.

4.2 Apparatus

The experiment was conducted on Dell Axim X51 PDA. The screen size was 3.5" and ran at a resolution of 240 × 300 pixels.

Participants accomplished the experiment using the following two virtual keyboards:

The first one is a traditional virtual keyboard (without accordion folds) with a folding angle of 180° and an oblique angle of 0° (No-accordion). The second virtual keyboard is 3DKey virtual keyboard with a folding angle of 120° and an oblique angle of 30° (120°-accordion). Its spreading is based on letter prediction as mentioned earlier.

For each virtual keyboard, the program reads a series of 10 phrases ranging from 16 to 43 characters [17]. The two virtual keyboards are built in .NET C#.

4.3 Procedure

The experiment consisted of two sessions: a training session followed by a testing session. The first session consisted of entering the sentence "the quick brown fox jumps over the lazy dog" using two virtual keyboards.

The testing session consisted of two blocks. A block is to enter phrases using traditional virtual keyboard, while another block is to enter phrases using 3DKey virtual keyboard. Hence each participant completed two sentence tasks using two virtual keyboards.

Participants were divided into two-person groups to perform the tasks in a different order. Five participants entered phrases with the traditional virtual keyboard first, followed by 3DKey virtual keyboard. The other half reversed the order.

Participants were instructed to enter the phrases as quickly and as accurately as possible. However, they could make errors and corrections, as in the real world.

The same phrases were used for two tasks but were in a different order so that user could not anticipate the phrase in the other task.

The phrases to be entered appeared on the PDA screen, just above text entry area where participants transcribed the text.

The experiment was conducted in our research laboratory. The total time to conduct the experiment was about 25 minutes.

4.4 Results and Discussion

In all, participants entered 22 phrases using the traditional and 3DKey virtual keyboards. The phrases were the same for all users in a trial so that variations in phrases can be excluded in statistical analysis. The order of testing two virtual keyboards is counterbalanced so that has no impact on results.

The variables measured for both virtual keyboards were (1) text entry speed expressed in words per minute (wpm) or characters per second (cps) (2) accuracy or error rate during test and (3) accuracy or error rate after text entry.

4.4.1 Text Entry Speed

The average text entry rate for ten participants across two testing blocks is shown in figure 5. The overall average text entry speeds were 17.79 wpm for traditional virtual keyboard and 24.5 wpm for 3DKey virtual keyboard, suggesting a 37.71 % performance advantage for 3DKey virtual keyboard. The difference was statistically significant ($F_{1,18} = 83.12$, $p < .0001$), as determined using an analysis of variance ANOVA.

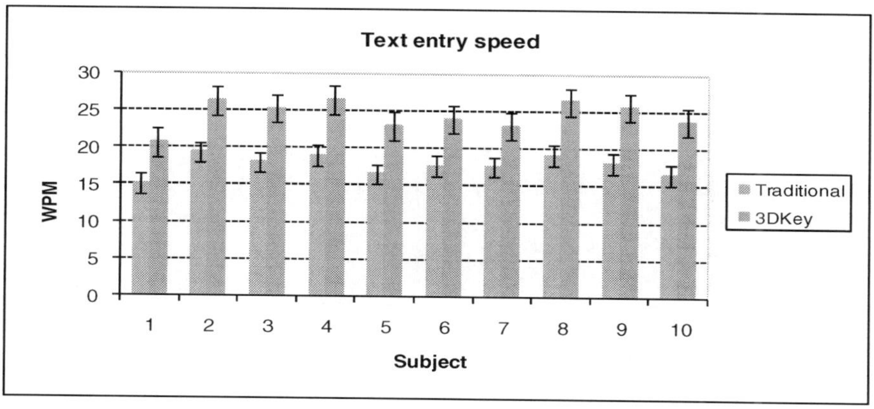

Fig. 5. Text entry speed for both virtual keyboards

There was a variation by participant. For traditional virtual keyboard, participant means ranged from 15.16 wpm to 19.42. For 3DKey virtual keyboard, the means ranged from 20.68 wpm to 26.53 wpm. This suggests that participants performed the task with different attitudes on balancing speed with accuracy.

4.4.2 Accuracy

Our task allowed corrections while writing. Thus, two kinds of errors were present in the data: those that the participant noticed and corrected and those that remained uncorrected. Hence error rate was measured using two metrics [18].

The first one is the *Corrected Error Rate* to compute the errors made during text entry. Figure 6 shows the average corrected error rate for ten participants across two testing blocks. The average corrected error rate for traditional virtual keyboard was 2.41 %, while that for 3DKey virtual keyboard was lower at 1.38 %. The difference was statistically significant ($F_{1,18} = 5.78$, $p < .05$).

The second metric is the *Not Corrected Error Rate* to measure the errors remained in transcribed string. Figure 7 shows the average not corrected error rate for ten participants across two testing blocks. The average not corrected error rate for traditional virtual keyboard was 3.40 %, while that for 3DKey virtual keyboard was lower at 2.35 %. The difference was statistically significant ($F_{1,18} = 7.48$, $p < .05$).

Figures 6 & 7 also show that remained errors were higher than corrected errors for the most of the participants across both testing blocks.

As there isn't a perfect prediction system until now, our 3DKey technique may spread a wrong part that didn't happen in our experiment. However in this case user has to click on accordion-folded keys that always seem bigger than traditional ones, i.e. regarding their perimeter.

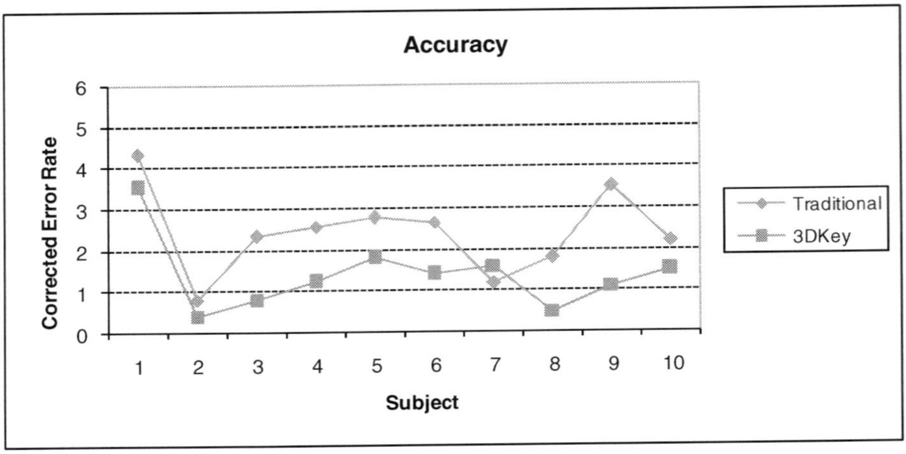

Fig. 6. Corrected error rate for both virtual keyboards

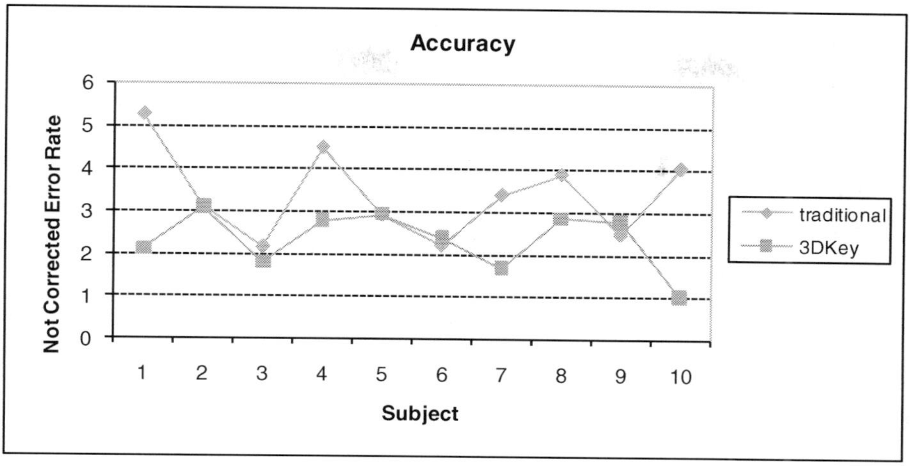

Fig. 7. Not corrected error rate for both virtual keyboards

5 Conclusion and Future Work

We have shown that the virtual keyboard based on accordion folding and predictive spreading virtual keyboard are more efficient than traditional virtual keyboard to make target acquisition easier for the text input on handheld devices. The proposed solution improved user text entry speed by 37.71 % over the traditional virtual keyboard and provided higher accuracy as well.

In the future, we plan to explore the effects of spreading the accordion-folded key when the stylus approaches it on user performance for text entry task.

3DKey could be an effective means allowing for a reduced initial size of interface widgets like icons of toolbars in an attempt to optimize screen space use.

We finally intend to test our accordion virtual keyboard for people with motor impairments who absolutely need a design reducing the fatigue and discomfort of a long pointing device distance.

References

1. McGffin, M., Balakrishnan, R.: Acquisition of expanding targets. In: CHI 2002, pp. 57–64. ACM Press, Minneapolis (2002)
2. Raynal, M., Truillet, P.: Fisheye keyboard: Whole keyboard displayed on PDA. In: HCI International 2007, pp. 452–459. Springer, Beijing (2007)
3. Al Faraj, K., Mojahid, M., Vigouroux, N.: BigKey: A virtual keyboard for mobile devices. In: HCI International 2009. Springer, San Diego (to appear, 2009)
4. MacKenzie, I.S., Soukoreff, R.W.: Text Entry for Mobile Computing: Models and Methods, Theory and Practice. Human-Computer Interaction 17(2), 147–198 (2002)
5. Zhai, S., Hunter, M., Smith, B.A.: The Metropolis keyboard: An exploration of quantitative for graphical keyboard design. In: UIST 2000, pp. 119–128. ACM Press, San Diego (2000)

6. Goldberg, D., Richardson, C.: Touch-Typing with a Stylus. In: INTERCHI, pp. 80–87. ACM Press, Amsterdam (1993)
7. Fleetwood, M.D., Byrne, M.D., Centgraf, P., Dudziak, K.Q., Lin, B., Mogilev, D.: An evaluation of text-entry in Palm OS: Graffiti and virtual keyboard. In: HFES 2002, pp. 617–621. Human Factors and Ergonomics Society, Baltimore (2002)
8. Perlin, K.: Quickwriting: Continuous Stylus-Based Text Entry. In: UIST 1998, pp. 216–251. ACM Press, San Francisco (1998)
9. Isokoski, P., Raisamo, R.: Quickwriting as a multi-device text entry method. In: NordiCHI 2004, pp. 105–108. ACM Press, Tampere (2004)
10. Mankoff, J., Abowd, G.D.: Cirrin: A Word-Level Unistroke Keyboard for Pen Input. In: UIST 1998, pp. 213–214. ACM Press, San Francisco (1998)
11. Ward, D.J., Blackwell, A.F., Mackay, D.J.C.: Dasher: A Data Entry Interface Using Continuous Gestures and Language Models. In: UIST 2000, pp. 129–137. ACM Press, San Diego (2000)
12. Zhai, S., Kristensson, P.O.: Shorthand Writing on Stylus Keyboard. In: CHI 2003, pp. 97–104. ACM Press, Ft. Lauderdale (2003)
13. Mackinlay, J.D., Robertson, G.G., Card, S.K.: Perspective wall: detail and context smoothy integrated. In: CHI 1991, pp. 173–176. ACM Press, New Orleans (1991)
14. Mayzner, M.S., Tresselt, M.E.: Tables of Single-Letter and Diagram Frequency Counts for Various Word-Length and Letter-Position Combinations. Psychonomic Monograph Supplements 1(2), 13–32 (1965)
15. Fitts, P.M.: The information capacity of the human motor system in controlling the amplitude of movement. Journal of Experimental Psychology 47(6), 381–391 (1954)
16. MacKenzie, I.S.: Fitts' Law as a Research and Design Tool in Human-Computer Interaction. Human-Computer Interaction 7(1), 91–139 (1992)
17. MacKenzie, I.S., Soukoreff, R.W.: Phrase set for evaluating text entry techniques. In: CHI 2003, pp. 754–755. ACM Press, Ft. Lauderdale (2003)
18. Soukoreff, R.W., MacKenzie, I.S.: Metrics for text entry research: An evaluation of MSD and KSPC, and a new unified error metric. In: CHI 2003, pp. 113–120. ACM Press, Ft. Lauderdale (2003)

Investigating Temporal-Spatial Characteristics of Mouse and Touch Input

Christian Müller-Tomfelde

CSIRO ICT Centre,
Cnr Vimiera and Pembroke Roads,
Marsfield NSW 2122, Australia
Christian.Mueller-Tomfelde@csiro.au

Abstract. This paper explores differences between user actions employing mouse and touch input devices when performing a collaborative task on a tabletop interface. We explore temporal and spatial characteristics of drag actions of users through mouse (indirect) and touch input (direct) devices. Our analysis is based on system-logged interaction data we collected in an exploratory study. The analysis reveals that touch users performed more drag actions than mouse users. Furthermore, touch users dragged artefacts on a tabletop for a shorter period of time than mouse users. At the same time, touch users dragged objects in the workspace shorter distances than mouse users. We also identify differences based on the temporal-spatial histograms of the drag actions. We discuss our findings based on observations we made during the collaborative task and interviews with participants after the study. The results may be related to the performed task and to ergonomic design issues of the setup. We describe the possible implications on co-located and remote collaboration.

Keywords: Direct and indirect input devices, synchronous co-located collaboration, tabletop, user study.

1 Introduction

Tabletop environments providing touch interaction are popular settings to support the collaborative work of co-located small teams [1, 2, 3, 4]. While the benefits of touch input devices for tabletops have been identified [5, 6], studies have been conducted to further understand the differences of touch and mouse input devices on individual task performance [7] and the implications of different interaction techniques on collaboration on tabletops [8]. Advantages and disadvantages have been documented to provide guidelines for design decisions for co-located collaboration at tabletops [5]. Differences between touch and mouse interactions have also been studied for unimanual and bimanual tasks of individuals [9]. The authors report the benefits for direct touch interaction for bimanual tasks and indicate that mouse devices might be more appropriate for individuals working on so called standard "single-point" interaction tasks.

We conducted an exploratory study on input device preferences and usage during co-located collaboration. The study revealed a balanced preference for mouse and

T. Gross et al. (Eds.): INTERACT 2009, Part I, LNCS 5726, pp. 645–657, 2009.

touch as input devices for the particular tabletop setup [10]. The system-logged interaction data of this exploratory study forms the basis of the detailed analysis in this paper. The contribution of this paper is twofold: firstly, we provide further insights to the characteristics of the temporal-spatial organisation of drag actions based on mouse and touch as input device during the collaborative task. These characteristics between mouse and touch users differs, despite the fact that there was no main effect of the input device on the task completion. Secondly, we discuss these findings with respect to observations made during the trials and to the particularities of the experimental setup. We discuss possible implications of our findings in the context of co-located and remote collaboration on tabletops.

2 Collaboration Study

In our exploratory study 22 participants (in 11 trials) were asked to solve jigsaw puzzle tasks with increasing assembly complexity. The study emphasises a quasi-realistic context with two work colleagues standing side by side at a tabletop to work in parallel (see Figure 1).

Fig. 1. In the exploratory study, participants were standing side-by-side using either mouse or touch input device to collaborate

More details about the setup are described in [10, 11]. The participants' task was to drag puzzle pieces on the tabletop surface to assemble several photo pictures. Both participants had to each solve one puzzle in front of them. The interface was designed to mimic that of real jigsaw puzzles or mosaics, except that it did not allow for rotation, lifting up or any sort of tangibility of the pieces. Solving one puzzle task lasted in average 7 min. In contrast to other studies (e.g. [9, 6]), we granted the participants the free choice to select and change their input device at any time during the study. As a consequence the input device in this study has to be considered as a dependent variable rather than an independent one. The experimental task was then increased in difficulty by mixing pieces between the two puzzles. This was implemented to trigger spontaneous coordination and communication amongst the team members as well as to find out how this might affect the usage of the input devices. The spatial layout of the physical task space may give the impression that each participant owned one puzzle and that individuals worked in parallel. However in all of the trials the participants worked collaboratively on the task, i.e., they communicated, observed each other workspaces and coordinated actions.

The goal of our study was to achieve, as much as possible, ecological validity of the task and setting in our lab environment. We collected qualitative and quantitative data of the participants' interactions through observations, and objective measures in the form of system-logged interaction data. The focus of this paper is on the objective measures and related observations to further understand the difference between mouse and touch device users in this tabletop setting.

3 Manipulating the Artefact

In order to further understand differences between the usage of direct and indirect input devices we explore the participants' behaviour at an input device level. We are focusing on drag actions, which we define as the action of a user dragging puzzles pieces on the tabletop. For instance, a mouse user can move the cursor on the screen at any time, but only drags an object when moving it after selecting the object by pressing the mouse button down. The period of moving the cursor towards a target object until pressing the mouse button is usually described using Fitts' law [12] (selection time). In contrast to this, we are focusing on the continuous drag actions after having selected the object and before releasing the object at a target position (similar to the docking task described in [9]). In the case of our touch input device, the position and movement of the finger could only be captured when it was in close proximity to the surface. Therefore, the selection time becomes difficult to compare between the devices and we concentrate on the manipulation of the artefact based on drag actions. It should be noted that the recorded drag actions are self-paced, as in [8, 13], rather than stimulus driven as in experiments, such as [9]. For our analysis, we generated the two measures, drag time and drag distance, from the interaction data.

3.1 Drag Time and Distance

We define drag time as the period of time of a drag action, i.e., the duration from the selection of a jigsaw puzzle piece by touch or mouse click until its release at a final position. The drag time starts with the selection of a puzzle piece, followed by its translation on the surface. The drag time stops with the release of the object at the final position. From the coordinates of a drag action we derive a distance measure. In a fist approach, we define the drag distance as the L2-norm of the coordinate vector from the start to the end point of a drag action. Other distance measures, e.g., along the trajectory of the path of action, might be useful to investigate in the future.

3.2 Collection of Interaction Data

We developed customised software to support up to four input devices (i.e., dual touch plus two mice) to concurrently control graphical elements for the experiment. Our application recorded all interactions with attributes such as time, device ID, position, state (e.g., move, drag), and events (e.g., button down or up). Based on this data we derived the overall time to complete the task and the period of time that participants actually drag puzzle pieces around. Further refinement of the interaction data allowed us to access all drag actions per interaction device.

4 Analysis

Based on the interaction data of 11 trials (N=22) we processed all drag actions with regard to their times, distances and input device type. The participants could be indentified as purely touch or mouse users, except in one trial where the two participants swapped the input device type during the trial. We excluded this trial to have an unequivocal classification. Thus, our results base on 10 trials:

- 2962 drag actions by mouse (9 participants) and
- 5497 drag actions by touch input device (11 participants).

We recorded 1.85 more drag actions with touch than with mouse input device. The average number of drag actions per participant was approximately 500 for direct and 330 for indirect input devices. The descriptive statistics for drag times and distances categorised by input device are shown in Table 1.

Table 1. Descriptive statistics of the drag times and drag distances of direct and indirect input devices

Device Type	Min	1st Qu.	Median	Mean	3rd Qu.	Max
	Drag time [s]					
Indirect	.078	.832	1.500	2.028	2.5630	93.610
Direct	.062	.438	0.875	1.161	1.578	11.420
	Drag distance [cm]					
Indirect	.048	4.312	11.72	15.05	23.69	86.71
Direct	.048	2.103	6.323	10.38	15.53	80.29

For both input device types the extreme small time values below 200 ms are likely be caused by artefacts of the detection. Manipulations with such a short execution time can not be considered to be deliberately executed actions [14] and were not used for this analysis. We can state that the median value of the drag times with mouse input device is approximately 0.5 seconds higher than that for touch. The median value of the mouse drag distances is approximately twice the value of that of touch.

5 Drag Time Histograms

The histograms of the drag times are shown in Figure 2a and 2b. The histograms are both skewed to the right, similar to those of human reaction time histograms. Histograms for the drag distances report a similar but slightly less positively skewed distribution. We must assume that the drag times and distances are not normally distributed and hence parametric significance tests such as t-tests are not applicable. A Wilcoxon rank-sum test of the drag times and drag distances between direct and indirect input device reveal significant differences (each $p < 0.001$) in the locations.

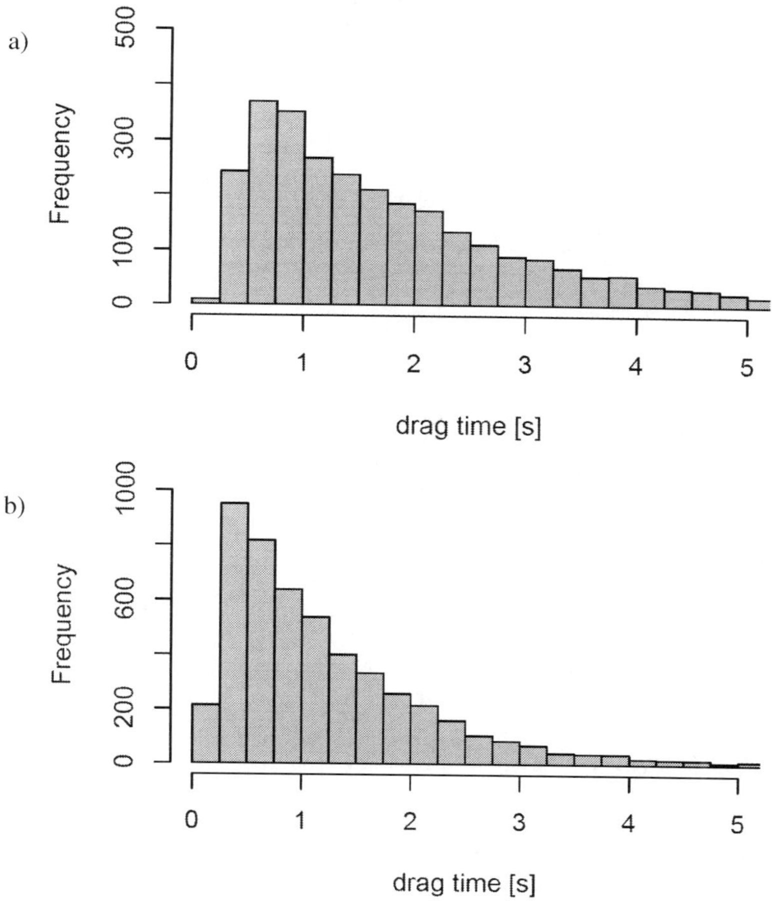

Fig. 2. Histograms of the drag times using either mouse or touch input device. Graph a) shows the histogram for indirect device (mouse) and b) the histogram for direct device (touch).

6 Temporal-Spatial Histograms

To understand more about the relationship between drag time and drag distance we plotted two-dimensional histograms (see Figure 3). These histograms show the distribution of drag actions of mouse and touch users in the temporal-spatial domain.

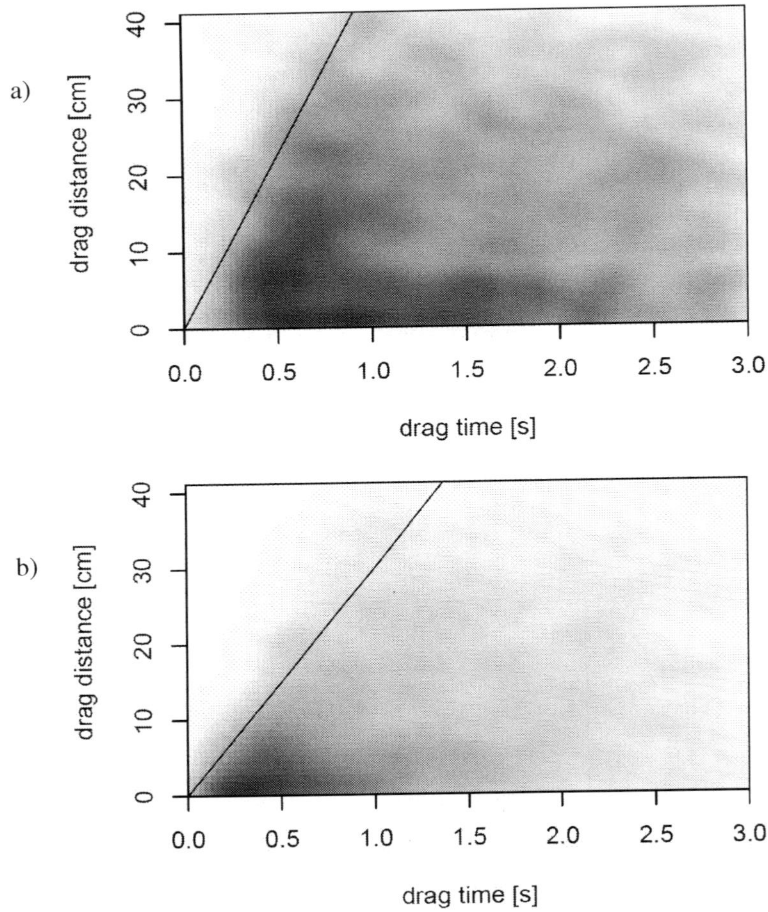

Fig. 3. Temporal-spatial histograms of a) indirect input (mouse) device drag actions and b) direct device (touch) drag actions. The lines represent the speed limits of drag actions.

Darker shaded areas have a higher frequency than lighter shaded areas. White areas signify minor or no occurrence of drag actions. Each histogram shows a distinct maximal drag speed of approximately 45 cm/s for indirect (represented by the line in Figure 3a) and 30 cm/s for direct input devices (Figure 3b).

Furthermore, the histogram of the indirect input device (Figure 3a) is more distributed in the temporal-spatial space than that of the direct input device. In particular, the histogram in Figure 3b (direct input) is much more focused on the area around and below 0.5 seconds with distances less than 7.5 cm. In contrast, the histogram of the indirect input (Figure 3a) has temporally long lasting drag actions with relatively short distances (less than 7.5 cm). Also many temporally short drag actions between (0.5 and 1 s) over a long distance, i.e., with high drag speed occurred. We also plotted the all drag actions of mouse and touch users in the two dimensional plain of the workspace to identify possible specific spatial patterns. However, we can report that the spatial organisation of drag actions of mouse and touch had no apparent differences.

7 Observations

We observed that all participants worked without any problems or complains on the task with either input device. Even the coordination of actions of both participants, i.e., the handing over of puzzle pieces from one to the other happened smoothly and without additional training [15, 16]. All participants concentrated and cooperated on the task and they shared their effort even more and developed strategies when they found out that puzzle pieces were mixed up (second sub trial). The communication amongst them increased as well as their gazes on the other's work area and number of coordinated actions.

Reviewing the video recordings of the trials we can report that the participants using the mouse exhibit clearly fewer physical body movements than touch users. The latter moved most of them time the arm of their dominant hand to manipulate the artefact in front of them on the display. Mouse users seem to remain still, only moving their hand resting on the rim of the table controlling the mouse (see Figure 1). Touch and mouse users moved their heads to follow the currently dragged puzzle piece or to better oversee the display seeking of a possible matching piece. Touch device users seem to be much more active. In trails with one mouse and one touch device user it appeared to the observers that only the touch user was active although they both were working highly concentrated on the task. The reduced physical body activity of participants using mouse devices comes also along with less physical effort during the task. Eventually all participants changed their general posture at the table, e.g., balancing their weight from on foot to the other. The participant however did not complained about standing at the table during the task.

We interviewed the participants after they completed the study. Participants who used direct touch input devices reported an almost similar experience as with a real puzzle (e.g., P1, trial 1). A touch user stated that "the touch is much more human" (P2, trial 5). One participant reported that with the touch device "it was a lot easier to get control" over the puzzle piece (P2, trial 7). Some mouse users were confident to work faster with the mouse than with the touch device (P2, trail 3) and P1 in trial 6 explained his input device preference that he "... uses [the] mouse mostly". One participant reported an ergonomic issue using the mouse without elbow support (P1, trial 3).

Both participants in trial 7 reported that they were not tempted to use the mouse even when they had to reach far away objects. This was also mentioned by P1 (trail 5) "it just didn't occurred to me". We observed however that some participants spontaneously changed temporally the input device but continue to work with their preferred input device after only a few manipulations. None of the participants mentioned that physical effort was an issue during the task. It was also not mentioned to be reason to choose one input device before the other.

We observed also a particular class of drag actions. Some of the participants acted beyond the instructed task and arranged the jigsaw pieces in the final stage of the task with high positioning precision. This happened, although the experimenters informed the participants at the beginning of the trial that precision does not matter for solving this task. This behaviour of "beautifying" the result of the work could be considered different to a normal drag action and might need to be removed from the data. While normal drag actions are carried out to reach the communicated goal of the experiment task, these beautifying actions serve more of an individual and aesthetic goal or desire. We observed that while these actions have short drag distances, they can also have long drag times. However, the impact on the findings are considered to minor, due to the fact that these particular actions happened only occasionally and had been carried out by users of both types of input device.

8 Discussion

We assume that our setting is typical for tabletop studies and that the task and collaboration are ecologically valid. However, the above described findings and observations strictly hold only for our specific setting of the study, such as the side-by-side position arrangement (other arrangements can be considered [17]). The presented quantitative differences in drag times and distances of touch and mouse input need to be discussed in the context of our observations and qualitative statements of the interviews of the participants. We discuss how the specific properties of the input devices might shape the way drag actions are carried out differently by the participants using an indirect or direct input device. Furthermore, the constructs of epistemic actions and complementary strategies as proposed by Kirsh [18, 19] might help to explain our findings and observations of the collaborative task.

8.1 Input Device Ergonomics

There are different ergonomic aspects of our experimental setting as depicted in Figure 1. We concentrate on the ergonomics of the input devices and assume that other aspects such as the posture and position arrangements of the participants have only indirect or minor influence on the reported findings. For instance, the standing posture just gives the touch users a larger area to act in (see [20]) and better visibility of the workspace. Our observations reveal that touch users require more physical effort than mouse users when reaching pieces and moving them around. Since the participants using the touch input devices never mentioned or even complained about the physical effort we must assume that this extra physical effort compared to those of mouse users is not apparent to the participants. Mouser users remained nearly motion less merely performing actions controlling the mouse and occasionally turning their heads slightly overseeing the partners' workspaces. Thus, their activity and intentions are less likely to become recognised by their partners than those of touch users. This provides plausibility for the fact that mouse users dragged pieces for a longer time because only small changes in the hand position are required. Instead, touch users performed drag actions confined to a particular region in the temporal-spatial histogram (see Figure 3b). Twice the number of the drag actions with touch than with mouse might compensate for these differences in temporal-spatial histogram of the drag actions. However it seems that the extra physical effort does not have an impact on the efficiency working on the task. We found no significant difference in the overall task completion time depending on the input device [10].

8.2 Epistemic Actions

Most of the participants had reported to have experience with solving jigsaw puzzles, and therefore it is likely that they pursued already established strategies to solve the puzzle task. Typical to this task is that users perform a visual search task that is accompanied and combined with so called "epistemic actions". This class of action is preformed to "uncover information that is hidden or hard to compute mentally" and therefore "change[s] the world in order to simplify the problem-solving task" [19]. In our example a typical epistemic action would be moving a puzzle piece towards potential matching pieces. By doing so, the visual search and the decision about whether two piece are matching or not becomes simplified. In case of a positive match the epistemic action becomes seamlessly transformed into a "pragmatic action". This action is executed directly to accomplish the goal of the task. Also "complementary strategies" might be exhibited, i.e., "any organizing activity which recruits external elements to reduce cognitive loads" [18]. The participants build subgroups of pieces with similar content or colour to structure and simplify process of solving the puzzle.

It has to be discussed how these actions and strategies become support or hindered by the digital artefact itself and by the different input device technologies. The fact that the puzzle pieces are displayed on the screen "only" and lack of any tangibility reduce the traditional handling of the pieces, e.g., with full hands. Therefore actions or strategy that requires full hand or bimanual interaction were impossible to perform in this setting. For instance, it is obvious that a pile of puzzle pieces can not simply distributed by just shuffling multiple pieces with a flat hand. Also a group of pieces can not be moved as a set to another location. Instead all pieces had to be moved individually with touch as well as with mouse input device.

However, the different input devices might support or inhibit epistemic actions and complementary strategies that led to our finding. We are focussing on the epistemic action of finding a matching piece by dragging it around. Our analysis of the drag actions suggests that it is possible that mouse users exhibited more of these epistemic actions than touch users. Mouse users not only drag objects longer but also show greater variety in the temporal-spatial distribution. It seems likely that persons using the mouse pick up a piece without having decided in advance where to place it due to the low physical effort required. In contrast touch user are to more consistent in their action (see Figure 3b) which suggests that they rather perform the drag action after they decided where to place the piece. Thus touch user minimise their physical effort and maximising efficiency of the drag actions. Instead of performing one long drag action in search for a match touch, users might also break up a search for a match into a sequence of short drag actions.

The key of the extension of drag actions in time and space with the mouse beyond those of touch actions however may lie in the very little physical effort that is required to manipulate the artefact with the mouse, similar to the effort in tradition desktop computer settings. We suggest that the different physical effort required by the specific input device to manipulate the artefact has an impact on the quality of the users' actions while solving the puzzle task. If an input device demands little physical effort more epistemic actions are likely to be performed.

8.3 Implications on the Collaboration

So far we discussed the difference of the drag actions for the individual performance ignoring the possible impact on the collaboration. We discuss the implication of our findings on the collaboration using the concept of workspace awareness and embodiment of actions. Workspace awareness is the understanding of another person's actions and "includes knowledge where and on what others are currently working and what they are doing next" [21]. It is supposed that workspace awareness supports the coordination during collaboration. Our findings allow us to conclude that touch device user provide more workspace awareness to their partners than mouse users. The shear amount of physical actions of touch users with theirs hands and arms provide richer peripheral awareness for their partners than to mouse users do. These physical actions show if and where the partner is working, and provides very well the information which puzzle piece is currently in focus. Recent findings also comparing touch and mouse actions presented in [22] support this conclusion. Other research comes also to similar conclusion comparing different interaction techniques [8]. The richer peripheral awareness created by touch users comes long with possible workspace occlusion and physical conflicts in case of multiple touch users actions in the same workspace area.

However when only focussing only changes in the workspaces created by drag actions another aspect of our findings comes into play. We consider now an environment, where two spatially distributed setting as used in our study form a shared workspace. This would lead to a similar environment as used in [23, 13] but without the rich remote action embodiments such as arm shadow [24]. The temporally longer drag actions in this distributed collaboration scenario could facilitate the communication and coordination better than touch. The longer drag actions provide more workspace awareness for remote collaborators since they can perceive more changes in the workspace. Our findings also show that drag actions with the mouse device have greater temporal-spatial variety than those of touch device users. This fact may imply that also more different classes of actions are performed. As argued in the section before, the particular epistemic actions with the mouse have the potential to better support awareness since they contain and convey to the remote site more meaning or intentionality than the touch actions.

To sum up the implication on collaboration, we can draw the following conclusion. In a straight comparison between the devices, the touch device is highly beneficial for co-located collaboration due to the natural and rich awareness of the users' physical actions with their arms and hands. In contrast, the mouse device bears the potential to better provide awareness in the collaboration with a remote partner because more meaningful changes in the workspace occur. An interesting research topic emerges here when developing an environment that combines the benefits of both input devices for distributed collaboration, i.e., when local mouse actions become remotely embodied with richer embodiments than standard mouse cursors.

9 Conclusion

We presented results from a detailed analysis of drag times and drag distances of touch and mouse interaction data collected during an earlier study. The analysis of these measures shows that touch users drag objects for shorter periods of time over shorter distances than mouse users. The temporal-spatial histograms of the drag actions reveal further characteristics of the specific input device. Mouse drag actions have greater variety in time and distance while touch drag actions are more focussed. These findings go beyond the existing knowledge about the characteristics of direct and indirect input device interaction. We discussed the finding in the context of the ergonomics of the input devices and of epistemic actions. The findings could be useful when developing new interaction techniques for distributed collaboration.

Acknowledgements

This research was conducted within the HxI Initiative [25], an Australian research initiative led by CSIRO, DSTO and NICTA [26]. The author thanks the test participants for allowing us to collect and publish the presented data. I also thank Claudia Schremmer in helping, organising and conducting the study and Anja Wessels for helping with the hands-on running of the experiment and the collection of experiment data.

References

1. Rauterberg, M., Fjeld, M., Krueger, H., Bichsel, M., Leonhardt, U., Meier, M.: BUILD-IT: a planning tool for construction and design. In: Proceedings of the SIGCHI conference on Human factors in computing systems (CHI 1998), pp. 177–178. ACM Press, New York (1998)
2. Rekimoto, J., Saitoh, M.: Augmented surfaces: a spatially continuous work space for hybrid computing environments. In: Proceedings of the SIGCHI conference on Human factors in computing systems (CHI 1999), pp. 378–385. ACM Press, New York (1999)
3. Streitz, N.A., Geißler, J., Holmer, T., Konomi, S., Müller-Tomfelde, C., Reischl, W., Rexroth, P., Seitz, P., Steinmetz, R.: i-LAND: an interactive landscape for creativity and innovation. In: Proceedings of the SIGCHI conference on Human factors in computing systems (CHI 1999), May 15-20, pp. 120–127. ACM Press, New York (1999)
4. Shen, C., Everitt, K., Ryall, K.: UbiTable: Impromptu face-to-face collaboration on horizontal interactive surfaces. In: Dey, A.K., Schmidt, A., McCarthy, J.F. (eds.) UbiComp 2003. LNCS, vol. 2864, pp. 281–288. Springer, Heidelberg (2003)
5. Scott, S.D., Grant, K.D., Mandryk, R.L.: System guidelines for co-located, collaborative work on a tabletop display. In: Proceedings of the eighth conference on European Conference on Computer Supported Cooperative Work (ECSCW 2003), Norwell, MA, USA, pp. 159–178. Kluwer Academic Publishers, Dordrecht (2003)
6. Ha, V., Inkpen, K., Mandryk, R., Whalen, T.: Direct intentions: the effects of input devices on collaboration around a tabletop display. In: Proceedings of the First IEEE International Workshop on Horizontal Interactive Human-Computer Systems (TABLETOP 2006), Adelaide, Australia, January 5-7, pp. 175–190. IEEE Computer Society, Los Alamitos (2006)
7. Huang, C.J.: Not just intuitive: examining the basic manipulation of tangible user interfaces. In: CHI 2004 extended abstracts on Human factors in computing systems (CHI 2004), pp. 1387–1390. ACM Press, New York (2004)

8. Nacenta, M.A., Pinelle, D., Stuckel, D., Gutwin, C.: The effects of interaction technique on coordination in tabletop groupware. In: Proceedings of Graphics Interface 2007 (GI 2007), pp. 191–198. ACM Press, New York (2007)
9. Forlines, C., Wigdor, D., Shen, C., Balakrishnan, R.: Direct-touch vs. mouse input for tabletop displays. In: Proceedings of the SIGCHI conference on Human factors in computing systems (CHI 2007), pp. 647–656. ACM Press, New York (2007)
10. Müller-Tomfelde, C., Schremmer, C., Wessels, A.: Exploratory study on concurrent interaction in co-located collaboration. In: Proceedings of the 2007 conference of the computer-human interaction special interest group (CHISIG) of Australia on Computer-human interaction: design: activities, artifacts and environments (OZCHI 2007), pp. 175–178. ACM Press, New York (2007)
11. Müller-Tomfelde, C.: Interacting with mouse and touch devices on horizontal interactive displays. International Journal Universal Access in the Information Society (in press, 2009)
12. Fitts, P.: The information capacity of the human motor system in controlling the amplitude of movement. Experimental Psychology, 381–391 (1997)
13. Pauchet, A., Coldefy, F., Lefebvre, L., Louis Dit Picard, S., Perron, L., Bouguet, A., Collobert, M., Guerin, J., Corvaisier, D.: TableTops: worthwhile experiences of collocated and remote collaboration. In: Proceedings of the Second Annual IEEE International Workshop on Horizontal Interactive Human-Computer Systems (TABLETOP 2007), Newport, Rhode Island, USA, October 10-12, pp. 27–34. IEEE Computer Society Press, Los Alamitos (2007)
14. Card, S., Moran, T., Newell, A.: The Psychology of Human-Computer Interaction. Lawrence Erlbaum, Hillsdale (1983)
15. Jun, L., Pinelle, D., Gutwin, C., Subramanian, S.: Improving digital handoff in shared tabletop workspaces. In: Proceedings of the 3rd IEEE International Workshop on Horizontal Interactive Human Computer Systems (TABLETOP 2008), October 1–3, pp. 9–16 (2008)
16. Müller-Tomfelde, C., Schremmer, C.: Touchers and Mousers: commonalities and differences in co-located collaboration with multiple input devices. In: Proceeding of the twenty-sixth annual SIGCHI conference on Human factors in computing systems (CHI 2008), pp. 1149–1152. ACM Press, New York (2008)
17. Tang, A., Tory, M., Po, B., Neumann, P., Carpendale, S.: Collaborative coupling over tabletop displays. In: Proceedings of the SIGCHI conference on Human Factors in computing systems (CHI 2006), pp. 1181–1190. ACM Press, New York (2006)
18. Kirsh, D.: Complementary strategies: why we use our hands when we think. In: Proceedings of the Conference of the Cognitive Science Society, Hillsdale, New Jersey. Lawrence Erlbaum, Mahwah (1995), `http://www.cogsci.ucsd.edu/~kirsh/Cogsci95/cogsci95.html` (cited 22.01.2009)
19. Kirsh, D., Maglio, P.: On distinguishing epistemic from pragmatic action. Journal on Cognitive Science, 513–549 (1994)
20. Toney, A., Thomas, B.H.: Considering reach in tangible and table top design. In: Proceedings of the First IEEE International Workshop on Horizontal Interactive Human-Computer Systems (TABLETOP 2006), Adelaide, Australia, January 5-7, pp. 57–58. IEEE Computer Society Press, Los Alamitos (2006)
21. Gutwin, C., Greenberg, S.: A descriptive framework of workspace awareness for real-time groupware. Computer Supported Cooperative Work (3), 411–446 (2002)
22. Hornecker, E., Marshall, P., Dalton, N.S., Rogers, Y.: Collaboration and interference: awareness with mice or touch input. In: Proceedings of the ACM 2008 conference on Computer supported cooperative work (CSCW 2008), pp. 167–176. ACM Press, New York (2008)

23. Tuddenham, P., Robinson, P.: Distributed Tabletops: Supporting remote and mixed-presence tabletop collaboration. In: Proceedings of the Second Annual IEEE International Workshop on Horizontal Interactive Human-Computer Systems (TABLETOP 2007), Newport, Rhode Island, USA, October 10-12, 2007, pp. 19–26. IEEE Computer Society Press, Los Alamitos (2007)
24. Tang, A., Neustaedter, C., Greenberg, S.: Videoarms: Embodiments for mixed presence groupware. In: Bryan-Kinns, N., Blanford, A., Curzon, P., Nigay, L. (eds.) Proc. of HCI on People and Computers XX. Springer, Heidelberg (2006)
25. HxI Initiative (2008), `http://www.hxi.org.au` (cited 05.01.2008)
26. Schremmer, C., Müller-Tomfelde, C.: HxI: research down under in distributed intense collaboration between teams. In: CHI 2008 extended abstracts on Human factors in computing systems (CHI 2008), pp. 3645–3650. ACM Press, New York (2008)

Adaptive Pointing – Design and Evaluation of a Precision Enhancing Technique for Absolute Pointing Devices

Werner A. König, Jens Gerken, Stefan Dierdorf, and Harald Reiterer

HCI-Group, University of Konstanz
Box-D73, Universität Konstanz, 78457 Konstanz, Germany
{koenigw,gerken,dierdorf,reiterer}@inf.uni-konstanz.de

Abstract. We present Adaptive Pointing, a novel approach to addressing the common problem of accuracy when using absolute pointing devices for distant interaction. First, we discuss extensively some related work concerning the problem-domain of pointing accuracy when using absolute or relative pointing devices. As a result, we introduce a novel classification scheme to more clearly discriminate between different approaches. Second, the Adaptive Pointing technique is presented and described in detail. The intention behind this approach is to improve pointing performance for absolute input devices by implicitly adapting the Control-Display gain to the current user's needs without violating users' mental model of absolute-device operation. Third, we present an experiment comparing Adaptive Pointing with pure absolute pointing using a laser-pointer as an example of an absolute device. The results show that Adaptive Pointing results in a significant improvement compared with absolute pointing in terms of movement time (19%), error rate (63%), and user satisfaction.

Keywords: Adaptive Pointing, bubble test, pointing precision, hand tremor, control-display gain, distant interaction, laser-pointer.

1 Introduction

With the steadily growing diversity of application domains beyond standard desktop usage, absolute pointing devices are becoming more and more favored. Absolute devices use a position-to-position mapping (mouse: velocity-to-velocity) as the transfer function between the input device and the display pointer [1]. As a result the user benefits from a more natural and convenient pointing experience [2] and easier hand-eye coordination compared with the decoupling of motor and display spaces and the non-linear pointer acceleration when using relative pointing devices. Due to the direct mapping of absolute pointing devices, the user can easily keep track of the cursor, since it is always in line with the user's finger, stylus, laser-pointer or any other absolute device.

Besides home entertainment (e.g. Nintendo Wii), there are various other application domains in, for example, the fields of ubiquitous computing, visual analytics, collaborative environments and interactive exhibitions, where users need the flexibility of absolute pointing devices to interact effectively. Especially in combination with

T. Gross et al. (Eds.): INTERACT 2009, Part I, LNCS 5726, pp. 658–671, 2009.

large, high-resolution displays, there is a need for input devices that provide more user mobility, allowing the user to work close to the display with detailed information and also to step back and manipulate the contents of the entire display space [3]. This trend is also reflected in research literature, with several authors proposing solutions for absolute input devices such as freehand pointing [3] or laser-pointer interaction [2,4].

However, a common problem shared by all absolute input devices operated from a distance, particularly in combination with high-resolution displays, is the pointing precision. Myers et al. concluded that "interaction techniques using laser-pointers tend to be imprecise, error-prone, and slow" [2]. Vogel et al. reported a similar result for their comparison of absolute, relative and hybrid mapping of hand movements. While the absolute technique was significantly faster than the hybrid and relative ones, the high error rates of the absolute mapping "prevent it from being a practical technique" [3]. Based on previous related work and our experience, we identified two main factors for this serious imprecision of absolute pointing devices used in midair: deviations are caused by **natural hand tremor** and limited **human pointing precision**. After discussing these two aspects in detail, we will present the Adaptive Pointing technique, an approach which continuously changes the CD gain of an absolute pointing device to enhance the pointing precision while preserving the behavior of an absolute pointing device.

1.1 Natural Hand Tremor

The task of maintaining a part of a limb in a constant position produces involuntary muscular contraction with rhythmical oscillations (8-40 Hz) referred to as physiological tremor [5]. When using freehand pointing or absolute pointing devices in midair without a stable rest, such natural tremor causes serious noise, which makes accurate pointing and selection more difficult or even impossible as the distance between display and user increases. A variety of approaches exist to reduce noise and so to steady the cursor, such as band-pass filters, dynamic moving windows (Myers et al. [2], Vogel et al. [3]), or using a Kalman filter (e.g. [4]) to smoothen the pointing behavior. While all approaches seem to increase the accuracy they also introduce a noticeable time lag, which reduces the responsiveness of the pointing device. To date, we are not aware of a systematic investigation that compares and ranks these smoothing approaches. All authors report a general improvement, but eliminating noise for pointing movements without introducing a certain amount of delay or reduction of responsiveness seems to be impossible for such reactive methods.ïBesides, it is questionable whether even the most perfect jitter compensation would, on its own, provide sufficient pointing accuracy. Thereby another factor has to be considered as well: human pointing precision.

1.2 Human Pointing Precision

Absolute pointing devices are characterized by a position-to-position mapping. The user expects that the cursor is in line with the device e.g. laser-pointer. Hence, the pointer motion in display space is proportional to the movement in motor space. When interacting from a greater distance, for example in a presentation situation or when using a high-density display, the effective pixel size on the display might fall below human pointing precision. In such a case, even if the tremor compensation worked perfectly, the user would not be able to move discretely one pixel at a time because of limited hand-eye coordination, restricted motor precision, and the necessary but unachievable fine control of the muscle groups involved in the movement (see [6] and [7] for a more detailed discussion). When using a relative input device such as the mouse, the human precision limit can be overcome by lowering the Control-Display gain (CD gain = $velocity_{Pointer}$ / $velocity_{Device}$) [8]. The CD gain modulates the mapping between the physical input device and the virtual display pointer. With a low-gain transfer function the pointer velocity in display space is several times slower than the actual velocity of the pointing device in motor space. Thus, low CD gain allows for precise targeting even in the case of high-density displays or distant interaction. On the downside, moving long distances is highly inefficient. This speed-accuracy trade-off can be solved by varying the CD gain during interaction. This approach is the basis for several interaction techniques that operate in motor-space and was also the fundamental design principle of our Adaptive Pointing technique.

We will discuss these different techniques according to a classification scheme we have developed. We thus distinguish between *target-oriented*, *manual-switching*, and *velocity-oriented* approaches. Target-oriented techniques basically use a metaphor approach based on magnetism or stickiness by lowering the CD gain when the pointer either enters a target (e.g. [9], [10]) or when it comes close to a target, thus creating a fisheye effect in motor space (e.g. [11], [12]). As a precondition, however, a semantic knowledge of the environment is required, and having to deal with large numbers of targets can be problematic.

The *manual-switching* approaches rely on the user to manually switch between absolute and relative pointing when appropriate. Forlines et al. [13] rely on this approach with their *HybridPointing* concept, which provided a two-mode interaction technique with manual switching for pen input on a large, high-resolution display. In this case the switching to relative mode was realized by tapping in a *Trailing Widget.* Lifting the pen off the display or clicking on the cursor reactivated the absolute mode. They also compared the *HybridPointing* technique with an exclusively absolute and an exclusively relative pen input. Overall, there was no significant main effect in terms of selection time, but a significant effect on error rate. Hybrid input was worst with 6.8% versus 4.3% for the absolute and 3.9% for the relative mode. The *Trailing Widget,* which was used for switching the mode, turned out to be "distracting" and sometimes "in the way". Vogel et al. [3] defined different hand postures to explicitly switch between absolute and relative mode in their freehand pointing technique. Hence, the user changes the CD gain manually between a constant value for absolute mode and a conventional acceleration function for relative mode. Vogel et al. compared this two-mode technique named *RayToRelative* with a solely absolute (*RayCasting*) and a solely relative mode (*Relative*). They reported that *RayCasting* was significantly faster (mean time 2843 ms vs. 3926 ms for Relative and 3744 ms for *RayToRelative*), particularly so for large targets and when clutching would have been required. However, there was a significantly higher error rate for the absolute *RayCasting* with a mean error of 22.5% compared with 3.5% (*Relative*) and 5.7% (*RayToRelative*). The mean error rate for absolute input even increased to 56% for the small target (16 mm) condition. Thus, the combination of absolute and relative mode turned out to be a good balance between accuracy and interaction speed. On the downside, the cognitive and physical load of switching explicitly between the two modes remained with the users.

The third group, the *velocity-oriented* approaches are motivated by the optimized-submovement model [14], which states that most aimed movements consist of an initial, large and fast movement towards the target followed by a few slower, corrective movements to compensate for over- or undershooting [15]. The movement velocity in motor space indicates in which phase of the movement the user is and which degree of precision or velocity in display space should be beneficial. This is the basis of all pointer-acceleration techniques already widely in use, for example by default in Mac OS X and Windows XP [16]. In research, different acceleration functions were investigated, for example discrete switches between constant gain levels dependent on the movement velocity, linear acceleration functions, or non-linear mappings. However, the experimental results concerning possible performance improvements in these diverse functions and also in comparison with constant CD gains are inconclusive (see [17] for a detailed discussion). Based on this approach, Frees et al. introduced the PRISM technique which dynamically adjusts the CD gain between the hand and the controlled object in a virtual 3D environment [18]. Evaluation results showed a clear improvement in pointing precision compared to a pure absolute mapping.

The results confirm the impression that combinations of absolute and relative input modes seem to be able to improve pointing precision – but only at a price. The drawback of all these approaches is that an absolute pointing device would no longer maintain the characteristically 1:1 mapping between the device position in motor space and the pointer position in display space. This however would lead to an unnatural and unpredictable behavior. The *manual-switching* approaches try to resolve this by letting the user choose between absolute and relative mapping while the *target-oriented* approaches rely on semantic knowledge of the environment, which might not be available. Precise pointing with an absolute input device therefore remains an unsolved problem. In the following section, we discuss our new approach to solving this issue, the Adaptive Pointing technique.

2 Adaptive Pointing

We introduce the Adaptive Pointing technique, which can also be classified as a velocity-oriented approach, relying on the optimized-submovement model of Meyer et al. [14] discussed above. However it differs from similar concepts such as PRISM by simulating absolute pointing behavior. The basic idea is to improve pointing performance for absolute input devices by implicitly adapting the CD gain to the current user's needs without violating the users' mental model of absolute-device operation. Users expect a 1:1 mapping between their device movement in motor space and the resulting pointer movement in display space when using an absolute pointing device. Adaptive Pointing appears to provide this pure absolute behavior but imperceptibly lowers the CD gain when higher precision is needed.

While PRISM works very well in the dedicated virtual environment for professional users, it has some obvious drawbacks when applied to a more general setting of (simulating) absolute pointing devices. Since the system explicitly visualizes the offset between display space and motor space movement, the device does no longer appear as an absolute pointing device to the user. This also reduces the intuitiveness and ease of use of the device, as the user has to understand at first how this gap between motor space and display space arises and how to deal with it. The absolute pointing behavior is furthermore flawed by the necessary offset reduction. PRISM increases the CD gain by the amount that is needed so that the offset is nullified within a period of about one second. This, however, should result in a noticeable "jumping" which would lead to an unnatural and unexpected behavior. Furthermore in case of movement direction changes, it might be that the pointer in display space is actually "in front" of the motor space movement. In such a case PRISM lets the users catch up the offset by themselves, which results in a non-movement of the pointer in display space. Again, this behavior results in a reduced ease of use and intuitiveness of the technique when applied to the more generic setting of an absolute pointing device.

Comparing the Adaptive Pointing with the manual-switching approaches, for example [3], [13], the user is not explicitly involved in the gain variation and thus does not need to decide which technique would be most suitable for the next task. Unlike target-oriented approaches such as [11] and [12], Adaptive Pointing does not need any knowledge of the displayed information or active elements. However, it can be easily combined with visual interaction techniques such as expanding targets [19] or Drag-and-Pop [20], as well as hand-tremor compensations (e.g. Kalman filter) if further pointing and selection improvement is desired.

2.1 Adaptive Gain

The Adaptive Pointing technique dynamically adjusts the CD gain depending on the movement velocity and the current offset between the motor-space position and display-space position. Fig. 1 shows the behavior for the velocity factor. As soon as a predefined minimal velocity threshold is met the CD gain is smoothly decreased. We describe this behavior in the following equations, but only for the horizontal case indicated by the index x. Vertical movement is calculated likewise. The first step of the iterative position mapping between motor and display space is the normalization of the velocity, which serves as an indicator of the users' need and as the main controlling factor (Eq. 1). The upper limit is v_{max}, which marks the threshold from where the CD gain decreases until the lower limit v_{min} is reached. Velocities below v_{min} and above v_{max} are also limited to a value range of 0 to 1 (Eq. 1). Since we want to ensure an absolute pointing behavior, it is important that the offset between the position in motor space and in display space is considered as well. Eq. 2 describes the offset calculation and the normalization is done likewise to the velocity normalization (Eq. 3). For further calculations we use the larger one of these two factors (Eq. 6). For the special case of a dwelling operation, another factor is added (Eq. 4 & Eq. 5) to stabilize the cursor even more. Since we want to avoid abrupt switches during the transition from constant gain (absolute mapping) to the varying gain (relative mapping), we use a modulated sine wave as damping function (Eq. 7). When the user decreases speed to aim at a target, the CD gain is smoothly adapted by the modulated sine wave until the minimum gain is reached or the user increases the movement speed again. When the CD gain is lowered, however, the pointer moves more slowly in display space than the input device in motor space. This results in an offset between the detected pointing position and the modulated pointer position. In case of either a high velocity or a large offset, the gain calculation reaches values above 1 and up to a predefined maximum.

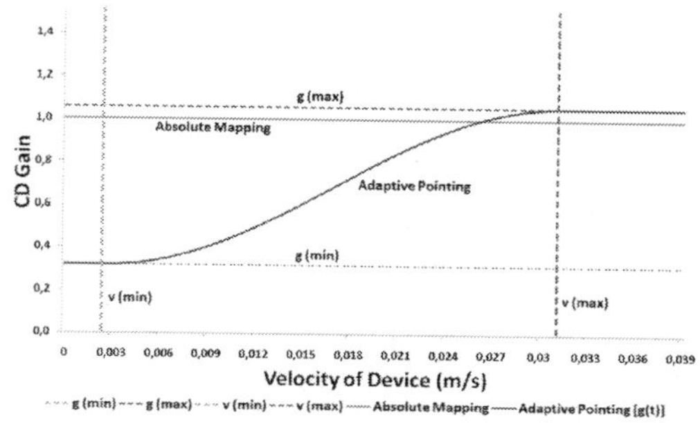

Fig. 1. Smooth transition between relative and absolute CD gain of Adaptive Pointing

In case that the pointer position in display-space lacks behind the position in motor space this results in a smooth catch-up. For the opposite case that the position in display space is "in front" of the position in motor space (e.g. due to a change of direction) we flip the part of the sine wave for which applies CD gain>1 at the CD gain=1.0 axis (Eq. 9). Thereby we reach a gain value slightly below 1 which allows a reverse catch-up of the offset. The new pointer position in display space is then calculated by applying the current CD gain g(t) as a factor to the last movement in motor space (Eq. 8) and adding this to the last position $x_{disp}(t\text{-}1)$ in display space (Eq. 10).

$$\hat{v}_x(t) = \begin{cases} 1 & if \quad v_x(t) > v_{max} \\ 0 & if \quad v_x(t) < v_{min} \\ \frac{v_x(t)-v_{min}}{v_{max}-v_{min}} & otherwise \end{cases} \quad (1)$$

$$d_x(t) = x_{mot}(t) - x_{disp}(t-1) \quad (2)$$

$$\hat{d}_x(t) = \begin{cases} 1 & if \quad |d_x(t)| > d_{max} \\ 0 & if \quad |d_x(t)| < d_{min} \\ \frac{|d_x(t)|-d_{min}}{d_{max}-d_{min}} & otherwise \end{cases} \quad (3)$$

$$w_x(t) = \frac{1}{n}\sum_{i=1}^{n}|x_{mot}(t) - x_{mot}(t-i)| \quad (4)$$

$$\hat{w}_x(t) = \begin{cases} 1 & if \quad w_x(t) > w_{max} \\ 0 & if \quad w_x(t) < w_{min} \\ \frac{w_x(t)-w_{min}}{w_{max}-w_{min}} & otherwise \end{cases} \quad (5)$$

$$m_x(t) = \hat{w}_x(t) \cdot \max\left(\hat{v}_x(t), \hat{d}_x(t)\right) \quad (6)$$

$$g_x(t) = g_{min} + \frac{1}{2}\left[\sin\left(m_x(t)\cdot\pi - \frac{\pi}{2}\right) + 1\right](g_{max} - g_{min}) \quad (7)$$

$$s_x(t) = x_{mot}(t) - x_{mot}(t-1) \quad (8)$$

$$\hat{g}_x(t) = \begin{cases} 1 - (g_x(t) - 1) & if \quad g_x(t) > 1 \ AND \ d_x(t) > 0 \ AND \ s_x(t) < 0 \\ 1 - (g_x(t) - 1) & if \quad g_x(t) > 1 \ AND \ d_x(t) < 0 \ AND \ s_x(t) > 0 \\ g_x(t) & otherwise \end{cases} \quad (9)$$

$$x_{disp}(t) = x_{disp}(t-1) + \hat{g}_x(t) \cdot s_x(t) \quad (10)$$

This approach allows a smooth and continuous pointer movement that is regulated by parameters for the maximum and minimum values for the CD gain, the movement velocity, and the offset between display- and motor-space. As pointed out before, this is an important difference to approaches like the PRISM technique, which furthermore does not consider the size of the offset but only the velocity of the movement. We applied the Adaptive Pointing to an infrared laser-pointer interaction system at a

221″ large high-resolution display (8.9 megapixels Powerwall) to explore the potential as well as the constraints of the novel interaction technique. This is obviously a very demanding setting for absolute pointing techniques, since the user has to point at, select and manipulate very small objects from a distance of several meters (e.g. the Windows start button is only 22mm in height on such a display). During iterative testing and configuration we found the following parameters most beneficial for this setting:

$v_{min} = 0.0028^{m}/_{s}$, $v_{max} = 0.0312^{m}/_{s}$, $d_{min} = 47px$, $d_{max} = 232px$, $g_{min} = 0.032$, and $g_{max} = 1.055$. Fig. 1 illustrates the resulting CD gain with respect to the velocity of the input device in motor space for the parameter set used.

3 Evaluation

To evaluate the Adaptive Pointing technique we conducted a controlled experiment with 24 participants. As a popular representative of an absolute pointing device we used an infrared laser-pointer interaction technology that is described in more detail in [21]. We compared the Adaptive Pointing technique with a Kalman filter enhanced absolute pointing in terms of efficiency, effectiveness and user satisfaction. In addition, we wanted to compare novices with experienced users of the laser-pointer interaction technology to assess whether the usefulness of the Adaptive Pointing technique diminishes with increasing familiarity with the device.

3.1 Materials and Participants

The experiment was conducted in front of the previously mentioned Powerwall (see Fig. 2), a wall-sized display with a resolution of 4640×1920 pixels and physical dimensions of 5.20×2.15 meters. The infrared (and thereby invisible) laser-pointer interaction technology is used to interact freely with the display. We applied a combination of static and dynamic Kalman filters for the absolute pointing condition; while for the Adaptive Pointing technique we relied solely on a static Kalman filter since the Adaptive Pointing technique replaces the dynamic component. In both cases we optimized the performance as well as the 'feeling' of the laser-pointer by iterative testing and configuration. The laser-pointer was equipped with a button, which was

Fig. 2. Comparing absolute input and Adaptive Pointing at a large, high-resolution display. Device: infrared laser-pointer, distance: 3 meters.

used to click on a target. Demographic data was collected via a pre-test questionnaire. A questionnaire/interview combination was used to assess users' subjective opinions about the Adaptive Pointing technique.

For the study we selected 24 subjects; 16 female and 8 male. Their ages ranged from 16 to 53 years (mean 26.75, st.dev. 8.81 years). Their fields of occupation varied greatly, embracing school pupils, university students and employees. Twelve participants formed the experienced group. They qualified for this group by having already used the laser-pointer with absolute pointing extensively in an earlier study (it took place on average 52.17 days earlier, 3.01 days st. dev.). None of the other twelve subjects (novice group) had ever used an interactive laser-pointer before.

3.2 Tasks

We used a 'bubble' task that essentially implements a discrete, multidirectional tapping paradigm to assess the pointing performance of the two different techniques (see Fig. 2). In such a task, users had to move the cursor (in the form of a cross-hair) onto a randomly appearing bubble target and click the button while over it. Between each trial users had to dwell on a homing position located in the center of the screen until the next target appeared. The task is largely along the lines of Fitts' Law experiments, as recommended by ISO-9241-9 with the differences being the use of a discrete tapping paradigm and the use of colors and sounds for motivational reasons (see [22] for a discussion). We used target widths (W) of 20, 40 and 80 pixels (22.4, 44.8 and 89.6 mm respectively). These appeared in home-to-target amplitudes (A) of 400, 1000, and 1800 pixels. An initial task fulfilled the dual roles of retention task for the experienced group and training task for the novice group. In this case we used target sizes of 40, 80 and 160 pixels and a different color setting to distinguish this training task from the experimental task. Participant used only the absolute pointing technique in this phase. Similar to [2] we used an additional dwelling task in order to assess the steadiness of the Adaptive Pointing technique, i.e. the stability with which one can hold a certain position. Users had to point at a 20-pixel target located in the center of the screen for five seconds, while measuring started one second after first crossing the target border. Each second was indicated with a short 'beep' sound.

3.3 Experimental Design

We used a 2x2x3 split-plot design, the first being a between-subjects factor (experience) and the latter two within-subjects factors (pointing technique, type of task). We fully counter-balanced the pointing-technique factor across the two experimental tasks (bubble + dwelling), leaving the training/retention task at the beginning unaffected, of course. This resulted in four different experimental groups to which we randomly assigned six participants each. The dependent variables were error rate (hit or miss), movement time (time between leaving the homing position and clicking on a target), and subjective rating of the technique (on a 6-point scale in terms of improvement or worsening, depending on the sequence of presenting the pointing techniques). We used of 3W(width)×3A(amplitude)×16trials×2blocks and an additional short familiarization phase of 3W×3A×5trials for each of the two pointing technique conditions. Together with 216 training/retention trials this sums up to 882 trials per participant and 21,168 trials in total. The dwelling task was repeated five times by each user for each pointing technique. Fig. 3 illustrates the exact procedure.

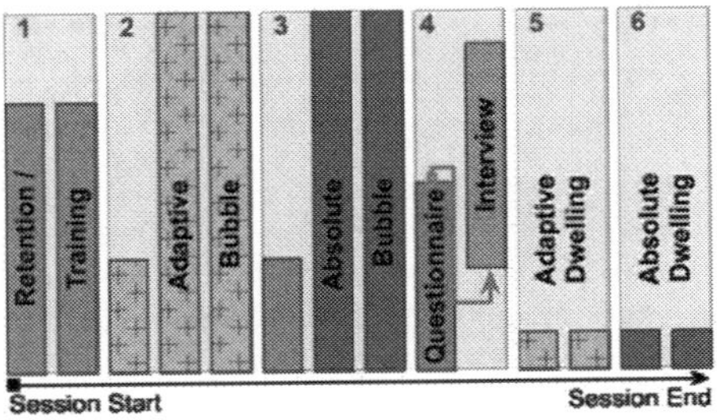

Fig. 3. Illustrating the (counter-balanced) experimental procedure – each pointing technique consisted of one familiarization block and two experimental blocks

It is important to note that participants were not informed of the condition change between absolute and adaptive pointing. Between each block, participants were able to relax for about one minute. After completing all tasks the participants were then compensated for their efforts with a payment of 8 Euros. Each session lasted about 70-90 min.

3.4 Hypotheses

Based on our goals and design principles for the Adaptive Pointing technique we formulated the following hypotheses for our experiment. We hereby focused on the general measures of movement time and error rate to be able to distinguish between accuracy and efficiency.

H1: Accuracy - aiming and hitting. Using the Adaptive Pointing technique will enable better aiming at and hitting of targets compared with using absolute pointing. This will become evident in a lower error rate during the bubble task and in lower deviations from the target during the dwelling task. When aiming at a target, users will slow down their movement and thereby enabling the Adaptive Pointing technique. When using absolute pointing, earlier studies suggest error rates of about 15% [21] and dwelling deviations between 7.3 and 8.9 mm [2].

H2: Moving. Regarding the movement time we expected the Adaptive Pointing technique to perform on a level comparable with absolute pointing. Since moving long distances is normally done at a higher speed [14], the CD gain should remain comparable with pure absolute pointing and therefore not affect the movement. However, since the measure 'movement time' includes the time for actually aiming and clicking, we expected the movement time for small targets to be lower compared with absolute pointing. The latter should need more time in the aiming phase in order to achieve a hit, especially when the targets are only 20 pixels in width.

H3: Imperceptibility. Since participants were not instructed of the change in conditions between absolute and adaptive pointing, we assumed that participants would either not recognize a change in the behavior of the laser-pointer or not ascribe it to the laser-pointer itself. The post-test questionnaire explicitly asked about any kinds of change noticed during the experiment in terms of accuracy, ease of use, and performance as well as the reasons that people claimed to be responsible for these changes.

One design rationale behind the Adaptive Pointing was to integrate an imperceptible change in CD gain, preserving the feeling of a pure absolute pointing device. According to a study by Sutter et al. [23], people tend to judge their hand movement mainly on the basis of the on-screen movement of the cursor and adapt their hand movement accordingly. This means that, as long as the discrepancy between cursor position and hand position is quite small, people will not recognize any discrepancy at all and therefore will not ascribe the different accuracies of per-se absolute pointing devices to the devices themselves.

H4: Experience. This last hypothesis assumed that people with more experience would 1) perform better than the novice group and 2) benefit less from the Adaptive Pointing in terms of the first two hypotheses. While the first point should be due to the larger amount of training producing positive results, as has been discovered before (see [22]), the second point reflects the thinking that a higher level of performance (due to training) naturally leads to less room for improvement.

4 Results

For further analysis and testing of our hypotheses we considered the 13,824 trials during the bubble task. In a first step, we removed 1.7% of these trials after identifying them as either accidental clicks or extreme outliers resulting in 13,578 trials used for analysis. Furthermore, one participant (in the experienced group) was completely excluded because of error rates higher than 25% regardless of the pointing technique. During the interview he stated that he didn't really try to hit the targets. Homogeneity of variances was met in all cases when contrasts or pair-wise comparisons were performed.

H4: experience: We begin the presentation of the results with our last hypothesis, which stated that experienced users would perform better, and benefit less from the Adaptive Pointing technique, when compared with the novice group. Results, however, show that both groups performed fairly equally. Table 1 shows that the small differences are non-significant.

Table 1. Comparing experience levels

	Error rate/std.err. (in %)	**Movement time / std. err. (in s)**
Novice	11.26/1.49	1.67/0.74
Expert	8.8/1.45	1.72/0.87
F-statistic	$F(1,21)=1.365$, $p=0.256$	$F(1,21)=0.430$, $p=0.519$

We therefore have to withdraw the hypothesis in favor of the null-hypothesis. This result is somewhat surprising. An analysis of the retention task in comparison to the earlier study reveals that although the performance of the experienced participants decreased about 5%, they were still superior to the novice group (about 16%), although the difference is not significant (p=0.069). Nevertheless, this might indicate that the increased difficulty of the bubble task made the training obsolete. In future studies we will investigate the influence of task difficulty on learning more in detail. Based on these findings we do not report the following findings with respect to different experience levels.

H1: accuracy (aiming & hitting): We first analyzed the error rate during the bubble task. A 2(exp.)×2(pointing technique) Repeated-Measures(RM)-ANOVA (measure: error rate) shows a significant main effect for pointing technique (F(2,20) =42.836, p=0.000). Post-hoc pair-wise comparisons (with Bonferroni adjustments) reveal that the error rates differ significantly in favor of the Adaptive Pointing technique (5.4% compared with 14.77%, std. err.: 0.7% for adaptive and 1.79% for absolute, p=0.000; confidence intervals (95%) for error rate: 3.93%-6.82% (adaptive) vs. 12.24%-17.13% (absolute)). Given the confidence intervals, this is a reduction of between 44.29% and 77.07% (mean: 63.44%). This is further strengthened by a very large effect size of eta_p^2=0.784. We analyzed the influence of the target widths in more detail (see Fig. 4). We can see that the difference is especially apparent for the 20- and 40-pixel targets (pair-wise comparison significant, p=0.000), while it is non-significant for the 80-pixel targets (p=0.653). The presentation sequence of the pointing techniques actually had a significant effect on error rate (F(1,18)=9.396, p=0.001). However, detailed analysis showed that it influenced the results in favor of the absolute pointing technique – while the Adaptive Pointing technique significantly decreased in performance when presented second (error rate: 7.22% compared with 3.73%, F(1,20)=8.256, p=0.009), the absolute condition benefited (error-rate: 11.08% compared with 18.79%, F(1,20)=19.304, p=0.000). Our results therefore tend to show a lower bound of the actual difference.

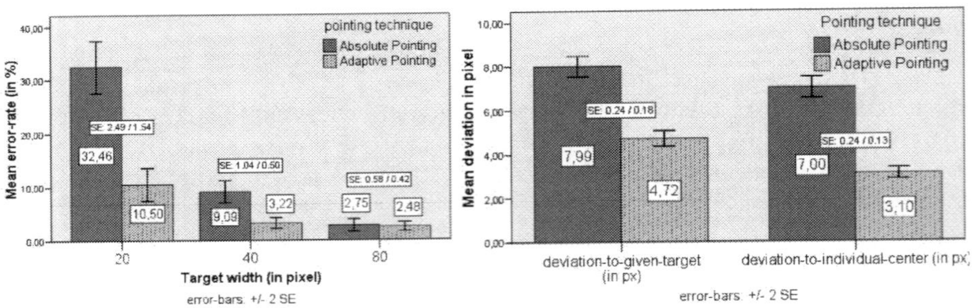

Fig. 4. Comparing error rate (bubble test, left) and dwelling deviations (dwelling test, right)

The dwelling task showed similar results. While users could point to the target with a mean deviation of 4.72 pixels when using the Adaptive Pointing technique, they only managed a mean deviation of 7.99 pixels with absolute pointing (see Fig. 4 on the right, main effect of pointing technique: F(1,23)=63.191, p=0.000). Since we used a 20-pixel target and not just a single dot we assumed participants might not have tried to point to the center but instead just to stay within the boundaries of the target. We therefore calculated the individual center of the pointing a-posteriori for each participant × trial and the deviation around this center. Results are similar again (Fig. 4 right, 3.1 px vs. 7.0 px, F(1,23)=119.559, p=0.000). In short, both the bubble test and the dwelling test strongly support the accuracy hypothesis.

H2: *moving:* The second hypothesis stated a decreased movement time for the Adaptive Pointing technique only for small targets due to the fact that this measurement also includes clicking on a target. Looking at the results shows that it did indeed take participants only 1.49 seconds to reach a target and click on it when using Adaptive Pointing compared with 1.84 seconds for absolute pointing. Accordingly, an RM-ANOVA shows a large main effect for pointing technique ($F(1,23)=58.468$, $p=0.000$, $eta_p^2=0.736$). Again, we analyzed the width × pointing technique interaction in detail to see the influence of the different target widths (see Fig. 5, left). This time, the differences between the two techniques remain significant (pair-wise comparisons, $p=0.000$) in all cases – the size of the effect, however, decreases with increasing target width. This is in line with the results of the previous hypothesis in that the benefit of Adaptive Pointing is particularly evident when having to click on small objects. To sum up, the results clearly support the stated hypothesis and show that Adaptive Pointing is more efficient even for larger target sizes of 80px (89.6mm).

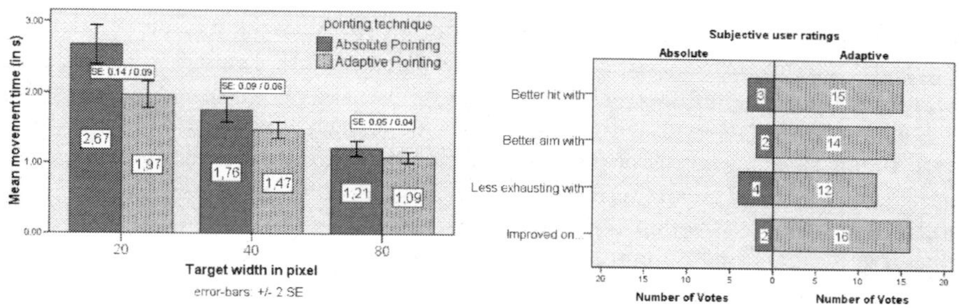

Fig. 5. Comparing movement times (left) and subjective user ratings (right)

H3: imperceptibility: The third hypothesis stated that users would not recognize the change in pointing technique during the experiment or at least would not ascribe it to the laser-pointer itself. Only three users did not recognize any change at all, clearly contradicting the first part of the hypothesis. The remaining 21 participants filled in a questionnaire asking them to define the change experienced during the experiment in more detail by agreeing with statements such as 'Usage got more/less tiresome', 'It was easier/harder to hit the targets', or 'I got better/worse'. Because we had varied the presentation sequence of the pointing techniques, we had a positive and a negative version of each statement. It is important to note that users could choose freely from the list of statements and were not asked to answer each of them. For analysis we then counted how many positive statements a technique received for each question. Negative statements were transformed into positive points for the competing technique. The resulting Fig. 5 (right) reveals that users clearly assigned the positive statements to the Adaptive Pointing technique. A Chi² test shows that the difference in distribution of the statements between techniques is significant for each case (getting better: $X^2(1,N=18)=10.889$, $p=0.001$; less tiresome: $X^2(1,N=16)=4.0$, $p=0.046$; easier to aim: $X^2(1,N=16)=9.0$, $p=0.003$; easier to hit: $X^2(1,N=18)=8.0$, $p=0.005$). When asked what might be responsible for the change that they had recognized, participants gave fatigue as the reason for getting worse (7 times) while changes to the laser-pointer itself

(7 times), results of practice (4 times) or an improvement in mental concentration (2 times) were made responsible for getting better. In addition to the above-mentioned statements, the 21 users who noticed a change had to give a total rating on a six-point scale, stating whether the change was for the worse or for the better. We transformed this scale so as ratings higher than 3.5 favored the Adaptive Pointing while values lower than 3.5 rated it as worse. The mean rating was 4.67 with a std. deviation of 1.197. A one-sample t-test (two-sided) reveals that this is a significant difference to the 3.5 test value ($t(20)=4.466$, $p=0.000$).

To sum up this hypothesis, our initial concern, namely that recognition would mean that the laser-pointer behaved unnaturally, turned out to be wrong. Our participants clearly ascribed positive characteristics to the Adaptive Pointing technique and rated it as significantly better compared with absolute pointing.

5 Discussion and Conclusion

The experiment provided some clear-cut results. In every single aspect, the Adaptive Pointing technique proved to be significantly better than a Kalman filter enhanced absolute pointing. We observed a mean reduction in error rate (effectiveness) of about 63%, an improvement in dwelling deviation of between 40% and 55%, as well as more efficient usage in terms of movement time (19% mean difference). Furthermore, users stated that they clearly preferred the Adaptive Pointing and assigned positive characteristics such as "better hitting" or "less exhausting" to it. Putting the results in perspective, we can for example compare the dwelling results with the study of Myers et al. [2]. In a similar setting they noted a deviation of between 7.3 mm and 8.9 mm, which corresponds approximately to our observed deviation of 7.99px (=8.95 mm) for absolute pointing, while Adaptive Pointing enabled a deviation of only 4.72px (=5.29 mm). With regards to efficiency and effectiveness, former approaches suffered a clear speed-accuracy trade-off [3], while our Adaptive Pointing performed better in both aspects. To conclude, we would like to cite our participants, firstly on the behavior of Adaptive Pointing: "No, it was no big readjustment by any means. It [Adaptive Pointing] was very helpful and happened without any problems. By itself."(ID12), and secondly on its effect: "In the beginning [absolute pointing] I found it exhausting but towards the end [Adaptive Pointing] I almost found it boring. Because then you hit almost every time." (ID24).

References

1. Hinckley, K.: Input technologies and techniques. In: Handbook of Human-Computer Interaction, pp. 161–176 (2008)
2. Myers, B.A., Bhatnagar, R., Nichols, J., et al.: Interacting at a distance: measuring the performance of laser-pointers and other devices. In: Proc. CHI 2002, pp. 33–40 (2002)
3. Vogel, D., Balakrishnan, R.: Distant freehand pointing and clicking on very large, high resolution displays. In: Proc. UIST 2005, pp. 33–42 (2005)
4. Oh, J., Stuerzlinger, W.: Laser-pointers as collaborative pointing devices. In: Proc: GI 2002 (2002)

5. Vaillancourt, E., Newell, K.M.: Amplitude changes in the 8–12, 20–25, and 40 hz oscillations in finger tremor. Clinical neurophysiology 111(10), 1792–1801 (2000)
6. Balakrishnan, R., MacKenzie, I.S.: Performance differences in the fingers, wrist, and forearm in computer input control. In: Proc. CHI 1997, pp. 303–310 (1997)
7. Card, S.K., Mackinlay, J.D., Robertson, G.G.: A morphological analysis of the design space of input devices. ACM Trans. Inf. Syst., 99–122 (1991)
8. Gibbs, B.: Controller design: Interactions of controlling limbs, time-lags and gains in positional and velocity systems. Ergonomics, 385–402 (1962)
9. Worden, A., Walker, N., Bharat, K., Hudson, S.: Making computers easier for older adults to use: area cursors and sticky icons. In: Proc. CHI 1997, pp. 266–271 (1997)
10. Cockburn, A., Firth, A.: Improving the acquisition of small targets. In: Proc. British Computer Society Conference on HCI 2003, pp. 181–196 (2003)
11. Baudisch, P., Cutrell, E., Hinckley, K., Eversole, A.: Snap-and-go: helping users align objects without the modality of traditional snapping. In: Proc. CHI 2005, pp. 301–310 (2005)
12. Blanch, R., Guiard, Y., Beaudouin-Lafon, M.: Semantic pointing: improving target acquisition with control-display ratio adaptation. In: Proc. CHI 2004, pp. 519–526 (2004)
13. Forlines, C., Vogel, D., Balakrishnan, R.: Hybridpointing: fluid switching between absolute and relative pointing with a direct input device. In: Proc. UIST 2006, pp. 211–220 (2006)
14. Meyer, D.E., Abrams, R.A., Kornblum, S., Wright, C.E., Smith, J.E.K.: Optimality in human motor performance: Ideal control of rapid aimed movements. Psychological Review, 340–370 (1988)
15. Balakrishnan, R.: "beating" fitts' law: virtual enhancements for pointing facilitation. Int. J. Hum.-Comput. Stud., 857–874 (2004)
16. Microsoft. Pointer ballistics for windows xp (2008), http://www.microsoft.com/whdc/archive/pointer-bal.mspx
17. Casiez, G., Vogel, D., Balakrishnan, R., Cockburn, A.: The impact of control-display gain on user performance in pointing tasks. Human-Computer Interaction 23(3) (2008)
18. Frees, S., Kessler, G.D., Kay, E.: PRISM interaction for enhancing control in immersive virtual environments. ACM Trans. Comput.-Hum. Interact. 14(1) (2007)
19. McGuffin, M., Balakrishnan, R.: Acquisition of expanding targets. In: Proc. CHI 2002, pp. 57–64 (2002)
20. Baudisch, P., Cutrell, E., Robbins, D., Czerwinski, M., Bederson, P.T.B., Zierlinger, A.: Drag-and-pop and drag-and-pick: Techniques for accessing remote screen content on touch- and pen-operated systems. In: Proc. Interact 2003, pp. 57–64 (2003)
21. König, W.A., Bieg, H.-J., Schmidt, T., Reiterer, H.: Position-independent interaction for large high-resolution displays. In: Proc. IHCI 2007 (2007)
22. Bieg, H.-J.: Laserpointer and eye gaze interaction - design and evaluation. Master's thesis, University of Konstanz (2008), http://hci.uni-konstanz.de/intehrdis/Bieg2008.pdf
23. Sutter, C., Muesseler, J., Bardos, L., Ballagas, R., Borchers, J.: The impact of gain change on perceiving one's own actions. In: Proc. M&C 2008 (2008)

The Perception of Cultural Differences in Online Self-presentation

Yifan Jiang, Oscar de Bruijn, and Antonella De Angeli

Manchester Business School, Booth Street West, Manchester, M15 6PB, UK
Yifan.Jiang@postgrad.mbs.ac.uk,
{Oscar.DeBruijn,Antonella.De-angeli}@mbs.ac.uk

Abstract. Online self-presentation, defined as the way people present themselves through profiles, blogs, photo albums, etc., forms the basis of much of the interpersonal relationship building taking place in social networking platforms such as Windows Live Space. However, little is known about how people make sense of this information, particularly if presenter and audience do not have a common cultural background. This study investigated the effectiveness of cross-cultural online communication by measuring the cross-cultural social perception of specially constructed online representations of a typical British and a typical Chinese person. The representations were based on a 7-dimensional characterization of cultural differences derived from a review of the literature. The findings suggested that cultural characterization embedded in online communication affects the social perception of others, that it can trigger stereotypes, and that it has consequences for establishing relationships. Implications for the design of social networking platforms are discussed.

Keywords: Cross-cultural communication, Online Self-presentation.

1 Introduction

Social networking platforms (e.g., Windows Live Spaces, Facebook) provide an opportunity for users to present themselves online and connect with each other [5]. These media have the potential, therefore, to substantially increase the amount of communication between people who do not share a cultural background. However, it is questionable whether much of this cross-cultural communication is effective in establishing relationships between people with different cultural backgrounds. Indeed, cross-cultural relationships are "*onerous to initiate, develop and maintain resulting from the interplay of a wide range of variables such as values, interest, personality traits, network patterns, communication styles, cultural knowledge, and relational and intercultural communication competence, intergroup attitudes, and so forth*" [2].

Our cultural background serves to help us interpret our own behaviour and that of others. Thus, culture determines in large part how we present ourselves to the outside world, and how we perceive others. Self-presentation is subject to different levels of intentional control. Verbal communication can be more closely controlled, we can decide what to disclose and how, whereas non-verbal communication (e.g., physical appearance, gestures, tone of voice, and other behaviour) may escape conscious

T. Gross et al. (Eds.): INTERACT 2009, Part I, LNCS 5726, pp. 672–685, 2009.

control. The way we are perceived by others will depend on the cues that they pick up from our verbal and non-verbal behaviour [7].

Online self-presentation is different from real life self-presentation. In online social networking sites, initial impressions of others are almost always based upon information they provide in their profiles, blogs and other forms of communication. These do not contain many of the non-verbal cues that are characteristic of offline communication. They are also substantially less spontaneous [11] [17], more static, and less immediately responsive to feedback. Evidence suggests that people adapt their style of self-presentation in offline communication according to the type of audience they are addressing [23]. The extent to which this can be achieved in online communication is often severely limited by the lack of affordances towards that end offered by online networking platforms. As a result, online self-presentation tends to emphasize a number of small cues based upon expectations of how audiences will react to these [4].

It appears therefore that the success of online communication for relationship building depends on the ability to anticipate the effects self-presentation has on others [15]. However, it seems likely that the perception of online self-presentation is substantially affected by the cultural background of the audience. In cross-cultural communication, therefore, it is unavoidable that presenters' anticipation of the effects of self-presentation is often inaccurate, as it is based on a cultural point of view that can be substantially different from that of the perceiver. In order to determine how cultural differences affects social networking, we have to investigate how cultural variation in self-presentation strategies affects the way people are perceived by others, and how these perceptions might affect cross-cultural encounters in online contexts.

2 Background

An important psychological framework, particularly relevant to the aim of this research, relates cultural differences in perception, emotion and motivation to specific forms of self-construal. The self-concept is a socio-cognitive construct used to denote all the knowledge people have about their self [1]. The self represents the most important set of cognitive representations available to a person, acting as an information processor, and mediating perception of the world. It filters, interprets and evaluates all the incoming stimuli in terms of their contribution to the individual's well-being.

Individuals of different cultures have different conceptions of the self, modulated on a continuum which varies according to the relationship between the self and others [18]. The interdependent self is grounded in one's connection with relevant others, whereas the independent self is grounded in autonomy, stability and uniqueness. Other people are still important to the independent self, but mainly for social comparison, remaining external to the self. In Eastern cultures (e.g., China) people tend to have a more interdependent self, whereas in Western cultures (e.g., Britain and the United States) people tend to have a more independent self. This theoretical distinction between independent and interdependent self, is explicit in several other cultural conceptualizations, including Hofstede's [9] cultural value dimension of collectivism versus individualism. This dialectic conception of self has important implications for the way people present themselves to others and how they communicate [24]. In particular, people with an interdependent self tend to describe themselves through roles and relationships (e.g., Father of X; Daughter of Y). They use an indirect communication style, and prefer to express self-criticism in order to maintain harmony. By contrast, people with an independent self express themselves through their inner thoughts and feelings [13]. These people use a direct communication style as they are driven by the realization of personal goals and the manifestation of individual capabilities.

Another way of framing the influence of the speaker's cultural background on communication style is by distinguishing between low-context and high-context communication cultures [8]. At the basis of this framework is the observation that the meaning of verbal communication often interacts with the context in which it occurs. In some societies, the cultural context in which most interpersonal interaction takes place is very strong due to their homogeneous make-up and long standing cultural traditions. In these societies, which include most Eastern societies, people can rely much more on a shared cultural context, and need not use explicit communication to make themselves understood. Other societies, in contrast, have a much more heterogeneous make-up and shorter cultural traditions. People in these societies, which include most Western societies, need to make their communication very explicit in order to be understood by others.

Differences in the perception of oneself may also have consequences for the way one perceives others. It is suggested that individuals with an interdependent self are more advertent to the needs of other people in order to maintain harmonious relationships, whereas individuals with an independent self care less about others' details due to their focus on themselves [14]. This suggests that the cultural background of the perceiver will determine what information they take into account when judging other people's self-presentations. A study amongst Korean people found that individuals with a more independent self preferred positive presentation styles to negative ones, whereas preferences of individuals with a more interdependent self were the other way around [10].

In summary, the literature on cultural differences suggests that culture affects the way people present themselves to others, the communication styles they use, and how they perceive other people. The study presented in this paper aims to investigate whether cultural differences in people's online self-presentation affect the way in which they are perceived and how this relates to the cultural background of the perceiver. Based on the background literature we developed two hypotheses about online communication:

H1: Differences in communication style and self-presentation in verbal communication will affect people's social perceptions.
H2: People from different cultures will base their opinions of others on different aspects of their self-presentation and communication style.

In order to test these hypotheses, people's social perception of pieces of online communication typical of British people and Chinese people were measured. This was achieved by independently manipulating the blog style and physical appearance embedded in a personal virtual space modeled on Windows Live Spaces. These manipulations created four different virtual spaces: Two in which the appearance matched the cultural style of the blog (congruent), and two in which the appearance did not match the cultural style of the blog (incongruent). These combinations lead to a third hypothesis:

H3: Congruent Combinations of appearance and blog style will be perceived as more socially desirable than incongruent combinations.

3 Related Work

Most of the work related to cultural differences in online communication has concentrated on cultural differences in presentation on Web sites and personal virtual spaces. An inventory of self-presentation on MSN Spaces (the forerunner of Windows Live Spaces) owned by either British or Chinese students studying at British Universities revealed strong cultural differences in line with the distinction between interdependent and independent self [3]. For example, spaces owned by Chinese students conformed more closely to a design standard, featured more extensive friend lists, and contained more pictures. Chinese students were also more accommodating, and more inclined to host filter blogs (blogs composed of filtered feeds from other people's blogs).

Other work has focused on the cues receivers of online communication use to form impressions of the people who produced the communication. As mentioned in the introduction, there may be several strategies for dealing with a lack of cues for social perception in online communication, one of which is a tendency of "*Internet users develop impressions of others, even with the limited cues available online, by adapting to the remaining cues in order to make decisions about others. Online users look to small cues in order to develop impression of others, such as a poster's email address, the links on a person' homepage, even the timing of email messages.*" [4]. These small cues may lead to the activation of stereotypes in an attempt to fill the gaps and create impressions of others that cover many more aspects of their personality then there is evidence for [6]. Of the cues that are available in online communication, a person's appearance is one that could easily trigger this application of stereotypes [16].

4 Method

4.1 Participants

A total of 80 students participated in the study as volunteers. Half of them were born in the UK and half of them were originally from China but studying in UK. The data obtained from two of the British-born participants were later excluded from the analyses because they indicated that their ethnicity was Chinese. The average age of the British participants was 24.18 (sd=5.60), and that of the Chinese participants was 23.93 (sd=3.75). Facebook (http://www.facebook.com) was used as the main social networking platform by 100% of the British participants, but only by 25% of the Chinese participants. The other 75% of the Chinese participants reported using mainly Windows Live Spaces (http://home.spaces.live.com). The gender composition of each group was exactly 50/50.

4.2 Apparatus

The manipulation of communication style was based on the seven dimensions of cultural differences between Western and Eastern societies described in Table 1, which were used to create two blogs. Each blog contained three diary entries reporting different aspects of student life. A British student and a Chinese student wrote the diaries together in English. They were given three hypothetical events, and discussed how they would deal with those events, focusing on their attitudes and behaviours. The first theme was about a supervisor who criticized a student's work. The British student complained about the supervisor by saying "*I was miffed because she did not agree with the research topic*", whereas the Chinese student showed respect for the supervisor by saying "*I appreciate his encouragement and supervision, I need to make every effort to please my supervisor*" (e.g., large vs. small power distance [9]). The theme of the second diary entry was the student's birthday. The British student's focus was on herself, "*I usually detest birthdays, because they mean I'm getting on … But who's to care? …. So I went out for lunch to celebrate and had a makeover …*", whereas the Chinese student's focus was on her friends and diverting attention away from herself, "*All of a sudden Bill, Catherine, Alex turned up at my house shouting "come and get your present"… I was dumbstruck and forgot to invite them into my house. My house is too small and not very clean*" (e.g., individualism vs. collectivism [9]). The theme of the third diary entry was about students working together on a group-work assignment. An attempt was made to make all of the cultural dimensions explicit in the differences between the diaries. Inevitably, this may have introduced other differences, such as language, but this was kept to a minimum by rigorous checks for grammatical correctness. Idiosyncratic expressions were avoided as much as possible without making the diaries sound stifled.

Table 1. Seven Dimensions of Cultural Differences between Eastern and Western Societies

Eastern Culture	Western Culture	Reference
Interdependent	Independent	[9], [18]
Indirect	Direct	[8], [18]
Reserved	Open	[8], [18]
Implicit	Explicit	[8]
Relationship-oriented	Task-oriented	[8], [9], [18]
Hierarchical	Social Equal	[9]
Long-term orientation	Short-term orientation	[9]

The manipulation of the appearance of the presenter was realized by the creation of two profiles: One containing a photo of a typical Caucasian face and typically British name (Emily Sutton), the other containing a photo of a typical Asian face and a typical Chinese name (Song Yang). The photos were selected from Rhodes *et al.* [22] on the basis that they were typical for their particular ethnic group and judged to be equally attractive. The profiles and blogs were styled on the format used by Windows Live Spaces. Combining the blogs and profiles created four personae: two with a congruent combination of blogs and profiles (e.g., Chinese style blog with Chinese appearance), and two with an incongruent combination of blogs and profiles (e.g., British style blog with Chinese appearance)[1].

4.3 Instruments

The perception of personae was measured in terms of the seven cultural dimensions of Table 1, the Interpersonal Attraction Scale [20] and the Source Credibility Scale [19]. Ratings on the cultural dimensions were obtained through five-point semantic differential scales between two bipolar adjectives with opposite meanings at each side (e.g., between 'direct' and 'indirect'). The Source Credibility Scale was designed to measure the extent to which a person was deemed to possess Competence (e.g., "unintelligent-intelligent"), 'Caring/Goodwill' (e.g., "self-centred-not self-centred"), and 'Trustworthiness' (e.g., "unethical-ethical"). Each subscale had six items which were also rated on five-point semantic differential scales. The Interpersonal Attraction scale was designed to measure a person's perceived Physical Attractiveness (e.g., "I think she is quite pretty"), Social Attractiveness (e.g., "I would like to have a friendly chat with her"), and Task Attractiveness (e.g., "you could count on her to get the job done"). Each subscale had six items which were rated on a 5-point Likert-type rating scale (1=strongly disagree, 5=strongly agree).

4.4 Procedure

Each participant was given one of the combinations of blogs and profile, and given 20 minutes to read the content of the blog and look at the profile. Immediately afterwards they were asked to fill out a questionnaire which included questions about their age, country of origin and online social networking habits, rating scales for the seven cultural dimensions, the Interpersonal Attraction Scale and Source Credibility Scale. A semi-structured interview was then conducted to further assess participants' perception of the persona (e.g. "where do you think the persona is originally from?") and their general experiences in on-line social networking. The total time spent by each participant was approximately 40 minutes.

5 Results

Multivariate Analysis of Variance (MANOVA) was used to test the effects of the independent variables on perceptions of the personae along the cultural dimensions. Univariate Analysis of Variance (ANOVA) was used to evaluate the effect of the independent variables on the scores on the subscales of the Interpersonal Attraction Scale and Source Credibility Scale. Scores on all of the subscales were calculated by adding the ratings on the six items making up each of the scales, as recommended by the original authors. As a result, the scores ranged from 6 (ratings of 1 on all six items) to 30 (ratings of 5 on all six items). Partial eta squared statistics (partial η^2)

---

[1] The examples of a congruent persona with a Chinese style blog and a Chinese appearance and a incongruent persona with a British style blog and a Chinese appearance are available in the following URLs: http://hiyahiyahiya1983.spaces.live.com/, http://goodbyemylover4ever.spaces.live.com/

were used as estimates of effect size. Partial η^2 was computed considering the variance attributable to the effect of interest plus error [21]. As a general guideline, η^2= .01 is considered small, η^2= .06 medium, and η^2= .14 large. Post-hoc tests for investigating significant interaction effects were done using Tukey HSD which controls the experiment-wise type I error [12]. Pearson's correlation coefficient was used to calculate the relationships between sub-scales and those between cultural dimensions and sub-scales.

5.1 Experimental Manipulation Check

The internal consistency of the seven cultural dimensions was measured as alpha=0.76 and all corrected-item correlation were larger than 0.38. It appears, therefore, that there is an underlying construct being measured by these dimensions. Multivariate analysis of participants' ratings on the cultural dimensions revealed a significant effect of Blog Style ($F(7,64)=24.00$, $p<.001$, partial $\eta^2=.72$) (Fig. 1). No other effects were significant. British blogs scored higher on all seven cultural dimensions (all *ps*<.001). Hence we can conclude that participants were able to distinguish between the blogs based on stereotypical cultural characteristics of their communication style. The other experimental manipulation involved the physical appearance, in which the independent variables on ratings of physical attractiveness of the personae were tested. No significant effects were found which ensured that physical attraction did not have to be considered in the interpretation of the effects on other variables found in this experiment.

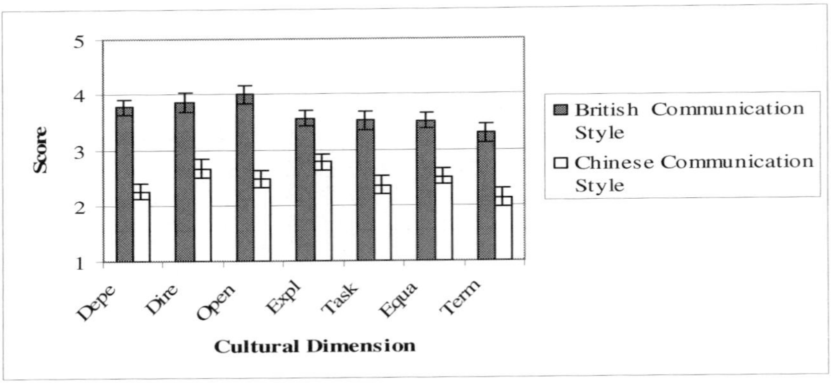

Fig. 1. Means ratings of the cultural dimensions for personae with British and Chinese communication styles (Error bars show the standard error)

Overall it was important to see if there was agreement amongst participants when attributing an origin to the persona they were asked to judge, and particularly how appearance and blog style affected this attribution. Table 2 shows the results. It can be seen that almost all participants thought that the congruent personae with British and Chinese appearances had their origins in the UK/Europe and China/Asia respectively.

However, their opinions about the origins of the incongruent personae were more diverse. In particular, the persona with British blog style and Chinese appearance was regarded by most Chinese participants and some British participants as a British Born Chinese (BBC) or a person from Hong Kong. In this case, appearance was more important than blog style in judging a person's origin for most British participants, while most Chinese participants took both appearance and blog style into account. This may be due to a lack of knowledge in the differences that exist between Chinese people, from different parts of China, from the British participants.

Table 2. Judgments about the Origins of the Personae (* BBC and people from Hong Kong were clustered together because they have a Chinese appearance but reflect behaviour that is more typical of British culture)

Blog/Appearance Combination	Participant's Origin	Attributed Origin			
		UK/Europe	China/Asia	BBC/Hong Kong	Other
Congruent (British blog style; British appearance)	British	10			
	Chinese	10			
Incongruent (British blog style; Chinese appearance)	British		5	4	
	Chinese	1	2	7	
Congruent (Chinese blog style; Chinese appearance)	British		9		1
	Chinese		10		
Incongruent (Chinese blog style; British appearance)	British	7			2
	Chinese	8	1		1

5.2 Test of Hypotheses

Overall, participants' answers exhibited high reliability. The Cronbach alpha reliability for the Interpersonal Attraction Scales was calculated as 0.85 for Social Attraction, 0.80 for Physical Attraction and 0.80 for Task Attraction. The Cronbach alpha reliability for the Source Credibility scales was calculated as 0.71 for Competence, 0.73 for Caring/Goodwill, and 0.76 for Trustworthiness.

5.2.1 Social Attraction

There was a significant main effect of Blog Style on participants' judgment of Social Attraction ($F(1,70)=4.27$, $p<.05$, partial $\eta^2=.05$). There was also a significant two-way interaction between Nationality and Blog Style ($F(1,70)=11.35$, $p<.01$, partial $\eta^2=.14$)(Fig. 2). Post-hoc analysis revealed that the British blog style was judged more socially attractive by British than by Chinese participants. In addition, Chinese participants who judged personae with a British blog style gave lower ratings than those who judged personae with a Chinese style (*ps*<.01). No such difference was found between groups of British participants. The judgment of Chinese participants appeared to be affected by blog style, but not the judgment of British participants.

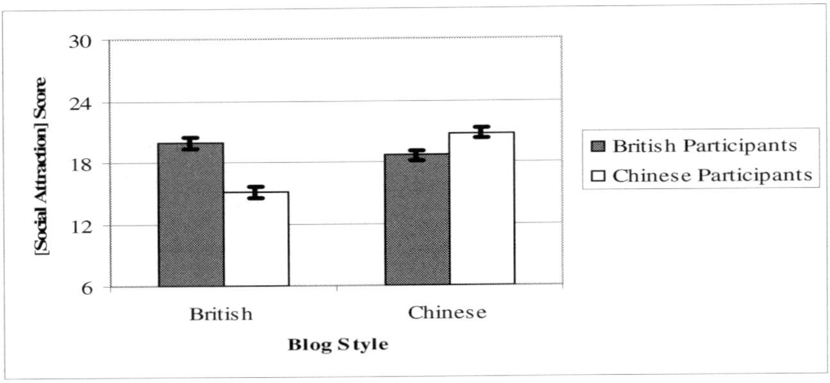

Fig. 2. The two-way interaction between Nationality and Blog Style on the perception of "Social Attraction" (Error bars show the standard error)

5.2.2 Task Attraction

There was a significant effect of Blog Style on participants' judgments of "Task Attraction" (F(1,70)=5.26, $p<.05$, partial $\eta^2=.07$). There was also a significant two-way interaction effect between Blog Style and Appearance (F(1,70)=4.53, $p<.05$, partial $\eta^2=.06$)(Fig. 3). Post-hoc analysis revealed that the incongruent persona with a Chinese appearance and British blog style received higher scores on this scale than the congruent persona with a Chinese appearance and Chinese blog style ($p<.05$). No difference was found in the scores received by the personae with a British appearance.

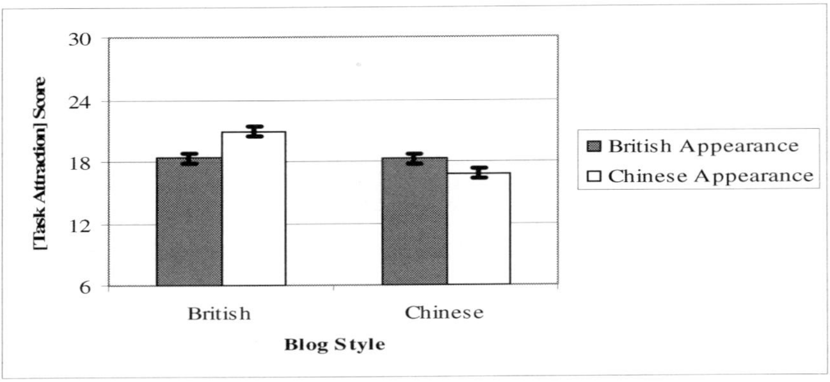

Fig. 3. The two-way interaction effect of Blog Style and Appearance on the perception of the "Task Attraction" (Error bars show the standard error)

5.2.3 Competence

There was a significant effect of Blog Style on participants' judgments of "Competence" (F(1,70)=32.03, $p<.01$, partial $\eta^2=.31$). There was also a significant three-way interaction among Nationality, Blog Style and Appearance (F(1,70)=4.01, $p<.05$, partial $\eta^2=.05$)(Fig. 4). Post-hoc analysis revealed that the congruent persona with a

British blog style and British appearance received higher scores than the incongruent persona with a British blog style but Chinese appearance when rated by British participants ($p<.01$). The congruent persona with Chinese blog style and Chinese appearance received lower scores than the incongruent persona with British blog style and Chinese appearance when rated by Chinese participants ($p<.05$). This suggests that British participants based their perception of competence on both appearance and communication style of online persona, whereas verbal cues had a bigger impact on the ratings of Chinese participants.

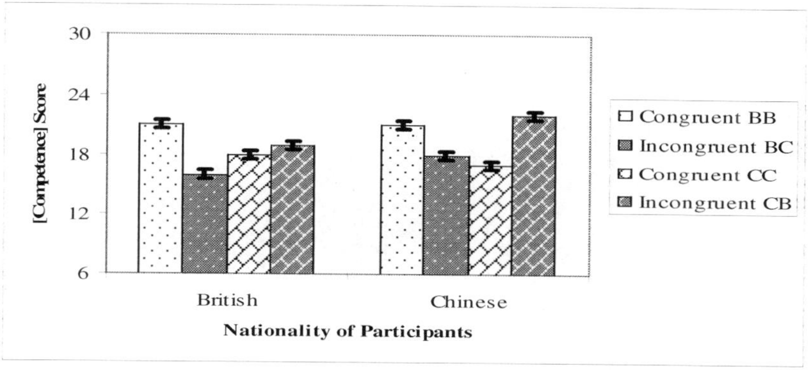

Fig. 4. The three-way interaction effect on the perception of the "Competence" of the personae (Error bars show the standard error)

5.2.4 Caring/Goodwill

There was a significant effect of Blog Style on participants' judgment of "Caring/Goodwill" ($F(1,70)=23.89$, $p<.01$, partial $\eta^2=.25$). There was a significant two-way interaction between Nationality and Blog Style ($F(1,70)=5.10$, $p<.05$, partial $\eta^2=.06$)(Fig. 5). Post-hoc Analysis revealed that the goodwill of personae with a

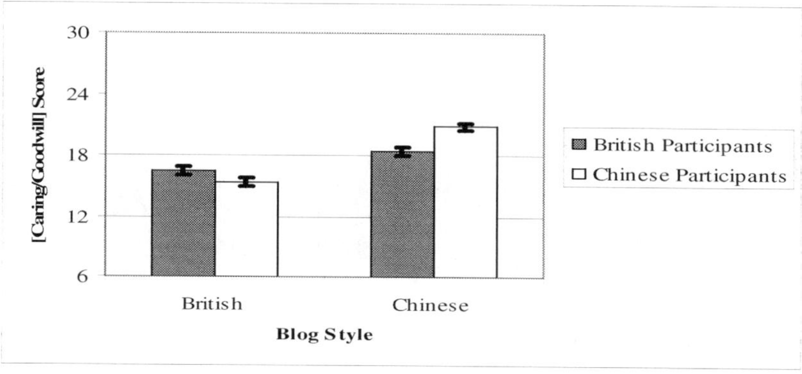

Fig. 5. The two-way interaction effect on the perception of the "Caring/Goodwill" of the personae (Error bars show the standard error)

Chinese presentation style was judged to be higher than that of personae with a British presentation style by Chinese participants (*ps*<.01), but no such difference was found for British participants. Again the judgments of Chinese participants appeared to be affected by the blog style, but not those of British participants.

5.2.5 Trustworthiness

There was a significant three-way interaction among Nationality, Blog Style and Appearance ($F(1,70)=5.58$, $p<.05$, partial $\eta^2=.07$)(Fig. 6). Although post-hoc analysis revealed no significant pair-wise differences, there was a trend that congruent personae were rated as more trustworthy than incongruent personae when judged by British participants, whereas a slight opposite trend was observed for Chinese participants.

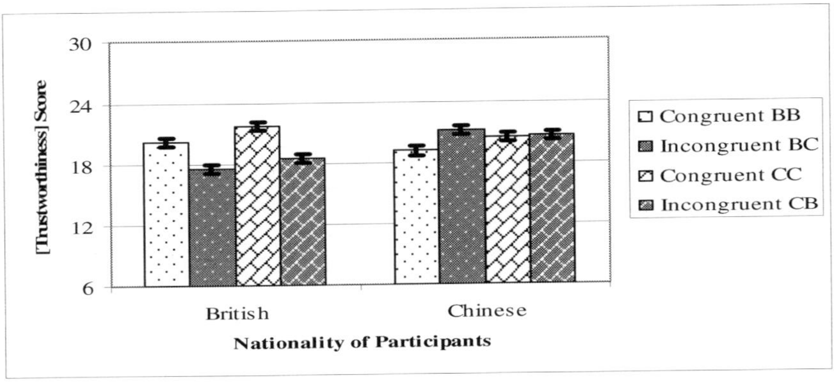

Fig. 6. The three-way interaction effect on the perception of the "Trustworthiness" of the personae (Error bars show the standard error)

5.3 Correlations

Correlations were calculated between ratings on the Interpersonal Attraction scales and Source Credibility scales for both British and Chinese participants separately. For British participants there were no significant relationships (*ps*>.05) Chinese participants tended to see more competent personae as less socially attractive ($r=-.49$, $p<.01$), and preferred making friendships with more caring personae ($r=.54$, $p<.01$). Remarkably, however, physical attraction was somewhat related to task attraction for Chinese participants ($r=.34$, $p<.05$).

Table 3 shows the correlations between ratings of the personae on the seven cultural dimensions and ratings on the Interpersonal Attraction and Source Credibility Scales. From this table it is clear that Chinese participants perceived personae with the British style of communication to be more competent, but also less caring based on all cultural dimensions. Chinese participants also base their judgments of social attractiveness on the interdependence, hierarchy, and relationship and long-term orientation of the blog style. All of these appear more in Chinese style blogs. British participants tended to associate an independent blog style with more competence, an explicit communication style with more socially attractive, as well as associated blog styles that were more direct, and more focused on social equality and short-term relations with higher task attractiveness. All of these appear more in British style blogs.

Table 3. Significant Correlations between 7-Cultural Dimensions and Scales among British and Chinese participants (**=significant at the 0.01 level; *=significant at the 0.05 level)

Cultural Dimension	Nationality	Scale	r
Interdependent vs. Independent	British	Competence	.48**
	Chinese	Social Attraction	-.68**
		Competence	.52**
		Caring/Goodwill	-.68**
Indirect vs. Direct	British	Task Attraction	.34*
	Chinese	Competence	.35*
		Caring/Goodwill	-.52**
Reserved vs. Open	British		
	Chinese	Competence	.49**
		Caring/Goodwill	-.48**
Implicit vs. Explicit	British	Social Attraction	.34*
	Chinese	Competence	.40**
		Caring/Goodwill	-.44**
Relationship-oriented vs. Task-oriented	British		
	Chinese	Social Attraction	-.43**
		Competence	.56**
		Caring/Goodwill	-.50**
Hierarchical vs. Social Equal	British	Task Attraction	.33*
	Chinese	Social Attraction	-.36*
		Competence	.56**
		Caring/Goodwill	-.36*
Long-term vs. Short-term Relations	British	Task Attraction	.50**
	Chinese	Social Attraction	-.39*
		Task Attraction	.38*
		Competence	.44**
		Caring/Goodwill	-.39*

6 Discussion

The nature of the interaction between variation in blog style of presenters and cultural background of audiences was clearly illuminated by this study. In particular, most of the cultural characteristics of the Chinese blog style were deemed by Chinese participants to contribute to creating more socially attractive and caring personae. This is consistent with the first hypothesis, stating that differences in communication style and self-presentation in verbal communication will affect people's social perceptions. Moreover, Chinese participants expressed a preference for interacting with people from their own-social group. It also indicated that the desirability of initiating online relationship can be varied between people from different cultures and that it is based on different aspects of self-presentation and communication style (H2).

There was also a clear interaction between the blog style of personae and their appearance on social perception of the participants, and on perceptions of task attractiveness in particular. Surprisingly, incongruent personae tended to be judged as more attractive to work with than congruent personae. This could be explained by taking into consideration the origins attributed to these personae. In particular, incongruent persona with Chinese appearance and British blog style were deemed to be British-born Chinese or from Hong Kong. Participants may have applied cultural stereotypes of these people that suggest they are high achievers which would make them more attractive to work with. For example, participants may have used their knowledge of the fact that British born children with Chinese ethnicity tend to achieve very high standards in education (e.g., they have the highest percentage of pupils achieving 5 good GCSEs, which are exams taken at age 16) compared to children from other ethnic groups including White British [25].

7 Conclusions

The results of this study provided support for the first two hypotheses, but no unequivocal support for the third hypothesis was found. This suggests that cultural differences embedded in online communication can dramatically impact the impressions it creates in people, and that these impressions depend on their cultural background. Indeed, people from different cultural backgrounds rely on different cues when forming impressions of others. British people may pay less attention to verbal cues than Chinese people, who tend to focus more on the detailed content of communication. The emphasis on individualism apparent in Western cultures may make them more suspicious of inconsistencies between appearance and content, whereas people from Eastern cultures may be prone to explain such anomalies away by evaluating individuals in relation to in-group and out-groups. This result is consistent with Hall's [8] high and low context theory. Effective communication in high context cultures requires a high degree of common ground between presenters and receivers. Furthermore, cross-cultural experience may play an important role in the findings. Historically the UK has a vast multi-cultural experience, which may affect British participants' responses. Similarly, the Chinese participants may be influenced by British culture, as they have relocated to the UK. Alternative explanations cannot be ruled-out, however, such as the increasing importance of political correctness in cross-cultural encounters typical of British society.

The results may have a number of implications for the design of social networking platforms. Social networking platforms may need to be designed to satisfy cultural differences, due to what we have shown to be important variances in preferences and presentation amongst users. In addition, people should be made aware of the different ways in which their self-presentation can be interpreted differently by people with different cultural backgrounds. Such awareness may increase the effectiveness of cross-cultural online relationship building. While this study only focuses on the role of cultural differences on influencing the initialization of cross-cultural online relationship, it would also be valuable to analyze their effects in maintaining and developing offline to online relationships.

References

1. Banaji, M.: The Self in Social Contexts. Annual Review of Psychology 45(1), 297–332 (1994)
2. Chen, Y.W.: Intercultural Friendship from the Perspective of East Asian International Students. China Media Research 2(3), 43–58 (2006)

3. De Angeli, A.: Cultural variations in virtual spaces design. AI & Society (to appear)
4. Ellison, N., Heino, R., Gibbs, J.: Managing Impressions Online: Self-Presentation Processes in the Online Dating Environment. Journal of Computer-Mediated Communication 11(2), 415–441 (2006)
5. Ellison, N., Steinfield, C., Lampe, C.: The benefits of Facebook "friends": Exploring the relationship between college students' use of online social networks and social capital. Journal of Computer-Mediated Communication 12(3), 1143–1168 (2007)
6. Fiske, S.T.: Stereotyping, prejudice, and discrimination at the seam between the centuries: Evolution, culture, mind and brain. European Journal of Social Psychology 30, 299–322 (2000)
7. Goffman, E.: The Presentation of Self in Everyday Life. Doubleday, New York (1959)
8. Hall, E.T.: Beyond culture. Doubleday, New York (1976)
9. Hofstede, G.: The Business of International Business is Culture. International Business Review 3(1), 1–14 (1994)
10. Kim, J., Kim, M.-S., Kam, K.Y., Shin, H.-C.: Influence of self-construals on the perception of different self-presentation styles in Korea. Asian Journal of Social Psychology 6, 89–101 (2003)
11. Kimmerle, J., Cress, U.: Group awareness and self-presentation in computer-supported information exchange. International Journal of Computer-Supported Collaborative Learning 3(1), 85–97 (2008)
12. Kirk, R.E.: Experimental Design: Procedures for the Behavioral Sciences. Pacific Grove: Brooks/Cole (1995)
13. Kitayama, S., Markus, H.R., Matsumoto, H., Norasakkunkit, V.: Individual and collective processes in the construction of the self: Self-enhancement in the United States and self-criticism in Japan. Journal of Personality and Social Psychology 72, 1245–1267 (1997)
14. Kitayama, S., Markus, H.R., Kurokawa, M.: Culture, emotion, and well-being: Good feelings in Japan and the United States. Cognition & Emotion 14, 93–124 (2000)
15. Lampe, C., Ellison, N., Steinfeld, C.: A familiar Face(book): Profile elements as signals in an online social network. In: Proceedings of Conference on Human Factors in Computing Systems, pp. 435–444. ACM Press, New York (2007)
16. Leary, M.R.: Self Presentation – Impression Management and Interpersonal Behaviour. Boulder, CO. Westview (1996)
17. Lee, H.: Privacy, Publicity, and Accountability of Self-Presentation in an On-Line Discussion Group. Sociological Inquiry 76(1), 1–22 (2006)
18. Markus, H.R., Kitayama, S.: Culture and the self: Implications for cognition, emotion, and motivation. Psychological Review 98, 224–253 (1991)
19. McCroskey, J.C., Holdridge, W., Toomb, J.K.: An instrument for measuring the source credibility of basic speech communication instructors. The Speech Teacher 23, 26–35 (1974)
20. McCroskey, J.C., McCain, T.A.: The measurement of interpersonal attraction. Speech Monographs 41, 261–266 (1974)
21. Pallant, J.: SPSS survival manual. Allen & Unwin (2007)
22. Rhodes, G., Lee, K., Palermo, R., Weiss, M., Yoshikawa, S., Clissa, P., et al.: Attractiveness of own-race, other-race, and mixed-race faces. Perception 34, 319–340 (2005)
23. Schau, H.J., Gilly, M.C.: We are what we post? Self-presentation in personal web space. Journal of Consumer Research 30(3), 385–404 (2003)
24. Triandis, H.: The self and social behaviour in differing cultural contexts. Psychological review 96(3), 506–520 (1989)
25. UK Department for Education and Skills. National Curriculum Assessments and GCSE/GNVQ attainment by pupil characteristics, in England, 2002 (final) and 2003 (provisional), SFR 04/2004 (2004), http://www.dfes.gov.uk/rsgateway/DB/SFR/s000448/NPD_sfr_text_Finished3.pdf

Anchoring Design in Rural Customs of Doing and Saying

Nicola J. Bidwell

James Cook University, Australia & Centre for ICT4D, Cape Town, South Africa

Abstract. An increasing range of initiatives aim to enable rural communities in developing regions to generate their own, non-text based, digital content to share local stories, information and concerns. Video, photos and audio offer new resources for practices that give communities' a sense of identity and continuity and that members acquire in relationships with each other, their environment and history via speech, gesture, song, music, drama, ritual, skills or crafts. However, these contexts pose challenges for designing interactions within frameworks that have a heritage of text and indirect orality and which emphasize particular communication dynamics and structures. We seek to create new design directions based on insights into local ways of 'doing and saying' gained in interactions with people living under traditional law and custom in the Xhosa Kingdom of Pondoland, South Africa. This paper distils themes from an ethnography when the author lived according to local norms and constraints and cogenerated design activities, situated in the community's priorities, customary power relations and consensus-based practice. We reflect on communication in ordinary and extraordinary activities, and sociotechnical 'experiments' from using social networking websites to storytelling with blogs. We describe how indexicality dynamically shares context and entwines a person's identity with physical setting; and, how practices, such as prolonged discussion, diachronic repetition and synchronous utterance, build rapport, collective memory and cohesion. We propose that these practices inspire ways that local social structures can impact on activities to design systems of organization for information sharing, with occasional reference to our observations of other rural peoples in north Mozambique and north Australia.

Keywords: Rural, Africa, Localizing design, Identity, Ethnography.

1 Introduction

An increasing range of initiatives aim to enable rural communities in developing regions to generate their own, non-text based, digital content to share local stories, information and concerns. Video and photos, sometimes linked to audio, offer new resources for practices that bestow a sense of identity and continuity to communities or groups and that members acquire through relationships with each other and with their environment and history via speech, gesture, song, music, drama, ritual, skills or crafts. To realise the opportunities for expression and communication that media and platforms can bring rural people we need to respond to the ways that knowledge is

T. Gross et al. (Eds.): INTERACT 2009, Part I, LNCS 5726, pp. 686–699, 2009.

created and recreated beyond the 'market' [3] of contemporary communication. Technologies, from Web 2.0, online social networks to SMS, emerge in a market of symbols, concepts and structural forms with a heritage in text and indirect orality, such as radio, television. This market affects all cultures to some extent, but in places with low technology ambiance, such as in rural Africa, a 'primary orality' [12] pervades. Transmitting oral and performed knowledge, directly, involves constantly recreating, accumulating and dividing it across a group according to social systems and protocols and power relations. This *intangible* [18] stuff poses a challenge for designers tackling oral and performed knowledge within their own culture let alone when crossing into social fields without the same provenance of text and indirect orality. Yet, finding hooks in such social fields to tether design directions determines not only technology's contribution to developing regions (ICT4D), cultural diversity and heritage, but also our own creativity.

In this paper I discuss insights into oral and performed information sharing gained as we sought to anchor new design endevours in a rural African village living under traditional law. Tethering design to users' view of collectivity is core to inventing tools for locally generated content but is not straight-forward; for instance, Indigenous people in America struggle to translate their meaning of collectivity into western interaction [10]. Many technologists use generalised models of cultural dispositions to tune their methods to local expectations and values, for example Hofstede's dimensions alert us to African cultural tendencies towards collectivism, rather than individualism, and acceptance of unequal power distributions (e.g. [19, 20]). But theories are not conduits into a social field as they do not depict how meanings are constituted, and transformed, by a specific community. To create vehicles for local content sharing in rural Africa we need to find anchor points in activities that organise information and respond to the ways collectivity is enacted in these practices.

Context carries the burden of meaning in communication [1] and determines semantics, whether people convey meaning by drawing on the intangible, the concrete or the abstract. Browning has explored ways that meaning in rural places is grounded, within a corpus of locational, temporal, historical and social contexts, by drawing on properties of indexicality [4]. Indexicality [4] provides actions and utterances with salience and, reflexively, augments context during interactions. For example, consider understanding the meaning of terrain burnt by fire to a leisure walker [4] a farmer or an Indigenous Elder whose Traditional Knowledge (TK) about fire maintains species diversity [2]. We 'handle' and interpret this typical Australian feature in ways that depend on context; thus, items, categories and relations gain significance in context and shape the market in which creativity emerges. This may contribute to dissonance when software created 'elsewhere' [15] is introduced. For instance, a Kuku-Thaypan Elder expressed regret that a GPS-based system, designed to assist persisting TK, did not support the indexical practices of 'walking country' in which physical locations entwine with communication protocols, ancient stories and ritual [2]. Social practice tends to emerge from practical, rather than cognitive, concurrence and people are mostly unaware of the actions and interactions that yield meaning through indexical processes. The roles of items, categories and relations in interactions, between people or between a person and artifacts, evolve and gain significance tacitly, such that their potency is sanctioned by the success of the interaction. Indexical processes lay at the heart of approaches that ethnographers use to negotiate meaning, depict another's reality and explain practices in inaccessible contexts to designers.

Interaction is not a static set of norms and techniques but is situated in prior occasions, the immediate moment and a relational totality [4] via regulated improvisation. Our cultural habituation enables us to participate in daily activities and social interactions competently and contingently and also to act strategically and creatively. The more adeptly we improvise in social interactions the more power we have in their market; thus designers often leverage local social competence in ICT4D as a conduit for engaging people in the dialectic processes of design. The social power of 'senior-level champions' [9] and 'Human Access Points' [12] can help to domesticate an introduced technology but may also limit creativity to their particular indexical emphases and the scope of technology that they can envisage

We seek to create new design directions based on ways of 'doing and saying' and local needs in a remote, impoverished and technologically marginalized village in the Eastern Cape of South Africa. I situated research in the customary power structures and everyday practices that organise information in a social field dominated by primary orality, by residing in the patrilineal kinship group of a Headman. I start by introducing the setting and our approach to collecting data and, then, outline activities and interactions in, around and about the village of Lwandile in which I gained insights into priorities and oral and performed practices. I conclude by proposing that the ways these practices express collectivity is relevant to designing technologies for information sharing, with occasional reference to observations of Indigenous people in Quirimbas Archipelago, north Mozambique and north Australia.

2 Situated in the Village of Lwandile

The village of Lwandile is the home of 72 year-old Hlathinkhulu Sithelo who is the senior of twelve Headman with authority over 20, 000 people dispersed across 50km2 of Lower Ndungunyeni. This area was settled at least eight generations ago by the Khonjwayo, one of six Chiefdoms descending from the monarchy of a distinct Xhosa tribal cluster in the Kingdom of Western Pondoland. Chiefdoms are territorial not pure kinship, thus the Khonjwayo share many kin but their ancestry also includes indigenous Khoikhoi and San, shipwrecked Europeans and exiles of the Apartheid era. Due to topology, local resistance to colonists, famine and invasion and subsequent neglect by successive regimes Ndungunyeni remains distinct and preserves traditions in habitation and communal landuse. Families live in umzi, informally distributed across hilly common grazing land and interconnected by paths to water. An umzi houses 4-5 adults and 2-7 children in cluster of thatched, mud-brick rondavels fronted by a garden and fenced kraal for livestock (Fig. 1b). With little paid employment locally many villagers temporarily migrate to cities so that, except at holidays, half of Lwandile's permanent population is under 15 years and women or pensioners head households. Even with remittances from emigrants and pensions most families survive on less that 10% of the national, median income for a working white man, although H. Sithelo receives a government salary of $250 per month which is in the top 10% of incomes in Lwandile. Traditionally a cattle culture, these days most families own a few of a range of animals and subsistence farm arable land for crops (e.g. maize). Rondavals last 40 years and most permanent built infrastructure reflects the Headsman's influence, such as a church built decade ago behind his umzi and a rocky, ungraded road to his umzi cleared by the municipality and along which the clinic was built. A few umzis, including the Headman's, have a solar panel but none have a mains water supply or grid electricity and solar power serves the clinic and, until the battery was stolen, the school as well.

2.1 Data Collection and Analysis

My analysis draws on ethnography in events that arose as I interacted with the setting and attempted to live according to local norms in situ. By residing in H. Sithelo's umzi and using only local, shared transport I was exposed to the geographic isolation of rural life and constraints on technology use (e.g. the limits of solar generated electricity to charge a deep cycle battery). I was also afforded social access and security due to the affectionate respect H. Sithelo, who is known locally as 'Tata' (father) commands. As a foreigner and the only white woman in a wide area, I would have been vulnerable to local psychopathologies, related to HIV and alcohol and, allegedly non-local, bands of criminals. I recorded data using handwritten notes, 650 photographs, of which villagers took 200 and 12 hours of video, though digital recording was limited by electricity. I transcribed video, compiled 'thick' textual descriptions and iteratively integrated all records to derive themes hermeneutically. Unlike classic ethnography, which gathers qualitative data without targeted intervention, I aimed to co-generate a design approach by interpreting priorities and discovering opportunities for design in the ad-hoc details in daily life and by establishing relationships and undertaking 'sociotechnical experiments' [19]. Thus, here I depict my progression in the social field as four phases of activities and interactions, written in the first person to distinguish various actors and reflexivity.

2.2 Phase 1: Deriving A Research Rationale

I was introduced to Lwandile by Arjan, a Dutch volunteer in a Non-governmental organisation (NGO) who had championed a university technology project to link Lwandile clinic to Canzibe hospital [17]. While the remote healthcare system had not been a success he hoped the Wi-Fi bridge could be used to communicate with the "outside world" about foreigners' exploitation of the land and community. So he approached Thulani, the Headman's eldest son, who had bought the first cell phone to Lwandile in 2003, had recently sent his first email using a Nokia E60i Smartphone, donated by the university and was eager to host me on his father's umzi. I visited twice before moving in, first to be formally presented and gain insights into priorities and later to bring equipment to put in a room the Sithelos had furnished for me. In discussion with design collaborators I based a research rationale on initial observations and Thulani's interest in using technology to attract attention and funds for social upliftment initiatives. Thus, I sought to gather data on ways local leaders interface with the community and local and remote agencies on development projects.

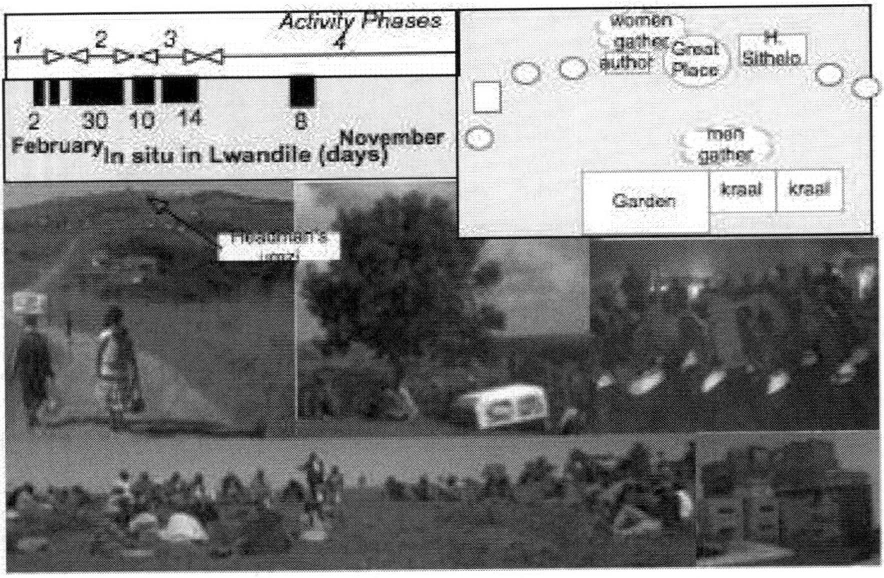

Fig. 1. Phases of activities (a) Layout of umzi (b) Road to H. Sithelo's umzi at top of hill (c) Men gather under the meeting tree (d) Dancers and dignitaries (taken by Sixolile) (e) H. Sithelo gestures at the meeting at Mngciebe (f) Palace Archives (g)

2.3 Phase 2: Acclimatizing to the Social Field

The first extended in situ phase lasted a month (Fig. 1) and most observation occurred around domestic and community life in H. Sithelo's umzi. The umzi comprises: the 'Great Place', used for community meetings; 6 other rondavals, formally used by male family members before they established their own umzi, and now used by visitors; a 4 room 'flat' (small square building) inhabited by H. Sithelo, his wife, youngest daughter Bulelwa, Bulelwa's infant, and two other grandchildren; and, a smaller flat where I lived in one room and the other room was occupied by various guests or the Sithelo's 20-year-old son when he was not at technical college. I gathered data through impromptu contextual interview while interacting with the family, in particular the elder sons, Thulani and Sixolile and participating in female duties (e.g. fetching water) and more passively observed villagers' visits to the umzi in connection with H. Sithelo's duties (e.g. resolving disputes, interfacing with police, signing permits for hunting and resources). I also recorded active events, such as walks to Sunday football matches, a meeting in the Great Place with the NGO's founder, a Transkei-raised Afrikaner (Johann), and walking through a forest near Mngciebe with Thulani and Johann as they discussed community projects.

In the first two weeks of Phase 2 (Fig 1a) I also undertook technology 'experiments' with Thulani and adjusted infrastructure. We moved the wireless router from its unused position in H. Sithelo's flat to my room and I introduced Thulani to various Internet facilities such as searching for information related to his interests, social networking (e.g. Facebook) and using photos to tell stories. I created a blog, www.topository.org, and uploaded a photo and Thulani enthusiastically received a digital camera and a laptop, to type text to accompany his photos. I also demonstrated the Internet to children, residents and visitors to the umzi who visited my room through curiosity, on errands or to charge cell-phones. In the first week Thulani said he needed to mobilize a Community Trust, comprising headmen from four villages, to advance his initiatives and decisively identified development projects on which to focus our activities. These related to using land near Mngciebe for agricultural food production and training and tourism and using technology to request funds (e.g. a blog to interest people overseas seeking to sponsor local initiatives).

We had preliminary success in oral storytelling around Thulani's photos of his daily life but, after a week, he lost interest in technology activities. He often forgot to bring the camera, did not type anything at his home, mentioning being unable to charge the laptop, and seemed bored when we used the Internet in other ways that I related to his development projects. He more eagerly discussed his beliefs about raising and using overseas funding, his plans and ability to marshal local support, his life and his culture. After the first two weeks there were 9 days when Thulani did not visit, appear at scheduled meetings, respond to SMS messages or organize activities we planned. I had scheduled time away at the end of a month in Lwandile and raised concerns with Thulani about lack of insight into the ways leadership interfaces with each other and local people on development projects. Thulani noted that mobilizing the Trust was slow as many members were old and inactive so I asked whether involving other villagers in technology activities would be advisable and Thulani agreed to ask his sister, Bulelwa, to act his secretary. This critical reflection relieved tension and Thulani accompanied me on the long trip to the bus and regularly contacted me in the week that I was away.

2.4 Phase 3: Looking for Anchor Points

A second in situ phase lasted one month, split midway when the Sithelos left the village to attend a funeral. It commenced with a transition in familiarity that led to my deeper involvement in Thulani's efforts which significantly expanded the dataset and refined the project's future. Diverse everyday data in Lwandile included impromptu discussions in the spaza, walks with various members of the Sithelo's extended family encountered in the village and sporadic visits to my room by local teenagers and people on business in the umzi, such as villagers, Lwandile's local Councilor and Thulani's brother-in- law, a Chief of another district. Further afield, I spoke to local people in tourist areas and white NGO volunteers in HIV awareness and ICT. Participant driven activities also became richer and began as soon as I returned and Thulani clarified his priorities by revealing that his aims for various local initiatives included pursuing the Sithelo's right to the Chieftainship. Thulani explained that 5 generations ago ancestors of the incumbent Chief had gained Chieftainship when the British deposed his Great Great Great Grandfather. This disempowerment led to local apathy, such as the Trust's inertia, and Thulani said that the Headmen under H. Sithelo's authority were "*crying for dignity*", which he sought to restore by lodging a claim, with the monarchy, for Khonjwayo Chieftainship. Meanwhile, to advance development projects he would mobilize activists related to the Trust. Shortly after the Chieftainship discussion Thulani and I traversed forested and rocky hills to visit Johann at

Mdumbi, accompanied Thulani and H. Sithelo, on horseback, to a hill-top community meeting in Mngciebe and a school's official opening. I also joined Thulani in the Great Place for meetings with younger activists in the Trust (35 to 39 years) who decided to form an independent non-profit organization: The Federation of Rural Coastal Communities (FRCC). The four men of the FRCC include Thulani; Mfundiso, a sub-Headsman's son and a teacher; Bongile, a teacher; and, Xolile who also Chairs another grassroots association. Further, afield I went with Thulani to consult Mthatha Municipal Archives and accompanied Thulani and H. Sithelo to the Palace to search for records, meet the Queen and attend a meeting.

Greater involvement in activities relating to Thulani's priorities increased opportunities to situate technology 'experiments'. From early in Phase 3 I embarked upon 15 'tutorials' with Bulelwa, who had a certificate in MS Word and Excel, which she had achieved without using a computer. Bulelwa, with her swaddled infant bound to her back, spent about an hour a day in my room learning to set-up solar power, explore the Internet for information of interest to her and send emails (e.g. to enquire about support for university study on social work). Meanwhile, Thulani and I discussed how the Internet might help in researching ancestry and emailed a contact in The National Archives & Records Services (NARS). Matome at NARS replied with suggestions on finding records and the possibility of bringing his department's new outreach program, 'Taking the Archives to the People', to Lwandile. The newly formed FRCC decided this was a rare opportunity to bring useful information to the community and discussed including it within an event on cultural and natural heritage, development and oral traditions. Email exchanges, related to research on Thulani's lineage and to the event, and a donation in response to a comment on my Facebook 'status update', to pay for fuel for a generator, illustrated the relevancy of ICT. The FRCC had reservations about technology until Thulani demonstrated using his E60i and raised ideas about business models to fund mobile communications.

With better insight into the relations between ancestry and development we co-generated activities to accumulate data on 'digital storytelling'. Bulelwa used a donated camera and uploaded records of 'Life in Lwandile' to the blog and Sixolile used the camera at a three-day party to honour the Queen. I videoed Sixolile viewing and describing his photos on the laptop, and he used the two media with great expression, the next day returning with a newspaper article about the party to further explain customary law. I also videoed Sixolile in walks crisscrossing Lwandile and in an interview with H. Sithelo with Sixolile translating and observed more impromptu digital storytelling by Thulani when we attended the opening of a new school.

2.5 Phase 4: Discovering Anchor Points

The last phase of activity analysed here started when I left Lwandile at the end of Phase 3 for research in Mozambique (Fig 1). To begin with I communicated remotely while the FRCC coordinated hosting the NARS Outreach team and a workshop in Lwandile, contacted municipal authorities and fund-raised. While invited to influence the structure and program I withheld comments, other than in support, to gain insight into the FRCC's approach. Two months into Phase 4, I returned to Lwandile for 8 days to gather data before, during and after the workshop. The 3.5-day workshop was structured around seven spoken presentations by: NARS; The Provincial Departments of Land Affairs and Environment; The Provincial House of Traditional Leaders; an emissary of Chief Gwadiso; and, Rosette, the local elected Councilor. Presentations were interleaved with protracted debate on archiving, local history, natural and cultural heritage, natural resource management, sustainable development and legislation on collectively owned land. Sessions also included a group exercise, critique and requests for future events, extensive votes of thanks and a film: Sarafina!

Early in Phase 4, I also introduced Xolile and Thulani to an American researcher (S) who was consulting for an IT company and they met briefly in Mthatha which enabled them to raise funds to register the FRCC. S encouraged Thulani to take an interest in Facebook but he did not download the 'how to' S created for him; so on my return to Lwandile we set up an Facebook account and created a Group to serve the FRCC. We also spent an hour creating blog entries with Bulelwa who had uploaded new photos to the laptop. In planning the workshop and the meeting with S, Xolile, the Secretary of FRCC, emailed or copied me into 24 emails to exchange information or seek advice. Wider communication was a persistent problem preventing the FRCC from creating a media draft, publicising the workshop as planned or co-ordinating transport. Hence, only 25% of their expected 200 to 300 participants attended. Thulani continued to use the lap-top but emailed me less regularly than Xolile, sending 9 emails before the workshop. Since the workshop, we set up email for Bongile, who has yet to use it, and Xolile presented a paper about the workshop at an oral history conference. I also received 11 messages and several invitations through Facebook, 18 emails from Thulani, Xolile and Bongiwe and have phoned Thulani and Sixolile. The FRCC's Facebook group (http://www.facebook.com/group.php? gid=35995351952) has 41 members, most of whom are Xhosa people connected through Bongwe, studying in Cape Town (35%); collaborators (e.g. authors in this project and the NGO in Mdumbi) (23%); and, 'friends' overseas introduced by S (27%). There are equal proportions of Xhosa people and non-Xhosa, and most of the latter do not live in Africa.

3 Reflections on Information Sharing

The hooks, in Lwandile's social fields, to which we can tether new design directions for sharing local information in development initiatives emphasise orality and performance. My analysis here refines insights about these anchors as a step in focusing activities to involve villagers in designing technologies. A starting point is the rarity of ambient text and literacy in everyday information sharing; for example, there is only one road sign, 'Lwandile', few labeled food products or posters, no local postal service, few people have poste restante addresses, or books, and, with limited written materials in Lwandile and Mgneibe school, children often learn by rote. Up to half of 9-year-olds cannot read, as many villagers speak only Xhosa but young children learn to read in English, and education is often truncated as less than 70% of those starting school at 7 years continue to 15, often assuming family duties when orphaned or married. Observations of people casually interacting with text, such as scouring job advertisements in English language newspapers brought from Mthatha or graffiti on school desks, were seldom and most observations of literacy were domain-specific and accompanied by some formality. For instance, Mfundiso re-wrote attendance lists at every meeting until they were perfect and teenage girls taking notes at the workshop did so with care. History recorded in text seems uninteresting, for example a unique poster display of newspaper articles on Apartheid attracted little attention at the workshop and the archives in Mthatha and at Limbode castle do not appear organized or regularly consulted (Fig 1g). Social practice, and preferences for media when present (e.g. TV, radio), emphasize orality, song and dance. People often sing while tending gardens or life-stock and start each day with hymns, choral group is a regular activity and the rarity of electricity means that any event with an amplifier attracts people to dance informally or in performance (e.g. at the workshop, the school opening). Many villagers over 15 years own or share a cell-phone, which they prefer to use to speak than SMS but do so rarely as airtime is unaffordable and not easily purchased locally. Thus, to create design activities for the community we are cautious not to emulate methods for text-based literacy.

Orality in Lwandile reflects durable traditions and, perhaps, the interplay between oppression in South Africa, historically, and the hegemonic effects of Western literacy and media. In village life people are not stigmatized as illiterate and associate status and dignity with other attributes, such as being in a Gospel choir or wage-earning (e.g. H. Sithelo ran away from school to work) but, as national speakers at the workshop reiterated, relying on orality is a disadvantage in modern, democratic and legislative South Africa. Villagers were stirred by NARS speakers' warnings that "*No-one will know your history if you are not protecting*". However, they perceive their obligation to preserving their heritage according to customs rather than by text-based recording. This suggests we need to attend to elements of these practices before re-purposing Western styles of recording for illiteracy or local language.

3.1 Embodiment in Physical Settings Orients Information

Villagers find the axes that outsiders use to orient information on Lwandile insufficient and indeed, collectivist culture has been associated with "high–context communication" where people ascribe meaning by reference to local context more than to abstractions [6]. The FRCC's workshop integrated natural and cultural heritage and development topics more holistically than if structured according to Western, urbanized, catagorisations and the narratives used by representatives of the national/provincial and traditional institutions differed. For instance, abstractions about land legislation, which in practical application derive from traditional mechanisms, incited contentions that they did not convey the meanings that entwine identity with a physical setting in which kin have resided for generations.

Lwandile's topological isolation and a daily-life spent outdoors means villagers are not anonymous and from birth to burial, and beyond, their identity becomes etched into the land. Even villagers migrating for work often return to Lwandile to retire or are buried in their umzi so ancestors' graves are close to home (e.g. 40% of the Sithelo clan reside in cities far away, but will be buried locally). Xhosa names are indexical to place, both in meaning (e.g. Hlathinkhulu means '*of big forest*') and as a located symbol. The language carries in the open-air and I began to acutely associate name sounds with umzis, for instance by hearing a grand-parent's frequent call to a child for an errand. The relevance of origin explains the Facebook Group: *Khanizi thuthe bantu!* where 2453 people have joined to write and discuss Xhosa, Zulu or Tswana clan names "*so that we may all know where we come from*". Names encode social relationships and ancestry symbolically and syntactically: a last name may be an ancestor's first name and first names are often phrases that tell a family story (e.g. Xolile: "*thank for this long waited child*"). This language morphology may help those villagers who can recite ancestors' names across generations and contribute to many people's eagerness to explain the meaning of their names.

As one middle-aged woman explained, the provincial representative's statements about ownership documents, such as "*This is your land .... here is your title and here is your land and heritage*", do not tell of the way name and place bond a community through practice. This resonates with our experience of the need to link digital resources to the topological, social and metaphysical infrastructures of land in Indigenous Australian culture to contextualise information at "*right spot, right time*" and the difficulty of doing so when the nature of the semantic inscription in landscape is so difficult for a designer to discern; for example, in a terrain of similar rondavals, merging into similar hills rolling in, all directions, to the horizon. Thus, the axes that orient villagers to information may be more perceptible by accompanying them in the actions that embody them. The landscape progresses the narrative of stories, prompts recollects and indexes villagers' practices. H. Sithelo chose to be interviewed under the tree in front of the Great Place (Fig. 1d) which commands a panoramic view and gestures across the hills of Lwandile when reminiscing sending a messenger on a horse; Thulani animated stories of his youth by indicating a forest; and, Bulelwa took a photo of the guava tree her brother planted. The furniture of rural life shaping interactions in conversations along roads and paths, across fences and at meeting places is as much outdoors (hills, water sources, farm animals, football field) as it is built (homes, Spazas, churches, shebeens). The features of, and material used, in storytelling join to expectations which seem bound to community, for instance, people were in 90% of Thulanis' photos of his construction work, domestic and village life.

When participants joined in songs several times a day at the workshop there was a sense of solidarity, but in contrast to national representatives' emphasis on a concept of African identity, villagers stressed being Khonjwayo. Such identification affords security (e.g. only gardens along the main road are gated and doors are locked only on departure for distant travel) and involves proximity (e.g. six Sithelos prefer to sleep in only one of the dwellings in the umzi). It also requires access, for example the Sithelo clan has several proximal umzi but the incumbent Headman always lives on the highest hill where villagers' can congregate for songs before work or for meetings (e.g. with the Councilor). Simultaneously, creating and expressing belonging separates villagers' intimate locale from more contemporary structures. For example, people were at ease telling me they went to the clinic or one of Lwandile's churches but not that they consulted any of Lwandile's many sangomas, who provide traditional herbal medicine and spiritual counselling. I also encountered signals for privacy around death, a fairly frequent occurrence, for instance the only time I felt unwelcome in the Sithelo's flat was on interrupting a meeting about a death and Thulani was emphatic that his photos of funerals (comprising 9% of his collection) must not be published. Boundaries between modern and traditional institutions (e.g. [5]) are re-interpreted in language and Internet use. Villagers prefer the rhythm, melody and richness of Xhosa's multi-syllabic words but may mix English into speech, particularly for numbers, institutions, biblical words and to translate their names (e.g. Thulani calls himself Patrick to outsiders) and apply that to their use of the internet (e.g. searching web-based resources on HIV in English). The use of social networking sites also exhibits a boundary between the local and the remote, consider how Thulani uses Facebook to link to people overseas, few of whom he knows, but not to Xhosa 'friends'; in contrast with rural users in the West [8].

3.2 Participation in Information Contributes to Collectivity

Design activities need to be compatible with those features of primary orality and performance that construct traditional identity. For instance, they should not threaten social structures in the way people in Lwandile, and on the remote African island of Ibo, attribute to American movies even though few people have access to television.

Customs suggest that villagers appreciate that knowledge is distributed across human repositories in oral traditions and participation in discourse contributes to collectivity. Headmen enact decisions about collectively owned resources based on prolonged, transparent debate to achieve consensus and Thulani believes that resolution emerges by listening to multiple perspectives not by overt coercion. Perhaps this view of consensus explains why Thulani associated the FRCC with a distant US, politically- oriented "*I bet I can find 1000,000 people who* ..." group. Traditions where leaders deferred to the general opinion of a court seem to be echoed in the ways meetings involving the Headman are 'chaired' by whoever raises an issue and mobilize experience spanning different views. For example, 20% of the 50 men attending the Mngciebe community meeting spoke and meetings of the FRCC, or between Thulani and the NGO, or at the workshop involved disparate perspectives and ideologies. The time spent listening and the significance of a presenter's role in cohesion is illustrated by the content of Thulani and Sixolile's photos, where 83% at the school opening, 53% at funerals and 48% at the kings party were of speakers or singers. Participation in discourse may involve 'handling' content within ritualised genres with defined linguistic structure or gesture, such as protocols of thanks or greetings. This handling provides significance to items and relations and shapes the context of consensus. For instance, patronage and "*friendship made by speaking*" is a rhetoric that shapes significance as shown when Thulani drew the Education Minister into a photo narrative. The Principal of Lwandile School asked Thulani and I to take photos of the poorly resourced and cramped classrooms in which staff "*diligently*" teach. Later at the opening of a pristine, new school Thulani took many photos of Chief Gwadiso and the Minister and, when they were encircled by apparatchiks, showed his photos of them and, then, of the decrepit school.

In designing for local information sharing in Lwandile we need to consider the role of etiquettes of ingratiation and participation in information structure and be wary about a structure that forces a singular flow of linear narrative, for example bound to the unidirectional timeline of video or a chronology of photos. This often happens in digital storytelling projects and is vital for marginalized voices to speak into Western markets (e.g. via YouTube) [2]) but not best suited to local information use where building rapport is prioritised over efficiency in information economies. While villagers' narratives often had a conventional story arc, for instance in re-telling the Sithelo's genology, building consensus from different viewpoints around a theme requires connections in various directions from disparate parts. Various Web 2.0 productivity tools enable people to annotate media content, such as by adding their own narration to on-line image slide shows, often providing diverging commentaries in the multi-vocal market of the Web, with its provenance of text and indirect orality. However, if operating within a group of interdependent voices, the orthogonal relationships interrupting a linear story may support consensus and common goals. Villagers often said, with pride, "*we share what we have*" and that neighbourly assistance was "*what it means to be African ... it's our identity*", sometimes refering to *Ubuntu*' which translates to "*the being human of a human being is noticed through his or her being human through human beings*" [14]. Villagers exchanged effort in many ways and survive, like rural communities globally, by co-operation however their reiteration of reciprocity as uniquely African suggests that they do not recognise interdependence as a Western trait. Rather they link autonomy to democracy, which they also attribute to social dysfunction. Pursuing unanimity through prolonged discussion may be a consequence of oral narrative's inherent malleability to history and politics and unify the community to maintain elder and patriarchal authority. Placing a unitary authoritarial narrative over information may disenfranchise the villagers, for example consider how the version of Sithelo genealogy within Lwandile differs markedly from that recited by Chief Gwadiso's emissary. We might expect convergence to a linear story while a traditional leader acts in the community's interests, much like years ago leaders stabilized tribal territories by bestowing economic protection in return for allegiance. Today the community supports a leader's success if it profits (e.g. Thulani's construction business provides jobs) and affirms community identity (e.g. Thulani's logo for the FRCC is four hands shaking above his own building tools) but withdraws support from a leader who prioritizes his individuality (e.g. villagers describe Chief Gwadiso as "*too greedy*").

3.3 Repetition to Create Consensus and Empathy

Translating a network of information to create tools for sharing presents difficulties for designers who may not necessarily recognize the rules that signify an item exists at an intersection. For example, an outsider might not realize, conceptually, that there are commonalities or interdependencies in information items. However, in codifying interdependencies across villagers' perspectives we note the role of repetition in group cohesion [16] and managing oral and performed interaction. Repetition may be a defining trait of oral traditions [13] to enable learning by rehearsal to yield collective memory (e.g. workshop participants were eager to show that they memorised dates, Thulani commented that it is usual to remember many phone numbers). Repetition shares context across generations by re-embodying the past through the particular phrasings of speech, actions or interactions with land, such as in retaining TK when Elders demonstrate fire practice to younger clan members. This longitudinal, or diachronic, repetition can involve people in meaning by connecting the immediate moment with prior occasions, setting the scene or emphasising part of a scene [16]. Repeating phrases and gestures across time enabled me to establish trust by authenticating significant items in momentary interactions. But repetition may also transmit core concepts that are inaccessible to rational logic; consider being invited to join an intimate circle of women on Ibo dancing to drum beats in a darkened ruin. The women shared a pattern unfamiliar to me; yet, in conforming to the repetitious movement, there was some 'primal' connection in sensory experience. Dance lacks the linearity of stories, and **is** life rather than a depiction, often mixed with spirituality, for instance African and indigenous Australian ceremonial dancers experience a transcendent reality to connect with ancestry. It appears Lwandile villagers are aware of such collective embodiment of information. For instance, the statement about heritage: *"people who are very, very eager to learn more, very eager to* ***do it*** *with whatever they have"* did not appear to be a mistranslation but to refer to embodying information through actions.

The hooks in Lwandile's social fields to which we tether design directions need to account for gendered participation in information and the different roles of repetition in managing oral and performed interaction. For example, only men made speeches at the Mngciebe meeting of 50 men and 12 women (Fig. 1f) and, only males asked questions or orated amongst the 24 male and 46 females in the main workshop sessions, while females prepared dinner or listened and took notes. At meetings in Lwandile in mixed groups people listen quietly until a speaker finishes before contributing (Fig 1f), and men tended to stand out vocally often using synchronic repetition to enhance dramatic qualities, for instance at the Mngciebe meeting men frequently gesticulated to parts of the land in similar ways when negotiating the price they should charge outsiders for sand. In contrast, women Lwandile are inclined to conform and to harmonize in their daily songs. We also observe a tendency for speech to overlap in Quimana women's conversation on Ibo with their increased involvement in discussions about the changes the island has undergone, whereas men on Ibo always spoke *asynchronously*. Perhaps these nuances reflect the need to manage interaction differently, for example in Lwandile women talk in clusters often sitting on the ground behind the Great Place or during their daily tasks (e.g. collecting water, washing laundry, visiting the clinic) while men tended to talk sit in small lines or stand overlooking the under a tree in front of the Great Place (Fig. 1 b) & d). Hardy has started applying features of synchronous speech in designing technologies inspired by her observations that Indigenous women perceive finishing or inserting a phrase in another's sentence as empathic rather than as interruptive [4].

4 Conclusion

We do not imagine that the properties of indexicality that we have identified in villagers' priorities and oral and performed practices are complete, unique to African rural living or are necessarily the most primary for collectivity in rural communities. Instead, we propose they can inspire concrete ways for local social structures to impact on activities to design systems of information organization, by allowing designer's to handle items important to local communication that may be less obvious in the market of symbols, concepts and structural forms that sustain communications tuned by a heritage of indirect orality and text. We suggest our handling can help us to develop an appropriate sensitivity to associations between the identity of the user and the meaning of collectivity inscribed in unbuilt physical settings. For example, our current activities to involve villagers in designing technologies respond to relationships between physical settings, group cohesion, collective memory and consensus-building communication practices, such as repetition.

References

1. Attewell, P.: Ethnomethodology Since Garfinkel. Theory and Society 1179(2), 179–210 (1974)
2. Bidwell, N.J., Standley, P.M., George, T., Steffensen, V.: The Landscape's Apprentice: Lessons for Design from Grounding Documentary. In: Proc. Designing Interactive Systems DIS 2008, Cape Town (2008)
3. Bourdieu, P.: Language and Symbolic Power. Harvard University Press (1991)
4. Browning, D., Bidwell, N.J., Hardy, D., Standley, P.: Rural Encounters: Cultural Translations Through Video. In: Proc. OZCHI 2008, pp. 148–155 (2008)
5. Byrne, E & Sahay, S (2006) Activity theory as an analytical tool: a case study of IS development for an anti-retroviral treatment clinic in South Africa. *Proc. South African* institute of computer scientists and information technologists. ACM Int. Conf. Proc. (24) 7
6. Erez, M. and Earley, P.C. (1993), *Culture, Self-identity, and Work*, Oxford
7. Garfinkel, H.: Studies in Ethnomethodology. Prentice Hall, Englewood Cliffs (1967)
8. Gilbert, E., Karahalios, K., Sandvig, C.: The Network in the Garden: An Empirical Analysis of Social Media in Rural Live. In: Proc. CHI 2008, vol. 12, pp. 1603–1612 (2008)
9. Heeks, R.: Information Systems & Developing Countries: Failure, Success, & Local Improvisations. The Information Society 18, 101–112 (2002)
10. Kim, U., Yang, G., Hwang, K.: Indigenous and Cultural Psychology. Springer, Heidelberg (2006)
11. Marsden, G., Maunder, A., Parker, M.: People are people, but technology is not technology. Phil. Trans. R. Soc. A (2008)
12. Ong, W.: Orality and literacy: The technologizing of the word. Methuen, London (1982)
13. Rosenberg, B.A.: The Complexity of Oral Tradition. Oral Tradition 2, 73–90 (1987)
14. Shutte, A.: Philosophy for Africa. Marquette University Press, Milwaukee (1993)
15. Suchman, L.: Located Accountabilities in Technology Production. Scandinavian J. of Information Systems Archive 2(14), 91–105 (2003)
16. Tannen: Talking voices: repetition, dialog, and images in conversational discourse. Cambridge University Press, Cambridge (1989)
17. Tucker, W., Blake, E.: The Role of Outcome Mapping in Developing a Rural Telemedicine System. In: Cunningham, P., Cunningham, M. (eds.) Proc. IST-Africa 2008, IIMC Int. Information Management Corp. (2008)
18. `http://www.unesco.org/culture/`
19. Walker, K., Underwood, J., M-Waema, T., Dunckley, L., et al.: A Resource Kit for Participatory Socio-Technical Design in Rural Kenya. In: Proc. CHI 2008, pp. 2709–2714. ACM Pr., New York (2008)
20. Winschiers, H., Fendler, J.: Assumptions considered harmful. In: Aykin, N. (ed.) HCII 2007. LNCS, vol. 4559, pp. 452–461. Springer, Heidelberg (2007)

Faces of Privacy: Effect of Culture and Context

Kari-Jouko Räihä and Saila Ovaska

Unit for Computer Human Interaction (TAUCHI), Department of Computer Sciences
FIN-33014 University of Tampere, Finland
{kari-jouko.raiha,saila.ovaska}@cs.uta.fi

Abstract. We repeated in Finland a study on privacy concerns originally carried out in the USA. The results suggest that there are cultural differences in the willingness of people to reveal privacy-sensitive information.

Keywords: Privacy, regulation mechanisms, cultural differences.

1 Introduction

It has been suggested [1] that mobile context-aware telephones could be designed to show the location information of the callee, who could set the phone to automatically dismiss the call still providing some information about his or her current situation. However, for different callers there would be a need to show different level of detail. For instance, a call from the boss requires more precise detail than a call from a merchant, especially if it comes during working hours. Also the presence of other people is an important message to the caller. Lederer and his colleagues combined these aspects into a metaphorical "Face" shown to the caller [1].

We repeated the data collection of [2] in Finland. We point at preliminary findings about possible cultural variation: based on the data collected, we expect that privacy regulation mechanisms may need to be culturally varied.

2 The Study

Data collection in the original study [2] was done with a web questionnaire. The questionnaire introduced a background scenario where the respondent was asked to imagine having a mobile phone with identity and profile information that could be disclosed to the callers with various levels of accuracy:

- Three faces: True, Vague, Blank, each revealing a different level of detail. For instance, a True face would reveal the actual identity of the person, a Vague face would show a pseudonym, and a Blank face would be anonymous. Similar distinctions applied to profile (contact information and interests), activity, and location.

Furthermore, the subjects were asked to fill in the face matching their preferences in 2x4 = 8 different contexts.

- Two situations: Working Lunch, Social Evening
- Four inquirers: Spouse/significant other, Employer, Stranger, Merchant.

T. Gross et al. (Eds.): INTERACT 2009, Part I, LNCS 5726, pp. 700–703, 2009.

The original study was part of a more extensive user-centered design process [3]. The web survey was preceded by interviews and followed by prototype evaluations to guide the design of the privacy regulation mechanism. In addition to serving this ultimate purpose, the specific question answered through the web survey was: *Which is more important, the inquirer or the situation in which the information is disclosed?*

This question was introduced to students in an advanced HCI class in Finland in 2004 and 2005. They were asked to interview 3-5 friends or acquaintances and report by email the faces chosen by the respondents and possible comments they had. The students of the class came from different ethnic backgrounds. Based on a preliminary analysis of the data collected in 2004 we asked the course in 2005 to report also the cultural background of the persons they interviewed. The demographic variables collected were gender, nationality, occupation, and age group. Students were used for data collection to teach them about privacy issues and to increase the sample size.

3 The Results and Analysis

The fundamental design-oriented question of interest in the original study [2] was whether people would use the faces at all, i.e., how many faces would they use overall. The resulting mean number of faces presented across situations and inquirers is shown in Table 1, both for the original study and our students. From the three possible faces, the respondents selected on average more than two different faces to display in the described events.

Table 1. Mean number of different faces used overall in the eight contexts

	Original study (n=130)	Our study (n=246)
Working lunch	2.72 (sd 0.84)	2.37 (sd 0.59)
Social evening	2.58 (sd 0.89)	2.35 (sd 0.59)

The main observation from these results is that within a given situation, subjects did vary faces across inquirers. Our numbers are lower than the original ones, but still indicate the interest in using a variety of faces.

Lederer et al. [2] found that for a given inquirer, subjects generally did not vary faces across situations. Their conclusion was that the inquirer's identity is a stronger determinant of privacy preferences than the user's situation. Table 2 summarizes the data when responses for both situations were pulled together.

Table 2. Face variation based on situation

	Original study		Our study in 2004	
Inquirer	Same Face	Different Face	Same Face	Different Face
Spouse	83.8%	16.2%	84.6%	15.4%
Employer	54.6%	45.4%	37.8%	66.2%
Stranger	77.7%	22.3%	80.9%	19.1%
Merchant	86.2%	13.6%	79.3%	20.7%

The results are similar, but there are marked differences as well, particularly in the case where the inquirer is the employer or merchant. Figure 1 shows a more detailed distribution of the different faces for these two cases.

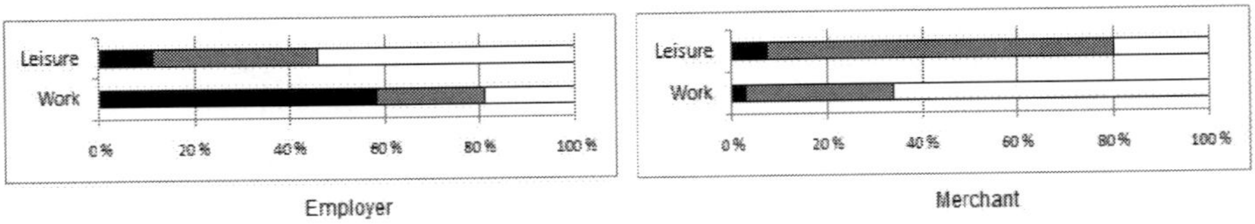

Fig. 1. Distribution of faces based on inquirer (shown below) and situation (shown next to the bar). Black color denotes the True face, grey denotes the Vague face, and white the Blank face.

It is obvious that the "same face to same inquirer independently of situation" does not hold for our respondents. They were willing to reveal the True face to the employer only at work, not during leisure. Similarly, merchants would have mainly received a Blank face while the respondents were at work, but a Vague face during leisure. Targeted advertisements were considered potentially valuable if they were not distracting and if they did not require too detailed information about the receiver.

We then analyzed the effects of the demographic variables. The first variable we considered was gender. The distributions of the responses were similar by male and female respondents. There was only one case, shown in Figure 2 (left), where there was a difference by more than just a few percentages in the replies. Female employees were somewhat less willing to put up their true face to the employer. This was the case independently of whether the situation was at work or at leisure.

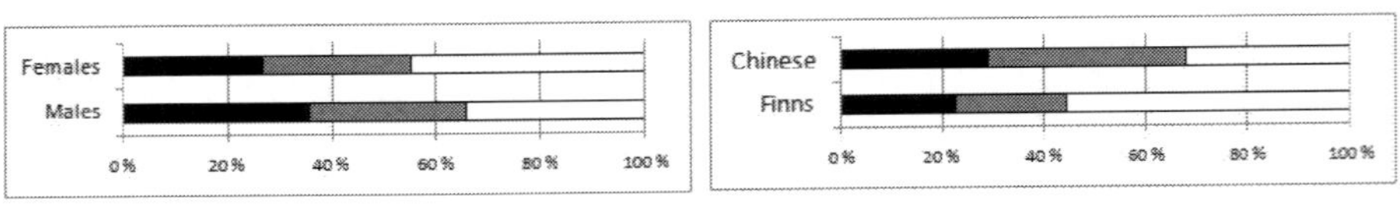

Fig. 2. Distribution of faces that female and male respondents would have shown to the employer (left), and Chinese and Finnish respondents would have shown at leisure (right)

Another interesting variable is the nationality of the respondents. The potential effect of nationality became clear only after reviewing the replies collected in 2004, and the nationality of respondents was systematically collected only in 2005; therefore the nationality-based analysis is based on a smaller sample than the ones above (n=208).

The majority of respondents (n=109) were Finns, so a natural first analysis was between Finns and non-Finns. The differences in the distributions were minor, but the non-Finns showed a lot of variation. The biggest subpopulation was formed by Chinese respondents (n=25), and we compared the Finnish and Chinese respondents in more detail. Figure 2 (right) shows an example of typical results.

The biggest differences were that Chinese respondents would never show a Blank face to their spouse (as opposed to 6.4 % of the Finns), and that the Chinese respondents would never show a True face to merchants (as opposed to 5.6 % of all the other respondents). For strangers, 76.1 % of the Finns would show a Blank face, whereas for Chinese the corresponding figure was 48.0 %.

4 Discussion

We requested our students to ask for explanations to the choices their respondents made. These revealed further variation and show clearly that the average and summary information given above must be taken only as indicative.

For instance, although Finns are considered as somewhat reserved (and indeed, did on average not have a problem with putting up a Blank face), there were exceptions. One Finnish respondent commented that "*I've got nothing to hide*," and another went even further: "*I have to reveal, it's in my personality*". When discussed in class, a student asked in disbelief: "Was that really a Finn?"

Another observation was that the faces chosen for the scenario were considered too general. People would have liked to know more about the inquirer. They would have been happy to put up at least a Vague face to merchants, had they known that the merchandise offered was potentially beneficial for them (e.g., an announcement of an interesting discount). They also might have put up a more revealing face than a Blank face to a stranger had they known something about the age and gender of the inquirer.

The results in Section 3 hint at the Chinese respondents being careful not to reveal too much of their identity when it was not necessary, but also not to put up a perhaps impolite Blank face. Finns, respectively, seemed less conscious and less considerate.

5 Conclusions

We repeated a study of privacy conceptions originally carried out in the USA. Our results show that one should be careful with general conclusions. A detailed analysis shows that the overall result of [2] does not hold in all cases. Culture was found to have a notable effect, and gender had an effect to a smaller degree. We are currently working on a more detailed analysis of the verbal comments of the participants.

Acknowledgments. We thank Scott Lederer for giving us access to the data set of the original study. This work was supported by Nordunet in the PriMa project (Privacy in the Making).

References

1. Lederer, S., Hong, J.I., Dey, A.K., Landay, J.A.: Personal Privacy through Understanding and Action: Five Pitfalls for Designers. Personal and Ubiquitous Computing 8(6), 440–454 (2004)
2. Lederer, S., Mankoff, J., Dey, A.K.: Who Wants to Know What When? Privacy Preference Determinants in Ubiquitous Computing. In: CHI 2003 Extended Abstracts on Human Factors in Computing Systems CHI 2003, pp. 724–725. ACM, New York (2003)
3. Lederer, S., Mankoff, J., Dey, A.K., Beckmann, C.: Managing Personal Information Disclosure in Ubiquitous Computing Environments. Technical Report CSD-03-1257. Univ. of California, Berkeley (2003), `http://www.eecs.berkeley.edu/Pubs/TechRpts/2003/5250.html` (retrieved January 28, 2009)

Fair Partnerships – Working with NGOs

Shikoh Gitau and Gary Marsden

ICT4D Research Centre, University of Cape Town, South Africa
{sgitau,gaz}@cs.uct.ac.za

Abstract. This paper highlights how Non-Governmental Organizations (NGOs) can be utilized during the design of Information Communication Technologies for Development (ICT4D). We use the design process of a voter education system as a case study, which incorporated three NGOs from two African countries. Of key interest to us are the ways in which we can avoid exploiting these NGOs and make sure the ICT intervention meets their goals, as well as those of the researchers.

Keywords: Public Display, ICT4D, Participatory Design, Contextual Design, Mobile Phones, Africa, developing world, NGOs.

1 Introduction

Some of the challenges facing the design of technology relevant for developing community include: understanding the users in their context; opportunity identification; determining design requirements as well as evaluating the impact caused by the resulting technology. These are mainly caused by differences between the researcher (mostly coming from a developed context) and the community of interest; the differences can be in terms of language, culture, attitudes and locality (where designers and users are separated geographically during some stages in the design process). These disconnects have had costly effects in ICT4D projects, with close to 70% of all initiated projects failing within the first few years of conception [1]. Hence there is a need for an alternative means to approach the design of ICT4D.

Non-Governmental Organizations (NGOs) are an instrumental and integral part in Africa's development agenda; they exist as non-profit citizen groups, organized on a local, national or international level. NGOs have enjoyed high levels of trust and acceptance in developing communities, and are now used to provide information, analysis and expertise about these communities. They also help with the implementation of government projects and monitoring of agreements and policies. Using an NGO for community liaison is therefore an attractive prospect for ICT researchers wishing to create technologies for developing world communities, and reports of such partnerships are common, e.g. [2]. However, instead of using the NGO just as a liaison element in development projects, with roles limited to 'access point' or 'contact', we believe that it is important for these NGOs to be incorporated in a more integral role both in the development and evaluation processes for the project as they will remain in the community long after the technologist or researchers have left. We believe this type of evaluation mechanism is absolutely critical in working with an

T. Gross et al. (Eds.): INTERACT 2009, Part I, LNCS 5726, pp. 704–707, 2009.

NGO as it will allow them to measure *in their own terms* any improvements the ICT intervention has made and determine what needs to be done to afford more impact.

In the rest of this paper we will report on working with three NGOs in the domain of voter education in Africa as part of a project to create new forms of multimedia voter education material. Voter education (VE) is a term used to refer to the process of disseminating materials and programmes designed to inform the electorate about the specifics and mechanics of the voting process for a particular election and aimed to enlighten them or convince them to participate in the election.

Three NGOs participated in this study, all of whom are involved in democracy and governance issues in Africa; specifically Kenya and South Africa. In Kenya we worked with the Centre for Multiparty Democracy-Kenya and Media Focus on Africa. In South Africa we worked with the Institute for Democracy in South Africa.

2 Methodology

Before the design process could begin, we needed to understand the voter education process from the NGO's perspective and context, as well as conduct document ethnography where we followed the voter information development process. We first sent out an initial questionnaire to the NGOs whose aims were to capture basic demographic information as well as the technical competency of their staff. This information allowed us to plan our study such that it would suit the NGO's schedules and technical abilities. Thereafter, we carried out a contextual inquiry study, where we took an 'apprentice mode' within the communication office that is in charge of the voter education process.

A contextual inquiry allows the designer to learn more about the user by observing them in their daily routine; this is especially important in circumstances where the designer has little or no understanding of the user's domain. We therefore observed the NGO staff as they carried out their day to day tasks throughout the voter education process in addition other tasks within their mandate. We followed these observations with unstructured interviews to clarify some of the observations that were made but were not explicit. This triangulation of techniques allowed us to capture information that we had missed previously and clarify observations made and inquire deeply into given actions.

We made notes for both the observation sessions as well as the interviews and digital photos were also taken of some the key moments.

3 Findings

The study found that voter education is a very complex but deliberate process that went beyond the mere dissemination of voter information material. We noted that each piece of information – the message – was tailored towards a particular segment of voters according to their demographic data. Voter education messages were disseminated either directly through face to face encounters (such as workshops), door to door visits or through broadcast media including print media, television, and radio. The radio was the dominant media, taking over 50% of the total VE budget dues to its wide spread use in both these countries.

NGOs monitored the impact of the VE process through a fortnightly survey, whose result determined whether a message achieved its intent, whether it should continue running or if it should be changed for a different segment of voters or moved to a different media.

During the study, we introduced the Big Board (BB)[3]as complimentary media for voter education that allowed sharing of multimedia using large public displays and mobiles phones via Bluetooth transfer. Using a participatory design approach, we designed a PC based application, that would allow the NGO staff to create, manipulate and upload media onto the BB, that will then be accessed by voters on their mobile phones. This media could be adjusted and cycled to fit the various voters needs, through a simple drag and drop interface (a technique familiar to the NGO staff). The application, as envisioned by the NGO would facilitate in cutting down on operational cost incurred from outsourced services but still enable a widespread reach via mobile phones with the assumed viral spread of the messages. Through various iterations, observations and task based analysis we ensured that the NGO staff could comfortably use this application to upload media onto the BB.

The cooperation with NGOs during the study not only ensured that we could develop appropriate solutions for information dissemination by providing us with an understanding of the voters and voter education processes; but their ability to measure the envisoned impact (through their standard monitoring tools) allowed them and us to have the confidence that they could evaluate the effectiveness of the BB system during a voter education process.

4 Discussion

This is a research that, if we had attempted to do on our own, would certainly have led to failure. We discovered that voter education turned out to be more complex than we had initially envisioned, where demographics, illiteracy, trust and integrity are critical aspects that are largely opaque to the outsider. Furthermore, we did not have the capacity in terms of staff and funding to properly explore these issues to a point where we could make a contribution.

So, once again we see the value of having a 'human-access point' into the community [4]. We could leverage their deep understanding of the people and their needs to help create solutions in developing community settings. What is less clear, however, is what the NGO gets out of their collaboration with us. If we are not to be accused of propagating imperialism in Africa once more (this time in the form of culture or technology) then joint research of this nature must be an equal partnership. From our experience we propose that this equality should not be in the form of task-sharing (it is pointless for the NGO to learn how to write software, just as it would be for us to learn all the laws relating to the conduct of elections). Instead, we recommend that each party have in place a meaningful evaluation method that can be applied at the end intervention. In this way, we believe that the research partnership can be kept 'honest' as there is a clear understand of what constitutes success for each party.

5 Conclusion

Ostensibly, this research is about the creation of a voter education system in Africa. A wider learning in the field of HCI4D (for the lack of a better term) is the way in which NGOs should be engaged in this type of research partnership. Many papers report on the data and advantages of working with established NGOs and human-access points ([4] for example) but do not report on how the NGO feels about the intervention. However, in at least one case we are aware of, an NGO partner was unhappy at the intervention.

Our experience suggests that these problems can be avoided by making sure the NGO has an evaluation method in place that can inform them of the impact of your intervention in their domain. In fact, we would argue that such a partnership must not be entered into until such evaluation methods exist. By this token, we can ensure equal benefit to both the research community and the NGO.

Acknowledgments. We would like to thank the three NGOs involved in this work for the patient support of our blundering attempts. We would also like to thank Microsoft Research Cambridge who funded the research.

References

1. Heeks, R.: Information Systems and Developing Countries: Failure, Success, and Local Improvisations. The Information Society 18(2), 101–112 (2002)
2. Chetty, M., & Grinter, R. HCI4D: HCI Challenges. In: Proceedings CHI 2007, pp. 2327–2332 (2007)
3. Maunder, A., Marsden, G., Harper, R.: SnapAndGrab – Accessing and sharing contextual multi-media content using Bluetooth enabled cameraphones and large situated displays. In: Proceedings CHI 2008, pp. 2319–2323 (2008)
4. Marsden, G.: Towards Empowered Design. IEEE Computer 41(6), 42–47 (2008)

An Evaluation Framework for Mobile User Interfaces

Marco de Sá and Luís Carriço

LaSIGE & Department of Informatics, University of Lisboa, Portugal
{marcosa,lmc}@di.fc.ul.pt

Abstract. We present the extensions to a software framework which supports the construction and evaluation of mixed-fidelity prototypes for mobile devices. The framework is available for desktop and mobile devices and allows designers and users to test the prototypes on actual devices. Additionally, the extensions aim at allowing designers to gather usage information, both passively and actively, tailoring the used techniques to users or project's goals. It supports contextual and ubiquitous evaluation also including in-situ prototyping and participatory design on-the-go. We address the evaluation's features and their contribution to the field of mobile interaction design, presenting real-life case studies and achieved results.

Keywords: Mobile devices, In-Situ Evaluation, Ethnography, Prototyping.

1 Introduction

Designing for mobile devices is an increasingly demanding challenge. Besides the hardware constraints that are imposed by their size, interaction modalities, diversity and portability, their pervasiveness and multi-purpose functionality imply an entire new set of usage paradigms. Accordingly, specific design methods and techniques for mobile devices have been emerging and receiving special attention by researchers, leading to the appearance of different approaches for a wide range of problems [1,10,11,21,24]. Given the differences from fixed technologies, most efforts are directed to prototyping and evaluation. These suggest the need for detailed and carefully built prototypes that offer a more resembling picture of final solutions and their characteristics [9,19] , even at the earliest stages of design. Another important benefit that results from using such techniques and carefully built prototypes is the ability to use them in realistic settings. In fact, the majority of research results within this area point the necessity of conducting evaluation out-of-the-lab [1,7,8,17], on the actual settings where the final applications will be used, since the beginning of the design process [24]. Besides providing users with more realistic experiences, this approach allows designers and evaluators to see users interact with the devices within scenarios that will likely be real settings for the final applications. This leads to the detection of more design and usability issues and allows for a better understanding of how users interact with the applications in the real-world [24].

However, despite the increasing amount of attention towards in-situ contextual evaluation, support for this type of procedure is still relatively scarce [12,24]. Existing examples usually point guidelines on how to emulate real world settings within labs

T. Gross et al. (Eds.): INTERACT 2009, Part I, LNCS 5726, pp. 708–721, 2009.

[1,21] or conduct role playing simulations. This contrasts with the aforementioned solid evidence and body of work that emphasize the advantages of out-of-the-lab evaluation [4,8,11,17,19]. As some experiences have shown, the lack of in-situ real world evaluation is a result of the relative inexistence of appropriate techniques to support such endeavor [12,24] and, when adequate techniques are available, the added effort that these require.

These issues led us to conduct a series of experiments with low-fidelity prototypes and ubiquitous data gathering and evaluation techniques [24]. Throughout these, the learnt lessons pointed directions and techniques that proved to be adequate while supporting mobile design and, in particular, mobile evaluation [24]. Nevertheless, despite the exciting results, some of these techniques still required added effort and placed a heavy burden on users. Naturally, this provided the motivation, which, propelled by the inspirational results, set the ground for the design of tools to support and share ways on how to apply, on an easier fashion, the same techniques.

In this paper we present the evolution and added features of a framework that acknowledges the inevitable differences between fixed and mobile technologies and respective design requirements and aims at supporting mobile design. The framework provides the necessary features to support the creation and design of mixed fidelity prototypes and their usage on real devices for testing sessions with real users on real locations. However, now, and more importantly, it has been updated to cover the evaluation of mobile applications and design experiments in realistic settings using the set of techniques that had a strong and positive impact on the aforementioned experiences. Our contribution in this paper is the description of how the experiences and techniques that inspired the framework's upgrade were materialized and integrated with the prototyping stage, allowing designers to tailor the evaluation process to the project's need or the target end-users.

We discuss how the combination of emerging ubiquitous evaluation techniques were introduced within our tool, supporting shorter design cycles and experimentation at very early stages, mitigating the burden placed on users and designers. We succinctly describe the overall framework and its goals focusing on the evaluation features that it integrates. We proceed with the description of some of the case studies in which the framework has been used, highlighting the impact it had on the design process. Finally, we discuss results, present conclusions and draw future goals.

2 Inspiration/Motivation

The evaluation of user interfaces and interactive applications is a crucial part of the design process. It provides the opportunity to understand if the user interface is suitable to be used while users are trying to achieve certain goals within a certain context, opening doors for corrections and improvements. When it comes to mobile devices, the settings and contexts in which users interact with the applications while trying to get something done, may vary infinitely, depending on the device, the user's location and surroundings (e.g., lighting conditions, noise, social context, posture). Moreover, some activities span through various settings, which might affect how users interact with the device/application, even during a set of actions that lead to one specific goal [24]. Consequentially, evaluation gains even more relevance in a mobile context and, as many experiences, including our own, have pointed, benefits greatly if undertaken in-situ, out of the lab, in the real world [17,19,21,23,24].

However, this introduces additional challenges, which are still difficult to overcome. The techniques that are usually applied for fixed technologies (e.g., user observation, WOz simulations) are demanding when applied away from laboratory settings, on moving contexts, sometimes even inadequate and frequently avoided [12,24]. Our experiences demonstrated that prototypes need to be realistic and to provide a tangible experience. Methods that require the designer's presence hinder the process by affecting the experience and because of the time/effort they imply. Nevertheless, techniques such as the Experience Sampling Method (ESM)[4] and diary studies[22], and even usage registration (e.g., actually writing and marking clicks/taps on the cards when interacting with them, provided good results. However, even these require user's cooperation and can be demanding during real-world tests.

Recent works, addressing these issues and aiming at further improving and supporting mobile evaluation, have introduced technological methods to gather usage data remotely through active (e.g., , ESM, Diary Studies) and passive modes (e.g., Logging), enabling evaluation on real settings. For instance, with close goals to our framework regarding evaluation, the Momento [3], and the MyExperience [8] systems provide support for remote data gathering. The first relies on text messaging and media messaging to distribute data. It gathers usage information and prompts questionnaires as required, sending them to a server where an experimenter manages the received data through a desktop GUI. On the second, user activities on Mobile Phones are logged and stored on the device. These are then synchronized depending on connection availability. The logging mechanism detects several events and active evaluation techniques can be triggered according to contextual settings. The Topiary system [15] follows a similar approach and aims at supporting the evaluation of context-based applications.

Our approach also addresses these issues and takes into account previous results, but inspired by lessons learned and the available literature [7,11,17,19,24] aims at integrating the in-situ prototyping and evaluation stages seamlessly, facilitating user involvement and the design process. None of the existing work integrates the in-situ prototyping and evaluation on real devices, also including means to adjust the prototypes while evaluating them or to analyze them (e.g., various alternatives to one user interface), individually or simultaneously, on intuitive and simple to review modes. Furthermore, most are focused on specific issues or domains and depend on server-client architectures, requiring a constant connection or frequent synchronizations. Additionally, none combines various techniques into the same tool, allowing designers to tailor evaluation to their needs.

Our goal is to focus the interactions that directly relate to prototypes on early design stages, facilitating their on-the-spot analysis through several mechanisms and to combine them with qualitative data easily gathered by end-users. For this, the evaluation methods are automatically integrated within a mixed-fidelity prototyping tool that conveys the two stages, bridging the gap between prototyping and in-situ evaluation. Our contribution over previous work is the integration of several data gathering and analysis techniques that can be used seamlessly on mobile devices, facilitating user involvement and the design process. We support the creation, use and evaluation of prototypes on real devices, also including means to adjust them (e.g., low and high-fidelity with video and audio) in-situ, while evaluating or analyzing them (e.g., various alternatives to one user interface), on a video-like mode.

2.1 Background

To cope with early design stage difficulties, especially during prototyping and evaluation, the framework's features cover both stages, supporting an iterative and participatory design that facilitates the transition between the two stages. Its umbrella goal is to support the early design of applications for mobile devices. Rather than including complex features and supporting the creation of very detailed software prototypes, we aim at supporting rapid prototyping and in-situ evaluation, focusing techniques and features that have been proved to be highly effective in these settings [24]. Like existing tools [6,13,14] it provides designers with means to quickly create prototypes. At this stage, the framework's main features allow designers to create mixed-fidelity prototypes (e.g., sketch-based or visual component based), targeting different concerns, and configure their behavior (e.g., navigation between screens/cards, play audio and video files; allow end-users to interact with traditional components – text-boxes, combo-boxes). These prototypes can be easily copied into a mobile device where end-users can interact with them [25].

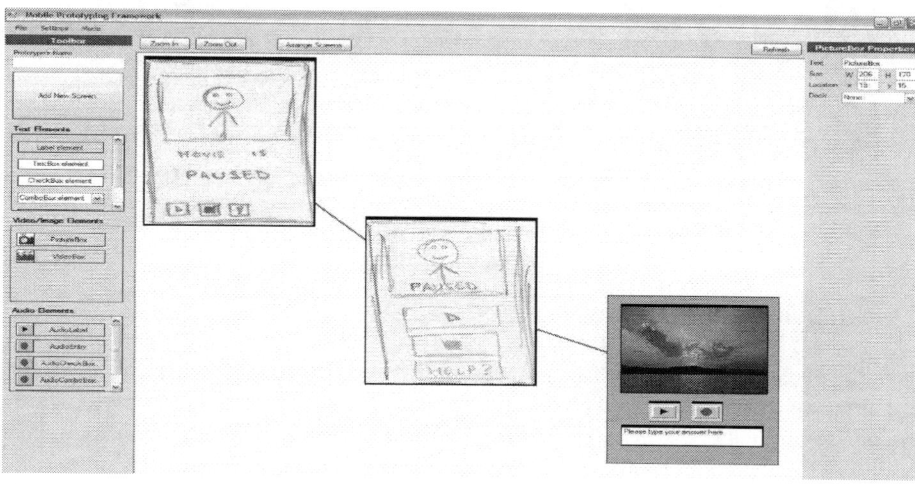

Fig. 1. Prototype editor. Cards/Screens can be dropped and moved inside the working area and composed by sketches (the first two screens) or interactive elements (right bottom – with a video container, two buttons and a text-box).

Additionally, direct prototyping on the mobile devices is also supported, enabling designers and end-users to update and re-arrange simple details, improving the prototypes on real settings, out of the lab. The major advantage of using actual devices, with components and interaction modalities available to the used device, is that problems regarding the device's characteristics (e.g., size, weight, screen resolution, shape) emulation are solved [19], avoiding the cargo cult syndrome [9] (e.g., misleading users) and providing end-users with a much more tangible and realistic usage experience and better evaluation results.

Figure 1 depicts the framework's prototyping interface. Designers can visually create each screen/card using sketch based images and augmenting them with behavior (e.g., defining rules - click areas emulating buttons) which allow end-users to navigate through the prototype (without the user acting as a Wizard-of-Oz) on the mobile device. Alternatively, or in concert with sketches, graphical components can be dragged and dropped on each card (e.g., picture-boxes, labels, buttons, text-boxes, track-bars). Each prototype's specification is saved into an XML file. The counterpart for the prototyping tool (Figure 1) is the runtime environment that is responsible for recreating the prototypes on the targeted devices (Figure 2, left). Currently we have a runtime environment for Windows Mobile, Palm OS and SymbianOS. A Windows version was also created to allow testing on TabletPCs.

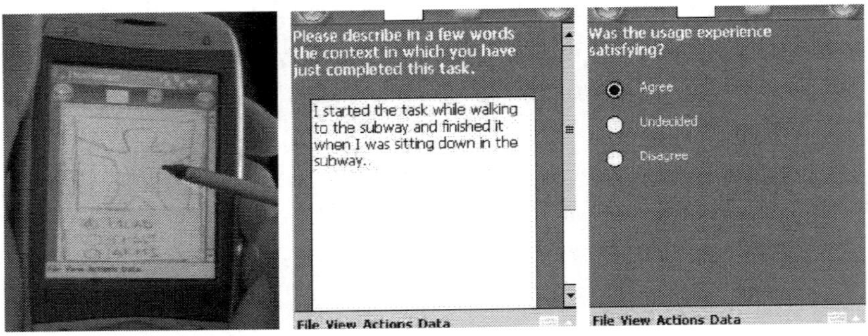

Fig. 2. a) User with an interactive low-fidelity prototype on an actual mobile device. b) Active data gathering. Questionnaires can be completed and browsed on the device.

3 Extensions and Requirements

In order to facilitate data gathering during real world evaluation sessions, using the techniques we applied on to the preceding experiences, our framework had to be extended, combining different approaches that could be used in concert or alternatively. Additionally, means to easily analyze the gathered data, even on-the-spot, during in-situ trials, were necessary. Overall, these goals can be supported by (a) retrieving reliable usage information without intrusive equipment, without the designer or usability engineer's presence and using seamless/passive techniques; (b) supporting the analysis of usage patterns and usability concerns through the visualization of the user's activities; (c) integrating alternative methods that provide qualitative data extending the scope of the evaluation process.

These goals emerge as a consequence from the framework's prototyping features and successful experiences they provided [24]. Directly embedding these techniques on the developed prototypes, created with the framework, should facilitate the overall design process flow. Globally, this can be achieved through the following features:

1. Gather data through passive and active techniques. On the former, every action that the user takes is automatically logged with customized granularities. On the latter, the use of methods such as probing, ESM [4] and diary studies [22], integrated within the tool, provide another source of data and usability information.
2. Contextual card tagging and sorting. Each screen/card can be tagged and numbered in-situ, defining a sequence that fits the user's needs in a particular setting/context. This allows designers to select optimal configuration and arrangements for the applications or user interfaces that are being designed.
3. Analysis functionalities - The analysis of gathered data is paramount during the design and evaluation process. Accordingly, we include data analysis features on the desktop editor and on a mobile version for in-situ evaluation/analysis.
4. Multimodalities are a key factor on mobile devices, providing redundant output/input channels that cope with the adversities of the usage context or offer support for disabled users. Since our framework supports the prototyping and simulation of multimodal applications (e.g., including voice capturing, audio and video elements) these modalities can play a paramount role for evaluation purposes.

4 Tailoring the In-Situ Evaluation

Besides combining the aforementioned techniques and integrating them with the prototyping features, particular care was directed into facilitating their utilization and adjustment. The following sections detail how they were applied and enhanced.

4.1 Passive Techniques – Intelligent Logging Engine

Integrated within the runtime environment, the tool in which users can interact with the prototypes, there is a logging engine which is responsible for the passive data gathering (i.e., without the user's explicit intervention) mechanisms. Its goal is to collect usage data without any intervention or even awareness by the user. Accordingly, it stores every event that is triggered by the user's interaction with the prototype and device or by the time constraints associated to each element/screen. Events range from each screen tap, each button press or even each character that was typed. Events are saved with a timestamp, allowing its reproduction for the re-enactment of the usage behavior. Details such as the type of interaction, location of the screen tap, etc., are also stored for every event. In summary, it generates a detailed and structured description of every occurrence while the prototype was used.

However, considering mobile devices' limited memory and battery, the granularity of the logged events can be easily configured both during usage and during the prototype's construction. Limiting the amount of logged events reduces the size of logs and the processing that logging requires. Moreover, the adjustment of the logging granularity can also be used to match the gathered data with evaluation and analysis' purposes. For instance, if the evaluator is particularly interested in understanding how the user navigates between the existing screens that compose the prototype, but has no interest in collecting data regarding the locations of taps on the screen, the latter event can be ignored. This mechanism creates logs that are focused to particular events.

These configuration options are also important when taking into account the several modalities that are available within a particular prototype. Here, the selection of events, which pertain to specific modalities (e.g., play, pause of an audio track or video, voice commands) is also paramount in order to facilitate analysis of usage logs (e.g., if the application is to be used by a visually impaired user, the designer might enable logging only for the audio modality and the user's voice commands). Overall, the logging engine supports configurable data gathering that can be focused on the evaluation goals without adding effort or requiring users' intervention.

4.2 Active Techniques

To support active data gathering users, while interacting with the prototypes assume an active role and are responsible for providing usage or context information for posterior analysis. This type of data gathering has been widely used on mobile devices, through techniques such as the ESM [4] or Diary Studies [23]. The main medium utilized to gather information with these techniques is questionnaires. For the former, at particular times, users are required to fill-in a questionnaire, responding to questions that pertain to the action that they are performing. On the second (diary studies) users are free to annotate any information that they find relevant such as their location, surroundings, etc. This provides qualitative data regarding the usability of the system that is being used. Naturally, users are usually required to carry paper questionnaires along with them while performing their activity, which often leads to users not remembering to complete the questionnaires or hinders the activity at hands [25]. Moreover, ESM questionnaires are generally directed to specific issues and diary studies are strongly dependent of what users find meaningful, which many times is not what designers are interested in. Here, the digital support plays a key role since questionnaires can be prompted automatically when necessary [26].

To facilitate and enhance these two techniques, the framework supports active data gathering by offering means for designers to create and include, within their prototypes, questionnaires that can be completed by users during in-situ evaluation sessions. Using the same mechanism and interactive elements that are used to build the high-fidelity prototypes, questionnaires can be easily configured to focus the details and goals of the evaluation or target users and include whichever questions designers find relevant.

Tailoring the Experience Sampling Method. Taking advantage of a behavior engine and respective conditions and actions, the framework provides means for designers to define specific conditions or settings in which these questionnaires can or should be presented to users. This technique, if well used, provides support for intelligent ESM and pro-active Diary Studies since usability questionnaires can be prompted according not only to time, but also location or behavior triggers. For instance, if the user misses a specific screen location or button several times, tapping a nearby location, or is taking more than 1 minute to respond to a question, a questionnaire can be automatically popped up. Here the end-user can be requested to explain the reason behind the low accuracy or describe the setting in which s/he was working (e.g., while jogging, seating on the sofa at home). Also, if targeting navigational issues or the application/user interface's structure, questionnaires can be configured to appear when certain cards/screens are reached (e.g., after the "send SMS" interface). Rule/behavior definition is wizard-based and does not require programming knowledge.

Enhanced Data Gathering. The various input and output modalities that the framework offers allow designers to gather data in diverse formats. For instance, when a questionnaire is popped, and in order to allow the user to continue with his/her activity while completing it, instead of typing the answers on the device, these can be given by voice, depending on the user's activity or preference. Besides increasing the flexibility and ease of responding to usability questionnaires it also provides richer data allowing designers to have an idea of the environment in which the user is interacting with the prototype (e.g., quiet/noisy, alone or accompanied by other users). For instance, if the user completes the questionnaire by recording his/her answers with an audio recording element (see figure 1, screen on the right bottom), the surrounding noises can or might also be recorded. Another positive consequence from using several modalities to collect data is the resulting accessibility it provides for users with impairments. For example, if testing a tool for blind users, they can be requested to easily collect usability data by recording thoughts instead of writing.

Furthermore, if needed, users are also able to film or take pictures (whenever the device includes a camera) of the environment in which the activity is taking place or where the usability issue was detected.This contextual information is extremely valuable, providing information on the user's location and the environment and can be used in a posterior analysis relating it with the data that is gathered through logging.

Screen/Card Annotation and Tagging. Text, audio or video (if the device has a microphone or camera) annotations can be added to every screen while using the prototypes. Annotations can store thoughts, opinions or users' impressions, pictures or the usage context, or any other information that the user whishes to collect (e.g., diary studies). The aim is to compensate for the absence of ESM questionnaires that focused a detected issue while the user interacted with the prototype and to allow users to freely provide evaluation data about the usage experience, even if not requested to do so. Screens can be tagged with sequence numbers in-situ and their sequence can be easily modified. This supports contextual card-sorting, adjusting the navigation sequence or desired workflow to the requirements of particular situations.

5 Analysis Tools

The framework includes two different approaches to the analysis of data which are directly correlated with the supported data-gathering techniques.

5.1 ESM/Diary Studies Results

All the data that is gathered by end-users, through ESM, diary studies, annotations and questionnaires can be directly reviewed and browsed on the runtime environment. As seen in figure 2 (middle and right), results of completed questionnaires are stored on the mobile device and can be loaded together with the questionnaires. Interaction logs that are automatically stored can also be consulted directly on the mobile device. All the results are stored in XML files and can also be reviewed in any text editor.

Fig. 3. Log Player – Interaction heat maps on two different approaches for the same tool

5.2 Log Player

In order to evaluate the users' behavior towards the user interface on real scenarios, we intended to replace, as far as possible, direct observation with a similar mechanism. The log player resembles a "movie player" which re-enacts every action that took place while the user was interacting with the prototype (figure 3). Adjusting the speed in which events are (re)played is also possible (e.g., fast-forward; double speed). Events can be played sequentially and according to the time-stamps that were recorded or they can be aggregated and searched by type (e.g., heat maps that show all the taps in a screen or browsing every "next screen" event). Although these logs are limited to direct interaction with the device, they still present enough detail to indicate whether a button needs to be enlarged, if the screen arrangement should be changed or what type of element or modality is preferable in certain situations [26].

The log-player tool also includes a communication module that allows the player to be connected to another mobile device while a user is interacting with a prototype. Here, the logging mechanism forwards every event to the monitoring device, allowing the designer to remotely review, in real-time, the user's interaction with the prototype. For instance, if the prototype is running on a Smart Phone with a GPRS connection or within the range of a Wi-Fi network, the designer is able to monitor and gather data on real-time on the user's interaction with the prototype directly on his/her desktop computer or even another mobile device.

6 Case Studies

The framework has been used to design and evaluate several prototypes on various domains (e.g., psychotherapy, physiotherapy, personal training, education, rich digital books). Throughout this process, both designers and end-users created and used their own prototypes on various locations, gathering data through the various techniques that are supported by the framework. Experiments occurred during the initial stages of design.

In order to assess the benefits of using our framework, and to further improve it, end-users participated in the evaluation sessions in two different stages. In the first stage, traditional [2] and updated techniques [24], focusing on mobile concerns, were used. In the second set of sessions, the framework was used. End-users and designers were interviewed after each session. When using the framework, end-users were also requested to use the included annotation features (and some questionnaires that were included in each prototype) to provide their opinion of the overall experience and suggestions. Designers responded to questionnaires after analyzing the resulting data from the tests that were conducted.

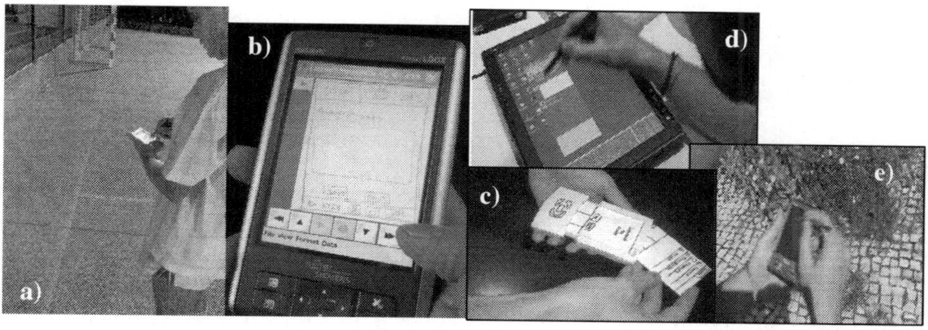

Fig. 4. Users interacting with mobile prototypes on different devices and different settings

A total of 5 designers and 50 end-users with diverse ages and backgrounds were involved in these experiences. From these 50 end-users, around 15 participated in the psychotherapy case study while the remaining were divided by the other experiences. Evaluation sessions took place in several settings (e.g., psychotherapy - therapist's office – fig. 4(d); personal training – soccer field – fig. 4 (a); education – university and gardens fig.4(e)). Different mobile devices were also used (e.g., TabletPCs, PDAs, SmartPhones with and without keyboards).

Throughout the tests that took place with evaluating the framework, the main concern was to understand the differences and advantages, for designers and end-users, between the use of traditional low-fidelity (figure 4(c)) and software prototypes with gathering techniques on the evaluation framework. When traditional techniques were used, paper cards/sketches were changed by a designer, using the WOz technique or by the user, when trying out the prototypes by him/herself. With these low-fidelity prototypes, ESM, end-users' and designers' questionnaires and registries were supported by paper and pen. Some experiments were filmed for posterior analysis and to detect issues that could be improved on the framework.

7 Results – Usability, Accessibility and Multi-modalities

Globally, designers' reactions to the evaluation framework were very positive. The ability to run their prototypes on actual devices (sometimes on the users' devices) was particularly appreciated. As stated by one of the designers:

"Mobile prototypes, especially phones, are very personal devices and users interact with their own differently than when using an unknown device, so seeing and getting usage information of users interacting with their devices was very positive."

ESM questionnaires that could be triggered and configured to request users for information at specific times were also very useful. However, the definition of the triggers and conditions took some time to be easily manipulated by the involved designers. Moreover, the construction of the questionnaires, especially when using audio and video recorders was somewhat difficult to understand and use. When asked about the active data gathering techniques, one of the designers said:

"It's a bit difficult to test sounds and videos on top of the sketches. Initially I also had trouble when creating questionnaires that didn't use text-boxes. The best feature was being able to add questionnaires to each screen and define when and if they should pop up."

Nevertheless, the analysis of the resulting data was stated to be very easy and natural since it followed the same mechanisms used to interact with the prototypes. In particular, the captured videos and photos (albeit very few) gave designers a very clear idea of the context in which users were while using the prototypes.

Experiences with the log-player also led to interesting findings. Usage patterns and the adequacy of some modalities were noticeable while reviewing the logs. For instance, track-bars, although not requiring text input, raised some difficulties mainly given the small size of the interactive counter. Moreover, when completing a task, if users were seated, they usually used the device's QWERTY keyboard (when available). However, once walking they preferred to use the virtual keyboard, using one hand to hold the device and the other to tap on the virtual keyboard, alternating with any other activity that required their hand. Curiously, once seated again, they would not return to the physical keyboard. Also, while walking, accuracy towards buttons was much lower. Audio input was also avoided when users were accompanied. However, audio output was preferred in most situations [26].

Figure 3 shows screenshots of the log player being used to evaluate a low-fidelity prototype for a movie player designed by a teacher during a brainstorming/evaluation session that took place at a public university. The images show the two prototypes being analyzed on the log player. Since all the logs have time-stamps and are cataloged by date, it was simple to correlate the logs and the locations/settings from which they resulted. Moreover, even specific portions of each evaluation session could be identified (e.g., at the beginning of the test, the user was seated; at the end of the evaluation test, the user was walking to another class). These situations were mapped to parts of the log where we noticed different accuracies regarding button selection and interaction, which allowed us to see that most of the missed taps on the screen referred to the situations where users were walking. As expected, while they were seated, accuracy was much higher. However, the log analysis provided a fairly precise idea of the necessary size and location for each button. With the first prototype, the log shows that users had difficulties while using the video controls. With the second version of the same prototype, with larger buttons, accuracy was much higher. Results showed that components placed near screen edges raised usage difficulties, especially when users interacted with their fingers instead of the stylus.

So far, all the involved designers considered the revision of users' behavior, without the need for direct observation, extremely useful. In fact, when combined with the questionnaire results this allowed the detection of several issues which translated directly into UI improvements. Results were particularly interesting since they focused not only on a wide variety of contexts but also allowed the detection of problems that emerged while transiting between contexts. However, interestingly, the most noteworthy and positive results were found when interviewing users.

The use of actual devices and prototypes that could be interacted with and used was very appealing to users and provided a much more tangible and realistic experience, especially when compared to the traditional low-fidelity prototypes.

"I only really understood what they (the designers) were showing us when I was able to use the PDA and the buttons started to actually do something."

Moreover the ability to participate on the prototyping process, even during field tests, was one of the favorite features.

"It was really nice to be able to propose ideas to them and show what would be a better fit for me by drawing it on the mobile device and bringing it to life right there. It made me want to become a designer."

Finally, when designers were able to create questionnaires with different modalities (e.g., video and audio recorders), users provided more and richer data. As commented by most users, this was a reflection of the easiness to speak or photograph when using the prototype instead of stopping and writing thoughts or detected issues.

"Compared with the paper version, it was much easier to record what I had in mind or photograph what was going around than writing it down."

Moreover, as previously mentioned, it allowed users with disabilities (on the rich digital book player case) to test the prototypes since the beginning and to provide usability data as well, regardless of the used device.

Globally, the results of the experiments and on users' opinions validated the positive influence of the prototyping and evaluation framework on the design process. Some of the findings that emerged when using the evaluation and analysis features resulted in modifications that were specific to the domains of each case study while others confirmed generic guidelines that can apply to most mobile devices when used ubiquitously (e.g., element location, content per screen, preferred modalities).

7.1 Design Perspectives and Guidelines

From the design process perspective, we believe the use of the evaluation framework can support and enhance the design of mobile applications and user interfaces. The main reasons and discussion topics that resulted from the case studies and evaluation sessions indicate that:

- Evaluation in-situ provides shorter design cycles. By gathering data, analyzing and adjusting prototypes on the field, designers are able to redefine, adjust concepts or approaches and test them very quickly and directly on the used device.
- Users grasp ideas and concepts better. The use of actual devices and interactive prototypes, that do not depend on the designer to work or change cards, provide a better usage experience and end-users and allows them to understand what designers are trying to convey more quickly.
- Data gathering works better when using multimodalities. Video and voice recording allowed users to quickly register their thoughts, opinions or answer ESM questionnaires without requiring them to stop what they were doing.
- Since data gathering is easier, users provide richer data. When compared with initial experiences using traditional techniques, users collected much more data.

The ability to film/photograph brings great benefits. Capturing a video or taking a photo of the surrounding environment is much easier than writing down a description of the user's context and provides much more detail.

- Intelligent ESM provides means to focus different or specific details. The ability to detect the user's activities and define questionnaires that can be displayed according to the user's behavior allows designers to focus key issues (e.g., user takes too long when viewing a screen or frequently misses a button).
- Automatic Wizard-of-Oz facilitates designer's work and reduces the need to follow or ask users to change the screens/cards by themselves, facilitating the process and, once again, providing better and more realistic usage experiences.
- Logging provides information on various details for low and high-fidelity prototypes. Furthermore, the ability to review how users interact with a prototype provides paramount information regarding usability issues.
- Overall, since it requires no programming knowledge the framework allowed users to actively participate on the evaluation, creating and adjusting their own prototypes, providing a softer and sounder transition between design fidelities.

8 Conclusions and Further Research Directions

This paper presented extensions to a framework which aim at taking advantage of some emerging techniques by offering support for in-situ mobile evaluation. The framework includes several methods and approaches into tools that support and integrate prototyping and evaluation, providing a tighter fit between these two stages and resulting in shorter design cycles on the initial design stages.

The experiences and case studies in which the tools were used confirmed the benefits that it provides for the design of mobile applications and user interfaces, especially during the initial stages of design. Besides facilitating the gathering of data on ubiquitous settings, it promoted user involvement and provided better and more realistic usage experiences which resulted in richer evaluation and field sessions.

Although we do not aim at replacing direct user observation or other contextual techniques, we believe that the presented framework can play an important part on the quick design and testing of design concepts and user interfaces. The encountered limitations, especially the development of ESM questionnaires and their integration within the prototypes, will be the focus of further evaluation and adjustments.

Finally, we are integrating the framework into a new group version which includes a large screen display module where several logs can be seen simultaneously. It enables teams to review logs simultaneously, comparing a user or a prototype's performance in various settings. The group log player also allows designers to monitor several users, even detecting interactions between each other. These will allow for the evaluation of team work and collaboration within mobile settings.

References

1. Barnard, et al.: Capturing the effects of context on human performance in mobile computing systems. Personal and Ubiquitous Computing 11(46)
2. Beyer, H., Holtzblatt, K.: Contextual Design: Customer Centered Approach to Systems Design. Academic Press, San Francisco (1998)

3. Carter, S., et al.: Momento:Support for Situated Ubicomp Experimentation. In: CHI 2007. ACM, New York (2007)
4. Consolvo, S., Walker, M.: Using the Experience Sampling Method to Evaluate Ubicomp Applications. IEEE Pervasive Computing, 2003 2(2), 24–31 (2003)
5. Costabile, M.F., Fogli, D., et al.: Building Environments for End-User Development and Tailoring. In: IEEE Symposia on Human Centric Computing Languages and Environmnets (2003)
6. Davis, R., et al.: SketchWizard: Wizard of Oz Prototyping of Pen-Based User Interfaces. In: Procs. UIST 2007. ACM Press, New York (2007)
7. Duh, H., et al.: Usability Evaluation for Mobile Device: A Comparison of Laboratory and Field Tests. In: Mobile HCI 2006. ACM Press, New York (2006)
8. Froehlich, J., et al.: MyExperience: A System for In Situ Tracing and Capturing of User Feedback on Mobile Phones. In: MobiSys 2007, pp. 57–70. ACM Press, New York (2007)
9. Holmquist, L.: Prototyping:generating ideas or cargo cult designs?Interactions. ACM Press, New York (2005)
10. Jones, M., Marsden, G.: Mobile Interaction Design. John Wiley & Sons, England (2006)
11. Kjeldskov, J., Stage, J.: New Techniques for Usability Evaluation of Mobile Systems. International Journal of Human Computer Studies (2003)
12. Kjeldskov, J., Graham, C.: A Review of Mobile HCI Research Methods. In: Chittaro, L. (ed.) Mobile HCI 2003. LNCS, vol. 2795, pp. 317–335. Springer, Heidelberg (2003)
13. Klemmer, S.R., et al.: SUEDE: A Wizard of Oz Prototyping Tool for Speech User Interfaces. In: Proc. of UIST 2000, San Diego, California, USA, pp. 1–10. ACM Press, New York (2000)
14. Landay, J.: SILK: Sketching Interfaces Like Krazy. In: CHI 1996, pp. 398–399. ACM Press, New York (1996)
15. Li, Y., Hong, J., Landay, J.: Topiary - Design Challenges and Principles for Wizard of Oz Testing of Location-Enhanced Applications. In: Pervasive Computing, pp. 70–75. IEEE Press, Los Alamitos (2007)
16. Lin, J., et al.: Denim: Finding a Tighter Fit Between Tools and Practice for Web Site Design. In: CHI 2000. ACM, New York (2000)
17. Nielsen, C.M., et al.: It's Worth the Hassle! The Added Value of Evaluating the Usability of Mobile Systems in the Field. In: NordiCHI 2006. ACM Press, New York (2006)
18. Oulasvirta, A., Nyyssönen, T.: Flexible hardware configurations for studying mobile usability. Journal of Usability Studies (in press)
19. Sá, M., Carriço, L.: Low-fi Prototyping for Mobile Devices. In: CHI 2006, pp. 694–699. ACM Press, New York (2006)
20. Svanaes, D., Seland, G.: Putting the users center stage: role playing and low-fi prototyping enable end users to design mobile systems. In: Procs. CHI 2004, Austria. ACM Press, New York (2004)
21. Scholtz, J., Consolvo, S.: Toward a framework for evaluating ubiquitous computing applications. IEEE Pervasive Computing 2, 82–86 (2004)
22. Sohn, T., Li, K.A., Griswold, W.G., Hollan, J.D.: A diary study of mobile information needs. In: Procs. CHI 2008, Florence, Italy, ACM Press, New York (2008)
23. Thompson, K.E., Rozanski, E.P., Haake, A.R.: Here, there, anywhere: Remote usability testing that works. In: Proceedings of SIGITE 2004, Salt Lake City, USA. ACM Press, New York (2004)
24. Sá, M., Carriço, L.: Lessons from Early Stages Design of Mobile Applications. In: MobileHCI 2008, pp. 127–136. ACM Press, New York (2008)
25. Sá, M., et al.: A Mixed-Fidelity Prototyping Tool for Mobile Devices. In: AVI 2008, pp. 225–232. ACM Press, New York (2008)
26. Sá, M., et al.: A Framework for Mobile Evaluation. In: CHI 2008 (extended abstracts), pp. 2673–2678. ACM Press, New York (2008)

Exploring Cross-Device Web Use on PCs and Mobile Devices

Shaun K. Kane[1], Amy K. Karlson[2], Brian R. Meyers[2], Paul Johns[2], Andy Jacobs[2], and Greg Smith[2]

[1] The Information School, DUB Group, University of Washington, Seattle, WA 98195 USA
skane@u.washington.edu
[2] Microsoft Research, One Microsoft Way, Redmond, WA 98052 USA
{karlson,brianme,pauljoh,andyj,gregsmi}@microsoft.com

Abstract. In this paper, we explore whether sharing a user's web browsing activity across their computing devices can make it easier to find and access web sites on a mobile device. We first surveyed 175 smartphone users about their web use across multiple devices. We found that users shared web information between devices, but generally used cumbersome manual methods to do so. In a second study, we tracked the web sites visited by 14 participants on their PC and mobile phone, and used experience-sampling surveys to determine whether sharing sites across devices would be useful. We found that participants visited many of the same sites on both their mobile device and PC, and that participants were interested in viewing additional sites from their PC on their mobile device. Our results suggest that automatically sharing web activity information between devices has potential to improve the usability of the mobile web.

Keywords: Mobile web, cross-device user experience, activity logging, experience sampling method.

1 Introduction

Mobile web browsers have become a common feature of many smartphones and mobile devices. While some earlier mobile devices supported only specially formatted mobile web pages, many current mobile devices offer full-featured web browsers that allow access to any web page. These mobile web browsers provide users with the ability to quickly look up facts, exchange messages with friends, read news articles, find maps or directions, and access other information from anywhere and at any time.

Despite the benefits of mobile web access, mobile web usability is fundamentally limited by the constraints of the user's mobile device. Mobile devices typically have slow connections, small screens, and tiny keyboards. One particular challenge to using the mobile web is the difficulty of navigating to new web sites. Entering a web site address on a mobile device requires the user to type a significant amount of text on a small mobile device keyboard, which can be slow and error prone. This presents an obstacle to visiting new sites on the mobile web. Therefore, making it easier for mobile web users to access web pages has the potential to substantially improve the user experience of web browsing on mobile devices.

T. Gross et al. (Eds.): INTERACT 2009, Part I, LNCS 5726, pp. 722–735, 2009.

One approach to improving access to mobile web sites is to automatically suggest web pages that a user might wish to visit. Prior research has shown that a user's context, such as their location, can be a useful predictor of their information needs [1]. Prior mobile search prototypes have used location information to auto-complete mobile search queries and improve search efficiency [2]. However, this previous work has focused primarily on a single type of context—location—and has ignored other sources of contextual information. In this paper we introduce a new source of context to enrich the mobile web browsing experience: the web activities that a user performs on their other devices, including their home and work PCs. Examining a user's web activity on these other devices may reveal which sites they frequently visit, what topics they are currently interested in, or what activities they are planning.

To understand how PC and mobile web browsing are connected, we performed two studies with current mobile web users. In the first study, we surveyed 175 smartphone users about their web browsing habits. We found that users sometimes shared information between their devices, but generally did so using manual methods such as emailing themselves or copying URLs on paper. In a second study, we used activity-logging software to determine whether users viewed the same sites on their mobile devices as on their PCs. We also used experience-sampling surveys to ask participants whether specific web pages from their PC browsing history would be useful on their mobile device. We found that 75.4% of the domains that participants visited on their mobile devices were also visited on their PC, and that 17.4% of the PC web pages suggested in surveys would also be useful on the participant's mobile device. Overall, our results offer strong evidence that users' web browsing activities may be similar across their desktops, laptops and mobile devices. These results suggest that supporting web activities across multiple devices can reduce barriers to accessing web content when using constrained mobile device interfaces.

2 Related Work

2.1 Mobile Web Use

Prior studies have shown that users' mobile web needs and behaviors are closely related to their current activities and context. Sohn et al. [3] used mobile surveys to capture users' information needs while using their mobile devices, and found that users had a variety of information needs which were often driven by their current context. Demumieux and Losquin [4] installed a logging application on users' mobile phones, and found that users performed a variety of information activities on their mobile devices. Cui and Roto [5] examined users' mobile web access logs, and found that mobile web use could be classified into four categories: information seeking, communication, transactions, and personal space extension. Lee et al. [6] conducted a diary study in which users documented their experiences when using the mobile web, and found that users viewed a variety of sites in a variety of contexts. Other studies [7, 8] have identified mobile search patterns from web search query logs. Our research adopts a different perspective than these prior studies by exploring the relationship between users' web browsing activities and information needs on both a PC and a mobile device simultaneously.

Some research projects have leveraged the contextual nature of mobile web use to provide easier access to the mobile web, such as by dynamically suggesting web sites based on a user's context or stated interests. Kamvar and Baluja [2] developed a mobile search page that used location information to predict and auto-complete mobile search queries. Cohen et al. [9] developed a personalized pocket directory that allowed users to select categories of interest, and then populated these categories with suggested sites from a public web site directory. Panayiotou and Samaras [10] developed a personalized web portal that considered users' preferred topics and location, and then automatically downloaded relevant web sites. Our research extends this prior work by exploring how a user's web activity on other devices can be used to suggest web sites on a mobile device.

2.2 Computing on Multiple Devices

Recent studies by Oulasvirta and Sumari [11] and Dearman and Pierce [12] examined how knowledge workers perform tasks that span multiple devices. Knowledge workers may use a combination of desktops, laptops, and mobile devices to perform tasks throughout the day. These studies suggest that managing information across devices can be difficult, and recommend that designers provide better tools for sharing and synchronizing information across users' devices. These studies did not explore issues specific to web use as we do here.

Other projects have investigated the usefulness of syncing web information between devices. WebPod [13] used a portable USB storage device to share a user's browsing session, including open windows, web history, and bookmarks, between PCs. Mozilla Weave[1] performs a similar function over the network, allowing a user to resume a browsing session on a different PC. However, prior work has not fully explored what types of web information are most useful to share between PCs and mobile devices. Our research therefore attempts to identify which, if any, web information would be useful to share between a user's various devices, taking into account differences in how each device is used.

3 Study 1: A Survey of Multi-device Web Use

Is sharing web information between devices useful? To answer this question, we investigated whether users currently share web information between their devices, and what methods they use to do so. We conducted a survey of current smartphone users that focused on their present-day web usage habits on their PCs and mobile devices.

3.1 Method

Informants. We recruited 175 (146 male, 29 female) mobile phone users with a mean age of 36 years (Standard Deviation, *SD*=7.3). All informants were employees at a

[1] http://labs.mozilla.com/projects/weave/

technology company and used the web frequently on their mobile phones. Informants were randomly selected from a list of company employees, and were recruited via email. Informants who completed the survey were entered into a prize drawing.

Procedure. Informants completed a web-based survey from their home or office. The survey covered topics such as the types of web sites that they visited on their PCs and mobile devices, how they shared information between devices, and difficulties they encountered in using the web on their mobile devices. Completing the survey took between 15 and 30 minutes. Survey responses were stored in a database, and were later analyzed using Microsoft Excel.

3.2 Results

Web Browsing on PCs and Mobile Devices. Our informants' browsing habits differed considerably between their devices. Informants visited many more web sites on their PCs than on their mobile devices. The majority of informants (64.6%) viewed more than 10 web sites per day on their PC, while most informants (85.1%) viewed 5 or fewer sites per day on their mobile device.

We were also interested in how mobile web users accessed web sites on their mobile devices. Informants reported that they used bookmarks much more frequently than they typed in URLs. Most informants (59.4%) used bookmarks stored on their phone to load pages at least several times per week, and 28.6% used these bookmarks daily. In contrast, 41.7% of informants manually entered URLs several times per week, and only 14.3% manually entered URLs daily. Overall, we found that informants generally used bookmarks or links to access web content on their mobile device (Fig. 1), which is unsurprising given the difficulty of mobile text entry.

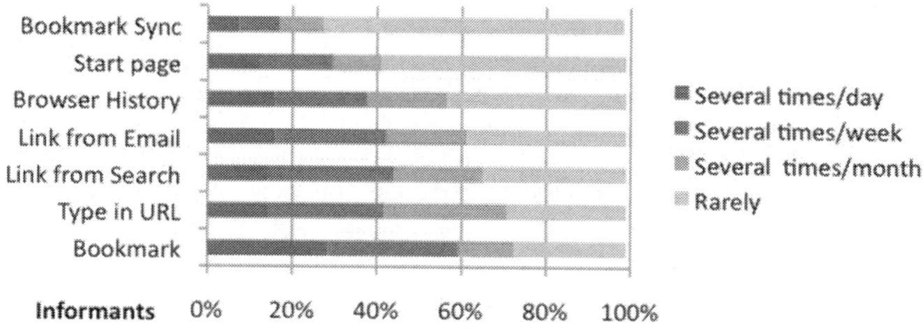

Fig. 1. Common methods used by our informants to load web pages on their mobile devices

Finally, we were interested in what types of sites informants viewed on their devices. We asked informants which categories of sites they viewed on each of their devices, using site categories adapted from prior research [14]. Informants viewed many different categories of sites on both devices, although they viewed more diverse categories on their PCs (Fig. 2).

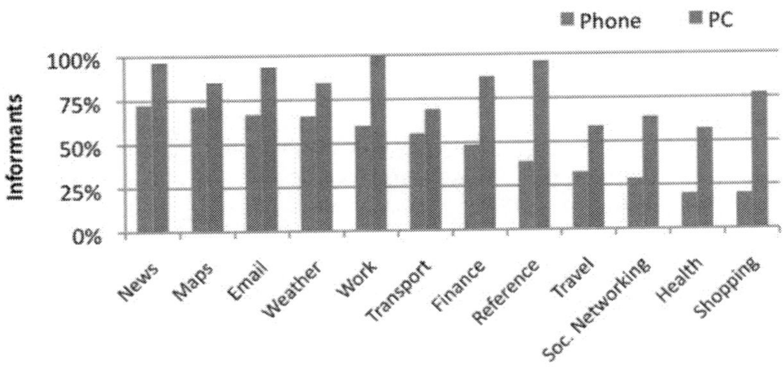

Fig. 2. Categories of web sites that our informants viewed regularly on their PCs and mobile devices

Transferring Information Between Devices. Many of our informants transferred web information between their PCs and mobile devices, but often used cumbersome manual methods to do so. Most informants (80.0%) did not use bookmark synchronization software, but instead emailed information to themselves (69.0%), or typed in a URL directly after writing it down or making a mental note (65.1%). This reliance on manual methods is surprising given that the vast majority of our informants used either Windows Mobile Smartphones (88.0%) or iPhones (7.4%), both of which offer automatic bookmark synchronization between devices. This result suggests that current synchronization services are not satisfactory and are mostly not used.

Informants also indicated the major difficulties that they encountered while browsing the web on their mobile devices. Poor web page layout (60.0%), small screen size (58.9%), poor network connections (47.4%), and difficulty entering text (45.7%) were informants' most common complaints about their current mobile web experience.

In conclusion, while informants did use the mobile web, their use was limited compared to their web use on the PC. Informants viewed relatively few sites on their mobile phones, and manually entered new URLs rarely (Fig. 1). Informants sometimes transferred information between their devices, but generally used cumbersome manual methods to do so.

4 Study 2: Logging Web Activity on Multiple Devices

Our survey revealed that mobile web users frequently share web information between devices, but generally do so by hand. Mobile web users might therefore benefit from techniques that enable easier sharing of web information between devices. However, our survey did not ask informants about the specific sites that they visited on each device, nor did it ask what additional sites informants would like to see on their mobile device. Therefore, we conducted a second study that focused on these issues.

This study was based on two primary research questions. First, are the web pages that users visit on their PCs related to the pages that they visit on their mobile devices? We used activity-logging software to capture the web pages visited by our participants on their PCs and mobile devices. This allowed us to capture much more detailed information than could be gathered through self-report. Then, we examined the URLs of web pages visited by participants on each device, and measured the degree to which these pages overlap.

Our second research question was: Are users interested in accessing web pages that they have previously viewed on their PC when using their mobile device? We used web surveys to ask whether participants were interested in viewing specific web pages, selected from their PC web browsing history, on their mobile device. Surveys were deployed using the experience-sampling method (ESM) [15], so that participants received surveys when they were away from their desk and likely to be carrying their mobile device. These surveys allowed us to explore which, if any, URLs from participants' PC browsing history would be useful on their mobile device.

4.1 Method

Participants. We recruited 14 participants (11 male, 3 female), with an average age of 33.2 years (*SD*=4.2). Participants were recruited through internal mailing lists at a technology company. All participants used Windows Mobile Smartphones and used the web browser on their phone for at least ten minutes per day. Participants were compensated for installing the software and for each week of participation. Participants were given additional compensation for completing more than 60% of the ESM surveys.

Apparatus. We installed web activity-logging applications on participants' work PCs and smartphones. On the PC, we installed PersonalVibe [16], a desktop activity-logging application that runs in the background of a Windows-based PC and records a user's activities. PersonalVibe generated a log of web page URLs, page titles, and view durations for every web page visited by each participant. On the mobile phone, we installed a new Windows Mobile activity-logging application, which also recorded a time-stamped log entry for each URL visited by the user from their phone. Logs were automatically uploaded daily to a central database.

We also deployed ESM surveys that asked participants whether specific URLs from their PC browsing history would be useful on their mobile device. Survey requests were sent by SMS or email, and included a link to a web-based survey page. This survey page asked participants to "check all of the web sites that would be interesting or useful to have on [their] phone today" (Fig. 3). Because it would require too much time to ask participants about every URL that they viewed, our survey software generated lists of 25 URLs per survey. However, it was not immediately clear how we should select pages to include in surveys, as we did not know which sites would be most useful to participants. Would participants prefer sites that they had viewed recently on their PC, or would they be interested in sites that they viewed most often on the PC? In order to answer this question, we developed a set of queries that were used to select pages from the web activity logs. These queries were intended to expose different aspects of web activity on the PC, including recently visited pages and frequently visited pages. Five queries were used to populate the surveys:

1. *Recently Visited.* Most recently visited web pages, ordered by time of the most recent visit.
2. *Frequently Visited.* Pages visited most frequently in the last 7 days, ordered by the number of visits.

3. *Search and Maps.* A combination of recent web search queries and map searches, ordered chronologically. Search and map sites were combined due to the low number of items in these data sets.
4. *Longest Viewed.* Pages viewed for the longest duration in the last 7 days, ordered by total time spent viewing the page.
5. *Grab Bag.* Randomly selected pages from PersonalVibe's web activity log.

Each survey contained the top 25 URLs from one of the five queries listed above, presented as a randomly ordered list (Fig. 3, left). Query order was counterbalanced such that participants received surveys from each query at different times per day. In addition to the surveys, we installed a bookmark in participants' mobile browsers that allowed them to view the top 10 items from each query as a web portal page (Fig. 3, right). This gave participants the opportunity to explore the URLs suggested in the surveys, although they were not required to do so.

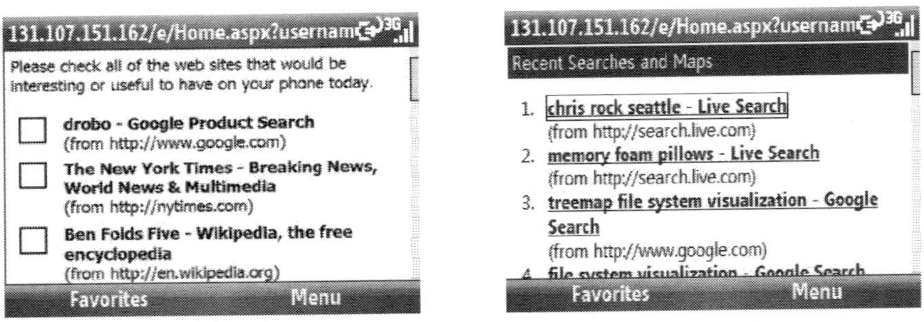

Fig. 3. Left: Example ESM survey on a Windows Mobile Smartphone. Right: Web portal view.

Adjustment to Data. In initial testing we discovered that the raw web activity logs contained pages that the participant did not intentionally visit, such as web page redirects. For this reason, web pages that the participant visited for less than 5 seconds were excluded from the web activity log. We also excluded intranet sites from the web activity logs, as these sites could not be reliably accessed by mobile devices.

Procedure. During the first week of the study, participants were instructed to go about their normal activities while the logging applications recorded their actions. Participants were aware that their computer and phone use was being monitored during this time, but we did not reveal our particular interest in web browsing.

After 7 consecutive days of activity logging, participants began receiving ESM survey requests. Participants received up to 6 survey requests per day. Survey requests were sent when PersonalVibe detected inactivity at the user's PC, indicating that the participant might be away from his or her desk, and therefore more likely to use their mobile browser. At this time, we also installed the web portal bookmark. Participants were never required to visit the portal page, although the survey web page did contain a link to the portal. Although we collected activity data during this second week, our analysis contains activity from the first week only, as participants' behavior might have changed once the surveys began.

Due to scheduling constraints, participants began the survey period on different days of the week, but always began on a weekday. Participants received survey requests for approximately 7 days, including weekends.

4.2 Results

Comparing Web Activity across Devices. During the logging period of the field study, we logged 15208 web page visits to 8087 unique URLs by 14 participants. As we found in the initial survey, log data revealed that participants browsed many more pages on their PCs than on their smartphones. Overall, participants made 10549 page visits on their PCs and 4659 on their smartphones. On the days they used their computer, participants visited a median of 71.5 pages (μ = 94.2) on their PC, including repeat visits. Participants visited a median of 25.0 (μ = 32.8) pages on their mobile device per day, including repeat visits.

Overall, participants generally visited different web pages on each of their devices, but visited many of the same web domains on both devices. Examining the overlap between devices, we found that participants visited a median of 73.7% (μ = 72.4%) of pages only on their PC, and 21.2% (μ = 23.2%) of pages only on their phone. The rest of the pages were visited on both devices. Of all pages visited on the PC, a median of 1.1% (μ = 2.0%) of pages were also visited on the mobile device. Of all pages visited on the mobile device, a median of 7.8% (μ = 10.5%) of pages were also visited on the PC. In examining this seemingly low overlap, we discovered that 82.8% of the 2216 unique pages viewed on a mobile device were mobile-formatted web pages. Therefore, even if participants viewed the same content on both their phone and their PC, the URLs would be different on each device, resulting in a low overlap. To account for this discrepancy, we manually mapped the URLs visited on the phone into the equivalent desktop web domain. We then measured the overlap between the mapped mobile domains and the original desktop domains to determine how often participants viewed information from the same web domain on both devices. Thus, if a participant read an MSNBC news article on their PC and then later read a different MSNBC article on their phone, we considered that a domain overlap, even if the page URL was not the same or if the phone was redirected to a mobile version of the MSNBC site. Using this metric, we found that a median of 75.4% (μ = 63.2%) of the domains visited on the phone were also visited on the PC, and a median of 13.1% (μ = 14.1%) of the domains visited on the PC were also visited on the phone.

Prior work has shown that PC users often revisit web pages throughout the course of a day [17], and we wished to see whether this effect was similar across devices. We found that a median of 36.7% page visits per day were revisits to pages viewed earlier in the same day. Examining each device separately showed that revisitation patterns were consistent across devices, with a median of 32.3% revisits per day on the PC and a median of 32.2% revisits on the mobile device. We also found 32 instances in which a URL was visited on one device, and then visited on the same day on the other device.

Due to the focus of this study, we did not collect detailed information about the content of sites that users visited, or about more complex revisitation patterns between devices. These analyses present a promising direction for future work.

ESM Survey Results. Our 14 participants completed a total of 411 surveys, with each participant completing a mean of 3.3 surveys per day (*SD*=1.0). During the survey period, participants performed a total of 9777 ratings of 3073 web pages. Of the 9777 pages suggested to any participant, 1288 (13.2%) were rated as being useful. On average, each participant performed 698.4 (*SD*=222.9) page ratings, and rated 92.0 (*SD*=71.4) of the suggested web pages as useful. Because we sometimes asked participants about a web page multiple times, it was possible that a participant would rate a page as useful in one instance, but not in another. This count, as presented above, is a conservative estimate of how many pages would be useful on the phone. Looking across surveys, participants rated a median of 192 distinct web pages each, and rated 33.5, or 17.4%, of these as useful at least once.

Although this overall usefulness rating is somewhat low, comparing the different queries used to populate the surveys shows that certain types of web information were perceived as more useful. We calculated an average usefulness rating for each of the five queries, grouped by participant, and evaluated these average ratings using a non-parametric Friedman test. This test showed a significant difference between the usefulness ratings of the different query types ($\chi 2_{(4,N=14)} = 18.17$, p=.001). A post-hoc pairwise Wilcoxon test, using Holm's sequential Bonferroni procedure [18], revealed no pairwise differences. However, looking only at the top 5 items from each query, we found that the Frequently Visited pages and Longest Viewed pages were significantly more useful than Search and Maps or Grab Bag pages, all at $p < 0.01$ (Fig. 5). Recommendations from participants' top 5 most Frequently Visited pages on the PC were useful 30% of the time, suggesting that optimizing these queries or allowing users to customize their own queries could produce a higher percentage of useful pages.

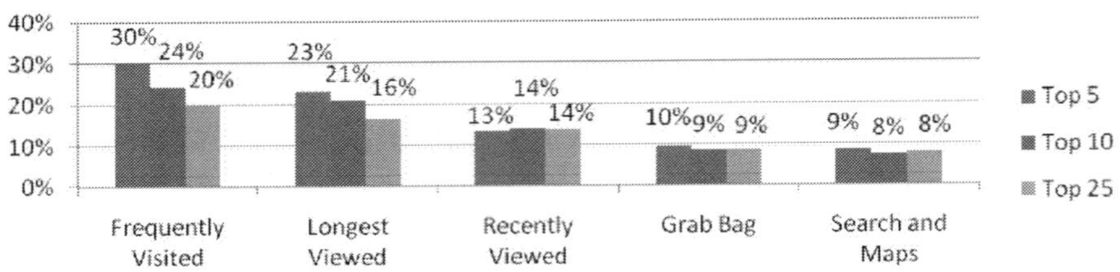

Fig. 4. Percentage of web pages rated as useful from each query type, averaged across participants. Higher is better.

We also looked at the categories of pages that paticipants rated as useful in the ESM surveys. We coded these pages manually using a modified version of the coding scheme used in Study 1 (as shown in Fig. 2)[2]. Overall, participants found News and Reference pages to be useful most often, but also found many Search, Shopping, and Social Networking pages to be useful. The number of pages chosen from each category are shown in Figure 5.

[2] The "Work" category from the original classification scheme was difficult to categorize without knowing details of the participants' work, and so we excluded this category. We added additional categories for Search and Entertainment based on examination of the data.

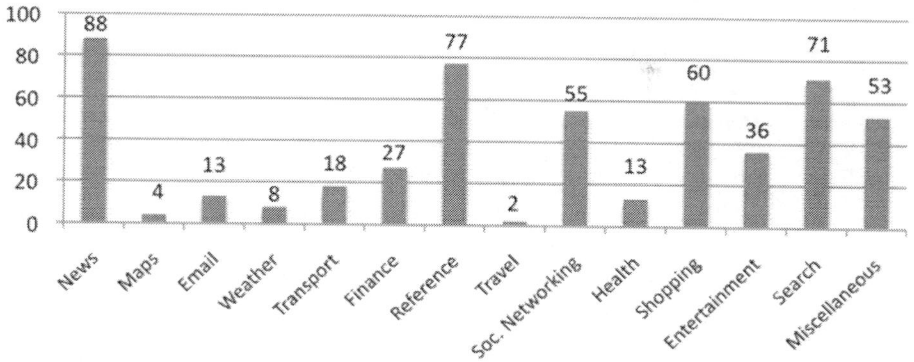

Fig. 5. Categories of the web pages that participants rated as useful in the ESM surveys. Categories were coded manually by the researchers.

In addition to completing the surveys, some participants also viewed the web portal page during the study, albeit rarely. Participants viewed the portal page a total of 110 times during the study, and clicked through to a destination page a total of 42 times. Overall, participants followed a link from the web portal on 38.8% of their visits. This suggests that participants are curious about the information presented by the portal, and might use such a portal if it were presented in a usable format.

Follow-up Survey. Eleven of the study participants (10 male, 1 female) with an average age of 33.4 years (*SD*=4.6) completed a web-based questionnaire that explored their responses to the ESM surveys. Participants were shown a list of web pages that they rated in surveys and were asked to describe why they rated the pages as useful or not useful. Their answers are summarized in Table 1. Pages were most often useful on a mobile device when they were updated frequently with new content, and were not useful if the page was difficult to view on the mobile device or if the participant was "finished" with that page.

Each participant was also presented with a subset of 10 pages that they had rated as useful in at least one of the ESM surveys. Participants were asked to rate how useful each page was on a 5-point Likert scale (1=Very useful, 2=Somewhat useful, 3=Neutral, 4=Somewhat useless, 5=Very useless), and asked whether they had bookmarked the page on their phone either before or during the study. Among pages that the participants had rated as useful, the mean usefulness rating was 2.48 (*SD*=0.8), 10.9% of these pages were already bookmarked prior to the study, and 10.0% were bookmarked during the study. Thus, while the pages varied in their overall usefulness, almost 90% of the pages that participants did find useful had not been bookmarked previously on the phone, suggesting that they would have been difficult to access without sharing URLs from the PC.

Table 1. Reasons why suggested web pages from the PC were/were not useful to participants

Reasons pages were useful	Ppts
Interested in tracking page updates	7
Useful when away from the PC	4
Interested in viewing later	2
Interested in sharing with friends	1

Reasons pages were not useful	Ppts
Poor rendering on mobile device	7
Page content only needed once	6
Page content useful only occasionally	2
Already use another version on phone	1

5 Discussion

Our work here focused on one specific challenge to mobile web browsing: the limited input capability of mobile devices. The severity of this issue was confirmed in our first study: nearly half (45.0%) of our survey informants said that entering URLs was a significant problem. We found that informants accessed web pages using direct-link strategies, such as bookmarks, more often than they entered URLs manually. In addition, informants reported visiting fewer web pages on the phone than on the PC. These results suggest that mobile browser enhancements that help users find and navigate to web pages could remove one of the barriers to the use of the mobile web. We have proposed addressing this problem by using information from a user's other devices to improve their experience on a mobile device. Since users frequently divide their work among multiple devices [11], combining information from these devices could yield useful information about users' habits and activities. This may be especially helpful when considering mobile devices, as a user's interactions with a PC, which are relatively unconstrained by input barriers, can be used to provide suggestions or predictions on a mobile device, where input is considerably more difficult.

Results from our second study confirm that sharing web information between devices is a promising strategy. First, our activity logs showed that most of the web domains that participants viewed on their mobile phones were also viewed on their PC. This indicates that users often consult the same information sources across all of their devices. Providing easier access to a user's common information sources might therefore improve usability across devices. Second, during the ESM survey period, participants found 17.4% of the web pages suggested from the PC browsing history to be useful, even though most of these pages had not been previously bookmarked on the phone. We take this number as a conservative estimate of the utility of shared URLs, as participants noted in post-survey feedback that they had marked many pages as not useful because of formatting concerns, and because some of suggested pages, such as frequently visited pages, were found to be considerably more useful than this average rate. Improving the queries used to select URLs from the PC, either through further experimentation or machine learning, could substantially improve the value of the shared URLs. We conclude from this evidence that a well-chosen subset of URLs from a user's PC can serve as a valuable launch point for a mobile web browser.

One remaining problem is how to select web pages from a PC to share with a mobile device. Improving our understanding of how mobile web users might utilize shared URLs will help us to identify when certain URLs will be useful. Our preliminary results suggest that users may in fact have multiple strategies for using shared URLs. For example, during the follow-up survey, 2 participants mentioned that they used their mobile device to look back at pages that they had already visited on the PC, either to finish reading an article or to look up information about a product that they were intending to purchase. Based on these comments, we might expect that mobile device users would like to revisit pages that they had previously seen on the PC. However, other participants noted that they had rated previously visited pages as not useful because they had already finished reading them. This suggests at least two possible uses for this proposed system: referring back to prior pages, and suggesting new pages or articles based on past history. Additional work is needed to understand the ways in which mobile device owners might use shared URLs, and how technology can support these multiple uses.

It is also important to consider that there may be some usability issues surrounding the integration of work, home, and mobile information spaces. In this study, we instrumented participants' work PCs, and linked this information with their personal mobile devices. In several cases, participants mentioned that they were not interested in having work-related URLs on their phone, although this was not always the case. Although we believe that sharing web information between devices will have a net benefit, future work in this area should explore ways to allow users to partition work and home life.

Finally, it is worth noting that participants frequently encountered difficulties when accessing web pages due to poor formatting on their mobile device screen. This issue can often be addressed by using specially formatted mobile pages, which most participants used, or by using mobile web transcoding sites such as Skweezer[3], which were used only by a few participants in our study. Properly formatting mobile web pages remains a significant problem, and technologies that attempt to improve mobile web browsing should consider providing options for reformatting web content for small screens.

6 Future Work

We identify two primary areas for extending this work. First, we intend to use the logging infrastructure that we developed in this study to explore other aspects of cross-device interaction. We have already begun to use this data to explore temporal patterns of use between devices [19]. We might extend this investigation to look at the content of web pages and how they relate across devices, or to include other information tasks such as e-mail and calendar use. We might also compare this data to other contextual features, such as a user's location or the time of day, in order to reveal deeper patterns of cross-device use. Finally, in this study we were only able to instrument participants' mobile devices and work PCs. Extending this research to include home PCs and other devices may reveal interesting interactions between home, work, and mobile devices.

We are also interested in exploring the development of tools that support mobile web use by sharing web history information between devices. In this study we considered how URLs themselves could be shared, but there are many other ways in which this information could be used to enrich mobile web browsing. Information about a user's web activities on other devices could be used to suggest or complete

[3] http://www.skweezer.com/

search queries, provide maps and directions, or recommend reading material during a long trip. Combining web history information with knowledge of a user's context presents further possibilities. For example, a mobile phone application might detect that the user is at a hardware store and present a summary of her recent searches related to home improvement. The infrastructure that we developed for this study will allow us to explore multiple possible designs for such a tool.

7 Conclusion

As mobile devices gain larger screens and faster network connections, they will increasingly be used to search and browse the mobile web. While advances in hardware are improving the mobile web user experience, interaction with the mobile web remains constrained by the limited input capabilities of mobile devices.

In this paper, we have proposed sharing information about a user's activities across multiple devices to improve interactions with a mobile device. This technique allows users to leverage the improved input capabilities of desktop and laptop PCs, and to potentially reduce input effort when interacting with a mobile device. The studies described in this paper have focused on sharing web page URLs, but this strategy may generalize to other types of information as well.

The studies presented here provide strong support for sharing web information between PCs and mobile devices. Our survey of 175 smartphone users showed that users already share web information between devices, but rely on cumbersome methods to do so. Our second study showed that many of the web sites that users visit on their mobile devices are also visited on their PCs, and that some additional sites that are visited on the PC only would be considered useful on a mobile device. These results suggest that, even with existing mobile web browsers, sharing specific web information between devices can improve the usability of the mobile web by allowing users to more easily access interesting and useful web sites while on the go.

Acknowledgements. We thank A.J. Brush and Gina Venolia for their assistance in planning the two studies.

References

1. Church, K., Smyth, B.: Understanding Mobile Information Needs. In: MobileHCI 2008, pp. 493–494. ACM Press, New York (2008)
2. Kamvar, M., Baluja, S.: The Role Of Context in Query Input: Using Contextual Signals to Complete Queries on Mobile Devices. In: MobileHCI 2007, pp. 405–412. ACM Press, New York (2007)
3. Sohn, T., Li, K.A., Griswold, W.G., Hollan, J.D.: A Diary Study of Mobile Information Needs. In: CHI 2008, pp. 433–442. ACM Press, New York (2008)
4. Demumieux, R., Losquin, P.: Gather Customer's Real Usage on Mobile Phones. In: MobileHCI 2005, pp. 267–270. ACM Press, New York (2005)
5. Cui, Y., Roto, V.: How People Use the Web on Mobile Devices. In: WWW 2008, pp. 905–914. ACM Press, New York (2008)

6. Lee, I., Kim, J., Kim, J.: Use Contexts for the Mobile Internet: A Longitudinal Study Monitoring Actual Use of Mobile Internet Services. International Journal of Human-Computer Interaction 18(3), 269–292 (2005)
7. Church, K., Smyth, B., Bradley, K., Cotter, P.: A Large Scale Study of European Mobile Search Behaviour. In: MobileHCI 2008, pp. 13–22. ACM Press, New York (2008)
8. Kamvar, M., Baluja, S.: A Large Scale Study Of Wireless Search Behavior: Google Mobile Search. In: CHI 2006, pp. 701–709. ACM Press, New York (2006)
9. Cohen, D., Herscovici, M., Petruschka, Y., Maarek, Y.S., Soffer, A.: Personalized Pocket Directories for Mobile Devices. In: WWW 2002, pp. 627–638. ACM Press, New York (2002)
10. Panayiotou, C., Samaras, G.: mPERSONA: Personalized Portals for the Wireless User: An Agent Approach. Mobile Networks and Applications 9(6), 663–677 (2004)
11. Oulasvirta, A., Sumari, L.: Mobile Kits and Laptop Trays: Managing Multiple Devices in Mobile Information Work. In: CHI 2007, pp. 1127–1136. ACM Press, New York (2007)
12. Dearman, D., Pierce, J.S.: "It's on My Other Computer!": Computing with Multiple Devices. In: CHI 2008, pp. 767–776. ACM Press, New York (2008)
13. Potter, S., Nieh, J.: WebPod: Persistent Web Browsing Sessions with Pocketable Storage Devices. In: WWW 2005, pp. 603–612. ACM Press, New York (2005)
14. Morrison, J.B., Pirolli, P., Card, S.K.: A Taxonomic Analysis of What World Wide Web Activities Significantly Impact People's Decisions and Actions. In: Extended Abstracts of CHI 2001, pp. 163–164. ACM Press, New York (2001)
15. Consolvo, S., Walker, M.: Using the Experience Sampling Method to Evaluate Ubicomp Applications. Pervasive Computing 2(2), 24–31 (2003)
16. Brush, A.J.B., Meyers, B.R., Tan, D.S., Czerwinski, M.: Understanding Memory Triggers for Task Tracking. In: CHI 2007, pp. 947–950. ACM Press, New York (2007)
17. Adar, E., Teevan, J., Dumais, S.T.: Large Scale Analysis of Web Revisitation Patterns. In: CHI 2008, pp. 1197–1206. ACM Press, New York (2008)
18. Holm, S.: A Simple Sequentially Rejective Multiple Test Procedure. Scandinavian Journal of Statistics 6(2), 65–70 (1979)
19. Karlson, A.K., Meyers, B.R., Jacobs, A., Johns, P., Kane, S.K.: Working Overtime: Patterns of Smartphone and PC Usage in the Day of an Information Worker. To appear in: Pervasive 2009. Springer, Heidelberg (2009)

Fancy a Drink in Canary Wharf?: A User Study on Location-Based Mobile Search

Alia Amin[1,*], Sian Townsend[2], Jacco van Ossenbruggen[1,3], and Lynda Hardman[1,4]

[1] Centrum Wiskunde & Informatica, Amsterdam, The Netherlands
[2] Google UK Ltd., London, United Kingdom
[3] VU University, Amsterdam, The Netherlands
[4] University of Amsterdam, The Netherlands

Abstract. We present a web-based diary study on location-based search behavior using a mobile search engine. To capture users' location-based search behavior in a ubiquitous setting, we use a web-based diary tool that collects users' detailed mobile search activity, their location and diary entries. This method enables us to capture users' explicit behavior (query made), their implicit intention (motivation behind search) and the context (spatial, temporal, and social) in which the search was carried out. The results of the study show that people tend to stick closely to regularly used routes and regularly visited places, e.g. home and work. We also found that most location-based searches are conducted while in the presence of others. We summarize our findings and offer suggestions to improve location-based search by using features such as location-based service mash-ups.

Keywords: Location-based search, local search, mobile search, diary study.

1 Introduction

While the World Wide Web allows access to information globally, local geographical aspects are nonetheless important in many web search tasks. In a generic search, such as searching for a movie trailer or a book, geographical aspects are irrelevant. This is not the case for location-based searches. For example, when a user is searching for the nearest pubs, the system is required to identify local pubs and only present those that are in the neighborhood. Unlike generic search, the geographical context is important for location-based search. Much research has shown consistent demand for location-based information on the desktop as well as on mobile devices [9,21,22]. Estimates on how often such search occurs have been disclosed by several major search engines: in [21], samples of queries from 2001 Excite desktop searches were examined and 19.7% of them were searching for places, people and things; around 9-10% of the queries collected in [22] on Yahoo! mobile search were identified to have geographical search intentions, whereas more than 15% of 1 million Google queries from PDA devices are for local services [9]. In addition to search engines, many web services offer search support for diverse location-based information, such as, local businesses

---

* This work was conducted while working as an intern at Google UK Ltd., London.

T. Gross et al. (Eds.): INTERACT 2009, Part I, LNCS 5726, pp. 736–749, 2009.

search and review (e.g. www.yelp.com), city guide (e.g. www.citysearch.com), or local traffic news (e.g. www.highways.gov.uk/traffic). These examples show a healthy market for location-based information providers.

Research on location-based information needs is still at an early stage and most reports are confined to the different domains of interest related to location-based search. For example, large scale mobile query analyses done by Google [9], Yahoo! [2] and an EU Mobile operator [5] consistently report that people make location-based queries on a wide range of domains of interests, such as food and drink (e.g. restaurants), shopping (e.g. stores) and travel (e.g. addresses). A small scale diary study on mobile information needs [20] reported that people search for generic information, such as looking for music, and for location-based information, such as looking for places of interest (POI), business hours, and movie times. In these types of searches it might be useful to consider location context as it has proven to improve the quality of query prediction in a mobile search application [10]. Unfortunately, past research on has not given any explanation as to *when, where* and *why* people conduct location-based search. Most research on mobile information needs do not focus on this topic e.g [2,5,9,20], and those that do, limit their approach to automatic query log analysis e.g. [18,19]. As far as we know, there is no user study that exclusively investigates people's location-based search motivations and context. In order to improve and optimize location-based services, it is necessary to understand people's location-based information needs and the context in which they occur.

We define location-based search as: *"Search for a business or place of interest that is tied to a specific geographical location."* This definition is somewhat broader than *Location-aware search* where it is implied that the system has knowledge of and exploits the searcher's location. We use this terminology to reflect the type of query that is collected from the search engine in this study. In this research, we investigate location-based search on mobile devices. The contribution of this paper is an in-depth investigation of location-based search behavior using the mobile search engine and includes the spatial, temporal, and social contexts in which this search occurs. We look into how the users' location and the people they were with influence the location-based search made on a mobile device. We collect comprehensive information from search engine log data, location data tracking and diary entries. Key findings include, first, that people specify location-based search at different levels of granularity, from simple to detailed queries, constructed by different types of information. Second, people tend to travel along regular routes in their environment and visit the same places of interest regularly, and the impacts on their search behavior. Third, most location-based searches on mobile devices are conducted in the company of other people, such as friends, family or colleagues.

This paper is structured as follows. In the next section, we describe our research method. We then present the results, including how people express location-based searches, the contexts in which the searches are conducted, and the search tools used when they do location-based search. This is followed by discussions on the key findings and design considerations to improve location-based services. We close with a summary and future work.

2 Research Method

We want to investigate how people express location-based information needs on a mobile device, what are the different situations when this search occurs and what are the search tools that people use to conduct location-based search. Our research questions are as follows:

What types of location-based search can be identified?
In what context (spatial, temporal, and social) are these searches initiated?
What are the information sources (e.g. maps) used for location-based searches?

Capturing users' behavior on a mobile platform is challenging because of the difficulty of unobtrusively collecting data in a ubiquitous environment. Previous research with the mobile phone relies on different methods, such as interview e.g. [8], log data analysis e.g. [2], (video) observation e.g. [14], experience sampling e.g. [7], diary study e.g. [3,20], or a combination of two or more methods [17]. Search logs provide data on users' realistic search engine usage. They do not, however, provide any insight into users' intentions. Identifying location-based information needs solely from log analysis is not easy because the intention might not always be expressed explicitly in the query by specifying an address or a city name [22]. Diary studies give the opportunity for users to express search goals. Our approach is to combine two methods: search logging and diary study in order to benefit from the strengths of both. Additionally, to understand how people perceive the spatial world around them and the places that are important to them, we use a method similar to that proposed in [13] in the form of a creative exercise where people describe and visualize their environment and the places they go. Next, we describe the web diary tool, the user study procedure and participant profile.

2.1 The Web-Based Diary Tool

The diary tool collects and links 3 types of data: users' search event logs from the Google mobile search engine, location tracking data from participant's device and diary entry data.

Search event log. Events occurring using Google mobile search[1] were collected (e.g., queries entered, clicks, scrolls, keystrokes) including the corresponding timestamps. We also collected SMS snippets. Participants were asked to send an SMS to a dedicated number whenever they identified an information need that was answered by some other information source (e.g. maps, other websites) or a need that could not be answered.

Location tracking. We logged the user's location (latitude and longitude), every time a search is made. The location data provides information on the participants' whereabouts when the search occurs.

Diary entry. Participants were required to log into the diary at the end of every day and to answer questions about their search activity. The participant's detailed search

[1] A software was installed on users' phones to enable us to log search events and location (latitude and longitude) while users were searching with the Google Mobile Search. http://www.google.com/mobile/

history throughout the day is made available. There are 2 steps of action in the diary tool. First, participants need to identify search tasks. In some cases, information needs can only be answered by a participant through conducting several queries in a search session. For example, a user might type several queries, such as *pubs, bars, Irish pubs,* for one search task: to find the nearest pubs. Thus, in the web-diary tool, we provide an option for the participant to group these queries from the same session into a single search task. Second, for every search task, participants need to answer several questions:

How important is this task?
Where were you?
What were you doing?
Who were you with?
Describe in detail what you needed to look for.
When was this need initiated?
What tool(s) did you use to find your answer?
Did you successfully accomplish your task?
Positive and negative experiences with the tool used?

The search event log provides information on the location-based information needs that occurred and the search history. The location tracking indicates where the search took place, and the answers provided by the participants from these questions give an overview on the condition and situation when the information need arose.

2.2 Procedure

The study is divided into four parts:

Pre-study interview. Participants were briefed about the procedure and were requested to provide background information about their daily activities and search experiences. Participants were free to search for any topic but were told that this study was investigating location-based search. Participants gave their consent to have their search activity logged and location tracking during the course of the study.

Digital diary study. The diary study lasted for 12 days. The duration of the study covered different types of days (6 work days, 6 days weekend/public holidays). During this period, participants were asked to make approximately 3 queries per day, as a loose guideline, with the search client on their phone, and to log into the diary website daily from their PC to answer questions related to the mobile searches made.

SMS Reminder. During the course of the diary study, an SMS was sent every 2 or 3 days as a reminder to make queries, and to log into the online diary daily.

Post-study interview. After the study, participants were invited for a semi-structured interview. They were asked additional questions relating to their mobile search experiences based on the answers provided on the diary website. Any unclear or missing diary entries were clarified. Finally, participants were given a creative exercise to sketch typical places where they usually go, and to specify the distance and means of travel to get there.

Participants

Twelve participants were recruited from the London area from which 9 participants (5 female, 4 male) successfully completed the whole study. We recruited participants who used Blackberry phones[2]. All nine participants were young professionals, aged between 27-35 years old (*M*=32.6, *SD*=2.5). We recruited participants with different occupations, such as a financial advisor, photographer, and retail sales person. All participants were regular users of mobile phones and PCs. Our participants use their phones for calls and SMS-es on a regular basis. In addition, they have a mobile Internet subscription and use it to access their emails, news and entertainment content (e.g. BBC), to plan journeys (e.g. maps, public transport schedules), to keep in touch (e.g. Facebook) and to do search (e.g. Google, Yahoo!).

3 Results

During the course of the study, we collected 347 location-based mobile search queries (see Table 1). These were organized by participants into 186 location-based search tasks (see Fig. 1B). Thus, in average, participants make 1.87 queries per location-based search task. Additionally, there were 13 search tasks (6.3%) which were not location-based search tasks, such as downloading images, music, or games (i.e. Transaction task[3]). We omit these and focus our analysis and discussion on location-based search tasks. The diary tool provides a rich context (who, where, when, why, and how) for each search task conducted. Queries and tasks were systematically analyzed as follows. First, we examine the queries from different perspectives to understand how people express location-based information needs, the different domains of interest and different types of search tasks. Second, we examine the answers provided from each diary entry to understand the spatial, temporal, and social context when location-based information needs arose. Third, we examine the tools that people use to find location-based information and the reasons behind unsuccessful location-based search. Finally, we use affinity diagram technique to understand emerging topics that lead to the discussions and design implications.

3.1 Types of Location-Based Queries

The queries were analyzed from 3 different perspectives. Each perspective offers a unique view on location-based search. We examined the query patterns to identify how people express location-based information needs (Syntactic view). Afterwards, we looked at the variety of domains to get an overview of peoples' interests and on the types of places people look for the most (Domain view). Finally, we look from the perspective of information seeking tasks, to understand the breadth of the search goal (Task view).

[2] Due to a technical restriction of our system.

[3] Transaction task is an information exchange task, e.g., online banking, downloading multimedia documents. Transactions are often associated with a user name and password combination [12].

Table 1. How people express location-based information needs (Total: 347 queries)

		Query	example
	67.7%	**Simple location-based query (235 queries)**	
a.	22.9%	Business	*the orange tree pub* [P4], *Charlie harmer + dry cleaning* [P5]
b.	4.3%	Business category	*Mexican restaurant* [P6]
c.	2.4%	Event	*cbeebies + tour* [P5]
d.	7.2%	Product/service	*smart 12 month lease* [P6], *vintage leather jacket* [P7]
e.	2.9%	Location	*Where is covent garden* [P3], *pennyhill park* [P4]
f.	10.1%	Local news, weather	*BBC weather* [P1]
g.	5.8%	Transport schedule, map	*train times* [P1], *tube map* [P4]
h.	12.1%	Url	*Streetmap.co.uk* [P4], *kidslovelondon.com* [P11]
	32.3%	**Detailed location-based query (112 queries)**	
i.	1.4%	Business and attribute	*tesco opening hours* [P1]
j.	13.0%	Business and location	*burger king charing cross* [P6], *nandos – se19* [P3]
k.	5.8%	Business category and location	*canary wharf bars* [P2], *model agencies in London* [P7]
l.	1.9%	Event and location	*moon walk 2008 london* [P7]
m.	6.8%	Product/service and location	*driving testing centre – hither green*[P3], *paint balling Victoria*[P11]
n.	3.4%	Multiple locations	*directions from green park to primrose hill* [P7]

3.1.1 Syntactic View

We manually analyzed each query to investigate how people express location-based queries (see Table 1). There are 6 different components of a location-based query: business name (e.g. Orange Tree pub), business category (e.g. Mexican restaurant), location name (e.g. Pennyhill Park), event name (e.g. Cbeebies tour), product or service (e.g. Smart 12 month lease), and web address (e.g. www.streetmap.co.uk). We found that participants express location-based information needs in different levels of granularity with these elements: (a) A *simple location-based query* consists of only one of these components (see Table 1, a-e). Additionally, some people make Navigational queries[4] to search for a website that contains location-based information (see Table 1, f-h), e.g. www.streetmap.co.uk, www.tfl.gov.uk/tube, or www.kidslovelondon.com. These sites usually offer dynamic and detailed information, such as tube schedules, the city's weather forecast, and local events. (b) A *detailed location-based query* consists of a combination of more than one element, e.g. business name and location name (see Table 1, i-n). From Table 1, we observe that location-based information need is expressed by specifying a business name (22.9%), a business name and location (13.0%), or a web address containing local information (12.1%).

3.1.2 Domain View

The queries were further analyzed to identify the domains of interest. Four main domains of interest that our participants looked for (see Fig. 1A): stores (27.0%): businesses that offers products/services, such as electronic stores, furniture stores, book stores; food & drink (24.5%): businesses such as restaurants, pubs, cafes; entertainment (13.7%): such as cinemas, theaters, concerts; and transportation (10.3%): public or private companies, such as train, bus, tube, taxi.

[4] Navigational query is a query where the intention is to reach a particular site [4].

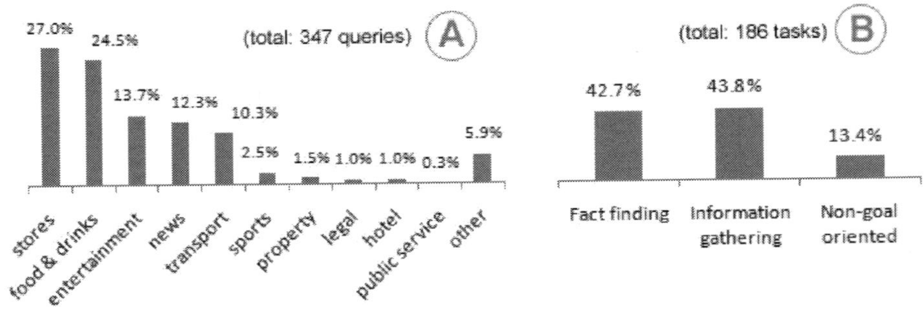

Fig. 1. A) Distribution of domains of interest. B) Types of location-based search task.

3.1.3 Task View

The diary entries provide rich descriptions of users' search tasks and motivation behind each search query. We found there are different location-based search tasks (see Fig. 1B) from specific to broad as explained by the Information Seeking Task taxonomy [1, 11, 12]. These tasks are:

(a) Fact Finding tasks. The task is goal oriented and focused: Users look for specific factual pieces of information. The search intention is usually straightforward e.g. looking up a phone number. We found 42.7% of the location-based search tasks fall into this category. Examples of participant's tasks are: Looking for service information: public transport timetable. *"I want to know the train times home to return to London."* [P1]. Looking for business information e.g. contact details. *"I needed the number for Pizza Express to order the food."* [P12]

(b) Information Gathering tasks. Users carry out several search tasks to fulfill a higher level goal. We found 43.8% of the search tasks belong in this category. Examples of participants' tasks are: making a decision where to go for dinner by exploring different businesses with different constraints, such as cost, distance and product. *"Looking for a Mexican restaurant for a surprise birthday party, found a good selection of restaurants with distance information and maps to easily locate."* [P6] . *"We were looking for a reasonably priced place to go and eat in central London as that would be convenient for everyone."* [P11]

From our search logs, we observe that Information Gathering search tasks tend to be *iterative* (the user goes through several rounds of searches), *exploratory* (the user tries out different alternative queries/search strategies), and *comparative* (comparing different search results before making a decision).

(c) Non-goal oriented information seeking tasks. Users' information needs are not goal driven. The motivation of the search activity is either to be informed or to see what is new or interesting. We found 13.4% search tasks that belong to this category, e.g. Keeping up-to-date with upcoming events. Users carry out serendipitous browsing to see if there are interesting events. *"I was just trying to find out if there were any packages for dinner & show or if there were any specials in restaurants, bars, clubs.. just to get an idea and see if I find something that stands out."* [P7]

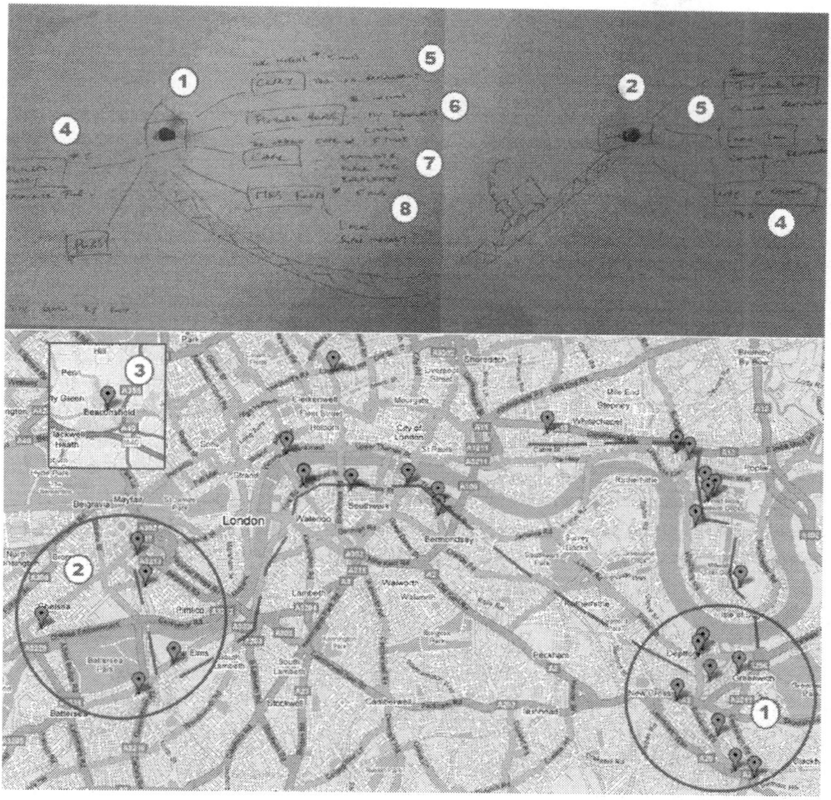

Fig. 2. *Upper half:* An example of a participant's sketch about his regular routes. *Lower half:* the related location tracking data. The markers represent approximate search locations. Multiple queries from one location are presented as one marker: (1) home area, (2) work area, (3) weekend holiday out of town, (4) pubs, (5) curry restaurant, (6) picture house cinema, (7) cafe, (8) supermarket. The dashed lines connecting areas (1) and (2) are the participant's daily train route.

3.2 The Context of Location-Based Search

The web-based diary tool gave us comprehensive information on where, when and how each location-based search occurs. We discuss each of these in the following subsections: spatial, temporal and social context.

3.2.1 Spatial Context

Participants' search activities and locations, while using the search engine, were logged throughout the study. We found that many searches are made either at home, at work, while travelling between the two, or at regularly visited places. With the exception of a weekend break, most of the time, participants' follow regularly used routes and regularly visited places (hotspots). Fig. 2 (lower half) shows a map visualization of searches made by a participant. Searches that have overlapping locations are represented by one point. The line connecting home (1) and work (2) represents a participant's daily travel routine with the train. At the post-study interview, we asked participants to make a sketch of the places they most frequently visit. For example, Fig. 2 (upper half) shows the corresponding sketches from the same participant. His regularly visited places are home, work, and several favourite businesses (pubs, restaurants, cinema, cafe) that are located within 5-15 minutes walking distance from home or work. By comparing the map visualization and the user sketches, we have a better understanding about our participants' spatial mobility, their hotspots, the distance between hotspots and their means of transport. From the 186 search tasks made by participants, the most common place to search was: at family/friends' home (6.5%); public places (8.5%), e.g. at the gym, at the pub/cafe; at work (12%); on the move (20%), e.g. on the public transport, inside a car; at home (53%), e.g. watching TV, lying in bed, preparing to go out. We discovered that the target location is more often related to their regularly visited places (e.g. work, home) rather than to the proximity of their current location, e.g. while on a way to work a participant searched for an optician close to home/work where he can easily stop by: *"I needed to find the closest opticians and deals nearest to home or work."* [P3].

3.2.2 Temporal Context

For every search task, participants were asked to specify whether the need for the information was spontaneous, related to something planned on that day, or arose in relation to something prior to that day. We found that more than half of the queries were a spontaneous need (66.1% of 186 tasks), prompted mainly by activities and situations. They were based on recently acquired needs to obtain information and required immediate answers. *"I needed to find a phone number for a client to contact him urgently."* [P5] . Less than a quarter of the queries were needs that were planned for the same day but had less sense of urgency (21.5% of 186 tasks), e.g. deciding where to go for lunch later. *"Wanted to book a table for lunch with a local Tapas restaurant."* [P1]. The remaining search tasks were needs for another day (12.4% of 186 tasks). These tasks are mainly exploratory search and not urgent at all. *"I was looking at a health farm for a weekend break."* [P4]

3.2.3 Social Context

Participants were asked about who they were with at the moment they conducted the searches. More than three quarters of the location-based search tasks were conducted in the presence of others (76.1% of 186 tasks), e.g. while with family, friends or colleagues. Most location-based searches were prompted by: conversations with people, *"We were talking about Rosarito and we wanted to know where that is."* [P7]; event planning, *"We were looking for somewhere to go for lunch on Easter Monday."* [P5]; recommendation by people, *"We have spoken about this wine tasting place and I wanted to go and have the experience."* [P11]; and necessity, *"We needed directions on how to get there."* [P11]. Less than a quarter of location-based search tasks were conducted alone (23.9% of 186 tasks), mostly driven by necessity. *"I wanted to see that day's weather."* [P5], *"I wanted to know how to get from Hyde Park Corner to the City Airport."* [P7].

Because of the common perception that a mobile device is a personal device, we were surprised to find most location-based searches are not merely a solitary activity but one that is strongly influenced and triggered by social interactions. Cui et al. [7] reported similar observation: that the mobile web acts as a *conversation enhancer*, such as to start a new topic, an ongoing discussion or settle a dispute. In our study, the mobile device plays a bigger role than merely as a communication tool and a conversation enhancer. Mobile search supports social activity, such as searching for ideas, collaborating on making plans, and sharing recommendations.

3.2.4 Decision Making

Related to the influence of spatial, temporal and social context, we investigated the decision making process in location-based search. In our post-study interview, 8-9 tasks were randomly chosen for every participant. For these tasks, participants were asked about the reason(s) behind choosing a certain business from the search result list. Table 2 shows the 9 most frequent reasons for choosing a certain place of interest. Most participants made the decision based on the availability of a specific product/service (23.7%), e.g. checking if the store sells a particular product. *"Needed to stock check a toy for my niece's 1st birthday."* [P1]. Many of the decision making processes in location-based searches were strongly influenced by social elements, such as recommended by other people (15.8%) *"Wanted to confirm the location of a pub. Had been given the name by a friend."* [P1], or decided together with other people (13.2%) e.g. *"It's a restaurant to go for our anniversary."* [P4], "

Table 2. Reasons to choose a place of interest from location-based search (Total: 76 tasks)

Reasons	
23.7%	has a particular product/service
15.8%	is recommended by other people
13.2%	is decided together *
7.9%	is close to where I am now
7.9%	It's my favorite place
6.6%	is close to my home
6.6%	is decided for work purpose
5.3%	is decided by someone else
3.9%	has the best offer (e.g. sale)
9.1%	Other (e.g. serendipity search)

* e.g. with friends, family, colleagues

3.3 Location-Based Information Sources

Where participants were unable to satisfy their information need with the Google service, they were asked to report any other tools they used. A number of various location-based information sources were used, such as: business directory, e.g. yell.com; event guide website, e.g. www.timeout.com; travel website, e.g. www.nationalrail.co.uk; news website, e.g. www.bbc.co.uk and information in public places, e.g. poster or map on the wall. Participants were also asked to note down if the search was successful or not. Of the 186 search tasks, 64.1% were successful, 24.3% were partially successful, and 11.7% were unsuccessful. Several reasons why location-based search on a mobile device was unsuccessful are, e.g. (a) Participant could not find local content or could not find up-to-date information. *"Mainly American sites, couldn't find the UK one easily and then couldn't get the phone number."* [P5]. *"A very old wrestling information came up. Like years old."* [P11]. (b) Difficult to conduct complex search with mobile interface. *"National Rail Enquires needed the same information entering 2/3 times which was annoying and time consuming."* [P1]. (c) Problems with mobile connection *"It timed out a few times so I gave up."* [P4], *"Before I could finish my search, my train went into a tunnel and therefore no mobile connection."* [P6]. When the search is unsuccessful, the participant has the choice to either abandon the search altogether, look for another information source, or develop a new problem solving strategy. *"On Mobile, if I don't find something quickly then I give up, I lose interest. It would be rare to go back (to refine query). I guess it's cos you're used to going back using the back button on your PC ...on mobile you just give up."* [P6], *"There was nowhere I wanted to go in the search so I just decided to drive to the area and decide then."* [P4].

4 Discussion

Our goal was to investigate location-based search needs and to understand the context in which they occurred. From the results, we distill a number of key findings:

Most location-based search is conducted in the presence of others. Although a mobile phone is a personal device, our study shows that more than three quarters of the searches are done in the presence of other people (76.1% of 186 tasks). In some cases, these searches are *group information needs* rather than individual needs. This is because location-based mobile search is closely tied to social/group activities, such as going out. We also discovered that decision making in location-based search (e.g. where to go, which businesses to choose from) is highly influenced by social factors, such as recommended by people they know or decided together with family/friends.

Search now vs. search later. Our study reveals that mobile information seeking behavior progresses over time. A study on the mobile consumer behavior in 2001 reported that even though the information needs were triggered at a particular moment, people prefer to do Information Gathering search activities at a later time with their desktop, because of the difficulty in acquiring comprehensive information and making product comparison on the mobile phone [15]. In our study, this is partially still the case. Comparison search is still a difficult task to do on a mobile device. However, accessing information on the mobile device has become easier. On many occasions, participants prefer to use their mobile device at home rather than using their desktop because of the *lower engagement threshold*. For example, one participant and his daughter used the mobile search to plan their day while having breakfast in the kitchen. On another occasion he used mobile search just before bedtime while discussing weekend plans with his wife. These quick searches were considered inconvenient to do with the desktop computer located in the other room. Moreover, as they can now access many things on conveniently through the mobile device, there is less need to plan or to do search ahead of time. One participant puts it: *"It will change a lot of things, you usually do your homework before (at home), now you can do it afterwards (on the road)."*

Resident vs. Tourist. It should be noted that there are differences between the users in this study and the users in studies on mobile tourism, e.g. [6]. In our study, participants are residents, are somewhat familiar with the city, conduct location-based search regularly, and search on a broad domain of interest from plumbing to paint balling. Tourists, however, are more likely to be unfamiliar with the city (need to orient themselves often), have fewer time restrictions, and search for specific domains of interest e.g. city landmarks and how to get to these places [6]. We expect differences between the two user roles with respect to location-based search types, and their spatial, temporal, and social context.

Study limitation. We acknowledge that there are several limitations to our study. First, our participants are Blackberry users. As pointed out in [9], users with Qwerty keyboards may have different search patterns compared to users with 12-keypad devices with regards to the distribution of number of words per query, domain of interest distribution, query distribution and session characteristics. Nevertheless, we expect users' location-based information needs and the aspects investigated in this study (information seeking tasks, the role of spatial, temporal and social context) are mobile device independent. Second, our study had a relatively homogeneous demographic profile. This should not come as a surprise. The reality is that smart phone and mobile Web penetration is highest amongst a fairly narrow group who tend to be young professionals. It would not have been logical to recruit a cross section of all mobile users since we wanted to ensure we only recruited people who already use and were thus familiar with mobile search. It should be acknowledged that the findings of this research may vary for different user segment. However, this research is among the first to report on location-based search actual usage.

5 Design Implications

Location-based search experience can be improved by taking into account users' motivation, search patterns and context. We present a list of issues that should be addressed in future system designs.

Detecting and predicting location-based information needs. As mentioned in [22], it is difficult for a search engine to identify whether a query is location-based without any location qualifier. In our study, we found that most of the time participants only specify business name, business category, event name or product name. Thus, based on our findings we recommend that whenever a search engine receives a query that contains one of these elements, the search engine should prioritize using location-based information.

Recommendation based on hotspots. We found that people move along regularly used routes and their location-based search interests are within their hotspots (as shown in Fig. 2). Moreover, users' interests in location-based information are usually within the proximity of their hotspots. Thus, a personalized search result that provides location-based information tailored to users' hotspots areas would be potentially valuable.

Location-based search query refinement. Features that help avoid making mistakes when typing unfamiliar business/place names and addresses is useful to have in search engines. Search engines can help users by providing query suggestions based on likely local business/place names, for example, a list of query refinements, similar to the *'Did you Mean?'* feature for business/place names that are phonetically or morphologically similar to what has been typed. Another useful feature to help users specify business names and places is to provide autocompletion suggestions of businesses nearby or favorite businesses from users' bookmark or search history.

Support iterative, exploratory and comparative search activity. Our results show that a large portion of our search tasks are Information Gathering tasks (43.8%, see Fig. 1B). Most search interfaces, however, do not provide features that support iterative, exploratory, and comparative search activities. Features that would help users in this task are: first, support users to collect, filter, organize, compare, save and share location-based search results; second, support exploration by allowing users to tweak a set of constraints, such as enable to filter points of interest by distance, business category, service price, in order to find the optimum search results.

Location-based services mash-ups. Integration of different services, such as business directory (restaurant, pub, store), places (car parks, bus stops), public transport system (train, bus, tube), navigation system (route, distance), other services (ATM, gas station, restroom) and map application is another way to help users in Information Gathering tasks. Integration of different services will help them decide where to go, match their schedules, estimate distance and travel time between places, and ultimately help users make better plans.

Recommendation based on social network. Recommendations made by people play an important role in prompting location-based search needs and the decision making processes. It would be helpful to provide several features: (a) enable people to search, recommend and share experiences on businesses and make this information easily accessible to people from their social networks; (b) to provide location-based recommendations based on the interests of the whole group, for example if people within a social network are detected to be in close proximity to each other, a search engine can recommend places of interest that incorporate the interests of all members of the group rather than just the searcher.

6 Conclusion and Future Work

We conducted an in-depth web-based diary study using different types of data collected from search event logs, location tracking and diary entries. We found that location-based searches are mostly based upon just-in-time information needs that are usually related to social activity. Our study also shows that participants have regularly used routes and regularly visited places (hotspots). We also found that the target locations for these searches are more often related to users' regularly visited places (e.g. work, home). Services that support location-based search need to take user's social and spatial context into account. There is still much work to be done on how to properly implement search recommendations based on users' hotspots and social networks, e.g. with respect to information privacy and security. Finally, as mobile web searching becomes more widely adopted, we believe that location-based search will be an even more prominent need that calls for alternative mobile search interfaces and new engaging ways to interact with location-based information.

Acknowledgments. We thank Google for the opportunity to conduct this research; Liviu Tancau and Terry Van Belle for the exceptional technical support; Jens Riegelsberger and Robin Jeffries for the feedback on a draft of this paper.

References

1. Amin, A., Hardman, L., van Ossenbruggen, J., van Nispen. A.: Understanding cultural heritage experts' information seeking tasks. In: Proc. JCDL 2008, pp. 39–47 (2008)
2. Baeza-Yates, R., Dupret, G.: Velasco. J.: A study of mobile search queries in Japan. In: Query Log Analysis: Social and Technological Challenges, at WWW 2007 (2007)
3. Brandt, J., Weiss, N., Klemmer, S.R.: txt 4 l8r: lowering the burden for diary studies under mobile conditions. In: Proc. CHI 2007, pp. 2303–2308 (2007)
4. Broder, A.: A taxonomy of web search. SIGIR Forum 36(2), 3–10 (2002)
5. Church, K., Smyth, B., Cotter, P., Bradley, K.: Mobile information access: A study of emerging search behavior on the mobile internet. ACM Trans. Web 1(1), 4 (2007)
6. Brown, B., Chalmers, M.: Tourism and mobile technology. In: Proc. ECSCW 2003, pp. 335–354. Kluwer Academic Publishers, Dordrecht (2003)
7. Consolvo, S., Walker, M.: Using the experience sampling method to evaluate ubicomp applications. IEEE Pervasive Computing 2(2), 24–31 (2003)
8. Cui, Y.: Roto. V.: How people use the web on mobile devices. In: Proc. WWW 2008, pp. 905–914 (2008)
9. Kamvar, M.: Baluja. S.: A large scale study of wireless search behavior: Google mobile search. In: Proc. CHI 2006, pp. 701–709 (2006)
10. Kamvar, M., Baluja, S.: The Role of Context in Query Input: Using contextual signals to complete queries on mobile devices. In: Proc. MobileHCI 2007 (2007)
11. Kellar, M., Watters, C., Shepherd, M.: A field study characterizing web-based information seeking tasks. Technical report, Dalhousie University Halifax (2005)
12. Kellar, M., Watters, C., Shepherd, M.: The impact of task on the usage of web browser navigation mechanisms. In: Proc. GI 2006, pp. 235–242. Canadian Information Processing Society (2006)
13. Lynch, K.: The image of the city. The MIT Press, Cambridge (1960)
14. Mark, G., Christensen, U., Shafae, M.: A methodology using a microcamera for studying mobile. In: IT Usage and Person Mobility, CHI 2001 Workshop on Mobile Communications: Understanding Users, Adoption & Design (2001)
15. O'Hara, K., Perry, M.: Shopping anytime anywhere. In: Proc. CHI 2001, pp. 345–346 (2001)
16. Palen, L., Salzman, M.: Voice-mail diary studies for naturalistic data capture under mobile conditions. In: Proc. CSCW 2002, pp. 87–95 (2002)
17. Riegelsberger, J., Nakhimovsky, Y.: Seeing the bigger picture: a multi-method field trial of google maps for mobile. In: Proc. CHI 2008, pp. 2221–2228 (2008)
18. Sanderson, M., Han, Y.: Search words and geography. In: Proc. GIR 2007, pp. 13–14 (2007)
19. Sanderson, M., Kohler, J.: Analyzing geographic queries. In: Workshop on Geographic Information Retrieval SIGIR (2004)
20. Sohn, T., Li, K.A., Griswold, W.G., Hollan, J.D.: A diary study of mobile information needs. In: Proc. CHI 2008, pp. 433–442 (2008)
21. Spink, A., Jansen, B., Wolfram, D., Saracevic, T.: From E-Sex to E-Commerce: Web Search Changes, pp. 107–109. IEEE Computer Society, Los Alamitos (2002)
22. Yi, J., Maghoul, F.: Pedersen. J.: Deciphering mobile search patterns: a study of yahoo! mobile search queries. In: Proc. WWW 2008, pp. 257–266 (2008)

Bringing Digital Storytelling to the Mobile

Thomas Reitmaier and Gary Marsden

University of Cape Town Centre in ICT4D
Cape Town, South Africa
Thomas.Reitmaier@uct.ac.za, gaz@cs.uct.ac.za

Abstract. Technology has changed the way in which people tell their stories. This paper introduces digital storytelling and looks at why the mobile is an ideal platform for creating digital stories. The iterative design approach chosen for our Mobile Digital Storytelling system is discussed. Results of a final experiment, comparing our system to an existing mobile system that supports digital storytelling, are presented, which suggest that our system has met its design goals of providing an effective and efficient user interface. Qualitative insights from user evaluations show that mobile digital storytelling has a future.

Keywords: User-centered design, digital storytelling, mobile devices, content creation, interaction design.

1 Introduction

Everybody has stories to tell. They can range from the banal, to the instructional, and on to rich and compelling stories. Although the content of these stories varies considerably, one aspect holds true for all of them—they are all stories and thus convey an experience.

Storytelling serves as "dialog between people, cultures, and times" [4]. Originally an oral tradition, it has evolved into a written practice, and has recently experienced a shift to the digital medium. Storytelling empowers people to "preserve, share, and reflect on life experiences" [4]. It has evolved from a strong oral background to utilizing new technological advances and media types as they have emerged [2].

1.1 Digital Storytelling

A broad definition of a digital story is that it is a series of pictures with a voice-over or describing text. A clear definition of a 'digital story', however, does not exist. Some researchers say that digital storytelling should involve a degree of critical reflection [4]. To them a digital story is much more than an annotated photo slideshow. The story, not the pictures, is the most important aspect. Others argue that the term 'digital story' is more of an umbrella, and encompasses both 'picture-driven' and 'story-driven' approaches [1].

1.2 Mobile Digital Storytelling

Bringing digital storytelling to the mobile, while challenging, offers great opportunities. It would allow users without access to a personal computer to create and share

T. Gross et al. (Eds.): INTERACT 2009, Part I, LNCS 5726, pp. 750–753, 2009.

their stories, thus giving them a digital voice. Digital stories are often personal stories, in tune with the personal nature of the mobile and the emotional attachment users have towards it [3]. This compatibility suggests that the mobile is an ideal and low cost digital storytelling platform.

Some of the challenges we faced while developing our mobile digital storytelling system are the limited computing resources of mobile phones and their limited interaction capabilities. By restricting ourselves to simpler digital stories, consisting of still images annotating a recorded audio narrative, our mobile digital storytelling system should run on lower end mobiles. We chose an iterative design approach, outlined in the next section, to tackle the limited interaction capabilities of mobiles.

2 Design Process

The design question was to develop an easy-to-use mobile system, which allows people to record their stories. Everybody has a story—not just people with access to computers— by bringing digital storytelling to the mobile we aim to extend its reach.

One of the few existing systems that supports mobile digital storytelling is the Mobile Multimedia Presentation Editor [2] by Jokela et al, seen in the left of Figure 1. After inspecting the Mobile Multimedia Presentation Editor, we decided to steer clear of their timeline interface and rather try to improve upon it. Timeline interfaces may be familiar to many of us from video-editing software, but they may be difficult to use, particularly in the storytelling context, for novice or casual computer users.

Fig. 1. The timeline interface of Mobile Multimedia Presentation Editor (left) and our Mobile Digital Storytelling storyline interface (right)

An approach based on the principles of Interaction Design was used to develop our Mobile Digital Storytelling system. In developing our system, we focused on three main activities, understanding user needs, developing prototypes, and user evaluation. Through iterative prototyping and user evaluation a final design emerged.

We created a prototype, which we improved and refined over four design iterations. In our background research, we established that two approaches could be taken towards creating a digital story, a story-driven (annotating narrative with pictures) and a picture-driven (adding narrative to pictures) approach. We decided to create two interfaces—one for each approach. User evaluations revealed that users preferred the picture-driven approach, which we will discuss from here on out.

In the first design iteration, we created a low-fidelity paper prototype, which we tested against usage scenarios and evaluated heuristically. Because of the interactive nature of our system we chose a user-less evaluation for this first design iteration.

We then incorporated the lessons learned from the first design iteration into the PowerPoint prototype of the second design iteration. We evaluated the usability of this prototype using six users. Because of time and cost constraints, the users we recruited for this evaluation were university students. To ensure sample population diversity, we recruited students from different parts of the university campus.

Keeping the lessons learned from previous design iterations in mind, we created a high-fidelity Flash Lite prototype, which runs on a mobile phone. In this prototype the system's interaction capabilities are more accurately modeled than in lower fidelity prototypes, giving an accurate model of the systems look, feel, and interactions. Again, we performed a formative user evaluation on the interface. As the interface was now more mature than the interfaces of previous iteration, we aimed to discover more subtle usability problems and thus decided to evaluate our system on eight student users, recruited from different university departments to ensure population diversity. The user evaluation performed on the Flash Lite prototype revealed mostly minor terminology related usability problems, which we addressed in the final design.

2.1 Final Design

The elements of the final interactive Flash Lite prototype can be seen in Figure 2. Pictures are added to the storyline, for which an annotating narrative is then recorded.

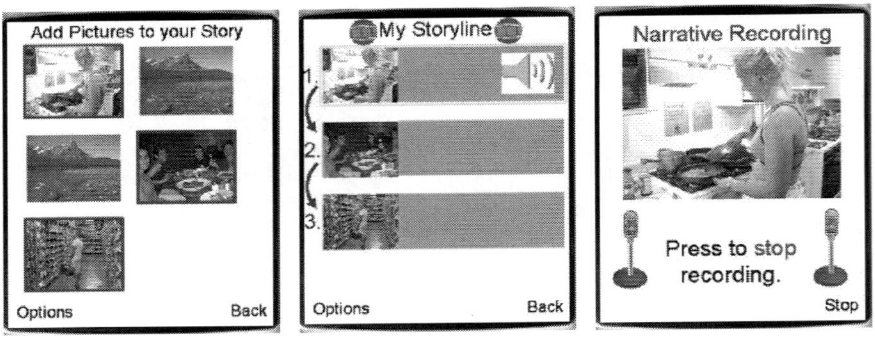

Fig. 2. Elements of the final interface design

In the previous iteration, mostly minor terminology related usability problems were discovered, which we addressed in this iteration. That led us to believe that an effective and easy to use design had emerged in our final prototype.

2.2 User Experiment

A summative evaluation was conducted in a usability lab to test the hypothesis that, given a pre-scripted story and annotating picture, users will be able to create a digital story more quickly using our Mobile Digital Storytelling system than using Mobile Multimedia Presentation Editor of Jokela et al.

The experimental results of the within-group experiment with counterbalancing testing the null-hypothesis show that all ten participants were able to perform the task of creating a digital story faster on our system (345 seconds on average) than on the Mobile Multimedia Presentation Editor (427 seconds on average). On average, the participants performed 82 seconds faster on our system—this constitutes a 23.9% improvement. A paired t-test performed ($t=10.043$) on the results showed a calculated p-value of less than 0.0001, which is statistically significant. The experiment indicates that, when creating digital stories, users perform better (faster) on our Mobile Digital Storytelling system than on the Mobile Multimedia Presentation Editor of Jokela et al.

3 Discussion and Conclusion

We were surprised that very few users in our evaluations had ever heard of digital storytelling. After discovering digital storytelling, in part through interacting with our prototypes, our users were delighted with the simplicity, flexibility, and power of the digital story. Almost all of the users could immediately come up with a scenario where they could use our system, which ranged from "telling a friend about the club I'm currently at" to "I'm sure that the people in the AIDS clinic I volunteer at would love it"—showing the potential of digital storytelling and our mobile system.

We have seen not only that mobile digital storytelling is viable and possible but also that our system is a significant improvement to an existing system—enabling even storytelling novices to create and explore the power of digital stories.

Possible future work includes, more ethnographic work on how people tell stories using pictures, exploring locative aspects of storytelling, enabling users to collaborate on their stories, and better utilizing the ad-hoc nature of the mobile for in situ storytelling.

References

1. Balabanovic, M., Chu, L.L., Wolff, G.J.: Storytelling with digital photographs, 564–571 (2000)
2. Jokela, T., Lehikoinen, J.T., Korhonen, H.: Mobile multimedia presentation editor: enabling creation of audio-visual stories on mobile devices, 63–72 (2008)
3. Jones, M., Marsden, G.: Mobile Interaction Design. John Wiley & Sons, Chichester (2006)
4. Landry, B.M., Guzdial, M.: Learning from Human Support: Informing the Design of Personal Digital Story-Authoring Tools. Journal of the International Digital Media and Arts Association 3(1), 106 (2006)

Exploring User Requirements for Non-visual Mobile Navigation Systems

Charlotte Magnusson[1], Kirsten Rassmus-Gröhn[1], Konrad Tollmar[1,2], and Hanna Stigmar[3]

[1] Certec, Department of Design Sciences, Lund University, Box 118, 221 00 Lund, Sweden
[2] Mobile Life, DSV, Stockholm University, Forum 100 SE-16440 Kista, Sweden
[3] GIS-centrum, Lund University, Sölvegatan 12, 223 62 LUND
kirre@certec.lth.se, charlotte.magnusson@certec.lth.se, konrad.tollmar@design.lth.se, hanna.stigmar@lantm.lth.se

Abstract. This paper describes an explorative user study of how two different user groups experience current, as well as envisioned new mobile navigation systems. Two groups have been the primary target in this study; a group of elderly people and a group of relatively young university students that were visually impaired. The study consisted of three parts: a focus group/test, a diary study and a design workshop where the users envisioned new kinds of interaction with mobile navigation systems by building and demonstrating low-fi prototypes. Information about user requirements for these types of applications is obtained and we observe features in the study design which are relevant for a wider range of mobile services.

Keywords: Mobile, Navigation, Non-visual, Digital Maps.

1 Introduction

The present study, which is part of the HaptiMap project (FP7-ICT-224675. Co-funded by the European Commission and also supported by VINNOVA, Sweden), investigates user requirements for the design of mainstream mobile navigational devices and mobile maps, with a particular focus on the non-visual modalities. The project targets several user groups: sighted, elderly and visually impaired persons.

A growing number of mobile applications (to a large degree map-based navigation systems) make heavy use of visual information while implicitly targeting usage situations where the visual channel is needed for other things than looking at a device [1]. Despite this interfaces used in mobile devices are usually based on traditional visual map design [2] and more flexible and usable interfaces for geospatial interaction have not yet been properly explored.

2 Exploring Non-visual Mobile Navigation Systems

This study targets several user groups and the design space to be investigated is complex. Furthermore, we do not look at assistive devices for a selected group, but are

T. Gross et al. (Eds.): INTERACT 2009, Part I, LNCS 5726, pp. 754–757, 2009.

interested in improving the design of mainstream products and services. We are in the process of investigating the user requirements relevant to this particular project, and the present article reports an early explorative study involving both elderly and visually impaired users.

In the design of our study were inspired by [3 - 6] and combined a focus group discussion, a contextual test/interview, a diary study and a user workshop where users design low-fi versions of potential services. Often this type of sequence is described as separate studies – but in our study design we decided to link the different parts together. Thus, the two initial activities were important on their own, but also expected to provide the necessary background for the user workshop.

The study consisted of three parts. The first was a discussion/focus group meeting where the groups also tested different navigational systems informally in a scenario walk. The second part consisted of a diary study performed over a week where the participant recorded his or her experiences of everyday routines when traveling. The final and third part of this study was the design workshop in which each group envisioned new kinds of interaction with mobile navigation systems by building and demonstrating low-fi prototypes and demonstrated these in a simulation walk [Fig 1].

Fig. 1. Demonstrating low-fi prototypes in a simulation walk

The study involved a group of eight persons; five elderly people between 67-78 (2 male / 3 female) with a general reduction in vision capabilities and a group of three relatively young university students that are visually impaired (1 male / 2 female).

Almost everyone in the group claimed that they performed daily trips, mostly by public transportation. Leisure was the most common reason to go for a trip (3-5 times/week) followed by shopping (3-5 times/week), and work (3-5 times/week, and of course in this group most participants do not work). Everyone in the group owns a PC and cell phone but only two persons own a GPS. They all use Internet daily but never mobile services and almost never navigation systems. Travel planning is mostly done via Internet and printed maps are brought on the trip. When going on a trip they all bring there their cell phone, and sometimes maps and time tables. But company is also needed in some cases since they can't always operate on their own.

3 Summary of Results and Discussion

Both our user groups turned out to have many requirements in common. Both groups pointed out the importance of landmarks and context information such as houses, house numbers and other things in the environment. Both groups were in general interested in hands-free and eyes-free solutions, although one of the visually impaired users wanted a device that had a fairly large screen which could act as a device that made it possible to see things further away. Both groups also liked speech information although it was seen as important that this should not be too disturbing. Confirmation that you are on the right track was also important for both groups as well as position accuracy. Both groups were also concerned about rerouting – if you indeed made a wrong turning you would prefer to get that information to being rerouted. Information about your orientation in the environment is another common requirement as (of course) correct and updated map information. The main difference between the groups was in fact the attitude to multifunctional devices – the elderly group wanted a simple device with few functions, while the younger visually impaired users were more concerned with the number of devices and preferred one device that could do everything. The diversity found (particularly within the group of visually impaired users) still highlights the importance of being able to tailor the interaction and the information to the needs of the particular user. As can be expected these results agree with the results from [7-11], although the comment in [10] about negative attitude towards technology among elderly users did not seem to apply to our user group. Our users also agreed with [12] on the importance of hands-free interaction. Added to this there were a number of detailed useful suggestions and observations.

If we consider the method used, we found that the sequence design used was very fruitful. The inclusion of existing technology in the focus group discussions provide a technological reference for the users, while the scenario walk provided the necessary context (during the walk comments were made that were not triggered in the preceding discussion). Concerning the diaries, the participants were concerned that the researchers should get as much as possible out of the diaries and suggested longer time for diary keeping. The workshop finally, showed that also for non-visual interaction design, low-fi workshops can be a useful tool for involving users in the design process (as expected from [13]). The workshop and discussion turned out to be a fruitful arena to get into detailed questions about the functionality of the system. During the simulated walk, both users and researchers were in the context of a way finding task (however artificial), which triggered questions and also made more plausible that both parties were talking about the same thing.

4 Conclusion

To conclude, we have shown that a more longitudinal study design consisting of a linked sequence combining a focus group discussion, a contextual test/interview, a diary study and a user workshop where users design low-fi versions of potential services can be a useful tool for the exploration of the user requirements for non-visual interaction designs intended for mobile navigation services. We note the importance of landmarks and information about objects in the environment. Other things seen to be important were hands-free and eyes-free operation, position accuracy, speech feedback, confirmation, routing design, correct user orientation in the environment and map content. Furthermore, we have seen that elderly sighted and visually impaired users appear to have many requirements in common in this study – although it should be noted that a request for hands-free and eyes-free solutions can also be a consequence of the mobile context (where hands and eyes are needed for other things).

References

1. Magnusson, C., Brewster, S., Sarjakoski, T., Roselier, S., Sarjakoski, L.T., Tollmar, K.: Exploring Future Challenges for Haptic, Audio and Visual Interfaces for Mobile Maps and Location Based Service. In: LocWeb 2009 Workshop, CHI 2009, Boston, MA, USA, April 4-April 9 (2009)
2. Dykes, J., MacEachren, A.M., Kraak, M.-J.: Exploring Geovisualization. In: Dykes, J., MacEachren, A.M., Kraak, M.-J. (eds.) Exploring geovisualization. Elsevier, Amsterdam (2005)
3. Svanæs, D., Seland, G.: Putting the Users Center Stage: Role Playing and Low-fi Prototyping Enable End Users to Design Mobile Systems. In: CHI 2004, Vienna, Austria (2004)
4. Sá, M., Carriço, L.: Low-Fi Prototyping for Mobile Devices. In: CHI 2006, Montréal, Canada, pp. 694–699. ACM, New York (2006)
5. Messeter, J., Brandt, E., Halse, J., Johansson, M.: Contextualizing mobile IT. In: Proceedings of the 5th Conference on Designing interactive Systems: Processes, Practices, Methods, and Techniques. DIS 2004, Cambridge, MA, USA, August 1-4. ACM, New York (2004)
6. Iacucci, G., Kuutti, K., Ranta, M.: On the move with a magic thing: role playing in concept design of mobile services and devices. In: Boyarski, D., Kellogg, W.A. (eds.) Proceedings of the 3rd Conference on Designing interactive Systems: Processes, Practices, Methods, and Techniques. DIS 2000, New York City, New York, United States, August 17-19. ACM, New York (2000)
7. May, A., Ross, T., Bayer, S., Tarkiainen, M.: Pedestrian navigation aids: information requirements and design implications. Personal Ubiquitous Comput. 7(6), 331–338 (2003)
8. Bradley, A., Dunlop, D.: An Experimental Investigation into Wayfinding Directions for Visually Impaired People. Personal Ubiquitous Comput. 9(6), 395–403 (2005)
9. Strothotte, T., Petrie, H., Johnson, V., Reichert, L.: MoBIC: user needs and preliminary design for a mobility aid blind and elderly travellers. In: Proceedings of the 2nd TIDE Congress, La Villette, Paris, April 26-28 (1995)
10. Goodman, J., Gray, P.: A Design Space for Location-Sensitive Aids for Older Users. In: HCI in Mobile Guides, Udine, Italy (2003)
11. Sjölinder, M.: Age-related decline and navigation in electronic environments, PhD thesis, Department of Psychology, Stockholm University (2006)
12. Heuten, W., Henze, N., Pielot, M., Boll, S.: Tactile Wayfinder: A Non-Visual Support System for Wayfinding. In: NordiCHI 2008, Lund, Sweden, October 20-22 (2008)
13. Magnusson, C., Brewster, S.: Proceedings of the workshop: Guidelines for Haptic Lo-Fi prototyping. NordiCHI 2008, Lund, Sweden (October 19 2008), http://www.english.certec.lth.se/haptics/Proceedings_lo_fi_workshop.pdf (accessed 2009-01-26)

Multi-display Composition: Supporting Display Sharing for Collocated Mobile Devices

Kent Lyons, Trevor Pering, Barbara Rosario, Shivani Sud, and Roy Want

Intel Research
2200 Mission College Blvd.
Santa Clara, CA 95054
{kent.lyons,trevor.pering,barbara.rosario,shivani.a.sud, roy.want}@intel.com

Abstract. Multi-display composition is a technique that enables several mobile devices to join together over a wireless network to form a larger logical display. This logical display can be created in an *ad hoc* manner for use when and where it is needed out of a group of users' existing mobile computers. In this work we present a multi-display composition system and discuss our implementation that supports dynamically extending the display across several devices. Furthermore, we present findings from a study of collocated groups of individuals using multi-display composition on two different types of mobile computers. We found mixed results with respect to the effect of the resulting display area. The use of two devices by a pair of participants tended to be rated more favorably than a corresponding group of four devices and participants. Furthermore, while providing additional screen real estate for smaller UMPCs, tablets were rated more favorably when using our system. Finally, we discuss usage themes that emerged from participants' use of the multi-display composition system.

1 Introduction

In recent years, personal computing has evolved from a primarily desktop activity to a highly mobile one. Laptop computers are an extremely popular computing platform, and the tremendous success of mobile phones indicates that the adoption rates that we observe for smart phones and Mobile Internet Devices (MIDs) will likely continue. While these mobile devices have ever increasing processing, storage, and network capabilities, they also tend to have limited input and output. One key challenge for enabling the full utilization of the capabilities of these devices will be overcoming the limitations of their interfaces. Dynamic Composable Computing is one approach for overcoming these limitations by enabling the impromptu assembly of a logical computer from the best available nearby wireless components [12] [19].

The display characteristics of a mobile computer are one of the most defining attributes of the device. The size of the display has implications for both the mobility and the form factor of the computer. For example, there are several laptop computers on the market that offer very similar computing capabilities, but are packaged differently and offer different screen sizes and resolutions. Tablet PCs often offer similar performance to laptops but are designed to be operated with a stylus. Ultra Mobile

T. Gross et al. (Eds.): INTERACT 2009, Part I, LNCS 5726, pp. 758–771, 2009.

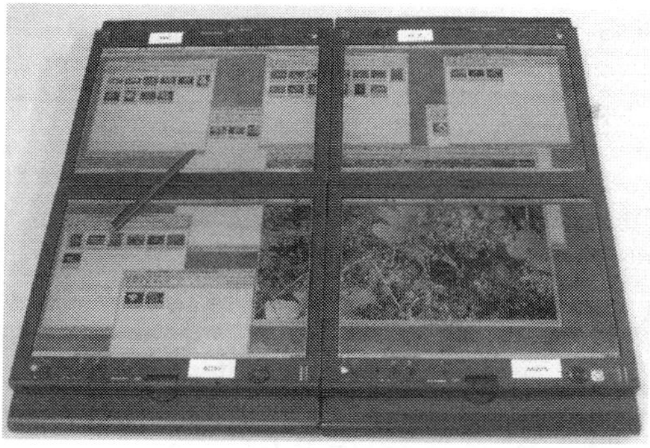

Fig. 1. Four individual tablet computers, linked only by a wireless network, forming a multi-display composition resulting in a single logical display

PCs (UMPCs) provide users with significant computing resources and run standard desktop operating systems and applications. However, these systems are designed to be more portable and as such have much smaller displays. Smart phones are smaller still and require highly tailored applications to accommodate the limited screen real estate. While in a modern version of each device the power of the processor subsystem scales moderately with physical size, the display limitation still provides the largest differentiating factor in user experience across these platforms.

In this work, we are exploring how the displays of several mobile computers can be wirelessly joined together to gain more display area. In particular, multi-display composition is a system that uses the screen real estate of multiple mobile devices to form a larger logical display. Originally, this technique was developed as a mechanism for overcoming the display size limitations of small devices like UMPCs and smart phones with the intent of providing a mechanism for obtaining enough screen space on which to run traditional legacy desktop applications. However, multi-display composition can also be applied to larger mobile computers. For example, Figure 1 shows the formation of a single logical display from four separate tablet PCs effectively resulting in an *ad hoc* tabletop display.

The contributions of this paper are twofold: First, we present the *ad hoc* multi-display composition technique which supports running legacy applications on a logical display formed by dynamically combining the display resources of several mobile computers. Second, we discuss the results from a study where groups of collocated individuals completed several tasks using a multi-display composition of two or four devices with two different types of mobile computers.

2 Related Work

Research into alternative display technologies reveals several techniques which could decouple the size of the display from the size of the mobile device. Technologies such as electronic ink and organic LEDs may eventually allow for the mass market production of displays that have a large area and high resolution while also being easily rolled or folded to fit in a pocket or bag for portability. Micro projectors [1] [2] and head mounted displays [15] [18] use miniature displays and optics to create large images out of very small packages. In addition to these novel display technologies, another approach to gaining more display area on a mobile device is to utilize multiple traditional LCDs. The Nintendo DS portable gaming system utilizes a clam–shell design with two smaller displays. The hinged design offers a small form–factor to support mobility while not in use. However, when open, the two displays can be used to increase the amount of available screen real estate. Similarly, Chen *et al.* demonstrated an electronic book reader with two displays that attach and fold against each other [3], and Siftables explores the use of several very small displays [11].

More directly related to multi-client composition is the work on ConnecTables [16] which demonstrated the ability to dynamically link two mobile computers together to gain increased screen area. Hinckley's work on Synchronous Gestures [6] and Stitching [7] brings a similar concept to tablet PCs and explores different mechanisms for initiating the link between the computers. This set of related work all relied upon custom applications to utilize the combined display resources of the mobile computers. Furthermore, these only demonstrate connecting two devices together. In contrast, as we will show with our multi-display system, we provide support to run legacy applications unmodified across multiple mobile displays and demonstrate the use of four displays in our study. Finally, our user study, in contrast to Hinckley *et al.*'s [7], is explicitly focused on the multi-display aspects of the system and uses groups of two or four participants with pre-existing social relationships.

3 Multi-display Composition

Multi-display composition performs its display sharing at the windowing system level, and as such, is related to a large body of work exploring the interplay between displays and high-speed networks. The X Window System and Virtual Network Computing (VNC) [14] are two well established examples of systems that support sending graphical data over the network to a remote computer system. In this work, we continue this trend of using network enabled displays but focus on how it can be applied to a group of *ad hoc* mobile devices. The advances in the capabilities of mobile computers have resulted in the ability to perform similar types of display sharing across wireless networks such as WiFi (e.g. IEEE 802.11n) and on devices such as laptops and tablets. Even smaller handhelds, such as UMPCs and MIDs, are gaining enough computational power for this type of display sharing.

By using a multi-display composition on mobile devices, several novel usage scenarios emerge. With a composition in which the displays of several devices mirror a single source display, a group of collocated users can each use their own device to access the same information. For example, instead of passing a camera phone between members of a group of people to view a captured photograph, a multi-display composition could let every person view the photo from their own phone similar to the system created by Clawson *et al.* [5]. Alternatively, several tablet computers can be placed on a table and used together to form one large aggregate display surface. With this extended multi-display composition, the displays of several mobile devices are bound together creating one display which spans the computers. When applied to a group of four tablets, an *ad hoc* tabletop display is formed (Figure 1). These examples utilize the devices from a group of individuals to create a larger display system. It is possible that a single individual may also have access to multiple mobile devices. For example, if Weiser's vision of ubiquitous tabs and pads comes to pass [20], a single user could form multi-display compositions using devices found serendipitously in the environment. We are already starting to see signs of this type of usage where people use both a laptop and mobile phone in combination [7] [9].

Our implementation of multi-display composition is built on top of the VNC remote display sharing protocol [14]. This protocol allows a user to see and interact with the framebuffer of one computer using another remote computer connected by an IP network. We extended the VNC protocol and created a custom X server that is headless and not attached to a physical framebuffer. By decoupling the display from the host device, we are able to extend the server so that the framebuffer can be arbitrarily re-sized at run-time and shared over the network.

This design choice is important in that it allows for any legacy X application to be used in this multi-display environment that can dynamically grow and shrink as needed; existing applications do not need to be rewritten or modified. The applications are rendered as usual into X's framebuffer, and the multi-display composition system manages all of the issues associated with dynamically adding or removing devices and distributing the framebuffer and applications' display across the devices. While we chose X and VNC as the basis of our system, several alternative implementations could also be explored where the display sharing is implemented at other layers in the windowing system. For example, two alternatives would be to share and distribute OpenGL [8] or the X protocol to multiple devices. Similarly instead of the custom X server, a modern compositing windowing system such as Mac OS X or Windows Vista already has the required decoupling between the rendering of windows and graphical information and the framebuffer.

Our VNC server extensions build on the TurboVNC[1] implementation of VNC. The performance of this software has been improved by using a high-speed vector optimized JPEG library. Our implementation incorporated these optimizations for the VNC server into LibVNCServer[2], an open source library that supports the creation of custom VNC servers. In turn, this library was linked against our custom X server with multi-client support. Several types of VNC clients were created. The native Linux and Windows optimized TurboVNC clients were modified to support the additions needed for multi-client mode. Furthermore, the Java version of the Tight VNC client was modified to provide solutions for other platforms.

The system is started by one mobile device running the server. The software creates a new X session, and a VNC client is attached to this server from the same device to show the first portion of the desktop. When a client connects in legacy VNC mode, the entire framebuffer is shared. In a multi-client display composition, this configuration allows for a single display to be mirrored on several other devices.

As additional clients connect in the new extended mode, the server dynamically grows its logical framebuffer by the size of the connecting device. The client's viewport is set to the newly created region to display its portion of the overall desktop. The user is then free to utilize the new screen real estate shown on the new device as if it

---

[1] http://www.virtualgl.org/About/TurboVNC

[2] http://libvncserver.sourceforge.net/

were part of the original display. The system can handle an arbitrary number of displays, limited only by the processing capability of the device acting as the server and the available bandwidth. We have tested the system with up to six displays in a grid over IEEE 802.11a and more devices could likely be supported. The policy for choosing a direction to grow the display (horizontally or vertically) and where to place the incoming display connection is currently programmed into the server. We have a prototype implementation of a mechanism that allows a user to manually reposition the viewports of each connected device, and in the future we want to explore the use of sensors to automatically determine the relative location of devices [10]. When devices of the same resolution are connected, the system fully tiles the space in a grid. Devices with heterogeneous display sizes are also placed into the grid using the resolution of the connecting device to grow the display as needed. However in this case, it is likely that there will be inaccessible portions of the display (just as when using two monitors of different resolutions in a multi-monitor configuration). Currently these portions of the display are rendered, but not visible. Solutions for managing existing multi-monitor systems would likely be useful to implement in this system to address this issue.

Finally, we are using the Composition Framework [12] [19] to manage the multi-display composition. The Composition Framework provides a mechanism for the system to discover the devices and sharable services connected to the same (wireless) network. It also provides a user interface for managing the sets of connections needed to form the multi-display composition. Previous work pilot testing the interface has shown that participants could effectively use it to create and manage compositions of different platform services.

4 Evaluation

As discussed above, we have a generic implementation of multi-display composition that runs on mobile devices connected to a wireless network. The Composition Framework supports the formation of *ad hoc* display compositions, and the geometry management of the system allows the display to dynamically grow and shrink across several devices as needed. Given the above implementation, we wanted to explore how the system might be used and if it effectively allowed for the sharing of multiple mobile display resources. We conducted an evaluation on the composition of a large logical display and decided to focus on pen-based mobile computers and how a group of users might come together to use a set of devices as an *ad hoc* display. In our study, participants used the multi-display system simulating a situation where each person would carry and contribute their own mobile device to work jointly on a task.

4.1 Participants

We recruited participants from our organization (primarily interns) by word of mouth. None of the participants had any previous experience with our system, and we recruited participants so that each person knew all of his or her group members for at least one month prior to the study. Each participant was compensated with a $50 gift card for a single 90 minute session. We recruited five groups of four people, and five groups of two, for a total of thirty participants. Eight of the participants were female. The median age of the participants was 23 (ranging from 19 to 31) and they knew each other a median of 2.75 months (ranging from 1 to 12 months). All of the participants reported extensive computer use with a median of 10.5 years of use (ranging from 6 to 21 years). Twenty-six of the participants used a laptop as their primary computer while the remaining four indicated they used a desktop. Only five participants indicated they had used a tablet more than once, and only one participant indicated daily use. All 30 participants had used some form of remote display sharing application (VNC, Windows Remote Desktop, NetMeeting, LiveMeeting, Citrix, X). Nine of the participants indicated they used it for sharing a display remotely with another individual, fourteen reported using remote display sharing to gain access to a remote system for individual use. Four participants used display sharing for both of these usages, and three did not specify their usage.

4.2 System Configuration

We used two different sets of mobile devices for the study: Lenovo X61 Tablet PCs and Sony Vaio UX71 UMPCs. As indicated above, we recruited two different group sizes (two and four people) and maintained a one-to-one mapping between the number of devices and the size of the group. The devices for the groups of four people were pre-configured in an array of two columns by two rows (2x2) (Figure 1), while the devices for the groups of two people were placed in a single row (2x1). For all of the configurations, the devices were positioned side-by-side in a landscape orientation with minimal space between them.

The X61 Tablets have resolution of 1400x1050. The active portion of the display measures 24.6x18.5cm resulting in a pixel density of approximately 140 dpi. Discounting screen real estate used by the system for window boarders and the taskbar, the 2x1 configuration has a total resolution of 2780x970, while the 2x2 has a resolution of 2780x1940. The UX71 UMPCs have a resolution of 1024x600. The active portion of the display measures 9.9x5.8 cm resulting in pixel density of approximately 260 dpi. Again, discounting screen real estate used by the system, the 2x1 configuration has a total resolution of 2028x520, while the 2x2 has a resolution of 2028x1040. The devices communicate through a dedicated 802.11a wireless access point.

In addition to the basic multi-display composition system, we implemented a mechanism to allow users to drag and drop between devices using the stylus. Even though the displays logically present a single screen, the bezels of the devices present a barrier that one would not be able to cross with a standard pen-based mechanism. In particular, it would be impossible to start a drag on one device and finish on another. Inspired by Rekimoto's Pick–and–Drop technique [13], we utilized a hardware button on the device's bezel to allow a user to enter a mode where they could lift the pen mid-drag and place it down on another device to finish the drag operation.

4.3 Tasks

We designed three tasks for the groups of participants to perform in our study: a sorting task of flower photographs, the use of a spreadsheet containing nutritional data, and an analysis of a graph of movie actors/actresses and movie titles (Figure 2). The primary purpose of the tasks was to have a structured way in which we could engage the participants with the system. Furthermore, the tasks represented examples that had the potential to benefit from the system's larger aggregate display size given the scale of the data involved. Finally, these tasks represent traditional desktop applications which might be started by an individual, then grown across a set of collaborators' devices. While we collected data on the group's performance of each individual task, we were primarily interested in the overall experience of the group using the system. As such, the tasks were chosen so they spanned a range of visual representations of data (images, text, and abstract graphics) as well as in the nature and amount of required interaction. Furthermore, the tasks were constructed so that they could be performed in a limited number of ways to reduce variation and dependence upon creative user input. For each type of task, three different versions (one practice, two test) were created to minimize learning effects.

For the flower image sorting task, participants were asked to sort pictures of 32 flowers into six categories using drag and drop. Seven windows were displayed with one window being the source of all images and the remaining six were destinations. Each window showed image thumbnails, and the image could be opened for closer inspection in a separate window by double clicking on the thumbnail. A total of 132 images were obtained with each image ranging in size between 1600x1200 and 4368x2912 pixels. The images for each category were randomly shuffled and divided evenly into three sets. Finally, two representative images were manually selected from each category to serve as examples and were provided to the participants to facilitate sorting. Participants were also aided by a paper printout which showed the examples printed in color and the final number of flowers for each category.

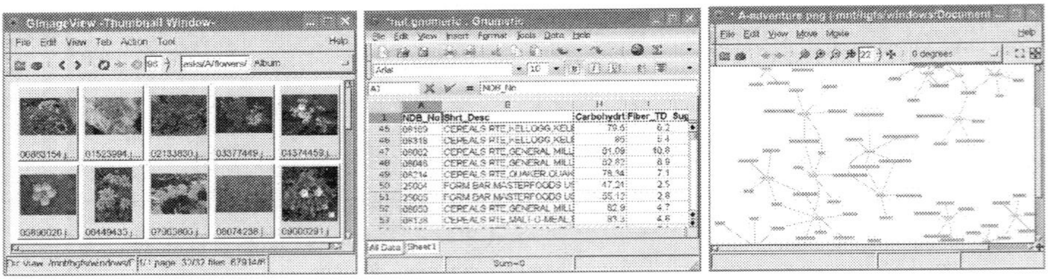

Fig. 2. Sample study data from the flower image sorting task (left) nutrition spreadsheet task (center) and movie graph task (right)

For the nutrition spreadsheet tasks, participants were asked to perform operations on the U.S. Department of Agriculture's abbreviated spreadsheet of nutritional information [17]. This spreadsheet contained 7520 rows of data, each representing a different type of food. The 51 columns of the spreadsheet contained various nutritional data about each food item. The groups of participants were asked to perform several operations on this data including sorting, copying rows of data, and searching for items with specific characteristics. A paper form was provided to the group with the instructions for the task and provided space to record answers.

For the final task, the group of participants interacted with a large undirected graph which contained information about actors, actresses, and the movies in which they performed. The source data is from the IEEE Infovis 2007 contest[3]. The data were filtered and rendered into static images of undirected graphs with two types of nodes. The first type contained the title of the movie, while the second type presented the name of an actor or actress. Edges linked people to the movie(s) in which they performed. This resulted in graphs with between 20 and 22 actor nodes, 76 and 95 movie nodes, and 114 and 121 edges. The rendered images were between 3007x2658 and 3194x3572 pixels. The groups of participants filled out a paper form asking them to list all of the movies which contained actors or actresses in exactly six movies, and to list the movies which had either two or three actors shown in the graph.

4.4 Procedure

The study began with the group members filling out a survey for demographic data and information about their computer usage. The system was described, and the participants were provided with some usages scenarios of how the system might be used and constructed from individuals' mobile devices. Next, a practice session began. Here a researcher showed the participants how to use the stylus, how the system presented a single logical display spread across the devices, and how to use the cross device drag and drop capability. Each participant was encouraged to interact with the system to gain some experience. Next, the experimenter explained each of the three tasks in detail and allowed the group to practice each task. This practice provided further time to become familiar with the system and ensured that the participants understood the tasks they were performing. After answering any questions, the practice session came to a conclusion.

At that point, the three tasks were performed on the first set of devices (either the UMPCs or the Tablets). The order of tasks was selected randomly, while the order of devices was counterbalanced across groups. The participants were given five minutes to complete as much of each task as quickly and accurately as possible. While five minutes is a short duration, we chose this amount to reflect our scenario of the group of individuals joining their displays for a short period of time to perform a given task.

After each task, the participants individually completed a questionnaire. The questionnaire asked them to list three positive and three negative aspects of using the system for the given task. Furthermore, it contained Likert questions (on a nine point scale) from the Questionnaire for User Interaction Satisfaction (QUIS) [4]. In particular it contained the questions about the Overall User Reactions and a subset of questions related to the display. Additionally, several questions were created in a similar style asking for ratings on the ability to participate in the task, feedback about the spacing between group members, etc.

After all three tasks and questionnaires were completed for the first type of display, the researcher swapped devices for the final part of the experiment. The researcher showed the participants the differences between the computers (how the devices had different types of pen input, etc.). After answering any questions, the last three tasks were performed by the group, again filling out the post-task questionnaires. At the conclusion of the study, the participants completed one more questionnaire asking them to rate each device and condition paring performed (six in total), to subjectively rate their satisfaction with the devices, and to comment on their overall experience.

[3] http://eagereyes.org/InfoVisContest2007Data.html

5 Findings

We analyzed the data collected during the study examining trends about the participants' perception of the system in the quantitative measures collected from the post-task Likert scale questionnaire and the exit questionnaire. We also report themes in usage and feedback about the multi-display composition system. In particular, we examine the positive and negative comments recorded on the post–task questionnaire. This information is further substantiated by the overall comments participants provided at the end of the study and by the observations recorded in the researcher's notes during the trials.

5.1 Overall Utility

Overall, the participants rated the extended multi-display composition system positively. Aggregated across all of the data, the QUIS Overall User Reaction score was moderately positive with a mean score of 6.05 (SD=1.72) from a range of 1 to 9 with higher values being more positive. Similarly, the absolute rankings of the devices provided at the end of the experiment about how helpful the system was for performing the tasks show similar results with a mean "helpfulness" rating of 7.08 (SD=1.29) (again on the 9 point scale).

Examining these results in more detail reveals differences based on the type of device and the size of the group (Figures 3 and 4). For the overall QUIS user reaction score, there was a significant difference found based on condition (Kruskal-Wallis, $p<0.001$). Further analysis reveals participants preferred the tablets (M=6.71, SD=1.47) relative to the UMPCs (M=5.38, 1.70) (Wilcoxon Signed Ranks, $p<0.001$) and groups of two rated the multi-display composition higher (M=6.72 SD=1.45) than groups of four (M=5.71 SD=1.76) (Mann-Whitney $p<0.001$). The responses about device preference from the exit interview follow the same pattern with a significant difference between the conditions (Kruskal-Wallis Test, $p<0.001$). Tablet conditions again rated more favorably (M=7.09 SD=1.29) than the UMPC conditions (M=4.94 SD=2.04) (Wilcoxon Signed Ranks Test, $p<0.001$), and the groups of two rated the task more favorably (M=6.82 SD=1.39) than groups of four (M=5.62 SD=2.16) (Mann-Whitney Test, $p<0.001$). These trends also continue for our other subjective measures with the tablets generally rated higher than the UMPCs and similarly, the groups of two rating the system more favorably than groups of four (Figures 5 – 10).

Examining differences between tasks also reveals significant differences. The overall QUIS user reaction score shows a significant difference based on task (Friedman, $p=0.024$). Further analysis shows there are pair wise differences between the nutrition spreadsheet task and the flower photograph sorting task as well as between the nutrition task and the movie graph task (Wilcoxon Signed Ranks: $p=0.007$ and $p=0.010$ respectively). The nutrition spreadsheet task was rated least favorably (photo: M=6.20 SD=1.62, nutrition: M=5.64 SD=1.63, movie: M=6.20, SD=1.85). Similar results are true for the helpfulness ratings collected with the exit questionnaire. There is an overall effect for task type (Friedman, $p=0.005$) and significant differences between the nutrition task and both the photo and movie tasks (Wilcoxon Signed Ranks: $p=0.001$ and $p=0.003$ respectively). Again the spreadsheet nutrition task was rated least favorably (photo: M=6.58 SD=2.49, nutrition: M=5.20 SD=2.43, movie: M=6.27, SD=2.60).

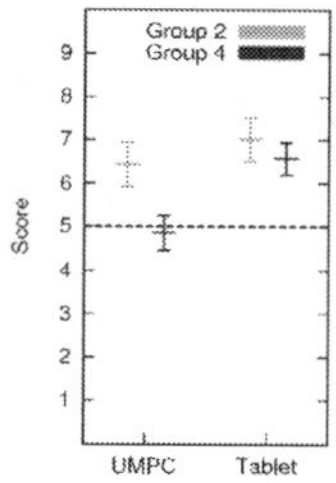

Fig. 3. QUIS Overall User Reaction scores (mean and 95% C.I.)

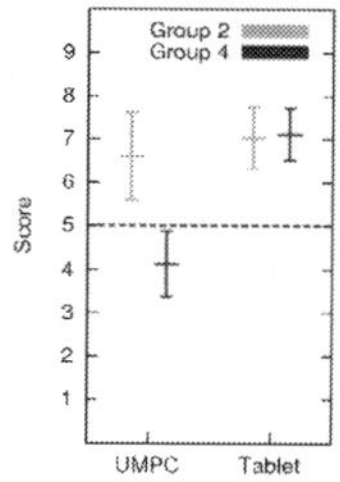

Fig. 4. Overall helpfulness of the display for a task

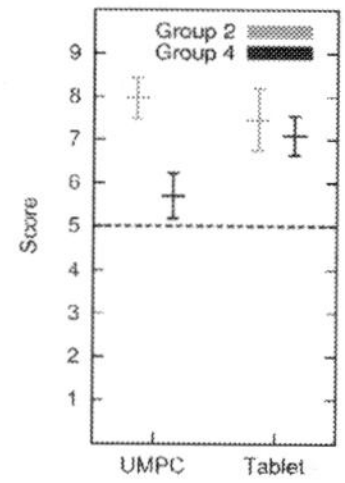

Fig. 5. Ability to participate in task

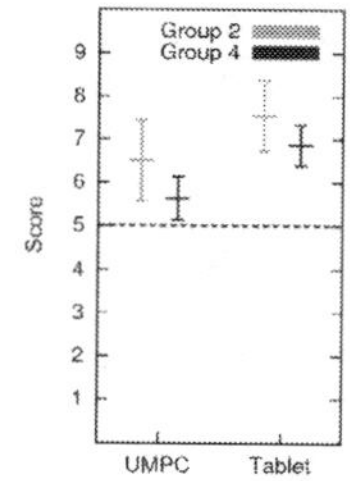

Fig. 6. Spacing between yourself and the other participants

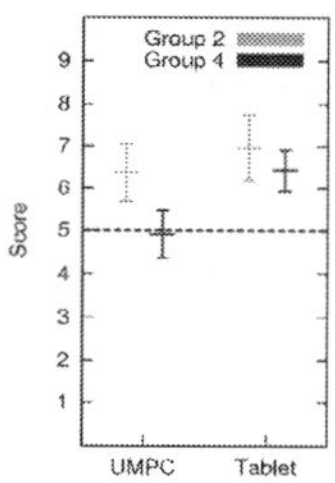

Fig. 7. Ability to provide input

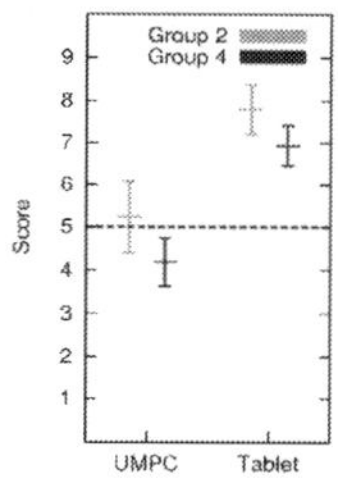

Fig. 8. Visibility of computer screen

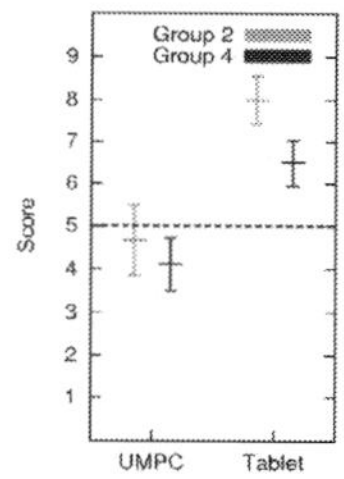

Fig. 9. Characters on the screen

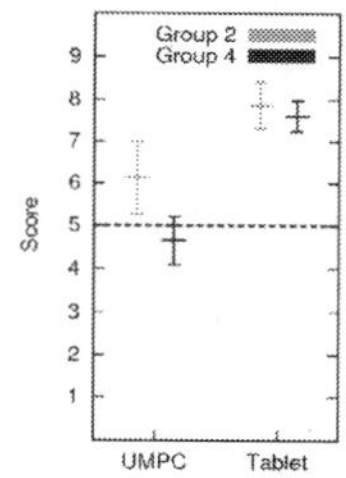

Fig. 10. Amount of info. Displayed

Together, these quantitative data show interesting results. While we originally aspired to create this system to increase the capabilities of UMPCs, it appears overall that it provides more benefit for tablets. Also, these data indicate that more pixels are not always better. While the use of four devices offered more screen area for the applications, it also meant there were four people trying to use the devices simultaneously, negating some of the advantages of having a larger display area.

5.2 Usage Themes

Given the overall trends in the quantitative data, we next turn to the qualitative information. This data was collected by asking the participants to list three positive and three negative aspects of the system after each task (for a total of six times per participant). The data from general comments provided by the participants at the end of the experiment and observation recorded during the study are further used to examine the usage patterns.

Display Size: One of the first positive comments participants often made was about having more screen real estate with the multi-display composition on the mobile devices. This aspect of the system was by design, but the participant comments and other data reveal several different ways the screen space was used. For the tasks that primarily utilized a single window (the spreadsheet and the movie tasks), nearly all of the groups immediately maximized the window to fill all of the available displays. Participants commented that this let them see more of the data and led to less scrolling. This held true even though most participants thought the space between displays taken up by the bezel was a negative aspect. For the photo sorting task, several groups used the screen space to spread out the windows to minimize overlapping. A few groups also commented on the advantage of the larger screen for seeing the larger view of a photograph. These comments held true for both the tablets and UMPCs: "the screens were small, but did fit a lot of things for a small screen".

Awareness: The participants also indicated that they appreciated the awareness of the group's activity that the system provided. The participants commented that they liked the ability to see what the others were doing, being able to quickly check with other group members about an activity, and to point out information on the composed display. Given that only one person could provide input at a given time, there was often the ability for the other group member(s) to help guide the navigation through the interface either looking ahead or for confirming the proper input. The shared display was also used for a common frame of reference where participants would point to the screen with either the stylus or a finger so that everyone could focus on the same information. This awareness was used for confirming a selection in the spreadsheet task, for pointing to a name in the movie task, and for building consensus about the type of a given flower in the photograph sorting task. This awareness results from using the multiple mobile computers as a single logical display, and would likely be absent if other display sharing models were used.

Collaboration: Many of the participants liked the ability to parallelize the task. Given the time limit of the tasks imposed by the study, there was an incentive for the groups to attempt to optimize for efficiency. In doing so, one common strategy adopted was to divide the tasks in different ways. The participants also leveraged the fact that the single logical display was spread across several physical devices, and used the device as a unit for dividing the task or interaction. For example, some of the groups of two very quickly adopted terminology such as "mine" and "yours" referring to either the device or data on the device directly in front of them or in front of their partner respectively. The division of labor also let participants manage the physical area of the display. Several participants commented negatively about the difficulty of reaching to the other side of the display to provide some needed input. While this was seen as a problem by some, others commented that the group nature of the task also provided a solution where "everyone clicked on their closest screen." And indeed, observations revealed that sometimes a participant would attempt to reach across all of the devices and fail to provide the needed input, so a closer person would finish the interaction. Some groups developed the strategy of having a person "assigned" either implicitly or explicitly to a region of the interface, for example operating the scroll bar or menus. While the participants commented on using this approach, observations indicated that these divisions were very flexible and fluid.

Input: Another form of shared interaction which occurred spontaneously in several groups centered on the functionality for performing a drag across device boundaries. During the flower sorting task which required many drag and drop operations, some of the groups developed a strategy where one person would start the drag, another would press the button on the tablet bezel to initiate the needed mode, and potentially a third person (for the groups of four) finished the drag on another device. Beyond this split operation, a few of the groups performed this task without speaking. The shared objective and visibility of the operations on the single logical display provided sufficient information for the group to successfully perform this operation in a very fluid fashion. Another issue revealed in the user comments and observations related to the single input nature of the system. The devices, the underlying windowing system, and applications were not multi-cursor aware. On the resistive touch screen of the UMPC, problems only occurred when multiple people touched the display. However, the tablets also tracked pen hover which could cause erratic mouse behavior when more than one person put their pen in the proximity of a device. While the tablets presented this problem, the overall trend of the tablets being rated more favorably continued when participants were asked to rate their ability to provide input to the system (Figure 7). As multi-touch devices such as the iPhone become more common, these issues may become less important.

Physical Aspects: Many participants commented about their position around the table and their ability to view the composition of displays. For example, some participants made comments about the "crowding of people". Others remarked about the viewing angle and effectively looking at the display from the side. It was also observed that some of the participants, especially in the groups of four, would stand up or kneel on their chair to be in a position where they could lean over the table. While participants commented that their spacing within the group was less than ideal, it appears not to have been too negative of a factor. The quantitative data reveals that participants rated the spacing favorably overall (M=6.50 SD=2.20). The overall trend of tablets being rated better than UMPCs, and groups of two having higher scores continues (Figure 6). Some participants also commented that some of the text was small or that the visibility could be improved. Here the quantitative data again shows that the UMPC performed worse than the tablet PC (Figures 8 and 9). In addition to the UMPC having fewer pixels and a smaller screen, it also has a higher pixel density. Together, those factors result in the bitmapped information appearing smaller on these devices. And while the multi-display system provided more pixels to see more content, it did not overcome this problem. This data reveals that an alternative approach for using multiple devices might be worth exploring. In particular, instead of just expanding the size of the virtual screen to fill all of available pixels, the system could use the extra screen real estate to also provide some magnification of the screen. Depending on the number of displays and magnification applied, the system could increase both the number of available pixels as well as the area used for each pixel.

6 Conclusions

Overall, our study provided insight that groups of participants were able to effectively use a multi-display composition involving several mobile devices as a unified display. The study revealed an interesting trade-off between the size of a composite display and correspondingly the number of participants in the group. Even though groups of four had more screen real estate to perform the tasks, they generally rated the use of the system less positively than the groups of two. There could be a number of factors leading to this result ranging from the need to coordinate more people, reduced visibility and the need to provide input to a physically larger device.

The trend in our results for the differences between devices is less surprising. Each tablet provides a larger individual display which is likely more usable that a smaller

UMPC display. And while the UMPCs were not the preferred devices, our data indicates that the system was still usable. When using smaller devices such as UMPCs or MIDs, an especially rich area for future work will be to explore how different configurations of multi-display composition (mirroring and extending) compare to more traditional collocated collaboration techniques on the same devices.

The spacing between the individuals in the group also presents an interesting finding. In previous work by Hinckley *et al.*, which also examined the joint use of two tablets by two individuals, the participants were reluctant to keep the devices in contact with each other [7]. While we did receive some negative feedback about the spacing between group members, the overall ratings for this issue were positive. Furthermore, none of the participants asked to separate the devices during our study. One possibility for the alternate findings is the different visual presentation and functionality of the two systems. It is possible that spreading the entire desktop across the computers increased the need or desire to keep the devices in direct physical proximity. Secondly, Hinckley *et al.* used pairs of participants who did not know each other before the study, whereas in our study there was a preexisting relationship of at least one month. Future work will be needed to better understand the dynamics of group interaction with the joint use of mobile devices.

In conclusion, we have presented multi-display composition, a technique for supporting the collocated display sharing of wireless mobile devices. We described our implementation of the system and discussed how it can be used to run legacy applications on a logical display formed from several mobile computers. Our study examined a specific usage scenario where a group of collocated users collaborate using an *ad hoc* display composed from pen-based computers. Our findings indicate that the system was generally rated favorably and groups of two people using tablet computers provided the most positive results. We also found several interesting themes of usage relating to the collaborative practices adopted by the groups using our system and some of the technical challenges that should be addressed. Overall, this work shows multi-display composition provides a useful technique for opportunistically overcoming the display limitations of mobile devices.

References

1. Blasko, G., Feiner, S., Coriand, F.: Exploring interaction with a simulated wrist-worn projection display. In: ISWC 2005, pp. 2–9. IEEE, Los Alamitos (2005)
2. Cao, X., Balakrishnan, R.: Interacting with dynamically defined information spaces using a handheld projector and a pen. In: Proceedings of UIST 2006, pp. 225–234. ACM, New York (2006)
3. Chen, N., Guimbretiere, F., Dixon, M., Lewis, C., Agrawala, M.: Navigation techniques for dual-display e-book readers. In: Proceeding of CHI 2008, pp. 1779–1788. ACM Press, New York (2008)
4. Chin, J.P., Diehl, V.A., Norman, K.L.: Development of an instrument measuring user satisfaction of the human-computer interface. In: Proceedings of CHI 1988, pp. 213–218. ACM Press, New York (1988)
5. Clawson, J., Voida, A., Patel, N., Lyons, K.: Mobiphos: a collocated-synchronous mobile photo sharing application. In: Proceedings of MobileHCI 2008, pp. 187–195. ACM Press, New York (2008)

6. Hinckley, K.: Synchronous gestures for multiple persons and computers. In: Proceedings of UIST 2003, pp. 149–158. ACM Press, New York (2003)
7. Hinckley, K., Ramos, G., Guimbretiere, F., Baudisch, P., Smith, M.: Stitching: pen gestures that span multiple displays. In: Proceedings of AVI 2004, pp. 23–31. ACM Press, New York (2004)
8. Humphreys, G., Houston, M., Ng, R., Frank, R., Ahern, S., Kirchner, P.D., Klosowski, J.T.: Chromium: a stream-processing framework for interactive rendering on clusters. In: Proceedings of SIGGRAPH 2002, pp. 693–702. ACM Press, New York (2002)
9. Hutchings, H.M., Pierce, J.S.: Understanding the whethers, hows, and whys of divisible interfaces. In: Proceedings of AVI 2006, pp. 274–277. ACM Press, New York (2006)
10. Kortuem, G., Kray, C., Gellersen, H.: Sensing and visualizing spatial relations of mobile devices. In: Proceedings of UIST 2005, pp. 93–102. ACM Press, New York (2005)
11. Merrill, D., Kalanithi, J., Maes, P.: Siftables: towards sensor network user interfaces. In: Proceedings of Tangible and embedded interaction, pp. 75–78. ACM Press, New York (2007)
12. Pering, T., Want, R., Rosario, B., Sud, S., Lyons, K.: Enabling pervasive collaboration with platform composition. In: Proceedings of Pervasive 2009 (2009)
13. Rekimoto, J.: Pick-and-drop: a direct manipulation technique for multiple computer environments. In: Proceedings of UIST 1997, pp. 31–39. ACM Press, New York (1997)
14. Richardson, T., Stafford-Fraser, Q., Wood, K.R., Hopper, A.: Virtual network computing. IEEE Internet Computing 2(1), 33–38 (1998)
15. Spitzer, M., Rensing, N., McClelland, R., Aquilino, P.: Eyeglass-based systems for wearable computing. In: Proceedings of the ISWC 1997. IEEE, Los Alamitos (1997)
16. Tandler, P., Prante, T., Müller-Tomfelde, C., Streitz, N., Steinmetz, R.: Connectables: dynamic coupling of displays for the flexible creation of shared workspaces. In: Proceedings of UIST 2001, pp. 11–20. ACM Press, New York (2001)
17. U.S. Department of Agriculture Agricultural Research Service. USDA National Nutrient Database for Standard Reference, Release 20 (2007), `http://www.nal.usda.gov/fnic/foodcomp/Data/SR20/dnload/sr20abxl.zip`
18. Vadas, K., Patel, N., Lyons, K., Starner, T., Jacko, J.: Reading on-the-go: a comparison of audio and hand-held displays. In: Proc. of MobileHCI 2006, pp. 219–226. ACM Press, New York (2006)
19. Want, R., Pering, T., Sud, S., Rosario, B.: Dynamic composable computing. In: Proceedings of HotMobile 2008 (February 2008)
20. Weiser, M.: The computer for the twenty-first century. Scientific American, 94–104 (1991)

Animated Transitions for Adaptive Small Size Mobile Menus

Jussi Huhtala[1], Jani Mäntyjärvi[1,2], Aino Ahtinen[1], Leena Ventä[1], and Minna Isomursu[2]

[1] Nokia Research Center, P.O. Box 300, FI-90230, OULU, Finland
[2] VTT Technical Research Centre of Finland, P.O. Box 1100, FI-90571, OULU, Finland
{jussi.huhtala,aino.ahtinen,leena.venta}@nokia.com,
{jani.mantyjarvi,minna.isomursu}@vtt.fi

Abstract. This paper explores how the user interface of a mobile device could support human perception and conception of changes in its environment. Animated transition effects may hold potential for visualizing changes in the resources available for the user through the context-aware user interface. Four different transition types are investigated. Each transition represents a different approach for visualizing changes in UI. The transitions are evaluated with 40 test subjects, half in India and half in Europe. Statistical analysis of the results indicates that animated transition effects have a clear positive effect on perception and conception of change.

Keywords: Mobile UI design, animation, transition.

1 Introduction

In ubiquitous computing, all computing devices are aware of their surrounding devices and their available resources. A mobile device could potentially act as a generic device for providing user interfaces (UIs) for a smart environment. When a user moves from a smart space to another, digital affordance available for the user through a mobile UI changes, too. This may set challenges for a user since (s)he has gotten accustomed to the UI structure of his/her device.

This paper explores how the user interface of the mobile device could visually support the user to perceive and comprehend the changes in the resources available. The purpose of this research is to study user perception of dynamic grid menus which have changing elements depending on the space a user experiences at the moment. This study assumes that there is technology available, which provides information on the new smart spaces and all available resources of a given place to a mobile device before the user arrives to this place [1].

Research on perception and motion on a screen is quite novel in the mobile UI domain. However, considerable research work has been carried out on human visual perception in the realm of desktop UI. Animations have been reported to improve user performance and user experience. In the research by Bladh et al. it has been found that short animations during navigation with 3D maps affect user performance and reduce task times when e.g. counting details on maps [2]. Klein & Bederson measured better

T. Gross et al. (Eds.): INTERACT 2009, Part I, LNCS 5726, pp. 772–781, 2009.

results in reading when scrolling animation was used [3]. The results of Baecker et al. show that small animated icons can convey functionality better than static icons of the same size. [4]. Baudish et al. present how animated effects have been used successfully to improve the user's ability to perceive changes on a computer desktop [5]. With careful design, the transitions can be designed and implemented so that they do not cause delays or disturb the task performance. Study by Hong et al. shows that flashing animation apparently helps users to locate single targets within a larger amount of information [6]. However, flashing has also been found to disturb the user if the information density is not high or flashing does not happen in a targeted item. Several studies concerning failures of visual awareness show that pictures separated by a blank frame cause a change blindness effect [7]. These results can help to understand visual perception in computer graphics and set a baseline for animation perception.

Studies on the use of animated transitions have usually been done in desktop environments. In related work, moving screens or elements are used to help with navigation and draw the attention of the user to selected user interface elements. The work presented here explores how animations could make the user more aware of the changes in the digital resources available in varying environments.

This paper is organized as follows: Animated transitions are explained in the next section, after which the experiments are described. Then, results are provided, and finally, concluding remarks are presented.

2 Animated Transitions

We used a demonstration application that visualized a hypothetical situation: A user moving from one space to another and a UI presenting the new resources available. The application presented twelve icons arranged in a grid type menu. The icons were selected to represent different digital resources. We used Crystal Project [8] icons designed for open source environments because they were not widely used in mobile devices. Some of them were widely known figures like the RSS feed icon and others represented general features like device icons (Figure 1). The selected 48 icons had

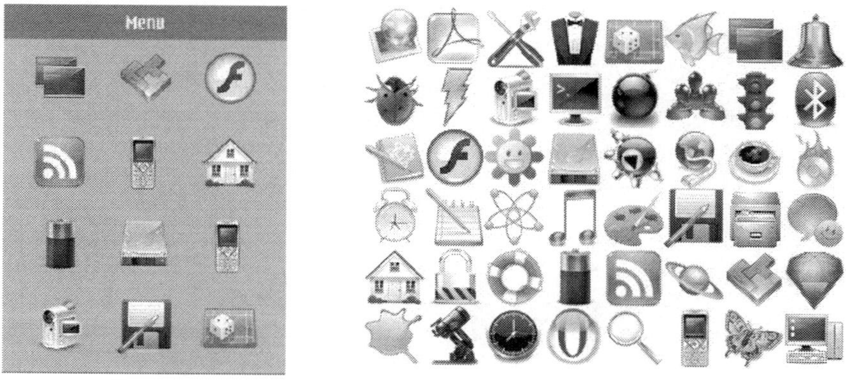

Fig. 1. Mobile grid menu and all icons used in the study

various overall colorings and outline shapes. Text was not used because we wanted to keep the visual information clear and reduce the effect of different linguistic backgrounds.

Four different transition types were chosen as options for presenting change. The first two transition types were not animated, and the last two represented different, both common, animated transition types. The transition types with their implementation are described in detail in the following.

Blank screen transition (change blindness effect) displays a grey screen for the duration of 1, 2, or 3 seconds between the screens. Variations of blank screen transitions are common, for example, in applications where a box with text "Updating…" is displayed on the screen while updating is in progress. Even partial covering of the screen can cause change blindness which makes it difficult to notice the change.

Direct change transition switches the icons immediately without any animation. Direct change does not give any visual cue that a change is about to happen.

Sliding animation accelerates the disappearing icon to the bottom right, representing the resource becoming unavailable. The new icon appears simultaneously by sliding into the menu from the upper left corner of the screen. The new icon slows its speed before placing itself in the grid to emphasize grounding and staying in place. The sliding animation is illustrated in Figure 2.

Blinking animation first pulses the icon representing the old resource to partial transparency two to six times, depending on the duration of transition, after which it disappears from the screen. After that, the icon representing the new available resource appears first as a white silhouette of the icon and then smoothly tones down to its normal coloring. The blinking effect is illustrated in Figure 3.

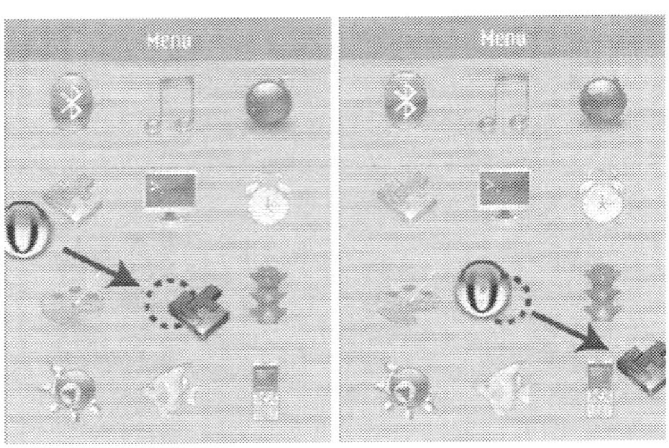

Fig. 2. Sliding animation

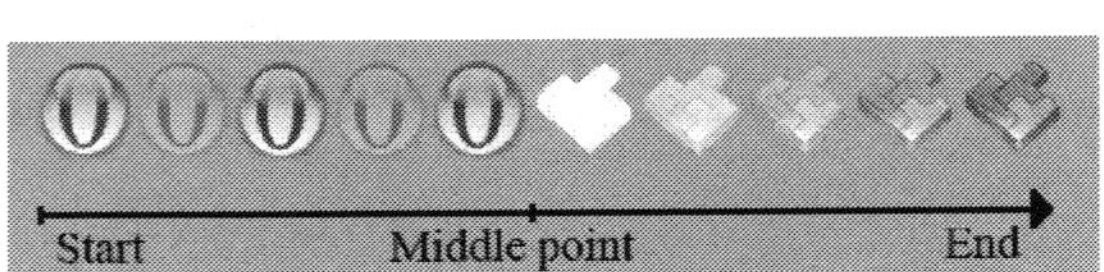

Fig. 3. Blinking animation

3 Experiment

The transition effects were explored from the viewpoints of user performance and subjective satisfaction.

The experiment was conducted with 40 voluntary participants. 20 of them were from Finland and 20 from India. The test subjects were between the ages of 20 and 40 years (average about 30 years). Most participants used mobile phones with graphical user interfaces regularly, and had a technical or office work background. 16 of the test subjects were female and 24 were male.

3.1 Experiment Settings

The demonstration application ran on the Nokia N95 mobile phone and the Flash Lite application. The test was performed indoors in a place where the illumination conditions were even, no distractions were present, and the users were able to physically move from one space to another. Data collection was done by a researcher who shadowed the subjects during the experiment. The experiment procedure was as follows:

The user was given a mobile device and a pen. The user held the pen in the hand they used for writing, and the mobile phone in the other hand. The following task was repeated 18 times by each user.

1. The user was requested to walk a couple of meters, and open the blank screen by pressing "Enter."
2. When the application started, the user first saw a grid menu with the resources of the "old location" on the mobile device screen for the duration of five seconds.
3. Then one of the four transitions was used to change two, four or six icons in different locations of the screen simultaneously. The transition times varied between one and three seconds.
4. The new combination of resource icons was displayed to the user for the duration of five seconds, after which the screen turned black (see timeline in Figure 4).
5. The researcher presented the data collection form to the user, who then used it to report the changes he or she had been able to perceive. The data collection form followed the structure presented in Figure 5.

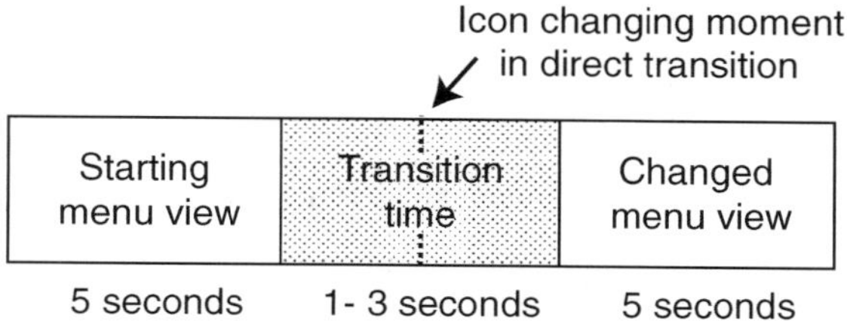

Fig. 4. Timeline of the application

As we used four different transition types, three different transition durations, and three different amounts of changing icons, there was a total of 36 different combinations to test. To maintain the participant's attention, each user tested only 18 of all the combinations. The application automatically randomized the icon graphics to make the icon grid look different each time. In addition, we allowed multiple similar icons on the screen because this is possible in real-world situations as well. The new icons after transition were always different from the ones they replaced.

The locations of the changing icons were randomized beforehand in three different sets of tasks to reduce the effect of easily recognized patterns. The distribution between sets was 7-6-7.

The data collection form shown in Figure 5 was presented to the test subject. Places where the user had perceived change were marked on the answer cells representing the grid menu. To prevent a learning effect, the transitions were not presented to the user beforehand. The order of tasks was also varied between users.

After the tasks, users gave subjective ratings from 1 (low) to 5 (high) to rank the visual appearance, clarity, and usefulness of the transition types. Also, subjective comments on the complexity of the task and general remarks were requested.

Rate the visual appearance

	Not visually appealing		Can't say		Visually appealing
Direct transition	1	2	3	4	5
Blank screen	1	2	3	4	5
Moving icons	1	2	3	4	5
Blinking icons	1	2	3	4	5

Rate the clearness

	Unclear		Can't say		Very clear
Direct transition	1	2	3	4	5
Blank screen	1	2	3	4	5
Moving icons	1	2	3	4	5
Blinking icons	1	2	3	4	5

Rate the usefulness

	Not useful		Can't say		Very useful
Direct transition	1	2	3	4	5
Blank screen	1	2	3	4	5
Moving icons	1	2	3	4	5
Blinking icons	1	2	3	4	5

Fig. 5. Part of answer sheet, and ratings sections in end question sheet

3.2 Analysis of Data

The data collection forms were analyzed through the procedure illustrated in Figure 6.

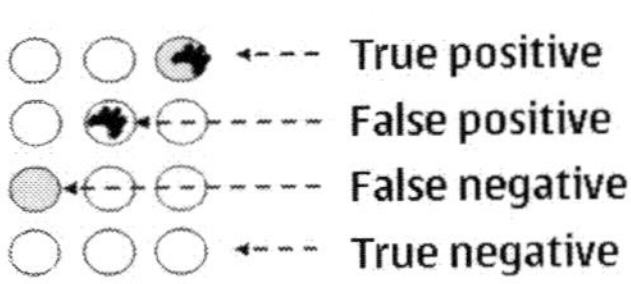

Fig. 6. Answer sheet shell and all four possible answers. Shaded circles are the locations where icons actually changed.

Precision and recall are commonly used to measure performance. Precision is the number of correctly marked locations divided by the number of all marked locations, and recall is the number of correctly marked locations divided by the total number of all actually changed icons.

$$\Pr ecision = \frac{tp}{tp + fp}, \quad \text{Re}call = \frac{tp}{tp + fn} \tag{1, 2}$$

We used Rijsbergen's F-measure [9] value to compare the different task groups. The harmonic mean of the Precision and the Recall values gave the probability of getting the correct answers from users. Then the F-measure values of different sets (transition types, durations, and amounts of icons) were compared.

$$F = 2 \cdot \frac{\Pr ecision \cdot \text{Re}call}{\Pr ecision + \text{Re}call} \tag{3}$$

The subjective ratings consisted of numerical ratings and free-form verbal comments. Mean values were counted from numerical ratings, as variation was very small and preferences consistent between users. Verbal comments were grouped into themes, and they were used to find explaining factors for the quantitative results.

4 Results

Here, we first discuss the results from performance analysis and move then to the analysis of subjective ratings.

4.1 Performance Evaluation

Effect of transition type

The F-measure values were analyzed by using one-way ANOVA tests using transition type (four groups), duration (three groups), and icon amount (three groups) as independent variables. After that, Tukey's post-hoc test was applied to compare significant groups.

Table 1. Sums of true positives, false positives, false negatives and true negatives

Transition	tp	fp	fn	tn
Direct	450	50	270	1390
Empty	159	160	561	1280
Blinking	666	21	54	1419
Sliding	642	39	78	1401

Animated transitions proved to be significantly more effective at supporting the subjects in perceiving the change in the resources (Figure 7). In multiple comparisons, no statistical difference was found between the animated transitions (blinking versus

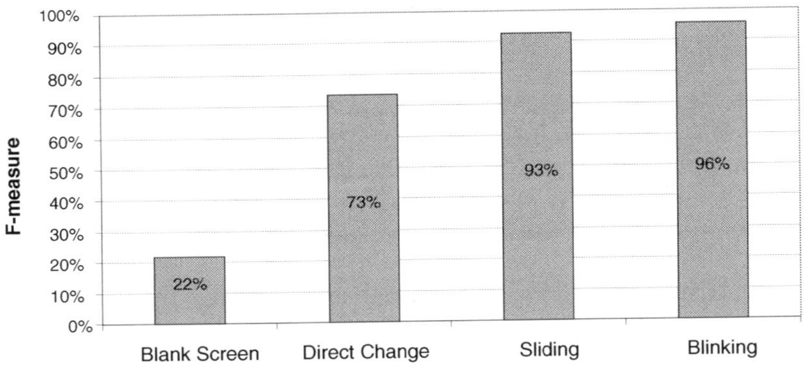

Fig. 7. Effect of transition types

sliding). However, comparisons of all other transition pairs were significant ($p<.05$). Results show that the chance of getting a right answer with the blank screen transition was remarkably low. Performance with direct transitions was significantly better, but still significantly poorer than with animated transitions.

Duration and amount

The ANOVA test did not show significant differences between duration groups or between amount groups.

Varying the duration of animations between one, two and three seconds did not have a significant impact on the results ($F(2, 717) = 0.518$, $p>.05$). One-second animations worked as well as three-second ones. This is in agreement with the menu transitions study of Bladh et al [2].

Varying the amount of simultaneously changing icons also had no statistically significant impact ($F(2,717) = 2.41$, $p>.05$). However, when comparing icon amounts and transition types together, there seemed to be a small tendency that blank screen was better with a larger amount of icons (Figure 8).

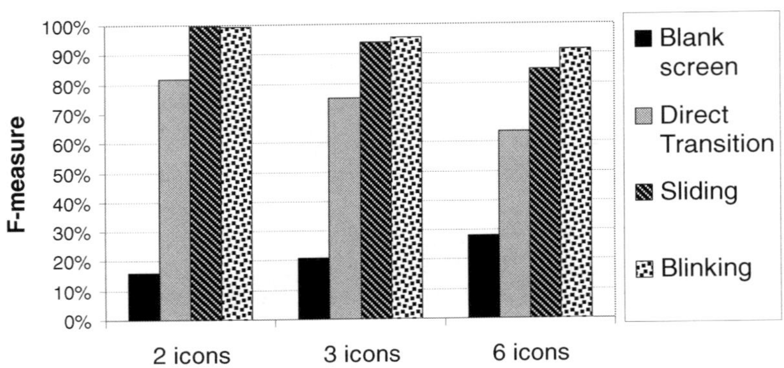

Fig. 8. Effect of icon amount with different transitions

4.2 Subjective Ratings

Our analysis shows that the subjective ratings of the test subjects follow the findings of the performance evaluation. In addition, there was little variation in ratings. The transitions resulting in the best user performance were also rated most visually appealing, clear and useful. Also, there was not much variation in individual ratings between visual appearance, clarity, and usefulness. This might indicate that the test subjects were not able to express their experience through dividing it into the three components presented.

Users commented that a blank screen between two screens required more active memorizing and resulted in more cognitive load than the other transition types. With blank screen transitions, the users sometimes stated that they did not see anything changing, or that everything changed. This might explain high error rates. Change blindness forced users to make assumptions and guesses, and perhaps also to use special memorizing techniques (Figure 9).

Opinions of direct transition were more neutral. Test subjects stated that several icons changing simultaneously was confusing, and they thought they blinked just when change occurred. It is possible that this situation can be compared to change blindness. With animated transitions, this kind of problem was not mentioned (Figure 10).

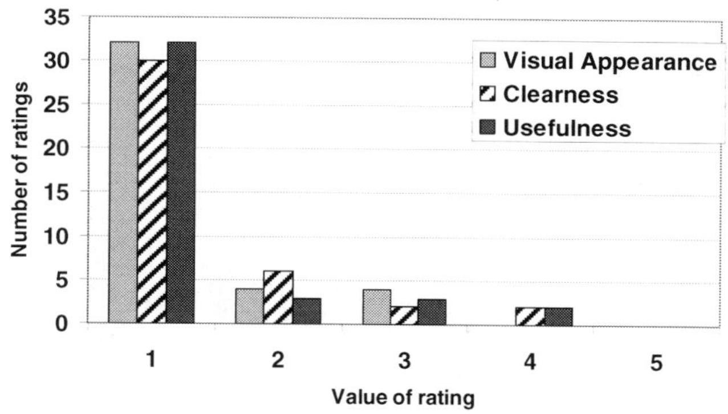

Fig. 9. Opinions of blank screen

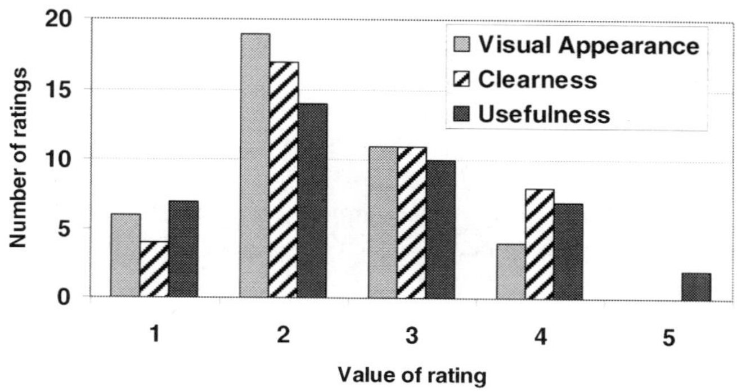

Fig. 10. Opinions of direct change

Blinking animation was the most liked, but no significant difference was noted from sliding animation (Figure 12). Blinking was mentioned as being enjoyable and clear, but also slightly annoying. Some stated that the white color effect could last longer (Figure 11).

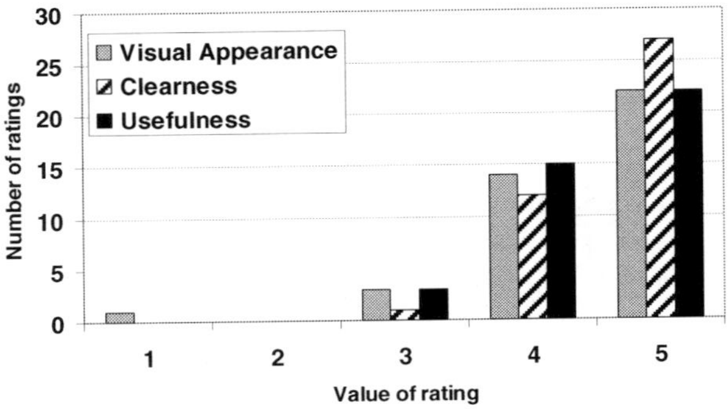

Fig. 11. Opinions of blinking animation

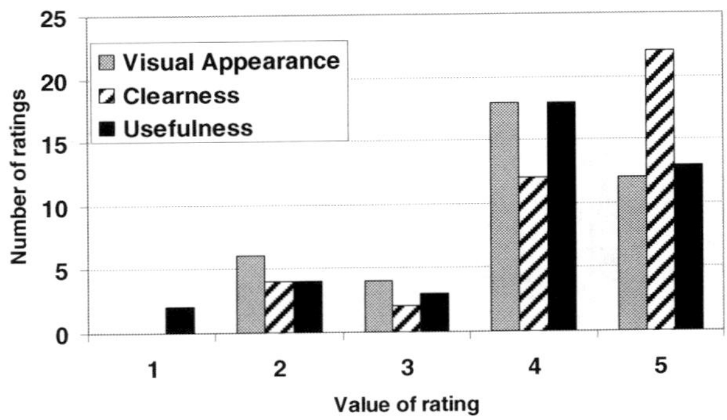

Fig. 12. Opinions of sliding animation

Sliding was liked, too, but multiple icons sliding on the screen simultaneously was perceived as confusing. Overlapping of icons was also perceived as disturbing. Sliding icons caught users' attention in a positive way. There were some slight differences in subjective ratings between blinking and sliding animations. Users rated visual appearance and usefulness a bit poorer for the sliding transition. However, this difference was not clearly supported by user comments. The most interesting detail was that the sliding animation was hoped to last for a shorter time, but the blinking one was hoped to last longer.

Users wished that the dynamic and static parts of menus should be marked clearly in the user interface. Some users mentioned that the icons should look different enough that they are not confused accidentally.

5 Concluding Remarks

The animated transitions resulted in significantly better user performance compared with non-animated transitions. Even though transition time did not have an effect on user performance, subjective experiences revealed interesting issues about timing. Users hoped that sliding animations would be faster, but blinking was hoped to last longer. Experimenting with more variation in animation timing could be a subject of further research.

Blinking was perceived as a little annoying, but it was seen as a clear indicator. Sliding icons were perceived as confusing when they overlapped other icons. More detailed comparison between moving and blinking animations would offer more information how to use the benefits of animation on small screens. It appears that human visual perception can accurately handle quite complex movement on the screen. The challenge in design is to attract the user's attention without losing the appeal of the user interface. The role of animation design, acceleration in animation, and color effects with blinking animation are interesting issues for future work.

Even though the test was performed in a mobile setting simulating real-life usage situations, the users seemed to have problems in understanding the concept of changing resources and adaptive UI. A truer level of experimental realism would be needed to evaluate issues beyond perception and comprehension, such as usability and utility.

References

1. Such an enabling technology could be e.g. NoTA, `http://www.notaworld.org`
2. Bladh, T., Carr, D.A., Kljun, M.: The Effect of Animated Transitions on User Navigation in 3D Tree-Maps. In: Proceedings of the Ninth International Confer-ence on Information Visualisation (IV 2005), pp. 297–305. IEEE Computer Society, Los Alamitos (2005)
3. Klein, C., Bederson, B.B.: Benefits of animated scrolling. In: Conference on Human Factors in Computing Systems (CHI 2005), pp. 1965–1968. ACM Press, New York (2005)
4. Baecker, R., Small, I., Mander, R.: Bringing icons to life. In: Conference on Human Factors in Computing Systems (CHI 1991), pp. 1–6. ACM Press, New York (1991)
5. Baudisch, P., Tan, D., Collomb, M., Robbins, D., Hinckley, K., Agrawala, M., Zhao, S., Ramos, G.: Phosphor: Explaining Transitions in the User Interface Using Afterglow Effects. In: Proceedings of UIST 2006, pp. 169–178. ACM Press, New York (2006)
6. Hong, W., Thong, J.Y.L., Tam, K.-Y.: Does Animation Attract Online Users' At-tention? The Effects of Flash on Information Search Performance and Perceptions. Information Systems Research. INFORMS 15(1), 60–86 (2004)
7. Mancero, G., Wong, W., Amaldi, P.: Looking but not seeing: implications for HCI. In: Proceedings of ECCE 2007, pp. 167–174. ACM, New York (2007)
8. The Crystal Project is released under GNU General Public License, `http://www.everaldo.com/crystal/`
9. Van Rijsbergen, C.J.: Information Retrieval. Butterworth-Heinemann, Newton (1979)

Investigating the Use of Voice and Ink for Mobile Micronote Capture

Adrienne H. Andrew[1], Amy K. Karlson[2], and A.J. Bernheim Brush[2]

[1] Computer Science and Engineering, University of Washington, Seattle WA 98195 USA
[2] Microsoft Research, One Microsoft Way, Redmond WA 98052 USA
aha@cs.washington.edu, {karlson,ajbrush}@microsoft.com

Abstract. Despite the potential benefits of digital note taking tools, research has found that people continue to use paper for creating micronotes, informal personal notes such as reminders and to-dos. Design recommendations from formative studies suggest that "natural" input modalities such as voice and digital ink could help to overcome the drawbacks of text entry on phones and PDAs. We conducted an 18-person lab study to understand the perceived and actual trade-offs that these non-traditional input methods offer for micronote capture. We found that people preferred ink (8 participants) and voice (8 participants) input over keyboard (2 participants) input. Half our participants varied the input method they used in different environments, while the rest did not. However, paper remains popular and was preferred by 8 participants when given the option. The 9 participants whose ink and voice micronotes were transcribed with higher error rates had a noticeably different experience using voice including slower capture times, and higher mental and physical demand survey responses. The percentage of participants that preferred ink, voice, and keyboard was the same for both transcription quality groups.

Keywords: Mobile input, voice input, digital ink, micronotes, mobile note taking.

1 Introduction

Despite the large number of technologies that are now available to help us digitally capture and manage small pieces of information, such as to-do lists and phone numbers, people continue to use paper for these notes. Micronotes, a term Lin et al. [1], adopted to "cover the host of personal jottings to ourselves that we all make every day" often manifest themselves on the scraps of paper that fill our desks, purses and bags. Digital versions take the form of a small piece of information emailed to yourself, or typed into Notepad or digital post-its. As such, micronotes (both physical and digital) are frequently distinguished from formal notes or tasks by their inability to fit easily into traditional Personal Information Management (PIM) tools. The result is that micronotes are often lost and difficult to maintain over time.

Researchers have been captivated by the potential benefits that digital capture might offer micronote creators in terms of editing, searching, sharing, and archiving. Several research studies have explored the content and purpose of micronotes [2], the lifecycle of micronotes [1], the management of micronotes [3,4] and how people use

T. Gross et al. (Eds.): INTERACT 2009, Part I, LNCS 5726, pp. 782–795, 2009.

(or do not use) PDAs for capturing and retrieving micronotes [1,4,5,6]. Their results highlight that a key barrier to digitizing micronotes is getting them in digital form in the first place; that is, people find that digital devices, even pervasive ones such as mobile phones, generally do not meet their needs during micronote creation. Design recommendations from these studies suggest numerous ways in which future tools might lower the barrier to digital micronote capture. Of particular interest to us, several studies recommend that support for input methods such as digital ink and voice could be valuable in making micronote capture natural and fast, while automatic transcription of the resulting pen-strokes and audio could assist people in retrieving, organizing and searching their captured notes [1,3,5,6,7].

Inspired by these design recommendations and to complement previous research, which has primarily focused on understanding current micronote taking practices, we conducted a controlled laboratory study to lend formal insight into micronote capture. Specifically, we were interested in understanding what factors might influence people's choice of input modality for capturing a micronote on a mobile device that supported digital ink and voice input in addition to standard keyboard entry. Our study was designed to allow us to explore the effect of three factors on participant preference: transcription quality, time to enter a note, and the physical environment. Eighteen participants created micronotes on a phone using digital ink, voice, and a virtual soft keypad for lists of varying length in three different settings: a lab, café, and while walking. The ink and voice micronotes of half our participants were transcribed with error rates similar to current day technology, while the micronotes of the other half were transcribed with near perfect accuracy that might be possible in the future.

Our participants preferred voice (8 participants) and ink (8 participants) over keyboard input (2 participants). Surprisingly, although participants in different transcription conditions did have measurably different experiences, particularly for voice input, the distribution of participant preferences across input modalities was the same in both conditions (e.g. 4 from each condition preferred voice, 4 preferred ink and 1 preferred keyboard). Even after trying the "natural" input modalities of ink and voice, paper remained appealing to 8 participants who ranked it as their most preferred input when given the option. Participant preference did not appear to be related to how fast they were at capturing notes using a particular modality, while the environment did seem to affect which modality some participants selected (e.g., using voice while walking, but using ink or keyboard in the nosy café). However half of our participants did not change their input modality based on the environment suggesting some had a strong personal preference. Our results lend evidence that note taking systems should offer integrated experiences to allow users flexibility in choosing an appropriate input modality based on their preferences and situational needs.

2 Related Work

Lin et al. [1] conducted one of the earliest studies investigating micronotes, identifying the lifecycle of a micronote. This includes trigger, record, transfer, maintain, refer, complete, discard, and archive. In our study we focus on the record stage and how people capture micronotes using mobile devices. Research by Lin and others (e.g., [1,3,5,8]) highlights the importance of being able to quickly access the capture device (for example, taking a mobile phone out of a pocket), start taking the note, and finish making the note. Several studies (e.g., [3,4,5,6,8]) have also found that some note-taking applications require people to specify detailed information about the note after entering it (e.g., a reminder time, date or importance rating) which are potential barriers to the quick capture of a micronote.

Previous research (e.g., [1,3,5,6]) has suggested that people can more quickly create a micronote using either voice or writing with a pen, rather than, for example, multi-tap on a cell phone. However, voice and ink input both have drawbacks in terms of post-entry consumption and management. For example, voice notes are easy to enter, but time-consuming to listen to. Ink is natural to enter on a touchscreen device, but handwriting can look messy and tends to be large so fewer notes can fit on a screen. Research by [1] and [2] suggests both voice and ink notes can benefit from post-processing that transforms them into digital characters (transcription), which then allows them to be searched, quickly visually inspected, organized and incorporated into reminder systems. As Lin et al. wrote, "In summary, the optimal mobile micronote system combines the ubiquitous convenience of paper, the intuitive writing process of a digital pen, and the computational functionality of a PDA" [1].

Of course mobile micronote tools are being developed. Commercial offerings include tools such as Jott [9], which allows users to call a number and follow structured voice prompts to leave a voice message which is then transcribed and made available to the user, and Microsoft's OneNote Mobile that accepts voice and digital ink input, as well as research prototypes (e.g., [1]). Evernote [10], which supports mobile note-taking using voice, pictures, and text, is one of the most compelling mobile micronote applications, but it does not support ink input or transcribe voice notes. The widespread continuing use of bits of paper, post-it notes and other scraps for many micronotes highlights the challenges of developing a digital micronote application that is widely adopted [3,8]. Given that previous studies have identified quick entry and natural input modalities as important, in this study we sought to better understand in a systematic way people's preference for using ink and voice to capture micronotes.

3 Study

We designed and executed a controlled quantitative study to answer research questions regarding how transcription quality, capture time, and environment affect user choice and preference for using Ink and Voice for entering micronotes on a touch-screen-based mobile device. Our three specific research questions were:

Q1: How accurately can users build a mental model of what input modality is fastest for them? Does transcription quality affect this?
Q2: Does the environment influence the choice of input modality or do participants seem to have a stable personal preference across environments?
Q3: What input modalities do participants prefer? Does transcription quality or speed of capture seem to influence users' preference?

To explore these questions we recruited eighteen participants (9 men, 9 women; ages 17 to 56, mean = 39, median = 46) from the general population to take part in our study in July 2008. We specifically recruited participants who used paper to capture micronotes at least once a week and owned a standard mobile phone (not a Smartphone or Pocket PC) so that they would not be biased by previous mobile micronote capture experiences. During the study, participants captured micronotes of three different lengths (short, medium, long) using Ink, Voice and a virtual Keyboard. The transcription quality of the Ink and Voice notes was a between-subjects condition. Participants in the CurrentDay (CD) condition received transcriptions with error rates similar to those produced by standard voice and ink recognizers [11,12], while those in the NearPerfect (NP) transcription condition received transcriptions that were close to perfect and represented possible future error rates. We split the men and women in the study across the two transcription conditions as equally as possible (CD: 5M, 4W; NP: 4M, 5W). We now describe VINO, a prototype mobile note taking application we built for our study and then our study procedure.

3.1 VINO Prototype

For the study we built the VINO (Voice and InkNOtes) note taking prototype. The note capture screen shown in Fig. 1a can be reached directly by using the hardware note-taking button or from an initial screen (not shown) listing all previously entered notes. From the capture screen the user can create a note in whatever modality she wishes—either by starting the recorder using the audio recording bar (top), writing in Ink (middle), or typing on the Keyboard (bottom). Once input has begun, the display swaps into either audio-capture mode, Ink-capture mode (Fig. 1b), or typing mode to maximize the space available for capturing the micronote, which is especially valuable during Ink input mode. After an Ink or Voice note has been captured, an editable transcription appears in a new tab (Fig. 1c), allowing the user to toggle between the original Ink or Voice note and its transcription. VINO does not currently support real-time transcription. All transcriptions were pre-computed for each user task because of the need to control for errors in our study, and we incorporated event logging capabilities and study control logic into the prototype.

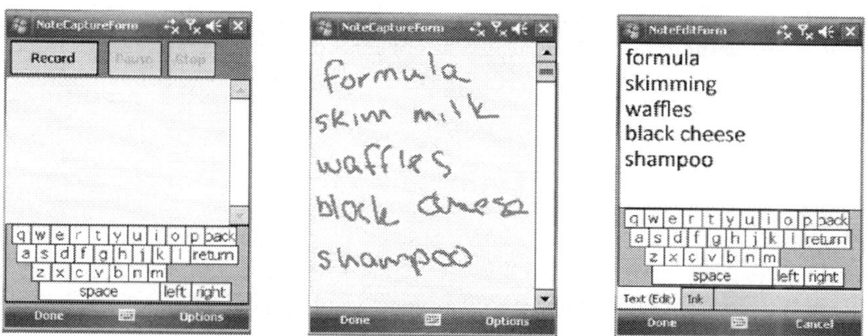

(a) (b) (c)

Fig. 1. The VINO note capture software. (a) The note capture screen supports voice (top), ink (middle) or keyboard entry (bottom); (b) ink entry mode; (c) the transcription screen for Voice or Ink notes.

To develop transcriptions for the CurrentDay and NearPerfect transcription conditions, six co-workers (3M, 3F) were recruited to speak and write (with digital Ink) all of the micronotes included in the study tasks. We then used standard Voice and Ink recognizers [11,12] to transcribe this data, and calculated error rates using a version of the Levenshtein distance function [13] modified to take into account the fact that the VINO text editor only allows insertions and deletions, not overwrites. This process helped us determine our error rates for the CurrentDay condition as 0.35 errors per character for Voice and 0.17 for Ink. For the NearPerfect condition, we decided upon error rates for Voice of 0.11 and 0.04 for Ink.

Using these rates, we introduced errors to the transcriptions we gave the participants using misrecognitions from the software-generated transcriptions whenever possible. To control for total number of errors across tasks in each condition, we occasionally created a transcription with the appropriate number of errors that was similar to but not exactly the same as any error generated by the transcription software. In a further attempt at realism, Voice transcriptions were always displayed as a single line, while Ink transcriptions showed the lists as 1, 3, or 5 lines, depending on the task length. Overall, this process allowed us to generate "fake" transcriptions that contained realistic errors, but which also had a controlled error rate. One aspect of errors we did not control for were "meaning-changing" errors. For example, with the micronote "bake cookies," a transcription of "bak cookie" is likely to be understood by the creator, while "bark copies" might not be. We calculated that 40% of the 168 transcriptions we used had potentially meaning-changing errors. The participants did not communicate any concern or disbelief about the transcriptions.

We built VINO using C# (.NET Compact Framework) and it runs on Windows Mobile PocketPCs—mobile phones with touchscreens that function similar to Personal Digital Assistants (PDAs). We conducted the study using an HTC Touch Cruise, which has a large screen with a flush bezel that is easy to write on, a hardware button that could be used to launch VINO, and a voice recorder. However, because the Touch Cruise lacks a physical keyboard, we built a custom soft keyboard for inclusion in VINO. We implemented our own keyboard to control when and how it was displayed to users and avoid the predictive word choices that the built-in keyboard automatically presents to users as we were concerned it might confuse users and potentially confound our results.

3.2 Procedure

The study was conducted in our lab and took roughly 1.5 hours. The study consisted of five phases:

Current Behavior: We interviewed the participant about her use of micronotes, and discussed the personal micronotes we asked her to bring to the lab.

Training (3 micronotes): We introduced the participant to the VINO software and the protocol that would be used for performing the study tasks by having her enter micronotes using all three input modalities (Ink, Voice, Keyboard) and lengths. We specified the text of each micronote for all trials, which were either Short (S), a 1-item 2-word list, Medium (M), a 3-item 4-word list or Long (L), a 5-item 7-word list. We ensured that all micronotes in each length category had the same number of characters. Research by Ludford et al. [14] showed that users in their study on location-based reminding created lists of things to do or get most of the time. Therefore, the micronotes we created for the study were lists of things to do (e.g., "wash windows") or get (e.g., "cloth, bucket, rubber gloves").

At the start of each task the participant was given a printed card showing the target micronote text, which was also displayed on the screen of the phone. The participant pressed a button on the screen to start the capture process, entered the content into VINO using the designated input method, and then pressed another button to indicate they were finished. The participant was then presented with a transcription of the note (Fig. 1c), which she corrected using the soft keyboard before submitting the final note. The participants were not aware that the transcriptions were pre-computed.

Participants were instructed to correct transcriptions to whatever degree "felt comfortable" in order to make the final transcription capture the essence of the list presented on the printed card. For consistency, we had considered asking participants to correct the transcription to exactly match the list given in the task. However, our two pilot participants reported that it felt arbitrary and contrived. Thus we decided to loosen the correction constraint, as this is closer to real world use where one might ignore a mistranslation that is clearly an error, but is still recognizable.

Input Trials (18 micronotes): The participant captured 2 micronotes for each note length (S, M, L) using each of the three input modalities (Ink, Voice, Keyboard). All 6 tasks for a particular input modality were performed together, but the presentation order of the input modalities was counterbalanced across participants. Tasks were randomized within each input modality. After each input modality, the participant filled out a NASA TLX-based survey about her experience.

Timed Competition (6 micronotes): The participant captured 6 micronotes (2 for each of the 3 note lengths) using whatever input modality she felt would allow her to capture a note fastest. We required that the final note match the task text exactly, and specified that the time to enter the note included the edit time. Participants could choose a different input modality for each of the 6 tasks. To motivate participants to choose the input modality they perceived to be fastest we told them that an additional gratuity would be awarded to the participant with the fastest average capture time.

Environment Phase (12 micronotes): We took the participant to a café located in our building to enter 6 micronotes (2 of each length) using her preferred input method, and then had her walk around the building while entering another 6 micronotes (2 of each length), again using whatever method she wished.

Wrap-up Phase: At the end of the study participants filled out a survey about which input methods they thought were fastest and which they preferred.

4 Results

Our 18 participants (M:9, F:9) ranged in age from 17 to 56 (mean = 39, med. = 46) and had wide variety of occupations including student, artist, fire-fighter, healthcare and technology related (e.g. programmer, IT specialist). Despite this diversity, capturing micronotes was a common occurrence for our participants and twelve told us they deliberately carried note-taking mechanisms with them. We asked participants how frequently they captured micronotes for a variety of methods with the options of never, once ever, monthly, weekly, daily, and several times per day. For our participants, paper was the most commonly used method for micronotes (med. = 'several times per day'). This was followed by the use of personal computers (med. = 'weekly'), but phone, PDA, and voice recorder all had a median response of 'never.' We were not surprised that our participants did not use their phones for micronote capture, given that we had explicitly recruited participants with standard mobile phones so they would not be biased for or against capturing micronote notes on their mobile phone. However, 17 of the 18 participants used their mobile phones daily or multiple times per day, so we know they are carrying mobile devices with them. We now describe results of our Input Trials, followed by the Timed Competition, capture by participants in different Environments, and their Preferences.

4.1 Input Trials

The Input Trials gave participants experience with all three input modalities.

4.1.1 Total Capture Time

To understand how the Ink, Voice and Keyboard input methods compared to each other, we first considered the total time it took participants to capture micronotes using each input modality. Fig. 2 shows the average total capture time for the three input modalities and two transcription conditions broken down by input and edit time.

We first compared capture times within transcription conditions by conducting a 3 (InputMode: Ink, Voice, Keyboard) x 3 (Length) RM-ANOVA for each transcription condition. However, other than the expected main effects of Length on capture time for both groups, no significant effects of InputMode were present for either NearPerfect or CurrentDay participants. So overall, capture times for participants in each condition were not significantly different across the three input modalities, which we found somewhat surprising.

Next, we compared how transcription quality affected total capture times, by comparing capture times between participants in the two transcription conditions for each input method. Looking at the right hand side of Fig. 2, we can see that participants performed comparably in the Keyboard condition across the two transcription conditions. Given that the Keyboard condition lacked a transcription/edit phase, this performance similarity is what we would have expected and gives us confidence that our random assignment of participants into the two transcription conditions avoided any unintentional speed bias.

For Ink and Voice, where we would have expected transcription quality to make a difference, we compared the capture times between the two transcription conditions. We conducted a one-way RM-ANOVA with a within-subjects factor of Length and a between-subjects factor of transcription quality (TxQuality) on the mean total micronote capture time for Ink and Voice. Both tests yielded the expected significant main effects for Length, but only Voice tasks showed significant effects of TxQuality ($F(1,16)=8.6$, $p=.01$), with NP participants completing Voice tasks faster than CD participants (29.9s. v. 43.2s).

4.1.2 Input and Edit Times

We also independently analyzed the time spent to input and edit the micronote. To explore input time, a 3 (InputMode) x 3 (Length) RM-ANOVA with a between-subjects factor of TxQuality was performed on mean input time. Significant main effects were found for InputMode (F(2,15)=53.89, p<.001) and again for Length (F(2,15)=62.71, p<.001). However, as per our design, TxQuality did not affect input times, which again gives us confidence that participants' input speeds were balanced across the transcription conditions. Post hoc tests on InputMode using Bonferroni correction revealed significant differences between input speeds of all modalities; Voice supported faster micronote input than Ink (11.15s v. 26.69s, p<.001), which in turn was faster than Keyboard (34.70s, p=.002).

Given that input times varied significantly by InputMode, but total capture times did not, we conclude that edit times were inversely proportional to input times for these three modalities. This interpretation is also supported by Fig. 2 which shows Voice edits generally took longer than Ink edits, which took longer than Keyboard edits. This is perhaps not surprising given our design incorporated more transcription errors in Voice tasks than in Ink tasks, as well as more errors in CurrentDay tasks than in NearPerfect tasks. However, given that we asked users to correct tasks to something they were "comfortable" with, we worried that participants might have chosen not to edit the transcriptions. To check this, we ran a 2 (InputMode: Ink, Voice) x 3 (Length) RM-ANOVA with a between-subject factor TxQuality on mean number of corrections. Keyboard was excluded from the analysis because it did not have an edit phase. Significant main effects for InputMode (F(1,16)=140.8,p<.001), TxQuality (F(1,16)=85.2, p<.001) and Length (F(2,15)=91.3, p<.001) were present.

Post hoc analyses found that users made significantly fewer corrections during Ink tasks than Voice tasks (3.6 v. 11.0, p<.001) and corrected fewer errors in the NearPerfect condition than the CurrentDay condition (3.5 v 11.1). Thus, our analysis shows that users indeed varied the amount of correction applied to tasks according to the number of errors present in the transcription, preserving the relative edit effort we had intentionally designed into the study. Equivalent analyses on edit times (vs. number of corrections) yielded the same findings.

4.1.3 Survey Responses

We surveyed participants after they had used each input modality using a NASA TLX-based survey. Participants answered questions on a 7-point Likert scale, with 1= 'Very Low' and 7='Very High' about mental demand (Voice: med.=2 Ink: med.=2, Keyboard: med.=3), physical demand (V:2, I:3, K:2.5), whether they became discouraged during the tasks (V:2, I:2, K:2), or had to work hard (V:3, I:2.5, K:2). We also asked how easy the input was to use[1] (V:2, I:3, K:3.5), to learn (V:2, I:2, K:1), and lastly how quickly they felt they could do the tasks (V:3, I:3, K:3). We conducted Friedman tests to compare the responses across the three input modalities and saw a statistically significant difference only for physical demand (χ^2 (2, N=18) = 11.36,

[1] Questions about ease of use and learning used the scale of 1='Not Easy' to 7= 'Very Easy' while the 'quickly' question had the scale 1='Very slowly' to 7='Very Quickly.' All three questions have been reverse coded for analysis to be consistent with other questions where lower scores indicate less effort and higher scores indicate more effort.

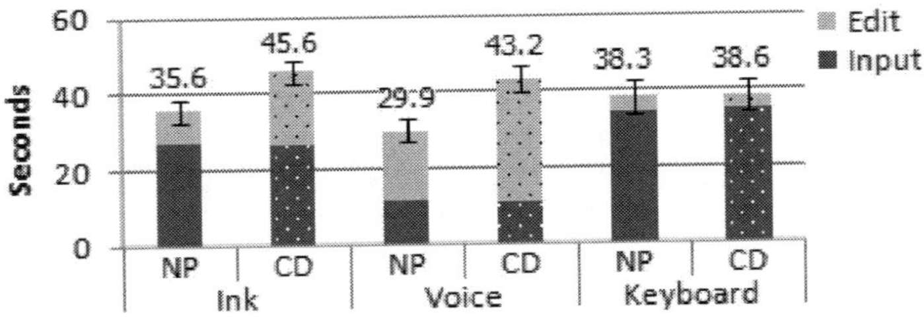

Fig. 2. Total capture time (input+edit) averaged across micronote lengths by input mode and transcription condition (NP=NearPerfect, CD=CurrentDay)

p=.003). Follow-up pairwise comparisons using a Wilcoxon test showed participants felt Voice required significantly less physical exertion than Ink (z=-2.97, p=0.003).

To compare responses of participants in the CurrentDay (CD) condition to those in the NearPerfect (NP) condition we conducted Mann-Whitney U tests for each of the survey questions. We saw statistically significant differences only for the Voice input modality, specifically for the questions on mental demand (NP:1, CD:3, z=-2.72 p=.007), physical demand (NP:1, CD:3, z=-3.00, p=.003), how discouraged participants were (NP:1, CD:4, z=-2.70, p=.007) and how hard they felt they had to work (NP:2, CD:5, z=-2.89, p=.004). Taken together these ratings suggest that differences in transcription quality for the Voice input did make a noticeable difference in the perceptual impact on the participants.

4.2 Timed Competition

The Timed Competition, which participants completed right after the Input Trials, was designed to help us answer our first research question and determine whether participants could build a correct mental modal of how long it took them to capture a micronote. For each of the 108 tasks in the Timed Competition (6 tasks for 18 participants), we calculated the input modality choice that would have been optimal for the participant to use based on the input modality that was fastest for them for tasks of the same length in the Input Trials.

Based on these calculations, 8 of the 18 participants, all from the NearPerfect condition, were expected to use Voice for all task lengths. Seven of the participants should have switched between 2 different modalities, and 3 were expected to switch between all 3 modalities. While 3 participants (NP:3, CD:0) used the optimal input modality for all tasks, our data suggests that most participants did not necessarily have a clear understanding of what input modality would be fastest for them for different task lengths. The remaining 15 participants (NP:6, CD:9) chose the non-optimal input modality in 51 tasks (47%). We were somewhat surprised that the incorrect choices were split relatively evenly between task lengths (Short:25%, Medium:37%, Long:37%) as we expected participants might have more trouble determining the optimal input mode for shorter tasks where capture times using different modalities might be more similar. However, we did find that participants in the CurrentDay condition appeared to have more trouble. Of the 51 incorrect choices, 63% of them were made by participants in the CurrentDay condition while only 37% where made by participants in the NearPerfect condition. Finally, when participants made a non-optimal choice they did not appear to favor any one particular input modality, using Voice 37%, Ink 37% and Keyboard 26% of the time. People in the CurrentDay condition who chose non-optimally chose Voice 41% (13), Ink 38% (12) and Keyboard 22% (7) of the time. NearPerfect participants used Voice 32% (6), Ink 37% (7) and Keyboard 32% (6) of the time.

Survey responses also support the notion that participants had trouble determining what method was fastest for them. On the final survey we asked participants to rank input modalities from fastest to slowest for capturing short lists and long lists. We compared participants' reported fastest methods to their actual performance in the timed trials and again found they correctly identified their fastest method correctly only 53% of the time.

4.3 Different Environments

Our second research question asked about the affect of environment on the participants' choice of input modality. While understanding realistic usage across different environments requires a field study, we felt it was valuable to take our lab study participants into two additional environments (café and walking) to explore in a structured way the impact of environment on their choice of input modality.

Of the 108 micronotes captured in the café (in both conditions), participants used Voice for 38% of the micronotes, Ink for 39%, and Keyboard for 23%. When walking, participants used Voice for 72%, Ink for 17% and Keyboard for 11%. Fig. 3 shows participants' input choices by transcription condition. Participants in the NearPerfect condition had a mostly even split between Ink and Voice inputs in the café, while CurrentDay participants chose more evenly among the three inputs. A few participants expressed concerns about Voice in public venues. Comments included "It would seem weird to command your phone while you are in a café or public place" (P9), and "you don't always want everybody to hear what you are saying" (P7).

The worse transcriptions that the CD participants received may have negatively affected the experience with Voice and Ink enough to encourage the use of Keyboard input. However, while walking, the majority of participants in both transcription conditions chose Voice input, so some users in both conditions switched from another input to Voice, presumably prioritizing Voice's low visual and physical demands over

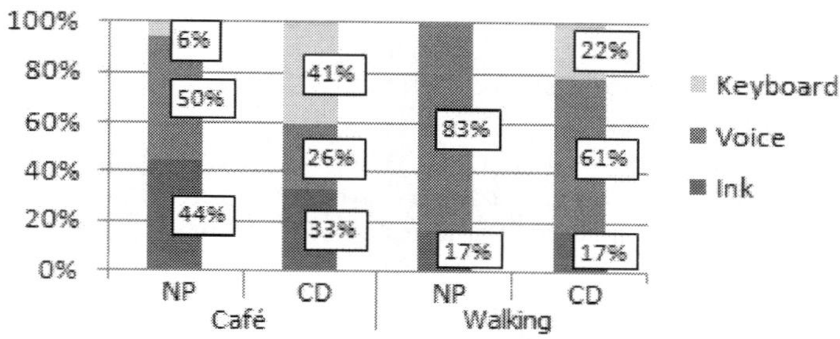

Fig. 3. Percentage of environment tasks captured with the three input modalities, by environment (Café v. Walking) and transcription quality group

other considerations while mobile. Despite the high visual and physical attention required for Keyboard input, Keyboard was not entirely abandoned by the CD participants during walking as it was by the NP participants. This again demonstrates the seemingly negative influence that the worse transcription quality had on CD participants' likelihood of choosing one of the more "natural" input methods.

We were also interested in how consistently participants used the same input modality in each environment. In this analysis we considered users to have a consistent input for an environment if they used a particular input method for at least 4 of the 6 tasks performed. Nine participants (NP:6, CD:3) did not change their preferred input method based on the environment; in 7 of these cases, the method chosen was the one they reported as their overall preferred capture method among the three studied, and in two cases the method chosen was the one they considered fastest, based on their Timed Competition data. Of the other 9, 4 (NP:1, CD:3) did not exhibit a consistent input method in one or both environments. The 5 remaining participants switched from another input method to Voice for walking.

To summarize, participants in the NP condition were more likely to choose Voice or Ink over Keyboard for micronote capture and tended to be more stable in their choices. In contrast, CD participants were more divided among three input methods in the café, had more participants who made inconsistent task-to-task choices, and had more participants switch input choice between environments. These fluctuations observed in the CD participants suggest that the worse transcription made it more difficult for them to determine or decide on a preferred input method. For both conditions, however, we saw that environment could influence choice, with users favoring the lower demands of Voice for capturing micronotes while walking.

4.4 Participant Preference

Our final research questions asked what input modalities participants prefer and whether it appeared that either transcription quality or speed of capture had an effect on participants' preferences. On the final survey we asked participants to rank the input modalities from most to least favorite. Responses strongly demonstrate participants' preference for Ink and Voice input over Keyboard. As Fig. 4a shows, 8 participants preferred Voice, 8 participants preferred Ink and 2 preferred Keyboard for micronotes when paper was not option. When asked what they liked about their favorite method, common responses for both Ink and Voice included ease of use (Voice:6 participants, Ink:2), accuracy of transcription (Voice:5, Ink:4), and speed (Voice:3, Ink: 2). Very surprisingly, the number of participants who preferred Voice, Ink and Keyboard between the NearPerfect and CurrentDay conditions was exactly the same when paper was not an option.

However, Fig. 4b highlights that Paper was still a very popular choice for micronotes. Given the option, 8 participants (4 from each condition), ranked Paper as their most preferred input method. Participants who originally favored Ink seemed most likely to prefer Paper (5 moved from Ink to Paper). Again transcription quality did not seem to greatly affect preferences as the same number of participants from both transcription conditions preferred paper.

We also examined whether participants' preferred input modality might correlate with the modality they felt they were fastest using. Given that half (8) the participants

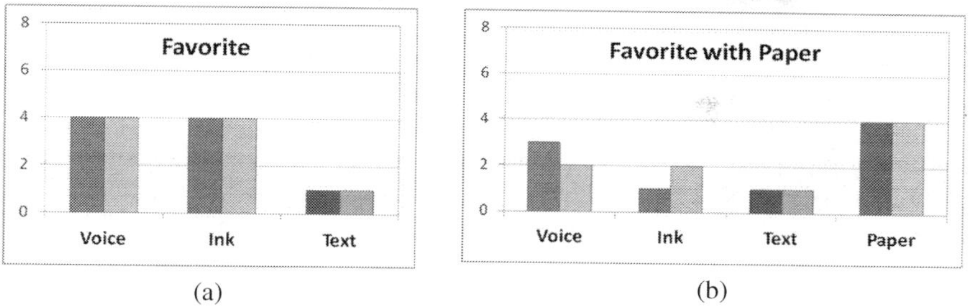

Fig. 4. Participants' favorite input modality (a) without and (b) with paper. Darker bars are users in the NearPerfect condition, lighter bars are CurrentDay.

felt that two different input methods were fastest for short vs. long tasks, it is impossible to draw conclusions about whether those participants' single preferred capture method was related to their perception of the fastest input method. But out of the 8 participants who felt that a single capture method was fastest for both long and short tasks, 7 chose that same method as their preferred capture method overall, providing some evidence that for those individuals, perceived capture speed influenced their stated modality preference.

We found it interesting that Ink was preferred as often as it was (8 participants) considering it was fastest on average for only one participant. Some of this discrepancy can be explained by the fact that 6 of those participants (incorrectly) *thought* Ink was fastest for at least some tasks, while 2 participants knew Ink was slower than others, but still preferred it overall. Even so, the relative popularity of Ink in the face of modest performance suggests that users appreciate a broader range of capture qualities beyond speed, such as similarity to paper-based note taking, and discreet capture. Comments on the final survey about Ink included "I like writing in my own handwriting" (P11), "seeing written words helps jog ideas and gives time to think" (P13), and "I always write/draw, so it's very familiar and amusing" (P16).

Finally, while not the focus of our study, participants provided several important pieces of feedback about the usability of the VINO prototype. First, while VINO required participants to input and then edit, some participants wanted to have the ink or voice transcription available immediately so they could see and correct any problems as they were inputting the micronote. Additionally, a few participants were very adamant about wanting to take notes in multiple different colors and easily changing colors mid-note. Lastly, a few participants felt the custom-keyboard was too small for older eyes and would have liked the text to be larger.

5 Discussion

We now discuss more broadly what our findings suggest for future mobile micronote capture technologies. First, participants' preferences, and their use of Ink and Voice input when given the option, strongly support the value of providing users with these "natural" input modalities for digitally capturing micronotes. More specifically, given that half our participants switched which input modality they used in different environments, as well as the almost equal split in preferences for Ink or Voice, we believe that our study highlights the importance of multi-modal micronote capture applications that allow users to select whatever capture modality is appropriate for their current context and needs. This is in contrast to separate end-to-end applications for different input modalities that seem to be the focus of current development (e.g., Jott supports only Voice input). Supporting Ink, Voice and Keyboard input equally, and allowing participants to switch between them as we prototyped with VINO, would better support the capture behaviors we observed where some participants switched depending on the environment. Even as predictive text entry improves and becomes widely available, we anticipate different input modalities will remain valuable due to the need for low attention interfaces in certain environments and participants' varied preferences.

While clearly some research on improving transcription quality would be beneficial, having micronotes with near perfect transcription did not appear to make participants in the NearPerfect condition less resistant to the allure of paper (4 of 9 preferred paper when given the option). One consideration is that in our study participants were forced to correct the transcription after entering the complete note. Given that some participants wanted to have the Voice and Ink transcription available immediately so they could see and correct problems, we believe two approaches to transcription would be interesting for further study. First, providing immediate transcription even with a likely reduction in accuracy, and second emphasizing 'just-in-time' transcription where users would only edit or view transcription if needed (e.g., often the unrecognized Ink note might be fine) and ideally at a place where it might be easier to correct such as on a desktop or laptop computer.

6 Concluding Remarks

Our study participants preferred natural input modalities of Voice and Ink to a virtual Keyboard for making micronotes on a mobile device; however paper remains appealing to many. While participants in our CurrentDay transcription condition did find the tasks more challenging in some respects, particularly for Voice input, having worse transcription did not change the distribution of participants' preferences across the input modalities. Nor did more participants in the NearPerfect condition favor digital micronote capture over paper compared to those in the CurrentDay condition, suggesting dramatically better transcription quality on its own will not cause people to adopt digital micronote capture technologies.

However, given that our participants are already carrying mobile phones that will only grow more powerful in the years to come, we do believe there is an opportunity for developing mobile micronote capture technology that meets people's needs. We feel strongly these applications must support multiple input methods including Voice and Ink so that users can switch between different modalities as they desire. While we focused on input methods for capture in our study, it is critical to remember the entire lifecycle that Lin et al. identified, as emphasizing the additional benefits that digital captured notes might have (e.g., easy to share, search) will no doubt be important in developing a digital micronote capture system that people find useful.

Going forward we believe there are two valuable research directions that would build on our findings. First, conducting a similar study with users of smartphones to better understand their past experience with existing technology and compare their responses to VINO with the results from this study. Second, building a more robust version of VINO, perhaps with offline transcription, that could be deployed for short field studies in order to further explore the appeal of a multi-modal capture application in the wild.

References

1. Lin, M., Lutters, W.G., Kim, T.S.: Understanding the micronote lifecycle: improving mobile support for informal note taking. In: Proceedings of the SIGCHI Conference on Human Factors in Computing Systems, pp. 687–694. ACM, New York (2004)
2. Bernstein, M., Van Kleek, M., Karger, D.R., Schraefel, M.C.: Information Scraps: How and Why Information Eludes our Personal Information Management Tools. ACM Transactions on Information Systems 26(4), 1–46 (2008)
3. Bernstein, M.S., Van Kleek, M., Schraefel, M.C., Karger, D.R.: Management of Personal Information Scraps. In: CHI 2007 Extended Abstracts on Human Factors in Computing Systems, pp. 2285–2290. ACM, New York (2007)
4. Dai, L., Lutters, W.G., Bower, C.: Why use memo for all?: restructuring mobile applications to support informal note taking. In: CHI 2005 Extended Abstracts on Human Factors in Computing Systems, pp. 1320–1323. ACM, New York (2005)
5. Campbell, C., Maglio, P.: Supporting notable information in office work. In: CHI 2003 Extended Abstracts on Human Factors in Computing Systems, pp. 902–903. ACM, New York (2003)
6. Hayes, G.R., Pierce, J.S., Abowd, G.D.: Practices for capturing short important thoughts. In: CHI 2003 Extended Abstracts on Human Factors in Computing Systems, pp. 904–905. ACM, New York (2003)
7. Zhou, L.: Natural Language Interface for Information Management on Mobile Device. Behavior & Information Technology 26(3), 197–207 (2007)
8. Falke, E.: The associative pda 2.0. In: CHI 2008 Extended Abstracts on Human Factors in Computing Systems, pp. 3807–3812. ACM, New York (2008)
9. Jott, `http://www.jott.com`
10. Evernote, `http://www.evernote.com`
11. Microsoft Ink API, `http://msdn.microsoft.com/en-us/library/microsoft.ink.aspx`
12. Microsoft Speech API, `http://msdn.microsoft.com/en-us/library/system.speech.recognition.aspx`
13. Soukoreff, R.W., MacKenzie, I.S.: Measuring errors in text entry tasks: an application of the Levenshtein string distance statistic. In: CHI 2001 Extended Abstracts on Human Factors in Computing Systems, pp. 319–320. ACM, New York (2001)
14. Ludford, P.J., Frankowski, D., Reily, K., Wilms, K., Terveen, L.: Because I carry my cell phone anyway: functional location-based reminder applications. In: Proceedings of the SIGCHI Conference on Human Factors in Computing Systems, pp. 889–898. ACM, New York (2006)

SmartActions: Context-Aware Mobile Phone Shortcuts

Akos Vetek, John A. Flanagan, Ashley Colley, and Tuomas Keränen

Nokia, P.O. Box 407, FIN-00045, Nokia Group, Helsinki, Finland
{akos.vetek,adrian.flanagan,ashley.colley,
tuomas.j.keranen}@nokia.com

Abstract. Mobile phones are often regarded as difficult to use due to their size restrictions. To improve on this, in this paper we described our approach using unsupervised learning to automate common tasks on a mobile phone, thereby requiring less key presses, by means of context-dependent quick-access shortcuts presented in the homescreen of the phone. We also briefly reviewed some of our user study findings, and raised the issue of possible privacy concerns with our implementation.

Keywords: Mobile interfaces, adaptive interfaces, context-dependent systems.

1 Introduction

Mobile phones have become ubiquitous and have now reached a stage where especially smartphones can provide users with a wide range of applications and services. Despite this, mobile phones are still often regarded as being difficult to use [1]. Due to the size restrictions of mobile phones, providing a more usable interface is hard to achieve. Context awareness can be used to facilitate the interaction of the user by recognizing the user context and determining and reacting to the user's needs in a given context by, for instance making available appropriate shortcuts, thus minimizing the user's interaction with the device through the UI.

Related work has focused on command-line prediction in a UNIX environment using a probabilistic bigram model to predict a user's next command [2] and also complete user commands [3]. More recently, Bridle and McCreath [4] investigated several approaches to induce shortcuts to automate making voice calls and sending text messages on a mobile phone. They found that some relatively simple approaches (e.g. most frequent commands) saved a considerable number of key presses, however such approaches presented the users with shortcuts that varied frequently. This is important as, in terms of usability, the aspect important in mobile phone design is not only efficiency (e.g. number of key presses) but predictability as well [5].

In this paper we describe our approach of inducing and applying both simple and complete shortcuts that automate a sequence of keypad presses. Our approach is based on context recognition, using an efficient unsupervised learning algorithm that requires no intervention from the user. The context-dependent shortcuts are displayed as a quickly glanceable list on the homescreen of the phone.

T. Gross et al. (Eds.): INTERACT 2009, Part I, LNCS 5726, pp. 796–799, 2009.

2 SmartActions Application

An intelligent mobile device should not only know what its user wants, but also where and when its user wants it. Such a device should learn how it is used, that the user sets the alarm every night before bed, that typically she quickly checks her e-mail before leaving for the office in the morning and maybe even sends a text message to her spouse in the evening before leaving the office.

To this end, SmartActions is an implementation of a context recognition algorithm on the Nokia N80, a 3rd edition S60 smartphone, driving an adaptive menu of lists of shortcuts. The list of items displayed in the menu adapts based on the current, recognized, user context and the applications associated with that context. The association between the context and the actions is learned from the user's previous use of applications in the same context. The context recognition is done using the K-Symbol String Clustering Map (K-SCM) [6], an efficient unsupervised clustering algorithm.

In the following two sub-sections the user interface and the operation of the K-SCM algorithm underlying the application will be described in more detail.

Fig. 1. a) A typical homescreen with SmartActions indicated by the brace. b) One of the shortcuts highlighted. c) The result of applying the shortcut with sender information filled in.

2.1 User Interface

The homescreen of 3rd edition S60 devices can be customized via plug-ins. Plug-ins can provide an overview of the current state and contents of the device, such as the list of upcoming calendar appointments or a summary of new email messages.

SmartActions makes use of this framework and presents a quickly glanceable list of the 5 most likely functions the user will use in the current context (as defined by time and location) embedded in the homescreen (Fig. 1). The list includes not only application launcher shortcuts, such as "*Launch Messaging*", but also real user-level actions, such as "*Call to Peter*", "*(send) SMS to Mary*" or "*(set) Profile: Silent*". A more complete list of the currently implemented shortcuts is presented in Table 1. These suggested actions can be selected in a single key press, typically saving around 5 key presses or more. Should none of the displayed items be appropriate, the user can initiate the intended functionality at no loss in efficiency, as usual via the S60 application grid, as the rest of the phone's UI is left untouched.

Table 1. List of possible SmartActions that can be learned with examples in brackets

List of possible SmartActions and examples
• Application launch (e.g. "*Launch File Manager*")
• Setting alarm ("*Set alarm*")
• Profile activation (e.g. "*Profile: Silent*")
• Establishing voice call to specified contact (e.g. "*Call to John Doe*")
• Sending SMS/MMS/email to specified contact (e.g. "*SMS to John Doe*")
• Opening browser with specified URL (e.g. "*www.ovi.mobi*")

2.2 Context Recognition and Shortcut Association Using K-SCM

An important challenge mobile phones provide for a learning system is the limited memory and processing power. This is especially crucial as any such approach must collect data and make predictions in an on-line and real-time manner.

With this in mind, we selected a modified version of the Symbol String Clustering Map (SCM), an algorithm for the unsupervised clustering of symbol string data based on adaptive learning [7]. The K-SCM algorithm improves on the SCM by requiring less memory and computational resources while giving the same result as the SCM [6]. The big benefit of unsupervised learning, as opposed to, for instance, ontology-based approaches, is that it requires no intervention from the user, and as such there is no need for any user settings at all.

As implemented in SmartActions, the inputs to the algorithm are: the location obtained from the GSM Cell ID parameters and the time and date encoded as symbol strings. The purpose of SmartActions is to learn different user contexts, in this case the context in terms of time and location, and to associate different applications that the user normally uses in these recognized contexts with the context. For example, if typically in the morning, at home, before leaving for work the user checks the news using the browser on the phone, SmartActions in this case would learn the context, "*at home in the morning*", with the location "*home*" determined from the GSM Cell ID, and the time "*morning*" from the clock. After several mornings the user would notice "*Launch Browser*" as one of the shortcuts on the homescreen, because the application has first of all learned the context "*at home in the morning*" and second of all learned to associate the use of the browser with this context. As the application is event driven, it does not learn all possible contexts, rather only those contexts where the user launches an application or otherwise interacts with the phone. As another example, at around "*midday when at work*" the user normally sends a text message to her spouse. This would correspond to a second context, SmartActions would learn the "*midday when at work*" context and associate the messaging application with this context. Hence around midday at work the messaging application would feature at the top of the list of suggested shortcuts in the homescreen.

In summary, the K-SCM algorithm is used so that contexts where the user interacts with the device are learned and those interactions are associated with the learned contexts.

3 Initial User Study Findings

Twelve participants (6 male) used the application for a period of 2.5-3 weeks. Data was collected through focus group interviews, questionnaires and a post-interview. Initial results indicate that users generally liked the idea of a learning application (5.3 on a scale 1-6, 6 being most positive) and found it easy to understand how SmartActions functioned (4.3/6), however they expressed privacy concerns as the list of shortcuts was deemed too visible in the case of "confidential" contacts. Even though our aim was to design a quickly accessible, completely automatic system without any user settings, this is prompting us to rethink the appropriateness of displaying such potentially confidential shortcuts on the homescreen in an always on manner, or to introduce some means of customization to allow the permanent removal of unwanted shortcuts. In general, finding the appropriate way to display the results of the learning algorithm to the user is critical in the success of such systems.

4 Conclusion and Future Work

We explored the use of unsupervised learning to automate common tasks on a mobile phone, by means of context-dependent quick-access shortcuts displayed in the homescreen of the device. We also presented initial user study results that indicated that the appropriate way to display the results of the learning algorithm to the user is critical in the success of such systems. Experimenting with alternative ways of presenting the shortcuts, along with extending the set of context parameters and studying their effects will form the core of future work.

References

1. Amant, R.S., Horton, T.E., Ritter, F.E.: Model-based evaluation of cell phone menu interaction. In: Proceedings of the SIGCHI conference on Human factors in computing systems, pp. 343–350 (2004)
2. Davison, B.D., Hirsh, H.: Probabilistic Online Action Prediction. In: Proceedings of the AAAI Spring Symposium on Intelligent Environments, pp. 148–154 (1998)
3. Korvemaker, B., Greiner, R.: Predicting Unix command lines: adjusting to user patterns. In: Proceedings of the Seventeenth National Conference on Artificial Intelligence, pp. 230–235 (2000)
4. Bridle, R., McCreath, E.: Inducing shortcuts on a mobile phone interface. In: Proceedings of the 11th international conference on Intelligent user interfaces, pp. 327–329 (2006)
5. Lindholm, C., Keinonen, T.: Mobile Usability: How Nokia Changed the Face of the Cellular Phone. McGraw-Hill, Inc., New York (2003)
6. Flanagan, J.A.: Unsupervised Clustering of Context Data and Learning User Requirements for a Mobile Device. Modeling and Using Context, 155–168 (2005)
7. Flanagan, J.A.: Unsupervised clustering of symbol strings. In: Proceedings of the International Joint Conference on Neural Networks, pp. 3250–3255 (2003)

Can You Feel It? – Using Vibration Rhythms to Communicate Information in Mobile Contexts

Sebastian Feige

Digital Media Group, TZI, University of Bremen,
Bibliothekstr. 1, 28359 Bremen, Germany
sfeige@tzi.de

Abstract. Development of interfaces for interaction in mobile scenarios faces the challenge of a broad variety of different possible user contexts. New approaches are needed, which demand a minimum of attention in situations where the user is engaged in other mobility tasks. In this paper, the results of an experiment targeting the recognition of vibration rhythms in real world mobile situations are depicted, suggesting further research on tactile mobile interfaces.

Keywords: HCI, mobility, tactile, perception, cognition, attention.

1 Introduction

Mobile devices are used in a broad variety of different situations – from sitting alone in a quiet café to engaging in a lively discussion with a friend while walking along a busy road. The cognitive resources being available for the interaction with a mobile application vary greatly depending on simultaneous mobility tasks [1]. Especially proactive services may interrupt users in mobile situations where their visual and acoustic senses are otherwise involved. In contrast, the tactile sense is often mainly unused. This is why using it to receive information in mobile scenarios is appealing.

Vibration rhythms offer an unobtrusive, socially acceptable possibility to use the skin as an additional channel for information. Allport *et al.* showed with their research from the early 1970's [2] that paying attention to information on multiple channels simultaneously is possible, if they use differing cognitive resources. In this paper, the results of an experiment are presented, which aimed at the recognition of vibration rhythms triggered by a wristband. In particular, it was looked for differences between a lab-condition and various typical mobile contexts.

2 Related Work

Tactile displays as a means of communicating information have been the topic of several studies. Brown & Kaaresoja [3] investigated the use of so-called "Tactons" to encode phone call information about caller and priority. In addition to different rhythms they used and compared the effectiveness of a vibration's "roughness" and "intensity", respectively, for a second dimension of information. They used a mobile phone which was held in the hand. While the recognition rate of the rhythms was above 90%, the

T. Gross et al. (Eds.): INTERACT 2009, Part I, LNCS 5726, pp. 800–803, 2009.

identification rates of priority encoded in roughness (55%) and intensity (75%) were not as high. As the experiment was solely conducted in a lab-environment, Brown and Kaaresoja suggest the investigation of recognition rates under real life conditions with the phone in a pocket and the user engaged in another task.

Among the approaches to assess the influence of real life mobile situations on recognition rates of tactile signals are experiments on a treadmill [4] and generic cognitive tasks in a controlled lab environment [5]. In contrast, an outdoor quasi-experimentation approach was utitilised for the experiment presented below, with the goal to simulate more realistic typical mobile use situations.

3 Experiment

Using tactile signals as a channel of information for everyday use requires a small, low-cost approach with generally interpretable tactile representations of low complexity. Pre-tests showed that using a mobile phone in a pocket is far from satisfying for recognising information through different vibration rhythms, because distinguishing between different kinds of vibration – if perceivable at all – was hardly possible. Additionally, lots of users don't carry their mobile phone in a pocket, but e.g. in their jacket, a bag, etc. To increase perceptibility, an approach with a fixed position of the vibration motor close to the user's skin was needed.

Inspired by devices like the BlueQ wristband[1] or mobile phone watches such as the M500[2], a prototype of a remote controlled wristband able to vibrate in different rhythms was built: An Arduino Nano microcontroller board, a bluetooth modem and a battery case were sewed into a stretchable wristband (fig. 1a). For the vibration, a LilyPad Vibeboard with a vibration motor running at a rated speed of 12000 rpm was sewed on the bottom side. Considering the recognition rates for intensity reported by Brown & Kaaresoja [3], the conducted experiment focussed on rhythm recognition.

Five different rhythms were selected for the experiments (fig. 1c). It is important to emphasise that these are not the result of a strictly systematic approach to find the very best rhythms but a sample suitable for the focus of this paper, which is to investigate situational influences on recognition rates. The utilised rhythms had been modified iteratively during pre-tests with colleagues from the lab until they showed to be discernable in a mostly distraction-free environment. For rhythm identification, numbers from 1 to 5 were used as generic identifiers. Identification rates when matching words or phrases to rhythms will be the focus of further research.

Fourteen persons aged 19 to 46 (avg: 26.2, sd: 8.4) volunteered for participation in the experiments. They were randomly assigned to either the experimental or the control group which were of equal size. First of all, a proband was primed, until she uttered she felt able to recognise the five rhythms.

Probands in the control group were asked to sit alone in a neutral room for 45 minutes and record perceived rhythms by pressing a button with the corresponding number on a PDA. The rhythms were randomly initiated at an average of every five minutes.

---

[1] http://www.engadget.com/2007/05/18/blueqs-unsightly-vibrating-bluetooth-wristband/
[2] http://www.mymobilewatch.com/watch_specification.php

Probands in the experimental group had to walk a route unhurriedly with the help of printed cards which guided them from spot to spot and sometimes posed a task. At seven pre-defined spots on the route, the supervisor, who followed the proband (fig. 1b), initiated random activation of one of the five rhythms with a PDA wirelessly connected to the vibration wristband. The exact moment was randomly determined within a timeframe of ten seconds to minimize potential situational bias. The spots on the route were chosen to represent different typical kinds of real world mobile environments (quiet/noisy, calm/crowded) or activities (conversing, eating, messaging with mobile phone, checking bus connections). To avoid ordering effects, the direction of the route was randomly chosen for each participant.

The deployed design is a between-groups design with (lab/mobile)-environment as independent and recognition rate as dependent variable.

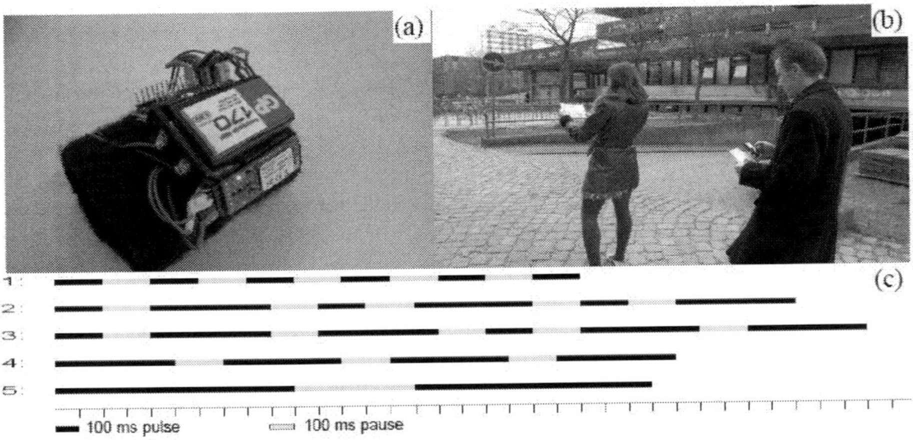

Fig. 1. (a) wristband prototype (b) navigating on mobile route (c) rhythms

4 Results

The main hypothesis was that the recognition rate in the experimental group would be lower than in the control group. A tendency for lower recognition in mobile contexts with a higher demand of cognitive resources was expected.

Interestingly, the recognition rate for both groups showed to be almost identical: After excluding the data of one proband, who failed to identify half of the rhythms in the control group (and was therefore treated as an outlier), the overall recognition rates were about 93% (sd: 11.5) in the control group and even 94% (sd: 16.2) in the experimental group. These results conform to those of Brown & Kaaresoja [3] for a mobile phone in the hand in a lab condition. As almost every rhythm was correctly identified by the probands in the experimental group, the data shows no significant differences between the selected situations. In both groups, no rhythm was completely missed.

According to Petrie *et al.* [6], negative effects of a mobile device result in a decrease of the user's walking speed. Although Preferred Walking Speed (PWS) was not explicitly used as a measure, it is worth mentioning that probands in the experimental group did not visibly slow down or even stop when perceiving a vibration rhythm while walking.

5 Conclusion and Future Work

Using a wristband capable of vibrating in different rhythms has promising potential to communicate information – even while users are busy with other tasks in real world mobile scenarios. Using a wristband instead of e.g. a mobile phone's own vibration motor seems to be able to bypass the problem of missing a vibration because of too much distance between vibration transducer and the user's skin.

Five different rhythms were quite easily discernable by most of the participants. Further research should closer investigate an optimal design for these rhythms and explore how capable users are of matching meaningful words or phrases to rhythms and what the best strategies are to support this. Moreover, a field test over a longer period of time, involving diverse real life mobile contexts would be valuable.

Acknowledgement. This work has been kindly funded by the Klaus Tschira Foundation as part of the graduate school "Advances in Digital Media".

References

1. Oulasvirta, A., Tamminen, S., Roto, V., Kuorelahti, J.: Interaction in 4-Second Bursts: The Fragmented Nature of Attentional Resources in Mobile HCI. In: CHI 2005: Proceedings of the SIGCHI conference on Human factors in computing systems, pp. 919–928. ACM Press, New York (2005)
2. Allport, A.D., Antonis, B., Reynolds, P.: On the Division of Attention: A Disproof of the Single Channel Hypothesis. The Quarterly Journal of Experimental Psychology 2(24), 225–235 (1972)
3. Brown, L.M., Kaaresoja, T.: Feel Who's Talking: Using Tactons for Mobile Phone Alerts. In: CHI 2006: Extended abstracts on Human factors in computing systems, pp. 604–609. ACM Press, New York (2006)
4. Hoggan, E., Brewster, S.: Designing Audio and Tactile Crossmodal Icons for Mobile Devices. In: Proceedings of the 9th International Conference on Multimodal Interfaces, pp. 162–169. ACM Press, New York (2007)
5. Jones, L.A., Kunkel, J., Piateski, E.: Vibrotactile Pattern Recognition on the Arm and Back. Perception 1(38), 52–68 (2009)
6. Petrie, H., Furner, S., Strothotte, T.: Design Lifecycles and Wearable Computers for Users with Disabilities. Presented at The First Workshop on Human-Computer Interaction with Mobile Devices, Glasgow, UK (1998)

An Evaluation of Product Identification Techniques for Mobile Phones

Felix von Reischach[1,2], Florian Michahelles[1], Dominique Guinard[1,2], Robert Adelmann[1], Elgar Fleisch[1,3], and Albrecht Schmidt[4]

[1] ETH Zürich, Switzerland
[2] SAP Research, Switzerland
[3] University of St. Gallen, Switzerland
[4] University of Duisburg-Essen, Germany
{freischach,fmichahelles,dguinard,efleisch}@ethz.ch,
robert.adelmann@inf.ethz.ch, albrecht.schmidt@icb.uni-due.de

Abstract. Among others, consumer products can be purchased in the Internet and in traditional stores. Each of the two has dedicated advantages. An online survey conducted within the frames of this work investigates these advantages. It motivates the transition of the advantages of online shopping, such as access to recommendations of other consumers, to the sales floor. Recent trends in mobile phone technology, for example the emergence of the mobile Internet, enable exactly this transition, potentially enriching the shopping experience in the real world. A key challenge though is a fast and convenient identification of products. This work compares five product identification modalities for mobile phones in a comparative study. The dependent variables evaluated are 'task completion time' and 'perceived ease of use'. Our study is the first that quantifies the advantage of automatic identification. The results indicate that automatically identifying a product scanning a tag can be up to eight times faster than entering a product name in a text field. Surprisingly, barcode recognition using a camera phone can be conducted almost as fast and convenient as scanning an RFID tag. Our work provides a benchmark for developers having to choose appropriate identification technology for their mobile application.

1 Introduction

Over the past years, the Internet has developed into a valuable tool for consumers searching for unbiased and extensive product information. With the goal to take a rational buying decision, consumers frequently access price comparisons, technical specifications, consumer reviews, or similar information in the web. Online shops utilize the availability of this information and integrate according functionalities into their websites, creating a better experience [1] and positively influencing sales [2]. But although revenues in online shops are increasing, physical stores still retain their attractiveness to customers. A reason for that is certainly that the overall shopping experience created in a shopping mall or a corner store is very different from shopping with a web browser.

T. Gross et al. (Eds.): INTERACT 2009, Part I, LNCS 5726, pp. 804–816, 2009.

The separation between products and related information, as mentioned above, leads to a phenomenon called "hybrid shopping" or "multi-channel shopping" [3]. As consumers want to leverage the transparency in the Internet and the shopping experience from their usual shopping, people go back and forth between searching for information on the Web and buying their products in real world shops. This leads to a fragmentation of the shopping process in time and space [4]. However, recent technology allows a time-wise and location-wise combination of Internet-based information and traditional shopping: Newer generations of handsets make the Internet portable, implicating that consumers can potentially access product-related information on the sales floor. When actually shopping, they can enjoy the advantages of both worlds: touch and see the products, while accessing a rich pool of product-related information. But although mobile Internet access is on the rise, product-related services have not been widely adopted by consumers yet. It seems that for their widespread diffusion a number of shortcomings regarding their usability have to be tackled. Among them are the limited possibilities to browse websites due to rather small displays and the cumbersome entry of text. Especially when in the context of shopping, the entry of longer text strings such as product name or product number seems to prevent people from accessing additional product information using their mobile device.

As an approach to this, research and practice have been investigating interaction techniques that facilitate the identification of products through mobile phones. On the one hand, mobile phones have been turned into barcode readers [5, 6]. Using the phone's camera and applying image recognition algorithms, common 1-dimensional barcodes as well as 2-dimensional barcodes can be identified. On the other hand, there are two technologies that turn mobile phones into readers of Radio Frequency Identification (RFID) tags. The first technology, Near Field Communication (NFC) [7], is a consumer-oriented transmission standard that allows reading of RFID tags by touching them with a mobile phone's antenna. Typical current NFC applications include mobile payment [8], smart posters [9] and ticketing [10]. Secondly, readers have been integrated into mobile phones that allow the identification of RFID tags at ultra high frequency (860-960 MHz) from a distance up to 50 cm [11]. This so called Electronic Product Code (EPC) standard [12] is typically applied for supply chain applications and is in discussion to replace the barcode on consumer products in the future [13]. It is not yet clear though whether NFC or EPC will succeed in the consumer goods industry [14].

Yet there have been several projects from both research [15, 16, 17, 18] and business practice[1] that take advantage of these new technical possibilities in the shopping context. However, to the best of our knowledge, none of the works has investigated the advantage of automatic identification compared to manual entry. And moreover, no work has focused on finding suitable product identification techniques for mobile shopping assistance. We investigate:

- How significant is the advantage of automatic product identification versus manual product identification?
- What is the most appropriate mobile identification technique for shopping applications?

[1] Among the first commercial mobile shopping assistants making use of automatic product identification techniques are CompareEverywhere, Scanlife, and Barcoo.

To tackle these questions we proceed as follows: Firstly, we distinguish from related literature. Secondly, we motivate our experiment with an online-survey that aims at investigating the potential of mobile product-related services in general. Thirdly, we describe the design and execution of a user study conducted with 17 participants. Fourthly, we present the results of this study. We conclude interpreting these results and giving guidelines for developers.

2 Related Work

This section links our survey to related literature and distinguishes our main contribution, the user study, from existing works.

In the early 2000s, the "hype-phase" of e-commerce, a number of studies and surveys were performed that investigate the behavior of consumers when shopping online. These are predominantly settled in the areas of business research, or more specifically, around the terms marketing, consumer research, and decision making theories. Häubl and Trifts [19], for example, have investigated the effects of interactive decision aids on online shopper's buying behavior. Another relevant work has been performed by Ward and Morganowsky [4], examining how the availability of marketing information channels (Internet, print, broadcast, catalog) affects the channel for purchasing the good. They propose a better management of this so called 'channel confilict'. More specifically, Senecal and Nantel [2] investigate the usage of online recommendation sources through consumers and their influence on online product choices. Our survey differentiates from this by collecting generating up-to-date data on what values consumers attribute to online shopping and shopping in traditional stores, what information sources they consult, and what they are willing to pay for product information on mobile phones.

When accessing product-related information on the mobile phone while shopping, a key requirement is a fast and convenient identification of products. Numerous researchers have suggested that mobile phones may be the ideal candidates for enriching real-world interactions with information from the Internet. We build up upon Ballagas et al. [20], who have explored and classified various mobile input modalities. Our work goes beyond this by comparing these modalities in a quantitative manner. In this, our approach is similar to the work of Broll et al. [21] as well as to the study of Rukzio et al. [22]. Both analyze and compare input techniques for interacting with the physical world. According to these studies, touching (e.g. NFC) and pointing (e.g. barcode identification, image recognition and EPC Tag Scan to some extent) are the preferred techniques if the object in question is within the reach of the user. We leveraged these results in our selection of modalities to be evaluated.

Our contribution extends the state of the art in two ways. Firstly, we specifically contribute a quantification of the advantage of automatic product identification techniques on mobile phones. While other studies have found out that there is an advantage in automatic identification on mobile phones, we aim at specifically determining: how big is this advantage? Secondly, our study aims at testing mobile identification techniques specifically for shopping applications. This is, for example, reflected in task 2, where the identification speed for several items is measured simulating a product comparison.

3 A Survey on the Potential of Mobile Product Information

In order to investigate the potential of mobile-Internet-enhanced shopping, we conducted a web-based survey. The questionnaire consisted of 20 questions and took about 20 minutes to complete. The participants were recruited via email (friends, colleagues, friends of friends, and RFID researchers). We received 136 complete responses (25% females) of people with mixed backgrounds from 15 countries on 4 continents. The age range was between 18 and 50+. The educational levels of the participants were heterogeneous, with 88% of the participants having a university degree or higher. The language of the survey was English. In the following, we describe selected results from a descriptive evaluation of the survey.

The survey investigates the shopping behavior for three types of products: digital cameras, books, and wine. In the selection, we build up on the work of Nelson [23] and King and Balasubramanian [24], who distinguish between so called 'search products' and 'experience products'. Search products are dominated by properties that can be evaluated prior purchase, such as the 'amount of megapixels' when looking for a digital camera. In contrast, experience goods are dominated by attributes that cannot be known until purchase and use of the product: an example is wine. A book is somewhere in between. It can be browsed, but hardly read and assessed completely before purchase. This classification influences the way we buy products, especially the information we base our buying decision on.

The first part of the survey investigates the following question: What are the advantages and disadvantages of buying products online vs. in a real shop? We asked this question for all three of the above product types. The participants answered in free text. The responses entered show that a large majority of people sees, among others, roughly the following advantages for physical shopping (numbers refer to the purchase of a digital camera, but were similar for all products; similar answers were grouped manually):

- you can touch and feel the product (64%)
- you can come back to the store in case of a problem with the product (57%)
- you have the product immediately / no shipping required (15%)

For online-shops the consumers reported the following benefits:

- easy price and product comparison and hence getting a better deal (60%)
- easy access to technical details, in-depth reviews and customer comments (52%)
- convenience of not having to go shopping in person (29%)

Looking at the advantages of online-shopping it becomes clear that two important benefits are based on the access to additional information. We wanted to know, whether people actually mix searching for product information in the Web and shopping in traditional stores. We asked: Have you ever searched for product information in the Internet, but finally purchased the product in a real store? Of all participants, 79% were positive. Asked for the products searched for, electronic devices and books were among the ones stated the most.

In order to get hints on what information consumers would appreciate on their mobile phone when shopping, we asked: On what information will you base your buying decision? Possible answers were: own experience, recommendations of friends and family members, technical features, visible features, commercial recommendations, price, recommendations of unknown Internet users, and independent consumer organizations and magazines. The answers differ significantly for each considered product type. When buying a digital camera, consumers predominantly rely on technical details (93%), price (85%) and recommendations of friends and family members (72%). When shopping for books, the own experience (86%) and recommendations of friends and family members (84%) is what counts by far the most. When shopping for wine, people rely predominantly on their own experience (87%), recommendations of friends and family members (64%) and price (64%). It seems that empowering users to share recommendations among friends and family members on the mobile phone provides a vast potential, especially for experience products.

Based on the preceding questions, indicating that mobile shopping applications have the potential to support consumers, we did a first step towards an assessment of their business potential and asked: How much would you pay for a rich collection of information about the product on your mobile phone in a real store (all three product categories)? The willingness to pay is similar among all products (digital camera, book, wine). For a digital camera, for example, the opinions are distributed as follows (selection from predefined answers):

- Nothing. This service should be generally free of charge (51%).
- Nothing. But I would accept advertisements (18%).
- I would be willing to pay roughly the value of a text message (19%).
- I could imagine to pay between 3 and 5 dollars (5%)

Some participants used the additional free text field we provided and entered other ways for compensation. Many proposed a flat rate tariff, others proposed to earn community credits though self-created recommendations and use these to pay, again others insisted the price should be relative to the item on hand.

Summarizing the survey results it becomes clear that people appreciate product information on their mobile phone. However, the product information must be easily accessible, which is not the case today. Besides mobile Internet flat rates and appropriate displays, easy identification is a fundamental element of the design of systems providing product information on mobile phones. This finding motivated our user study, which is described in the next section.

4 Usability Study: Design and Execution

The study consisted of two tasks and a follow-up interview. In the first task, the participants identified single products in a mixed sequence of five different identification techniques. In the second task the users simulated the comparison of three given products, identifying three products in a row. For time reasons we compared only the expectedly fastest manual identification technique to the expectedly fastest automatic identification technique. In the adjacent interview the participants rated each of the identification techniques regarding their 'perceived ease of use'.

4.1 Participants

We recruited 17 participants (6 females) for the study. Their average age was 27.5 years with mixed professional backgrounds (secretary staff, physicians, business people, IT people, engineers, and others). All participants owned a mobile phone and were familiar with text input on mobile devices. The study was executed on two consecutive days in September 2008.

4.2 Study Design

We utilized a within-subject study design. The dependent variable was the time required to identify a product (task completion time). In the experiment we used 4 different wine bottles (denoted as A, B, C, and D) as the products to be identified. The choice of products was motivated by the following reasons: the survey suggested that wine is a product predominantly bought in traditional shops and the individual products can be easily identified by name. Also, consumers rely on additional information for wine purchases, such as recommendations from friends and test institutes. The wine bottles were selected randomly in a supermarket from more than 300 different wine bottles offered, in order to achieve a sufficient randomization of the product name. Each of the bottles had an EAN13 barcode attached, and a product name label. In addition, we tagged each bottle with an NFC RFID tag and an EPC RFID tag. The appearance of the bottles is depicted in Fig. 1.

Fig. 1. Labels and tagging of the wine bottles used

The independent variables were the following identification techniques:

Manual Barcode Entry (MBE) denotes the manual entry of the number that is located below a barcode. We used a smart phone (Nokia N95), which is well suited for inputting numbers, with a simple application allowing the user to enter barcodes (EAN8, UPC12, EAN13), pressing a button for confirmation and receiving feedback that the product was identified. In the case of our study, all products were equipped with the 13-digit EAN13 barcodes. These are most commonly used for consumer products.

Manual Product Search (MPS) required the user to enter a search term for the given product into a text field. For this condition the iPhone was used, as it is widely used for accessing the mobile Internet. In contrast to many other phones it offers a fairly large on-screen keyboard. For comparability reasons, we only measured the time the used needed to enter a search term until he pressed the search button. We deliberately did not predefine the term to search for. We assume that one key disadvantage of today's practice is that consumers in most cases cannot search for product information in the web based on a tag on the product (an exception might be searching for books, based on the ISBN). Thus we believe that for quantifying the benefit of automatic identification, the time needed to find an appropriate search term should be included in the measurement.

For **Automatic Barcode Recognition (ABR)** the participants used a smart phone (Nokia N95) with a built-in camera. For the task a simple application based on a barcode recognition toolkit [6] was used. The barcode recognition software used is from our experience the most reliable barcode reader. Users had to scan the barcode by moving the product's barcode into the field of the lens coverage of the handset's camera at a distance of about 3 centimeters. They received feedback when the barcode was recognized.

NFC Tag Scan (NFC) was implemented with a simple Java application using JSR 257 on a Nokia 6131 NFC handset. The latter is a commercially available phone with an integrated NFC RFID reader. Performing the task required the user to touch a tag with mobile phone antenna. The reading range is about 5 cm. The user received a sound feedback as soon as the tag was recognized.

EPC Tag Scan (EPC) was done on a prototype phone (Nokia E61i with integrated EPC UHF RFID reader) using a simple Java application. To identify the product the user had to point the phone towards the product (reading range up to 50 cm, according to the manufacturer).

In the beginning, the participants received an oral introduction (roughly 10 minutes) to the different identification techniques and were encouraged to try them out. Users tested each technique a couple of times until they confirmed that they felt familiar with each. We briefly motivated the use of product identification techniques on mobile devices with potential application scenarios. After this, the participants completed two tasks. Following the study, we conducted an interview with each of the participants.

For each participant the study was recorded on video. In a later step we extracted the precise time recording for the identification techniques from the video[2]. We also transcribed all comments the participant made during the study.

4.3 Task 1 – Single Product Identification

The task for the participants was to use every identification technique (MBE, MPS, ABR, NFC, EPC) on each product (A, B, C, D). In total, each participant performed 20 identification tasks, their order was randomized. Overall, task 1 took about 10 minutes per participant.

Each of the 20 identifications was performed in the following steps: A mobile handset with the software supporting the respective identification technique was handed to the participant. The identification application was active in all cases. As soon as the participant confirmed readiness, the supervisor touched one of the four

[2] A video summarizing the study and the results is available at: http://www.youtube.com/watch?gl=DE&v=d1AgudZwPkM

bottles (simulating the discovery of an interesting product as described above) in order to indicate for which product the identification task should be performed. Touching the bottle is also used as a trigger to measure time. The participant then identified the product. As soon as the product was identified, time recording was stopped. The mobile phone was returned to a supervisor and reset.

4.4 Task 2 – Comparison of Multiple Products

In the second task we compared one manual and one automatic identification technique. We have selected Manual Barcode Entry (MBE) and NFC Tag Scan (NFC), as they have proven fastest and most convenient for the users.

Each participant performed the comparison task (for time reasons) only with three randomly chosen bottles (A, C, and D); once with each technique. Half of the participants began with technique MBE, before performing the task with technique NFC, and vice versa. As in task 1, each participant was given a handset with an active application which allowed identification with the respective technique. After a trigger signal, the participant identified the three bottles in a row. With the confirmation of the last identification (beep) the time recording was stopped.

We measured the time the participants needed for three subsequent identifications using each technique and evaluated all comments made during the experiment by video analysis.

4.5 Interview

After having performed the above tasks, we asked each participant to rate each identification technique on a Likert scale from 1 (very hard to use) to 5 (very easy to use). We concluded the interview with an informal discussion about the individual techniques encouraging participants to share their perceptions. Finally, we clarified the concrete intention of the study to the participants.

5 Usability Study: Results

The following paragraphs describe the results of the study. In addition to the clearly measurable variables 'task completion time' and 'perceived ease of use', we describe comments made by the participants and observations made during the experiments.

5.1 Automatic Techniques Up to Eight Times Faster, Barcode Almost as Fast as RF

Measuring the time per single product identification (task 1) indicates that automatic identification is significantly faster than manual techniques (see Figure 2). While this could have been expected, the experiments reveal that the fastest automatic identification technique (NFC) is roughly eight times faster per identification than the slowest user-mediated identification technique (MPS). From the comments during the study it becomes apparent that manual input is not considered an alternative when searching for product information on mobile phones. Participant P2 highlights this saying "why do you bother to do the test, it is clear nobody's gonna do this".

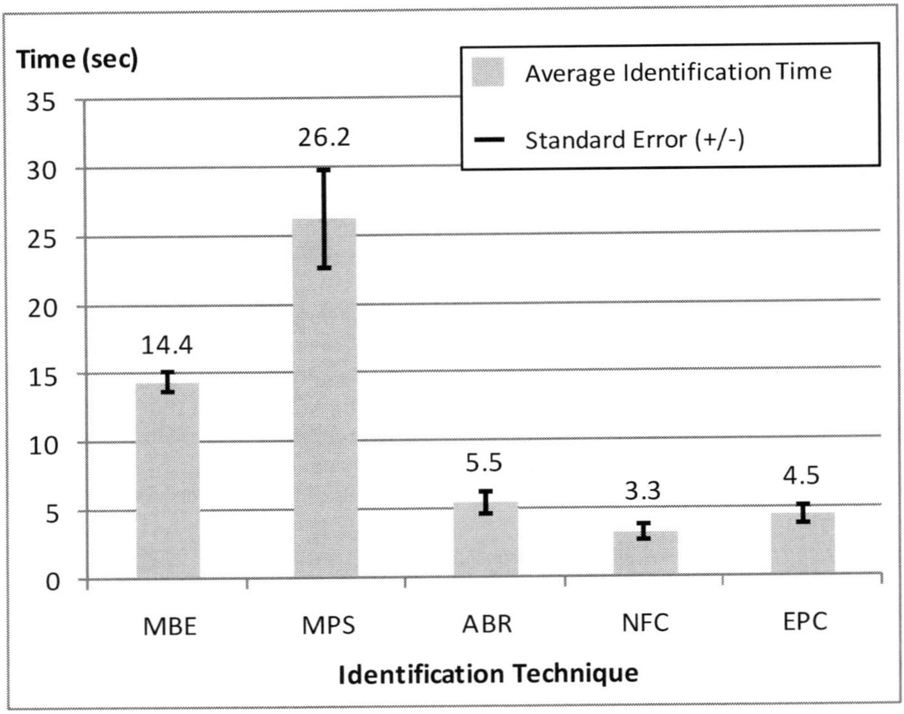

Fig. 2. Average Time per Identification by Technique

The fastest technique in the experiment is the NFC Tag Scan (NFC), taking the users 3.3 seconds in average to identify a product. Scanning NFC Tags is time-wise followed by EPC Tag Scans (EPC), which takes the user in average 4.5 seconds. In this context it is worth mentioning that, at the current technical level, NFC tag scan and the EPC tag scan interact with products in the same way – by touching the tag on the product with the antenna integrated in the phone. Although both RFID-based identification techniques (NFC, EPC) are the fastest, they are, surprisingly, relatively closely followed by the third automatic identification technique, the automatic barcode recognition (ABR, 5.4 seconds on average).

In contrast, manual barcode entry (MBE) takes approximately three times as long as recognizing the barcode automatically. Moreover, the technique that takes the users by far the longest time is entering product information on a search page (MPS), taking about eight times as long as scanning an NFC tag. The large temporal deviations of technique MPS are due to the fact that each participant could freely pick the term considered best suited to find information about the product on hand, leading to search terms of between 7 and 31 characters length. In addition, heavy iPhone users perform slightly better than those who have never used an iPhone before.

5.2 Approximately Linear Progression of 'Task Completion Time'

The time for three identifications in a row (task 2) was performed by means of manual barcode entry (MBE) and NFC tag scan (NFC). Comparing three products can be considered a typical task during a buying decision. While the automatic identification of three products takes 8.4 seconds on average, the manual identification is with 39.2 seconds significantly slower.

5.3 Correlation between 'Task Completion Time' and 'Perceived Ease of Use'

The results of the assessment of perceived ease of use are depicted in Figure 3.

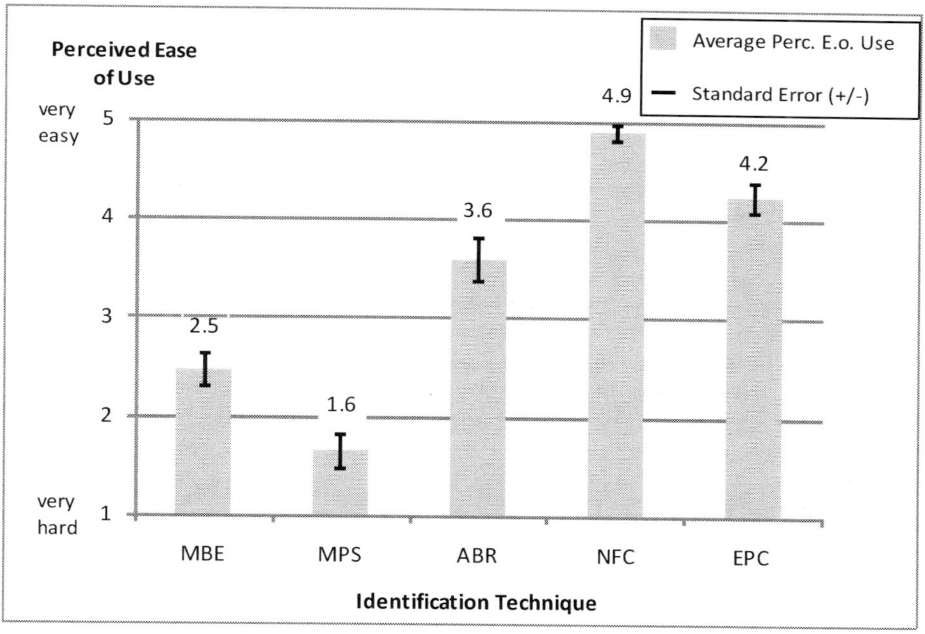

Fig. 3. Average Perceived Ease of Use per Identification Technique

The NFC tag scan (NFC) is perceived as the easiest-to-use identification technique with an average score of 4.9 and only two people not rating it at 5. The EPC tag scan (EPC) is slightly behind (4.2), with some more distance to barcode recognition. The manual identification techniques are according to the user ratings significantly harder to use.

Ordering the identification techniques by speed provides the same result as ranking them by user preference. This indicates a strong correlation between the time needed for identification using a particular technique and the perceived ease of use. Interestingly, three out of six female participants of the study do not perceive a significant difference regarding the ease of use of entering a barcode manually and recognizing it automatically.

5.4 Variable Attention Requirements per Technique

Observing the participants performing the tasks we noticed large differences in the attention a user needs to use the different techniques. In particular identification techniques NFC and EPC can be performed with little effort. Participants stated that they could imagine technique MBE, MPS, and ABR being serious hurdles for people with limited attention capabilities.

6 Discussion and Conclusion

Our survey shows that when shopping online, the access to additional information can potentially be valuable to consumers. The mobile phone offers possibilities to provide this information. More specifically, the survey shows what information consumers exactly base their buying decision on. Given these results, applications should provide easy mobile access rather to technical details and price comparisons for so called 'search products', and to recommendations of friends and family members and own experiences (for example with wine) for so called 'experience products'. To our knowledge, the survey is the first of its kind providing figures on the motivation of consumers to pay for additional product information on mobile phones. Roughly 70% of the consumers are not willing to pay for additional product information on their mobile phone. Consequently, entrepreneurs will have to think about appropriate business models for mobile product information systems. If the consumer does not pay, who else will pay? Our experience shows that for example retailers fear the transparency generated through mobile shopping assistants, but at the same time they gradually discover that it will be difficult to prevent consumers from using such systems. While our survey has provided insights for the given respondents group, future work will also have to investigate whether the results are different for the so called 'ringtone' generation below the age of 20, who have been underrepresented in our survey, but provide a target group for mobile services.

Our user study indicates a significant advantage of automatically recognizing an identifier compared to entering a search term or a 13-digit number in a text field (both are the only ways to interact with products using a mobile phones that are applied today). This lets us assume that product-related services will not widely be used as long as automatic identification is not available on mobile phones. A frequently disregarded issue is that automatic identification is even more important when interacting with more than one product, as simulated in task 2. While consumers might scan three products in a row (8.3 seconds) it is hard to believe that anybody will enter three barcodes manually (39.2 seconds).

Our figures show that barcode recognition can be time-wise performed almost as fast as scanning RFID tags, using one of the best mobile barcode scanners available. This fact, in combination with the pervasiveness of barcodes among today's products, makes the detection of barcodes a promising mobile identification technique in today's world, at least as long as the consumer goods industry does not switch to RFID on item-level. In addition, our results show that algorithms for detecting barcodes should take significantly less time than the 14.4 seconds the manual entry of a barcode takes in average. Given the differences in the performance of mobile barcode recognition today, this is not self-evident. A further point worth mentioning is that at current technical level, there is no barcode reader that works for a broad range of mobile platforms and handsets.

On a more abstract level we conclude that, despite the number of already commercially available mobile product-related services based on automatic identification, it needs to be worked on fast, reliable, and broadly applicable barcode readers for the identification of current products. Manual product identification as applied for example on the iPhone today (to our knowledge there is no 1d barcode reader on the iPhone that works without an additional lens on the camera) cannot be considered an alternative. In addition, novel revenue models have to be developed as a majority of consumers is not willing to pay for product information on their mobile phone.

As a next step we will propose an architecture for invoking different services from mobile phones, based on identified products.

Acknowledgements

This work has been partly funded by the Nokia NRC Pervasive Communications Laboratory in Lausanne (Switzerland), by the research project SemProM (funded by the German Government), and by the Auto-ID Labs initiative.

References

1. Szymanski, M., Hiseb, R.T.: E-Satisfaction: An Initial Examination. Journal of Retailing 76(3), 309–322 (2000)
2. Senecal, S., Nantel, J.: The Influence of Online Product Recommendations on Consumers' Choices. Journal of Retailing 80(2), 159–169 (2004)
3. Cassar, K. (2008): The Online and In-Store Crossover Conundrum. In: Nielsen Consumer Insight Magazine (2008), `http://www.nielsen.com/consumer_insight/issue10/ci_story1.html` (checked January 2008)
4. Ward, M.R., Morganowsky, M.: Consumer Acquisition of Product Information and Subsequent Purchase Channel Decisions. The Economics of the Internet and E-Commerce 11, 231–255 (2002)
5. Rohs, M., Gfeller, B.: Using Camera-Equipped Mobile Phones for Interacting with Real-World Objects. In: Ferscha, A., Hoertner, H., Kotsis, G. (eds.) Advances in Pervasive Computing, pp. 265–271. Austrian Computer Society (OCG) (2004)
6. Adelmann, R.: Mobile Phone Based Interaction with Everyday Products - On the Go. Conference on Next Generation Mobile Applications, Services and Technologies (2007)
7. NFC Forum NFC Data Exchange Format Technical Specification (2008), `http://www.nfc-forum.org`
8. Ondrus, J., Pigneur, Y.: An Assessment of NFC for Future Mobile Payment Systems. In: Conference on the Management of Mobile Business (2007)
9. Anokwa, Y., Borriello, G., Pering, T., Want, R.: A User Interaction Model for NFC Enabled Applications. Pervasive Computing and Communications Workshops (2007)
10. Geven, A., Strassl, P., Ferro, B., Tscheligi, M., Schwab, H.: Experiencing Real-World Interaction: Results from a NFC User Experience Field Trial. In: Conference on Human Computer Interaction with Mobile Devices and Services (2007)

11. Savolainen, J., Iraji, S., Hirvola, H.: EPC UHF RFID Reader: Mobile Phone Integration and Services. In: Consumer Communications and Networking Conference (2009)
12. Thiesse, F., Michahelles, F.: An Overview of EPC Technology. Sensor Review 26(2), 101–105 (2006)
13. Sarma, S.: Towards the 5¢ Tag, Massachussets Institute of Technology, Auto-ID Center White Paper (2001)
14. Wiechert, T., Thiesse, F., Michahelles, F., Schmitt, P., Fleisch, E.: Connecting Mobile Phones to the Internet of Things: A Discussion of Compatibility Issues between EPC and NFC. In: Americas Conference on Information Systems, AMCIS (2007)
15. von Reischach, F., Guinard, D., Michahelles, F., Fleisch, E.: A Mobile Product Recommendation System Interacting with Tagged Products. In: IEEE Conference on Pervasive Computing and Communications, PerCom 2009 (2009)
16. O'Hara, K., Perry, M.: Shopping Anytime Anywhere. In: CHI Extended Abstracts on Human Factors in Computing Systems (2001)
17. Resatsch, F., Sandner, U., Leimeister, J.M., Krcmar, H.: Do Point of Sale RFID-based Information Services Make a Difference? Analyzing Consumer Perceptions for Designing Smart Product Information Services in Retail Business. Electronic Markets 18(3), 216–231 (2008)
18. Zenebe, A., Ozok, A., Norcio, A.F.: Personalized Recommender Systems in E-commerce and M-commerce: A Comparative Study. In: Conference on Human-Computer Interaction (HCI International) (2005)
19. Häubl, G., Trifts, V.: Consumer Decision Making in Online Shopping Environments: The Effects of Interactive Decision Aids, Marketing Science (2000)
20. Ballagas, R., Borchers, J., Rohs, M., Sheridan, J.: The Smart Phone: A Ubiquitous Input Device. IEEE Magazine on Pervasive Computing 5(1), 70–77 (2006)
21. Broll, G., Siorpaes, S., Rukzio, E., Paolucci, M., Hamard, J., Wagner, M., Schmidt, A.: Comparing Techniques for Mobile Interaction with Objects from the Real World. In: Permid Workshop at the Pervasive Conference (2007)
22. Rukzio, E., Broll, G., Leichtenstern, K., Schmidt, A.: Mobile Interaction with the Real World: An Evaluation and Comparison of Physical Mobile Interaction Techniques. In: Conference on Ambient Intelligence, AmI (2007)
23. Nelson, P.: Information and Consumer Behavior. Journal of Political Economy 78(2), 311–329 (1970)
24. King, M.F., Balasubramanian, S.K.: The Effects of Expertise, End Goal, and Product Type on Adoption of Preference Formation Strategy. Journal of the Academy of Marketing Science 22(2), 146–159 (1994)

Presence, Routines, and Technology Discrepancy – Information Exchange between Parents and Preschool Teachers

Stina Nylander

Swedish Institute of Computer Science, Box 1263, 16429 Kista, Sweden
stny@sics.se

Abstract. We have interviewed four parents and a teacher at a Swedish preschool to investigate the practices for spreading information in preschool. Our findings suggest that frequent presence in the premises of the preschool is important to get information, and that parents rely heavily on routines to make it work. When either of these points fail, breakdowns occur. Discrepancies in parents' and teachers' IT use also complicates the information exchange.

1 Introduction

Family life and the elements of planning, coordination, and problem solving it encompasses have received a lot of attention in the HCI community in the recent years. Various studies have shed light on families organize their lives using various tools such as paper lists [11], home made organizing systems [10], and paper calendars [1], how they communicate and coordinate their information [3], and how this work could be supported by smart home systems [2]. This research has focused on the family as a unit and explored how family members communicate with each other, organize incoming information, and negotiate their everyday tasks. We add to this body of knowledge by looking at the information exchange between the family and an external unit, preschool. Families stay in contact with many external units such as schools, sports teams, authorities, doctors and the like. We have chosen preschool since it is a daily activity, involves different types of information in both directions, and breakdowns can have potentially cumbersome consequences such as a parent having to stay home from work unexpectedly.

The information exchange between parents and preschool teachers is frequent and important. Parents get a lot of practical information and information about their children's development from preschool teachers. They also need to convey information about the children to the teachers. A large part of the information exchange takes place in the premises of preschool where parents talk to teachers, pick up paper notes, reads notes posted on notice boards etc. Some information is conveyed over the phone while email is used very little in the studied preschool. Parents then bring the information home and incorporate it in their own organizing system to keep track of what is going on.

We have investigated the practices for information exchange between teachers and parents at a Swedish preschool through interviews with four parents of preschool

T. Gross et al. (Eds.): INTERACT 2009, Part I, LNCS 5726, pp. 817–829, 2009.

children, and a preschool teacher. Here we focus on the present handling of written information. Our findings suggest that the existing routines for keeping track of information rely heavily on presence (at home and in preschool) and that the information usually is non-portable. We also noted a discrepancy between the parents' and the teachers' use of information technology that seemed to influence the information exchange. We conclude the paper by presenting some implications for future design of information technology for family use.

2 The Studied Preschool

In Sweden, 80% of children aged 1-5 attended preschool in 2007. At the age of six, they start in "preschool class" which is a preparatory year between preschool and school. In average, children are 18 months old when they start preschool.

Two main professional groups work in preschool, preschool teachers and child care assistants. The preschool teachers have 3.5 years of university education in pedagogy, and children's development and learning, combined with a variety of specializations such as music, drama, science for children etc. The child care assistant education is given within high school. Formally, preschool teachers have the pedagogic responsibility while the child care assistants are in charge of the practical issues of taking care of children. In this paper, we will refer to both groups as teachers.

Parents pay a fee for their children to go to preschool. The fee is 3% of the parent's income with a ceiling of 1260 SEK/month for 2008. If a family has more than one child in preschool the fee for the second and third child is reduced. Children aged 4 and 5 have a right to 15 hours a week of preschool without charge. In Sweden, there are public preschools, private preschools and preschools run by parents, but they all operate with the same fees.

When it comes to technology and its use, the differences between various preschools are huge. The migration from paper to digital information in the administration work is basically completed by now, but many preschools have old computers, extremely slow Internet connections, no digital cameras or other technology. The differences are also large in how the existing technology is used in the pedagogic work with the children. Some preschools use digital cameras and camcorders to document the activities and let children watch and manipulate the pictures using the computers. Drawing software and games are also used with the children. The use of technology with the children of course depend on what kind of technology the preschool have access to, but also how comfortable teachers are with using it.

Here we do not focus on the specific organization of preschools or how the pedagogic activities are carried out, but exclusively on the information exchange between teachers and parents that are necessary to make everything work. The daily communication between parents and teachers about a child and the activities of the day, as well as the information about events, things to bring, meetings and other issues are present in all kinds of child care in many cultures. We therefore believe that the issues that we discuss in this paper are not only relevant for the case of Swedish preschools but also for a larger cultural context.

The preschool that was the target of this study takes care of 37 children divided into two groups, 16 children in a younger group (1-2 years old) and 21 children in an older group (3-5 years old). The younger group is attended to by three teachers, the older group has four teachers.

The preschool is equipped with computers and Internet access that are used for both administrative tasks and pedagogic activities with the children. Teachers use the computers for example to write notes and letters to parents, report their working hours, and to show parents pictures and movies of what the children are doing in preschool. The children use the computers for example for drawing, watching digital pictures that they have taken themselves (or the teachers have taken of them), and watching movies that the teachers take of certain activities in the preschool. Email is used within the organization for communication between teachers at different preschools, organization of teachers' conferences and spreading of administrative information. It is only used tentatively for communication between parents and teachers.

3 Related Work

Research from the past few years has shown that family life demands a great deal of effort to manage and coordinate [3]. Families need to keep track of information from various sources about events, responsibilities, people, and things. Paper calendars displayed in the kitchen or other central places in the home are common tools to help families [1, 7]. Taylor & Swan have also described how this is done using paper lists [11] and other home made organizing systems such as charts or notebooks [10] to achieve the flexibility needed in combination with the beauty, personalization, and functionality desired. The above approaches have in common that they have focused on the family and how they manage incoming information and keep track of it. Little attention has been given to the sources of the incoming information or to how the family informs others about itself. We would like to add to the body of knowledge on family coordination by studying how the family communicates with an external unit and how that information exchange works. Here, we have chosen preschool as the external unit.

Many attempts have been done to design and implement various applications that would support families with the wall calendar as the most frequently used application. The attempts bear witness of the difficulties to replace well established domestic routines based on traditional tools such as notice boards and paper calendars with information technology. Crabtree et al. [1] points out that it is not a good idea to replace a paper wall calendar with individual electronic calendars since the wall calendar has an important purpose of serving as a central point of information and awareness. Neustadter et al. show in their trials with the LINC prototype digital wall calendar that it is not trivial to replicate the flexibility and the ease of use of the paper calendar even though they have taken important steps in the process [7, 8].

Another body of work that is relevant for this work is the smart home domain. Davidoff et al. [2] have investigated how a smart home could support families to manage information. Another example is the smart bag [5] where an object is augmented with sensor technology to be able to help its owner remember what to pack and to bring the bag to the right event. In the particular case presented here we do not advocate anything like a smart home infrastructure but we definitely acknowledge the possibilities of information technology to be of help in family organization. Our case of preschool teachers and parents call for simple, robust and easy to use solutions, which leads us to envision trials with email and text messages, technologies already well integrated in participants' lives.

4 Method

The routines for information exchange between parents and preschool teachers have been examined through interviews. Four parents and one preschool teacher have been interviewed individually. The interviews lasted 45-60 minutes and were recorded. Three of the parents were interviewed at home while the fourth interview was conducted in a quiet restaurant. One or two children were present during the interviews that were conducted at home. The teacher was interviewed in the premises of the preschool. The parents were recruited at a parent-teacher meeting at the preschool that the author attended. The interviews focused on the routines of the preschool for giving information to the parents, how parents give information to the teachers, how the parents keep track of all the information, and where the breakdowns occur. A few questions were also asked about the parents' experience with technology such as the Internet, email, and cell phones.

We are aware of the drawbacks of self-reporting as a method of gathering data, especially in a case such as ours that is surrounded with strong social norms. However, we believe that parents have been honest enough. One of our participants reported having forgotten to pick up a child in time and received a phone reminder from preschool, and others reported several cases of forgotten stuff that should have been brought and other mistakes. In addition, the stories of the interviewed parents matched the story of the interviewed teacher well.

The interviews were complemented with a visit to the preschool where pictures of places and artifacts relevant to the information spreading process were taken.

4.1 Participants

Participant 1 (P1) was a married woman in her thirties with two children, one and three years old. At the time of the interview, she was on maternity leave with her youngest child, but her older child still attended preschool a few days a week. Since she was staying at home she took care of the dropping off and picking up at preschool, and also kept track of all information concerning preschool. Her primary tool for that was a day planner where she noted all important information. She reported that she used the Web and email frequently during her maternity leave, and would go back to her work where she uses the Web and email daily. Her cell phone was Web enabled and she had tried to surf from it once.

Participant 2 (P2) was a married woman in her thirties with one four year old child. Both she and her husband were working, and she took care of most of the dropping off and picking up their child at preschool, with some help from her mother-in-law that sometimes picked her child up from preschool. She was the one in the family that is responsible for keeping track of the information from preschool, and wrote things down in a day planner that she carried in her purse. The list of dates when the preschool is closing early was posted on the fridge, and she sometimes let notes from preschool lie visible in the kitchen so that her mother-in-law could read them. She used email daily in her work and had a Web enabled cell phone. She had tried occasionally to surf from the phone but it was not a habit.

Participant 3 (P3) was a married man in his forties with six children, three with his current wife (aged two, four, and six), and three teenagers from a previous marriage of which two lived every other week with his current family. The two youngest children attended the preschool described in this study. Both he and his wife worked, and they shared the responsibility of dropping off and picking up children. The family had a kitchen calendar with one column for each person in the family where important events and reminders were noted, which he referred to as the main information point in the house. He kept his own calendar in his cell phone, his wife had her calendar, and he reported that their personal calendars usually were not fully synchronized with each other. Besides the kitchen calendar the family also had a poster by the front door with things that needed to be remembered for each day of the week, such as sports clothes Monday, picnic lunch Tuesday etc. He used email daily both for work and private purposes (but used different computers for each purpose to keep them separated), and had a Web enabled cell phone but did not use it to surf the Web.

Participant 4 (P4) was a married woman in her forties with two children aged four and six, of which the youngest attend the preschool described here. Both she and her husband were working, and they shared the responsibility of dropping their children off and picking them up at preschool. Her husband dropped them off every morning, she picked them up three days a week, and the other two days the grandmothers picked them up one day each. She was the one responsible for keeping track of the information in the family and writing it down in the kitchen calendar or posting it on the message board. Usually, she also told her husband when something was going on since he rarely looked in the calendar. She had no personal day planner. She had a desk calendar at work where she also noted personal and family events. In her work she used email daily but she had never tried to surf from her phone.

5 Different Types of Information

The main information channels between parents and teachers are paper notes (mostly from teachers to parents) and face-to-face communication. Paper is used for information about dates, events, decisions and reminders. A monthly information letter with summaries of the past month's activities and important dates to come is distributed to the parents, complemented by reminder notes and extra notes when something comes up. Email is only used occasionally in the studied preschool. No routines have been established yet as to what information could be distributed electronically. The information exchanged between parents and teachers mainly concern three broad areas:

- the children and the activities in general – parents tell teachers in the morning if there is anything special with their children that day, teachers tell parents in the afternoon what has happened during the day. The main part of this information exchange is oral, but teachers usually write a summary of the day's activities in the school's wall calendar.
- logistics – parents inform teachers about when the children will be picked up, sick children that are not coming to school, doctor's appointments, vacation dates

and the like using face to face conversations, phone calls and paper notes. Teachers inform parents about things to bring, when preschool is closing early, diseases etc. using face to face conversations and paper notes.

- events – the preschool is taking the children to the theatre, parents are invited for the Easter party etc. This information is always conveyed in written form, in the monthly letter, separate notes or both.

Fig. 1. The toilet paper rolls that are used as mail boxes

6 Strategies to Make Information Exchange Work

Parents have tricks and strategies to keep track of information as well as teachers have strategies to make parents pay attention. Some strategies are used by both parents and teachers.

6.1 Strategy 1: Display Information in Prominent Places

Both teachers and parents display paper notes in prominent places to disseminate and remember important information. This strategy works well as long as the concerned persons frequent the places where the information is displayed.

The most important source of information for the parents is a toilet paper roll (see figure 1). Each child has paper roll attached to the wall besides the entrance which serves as a mail box. All the written information from the teachers is put in the roll. The interviewed parents reported that the first thing that they did when entering the preschool was to check if there was anything in their child's roll.

There are several message boards in use. At the entrance there is one with general information to parents, such as the pedagogic plan, documentation from PTA meetings, important phone numbers, the menu for the week etc. Each of the two child groups also has a message board where information about the daily activities is posted. Important information is posted on the front door so that no one can leave the building without noticing. Especially important information is also posted on the outside of the front door so that it is visible on arrival, for example the reminder that the preschool is closing early today.

Prominent places are also used to display information in the home. A wall calendar in the kitchen is a common way to organize information concerning various family members [1, 7]. Three of the interviewees reported that their family had one where everything was written down. One of them usually looked at the calendar in the evening, after dinner, another one looked at least every morning.

"I look at the calendar several times a day. Don't know why, guess I'm afraid to forget something." (P4)

Several participants also reported having other places for information in the kitchen in addition to the wall calendar, such as a notice board or notes posted on the fridge. This lies well in line with the findings of [3] that information tend to gather in the places where all the family gathers.

One family had a poster on the inside of the front door with a list of things that needed to be remembered or packed for each day of the week: fruit on Monday, sports clothes on Tuesday, picnic lunch on Wednesday etc. However, such a reminder easily gets ignored after a while:

"*Maybe we should move the poster around once in a while so that we notice it. Now we almost don't see it anymore*." (P3)

Remote access to some of the information concerning preschool could help teachers to disseminate information and parent to keep track of it. This will be further discussed in the section on Design Implications.

6.2 Strategy 2: Establish Routines

Routines are important tools for making the family-preschool puzzle work [12], and our participants relied on them for various related tasks. Many of the reported breakdowns related to deviations from routines.

All the interviewed families had their own fixed schedule for who was dropping off and picking up the children from preschool to avoid misunderstandings.

"My husband drops the kids off every morning, I pick them up three days and each grandmother picks them up one day." (P4)

Three of the interviewees said that their family had an explicit agreement that the person picking up the children also brings home any note that is found in the roll. Taking the note in the morning had proved to be a bad strategy.

"*I don't dare to take it in the morning, I did it once and it got lost and we missed something. It's better to take it directly home and write down the info in the wall calendar*" (P3)

However, there are often deviations from routines [2]. The most frequently mentioned example in the interviews was the monthly early closing of the preschool. This means that all children need to be picked up at 3.45pm at the latest, compared to 6pm. These dates are announced in a special note that is distributed in the beginning of the semester, it is mentioned in the monthly letter and it is posted on the front door on the actual day. Parents reported carefully noting these dates since they need to depart from their established routine of picking up their children. However, staff reported that in average one family per occasion (different families every time) was late to pick up their children the day when they close early, and needed a reminder by phone. A probable reason for this is of course that deviations from routines are always difficult, especially when they occur as seldom as once a month. However, it is very common that one parent drops the kids off and the other parent picks them up which breaks the principle of presence. The parent that sees the reminder in the morning is not the one that needs to come early in the afternoon. For some families, nannies and/or grandparents are also involved in picking children up from day care. Moreover, the usual case is that the parent picking up the children comes directly from work which means that they do not have access to the family's central kitchen calendar. Our findings suggest that the present methods for spreading information in the preschool in question do not fully handle deviations from established routines. These situations call for information adapted to the situation such as various kinds of contextual reminders which will be further discussed in the section on Design Implications.

6.3 Strategy 3: Use Information Technology

Our participants reported using information technology such as email and the Web daily both for work and private purposes. Two participants reported using mobile technology to help them manage their personal information. One of our participants reported that he, for personal purposes, used his cell phone as a calendar and that he frequently used the alarm function to be reminded about upcoming calendar events.

"An hour before you came the phone beeped and reminded me that you were coming, otherwise I would have forgotten completely." (P3)

Another participant reported that she did not use the calendar functionality in her cell phone but that she frequently used "mobile notes". With mobile notes she could make a note about an upcoming event and put it as a wall paper on the screen of the cell phone. Since she used the phone instead of a watch she looked at it repeatedly during the day and thus saw the reminder for the event.

"That way it is rubbed in." (P4)

The preschool, though, used very little electronic information in their communication with the parents. A few short-lived attempts with email reminders for the days when the preschool closes early had been made but no routines were established. All interviewed parents reported using email and the Web daily, and two of them reported that they would like the preschool to use email for certain information purposes.

6.4 Fallback Strategies, When All Else Fail...

Of course, even though strategies for disseminating information may be carefully designed and well implemented, they sometimes do fail. One example that came up during the study was the collection of vacation dates for all families before the summer (the study was conducted in late May so the topic of vacation was highly relevant). Forms for reporting the vacation dates had been distributed to the parents during April and posters to remind them to hand the forms in had been posted in the premises. However, many parents did not return the forms so teachers fell back to good old "chasing and reminding". They tried to keep in mind who had returned the form and reminded those who had not. This sometimes took the form of going to the office to check who needed to be reminded and, during that time the family had left so the teacher had to run after them out on the side walk. The interviewed preschool teacher reported that such things take a lot of time. Teachers also remind parents in more general situations such as when there is an event scheduled for tomorrow. One of our interviewed parents said that he did not know if teachers reminded everyone or just him about events, but he did not mind being reminded.

"It doesn't bother me [to be reminded about events or things to bring]. It would be worse if they said 'don't forget to pick up your kid', that would hurt more." (P3)

Participants also reported that they sometimes call other parents, or the preschool, to find out if something special is up, for example if they have been away for a few days.

"If the kids have been sick we usually call preschool to check if something is up for next week. If we have been away we check with other parents if there is something we need to know." (P3)

7 Breakdowns and Consequences

Breakdowns usually happen when deviations from routines occur, such as when the preschool closes early, or during periods of time when parents have a lot on their mind such as the weeks before Christmas. Consequences are mostly minor, (often due to the flexibility of the teachers) but none the less they cause irritation, frustration, and restrict the teachers' time with the children.

The most serious consequences of information breakdowns are those who steal time from the main tasks that teachers are to perform. For example, when parents do not provide requested information in time (such as vacation dates), teachers need to spend a lot of time keeping track of who has not provided the information and remind them in various ways. One such problem used to be parents that needed phone numbers to other parents because the children set up play dates themselves during the day. Thus, in the afternoon when many parents arrive at the same time and want to talk to the teachers about the day, they have to go into the office to get phone numbers. This was so frequent and time consuming that it was solved by posting a list with names and phone numbers at the entrance so parents can find the numbers without asking the teachers. The interviewed teacher reported that it is very important for all teachers to be able to spend time with the children. That is their main work task and also the most rewarding one. When the time with the children is restricted due to administrative work, extra information work or other tasks, teachers easily get frustrated and feel that they are not allowed to do their job. Therefore, they work hard to make the information exchange with parents as efficient as possible.

"When the time with the children shrinks the teachers get frustrated." (Teacher)

An example that came up over and over again in the interviews was the issue of preschool closing early one day a month to allow the teachers to plan their work. When parents are late it creates problems for the teachers since they do not leave children unattended. In these situations someone misses the planning session since they must take care of the child/ren that are not picked up in time. It was also described as an awkward situation since teachers did not feel that they could call parents and remind them until about 4pm. If the parents then were still at work it would often take them more than 30 minutes to arrive to preschool.

"Sometimes you don't want to call because it gets embarrassing. You call them after 15 minutes and they are still down town." (Teacher)

Parents mostly reported bad conscience and feelings of being a bad parent as consequences of information breakdowns.

"You do want to do things right." (P1)

Practical problems could usually be solved by quick expeditions back home to get things that were left behind or to the grocery store when the picnic lunch was forgotten.

"Luckily, Engströms [the nearest grocery store] opens at 8am." (P2)

Parents also reported that the preschool teachers work hard to keep the consequences from the children when breakdowns occur. For example, the children of course get lunch even if the parents have forgot to report that they are not sick anymore and will be back at preschool, and children do not get left behind when the preschool is closing early and parents forget about that. However, the interviewed parents reported that such breakdowns sometimes cause family internal arguments.

"We argue about whose fault it was." (P3)

8 Implications for Design

Our findings suggest that many issues of parent-teacher information exchange center around three areas: presence, deviation from routines and discrepancies in technology use. Below we will discuss their implication for future design of technology for preschool use.

8.1 Presence, Absence, and Remote Access to Information

The routines of spreading necessary information both to parents and to teachers rely heavily on physical presence in the facilities [9]. In many cases this works well since parents drop off and pick up their children every day, which allow them to both get information from and give information to the teachers. However, if a child is absent due to illness there is a problem. Very little information gets through if you are not coming to the school.

"Before Christmas last year we were sick a lot and we totally lost track of what was going on. I think we missed a lot that we didn't even know about." (P1)

The interviewed parents reported that they sometimes call the preschool or other parents to check if something has come up while they have been at home with sick children.

The other central place for information is the home. Most of the interviewed families had a wall calendar in the kitchen and a message board for notes. This information is accessible even when children are staying at home sick, but when the family is traveling or the parents go to work they lose access to the information. Picking up children in the afternoon is for example an activity that does not start from home. Parents go from work to the preschool to pick the children up which means that they cannot check the kitchen calendar during the day to see if there is something special to adapt to. Even though home and preschool are natural places for storing information they are not the only places where parents need information access. There is a workplace for each parent, homes and workplaces for potential other persons involved in the child care, and transit places such as subway trains and cars. Some of the children also have divorced parents and thus two "homes", many of them spending every other week at each home. Access to preschool information from other places than the home and the preschool could obviously be beneficial. Remote access to the information would also reduce problems that occur when children are sick and no one from the family comes to preschool for some time.

Another example of remote access to information concerns the handling of contact information. Keeping the contact information of all families up to date and available is a challenge. One of the reasons that the trials with manual email reminders about the early closing did not continue was that it was too cumbersome to collect email addresses to all parents and to keep the list up to date. We have also described above that it took so much time for teachers to help parents find phone numbers for each other that they finally posted a list on the wall so that parents could find the numbers themselves. An electronic record of contact information to which parents could get secure remote access and update their own information would be of great help and alleviate the teachers.

8.2 Deviations from Routines

When deviations from routines occur, which can happen frequently, extra support such as reminders is needed. The current practice includes written information in advance about the early closing, paper note on the front door the day previous to and the day of the closing, and oral reminders in the morning. However, as we described above, it is not always the person that gets reminded in the morning that will pick the child up early in the afternoon. Moreover, when deviating from an established routine, a reminder that occurs six or seven hours before the actual event might easily be forgotten. Situations like this could benefit from contextual reminders [5-7] through for example text messages to cell phones or email. A reminder to the right parent an hour or two before the child needs to be picked up would probably reduce the number of late pick-ups significantly. It would also relieve the teachers from awkward phone calls to remind parents that are running late. We also believe that especially text messages to cell phones would be well received by parents. For example two of our participants, P3 and P4, described how they already use their cell phones to remind them about important events. However, it is important that reminders can be set in advance and sent automatically since teachers do not have time to administer them in the afternoon.

8.3 Discrepancies in IT Use

It was obvious from the interviews that there is a discrepancy between how information technology is used in the preschool and how the interviewed parents used it in other parts of their lives. Information technology has only to a small extent entered the preschool while the parents were frequent users of email and the Web.

"For me I think maybe email would work better." (P1)

When the parents communicated with each other, for example about organizing activities, they often used email. For example, when the parents organized a day of fixing things in the preschool and cleaning the yard, the vote about which day to do it was made by email. When the date was set, a paper note was distributed to everyone since that is the official way to announce an event. P2 also reported that the minutes from the last meeting with teachers and parents were taken by a parent and then emailed to everyone.

We believe that information technology could help to improve the information exchange between parents and preschool teachers in several ways. As described above, it can be used to provide remote access to information, to create contextual reminders, and allow parents to update their own contact information. We also believe that it can help by already being an integrated part of our participants existing organization systems. They reported in the interviews that they use email and the Web daily for both work and private purposes. In this respect we believe that our participants are representative for the Swedish population in general, for example did more than 85% of Swedes aged 16-45 use the Internet daily in 2008 [4]. Tapping into this existing behavior to disseminate preschool information therefore has good opportunities to work.

Privacy and the careful handling of personal information is an important issue here. Preschool have strict guidelines on how they are allowed to store and handle personal information which are often based on the paper based procedures but still need to be respected when moving to information technology. We envisage written consent and at least password protection for contact information on the Web. Our experience so far does not support the need for keeping other personal information such as the children's progress and development on the Web.

We are also aware of the current low use of information technology in preschool. Many teachers have little experience and little education, and the equipment is often old. Extreme care need to be taken when introducing new technology and new use of the existing technology as to not burden teachers. We are trying to improve the information exchange to give teachers more time with the children. It is therefore crucial that the proposed solution does not eat up the liberated time.

9 Future Work

Based on the findings presented here we are continuing to work with teachers and parents at this preschool and five others in the Stockholm area to create information tools that fulfill the needs we have identified. We are planning a web interface for teachers to create simple web pages for the child groups that are accessible from computers and cell phones. That way, parents get remote access to information. The system will also support automatic email reminders in the first step, and automatic text message reminders to cell phones in the second step. To inform the design of this system further we plan to interview more parents and teachers from the different preschools in addition to the interviews presented here.

10 Conclusions

Based on interviews with parents and a preschool teacher, we have identified presence and routines as important foundations for the information exchange between parents and preschool teachers. Parents come to preschool daily and pick up paper notes, talk to teachers, and look at notice boards. They also often have schedules on who is dropping of and picking up the children on different days of the week. In the interviews we found that in case of absence from preschool, for example due to illness or travel, and when deviations from routines occur, there are often breakdowns in the parent-teacher information exchange. This has led us to consider ways of making the information remotely accessible, and provide reminders in situations that deviate from routines. Web access to some of the information from preschool would make it possible to check what is coming up for example from work or other places. We also believe that an increased use of information technology from the part of the teachers, to match that of the parents, would improve the information exchange.

Acknowledgements. We would like to thank the parents and preschool teachers that took time from their busy schedule to talk to us. Thanks also to Squace AB that supported this pilot study and will be a partner in future work in this area. This work has been funded by the Swedish Governmental Agency for Innovation (Vinnova).

References

1. Crabtree, A., Hemmings, T., et al.: Informing the Development of Calendar Systems for Domestic Use. In: Proceedings of ECSCW, pp. 119–138 (2003)
2. Davidoff, S., Lee, M.K., Yiu, C., Zimmerman, J., Dey, A.K.: Principles of smart home control. In: Dourish, P., Friday, A. (eds.) UbiComp 2006. LNCS, vol. 4206, pp. 19–34. Springer, Heidelberg (2006)
3. Elliot, K., Neustaedter, C., Greenberg, S.: Time, ownership and awareness: The value of contextual locations in the home. In: Beigl, M., Intille, S.S., Rekimoto, J., Tokuda, H. (eds.) UbiComp 2005. LNCS, vol. 3660, pp. 251–268. Springer, Heidelberg (2005)
4. Findahl, O.: Svenskarna och Internet 2008 (In Swedish. The Swedish people and the Internet 2008), World Internet Institute (2008)
5. Lee, M.K., Davidoff, S., et al.: Smart Bag: Managing Home and Raising Children. In: Proceedings of Designing Pleasurable Products and Interfaces, Helsinki, Finland, pp. 434–437 (2007)
6. Ludford, P.J., Frankowski, D., et al.: Because I Carry My Cell Phone Anyway: Functional Location-Based Reminder Applications. In: Proceedings of CHI 2006, Montréal, Canada, pp. 889–898. ACM Press, New York (2006)
7. Neustaedter, C., Bernheim Brush, A.J.: "LINC-ing" the Family: The Participatory Design of an Inkable Family Calendar. In: Proceedings of CHI, Montréal, Quebec, pp. 141–150. ACM Press, New York (2006)
8. Neustaedter, C., Bernheim Brush, A.J., et al.: A Digital Family Calendar in the Home: Lessons from Field Trials of LINC. In: Proceedings of Graphics Interface Conference, Montréal, Canada, pp. 199–206 (2007)
9. Nylander, S.: Presence as a Foundation for Information Exchange between Parents and Pre-School Teachers. In: Proceedings of CSCW Extended proceedings, San Diego, CA (2008)
10. Taylor, A.S., Swan, L.: Artful Systems in the Home. In: Proceedings of CHI, Portland, Oregon, pp. 641–650. ACM Press, New York (2005)
11. Taylor, A.S., Swan, L.: List Making in the Home. In: Proceedings of CSCW, Chicago, Illinois, pp. 542–545 (2004)
12. Tolmie, P., Pycock, J., et al.: Unremarkable Computing. In: Proceedings of CHI, Minneapolis, Minnesota, pp. 399–406. ACM Press, New York (2002)

TimeTilt: Using Sensor-Based Gestures to Travel through Multiple Applications on a Mobile Device

Anne Roudaut[1,2], Mathias Baglioni[1,2], and Eric Lecolinet[1]

[1] Telecom ParisTech – CNRS LTCI UMR 5141, 46 rue Barrault, 75013, Paris, France
[2] Alcatel-Lucent Bell Labs France, Villarceaux, Route de Villejust 91620, Nozay, France
{anne.roudaut,mathias.baglioni,
eric.lecolinet}@telecom-paristech.fr

Abstract. We present TimeTilt, a sensor-based technique that allows multiple windows switching on mobile devices, and which overcomes the limitations of mobile devices, i.e. their impoverished input bandwidth (often no keyboard, a small tactile screen and the drawbacks of one-handed interaction). TimeTilt, which is based on a lenticular metaphor, aims at both reducing the activation time when switching between views, and supporting a natural mapping between the gestures and the navigation. We draw a brief classification of sensor-based gestures that could be used in mobile conditions, and we present an experiment.

Keywords: Mobile devices, One-handed interaction, Multiple windows, Sensors, Gestures, Lenticular, Undo, Redo.

1 Introduction

More than simple communication systems, mobile devices provide a full set of multimedia services, helping people to manage medias anywhere. Although mobile device functionalities almost reach the ones of a laptop, they are constrained by their small form factor. Most familiar input devices have been removed (e.g. there is no mouse and often no keyboard) and the lack of screen real estate makes it impossible to display a large amount of information. Moreover, mobile devices are often operated with one hand, by interacting with the thumb [11] (e.g. when the user is standing in the metro). This causes occlusion on the screen and makes selection imprecise. The recent integration of motion sensors creates a great potential for designing new techniques: sensors fit very well with the graspable form of mobile devices and do not hamper touchscreen visualization and interaction. Several studies have been done in this field [7, 3], for instance for recognizing 3D shapes, for scrolling a list by tilting or for enriching games. However, in mobile conditions, users may perform involuntary gestures, and certain gestures may seem awkward to perform in public spaces. A compromise must then be found between gestures that are comfortable for users and compatible with their activities, and that do not hamper usual interaction techniques.

To address these issues, we present TimeTilt, a window management technique that relies on sensor-based interactions. This new technique does not interfere with standard interactions. This feature is especially welcome because it makes it possible to activate commands or trigger interaction techniques in the usual way, while changing

T. Gross et al. (Eds.): INTERACT 2009, Part I, LNCS 5726, pp. 830–834, 2009.

windows easily. This makes it for instance possible to drag and drop objects from a window to another one. In fact, changing windows quickly is useful in a variety of situations, such as switching between an overview and a zoomed view, between tabled views, etc. We first present TimeTilt and its properties. The two kinds of gestures used in this technique (smooth and jerk gestures) are described in the last part.

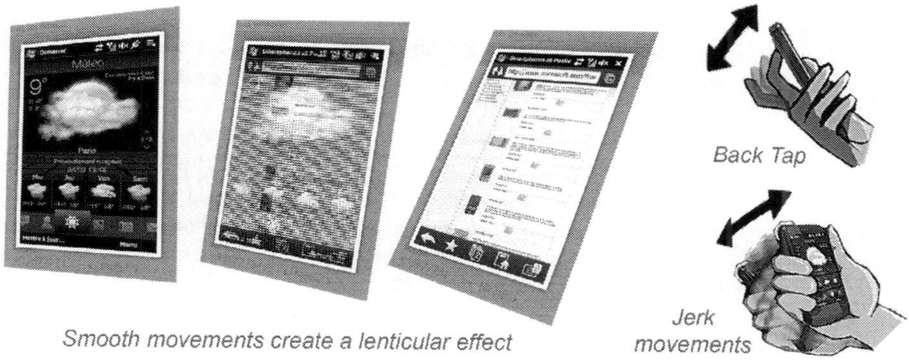

Fig. 1. TimeTilt helps to "travel in time" to reach previously opened windows. A tap on the back of the device triggers a continuous mode so that the user can navigate through windows by performing smooth gestures. A discrete mode can be activated with jerk movements.

2 TimeTilt Technique

While this is technically possible, mobile devices do not allow the user to switch easily between several windows. Because there is no room to display more than one window, the user must close the current window, find the other application (s)he now wants to interact with by navigating through the interface, and open it. Some applications may have their data stored in memory, but it is not always the case and the user must wait for the application to be loaded. TimeTilt was developed to solve this problem. Unlike desktop windows managers that have a spatial layout (with icons in the desktop bar), it is based on a temporal approach well suited for mobile devices. TimeTilt allows the user to tilt the device to “travel across time” and to navigate through open windows. When the desired window is found, the user just presses the screen to activate the corresponding application.

TimeTilt is based on a lenticular metaphor (Fig. 1). The lenticular effect (used in certain gift postcards) makes it possible for the user to see different images depending on the card orientation. The principle is to merge multiple images into the same sheet with a strips and lenses mechanism. As one’s viewing angle changes, one sequentially sees different strips of the image underneath the lenses, showing an animation. We used this effect to design a user-friendly technique that helps users to perform gestures (as advised in embodied user interface [4]). By analyzing the data provided by a G-sensor (i.e. accelerometers), TimeTilt takes into account three kinds of movements:

- A finger tap at the back of the device triggers/stops a continuous mode
- A smooth tilt of the device allows navigating *continuously* through windows (the lenticular metaphor animation provides a fluid transition between windows). When the user taps the screen, the current application is activated
- A jerk movement over the z-axis (forward or backward) performs a *discrete* action, activating the previous or a next opened window

Among these gestures, we distinguish two categories: the smooth ones as tilting the device for scrolling a list or navigate in a map [1, 5, 10, 12] and the jerk ones, which are sharper. The back tap is a jerk gesture because it creates a large acceleration variation, as we will see. TimeTilt leverages the three gestures in combination.

First, the back tap triggers a continuous mode *on demand*, without using standard inputs (as a physical key which may already trigger an action). The user chooses the beginning of the gesture to have always the screen visible. As showed in [9], users can navigate through 8 to 12 views by tilting the device. Moreover the activation tap is performed on the back of device, unlike [8] where users tap on the sides. This design is adapted to one-handed interaction because when interacting with the thumb, other fingers can activate commands from the back, as in recent studies [2].

Secondly, smooth gestures trigger a continuous mode that is well suited to switch between views. A user can easily navigate back-and-forth between, e.g., a map and an email application. They need not perform time-consuming steps that would distract his attention from the task.

Finally, jerk gestures offer a discrete mode that helps to quickly reach the last opened window: when interrupted by a phone call, the user can return to his previous task without searching in an application list (like in the iPhone) or without having to select small screen widgets with a stylus (as in Windows Mobile devices). This makes our technique well adapted to one-handed interaction.

In summary, this sensor-based gesture vocabulary contains three movements over the z-axis to support a natural mapping with the lenticular metaphor, which helps the user to understand and memorize the gestures. In the following, we present a use case of TimeTilt and then we explain how smooth and jerk gestures are recognized.

3 TimeTilt Use Case

Bob is searching on Google Map when he receives from a friend a message that indicates a date location. Bob copies the street address and taps on the back of his device. The messaging window freezes. From that position and according to a threshold, each rotation of the device around the z-axis displays the previous windows opened. Bob tilts the device forward to make the Google Map window appears and taps the screen. Bob pastes the street address in the Google Map research field, and the destination appears. He can then perform the reverse interaction and return to the messaging window to answer back to his friend.

4 Smooth and Jerk Gestures Features

The acceleration variation vector is a relevant value to distinguish smooth and jerk gestures because it does not depend on mobile orientation. Gestures can be recognized whatever the device position in the hand. Secondly, its values are almost flat during smooth gestures. Therefore, the challenge is to detect and identify jerk gestures. Because sensor hardware events are "continuous" (more precisely each 50ms in our implementation), there is neither start nor end of a gesture. To address this issue, our algorithm observes the acceleration variation and waits for a stable frame of 300ms. This value detects the jerk gestures studied in the experiment to be described below.

We conducted a preliminary study to collect jerk movements performed over the z-axis. The experiment aimed at finding the characteristics that are relevant to design a recognizer. Our 8 participants (2 female) were asked to perform gestures, while seated, with their preferred hand holding the device. There were six gestures to perform six times: 1) a back tap; 2) a back tap while holding the finger on the device before releasing; 3) a small jerk movement forward and 4) backward; 5) a sharper jerk movement forward and 6) backward. The experiment software was developed in C# (.Net Compact Framework) on a HTC Touch HD (Windows Mobile 6.1) with a 480x800px resistive touchscreen.

ANOVAs helps us indentify six relevant features for classifying jerk movement ($p<0{,}001$): 1) the global amplitude ($F_{5,35}=21.5$); 2) the maximum amplitude between two consecutive values ($F_{5,35}=12.2$); 3) the total duration ($F_{5,35}=29.7$); 4) the duration between the maximum and the minimum value ($F_{5,35}=4.3$, $p<0.003$); 5) the number of sign changes ($F_{5,35}=5.6$); 6) the sign of the first acceleration episode ($F_{5,35}=15.7$). Post-hoc multiple means comparison tests showed that back taps are faster, with a strong acceleration that does not seem to occur when performing the other jerk movements. We also observed that the shape of these gestures differed to a sufficient extend to avoid confusion with the natural gestures performed by the user. Finally, further analysis showed that although values differ from a user to another, patterns are similar enough for allowing proper recognition.

In the future we plan to discriminate more gestures, and to combine several sensors (e.g. with microphones as in [6]). We will compare TimeTilt with alternative methods to evaluate its performances and the satisfaction of users. We also want to increase TimeTilt capabilities by applying it for repeated undo/redo actions, or by enabling gestures over the x-axis with a “fan” metaphor to switch between tabs for instance.

References

1. Barlett, J.F.: Rock‘n scroll is here to stay. IEEE Comp. Graph. Ap., 40-45 (May/June 2000)
2. Baudisch, P., Chu, G.: Back-of-device Interaction allows creating very small touch devices. In: CHI 2009 (to appear, 2009)
3. Dachselt, R., Buchholz, R.: Throw and Tilt - Seamless Interaction across Devices Using Mobile Phone Gestures. In: GI 2008, pp. 272–278 (2008)
4. Fishkin, K.P., Gujar, A., Harrison, B.L., Moran, T.P., Want, R.: Embodied user interfaces for really direct manipulation. Commun. ACM 43(9), 74–80 (2000)
5. Harisson, B., Fishkin, K., Gujar, A., Mochon, C., Want, R.: Squeeze Me, Hold Me, Tilt Me! An exploration of manipulative user interfaces. In: CHI 1998, pp. 17–24 (1998)
6. Harrison, C., Hudson, S.E.: Scratch Input: Creating Large, Inexpensive, Unpowered and Mobile finger Input Surfaces. In: UIST 2008, pp. 205–208 (2008)

7. Hinckley, K., Pierce, J., Sinclair, M., Horvitz, E.: Sensing techniques for mobile interaction. In: UIST 2000 (2000)
8. Linjama, J., Kaaresoja, T.: Novel, minimalist haptic gesture interaction for mobile devices. In: NordiCHI 2004, pp. 457–458 (2004)
9. Rahman, M., Gustafson, S., Irani, P., Subramanian, S.: Tilt Techniques: Investigating the Dexterity of Wrist-based Input. In: CHI 2009 (to appear, 2009)
10. Rekimoto, J.: Tilting operations for small screen interfaces. In: UIST 1996, pp. 167–168 (1996)
11. Roudaut, A., Lecolinet, E., Huot, S.: Taptap and MagStick: Improving One-Handed Target Acquisition on Small Touch-screens. In: ACM AVI 2008, pp. 146–153 (2008)
12. Small, D., Ishii, H.: Design of spatially aware graspable displays. In: CHI 1997, pp. 367–368 (1997)

NFC-Based Mobile Interactions with Direct-View Displays

Khoovirajsingh Seewoonauth[1], Enrico Rukzio[1], Robert Hardy[1], and Paul Holleis[2]

[1] Computing Department, Lancaster University, UK
{hardyr,rukzio}@comp.lancs.ac.uk
[2] DoCoMo Euro-Labs, Germany
holleis@docomolab-euro.com

Abstract. Two NFC-based interactions are described in the paper. The first interaction technique is referred to as Touch & Connect: a process by which an NFC tag is used to rapidly pair a mobile device with a computer. The second interaction technique is referred to as Touch & Select, and considerably extends the Touch & Connect concept by allowing the use of an NFC-enabled mobile phone to directly touch at, and select, an object on the computer screen. We achieve this by attaching a grid of NFC tags to the back of the screen. A picture browsing application has been developed in order to compare Touch & Connect and Touch & Select with the currently available Bluetooth-based approach. Our most salient findings show a considerable task time decrease for Touch-and-Connect (31%) and Touch-and-Select (43%) over the standard Bluetooth approach for picture browsing tasks.

1 Introduction and Overview

The most prominent method of transferring data between a mobile device and computer is using Bluetooth. However, this involves performing various actions and can consume considerable time when pairing the devices for the first time. We provide a concept and a first implementation of two very quick and easy to use ways of sharing data between a mobile device and a computer system such as a laptop. Both interactions use passive NFC (Near-Field Communication) tags that allow a small amount of data to be read / written to them. In order to test the new types of interaction, with respect to each other and to other possibilities, a picture sharing application was developed. The application allows the downloading and uploading of pictures between the laptop and the mobile device. In addition, the laptop display can be used to enlarge and view pictures in full resolution.

2 Related Work

Existing work has mainly focused on augmenting static user interfaces such as maps [1] or posters [2] with NFC tags. The disadvantage of this approach is that only the mobile phone can provide feedback. This approach was then extended through the use of NFC with front-projection displays. As shown in [3], a grid of tags can then be

T. Gross et al. (Eds.): INTERACT 2009, Part I, LNCS 5726, pp. 835–838, 2009.

used to connect virtual content to the tags and display dynamic visual feedback. However, besides difficulties with the image quality of projections in bright light conditions, a big disadvantage of such a setup is the occlusion of the image, which is caused by people and objects (such as the phone used to touch the tags). By extending NFC deployment to direct-view displays (as presented in this paper), visual feedback can be maintained in almost all light conditions. Consequently, the problem with occlusion is also nearly negligible. The tag mesh is attached to the screen itself, thus improving portability and requiring considerably less physical space. Moreover, in contrast to projection, there are also no deployment issues with regards to calibration.

3 Implementation and Use

The presented system is the first to implement an interaction technique in which a mobile phone can directly interact with a direct-view display through intuitive touch interaction without the problems that would exist when using a front-projection display. We used a MacBook laptop and a Nokia 6131 NFC phone for the implementation of the prototypes.

3.1 Touch and Connect

Touch & Connect is a technique in which a Bluetooth connection between a mobile phone and laptop is established by simply touching the laptop with the mobile device. The NFC tag, used for initiating the connection, can additionally be employed for transferring extra data between the devices.

For this prototype, an NFC tag is attached to the laptop's armrest and stores the laptop's Bluetooth MAC address which is then used to avoid the time required for searching available Bluetooth devices. Subsequent connections to the NFC tag are then used to initiate actual data transfers between the devices. This also eliminates problems concerning searching for previously paired devices as the device names can be ambiguous. Using the NFC tag when transferring data, the user can directly specify the target device which can be automatically inferred by the application.

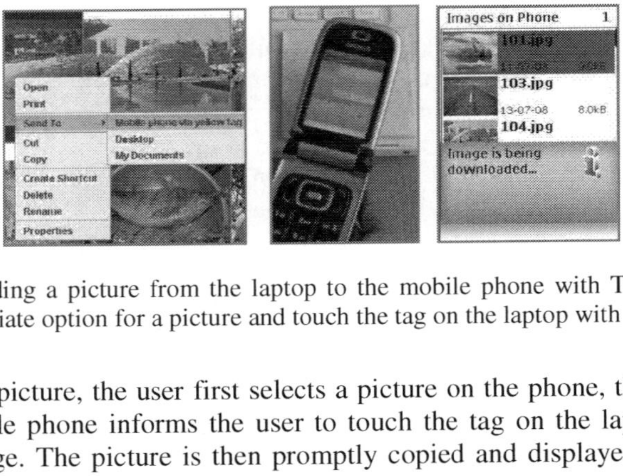

Fig. 1. Downloading a picture from the laptop to the mobile phone with Touch & Connect: select the appropriate option for a picture and touch the tag on the laptop with the phone

To upload a picture, the user first selects a picture on the phone, then chooses upload. The mobile phone informs the user to touch the tag on the laptop in order to upload the image. The picture is then promptly copied and displayed on the laptop.

Reversely, in order to download an image to the phone, it is selected using the mouse in the picture browsing application on the laptop. Then, the user chooses "Send To Mobile Phone via Yellow Tag" (Fig. 1, left). The user then touches the yellow tag on the laptop (Fig. 1, center) to copy the image to the phone (Fig. 1, right).

3.2 Touch and Select

The concept of Touch & Connect is extended by transferring information and data via multiple tags. The major advantage is that the user can specify the screen location where information is to be sent or read. It can also simultaneously provide multiple options to the user. As shown in Fig. 2 (left), the Touch & Select prototype features a laptop display; the back of which was augmented with a mesh of 7x4 NFC tags. Each tag stores its location in the mesh together with the Bluetooth address that resolves to the laptop Bluetooth device. The location coordinates are shown in Fig. 2 (center). The mobile phone can read this information when touching the front of the laptop display (see Fig. 2, right). Through this the user can select any object (e.g. a picture or folder) shown on the laptop display by touching it with the mobile phone.

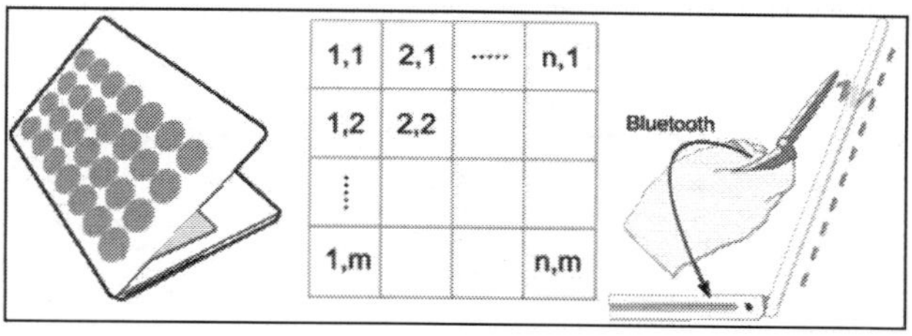

Fig. 2. Touch and Select. *Left*: NFC tag grid attached to the back of a laptop screen. *Center*: location information stored in the tags. *Right*: interaction with the NFC tags on the laptop.

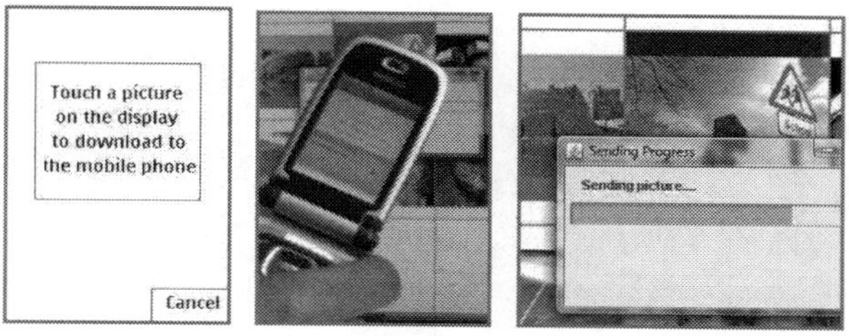

Fig. 3. Downloading a picture from the laptop to the mobile phone with Touch & Select

The picture browsing application has been implemented in such a way that each photo item corresponds in its position to a tag in the back of the display. Even though this mapping suggests itself for this application, we argue that this is also possible for other types of applications based on sharing of information. With smaller tags coming on the market, the grid granularity can be increased such that a more precise location of the phone can be tracked. To upload a picture with Touch & Select, the user first selects it on the phone and chooses upload. The mobile phone then informs the user that an empty square on the display can be touched in order to upload the image. When a user touches the display, the corresponding picture is uploaded and shown on the screen of the laptop. The advantage of this method, besides being able to quickly transfer the file, is that a concrete location (or potentially application) can directly be chosen on the screen. Similarly, in order to download an image, the user switches to download mode on the mobile phone (Fig. 9, left) and selects the picture on the laptop by touching it with the mobile phone (Fig. 9, center). The picture is then copied to the mobile phone (Fig. 9, right) and displayed there. Again, the advantage is that the image can directly be selected using the phone and no additional interaction is necessary saving extra steps and considerably increasing the speed for this interaction.

3.3 Comparative Study and Outlook

In order to compare the new techniques with existing methods, we also implemented picture transfer via the standard Bluetooth method using the same picture sharing application interface as described above. The user selects a picture on the phone and selects "Send via Bluetooth". The phone then searches for available Bluetooth devices and presents a corresponding list. After choosing the entry for the laptop, the image is copied and displayed in the picture browsing application running on the laptop. Downloading is implemented accordingly.

In a study (with 19 participants) we compared Touch & Connect and Touch & Select with conventional Bluetooth-based file transfers [4]. This study showed that Touch & Select is significantly better than Touch & Connect, which is again significantly better than the currently used Bluetooth-based approach when considering user preferences, task completion time, usability satisfaction, task load and qualitative feedback from the study participants. Specifically, task completion time for uploading and downloading pictures was 31% (using Touch & Connect) and 43% (using Touch & Select) faster than the conventional Bluetooth-based approach.

The presented interaction techniques – Touch & Connect and Touch & Select – significantly simplify the way data can be transferred between a mobile phone and a computer.

Embedding NFC tags into TFT / LCD / Plasma / rear-projection displays has the possibility to provide many opportunities for developing novel and exciting interaction techniques enhancing the human computer interface by using the mobile phone as a smart input device. Further application areas that could be investigated include mobile device synchronization, general file transfer, and uploading contextual information from the phone. With regards to further deployment options, the tag mesh could be augmented to digital picture frames and public displays.

References

1. Reilly, D., Rodgers, M., Argue, R., Nunes, M., Inkpen, K.: Marked-up Maps: Combining Paper Maps and Electronic Information Resources. PUC 10(4), 215–226 (2006)
2. Rukzio, E., Broll, G., Leichtenstern, K., Schmidt, A.: An Evaluation and Comparison of Physical Mobile Interaction Techniques. In: AmI 2007 (2007)
3. Hardy, R., Rukzio, E.: Touch & Interact: Touch-based Interaction with a Tourist Application. In: MobileHCI 2008, pp. 531–534 (2008)
4. Seewoonauth, K., Rukzio, E., Hardy, R., Holleis, P.: Touch & Connect and Touch & Select: Interacting with a Computer by Touching it with a Mobile Phone. In: MobileHCI 2009 (2009)

Design and Evaluation of an Adaptive Mobile Map-Based Visualisation System

Bradley van Tonder and Janet Wesson

Department of Computer Science and Information Systems,
Nelson Mandela Metropolitan University, PO Box 77000, Port Elizabeth,
South Africa, 6031
{Bradley.vanTonder,Janet.Wesson}@nmmu.ac.za

Abstract. Mobile visualisation of map-based information is a difficult task. Designers of such systems must contend with the limitations of mobile devices in terms of hardware, screen size and input mechanisms. These problems are exacerbated by the nature of spatial data, where a large information space needs to be presented and manipulated on a small screen. In this paper, a prototype adaptive mobile map-based visualisation system, called MediaMaps, is presented. MediaMaps allows users to capture, location-tag, sort and browse multimedia in a map-based view. MediaMaps was designed to adapt the information visualised, the map-based visualisations and the supporting user interface. The results of an international field study, in which participants used MediaMaps on their personal mobile phones for a three-week period, are also presented. These results show that the adaptations implemented achieved high levels of accuracy and user satisfaction and successfully addressed some of the limitations of mobile map-based visualisation.

Keywords: Mobile map-based visualisation, adaptive interfaces, usability evaluation.

1 Introduction

Mobile devices have emerged in the last decade as a powerful new platform for the development of visualisation systems. These applications take advantage of two key features that distinguish mobile visualisation from desktop visualisation, namely the mobility of the platform and the ability to sense a wide range of variables influencing the user's context. Mobile visualisation systems, however, face a number of limitations in terms of resources, screen size and interaction mechanisms [1].

The problems associated with mobile visualisation are exacerbated in mobile map-based visualisation (MMV) systems, where a large information space must be visualised on a small screen. Several techniques have been developed to address these problems, including modified versions of desktop visualisation techniques and techniques which adapt various aspects of MMV systems.

Adaptive User Interfaces (AUIs) can provide potential benefits for addressing the limitations of mobile devices [2]. Adaptation of the user interface has been identified as an important aspect to be considered in the design of mobile visualisation systems

T. Gross et al. (Eds.): INTERACT 2009, Part I, LNCS 5726, pp. 839–852, 2009.

[3]. Adaptation techniques include adaptation of the information visualised, the presentation of the map-based visualisations and the supporting user interface [4].

Usability evaluations and field studies of adaptive MMV systems are still rare. In this paper, the design and evaluation of an MMV system for capturing, location-tagging, organising and browsing multimedia collections is presented. This system, called MediaMaps, allows users to view map-based visualisations of their multimedia collections and implements information, visualisation and interface adaptation.

This paper is organised as follows. Section 2 presents related work concerning the problems associated with mobile visualisation and MMV and existing techniques for addressing these problems. Section 3 describes the design and implementation of MediaMaps, as well as the different forms of adaptation which were incorporated into the system. In Section 4, the results of a three-week international field study, in which participants used MediaMaps on their personal mobile phones, are presented.

2 Related Work

The problems and shortcomings associated with mobile visualisation and MMV are now described in more detail, followed by a brief discussion of existing techniques which have been developed to address these problems.

2.1 Problems and Shortcomings

Several problems and shortcomings related to mobile visualisation and MMV originate from the nature of mobile devices. The most obvious problem is the limited screen space available on mobile devices [1, 5]. This is particularly problematic for MMV, in which a large information space needs to be visualised using the limited screen real estate available. Screen clutter can often result [6].

Another significant problem relates to the limited input mechanisms provided by mobile devices. These input mechanisms result in additional constraints on the interaction design of MMV systems [5, 7]. MMV systems typically allow the user to manipulate the map-based visualisations provided and support a wide range of fairly complex tasks [4]. The limited input mechanisms currently provided by mobile devices can be especially problematic in these systems. Mobile devices also provide limited processing power, memory and network bandwidth [1].

2.2 Adaptive Mobile Map-Based Visualisation

MMV systems can benefit significantly from personalisation techniques [8]. Several MMV systems have already been developed which incorporate adaptation. Existing research can be classified according to the variables which influence adaptation and the elements of the MMV system which are adapted.

Four classes of input variables have been identified in existing research [4, 8]:

- *Device:* The system can adapt to the differing capabilities of different devices.
- *Context:* The system can adapt to the user's context, including variables such as location, movement and ambient light.

- *Task:* The system can adapt to the user's current activity. This could refer to a system task, or to an activity the user is conducting external to the system.
- *User:* The system can adapt to the user profile, or to the user's preferences, as determined by modelling the user's behaviour.

Adaptation has been incorporated into MMV systems in several ways. The following four broad classes of adaptation have been identified [4]:

- *Information:* The information selection and organisation can be adapted.
- *Visualisation:* The presentation of information can be adapted.
- *User Interface:* The supporting user interface can be adapted in a variety of ways, including the availability of functions and shortcuts.
- *Device:* Various aspects of the MMV system can adapt according to the device's capabilities.

Information adaptation has been implemented to adapt the amount, classification and level of detail of information [8, 9, 10]. Visualisation adaptation has been used to adapt the orientation, layout, section, scale, generalisation and graphical elements of map-based visualisations [4]. Adaptations of this type have ranged from simple adaptations of the map symbols used [11], to advanced techniques such as Focus Maps which uses generalization and colour to emphasise map regions considered relevant to the user's current task [12]. Interface adaptations are comparatively rare, but some have been implemented successfully in MMV systems [7]. Device adaptations are generally more low-level and ensure that the MMV system is able to run on different mobile devices [9, 10].

The next section describes the design and implementation of a prototype MMV system which includes information, visualisation and user interface adaptation.

3 MediaMaps

A prototype MMV system, called MediaMaps, was developed to incorporate the adaptation input variables and adaptation effects identified in Section 2.2. Device adaptation was excluded as it has been well-covered in existing research [9, 10] and is a technical issue which does not involve the user's behaviour or preferences.

3.1 Functional Requirements

MediaMaps provides the following basic functionality:

- *Capturing* and *location tagging* of multimedia (photos, videos and sound) (Figure 1).
- *Organising* multimedia into collections based on time and location (Figure 1).
- *Map-based visualisation* of multimedia collections and items (Figure 2).
- *Search* functionality allowing users to search by criteria such as date or location name (Figure 3).

Several systems have been developed to visualise photo collections on mobile devices. Many of these have incorporated context variables, including time and location, to allow users to browse their photo collections according to different dimensions [13, 14]. Zurfer, a mobile Flickr client, was also recently developed to allow users to browse both their own photos and those of their friends, organised into channels (based on spatial, topic or social dimensions) [15]. Existing mobile visualisation systems have, however, rarely made use of maps.

3.2 Design and Implementation

A model-based design approach was used to design MediaMaps, based on an existing model [16]. MediaMaps incorporates three components which facilitate adaptation, namely the User Monitoring and Modelling Component (UMMC), the Knowledge Base and the Adaptation Engine. MediaMaps was implemented using Java ME.

User Monitoring and Modelling Component (UMMC)
The UMMC monitors user interaction with the system and the values of context variables (the current time and the user's location). This information is processed using a user modelling component and stored in the User and Context Models. Privacy concerns are not an issue, as interaction data is stored locally on the user's personal mobile phone.

Knowledge Base
The Knowledge Base contains four different models which influence adaptation. These are the User and Context Models, as well as a Task Model and a System Model. The User Model stores user preferences relating to the different forms of adaptation implemented in MediaMaps. The Task Model is used to identify when the user is performing a new task (so that the system is able to adapt accordingly). The System Model is used to store the current values of the different adaptable parameters of the system. This acts as a central repository, ensuring that a consistent system state is maintained, as both the system and the user are able to perform changes to these parameters.

Adaptation Engine
The Adaptation Engine contains three components to manage each of the three forms of adaptation implemented in MediaMaps. The Information, Visualisation and Interface Manager components consult the Knowledge Base in order to ensure that the adaptations performed match the user's preferences, context and current task. These three forms of adaptation are discussed in more detail in the following sections.

3.3 Information Adaptation

Clutter is a significant problem in MMV systems [6]. The filtering of information according to user preferences was therefore considered to be a useful adaptation. This filtering is performed similarly to the visualisation adaptation in MediaMaps and is discussed in the next section. The limited interaction techniques currently available on mobile devices, combined with the increasing volumes of media items being stored, create a need for better ways of organising and retrieving multimedia on such devices. Furthermore, if a user's entire media collection is visualised in a single map-based view, screen clutter is likely to be severe. The sorting of media items into collections can help to minimise this clutter problem.

The real-time event detection (RED) algorithm, proposed by Chen and Chen [17], was used to implement information adaptation in MediaMaps. The RED algorithm allows photos to be sorted, creating collections based on time and location. The RED algorithm follows on a large amount of related work that attempts to organise photo collections based on a variety of variables, including time and location [18, 19, 20, 21]. Most existing algorithms are unsuitable in a mobile environment, as they are resource intensive and may result in significant delays before photos are sorted.

The RED algorithm provides for incremental sorting of photos in real-time (as they are captured). The RED algorithm was specifically designed for use in the resource-constrained environments of mobile phones. Photos can be classified as they are captured, allowing for immediate user feedback. This also means that the algorithm has the capability to adapt, with user responses to system recommendations used to improve the accuracy of the algorithm.

The RED algorithm organises the user's photo collection into "events", with the algorithm determining where the boundaries between these events lie. Chen and Chen hypothesised that, given certain assumptions, a particular user's photo capturing behaviour can be matched to a Poisson distributed statistical process.

The time gap between the current event and the previous event is used to decide which of the following three regions the current photo belongs to:

- R_o: Identified as belonging to the current (old) event.
- R_l: Falls into an intermediate area between a new or old event.
- R_n: Identified as belonging to a new event.

If a newly captured photo falls into R_l, the distance between the location of the current photo and the preceding photo is used to determine whether a photo belongs to the current event or to a new event. The RED algorithm relies on three parameters that can be tuned according to user behaviour and feedback, μ_d (mean distance between photos), σ_d (standard deviation) and λ (arrival rate per hour). These three parameters are adjusted in order to compensate for errors made by the algorithm. For example, if a new photo is identified as belonging to R_o (current event), but actually belongs to a new event, then the arrival rate, λ, needs to be increased to reflect the higher than expected rate of arrival of new events. For a detailed discussion of how the RED algorithm compensates for erroneous classifications, refer to [17].

The RED algorithm was used in MediaMaps to organise different multimedia types (including photo, video and sound recordings) into collections. Every time a user captures a media item, the system determines whether it belongs to the current collection, or to a new collection. The user is required to provide feedback regarding this recommendation (Figure 1). This feedback is used to update the algorithm's parameters. This feedback step can be removed once the system has learned the user's preferences. The version of MediaMaps used in the evaluation described in this paper required feedback for every media item captured.

The user's behaviour is monitored and recorded by the UMMC. The Context Model, which is updated with the user's position, is used to supply the location information for the algorithm. The parameters λ, σ_d and μ_d are stored in the User Model and the Information Manager is used to perform changes to the underlying structure of the data.

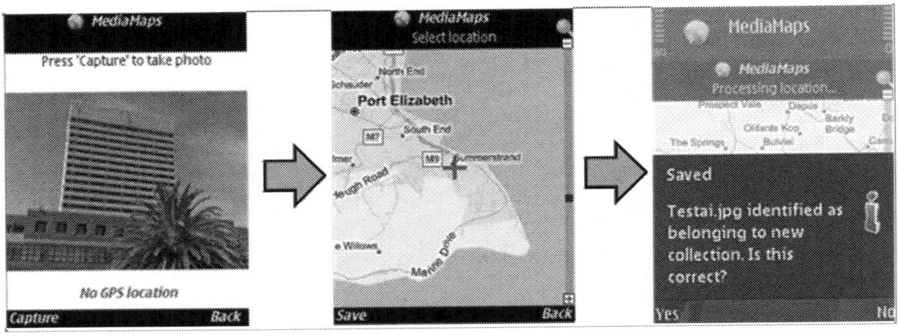

Fig. 1. Sorting media items into collections in MediaMaps. Manual location tagging is used in this case as the user's GPS location is unavailable.

3.4 Visualisation Adaptation

Several simple, yet important visual and information-related parameters were selected to be included in the adaptation process. The following parameters have previously been identified as important parameters to be adapted in MMV systems [4] and are adapted in MediaMaps:

- The zoom-level being visualised;
- The map-type being displayed;
- The latitude and longitude at which the map is centred;
- The time period being visualised; and
- The media types to be visualised.

One of the most significant problems of standard zooming and panning techniques is that the user often needs to perform many zooming and panning operations to find information of interest [22]. To overcome this, the map-based visualisations in MediaMaps are adapted according to previous user behaviour. This was done in order to save the user from having to perform the same view customisation operations each time a particular collection is viewed.

Naïve Bayesian classifiers were used to implement visualisation adaptation in MediaMaps. This technique assumes that different input variables are independent of one another. Despite the fact that this is typically not the case, this technique has proven accurate for several domains. Bayesian classifiers have previously been used in adaptive mobile applications [23] and were selected because of their simplicity and low resource requirements (while still providing potentially high levels of accuracy).

User behaviour is observed and recorded, with the current mode and the collection being viewed used as inputs in order to determine how to adjust these parameters. The UMMC observes and records user interaction information. This interaction data is then processed by the UMMC at system start-up in order to extract user preferences for different collections and visualisation modes. These preferences are recorded in the User Model. Older interaction data is progressively discarded to minimise the amount of interaction data that needs to be processed by the system. This also ensures that the adaptations keep pace with the user's changing preferences over time.

The Visualisation and Information Managers are responsible for ensuring that the visualisation and information are adapted according to the user's preferences whenever a new visualisation is rendered. The Task Model is consulted to determine when a new visualisation is to be rendered in order to invoke these components.

Figure 2 shows the same data set (the icons indicate media collections) before and after adaptation. The map style, zoom level and location have all been adapted.

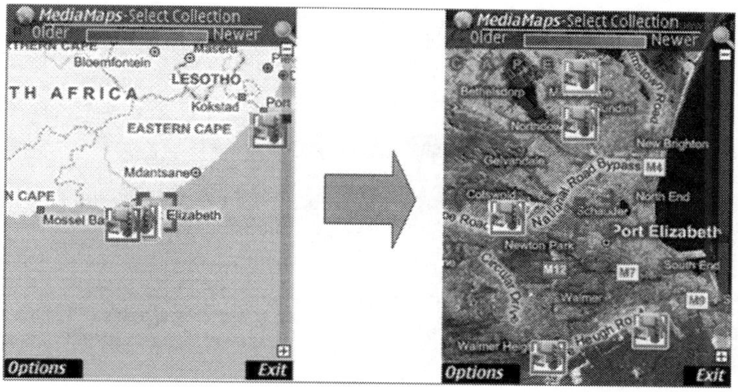

Fig. 2. Visualisation adaptation. The same data set is shown before and after adaptation.

3.5 Interface Adaptation

Interface adaptation in MediaMaps is limited to ordering of list options. Previous research has shown that the ordering of menus and lists in small screen devices can provide even greater efficiency benefits than in desktop systems [24]. Early user testing of MediaMaps showed that the users spent a significant amount of time browsing lists of options that can potentially grow quite large. As a result, it was decided to adapt the ordering of lists of options in MediaMaps based on how recently and frequently the different items are selected.

A variation of the algorithm used by Findlater and McGrenere [24] was used, which relies on the following three rules to order menu options:

1. The top section contains the most recently selected item and the two most frequently selected items
2. If there is duplication amongst these items, then the third most frequently selected item is included in the top section.
3. The items appear in the same relative order in the top section as they would in the bottom section of the list.

List items are moved to the top section, rather than replicated. Informal evaluation revealed that replicating items on short lists resulted in user confusion regarding which item to select. A grey background is used in order to draw users' attention to the fact that the top three items are adapted according to their behaviour (Figure 3). This interface adaptation is applied to all lists of options within the system, including the list of collections, list of saved views and lists of locations. Frequency data and the

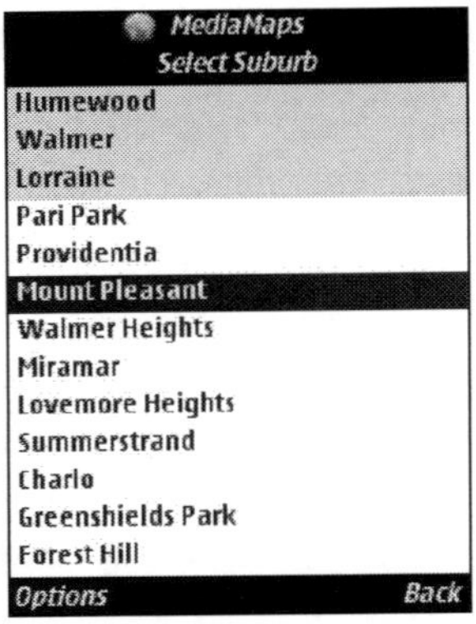

Fig. 3. Location search in MediaMaps, with recently and frequently selected items at the top

most recent selection for each list are stored in the User Model. The Task Model is used to determine when the user is accessing a list view and the Interface Manager is invoked in order to ensure that the appropriate options are in the top section of the list.

4 Evaluation

Preliminary user testing was conducted in order to evaluate the usability of the system and to ensure that no significant usability problems existed. The results of this evaluation revealed that MediaMaps was highly effective at supporting users in completing major system tasks. High levels of user satisfaction were also reported. Several minor usability problems were discovered and corrected. A longer term field study was then conducted to evaluate several aspects of the adaptations implemented. The results of this evaluation are discussed below.

4.1 Objectives

The field study was conducted to evaluate the following aspects of MediaMaps:

- *Performance:* Were the adaptations performed accurate?
- *User satisfaction:* Did users find MediaMaps easy to use? Were the adaptations performed perceived as useful?

These aspects were evaluated to determine whether the adaptations addressed the problems and shortcomings of MMV which were previously identified (Section 2.1).

4.2 Participants

International participants were recruited through a bidding process [25]. Twenty-six bids were accepted, although only 20 test participants (14 male, 6 female) completed the field study satisfactorily. Non-completion occurred for several reasons, including technical problems with the participants' phones and insufficient use of the system to warrant useful feedback. An average of $46.50 was paid per test participant. Participants were recruited from twelve different countries on four continents. Figure 4 shows the demographic profile of the test participants.

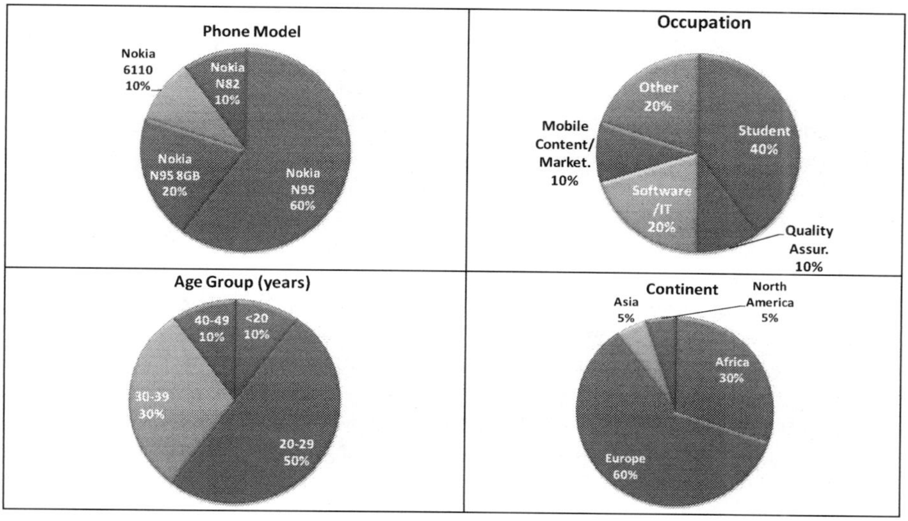

Fig. 4. Demographic profile of field study participants (n=20)

4.3 Procedure

Test participants were required to use MediaMaps on their personal mobile phones over a three week period. The participants were free to use MediaMaps as desired, but were encouraged to use the system as their primary means of capturing and browsing media for the duration of the test period. Participants were contacted in person, by email and instant messaging (where necessary) in order to ensure the system was being used as intended and to sort out any issues, particularly concerning installation.

At the end of the test period, users were required to complete a user satisfaction questionnaire based on the Questionnaire for User Interface Satisfaction (QUIS) [26]. A five point Likert scale was used with antonyms at extremes of each scale. A qualitative feedback section was also included to elicit positive and negative feedback, as well as suggestions for improvement. A logging mechanism was integrated into the system to record user and system behaviour.

4.4 Performance Results

Interaction log files were recorded to analyse the accuracy of the information and interface adaptations implemented in MediaMaps. Precision, Recall and F-Score metrics are commonly used to evaluate algorithms for detecting event boundaries in photo collections [18, 20]. Precision refers to the ratio between the number of correctly detected event boundaries and the total number of event boundaries detected. Recall can be expressed as the ratio between correctly detected event boundaries and the actual number of event boundaries which exist. The F-score combines these two into a single metric (*F-Score = (2 x Precision x Recall) / (Precision + Recall)*). A general accuracy percentage was also calculated. A recommendation was regarded as accurate if it was accepted by the participant.

Table 1 shows the results obtained for Precision, Recall, F-Score and general accuracy. Cumulative results (across all participants) and average results (in which all participants received equal weighting) are shown. The average results for all four metrics were above 80%. The accuracy of the algorithm was also analysed according to the three regions into which the RED algorithm classifies new media items (Section 3.3). It is interesting to note that the algorithm achieved high levels of accuracy (85.55%) in R_l where temporal information was inconclusive and location information was used to aid in the decision making process. Although this represents only seven percent of media items captured, it is nevertheless encouraging to note that the use of location information proved useful for ensuring accurate classifications.

The accuracy of the RED algorithm improved in response to user feedback. A significant correlation co-efficient of 0.79 (α=0.05) was calculated between the number of media items captured and the accuracy of the recommendations provided.

Table 1. Accuracy results for the RED algorithm implemented in MediaMaps

Theme	*Cumulative*	Average
Accuracy	89.34%	87.44%
Precision	81.52%	84.81%
Recall	76.53%	81.14%
F-Score	78.95%	83.33%

Accuracy information was also calculated for the interface adaptation algorithm. List option selections were split into three categories, namely pre-adaptive selections (when lists were too short to warrant adaptation), adaptive selections and non-adaptive selections. These results showed that (on average) options were selected from the adaptive section of the lists 76.78% of the time. Participant perceptions regarding the usefulness of the adaptation of list ordering were found to be positively correlated to the amount of time spent using MediaMaps. A statistically significant correlation co-efficient of 0.62 (α=0.05) was calculated.

4.5 Satisfaction Results

The results of the user satisfaction questionnaire are summarised in Table 2. All three forms of adaptation (Section D-F) were highly rated by participants (median=4.00). Participants were also highly satisfied with the support provided for searching for media items (Section C).

Table 2. User satisfaction results summarised by section (*n*=20)

Section	Mean	Median	Mode	Std. Dev.
B. Capturing Media	3.67	4.00	4.00	1.12
C. Searching for Media	3.90	4.00	5.00	1.11
D. Sorting Media (information adaptation)	3.83	4.00	4.00	1.02
E. List Sorting (interface adaptation)	3.72	4.00	5.00	1.25
F. Map View Adaptation (visualisation adaptation)	3.55	4.00	4.00	1.17

The perceived usefulness of all three forms of adaptation in MediaMaps was highly rated by participants (where 1 = Not useful and 5 = Useful) (Table 3). Information adaptation, in which media items were sorted into collections based on time and location, was particularly highly rated. The perceived usefulness of all three forms of adaptation received median ratings of at least 4. The results of Likert scale ratings also showed that participants found all three forms of adaptation to be logical.

Table 3. User satisfaction results for perceived usefulness (*n*=20)

Adaptation Type	Mean	Median	Mode	Std. Dev.
Information Adaptation (sorting of media items into collections)	4.20	4.50	5.00	0.95
Interface Adaptation (ordering of list options)	3.80	4.00	5.00	1.24
Visualisation Adaptation (adaptation of map visualisation parameters)	3.75	4.00	4.00	1.02

Qualitative feedback revealed that the system was used in a wide variety of situations and contexts. The field study took place during the northern hemisphere summer holidays and as a result, many of the participants used MediaMaps while on holiday and/or travelling between different cities and countries. General user satisfaction feedback was very positive regarding the usefulness, ease of use, learnability and enjoyment of MediaMaps.

Qualitative feedback regarding information adaptation supported the quantitative data, with many positive comments received. Sixty percent of participants specifically praised the information adaptation. The following positive comments regarding the information adaptation are examples of those received:

- *"Excellent management capabilities for media items."*
- *"Very good system for organising your digital library."*
- *"Concept of collections and automated decisions very useful"*

Participants also responded positively to the interface adaptation, commenting favourably on the *"faster access to recent/frequent media collections"*. Visualisation adaptation was regarded as useful in the manual location-tagging map (Figure 1), with users not having to perform the same view customisation options repeatedly.

The only negative feedback received related to a lack of flexibility in the process of sorting media items into collections. Some participants wanted the ability to move items between collections after initial sorting, the ability to change the location associated with an image (in the case of incorrect manual tagging) and the ability to perform manual location-tagging at their own convenience. Some participants felt it unnecessary to create multiple collections for the same location on different dates. Many of these issues would be difficult to address without making significant changes to the RED algorithm.

Previous systems for browsing media collections on mobile devices have avoided the use of map-based interfaces [14, 15]. It was therefore interesting to note that participants regarded the ability to view map-based visualisations of their media as highly useful (mean=4.25, median=4.50 and mode=5.00). Participants were also highly satisfied with the ease with which they were able to locate previously captured media using MediaMaps (mean=4.00, median=4.00 and mode=5.00).

4.6 Analysis of Results

The objective of the field study was to determine whether the information, visualisation and interface adaptations implemented in MediaMaps addressed some of the problems of MMV. Information adaptation was implemented in the form of an adaptive algorithm for sorting media items into collections. This was done to minimise user effort in organising media collections (using the limited interaction mechanisms available) and to reduce clutter that would otherwise result if a user's entire media collection was visualised in a single view. The high accuracy of the recommendations provided by the RED algorithm, combined with the positive participant feedback regarding the perceived usefulness of this form of adaptation, suggest that the information adaptation performed was indeed useful. Further supporting evidence regarding the usefulness of this form of adaptation is provided by the fact that participants were able to easily locate previously captured and sorted media items. The accuracy results achieved are particularly impressive if compared with those achieved by more resource-intensive algorithms, which do not allow media to be sorted in real time. Such algorithms have been shown to achieve only slightly superior accuracy, although tested on different media collections [18, 20]. The RED algorithm was also shown to adapt to user feedback and improve accuracy.

Chen and Chen evaluated the RED algorithm on a desktop computer. This research therefore represents the first time that the RED algorithm has been implemented and evaluated in a mobile context.

Visualisation adaptation was performed in order to reduce the amount of interaction required to perform view customisation operations such as zooming and panning. User satisfaction feedback showed that participants considered this form of adaptation to be very useful. Benefits were achieved in terms of efficiency and the amount of interaction required using the available interaction mechanisms.

Interface adaptation (list ordering) was implemented to improve user efficiency in selecting options from potentially long lists of options. Interaction logs showed that participants selected options from the adaptive portions of lists on average 76.78% of the time. This implies efficiency gains, as participants did not have to browse long lists searching for their desired option. Quantitative and qualitative user satisfaction feedback showed that the participants viewed this form of adaptation as highly useful, with perceived usefulness increasing the longer the participants used MediaMaps.

5 Conclusions

This paper discussed the design and evaluation of an adaptive MMV system, called MediaMaps. MediaMaps provides automatic facilities for location tagging and organising media into collections on a mobile phone and allows users to view map-based visualisations of these collections. Existing adaptation techniques were modified for a mobile platform and extended to supported information, visualisation and interface adaptation. An international field study was conducted to evaluate the accuracy and perceived usefulness of the adaptation techniques and the participants' satisfaction with the system. The results of this study clearly show that the adaptation techniques were highly accurate and that the participants found the adaptations to be useful, efficient and easy to understand.

The evaluation of the RED algorithm used to perform information adaptation showed that this algorithm effectively supported the participants in organising and visualising their media collections. The accuracy of the RED algorithm was also shown to improve in response to user feedback. The problems inherent with the limited interaction mechanisms provided by mobile devices were minimised and effective use of the limited screen space was made by organising and visualising media collections based on time and location. The visualisation adaptation reduced the need for repetitive view customisation operations to be performed, while the interface adaptation minimised the amount of interaction necessary.

This paper thus provides empirical evidence that adaptation can provide significant benefits for mobile map-based visualisation. Future work will include changes to MediaMaps to address system limitations identified during the field study.

References

1. Chittaro, L.: Visualizing Information on Mobile Devices. IEEE Computer 39(3), 40–45 (2006)
2. Al-bar, A., Wakeman, I.: A Survey of Adaptive Applications in Mobile Computing. In: Proc. International Conference on Distributed Computing Systems (ICDCSW 2001), pp. 246–251. IEEE Computer Society Press, Los Alamitos (2001)
3. Karstens, B., Kreuseler, M., Schumann, H.: Visualization of Complex Structures on Mobile Handhelds. In: Proc. International Workshop on Mobile Computing (2003)
4. Reichenbacher, T.: Mobile Cartography - Adaptive Visualisation of Geographic Information on Mobile DevicesInstitut für Photogrammetrie und Kartographie, Technischen Universitat, Munchen (2004)
5. Björk, S., Redström, J., Ljungstrand, P., Holmquist, L.E.: PowerView: Using information links and information views to navigate and visualize information on small displays. In: Thomas, P., Gellersen, H.-W. (eds.) HUC 2000. LNCS, vol. 1927, pp. 46–62. Springer, Heidelberg (2000)
6. Baudisch, P., Rosenholtz, R., Halo, R.H.: A Technique for Visualizing Off-Screen Locations. In: Proc. SIGCHI Conference on Human Factors in Computing Systems (CHI 2003), pp. 481–488. ACM Press, New York (2003)
7. Carmo, M.B., Afonso, A.P., Pombinho de Matos, P., Vaz, A.: MoViSys – A visualization system for geo-referenced information on mobile devices. In: Sebillo, M., Vitiello, G., Schaefer, G. (eds.) VISUAL 2008. LNCS, vol. 5188, pp. 167–178. Springer, Heidelberg (2008)
8. Looije, R., te Brake, G., Neerincx, M.: Usability Engineering for Mobile Maps. In: Proc. International Conference on Mobile Technology, Applications, and Systems (Mobility 2007), pp. 532–539 (2007)

9. Chalmers, D., Sloman, M., Dulay, N.: Map Adaptation for Users of Mobile Systems. In: Proc. World Wide Web Conference (WWW 2001), pp. 735–744. ACM Press, New York (2001)
10. Fresco, R., Marucci, L., Signore, O.: Adaptive Hypermedia for User-Centred Geovisualization in Multiplatform Environments. In: Proc. ACM Conference on Hypertext and Hypermedia (HyperText 2003), pp. 20–21. ACM Press, New York (2003)
11. Nivala, A.-M., Sarjakoski, L.: Adapting Map Symbols for Mobile Users. In: Proc. International Cartographic Conference, ICC 2005 (2005)
12. Zipf, A., Richter, K.-F.: Using Focus Maps to Ease Map Reading: Developing Smart Applications for Mobile Devices. Künstliche Intelligenz (KI) (Artificial Intelligence). Special Issue: Spatial Cognition (4), 35–37 (2002)
13. Harada, S., Naaman, M., Song, Y.J., Wang, Q., Paepcke, A.: Lost in Memories: Interacting With Photo Collections On PDAs. In: Proc. the Joint ACM/IEEE Conference on Digital Libraries (JCDL 2004), pp. 325–333. ACM Press, New York (2004)
14. Pauty, J., Couderc, P., Banâtre, M.: Using Context to Navigate Through a Photo Collection. In: Proc. International Conference on Human Computer Interaction with Mobile Devices & Services (Mobile HCI 2005), pp. 145–152. ACM Press, New York (2005)
15. Naaman, M., Nair, R., Kaplun, V.: Photos on the Go: A Mobile Application Case Study. In: Proc. SIGHCI Conference on Human Factors in Computing Systems (CHI 2008), pp. 1739–1748. ACM Press, New York (2008)
16. van Tonder, B., Wesson, J.: Using Adaptive Interfaces to Improve Mobile Map-based Visualisation. In: Cilliers, C., Barnard, L., Botha, R. (eds.) Proc. SAICSIT 2008, pp. 257–266. ACM Press, New York (2008)
17. Chen, W., Chen, M.: Event detection in real time on a personal camera phone image collection. Multimedia Systems (12), 479–492 (2007)
18. Naaman, M., Jiun Song, Y., Paepcke, A., Garcia-Molina, H.: Automatic Organization for Digital Photographs with Geographic Coordinates. In: Proc. CM/IEEE-CS Joint Conference on Digital Libraries (JCDL 2004), pp. 53–62. ACM Press, New York (2004)
19. Platt, J.C., Czerwinski, M., Field, B.A.: PhotoTOC: Automatic Clustering for Browsing Personal Photographs. In: Proc. the Fourth International Conference on Information, Communications and Signal Processing, pp. 6–10 (2003)
20. Cooper, M., Foote, J., Girgensohn, A., Wilcox, L.: Temporal Event Clustering for Digital Photo Collections. ACM Transactions on Multimedia Computing, Communications and Applications 1(3), 269–288 (2005)
21. Pigeau, A., Gelgon, M.: Building and Tracking Hierarchical Geographical & Temporal partitions for Image Collection Management on Mobie Devices. In: Proc. the International Conference on Multimedia, pp. 141–150 (2005)
22. Kaptelinin, V.: A Comparison of Four Navigation Techniques in a 2D Browsing Task. In: Proc. SIGCHI Conference on Human Factors in Computing Systems (CHI 1995), pp. 282–283. ACM Press, New York (1995)
23. Boström, F., Floréen, P., Liu, T., Nurmi, P., Oikarinen, T.-K., Vetek, A., Boda, P.: Capricorn - An Intelligent User Interface for Mobile Widgets. In: Proc. the International Conference on Intelligent User Interfaces (IUI 2008), pp. 417–418. ACM Press, New York (2008)
24. Findlater, L., McGrenere, J.: Impact of Screen Size on Performance, Awareness and User Satisfaction With Adaptive Graphical User Interfaces. In: Proc. SIGCHI Conference on Human Factors in Computing Systems (CHI 2008), pp. 1247–1256. ACM Press, New York (2008)
25. Mob4Hire. Mob4Hire - Crowdsourced Mobile Application Testing, `http://www.mob4hire.com`
26. Chin, J.P., Diehl, V.A., Norman, K.L.: Development of an Instrument Measuring User Satisfaction of the Human Computer Interface. In: Proc. SIGCHI 1988, pp. 213–218. ACM Press, New York (1988)

Exploring Multimodal Navigation Aids for Mobile Users

Teija Vainio

Tampere University of Technology, Human-Centered Technology
P.O. Box 589, 33101 Tampere, Finland
teija.vainio@tut.fi

Abstract. When navigating in real physical environments, as human beings we tend to display systematic or near-systematic errors with distance, direction and other navigation issues. To avoid making these errors, we choose different stratategies to find our way. While there have been a lot of HCI studies of navigation design guidelines for using maps or speech-based or tactile-based guidance in mobile devices, in this paper we introduce an initial study of multimodal navigation design utilising the design practice of episodes of motion originated from urban planning. The implications of designing cues and providing rhythm, as the design guidelines of episodes of motions suggests, are explored in this study with the subjects being pedestrians with wayfinding tasks in an urban area. The main contributions of this paper are in evaluating the design implications in the context of mobile wayfinding tasks and in reflecting the results according to human wayfinding behaviour. It is concluded that by designing predictive clues and rhythm into mobile multimodal navigation applications, we can improve navigation aids for users.

Keywords: Mobile navigation, multimodality, design.

1 Introduction

We must understand the nature of human wayfinding behaviour [10] such as typical navigation errors and strategies to avoid these errors to be able to understand how to support the wayfinding of mobile users. When developing tools to support wayfinding tasks of mobile users, we should pay attention that while users are using mobile wayfinding tools, usage should be consistent with user's own strategies to find a way.

Typical human navigation errors can be classified into three main categories: *errors of distance, errors of direction*, and *other errors* [25]. Errors with estimating the distance tend to be related to the amount of turns, landmarks or intersections: the more objects there are, the longer the distance estimated whereas when a mistake is related to the direction of a route, it could be caused, for example, by a person mentally rotating north-south and east-west axes, more in line with geographical axes that are on a different angle than these actual north-south axes. The third type of errors may include such issues as incorrectly estimating sizes, shapes or perspectives [25]. It is argued here that when developing novel navigation aids, the primary focus should be on supporting users to solve typical navigation errors.

T. Gross et al. (Eds.): INTERACT 2009, Part I, LNCS 5726, pp. 853–865, 2009.

To avoid making different kinds of navigation errors, we as human beings tend to choose different types of strategies to finding our way in a real environment. Some people tend to favour a *route strategy*, i.e., they focus upon specific instructions on how to get from one place to another, whereas some find their way with an *orientation strategy,* i.e., monitoring their own position relative to reference points in the environment [14]. In recent studies related to navigation performance and wayfinding strategies it has been shown, for example, that the directions provided influence the efficiency of navigation, and the gender of the navigator is also influential [16]. Therefore, to be able to support users to avoid or to solve typical navigation errors and to develop useful navigation aids, one must understand what kind of strategies users have when making decisions how to find their way and how do gender and mode of given instructions have an effect on navigation tasks.

Although people still quite often solve their wayfinding tasks while they are on the move, either with maps printed on paper or displayed on the screen of a mobile navigation device, i.e., with a visual modality, the focus of navigation HCI research has also turned towards other human modalities, such as audio modality [2], [13] or tactile modality [3], [9]. These multimodal aids convey information through non-speech audio [10] or thematic maps [30], [32] or give feedback to visually impaired users [9] regarding how to navigate. Nonetheless, designing multimodal applications has its own challenges due to a fact that multimodal interaction occurs not only as a one-way or one-level interaction.

One key design challenge is to distinguish between when users are and are not interacting multimodally. When the focus is upon one modality at a time, it is called *unimodality* instead of *multimodality*. Furthermore, when users are interacting multimodally, recent studies have shown that users have different patterns, i.e., they interact *simultaneously* or they integrate their interaction *sequentially* [23]. However, very few studies have explored the design issues of multimodal navigation aids for mobile users by reflecting the design through typical human wayfinding behaviour such as wayfinding strategies. Hence, in order to be able to design multimodal navigation aids, one should understand the possible impacts of these factors.

It is argued here that there is no sense in designing only navigation aids based on conventional maps, see e.g. [26], and therefore more novel practices should be explored when designing navigation aids. We suggested that one possibility that can be examined is utilise design practices originating from urban planning. For several centuries, designers, urban planners and architects have developed aids for individuals navigating in real physical environments whereas, mobile HCI practitioners and researchers have studied how to support navigation with mobile devices and applications for only a few decades. Thus, for HCI professionals there are many possibilities in exploring existing design guidelines originally developed for urban planners to then support users to navigate better. Whilst there have been a lot of studies of navigation design guidelines based on Kevin Lynch's imageability [17], in this paper we propose an initial study of navigation design guidelines utilising the theory of designing *episodes of motion* [27].

Thus, this study investigates the relationships between two of the design principles of episodes of motion, namely the design of *rhythm* and *cues*, and users' wayfinding strategies within three different modalities: visual, audio and tactile. In this study, we define a cue as a unit of route information provided through the navigation system, not awareness information of others, see e.g. [20] or the environmental cues. A rhythm is defined here as route information that is provided through the navigation system regularly according period of distances.

For HCI practitioners and academics, this study presents a novel multidisciplinary design approach in order to support human navigation. In addition, for developers of mobile navigation applications, the results present an encouraging perspective in order to integrate design practices that take into account the wayfinding task in an urban environment. In addition, practical design concepts of providing cues and presenting rhythm are presented.

This paper is structured as follows. In the following section, we first present a more detailed overview of related multimodal or unimodal navigation research before presenting arguments for combining navigation design issues and urban planning practices in the section 'Designing cues and rhythm to support wayfinding'. Then, we describe the experiment and present the results. Finally, we discuss the findings and conclude the research, outlining our future work on navigation aid design.

2 Related Work

When exploring human navigation in a real environment with mobile applications designed to support wayfinding tasks, the focus in recent research seems to be upon issues of context (indoor, outdoor, in-vehicle, pedestrian). The user-related key concepts seem to focus upon the impact of visual ability [9] and the impact of indoor or outdoor navigation [5], as well as whether the navigators are acting as a driver [26] or as a pedestrian [14]. The main findings of non-desktop navigation research are related to interaction design, e.g., [13], [20], context [24] and adaptability, e.g., [1].

However, in mobile contexts, users' internal factors are different and external factors are dynamic and unpredictable. Furthermore, Tamminen et al. [24] argued that in relation to a mobile context, users solve navigation problems with social solutions, both national and within the mobile context, and there are temporal tensions, such as acceleration, declaration, hurrying, normal and waiting. Regarding the user interface, modality selection and interruption management are two of the main issues. [24] In relation to solving temporal tensions, it is argued here that repeating regularly navigation guidance, i.e., according certain rhythm, users are able to update their knowledge en-route.

In research on navigation tools, the tools are typically based on three major modalities: visual, audio or tactile. However, most studies are describing unimodality systems emphasizing either visual, tactile or audion modality. Recent studies related to multimodality in mobile devices have stated that multimodality can enhance the usability of mobile devices and that multimodal interaction can be superior to classical unimodal interaction in complicated tasks [14]. It has been stated also that users have a strong preference for multimodal interaction when they are interacting multimodally for a map-based task [7]. Furthermore, the research of geographic information systems (GIS) has their potential in a mobile context, for example, when personalising maps in multimodal mobile GIS [30].

Navigation research on multimodal aids has been focused upon two main streams: unimodal navigation support and characteristics of multimodality in interaction. Hence, very few studies take into account variety of wayfinding strategies, and their impacts on navigation performance. Furthermore, only few studies present design guidelines for mobile multimodal navigation system. This study takes another approach. It is argued here that when we are designing navigation tools to be used in real environments there are lessons to be learnt from other disciplines that have a longer tradition in designing navigation support in physical environments, i.e., urban planning and environmental psychology. Theories and practices of urban planning have been utilised in navigation, but mainly when examining navigation in virtual three-dimensional worlds [6]. Furthermore, it seems that majority of the navigation HCI research is utilizing one particular urban planning practice, i.e., Lynch's imageability [17]. We acknowledged Lynch's excellent ideas that give a solid ground also for designers in the field of navigation HCI research. However, it is argued here that there is no need to have a tunnel vision of urban planning design praxis and thereby HCI researchers and designers should extend their view beyond imageability [17] when exploring multidisciplinary design methods.

3 Designing Cues and Rhythm to Support Wayfinding

In some well-known urban planning design principles, such as in Lynch's [17] imageability, focusing on the design of a series of places and the design of the user's experience moving in the physical environment are emphasised. In regard to the area of designing the user's experience of moving in the physical environment, Stenros and Aura [27] presented the idea of designing *episodes of motion*. Concerning the experience of moving from one place to another, Stenros and Aura [27] presented the following principles for designing episodes of motion:

- Design routes so that they can be recognised as *part of the entire larger system*, e.g., as part of a city.
- Indicate with some kinds of *clues* how the route is going to continue after the episode.
- Design *variation* within a single episode to make the episode interesting.
- Design a *rhythm* in an episode to make it easy for users to perceive the environment
- Design *open views and spaces* in a route to support the user in better visualising the overall spaces.

Regarding the design principles of episodes of motion, providing cues and designing rhythm were chosen for deeper analysis in this study. These design principles are reflected through three modalities, i.e., visual, audio and tactile modalities in the wayfinding tasks of mobile pedestrians.

In this study, it was predicted that people reporting greater preference for a particular modality of guidance would be more efficient navigators. Moreover, people reporting greater preference for a route strategy would be more efficient navigators with guidance according regular rhythm. Finally, it was expected that wayfinding efficiency would vary as a function of the modality of navigation support and gender.

This study investigates the following:

1. Two types of navigation guidance in three different modalities, namely (a) predictive cues, (b) guidance with regular rhythm within guidance provided through (i) visual, (ii) audio or (iii) tactile modality.
2. Is the most efficient and the most perceived type of guidance obtained when (a) referenced to the person's wayfinding strategy, or (b) referenced to the person's gender?

4 Methods

The study presented in this paper is a part of the author's PhD research concerning design issues of navigation aids for mobile users. In this study, both quantitative and qualitative methods were used to gather and analyse the data. Before conducting field experiments to examine multimodal navigation aids, the preliminary study identifying users' attitudes of usefulness providing two types of guidance (cues and rhythm) in three modalities (visual, audion and tactile) was carried out. The more detailed description and the results of the preliminary study are reported in our other publications, see e.g. [28]. In the field experiment impacts of two types of guidance (cues and rhythm) in three different modalities (visual, audion and tactile) in relation user's wayfinding strategies and gender issues were explored.

4.1 Field Experiment

The field experiment consisted of two parts. In the first part, in addition to background information, wayfinding strategies of the participants were analysed. Wayfinding strategies were studied because it is assumed that different users with different wayfinding strategies need different types of guidance. Furthermore, the participants took part in a Mental Rotation Test (MRT) with a version of Cooper and Shepard's mental rotation paradigm [18], which analysed the participants' ability to rotate objects mentally. The MRT was carried out to identify possible differences in reading visual maps among the participants.

In the second part of the field experiment, the field test was conducted in an urban area using the Wizard Of Oz (WOZ) technique. The field study procedure was adapted from Brewster et al. [3]. The participants were asked to complete seven wayfinding tasks and the researcher, simulating a computer, provided the navigation guidance. After each task, participants evaluated the task loads of each task subjectively. They were then interviewed after they completed all seven wayfinding tasks. During the wayfinding tasks, time of performance and number of navigation errors were recorded.

The visual modality was conducted with three types of paper maps without textual information: an overview map, maps describing part of the route and given to the participant either before the forthcoming need to turn left/right or as part of their regular rhythm. The guidance in the audio modality was given by the researcher either before the forthcoming need to turn left/right or according to the regular rhythm ("turn left/turn right/go straight forward"). The tactile guidance was given by shoulder tapping either before the forthcoming need to turn left/right or according to the regular rhythm by tapping on the right/left shoulder and between the shoulders.

The second part of the experiment consisted of seven wayfinding tasks (see Table 1). The routes and modalities were counterbalanced. The order of the wayfinding tasks was organised according to the principles of the Latin Square in order to exclude learning effects (see Table 1).

Table 1. The order of modalities in relation to routes and ordinal number of an experiment

	Route 1	Route 2	Route 3	Route 4	Route 5	Route 6	Route 7
Visual modality: an overview map	1, 8, 15	2, 9, 16	3, 10 17	4, 11, 18	5, 12, 19	6, 13, 20	7, 14, 21
Visual modality: maps with cues	4, 11, 18	7, 14, 21	5, 12, 19	1, 8, 15	6, 13, 20	2, 9, 16	3, 10 17
Visual modality: maps with rhythm	5, 12, 19	6, 13, 20	7, 14, 21	2, 9, 16	3, 10 17	4, 11, 18	1, 8, 15
Audion modality: voice with cues	2, 9, 16	3, 10 17	6, 13, 20	7, 14, 21	4, 11, 18	1, 8, 15	5, 12, 19
Audion modality: voice with rhythm	7, 14, 21	4, 11, 18	1, 8, 15	5, 12, 19	2, 9, 16	3, 10 17	6, 13, 20
Tactile modality: taction with cues	6, 13, 20	1, 8, 15	2, 9, 16	3, 10 17	7, 14, 21	5, 12, 19	4, 11, 18
Tactile modality: taction with rhythm	3, 10 17	5, 12, 19	4, 11, 18	6, 13, 20	1, 8, 15	7, 14, 21	2, 9, 16

Each route was approximately 480 metres with four to five turns. The names of the streets were removed from the paper maps to simulate the unfamiliarity of the environment. The actual task given to the participants was to "find your way as fast as you can by walking at your normal speed". Navigation guidance was given in the form of a paper map (visual modality), with the voice (audio modality), or with haptic output (tactile modality). Furthermore, for each modality, the wayfinding instructions were given either as predicting cues or according to a regular rhythm.

While the participants were conducting the seven wayfinding tasks by walking, they were asked two questions. Examples of the questions were "What time is it?",

"Did you notice any mailboxes on the streets?", "What kind of colours were those flowers on the left side of the street?" or "How many cars are parked in that parking area?" The aim of these interrupting questions was to simulate the context that pedestrians have when navigation is not their primary task while they are moving. Interruption management and modality selection are argued to be two key issues in mobile contexts [24]. Furthermore, the cognitive resources of mobile users are in the real contexts reserved for multiple actions simultaneously: monitoring, selecting and reacting to the context and events [20]. After each wayfinding task, the participants filled out the seven-point Nasa Task Load Index [19] to evaluate the subjective task load of each task (mental, physical and temporal demand).

After completing the tasks, participants were interviewed. Participants were asked to rank the most useful and the least useful modality for navigation support. They were then asked if they recognised any differences between the navigation support within one modality to find out if they separated predictive cues and rhythm from each other, and if they did, which one was better. Finally, they were each asked for ideas about how the multimodal navigation tool might be improved in order to be more useful.

4.1.1 Data Analysis

Walking times were converted to walking speed in metres per minute. The ratio of navigation performance was calculated for each participant for each mode of guidance. These ratios were used as relative indicators of performance improvement for each participant. Standard t-tests and a one-way ANOVA were performed in order to determine the significance of navigation performance for each mode of guidance. The participants' subjective evaluations of task load were used to present the most demanding and least demanding modes of guidance. Standard t-tests and a one-way analysis of variance (ANOVA) were performed in order to find possible differences.

4.1.2 Participants

There were 21 volunteer participants (14 female, 7 male) in the experiment. Of the participants, 37% were aged 18–25 years, 32% were aged 26–35 years, 21% were aged 36–45 years, and the rest of the participants (10%) were over 46 years. Most of the participants were non-IT professionals, 40% were students and 15% were researchers. The occupations of the rest of the participants (40%) were other than those specified. The participants were recruited by email and rewarded for their time for 15 euros.

The participants of the field experiment were not the same participants that we had in our preliminary study. Furthermore, based on the results of our preliminary study [28], we selected participants who were unfamiliar with the environment for our field experiment.

4.1.3 Research Design

The study involved a mixed factorial that included a between-subject comparison of individual differences in type of wayfinding strategies (orientation strategy, route strategy) and navigation performance in addition to the within-subject comparison type of navigation support (predictive cues, support with regular rhythm).

5 Results

Our previous results indicate that in general, there are no significant differences between usefulness of providing cues or rhythm as a navigation aids in different modalities whereas when the environment is familiar for users, navigation aids provided with regular rhythm is not preferred as useful navigation aids .Thus, familiarity of the environment seem to be a key factor for users when evaluating usefulness of navigation aids. [28] This finding is consistent with earlier studies exploring spatial familiarity [8].

The results of the field experiment are presented according to the relative walking speed, i.e., objective data, and according to the results of experienced workload measured with the NASA Task Load Index [19], i.e., subjective data. Due to the small number of participants (n=21), results based on formal statistical analysis are limited. However, they provide indications and potential trends for multimodal design.

The total number of navigation errors was 21, and 11 of the participants made these errors. All the errors occurred when participants choose the direction, and 84% of the errors were made with the paper maps. The most common error was confusing north and south. The remaining 16% of the errors were made with the audio modality with cues, when the participants mixed up the left and right turns. The results of Mental Rotation Test indicated no significance differences between the participants.

5.1 Rhythms versus Cues

After each navigation task, the participants filled out a seven-point scale NASA Task Load Index [19]. The load index was ranked for each participant to find out the tasks that participants found most stressful and having least stressful (see Table 3). According to these data, navigating with a paper-based map was the most difficult from which to find their way.

5.1.1 Objective Data

The average walking speeds were calculated on each route and the fastest and slowest performances (modality with predicting cues or guidance with regular rhythm) were ranked for each participant. Table 2 summarises the fastest and slowest performances. Based on analysed data, it can be argued that designing cues or rhythms in the visual modality does not improve the performance of users in wayfinding tasks. However, guidance using the audio modality with the regular rhythm seemed to be slightly better (over 21%) than having audio with predicting cues (less than 16%). Meanwhile, the tactile guidance predicting cues led to better performance (over 21%) than providing guidance with a regular rhythm (see Table 2).

One-way ANOVA statistical analysis was performed and the results indicate no statistical significance between the relative walking speed and guidance mode. However, a statistically significant effect was found between gender and relative walking speed with guidance from visual rhythm, and between gender and relative walking speed with tactile guidance from rhythm ($p < 0.05$).

To summarise, the results between guidance modes indicate certain trends. The main trend appears to be that the best performance was achieved by tactile guidance with predicting cues, and the worst performance was by visual guidance with predicting cues. Statistically significant results were found between gender and walking speed with guidance either from visual or tactile rhythm.

Table 2. Relationships between relative walking speed and types of guidance

	Fastest performance (%)	Slowest performance (%)
Visual modality with an overview map	15.8	21.1
Visual modality with predictive cues	0	36.8
Visual modality with regular rhythm	5.2	26.3
Audio modality with predictive cues	15.8	5.2
Audio modality guidance with regular rhythm	21.1	5.2
Tactile modality guidance with predictive cues	21.1	0
Tactile modality guidance with regular rhythm	15.8	5.2
Total	100	100

5.1.2 Subjective Data

One of the key results is that when participants were asked after completing the seven wayfinding tasks if they noticed differences between the instructions they were given in the different modalities, of the participants 60% did not remember any differences between being given predictive cues or instructions with a regular rhythm. When evaluating task load in three different modalities with two types of guidance (cues/rhythm), tactile modality with predictive cues was experienced the least stressful and an overview map the most stressful type of navigation guidance (see Table 3). Furthermore, a statistically significant difference ($p < 0.05$) between gender and experiencing task load in audio with rhythm was found.

Table 3. Subjective estimation of the workload using the NASA Task Load Index

	Least stressful (%)	Most stressful (%)
Visual modality with an overview map	2	28
Visual modality with predictive cues	21	15
Visual modality with regular rhythm	3	20
Audio modality with predictive cues	8	20
Audio modality with regular rhythm	20	15
Tactile modality with predictive cues	32	0
Tactile modality with regular rhythm	15	3
Total	100	100

There were no statistically significant differences in experienced task load between different modalities, but between gender and experienced task load there were statistically significant difference in audion modality with regular rhythm.

5.2 Impacts of Wayfinding Strategies

In relation to our second research question, we analyze the data according the participant's wayfinding strategies. According to the participants, the least stressful guidance was the tactile modality with predictive cues regardless of the participant's wayfinding strategy (see Table 4).

Table 4. Relationships between wayfinding strategy and types of guidance

	Fastest performance	Slowest performance	Least stressful	Most stressful
Participants emphasising orientation strategy	Audio or tactile modality with cues 60%	Visual modality with cues 40%	Tactile modality with cues 40%	Visual modality (an overview map) 45%
Participants emphasising route strategy	Visual, audio or tactile modality rhythm 54%	Visual modality with cues 45%	Tactile modality with cues 31%	Vision modality (an overview map) 34%

There was a statistically significant ($p < 0.05$) difference between how participants who emphasised orientation strategy evaluated task load with guidance from tactile cues. In addition, there was a statistically significant ($p < 0.05$) difference between how participants who emphasised route strategy evaluated task load with guidance from tactile cues.

6 Discussion

Our results introduce promising design implications for the development of multimodal navigation aids to support the wayfinding of mobile users. Multidisciplinary approaches, such as design practices from urban planners, have potential when mobile human-computer interaction is investigated. In this study, the possible benefits of predictive cues or rhythm in three different modalities of navigation guidance were examined.

It is stated here that a number of important lessons from the study described in this paper can be drawn:

1. Designing cues or rhythm can be beneficial particularly when mobile users interact with tactile or audion modality. There was no clear evidence that visual cues or visual guidance with regular rhythm would be useful.
2. There is a difference between male and female navigators in relation to relative walking speed and having visual or tactile guidance with regular rhythm.
3. There is a difference between male and female navigators how participants experience the workload in audion modality with rhythm.
4. Wayfinding strategy has an impact on how human experience the workload of tactile guidance with cues

Our findings concerning the navigation performance and gender issues are consistent with earlier findings in navigation HCI studies, see e.g., [10], [15], [16]. However, only a few if any previous studies in the field of mobile HCI have explored the impacts of wayfinding strategies and gender issues in relation to navigation performance. Thus, besides the design practices resulting from this study and presented above, it must be noted that evaluation method that was conducted in this study has its own potential. When evaluating wayfinding tasks, the NASA Task Load Index is one suitable indicator for understanding and measuring the subjective workload, but particularly when the focus of research is on human wayfinding, wayfinding strategies should be explored.

7 Conclusion

This paper reported on design issues to investigate navigation performance in mobile multimodal navigation aids. The results show a good potential with designing cues and rhythm in tactile and audio guidance. In particular, the results also show that with visual modality, cues and rhythm were less beneficial than with audion or tactile modality

In the field of traffic planning, the concept of fluent traffic is useful to acknowledge when we are exploring and designing human computer interaction within mobile navigation services. *Fluent navigation* in the context of human computer interaction and particularly in the context of this study can be defined as easy and as smooth navigation performance as possible including relative fast walking speed with only a few navigation errors. It is also including user's subjective experience of navigation performance with minimum workload.

When providing different modalities for pedestrians to receive wayfinding instructions in urban areas, providing both predicting cues and giving instructions according to a regular rhythm should be alternatives for users to choose from. According to our results, users do not differentiate between these instructions in every case, but there are still differences when measuring the walking speed or experienced work load.

A couple of potential directions for potential future research are emerging. The first concerns studying navigation with pedestrians in more detail using some other urban planning design practice than episodes of motion to support mobile users in wayfinding. The second direction of future research could focus upon investigating how to better support different wayfinding strategies in unfamiliar environments.

In conclusion, the results show that when designing cues and rhythm into mobile navigation systems, we can support wayfinding task when pedestrians are interacting with audion or tactile modality. Furthermore, when exploring wayfinding with mobile users in general, the possible impacts of wayfinding strategies should be explored.

Acknowledgments. The author would like to acknowledge professors Kaisa Väänänen-Vainio-Mattila and Sari Kujala at the Tampere University of Technology, the partners of TOPI project at the University of Tampere, Dr Matt Jones and researcher Satu Jumisko-Pyykkö for their contributions.

References

1. Baus, J., Krüger, A., Wahlster, W.: A resource-adaptive mobile navigation system. IUI 2002. In: Proc. of the 7th International Conference on Intelligent User Interfaces (2002)
2. Baus, J., Wasinger, R., Aslan, I., Krüger, A., Maier, A., Schwartz, T.: Auditory perceptible landmarks in mobile navigation. In: Proc. of the 12th International Conference on Intelligent User Interfaces, IUI 2007 (2007)

3. Brewster, S., Chohan, F., Brown, L.: Tactile feedback for mobile interactions. In: Proceedings of the SIGCHI Conference on Human Factors in Computing Systems. CHI 2007, San Jose, California, USA, April 28 - May 03, pp. 159–162. ACM, New York (2007)
4. Brewster, S., Lumsden, J., Bell, M., Hall, M., Tasker, S.: Multimodal 'eyes-free' interaction techniques for wearable devices. In: Proc. of the SIGCHI Conference on Human Factors in Computing Systems, pp. 473–480 (2003)
5. Butz, A., Baus, J., Krüger, A., Lohse, M.: A hybrid indoor navigation system. In: Proceedings of the 6th international Conference on intelligent User interfaces. IUI 2001, Santa Fe, New Mexico, United States, January 14-17, pp. 25–32. ACM, New York (2001)
6. Charitos, D.: Designing Space in Virtual Environments for Aiding Wayfinding Behaviour. In: Proceedings of the 4th UK Virtual Reality Special Interest Group Conference, Brunel University, Brunel University Printing Services (1997)
7. Cohen, P., McGee, D., Clow, J.: The efficiency of multimodal interaction for a map-based task. In: Proceedings of the Sixth Conference on Applied Natural Language Processing. Applied Natural Language Conferences, Seattle, Washington, April 29 - May 04, pp. 331–338. Morgan Kaufmann Publishers, San Francisco (2000)
8. Gale, N., Golledge, R.G., Halperin, W.C., Couclelis, H., Niehaus, R.D.: Exploring Spatial Familiarity. The Professional Geographer 42(3), 299–313
9. Ghiani, G., Leporini, B., Paternò, F.: Vibrotactile feedback as an orientation aid for blind users of mobile guides. In: Proc. of the 10th International Conference on Human-Computer interaction with Mobile Devices and Services, pp. 431–434 (2008)
10. Golledge, R.D. (ed.): Wayfinding Behavior: Cognitive Mapping and Other Spatial Processes. John Hopkins Press, Baltimore
11. Heuten, W., Wichmann, D., Boll, S.: Interactive 3D sonification for the exploration of city maps. In: Proc. of the 4th Nordic Conference on Human-Computer interaction: Changing Roles, pp. 155–164 (2006)
12. Hoggan, E., Brewster, S.: Designing audio and tactile crossmodal icons for mobile devices. In: Proc. of the 9th International Conference on Multimodal Interfaces, pp. 162–169 (2007)
13. Holland, S., Morse, D., Gedenryd, H.: AudioGPS: Spatial Audio Navigation with a Minimal Attention Interface. Personal Ubiquitous Comput 6(4), 253–259 (2002)
14. Jöst, M., Häußler, J., Merdes, M., Malaka, R.: Multimodal interaction for pedestrians: an evaluation study. In: Proceedings of the 10th International Conference on Intelligent User Interfaces (2005)
15. Lawton, C.: Gender differences in wayfinding strategies: relationship to spatial ability and spatial anxiety. Journal of Sex Roles 30(11-12), 765–779 (1994)
16. Lawton, C.A., Kallai, J.: Gender differences in wayfinding strategies and anxiety about wayfinding: a cross-cultural comparison. Sex Roles 47, 389–401
17. Lynch, K.: Image of the City. The Technology Press & Harvard University Press, Cambridge (1960)
18. Mental Rotation Experiment Software (MENTROT), `http://artsci.wustl.edu/~rabrams/psychlab/mentrot.htm`
19. NASA Task Load Index (TLX), `http://www.cc.gatech.edu/classes/AY2005/cs7470_fall/papers/TLXScale.pdf`
20. Oulasvirta, A., Tamminen, S., Roto, V., Kuorelahti, J.: Interaction in 4-second bursts: the fragmented nature of attentional resources in mobile HCI. In: Proceedings of the SIGCHI Conference on Human Factors in Computing Systems. CHI 2005, Portland, Oregon, USA, April 02-07, pp. 919–928. ACM, New York (2005)

21. Oulasvirta, A., Petit, R., Raento, M., Tiitta, S.: Interpreting and acting on mobile awareness cues. Human-Computer Interaction. Human-Computer Interaction 22(1), 97–135 (2007)
22. Oviatt, S.: Multimodal system processing in mobile environments. In: Proc. of the 13th Annual ACM Symposium on User interface Software and Technology, pp. 21–30 (2000)
23. Oviatt, S., Coulston, R., Lunsford, R.: When do we interact multimodally?: cognitive load and multimodal communication patterns. In: Proc. of the 6th International Conference on Multimodal Interfaces, pp. 129–136 (2004)
24. Tamminen, S., Oulasvirta, A., Toiskallio, K., Kankainen, A.: Understanding mobile contexts. Personal Ubiquitous Comput. 8(2), 135–143 (2004)
25. Tversky, B.: Navigating by Mind and by Body. In: Freksaet, et al. (eds.) Spatial Cognition III, pp. 1–10. Springer, Heidelberg (2003)
26. Schraggen, J.M.C.: An experimental comparison betweendifferent types of in-car navigation information (Tech. Rep. No. IZF 1991 B-1). Soesterberg, The Netherland TNO Institute for Perception (1991)
27. Stenros, H., Aura, S.: Time, Motion and Architecture. Weilin + Göös, Espoo (1987)
28. Vainio, T.: Exploring cues and rhythm for designing multimodal tools to support mobile users in way-finding. In: CHI 2009 Extended Abstracts on Human Factors in Computing Systems. CHI 2009, Boston, MA, USA, April 4-9, pp. 3715–3720. ACM, New York (2009)
29. Wahlster, W.: Smartweb: multimodal web services on the road. In: Proc. of the 15th International Conference on Multimedia, p. 16 (2007)
30. Wilson, D., Doyle, J., Weakliam, J., Bertolotto, M., Lynch, D.: Personalised maps in multimodal mobile GIS. Int. J. Web Eng. Technol. 3(2), 196–216 (2007)
31. Zhao, H.: Interactive sonification of geo-referenced data. In: CHI 2005: Extended Abstracts on Human Factors in Computing Systems, pp. 1134–1135 (2005)
32. Zhao, H., Smith, B.K., Norman, K., Plaisant, C., Shneiderman, B.: Interactive sonification of choropleth maps. IEEE MultiMedia 12(2), 26–35 (2005)

Feature Use in Mobile Video Creation

Arto Puikkonen[1], Jonna Häkkilä[2], Rafael Ballagas[3], and Jani Mäntyjärvi[4]

[1] Nokia Research Center, Visiokatu 1,
33720 Tampere, Finland
[2] Nokia Research Center, Yrttipellontie 1,
90401 Oulu, Finland
[3] Nokia Research Center, 955 Page Mill Road,
94304-1013 Palo Alto, USA
[4] VTT, Kaitoväylä 1,
90570 Oulu, Finland
{arto.puikkonen,tico.ballagas,jonna.hakkila}@nokia.com,
jani.mantyjarvi@vtt.fi

Abstract. Today's mobile phones are also video cameras. People are using these ubiquitous cameras to document everyday surroundings as well as create more artistic videos. This paper examines emergent mobile film making patterns by tracking video composition and recording activities in ecologically valid contexts of use. We report the findings of a user study on user created mobile videos, where the actions of 11 active mobile video users were documented for 2 weeks. The collected material included diaries, device logs, and altogether 255 videos. Our findings characterize the features of a typical mobile video. Additionally, our study uncovers common practices, user motivations and pitfalls during filming and editing in the mobile context.

Keywords: Mobile video, mobile multimedia, user created content, user studies.

1 Introduction

Video has become an integral part of the way we capture, and share experiences. The emergence of popular online video sharing websites has significantly lowered the threshold for distributing video content, and people are now able to capture video in more circumstances than ever before and share it instantaneously. Earlier research reveals that the lightweight video work, meaning the use of mobile phone for shooting the videos, included more spontaneous and 'just for fun' filming in comparison to the use of conventional video cameras [3]. Other studies related to mobile videos include collaborative live video creation [1] and the practices on consuming videos [4] or mobile TV content [2], where for instance gift giving practices (e.g. recording content for a friend) were exposed [2]. To the authors' knowledge, this is the first study focusing on charting the technical and editing features used in everyday practices with user created mobile phones videos. Due the limited length, this paper has concentrated on the structure and feature use findings. In their further work, the authors will seek to look deeper into the context and content side of mobile phone video creation.

T. Gross et al. (Eds.): INTERACT 2009, Part I, LNCS 5726, pp. 866–869, 2009.

2 Study Setting and Resulting Videos

For a study in summer 2008, a total of 12 participants (10 male, 2 female) were recruited with a variety of occupations and all from Finland for a study. The average age was 30 years, from 16 to 45. One of the participants, #10, dropped out during the study. Each participant received a Nokia N95 mobile phone for 2 weeks, which includes a camera for video. The phones were equipped with key logging software, which gathered all key presses with a time stamp within the camera, gallery and editor application. For the 2 weeks, the participants were asked to use the given mobile phone just as they use their own. The participants were also provided with a small paper diary about filming and transferring, which the participants were asked to fill in whenever such an event occurred. In the end, each participant was interviewed. All the videos were analyzed for content, context, structure and feature use. This analysis was supported by analyzing the logger, interview and diary data.

The participants filmed a total of 266 videos with the provided mobile phones, resulting in the average of 24.2 videos, minimum being 4 and maximum 90 clips. Three (#1, 4, 11) removed 11 videos during the study. In addition, 10 videos were accidental extremely short ones, making the total amount of analyzed videos 245. (See Fig. 1)

Fig. 1. Example screenshots from user created videos

3 Feature Use Related to Filming Mobile Videos

A vast amount of videos, (222/245), were single clip. Only two participants created videos with multiple clips (#9, 11). Out of the 42 videos by user #9, 17 had multiple clips and for user #11, 6/28 had multiple clips. The average amount of clips for each multiclip video was 2.6 varying from 2 to 4 clips, 3 being the most frequent. With clip length in multiclip videos, the average length was 29.5 seconds.

Interestingly, all multiclip videos were created by using the phones provided pause function, which enables you to halt and resume filming when desired. When asked in the end interview also users #5 and #7 stated that they sometimes use this function. The motivation is getting a rough editing with little effort, as further editing was unlikely. "I just want to cut out stuff so it makes it easier to edit it later or that it is already edited as I probably won't have the energy to edit it later on." (#7). It was stated that this kind of editing had its downsides, but is most often used due to its level of ease. "It leaves extra bits in it." (#7)

The other 7 participants stated that they do not use this feature. Reasons for not creating multiclip videos divide into two categories. Five of the users expressed that they want the videos to be single entities as the videos are consumed as single entities.

"Do not need it as they are for single items." (#6) For the rest, the reason is the unexpected nature of the filmed target, which then would require more user attention.

Besides the pause feature, zoom typically is the easiest feature to access in mobile phones. Not surprisingly, 8 of the participants used zoom during the study and also 1 other stated using zoom occasionally. In total, zoom was used with 71 videos out of the 234 videos they created altogether. But commonly among all participants the opinion about the zoom was negative, and considered mainly as 'a necessary evil'.

Zooming was more preferred during filming instead of before filming. Out of 71 videos with zoom, 70% (50) videos had zooming during filming. 65% (46) had forward zooming and 55% (39) videos backward zooming. 49% (35/71) of the videos included zooming prior to filming. During interviews and by analyzing the videos, it became clear that people were less rushed in these circumstances and thus had more time to spend on video composition.

A significant factor discouraging the use of zoom is the perceived decrease in video quality. Many of the videos are eventually consumed on larger screens where the downside of reduced quality is very apparent. Even for those that consume video on mobile phones, the use of zoom is seen as very unpleasant as the decrease in quality is apparent when filming. These issues make the use of zoom even more unpleasant for many and limits the use to situations where it is very necessary.

When probed about the situations where zoom was necessary, the response was distance to the target. In these situations, it is either impossible to get closer, getting closer would have an undesired impact on the target, or getting closer would be socially awkward. In addition, two users reported that using the zoom is an easy way to get some life into the video, if the target itself is not lively enough.

In general, when examining the actions done during filming, the remarkable observation was the lack of them. During the study, none of the users changed any video settings of the device that are available through the menus in the UI. Even for video resolution, the common consensus was that it is initially changed to the desired quality and left that way for good. When asked about the use of the other settings, no user changed from the default. Reasons for using default settings divide into two categories. For some, the default settings for white balance and color tone are seen as the best alternative in almost every situation. For others, the reason is simply not knowing what setting would be the best or even what the effect of these settings is. Thus the defaults are the "easy way out" for a good quality end-result.

As every day situations often have a sporadic nature, changing the settings before filming is out of the question if it delays capture. The only situations, where settings are changed, are nighttime situations when being fast is not required. This event did not occur during the study, but was found during interviews (#4, 6). For both the night mode feature provided needed improvement, when the received quality is generally poor. However, for both, avoiding filming in poor lighting was still the preferred option.

Many of today's mobile phones offer editing capabilities, such as the possibility to merge videos, give the file a name, and replace audio. Similarly as none of the multi-clip videos during the study were done by using the merging feature, the use of other features after the filming was also minimal. The logger data showed that no-one had used the editor, none of the videos had been given names and none had changed the audio using the provided features. When this behavior was presented to participants, it was clear that this also represented their practices in every day life.

Out of the 11, only 3 (#5, 11, 12) stated that they had ever tried to use a video editor on a mobile phone. Out of the 3 that have tried the editor, none have used it more than a few times. For all three, the experience was seen as slow, cramped controls and requiring too much effort. "You can't do stuff like that with a small screen when even the PC screen sometimes feels too small for editing." (#11) All three that have tried the editor provided by a mobile phone actively utilize an editor provided by a PC.

For the 7 participants that have not even tried to use the editor, the reasoning can be divided into two categories. The 4 (# 2, 3, 7, 8) that have tried and used editors on a PC stated that the mere idea of editing on a mobile phone is seen as too complicated. This level of complication is compared to their experiences with PC editing that is also seen as challenging. The 3 (#1, 4, 6) that haven't tried editing on any device stated that there is no need to edit on a mobile as there is no need to edit on a PC either. "I really don't see it as important as I don't need editing." (#1) The reasons for not seeing the editing as important for the three were "My videos are not movie-like, only documents of events." (#1), "I don't have time for that." (#4) and "They are just individual clips." (#6)

When asked about the possibility to give names to video files, none of the users were interested in the feature. In fact, none of the users give names to the files at any point of the video life, until it is a complete edited entity. When it is an edited complete version, users 5 and 12, who actively edit videos, sometimes give the end versions names. Naming files is typically done where editing is done, which is on a PC. During the study user 12 created one edited complete version and gave that a name. The name of the file was the name of the lake where the video was filmed.

As a conclusion, mobile phone videos form an important part in capturing a variety of everyday events. As the current solutions may be fairly suitable for some users, the more active users clearly experience technical limitations when using a mobile phone to capture the things that surround them.

References

1. Engström, A., Esbjörnsson, M., Juhlin, O.: Mobile Collaborative Live Video Mixing. In: Proceedings of MobileHCI 2008, pp. 157–166. ACM Press, New York (2008)
2. Harper, R., Regan, T., Izadi, S., Mosawi, K.A., Rouncefield, M., Rubens, S.: Trafficking: design for the viral exchange of TV content on mobile phones. In: In Proc.of MobileHCI 2000, vol. 309, pp. 249–256. ACM, New York (2000)
3. Kirk, D., Sellen, A., Harper, R., Wood, K.: Understanding Videowork. In: Proc. CHI 2007, pp. 61–70 (2007)
4. O'Hara, K., Mitchell, A.S., Vorbau, A.: Consuming Video on Mobile Devices. In: Proc. CHI 2007, pp. 857–866 (2007)

Glaze: A Visualization Framework for Mobile Devices

Roberto Sousa, Valentina Nisi, and Ian Oakley

Dept de Matemática e Engenharias, Universidade da Madeira, Funchal, Portugal
robertonssousa@gmail.com, valentina.nisi@gmail.com, ian@uma.pt

Abstract. The processing power of mobile devices is increasing steadily; their screen size suffers more fundamental limits. Given this contrast, we identify mobile information visualization which maximizes the effectiveness of small screen displays as a key area for future development. To achieve this, we present an overview of Glaze, a plug-in based visualization framework for mobile devices based on the information visualization reference model. We discuss two prototype visualizations implemented using Glaze and designed based on the output of concept generation interviews with users.

Keywords: Visualizations, Mobile Devices, Multimedia, Framework.

1 Introduction

Mobile phones are now a part of many aspects of everyday life. Modern Smartphones can not only make calls, but also play music, take and store photos, browse the Internet and send email. They are arguably on the cusp of becoming truly personal computers capable of capturing, maintaining and storing large amounts of valuable information for their users. They are also becoming increasingly able to detect information about their environment. Sensors such as cameras, accelerometers, GPS and magnetometers now appear in high end devices; past trends suggest they will migrate to lower-end handsets in the near future.

The application areas opened up by such mobile data processing and sensing capabilities are broad. Navigation has been extensively explored and many map based commercial systems exist (e.g. Nokia Maps). The research community is exploring other metaphors such as augmented reality (Narzt, et al., 2003) or non-visual directional cues (Erp et al., 2007). Other sensors are more focused on user interaction. For example, the sensing of pose to control the orientation of graphical displays (Hinckley et al., 2005), motion as input to dynamic simulations (Cho et al., 2007) and camera input to perform cursor-like navigation and selection (Rohs, 2005).

One area at the convergence of these new technologies is that of information visualization. This is of particular relevance to mobile devices because of their limited display capacity – the small screens of handheld devices provide a clear imperative to design visual information carefully and with the goal of presenting it most effectively. Although this is true of the information and content natively stored on a phone (such as message, contacts and photos), it is also relevant when considering the diverse information captured by sensors. This often relates to multi-dimensional spaces, such as maps, or other rich contextual data sets, such as the markers used in augmented

T. Gross et al. (Eds.): INTERACT 2009, Part I, LNCS 5726, pp. 870–873, 2009.

reality. This paper identifies a need for flexible frameworks to support the development of advanced sensor-enabled visualizations on mobile devices and describes Glaze, a first attempt to produce such a framework. The remainder of this paper is structured as follows: Section 2 provides an overview of Glaze; Section 3 introduces particular scenarios and visualizations that we have implemented; and Section 4 contains conclusions and speculations on the future of this work.

2 Glaze Framework

Existing mobile visualization frameworks typically address specific problems such as viewing networks (Kim et al., 2008) or volume data (Zhou et al., 2006). Glaze on the other hand is a general mobile visualization framework intended to support a wide range of sensor inputs and output visualizations. To this end, it was kept intentionally minimalist in structure and its architecture was based on the information visualization reference model described by Card et al. (1999) and shown in Figure 1. It was developed using C++ for the Nokia N95 (running Symbian 9.2 and S60 Rel 3.1) but features an extensible structure of plug-ins to facilitate its use with different input and output capabilities or operating systems. The overall design approach was to effectively separate responsibilities to ease development and maximize the future portability of the code.

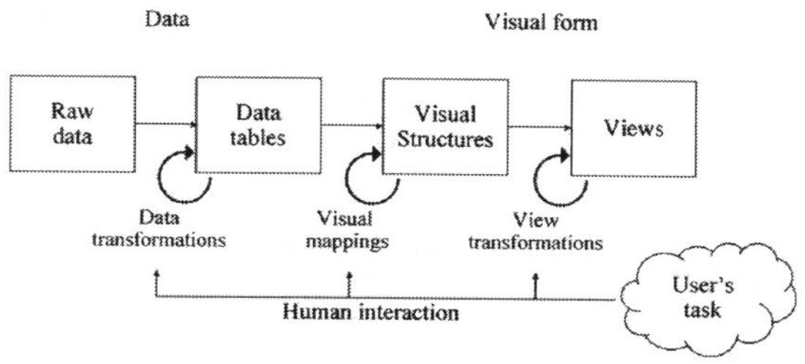

Fig. 1. Information Visualization Reference Model (from Card et al., 1999)

The framework has four components: the core, input, visualization and front-end. The core simply manages the application and implements the processes described in the information visualization reference model. The latter three components are plug-in based and can also be configured using XML, at the discretion of the developer. Plug-ins intended for a single purpose might offer no (or only superficial) customization options, while more sophisticated ones can introduce new schemas to control key aspects of their behavior. One immediate implication of this structure is that it allows the creation of generic visualization templates (such as fish-eyes) which can be tailored to particular data sets and scenarios defined within the XML. Components are based on the three mapping and transformation processes in Card et al.'s model and are described in more detail below.

The input component is responsible for reading and abstracting the raw data into a developer specified format suitable for further processing. Developers are able to write input plug-ins for different sensors (such as cameras, accelerometers or GPS) or files without modifying other parts of the system.

Fig. 2. Two Glaze visualizations: Nightvision (left), Information Overlay (right)

The visualization component is responsible for mapping data from input component to visual elements and specifying how these objects can be viewed and interacted with. This is a substantial task and the minimalist approach in Glaze means it is largely unconstrained: the developer of a plug-in has considerable flexibility in performing this task. The disadvantage of this approach is that it increases the complexity of constructing new visualization components. Finally, the front-end is responsible for initializing and updating the graphic side of the visualization and also of rendering the scene to the screen. It simplifies development by providing and encapsulating basic services such as device initialization and screen rendering. This explicit separation ensures that Glaze is independent from a particular rendering API; the developer can choose which API to work with by simply re-implementing the front-end. Finally, this separation also allows for visualization aggregation with API's that support a render to texture functionality. This enables the display of multiple visualizations on the screen at the same time (or the use of one visualization as the input to another) and considerably increases the expressiveness of the system. Basically, on-screen visualizations can be "mashed-up" or combined in an ad-hoc manner simply through editing the XML configuration files.

3 Test Applications

To gather potential uses of an advanced visualization system for mobile devices, we conducted a series of 18 semi-structured interviews with users. These involved deliberately open ended questions intended to elicit device features and applications unrelated to current technological capabilities and limitations. From this data set, we selected two candidate targets for visualization development based on their novelty, potential utility and the frequency with which they were requested. These were Night Vision and Information Overlay, both also illustrated in Figure 2.

The Night Vision system uses GPS and an external digital compass to compute the position and orientation of the user. It displays a 3D model of the area around a user mapped so that the position and orientation of the virtual scene match that of the real world. This allows users to easily see the structure and organization of their surroundings and navigate in low light environments. Information Overlay again uses the GPS, camera and an external compass to overlay relevant information about objects around the user on visual scene captured by the viewfinder. We have also developed several generic visualizations, such as a tagcloud and a 1D fish eye view.

4 Conclusions and Future Work

Glaze was designed to be highly general and flexible for both developers and users. It provides a minimal software structure to constrain a visualization developer's task to a systematic set of modular problems. It also provides a mechanism for end users to customize the system by combining and mixing the on-screen visualization components. This provides the ability to "mash-up" different visualizations, but also to use the output of one as the input to another. For example, a location aware map visualization could be configured as the input to a 2D fish-eye to create a richer display with a higher information density.

Future work will focus on both user evaluation and further developing the system. For example, basic input modules for the N95's camera, accelerometer and GPS have been implemented. We also plan to conduct several user studies both to provide further ideation as to novel visualizations and also to systematically evaluate those we create. In short, given the growing processing power and limited screen size of mobile devices, this paper has identified effective information visualization to be an important area for development. By introducing Glaze, a general visualization framework for handhelds, it hopes to usher in a new range of expressive, attractive and user-customizable mobile interfaces.

References

1. Card, S.K., Mackinlay, J.D., Shneiderman, B.: Readings in information visualization: using vision to think. Morgan Kaufmann Publishers Inc., San Francisco (1999)
2. Cho, S., Choi, C., Sung, Y., Lee, K., Kim, Y., Murray-Smith, R.: Dynamics of tilt-based browsing on mobile devices. In: CHI 2007 (2007)
3. Erp, J.B., Veen, H.A., Jansen, C., Dobbins, T.: Waypoint navigation with a vibrotactile waist belt. ACM Trans. Appl. Percept. 2, 2 (2005)
4. Hinckley, K., Pierce, J., Horvitz, E., Sinclair, M.: Foreground and Background Interaction with Sensor-enhanced Mobile Devices. ACM TOCHI Special Issue on Sensor-Based Interaction, 12 (1) (2005)
5. Narzt, W., Pomberger, G., Ferscha, A., Kolb, D., Müller, R., Wieghardt, J., Hörtner, H., Lindinger, C.: Pervasive Information Acquisition for Mobile AR-Navigation Systems. In: 5th IEEE Workshop on Mobile Computing Systems & Applications (2003)
6. Rohs, M.: Real-world interaction with camera phones. In: Murakami, H., Nakashima, H., Tokuda, H., Yasumura, M. (eds.) UCS 2004. LNCS, vol. 3598, pp. 74–89. Springer, Heidelberg (2005)
7. Kim, J., Hsu, W.-J., Moon, S., Kumar, U., Helmy, A.: Visualization and Representation of Mobile Network Users. In: 5th Annual IEEE Communications Society Conference, San Francisco, pp. 588–590 (2008)
8. Zhou, H., Qu, H., Wu, Y., Chan, M.-Y.: Volume visualization on mobile devices. In: 14th Pacific Conference on Computer Graphics and Applications, pp. 76–84. National Taiwan University Press, Taiwan (2006)

A Collaborative Approach to Minimize Cellphone Interruptions

Ashraf Khalil[1] and Kay Connelly[2]

[1] Abu Dhabi University, College of Engineering & Computer Science, United Arab Emirates
ashraf.khalil@adu.ac.ae
[2] Indiana University, School of Informatics, Bloomington, Indiana 47405, USA
connelly@indiana.edu

Abstract. In this paper, we present a collaborative approach to minimizing inappropriate cellphone interruptions. The approach uses Bluetooth technology to discover and communicate with the surrounding cell phones in order to read their notification profiles. The profile of the majority is assumed to be the most suitable setting for the current social environment. Cellphones running the collaborative service can automatically update their profile according to the majority profile or at least alert the user to do so. We have conducted a user study to examine the acceptability and the usefulness of the collaborative service and to incorporate users' feedback into the early design process.

1 Introduction

Mobile phones offer great accessibility and flexibility. No longer do people have to remain in a fixed location to carry on conversations over the phone. The benefits offered by cell phones, such as flexibility and accessibility, seem to inevitably come with the cost of increased interruption and interaction demands. Examples of inappropriate cell phone interruptions are when a cell phone ring disrupts a group activity, such as a class, meeting or movie. In large part, this mismatch between the user's context and the cell phone's behavior occurs because owners do not remember to frequently update their cell phone configuration according to the current context. The tremendous growth of cell phones' usage and their location-free nature have only magnified this problem.

Interruption caused by inappropriate notification such as ringing in a meeting can cause inconvenience, disruption and embarrassment for the owner. The effect of interruptions has been shown to be disruptive to task performance even when the interruption is ignored [1]. Interruption is not limited to the owner of the cell phone only but extends to the surrounding environment as well. Kern et al. have introduced and validated a model for interruptability wherein they distinguish between interruption of a user's environment (social interruptability) and interruption of a user him or herself (personal interruptability) [2].

2 Motivation

In this paper we describe an approach aimed at minimizing cell phone interruption: a collaborative technique that accepts the configuration of the majority of the surrounding cell phones as the appropriate configuration and adapts accordingly. The

T. Gross et al. (Eds.): INTERACT 2009, Part I, LNCS 5726, pp. 874–877, 2009.

collaborative approach uses Bluetooth technology for discovering and communicating with the surrounding cell phones. The main idea behind this approach is the observation that most people in any given situation have their cell phones configured to the correct setting, or profile, for that situation. The collaborative approach capitalizes on the explosion of cell phones that are equipped with short-range Bluetooth capability, which enables them to communicate with other cell phones in the vicinity. For instance if a user in a meeting has forgotten to turn his cell phone ringer off, his cell phone can contact other cell phones in the same room and learn that most of them have their ringer off. Consequently, the cell phone can safely assume that it should also have its ringer off, and when the meeting is over the cell phone can return to its default state (ringer on) without the user having to take action. Cell phones that are equipped with Bluetooth connectivity can use that observation to automatically set their profile to fit the majority profile without user's explicit intervention or at least to remind the owner to manually switch to the right setting.

Bluetooth has many properties than make it ideal for collaborative configuration. In general, Bluetooth technology fits social interactions well and many applications and tools have been developed for social purposes [3]. Serendipity is a tool developed by the MIT Media lab that allows two different devices within the range of Bluetooth to communicate with each other if their personal profiles match [4].

3 Methodology

A user study was conducted in order to examine the acceptability and usefulness of the collaborative service and to incorporate users' feedback into the early design process. Due to the futuristic nature of the collaborative service, 10 participants were introduced to the service and were asked to 'pretend' it exists on their mobile phones. The participants, 2 of whom were males, were ages 19-30, were mostly students and all had either a full-time or part-time job. All participants had owned cell phones over a year.

The study was based on a five-day diary in which participants were asked to record relevant activities they engaged in each day, specifically those involving surrounding people, and describe those situations in which they think the collaborative service would be useful. The descriptions were to include the activity, location, number of surrounding people, their relationship with those people, and any other relevant context information. Semi-structured interviews were conducted at the end of the study in order to get their overall feedback, reactions and attitude towards the collaborative service.

4 Findings

4.1 Acceptability and Usefulness

On average participants reported 1 to 5 different situations per day, with an average of 3, in which they could envision using the collaborative service. The diverse situations included official meetings, work, family gatherings, dinner, class, and exhibits. This indicates that participants considered the usefulness of the collaborative service in many situations both formal and informal. In the end-of-study interview, participants were also asked to rate the usefulness of the service on a scale of 1 to 5, with 5 being the most useful. All participants rated the service 3 or higher with an overall average of 4. This high level of perceived usefulness is translated as a high level of usability, supported by the fact that all participants reported that they would use the service if their cell phones came equipped with it.

4.2 User Control

During the interview, we asked participants which if any specific features of the collaborative service they would like to have control over so they could personalize the service according to their particular needs. Participants reported a desire to control the following features:

- Turning the service on and off whenever they wish to.
- Controlling the frequency of scanning for new surrounding cellphones so that new situations can be discovered whenever possible. This parameter is a trade-off between conserving the battery power and discovering new social environments that require different cell phone configurations. Naturally, this will be different from one user to another depending on their lifestyle. For example, a student with a busy class schedule might need to set the discovery frequency higher than would an IT consultant who spends most of his day in the office with some sporadic meetings. The perceived cost of inappropriate interruption also plays an important role in deciding on the value for this parameter. Cell phone interruptions that might disturb a large group of people during an important meeting, such as in a classroom or a movie theater, are essential to avoid. Thus, a user might decide to increase the discovery frequency more than he or she would normally. Sixty percent of participants reported that they would choose 5 minutes as the default value between scans with an overall average of 30 minutes.
- Controlling the configuration transitions and notifications. Seventy percent of the participants reported that they would only use the service for a profile change going from loud (ringing) to quiet (vibration) but not the other way around. They reported that avoiding inappropriate interruption is their priority. One participant reported that she would use the service for both transitions while the rest reported that it would depend on the situation. As for the style of profile transition and whether it should be automatic or should notify the user and let her decide how to proceed, half of the participants reported that they would like to be notified of the profile change. The remaining half of the participants opted for automatic transition.

4.3 Privacy and Trust

Participants were asked during the interview whether they mind sharing their cellphone notification profile with the surrounding people. All but one answered negatively. The participant who reported some privacy concerns commented that “It is a bit disconcerting. It makes me think of conspiracy theory”. All participants reported that they would trust the profiles of the surrounding people in the same way regardless of their social relations to them. One participant commented that “I would have the same level of trust regardless, because friends could have the wrong setting”.

5 Conclusion

We have introduced a novel collaborative approach that aims at improving the awareness of cellphones to the social context by minimizing inappropriate interruptions. Our approach is most useful in cases where a user forgets to change the notification profile of his or her cellphone. The diverse usage scenarios, together with the high acceptability rate reported by the users during the usability study, reflect that our proposed collaborative approach is both feasible and desirable.

It is essential to incorporate the above mentioned personalization features into the design of the collaborative service since different people are subjected to different social interactions and environments. Personalization provides them with the tools to customize the service according to their specific needs. Another important advantage of personalization is that it provides users with a sense of control over their devices and hence makes them more comfortable in using the collaborative service.

It is important to indicate that the collaborative approach is basically independent of the underlying communication technology as long as it supports the same features that are supported by Bluetooth, including short-range, automatic discovery, low power consumption and widespread adoption. However, from the current market share and the market trend over the last couple of years, it is very reasonable to assume that the majority of cell phones will be equipped with Bluetooth capability within the coming few years.

References

1. Cutrell, E., et al.: Notification, Disruption, and Memory: Effects of Messaging Interruptions on Memory and Performance. In: Proceedings of Interact (2001)
2. Kern, N., et al.: A model for human interruptability: experimental evaluation and automatic estimation from wearable sensors. In: Proceedings of IEEE International Symposium on Wearable Computers (2004)
3. Beale, R.: Supporting social interaction with the smartphone - designing pervasive systems. IEEE Pervasive Computing 4(2) (2005)
4. Eagle, N., et al.: Social Serendipity: Mobilizing Social Software. IEEE Pervasive Computing 4(2) (2005)

Augmented Interactions: A Framework for Adding Expressive Power to GUI Widgets

Jared Cechanowicz and Carl Gutwin

Department of Computer Science, University of Saskatchewan
110 Science Place, Saskatoon, Canada, S7N 5C9
{jared.cechanowicz,carl.gutwin}@usask.ca

Abstract. The basic elements of WIMP interfaces have proven to be robust components for building interactive systems, but these standard interactors also have limitations. On many occasions, researchers have introduced augmented GUI elements that are capable of more expressive interactions and that are better suited to user tasks. Although many of these novel designs have been effective, augmented interactors are still invented in an ad-hoc fashion, and there is no systematic way of thinking about or designing augmentations. As a result, there is little understanding of the principles underlying augmentation, the relationships between different designs, or the possibilities for creating new interactors. In this paper we present a framework that specifies elemental interactions with WIMP components and identifies the possible ways in which augmentations can occur. We show the explanatory and generative power of the framework by analysing existing and novel augmented interactions.

1 Introduction

The basic interactors of Windows-Icons-Menus-Pointer (WIMP) interfaces have proven over many years to be a robust and successful set of building blocks for developing interactive systems. As a result, the past 30 years have seen the standard desktop graphical user interface (GUI) change very little. While designs based on this model have been successful, a number of flaws have been identified (e.g., [2,4,16]). For example, desktop interfaces often require a large number of GUI widgets, with each widget mapped to a single system command. As a result, higher-level tasks like navigating and searching are not well supported, requiring that the user activate multiple controls, or manipulate a single control multiple times.

Numerous new controls, augmented controls, and novel interaction techniques have been developed that perform common desktop tasks better than standard WIMP interactors (e.g., [1,5,8,9,11,15,19,20,28]). As well, a number of augmented interactions that address WIMP limitations have been adopted as standard GUI idioms. For example, double-clicking is an augmentation of the basic click selection action, making use of a timeout period to increase the number of states that can be specified by the user; similarly, Shift-clicking is an augmentation that uses a key press to add a second mode to basic selection. Researchers have also introduced numerous augmentations, often based on an existing interaction or GUI widget. For example, OrthoZoom [1] is an augmented scroll thumb that uses the unused horizontal dimension of mouse movement to control

T. Gross et al. (Eds.): INTERACT 2009, Part I, LNCS 5726, pp. 878–891, 2009.

document zoom while the scroll thumb is activated. By enabling zooming as well as scrolling, higher-level navigation tasks are supported, and switching between separate scrolling and zooming widgets is no longer required. This augmentation, and others like it, have been shown to provide numerous benefits, including increases in user performance, better fit to high-level user tasks, and reduction in unnecessary screen clutter.

Although many different augmentations have been proposed, the design of these augmentations has most often been carried out in an ad-hoc fashion, and has usually focused on solving a particular interaction problem for a particular task. As a result, there is no standardized way of designing augmentations, and no way for designers to analyze or discuss the principles underlying an augmentation, relationships between different designs, or different design possibilities for creating new interactions.

In this paper we present a framework that is intended to provide this foundation for designers of augmented interactions. The framework identifies the core elements of an interaction in a WIMP interface, identifies the action primitives that can be used in an interaction, and specifies the types of augmentation that can be contemplated. The framework sets augmented interactions into a context of user tasks at the high level, and characteristics of input devices at the low level. The framework has both explanatory and generative power. We analyse and characterize several existing augmentations using the language and principles of the framework, and also use it to generate new augmented interactions that have not been seen before. The contributions of this work are: first, the idea that augmented interactions follow standard underlying principles; second, the framework that gathers these principles together in a form that is useful to designers; and third, a demonstration of the framework's power through several example designs. Our work shows that an understanding of the principles underlying augmented interaction can be a useful design tool, and can aid in the evolution of the GUI.

2 A Framework for Augmented Interaction

In order to simplify the process of designing augmented interactions for WIMP interfaces, we present a conceptual framework that is based on a high-level view of a user's interaction with a GUI. The framework has at its core the idea of an *interaction*, which we define as a combination of an *object* in the interface with one or more *actions*, each of which have a characteristic degree of freedom. Interactions are undertaken in service of a user *task*, and are supported by *input mechanisms* that provide the actual input data. In the following sections we describe each part of the framework in more detail, starting with the idea of an interaction.

2.1 Interaction: Object + Actions

A WIMP interaction can be defined as a user's manipulation of an on-screen entity. We formalize this with the concepts of the GUI *object* and the interface *action*; therefore, an interaction can be specified as one or more actions applied to an object.

WIMP Objects: Data and Controls

An object is an entity in a WIMP interface that has a visible representation. There are two basic object types in WIMP based GUIs: data objects and controls.

Data objects are the visual representations of the data of interest: icons in a file explorer, text and links in a web browser, or custom objects in a visual workspace.

Controls are graphical instruments that allow manipulation of data [2]. Since controls lie between the user's actions and the actual data, they are indirect instruments in a GUI. Traditional widgets such as buttons and sliders are the most common examples of controls; however, some types of data objects can also be given control capabilities (such as the links on a web page, which act both as data on the page, and as buttons that invoke navigation actions).

Actions in WIMP interfaces

Actions are the manipulations that are possible with a data object or control, and can be characterized by the degrees of freedom of the data that is being manipulated.

- *1D-Discrete*. The action is used to specify one of multiple states. For example, clicking on an icon in a file browser implies specifying which of two states the icon is in. 1D-D actions are often implemented with two-state devices such as mouse buttons, but devices with more than two states can also be employed [30].
- *1D-Continuous*. These actions allow specification of a single continuous value. For example, scrolling a document in one dimension is a 1D-continuous action. 1D-C actions can receive input from devices that are one-dimensional, but can also use a single dimension of a more powerful device (e.g., 1D scrolling using a 2D mouse).
- *2D-Continuous*. These actions allow simultaneous specification of two continuous values. An example action is 2D movement of a cursor; input is commonly received from any of several 2D pointing devices.
- *Higher-dimensional actions*. 3D and higher-degree actions are needed in some applications. However, they are not common in WIMP interfaces, and we do not consider these actions further, other to note that there are a number of high-degree-of-freedom input devices whose extra dimensions could be used in the augmentations described below.

Higher-level manipulations can be specified using these action primitives. For example, the common idiom of *dragging* can be characterized as an interaction made up of two actions: a 1D-D action (to select the object) plus a 2D-C action (to move it across the screen). Similarly, the idiom of 'Shift-clicking' can be characterized as a combination of two 1D-D actions: one for the shift, and one for the click.

2.2 Augmentation

An augmentation is a modification that is made to an action to increase expressive power; we identify several possible augmentations.

- *Adding states to a 1D-Discrete action*. A simple augmentation involves increasing the number of states that are possible for an interaction: for example, adding a state to an on-screen button changes it from a two-state widget to a three-state widget (e.g., pop-through buttons [30]).
- *Adding a 1D-Discrete action to an existing action*. Adding a discrete dimension to an existing action allows a multiplication of the expressiveness of the original – essentially adding modes to the interaction. Examples include common techniques such as Shift-clicking or Control-dragging, as well as research techniques such as Pressure Marks [26], which changes drag behaviour based on pressure level.

- *'Upgrading' a 1D-Discrete action to 1D-Continuous.* This allows the conversion of state-based manipulations to continuous manipulation. For example, a scroll button uses a 1D-D action; changing to a 1D-C action allows the scroll button to support variable-rate scrolling [2], given an appropriate 1D-C input source.
- *Adding a 1D-Continuous action to a 1D-Discrete action.* This augmentation can allow a continuous-value specification at the same time as a discrete selection. For example, Benko and colleagues developed techniques for continuous parameter control using finger position on a multitouch screen with bi-manual interactions [5].
- *Adding a secondary 1D-Continuous action.* Multiple dimensions can be controlled simultaneously with the addition of other 1D-C actions. For example, OrthoZoom [1] adds support for zooming (a secondary 1D-C action) to an existing 1D-C action (scrolling). Note that adding a second 1D-C action need not convert the interaction to a true 2D manipulation (e.g. horizontal and vertical scrolling); rather, it can remain a composite of two 1D manipulations [20] (as with OrthoZoom).
- *Adding a 1D-Continuous action to a 2D-Continuous action.* There are many ways that 2D movement can be augmented with an additional degree of freedom. For example, 1D-C pressure sensitivity is already used to control line thickness in many Tablet PC applications; pressure has also been used to control cursor size [26] and zoom during 2D pointer movement [23].
- *Adding a 2D-Continuous action to a 2D-Continuous action.* These augmentations add a second 2D capability to an interaction. Current examples generally involve the addition of a second 2D position controller – as seen in multi-touch displays which allow multiple fingers to simultaneously move, rotate, and scale objects.

As stated earlier, an interaction is made up of a GUI object and a set of actions. By adding to or modifying the actions related to an object, extra dimensions are added to the interaction which must be controlled by some input mechanism. In the following section we discuss input mechanisms as they relate to actions, and later discuss some additional rules for pairing input mechanisms and actions.

2.3 Input Mechanisms

Although a variety of input mechanisms can be used to control augmented actions, not every device is suited to every action, and choosing appropriate input is more complex than simply pairing devices and actions by the dimensions they control. The following paragraphs set out some of the issues in matching input device to actions.

Input Mechanism Properties

The properties of the input mechanism can guide the pairing of input mechanism and action, and here we highlight five properties that have been identified in previous research on input issues (e.g., [14,16,17]).

- *Physical Property Sensed.* Common properties sensed by input devices include position and force. Positional devices generally map best to positional tasks, and force has traditionally been used as a mapping for rate [14,17]. However, exceptions can be found: the mouse is used for rate control in Microsoft Windows, and pressure has been used for single-DoF positional control [7,22].

- *Absolute vs. Relative Mapping*. Absolute devices like sliders, and pressure sensors have a fixed 'zero' location, whereas a mouse and scroll wheel only sense relative movements. Relative devices are advantageous because they can be mapped to very large virtual spaces; however, they also require clutching. Absolute devices are best mapped to finite virtual spaces [17].
- *Continuous vs. Discrete Input*. Continuous devices like mice, foot pedals and pressure sensors map best to continuous tasks, but can also be quantized depending on the desired granularity [14]. Discrete devices provide the user with physical affordances, such as mechanical clicks and detents.
- *Reflexivity*. This is a property of absolute force-sensing devices like pressure sensors and isometric joysticks; these devices return to their zero position when released by the user. Reflexive devices avoid the 'nulling' problem [6] that can occur when an action is begun with the device not 'zeroed'.
- *Bi-directionality*. This is a property of relative devices like mice and scroll wheels; input can be specified as both positive and negative along a single axis. Some absolute devices have implemented bi-directionality by including a mode switch [25], or a second sensor [7].

Sources of Input

Depending on the properties of the action that must be supported, a number of input devices may be suitable for controlling the action. In situations where additional devices are impractical to add to the system, other input schemes can be employed. We have identified five ways that additional input capability can be obtained:

- *Overload the existing input capability with modes*. In this scheme, a discrete DoF facilitates a mode switch for another input. For example, holding down a modifier key (such as Shift or Control) could change the behavior of continuous actions (e.g., scrolling pages instead of lines with the scroll wheel) or discrete actions (e.g., open a link in a new tab instead of in the current window). FlowMenu [10] for example makes use of modes to increase the input capabilities of a stylus.
- *Use time as a DoF*. In this scheme time is used as a DoF. Time can be quantized and used to indicate discrete actions (e.g., 'hover help' activates after a time delay), as a continuous parameter for acceleration functions (e.g., scrolling accelerates the longer a scroll button is activated), and for mode switching (e.g., the difference between two clicks and a double-click). Time is commonly used in WIMP interfaces, and many gestural input systems use time as a DoF.
- *Use constraints*. In this scheme constraints are added to an interaction in order to create more complex behavior. For example, Kruger and colleagues [20] developed a constraint-based system called RotateNTranslate that allowed rotation to be calculated automatically from translation information. Similarly, Speed-Dependent Automatic Zooming calculates zoom level from the user's scrolling speed [15].
- *Leverage unused degrees of freedom*. In this scheme an unused DoF in the input device is used to control the augmented action. For example, Zliding [25] utilizes the unused pressure DoF to control zooming while sliding or scrolling with a stylus.
- *Add new degrees of freedom*. A final approach is to add new input capabilities to the input device to provide the needed degrees of freedom. Some upgrades take an existing device and transform it into a higher DoF device, as with the 6DoF VideoMouse [13]. Other upgrades to devices come in the form of independent input

devices, as with pressure augmented mice [7] and the addition of the scroll wheel. Degrees of freedom can also be added to a system through independent modalities, including gaze [21], bimanual input [19] or continuous voice input [11].

At a minimum, an input mechanism must meet the dimension requirements of the interaction. However, higher-dimension input can be used for lower-dimension actions: for example, 1D-Continuous input could be quantized to provide a 1D-Discrete action, as frequently occurs when time is used as an input dimension.

2.4 User Task

Although specific tasks for augmented interactions will vary, there are several general reasons for wanting additional expressiveness during an interaction. We have identified four in particular:

- *Integrate interactions that make sense together or are part of a higher level task.* In some situations, additional tasks can be naturally combined with existing tasks. For example, scrolling and zooming are naturally combined into a navigation interaction [1,15], as are rotation and translation [20].
- '*Working with your hands full.*' In some cases it is important to provide alternate mechanisms for interaction when a primary mechanism is in use. For example, 'spring-loaded folders' allow users to open folders while dragging a file.
- *Integrate multiple single actions into a continuous control.* Frequent and repetitive single actions can often be reconsidered as continuous manipulations; for example, multiple presses of a 'Back' button could be converted into a multi-level 'Reach Back' button that goes back a variable distance. Ramos and colleagues' Pressure Widgets provide a similar interaction [24].
- *Allow richer input.* There are several situations where additional expressiveness could allow users to be more judicious in the execution of their tasks. Different types of richness include being able to express variable levels of selection (e.g., 'lightly selected,' 'strongly selected'), express variable levels of confidence in an action [8], or choose variable levels of preview. Many real-world examples exist – such as the way that the volume of a spoken command reflects its urgency: "open the door" versus "OPEN THE DOOR."

2.5 Augmentation Guidelines

The process of creating an augmented interaction, then, involves first identifying the action primitives that currently exist in the interaction of interest, augmenting the actions, and choosing input mechanisms for controlling those actions. The framework makes it possible to consider augmentations as the application of simple changes to existing primitives, but the task that the interaction supports determines whether an augmentation is useful or needed.

In addition, although any number of augmented interactions are possible, not all augmentations would be effective or useful. When designing an augmented interaction, one can begin by describing the existing interaction in terms of the framework components: object, action(s), user task and input mechanism. By analyzing the interaction in terms of its parts, possible augmentations may reveal themselves. Comparing two similar augmented interactions in this manner can also reveal strengths and weaknesses in their respective designs, and potentially identify the more promising design. We have identified several issues that designers should consider when assessing the potential value of an augmented interaction:

- *Leverage natural mappings.* How a device is used can sometimes map naturally to the interaction itself. For instance, the rotation dimension of a Polhemus tracker maps easily to the rotation of an object, stylus hover maps to layers above the surface [9], and multi-state buttons can be used to indicate definiteness and confidence [8]. In addition, the direction of movement of the device and on-screen object / feedback should be compatible if possible [2].
- *Higher DoF is not always better.* Higher DoF actions can be useful in some situations, but troublesome in others. For instance, 2D drawing is accomplished with a mouse or stylus, but drawing a straight line (1D drawing) is difficult. As a result, programs include modes for locking an input dimension (holding Shift allows straight lines to be drawn). Even if the extra dimensions of the device are not used, a device that matches the degrees of freedom of the action is better suited to the task [2,16] (a 2D mouse performs better than a 6DoF device or two 1DoF devices in 2D pointing tasks).
- *Combine closely related interactions.* Some object parameters are naturally related (e.g. size and position, rotation and position) and suited to being combined in a single interaction [16]. OrthoZoom [1] and SDAZ [15] combine scrolling and zooming which are both important to navigating and reading documents.
- *Integrality vs. Separability.* When choosing an input mechanism, it may be unclear whether a higher-DoF device or two lower-DoF devices are more suitable. The principles of Integrality and Separability can assist when making this decision. Tightly coupled properties (e.g. size and position) are best controlled with a single high DoF input device, while separable properties (e.g. size and hue) are best controlled with two separate lower DoF devices [16].
- *Feedback.* All interactions should provide some form of feedback related to the state of the input device controlling the action. Some absolute devices, like foot pedals and sliders, already give some feedback to the user (both visually and through proprioception); however, visual feedback presented on or near the augmented GUI object is also important since the user's visual attention is on the object at the time of activation. Visual feedback is particularly important for pressure sensing devices [7,24]. Feedback through other modalities such as haptics [22] and pseudo-haptics [23] has proven useful in some cases for promoting user awareness of GUI objects.

3 Examples Using the Framework

In order to show the generality, expressive power, and generative capabilities of the framework, this section characterizes several augmented interactions using the concepts described above. We start with interactions that are commonly known in many GUIs, then characterize augmentations that have appeared in research literature, and finally present two interactions that are novel. These examples show that the framework is able to summarize a very wide range of existing augmentations, allowing them to be compared and discussed at an abstract level. In addition, the final examples show that the framework is valuable in the design of new augmentations.

3.1 Characterizing Common Augmented Interactions with the Framework

Here we look at two kinds of common augmented interactions: those using a keypress as a mode switch, and those using a time threshold to trigger enhanced behaviour.

Shift-clicking adds a mode to an existing selection action. The original action is a 1D-Discrete selection (often using the two states of the mouse button as input), and the augmentation uses a keyboard key, also a 1D-Discrete input device with two states: these two states imply two modes for the selection. (Users generally do not think of ordinary clicking as a mode, but *not* pressing the Shift key just means that the key is in its home state). Augmenting a selection action with Shift mirrors the key's original use as a single-mode augmentation of other keyboard actions (i.e., to provide capitals), but if the original action is carried out with an input device like the mouse, any key on the keyboard can be used as the augmentation input (as has been seen with variations such as Control-click or Alt-click; versions such as 'A'-click or 'B'-click are also possible, as long as these keys are not being used for text input).

Shift-dragging uses the same augmentation as shift-clicking, but with a different base action – dragging an object with the 2D-Continuous pointing device. The additional mode is often used to restrict the degrees of freedom of the base action from two dimensions to one – for example, limiting translation to use only horizontal or vertical movement. The augmentation can, of course, be used to increase capability rather than to restrict – for example, some pixel drawing programs use Shift-dragging to switch temporarily to the eraser tool.

Double-clicking is an augmentation of a single-click selection action (a 1D-Discrete action using the mouse button as an input device). The augmentation uses a second single click, separated with a time threshold (a 1D continuous input, discretized into two regions). This augmentation strategy provides a simple unary specification system, and can be extended: for example, triple-clicking is used in many applications (such as the Firefox browser), and higher numbers are possible.

Hover help augmentations also use time as the input mechanism. The base action is made up of two constraints – that the pointer (controlled by a 2D-Continuous input device) does not move, and that the pointer is located over a help-sensitive object. The time augmentation controls the appearance of the help balloon, which pops up if the pointer is held motionless for a certain time threshold (a 1D-Discrete action).

Spring-loaded folders are another 1D-Discrete augmentation using time as the input mechanism. Spring loading allows a user to open a folder in a file browser without releasing the mouse button, and is an example of the 'working with your hands full' user task (see §2.4 above) that can be seen in standard file browsers in Macintosh OS/X and Windows Vista. The base action is a 2D-Continuous drag operation, with the added constraint that the pointer stops over a closed folder icon. The augmentation is a 1D-Discrete time threshold (as with hover help); once the threshold is reached, the folder under the pointer opens automatically. Using spring-loaded folders, however, reveals a usability issue when time is used as an extra DoF: setting an appropriate time threshold can be difficult, and folders can open too quickly (e.g., while the user is still reading the folder name or deciding whether this is the correct choice). The problem arises because time does not explicitly indicate user intention, and is often used for other purposes (such as reading the folder name). The framework's characterization of this interaction makes it clear that several other 1D-Discrete input mechanisms could be used instead of a time threshold; thus, the usability problem could be solved by using a mechanism that has a more explicit action that can be better interpreted as user intention (e.g., a keyboard key, or the secondary mouse button).

3.2 Characterizing Augmentations Proposed in Previous Research

Here we analyse several augmented interactions that have been proposed or evaluated in previous research literature. The framework allows characterization of a wide range of different designs, and also allows simple comparison of similar techniques.

Rate-controlled scroll buttons. Ordinary scroll buttons are widgets that control scrolling for a single axis of a document; clicking the button scrolls by one line, and holding the button scrolls at a fixed rate. The base action, therefore, is a simple 1D-Discrete action (selecting the widget with a two-state input device like a mouse button). The fixed scroll rate, however, is often not optimal for the user's task. To increase the expressiveness of the control, researchers have proposed augmenting scroll buttons to allow the user to control the scroll rate. This involves adding a 1D-Continuous action to specify the rate. There are several 1D-Continuous input mechanisms that can be used for this action: previous researchers have suggested a pressure sensor [3,24], but others are also possible, including pointer distance from the widget, or dwell time on the widget.

Combined zooming and scrolling. Researchers have invented techniques for controlling scrolling and zooming at the same time. In the OrthoZoom technique [1], one dimension of the 2D pointer controls document location (i.e., normal scrolling with the scroll thumb), and the other dimension (which is unused during scrolling) controls zoom level. In the Zliding technique [25], zooming with a pressure sensor augments ordinary scrolling. In these techniques, the base action of scrolling is a 1D-Continuous action on the scroll-thumb widget, and the augmentation adds a second 1D-Continuous action (the orthogonal dimension of the pointer or the pressure sensor) to control zoom. A third design that combines zooming and scrolling, but one that does not put zoom level under user control, is Speed-Dependent Automatic Zooming (SDAZ) [15]. In this technique, the zoom level is automatically calculated from the scrolling speed; although the augmentation still uses a 1D-Continuous action, there is no user control and the manipulation of the DoF happens entirely within the system.

Pop-through mouse buttons are a hardware augmentation of regular mouse buttons [30] that provide a second button click beneath the normal click mechanism. This converts a mouse button from a 1D-Discrete input device with two states, to one with three states (up, first click, second click). Pop-through buttons provide a novel input mechanism to match the addition of a 1D-Discrete action on an existing 1D-Discrete mouse-click-based action (such as the augmentation used in spring-loaded folders).

Bi-manual input. Several researchers have explored techniques that use two hands for input. For example, the non-dominant hand can control panning (a 2D-Continuous action), while the dominant hand performs detailed operations with the mouse [19]. Bimanual panning is an example of an augmentation that happens at the level of the workspace itself, and operates as a general capability that can occur along with any other operation (i.e., it is not specific to a particular interaction technique or widget).

Non-speech voice input has been suggested as a way to enrich standard desktop interactions. For example, Harada *et al* demonstrate 'Voicepen,' a drawing tool in which parameters such as line width or opacity are continuously controlled by the pitch or loudness of the user's voice [11]. The base action in this example (line drawing) is a 2D-Continuous action; the augmentations are separate 1D-Continuous inputs that control the different line parameters. The motivation for the augmentation is to increase the expressivity of standard drawing. This example is a good illustration of how the framework can assist designers with the comparison and evaluation of novel interactions. In the case of Voicepen, the framework's characterization suggests that the new input modality of non-speech vocalization could be compared to more traditional 1D-Continuous input mechanisms such as a slider or a mouse wheel.

3.3 Characterizing Novel Augmentations

To show the framework's value in helping designers explore new regions of design space, here we present two novel augmented interactions: one that allows users to control the size and detail of object previews, and one that allows users to specify an action with different degrees of confidence.

Variable-size previews. In this example, we show how the framework helped identify design opportunities in presenting richer previews (adding a 1D-Continuous action to control preview detail). Ordinary web links and icons represent underlying data, but do not fully describe it: for example, a file icon shows the type and name of a file, but not its contents; hyperlinks show even less, often indicating only that a link exists. To provide more information, some kinds of data objects provide previews of their content; however, these previews are usually provided at a single fixed size. We augmented the preview capabilities of ordinary object selection (a 1D-Discrete base action) to provide user control over preview size (Figure 1). This allows the user to select how much preview information is appropriate. We implemented this augmentation with a pressure-sensitive mouse; as the user presses harder on the button, additional detail is provided through a thumbnail image and a status-bar display. Pressure is a 1D-Continuous input mechanism, and matches the nature of the input action (i.e., requesting variable detail of preview). Other input mechanisms are also possible for this augmentation (e.g., a scroll wheel), but pressure maps well to an abstract idea like user interest [8], providing a natural mapping for the interaction.

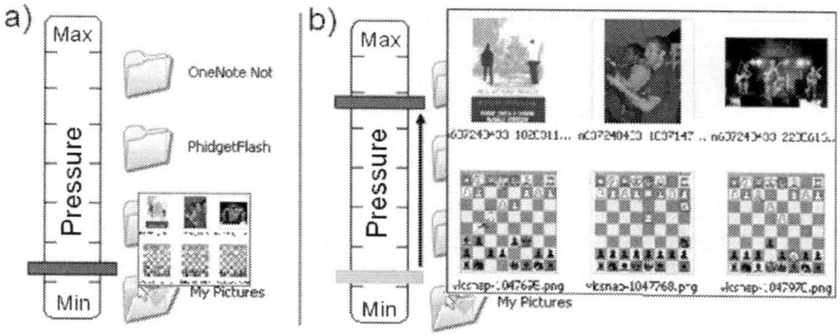

Fig. 1. a) Variable preview of a file folder. b) As pressure increases, thumbnail size increases.

Rich activations. Our second novel example involves the enrichment of user capabilities in a file explorer, through 1D-Discrete augmentations. Some actions in GUIs are possibly dangerous, such as opening system folders, or downloading items from the web that have been identified as potentially harmful. User preferences and system security settings often require that users confirm such activations through a confirmation dialog box, or may even require that users activate several menus to alter their preferences or security settings. This can result in user frustration, especially when a user's task is interrupted and when objects that the user knows are safe have been marked as potentially harmful. We augmented these activation actions with a 'degree of confidence' parameter that allows users to avoid unneeded confirmation dialogs. We used pressure for this new parameter's input, since pressure can be quantized into several different levels, and since (as described above) pressure maps well to degree of interest or confidence. With this augmentation, system folders can be opened without the dialog if the user applies pressure beyond a fixed threshold (Figure 2). Similarly, the user's confidence in activating web content can be communicated to the system through either a hard or a soft press of the mouse button.

This augmentation can also be applied to drag-and-drop operations (Figure 3). In this technique, the user can place content into a folder with a variable degree of confidence: for example, a user could drop a music file into a 'video only' folder by pressing harder before the drop action.

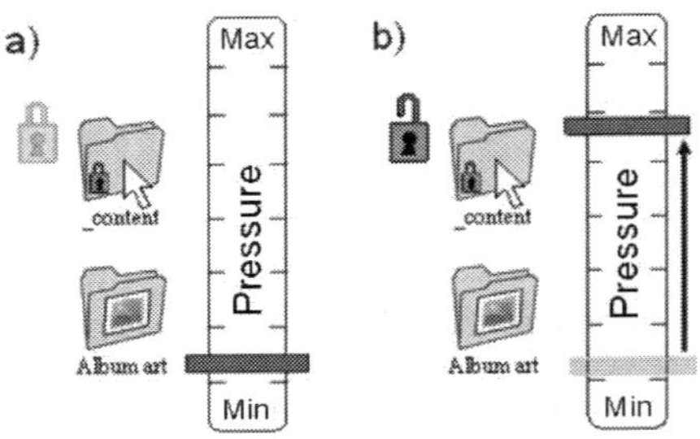

Fig. 2. a) A secure folder that requires enhanced activation. b) With enough pressure, the folder opens.

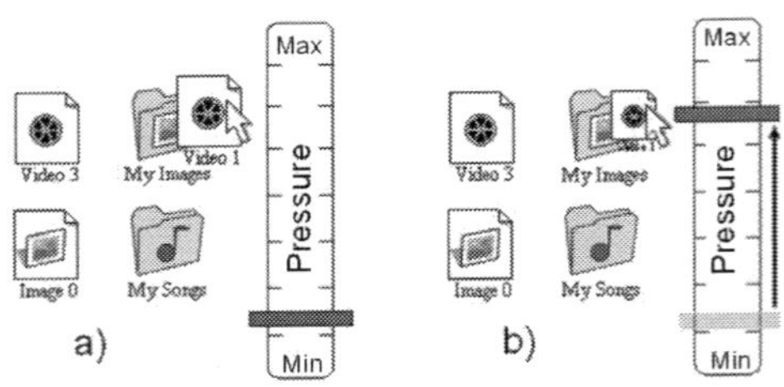

Fig. 3. a) The folder is set to only accept image files. b) With additional pressure, the icon shows that the defaults are overridden.

4 Discussion

Here we discuss the relationship of our framework to other formalisms and models of interface development, and comment on issues related to the design and use of augmented interactions more generally.

First, a number of other models exist for designing and developing interactions, including Direct Manipulation [29], Instrumental Interaction [2], and Reality-Based Interaction [18]. In addition, formalisms exist for specifying and notating interactions: for example, Buxton's three-state model [6] or the User Action Notation (UAN) [12].

Our augmented interactions framework is not meant to replace other design models; rather it is a tool for comparing and designing interactions that are developed in the context of other interaction models. Although we have presented this framework in the context of WIMP interfaces, the ideas can easily be applied to other interface-design paradigms. For example, an interface like CPN/Tools [3] does not include scroll bars, pull-down menus, or the notion of selection (instead, it includes a number of post-WIMP interactors like toolglasses, marking menus and floating palettes, as well as elements of direct manipulation). However, the augmented interactions framework could still be employed within this context: toolglasses could include multiple modes, or their size could be modifiable with an augmented interaction; floating palettes include buttons that could be augmented; and the direct manipulation actions in this interface could also be augmented using our approach.

The main contribution of our framework is that it looks explicitly at the issue of augmenting interaction, which extends what other formalisms are intended to do. For example, Buxton's three-state model can characterize and notate existing interactions, but does not set out what is possible for augmentation. Similarly, UAN is a notation for what does occur rather than a specification of what is possible; that is, a statement of action with a design rather than specification of the design space for a particular interactor. We note, however, that Buxton's model or UAN could be paired with our framework as notation.

Second, our experiences with augmented interactions suggest several questions regarding wider-scale deployment of these new techniques.

Will input hardware support the new designs? Additional degrees of freedom are gradually being added to input devices: scroll wheels are now standard, and commercial devices such as the IBM ScrollPoint mouse and the Xbox 360 controller support pressure input. Devices like isometric joysticks, pressure sensors, and multi-touch screens are widely available. As more powerful input devices become more readily available, more applications can make use of their capabilities.

Will new designs break existing interaction styles? One advantage of the framework is that it allows an augmentation to be broken into components so that designers can consider whether new actions can be supported with existing input devices. As shown in the examples, many augmentations can be designed such that the original interaction is preserved, and the augmentation can be used optionally (like a shortcut) by those who wish to do so.

Is the framework 'just for shortcuts'? Although shortcuts are a common modification, it is clear from the examples given above that the framework is able to characterize more than simply shortcuts. For example, adding rate control to a scroll button (a 1D-Continuous augmentation to a 1D-Discrete action) provides a degree of control over scrolling that was not possible before; similarly, the ability to represent combined actions (such as scrolling and zooming) shows that the framework can help designers think about higher-level design ideas such as the integration of different kinds of behaviour in the same control.

5 Conclusions and Future Work

Augmentations to standard GUI interactions are now becoming common, both in research literature and commercial products; however, most augmentations are designed in an ad-hoc fashion. We presented a framework for understanding and designing augmented GUI interactions that can aid in comparing, evaluating, and building GUI augmentations. The framework is able to categorize and describe a wide range of previously developed augmented interactions. We also presented augmentations that are novel, showing the power of the framework to help in the exploration of design space and in the identification of new design opportunities.

Our work in the area of augmented interactions will continue in three ways. First, further development and refinement of the framework will add detail to the basic dimensions described here. Second, quantitative evaluations of some of our designs will be carried out to measure the benefit of various augmentations and to test the comparative power of the framework. Third, we will explore possibilities in toolkit support for augmented interactions, so that designers can quickly and easily include augmented interactions in new applications, and also retrofit existing systems.

References

1. Appert, C., Fekete, J.: OrthoZoom scroller: 1D multi-scale navigation. In: ACM Human Factors in Computing Systems, pp. 21–30 (2006)
2. Beaudouin-Lafon, M.: Instrumental interaction: an interaction model for designing post-WIMP user interfaces. In: ACM Human Factors in Computing Systems, pp. 446–453 (2000)
3. Beaudouin-Lafon, M., Lassen, H.: The Architecture and Implementation of CPN2000, a Post-WIMP Graphical Application. In: ACM Symposium on User Interface Software and Technology, pp. 181–190 (2000)
4. Beaudouin-Lafon, M.: Designing interaction, not interfaces. In: ACM Advanced Visual Interfaces, pp. 15–22 (2004)
5. Benko, H., Wilson, A.D., Baudisch, P.: Precise selection techniques for multi-touch screens. In: ACM Human Factors in Computing Systems, pp. 1263–1272 (2006)
6. Buxton, W.: Lexical and pragmatic considerations of input structures. ACM Comput. Graph. 17(1), 31–37 (1983)
7. Cechanowicz, J., Irani, P., Subramanian, S.: Augmenting the mouse with pressure sensitive input. In: ACM Human Factors in Computing Systems, pp. 1385–1394 (2007)
8. Forlines, C., Shen, C., Buxton, B.: Glimpse: a novel input model for multi-level devices. In: ACM Human Factors in Computing Systems, pp. 1375–1378 (2005)
9. Grossman, T., Hinckley, K., Baudisch, P., Agrawala, M., Balakrishnan, R.: Hover widgets: using the tracking state to extend the capabilities of pen-operated devices. In: ACM Human Factors in Computing Systems, pp. 861–870 (2006)
10. Guimbretiére, F., Winograd, T.: FlowMenu: combining command, text, and data entry. In: ACM User Interface Software and Technology, pp. 213–216 (2000)
11. Harada, S., Saponas, T.S., Landay, J.A.: Voicepen: augmenting pen input with simultaneous non-linguistic vocalization. In: International Conference on Multimodal Interfaces, pp. 178–185 (2007)
12. Hartson, H., Siochi, A., Hix, D.: The UAN: A User-Oriented Representation for Direct Manipulation Interface Designs. ACM ToIS 8(3), 181–203 (1990)
13. Hinckley, K., Sinclair, M., Hanson, E., Szeliski, R., Conway, M.: The VideoMouse: a camera-based multi-degree-of-freedom input device. In: ACM User Interface Software and Technology, pp. 103–112 (1999)
14. Hinckley, K.: Input Technologies and Techniques. In: Sears, A., Jacko, J. (eds.) The Human-Computer Interaction Handbook, pp. 3–11. CRC Press, Boca Raton (2002)
15. Igarashi, T., Hinckley, K.: Speed-dependent automatic zooming for browsing large documents. In: ACM User Interface Software and Technology, pp. 139–148 (2000)

16. Jacob, R.J., Sibert, L.E., McFarlane, D.C., Mullen, M.P.: Integrality and separability of input devices. ACM ToCHI 1(1), 3–26 (1994)
17. Jacob, R.: The future of input devices. ACM Comput. Surv. 28(4), 138–159 (1996)
18. Jacob, R., Girouard, A., Hirshfield, L., Horn, M., Shaer, O., Solovey, E., Zigelbaum, J.: Reality-based interaction: a framework for post-WIMP interfaces. In: ACM Human Factors in Computing Systems, pp. 201–210 (2008)
19. Kabbash, P., Buxton, W., Sellen, A.: Two-handed input in a compound task. In: ACM Human Factors in Computing Systems, pp. 230–238 (1994)
20. Kruger, R., Carpendale, S., Scott, S., Tang, A.: Fluid integration of rotation and translation. In: ACM Human Factors in Computing Systems, pp. 601–610 (2005)
21. Lucas, J., Kim, J., Bowman, D.: Resizing beyond widgets: object resizing techniques for immersive virtual environments. In: ACM Human Factors in Computing Systems, pp. 1601–1604 (2005)
22. Miller, T., Zeleznik, R.: The design of 3D haptic widgets. In: ACM Interactive 3D Graphics, pp. 97–102 (1999)
23. Mandryk, R., Rodgers, M., Inkpen, K.: Sticky widgets: pseudo-haptic widget enhancements for multi-monitor displays. In: ACM Human Factors in Computing Systems, pp. 1621–1624 (2005)
24. Ramos, G., Boulos, M., Balakrishnan, R.: Pressure widgets. In: ACM Human Factors in Computing Systems, pp. 487–494 (2004)
25. Ramos, G., Balakrishnan, R.: Zliding: fluid zooming and sliding for high precision parameter manipulation. In: ACM User Interface Software and Technology, pp. 143–152 (2005)
26. Ramos, G.A., Balakrishnan, R.: Pressure marks. In: ACM Human Factors in Computing Systems, pp. 1375–1384 (2007)
27. Rekimoto, J., Schwesig, C.: PreSenseII: bi-directional touch and pressure sensing interactions with tactile feedback. In: ACM Human Factors in Computing Systems, pp. 1253–1258 (2006)
28. Ren, X., Ying, J., Zhao, S., Li, Y.: The Adaptive Hybrid Cursor: A Pressure-based Target Selection Technique for Pen-based Interfaces. In: IFIP Conference on Human-Computer Interaction, pp. 310–323 (2007)
29. Shneiderman, B.: Direct Manipulation: a Step Beyond Programming Languages. IEEE Computer 16(8), 57–69 (1983)
30. Zeleznik, R., Miller, T., Forsberg, A.: Pop-through mouse button interactions. In: ACM User Interface Software and Technology, pp. 195–196 (2001)

Model-Based Design of Multi-device Interactive Applications Based on Web Services

Fabio Paternò, Carmen Santoro, and Lucio Davide Spano

ISTI-CNR, HIIS Lab, Via Moruzzi 1,
56124 Pisa, Italy
{Fabio.Paterno,Carmen.Santoro,Lucio.Davide.Spano}@isti.cnr.it

Abstract. Creating an interactive application based on pre-existing functionalities poses a number of novel issues in the design process. We discuss a method and an associated model-based language, which aim to address such issues in multi-device contexts. One specific aspect of this method is the ability to obtain user interfaces for accessing multiple services. In addition, the possibility to specify interactive objects, Web services accesses and scripts allows designers to describe Rich Internet Applications as well.

Keywords: Model-Based Design, Multi-device Environments, User Interface Design, Web Services.

1 Introduction

Model-based approaches for UI design are characterised by the use of some representations (models) of the aspects that are supposed to be relevant in the UI software lifecycle. This involves the identification and representation of the characteristics that are meaningful at each design stage, and mainly highlights one of the most difficult parts of the work: identifying what characterizes a UI without having to deal with a plethora of low-level implementation details that can distract the designer from the most important issues. After having identified such characteristics, the next issue is specifying them through suitable languages that can enable simple integration within software environments, so as to facilitate the work of the designers.

The design of interactive multi-platform systems has further stimulated interest in model-based approaches in HCI. In the design and development of such systems the use of model-based approaches has revealed to be useful, especially through the capture and modelling of different levels of abstractions in which it is possible to gradually move from aspects that are technology-neutral to more concrete, platform-dependent detailed aspects. In such a way it is possible to start with a general abstract vocabulary and then obtain concrete languages for each type of platform by just refining the abstract language.

However, recently, the design of multi-platform systems has become even more challenging. Indeed, not only must the same interactive application be accessible from different devices within different contexts of use, but also the way in which such interactive applications are built/created has changed, since there is the need to reuse existing code to reduce development time and effort. An example of this can be seen

T. Gross et al. (Eds.): INTERACT 2009, Part I, LNCS 5726, pp. 892–905, 2009.

in the role that Web services are playing in the development of interactive applications. Indeed, the increasing availability of functional units within Web services has driven the need to develop methods that are able to exploit such pre-existing functionalities by including them into more composite interactive applications. In particular, some heterogeneous issues have to be faced by the designers in this case. First, the need to exploit some (generally small) legacy functionalities that were developed without accounting for human interaction, since they were basically intended to support computer-to-computer (service-to-service) communication. Therefore, the first issue is how to obtain the UI for such functionalities, possibly in a semi-automatic way, so that it can ease the designer's work. Secondly, even when a UI for such portions of functionalities is available, there is the issue of including and integrating pre-existing user interfaces associated with functionalities into new, composite ones, and possibly support the designer during such composition.

In the paper, after discussing some related work we describe the main features of our approach for designing user interfaces for Web services. We also introduce the dimensions of a design space for composing user interfaces in such context. Afterwards, we express the requirements that have driven the development of MARIA, an XML-based language for describing user interfaces at various abstraction levels. Then, we detail an example to show more concretely how the proposed approach is able to support the design of user interfaces for applications exploiting Web Services in multi-device environments. Lastly, some conclusions and directions for future work are provided.

2 Related Work

Several model-based approaches have been put forward in the field of multi-device UIs. A sign of the maturity of this area can be seen by the recent interest in defining connected international standards (e.g.: new W3C Group on Model-based User Interfaces: http://www.w3.org/2005/Incubator/model-based-ui/) and their adoption in industrial settings (e.g.: dedicated Working Group in the NESSI NEXOF-RA IP, http://www.nexof-ra.eu/).

In particular, a number of approaches have been proposed to support descriptions of logical user interfaces. UIML [1] was one of the first model-based languages targeting multi-device interfaces. It structures the user interface in: structure, style content, behavior. However, it has not been applied to obtain rich multimodal-user interfaces. XForms [http://www.w3.org/MarkUp/Forms/] is a W3C initiative, and represents a concrete example of how the research in model-based approaches has been incorporated into an industrial standard. XForms is an XML language for expressing the next generation of Web forms, through the use of abstractions to address new heterogeneous environments. The language includes both abstract and concrete descriptions (control vocabulary and constructs are described in abstract terms, while presentation attributes and data types in concrete terms). XForms supports the definition of a data layer within the form, and is mainly used for expressing form-based UIs, though it does not seem particularly suitable for supporting other interaction modalities, such as voice. UsiXML (USer Interface eXtensible Markup Language) [3] is an XML-compliant markup language, which aims to describe the UI for multiple contexts of use. UsiXML is decomposed into several meta-models describing different aspects of the UI. There is also a transformation model that is used to define model-to-model transformations. The authors use graph transformations to support model transformations, which is an interesting academic approach, albeit with some performance issues. TERESA XML [5] defines several abstraction levels for expressing the characteristics of a user interface. Among such levels, one (the concrete interface) is specified through a number of platform-dependent languages. These are refinements of the abstract level, which describes the user interface using a platform-neutral vocabulary: interactors (describing single interaction objects), composition operators (indicating how to compose interactors), presentations (indicating the elements that can be perceived at a given time). Various modalities are supported through this approach. However, it does not support data or event models.

One issue with such model-based approaches is that they have not sufficiently addressed the recent increasing trend in software design towards building atomic software components, called Web services, which are available in distributed settings. Thus, applications have to be assembled starting from such pre-existing building blocks. Especially for enterprises this offers several advantages in terms of code reuse, increase productivity and leveraging integration processes. Some work has been dedicated to the generation of user interfaces for Web services [7, 8] but without exploiting model-based approaches. Previously, there have been approaches investigating the possibility of automatic generation with model-based support for applications based on Web services [4]. but such approaches work well only with not too complex cases and when the application domain is well-known. In [9] there is a proposal to extend service descriptions with user interface information. For this purpose the WSDL description is converted to OWL-S format, which is combined with a hierarchical task model and a layout model. We follow a different approach, which aims to support the access to the WSDL without requiring its substantial modification in order to generate the corresponding user interfaces, still exploiting logical interface descriptions. Therefore, model-based approaches have to cope with further requirements. There is less need to design an application from scratch, but they have to support interactive application development starting with small functionalities (services) that are already available, even if these were not built with that particular application in mind. In addition, there is a need to access the same service through an increasing number of device types (in particular mobile) available in the mass market, sometimes able to exploit a variety of sensors (e.g. accelerometers, tilt sensors, electronic compass), localization technology (such as RFIDs, GPS) and interaction modalities (multi-touch, gestures, camera-based interaction). This has further urged the identification of suitable universal declarative languages able to address such composite number of aspects in a comprehensive specification.

3 The Approach

A top-down approach essentially consists in breaking down and progressively refining an overall system into its sub-systems, thus it is particularly effective when the design starts from scratch. In such cases the designer has an overall picture of the system to be designed and can refine it gradually, without any particular constraints.

However, when the designer wants to include already existing pieces of software as services, this necessarily requires that a bottom-up approach is considered in the design process in order to include and exploit not only such legacy, fine-grained functionalities, but also composite and higher level functionalities obtained by assembling the elementary ones. Therefore, the best option seems to be a *hybrid* solution in which a mix of bottom-up and top-down approaches is used.

Automatic or semi-automatic *composition* of user interfaces associated with various services is one important issue in this context. Indeed, the design and development of an interactive application based on pre-existing Web services is by definition driven by a composition-oriented approach. Not only must functionalities be composed (for this purpose various approaches already exist, e.g. BPEL, WS-BPEL) in order to provide arbitrarily complex functionalities, but also the corresponding user interface specifications associated with the elementary services (which can be provided through specific annotations) can be composed as well. In order to better understand how this composition activity can be carried out, we have identified a design space for this specific activity (see Figure 1).

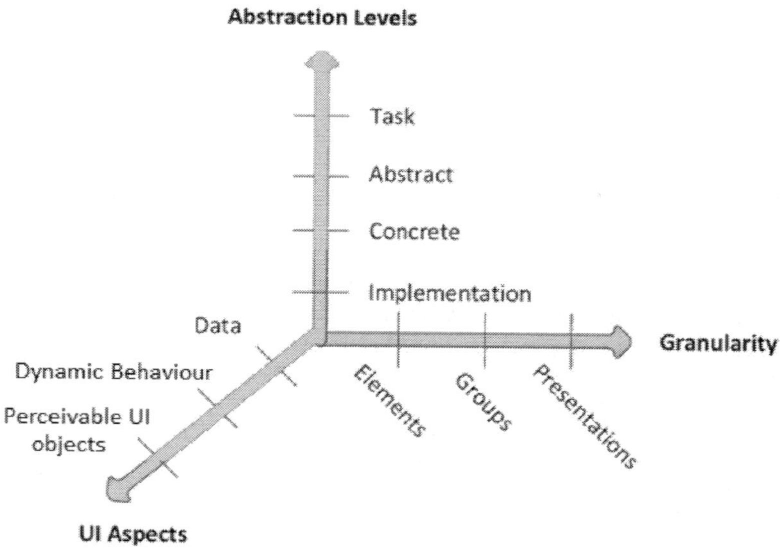

Fig. 1. The Design Space for UI Composition

Three main aspects have been identified as important in order to compose user interfaces: the abstraction level of the user interface description, the granularity of the user interface considered, and the types of aspects that are affected by the UI composition. Regarding the *abstraction level*, since a user interface can be described at various abstraction levels (task and objects, abstract, concrete, and implementation), it is straightforward that the user interface composition can occur at each of them. The *granularity* refers to the size of elements to be composed: indeed, we can compose single user interface elements (for example a selection object with an object for editing a value), groups of objects (for instance a navigation bar with a list of news), we can also compose various types of interface elements and groups to obtain an entire presentation, and we can compose presentations in order to obtain the user interface for an entire application. It is worth pointing out that by the term 'presentation' we refer to the set of user interface elements that can be perceived at a given time, a common example being a graphical Web page.

Lastly, we have to distinguish the compositions depending on the main *UI aspects* they affect, which are: i) the dynamic behaviour of the user interface, which means the possible dynamic sequencing of user actions and system feedback (e.g.: when some elements of the UI appear or disappear depending on some conditions); ii) the perceivable UI objects (for example in graphical user interface we have to indicate the spatial relationships among the composed elements); iii) the data that are manipulated by the user interface.

More specifically, in the proposed approach first a bottom-up step is envisaged, in order to analyse the Web services providing functionalities useful for the new application. We then specify the application task model in ConcurTaskTrees (CTT) [6], a standard de facto for task model specification (http://giove.isti.cnr.it/ctte.html).

The Web services can be seen as a particular type of task (system tasks, namely tasks whose performance is entirely allocated to the application), and the temporal relationships that are specified in a task model indicate how to compose such functionalities. The specification of the task model should be driven by the user requirements, and it also implies some constraints on how to express such model. Indeed, in order to address the right level of granularity, not only will a Web service be associated with an application task, but it is useful that each operation of the Web service be associated to a specific system task. Thus, if a Web service supports three operations, then there would be three basic system tasks, with the parent task being another application task (corresponding to the web service itself). Such system tasks are related to the user and interaction tasks in the overall task model.

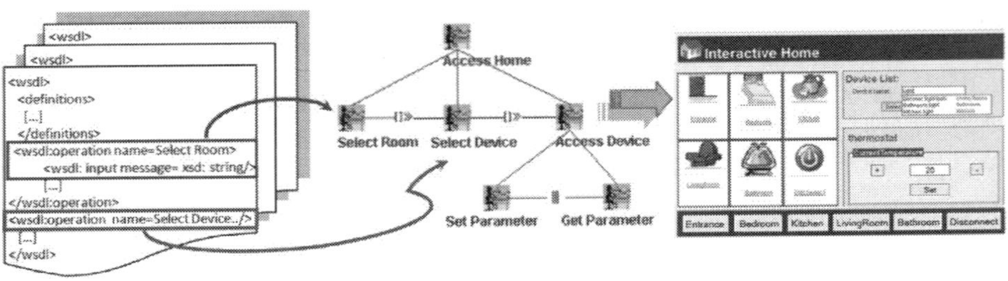

Fig. 2. The Approach

After having performed this step, we have obtained a level of composition, which also involves the functionalities associated with the Web services. The result is a structured model in which such functionalities have been progressively organised in a hierarchical task model, which includes system tasks associated with Web services and their operations. At this point, once we have obtained the task model it is possible (through a top-down step) to generate the various UI logical descriptions, and then refine them up to the implementation, by using the MARIA language (the final phase in Figure 2).

4 MARIA

Based on the lessons learned from the analysis of the state of the art and previous experiences conducted by various groups with TERESA (see [2] for a test in an industrial setting), we have identified a number of requirements for a new language suitable to support user interfaces in ubiquitous environments.

In particular, the following requirements have been identified for the new language:

- providing the designer with higher control of the user interface produced, also through an event model;
- a more flexible dialogue and navigation model, also supporting parallel interactions;
- a flexible data model, which allows the association of various types of data to the various interactors;
- support for recent dynamic techniques, such as ajax scripts;
- streamlining the specifications of the abstract and concrete languages, in order to make the specifications shorter and more readable.

4.1 Main Features

A number of features have been included in the language:

a) *introduction of data model*

We have introduced an abstract description of the underlying data model of the user interface, needed for representing the data (types, values, etc.) handled by the user interface. Indeed, by means of defining an abstract data model, the interactors (the elements composing an abstract [concrete] user interface) can be bound to a specific type or an element of a type defined in the abstract [concrete] data model. The introduction of a data model also allows for more control over the admissible input that can be provided to the various interactors. In MARIA XML, the data model is described using the XSD type definition language. Therefore, the introduction of the data model can be useful for: doing some correlations between the values of interface elements (for instance, the value of one element can vary depending on the value of another element), conditional presentation connections (triggering the activation of a presentation depending on a certain value associated to an interactor), conditional layout of interface parts (showing or not a portion of a presentation depending on the value associated with a UI element), specifying the format of the input values (depending on the data type it is possible to specify a certain acceptable template for input values associated with that data type), application generation from the interface description (having information on the values associated with a UI description enables the actual generation of a working application).

b) *Introduction of an event model*

In addition, an event model has been introduced at different abstract/concrete levels of abstractions. The introduction of an event model allows for specifying at different abstraction levels how the user interface is able to respond to events triggered by the user. In MARIA XML two types of events have been introduced:

i) *Property change events*: events that change the status of some UI properties (e.g. when a user selects an element in a drop-down menu then the text label of a text field changes accordingly).

ii) *Activation events:* some interactors can raise events with the purpose of activating some application functionality (e.g. access to a database or to a web service).

c) *Support for Ajax scripts, which allow continuously updating of fields*
Another aspect that has been included in MARIA is the possibility of supporting continuously updating of fields at the abstract level. To this aim we have added an attribute to the interactors: continuosly-updated= "true"["false"]. At the concrete level more detail on this feature should be provided, depending on the technology used for the final UI (Ajax for web interfaces, callback for standalone application, etc.). For instance, with Ajax asynchronous mechanisms, there is a behind-the-scene communication between the client and the server about what has to be modified in the presentation, without an explicit request from the user. When it is necessary the client redraws the relevant part rather than redrawing the entire presentation from scratch.

d) *Dynamic set of user interface elements*
Another feature that has been included in MARIA XML is the possibility to express the need to dynamically change only a part of the UI. This has been specified in such a way to be able to affect both how the UI elements are arranged in a single presentation, and how it is possible to navigate between the different presentations. Therefore, the content of a presentation can dynamically change (this is also useful for supporting Ajax techniques). In addition, it is also possible to specify a dynamic behaviour that changes depending on specific conditions: this has been implemented thanks to the use of conditional connections between presentations.

In the next sections we provide a more detailed description of concepts/models that have been included in MARIA, both for the Abstract UI and the Concrete UI.

4.2 MARIA – Abstract Level

The advantage of using an abstract description of a user interface is that designers can reason in abstract terms without being tied to a particular platform/modality/ implementation language. In this way, they have the possibility to focus on the *semantic* of the interaction (namely: what the intended goal of the interaction is), regardless of the details and specificities of the particular environment considered. Figure 3 shows the main elements of the abstract user interface meta-model (some details have not been shown for readability reasons). An interface is composed of one data model and one or more presentations. The presentation includes a data model and a dialog model, which contains information about the events that can be triggered by the presentation in a given time. The dynamic behaviour of the events is specified using the CTT temporal operators. When an event occurs, it produces a set of effects (such as performing operations, calling services etc.) and can change the set of currently enabled events (e.g. an event occurring on an interactor can affect the behavior of another interactor, by e.g. disabling the availability of an event associated to another interactor). The dialog model can also be used to describe parallel interactions between the user and the interface. A *connection* indicates what the next active presentation will be when a given interaction is performed and it can be either an elementary connection, or a complex connection (when a Boolean operator composes several connections) or a conditional connection (when various conditions on connections are specified).

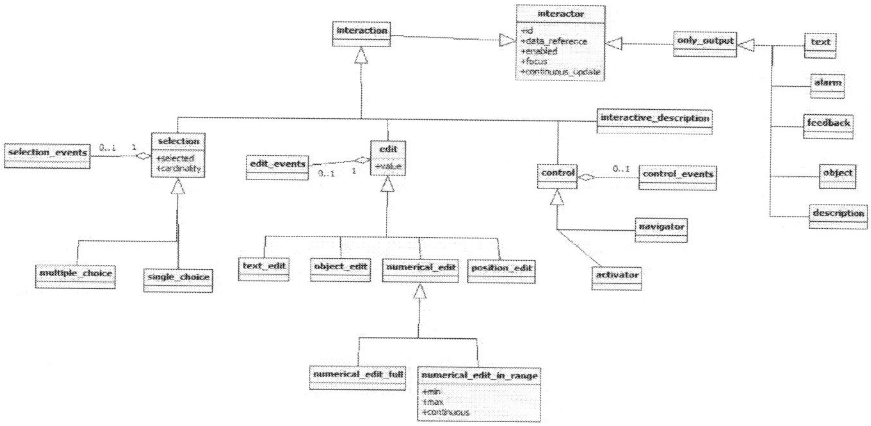

Fig. 3. An overview of the AUI metamodel

There are two types of *interactor composition*: *grouping* or *relation*, the latter has at least two elements (interactor or interactor compositions) that are in relation to each other. An interactor can be either an interaction object or an only_output object. The first one can assume one of the following types: selection, edit, control, interactive description, depending on the type of activity the user is supposed to carry out through such objects. An only_output interactor can be object, description, feedback, alarm, text, depending on the supposed information that the application provides to the user through this interactor. The selection object is refined into *single_choice* and *multiple_choice* depending on the number of selections the user can perform. The further refinement of each of these objects can be done only by specifying some platform dependent characteristics, therefore it is specified at the concrete level (see next section for some examples). All the interaction objects have associated events in order to manage the possibility for the user interface to model how to react after the occurrence of some events in their UI. The events differ depending on the type of object they are associated with.

4.3 MARIA – Concrete Level

The concrete description is aimed at providing a platform-dependent but implementation language-independent description of the user interface. It assumes that there are certain available interaction resources that characterise the set of devices belonging to the considered platform. Moreover, it provides an intermediate description between the abstract description and that supported by the available implementation languages for that platform. Thus, for example, if at the abstract level there is a single selection object at the concrete level, this can be refined into a radio-button or a drop-down menu or a list (in case of a graphical platform) but it can also be refined into a vocal selection or gesture-based selection if different platforms are addressed.

In order to enhance the readability of the language and also for consistency reasons (cross-references between different models enabling more consistency because they avoid to replicate the same data in two different places), we decided to furnish the concrete user interface only with the details of the concrete elements, leaving the specification of the higher hierarchy in the abstract meta-model. At this level differences associated with the specific characteristics of the platform will be modelled. For instance, when focusing on a iPhone platform the concrete user interface language has to express the fact that interaction is carried out through the use of not only a simple touch-based interface (which is also to some extent available on PDA), but it also has to handle *multi-touch* events. Therefore, on this platform, there is the need of introducing and modelling a different group of events, the so-called *touch property events*, which includes *touch start* (activated when a finger tap the screen surface), *touch move* (triggered when a finger moves on the surface), *touch end* (activated when a finger leaves the screen surface). In addition, the *zoom gesture event* (which is done through a multi-touch interaction) notifies that a zoom command has been recognized by the system and contains the scale factor that should be considered for zooming. Another peculiar characteristics of the iPhone is the existence of an accelerometer. In this case, the concrete user interface language has to support the specification of the current screen orientation and also to support the associated events.

More generally, the flexibility introduced at the abstract level is reflected also at the concrete level. Thus, for example, there is no more a rigid separation between interface elements for activating functions and elements supporting a selection (as it happened in traditional model-based approaches) but it is possible to model a radio-button, which is associated with different functionalities depending on the selected element.

5 Example Application

As an example application of the features of MARIA XML we consider a home application in which users can control some interactive devices and appliances. In this home application we focus on a specific subset of functionality for demonstrating some of the MARIA XML features. In particular, we focus on i) the possibility to provide suggestions for searching a device through a text editing interactor (for example, the user enters a part of the device name and some suggestions for the completion appear) and ii) displaying information on a set of appliances in a part of the presentation while the user can dynamically add or remove elements from the appliance set.

Regarding the first aspect, let us consider in the home scenario a web service which, given a string, returns a list of suggestions for selecting an appliance that matches the input string. For modelling such a situation we need at the abstract level: an edit interactor for receiving the input string from the user; when the user enters the text, we need to express that the web service has to be invoked and a selection interactor must be populated with the web service output.

To explain how it is possible to model such interaction at the abstract level, we use the following MARIA XML features:

- Abstract events on interactors (to detect the change in the input string);
- Syntax for expressing external functions calls;
- Binding between the UI model and the data model within the UI definition.

First of all we need to "import" the Web service into the UI definition. This is possible using the external functions introduced before. An external function is an abstract representation of services and functionalities that are not defined in the UI (such as Web services or database access). When an abstract function is declared, it can be called by the abstract scripts to express how the interface should use the output of these functions. The following XML excerpt shows a possible abstract representation of the suggestion service:

```
<aui:external_functions>
    . . .
  <aui:function name="getSuggestions" type="web_service">
   <aui:output type="UserSession/suggestions" />
   <aui:input type="xs:string" name="inputString"/>
  </aui:function>
    . . .
<aui:external_functions>
```

The external_functions tag contains all the external function declarations. A single function is declared specifying: a name (e.g. getSuggestions); its type (such as Web service, database, code etc); its output type (in this case we presume a data type UserSession in the data model that contains an element *suggestions,* which is the suggestion list and corresponds to the external function output type); its parameters (in this case the input string).

Now we can describe that when the input string changes, the external function must be called and the suggestions must be displayed. To this end, we use the value changed event of the text_edit interactor. When this event occurs, the function is called using an abstract script, and the *hidden* property of the choice interactor (a single choice in this case) is changed to false. The following excerpt is the definition of the text edit interactor:

```
<aui:text_edit id="device_search">
 <aui:events>
  <aui:value_change>
   <aui:handler>
    <aui:script>
    <![CDATA[
       data:UserSession/suggestions
=external:getSuggestions(ui:device_search.value); ]]>
 [...]
   <aui:handler>
    <aui:change_property interactor_id="device_suggestions"
              property_name="hidden" property_value="false" />
   </aui:handler>
 [...] </aui:text_edit>
```

The previous definition states that when the input text, which is specified by using an abstract object of type text_edit with id="device_search", changes (this is specified by the fact that the event type is "value_change"), the field suggestions of the UserSession data type (see "UserSession/suggestions" field in the previous excerpt) is populated with the output of the external function getSuggestions, invoked by passing the input text value, see "external:getSuggestions(ui:device_search.value);" in the excerpt above. After the function call, the device_suggestion interactor (a single choice interactor) has to be shown. This interactor is bound to the same data field populated by the external function invocation so, when this field changes, the interactor is also updated with the new options. The following excerpt contains the single_choice interactor definition:

```
  <aui:single_choice  id="device_suggestions"
data_reference="UserSession/suggestions" >
    <aui:events>
     <aui:selection_change>
      <aui:handler>
       <aui:change_property interactor_id="device_select_activator"
                    property_name="enabled"
                    data_value="true" />
       <aui:change_property interactor_id="device_monitor_activator"
                    property_name="enabled"
                    data_value="true" />
       <aui:change_property interactor_id="device_search"
                    property_name="value"
                    data_value="ui:device_suggestions.selected" />
       <aui:change_property interactor_id="device_suggestions"
                    property_name="hidden"  property_value="true" />
  [...]
   </aui:single_choice>
```

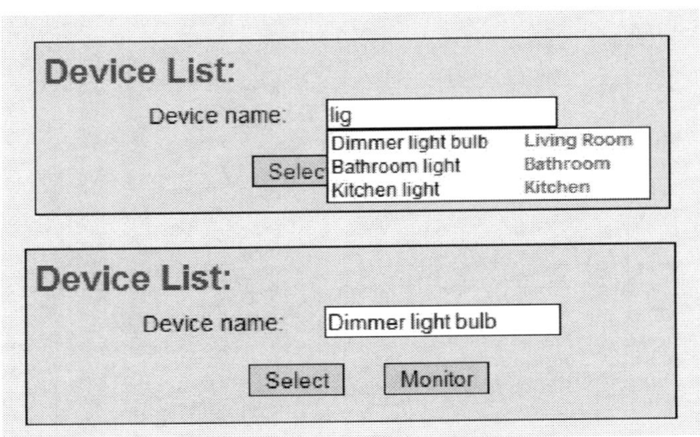

Fig. 4. The interaction modelled in the example

The interactor is bound to the data using the data_reference attribute. When the selected element changes, it enables two activators (activator is the interactor type that models interface elements dedicated to activate functionalities): one for getting the control panel for the device and the other for monitoring it (see *Select* and *Monitor* buttons in Figure 4). Then it completes the input text of the text_edit presented before (setting the value attribute with its selected value) and hides itself. Note that the specification is completely abstract, it is not specified how the service is called, how the interactors are hidden or shown and what the UI platform is.

We can refine the interface definition to various concrete platforms and final implementations. The interface can be adapted to the target platform capabilities (screen size, processor speed etc) and interaction techniques (mouse, multitouch, vocal commands

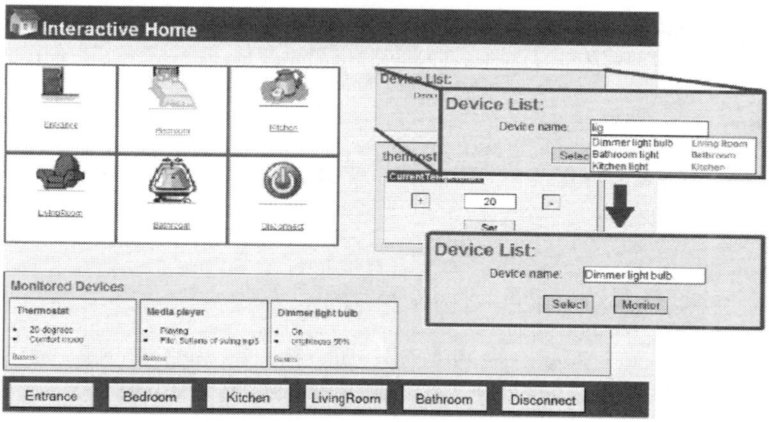

Fig. 5. Example implementation for desktop platform

Fig. 6. Example implementation for the iPhone platform

etc). Figures 5 and 6 show two possible final implementations (obtained passing through a model-to-code generation step) of the same abstract user interface for two devices (desktop and iPhone).

However, the differences between a desktop computer and the iPhone can require a different number of presentations for the same content and also different locations of the groups in the screen (in figure 6 the controls for the selected device and the list of monitored status in the iPhone is in a different page and the groups have a flow layout). However, the suggestion mechanism is the same in both devices (although it can be implemented in different ways) and this aspect is reflected in the abstract description.

6 Conclusions, Future Work and Acknowledgments

In this paper we present our method for developing interactive applications based on the access to Web services. The described approach exploits a multi-layer framework of languages for describing UIs through a mix of bottom-up and top-down phases. This allows designers to develop service front-ends for Web services, which were originally developed without exactly knowing the interactive applications that will access them. We have also discussed how the MARIA language is able to support specification of flexible interactions exploiting such Web services and scripts, for then generate implementations for different types of devices. This type of interactions are becoming widely used in Web 2.0 and Rich Internet Applications.

We are developing an authoring environment to support the various phases of the method presented, including the association of system tasks with Web services and their operations, and ease the use of MARIA and the associated transformations. We also plan to integrate in MARIA some concepts of the WAI-ARIA (Accessible Rich Internet Applications, http://www.w3.org/WAI/intro/aria) in order to support generation of user interfaces accessible to disabled people, such as blind people interacting through screen readers.

We gratefully acknowledge support from the EU ServFace Project (http://www.servface.eu).

References

1. Abrams, M., Phanouriou, C., Batongbacal, A., Williams, S., Shuster, J.: UIML: An Appliance-Independent XML User Interface Language. In: Proceedings of the 8th WWW conference (1999)
2. Chesta, C., Paterno, F., Santoro, C.: Methods and Tools for Designing and Developing Usable Multi-Platform Interactive Applications. Psychnology 2(1), 123–139 (2004)
3. Limbourg, Q., Vanderdonckt, J., Michotte, B., Bouillon, L., Lopez-Jaquero, V.: USIXML: A Language Supporting Multi-path Development of User Interfaces. In: EHCI/DS-VIS 2004, pp. 200–220 (2004)
4. Mori, G., Paternò, F., Spano, L.D.: Exploiting web services and model-based user interfaces for multi-device access to home applications. In: Graham, T.C.N., Palanque, P. (eds.) DSV-IS 2008. LNCS, vol. 5136, pp. 181–193. Springer, Heidelberg (2008)
5. Paternò, F., Santoro, C., Mantyjarvi, J., Mori, G., Sansone, S.: Authoring Pervasive Multi-Modal User Interfaces. International Journal of Web Engineering and Technology, Inderscience Publishers 4(2), 235–261 (2008)

6. Paternò, F.: Model-Based Design and Evaluation of Interactive Applications. Springer, Heidelberg (1999)
7. Song, K., Lee, K.-H.: Generating multimodal user interfaces for Web services. Interacting with Computers 20(4-5), 480–490 (2008)
8. Spillner, J., Braun, I., Schill, A.: Flexible Human Service Interfaces. In: Proceedings of the 9th International Conference on Enterprise Information Systems, pp. 79–85 (2007)
9. Vermeulen, J., Vandriessche, Y., Clerckx, T., Luyten, K., Coninx, K.: Service-interaction Descriptions: Augmenting Services with User Interface Models. In: Proceedings Engineering Interactive Systems 2007, Salamanca. Springer, Heidelberg (2007)

Speed-Accuracy Tradeoff in Trajectory-Based Tasks with Temporal Constraint

Xiaolei Zhou[1], Xiang Cao[2], and Xiangshi Ren[1]

[1] Kochi University of Technology, Kochi 782-8502, Japan
zxljapan@gmail.com, ren.xiangshi@kochi-tech.ac.jp
[2] Microsoft Research Cambridge, Cambridge CB3 0FB, United Kingdom
xiangc@microsoft.com

Abstract. Speed-accuracy tradeoff is a common phenomenon in many types of human motor tasks. In general, the more accurately the task is to be accomplished, the more time it takes, and vice versa. In particular, when users attempt to complete the task with a specified amount of time, the accuracy of the task can be considered as a dependent variable to measure user performance. In this paper we investigate speed-accuracy tradeoff in trajectory-based tasks with temporal constraint, through a controlled experiment that manipulates the movement time (*MT*) in addition to the tunnel amplitude (*A*) and width (*W*). A quantitative model is proposed and validated to predict the task accuracy in terms of lateral standard deviation (*SD*) of the trajectory.

Keywords: Human performance model, speed-accuracy tradeoff, temporal constraint, trajectory-based tasks.

1 Introduction

An important research branch of human-computer interaction is to develop predictive models for human performance in fundamental interaction tasks. One of such tasks is the trajectory-based "steering" task, in which the user uses the input device such as a stylus to produce a trajectory ("stroke") through a "tunnel" with set amplitude (length) *A* and width *W*. The movement time (*MT*) of the steering tasks has been modeled by the steering law [1]: $MT = a + b\ (A/W)$, where *a* and *b* are empirically determined constants, and *A/W* (index of difficulty or *ID*) characterizes the difficulty of the task. The steering law has been verified with several input devices [2], in different scales [3] and in simulated driving tasks [25].

The steering law models the relationship between the movement time of trajectory-based tasks and the task difficulty, determined by the tunnel amplitude *A* and tunnel width *W*. In the steering law, the movement time *MT* is the dependent variable. The more accurate the task is required (the narrower the tunnel width *W* is), the longer the resulting movement time is. However, if we want to consider the opposite direction, i.e. inferring the actual trajectory accuracy given a specific movement time (or speed), the steering law does not enable us to make this prediction.

Given the bidirectional relationship between time and accuracy, it is worthwhile to establish a model that predicts the trajectory accuracy by considering the movement

T. Gross et al. (Eds.): INTERACT 2009, Part I, LNCS 5726, pp. 906–919, 2009.

time as an independent variable. Such a model will supplement the steering law, and enrich our understanding of the speed-accuracy tradeoff in trajectory-based tasks. On the other hand, a prediction model of the trajectory accuracy also has practical implications. For example, pen gestures have been widely used to trigger commands. Such a model may allow us to estimate the deviation of the actual gesture stroke from the standard template at different drawing speeds, and improve the recognition and interpretation of the gestures. In a real world scenario, we may determine the optimal road width according to the marked driving speed.

Although speed-accuracy tradeoffs have been widely studied [14], [15], [17], [20], [23], these works have mostly focused on target acquisition tasks. In this paper, we sought to investigate the speed-accuracy tradeoff in trajectory-based tasks through a controlled experiment, and derive a quantitative model for predicting accuracy.

Previous studies on speed-accuracy tradeoffs have involved experimental protocols with two types of constraints: spatial constraint and temporal constraint, which differentiate the nature of the task. For example, in rapid aimed hand movements with spatial constraints, participants are required to move as quickly as possible to reach the target with width W placed at distance A. The movement time is measured to reflect the task performance. This is a target acquisition task (also known as *time-minimization task*) and has been modeled by Fitts' law [6]. In rapid aimed hand movements with temporal constraints, participants are required to reach the target with a specified movement time. This is a paced reaching task (also known as a *time-matching movement task*) [20]. In this type of tasks, movement time is controlled and spatial variability of the movement is measured to reflect the accuracy. Similarly, in trajectory-based movements with spatial constraints, participants are required to produce a trajectory through a tunnel with length A and width W as quickly as possible. This is the standard steering task and has been modeled by the steering law [1]. However, if participants are required to produce a trajectory through a tunnel with length A and width W with a specified movement time, does regularity exist in the relationship between the trajectory accuracy and the task parameters? What kind of speed-accuracy tradeoff can be observed from trajectory-based task with temporal constraint? What are the differences between trajectory-based movements with temporal constraint and with spatial constraint? We sought to answer these questions in this paper.

2 Related Work

Depending on the stimulus of the task (target or trajectory) and the type of the constraint (spatial or temporal), research on the speed-accuracy tradeoffs can be divided into four categories as follows:

2.1 Target-Based Tasks with Spatial Constraint

One of the most famous and commonly used models in HCI is Fitts' law[1] [6]. Fitts' law describes a logarithmic speed-accuracy tradeoff formulation in target acquisition

[1] $MT = a + b \log_2 (A/W)$, where A is the amplitude of the movement, W is the target width (i.e. the required accuracy), and MT (the dependent variable) is the movement time taken to acquire the target. a and b are empirically determined constants.

tasks with spatial constraint. Subsequently, the logarithmic speed accuracy tradeoff has been empirically validated for a wide variety of individual body joints [11], activities [11], and environmental conditions [8], [9]. Several variations of Fitts' law have also been presented by Welford [21] and Mackenzie [12].

Based on the traditional Fitts' law, Zhai et al. [26] investigated the speed-accuracy tradeoff based on participants' operational biases toward speed or accuracy, and attempted to derive a model incorporating both objective task parameters and subjective biases. However, a simple and linear model was not found by the empirical studies. Consequently, Ren et al. [19] established the SH-Model involving both the system and subjective factors based on the distribution of the actual movement time.

2.2 Target-Based Tasks with Temporal Constraint

Schmidt's law[2] [20] is closely related to Fitts' law. In their study, movement amplitude and time were manipulated, and the standard deviation of end points distribution was measured. Schmidt's law described a strong linear relationship between the movement speed and the standard deviation of the end points distribution.

In order to investigate the coexistence of spatial and temporal constraints in one motor task, Zelaznik et al. [24] manipulated movement time, amplitude and target width ($W > 0$) and discovered a similar linear speed-accuracy tradeoff. The target width did not affect the nature of the speed-accuracy tradeoff relationship.

In addition to researches that look at end point distribution, Wobbrock et al. [22] derived a predictive model for error rate through an experiment that manipulated target size, target distance and movement time. A logarithmic speed-accuracy tradeoff was found instead.

2.3 Trajectory-Based Tasks with Spatial Constraint

The steering law [1], described at the beginning of this paper, is the widely accepted model for trajectory-based tasks with spatial constraint. The movement time follows a linear relationship with the index of difficulty.

Subsequently, extensive researches have been done based on the steering law, such as models for steering through corners [16], steering within above-the-surface interaction layers using the tracking state of the stylus [7], and study of subjective biases toward speed or accuracy in steering tasks [27]. In addition, a pen stroke gesture model for predicting completion time of free hand trajectory drawing tasks has also been proposed [5].

2.4 Trajectory-Based Tasks with Temporal Constraint

So far, trajectory-based task with temporal constraint has not been investigated and modeled. Our aim in this paper is to investigate the trajectory accuracy when the movement time is considered as an independent variable in trajectory-based tasks,

---

[2] $W_e = b\ (A/MT)$, where W_e represents the standard deviation of end points, A is the amplitude of the movement, and MT (an independent variable) is the movement time as specified by the metronome. Therefore A/MT characterizes the average movement speed. In this experiment, the target is a single line with zero width ($W = 0$).

which will fill the void in human performance modeling research. In actual HCI applications, such a model may guide us to determine the optimal tunnel width given the speed requirements for particular trajectory-based interactions, such as navigating a hierarchical menu. Our model for trajectory accuracy may also have implications in scenarios beyond human-computer interaction, for example to determine optimal road widths for different driving speeds in traffic planning.

3 Problem Definition and Hypothesis

In this paper, we investigate the trajectory-based task of steering through a straight tunnel with temporal constraint (Fig.1). The user is required to complete the task with a specified movement time (within a tolerance range). Although the tunnel does have a finite width *W* that the user supposedly stays within, this spatial constraint is not strictly enforced, i.e. the user may move outside the sides of the tunnel without failing the task.

We are interested in establishing a quantitative model for the trajectory accuracy described by the amount of lateral deviation throughout the trajectory produced. In practice this is represented by *SD*, the standard deviation of the y-coordinates (in the case of a horizontal tunnel) along the entire trajectory. The larger *SD* is, the less accurate the trajectory is. Note that in contrast to the target acquisition task where accuracy is measured by the statistical distribution of a set of trials, here *SD* describes the accuracy of a single steering movement trajectory.

In both Schmidt et al.'s study ($W = 0$) [20] and Zelaznik et al.'s study ($W > 0$) [24] on target acquisition tasks with temporal constraint, the standard deviation of the end point distribution is linearly related to the average movement speed. The effect of the target width on the accuracy was small, hence not included in their speed-accuracy tradeoff models. This might be explained as that in the target acquisition task, the target width only constrains the final corrective submovement but not the initial ballistic submovement (as discussed by Meyer et al. [13]). In contrast, in trajectory-based tasks the tunnel width constrains the entire movement, as the user is expected to produce a trajectory that stays within the tunnel all the time. Consequently, we hypothesize that in trajectory-based tasks with temporal constraint, not only is *SD* related to the average movement speed (*A*/*MT*), but also the tunnel width *W* will have a considerable influence on *SD*. In order to provide a holistic understanding of all affecting factors, our speed-accuracy model for trajectory-based tasks should incorporate impacts of both factors. The correctness of this hypothesis will be verified through our experiment.

4 Experiment

4.1 Apparatus

The experiment was conducted on an IBM ThinkPad X41 Tablet PC with a 12.1-inch screen at the resolution of 1024 × 768, and a stylus as the input device. The experimental software was developed in Java.

4.2 Task

The experiment used a basic trajectory-based task, which is steering through a horizontal straight tunnel with amplitude *A* and width *W* (Fig.1). The participant was required to move the stylus from the start line rightward to the end line through the tunnel, with a specified movement time (denoted as *movement time goal* or *MT goal* hereafter to distinguish from the *actual movement time* observed). A percentage *temporal error tolerance* parameter determined the acceptable range for the actual movement time. For example, if *movement time goal* was 200ms and *temporal error tolerance* was 10%, the actual movement time was allowed to range between 180ms and 220ms to be accepted. The participants were instructed that their movement time should be anywhere within the specified range.

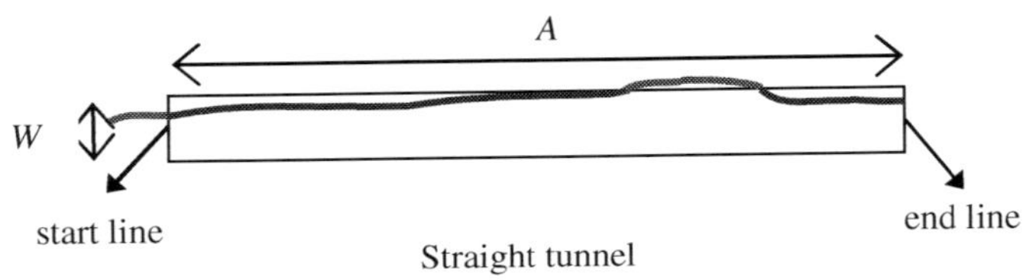

Fig. 1. Experimental task

Before the experiment began, the instructions were explained to the participants, who then conducted training trials until they fully understood the requirements and felt comfortable with the task. At the beginning of each trial, the tunnel to be steered was presented in black. After placing the stylus tip to the left of the start line, the subject began to move the stylus rightward. A green line was displayed to show the stylus trajectory produced by the participant. When the stylus crossed the start line, the trajectory line turned blue to signal that the task had begun. When the stylus crossed the end line, the task ended, and the actual movement time taken was displayed as feedback to the participant.

If the actual movement time was within the acceptable range, the trial was considered successful. Otherwise, the trial needed to be repeated until the actual movement time was within the acceptable range. For unsuccessful trials, the system indicated the percentage by which the trial was too fast or too slow, to help the participant adjust the movement time to meet the requirement.

Lifting the stylus between the start line and the end line was considered invalid and the trial needed to be repeated. The participant was instructed to try to keep the stylus within the upper and lower borders of the tunnel throughout the task. If the stylus was outside the tunnel borders during the trial, the trajectory part outside the borders was displayed in red as a warning (Fig.1), but the trial was not considered invalid.

4.3 Measurements

For each successful trial, the stylus position along the trajectory was sampled in intervals of 10ms. Based on these sample points, we calculated *SD* (*Standard Deviation* of y-coordinates of the sample points), and *OPM* (*Out of Path Movement*, percentage of sample points outside the tunnel) [10]. Calculated from the same set of data, both *SD* and *OPM* describe the accuracy of the trajectory, but from slightly different perspectives. *SD* describes the original user behavior (lateral deviation) under the current stimuli, and provides understandings about the fundamental human capabilities; while *OPM* evaluates how the user behavior satisfies the accuracy requirement (tunnel width) set by the particular task, and its implications are more on the user interaction side. For both *SD* and *OPM*, higher values indicate lower accuracy.

In addition to the accuracy metrics, we recorded the *actual movement time* (or *actual MT*) for each successful trial to understand participants' performance on matching the *MT goal*. The *actual MT* is the time taken to move the stylus between the start line and the end line.

4.4 Design and Procedure

The experiment employed a mixed factorial design and combined within- and between-subject factors. The within-subject factors were *A* (300, 600, 800 pixels), *W* (10, 25, 40, 55, 70 pixels), and *MT goal* (300, 500, 2000, 3500, 5000ms). The values of *MT goal* were chosen according to the preliminary results of a pilot study, and values of *A* and *W* were chosen according to previous studies in [1] and [2].

The between-subject factor was *temporal error tolerance* (10%, 20%, and 40%). Zelaznik et al. [24] adopted 3 levels of temporal error tolerance to investigate the effect of temporal precision on the nature of the speed-accuracy tradeoff. To be consistent, in our experiment we also chose these 3 levels in order to investigate whether and how different levels of *temporal error tolerance* might affect the human performance and the nature of speed-accuracy tradeoff.

The participant was first briefed on the purpose of the experiment. Then 5 experiment sessions corresponding to the 5 *MT goal* conditions were tested in sequence. Within each session, the participant performed 3 successful trials for each combination of *A* and *W* respectively. Before each session began, the participant was informed of the current *MT goal* and the relevant acceptable range of the *actual movement time*, and was allowed to perform practice trials until s/he felt comfortable.

The order of the *MT goal* conditions was counterbalanced using a Latin square pattern across participants. The order of the *A* and *W* conditions was randomized within each *MT goal* condition.

4.5 Participants

Thirty righted-handed people, aged from 21 to 34, participated in the experiment. They were assigned randomly to one of three *temporal error tolerance* groups (10%, 20% and 40%), with 10 participants (8 males and 2 females) per group.

Therefore, the total number of successful trials performed was: 3 (trials) × 3 (tunnel amplitude *A*) × 5 (tunnel width *W*) × 5 (*MT goal*) × 3 (*temporal error tolerance* group) × 10 (participants per group) = 6,750.

5 Results

5.1 Actual Movement Time (Actual *MT*)

The *actual movement time* (*actual MT*) varied significantly with both the between-subject factor *temporal error tolerance* ($F_{2, 27} = 8.97$, $p = .001$), and all the within-subject factors: *MT goal* ($F_{4, 108} = 6584.77$, $p < .001$), *W* ($F_{4, 108} = 13.01$, $p < .001$), and *A* ($F_{2, 54} = 249.24$, $p < .001$). The mean *actual MT* for the 10%, 20% and 40% *temporal error tolerance* groups were 2250, 2226 and 2089ms respectively. A significant interaction between *temporal error tolerance* and *MT goal* was observed on *actual MT* ($F_{8, 108} = 6.35$, $p < .001$) (Fig.2). For 10% and 20% groups, the mean *actual MT* values approximated the *MT goals*. However, such was not the case for the 40% group. The mean *actual MTs* for the 300ms to 5000ms conditions were 312, 495, 1910, 3205, and 4522ms respectively. Post hoc pair-wise comparisons showed that *actual MTs* were almost equivalent with the *MT goals* for the 10% and 20% groups. However, for the 40% group, the *actual MTs* were equivalent with the other two groups only under the 300ms and 500ms condition, and significantly lower *actual MTs* were observed than the other two groups under the 2000, 3500 and 5000ms conditions ($p < 0.05$).

Similar to the results obtained by Zelaznik [24], the results of *MT* for the 40% group indicated a range effect [18]: longer-duration tasks exhibit an *actual MT* shorter than the *MT goal*, indicating the participant moving at a more natural speed, faster than the speed dictated. The looser temporal constraint in the 40% group allowed this range effect to be observed, while the tighter constraints in the other two groups effectively eliminated the range effect.

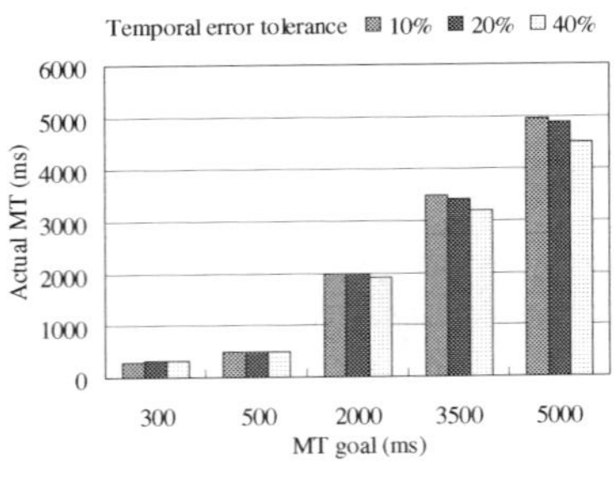

Fig. 2. Actual *MT* vs. *MT* goal for each temporal error tolerance

Another phenomenon was the significant interaction for *temporal error tolerance* × *W* ($F_{8, 108} = 4.36$, $p < .001$), and *temporal error tolerance* × *A* ($F_{4, 54} = 57.39$, $p < .001$). In the 10% *temporal error tolerance* group, *W* did not have a significant effect on *actual MT* ($F_{4, 36} = 1.68$, $p = .176$). However, in both of the other two groups, *W* had significant effects on *actual MT* ($F_{4, 36} = 4.91$, $p = .003$ for 20% group; $F_{4, 36} = 8.49$, $p < .001$ for 40% group), in that *actual MT* decreased as *W* increased. Similarly, the 10% group pair-wise comparisons revealed no significant difference in the *actual MT* between the $A = 600$ pixels and $A = 800$ pixels conditions ($p = 0.673$). But in both the

20% and the 40% group, significant differences of *actual MT* were found among all three levels of *A* ($p = 0.003$), showing that *actual MT* increased as *A* increased. In the 20% and 40% groups the effects of *A* and *W* displayed the similar trends discovered by the steering law research [1], i.e., *MT* increases with *A* and decreases with *W*. Not surprisingly, because of the temporal constraints, the trends shown in our experiment were not strong enough to follow the linear relationship dictated by the steering law. Nevertheless, this is an interesting finding that even when people intentionally attempt to match a specific movement time, the underlying motor control mechanism still regulates the motion subconsciously within the allowable range and cannot be completely overridden. Again, in the 10% group, the strict temporal constraint prevented the trends from being observable.

5.2 Trajectory Accuracy (*SD*)

SD measures the lateral deviation of the trajectory, as an indication of the trajectory accuracy. The grand mean of *SD* was 2.85 pixels. *SD* did not vary significantly with the between-subject factor *temporal error tolerance* ($F_{2, 27} = 1.36$, $p = .275$), but varied significantly with all the within-subject factors: *MT goal* ($F_{4, 108} = 121.04$, $p < .001$), *W* ($F_{4, 108} = 82.22$, $p < .001$), and *A* ($F_{2, 54} = 292.42$, $p < .001$). *SD* decreased as *MT goal* increased, showing that a longer movement time enabled participants to be more accurate. *SD* increased as *W* increased, showing that a wider tunnel allowed for less accurate movement. *SD* also increased as *A* increased, showing that a longer path (hence higher movement speed when other factors remain the same) resulted in less accurate movement. Table 1 summarizes these.

Table 1. Main effects on *SD*

MT goal (ms)	300	500	2000	3500	5000
SD (pixels)	4.15	3.50	2.40	2.16	2.04

W (pixels)	10	25	40	55	70
SD (pixels)	2.33	2.50	2.86	3.19	3.38

A (pixels)	300	600	800
SD (pixels)	1.87	2.92	3.76

Since no significant difference of *SD* was observed among the three *temporal error tolerance* groups, we combined the data sets from the three groups in further analysis. No significant interaction for *MT goal* × *W* ($p = .059$) was observed on *SD*, as shown in Fig.3 by the fact that the five regression lines are almost parallel, meaning that the effects of *MT goal* and *W* were independent. In addition, the correlations (R^2) between *SD* and *W* are high (0.875 ~ 0.985) for each *MT goal*, showing that *SD* follows a strong linear relationship with *W* when other variables are factored out.

Similarly, no significant interaction between *W* and *A* were observed on *SD*, indicating that the effects of *W* and *A* were independent as well.

A significant interaction between *MT goal* and *A* ($F_{8, 72} = 45.216$, $p < .001$) was observed on *SD* (Fig.4). The effect of *A* increased as *MT goal* decreased, as shown by the slopes of the regression lines. This is an intuitive observation if we consider the

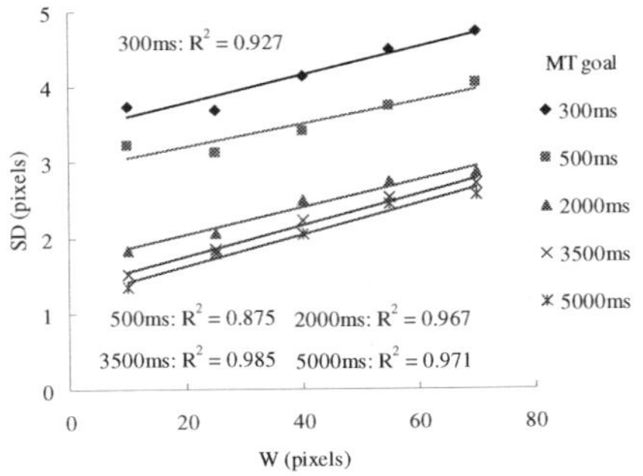

Fig. 3. Mean *SD* vs. *W* for each *MT goa.*

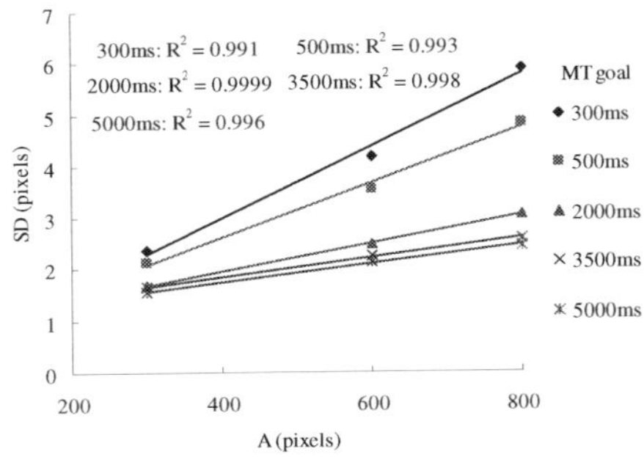

Fig. 4. Mean *SD* vs. *A* for each *MT goal*

average movement speed that is *A/MT*. Smaller *MT goal* resulted in larger changes on the anticipated movement speed for the same amount of change over *A*, and in turn larger changes on the movement accuracy. Similar to *W*, the correlations (R^2) between *SD* and *A* are high for each *MT goal* in Fig.4, showing that *SD* follows a strong linear relationship with *A* when other variables are factored out.

5.3 Out of Path Movement (*OPM*)

OPM measures the percentage of the trajectory outside the tunnel, indicating how well the spatial constraint was satisfied. The grand mean of *OPM* was 3.4%. *OPM* did not vary significantly with the between-subject factor *temporal error tolerance* ($F_{2, 27} = 1.77$, $p = .189$), but varied significantly with all within-subject factors: *MT goal* ($F_{4, 108} = 148.53$, $p < .001$), *W* ($F_{4, 108} = 315.58$, $p < .001$), and *A* ($F_{2, 54} = 128.88$, $p < .001$). Table 2 summarizes mean *OPM* under different conditions. Similar to *SD*, *OPM* decreased as *MT goal* increased, and increased as *A* increased. However, different from *SD, OPM* decreased as *W* increased. It was easier for participants to keep the stylus inside a wider tunnel, despite that the produced trajectory itself becomes more relaxed (resulting in higher *SD*).

Table 2. Main effects on *OPM*

MT goal (ms)	300	500	2000	3500	5000
OPM (%)	8.6	6.6	1.3	0.5	0.2

W (pixels)	10	25	40	55	70
OPM (%)	14.3	2.3	4.0	0.2	0.1

A (pixels)	300	600	800
OPM (%)	1.3	3.3	5.7

Given that no significant difference of *OPM* was observed among the three *temporal error tolerance* groups, we combined the data set from these three groups in further analysis on *OPM*. Significant interaction between *MT goal* and *W* ($F_{16, 144} = 190.31$, $p < .001$) was observed on *OPM*. The effect of *W* increased as *MT goal* decreased. As known from the analysis of *SD*, smaller *MT goal* resulted in larger lateral deviation (*SD*) in the trajectory, which contributed to the variety of *OPM* values that depended heavily on the tunnel width. However when *MT goal* is larger, the resulting smaller *SD* meant most of the trajectory would stay inside the tunnel, and in turn caused the uniformly small *OPM*. This finding is similar to the study results on subjective bias in steering tasks [27]. Significant interactions also exist in $A \times MT$ *goal* ($F_{8, 72} = 35.31$, $p < .001$) and $A \times W$ ($F_{8, 72} = 115.86$, $p < .001$).

6 Model Deduction and Verification

Based on the experimental results, we now attempt to establish a speed-accuracy tradeoff model that quantitatively predicts *SD* from *A*, *W* and *MT goal*. Based on our analysis of *SD*, we concluded that:

- *SD* is significantly affected by tunnel width *W*, tunnel amplitude *A* and *MT goal*.
- *SD* increases as *A* and *W* increase, and decreases as *MT goal* increase.
- The relationship between *SD* and *W* is linear when other variables remain constant. Same for the relationship between *SD* and *A*.
- The effects of *W* and *MT goal* on *SD* are independent of each other (i.e. additive). Same for the effects of *W* and *A*. The effects of *A* and *MT goal* on *SD* are not independent (i.e. not additive).

Considering all these properties, we speculated the following model to describe the speed-accuracy tradeoff in trajectory-based tasks with temporal constraint:

$$SD = a + bW + c\,(A/MT)\,. \qquad (1)$$

where *W* is the tunnel width, *A* is the tunnel amplitude, *MT* is the specified movement time (i.e. *MT goal*), and *SD* is the lateral standard deviation of the trajectory. *a*, *b* and *c* are empirically determined constants. *A*/*MT* represents the average movement speed.

To verify the above model, we fit it to our experimental data using least-square regression. In addition to fitting to the entire data set, we also fit the model to the data from each *temporal error tolerance* group individually to test its performance under different conditions. Table 3 summarizes the regression coefficients and R^2 values.

Table 3. Regression results of the proposed model (1)

temporal error tolerance	*a*	*b*	*c*	R^2
All	1.08	0.0185	1.44	0.857
10%	0.985	0.0209	1.20	0.800
20%	1.25	0.0164	1.41	0.826
40%	1.02	0.0181	1.71	0.880

The model had a good fit with the entire data set ($R^2 = 0.857$), as well as with data from all individual *temporal error tolerance* groups ($R^2 \geq 0.800$). This confirmed the validity of our model.

This model also confirmed our initial hypothesis that in trajectory-based tasks with temporal constraint, *SD* is not only related to the average movement speed (*A*/*MT*), but also related to the tunnel width *W*. In order to further consolidate our model by comparing its performance with simpler alternatives, we tested an alternate model that ignored the effect of *W* in model (1), i.e.:

$$SD = a' + b' (A/MT) . \tag{2}$$

Regression results showed that the R^2 values for model (2) are lower (R^2 = 0.813 for 40% group, and < 0.77 for all other conditions) than those of model (1) in all cases, therefore not considered a valid model. Detailed results are omitted given the space limitation. Unlike in target acquisition tasks, the effect of *W* on *SD* cannot be ignored in trajectory-based tasks. As such, we conclude that model (1) best describes the speed-accuracy tradeoff in trajectory-based tasks with temporal constraint.

7 Discussion

In our model, *SD* measures the "average" accuracy throughout the entire trajectory. This is consistent with our original problem setup of a straight tunnel with uniform width *W*, and *A*/*MT* is the "average" movement speed. However, if we consider the more general case in which both the tunnel width and the movement speed can vary throughout the trajectory, we could let W_P and V_P represent the local tunnel width and instant movement speed at a given point on the trajectory. As a result, $SD_P = a + bW_P + cV_P$ might be used to predict the local expected lateral deviation at the point. This might help us design and analyze interactions using trajectories or tunnels of various shapes and properties, and understand them at a finer level.

Our experiment used a setup with relatively strict temporal constraint and non-strict spatial constraint to investigate trajectory-based tasks and the degree that people can conform to this constraint (hence the metric *OPM*). Real-world trajectory-based tasks often have this non-strict spatial constraint property, such as tracing a drawing. Nevertheless, the visual stimulus of the spatial constraint affects the precision of the movement, as is reflected in the model. In our future investigation, we could naturally study the other variant where the spatial constraint is strictly enforced. Conversely, we may consider the case there is no explicit spatial constraint at all (i.e. tunnel width $W = 0$), which essentially becomes a line tracing task. Fortunately, we might predict the user performance under this case by setting $W = 0$ in our current model, which then becomes $SD = a + c\ (A/MT)$. This means the lateral deviation is linearly related to the movement speed only, a similar result to Schmidt's law [20]. Obviously, this prediction would need real experimental data to be validated.

Throughout this paper we have been referring to previous research on speed-accuracy tradeoff in target acquisition tasks as an analogy. However, we also want to emphasize the differences between trajectory-based tasks and target acquisition tasks, especially in terms of the notion of accuracy. In a target acquisition task, the movement accuracy is solely determined by the destination (end point) of the movement, for which we call the "destination accuracy". The spatial error in the destination is mainly caused by the ballistic nature of the movement, and is collinear to the movement. In contrast, in a trajectory-based task, the movement accuracy is determined by the entire process (trajectory) of the movement, for which we call the "process accuracy". The spatial error in the trajectory is mainly caused by the motor instability in the movement, and is perpendicular to the movement. These differences also contributed to the different forms of speed-accuracy tradeoff models for the two types of tasks. Similar comparisons can be made with other motor control tasks, For example, in a crossing task, destination accuracy and perpendicular errors coexist, which may result in yet another form of speed-accuracy tradeoff.

Since participants could not possibly finish a task with the specified movement time exactly, *temporal error tolerance* was introduced to define the range of acceptable movement time. Although our choice of testing multiple levels of *temporal error tolerance* did not result in observable effects on the trajectory accuracy, it did provide interesting observations on user behaviors in terms of the actual movement time taken. In particular, from the groups with higher *temporal error tolerance* values, we observed that the steering law as a fundamental motor control mechanism still affects the movement time, even when people consciously follow an explicit temporal requirement. We suspect that a similar effect might be present in other types of motor control tasks as well. This suggests that in time-critical applications, we can not overlook the inherent properties of the tasks and expect users to be able to perform at an arbitrary rate, even when accuracy is not the priority. On the other hand, we used a post hoc feedback mechanism about the user's temporal performance. How real-time feedback mechanisms (e.g. progressively filling the tunnel with color to indicate the elapsing of time) might affect the users' behaviors remains an interesting topic for further study.

8 Conclusion and Future Work

As the result of our investigation, we can now answer the questions we raised in the beginning: In trajectory-based tasks with temporal constraints, regularity does exist in the relationship between the trajectory accuracy and the task parameters, which is described by the speed-accuracy tradeoff model:

$$SD = a + bW + c\,(A/MT)$$

where W is the tunnel width, A is the tunnel amplitude, MT is the specified movement time, and SD represents the lateral standard deviation of the trajectory. SD forms a linear relationship with both the tunnel width W and average movement speed (A/MT).

Regarding the comparison between temporally and spatially constrained trajectory-based movements, both of them reflect a linear speed-accuracy tradeoff. As investigated by [27], in spatially-constrained tasks with subjective biases, the lateral deviation of trajectory (SD) is affected by the tunnel width W and the subjective bias. In comparison, in temporally-constrained tasks the accuracy of trajectory (SD) is affected by both the tunnel width W and the average steering speed (A/MT).

In the future, we plan to extend our investigation to trajectory-based tasks with zero tunnel width, non-uniform tunnel width, as well as trajectories of other shapes such as a circle. We also plan to test our model using other input devices, other forms of temporal feedback, or other reward-penalty mechanisms for the temporal constraint.

In addition to spatial accuracy, we are interested in investigating the temporal accuracy, which describes human capabilities in matching the temporal constraints. Finally, we plan to investigate individual differences in terms of perception, estimation, and preference of the time constraints, especially for different age groups.

References

1. Accot, J., Zhai, S.: Beyond Fitts' Law: Models for Trajectory-Based HCI Tasks. In: Proc. CHI 1997, pp. 295–302. ACM Press, New York (1997)
2. Accot, J., Zhai, S.: Performance evaluation of input devices in trajectory-based tasks: an application of the steering law. In: Proc. CHI 1999, pp. 466–472. ACM Press, New York (1999)
3. Accot, J., Zhai, S.: Scale effects in steering law tasks. In: Proc. CHI 2001, pp. 1–8. ACM Press, New York (2001)
4. Annett, J., Golby, C.W., Kay, H.: The measurement of elements in an assembly task: The information output of the human motor system. Quarterly Journal of Experimental Psychology 10, 1–11 (1958)
5. Cao, X., Zhai, S.: Modeling human performance of pen stroke gestures. In: Proc. CHI 2007, pp. 1495–1504. ACM Press, New York (2007)
6. Fitts, P.M.: The Information Capacity of the Human Motor System in Controlling the Amplitude of Movement. Journal of Experimental Psychology 47, 381–391 (1954)
7. Kattinakere, R.S., Grossman, T., Subramanian, S.: Modeling steering within above-the-surface interaction layers. In: Proc. CHI 2007, pp. 317–326. ACM Press, New York (2007)
8. Kerr, R.: Movement time in an underwater environment. Journal of Motor Behavior 5, 175–178 (1973)
9. Kerr, B.A., Langolf, G.D.: Speed of aiming movements. Quarterly Journal of Experimental Psychology 29, 475–481 (1977)
10. Kulikov, S., Mackenzie, I., Stuerzlinger, W.: Measuring the effective parameters of steering motions. In: Proc. CHI 2005, pp. 1569–1572. ACM Press, New York (2005)
11. Langolf, G.D., Chaffin, D.B., Foulke, J.A.: An investigation of Fitts' law using a wide range of movement amplitudes. Journal of Motor Behavior 8, 113–128 (1976)
12. MacKenzie, I.S.: A note on the information-theoretic basis for Fitts' law. Journal of Motor Behavior 21, 323–330 (1989)
13. Meyer, D.E., Abrams, R.A., Kornblum, S., Wright, C.E., Smith, J.E.K.: Optimality in human motor performance: Ideal control of rapid aimed movements. Psychological Review 95(3), 340–370 (1988)
14. Meyer, D.E., Smith, J.E.K., Kornblum, S., Abrams, R.A., Wright, C.E.: Speed-accuracy tradeoffs in aimed movements: Toward a theory of rapid voluntary action. In: Jeannerod, M. (ed.) Attention and Performance, vol. XIII, pp. 173–226. Lawrence Erlbaum, Hillsdale (1990)
15. Meyer, D.E., Smith, J.E.K., Wright, C.E.: Models for the speed and accuracy of aimed movements. Psychological Review 89(5), 449–482 (1982)
16. Pastel, R.: Measuring the difficulty of steering through corners. In: Proc. CHI 2006, pp. 1087–1096. ACM Press, New York (2006)
17. Plamondon, R., Alimi, A.M.: Speed/accuracy trade-offs in target-directed movements. Behavior and Brain Sciences 20(2), 279–349 (1997)
18. Poulton, E.C.: Range effects in experiments on people. American Journal of Psychology 88, 3–32 (1975)

19. Ren, X., Kong, J., Jiang, Q.: SH-Model: A Model Based on both System and Human Effects for Pointing Task Evaluation. Journal of Information Processing Society of Japan (IPSJ) 46(5), 1343–1353 (2005)
20. Schmidt, R.A., Zelaznik, H., Hawkins, B., Frank, J.S., Quinn, J.T.: Motor-output variability: A theory for the accuracy of rapid motor acts. Psychological Review 86, 415–451 (1979)
21. Welford, A.T.: Fundamentals of skill. Methuen, London (1968)
22. Wobbrock, J.O., Cutrell, E., Harada, S., Mackenzie, I.S.: An error model for pointing based on Fitts' law. In: Proc. CHI 2008, pp. 1613–1622. ACM Press, New York (2008)
23. Wright, C.E., Meyer, D.E.: Conditions for a linear speed-accuracy trade-off in aimed movements. Quarterly Journal of Experimental Psychology 35A(2), 279–296 (1983)
24. Zelaznik, H.N., Mone, S., McCabe, G.P., Thaman, C.: Role of temporal and spatial precision in determining the nature of the speed-accuracy trade-off in aimed-hand movements. Journal of Experimental Psychology: Human Perception and Performance 14(2), 221–230 (1988)
25. Zhai, S., Accot, J., Woltjer, R.: Human Action Laws in Electronic Virtual Worlds - an empirical study of path steering performance in VR. Presence 13(2), 113–127 (2004)
26. Zhai, S., Kong, J., Ren, X.: Speed-accuracy tradeoff in Fitts' tasks - on the equivalency of actual and nominal pointing precision. International Journal of Human-Computer Studies 61(6), 823–856 (2004)
27. Zhou, X., Ren, X.: An Investigation of Subjective Operational Biases in Steering Tasks Evaluation. To appear in Behaviour & Information Technology. Taylor & Francis (in press)

Author Index

FSC
www.fsc.org
MIX
Papier | Fördert gute Waldnutzung
FSC® C083411

Kolibri 360 GmbH
Ferdinand-Jühlke-Straße 7
99095 Erfurt, Deutschland
produktsicherheit@kolibri360.de